Witness to America

A Documentary History of the United States from It's Discovery to Modern Times

Edited By
Henry Steele Commager
and
Allan Nevins

BARNES
&NOBLE
BOOKS
NEW YORK

To
N.T. McC. C.
A.N.
M.N.
H.S.C., Jr.

Originally published as *The Heritage of America*.

A Lou Reda Book.
1996 edition published by Barnes & Noble Books.
by arrangement with Lou Reda Productions.

1996 Barnes & Noble Books

ISBN 1-56619-967-0

Printed and bound in the United States of America.
M 9 8 7 6 5 4 3 2 1
RRDC

Introduction

FEW men realize how much history has been made in America since the first explorers and colonists reached its shores; how broad, how richly multiform, how full of adventure, drama, and color this history has been. Few realize, again, how much of this history has been written by actual participants and observers; how many thousands of racy, vivid, and veracious narratives have been penned by the settlers, the soldiers, the traders, the boatmen, the gold hunters, the fur trappers, the railroad builders, the merchants, the educators, the preachers, the politicians. The writers of such narratives range from Presidents to pioneers, from millionaires to mule drivers, from admirals to aviators. In general usage the connotation of the word history tends always to become too formal, and many men tend to think of it too much as a subject connected with the dusty library and the full-dress treatise. That is an error which cannot be too often corrected. History is not a matter of libraries but of life; the best of it is not stiffly secondhand, but is matter pulsing with the hopes and despairs, the ardors and endurances, the joys and sorrows of plain people everywhere. The editors of this volume hope that it will do something to demonstrate this fact. They hope that it will contribute to an understanding of the variety, the vitality, and the absorbing interest of that immense part of our historical literature which has come from the pens of the men and women who helped to make history.

From the great treasure house of firsthand narratives of American life many volumes like this might be selected. Our book is meant to be but a sampling of the feast that lies spread for all who will come to partake of it. We hope that many who are within reach of books will be led by these pages to explore further for themselves. For those others who do not find large libraries available, we hope this book will serve a special purpose, for it will supply typical extracts from a large body of writers, some of whom are not easily found. We make no claim that this is the best possible collection. No collection can be "best" for any but a limited group. We offer it merely as a catholic and fairly comprehensive garner, representative of what we ourselves have found most illuminating and delightful, and in our opinion adapted to seize the interest and awaken the imagination of a large body of readers. In choosing selections we have applied various touchstones. But the principal test, beyond our insistence upon a reasonable accuracy and authenticity, has always been that of broad human interest. The volume is not for the specialist, and does not fall into or even touch that category of "collected documents" or "source books" of which large numbers already exist. At the same time, we hope that it will afford instruction to students as well as pleasure to general readers.

No collection of personal narratives, no matter how extensive, can ever form a really connected history of America. Many personal narratives present a tangential interest. Dealing with a more or less unique experience, they lie somewhat apart from the general stream of affairs, or traverse it at an angle. But we have tried hard to give this book as much coherence and integration as possible. We have divided it into sections, each representing a different phase or era of American life; and within each section we have tried to place a group of narratives that have some relation to each other, and that taken together really give some conception of this phase or era. Enough editorial matter has been supplied to form a background, and to offer a measure of continuity. We believe that the book can be read from beginning to end without any sense of undue roughness, any consciousness of glaring gaps; and that is surely sufficient. Had we increased the amount of editorial matter, we would have found ourselves writing another general history of America, and there are assuredly enough general histories of an elementary nature already.

Our guiding rule in dealing with the text of these narratives has been to serve the general reader and the ordinary student, not to minister to the pedant. We have tried to insist upon verbal accuracy. We have made spelling and punctuation conform to modern usage, however, and we have omitted ellipsis marks in the interest of readability. At the end of the volume we offer a full bibliography, so that those who wish to obtain the text of any selection in its original form may do so. To the many publishers and authors who have cordially co-operated with us, and whose favors are specifically acknowledged elsewhere in this book, we desire here to express our warm gratitude. We of course wish it understood that none of the views expressed by the various writers included in the volume is necessarily our own; indeed, we have tried to obtain a wide variety of views, by no means excluding some of an extreme or eccentric character.

We gratefully acknowledge the services of Miss Margaret Carroll in helping to select and prepare for the press the contents of this volume.

HENRY STEELE COMMAGER
ALLAN NEVINS

New York City,

Contents

IV · White Men and Red

V · The Struggle for the Continent

VI · The Coming of the Revolution

VII · The Winning of Independence

VIII · Confederation and Constitution

IX · Launching the New Government

X · The War of 1812

XI · The Hardy Frontiersman

XII · New Settlements in the Wilderness

XIII · Sailing and Whaling

XIV · Steamboat Days

XV · Social Life in the Early Republic

XVI · Man the Reformer

XVII · The South and Slavery

XVIII · Abolition and Fugitive Slaves

XIX · Westward the Course of Empire

XX · The Mining Kingdom

XXI · Texas and the Mexican War

XXII · Politics

XXVI · Reconstruction

XXVII · The Last West

XXVIII · The Rise of the City

XXIX · School and Society

XXX · Business and Labor

XXXI · Cuba Libre

XXXII · *The Progressive Era*

XXXIII · *Modern Politics*

XXXIV · *The World War*

XXXV · From Normalcy to New Deal

XXXVI · The Second World War

I

Opening Up the Continent

1. Leif Ericson Sails to Vineland

Columbus' voyages were not the first made to the American continents. In a geographical sense Greenland is part of America, and the Northmen began colonizing Greenland in the tenth century. Moreover, a true pre-Columbian discovery of the great mainland occurred in the year 1000 A.D. That summer Leif, the son of Eric the Red, set out from Greenland with thirty-five men to examine the lands to the south. "He was a large man and strong," says the saga, "of noble aspect, prudent and moderate in all things." He sailed south till he reached a bleak, stony land which was probably Labrador or northern Newfoundland; then on to a wooded coast which seems to have been Cape Breton Island or Nova Scotia, and which he called Markland; and then still farther south to a country — Vineland — so pleasant, warm, and full of fish that he resolved to spend the winter in it. His brother Thorvald made a voyage later in his track, while a wealthy Icelander directed an unsuccessful attempt to establish a colony in Vineland. The ships of the Northmen were probably stauncher and safer, and were certainly faster, than those of Columbus; but the Northmen lacked the geographical knowledge that would have enabled them to make real use of their discoveries, while Europe in the year 1000 had not reached a stage of progress which made the settling of America possible.

THERE was now much talk about voyages of discovery. Leif, the son of Eric the Red, of Brattahild, went to Biarni Heriulfson, and bought the ship of him, and engaged men for it, so that there were thirty-five men in all. Leif asked his father Eric to be the leader on the voyage, but Eric excused himself, saying that he was now pretty well stricken in years, and could not now, as formerly, hold out all the hardships of the sea. Leif said that still he was the one of the family whom good fortune would soonest attend, and Eric gave in to Leif's request, and rode from home so soon as they were ready, and it was but a short way to the ship. The horse stumbled that Eric rode, and he fell off and bruised his foot. Then said Eric, "It is not ordained that I should discover more countries than that which we now inhabit, and we should make no further attempt in company." Eric went home to Brattahild, but Leif repaired to the ship, and his comrades with him, thirty-five men. There was a German on the voyage who was named Tyrker.

Now prepared they their ship, and sailed out into the sea when they were ready, and then found that land first which Biarni had found last. There sailed they to the land, and cast anchor, and put off boats and went ashore, and saw there no grass. Great icebergs were over all the up country, but like a plain of flat stones was all from the sea to the mountains, and it appeared to them that this land had no good qualities. . . .

Then went they on board, and after that sailed out to sea, and found another land. They sailed again to the land and cast anchor, then put off boats and went on shore. This land was flat and covered with wood, and white sands were far around where they went, and the shore was low. Then said Leif: "This land shall be named after its qualities, and called Markland [woodland]." They then immediately returned to the ship.

Now sailed they thence into the open sea with a northeast wind, and were two days at sea before they saw land, and they sailed thither and came to an island which lay to the eastward of the land, and went up there and looked round them in good weather, and observed that there was dew upon the grass. And it so happened that they touched the dew with their hands, and raised the fingers to the mouth, and they thought that they had never before tasted anything so sweet.

After that they went to the ship and sailed into a sound which lay between the island and a promontory which ran out to the eastward of the land, and then steered westward past the promontory. It was very shallow at ebb tide, and their ship stood up so that it was far to see from the ship to the water. But so much did they desire to land that they did not give themselves time to wait until the water again rose under their ship, but ran at once on shore at a place where a river flows out of a lake. But so soon as the waters rose up under

the ship, then took they boats, and rowed to the ship, and floated it
up the river, and thence into the lake, and there cast anchor, and
brought up from the ship their skin cots, and made there booths.

After this they took counsel and formed the resolution of remaining
there for the winter, and built there large houses. There was no want
of salmon either in the river or in the lake, and larger salmon than
they had before seen. The nature of the country was, as they thought,
so good that cattle would not require house feeding in winter, for
there came no frost in winter, and little did the grass wither there.
Day and night were more equal than in Greenland or Iceland, for
on the shortest day the sun was above the horizon from half past
seven in the forenoon till half past four in the afternoon. . . .

It happened one evening that a man of the party was missing, and
this was Tyrker the German. This Leif took much to heart, for
Tyrker had been long with his father and him, and loved Leif much
in his childhood. Leif now took his people severely to task, and prepared to seek for Tyrker, and took twelve men with him. But when
they had got a short way from the house, then came Tyrker towards
them and was joyfully received. Leif soon saw that his foster father
was not in his right senses. . . . Then said Leif to him: "Why were
thou so late, my fosterer, and separated from the party?" He now
spoke first for a long time in German, and rolled his eyes about to
different sides, and twisted his mouth, but they did not understand
what he said. After a time he spoke Norsk. "I have not been much
farther off, but still I have something new to tell of; I found vines
and grapes." "But is that true, my fosterer?" quoth Leif. "Surely is
it true," replied he, "for I was bred up in a land where there is no
want of either vines or grapes."

They slept for the night, but in the morning Leif said to his
sailors: "We will now set about two things, in that the one day we
gather grapes, and the other day cut vines and fell trees, so from
thence will be a loading for my ship." And that was the counsel
taken, and it is said their longboat was filled with grapes. Now was
a cargo cut down for the ship, and when the spring came they got
ready and sailed away; and Leif gave the land a name after its
qualities, and called it Vineland.

They sailed now into the open sea, and had a fair wind until they
saw Greenland, and the mountains below the glaciers. . . .

Now there was much talk about Leif's voyage to Vineland; and Thorvald, his brother, thought that the land had been much too little explored. Then said Leif to Thorvald: "Thou canst go with my ship, brother, if thou wilt, to Vineland, but I wish first that the ship should go and fetch the timber which Thorer had upon the rock." And so it was done.

Now Thorvald made ready for this voyage with thirty men, and took counsel thereon with Leif, his brother. Then made they their ship ready, and put to sea . . . until they came to Leif's booths in Vineland. There they laid up their ship, and spent a pleasant winter, and caught fish for their support.

But in the spring, said Thorvald, they should make ready the ship, and some of the men should take the ship's longboat round the western part of the land, and explore there during the summer. To them the land appeared fair and woody, and but a short distance between the wood and the sea, and white sands; there were many islands and much shallow water. They found neither dwellings of men or beasts, except upon an island to the westward, where they found a corn shed of wood, but many works of men they found not. And they then went back and came to Leif's booths in the autumn.

Voyages of the Northmen to America

2. Christopher Columbus Discovers America

No one knows what Columbus expected or wished to find when he set out on his immortal voyage. We do know that he was obsessed by the idea that the world was round, and that by sailing west he could reach the East. But did he expect to find old lands or new? Did he hope to find a shorter route to Oriental goods and spices, or vast populations to convert to Christianity, or new domains to be governed by Spain? At any rate, the Spanish sovereigns gave him a letter to the Grand Khan, and he returned from his first voyage reporting that he had reached Cipango or Japan and the Spice Islands. Columbus remains a shadowy per-

sonality; his birth, training, and ambitions all the subject of violent controversy. But it is certain that he was dominated by the sense of a high mission, and in character and intellect had many elements of greatness. With ninety men, his three frail vessels left Palos before sunrise on August 3, 1492. Refitting at the Canaries, they did not sail again until September 6. As the voyage lengthened the temper of the sailors grew more dangerous, and it was fortunate for Columbus that early in October signs of land thickened.

WEDNESDAY, 10th of October. — The course was west-south-west, and they went at the rate of ten miles an hour, occasionally twelve miles, and sometimes seven. During the day and night they made fifty-nine leagues, counted as no more than forty-four. Here the people could endure no longer. They complained of the length of the voyage. But the Admiral cheered them up in the best way he could, giving them good hopes of the advantages they might gain from it. He added that, however much they might complain, he had to go to the Indies, and that he would go on until he found them, with the help of our Lord.

Thursday, 11th of October. — The course was west-southwest, and there was more sea than there had been during the whole of the voyage. They saw sandpipers, and a green reed near the ship. Those of the caravel *Pinta* saw a cane and a pole, and they took up another small pole which appeared to have been worked with iron; also another bit of cane, a land plant, and a small board. The crew of the caravel *Niña* also saw signs of land, and a small branch covered with berries. Everyone breathed afresh and rejoiced at these signs. The run until sunset was twenty-six leagues.

After sunset the Admiral returned to his original west course, and they went along at the rate of twelve miles an hour. Up to two hours after midnight they had gone ninety miles, equal to twenty-two and a half leagues. As the caravel *Pinta* was a better sailer, and went ahead of the Admiral, she found the land, and made the signals ordered by the Admiral. The land was first seen by a sailor named Rodrigo de Triana. But the Admiral, at ten in the previous night, being on the castle of the poop, saw a light, though it was so uncertain that he could not affirm it was land. He called Pedro

Gutierrez, a gentleman of the King's bedchamber, and said that there seemed to be a light, and that he should look at it. He did so, and saw it. The Admiral said the same to Rodrigo Sanchez of Segovia, whom the King and Queen had sent with the fleet as inspector, but he could see nothing, because he was not in a place whence anything could be seen. After the Admiral had spoken he saw the light once or twice, and it was like a wax candle rising and falling. It seemed to few to be an indication of land, but the Admiral made certain that land was close. When they said the *Salve,* which all the sailors were accustomed to sing in their way, the Admiral asked and admonished the men to keep a good lookout on the forecastle, and to watch well for land; and to him who should first cry out that he saw land, he would give a silk doublet, besides the other rewards promised by the sovereigns, which were ten thousand maravedis to him who should first see it. At two hours after midnight the land was sighted at a distance of two leagues. They shortened sail, and lay by under the mainsail without the bonnets.

Friday, 12th of October. — The vessels were hove to, waiting for daylight; and on Friday they arrived at a small island of the Lucayos, called, in the language of the Indians, Guanahani [Watling Island; named San Salvador by Columbus]. Presently they saw naked people. The Admiral went on shore in the armed boat, and Martin Alonso Pinzon, and Vicente Yañez, his brother, who was captain of the *Niña.* The Admiral took the royal standard, and the captains went with two banners of the green cross, which the Admiral took in all the ships as a sign, with an F and a Y [Fernando and Ysabel] and a crown over each letter, one on one side of the cross and the other on the other. Having landed, they saw trees very green, and much water, and fruits of diverse kinds. The Admiral called to the two captains, and to the others who leaped on shore, and said that they should bear faithful testimony that he, in presence of all, had taken, as he now took, possession of the said island for the King and for the Queen, his lords, making the declarations that are required, as is more largely set forth in the testimonies which were then made in writing.

Presently many inhabitants of the island assembled. What follows is in the actual words of the Admiral in his book of the first navigation and discovery of the Indies. "I," he says, "that we might form great friendship, for I knew that they were a people who could be more easily freed and converted to our holy faith by love than by force, gave to some of them red caps, and glass beads to put round their necks, and many other things of little value, which gave them great pleasure, and made them so much our friends that it was a marvel to see. They afterwards came to the ship's boats where we were, swimming and bringing us parrots, cotton threads in skeins, darts, and many other things; and we exchanged them for other things that we gave them, such as glass beads and small bells. In fine, they took all, and gave what they had with good will. It appeared to me to be a race of people very poor in everything. They go as naked as when their mothers bore them, and so do the women, although I did not see more than one young girl. All I saw were youths, none more than thirty years of age. They are very well made, with very handsome bodies, and very good countenances. Their hair is short and coarse, almost like the hairs of a horse's tail. They wear the hairs brought down to the eyebrows, except a few locks behind, which they wear long and never cut. They paint themselves black, and they are the color of the Canarians, neither black nor white. Some paint themselves white, others red, and others of what color they find. Some paint their faces, others the whole body, some only round the eyes, others only on the nose. They neither carry nor know anything of arms, for I showed them swords, and they took them by the blade and cut themselves through ignorance. They have no iron, their darts being wands without iron, some of them having a fish's tooth at the end, and others being pointed in various ways. They are all of fair stature and size, with good faces, and well made. I saw some with marks of wounds on their bodies, and I made signs to ask what it was, and they gave me to understand that people from other adjacent islands came with the intention of seizing them, and that they defended themselves. I believed, and still believe, that they come here from the mainland to take them prisoners. They should be good servants and intelligent, for I observed that they quickly took in what was said to them, and I believe that they would easily be made Christians, as it appeared to me that they had no religion. I, our Lord being pleased, will take hence, at the time of my departure, six natives for your Highnesses, that they may learn to speak. I saw no beast of any kind, except parrots, on this island." The above is in the words of the Admiral.

Journal of Christopher Columbus

3. De Soto Finds the Mississippi and Is Buried beneath It

Hernando de Soto had served with Pizarro in the conquest of Peru and the looting of its incredible riches. Returning home, he was able in 1537 to obtain the royal appointment as Governor of Cuba, with authority to conquer all the unknown lands north of the Gulf of Mexico. Nobody but Pánfilo de Narváez had made a serious attempt to penetrate these lands, and De Narváez, setting forth in 1528, had lost his life and those of all but four of his four hundred followers. De Soto talked with one of these four survivors, Cabeza de Vaca, before he left Spain. He believed there must be kingdoms to conquer in the vast unknown expanse, and was especially excited by De Vaca's gossip about the Seven Cities. In the spring of 1539 he gathered at Havana nine vessels and 570 men. A little later he was fighting his way through the hostile tribesmen of the Creek Confederacy in what is now Alabama. In December, 1541, he reached the Yazoo, and there spent the winter. When spring came in 1542 he and his men crossed the Mississippi and wandered northward as far as present-day Missouri, looking in vain for El Dorado. Then they turned disconsolately southward again.

THREE days having gone by since some maize had been sought after, and but little found in comparison with the great want there was of it, the Governor became obliged to move at once, notwithstanding the wounded had need of repose, to where there should be abundance. He accordingly set out for Quizquiz, and marched seven days through a wilderness having many pondy places, with thick forests, all fordable, however, on horseback, except some basins or lakes that were swum. He arrived at a town of Quizquiz without being descried, and seized all the people before they could come out of their houses. Among them was the mother of the cacique;

and the Governor sent word to him, by one of the captives, to come and receive her, with the rest he had taken. The answer he returned was that if his lordship would order them to be loosed and sent, he would come to visit and do him service.

The Governor, since his men arrived weary and likewise weak for want of maize, and the horses were also lean, determined to yield to the requirement and try to have peace; so the mother and the rest were ordered to be set free, and with words of kindness were dismissed. The next day, while he was hoping to see the chief, many Indians came with bows and arrows to set upon the Christians, when he commanded that all the armed horsemen should be mounted and in readiness. Finding them prepared, the Indians stopped at the distance of a crossbowshot from where the Governor was, near a river bank, where, after remaining quietly half an hour, six chiefs arrived at the camp, stating that they had come to find out what people it might be, for that they had knowledge from their ancestors that they were to be subdued by a white race; they consequently desired to return to the cacique to tell him that he should come presently to obey and serve the Governor. After presenting six or seven skins and shawls brought with them, they took their leave and returned with the others who were waiting for them by the shore. The cacique came not, nor sent another message.

There was little maize in the place, and the Governor moved to another town, half a league from the great river [the Mississippi], where it was found in sufficiency. He went to look at the river, and saw that near it there was much timber of which piraguas might be made, and a good situation in which the camp might be placed. He directly moved, built houses, and settled on a plain a crossbowshot from the water, bringing together there all the maize of the towns behind, that at once they might go to work and cut down trees for sawing out planks to build barges. . . .

The next day the cacique arrived, with two hundred canoes filled with men having weapons. They were painted with ocher, wearing great bunches of white and other plumes of many colors, having feathered shields in their hands, with which they sheltered the oarsmen on either side, the warriors standing erect from bow to stern, holding bows and arrows. The barge in which the cacique came had an awning at the poop under which he sat; and the like had the barges of the other chiefs; and there, from under the canopy where the chief man was, the course was directed and orders issued to the rest. All came down together and arrived within a stone's cast of the ravine, where the cacique said that he had come to visit, serve, and obey him, for he had heard that he was the greatest of lords, the most powerful on all the earth and that he must see what he would have him do. The Governor expressed his pleasure, and besought him to land that they might the better confer; but the chief gave no reply, ordering three barges to draw near, wherein was great quantity of fish, and loaves like bricks, made of the pulp of plums, which De Soto receiving, gave him thanks and again entreated him to land.

Making the gift had been a pretext to discover if any harm might be done, but finding the Governor and his people on their guard, the cacique began to draw off from the shore, when the crossbowmen who were in readiness, with loud cries, shot at the Indians, and struck down five or six of them. They retired with great order, not one leaving the oar, even though the one next to him might have fallen, and covering themselves, they withdrew. Afterwards they came many times and landed; when approached, they would go back to their barges. These were fine-looking men, very large and well formed; and what with the awnings, the plumes, and the shields, the pennons, and the number of people in the fleet, it appeared like a famous armada of galleys.

During the thirty days that were passed there, four piraguas were built, into three of which, one morning, three hours before daybreak, the Governor ordered twelve cavalry to enter — four in · each — men in whom he had confidence that they would gain the land notwithstanding the Indians, and secure the passage, or die; he also sent some crossbowmen on foot with them, and in the other piragua oarsmen to take them to the opposite shore.

So soon as they had come to shore the piraguas returned; and when the sun was up two hours high, the people had all got over. The distance was near half a league; a man standing on the shore could not be told, whether he were a man or something else, from the other side. The stream was swift and very deep; the water, always flowing turbidly, brought along from above many trees and much timber, driven onward by its force. There were many fish of several sorts, the greater part differing from those of the fresh waters of Spain.

The Governor, conscious that the hour approached in which he should depart this life, commanded that all the King's officers should be called before him, the captains and the principal personages, to whom he made a speech. He said that he was about to go into the presence of God, to give account of all his past life. To prevent any divisions that might arise as to who should command, he asked that they be pleased to elect a principal and able person to be governor, one with whom they should all be satisfied, and, being chosen, they would swear before him to obey; that this would greatly satisfy him, abate somewhat the pains he suffered, and moderate the anxiety of leaving them in a country they knew not where.

Baltasar de Gallegos responded in behalf of all. Thereupon the Governor nominated Luys Moscoso de Alvarado to be his captain general; when by all those present was he straightway chosen and sworn Governor.

The next day, the 21st of May, departed this life the magnanimous, the virtuous, the intrepid captain, Don Hernando de Soto, Governor of Cuba and Adelantado of Florida. He was advanced by fortune in the way she is wont to lead others, that he might fall the greater depth; he died in a land, and at a time, that could afford him little comfort in his illness. . . . Luys de Moscoso determined to conceal what had happened from the Indians, for De Soto had given them to understand that the Christians were immortal; besides, they held him to be vigilant, sagacious, brave; and, although they were at peace, should they know him to be dead, they, being of their nature inconstant, might venture on making an attack. And they were credulous of all that he had told them, for he made them believe that some things which went on among them privately he had discovered without their being able to see how, or by what means; and that the figure which appeared in a mirror he showed, told him whatsoever they might be about, or desired to do; whence neither by word nor deed did they dare undertake anything to his injury.

So soon as the death had taken place, Luys de Moscoso directed the body to be put secretly into a house, where it remained three days; and thence it was taken at night, by his order, to a gate of the town, and buried within. The Indians who had seen him ill, finding him no longer, suspected the reason; and passing by where he lay, they observed the ground loose, and, looking about, talked among themselves. This coming to the knowledge of Luys de Moscoso, he ordered the corpse to be taken up at night, and among the shawls that enshrouded it having cast abundance of sand, it was taken out in a canoe and committed to the middle of the stream. The cacique of Guachoya asked for him, saying: "What has been done with my brother and lord, the Governor?" Luys de Moscoso told him that he had ascended into the skies, as he had done on many other occasions, but as he would have to be detained there some time, he had left him in his stead. The chief, thinking within himself that he was dead, ordered two well-proportioned young men to be brought, saying that it was the usage of the country when any lord died to kill some persons, who should accompany and serve him on the way, on which account they were brought; and he told him to command their heads to be struck off that they might go accordingly to attend his friend and master. Luys de Moscoso replied to him that the Governor was not dead, but only gone into the heavens, having taken with him of his soldiers sufficient number for his need.

Narrative of the Expedition of Hernando de Soto
by the Gentleman of Elvas

4. Marquette and Joliet Float down the Mississippi

As De Soto represented the southern incursion into what is now the United States, so Marquette represented the incursion from the north. He was, of course, not the first great French explorer of North America. Cartier, Champlain, and Jean Nicolet had all preceded him. But he, La Salle, and Joliet were the first to push past the hostile Iroquois and penetrate to the very heart of present-day America; they were the men who laid the foundation of French hopes of a great empire in the Mississippi Valley. Father Jacques Marquette, who was not quite thirty when he reached Canada in 1666 as a Jesuit missionary, was sent two years later to the upper lakes of the St. Lawrence. Then in 1673 he was chosen with Joliet to explore the Mississippi, of which stories had reached the French from the prairie tribes. The two heroic men descended the river as far as the mouth of the Arkansas before they turned back.

ON THE 17th day of May, 1673, we started from the mission of St. Ignatius at Michilimakinac, where I then was. The joy that we felt at being selected for this expedition animated our courage and rendered the labor of paddling from morning to night agreeable to us. And because we were going to seek unknown countries, we took every precaution in our power, so that, if our undertaking were hazardous, it should not be foolhardy. To that end we obtained all the information that we could from the savages who had frequented those regions; and we even traced out from their reports a map of the whole of that new country; on it we indicated the rivers which we were to navigate, the names of the people and of the places through which we were to pass, the course of the great river, and the direction we were to follow when we reached it.

With all these precautions, we joyfully plied our paddles on a portion of Lake Huron, on that of the Illinois, and on the Bay des Puants.

The first nation that we came to was that of the Folle Avoine [Menominee]. I entered their river to go and visit these peoples to whom we have preached the Gospel for several years — in consequence of which, there are several good Christians among them.

I told these people of the Folle Avoine of my design to go and discover those remote nations, in order to teach them the mysteries of our holy religion. They were greatly surprised to hear it, and did their best to dissuade me. They represented to me that I would meet nations who never show mercy to strangers, but break their heads without any cause; and that war was kindled between various peoples who dwelt upon our route, which exposed us to the further manifest danger of being killed by the bands of warriors who are ever in the field. They also said that the great river was very dangerous, when one does not know the difficult places; that it was full of horrible monsters, which devoured men and canoes together; that there was even a demon, who was heard from a great distance, who barred the way and swallowed up all who ventured to approach him; finally, that the heat was so excessive in those countries that it would inevitably cause our death.

I thanked them for the good advice that they gave me, but told them that I could not follow it, because the salvation of souls was at stake, for which I would be delighted to give my life; that I scoffed at the alleged demon; that we would easily defend ourselves against those marine monsters; and, moreover, that we would be on our guard to avoid the other dangers with which they threatened us. After making them pray to God, and giving them some instruction, I separated from them.

Here we are at Maskoutens. This word may, in Algonquin, mean "the Fire Nation" — which, indeed, is the name given to this tribe. Here is the limit of the discoveries which the French have made, for they have not yet gone any farther. . . .

No sooner had we arrived than we, Monsieur Joliet and I, assembled the elders together; and he told them that he was sent by Monsieur our Governor to discover new countries, while I was sent by God to illumine them with the light of the holy Gospel. He told them that, moreover, the Sovereign Master of our lives wished to be known by all the nations; and that in obeying His will I feared not the death to which I exposed myself in voyages so perilous. He informed them that we needed two guides to show us the way; and we gave them a present, by it asking them to grant us the guides. To this they very civilly consented; and they also spoke to us by means of a present, consisting of a mat to serve us as a bed during the whole of our voyage.

On the following day, the 10th of June, two Miamis who were given us as guides embarked with us, in the sight of a great crowd, who could not sufficiently express their astonishment at the sight of seven Frenchmen, alone and in two canoes, daring to undertake so extraordinary and so hazardous an expedition.

We knew that, at three leagues from Maskoutens, was a river which discharged into the Mississippi. We knew also that the direction we were to follow in order to reach it was west-southwesterly. But the road is broken by so many swamps and small lakes that it is easy to lose one's way, especially as the river leading thither is so full of wild oats that it is difficult to find the channel. For this reason we greatly needed our two guides, who safely conducted us to a portage of twenty-seven hundred paces, and helped us to transport our canoes to enter that river, after which they returned home, leaving us alone in this unknown country, in the hands of Providence.

Thus we left the waters flowing to Quebec, four or five hundred leagues from here, to float on those that would thenceforward take us through strange lands.

The river on which we embarked is called Wisconsin. It is very wide; it has a sandy bottom, which forms various shoals that render its navigation very difficult. It is full of islands covered with vines. On the banks one sees fertile land, diversified with woods, prairies, and hills. There are oak, walnut, and basswood trees, and another kind whose branches are armed with long thorns. We saw there neither feathered game nor fish, but many deer, and a large number of cattle. Our route lay to the southwest, and after navigating about thirty leagues we saw a spot presenting all the appearances of an iron mine; and, in fact, one of our party who had formerly seen such mines assures us that the one which we found is very good and very rich. It is covered with three feet of good soil and is quite near a chain of rocks, the base of which is covered by very fine trees. After proceeding forty leagues on this same route, we arrived at the mouth of our river; and, at forty-two and a half degrees of latitude, we safely entered the Mississippi on the 17th of June, with a joy that I cannot express.

Here we are then, on this so renowned river, all of whose peculiar features I have endeavored to note carefully. The Mississippi takes its rise in various lakes in the country of the northern nations. It is narrow at the place where Miskous [the Wisconsin] empties; its current, which flows southward, is slow and gentle. To the right is a large chain of very high mountains, and to the left are beautiful lands; in various places the stream is divided by islands. From time to time, we came upon monstrous fish, one of which struck our canoe with such violence that I thought that it was a great tree about to break the canoe to pieces. On another occasion, we saw on the water a monster with the head of a tiger, a sharp nose like that of a wildcat, with whiskers and straight, erect ears; the head was gray and the neck quite black; but we saw no more creatures of this sort. When we cast our nets into the water we caught sturgeon, and a very extraordinary kind of fish. It resembles the trout, with this difference, that its mouth is larger. Near its nose — which is smaller, as are also the eyes — is a large bone, shaped like a woman's busk, three fingers wide and a cubit long, at the end of which is a disk as wide as one's hand. This frequently causes it to fall backward when it leaps out of the water. When we reached the parallel of forty-one degrees, twenty-eight minutes, following the same direction, we found that turkeys had taken the place of game; and the pisikious, or wild cattle [buffalo], that of the other animals.

We continued to advance, but, as we knew not whither we were going — for we had proceeded over one hundred leagues without discovering anything except animals and birds — we kept well on our guard. On this account, we make only a small fire on land, toward evening, to cook our meals; and, after supper, we remove ourselves as far from it as possible, and pass the night in our canoes, which we anchor in the river at some distance from the shore. This does not prevent us from always posting one of the party as a sentinel for fear of a surprise. Proceeding still in a southerly and south-southwesterly direction, we find ourselves at the parallel of forty-one degrees, and as low as forty degrees and some minutes — partly southeast and partly southwest — after having advanced over sixty leagues since we entered the river, without discovering anything.

Finally on the 25th of June we perceived on the water's edge some tracks of men, and a narrow and somewhat beaten path leading to a fine prairie. We stopped to examine it; and, thinking that it was a road which led to some village of savages, we resolved to go and reconnoiter it. We therefore left our two canoes under the guard of our people, strictly charging them not to allow themselves to be surprised, after which Monsieur Joliet and I undertook this investigation — a rather hazardous one for two men who exposed themselves alone to the mercy of a barbarous and unknown people. We silently followed the narrow path, and, after walking about two leagues, we discovered a village on the bank of a river, and two others on a hill distant about half a league from the first. Then we heartily commended ourselves to God, and, after imploring His aid, we went farther without being perceived, and approached so near that we could even hear the savages talking. We therefore decided that it was time to reveal ourselves. This we did by shouting with all our energy, and stopped without advancing any farther. On hearing the shout, the savages quickly issued from their cabins, and having probably recognized us as Frenchmen, especially when they saw a black gown — or, at least, having no cause for distrust, as we were only two men, and had given them notice of our arrival — they deputed four old men to come and speak to us. Two of these bore tobacco pipes, finely ornamented and adorned with various feathers. They walked slowly, and raised their pipes toward the sun, seemingly offering them to it to smoke — without, however, saying a word. They spent a rather long time in covering the short distance between their village and us. Finally, when they had drawn near, they stopped to consider us attentively. I was reassured when I observed these ceremonies, which with them are performed only among friends; and much more so when I saw them clad in cloth, for I judged thereby that they were our allies. I therefore spoke to them first, and asked who they were. They replied that they were Illinois; and, as a token of peace, they offered us their pipes to smoke. They afterward invited us to enter their village, where all the people impatiently awaited us.

The Jesuit Relations, Vol. LIX

II

Planting Colonies in the New World

5. John Smith Founds Jamestown and Is Saved by Pocahontas

The nation that was to give its language and civilization to most of North America planted its first permanent settlement in Virginia under a company of gentlemen and merchants, the Virginia Company, which John Smith claimed to have been largely instrumental in promoting. He was a figure worthy of the English race which found in him its first great American representative: intrepid before danger, stubbornly indomitable under hardship, resourceful in emergencies, full of energy, zest, and enterprise. As 1606 drew to a close he and 143 other colonists sailed from London with their orders sealed in a box; the following May they disembarked 105 strong at Jamestown. Smith was one of the council of seven appointed to administer the colony during its first year, and was worth all the others put together. Some of his stories may have grown in the telling, though even the Pocahontas episode has no inherent improbability; but that his exertions in getting food from the Indians saved the starving settlers, that his other measures showed admirable judgment, there can be no doubt. His brief career in Virginia was not more important than the contributions he made toward the founding of New England, but it is so spectacular that the American imagination has never tired of dwelling upon it.

I

AFTER many crosses in The Downs by tempests, we arrived safely upon the southwest part of the great Canaries; within four or five days after we set sail for Dominica, the 26th of April [1607]. The first land we made, we fell with Cape Henry, the very mouth of the Bay of Chesapeake, which at that present we little expected, having by a cruel storm been put to the northward. Anchoring in this bay, twenty or thirty went ashore with the Captain, and in coming aboard they were assaulted with certain Indians which charged them within pistolshot, in which conflict Captain Archer and Mathew Morton were shot. Whereupon Captain Newport, seconding them, made a shot at them which the Indians little respected, but having spent their arrows retired without harm. And in that place was the box opened wherein the Council for Virginia was nominated. And arriving at the place where we are now seated, the Council was sworn and the president elected . . . where was made choice for our situation a very fit place for the erecting of a great city. All our provision was brought ashore, and with as much speed as might be we went about our fortification. . . .

Captain Newport, having set things in order, set sail for England the 22d of June, leaving provision for thirteen or fourteen weeks. The day before the ship's departure, the king of Pamaunkee sent the Indian that had met us before, in our discovery, to assure us of peace. Our fort being then palisaded round, and all our men in good health and comfort, albeit that through some discontented humors it did not so long continue. God (being angry with us) plagued us with such famine and sickness that the living were scarce able to bury the dead — our want of sufficient and good victuals, with continual watching, four or five each night at three bulwarks, being the chief cause. Only of sturgeon had we great store, whereon our men would so greedily surfeit as it cost many lives. . . . Shortly after it pleased God, in our extremity, to move the Indians to bring us corn, ere it was half ripe, to refresh us when we rather expected they would destroy us. About the 10th of September there were about forty-six of our men dead. . . .

Our provisions being now within twenty days spent, the Indians brought us great store both of corn and bread ready-made, and also there came such abundance of fowls into the rivers as greatly refreshed our weak estates, whereupon many of our weak men were presently able to go abroad. As yet we had no houses to cover us, our tents were rotten, and our cabins worse than nought. Our best commodity was iron, which we made into little chisels. The president and Captain Martin's sickness constrained me to be cape merchant, and yet to spare no pains in making houses for the company, who, notwithstanding our misery, little ceased their malice, grudging and muttering.

As at this time most of our chiefest men were either sick or discontented, the rest being in such despair as they would rather starve and rot with idleness than be persuaded to do anything for their own relief without constraint, our victuals being now within eighteen days spent, and the Indian trade decreasing, I was sent to the mouth of the river, to Kegquouhtan and Indian town, to trade for corn and try the river for fish; but our fishing we could not effect by reason of the stormy weather. With fish, oysters, bread, and deer they kindly traded with me and my men.

JOHN SMITH, A True Relation

II

And now [1608], the winter approaching, the rivers became so covered with swans, geese, ducks, and cranes, that we daily feasted with good bread, Virginia peas, pumpkins, and putchamins, fish, fowl, and divers sorts of wild beasts as fat as we could eat them: so that none of our tuftaffety humorists desired to go for England.

But our comedies never endured long without a tragedy; some idle exceptions being muttered against Captain Smith for not discovering the head of Chickahamania River, and taxed by the Council to be too slow in so worthy an attempt. The next voyage he proceeded so far that with much labor by cutting of trees asunder he made his passage; but when his barge could pass no farther, he left her in a broad bay out of danger of shot, commanding none should go ashore till his return: himself with two English and two savages went up higher in a canoe; but he was not long absent but his men went ashore, whose want of government gave both occasion and opportunity to the savages to surprise one George Cassen, whom they slew, and much failed not to have cut off the boat and all the rest.

Smith, little dreaming of that accident, being got to the marshes at the river's head, twenty miles in the desert, had his two men slain, as is supposed, sleeping by the canoe, whilst himself by fowling sought them victual: finding he was beset with 200 savages, two of them he slew, still defending himself with the aid of a savage his guide, whom he bound to his arm with his garters, and used him as a buckler, yet he was shot in his thigh a little, and had many arrows that stuck in his clothes; but no great hurt, till at last they took him prisoner. When this news came to Jamestown, much was their sorrow for his loss, few expecting what ensued.

Six or seven weeks those barbarians kept him prisoner, many strange triumphs and conjurations they made of him, yet he so demeaned himself amongst them, as he not only diverted them from surprising the fort but procured his own liberty, and got himself and his company such estimation amongst them that those savages admired him more than their own Quiyouckosucks.

The manner how they used and delivered him is as follows. . . .

He demanding for their captain, they showed him Opechan-kanough, king of Pamaunkee, to whom he gave a round ivory double compass dial. Much they marveled at the playing of the fly and needle, which they could see so plainly and yet not touch it because of the glass that covered them. But when he demonstrated by that globe-like jewel the roundness of the earth and skies, the sphere of the sun, moon, and stars, and how the sun did chase the night round about the world continually; the greatness of the land and sea, the diversity of nations, variety of complexions, and how we were to them antipodes, and many other such like matters, they all stood as amazed with admiration. Notwithstanding, within an hour after they tied him to a tree, and as many as could stand about him prepared to shoot him: but the king holding up the compass in his hand, they all laid down their bows and arrows, and in a triumphant manner led him to Orapaks, where he was after their manner kindly feasted, and well used.

At last they brought him to Werowocomoco, where was Powhatan, their emperor. Here more than two hundred of those grim courtiers stood wondering at him, as he had been a monster; till Powhatan and his train had put themselves in their greatest braveries. Before a fire upon a seat like a bedstead, he sat covered with a great robe, made of raccoon skins, and all the tails hanging by. On either hand did sit a young wench of sixteen or eighteen years, and along on each side the house, two rows of men, and behind them as many women, with all their heads and shoulders painted red, many of their heads bedecked with the white down of birds, but every one with something, and a great chain of white beads about their necks. At his entrance before the king, all the people gave a great shout. The queen of Appamatuck was appointed to bring him water to wash his hands, and another brought him a bunch of feathers, instead of a towel to dry them. Having feasted him after their best barbarous manner they could, a long consultation was held, but the conclusion was, two great stones were brought before Powhatan: then as many as could laid hands on him, dragged him to them, and thereon laid his head, and being ready with their clubs to beat out his brains, Pocahontas, the king's dearest daughter, when no entreaty could prevail, got his head in her arms, and laid her own upon his to save his from death: whereat the emperor was contented he should live to make him hatchets, and her bells, beads, and copper; for they thought him as well of all occupations as themselves. For the king himself will make his own robes, shoes, bows, arrows, pots; plant, hunt, or do anything so well as the rest.

Two days after, Powhatan having disguised himself in the most fearfulest manner he could, caused Captain Smith to be brought forth to a great house in the woods, and there upon a mat by the fire to be left alone. Not long after, from behind a mat that divided the house was made the most dolefulest noise he ever heard; then Powhatan, more like a devil than a man, with some two hundred more as black as himself, came unto him and told him now they were friends, and presently he should go to Jamestown, to send him two great guns, and a grindstone, for which he would give him the county of Capahowosick, and for ever esteem him as his son Nantaquoud.

JOHN SMITH, The Generall Historie of Virginia

6. The Pilgrims Arrive Safely at Plymouth

The Pilgrims in the Mayflower, *like John Smith's fellow settlers at Jamestown, were the pioneers of a mighty host; and we know now that the two great streams of migration, that to Massachusetts and that to Virginia, were not so unlike as was long supposed. Yet the Pilgrims and the Puritans did have some special characteristics. King James I yearned toward absolute sovereignty. He objected vigorously to the sect of Separatists who denied the supremacy of the crown over church affairs and demanded the right to organize their own congregations under their own ministers, without regard to king or bishop. "I will make them conform," exclaimed James at the Hampton Court conference, "or I will harry them out of the land." Leave the land, the Separatists or Congregationalists of Scrooby did, going first to Holland in 1607–1608, and then in 1617 deciding to found a Puritan state in America. Three years later an advance guard of the Leyden congregation left Delfthaven in the* Speedwell, *to be joined at Southampton by friends from London in the* Mayflower. *But the former boat leaked and it was the* Mayflower *alone that sailed from Plymouth in Devon on September 6, 1620, with about a hundred people aboard. This little handful had a religious fervor, a high-minded idealism, and an iron strength of character which left a clear impress on the nation they helped to found.*

THEIR REMOVAL TO LEYDEN

FOR THESE and some other reasons they removed to Leyden, a fair and beautiful city, and of a sweet situation, but made more famous by the university wherewith it is adorned, in which of late had been so many learned men. But wanting that traffic by sea which Amsterdam enjoys, it was not so beneficial for their outward means of living and estates. But being now here pitched they fell to such trades and employments as they best could, valuing peace and their spiritual comfort above any other riches whatsoever. And at length they came to raise a competent and comfortable living but with hard and continual labor. . . .

SHOWING THE REASONS AND CAUSES OF
THEIR REMOVAL

After they had lived in this city about some eleven or twelve years, and sundry of them were taken away by death and many others began to be well stricken in years, the grave mistress Experience having taught them many things, those prudent governors, with sundry of the sagest members, began both deeply to apprehend their present dangers and wisely to foresee the future and think of timely remedy. In the agitation of their thoughts and much discourse of things hereabout, at length they began to incline to this conclusion, of removal to some other place — not out of any new-fangledness or other such like giddy humor by which men are oftentimes transported to their great hurt and danger, but for sundry weighty and solid reasons, some of the chief of which I will here briefly touch. And first, they saw and found by experience the hardness of the place and country to be such as few in comparison would come to them, and fewer that would bide it out, and continue with them. For many that came to them and many more that desired to be with them could not endure that great labor and hard fare, with other inconveniences which they underwent and were contented with.

Secondly, they saw that though the people generally bore all these difficulties very cheerfully and with a resolute courage, being in the best and strength of their years, yet old age began to steal on many of them (and their great and continual labors, with other crosses and sorrows, hastened it before the time), so as it was not only probably thought, but apparently seen, that within a few years more they would be in danger to scatter, by necessities pressing them, or sink under their burdens, or both.

Thirdly, as necessity was a taskmaster over them, so they were forced to be such, not only to their servants but in a sort to their dearest children; the which as it did not a little wound the tender hearts of many a loving father and mother, so it produced likewise sundry sad and sorrowful effects. But that which was more lamentable, and, of all sorrows, most heavy to be borne, was that many of their children, by these occasions and the great licentiousness of youth in that country, and the manifold temptations of the place, were drawn away by evil examples into extravagant and dangerous courses, getting the reins of their necks and departing from their parents. Some became soldiers, others took upon them far voyages by sea, and others some worse courses, tending to dissoluteness and the danger of their souls, to the great grief of their parents and dishonor of God. So that they saw their posterity would be in danger to degenerate and be corrupted

Lastly (and which was not least), a great hope and inward zeal they had of laying some good foundation, or at least to make some way thereunto, for the propagating and advancing the gospel of the kingdom of Christ in those remote parts of the world; yea, though they should be but even as stepping-stones unto others for the performing of so great a work.

The place they had thoughts on was some of those vast and un-peopled countries of America, which are fruitful and fit for habitation, being devoid of all civil inhabitants, where there are only savage and brutish men, which range up and down, little otherwise than the wild beasts of the same. This proposition being made public and coming to the scanning of all, it raised many variable opinions amongst men, and caused many fears and doubts amongst themselves. Some, from their reasons and hopes conceived, labored to stir up and encourage the rest to undertake and prosecute the same; others, again, out of their fears, objected against it and sought to divert from it, alleging many things, and those neither unreasonable nor unprobable, as that it was a great design and subject to many unconceivable perils and dangers; as, besides the casualties of the seas (which none can be freed from) the length of the voyage was such as the weak bodies of women and other persons worn out with age and travel (as many of them were) could never be able to endure. And yet if they should, the miseries of the land which they should be exposed unto would be too hard to be borne, and likely, some or all of them together, to consume and utterly to ruinate them. For there they should be liable to famine, and nakedness, and the want, in a manner, of all things. The change of air, diet, and drinking of water, would infect their bodies with sore sicknesses and grievous diseases. And also those which should escape or overcome these difficulties should yet be in continual danger of the savage people, who are cruel, barbarous, and most treacherous, being most furious in their rage, and merciless where they overcome, not being content only to kill and take away life, but delight to torment men in the most bloody manner that may be, flaying some alive with the shells of fishes, cutting off the members and joints of others by piecemeal, and broiling on the coals, eat the collops of their flesh in their sight whilst they live; with other cruelties horrible to be related. And surely it could not be thought but the very hearing of these things could not but move the very bowels of men to grate within them, and make the weak to quake and tremble. It was further objected that it would require greater sums of money to furnish such a voyage and to fit them with necessaries than their consumed estates would amount to; and yet they must as well look to be seconded with supplies as presently to be transported. Also many precedents of ill success and lamentable miseries befallen others in the like designs were easy to be found, and not forgotten to be alleged; besides their own experience, in their former troubles and hardships in their removal into Holland, and how hard a thing it was for them to live in that strange place, though it was a neighbor country and a civil and rich commonwealth.

It was answered that all great and honorable actions are accompanied with great difficulties, and must be both enterprised and overcome with answerable courages. It was granted the dangers were great but not desperate; the difficulties were many but not invincible. For though there were many of them likely, yet they were not certain; it might be sundry of the things feared might never befall; others, by provident care and the use of good means, might in a great measure be prevented; and all of them, through the help of God, by fortitude and patience, might either be borne or overcome. True it was that such attempts were not to be made and undertaken without good ground and reason, not rashly or lightly, as many have done for curiosity or hope of gain, etc. But their condition was not ordinary; their ends were good and honorable, their calling lawful and urgent; and therefore they might expect the blessing of God in their proceeding. Yea, though they should lose their lives in this action, yet might they have comfort in the same, and their endeavors would be honorable. . . . After many other particular things answered and alleged on both sides, it was fully concluded by the major part to put this design in execution and to prosecute it by the best means they could.

OF THEIR DEPARTURE FROM LEYDEN, WITH THEIR ARRIVAL AT SOUTHAMPTON

At length, after much travel and these debates, all things were got ready and provided. A small ship was bought and fitted in Holland, which was intended as to serve to help to transport them so to stay in the country and attend upon fishing and such other affairs as might be for the good and benefit of the colony when they came there. Another was hired at London, of burden about ninescore, and all other things got in readiness. So, being ready to depart, they had a day of solemn humiliation, their pastor taking his text from Ezra viii, 21. *And there at the river, by Ahava, I proclaimed a fast, that we might humble ourselves before our God, and seek of him a right way for us, and for our children, and for all our substance.* Upon which he spent a good part of the day very profitably, and suitable to their present occasion. The rest of the time was spent in pouring out prayers to the Lord with great fervency mixed with abundance of tears. And the time being come that they must depart, they were accompanied with most of their brethren out of the city unto a town sundry miles off called Delfthaven, where the ship lay ready to receive them. So they left the goodly and pleasant city which had been their resting place near twelve years; but they knew they were pilgrims and looked not much on those things but lifted up their eyes to the heavens, their dearest country, and quieted their spirits. When they came to the place they found the ship and all things ready; and such of their friends as could not come with them followed after them, and sundry also came from Amsterdam, to see them shipped and to take their leave of them. That night was spent with little sleep by the most, but with friendly entertainment and Christian discourse and other real expressions of true Christian love. The next day, the wind being fair, they went aboard, and their friends with them, where truly doleful was the sight of that sad and mournful parting; to see what sighs and sobs and prayers did sound amongst them, what tears did gush from every eye, and pithy speeches pierced each heart, that sundry of the Dutch strangers that stood on the quay as spectators could not refrain from tears. Yet comfortable and sweet it was to see such lively and true expressions of dear and unfeigned love. But the tide (which stays for no man) calling them away that were thus loath to depart, their reverend pastor, falling down on his knees (and they all with him), with watery cheeks commended them with most fervent prayers to the Lord and His blessing. And then with mutual embraces and many tears they took their leaves one of another, which proved to be the last leave to many of them. . . .

Being thus arrived in a good harbor and brought safe to land, they fell upon their knees and blessed the God of Heaven who had brought them over the vast and furious ocean and delivered them from all the perils and miseries thereof, again to set their feet on the firm and stable earth, their proper element.

But here I cannot but stay and make a pause and stand half amazed at this poor people's present condition; and so I think will the reader too, when he well considers the same. Being thus past the vast ocean and a sea of troubles before in their preparation (as may be remembered by that which went before), they had now no friends to welcome them, nor inns to entertain or refresh their weatherbeaten bodies, no houses or much less towns to repair to, to seek for succor. It is recorded in Scripture as a mercy to the apostle and his shipwrecked company, the barbarians showed them no small kindness in refreshing them, but these savage barbarians, when they met with them (as after will appear) were readier to fill their sides full of arrows than otherwise. And for the season, it was winter, and they that know the winters of that country know them to be sharp and violent and subject to cruel and fierce storms, dangerous to travel to known places, much more to search an unknown coast. Besides, what could they see but a hideous and desolate wilderness full of wild beasts and wild men? And what multitudes there might be of them they knew not. If it be said they had a ship to succor them, it is true; but what heard they daily from the master and company but that with speed they should look out a place with their shallop where they would be at some near distance; for the season was such as he would not stir from thence till a safe harbor was discovered by them where they would be and he might go without danger; and that victuals consumed apace but he must and would keep sufficient for themselves and their return. Yea, it was muttered by some that if they got not a place in time they would turn them and their goods ashore and leave them. Let it also be considered what weak hopes of supply and succor they left behind them that might bear up their minds in this sad condition and trials they were under; and they could not but be very small. It is true, indeed, the affections and love of their brethren at Leyden was cordial and entire towards them, but they had little power to help them or themselves; and how the case stood between them and the merchants at their coming away hath already been declared. What could now sustain them but the spirit of God and His grace? May not and ought not the children of these fathers rightly say: *Our fathers were Englishmen which came over this great ocean, and were ready to perish in this wilderness; but they cried unto the Lord, and he heard their voice and looked on their adversity, etc. Let them therefore praise the Lord, because he is good and his mercies endure forever. Yea, let them which have been redeemed of the Lord show how he hath delivered them from the hand of the oppressor. When they wandered in the desert wilderness out of the way, and found no city to dwell in, both hungry and thirsty, their soul was overwhelmed in them. Let them confess before the Lord his loving kindness, and his wonderful works before the sons of men.*

WILLIAM BRADFORD, History of Plimoth Plantation

7. Richard Mather Sails to Cape Cod

After the Pilgrims, came the great Puritan exodus which within twenty years gave New England a population of 26,000 people. It was caused by the rise of the Stuart despotism in England, and ended by its fall — that is, by the meeting of the Long Parliament in 1640 to place sharp curbs upon Charles I. This exodus sent to America not only much the largest European population which either continent had yet received, but a population of remarkable qualities. It was purely and exclusively English; it was profoundly religious; it was deeply attached to the idea of democratic self-government; it was hardy, energetic, highly intelligent, and remarkably prolific. In short, better seed for a new land could not have been found. Typical of their fine qualities and also of their dogmatism was Richard Mather, founder of a famous American family, who went to Brasenose at Oxford, took Anglican orders, turned to Puritanism, and in 1635 sailed from Bristol to Massachusetts, where he became minister of the church at Dorchester.

WE CAME from Warrington on Thursday, April 16 [1635], and came to Bristol on the Thursday following, viz. April 23, and had a very healthful, safe, and prosperous journey all the way, blessed be the name of God for the same, taking but easy journeys because of the children and footmen, displacing one hundred and nineteen or one hundred and twenty miles in seven days. . . .

Nevertheless we went not aboard the ship until Saturday, the 23d of May, so that the time of our staying in Bristol was a month and two days, during all which time we found friendship and courtesy at the hands of divers godly Christians in Bristol. Yet our stay was grievous unto us when we considered how most of this time the winds were easterly and served directly for us. But our ship was not ready, so ill did our owners deal with us.

Going aboard the ship in King Road the 23d of May, we found things very unready, and all on heaps, many goods being not stowed but lying on disordered heaps here and there in the ship. This day there came aboard the ship two of the searchers and viewed a list of all our names, ministered the oath of allegiance to all at full age, viewed our certificates from the ministers in the parishes from whence we came, approved well thereof, and gave us tickets — that is, licenses under their hands and seals, to pass the seas — and cleared the ship, and so departed.

Thursday morning [May 28], the wind serving for us, and our master and all the sailors being come aboard, we set sail and began our sea voyage with glad hearts that God had loosed us from our long stay wherein we had been holden, and with hope and trust that He would graciously guide us to the end of our journey. We were, that set sail together that morning, five ships: three bound for Newfoundland, viz. the *Diligence,* a ship of one hundred and fifty ton; the *Mary,* a small ship of eighty ton, and the *Bess;* and two bound for New England, viz. the *Angel Gabriel* of two hundred and forty ton, the *James* of two hundred and twenty ton.

Monday morning [June 22], the wind serving with a strong gale at east, we set sail from Milford Haven where we had waited for wind twelve days, and were carried forth with speedy course, and about noon lost all sight of land. The wind being strong, the sea was rough this day, and most of our passengers were very sick and ill through much casting.

Tuesday, the wind still easterly, and a very rainy day. We were carried forward apace and launched forth a great way into the deep, but our people were still very sick. This day at evening we lost sight of the three ships bound for Newfoundland, which had been in company with us from King Road.

Thursday morning [July 23], a fine gale of wind at north and by east. Now we saw this morning abundance of porpoises and grampuses, leaping and spewing up water about the ship. About eight or nine of the clock the wind blew more stiffly and we went about eight or nine leagues a watch. Toward evening our seamen deemed that we were near to some land, because the color of the water was changed, but sounding with a line of an hundred and sixty fathom, they could find no bottom. It was a very cold wind, like as if it had been winter, which made some to wish for more clothes.

Friday, wind still northerly, but very faint. It was a great foggy mist, and exceeding cold as it had been December. One would have wondered to have seen the innumerable numbers of fowl which we saw swimming on every side of the ship, and mighty fishes rolling and tumbling in the waters, twice as long and big as an ox. In the afternoon we saw mighty whales spewing up water in the air like the smoke of a chimney, and making the sea about them white and hoary.

[July 26.] The fifth Sabbath from Milford Haven and the tenth on shipboard; a fair sunshiny summer day, and would have been very hot, had not God allayed the heat with a good gale of southerly wind, by which also we were carried on in our journey after seven leagues a watch. I was exercised [preached] in the forenoon and Mr. Maude in the afternoon. In the afternoon the wind grew stronger, and it was a rough night for wind and rain, and some had our beds that night ill wet with rain leaking in through the sides of the ship.

Monday [July 27], wind still strong at south. This day we spent much time in filling divers tuns of emptied cask with salt water; which was needful, because much beer, fresh water, beef, and other provisions being spent, the ship went not so well, being too light for want of ballast. When this work was done we set forth more sail, and went that evening and all the night following with good speed in our journey.

Tuesday morning, a great calm, and very hot all that forenoon; our people and cattle being much afflicted with faintness, sweating, and heat; but (lo the goodness of our God) about noon the wind blew at north and by east, which called us from our heat and helped us forward in our way. This afternoon there came and lit upon our ship a little land bird with blue-colored feathers, about the bigness of a sparrow, by which some conceived we were not far from land.

Thursday, wind still westerly against us all the forenoon, but about one of the clock the Lord remembered us in mercy, and sent us a fresh gale at south; which though weak and soft yet did not only much mitigate the heat, but also helped us something forward in our way. In the evening about sunsetting, we saw with admiration and delight innumerable multitudes of huge grampuses rolling and tumbling about the sides of the ship, spewing and puffing up water as they went, and pursuing great numbers of bonitos and lesser fishes; so marvelous to behold are the works and wonders of the Almighty in the deep.

Saturday morning [August 1], a cool wind at north, whereby we went on in our course an hour or two, though very slowly because of the weakness of the wind. Afterwards it became a great calm; and our seamen sounded about one of the clock and found ground at sixty fathom. Presently after, another little land bird came and lit upon the sails of the ship. In the cool of the evening (the calm still continuing) our seamen fished with hook and line and took cod as fast as they could haul them up into the ship.

[August 3.] But lest we should grow secure and neglect the Lord through abundance of prosperity, our wise and loving God was pleased on Monday morning about three of the clock, when we were upon the coast of land, to exercise us with a sore storm and tempest of wind and rain; so that many of us passengers with wind and rain were raised out of our beds, and our seamen were forced to let down all the sails; and the ship was so tossed with fearful mountains and valleys of water, as if we should have been overwhelmed and swallowed up. But this lasted not long, for at our poor prayers the Lord was pleased to magnify His mercy in assuaging the winds and seas again about sunrising. But the wind was become west against us, so that we floated upon the coast, making no dispatch of way all that day and the night following; and besides there was a great fog and mist all that day, so that we could not see to make land, but kept in all sail, and lay still, rather losing than gaining, but taking abundance of cod and halibut, wherewith our bodies were abundantly refreshed after they had been tossed with the storm.

Tuesday, the fog still continued all forenoon; about noon the day cleared up, and the wind blew with a soft gale at south, and we set sail again, going on in our course, though very slowly because of the smallness of the wind. At night it was a calm and abundance of rain.

Saturday morning [August 8] we had a good gale of wind at west-southwest; and this morning our seamen took abundance of mackerel, and about eight of the clock we all had a clear and comfortable sight of America and made land again at an island called Menhiggin, an island without inhabitants about thirty-nine leagues northward or northeast short of Cape Anne. A little from the island we saw more northward divers other islands called St. George Islands, and the mainland of New England all along northward and eastward as we sailed. This mercy of our God we had cause more highly to esteem of, because when we first saw land this morning there was a great fog; and afterward when the day cleared up we saw many rocks and islands almost on every side of us, as Menhiggin, St. George Islands, Pemmequid, etc. Yet in the midst of these dangers our God preserved us, though, because of the thick fog we could not see far about us to look unto ourselves. In the afternoon, the wind continuing still westward against us, we lay off again to the sea southward, and our seamen and many passengers delighted themselves in taking abundance of mackerel.

Wednesday morning [August 12], the wind serving with a fresh gale at north and by east, we set sail from Richmond's Island for Massachusetts Bay, and went along the coast by Cape Porpoise still within sight of land. This day the wind was soft and gentle, and as we went along our seamen and passengers took abundance of mackerel. Towards night it became a calm, so that then we could dispatch little way.

[August 15.] But yet the Lord had not done with us, nor yet had let us see all His power and goodness which He would have us take knowledge of; and therefore on Saturday morning about break of day, the Lord sent forth a most terrible storm of rain and easterly wind, whereby we were in as much danger as I think ever people were, for we lost in that morning three great anchors and cables, of which cables one having cost fifty pounds never had been in any water before; two were broken by the violence of the waves, and the third cut by the seamen in extremity and distress to save the ship and their and our lives. And when our cables and anchors were all lost, we had no outward means of deliverance but by losing sail, if so be we might get to the sea from amongst the islands and rocks where we anchored. In this extremity and appearance of death, as distress and distraction would suffer us, we cried unto the Lord and He was pleased to have compassion and pity upon us; for by His overruling providence and His own immediate good hand, He guided the ship past the rock, assuaged the violence of the sea, and the wind and rain, and gave us a little respite to fit the ship with other sails.

This day [August 16] we went on towards Cape Anne, as the wind would suffer, and our poor sails further, and came within sight thereof the other morning, which Sabbath being the thirteenth we kept on shipboard was a marvelous pleasant day, for a fresh gale of wind and clear sunshine weather. This day we went directly before the wind and had delight all along the coast as we went, in viewing Cape Anne, the bay of Saugus, the bay of Salem, Marble-head, Pullin Point, and other places, and came to anchor at low tide in the evening at Nantascot in a most pleasant harbor like to which I had never seen, amongst a great many islands on every side. I was exercised [preached] on shipboard both ends of the day. After the evening's exercise, when it was flowing tide again, we set sail and came that night to anchor again before Boston, and so rested that night with glad and thankful hearts that God had put an end to our long journey, being a thousand leagues, that is three thousand miles English, over one of the greatest seas in the world.

Richard Mather's Journal

8. Wouter Van Twiller Rules in New Amsterdam

While the English colonies in Virginia and Massachusetts were growing sturdily, the Dutch were making stormier, slower headway in New Amsterdam, where they had planted their first party of permanent settlers in 1623. The Dutch were in some respects good colonizers. But they never learned, as the English did, to transfer self-government to the New World, and self-government is indispensable to a vigorous community. Rulers like Wouter Van Twiller, William Kieft, and Peter Stuyvesant tried to keep an iron hand upon the conduct of affairs, and found themselves involved in constant bickering. Of these three, Wouter — "Walter the Doubter" — was the weakest. Yet Irving's portrait or, rather, caricature of him unquestionably does some injustice to this ill-educated Amsterdam clerk, promoted (chiefly by marriage) to be governor of New Amsterdam; he had more sense and character than the humorist indicates. But within limits, as John Fiske states, Irving gives a correct impression of the burly Dutchman's weak-nesses. He came in 1633, and held office less than five years.

IN THE year of our Lord 1629, Mynheer Wouter Van Twiller was appointed governor of the province of Nieuw Nederlandts, under the commission and control of their High Mightinesses the Lords States General of the United Netherlands, and the privileged West India Company.

This renowned old gentleman arrived at New Amsterdam in the merry month of June, the sweetest month in all the year; when Dan Apollo seems to dance up the transparent firmament — when the robin, the thrush, and a thousand other wanton songsters make the woods to resound with amorous ditties, and the luxurious little boblincoln revels among the clover blossoms of the meadows — all which happy coincidence persuaded the old dames of New Amsterdam, who were skilled in the art of foretelling events, that this was to be a happy and prosperous administration.

The renowned Wouter (or Walter) Van Twiller was descended from a long line of Dutch burgomasters who had successively dozed away their lives and grown fat upon the bench of magistracy in Rotterdam, and who had comported themselves with such singular wisdom and propriety that they were never either heard or talked of — which, next to being universally applauded, should be the object of ambition of all magistrates and rulers. There are two opposite ways by which some men make a figure in the world, one by talking faster than they think and the other by holding their tongues and not thinking at all. By the first, many a smatterer acquires the reputation of a man of quick parts; by the other, many a dunderpate, like the owl, the stupidest of birds, comes to be considered the very type of wisdom. This, by the way, is a casual remark, which I would not, for the universe, have it thought I apply to Governor Van Twiller. It is true he was a man shut up within himself like an oyster and rarely spoke except in monosyllables, but then it was allowed he seldom said a foolish thing. So invincible was his gravity that he was never known to laugh or even to smile through the whole course of a long and prosperous life. Nay, if a joke were uttered in his presence that set light-minded hearers in a roar, it was observed to throw him into a state of perplexity. Sometimes he would deign to inquire into the matter, and when, after much explanation, the joke was made as plain as a pikestaff, he would continue to smoke his pipe in silence, and at length, knocking out the ashes, would exclaim: "Well! I see nothing in all that to laugh about."

With all his reflective habits, he never made up his mind on a subject. His adherents accounted for this by the astonishing magnitude of his ideas. He conceived every subject on so grand a scale that he had not room in his head to turn it over and examine both sides of it. Certain it is that if any matter were propounded to him on which ordinary mortals would rashly determine at first glance, he would put on a vague, mysterious look; shake his capacious head; smoke some time in profound silence, and at length observe that he "had his doubts about the matter"; which gained him the reputation of a man slow of belief and not easily imposed upon. What is more, it gained him a lasting name: for to this habit of the mind has been attributed his surname of Twiller, which is said to be a corruption of the original Twijfler, or, in plain English, *Doubter*.

The person of this illustrious old gentleman was formed and proportioned as though it had been molded by the hands of some cunning Dutch statuary as a model of majesty and lordly grandeur. He was exactly five feet six inches in height, and six feet five inches in circumference. His head was a perfect sphere, and of such stupendous dimensions that Dame Nature, with all her sex's ingenuity, would have been puzzled to construct a neck capable of supporting it; wherefore she wisely declined the attempt, and settled it firmly on the top of his backbone just between the shoulders. His body was oblong and particularly capacious at bottom; which was wisely ordered by Providence, seeing that he was a man of sedentary habits, and very averse to the idle labor of walking. His legs were short, but sturdy in proportion to the weight they had to sustain; so that when erect he had not a little the appearance of a beer barrel on skids. His face, that infallible index of the mind, presented a vast expanse, unfurrowed by any of those lines and angles which disfigure the human countenance with what is termed expression. Two small gray eyes twinkled feebly in the midst like two stars of lesser magnitude in a hazy firmament, and his full-fed cheeks, which seemed to have taken toll of everything that went into his mouth,

were curiously mottled and streaked with dusky red like a Spitzen-
berg apple.

His habits were as regular as his person. He daily took his four
stated meals, appropriating exactly an hour to each; he smoked and
doubted eight hours, and he slept the remaining twelve of the four-
and-twenty. Such was the renowned Wouter Van Twiller — a true
philosopher, for his mind was either elevated above, or tranquilly
settled below, the cares and perplexities of this world. He had lived
in it for years without feeling the least curiosity to know whether
the sun revolved round it, or it round the sun; and he had watched
for at least half a century the smoke curling from his pipe to the
ceiling, without once troubling his head with any of those numerous
theories by which a philosopher would have perplexed his brain in
accounting for its rising above the surrounding atmosphere.

In his council he presided with great state and solemnity. He sat
in a huge chair of solid oak, hewn in the celebrated forest of the
Hague, fabricated by an experienced timberman of Amsterdam,
and curiously carved about the arms and feet into exact imitations of
gigantic eagle's claws. Instead of a scepter he swayed a long Turkish
pipe, wrought with jasmin and amber, which had been presented to
a stadtholder of Holland at the conclusion of a treaty with one of
the petty Barbary powers. In this stately chair would he sit and this
magnificent pipe would he smoke, shaking his right knee with a
constant motion, and fixing his eye for hours together upon a little
print of Amsterdam, which hung in a black frame against the opposite wall of the council chamber. Nay, it has even been said that
when any deliberation of extraordinary length and intricacy was
on the carpet, the renowned Wouter would shut his eyes for full
two hours at a time that he might not be disturbed by external objects — and at such times the internal commotion of his mind was
evinced by certain regular guttural sounds, which his admirers declared were merely the noise of conflict made by his contending
doubts and opinions.

WASHINGTON IRVING, A History of New York

III

Life in the American Colonies

9. The Puritans Hunt Witches in Salem

Few episodes in colonial history are more tragic than the witchcraft prosecutions of 1692 in Massachusetts. Altogether, nineteen men and women were executed by a special court set up by Sir William Phips, the charge being that they had conspired with the devil to bewitch their neighbors. Belief in witchcraft had for centuries been general among both Catholics and Protestants; in the previous three hundred years thousands of supposed witches and wizards had been executed in England, and tens of thousands in Europe as a whole. But the great delusion in Massachusetts came when liberal men elsewhere were shaking themselves free from this kind of superstition. Cotton Mather did much by his writings and preaching to create the atmosphere which made the Salem executions possible, and publicly defended some of the sentences. But it was not long before a sharp reaction in sentiment occurred, and the legislature decreed a public fast by way of penance for the wrong that had been done.

THE TRIAL OF MARTHA CARRIER

MARTHA CARRIER was indicted for the bewitching of certain persons, according to the form usual in such cases pleading not guilty to her indictment. There were first brought in a considerable number of the bewitched persons, who not only made the court sensible of an horrid witchcraft committed upon them, but also deposed that it was Martha Carrier or her shape that grievously tormented them by biting, pricking, pinching, and choking of them. It was further deposed that while this Carrier was on her examination before the magistrates, the poor people were so tortured that every one expected their death upon the very spot, but that upon the binding of Carrier they were eased. Moreover the look of Carrier then laid the afflicted people for dead; and her touch, if her eye at the same time were off them, raised them again. Which things were also now seen upon her trial. And it was testified that upon the mention of some having their necks twisted almost round by the shape of this Carrier, she replied: "It's no matter though their necks had been twisted quite off."

Before the trial of this prisoner several of her own children had frankly and fully confessed, not only that they were witches themselves, but that this their mother had made them so. This confession they made with great shows of repentance, and with much demonstration of truth. They related place, time, occasion; they gave an account of journeys, meetings, and mischiefs by them performed, and were very credible in what they said. Nevertheless, this evidence was not produced against the prisoner at the bar, inasmuch as there was other evidence enough to proceed upon.

Benjamin Abbot gave in his testimony that last March was a twelvemonth this Carrier was very angry with him upon laying out some land near her husband's. Her expressions in this anger were that she "would stick as close to Abbot as the bark stuck to the tree; and that he should repent of it afore seven years came to an end, so as Doctor Prescot should never cure him." These words were heard by others besides Abbot himself, who also heard her say she "would hold his nose as close to the grindstone as ever it was held since his name was Abbot." Presently after this he was taken with a swelling in his foot, and then with a pain in his side, and exceedingly tormented. It bred into a sore, which was lanced by Doctor Prescot, and several gallons of corruption ran out of it. For six weeks it continued very bad, and then another sore bred in his groin, which was also lanced by Doctor Prescot. Another sore then bred in his groin, which was likewise cut, and put him to very great misery. He was brought unto death's door, and so remained until Carrier was taken and carried away by the constable, from which very day he began to mend and so grew better every day, and is well ever since.

Sarah Abbot also, his wife, testified that her husband was not only all this while afflicted in his body, but also that strange, extraordinary, and unaccountable calamities befell his cattle, their death being such as they could guess at no natural reason for.

Allin Toothaker testified that Richard, the son of Martha Carrier, having some difference with him, pulled him down by the hair of the head. When he rose again he was going to strike at Richard Carrier, but fell down flat on his back to the ground and had not power to stir hand or foot, until he told Carrier he yielded; and then he saw the shape of Martha Carrier go off his breast.

This Toothaker had received a wound in the wars, and he now testified that Martha Carrier told him he should never be cured. Just afore the apprehending of Carrier, he could thrust a knitting needle into his wound, four inches deep; but presently after her being seized, he was thoroughly healed.

He further testified that when Carrier and he sometimes were at variance, she would clap her hands at him, and say he "should get nothing by it." Whereupon he several times lost his cattle by strange deaths, whereof no natural causes could be given.

One Foster, who confessed her own share in the witchcraft for which the prisoner stood indicted, affirmed that she had seen the prisoner at some of their witch meetings, and that it was this Carrier who persuaded her to be a witch. She confessed that the devil carried them on a pole to a witch meeting; but the pole broke, and she hanging about Carrier's neck, they both fell down, and she then received an hurt by the fall whereof she was not at this very time recovered.

One Lacy, who likewise confessed her share in this witchcraft, now testified that she and the prisoner were once bodily present at a witch meeting in Salem Village; and that she knew the prisoner to be a witch, and to have been at a diabolical sacrament, and that the prisoner was the undoing of her and her children, by enticing them into the snare of the devil.

Another Lacy, who also confessed her share in this witchcraft, now testified that the prisoner was at the witch meeting, in Salem Village, where they had bread and wine administered unto them.

In the time of this prisoner's trial, one Susanna Sheldon in open court had her hands unaccountably tied together with a wheel band, so fast that without cutting it could not be loosed. It was done by a specter, and the sufferer affirmed it was the prisoner's.

Memorandum. This rampant hag, Martha Carrier, was the person of whom the confessions of the witches, and of her own children among the rest, agreed that the devil had promised her she should be Queen of Hell.

COTTON MATHER, The Wonders of the Invisible World

THE TRIAL OF GOODWIFE COREY

On Monday, the 21st of March, the magistrates of Salem appointed to come to examination of Goodwife Corey. And about twelve of the clock they went into the meeting house, which was thronged with spectators. Mr. Noyes began with a very pertinent and pathetic prayer, and Goodwife Corey being called to answer to what was alleged against her, she desired to go to prayer, which was much wondered at, in the presence of so many hundred people. The magistrates told her they would not admit it; they came not there to hear her pray, but to examine her in what was alleged against her. The worshipful Mr. Hathorne asked her why she afflicted those children. She said she did not afflict them. He asked her, "Who did then?" She said, "I do not know; how should I know?"

The number of the afflicted persons were about that time ten, viz. four married women: Mrs. Pope, Mrs. Putnam, Goodwife Bibber, and an ancient woman named Goodall; three maids: Mary Walcut, Mercy Lewes, at Thomas Putnam's, and a maid at Dr. Griggs's; there were three girls from nine to twelve years of age, each of them, or thereabouts, viz. Elizabeth Parris, Abigail Williams, and Ann Putnam.

These were most of them at Goodwife Corey's examination, and did vehemently accuse her in the assembly of afflicting them, by biting, pinching, strangling, etc.; and that they did in their fit see her likeness coming to them, and bringing a book to them. She said she had no book. They affirmed she had a yellow bird that used to suck betwixt her fingers; and being asked about it, if she had any familiar spirit that attended her, she said she had no familiarity with any such thing, she was a gospel woman, which title she called herself by. And the afflicted persons told her ah, she was a gospel witch. Ann Putnam did there affirm that one day when Lieutenant Fuller was at prayer at her father's house, she saw the shape of Goodwife Corey and she thought Goodwife N., praying at the same time to the Devil. She was not sure it was Goodwife N., she thought it was, but very sure she saw the shape of Goodwife Corey. The said Corey said they were poor, distracted children, and no heed to be given to what they said. Mr. Hathorne and Mr. Noyes replied it was the judgment of all present they were bewitched, and only she, the accused person, said they were distracted.

It was observed several times that if she did but bite her underlip in time of examination, the persons afflicted were bitten on their arms and wrists and produced the marks before the magistrates, ministers, and others. And being watched for that, if she did but pinch her fingers, or grasp one hand hard in another, they were pinched, and produced the marks before the magistrates and spectators. After that, it was observed that if she did but lean her breast against the seat in the meeting house (being the bar at which she stood), they were afflicted. Particularly Mrs. Pope complained of grievous torment in her bowels as if they were torn out. She vehemently accused said Corey as the instrument, and first threw her muff at her, but that not flying home, she got off her shoe, and hit Goodwife Corey on the head with it. After these postures were watched, if said Corey did but stir her feet, they were afflicted in their feet, and stamped fearfully. The afflicted persons asked her why she did not go to the company of witches which were before the meeting house mustering. Did she not hear the drum beat? They accused her of having familiarity with the Devil, in the time of examination, in the shape of a black man whispering in her ear; they affirmed that her yellow bird sucked betwixt her fingers in the assembly; and, order being given to see if there were any sign, the girl that saw it said it was too late now; she had removed a pin and put it on her head, which was found there sticking upright.

They told her she had covenanted with the Devil for ten years; six of them were gone, and four more to come. She was required by the magistrates to answer that question in the catechism, "How many persons be there in the Godhead?" She answered it but oddly, yet there was no great thing to be gathered from it; she denied all that was charged upon her, and said they could not prove her a witch. She was that afternoon committed to Salem prison; and after she was in custody, she did not so appear to them and afflict them as before.

DEODAT LAWSON, Brief and True Narrative

THE EXECUTIONS

August 5 [1692]. — The court again sitting, six more were tried on the same account, viz., Mr. George Burroughs, sometime minister of Wells, John Procter and Elizabeth Procter, his wife, with John Willard of Salem village, George Jacobs, Senior of Salem, and Martha Carrier of Andover. These were all brought in guilty, and condemned, and were all executed August 19, except Procter's wife, who pleaded pregnancy.

Mr. Burroughs was carried in a cart with the others through the streets of Salem to execution. When he was upon the ladder he made a speech for the clearing of his innocency with such solemn and serious expressions as were to the admiration of all present. His prayer (which he concluded by repeating the Lord's Prayer) was so well worded and uttered with such composedness and such (at least seeming) fervency of spirit as was very affecting, and drew tears from many (so that it seemed to some that the spectators would hinder the execution). The accusers said the Black Man stood and dictated to him. As soon as he was turned off, Mr. Cotton Mather, being mounted upon a horse, addressed himself to the people, partly to declare that he was no ordained minister and partly to possess the people of his guilt, saying that the Devil has often been transformed into an angel of light. And this did somewhat appease the people, and the executions went on. When he was cut down, he was dragged by the halter to a hole, or grave, between the rocks, about two foot deep; his shirt and breeches being pulled off and an old pair of trousers of one executed put on his lower parts, he was so put in, together with Willard and Carrier, one of his hands and his chin and a foot of one of them being left uncovered.

John Procter and his wife being in prison, the sheriff came to his house and seized all the goods, provisions, and cattle that he could come at, and sold some of the cattle at half price, and killed others, and put them up for the West Indies; threw out the beer out of a barrel, and carried away the barrel; emptied a pot of broth, and took away the pot, and left nothing in the house for the support of the children. No part of the said goods are known to be returned. Procter earnestly requested Mr. Noyes to pray with and for him, but it was wholly denied, because he would not own himself to be a witch.

ROBERT CALEF, More Wonders of the Invisible World

10. Nathaniel Bacon Rebels against Governor Berkeley

No less a person than a cousin of Lord Bacon headed the first important American rebellion. Nathaniel Bacon was a highly educated man, trained at Cambridge University and Gray's Inn. Settling in Virginia and gaining a seat on the Council, he witnessed with growing irritation the wrongs under which the common people of the colony labored. The king had made lavish grants of land to favorites. Lord Berkeley, the royal governor, seemed to have set up a political machine which was managing affairs for the benefit of a special group. Small farmers and planters complained that taxation was excessive and unfairly distributed; frontiersmen believed that the government and the rich tidewater landholders were not doing enough to furnish protection against the Indians. In 1676 a new set of Indian outrages brought the popular discontent to a head, and the people turned to the impetuous Bacon—wrathful because the savages had slain his overseer—for leader. His aims were twofold: to teach the Indians an enduring lesson, and then to wring reforms from the governor and the tidewater interests.

IN THESE frightful times the most exposed small families withdrew into our houses, which we fortified with palisades and redoubts; neighbors in bodies joined their labors from each plantation to others alternately, taking their arms into the fields, and setting sentinels; no man stirred out of door unarmed. Indians were ever

and anon espied, three, four, five, or six in a party, lurking throughout the whole land, yet (what was remarkable) I rarely heard of
any houses burnt, though abundance was forsaken, nor ever of any
corn or tobacco cut up, or other injury done, besides murders, except
the killing a very few cattle and swine.

Frequent complaints of bloodsheds were sent to Sir William
Berkeley (then governor) from the heads of the rivers, which were
as often answered with promises of assistance.

These at the heads of James and York Rivers (having now most
people destroyed by the Indians' flight thither from Potomac) grew
impatient at the many slaughters of their neighbors and rose for
their own defense, who choosing Mr. Bacon for their leader sent
oftentimes to the Governor, humbly beseeching a commission to
go against those Indians at their own charge, which his Honor as
often promised, but did not send. . . .

During these protractions and people often slain, most or all the
officers, civil and military, with as many dwellers next the heads of
the rivers as made up three hundred men, taking Mr. Bacon for their
commander, met, and concerted together the danger of going without a commission on the one part, and the continual murders of
their neighbors on the other part (not knowing whose or how many
of their own turns might be next) and came to this resolution, viz.,
to prepare themselves with necessaries for a march, but interim to
send again for a commission, which if could or could not be obtained by a certain day, they would proceed, commission or no commission.

This day lapsing and no commission come, they marched into the
wilderness in quest of these Indians, after whom the Governor
sent his proclamation, denouncing all rebels who should not return
within a limited day, whereupon those of estates obeyed. But Mr.
Bacon with fifty-seven men proceeded until their provisions were
near spent, without finding enemies; when coming nigh a fort of
friendly Indians, on the other side a branch of James River, they desired relief, offering payment, which these Indians kindly promised
to help them with on the morrow, but put them off with promises
until the third day, so as having then eaten their last morsels they
could not return, but must have starved on the way homeward.
And now 'twas suspected these Indians had received private mes-

sages from the Governor, and those to be the causes of these delusive procrastinations; whereupon the English waded shoulder-deep through that branch to the fort palisades, still entreating and tendering pay, for victuals; but that evening a shot from the place they left on the other side of that branch killed one of Mr. Bacon's men, which made them believe those in the fort had sent for other Indians to come behind them and cut them off.

Hereupon they fired the palisades, stormed and burnt the fort and cabins, and (with the loss of three English) slew one hundred and fifty Indians.

From hence they returned home, where writs were come up to elect members for an Assembly, when Mr. Bacon was unanimously chosen for one, who coming down the river was commanded by a ship with guns to come on board, where waited Major Hone, the high sheriff of Jamestown, ready to seize him, by whom he was carried down to the Governor and by him received with a surprising civility in the following words: "Mr. Bacon, have you forgot to be a gentleman?" "No, may it please your Honor," answered Mr. Bacon; then replied the Governor, "I'll take your parole," and gave him his liberty. . . . The morning I arrived to Jamestown, after a week's voyage, was welcomed with the strange acclamations of "All's over, Bacon is taken," having not heard at home of the southern commotions, other than rumors like idle tales, of one Bacon risen up in rebellion, nobody knew for what, concerning the Indians.

The next forenoon, the Assembly being met in a chamber over the general court and our speaker chosen, the Governor sent for us down, where his Honor with a pathetic emphasis made a short, abrupt speech wherein were these words:

"If they had killed my grandfather and grandmother, my father and mother and all my friends, yet if they had come to treat of peace, they ought to have gone in peace," and sat down; the two chief commanders at the forementioned siege, who slew the four Indian great men, being present and part of our Assembly.

The Governor stood up again and said: "If there be joy in the presence of the angels over one sinner that repenteth, there is joy now, for we have a penitent sinner come before us. Call Mr. Bacon." Then did Mr. Bacon upon one knee at the bar deliver a sheet of paper confessing his crimes, and begging pardon of God, the King, and the Governor; whereto (after a short pause) he answered, "God forgive you, I forgive you," thrice repeating the same words; when Colonel Cole (one of the Council) said, "And all that were with him?" "Yea," said the Governor, "and all that were with him," twenty or more persons being then in irons, who were taken coming down in the same and other vessels with Mr. Bacon.

The Governor had directed us to consider of means for security from the Indian insults and to defray the charge. Whilst some days passed in settling the quotas of men, arms and ammunition, provisions, etc. each county was to furnish, one morning early a bruit ran about the town, "Bacon is fled, Bacon is fled." Bacon was escaped into the country, having intimation that the Governor's generosity in pardoning him and his followers, and restoring him to his seat in Council, were no other than previous wheedles to amuse him and his adherents and to circumvent them by stratagem, forasmuch as the taking Mr. Bacon again into the Council was first to keep him out of the Assembly, and in the next place the Governor knew the country people were hastening down with dreadful threatenings to doubly revenge all wrongs should be done to Mr. Bacon or his men, or whoever should have had the least hand in them.

In three or four days after this escape, upon news that Mr. Bacon was thirty miles up the river, at the head of four hundred men, the Governor sent to the parts adjacent, on both sides James River, for the militia and all the men could be got to come and defend the town. Expresses came almost hourly of the army's approaches, who in less than four days after the first account of them, at two of the clock, entered the town, without being withstood, and formed a body upon a green, not a flight shot from the end of the state house, of horse and foot, as well regular as veteran troops, who forthwith possessed themselves of all the avenues, disarming all in town, and coming thither in boats or by land.

In half an hour after this the drum beat for the House to meet, and in less than an hour more Mr. Bacon came with a file of fusiliers on either hand, near the corner of the state house, where the Governor and Council went forth to him. We saw from the window the Governor open his breast, and Bacon strutting betwixt his two files of men, with his left arm on Kenbow, flinging his right arm every way, both like men distracted; and if, in this moment of fury, that enraged multitude had fallen upon the Governor and Council, we of the Assembly expected the same immediate fate. I stepped down, and amongst the crowd of spectators found the seamen of my sloop, who prayed me not to stir from them, when, in two minutes, the Governor walked towards his private apartment, a quoit's cast distant, at the other end of the state house, the gentlemen of the Council following him; and after them walked Mr. Bacon with outrageous postures of his head, arms, body, and legs, often tossing his hand from his sword to his hat, and after him came a detachment of fusiliers (muskets not being there in use), who with their locks bent presented their fusils at a window of the Assembly chamber filled with faces, repeating with menacing voices, "We will have it, we will have it," half a minute, when as one of our House, a person known to many of them, shook his handkerchief out at the window, saying, "You shall have it, you shall have it," three or four times; at these words they set down their fusils, unbent their locks, and stood still until Bacon coming back, they followed him to their main body. In this hubbub a servant of mine got so nigh as to hear the Governor's words, and also followed Mr. Bacon and heard what he said, who came and told me that when the Governor opened his breast, he said: "Here! shoot me. 'Fore God, fair mark! shoot!" often rehearsing the same, without any other words; whereto Mr. Bacon answered: "No, may it please your Honor, we will not hurt a hair of your head, nor of any other man's; we are come for a commission to save our lives from the Indians, which you have so often promised, and now we will have it before we go."

But when Mr. Bacon followed the Governor and Council with the forementioned impetuous (like delirious) actions, whilst that party presented their fusils at the window full of faces, he said: "Damn my blood, I'll kill Governor, Council, Assembly, and all, and then I'll sheathe my sword in my own heart's blood"; and afterwards 'twas said Bacon had given a signal to his men who presented their fusils at those gazing out at the window, that if he should draw his sword they were on sight of it to fire, and slay us; so near was the massacre of us all that very minute, had Bacon in that paroxysm of frantic fury but drawn his sword before the pacific handkerchief was shaken out at window.

In an hour or more after these violent concussions, Mr. Bacon came up to our chamber and desired a commission from us to go against the Indians. Our speaker sat silent, when one Mr. Blayton, a neighbor to Mr. Bacon and elected with him a member of Assembly for the same county (who therefore durst speak to him), made answer: " 'Twas not in our province or power, nor of any other, save the King's viceregent, our governor." He pressed hard nigh half an hour's harangue on the preserving our lives from the Indians, inspecting the public revenues, the exorbitant taxes, and redressing the grievances and calamities of that deplorable country, whereto having no other answer, he went away dissatisfied.

Little expecting to hear of more intestine broils, I went home to Potomac, where reports were afterwards various. We had account that General Bacon was marched with a thousand men into the forest to seek the enemy Indians, and in a few days after our next news was that the Governor had summoned together the militia of Gloucester and Middlesex Counties to the number of twelve hundred men, and proposed to them to follow and suppress that rebel Bacon; whereupon arose a murmuring before his face, "Bacon, Bacon, Bacon," and all walked out of the field, muttering as they went, "Bacon, Bacon, Bacon," leaving the Governor and those that came with him to themselves, who being thus abandoned wafted over Chesapeake Bay thirty miles to Accomac.

Mr. Bacon, hearing of this, came back part of the way, and sent out parties of horse patrolling through every county, carrying away prisoners all whom he distrusted might any more molest his Indian persecution, yet giving liberty to such as pledged him their oaths to return home and live quiet; the copies or contents of which oaths I never saw, but heard were very strict, though little observed.

The Governor made a second attempt, coming over from Accomac with what men he could procure in sloops and boats forty miles up the river to Jamestown, which Bacon hearing of, came again down from his forest pursuit, and finding a bank not a flight shot long cast up thwart the neck of the peninsula there in Jamestown, he stormed it, and took the town, in which attack were twelve men slain and wounded. but the Governor with most of his followers fled back down the river in their vessels.

Here, resting a few days, they concerted the burning of the town, wherein Mr. Lawrence and Mr. Drumond, owning the two best houses save one, set fire each to his own house, which example the soldiers following, laid the whole town (with church and state house) in ashes, saying the rogues should harbor no more there.

On these reiterated molestations, Bacon calls a convention at Middle Plantation, fifteen miles from Jamestown, in the month of August, 1676, where an oath with one or more proclamations were formed, and writs by him issued for an Assembly. The oaths or writs I never saw, but one proclamation commanded all men in the land on pain of death to join him, and retire into the wilderness upon arrival of the forces expected from England, and oppose them until they should propose or accept to treat of an accommodation, which we who lived comfortably could not have undergone, so as the whole land must have become an Aceldama if God's exceeding mercy had not timely removed him.

During these tumults in Virginia a second danger menaced Maryland by an insurrection in that province, complaining of their heavy taxes, etc., where two or three of the leading malcontents (men otherwise of laudable characters) were put to death, which stifled the further spreading of that flame. Mr. Bacon (at this time) pressed the best ship in James River, carrying twenty guns, and putting into her his lieutenant general, Mr. Bland, and under him the fore-mentioned Captain Carver, formerly a commander of merchants' ships, with men and all necessaries, he sent her to ride before Accomac to curb and intercept all smaller vessels of war commissioned by the Governor, coming often over and making depredations on the western shore, as if we had been foreign enemies.

Now returning to Captain Carver, the Governor sent for him to come on shore, promising his peaceable return, who answered, "He could not trust his word, but if he would send his hand and seal, he would adventure to wait upon his Honor," which was done, and Carver went in his sloop well armed and manned with the most trusty of his men, where he was caressed with wine, etc., and large promises, if he would forsake Bacon, resign his ship, or join with him; to all which he answered that if he served the devil he would be true to his trust, but that he was resolved to go home and live quiet.

In the time of this reception and parley, an armed boat was pre-

pared with many oars in a creek not far off, but out of sight, which
when Carver sailed, rowed out of the creek, and it being almost calm
the boat outwent the sloop, whilst all on board the ship were upon
the deck, staring at both, thinking the boat's company coming on
board by Carver's invitation to be civilly entertained in requital of
the kindness they supposed he had received on shore, until coming under the stern, those in the boat slipped nimbly in at the gun-
room ports with pistols, etc., when one courageous gentleman ran
up to the deck, and clapped a pistol to Bland's breast, saying, "You
are my prisoner," the boat's company suddenly following with
pistols, swords, etc., and after Captain Larimore (the commander
of the ship before she was pressed) having from the highest and
hindmost part of the stern interchanged a signal from the shore by
flirting his handkerchief about his nose, his own former crew had
laid handspikes ready, which they (at that instant) caught up, etc.,
so as Bland and Carver's men were amazed, and yielded.

Carver, seeing a hurly-burly on the ship's deck, would have gone
away with his sloop, but having little wind and the ship threatening
to sink him, he tamely came on board, where Bland and he with
their party were laid in irons and in three or four days Carver was
hanged on shore. . . . Mr. Bacon now returns from his last expedition sick of a flux, without finding any enemy Indians, having
not gone far by reason of the vexations behind him; nor had he one
dry day in all his marches to and fro in the forest, whilst the plantations (not fifty miles distant) had a summer so dry as stinted the
Indian corn and tobacco, etc., which the people ascribed to the
powwowings (i.e. the sorceries of the Indians). In a while Bacon
dies and was succeeded by his Lieutenant General and so all
submitted and were pardoned, exempting those nominated and
otherwise proscribed, in a proclamation of indemnity, the principal of whom were Lawrence and Drumond.

Mr. Bland was then a prisoner, having been taken with Carver, as
before is noted, and in a few days Mr. Drumond was brought in,
when the Governor, being on board a ship, came immediately to
shore and complimented him with the ironical sarcasm of a low
bend, saying: "Mr. Drumond! you are very welcome; I am more
glad to see you than any man in Virginia. Mr. Drumond, you shall
be hanged in half an hour"; who answered, "What your Honor

pleases"; and as soon as a council of war could meet, his sentence be dispatched and a gibbet erected (which took up near two hours), he was executed.

The last account of Mr. Lawrence was from an uppermost plantation, whence he and four others, desperadoes, with horses, pistols, etc., marched away in a snow ankle-deep, who were thought to have cast themselves into a branch of some river, rather than to be treated like Drumond.

Bacon's body was so made away, as his bones were never found to be exposed on a gibbet as was purposed, stones being laid in his coffin, supposed to be done by Lawrence.

Near this time arrived a small fleet with a regiment from England, Sir John Berry, admiral; Colonel Herbert Jefferyes, commander of the land forces; and Colonel Morrison, who had one year been a former governor. There, all three joined in commission with or to Sir William Barclay, soon after when a general court and also an Assembly were held, where some of our former Assembly (with so many others) were put to death, divers whereof were persons of honest reputations and handsome estates, as that the Assembly petitioned the Governor to spill no more blood; and Mr. Presley, at his coming home, told me he believed the Governor would have hanged half the country if they had let him alone. The first was Mr. Bland, whose friends in England had procured his pardon to be sent over with the fleet, which he pleaded at his trial was in the Governor's pocket, but he was answered by Colonel Morrison that he pleaded his pardon at sword's point, which was looked upon an odd sort of reply, and he was executed; as was talked, by private instructions from England, the Duke of York having sworn, "By God, Bacon and Bland should die."

The Governor went in the fleet to London, leaving Colonel Jefferyes in his place, and by next shipping came back a person who waited on his Honor in his voyage (and until his death), from whom a report was whispered about, that the King did say, "That old fool has hanged more men in that naked country than he had done for the murder of his father"; whereof the Governor hearing died soon after, without having seen his Majesty — which shuts up this tragedy.

The Virginia Rebellion in the Seventeenth Century, by T.M.

11. The Men of Maine

Maine was more difficult to colonize than other parts of coastal New England; its isolated inhabitants early developed traits peculiar to them. The principal promoter of settlement was Sir Ferdinando Gorges, who shared with John Mason a wide grant of land north of Massachusetts, and who soon took everything between the Piscataqua and the Kennebec rivers for his share. But aggressive Puritan emigrants from Massachusetts moved into the territory and became the dominant element. By 1650 the Bay Colony had annexed all the scattered Maine settlements. One of the men most irritated by this expansion of Massachusetts was John Josselyn, whose brother was a principal representative in New England of the aggrieved Gorges and Mason heirs. In writing of his voyages he spoke highly of the sturdy men of Maine, and with sly hostility of their neighbors; it is clear that the Maine men he did not like were those who had come up from the south.

THE PEOPLE in the province of Maine may be divided into magistrates, husbandmen or planters, and fishermen; of the magistrates some be royalists, the rest perverse spirits, the like are the planters and fishers, of which some be planters and fishers both, others mere fishers.

Handicraftsmen there are but few, the cooper, smiths and carpenters are best welcome amongst them, shopkeepers there are none, being supplied by the Massachusetts merchant with all things they stand in need of, keeping here and there fair magazines stored with English goods, but they set excessive prices on them; if they do not gain cent per cent, they cry out that they are losers. Hence English shoes are sold for eight and nine shillings a pair; worsted stockings of three shillings sixpence a pair for seven and eight shillings a pair; dowlas that is sold in England for one- or two-and-twenty pence an ell, for four shillings a yard; serges of two shillings or three shillings a yard, for six and seven shillings a yard; and so all sorts of commodities both for planters and fishermen.

The planters are or should be restless painstakers, providing for their cattle, planting and sowing of corn, fencing their grounds, cutting and bringing home fuel, cleaving of clawboard [clapboard] and pipe staves; fishing for fresh-water fish and fowling takes up most of their time, if not all; the diligent hand maketh rich, but if they be of a dronish disposition, as some are, they become wretchedly poor and miserable, scarce able to free themselves and family from importunate famine, especially in the winter for want of bread.

They have a custom of taking tobacco, sleeping at noon, sitting long at meals, sometimes four times in a day, and now and then drinking a dram of the bottle extraordinarily: the smoking of tobacco, if moderately used, refresheth the weary much, and so doth sleep.

> A traveler five hours doth crave
> To sleep, a student seven will have,
> And nine sleeps every idle knave.

The physician allows but three draughts at a meal, the first for need, the second for pleasure, and the third for sleep; but little observed by them, unless they have no other liquor to drink but water. In some places where the springs are frozen up, or at least the way to their springs made unpassable by reason of the snow and the like, they dress their meat in aqua caelestis, i.e. melted snow. At other times it is very well cooked, and they feed upon (generally) as good flesh, beef, pork, mutton, fowl, and fish as any is in the whole world besides.

Their servants, which are for the most part English, when they are out of their time, will not work under half a crown a day, although it be for to make hay, and for less I do not see how they can, by reason of the dearness of clothing. If they hire them by the year, they pay them fourteen or fifteen pound, yea, twenty pound at the year's end in corn, cattle, and fish; some of these prove excellent fowlers, bringing in as many as will maintain their master's house, besides the profit that accrues by their feathers. They use (when it is to be had) a great round shot, called Barstable shot (which is best for fowl), made of a lead blacker than our common lead; to six pound of shot they allow one pound of powder; cannon powder is esteemed best.

The fishermen take yearly upon the coasts many hundred kentles of cod, hake, haddock, pollack, etc., which they split, salt, and dry at their stages, making three voyages in a year. When they share their fish (which is at the end of every voyage) they separate the best from the worst; the first they call merchantable fish, being sound, full-grown fish and well made up, which is known when it is clear like a lanthorn horn and without spots; the second sort they call refuse fish — that is, such as is salt-burnt, spotted, rotten, and carelessly ordered: these they put off to the Massachusetts merchants; the merchantable for thirty and two-and-thirty ryals a kentle [a hundred-and-twelve-pound weight]; the refuse for nine shillings and ten shillings a kentle.

The merchant sends the merchantable fish to Lisbon, Bilbao, Bordeaux, Marseilles, Toulon, Rochelle, Rouen, and other cities of France, to the Canaries with clawboard and pipe staves, which is there and at the Caribs a prime commodity; the refuse fish they put off at the Carib Islands, Barbados, Jamaica, etc., who feed their Negroes with it.

To every shallop belong four fishermen — a master or steersman, a midshipman, and a foremastman — and a shore man who washes it out of the salt, and dries it upon hurdles pitched upon stakes breast-high and tends their cookery; these often get in one voyage eight or nine pound a man for their shares, but it doth some of them little good for the merchant to increase his gains by putting off his commodity in the midst of their voyages, and at the end thereof comes in with a walking tavern, a bark laden with the legitimate blood of the rich grape, which they bring from Fayal, Madeira, Canaries, with brandy, rum, the Barbados strong water, and tobacco. Coming ashore he gives them a taster or two, which so charms them that for no persuasions that their employers can use will they go out to sea, although fair and seasonable weather, for two or three days — nay, sometimes a whole week — till they are wearied with drinking, taking ashore two or three hogsheads of wine and rum to drink off when the merchant is gone. If a man of quality chance to come where they are roistering and gulling in wine with a dear felicity, he must be sociable and rollypooly [rolypoly, i.e., he must play the game] with them, taking of their liberal cups as freely, or else be gone, which is best for him. When the day of payment comes, they may justly complain of their costly sin of drunkenness, for their shares will do no more than pay the reckoning; if they save a kentle or two to buy shoes and stockings, shirts, and waistcoats with, 'tis well; otherwise they must enter into the merchant's books for such things as they stand in need of, becoming thereby the merchant's slaves, and when it riseth to a big sum are constrained to mortgage their plantation if they have any; the merchant when the time is expired is sure to seize upon their plantation and stock of cattle, turning them out of house and home, poor creatures, to look out for a new habitation in some remote place, where they begin the world again. The lavish planters have the same fate, partaking with them in the like bad husbandry.

JOHN JOSSELYN, An Account of Two Voyages to New England

12. William Byrd Discovers Lubberland

If sophisticated observers could deride the simple, hardy, and not altogether puritanical people of Maine, much more could they make fun of the lazy and ignorant inhabitants of the backwoods of North Carolina. Some coastal settlements of that province, notably Edenton, could vie with any in the country in elegance. But the back country was filled — so Virginians and South Carolinians alleged — by an uncouth, indolent, and loutish race. William Byrd II of "Westover" had some reason for looking down on such folk. Educated in England, a member of the Royal Society, the possessor at his estate on the James of one of the largest libraries in America, he was a man of taste, whose Writings *contain some very amusing and instructive matter. His travels in North Carolina excited his satirical inclinations, and much of what he says is highly unfair. But it was at least authentic humor. The North Carolinians, he wrote, "keep so many sabbaths every week that their disregard of the seventh day has no manner of cruelty in it either to servants or cattle."*

SURELY there is no place in the world where the inhabitants live with less labor than in North Carolina. It approaches nearer to the description of Lubberland than any other, by the great felicity of the climate, the easiness of raising provisions, and the slothfulness of the people. Indian corn is of so great increase that a little pains will subsist a very large family with bread, and then they may have meat without any pains at all, by the help of the low grounds, and the great variety of mast that grows on the highland. The men, for their parts, just like the Indians, impose all the work on the poor women. They make their wives rise out of their beds early in the morning, at the same time that they lie and snore, till the sun has risen one-third of his course and dispersed all the unwholesome damps. Then, after stretching and yawning for half an hour, they light their pipes, and, under the protection of a cloud of smoke, venture out into the open air; though, if it happens to be never so little cold, they quickly return shivering into the chimney corner. When the weather is mild, they stand leaning with both their arms upon the cornfield fence, and gravely consider whether they had best go and take a small heat at the hoe, but generally find reasons to put it off till another time. Thus they loiter away their lives, like Solomon's sluggard, with their arms across, and at the winding up of the year scarcely have bread to eat. To speak the truth, it is a thorough aversion to labor that makes people file off to North Carolina, where plenty and a warm sun confirm them in their disposition to laziness for their whole lives.

Provisions here are extremely cheap and extremely good, so that people may live plentifully at a trifling expense. Nothing is dear but law, physic, and strong drink, which are all bad in their kind, and the last they get with so much difficulty, that they are never guilty of the sin of suffering it to sour upon their hands. Their vanity generally lies not so much in having a handsome dining room, as a handsome house or office; in this kind of structure they are really extravagant. They are rarely guilty of flattering or making any court to their governors, but treat them with all the excesses of freedom and familiarity. They are of opinion their rulers would be apt to grow insolent, if they grew rich, and for that reason take care to keep them poorer, and more dependent, if possible, than the saints in New England used to do their governors. They have very little corn, so they are forced to carry on their home traffic with paper money. This is the only cash that will tarry in the country, and for that reason the discount goes on increasing between that and real money, and will do so to the end of the chapter.

WILLIAM BYRD, A Journey to the Land of Eden

13. Sarah Knight Travels from Boston to New York

Just as amusing as William Byrd's work, equally satirical, and even more vivid is the record which Sarah Kemble Knight, a Boston schoolmistress and woman of affairs, wrote of her journey to New York at a period when such a trip was a serious venture for an unaccompanied woman. She was nearly forty at the time, and clearly a person of vigor. Underneath her sharp condemnation of the abuses and shortcomings from which she suffered is evident a vein of good humor and tolerance. We are not astonished to learn that after she settled at New London, Connecticut, she was indicted and fined for selling liquor to the Indians. Her diary was not written for fame, but for her own amusement, and did not see print until more than a century after her eventful journey.

MONDAY, October the 2d, 1704. — About three o'clock afternoon, I began my journey from Boston to New Haven; being about two hundred mile. My kinsman, Captain Robert Luist, waited on me as far as Dedham, where I was to meet the western post.

I visited the Reverend M. Belcher, the minister of the town, and tarried there till evening, in hopes the post would come along. But he not coming, I resolved to go to Billings' where he used to lodge, being twelve miles farther. But being ignorant of the way, Madam Belcher, seeing no persuasions of her good spouse's or hers could prevail with me to lodge there that night, very kindly went with me to the tavern, where I hoped to get my guide, and desired the hostess to inquire of her guests whether any of them would go with me. I told her no, I would not be accessory to such extortion.

"Then John shan't go," says she; "no, indeed, shan't he"; and held forth at that rate a long time, that I began to fear I was got among the quaking tribe, believing not a limber-tongued sister among them could outdo Madam Hostess.

Upon this, to my no small surprise, son John arose, and gravely demanded what I would give him to go with me. "Give you?" says I. "Are you John?" "Yes," says he, "for want of a better"; and behold! this John looked as old as my host, and perhaps had been a man in the last century. "Well, Mr. John," says I, "make your demands." "Why, half a piece of eight and a dram," says John. I agreed, and gave him a dram (now) in hand to bind the bargain.

My hostess catechized John for going so cheap, saying his poor wife would break her heart. . . .

When we had ridden about an hour, we came into a thick swamp, which by reason of a great fog, very much startled me, it being now very dark. But nothing dismayed John: he had encountered a thousand and a thousand such swamps, having a universal knowledge in the woods; and readily answered all my inquiries, which were not a few.

In about an hour, or something more, after we left the swamp, we came to Billings', where I was to lodge. My guide dismounted and very complacently helped me down and showed the door, signing to me with his hand to go in; which I gladly did—but had not gone many steps into the room, ere I was interrogated by a young lady I understood afterwards was the eldest daughter of the family, with these, or words to this purpose; viz., "Law for me!—what in the world brings you here at this time of night? I never see a woman on the road so dreadful late in all the days of my versal life. Who are you? Where are you going? I'm scared out of my wits!" — with much more of the same kind. I stood aghast, preparing to reply, when in comes my guide — to him Madam turned, roaring out: "Lawful heart, John, is it you? — how de do! Where in the world are you going with this woman? Who is she?" John made no answer, but sat down in the corner, fumbled out his black junk, and saluted that instead of Deb; she then turned again to me and fell anew into her silly questions, without asking me to sit down.

I told her she treated me very rudely, and I did not think it my duty to answer her unmannerly questions. But to get rid of them, I told her I came there to have the post's company with me tomorrow on my journey, etc. Miss stared awhile, drew a chair, bade me sit, and then ran up stairs and put on two or three rings (or else I had not seen them before), and returning, set herself just before me, showing the way to Reading, that I might see her ornaments, perhaps to gain the more respect. But her granam's new rung sow, had it appeared, would have affected me as much. I paid honest John with money and dram according to contract, and dismissed him, and prayed Miss to show me where I must lodge. She conducted me to a parlor in a little back lean-to, which was almost filled with the bedstead, which was so high that I was forced to climb on a chair to get up to the wretched bed that lay on it; on which having stretched my tired limbs, and laid my head on a sad-colored pillow, I began to think on the transactions of the past day.

Tuesday, October the 3d, about eight in the morning, I with the post proceeded forward without observing anything remarkable; and about two, afternoon, arrived at the post's second stage, where the western post met him and exchanged letters. Here, having called for something to eat, the woman brought in a twisted thing like a cable, but something whiter; and, laying in on the board, tugged for life to bring it into a capacity to spread; which having with great pains accomplished, she served in a dish of pork and cabbage, I suppose the remains of dinner. The sauce was of deep purple, which I thought was boiled in her dye kettle; the bread was Indian, and everything on the table service agreeable to these. I, being hungry, got a little down; but my stomach was soon cloyed, and what cabbage I swallowed served me for a cud the whole day after.

Having here discharged the ordinary for self and guide (as I understood was the custom), about three afternoon went on with my third guide. . . .

Being come to Mr. Haven's, I was very civilly received and courteously entertained, in a clean, comfortable house; and the good woman was very active in helping off my riding clothes, and then asked what I would eat. I told her I had some chocolate, if she would prepare it; which with the help of some milk, and a little clean brass kettle, she soon effected to my satisfaction. I then betook me to my apartment, which was a little room parted from the kitchen by a single board partition; where, after I had noted the occurrences of the past day, I went to bed, which, though pretty hard, yet neat and handsome. But I could get no sleep, because of the clamor of some of the town topers in next room, who were entered into a strong debate concerning the signification of the name of their country, viz. Narragansett. One said it was named so by the Indians, because there grew a brier there, of a prodigious height and bigness, the like hardly ever known, called by the Indians narragansett; and quotes an Indian of so barbarous a name for his author, that I could not write it. His antagonist replied no — it was from a spring it had its name, which he well knew where it was, which was extreme cold in summer, and as hot as could be imagined in the winter, which was much resorted to by the natives, and by them called narragansett (hot and cold), and that was the original notice, which he uttered with such a roaring voice and thundering of their place's name — with a thousand impertinences not worth blows with the fist of wickedness on the table, that it pierced my very head. I heartily fretted, and wished them tongue-tied; but with as little success as a friend of mine once, who was (as she said) kept a whole night awake, on a journey, by a country lieutenant and a sergeant, ensign, and a deacon, contriving how to bring a triangle into a square. They kept calling for t'other gill, which, while they were swallowing, was some intermission; but, presently, like oil to fire, increased the flame. I set my candle on a chest by the bedside, and sitting up, fell to my old way of composing my resentments, in the following manner:

> I ask thy aid, O potent Rum!
> To charm these wrangling topers dumb.
> Thou hast their giddy brains possest —

The man confounded with the beast —
And I, poor I, can get no rest.
Intoxicate them with thy fumes:
O still their tongues till morning comes!

And I know not but my wishes took effect; for the dispute soon ended with t'other dram; and so good night!

Wednesday, October 4th. — About four in the morning we set out for Kingston with a French doctor in our company. He and the post put on very furiously, so that I could not keep up with them, only as now and then they would stop till they saw me. This road was poorly furnished with accommodations for travelers, so that we were forced to ride twenty-two miles by the post's account, but nearer thirty by mine, before we could bait [feed] so much as our horses, which I exceedingly complained of. But the post encouraged me, by saying we should be well accommodated anon at Mr. Devil's, a few miles farther. But I questioned whether we ought to go to the devil to be helped out of affliction. However, like the rest of deluded souls that post to the infernal den, we made all possible speed to this devil's habitation; where alighting, in full assurance of good accommodation, we were going in. But meeting his two daughters, as I supposed twins — they so nearly resembled each other, both in features and habit, and looked as old as the devil himself, and quite as ugly — we desired entertainment, but could hardly get a word out of them, till with our importunity, telling them our necessity, etc., they called the old sophister, who was as sparing of his words as his daughters had been, and no, or none, were the replies he made us to our demands. He differed only in this from the old fellow in t'other country: he let us depart.

Thus leaving this habitation of cruelty, we went forward; and arriving at an ordinary about two miles farther, found tolerable accommodation. But our hostess, being a pretty full-mouthed old creature, entertained our fellow traveler, the French doctor, with innumerable complaints of her bodily infirmities; and whispered to him so loud that all the house had as full a hearing as he: which was very diverting to the company (of which there was a great many), as one might see by their sneering. But poor weary I slipped out to enter my mind in my journal, and left my great landlady with her talkative guests to themselves.

Thursday, October the 5th, about three in the afternoon, I set forward with neighbor Polly and Jemima, a girl about eighteen years old, who he said he had been to fetch out of the Narragansetts, and said they had rode thirty miles that day, on a sorry lean jade, with only a bag under her for a pillion, which the poor girl often complained was very uneasy.

About seven that evening we came to New London ferry; here, by reason of a very high wind, we met with great difficulty in getting over — the boat tossed exceedingly, and our horses capered at a very surprising rate, and set us all in a fright, especially poor Jemima, who desired her father to say "So, Jack" to the jade, to make her stand. But the careless parent taking no notice of her repeated desires, she roared out in a passionate manner: "Pray sooth, father; are you deaf? Say 'So, Jack' to the jade, I tell you." The dutiful parent obeys, saying "So, Jack; so, Jack," as gravely as if he'd been to saying catechize after young Miss, who with her fright looked of all colors in the rainbow.

Being safely arrived at the house of Mrs. Prentice's in New London, I treated neighbor Polly and daughter for their diverting company, and bade them farewell; and between nine and ten at night waited on the Reverend Mr. Gurdon Saltonstall, minister of the town, who kindly invited me to stay that night at his house, where I was very handsomely and plentifully treated and lodged; and made good the great character I had before heard concerning him, viz., that he was the most affable, courteous, generous, and best of men.

Friday, October 6th. — I got up very early, in order to hire somebody to go with me to New Haven, being in great perplexity at the thoughts of proceeding alone; which my most hospitable entertainer observing, himself went and soon returned with a young gentleman of the town, whom he could confide in to go with me. . . . The roads all along this way are very bad, encumbered with rocks and mountainous passages, which were very disagreeable to my tired carcass; but we went on with a moderate pace which made the journey more pleasant. But after about eight miles riding, in going over a bridge under which the river ran very swift, my horse stumbled and very narrowly 'scaped falling over into the water, which extremely frightened me. But through God's goodness I met with no harm, and mounting again, in about half a mile's riding, came to an ordinary, was well entertained by a woman of about seventy and vantage, but of as sound intellectuals as one of seventeen.

Saturday, October 7th. — About two o'clock afternoon we arrived at New Haven, where I was received with all possible prospects and civility. Here I discharged Mr. Wheeler with a reward to his satisfaction, and took some time to rest after so long and toilsome a journey; and informed myself of the manners and customs of the place, and at the same time employed myself in the affair I went there upon.

They are governed by the same laws as we in Boston (or little differing), throughout this whole colony of Connecticut, and much the same way of church government, and many of them good, sociable people, and I hope religious too: but a little too much independent in their principles, and, as I have been told, were formerly in their zeal very rigid in their administrations towards such as their laws made offenders, even to a harmless kiss or innocent merriment among young people, whipping being a frequent and counted an easy punishment, about which as other crimes, the judges were absolute in their sentences.

Their diversions in this part of the country are on lecture days and training days mostly; on the former there is riding from town to town. And on training days the youth divert themselves by shooting at the target, as they call it (but it very much resembles a pillory), where he that hits nearest the white has some yards of red ribbon presented him, which being tied to his hatband, the two ends streaming down his back, he is led away in triumph, with great applause, as the winners of the Olympic games. They generally marry very young: the males oftener, as I am told, under twenty than above: they generally make public weddings, and have a way something singular (as they say) in some of them, viz., just before joining hands the bridegroom quits the place, who is soon followed by the bridesmen, and as it were dragged back to duty — being the reverse to the former practice among us, to steal mistress bride. And they generally lived very well and comfortably in their families. But too indulgent (especially the farmers) to their slaves: suffering too great familiarity from them, permitting them to sit at the table and eat with them (as they say to save time), and into the dish goes the black hoof as freely as the white hand. They told me that there was a farmer lived near the town where I lodged who had some difference with his slave, concerning something the master had promised him and did not punctually perform, which caused some hard words between them; but at length they put the matter to arbitration and bound themselves to stand to the ward of such as they named — which done, the arbitrators, having heard the allegations of both parties, ordered the master to pay forty shillings to blackface and acknowledge his fault. And so the matter ended, the poor master very honestly standing to the award. . . .

Being at a merchant's house, in comes a tall country fellow, with his alfogeos [cheeks] full of tobacco; for they seldom loose their cud, but keep chewing and spitting as long as their eyes are open — he advanced to the middle of the room, makes an awkward nod, and spitting a large deal of aromatic tincture, he gave a scrape with his shovel-like shoe, leaving a small shovelful of dirt on the floor, made a full stop, hugging his own pretty body with his hands under his arms, stood staring round him, like a cat let out of a basket. At last, like the creature Balaam rode on, he opened his mouth and said, "Have you any ribinen for hatbands to sell, I pray?" The questions and answers about the pay being past, the ribbon is brought and opened. Bumpkin Simpers cries, "It's confounded gay, I vow"; and beckoning to the door, in comes Joan Tawdry, dropping about fifty curtsies, and stands by him; he shows her the ribbon. "Law, you," says she, "it's right gent, do you take it, 'tis dreadful pretty." Then she inquires, "Have you any hood silk, I pray?" which being brought and bought, "Have you any thread silk to sew it with?" says she; which being accommodated with, they departed. They generally stand after they come in a great while speechless, and sometimes don't say a word till they are asked what they want, which I impute to the awe they stand in of the merchants, who they are constantly almost indebted to, and must take what they bring without liberty to choose for themselves; but they serve them as well, making the merchants stay long enough for their pay.

December 6th. — Being by this time well recruited and rested after my journey, my business lying unfinished by some concerns at New York depending thereupon, my kinsman, Mr. Thomas

Trowbridge, of New Haven, must needs take a journey there before it could be accomplished; I resolved to go there in company with him and a man of the town which I engaged to wait on me there. Accordingly, December 6th, we set out from New Haven, and about eleven same morning came to Stratford ferry; which crossing, about two miles on the other side baited our horses and would have eat a morsel ourselves, but the pumpkin and Indian mixed bread had such an aspect, and the barelegged punch so awkward or rather awful a sound, that we left both, and proceeded forward, and about seven at night came to Fairfield, where we met with good entertainment and lodged; and early next morning set forward to Norrowalk, from its half-Indian name "North-walk", where about twelve at noon we arrived, and had a dinner of fried venison, very savory. Landlady, wanting some pepper in the seasoning, bid the girl hand her the spice in the little "gay" cup on the shelf. From hence we hastened towards Rye, walking and leading our horses near a mile together, up a prodigious high hill; and so riding till about nine at night, and there arrived and took up our lodgings at an ordinary, which a French family kept. Here being very hungry, I desired a fricassee, which the Frenchman, undertaking, managed so contrary to my notion of cookery, that I hastened to bed supperless; and being shown the way up a pair of stairs which had such a narrow passage that I had almost stopped by the bulk of my body, but arriving at my apartment found it to be a little lean-to chamber, furnished among other rubbish with a high bed and a low one, a long table, a bench, and a bottomless chair. Little Miss went to scratch up my kennel, which rustled as if she had been in the barn among the husks, and suppose such was the contents of the ticking. Nevertheless, being exceeding weary, down I laïd my poor carcass (never more tired), and found my covering as scanty as my bed was hard. Anon I heard another rustling noise in the room — called to know the matter — little Miss said she was making a bed for the men; who, when they were in bed, complained their legs lay out of it by reason of its shortness. My poor bones complained bitterly, not being used to such lodgings, and so did the man who was with us; and poor I made but one groan, which was from the time I went to bed to the time I rose, which was about three in the morning, sitting up by the fire till light, and, having discharged our ordinary — which was as dear as if we had had far better fare — we took our leave of Monsieur and about seven in the morning came to New Rochelle, a French town, where we had a good breakfast. And on the strength of that about an hour before sunset got to York.

The Journals of Madam Knight

14. German Redemptioners Take Ship to Pennsylvania

The problem of refugees is as old as the fact of man's inhumanity to man. Early in the eighteenth century many thousands of Germans from the Palatinate and other parts of the Rhineland took shelter in England, with grave embarrassment to the authorities. In 1710 three thousand were sent on to New York under the care of Robert Hunter, governor of that province. Some went to the Mohawk Valley; some reached the Susquehanna and other parts of Pennsylvania. Swiss Mennonites meanwhile came into the district about Lancaster, Pennsylvania. The hospitable province of the Penns was especially congenial to emigrants, and the main stream of German settlers poured into it; for thirty years beginning in 1727 an average of about two thousand a year came over. They made thrifty, enterprising farmers and loyal subjects of the king. Many were so poor that they could not pay their passage. They therefore became "redemptioners," selling their services for a term of years to obtain transportation and initial support. Any voyage in those days, as Dr. Johnson recognized when he compared ships with prisons, was a misery, but the poverty-stricken immigrants got especially rough treatment.

WHEN the ships have for the last time weighed their anchors near the city of Kaupp [Cowes] in Old England, the real misery begins with the long voyage. For from there the ships, unless they have good wind, must often sail eight, nine, ten to twelve weeks before they reach Philadelphia. But even with the best wind the voyage lasts seven weeks.

But during the voyage there is on board these ships terrible misery, stench, fumes, horror, vomiting, many kinds of seasickness, fever, dysentery, headache, heat, constipation, boils, scurvy, cancer, mouth rot, and the like, all of which come from old and sharply-salted food and meat, also from very bad and foul water, so that many die miserably.

Add to this want of provisions, hunger, thirst, frost, heat, damp-ness, anxiety, want, afflictions and lamentations, together with other trouble, as *e.g.,* the lice abound so frightfully, especially on sick people, that they can be scraped off the body. The misery reaches a climax when a gale rages for two or three nights and days, so that every one believes that the ship will go to the bottom with all human beings on board. In such a visitation the people cry and pray most piteously.

Among the healthy, impatience sometimes grows so great and cruel that one curses the other, or himself and the day of his birth, and sometimes come near killing each other. Misery and malice join each other, so that they cheat and rob one another. One always reproaches the other with having persuaded him to undertake the journey. Frequently children cry out against their parents, hus-bands against their wives, and wives against their husbands; brothers and sisters, friends and acquaintances, against each other. But most against the soul-traffickers.

No one can have an idea of the sufferings which women in con-finement have to bear with their innocent children on board these ships. Few of this class escape with their lives; many a mother is cast into the water with her child as soon as she is dead. One day, just as we had a heavy gale, a woman in our ship, who was to give birth and could not give birth under the circumstances, was pushed through a loophole [porthole] in the ship and dropped into the sea, because she was far in the rear of the ship and could not be brought forward.

Children from one to seven years rarely survive the voyage; and many a time parents are compelled to see their children mis-erably suffer and die from hunger, thirst, and sickness, and then to see them cast into the water. I witnessed such misery in no less than thirty-two children in our ship, all of whom were thrown into the sea. The parents grieve all the more since their children find no resting place in the earth, but are devoured by the monsters of the sea. It is a notable fact that children who have not yet had the measles or smallpox generally get them on board the ship, and mostly die of them.

When the ships have landed at Philadelphia after their long voyage, no one is permitted to leave them except those who pay for their passage or can give good security; the others, who cannot pay, must remain on board the ships till they are purchased and are released from the ships by their purchasers. The sick always fare the worst, for the healthy are naturally preferred and purchased first; and so the sick and wretched must often remain on board in front of the city for two or three weeks, and frequently die, whereas many a one, if he could pay his debt and were permitted to leave the ship immediately, might recover and remain alive.

The sale of human beings in the market on board the ship is carried on thus: Every day Englishmen, Dutchmen, and High German people come from the city of Philadelphia and other places, in part from a great distance, say twenty, thirty, or forty hours away, and go on board the newly-arrived ship that has brought and offers for sale passengers from Europe, and select among the healthy persons such as they deem suitable for their business, and bargain with them how long they will serve for their passage money, which most of them are still in debt for. When they have come to an agreement, it happens that adult persons bind themselves in writing to serve three, four, five, or six years for the amount due by them, according to their age and strength. But very young people, from ten to fifteen years, must serve till they are twenty-one years old.

Many parents must sell and trade away their children like so many head of cattle, for if their children take the debt upon themselves, the parents can leave the ship free and unrestrained; but as the parents often do not know where and to what people their children are going, it often happens that such parents and children, after leaving the ship, do not see each other again for many years, perhaps no more in all their lives.

It often happens that whole families, husband, wife, and children, are separated by being sold to different purchasers, especially when they have not paid any part of their passage money.

When a husband or wife has died at sea, when the ship has made more than half of her trip, the survivor must pay or serve not only for himself or herself, but also for the deceased. When both parents have died over halfway at sea, their children, especially when they are young and have nothing to pawn or to pay, must stand for their own and their parents' passage, and serve till they are twenty-one years old. When one has served his or her term, he or she is entitled to a new suit of clothes at parting; and if it has been so stipulated, a man gets in addition a horse, a woman, a cow.

Work and labor in this new and wild land are very hard and manifold, and many a one who came there in his old age must work very hard to his end for his bread. I will not speak of young people. Work mostly consists in cutting wood, felling oak trees, rooting out, or as they say there, clearing large tracts of forest. Such forests, being cleared, are then laid out for fields and meadows. From the best hewn wood, fences are made around the new fields; for there all meadows, orchards, and fruit fields are surrounded and fenced in with planks made of thickly-split wood, laid one above the other, as in zigzag lines, and within such inclosures horses, cattle, and sheep are permitted to graze. Our Europeans who are purchased must always work hard, for new fields are constantly laid out; and so they learn that stumps of oak trees are in America certainly as hard as in Germany.

Gottlieb Mittelberger's Journey to Pennsylvania in the Year 1750

15. Benjamin Franklin Arrives in Philadelphia

It was a memorable day for Pennsylvania and all America when in October, 1723, a seventeen-year-old printer named Benjamin Franklin, who had just quarreled with his half-brother in Boston and left his employ, arrived in Philadelphia

Within seven years he was married, sole owner of a flourishing business, and publisher of the Pennsylvania Gazette; *within twenty years he was one of the leaders of the province. Even at seventeen he had schooled himself thoroughly in Addison's writings, and the clear, flowing Addisonian style, as this selection shows, remained one of his important possessions.*

I HAVE been the more particular in this description of my journey, and shall be so of my first entry into that city, that you may in your mind compare such unlikely beginnings with the figure I have since made there. I was in my working dress, my best clothes being to come round by sea. I was dirty from my journey; my pockets were stuffed out with shirts and stockings, and I knew no soul nor where to look for lodging. I was fatigued with traveling, rowing, and want of rest; I was very hungry; and my whole stock of cash consisted of a Dutch dollar and about a shilling in copper. The latter I gave the people of the boat for my passage, who at first refused it, on account of my rowing; but I insisted on their taking it. A man being sometimes more generous when he has but a little money than when he has plenty, perhaps through fear of being thought to have but little.

Then I walked up the street, gazing about till near the market house I met a boy with bread. I had made many a meal on bread, and, inquiring where he got it, I went immediately to the baker's he directed me to, in Second Street, and asked for biscuit, intending such as we had in Boston; but they, it seems, were not made in Philadelphia. Then I asked for a threepenny loaf, and was told they had none such. So not considering or knowing the difference of money, and the greater cheapness nor the names of his bread, I bad him give me threepennyworth of any sort. He gave me, accordingly, three great puffy rolls. I was surprised at the quantity, but took it, and having no room in my pockets, walked off with a roll under each arm, and eating the other. Thus I went up Market Street as far as Fourth Street, passing by the door of Mr. Read, my future wife's father; when she, standing at the door, saw me, and thought I made, as I certainly did, a most awkward, ridiculous appearance.

Then I turned and went down Chestnut Street and part of Walnut Street, eating my roll all the way, and, coming round, found myself again at Market Street wharf, near the boat I came in, to which I went for a draught of the river water; and, being filled with one of my rolls, gave the other two to a woman and her child that came down the river in the boat with us, and were waiting to go farther.

Thus refreshed, I walked again up the street, which by this time had many clean-dressed people in it, who were all walking the same way. I joined them, and thereby was led into the great meeting house of the Quakers near the market. I sat down among them, and, after looking round awhile and hearing nothing said, being very drowsy through labor and want of rest the preceding night, I fell fast asleep, and continued so till the meeting broke up, when one was kind enough to rouse me. This was, therefore, the first house I was in, or slept in, in Philadelphia.

The Autobiography of Benjamin Franklin

16. George Mason Lives in State at Gunston Hall

Great-grandson of a Cavalier who emigrated to Virginia after Cromwell's men won the battle of Worcester, George Mason inherited some five thousand acres on the Potomac below Alexandria, thus becoming a close neighbor of George Washington. Few Americans of the time had as good an education as his, for his mother hired private tutors and he immersed himself in a library of some fifteen hundred volumes. Although he devoted himself to supervising his estates, declining to employ a manager, he was thoroughly trained in law and government, and Virginia found his services as constitutionalist and legislator invaluable. At the age of thirty, in 1755, he began building one of the famous mansions of tidewater Virginia, Gunston Hall, its architect a skilled craftsman from Oxford. Here he lived the life of gentleman, statesman, and practical planter.

GUNSTON HALL is situated on a height on the right bank of the Potomac River within a short walk of the shores, and commanding a full view of it, about five miles above the mouth of that branch of it on the same side called the Occoquan. When I can first remember it, it was in a state of high improvement and carefully kept. The south front looked to the river; from an elevated little portico on this front you descended directly into an extensive garden, touching the house on one side and reduced from the natural irregularity of the hilltop to a perfect level platform, the southern extremity of which was bounded by a spacious walk running eastwardly and westwardly, from which there was by the natural and sudden declivity of the hill a rapid descent to the plain considerably below it. On this plain adjoining the margin of the hill, opposite to and in full view from the garden, was a deer park, studded with trees, kept well fenced and stocked with native deer domesticated. On the north front, by which was the principal approach, was an extensive lawn kept closely pastured, through the midst of which led a spacious avenue, girded by long double ranges of that hardy and stately cherry tree, the common blackheart, raised from the stone, and so the more fair and uniform in their growth, commencing at about two hundred feet from the house and extending thence for about twelve hundred feet; the carriageway being in the center and the footways on either side, between the two rows forming each double range of trees, and under their shade.

To the west of the main building were first the schoolhouse, and then at a little distance, masked by a row of large English walnut trees, were the stables. To the east was a high paled yard, adjoining the house, into which opened an outer door from the private front, within or connected with which yard were the kitchen, well, poultry houses, and other domestic arrangements; and beyond it on the same side were the corn house and granary, servants' houses (in those days called Negro quarters), hay yard and cattle pens, all of which were masked by rows of large cherry and mulberry trees. And adjoining the inclosed grounds on which stood the mansion and all these appendages on the eastern side was an extensive pasture for stock of all kinds running down to the river, through which led the road to the Landing, emphatically so called, where all persons or things water-borne were landed or taken off, and where were kept the boats, pettiaugers [piraguas], and canoes, of which there were always several, for business transportation, fishing, and hunting, belonging to the establishment. Farther north and on the same side was an extensive orchard of fine fruit trees of a variety of kinds. Beyond this was a small and highly-fenced pasture devoted to a single brood horse. The occupant in my early days was named Vulcan, of the best stock in the country, and a direct descendant of the celebrated Old James. The west side of the lawn or inclosed grounds was skirted by a wood, just far enough within which to be out of sight was a little village called Log Town, so called because most of the houses were built of hewn pine logs. Here lived several families of the slaves serving about the mansion house; among them were my father's body servant James, a mulatto man and his family, and those of several Negro carpenters.

The heights on which the mansion house stood extended in an east-and-west direction across an isthmus and were at the northern extremity of the estate to which it belonged. This contained something more than five thousand acres and was called Dogue's Neck, water-locked by the Potomac on the south, the Occoquan on the west, and Pohick Creek on the east. The isthmus on the northern boundary is narrow and the whole estate was kept completely inclosed by a fence on that side of about one mile in length, running from the head of Holt's to the margin of Pohick Creek. This fence was maintained with great care and in good repair in my father's time, in order to secure to his own stock the exclusive range within it, and made of uncommon height to keep in the native deer which had been preserved there in abundance from the first settlement of the country and indeed are yet there in considerable numbers. The land south of the heights and comprising more than nine-tenths of the estate was an uniform level elevated some twenty feet above the surface of the river, with the exception of one extensive marsh and three or four water courses, which were accompanied by some ravines and undulations of minor character — and about two-thirds of it were yet clothed with the primitive wood; the whole of this level tract was embraced in one view from the mansion house. In different parts of this tract and detached from each other, my father worked four plantations with his own slaves, each under an overseer, and containing four or five hundred acres of open land. The crops were principally Indian corn and tobacco, the corn for the support of the plantations and the home house, and the tobacco for sale. There was but little small grain made in that part of the country in those days. He had also another plantation worked in the same manner, on an estate he had in Charles County, Maryland, on the Potomac about twenty miles lower down, at a place called Stump Neck.

It was very much the practice with gentlemen of landed and slave estates in the interior of Virginia, so to organize them as to have considerable resources within themselves; to employ and pay but few tradesmen, and to buy little or none of the coarse stuffs and materials used by them; and this practice became stronger and more general during the long period of the Revolutionary War, which in great measure cut off the means of supply from elsewhere. Thus my father had among his slaves carpenters, coopers, sawyers, blacksmiths, tanners, curriers, shoemakers, spinners, weavers and knitters, and even a distiller. His woods furnished timber and plank for the carpenters and coopers, and charcoal for the blacksmith; his cattle, killed for his own consumption and for sale, supplied skins for the tanners, curriers, and shoemakers, and his sheep gave wool and his fields produced cotton and flax for the weavers and spinners, and his orchards fruit for the distiller. His carpenters and sawyers built and kept in repair all the dwelling houses, barns, stables, plows, harrows, gates, etc., on the plantations and the outhouses at the home house. His coopers made the hogsheads the tobacco was prized in and the tight casks to hold the cider and other liquors. The tanners and curriers with the proper vats, etc., tanned and dressed the skins as well for upper as for lower leather to the full amount of the consumption of the estate, and the shoemakers made them into shoes for the Negroes. A professed shoemaker was hired for three or four months in the year to come and make up the shoes for the white part of the family. The blacksmith did all the iron work required by the establishment, as making and repairing plows, harrows, teeth chains, bolts, etc., etc. The spinners, weavers, and knitters made all the coarse cloths and stockings used by the Negroes, and some of finer texture worn by the white family, nearly all worn by the children of it. The distiller made every fall a good deal of apple, peach, and persimmon brandy. The art of distilling from grain was not then among us, and but few public distilleries. All these operations were carried on at the home house, and their results distributed as occasion required to the different plantations. Moreover all the beeves and hogs for consumption or sale were driven up and slaughtered there at the proper seasons, and whatever was to be preserved was salted and packed away for after distribution.

My father kept no steward or clerk about him. He kept his own books and superintended, with the assistance of a trusty slave or two, and occasionally of some of his sons, all the operations at or about the home house above described, except that during the Revolutionary War, and when it was necessary to do a great deal in that way to clothe all his slaves, he had in his service a white man, a weaver of the finer stuffs, to weave himself and superintend the Negro spinning-women. To carry on these operations to the extent required, it will be seen that a considerable force was necessary, besides the house servants, who for such a household, a large family and entertaining a great deal of company, must be numerous — and such a force was constantly kept there, independently of any of the plantations, and besides occasional drafts from them of labor for particular occasions. As I had during my youth constant intercourse with all these people, I remember them all and their several employments as if it was yesterday.

KATE M. ROWLAND, The Life of George Mason

IV

White Men and Red

17. John Lawson Visits the Indians of North Carolina

European readers had an insatiable interest in the Indians of North America. One of the men who tried to satisfy it was the English traveler John Lawson, who arrived in the Southern colonies in 1700, and after a thousand-mile journey among the savages, wrote a book, half of which was devoted to them and their customs. Vivid, sprightly, and accurate, it has been much used by both ethnologists and historians. In it Lawson gave a favorable description of the climate, products, and people of North Carolina. It is sad to record that the Indians whom he celebrated seized him and put him to death in 1711.

THE INDIANS of North Carolina are a well-shaped, clean-made people, of different statures, as the Europeans are, yet chiefly inclined to be tall. They are a very straight people, and never bend forwards or stoop in the shoulders, unless much overpowered by old age. Their limbs are exceeding well shaped. As for their legs and feet, they are generally the handsomest in the world. Their bodies are a little flat, which is occasioned by being laced hard down to a board in their infancy. This is all the cradle they have, which I shall describe at large elsewhere. Their eyes are black, or of a dark hazel; the white is marbled with red streaks, which is ever common to these people, unless when sprung from a white father or mother. Their color is of a tawny, which would not be so dark did they not daub themselves with bear's oil and a color like burnt cork. This is begun in their infancy and continued for a long time, which fills the pores and enables them better to endure the extremity of the weather. They are never bald on their heads, although never so old, which, I believe, proceeds from their heads being always uncovered, and the greasing their hair, so often as they do, with bear's fat, which is a great nourisher of the hair, and causes it to grow very fast.

Their eyes are commonly full and manly, and their gait sedate and majestic. They never walk backward and forward as we do, nor contemplate on the affairs of loss and gain, the things which daily perplex us. They are dexterous and steady, both as to their hands and feet, to admiration. They will walk over deep brooks and creeks on the smallest poles, and that without any fear or concern. Nay, an Indian will walk on the ridge of a barn or house and look down the gable end, and spit upon the ground as unconcerned as if he was walking on terra firma. In running, leaping, or any such other exercise, their legs seldom miscarry and give them a fall; and as for letting anything fall out of their hands, I never yet knew one example. They are no inventors of any arts or trades worthy mention; the reason of which I take to be that they are not possessed with that care and thoughtfulness, how to provide for the necessaries of life as the Europeans are; yet they will learn anything very soon. I have known an Indian stock guns better than most of our joiners, although he never saw one stocked before; and besides, his working tool was only a sorry knife. I have also known several of them that were slaves to the English, learn handicraft trades very well and speedily. I never saw a dwarf amongst them, nor but one that was humpbacked. Their teeth are yellow with smoking tobacco, which both men and women are much addicted to. They tell us that they had tobacco amongst them before the Europeans made any discovery of that continent. It differs in the leaf from the sweet-scented and oronoco, which are the plants we raise and cultivate in America. Theirs differs likewise much in the smell, when green, from our tobacco before cured. They do not use the same way to cure it as we do, and therefore the difference must be very considerable in taste; for all men (that know tobacco) must allow that it is the ordering thereof which gives a hogo to that weed rather than any natural relish it possesses when green. Although they are great smokers, yet they never are seen to take it in snuff or chew it.

As there are found very few or scarce any deformed or cripples amongst them, so neither did I ever see but one blind man; and then they would give me no account how his blindness came. They had a use for him, which was to lead him with a girl, woman, or boy by a string; so they put what burdens they pleased upon his back and made him very serviceable upon all such occasions. No people have better eyes, or see better in the night or day than the Indians. Some allege that the smoke of the pitch pine which they chiefly burn, does both preserve and strengthen the eyes; as perhaps it may do, because that smoke never offends the eyes, though you hold your face over a great fire thereof. This is occasioned by the volatile part of the turpentine, which rises with the smoke, and is of a friendly, balsamic nature; for the ashes of the pine tree afford no fixed salt in them.

They let their nails grow very long, which, they reckon, is the use nails are designed for, and laugh at the Europeans for paring theirs, which, they say, disarms them of that which Nature designed them for.

They are not of so robust and strong bodies as to lift great burdens and endure labor and slavish work as the Europeans are; yet some that are slaves prove very good and laborious; but, of themselves, they never work as the English do, taking care for no further than what is absolutely necessary to support life. In traveling and hunting they are very indefatigable, because that carries a pleasure along with the profit. I have known some of them very strong; and as for running and leaping, they are extraordinary fellows, and will dance for several nights together with the greatest briskness imaginable, their wind never failing them.

Their dances are of different natures, and for every sort of dance they have a tune, which is allotted for that dance; as, if it be a war dance, they have a warlike song, wherein they express, with all the passion and vehemence imaginable, what they intend to do with their enemies; how they will kill, roast, scalp, beat, and make captive such and such numbers of them; and how many they have destroyed before. All these songs are made new for every feast; nor is one and the same song sung at two several festivals. Some one of the nation (which has the best gift of expressing their designs) is appointed by their king and war captains to make these songs.

Their chiefest game is a sort of arithmetic which is managed by a parcel of small split reeds the thickness of a small bent; these are made very nicely so that they part and are tractable in their hands. They are fifty-one in number, their length about seven inches; when they play, they throw part of them to their antagonist; the art is to discover upon sight how many you have and what you throw to him that plays with you. Some are so expert at their numbers that they will tell ten times together what they throw out of their hands. Although the whole play is carried on with the quickest motion it is possible to use, yet some are so expert at this game as to win great Indian estates by this play. A good set of these reeds, fit to play withal, are valued and sold for a dressed doeskin.

They have several other plays and games, as with the kernels or stones of persimmons, which are in effect the same as our dice, because winning or losing depend on which side appear uppermost and how they happen to fall together.

Another game is managed with a baton and a ball and resembles our trapball; besides, several nations have several games and pastimes which are not used by others.

These savages live in wigwams or cabins built of bark, which are made round like an oven to prevent any damage by hard gales of wind. They make the fire in the middle of the house, and have a hole at the top of the roof right above the fire to let out the smoke. These dwellings are as hot as stoves, where the Indians sleep and sweat all night. The floors thereof are never paved nor swept, so that they have always a loose earth on them. They are often troubled with a multitude of fleas, especially near the places where they dress their deerskins, because that hair harbors them; yet I never felt any ill, unsavory smell in their cabins, whereas, should we live in our houses as they do we should be poisoned with our own nastiness, which confirms these Indians to be, as they really are, some of the sweetest people in the world.

The bark they make their cabins withal is generally cypress, or red or white cedar; and sometimes, when they are a great way from any of these woods, they make use of pine bark, which is the worser sort. In building these fabrics they get very long poles of pine, cedar, hickory, or any other wood that will bend; these are the thickness of the small of a man's leg at the thickest end, which they generally strip of the bark and warm them well in the fire, which makes them tough and fit to bend. Afterwards, they stick the thickest ends of them in the ground about two yards asunder, in a circular form, the distance they design the cabin to be (which is not always round but sometimes oval); then they bend the tops and bring them together, and bind their ends with bark of trees that is proper for that use, as elm is, or sometimes the moss that grows on the trees and is a yard or two long and never rots; then they brace them with other poles to make them strong; afterwards cover them all over with bark, so that they are very warm and tight, and will keep firm against all the weathers that blow. They have other sorts of cabins without windows, which are for their granaries, skins, and merchandises, and others that are covered overhead; the rest left open for the air. These have reed hurdles, like tables, to lie and sit on in summer, and serve for pleasant banqueting houses in the hot season of the year. The cabins they dwell in have benches all round, except where the door stands; on these they lay beasts' skins and mats made of rushes, whereon they sleep and loll. In one of these several families commonly live, though all related to one another.

JOHN LAWSON, History of Carolina

18. The Death of King Philip

Ablest and craftiest of all the New England Indians was Philip, sachem of the Wampanoags. As the white men bought more and more of the Indian land, restricting the tribe to narrower areas and diminished game, unrest grew. Finally in 1675 Philip began the most disastrous Indian war in the history of New England; a war in which twelve towns were destroyed and several thousand whites killed. Hostilities began near Narragansett Bay, but spread through Massachusetts and as far west as the Connecticut River. Before they were ended in the following year the colonists had spent a hundred thousand pounds. Philip's head was long exhibited by the vengeful colonists at Plymouth.

CAPTAIN CHURCH being now at Plymouth again, weary and worn, would have gone home to his wife and family; but the government being solicitous to engage him in the service until Philip was slain, and promising him satisfaction and redress for some mistreatment that he had met with, he fixes for another expedition.

He had soon volunteers enough to make up the company he desired, and marched through the woods until he came to Pocasset. And not seeing or hearing of any of the enemy, they went over the ferry to Rhode Island, to refresh themselves. The Captain, with about half a dozen in his company, took horses and rid about eight miles down the island to Mr. Sanford's, where they spied two horsemen coming a great pace. Captain Church told his company that "those men (by their riding) come with tidings." When they came up, they proved to be Major Sanford and Captain Golding, who immediately asked Captain Church what he would give to hear some news of Philip. He replied that was what he wanted. They told him they had rid hard with some hopes of overtaking him, and were now come on purpose to inform him that there were just now tidings from Mount Hope. An Indian came down from thence (where Philip's camp now was) and hallooed, and made signs to be fetched over. And being fetched over, he reported that he was fled from Philip, and told them also that Philip was now in Mount Hope Neck. Captain Church thanked them for their good news and said he hoped by tomorrow morning to have the rogue's head. The horses that he and his company came on, standing at the door, his wife must content herself with a short visit, when such game was ahead. They immediately mounted, set spurs to their horses, and away.

The two gentlemen that brought him the tidings told him they would gladly wait upon him to see the event of this expedition. He thanked them, and told them he should be as fond of their company as any men's; and they went with him. And they were soon at Trip's ferry (with Captain Church's company), where the deserter was, who was a fellow of good sense, and told his story handsomely. He offered Captain Church to pilot him to Philip and to help to kill him, that he might revenge his brother's death. Told him that

Philip was now upon a little spot of upland that was in the south end of the miry swamp just at the foot of the mount, which was a spot of ground that Captain Church was well acquainted with.

By that time they were got over the ferry and came near the ground, half the night was spent. The Captain commands a halt, and bringing the company together, he offered Captain Golding that he should have the honor (if he would please accept of it) to beat up Philip's headquarters. He accepted the offer and had his allotted number drawn out to him, and the pilot. Captain Church's instructions to him were to be very careful in his approach to the enemy and be sure not to show himself until by daylight they might see and discern their own men from the enemy; told him also, that his custom in the like cases was to creep with his company on their bellies until they came as near as they could; and that as soon as the enemy discovered them, they would cry out, and that was the word for his men to fire and fall on. He directed him that when the enemy should start and take into the swamp, they should pursue with speed; every man shouting and making what noise he could; for he would give orders to his ambuscade to fire on any that should come silently.

Captain Church, knowing that it was Philip's custom to be foremost in the flight, went down to the swamp, and gave Captain Williams of Scituate the command of the right wing of the ambush, and placed an Englishman and an Indian together behind such shelters of trees etc. as he could find, and took care to place them at such distance that none might pass undiscovered between them; charged them to be careful of themselves, and of hurting their friends, and to fire at any that should come silently through the swamp. But it being somewhat farther through the swamp than he was aware of, he wanted men to make up his ambuscade.

Having placed what men he had, he took Major Sanford by the hand and said, "Sir, I have so placed them that it is scarce possible Philip should escape them." The same moment a shot whistled over their heads, and then the noise of a gun towards Philip's camp. Captain Church at first thought it might be some gun fired by accident; but before he could speak, a whole volley followed, which was earlier than he expected. One of Philip's gang going forth to ease himself, when he had done, looked round him, and Captain

Golding thought that the Indian looked right at him (though probably it was but his conceit); so fired at him; and upon his firing, the whole company that were with him fired upon the enemy's shelter before the Indians had time to rise from their sleep, and so overshot them. But their shelter was open on that side next the swamp, built so on purpose for the convenience of flight on occasion. They were soon in the swamp, and Philip the foremost, who, starting at the first gun, threw his *petunk* and powder horn over his head, catched up his gun and ran as fast as he could scamper, without any more clothes than his small breeches and stockings, and ran directly upon two of Captain Church's ambush. They let him come fair within shot, and the Englishman's gun missing fire, he bid the Indian fire away, and he did so to the purpose; sent one musket bullet through his heart, and another not above two inches from it. He fell upon his face in the mud and water with his gun under him.

By this time the enemy perceived they were waylaid on the east side of the swamp and tacked short about. One of the enemy, who seemed to be a great, surly old fellow, hallooed with a loud voice, and often called out, "*Iootash, Iootash.*" Captain Church called to his Indian, Peter, and asked him who that was that called so. He answered it was old Annawon, Philip's great captain, calling on his soldiers to stand to it and fight stoutly. Now the enemy finding that place of the swamp which was not ambushed, many of them made their escape in the English tracks.

The man that had shot down Philip ran with all speed to Captain Church and informed him of his exploit, who commanded him to be silent about it and let no man more know it until they had driven the swamp clean. But when they had driven the swamp through, and found the enemy had escaped, or at least the most of them, and the sun now up, and so the dew gone that they could not easily track them, the whole company met together at the place where the enemy's night shelter was, and then Captain Church gave them the news of Philip's death. Upon which the whole army gave three loud huzzas. . . .

This being on the last day of the week, the Captain with his company returned to the island, tarried there until Tuesday, and then went off and ranged through all the woods to Plymouth, and received their premium, which was thirty shillings per head, for the enemies which they had killed or taken, instead of all wages; and Philip's head went at the same price. Methinks it is scanty reward and poor encouragement, though it was better than what had been some time before. For this march they received four shillings and sixpence a man, which was all the reward they had, except the honor of killing Philip. This was in the latter end of August, 1676.

THOMAS CHURCH, The History of
King Philip's War

19. Mary Rowlandson Is Taken into Captivity

It was during King Philip's War that Indians who attacked Lancaster, on the Massachusetts frontier, carried away captive a woman of singular resolution, energy, and intellect, with her three children. Mary White Rowlandson, who was probably born in England, was about forty years old at this time, and wife of the first minister of Lancaster. Her courage, physical vigor, and skill in making shirts and stockings for her captors won for her good treatment during the eleven weeks that the savages carried her about in northern Massachusetts and southern New Hampshire. Eventually the influence of John Hoar and a payment of twenty pounds brought her back to her friends. Her Narrative, published in Cambridge in 1682 and immediately reprinted in England, has gone through almost two-score editions. Written in graphic English, it is interesting as an adventure story, a picture of Indian life and character, and a reflection of the religious temper of the Puritan settlers.

THE DOLEFUL ONSLAUGHT OF THE INDIANS

ON THE 10th of February, 1675, came the Indians with great numbers upon Lancaster. Their first coming was about sunrising.

Hearing the noise of some guns, we looked out; several houses were burning, and the smoke ascending to heaven. There were five persons taken in one house; the father and the mother and a suckling child they knocked on the head; the other two they took and carried away alive. There were two others, who, being out of their garrison upon some occasion, were set upon; one was knocked on the head, the other escaped. Another there was who, running along, was shot and wounded, and fell down; he begged of them his life, promising them money (as they told me), but they would not hearken to him, but knocked him in the head, and stripped him naked, and split open his bowels. Another seeing many of the Indians about his barn ventured and went out, but was quickly shot down. There were three others belonging to the same garrison who were killed; the Indians, getting up upon the roof of the barn, had advantage to shoot down upon them over their fortification. Thus these murderous wretches went on burning and destroying before them.

At length they came and beset our own house, and quickly it was the dolefulest day that ever mine eyes saw. The house stood upon the edge of a hill; some of the Indians got behind the hill, others into the barn, and others behind anything that could shelter them; from all which places they shot against the house, so that the bullets seemed to fly like hail, and quickly they wounded one man among us, then another, and then a third. About two hours (according to my observation in that amazing time) they had been about the house before they prevailed to fire it (which they did with flax and hemp which they brought out of the barn, and there being no defense about the house, only two flankers at two opposite corners, and one of them not finished); they fired it once, and one ventured out and quenched it, but they quickly fired it again, and that took. Now is the dreadful hour come that I have often heard of (in time of the war, as it was the case of others), but now mine eyes see it. Some in our house were fighting for their lives, others wallowing in their blood, the house on fire over our heads, and the bloody heathen ready to knock us on the head if we stirred out. Now might we hear mothers and children crying out for themselves and one another, "Lord, what shall we do!" Then I took my children (and one of my sisters hers) to go forth and leave the house, but, as soon as we came to the door and appeared, the Indians shot so thick that the bullets rattled against the house as if one had taken a handful of stones and threw them, so that we were forced to give back. We had six stout dogs belonging to our garrison, but none of them would stir, though another time if any Indian had come to the door, they were ready to fly upon him and tear him down. The Lord hereby would make us the more to acknowledge His hand, and to see that our help is always in Him. But out we must go, the fire increasing, and coming along behind us roaring, and the Indians gaping before us with their guns, spears, and hatchets to devour us. No sooner were we out of the house but my brother-in-law (being before wounded in defending the house, in or near the throat) fell down dead, whereat the Indians scornfully shouted and hallooed, and were presently upon him, stripping off his clothes. The bullets flying thick, one went through my side, and the same (as would seem) through the bowels and hand of my dear child in my arms. One of my elder sister's children (named William) had then his leg broke, which the Indians perceiving they knocked him on the head. Thus were we butchered by those merciless heathen, standing amazed, with the blood running down to our heels. My eldest sister being yet in the house, and seeing those woeful sights, the infidels hauling mothers one way and children another, and some wallowing in their blood; and her elder son telling her that her son William was dead, and myself was wounded, she said, "And, Lord, let me die with them"; which was no sooner said, but she was struck with a bullet, and fell down dead over the threshold. I hope she is reaping the fruit of her good labors, being faithful to the service of God in her place.

I had often before this said, that if the Indians should come, I should choose rather to be killed by them than taken alive, but when it came to the trial, my mind changed; their glittering weapons so daunted my spirit, that I chose rather to go along with those (as I may say) ravenous bears, than that moment to end my days. And that I may the better declare what happened to me during that grievous captivity, I shall particularly speak of the several removes we had up and down the wilderness.

THE FIRST REMOVE

Now away we must go with those barbarous creatures, with our bodies wounded and bleeding, and our hearts no less than our bodies. About a mile we went that night, up upon a hill, within sight of the town, where they intended to lodge. There was hard by a vacant house (deserted by the English before, for fear of the Indians). I asked them whether I might not lodge in the house that night, to which they answered, "What, will you love Englishmen still?" This was the dolefulest night that ever my eyes saw. Oh, the roaring and singing, and dancing, and yelling of those black creatures in the night, which made the place a lively resemblance of hell. And as miserable was the waste that was there made, of horses, cattle, sheep, swine, calves, lambs, roasting pigs, and fowl (which they had plundered in the town), some roasting, some lying and burning, and some boiling, to feed our merciless enemies, who were joyful enough, though we were disconsolate. To add to the dolefulness of the former day and the dismalness of the present night, my thoughts ran upon my losses and sad, bereaved condition. All was gone, my husband gone (at least separated from me, he being in the Bay; and to add to my grief, the Indians told me they would kill him as he came homeward), my children gone, my relations and friends gone, our house and home, and all our comforts within door and without, all was gone (except my life), and I knew not but the next moment that might go too.

There remained nothing to me but one poor, wounded babe, and it seemed at present worse than death, that it was in such a pitiful condition, bespeaking compassion, and I had no refreshing for it, nor suitable things to revive it. Little do many think what is the savageness and brutishness of this barbarous enemy, — aye, even those that seem to profess more than others among them — when the English have fallen into their hands.

THE SECOND REMOVE

But now (the next morning) I must turn my back upon the town, and travel with them into the vast and desolate wilderness, I knew not whither. It is not my tongue or pen can express the sorrows of my heart, and bitterness of my spirit, that I had at this departure; but God was with me in a wonderful manner, carrying me along and bearing up my spirit, that it did not quite fail. One of the Indians carried my poor wounded babe upon a horse; it went moaning all along, "I shall die, I shall die." I went on foot after it, with sorrow that cannot be expressed. At length I took it off the horse, and carried it in my arms, till my strength failed and I fell down with it. Then they set me upon a horse with my wounded child in my lap, and there being no furniture on the horse's back, as we were going down a steep hill, we both fell over the horse's head, at which they, like inhuman creatures, laughed, and rejoiced to see it, though I thought we should there have ended our days, as overcome with so many difficulties. But the Lord renewed my strength still, and carried me along, that I might see more of His power, yea, so much that I could never have thought of, had I not experienced it.

After this it quickly began to snow, and when night came on they stopped; and now down I must sit in the snow by a little fire, and a few boughs behind me, with my sick child in my lap and calling much for water, being now (through the wound) fallen into a violent fever. My own wound also growing so stiff that I could scarce sit down or rise up, yet so it must be, that I must sit all this cold winter night, upon the cold snowy ground, with my sick child in my arms, looking that every hour would be the last of its life; and having no Christian friend near me, either to comfort or help me. Oh, I may see the wonderful power of God, that my spirit did not utterly sink under my affliction; still the Lord upheld me with His gracious and merciful spirit, and we were both alive to see the light of the next morning.

THE THIRD REMOVE

Thus nine days I sat upon my knees with my babe in my lap, till my flesh was raw again. My child being even ready to depart this sorrowful world, they bade me carry it out to another wigwam (I suppose because they would not be troubled with such spectacles), whither I went with a very heavy heart and down I sat with the picture of death in my lap. About two hours in the night, my sweet babe like a lamb departed this life, on February 18, 1675, it being about six years and five months old. It was nine days from the first wounding in this miserable condition, without any refreshing of one nature or other, except a little cold water. I cannot but take notice how at another time I could not bear to be in the room where any dead person was, but now the case is changed. I must and could lie down by my dead babe, side by side all the night after. I have thought since of the wonderful goodness of God to me in preserving me in the use of my reason and senses in that distressed time, that I did not use wicked and violent means to end my own miserable life.

In the morning when they understood that my child was dead they sent for me home to my master's wigwam (by my master in this writing must be understood Quanopin, who was a Sagamore, and married King Philip's wife's sister; not that he first took me, but I was sold to him by another Narraganset Indian, who took me when first I came out of the garrison). I went to take up my dead child in my arms to carry it with me, but they bid me let it alone. There was no resisting, but go I must and leave it. When I had been at my master's wigwam, I took the first opportunity I could get to go look after my dead child. When I came I asked them what they had done with it. Then they told me it was upon the hill. Then they went and showed me where it was, where I saw the ground was newly digged, and there they told me they had buried it. There I left that child in the wilderness, and must commit it and myself also in this wilderness condition to Him who is above all. God having taken away this dear child, I went to see my daughter Mary, who was at this same Indian town, at a wigwam not very far off, though we had little liberty or opportunity to see one another. She was about ten years old, and taken from the door at first by a praying Indian and sold afterward for a gun. When I came in sight. she would fall a-weeping, at which they were provoked and would not let me come near her, but bade me be gone, which was a heart-cutting word to me. I had one child dead, another in the wilderness. I knew not where; the third they would not let come near to me.

So I took my leave of them, and in coming along my heart melted into tears, more than all the while I was with them, and I was almost swallowed up with the thoughts that ever I should go home again. About the sun's going down, Mr. Hoar, myself, and the two Indians, came to Lancaster, and a solemn sight it was to me. There had I lived many comfortable years amongst my relations and neighbors; and now not one Christian to be seen, nor one house left standing. We went on to a farmhouse that was yet standing, where we lay all night; and a comfortable lodging we had, though nothing but straw to lie on. The Lord preserved us in safety that night, and raised us up again in the morning, and carried us along, that before noon we came to Concord. Now was I full of joy and yet not without sorrow — joy to see such a lovely sight, so many Christians together, and some of them my neighbors. There I met with my brother and my brother-in-law, who asked me if I knew where his wife was. Poor heart! he had helped to bury her and knew it not; she, being shot down by the house, was partly burned, so that those who were at Boston at the desolation of the town and came back afterward and buried the dead did not know her. Yet I was not without sorrow, to think how many were looking and longing, and my own children amongst the rest, to enjoy that deliverance that I had now received; and I did not know whether ever I should see them again. Being recruited with food and raiment, we went to Boston that day, where I met with my dear husband; but the thoughts of our dear children, one being dead and the other we could not tell where, abated our comfort each to other.

MARY ROWLANDSON, *Narrative*

20. John Giles Is Captured by the Indians

King William's War against the French and Indians brought fresh sufferings upon the English settlers. In lower New Hampshire in 1689 the savages slew Thomas Giles, who had been chief justice of the county of Cornwall under the government of the Duke of York, and carried off his son John. The latter lived to become author of one of the most famous narratives of Indian captivity, and Indian interpreter for the Massachusetts government.

ON THE second day of August, 1689, in the morning, my honored father, Thomas Giles, Esq., went with some laborers, my two elder brothers, and myself, to one of his farms which lay upon the river about three miles above Fort Charles, adjoining Pemmaquid Falls, there to gather in his English harvest, and we labored securely till noon. After we had dined, our people went to their labor, some in one field to their English hay, the others to another field of English corn. My father, the youngest of my two brothers, and myself tarried near the farmhouse in which we had dined till about one of the clock, at which time we heard the report of several great guns at the fort. Upon which my father said he hoped it was a signal of good news, and that the great council had sent back the soldiers to cover the inhabitants (for on report of the revolution they had deserted). But to our great surprise, about thirty or forty Indians, at that moment, discharged a volley of shot at us from behind a rising ground, near our barn. The yelling of the Indians, the whistling of their shot, and the voice of my father, whom I heard cry out, "What now! what now!" so terrified me (though he seemed to be handling a gun) that I endeavored to make my escape. My brother ran one way and I another, and, looking over my shoulder, I saw a stout fellow, painted, pursuing me with a gun, and a cutlass glittering in his hand which I expected every moment in my brains. I soon fell down, and the Indian seized me by the left hand. He offered me no abuse, but tied my arms, then lifted me up and pointed to the place where the people were at work about the hay and led me that way. As we went, we crossed where my father was, who looked very pale and bloody, and walked very slowly. When we came to the place, I saw two men shot down on the flats, and one or two more knocked on their heads with hatchets, crying out "O Lord!" etc. There the Indians brought two captives, one a man, and my brother James, who, with me had endeavored to escape by running from the house when we were first attacked.

After doing what mischief they could, they sat down and made us sit with them. After some time, we arose, and the Indians pointed for us to go eastward. We marched about a quarter of a mile, and then made a halt. Here they brought my father to us. They made proposals to him, by old Moxus, who told him that those were strange Indians who shot him, and that he was sorry for it. My father replied that he was a dying man, and wanted no favor of them but to pray with his children. This being granted him, he recommended us to the protection and blessing of God Almighty, then gave us the best advice, and took his leave of this life, hoping in God that we should meet in a better. He parted with a cheerful voice, but looked very pale, by reason of his great loss of blood, which now gushed out of his shoes. The Indians led him aside! — I heard the blows of the hatchet, but neither shriek nor groan! I afterwards heard that he had five or seven shot holes through his waistcoat or jacket and that he was covered with some boughs.

The Indians led us, their captives, on the east side of the river, towards the fort, and when we came within a mile and a half of the fort and town and could see the fort, we saw fire and smoke on all sides. Here we made a short stop, and then moved, within or near the distance of three-quarters of a mile from the fort, into a thick swamp. There I saw my mother and my two little sisters and many other captives who were taken from the town. My mother asked me about my father. I told her he was killed, but could say no more for grief. She burst into tears, and the Indians moved me a little farther off, and seized me with cords to a tree.

JOHN GILES, Memoirs of Odd Adventures

21. James Smith Is Adopted by the Delawares

The pioneer James Smith, of the sturdy Ulster Scottish stock which contributed so much to the making of America, was only about eighteen years old when, having left his frontier home in Pennsylvania to help build a military road from Shippensburg, Pa., to the Youghiogheny River, he was captured by the Indian allies of the French. Death by torture confronted him, but he was saved by being adopted into an Indian family. It was only after four years of wanderings through the wilderness of Ohio and Canada that he escaped near Montreal in 1759, and made his way to territory under the British flag. After the end of the Revolutionary War he became one of the leading citizens of Kentucky, well known for his political and religious activities. He was a good warrior with both pen and sword, fighting the Shaker sect by pamphlets as he had repeatedly fought the Indians with blade and musket. But he is best remembered for his vivid story of his adoption and captivity, published in Kentucky in 1799.

IN MAY, 1755, the province of Pennsylvania agreed to send out three hundred men in order to cut a wagon road from Fort Loudon to join Braddock's road, near the Turkey Foot, or three forks of Yohogania. My brother-in-law, William Smith, Esq., of Conococheague, was appointed commissioner to have the oversight of these road cutters. . . .

We went on with the road without interruption until near the Allegheny Mountain, when I was sent back in order to hurry up some provision wagons that were on the way after us. I proceeded down the road as far as the crossings of Juniata, where, finding the wagons were coming on as fast as possible, I returned up the road again towards the Allegheny Mountain, in company with one Arnold Vigoras. About four or five miles above Bedford, three Indians had made a blind of bushes, stuck in the ground as though they grew naturally, where they concealed themselves about fifteen yards from the road. When we came opposite to them, they fired upon us, at this short distance, and killed my fellow traveler, yet their bullets did not touch me; but my horse, making a violent start, threw me, and the Indians immediately ran up and took me prisoner. The one that laid hold on me was a Canafatauga; the other two were Delawares. One of them could speak English and asked me if there were any more white men coming after. I told them not any near that I knew of. Two of these Indians stood by me whilst the other scalped my comrade; then they set off and ran at a smart rate through the woods for about fifteen miles, and that night we slept on the Allegheny Mountain, without fire.

The next morning they divided the last of their provision which they had brought from Fort Duquesne and gave me an equal share, which was about two or three ounces of moldy biscuit — this and a young ground hog, about as large as a rabbit, roasted and also equally divided, was all the provision we had until we came to the Loyal Hannan, which was about fifty miles; and a great part of the way we came through exceeding rocky laurel thickets without any path. When we came to the west side of Laurel Hill, they gave the scalp halloo, as usual, which is a long yell or halloo for every scalp or prisoner they have in possession; the last of these scalp halloos was followed with quick and sudden, shrill shouts of joy and triumph.

As I was at this time unacquainted with this mode of firing and yelling of the savages, I concluded that there were thousands of Indians there, ready to receive General Braddock; but what added to my surprise, I saw numbers running towards me, stripped naked, excepting breechclouts, and painted in the most hideous manner, of various colors, though the principal color was vermilion or a bright red; yet there was annexed to this, black, brown, blue, etc. As they approached, they formed themselves into two long ranks, about two or three rods apart. I was told by an Indian that could speak English that I must run betwixt these ranks, and that they would flog me all the way as I ran, and if I ran quick it would be so much the better, as they would quit when I got to the end of the ranks. There appeared to be a general rejoicing around me, yet I could find nothing like joy in my breast; but I started to the race with all the resolution and vigor I was capable of exerting, and found that it was as I had been told, for I was flogged the whole way. When I had got near the end of the lines, I was struck with something that appeared to me to be a stick or the handle of a tomahawk, which caused me to fall to the ground. On my recovering my senses, I endeavored to renew my race, but as I arose, someone cast sand in my eyes, which blinded me so that I could not see where to run. They continued beating me most intolerably until I was at length insensible. But before I lost my senses, I remember my wishing them to strike the fatal blow, for I thought they intended killing me but apprehended they were too long about it.

The first thing I remember was my being in the fort, amidst the

French and Indians, and a French doctor standing by me, who had opened a vein in my left arm; after which the interpreter asked me how I did. I told him I felt much pain; the doctor then washed my wounds and the bruised places of my body with French brandy. As I felt faint and the brandy smelt well, I asked for some inwardly, but the doctor told me, by the interpreter, that it did not suit my case. I was then sent to the hospital and carefully attended by the doctors, and recovered quicker than what I expected.

Some time after I was there, I was visited by the Delaware Indian already mentioned who was at the taking of me and could speak some English. Though he spoke but bad English, yet I found him to be a man of considerable understanding. I asked him if I had done anything that had offended the Indians which caused them to treat me so unmercifully. He said no, it was only an old custom the Indians had, and it was like how-do-you-do; after that, he said, I would be well used. I asked him if I should be admitted to return with the French. He said no — and told me that as soon as I recovered, I must not only go with the Indians, but must be made an Indian myself. I asked him what news from Braddock's army. He said the Indians spied them every day, and he showed me by making marks on the ground with a stick that Braddock's army was advancing in very close order and that the Indians would surround them, take trees, and (as he expressed it) "shoot um down all one pigeon."

Some time after this, I heard a number of scalp halloos and saw a company of Indians and French coming in. I observed they had a great many bloody scalps, grenadiers' caps, British canteens, bayonets, etc. with them. They brought the news that Braddock was defeated. After that another company came in which appeared to be about one hundred, and chiefly Indians, and it seemed to me that almost every one of this company was carrying scalps; after this came another company with a number of wagon horses, and also a great many scalps. Those that were coming in, and those that had arrived, kept a constant firing of small arms, and also the great guns in the fort, which were accompanied with the most hideous shouts and yells from all quarters; so that it appeared to me as if the infernal regions had broke loose.

About sundown, I beheld a small party coming in with about a dozen prisoners, stripped naked, with their hands tied behind their backs, and their faces and part of their bodies blacked — these prisoners they burned to death on the bank of the Allegheny River opposite to the fort. I stood on the fort wall until I beheld them begin to burn one of these men; they had him tied to a stake and kept touching him with firebrands, red-hot irons, etc., and he screaming in a most doleful manner, the Indians in the meantime yelling like infernal spirits. As this scene appeared too shocking for me to behold, I retired to my lodging, both sore and sorry. . . .

A few days after this the Indians demanded me and I was obliged to go with them. I was not yet well able to march, but they took me in a canoe up the Allegheny River to an Indian town that was on the north side of the river, about forty miles above Fort Duquesne. Here I remained about three weeks, and was then taken to an Indian town on the west branch of Muskingum, about twenty miles above the forks, which was called Tullihas, inhabited by Delawares, Caughnewagas, and Mohicans.

The day after my arrival at the aforesaid town, a number of Indians collected about me, and one of them began to pull the hair out of my head. He had some ashes on a piece of bark in which he frequently dipped his fingers in order to take the firmer hold, and so he went on, as if he had been plucking a turkey, until he had all the hair clean out of my head, except a small spot about three or four inches square on my crown; this they cut off with a pair of scissors, excepting three locks, which they dressed up in their own mode. Two of these they wrapped round with a narrow beaded garter made by themselves for that purpose, and the other they plaited at full length and then stuck it full of silver brooches. After this they bored my nose and ears, and fixed me off with earrings and nose jewels; then they ordered me to strip off my clothes and put on a breechclout, which I did; then they painted my head, face, and body in various colors. They put a large belt of wampum on my neck, and silver bands on my hands and right arm; and so an old chief led me out in the street and gave the alarm halloo, *oo-wigh,* several times repeated quick, and on this, all that were in the town came running and stood round the old chief, who held me by the hand in the midst. As I at that time knew nothing of their mode of adoption, and had seen them put to death all they had taken, and as I never could find that they saved a man alive at Braddock's defeat, I made no doubt but they were about putting me to death in some cruel manner. The old chief, holding me by the hand, made a long speech, very loud, and when he had done he handed me to three young squaws, who led me by the hand down the bank into the river until the water was up to our middle. The squaws then made signs to me to plunge myself into the water, but I did not understand them; I thought that the result of the council was that I should be drowned, and that these young ladies were to be the executioners. They all three laid violent hold of me, and I for some time opposed them with all my might, which occasioned loud laughter by the multitude that were on the bank of the river. At length, one of the squaws made out to speak a little English (for I believe they began to be afraid of me) and said, "No hurt you"; on this, I gave myself up to their ladyships, who were as good as their word, for though they plunged me under water and washed and rubbed me severely, yet I could not say they hurt me much.

These young women then led me up to the council house, where some of the tribe were ready with new clothes for me. They gave me a new, ruffled shirt, which I put on, also a pair of leggings done off with ribbons and beads, likewise a pair of moccasins, and garters dressed with beads, porcupine quills, and red hair — also a tinsel-laced cap. They again painted my head and face with various colors, and tied a bunch of red feathers to one of these locks they had left on the crown of my head, which stood up five or six inches. They seated me on a bearskin, and gave me a pipe, tomahawk, and pole-catskin pouch, which had been skinned pocket fashion, and contained tobacco, killegenico or dry sumach leaves, which they mix with their tobacco, also spunk, flint, and steel. When I was thus seated, the Indians came in dressed and painted in their grandest manner. As they came in they took their seats and for a considerable time there was a profound silence; every one was smoking, but not a word was spoken among them. At length one of the chiefs made a speech which was delivered to me by an interpreter, and was as followeth: "My son, you are now flesh of our flesh and bone of our bone."

Account of the Remarkable Occurrences in the Life
and Travels of Colonel James Smith

V

The Struggle for the Continent

22. George Washington Warns Off the French

One October morning in 1753, a young Virginian rode off, quite innocently, upon an errand that was to mark the virtual beginning of the Seven Years' War in America — the war which decided that an English and not a French civilization should dominate the continent. The French were building forts along the Ohio. Settlers sent out by the Ohio Company were being killed by the Indians or taken prisoners by the French. Governor Dinwiddie of Virginia determined to send Washington, in the King's name, to tell the French Commandant that his invasion had aroused "surprise and concern," and that he must withdraw from British soil. At Fort Le Bœuf the young major of Virginia militia was rebuffed by the French officer in charge. But he brought back valuable information about the French intentions and strength; and Dinwiddie, forwarding this report to London, saw to it that he was promoted to be lieutenant-colonel. A little later he was busy enlisting and drilling men for service against these French trespassers. One of the greatest of American careers had fully opened.

WEDNESDAY, October 31, 1753.—I was commissioned and appointed by the Honorable Robert Dinwiddie, Esq., Governor etc. of Virginia, to visit and deliver a letter to the commandant of the French forces on the Ohio, and set out on the intended journey the same day. The next I arrived at Fredericksburg, and engaged Mr. Jacob Vanbraam to be my French interpreter, and proceeded with him to Alexandria, where we provided necessaries. From thence we went to Winchester, and got baggage, horses, etc., and from thence we pursued the new road to Wills Creek, where we arrived the 14th of November. . . .

Shingiss [Delaware chief] attended us to the Loggs Town, where we arrived between sunsetting and dark, the 25th day after I left Williamsburg. We traveled over some extreme good and bad land to get to this place.

As soon as I came into town, I went to Monacatootha (as the Half-King was out at his hunting cabin on Little Beaver Creek, about fifteen miles off) and informed him by John Davison, my Indian interpreter, that I was sent a messenger to the French general, and was ordered to call upon the sachems of the Six Nations to acquaint them with it. I gave him a string of wampum and a twist of tobacco, and desired him to send for the Half-King, which he promised to do by a runner in the morning, and for other sachems. I invited him and the other great men present to my tent, where they stayed about an hour and returned.

[November] 25th. — I inquired into the situation of the French on the Mississippi — their number, and what forts they had built. They informed me that there were four small forts between New Orleans and the Black Islands garrisoned with about thirty or forty men, and a few small pieces in each.

About three o'clock this evening the Half-King came to town. I went up and invited him privately to my tent and desired him to relate some of the particulars of his journey to the French commandant, and reception there, also to give me an account of the ways and distance. He told me that the nearest and levelest way was now impassable, by reason of many large, miry savannas; that we must be obliged to go by Venango, and should not get to the near fort under five or six nights' sleep, good traveling. When he went to the fort, he said, he was received in a very stern manner by the late commander, who asked him very abruptly what he had come about and to declare his business.

26th. — As I had orders to make all possible dispatch, and waiting here was very contrary to my inclinations, I thanked him in the most suitable manner I could, and told him that my business required the greatest expedition and would not admit of that delay. He was not well pleased that I should offer to go before the time he had appointed, and told me that he could not consent to our going without a guard for fear some accident should befall us and draw a reflection upon him. And accordingly he gave orders to

King Shingiss, who was present, to attend on Wednesday night with the wampum, and two men of their nation to be in readiness to set out with us next morning. As I found it was impossible to get off without affronting them in the most egregious manner, I consented to stay.

30th. — Last night the great men assembled to their council house to consult further about this journey, and who were to go; the result of which was that only three of their chiefs with one of their best hunters should be our convoy.

We set out about nine o'clock with the Half-King Jeskakake, White Thunder, and the hunter, and traveled on the road to Venango, where we arrived the 4th of December without anything remarkable happening but a continued series of bad weather.

We found the French colors hoisted at a house from which they had driven Mr. John Frazier, an English subject. I immediately repaired to it to know where the commander resided. There were three officers, one of whom, Captain Joncaire, informed me that he had the command of the Ohio, but that there was a general officer at the near fort, where he advised me to apply for an answer. He invited us to sup with them, and treated us with the greatest complaisance.

The wine, as they dosed themselves pretty plentifully with it, soon banished the restraint which at first appeared in their conversation, and gave a license to their tongues to reveal their sentiments more freely.

They told me that it was their absolute design to take possession of the Ohio, and, by G — , they would do it. For that, although they were sensible the English could raise two men for their one, yet they knew their motions were too slow and dilatory to prevent any undertaking of theirs. They pretend to have an undoubted right to the river from a discovery made by one La Salle sixty years ago, and the rise of this expedition is to prevent our settling on the river or waters of it, as they had heard of some families moving out in order thereto.

[December] 5th. — Rained excessively all day, which prevented our traveling.

6th. — The Half-King came to my tent, quite sober, and insisted very much that I should stay and hear what he had to say to the

French. I fain would have prevented his speaking anything till he came to the commandant, but could not prevail. He told me that at this place a council fire was kindled, where all their business with these people was to be transacted, and that the management of the Indian affairs was left solely to Monsieur Joncaire. As I was desirous of knowing the issue of this, I agreed to stay.

About ten o'clock they met in council. The king spoke much the same as he had before done to the general, and offered the French speech belt, which had before been demanded, with the marks of four towns on it, which Monsieur Joncaire refused to receive, but desired him to carry it to the fort of the commander.

7th. — At eleven o'clock we set out for the fort, and were prevented from arriving there till the 11th by excessive rains, snows, and bad traveling through many mires and swamps. These we were obliged to pass to avoid crossing the creek, which was impassable either by fording or rafting, the water was so high and rapid.

12th. — I prepared early to wait upon the commander, and was received and conducted to him by the second officer in command. I acquainted him with my business, and offered my commission and letter.

13th. — The chief officers retired to hold a council of war, which gave me an opportunity of taking the dimensions of the fort and making what observations I could.

I could get no certain account of the number of men here, but, according to the best judgment I could form, there are an hundred exclusive of officers, of which there are many. I also gave orders to the people who were with me to take an exact account of the canoes which were hauled up to convey their forces down in the spring. This they did, and told fifty of birchbark and one hundred and seventy of pine, besides many others which were blocked out in readiness to make.

14th. — As I found many plots concerted to retard the Indians' business and prevent their returning with me, I endeavored all that lay in my power to frustrate their schemes and hurry them on to execute their intended design. They accordingly pressed for admittance this evening, which at length was granted them, privately, with the commander and one or two other officers. The Half-King told me that he offered the wampum to the commander, who evaded taking it, and made many fair promises of love and friendship; said he wanted to live in peace and trade amicably with them, as a proof of which he would send some goods immediately down to the Loggs Town for them. But I rather think the design of that is to bring away all our straggling traders they meet with, as I privately understood they intended to carry an officer etc., with them. And what rather confirms this opinion — I was inquiring of the commander by what authority he had made prisoners of several of our English subjects. He told me that the country belonged to them; that no Englishman had a right to trade upon those waters; and that he had orders to make every person prisoner who attempted it on the Ohio, or the waters of it.

15th. — The commandant ordered a plentiful store of liquor, provision, etc., to be put on board our canoe, and appeared to be extremely complaisant though he was exerting every artifice which he could invent to set our own Indians at variance with us, to prevent their going till after our departure — presents, rewards, and everything which could be suggested by him or his officers. I can't say that ever in my life I suffered so much anxiety as I did in this affair. I saw that every stratagem which the most fruitful brain could invent was practised to win the Half-King to their interest, and that leaving him here was giving them the opportunity they aimed at.

As I was very much pressed by the Indians to wait this day for them, I consented, on a promise that nothing should hinder them in the morning.

16th. — The French were not slack in their inventions to keep the Indians this day also, but as they were obligated according to promise to give the present, they then endeavored to try the power of liquor, which I doubt not would have prevailed at any other time than this. But I urged and insisted with the Half-King so closely upon his word that he refrained and set off with us as he had engaged.

23d. — Our horses were now so weak and feeble and the baggage so heavy (as we were obliged to provide all the necessaries which the journey would require) that we doubted much their performing it. Therefore, myself and others (except the drivers, who were obliged to ride) gave up our horses for packs to assist along with the baggage. I put myself in an Indian walking dress, and continued with them three days till I found there was no probability of their getting home in any reasonable time. The horses grew less able to travel every day; the cold increased very fast; and the roads were becoming much worse by a deep snow, continually freezing. Therefore, as I was uneasy to get back to make report of my proceedings to his Honor the Governor, I determined to prosecute my journey the nearest way through the woods on foot.

Accordingly I left Mr. Vanbraam in charge of our baggage, with money and directions to provide necessaries from place to place for themselves and horses, and to make the most convenient dispatch in traveling.

I took my necessary papers, pulled off my clothes, and tied myself up in a matchcoat. Then with gun in hand and pack at my back, in which were my papers and provisions, I set out with Mr. Gist, fitted in the same manner, on Wednesday the 26th.

The day following, just after we had passed a place called the Murdering Town, we fell in with a party of French Indians who had lain in wait for us. One of them fired at Mr. Gist or me, not fifteen steps off, but fortunately missed. We took this fellow into custody and kept him till about nine o'clock, then let him go, and walked all the remaining part of the night without making any stop, that we might get the start so far as to be out of the reach of their pursuit the next day, since we were well assured that they would follow our track as soon as it was light. The next day we continued traveling till quite dark and got to the river about two miles above Shannapins. We expected to have found the river frozen, but it was not, only about fifty yards from each shore. The ice, I suppose, had broken up above, for it was driving in vast quantities.

There was no way for getting over but on a raft, which we set about with but one poor hatchet and finished just after sunsetting. This was a whole day's work. Then set off. But before we were halfway over, we were jammed in the ice in such a manner that we expected every moment our raft to sink and ourselves to perish.

Tuesday, the 1st day of January, we left Mr. Frazier's house and arrived at Mr. Gist's at Monongahela the 2d, where I bought a horse, saddle, etc. The 6th we met seventeen horses loaded with materials and stores for a fort at the forks of the Ohio, and the day after some families going out to settle. This day we arrived at Wills Creek, after as fatiguing a journey as it is possible to conceive, rendered so by excessive bad weather. From the 1st day of December to the 15th there was but one day on which it did not rain or snow incessantly; and throughout the whole journey we met with nothing but one continued series of cold, wet weather, which occasioned very uncomfortable lodgings, especially after we had quitted our tent, which was some screen from the inclemency of it.

On the 11th I got to Belvoir, where I stopped one day to take necessary rest, and then set out and arrived in Williamsburg the 16th, when I waited upon his Honor the Governor with the letter I had brought from the French commandant, and to give an account of the success of my proceedings. This I beg leave to do by offering the foregoing narrative, as it contains the most remarkable occurrences which happened in my journey.

The Writings of George Washington

23. Franklin Supplies Wagons for General Braddock

The Virginia militia were of course unable to check the French in the West, though at Fort Necessity Washington heard the bullets whistle, and wrote that he liked the sound. It was decided in London to send over an expeditionary force under the sixty-year-old General Edward Braddock. This force suffered in America from administrative confusion and lack of resources. The Quaker and German farmers of Pennsylvania selfishly refused to aid it until Franklin intervened, engaging to procure horses and wagons, and bringing in all that were needed. In the end he lost money and reputation by his patriotic but unfortunate service. This fact may have prejudiced his recollections of Braddock. In July, 1755, that brave though boastful officer led two gallant British regiments and a large number of Americans across the Monongahela on a terrible march to disaster and death.

IN CONVERSATION with him one day he was giving me some account of his intended progress. "After taking Fort Duquesne," says he, "I am to proceed to Niagara; and, having taken that, to Frontenac, if the season will allow time, and I suppose it will, for Duquesne can hardly detain me above three or four days; and then I see nothing that can obstruct my march to Niagara." Having before revolved in my mind the long line his army must make in their march by a very narrow road, to be cut for them through the woods and bushes, and also what I had read of a former defeat of fifteen hundred French, who invaded the Iroquois country, I had conceived some doubts and some fears for the event of the campaign. But I ventured only to say: "To be sure, sir, if you arrive well before Duquesne with these fine troops, so well provided with artillery, that place, not yet completely fortified, and, as we hear, with no very strong garrison, can probably make but a short resistance. The only danger I apprehend of obstruction to your march is from ambuscades of Indians, who, by constant practice, are dexterous in laying and executing them; and the slender line, near four miles long, which your army must make, may expose it to be attacked by surprise in its flanks, and to be cut like a thread into several pieces, which, from their distance, cannot come up in time to support each other."

He smiled at my ignorance, and replied: "These savages may, indeed, be a formidable enemy to your raw American militia, but upon the King's regular and disciplined troops, sir, it is impossible they should make any impression." I was conscious of an impropriety in my disputing with a military man in matters of his profession, and said no more. The enemy, however, did not take the advantage of his army which I apprehended its long line of march exposed it to, but let it advance without interruption till within nine miles of the place; and then, when more in a body (for it had just passed a river where the front had halted till all had come over), and in a more open part of the woods than any it had passed, attacked its advance guard by a heavy fire from behind trees and bushes, which was the first intelligence the general had of an enemy's being near him. This guard being disordered, the general hurried the troops up to their assistance, which was done in great confusion, through wagons, baggage, and cattle; and presently the fire came upon their flank. The officers, being on horseback, were more easily distinguished, picked out as marks, and fell very fast; and the soldiers were crowded together in a huddle, having or hearing no orders, and standing to be shot at till two-thirds of them were killed; and then, being seized with a panic, the whole fled with precipitation.

The wagoners took each a horse out of his team, and scampered; their example was immediately followed by others, so that all the wagons, provisions, artillery, and stores were left to the enemy. The general, being wounded, was brought off with difficulty; his secretary, Mr. Shirley, was killed by his side; and out of eighty-six officers, sixty-three were killed or wounded, and seven hundred and fourteen men killed out of eleven hundred. These eleven hundred had been picked men from the whole army; the rest had been left behind with Colonel Dunbar, who was to follow with the heavier part of the stores, provisions, and baggage. The flyers, not being pursued, arrived at Dunbar's camp, and the panic they brought with them instantly seized him and all his people; and though he had now above one thousand men, and the enemy who had beaten Braddock did not at most exceed four hundred Indians and French together, instead of proceeding and endeavoring to recover some of the lost honor, he ordered all the stores, ammunition, etc., to be destroyed, that he might have more horses to assist his flight toward the settlements and less lumber to remove. He was there met with requests from the governors of Virginia, Maryland, and Pennsylvania, that he would post his troops on the frontiers so as to afford some protection to the inhabitants; but he continued his hasty march through all the country, not thinking himself safe till he arrived at Philadelphia, where the inhabitants could protect him. This whole transaction gave us Americans the first suspicion that our exalted ideas of the prowess of British regulars had not been well founded.

The Autobiography of Benjamin Franklin

24. Montcalm and Wolfe Fight
on the Heights of Abraham

The capture of Quebec meant the conquest of Canada. William Pitt, British Prime Minister, gave command of the expedition against it to a young man of thirty-two, already distinguished in fighting in Europe and America. James Wolfe mustered his 9,000 men at Louisbourg, and in June of 1759 brought them up the St. Lawrence to the great French fortress, high on its cliffs. There he found himself faced by a much older French leader, the Marquis de Montcalm, who had indeed received a commission the year that Wolfe was born. The French forces were superior in numbers. For more than two months Montcalm, remaining on the defensive, baffled the besiegers. Finally, however, he was outwitted, and the British troops scaled the heights. The battle which followed, in which both commanders displayed exceptional gallantry and were mortally wounded, was one of the most memorable in modern history; and in Parkman's classic pages it has received a treatment worthy of the magnificent theme.

For FULL two hours the procession of boats, borne on the current, steered silently down the St. Lawrence. The stars were visible, but the night was moonless and sufficiently dark. The General was in one of the foremost boats, and near him was a young midshipman, John Robinson, afterwards professor of natural philosophy in the University of Edinburgh. He used to tell in his later life how Wolfe, with a low voice, repeated Gray's "Elegy in a Country Churchyard" to the officers about him. Probably it was to relieve the intense strain of his thoughts. Among the rest was the verse which his own fate was soon to illustrate, "The paths of glory lead but to the grave."

"Gentlemen," he said, as his recital ended, "I would rather have written those lines than take Quebec." None were there to tell him that the hero is greater than the poet.

As they neared their destination, the tide bore them in towards the shore, and the mighty wall of rock and forest towered in darkness on their left. The dead stillness was suddenly broken by the sharp "*Qui vive!*" of a French sentry, invisible in the thick gloom. "*France!*" answered a Highland officer of Fraser's regiment from one of the boats of the light infantry. He had served in Holland. and spoke French fluently.

"*A quel régiment?*"

"*De la Reine,*" replied the Highlander. He knew that a part of that corps was with Bougainville. The sentry, expecting the convoy of provisions, was satisfied, and did not ask for the password.

Soon after, the foremost boats were passing the heights of Samos, when another sentry challenged them, and they could see him through the darkness running down to the edge of the water, within range of a pistolshot. In answer to his questions, the same officer replied, in French: "Provision boats. Don't make a noise; the English will hear us." In fact, the sloop of war *Hunter* was anchored in the stream not far off. This time, again, the sentry let them pass. In a few moments they rounded the headland above the Anse du Foulon. There was no sentry there. The strong current swept the boats of the light infantry a little below the intended landing place. They disembarked on a narrow strand at the foot of heights as steep as a hill covered with trees can be. The twenty-four volunteers led the way, climbing with what silence they might, closely followed by a much larger body. When they reached the top they saw in the dim light a cluster of tents at a short distance, and immediately made a dash at them. Vergor leaped from bed. and tried to run off, but was shot in the heel and captured. His men, taken by surprise, made little resistance. One or two were caught, and the rest fled.

The main body of troops waited in their boats by the edge of the strand. The heights near by were cleft by a great ravine choked with forest trees, and in its depths ran a little brook called Ruisseau Saint-Denis, which, swollen by the late rains, fell plashing in the stillness over a rock. Other than this no sound could reach the strained ear of Wolfe but the gurgle of the tide and the cautious climbing of

his advance parties as they mounted the steeps at some little distance from where he sat listening. At length from the top came a
sound of musketshots, followed by loud huzzas, and he knew that
his men were masters of the position. The word was given; the
troops leaped from the boats and scaled the heights, some here,
some there, clutching at trees and bushes, their muskets slung at
their backs. Tradition still points out the place, near the mouth of
the ravine, where the foremost reached the top. Wolfe said to an
officer near him, "You can try it, but I don't think you'll get up."
He himself, however, found strength to drag himself up with the
rest. The narrow slanting path on the face of the heights had been
made impassable by trenches and abatis, but all obstructions were
soon cleared away, and then the ascent was easy. In the gray of the
morning the long file of red-coated soldiers moved quickly upward,
and formed in order on the plateau above. . . .

The day broke in clouds and threatening rain. Wolfe's battalions
were drawn up along the crest of the heights. No enemy was in sight,
though a body of Canadians had sallied from the town and moved
along the strand towards the landing place, whence they were quickly
driven back. He had achieved the most critical part of his enterprise;
yet the success that he coveted placed him in imminent danger. On
one side was the garrison of Quebec and the army of Beauport,
and Bougainville was on the other. Wolfe's alternative was victory
or ruin, for if he should be overwhelmed by a combined attack,
retreat would be hopeless. His feelings no man can know, but it
would be safe to say that hesitation or doubt had no part in them.

He went to reconnoiter the ground, and soon came to the Plains of
Abraham, so called from Abraham Martin, a pilot known as Maître
Abraham, who had owned a piece of land here in the early times
of the colony. The Plains were a tract of grass, tolerably level in
most parts, patched here and there with cornfields, studded with
clumps of bushes, and forming a part of the high plateau at the eastern end of which Quebec stood. On the south it was bounded by
the declivities along the St. Lawrence, on the north by those along
the St. Charles, or rather along the meadows through which that
lazy stream crawled like a writhing snake. At the place that Wolfe
chose for his battlefield the plateau was less than a mile wide.

Thither the troops advanced, marched by files till they reached the ground, and then wheeled to form their line of battle, which stretched across the plateau and faced the city. It consisted of six battalions and the detached grenadiers from Louisbourg, all drawn up in ranks three deep. Its right wing was near the brink of the heights along the St. Lawrence, but the left could not reach those along the St. Charles. On this side a wide space was perforce left open, and there was danger of being outflanked. To prevent this, Brigadier Townshend was stationed here with two battalions, drawn up at right angles with the rest, and fronting the St. Charles. The battalion of Webb's regiment, under Colonel Burton, formed the reserve; the third battalion of Royal Americans was left to guard the landing; and Howe's light infantry occupied a wood far in the rear. Wolfe, with Monckton and Murray, commanded the front line, on which the heavy fighting was to fall, and which, when all the troops had arrived, numbered less than thirty-five hundred men.

Quebec was not a mile distant, but they could not see it; for a ridge of broken ground intervened, called Buttes-à Neveu, about six hundred paces off. The first division of troops had scarcely come up when, about six o'clock, this ridge was suddenly thronged with white uniforms. It was the battalion of Guienne, arrived at the eleventh hour from its camp by the St. Charles. Some time after, there was hot firing in the rear. It came from a detachment of Bougainville's command attacking a house where some of the light infantry were posted. The assailants were repulsed, and the firing ceased. Light showers fell at intervals, besprinkling the troops as they stood patiently waiting the event.

Montcalm had passed a troubled night. Through all the evening the cannon bellowed from the ships of Saunders, and the boats of the fleet hovered in the dusk off the Beauport shore, threatening every moment to land. Troops lined the intrenchments till day, while the General walked the field that adjoined his headquarters till one in the morning, accompanied by the Chevalier Johnstone and Colonel Poulariez. Johnstone says that he was in great agitation, and took no rest all night. At daybreak he heard the sound of cannon above the town. It was the battery at Samos firing on the English ships. He had sent an officer to the quarters of Vaudreuil, which were much nearer Quebec, with orders to bring him word at once should anything unusual happen. But no word came, and about six o'clock he mounted and rode thither with Johnstone. As they advanced, the country behind the town opened more and more upon their sight; till at length, when opposite Vaudreuil's house, they saw across the St. Charles, some two miles away, the red ranks of British soldiers on the heights beyond.

"This is a serious business," Montcalm said, and sent off Johnstone at full gallop to bring up the troops from the center and left of the camp. Those of the right were in motion already, doubtless by the Governor's order. Vaudreuil came out of the house. Montcalm stopped for a few words with him; then set spurs to his horse, and rode over the bridge of the St. Charles to the scene of danger. He rode with a fixed look, uttering not a word.

The army followed in such order as it might, crossed the bridge in hot haste, passed under the northern rampart of Quebec, entered at the palace gate, and pressed on in headlong march along the quaint narrow streets of the warlike town: troops of Indians in scalp locks and war paint, a savage glitter in their deep-set eyes; bands of Canadians whose all was at stake — faith, country, and home; the colony regulars; the battalions of old France, a torrent of white uniforms and gleaming bayonets, La Sarre, Languedoc, Roussillon, Béarn — victors of Oswego, William Henry, and Ticonderoga. So they swept on, poured out upon the plain, some by the gate of St. Louis and some by that of St. John, and hurried, breathless, to where the banners of Guienne still fluttered on the ridge.

Montcalm was amazed at what he saw. He had expected a detachment, and he found an army. Full in sight before him stretched the lines of Wolfe: the close ranks of the English infantry, a silent wall of red, and the wild array of the Highlanders, with their waving tartans, and bagpipes screaming defiance. Vaudreuil had not come; but not the less was felt the evil of a divided authority and the jealousy of the rival chiefs. Montcalm waited long for the forces he had ordered to join him from the left wing of the army. He waited in vain. It is said that the Governor had detained them, lest the English should attack the Beauport shore. Even if they did so and succeeded, the French might defy them, could they but put Wolfe to rout on the Plains of Abraham. Neither did the garrison of Quebec come to the aid of Montcalm. He sent to Ramesay, its commander, for twenty-five fieldpieces which were on the palace battery. Ramesay would give him only three, saying that he wanted them for his own defense. There were orders and counterorders — misunderstanding, haste, delay, perplexity.

Montcalm and his chief officers held a council of war. It is said that he and they alike were for immediate attack. His enemies declare that he was afraid lest Vaudreuil should arrive and take command; but the Governor was not a man to assume responsibility at such a crisis. Others say that his impetuosity overcame his better judgment; and of this charge it is hard to acquit him. Bougainville was but a few miles distant, and some of his troops were much nearer; a messenger sent by way of Old Lorrette could have reached him in an hour and a half at most, and a combined attack in front and rear might have been concerted with him. If, moreover, Montcalm could have come to an understanding with Vaudreuil, his own force might have been strengthened by two or three thousand additional men from the town and the camp of Beauport; but he felt that there was no time to lose, for he imagined that Wolfe would soon be reinforced, which was impossible, and he believed that the English were fortifying themselves, which was no less an error. He has been blamed not only for fighting too soon, but for fighting at all. In this he could not choose. Fight he must, for Wolfe was now in a position to cut off all his supplies. His men were full of ardor, and he resolved to attack before their ardor cooled. He spoke a few words to them in his keen, vehement way. "I remember very well how he looked," one of the Canadians, then a boy of eighteen, used to say in his old age; "he rode a black or dark bay horse along the front of our lines, brandishing his sword, as if to excite us to do our duty. He wore a coat with wide sleeves, which fell back as he raised his arm, and showed the white linen of the wristband."

The English waited the result with a composure which, if not quite real, was at least well feigned. The three fieldpieces sent by Ramesay plied them with canister shot, and fifteen hundred Canadians and Indians fusilladed them in front and flank. Over all the plain, from behind bushes and knolls and the edge of cornfields, puffs of smoke sprang incessantly from the guns of these hidden marksmen. Skirmishers were thrown out before the lines to hold them in check, and the soldiers were ordered to lie on the grass to avoid the shot. The firing was liveliest on the English left, where bands of sharp-shooters got under the edge of the declivity, among thickets, and behind scattered houses, whence they killed and wounded a considerable number of Townshend's men. The light infantry were called up from the rear. The houses were taken and retaken, and one or more of them was burned.

Wolfe was everywhere. How cool he was, and why his followers loved him, is shown by an incident that happened in the course of the morning. One of his captains was shot through the lungs, and on recovering consciousness he saw the General standing at his side. Wolfe pressed his hand, told him not to despair, praised his services, promised him early promotion, and sent an aide-de-camp to Monckton to beg that officer to keep the promise if he himself should fall.

It was towards ten o'clock when, from the high ground on the right of the line, Wolfe saw that the crisis was near. The French on the ridge had formed themselves into three bodies, regulars in the center, regulars and Canadians on right and left. Two field-pieces, which had been dragged up the heights at Anse du Foulon, fired on them with grapeshot, and the troops, rising from the ground, prepared to receive them. In a few moments more they were in motion. They came on rapidly, uttering loud shouts, and firing as soon as they were within range. Their ranks, ill ordered at the best, were further confused by a number of Canadians who had been mixed among the regulars, and who, after hastily firing, threw themselves on the ground to reload. The British advanced a few rods, then halted and stood still. When the French were within forty paces, the word of command rang out, and a crash of musketry answered all along the line. The volley was delivered with remarkable precision. In the battalions of the center, which had suffered least from the enemy's bullets, the simultaneous explosion was afterwards said by French officers to have sounded like a cannon shot. Another volley followed, and then a furious clattering fire that lasted but a minute or two. When the smoke rose, a miserable sight was revealed: the ground cumbered with dead and wounded, the advancing masses stopped short and turned into a frantic mob, shouting, cursing, gesticulating. The order was given to charge.

Then over the field rose the British cheer, mixed with the fierce yell of the Highland slogan. Some of the corps pushed forward with the bayonet; some advanced firing. The clansmen drew their broadswords and dashed on, keen and swift as bloodhounds. At the English right, though the attacking column was broken to pieces, a fire was still kept up, chiefly, it seems, by sharpshooters from the bushes and cornfields, where they had lain for an hour or more. Here Wolfe himself led the charge, at the head of the Louisbourg grenadiers. A shot shattered his wrist. He wrapped his handkerchief about it and kept on. Another shot struck him, and he still advanced, when a third lodged in his breast. He staggered, and sat on the ground. Lieutenant Brown, of the grenadiers, one Henderson, a volunteer in the same company, and a private soldier, aided by an officer of artillery who ran to join them, carried him in their arms to the rear. He begged them to lay him down. They did so, and asked if he would have a surgeon. "There's no need," he answered; "it's all over with me." A moment after, one of them cried out, "They run; see how they run!" "Who run?" Wolfe demanded, like a man roused from sleep. "The enemy, sir. Egad, they give way everywhere!" "Go, one of you, to Colonel Burton," returned the dying man; "tell him to march Webb's regiment down to Charles River, to cut off their retreat from the bridge." Then, turning on his side, he murmured, "Now, God be praised, I will die in peace!" and in a few moments his gallant soul had fled.

Montcalm, still on horseback, was borne with the tide of fugitives towards the town. As he approached the walls a shot passed through his body. He kept his seat; two soldiers supported him, one on each side, and led his horse through the St. Louis gate. On the open space within, among the excited crowd, were several women, drawn, no doubt, by eagerness to know the result of the fight. One of them recognized him, saw the streaming blood, and shrieked, "*O mon Dieu! mon Dieu! le Marquis est tué!*" "It's nothing, it's nothing," replied the death-stricken man; "don't be troubled for me, my good friends."

FRANCIS PARKMAN, Montcalm and Wolfe

VI

The Coming of the Revolution

25. Mohawks Spill Tea in Boston Harbor

George III insisted upon a duty on tea imported by Americans. The revenue was trifling, but he regarded this tax as a matter of principle. When the colonists smuggled the commodity in from Holland, the king and his ministers took steps to cheapen English tea to such a level that Americans would find it lower priced, even with the duty added, than the smuggled substitute. They believed that the colonists would then buy. But the Americans were as firm upon a question of principle as the king. Popular wrath was aroused and committees representing Boston and five other towns resolved in November, 1773, to allow none of the tea to be landed. Under the leadership of Sam Adams Boston merchants and shopkeepers took matters into their own hands. Conservatives were scandalized by the destruction of property but John Adams wrote, "This is the most magnificent movement of all."

THE TEA destroyed was contained in three ships, lying near each other, at what was called at that time Griffin's wharf, and were surrounded by armed ships of war; the commanders of which had publicly declared, that if the rebels, as they were pleased to style the Bostonians, should not withdraw their opposition to the landing of the tea before a certain day, the 17th day of December, 1773, they should on that day force it on shore, under the cover of their cannon's mouth. On the day preceding the seventeenth, there was a meeting of the citizens of the county of Suffolk, convened at one of the churches in Boston, for the purpose of consulting on what measures might be considered expedient to prevent the landing of the tea, or secure the people from the collection of the duty. At that meeting a committee was appointed to wait on Governor Hutchinson, and request him to inform them whether he would take any measures to satisfy the people on the object of the meeting. To the first application of this committee, the Governor told them he would give them a definite answer by five o'clock in the afternoon. At the hour appointed, the committee again repaired to the Governor's house, and on inquiry found he had gone to his country seat at Milton, a distance of about six miles. When the committee returned and informed the meeting of the absence of the Governor, there was a confused murmur among the members, and the meeting was immediately dissolved, many of them crying out, "Let every man do his duty, and be true to his country"; and there was a general huzza for Griffin's wharf. It was now evening, and I immediately dressed myself in the costume of an Indian, equipped with a small hatchet, which I and my associates denominated the tomahawk, with which, and a club, after having painted my face and hands with coal dust in the shop of a blacksmith, I repaired to Griffin's wharf, where the ships lay that contained the tea. When I first appeared in the street, after being thus disguised, I fell in with many who were dressed, equipped, and painted as I was, and who fell in with me, and marched in order to the place of our destination. When we arrived at the wharf, there were three of our number who assumed an authority to direct our operations, to which we readily submitted. They divided us into three parties, for the purpose of boarding the three ships which contained the tea at the same time. The name of him who commanded the division to which I was assigned was Leonard Pitt. The names of the other commanders I never knew. We were immediately ordered by the respective commanders to board all the ships at the same time, which we promptly obeyed. The commander of the division to which I belonged, as soon as we were on board the ship, appointed me boatswain, and ordered me to go to the captain and demand of him the keys to the hatches and a dozen candles. I made the demand accordingly, and the captain promptly replied, and delivered the articles; but requested me at the same time to do no damage to the ship or rigging. We then were ordered by our commander to open the hatches, and take out all the chests of tea

and throw them overboard, and we immediately proceeded to execute his orders; first cutting and splitting the chests with our
tomahawks, so as thoroughly to expose them to the effects of the
water. In about three hours from the time we went on board, we
had thus broken and thrown overboard every tea chest to be found
in the ship, while those in the other ships were disposing of the
tea in the same way, at the same time. We were surrounded by
British armed ships, but no attempt was made to resist us. We then
quietly retired to our several places of residence, without having
any conversation with each other, or taking any measures to discover who were our associates; nor do I recollect of our having had
the knowledge of the name of a single individual concerned in that
affair, except that of Leonard Pitt, the commander of my division,
whom I have mentioned. There appeared to be an understanding
that each individual should volunteer his services, keep his own
secret, and risk the consequences for himself. No disorder took
place during that transaction, and it was observed at that time,
that the stillest night ensued that Boston had enjoyed for many
months.

During the time we were throwing the tea overboard, there were
several attempts made by some of the citizens of Boston and its
vicinity to carry off small quantities of it for their family use. To
effect that object, they would watch their opportunity to snatch
up a handful from the deck, where it became plentifully scattered,
and put it into their pockets. One Captain O'Connor, whom I well
knew, came on board for that purpose, and when he supposed he
was not noticed, filled his pockets, and also the lining of his coat.
But I had detected him, and gave information to the captain of
what he was doing. We were ordered to take him into custody, and
just as he was stepping from the vessel, I seized him by the skirt
of his coat, and in attempting to pull him back, I tore it off; but
springing forward, by a rapid effort, he made his escape. He had,
however, to run a gauntlet through the crowd upon the wharf;
each one, as he passed, giving him a kick or a stroke.

Another attempt was made to save a little tea from the ruins of
the cargo by a tall, aged man who wore a large cocked hat and white
wig, which was fashionable at that time. He had slightly slipped
a little into his pocket, but being detected, they seized him, and tak-

ing his hat and wig from his head, threw them, together with the tea, of which they had emptied his pockets, into the water. In consideration of his advanced age, he was permitted to escape, with now and then a slight kick.

The next morning, after we had cleared the ships of the tea, it was discovered that very considerable quantities of it were floating upon the surface of the water; and to prevent the possibility of any of its being saved for use, a number of small boats were manned by sailors and citizens, who rowed them into those parts of the harbor wherever the tea was visible, and by beating it with oars and paddles, so thoroughly drenched it, as to render its entire destruction inevitable.

GEORGE HEWES, A Retrospect of the Boston Tea-Party

26. John Adams Journeys to the Continental Congress

The punitive acts of Parliament against the province of Massachusetts which followed the destruction of the tea resulted in the adoption by the colonies of a plan for a general congress. Delegates were chosen by all the colonies except Georgia, and met in Philadelphia in September of 1774. John Adams, who had graduated from Harvard almost twenty years earlier, was one of the leading attorneys of Boston. He and Josiah Quincy, Jr., had defended the British soldiers arrested after the "Boston Massacre," obtaining the acquittal of all but two; and he had been prominent in the Massachusetts Legislature. A man of positive views, with a stiff, cold personality, and a rather suspicious temper, he took a radical attitude toward the issues between the colonies and the British government. His diary shows how little New Englanders were acquainted with New York and Pennsylvania, and how curious they were as to life therein.

BOSTON. August 10, 1774. — Wednesday. The Committee for the Congress took their departure from Boston, from Mr. Cushing's house, and rode to Coolidge's, where they dined in company with a large number of gentlemen, who went out and prepared an entertainment for them at that place. A most kindly and affectionate meeting we had, and about four in the afternoon we took our leave of them, amidst the kind wishes and fervent prayers of every man in the company for our health and success. This scene was truly affecting, beyond all description affecting. I lodged at Colonel Buck's.

16. Tuesday. — At four we made for New Haven. Seven miles out of town, at a tavern, we met a great number of carriages and of horsemen who had come out to meet us. The sheriff of the county, and constable of the town, and the justices of peace, were in the train. As we were coming, we met others to the amount of I know not what number, but a very great one. As we came into the town, all the bells in town were set to ringing, and the people, men, women, and children, were crowding at the doors and windows as if it was to see a coronation. At nine o'clock the cannon were fired, about a dozen guns, I think.

These expressions of respect to us are intended as demonstrations of the sympathy of this people with the Massachusetts Bay and its capital, and to show their expectations from the Congress, and their determination to carry into execution whatever shall be agreed upon. No governor of a province nor general of an army was ever treated with so much ceremony and assiduity as we have been throughout the whole colony of Connecticut hitherto, but especially all the way from Hartford to New Haven inclusively.

20. Saturday. — We breakfasted at Day's, and arrived in the city of New York at ten o'clock, at Hull's, a tavern, the sign the Bunch of Grapes. We rode by several very elegant country seats before we came to the city. This city will be a subject of much speculation to me.

The streets of this town are vastly more regular and elegant than those of Boston, and the houses are more grand, as well as neat. They are almost all painted, brick buildings and all. In our walks they showed us the house of Mr. William Smith, one of their Council, and the famous lawyer, Mr. Thomas Smith, etc., Mr. Rivington's store, etc.

22. Monday. — This morning we took Mr. McDougall into our coach and rode three miles out of town to Mr. Morin Scott's to breakfast — a very pleasant ride. Mr. Scott has an elegant seat there, with Hudson's River just behind his house and a rural prospect all around him. Mr. Scott, his lady and daughter, and her husband, Mr. Litchfield, were dressed to receive us. We sat in a fine airy entry till called into a front room to breakfast. A more elegant breakfast I never saw — rich place, a very large silver coffeepot, a very large silver teapot, napkins of the very finest materials, toast, and bread, and butter in great perfection. After breakfast a plate of beautiful peaches, another of pears, and another of plums, and a muskmelon were placed on the table.

Mr. Scott, Mr. William Smith, and Mr. William Livingston are the triumvirate who figured away in younger life against the Church of England, who wrote the *Independent Reflector,* the *Watch Tower,* and other papers. They are all of them children of Yale College. Scott and Livingston are said to be lazy; Smith improves every moment of his time. Livingston is lately removed into New Jersey and is one of the delegates for that province.

23. Tuesday. — The way we have been in, of breakfasting, dining, drinking coffee, etc., about the city, is very disagreeable on some accounts. Although it introduces us to the acquaintance of many respectable people here, yet it hinders us from seeing the college, the churches, the printers' offices and booksellers' shops, and many other things which we should choose to see.

With all the opulence and splendor of this city, there is very little good breeding to be found. We have been treated with an assiduous respect, but I have not seen one real gentleman, one well-bred man, since I came to town. At their entertainments there is no conversation that is agreeable; there is no modesty, no attention to one another. They talk very loud, very fast, and all together. If they ask you a question, before you can utter three words of your answer, they will break out upon you again, and talk away.

29. Monday. — We crossed the ferry over Delaware River to the province of Pennsylvania. . . . After dinner we stopped at Frankfort, about five miles out of town. A number of carriages and

gentlemen came out of Philadelphia to meet us — Mr. Thomas Mifflin, Mr. McKean, of the lower counties, one of their delegates, Mr. Rutledge of Carolina, and a number of gentlemen from Philadelphia, Mr. Folsom and Mr. Sullivan, the New Hampshire delegates. We were introduced to all these gentlemen, and most cordially welcomed to Philadelphia. We then rode into town, and dirty, dusty, and fatigued as we were, we could not resist the importunity to go to the tavern, the most genteel one in America. Here we had a fresh welcome to the city of Philadelphia, and after some time spent in conversation, a curtain was drawn, and in the other half of the chamber a supper appeared as elegant as ever was laid upon a table. About eleven o'clock we retired.

31. Wednesday. — Made a visit to Governor Ward of Rhode Island at his lodgings. There we were introduced to several gentlemen. Mr. Dickinson, the farmer, of Pennsylvania, came in his coach with four beautiful horses to Mr. Ward's lodgings to see us. He was introduced to us, and very politely said he was exceedingly glad to have the pleasure of seeing these gentlemen; made some inquiry after the health of his brother and sister, who are now in Boston; gave us some account of his late ill health and his present gout. This was the first time of his getting out. Mr. Dickinson has been subject to hectic complaints. He is a shadow, tall, but slender as a reed, pale as ashes; one would think at first sight that he could not live a month, yet upon a more attentive inspection, he looks as if the springs of life were strong enough to last many years. We dined with Mr. Lynch, his lady and daughter, at their lodgings, Mrs. McKenzie's; and a very agreeable dinner and afternoon we had, notwithstanding the violent heat. We were all vastly pleased with Mr. Lynch. He is a solid, firm, judicious man. He told us that Colonel Washington made the most eloquent speech at the Virginia Convention that ever was made. Says he, "I will raise one thousand men, subsist them at my own expense, and march myself at their head for the relief of Boston."

The Diary of John Adams

27. "Give Me Liberty or Give Me Death!"

Patrick Henry, prominent as a radical in opposing the measures of the British government, had sat in the First Continental Congress. As a member in 1775 of the revolutionary convention of Virginia, he believed war inevitable, and offered resolutions for arming the militia. Conservatives opposed this measure as premature. Henry then burst into this classic bit of eloquence. It was not written out or reported at the time, and the form undoubtedly owes something to Henry's biographer, William Wirt; but the substance and much of the phraseology is his own.

M R. PRESIDENT: It is natural for man to indulge in the illusions of hope. We are apt to shut our eyes against a painful truth, and listen to the song of that siren till she transforms us into beasts. Is this the part of wise men, engaged in a great and arduous struggle for liberty? Are we disposed to be of the number of those who, having eyes, see not, and having ears, hear not, the things which so nearly concern their temporal salvation? For my part, whatever anguish of spirit it may cost, I am willing to know the whole truth; to know the worst, and to provide for it.

I have but one lamp by which my feet are guided, and that is the lamp of experience. I know of no way of judging of the future but by the past. And, judging by the past, I wish to know what there has been in the conduct of the British ministry for the last ten years to justify those hopes with which the gentlemen have been pleased to solace themselves and the House? Is it that insidious smile with which our petition has been lately received? Trust it not, sir; it will prove a snare to your feet. Suffer not yourselves to be betrayed with a kiss. Ask yourselves how this gracious reception of our petition comports with those warlike preparations which cover our waters and darken our land. Are fleets and armies necessary to a work of love and reconciliation? Have we shown ourselves so unwilling to be reconciled that force must be called in to win back our love? Let us not deceive ourselves, sir. These are the implements of war and subjugation, the last arguments to which kings resort.

I ask the gentlemen, sir, what means this martial array, if its purpose be not to force us to submission? Can the gentlemen assign any other possible motive for it? Has Great Britain any enemy in this quarter of the world, to call for all this accumulation of navies and armies? No, sir, she has none. They are meant for us; they can be meant for no other. They are sent over to bind and rivet upon us those chains which the British ministry have been so long forging. And what have we to oppose to them? Shall we try argument? Sir, we have been trying that for the last ten years. Have we anything new to offer upon the subject? Nothing. We have held the subject up in every light of which it is capable; but it has been all in vain.

Shall we resort to entreaty and humble supplication? What terms shall we find which have not been already exhausted? Let us not, I beseech you, sir, deceive ourselves longer. Sir, we have done everything that could be done, to avert the storm which is now coming on. We have petitioned, we have remonstrated, we have supplicated; we have prostrated ourselves before the throne, and have implored its interposition to arrest the tyrannical hands of the ministry and Parliament. Our petitions have been slighted; our remonstrances have produced additional violence and insult; our supplications have been disregarded; and we have been spurned, with contempt, from the foot of the throne. In vain, after these things, may we indulge the fond hope of peace and reconciliation. There is no longer any room for hope.

If we wish to be free; if we mean to preserve inviolate those inestimable privileges for which we have been so long contending; if we mean not basely to abandon the noble struggle in which we have been so long engaged, and which we have pledged ourselves never to abandon until the glorious object of our contest shall be obtained — we must fight! I repeat it, sir, we must fight! An appeal to arms, and to the God of hosts, is all that is left us.

They tell us, sir, that we are weak — unable to cope with so formidable an adversary. But when shall we be stronger? Will it be the next week or the next year? Will it be when we are totally disarmed, and when a British guard shall be stationed in every house? Shall we gather strength by irresolution and inaction? Shall we acquire the means of effectual resistance by lying supinely on our backs, and hugging the delusive phantom of hope, until our enemies shall have bound us hand and foot? Sir, we are not weak, if we make a proper use of those means which the God of nature hath placed in our power. Three millions of people, armed in the holy cause of Liberty, and in such a country as that which we possess, are invincible by any force which our enemy can send against us.

Besides, sir, we shall not fight our battles alone. There is a just God, who presides over the destinies of nations, and who will raise up friends to fight our battles for us. The battle, sir, is not to the strong alone; it is to the vigilant, the active, the brave. Besides, sir, we have no election. If we were base enough to desire it, it is now too late to retire from the contest. There is no retreat but in submission and slavery! Our chains are forged. Their clanking may be heard on the plains of Boston! The war is inevitable — and let it come! I repeat it, sir, let it come!

It is vain, sir, to extenuate the matter. The gentlemen may cry, Peace, peace! but there is no peace. The war has actually begun! The next gale that sweeps from the north will bring to our ears the clash of resounding arms! Our brethren are already in the field! Why stand we here idle? What is it that the gentlemen wish? What would they have? Is life so dear or peace so sweet as to be purchased at the price of chains and slavery? Forbid it, Almighty God. I know not what course others may take, but as for me, give me liberty or give me death!

WILLIAM WIRT, Life of Patrick Henry

28. Colonel Washington Scouts the Idea of Independence

Jonathan Boucher, a conservative-minded clergyman of the Church of England in Maryland, undoubtedly gave a correct view of Washington's mind when he represented him, on his journey to the Second Continental Congress in 1775, as being still attached to Great Britain. Even after Lexington and Concord, most colonists hoped that with a redress of grievances the old relations with the crown could be restored; and Congress officially maintained this attitude long after it had sent Washington to take command at Cambridge.

I HAPPENED to be going across the Potomac to Alexandria with my wife and some other of our friends exactly at the time that General Washington was crossing it on his way to the northward, whither he was going to take the command of the Continental Army. There had been a great meeting of people, and great doings, in Alexandria on the occasion; and everybody seemed to be on fire, either with rum or patriotism or both. Some patriots in our boat huzzaed, and gave three cheers to the General as he passed us; whilst Mr. Addison and myself contented ourselves with pulling off our hats. The General (then only Colonel) Washington beckoned us to stop, as we did, just, as he said, to shake us by the hand. His behavior to me was now, as it had always been, polite and respectful, and I shall forever remember what passed in the few disturbed moments of conversation we then had. From his going on the errand he was, I foresaw and apprized him of much that has since happened; in particular that there would certainly then be a civil war, and that the Americans would soon declare for independency. With more earnestness than was usual with his great reserve, he scouted my apprehensions, adding (and I believe with perfect sincerity) that if ever I heard of his joining in any such measures I had his leave to set him down for everything wicked. Like Hazael, he might have said, "Is thy servant a dog that he should do this great thing?" So little do men know of themselves, and so dangerous is it to make one false step. Many a man, it may be, has gone through life without ever making any egregiously false step; but I question if an instance can be named when a man having made one false step made but one. When once a man goes one mile from the strict line of rectitude, he soon sees, or fancies he sees, reasons compelling him to go *twain.* This was the last time I ever saw this gentleman, who, contrary to all reasonable expectation, has since so distinguished himself as that he will probably be handed down to posterity as one of the first characters of the age.

JONATHAN BOUCHER, Reminiscences of an American Loyalist

29. Adams Nominates Washington Commander-in-Chief

John Adams, only less than his second cousin, Sam Adams, was from the beginning impatient for separation from England. He had great influence in the Continental Congress. Realizing that sectional harmony was indispensable, and that union of the colonies would be promoted if the commander of troops fighting on New England soil were a Virginian, he took the leading part in the presentation of Washington — whose superiority in experience over other aspirants was manifest — as commander-in-chief. This was in June, 1775, a full year before Adams seconded Richard Henry Lee's famous resolution that "these colonies are, and of right ought to be, free and independent States."

IN SEVERAL conversations, I found more than one very cool about the appointment of Washington, and particularly Mr. Pendleton was very clear and full against it. Full of anxieties concerning these confusions, and apprehending daily that we should hear very distressing news from Boston, I walked with Mr. Samuel Adams in the State House yard, for a little exercise and fresh air, before the hour of Congress, and there represented to him the various dangers that surrounded us. He agreed to them all, but said, "What shall we do?" I answered him that he knew I had taken great pains to get our colleagues to agree upon some plan, that we might be unanimous; but he knew that they would pledge themselves to nothing; but I was determined to take a step which should compel them and all the other members of Congress to declare themselves for or against something. "I am determined this morning to make a direct motion that Congress should adopt the army before Boston, and appoint Colonel Washington commander of it." Mr. Adams seemed to think very seriously of it, but said nothing.

Accordingly, when Congress had assembled, I rose in my place, and in as short a speech as the subject would admit, represented the state of the Colonies, the uncertainty in the minds of the people, their great expectation and anxiety, the distresses of the army, the danger of its dissolution, the difficulty of collecting another, and the probability that the British army would take advantage of our delays, march out of Boston, and spread desolation as far as they could go. I concluded with a motion, in form, that Congress would adopt the army at Cambridge and appoint a general; that though this was not the proper time to nominate a general, yet, as I had reason to believe this was a point of the greatest difficulty, I had no hesitation to declare that I had but one gentleman in my mind for that important command, and that was a gentleman from Virginia who was among us and very well known to all of us, a gentleman whose skill and experience as an officer, whose independent fortune, great talents, and excellent universal character, would command the approbation of all America, and unite the cordial exertions of all the colonies better than any other person in the Union. Mr. Washington, who happened to sit near the door, as soon as he heard me allude to him, from his usual modesty, darted into the library room. Mr. Hancock — who was our president, which gave me an opportunity to observe his countenance while I was speaking on the state of the colonies, the army at Cambridge, and the enemy — heard me with visible pleasure; but when I came to describe Washington for the commander, I never remarked a more sudden and striking change of countenance. Mortification and resentment were expressed as forcibly as his face could exhibit them. Mr. Samuel Adams seconded the motion, and that did not soften the president's physiognomy at all. The subject came under debate, and several gentlemen declared themselves against the appointment of Mr. Washington, not on account of any personal objection against him, but because the army were all from New England, had a general of their own, appeared to be satisfied with him, and had proved themselves able to imprison the British army in Boston, which was all they expected or desired at that time. Mr. Pendleton, of Virginia, [and] Mr. Sherman, of Connecticut, were very explicit in declaring this opinion; Mr. Cushing and several others more faintly expressed their opposition, and their fears of discontents in the army and in New England. Mr. Paine expressed a great opinion of General Ward and a strong friendship for him, having been his classmate at college, or at least his contemporary; but gave no opinion upon the question. The subject was postponed to a future day. In the meantime, pains were taken out-of-doors to obtain a unanimity, and the voices were generally so clearly in favor of Washington, that the dissentient members were persuaded to withdraw their opposition, and Mr. Washington was nominated, I believe by Mr. Thomas Johnson of Maryland, unanimously elected, and the army adopted.

The Diary of John Adams

30. A Shot Is Fired That Is Heard around the World

"What a glorious morning is this!"
exclaimed the exultant Sam Adams as he listened to the rattle of musketry on April 19, 1775. He realized that the events of that day made independence almost inevitable. Hostilities had almost begun in February, when General Thomas Gage sent a force by water to

Salem to search for powder. On April 19th he hurried a force at dawn to Concord, twenty miles from Boston, to destroy the military stores which had been collected there. This narrative from a British pen places the blame for the first shots squarely on the colonists; but the latter had witnesses who declared that the British had fired first.

ON THE evening of the 18th, about nine o'clock, I learned there was a large detachment going from this garrison, on which I immediately resolved to go with them, and meeting a few men in the street full accoutered, I followed them and embarked at the Magazine Guard and landed near Cambridge, where I joined Major Pitcairn, who I understood was to command next to Colonel Smith. Here we remained for two hours, partly waiting for the rest of the detachment and for provisions. About half an hour after two in the morning, on the 19th, we marched, Major Pitcairn commanding in front the light infantry. The tide being in, we were up to our middles before we got into the road. Continued for three miles without meeting with any person, when I heard Lieutenant Adair of the marines, who was a little before me in front, call out, "Here are two fellows galloping express to alarm the country," on which I immediately ran up to them, seized one of them and our guide the other, dismounted them, and by Major Pitcairn's directions, gave them in charge to the men. A little after, we were joined by Lieutenant Grant of the Royal Artillery, who told us the country, he was afraid, was alarmed, of which we had little reason to doubt as we heard several shots, being then between three and four in the morning (a very unusual time for firing), when we were joined by Major Mitchell, Captain Cochrane, Captain Lumm, and several other gentlemen who told us the whole country was alarmed and had galloped for their lives, or words to that purpose — that they had taken Paul [Revere], but were obliged to let him go after cutting his girths and stirrups. A little after, a fellow came out of a cross-road galloping. Mr. Adair and I called to him to stop, but he galloped off as hard as he could, upon which Mr. Simms, surgeon's mate of the Forty-Third Regiment, who was on horseback, pursued him and took him a great way in front. A little after, I met a very genteel man riding in a carriage they call a sulky, who assured me there were six hundred men assembled at Lexington with a view of opposing us. I think I should know the man again if I saw him, as I took very particular notice of his features and dress. I waited with him till Major Pitcairn came up with the division, to whom he repeated much the same as he did to me. Then going on in front again, I met, coming out of a crossroad, another fellow galloping. However, hearing him some time before, I placed myself so that I got hold of the bridle of his horse and dismounted him. Our guide seemed to think that this was a very material fellow and said something as if he had been a member of the provincial Congress. A little after this I mounted a horse I had, and Mr. Adair went into a chaise. It began now to be daylight and we met some men with a wagon of wood, who told us there were odds of a thousand men in arms at Lexington and added that they would fight us. Here we waited for some time, but seeing nothing of the divisions, I rode to the left about half a mile to see if I could fall in with them, but could see nothing of them. However, saw a vast number of the country militia going over the hill with their arms, to Lexington, and met one of them in the teeth whom I obliged to give up his firelock and bayonet, which I believe he would not have done so easily but from Mr. Adair's coming up. On this, we turned back the road we came and found the division who had halted in consequence of the intelligence the man in the sulky gave them, in order to make a disposition, by advancing men in front and on the flanks, to prevent a surprise. I went on with the front party, which consisted of a sergeant and six or eight men. I shall observe here that the road before you go into Lexington is level for about a thousand yards. Here we saw shots fired to the right and left of us, but as we heard no whizzing of balls, I conclude they were to alarm the body that was there of our approach. On coming within gunshot of the village of Lexington, a fellow from the corner of the road, on the right hand, cocked his piece at me, burnt priming [flashed in the pan]. I immediately called to Mr. Adair and the party to observe this circumstance, which they did, and I acquainted Major Pitcairn of it immediately.

We still went on farther when three shot more were fired at us, which we did not return, and this is sacred truth as I hope for mercy.

These three shot were fired from a corner of a large house to the right of the church. When we came up to the main body, which appeared to me to exceed four hundred in and about the village, who were drawn up in a plain opposite to the church, several officers called out, "Throw down your arms and you shall come to no harm," or words to that effect. Which, they refusing to do, instantaneously the gentlemen who were on horseback rode in amongst them, of which I was one, at which instant I heard Major Pitcairn's voice call out, "Soldiers, don't fire; keep your ranks; form and surround them." Instantly some of the villains, who got over the hedge, fired at us, which our men for the first time returned, which set my horse a-going, who galloped with me down a road above six hundred yards among the middle of them before I turned him. And in returning, a vast number who were in a wood at the right of the grenadiers fired at me, but the distance was so great that I only heard the whistling of the balls, but saw a great number of people in the wood. In consequence of their discovering themselves by firing, our grenadiers gave them a smart fire.

William Sutherland's Letter April 27, 1775

31. Jefferson Writes the Declaration of Independence

Although Jefferson can be said never to have made a real speech, he held a pen which gave him an enormous influence from young manhood to old age. He wrote elaborate resolutions for the first revolutionary convention of Virginia in 1774, later publishing them as a pamphlet under the title A Summary View of the Rights of America. *This work, of which numerous editions were printed in England, gave Jefferson a place among the most influential of American leaders. A little later he drafted Virginia's reply to the conciliatory proposals of Lord North, and followed this by writing the reply of Congress to the same proffer. The fame won by these documents pointed him out as the logical man to draft an explanation and defense of the action of the colonies in separating from England. As John Adams says, most of the ideas were old. In fact, some of the most essential were drawn from the writings of John Locke. But the immortal phraseology of the preamble was strictly Jefferson's.*

YOU INQUIRE why so young a man as Mr. Jefferson was placed at the head of the committee for preparing a Declaration of Independence? I answer: It was the Frankfort advice, to place Virginia at the head of everything. Mr. Richard Henry Lee might be gone to Virginia, to his sick family, for aught I know, but that was not the reason of Mr. Jefferson's appointment. There were three committees appointed at the same time, one for the Declaration of Independence, another for preparing articles of confederation, and another for preparing a treaty to be proposed to France. Mr. Lee was chosen for the Committee of Confederation, and it was not thought convenient that the same person should be upon both. Mr. Jefferson came into Congress in June, 1775, and brought with him a reputation for literature, science, and a happy talent of composition. Writings of his were handed about, remarkable for the peculiar felicity of expression. Though a silent member in Congress, he was so prompt, frank, explicit, and decisive upon committees and in conversation — not even Samuel Adams was more so — that he soon seized upon my heart; and upon this occasion I gave him my vote, and did all in my power to procure the votes of others. I think he had one more vote than any other, and that placed him at the head of the committee. I had the next highest number, and that placed me the second. The committee met, discussed the subject, and then appointed Mr. Jefferson and me to make the draft, I suppose because we were the two first on the list.

The subcommittee met. Jefferson proposed to me to make the draft. I said, "I will not." "You should do it." "Oh! no." "Why will you not? You ought to do it." "I will not." "Why?" "Reasons enough." "What can be your reasons?" "Reason first, you are a Virginian, and a Virginian ought to appear at the head of this business. Reason second, I am obnoxious, suspected, and unpopular. You are very much otherwise. Reason third, you can write ten times better than I can." "Well," said Jefferson, "if you are decided, I will do as well as I can." "Very well. When you have drawn it up, we will have a meeting."

A meeting we accordingly had, and conned the paper over. I was delighted with its high tone and the flights of oratory with which it abounded, especially that concerning Negro slavery, which, though I knew his Southern brethren would never suffer to pass in Congress, I certainly never would oppose. There were other expressions which I would not have inserted if I had drawn it up, particularly that which called the King tyrant. I thought this too personal, for I never believed George to be a tyrant in disposition and in nature; I always believed him to be deceived by his courtiers on both sides of the Atlantic, and in his official capacity, only, cruel. I thought the expression too passionate, and too much like scolding, for so grave and solemn a document; but as Franklin and Sherman were to inspect it afterwards, I thought it would not become me to strike it out. I consented to report it, and do not now remember that I made or suggested a single alteration.

We reported it to the committee of five. It was read, and I do not remember that Franklin or Sherman criticized anything. We were all in haste. Congress was impatient, and the instrument was reported, as I believe, in Jefferson's handwriting, as he first drew it. Congress cut off about a quarter of it, as I expected they would; but they obliterated some of the best of it, and left all that was exceptionable, if anything in it was. I have long wondered that the original draft had not been published. I suppose the reason is the vehement philippic against Negro slavery.

As you justly observe, there is not an idea in it but what had been hackneyed in Congress for two years before. The substance of it is contained in the declaration of rights and the violation of those rights in the Journals of Congress in 1774. Indeed, the essence of it is contained in a pamphlet, voted and printed by the town of Boston, before the first Congress met, composed by James Otis, as I suppose, in one of his lucid intervals, and pruned and polished by Samuel Adams.

JOHN ADAMS, Letter to Timothy Pickering, August 6, 1822

32. The United States Declare Independence

The best-known of American state papers, Jefferson's Declaration of Independence, is next to Lincoln's Second Inaugural Address also the noblest. It is of course the generalizations which give it nobility. Most of the specific statements on American grievances are decidedly partisan; some of them are historically open to controversy — even to grave question. But its statements upon the rights of man and the rights of Americans have inherent dignity, elevation, and truth. We may admit that Adams was right when he said that the general arguments of the Declaration were not fresh, and even that Rufus Choate spoke with some justice when he asserted that the paper was full of "glittering and high-sounding generalities." Asserting great basic truths, it was not intended to seek out novel ideas. But it set forth these truths with the logical force of John Locke, with a measured eloquence characteristic of the eighteenth century, and with a fervent idealism that was all Jefferson's own. Some of the phrases have been watchwords of democracy ever since.

In Congress, July 4, 1776,

THE UNANIMOUS DECLARATION OF THE THIRTEEN UNITED STATES
OF AMERICA,

When in the Course of human events, it becomes necessary for one people to dissolve the political bands which have connected them with another, and to assume among the Powers of the earth, the separate and equal station to which the Laws of Nature and of Nature's God entitle them, a decent respect to the opinions of mankind requires that they should declare the causes which impel them to the separation.

We hold these truths to be self-evident, that all men are created equal, that they are endowed by their Creator with certain unalienable Rights, that among these are Life, Liberty and the pursuit of Happiness. That to secure these rights, Governments are instituted among Men, deriving their just powers from the consent of the governed. That whenever any Form of Government becomes destructive of these ends, it is the Right of the People to alter or to abolish it, and to institute new Government, laying its foundation on such principles and organizing its powers in such form, as to them shall seem most likely to effect their Safety and Happiness. Prudence, indeed, will dictate that Governments long established should not be changed for light and transient causes; and accordingly all experience hath shown, that mankind are more disposed to suffer, while evils are sufferable, than to right themselves by abolishing the forms to which they are accustomed. But when a long train of abuses and usurpations, pursuing invariably the same Object evinces a design to reduce them under absolute Despotism, it is their right, it is their duty, to throw off such Government, and to provide new Guards for their future security. — Such has been the patient sufferance of these Colonies; and such is now the necessity which constrains them to alter their former Systems of Government. The history of the present King of Great Britain is a history of repeated injuries and usurpations, all having in direct object the establishment of an absolute Tyranny over these States. To prove this, let Facts be submitted to a candid world.

He has refused his Assent to Laws, the most wholesome and necessary for the public good.

He has forbidden his Governors to pass Laws of immediate and pressing importance, unless suspended in their operation till his Assent should be obtained; and when so suspended, he has utterly neglected to attend to them.

He has refused to pass other Laws for the accommodation of large districts of people, unless those people would relinquish the right of Representation in the Legislature, a right inestimable to them and formidable to tyrants only.

He has called together legislative bodies at places unusual, uncomfortable, and distant from the depository of their Public Records, for the sole purpose of fatiguing them into compliance with his measures.

He has dissolved Representative Houses repeatedly, for opposing with manly firmness his invasions on the rights of the people.

He has refused for a long time, after such dissolutions, to cause others to be elected; whereby the Legislative Powers, incapable of Annihilation, have returned to the People at large for their exercise; the State remaining in the mean time exposed to all the dangers of invasion from without, and convulsions within.

He has endeavoured to prevent the population of these States; for that purpose obstructing the Laws of Naturalization of Foreigners; refusing to pass others to encourage their migration hither, and raising the conditions of new Appropriations of Lands.

He has obstructed the Administration of Justice, by refusing his Assent to Laws for establishing Judiciary Powers.

He has made Judges dependent on his Will alone, for the tenure of their offices, and the amount and payment of their salaries.

He has erected a multitude of New Offices, and sent hither swarms of Officers to harass our People, and eat out their substance.

He has kept among us, in times of peace, Standing Armies without the Consent of our legislature.

He has affected to render the Military independent of and superior to the Civil Power.

He has combined with others to subject us to a jurisdiction foreign to our constitution, and unacknowledged by our laws; giving his Assent to their acts of pretended legislation:

For quartering large bodies of armed troops among us:

For protecting them, by a mock Trial, from Punishment for any Murders which they should commit on the Inhabitants of these States:

For cutting off our Trade with all parts of the world:

For imposing taxes on us without our Consent:

For depriving us in many cases, of the benefits of Trial by Jury:

For transporting us beyond Seas to be tried for pretended offences:

For abolishing the free System of English Laws in a neighbouring Province, establishing therein an Arbitrary government, and enlarging its Boundaries so as to render it at once an example and fit instrument for introducing the same absolute rule into these Colonies:

For taking away our Charters, abolishing our most valuable Laws, and altering fundamentally the Forms of our Governments:

For suspending our own Legislature, and declaring themselves invested with Power to legislate for us in all cases whatsoever.

He has abdicated Government here, by declaring us out of his Protection and waging War against us.

He has plundered our seas, ravaged our Coasts, burnt our towns, and destroyed the lives of our people.

He is at this time transporting large armies of foreign mercenaries to compleat the works of death, desolation and tyranny, already begun with circumstances of Cruelty & perfidy scarcely paralleled in the most barbarous ages, and totally unworthy the Head of a civilized nation.

He has constrained our fellow Citizens taken Captive on the high Seas to bear Arms against their Country, to become the executioners of their friends and Brethren, or to fall themselves by their Hands.

He has excited domestic insurrections amongst us, and has endeavoured to bring on the inhabitants of our frontiers, the merciless Indian Savages, whose known rule of warfare, is an undistinguished destruction of all ages, sexes and conditions.

In every stage of these Oppressions We have Petitioned for Redress in the most humble terms: Our repeated Petitions have been answered only by repeated injury. A Prince, whose character is thus marked by every act which may define a Tyrant, is unfit to be the ruler of a free People.

Nor have We been wanting in attention to our British brethren. We have warned them from time to time of attempts by their legislature to extend an unwarrantable jurisdiction over us. We have reminded them of the circumstances of our emigration and settlement here. We have appealed to their native justice and magnanimity, and we have conjured them by the ties of our common kindred to disavow these usurpations, which would inevitably interrupt our connections and correspondence. They too have been deaf to the voice of justice and of consanguinity. We must, therefore, acquiesce in the necessity, which denounces our Separation, and hold them, as we hold the rest of mankind, Enemies in War, in Peace Friends.

We, therefore, the Representatives of the united States of America, in General Congress, Assembled, appealing to the Supreme Judge of the world for the rectitude of our intentions, do, in the Name, and by Authority of the good People of these Colonies, solemnly publish and declare, That these United Colonies are, and of Right ought to be Free and Independent States; that they are Absolved from all Allegiance to the British Crown, and that all political connection between them and the State of Great Britain, is and ought to be totally dissolved; and that as Free and Independent States, they have full Power to levy War, conclude Peace, contract Alliances, establish Commerce, and to do all other Acts and Things which Independent States may of right do. And for the support of this Declaration, with a firm reliance on the Protection of Divine Providence, we mutually pledge to each other our Lives, our Fortunes and our sacred Honor.

VII

The Winning of Independence

33. Ethan Allen Captures Fort Ticonderoga

The embattled colonists needed cannon and stores; also they wished to seize the gateway to Canada. To encompass these two objects, hardy fighters from Connecticut, Massachusetts, and what shortly became Vermont joined in a spring march on Ticonderoga, key fortress of northern New York. Their leader was the Vermonter Ethan Allen, who tells the story spiritedly.

EVER since I arrived at the state of manhood, and acquainted myself with the general history of mankind, I have felt a sincere passion for liberty. The history of nations doomed to perpetual slavery in consequence of yielding up to tyrants their natural-born liberties, I read with a sort of philosophical horror; so that the first systematical and bloody attempt, at Lexington, to enslave America, thoroughly electrified my mind, and fully determined me to take part with my country. And, while I was wishing for an opportunity to signalize myself in its behalf, directions were privately sent to me from the then colony (now State) of Connecticut, to raise the Green Mountain Boys, and, if possible, with them to surprise and take the fortress of Ticonderoga. This enterprise I cheerfully undertook; and, after first guarding all the several passes that led thither, to cut off all intelligence between the garrison and the country, made a forced march from Bennington, and arrived at the lake opposite to Ticonderoga, on the evening of the 9th day of May, 1775, with two hundred and thirty valiant Green Mountain Boys; and it was with the utmost difficulty that I procured boats to cross the lake. However, I landed eighty-three men near the garrison, and sent the boats back for the rear guard, commanded by Colonel Seth Warner; but the day began to dawn, and I found myself under the necessity to attack the fort, before the rear could cross the lake; and, as it was viewed hazardous, I harangued the officers and soldiers in the manner following:

"Friends and fellow soldiers, you have, for a number of years past, been a scourge and terror to arbitrary power. Your valor has been famed abroad, and acknowledged, as appears by the advice and orders to me, from the General Assembly of Connecticut, to surprise and take the garrison now before us. I now propose to advance before you, and, in person, conduct you through the wicket gate; for we must this morning either quit our pretensions to valor, or possess ourselves of this fortress in a few minutes; and, inasmuch as it is a desperate attempt, which none but the bravest of men dare undertake, I do not urge it on any contrary to his will. You that will undertake voluntarily, poise your firelocks."

The men being, at this time, drawn up in three ranks, each poised his firelock. I ordered them to face to the right, and, at the head of the center file, marched them immediately to the wicket gate aforesaid, where I found a sentry posted, who instantly snapped his fusee at me; I ran immediately toward him, and he retreated through the covered way into the parade within the garrison, gave a halloo, and ran under a bombproof. My party, who followed me into the fort, I formed on the parade in such a manner as to face the two barracks which faced each other.

The garrison being asleep, except the sentries, we gave three huzzas, which greatly surprised them. One of the sentries made a pass at one of my officers with a charged bayonet, and slightly wounded him. My first thought was to kill him with my sword; but, in an instant, I altered the design and fury of the blow to a slight cut on the side of the head, upon which he dropped his gun, and asked quarter, which I readily granted him, and demanded of him the place where the commanding officer kept; he showed me a pair of stairs in the front of a barrack, on the west part of the garrison, which led up to a second story in said barrack, to which I immediately repaired, and ordered the commander, Captain de la Place, to come forth instantly, or I would sacrifice the whole garrison; at which the Captain came immediately to the door, with his breeches in his hand, when I ordered him to deliver me the fort instantly; he asked me by what authority I demanded it: I answered him, "*In the name of the great Jehovah and the Continental Congress.*" The authority of the Congress being very little known at that time, he began to speak again; but I interrupted him, and with my drawn sword over his head, again demanded an immediate surrender of the garrison; with which he then complied, and ordered his men to be forthwith paraded without arms, as he had given up the garrison. In the meantime some of my officers had given orders, and in consequence thereof, sundry of the barrack doors were beat down, and about one-third of the garrison imprisoned, which consisted of the said commander, a Lieutenant Feltham, a conductor of artillery, a gunner, two sergeants, and forty-four rank and file; about one hundred pieces of cannon, one thirteen-inch mortar, and a number of swivels. This surprise was carried into execution in the gray of the morning of the 10th of May, 1775. The sun seemed to rise that morning with a superior luster, and Ticonderoga and its dependencies smiled to its conquerors, who tossed about the flowing bowl, and wished success to Congress, and the liberty and freedom of America.

ETHAN ALLEN, Narrative of Captivity

34. William Humphrey Marches with Arnold to Quebec

Among the immortal marches of American forces against distant objectives — Benedict Arnold's march upon Quebec, George Rogers Clark's march upon Fort Kaskaskia, Frémont's march with the California Battalion upon Los Angeles — the first-named combines tragedy with heroism in an unforgettable way. Young Benedict Arnold, who had led a militia company from New Haven to Cambridge, and who had raised additional troops for the expedition against Ticonderoga, in which he reluctantly yielded first place to Ethan Allen, was ordered in the summer of 1775 to co-operate with General Richard Montgomery in an invasion of Canada.

He led his force of eleven hundred men out of Cambridge on September 17, 1775, and was soon advancing through the morasses and tangled woods of the Maine wilderness. Terrible hardships from cold, hunger, and disease killed many of his men and caused others to desert. When he reached Quebec winter was at hand, and the combined attack which he and Montgomery delivered on the last day of 1775 was a dismal failure.

OCTOBER 16, 1775.— This day, being very short of provisions and brought to one half-pint of flour per man, and waiting until nine o'clock for the rifle companies, in order to get some supplies, they not coming up, we proceeded on our way. Came to an Indian hut, where one Sabatis lived, as big a rogue as ever existed under heaven; still proceeded on our way, marched about four miles and encamped, and Colonel Arnold came up in the evening at about eight o'clock, and hearing of our want of bread, ordered four bateaux with thirty-two men of each division to return to the rear for a supply of provision in the morning.

Here our company had not five or six pounds of flour to fifty men. I was sent back with this detachment with a great deal of reluctance.

October 20.— This day it rained very hard — our boats not having got up, we packed up our cartridges in casks in order to be ready for an immediate embarkation here. Stayed this night, it being the third day that we have been obliged to lay by for a supply of provision.

October 21.— This day it rained very hard and was almost as heavy a storm as I ever was sensible of. Colonel Enos came up with us at about eleven o'clock, and expected to have found Colonel Arnold, but on his not finding him, returned back, drove up his rear in the afternoon. Major Bigelow, who had been down with our boats for provision, returned, with only two barrels of flour. We are very short of provisions, and there is no probability of getting any more until we get to Sertigan. Now we have no other view than either to proceed to Canada or to retreat. We concluded to send all those back who were not able to do actual duty. This night the river rose to a high degree, better than two feet and a half, which occasions the current to run very swift. Our encampment grew very uncomfortable, especially for those who had no tents, and not being used to soldiers' fare.

October 25. — We are absolutely in a dangerous situation; however, I hope for the best, but if we receive no supplies from the French side, we shall be poorly off.

This day there [were] a subaltern and forty-eight men of the sick went back with three bateaux. The river is narrow and exceeding swift, the going by land is very bad, the men are very much disheartened and desirous to return; however, if their bellies were full, I believe they would rather go forward — we are out and must go on. Colonel Arnold has sent Captain Hanchet with a party to purchase of the French if possible, and to clear the roads. Here a council of war determined that Colonel Enos should not go back.

October 28. — At four o'clock an express came from Colonel Arnold, with intelligence that the French [were] glad to receive us, and that they would supply us with provision — glad tidings to people that are brought to one half-pint of flour, and but very little meat. Today was delivered out all the meat we had in our battalion, which turned out two ounces of meat per man. An express passed us to go to his Excellency General Washington; a pilot was sent us to lead us the right way through the woods; two companies of the musketry are gone forward, but the three rifle companies stayed with us; this is the nineteenth carrying place.

October 30. — This day we proceeded through a swamp six miles and more in frozen water and mud half-leg-high — got into an alder swamp; steering east-southerly came to a small river which we forded; the water was middle-high and very cold. This river is about eight rods wide. From thence we proceeded to a hill and there shaped our course to another river that we crossed on a log — here several of our men had the luck to fall in. I must confess that I began to be concerned about our situation, having only four days' provision in this wilderness where there was no sign of any human being, but a swampy thicket of wood made only for an asylum of wild beasts.

November 1. — This day we proceeded on our way — our people grew very much fatigued and began to fall in the rear, being very much reduced with hunger and cold. I saw, with astonishment, a dog killed and even eat, his paunch, guts, and skin. Went about twelve miles and encamped.

November 2. — This day we proceeded on our way through much fatigue, sixteen miles. It is an astonishing thing to see every man without any sustenance but cold water — this, you must think, is weakening rather than strengthening. — Here a boy returns and tells us that there was provision within eight miles of us. I saw several, when they came to see the provision, shed tears, they were so much overjoyed at the sight of relief.

November 3. — This day we proceeded on our way and met the provision, got refreshed, then set out again; passed by a pair of falls and went one mile and encamped.

November 9. — This day proceeded six miles through settlements, then entered the woods, which is nine miles, went fifteen miles and stayed at St. Mary's parish at a house near the chapel of the same name; there dined, and set out again to Point Levy, where we arrived at eight o'clock. Found Colonel Arnold and our volunteers all well and in good spirits.

December 27. — This day stormy — the men were ordered to hold themselves in readiness to the shortest notice at about twelve at night, the army being divided according to the plan the General had laid. Part of our detachment proceeded to the hill, the other part stayed to attack the lower town under the command of Colonel Arnold; but, it clearing up, it was thought prudent to defer storming the garrison until a favorable opportunity.

December 28. — This day some of our men took four men that refused to turn out, and led them round with halters round their necks, from place to place, and treated them in such a manner as all such villains deserve. The General issued an order to the satisfaction of the soldiers in general, of the pleasure that he took in seeing the men so expert and alert in turning out in order to storm the city of Quebec.

December 30. — This day the enemy kept up a smart fire all day upon St. Roche's, but did little or no damage. This evening about ten o'clock, received orders that it was the General's determination to storm the city of Quebec; then we ordered our men to get their arms in readiness for to go and storm. It was very dark and snowed. The plan for executing the design is as follows: General Montgomery with the York troops to proceed round Cape Diamond to a place by the name of "The Potash" and make their attack there. Colonel Livingston, with a party of Canadians, to make a false attack upon Cape Diamond and St. John's Gate. An advance party of twenty-five men to proceed to D—— wharf. Colonel Arnold's detachment to attack the lower town. We were to receive a signal by three sky-rockets when to attack — but, not observing them, we was about half an hour too late. Captain Dearborn's company on account of being quartered on the other side of the Charles River, and the tide being high, not coming up, we proceeding without them, expecting them to drive up the rear, we forced and took the guard. Captain was drunk and not able to stand on his legs without assistance. . . . They fired very briskly upon us; we passed along the street, and they killed and wounded a number of our men. After we had gained the first barricade, we halted our men and tried to scale the second barrier — and, notwithstanding their utmost efforts, we got some of our ladders up and were obliged to retreat, our guns being wet, as not one in ten would fire. Then we concluded to retreat, which we did to first barrier that we had took, and when we came there, we found we could not retreat without losing all our men, or at least the most of them. There was killed of our party Lieutenant Humphrey and Lieutenant Cooper, together with Captain Hendricks, with a number of privates. And in General Montgomery's party there was killed the brave General Montgomery, his aide-de-camp Macpherson, Captain Cheesman, and some privates.

Colonel Campbell then took command and ordered them to retreat, so that the force of the garrison came upon us. Captain Lamb, among the rest, was wounded. There was no possibility of our retreating; they promising us good quarter, we surrendered ourselves. Colonel Arnold, being wounded in the front of the action, was carried off to the general hospital. Thus after a long and tedious march I have been unfortunate enough to become a prisoner.

WILLIAM HUMPHREY, Journal

35. Shaw Deplores Conditions in the American Army

Until almost the close of the year 1776 the war seemed to be, from the patriot point of view, a dismal failure. Washington lost the battle of Long Island, and was lucky to evacuate his army before it was captured by the British. His attempt to hold New York city failed, and Howe's capture of Fort Washington at the upper end of Manhattan Island compelled a further retreat. It is not strange that the morale of the American forces sank to a low ebb. From their discouragement, however, Washington's brilliant little victories over British outposts at Trenton and Princeton soon rescued them.

OCTOBER 11, 1776 [Fort Washington, New York].—The army still remain in tents. It will be late in the season before we get into huts or barracks. After our retreat from the city, our troops had a skirmish with the enemy and repulsed them. Though in itself it was a small affair, the consequences were great, as the check they received will probably be a means of keeping off an attack till the spring. This is devoutly to be wished, for the aspect of our affairs at present is not very flattering, I assure you. However, we hope soon to be in a very fine way, as the Congress, *at last,* seem to think the war must be carried on upon a large scale; eighty-eight battalions of seven hundred and odd men each, besides a proportionable number of artillery, with everything necessary to such an army as we must have, are to be raised. No more militia are to be called in; and, in my humble opinion, they are productive of more expense than the keeping an equal or larger number of regular troops, to say nothing of the little service they have been to us anywhere but in New England. Those from the Jerseys, and other places this way, on the appearance of the enemy, scampered off by whole companies and regiments, especially when the enemy's ships came before a fort of ours at Paulus

Hook, opposite the city of New York, about a mile and a quarter distant. So great a panic seized them that Captain Dana of our regiment was obliged to charge his cannon with grapeshot and threaten to fire on them; otherwise they would have abandoned the place before he could get the military stores off. These were your Southern heroes, fellows who affect to hold the Eastern Yankees in contempt; but I challenge them to produce an instance of cowardice in our people anyway equal to this of theirs. But I don't mean to enlarge on so ungrateful a subject. Comparisons are odious. There are, without doubt, good men among them; and it would be well if every distinction of this or that colony or province could be buried in that of *American*. I wish we had more Boston young fellows among us, for I think it rather disgraceful for so many of them to be idling at home these stirring times; and if they don't turn out, they will, when the war is over, appear very contemptible. . . .

November 18, 1776. — As for our army, God help it! — for at present it is in a disagreeable state; the militia gone and going home, the time of enlistment for our regular troops expiring, and little or nothing done towards raising new ones. The severities of the present campaign will discourage many from engaging again without large bounties, so that I do not think it improbable some of the states will be under a necessity of drafting men during the war. Very different this from the last, when many, without doubt, entered into the service merely for amusement. Ever since we left New England, we have been carrying on the war in an enemy's country, and firmly I believe, if Heaven had not something very great in store for America, we should ere this have been a ruined people. When I left the town of Boston with a view of joining our army, my enthusiasm was such as to induce me to think I should find as much public virtue among our people as is recorded of ancient Sparta or Rome. Numberless instances might be brought to show how miserably I was disappointed. Let it suffice to mention one. The militia whose times expired yesterday were desired to tarry for the good of their country *only four days,* and out of their whole number there were not sufficient to form one regiment who would engage. Scandalous! Tell it not in Britain. I cannot wish them a severer punishment than a due reward of their ingratitude. After the new army is raised, which must be done by some means or other, I hope we shall never be again so grossly infatuated as to expect any good can accrue from calling in the militia. Far be it from me to reflect on them as individuals. I speak of them as a body, which from its present constitution can be of no service to us; for, so long as men are under no obligation to stay after a limited time, at the expiration of which neither a regard for the welfare of their country nor a concern for their own honor can prevail on them, they must be not only ungrateful, but a dangerous part of society. You may perhaps, before this reaches you, be informed of Fort Washington's being in the hands of the enemy. They got possession of it the day before yesterday. We have not yet learnt the particulars, only that they made a feint of attacking some lines of ours below the fort, which induced the commanding officer to send a part of his force there. This the enemy took advantage of, by marching a number of troops they had previously prepared for the purpose between them and the fort, which, cutting off the communication, obliged them first — and shortly after, the fort, — to surrender, on what terms is not known. I was at General Lee's just after the news came. He was in a towering passion, and said that it was a splendid affair for Mr. Howe, who was returning chagrined and disgraced at being able to make no further progress this campaign, thus *to have his sores licked by us.* However, don't let us be discouraged, for we must expect greater rubs before an empire can be established.

The Journals of Major Samuel Shaw

36. The American Army Suffers at Valley Forge

Washington's army, defeated by Howe at the battle of Brandywine on September 11, 1777, was compelled to retire beyond Philadelphia while the British entered that city. The Continental Congress fled first to Lancaster and then to

York in Pennsylvania. Meanwhile the British fleet held Delaware
Bay and captured Forts Mercer and Mifflin. All the maritime areas
of Rhode Island, New York, Delaware, and Pennsylvania were thus
in the hands of the royal forces. For the darkest winter of the war,
Washington settled down with his fragmentary army at Valley
Forge. But somehow the army got through that winter and emerged
stronger and better disciplined than it had ever been.

SAND and forest, forest and sand, formed the whole way from
Williamsburg to the camp at Valley Forge. I do not remember how
many days I took to accomplish this difficult journey. Being badly
fed, as a natural consequence I walked badly, and passed at least
six nights under the trees through not meeting with any habitation.
Not knowing the language, I often strayed from the right road,
which was so much time and labor lost. At last, early in November
[1777], I arrived at Valley Forge.

The American army was then encamped three or four leagues
from Philadelphia, which city was then occupied by the British,
who were rapidly fulfilling the prophecy of Dr. Franklin.

That celebrated man — an ambassador who amused himself with
science, which he adroitly made to assist him in his diplomatic work
— said, when some friends came to Passy to condole with him on the
fall of Philadelphia: "You are mistaken; it is not the British army
that has taken Philadelphia, but Philadelphia that has taken the
British army." The cunning old diplomatist was right. The capital
of Pennsylvania had already done for the British what Capua did
in a few months for the soldiers of Hannibal. The Americans —
the "insurgents" as they were called — camped at Valley Forge; the
British officers, who were in the city, gave themselves up to pleasure;
there were continual balls and other amusements; the troops were
idle and enervated by inaction, and the generals undertook nothing
all the winter.

Soon I came in sight of the camp. My imagination had pictured
an army with uniforms, the glitter of arms, standards, etc., in short,
military pomp of all sorts. Instead of the imposing spectacle I expected, I saw, grouped together or standing alone, a few militiamen,
poorly clad, and for the most part without shoes — many of them

badly armed, but all well supplied with provisions, and I noticed that tea and sugar formed part of their rations. I did not then know that this was not unusual, and I laughed, for it made me think of the recruiting sergeants on the Quai de la Ferraille at Paris, who say to the yokels, "You will want for nothing when you are in the regiment, but if bread should run short you must not mind eating cakes." Here the soldiers had tea and sugar. In passing through the camp I also noticed soldiers wearing cotton nightcaps under their hats, and some having for cloaks or greatcoats coarse woolen blankets, exactly like those provided for the patients in our French hospitals. I learned afterwards that these were the officers and generals.

Such, in strict truth, was, at the time I came amongst them, the appearance of this armed mob, the leader of whom was the man who has rendered the name of Washington famous; such were the colonists — unskilled warriors who learned in a few years how to conquer the finest troops that England could send against them. Such also, at the beginning of the War of Independence, was the state of want in the insurgent army, and such was the scarcity of money, and the poverty of that government, now so rich, powerful, and prosperous, that its notes, called Continental paper money, were nearly valueless.

THE CHEVALIER DE PONTGIBAUD, A French Volunteer of the War of Independence

37. George Rogers Clark Conquers the Northwest

The British forts on the Wabash and Mississippi were small, but they enabled British agents to incite the Indians north of the Ohio River to attack American settlers in the West. To put an end to this George Rogers Clark, a Virginian settled in Kentucky, led a force westward in 1778 and took Kaskaskia and Cahokia. Little fighting was required, for the small British gar-

risons were dependent on the good will of the French settlers about.
When late in 1778 the British commander at Detroit, Henry Hamil-
ton, recovered Vincennes on the Wabash, Clark resolved upon instant
counter measures. Early in February, 1779, he set out from Kaskaskia
on the Mississippi to retake Vincennes and Fort Sackville, held by
only about eighty men.

EVERYTHING being ready, on the 5th of February [1779]
after receiving a lecture and absolution from a priest, we crossed the
Kaskaskia River with one hundred and seventy men and at a
distance of about three miles encamped until February 8. When we
again resumed the advance the weather was wet and a part of
the country was covered with several inches of water. Progress
under these conditions was difficult and fatiguing, although, fortunately, it was not very cold considering the time of year. My object now was to keep the men in good spirits. I permitted them to
shoot game on all occasions and to feast on it like Indians at a war
dance, each company taking turns in inviting the other to its
feast. A feast was held every night, the company that was to give
it being always supplied with horses for laying in a sufficient
store of meat in the course of the day. I myself and my principal
officers conducted ourselves like woodsmen, shouting now and
then and running through the mud and water the same as the men
themselves.

Thus, insensible of their hardships and without complaining, our
men were conducted through difficulties far surpassing anything we
had ever experienced before this, to the banks of the Little Wabash,
which we reached on February 13. There are here two streams
three miles apart, and the distance from the bank of one to the
opposite bank of the other is five miles. This whole distance we
found covered with some three feet of water, being never less than
two and frequently four feet in depth. I went into camp on an
elevation at the bank of the river and gave the troops permission
to amuse themselves. For some time I viewed with consternation
this expanse of water; then, accusing myself of irresolution, without holding any consultation over the situation or permitting any

one else to do so in my presence, I immediately set to work. I ordered a pirogue to be constructed at once and acted as though crossing the water would be only a bit of diversion. Since but few of the men could find employment at a time, pains were taken to devise amusement for the rest in order to keep up their spirits. However, the men were well prepared for the undertaking before us as they had frequently waded farther than we must now, although seldom in water more than half-leg-deep. . . .

On the evening of the 14th our boat was completed and I sent a crew of men to explore the drowned lands and find if possible some spot of dry land on the bank of the second little river. They found a place about half an acre in extent and marked the trees from it back to the camp. They returned with a very favorable report, having received private instructions from me in advance as to what they should say.

Fortunately for us the 15th chanced to be a warm, moist day, considering the season. The channel of the river where we were encamped was about thirty yards wide and the opposite bank was under three feet of water. Here we built a scaffold and the baggage was put upon it and ferried across, while our horses swam the channel and at the scaffold were again loaded with the baggage. By this time the soldiers had also been brought across and we took up our march, our boat being loaded with men who were sick.

We proceeded down below the mouth of the Embarrass, vainly attempting to reach the banks of the Wabash. Finding a dry spot, we encamped late at night and in the morning were gratified at hearing for the first time the morning gun of the British garrison. We resumed our march and about two o'clock in the afternoon of the 18th gained the banks of the Wabash, three leagues below the town, and went into camp.

On the 20th the water guard decoyed a boat ashore, having five Frenchmen and some provisions on board. These men were on their way down-river to join a party of hunters. They informed us that we had been discovered and that the inhabitants were well disposed toward us.

The men we had captured said it was impossible for us to make the town that night, or at all with our boats. Recalling what we had done, however, we thought otherwise, and pushing into the water, marched a league, frequently in water to our armpits, to what is called the upper Mamel. Here we encamped, our men still in good spirits from the hope of soon putting an end to their fatigue and realizing their desire to come into contact with the enemy.

This last march through the water was so far superior to anything our prisoners had conceived of that they were backward about saying anything further. They told us the nearest land was the Sugar Camp, a small league away on the bank of the river. A canoe was sent off to it and returned with the report that we could not pass. I now went myself, and sounding the water, found it as deep as my neck. I returned with the thought of having the men transported to the Sugar Camp in the canoes, which I knew would consume the entire day and the ensuing night, since the boats would pass but slowly through the bushes. To men half starved the loss of so much time was a serious matter, and I would now have given a good deal for a day's provisions or for one of our horses.

I returned but slowly to the troops in order to gain time for reflection. On our arrival all ran to hear our report and every eye was fixed on me. Unfortunately I spoke in a serious manner to one of the officers, and without knowing what I had said all were thrown into a state of alarm, running from one to another and bewailing their situation. For about a minute I stood looking upon their confusion and then, whispering to those close by to do as I did, I quickly scooped up some water with my hand, poured some powder into it, and blacking my face, raised the war whoop. I marched into the water. The party gazed at me for an instant and then like a flock of sheep fell in, one behind the other, without saying a word I ordered the men who were near me to strike up one of their favorite songs. It soon passed down the line, and all went on cheerfully. I now intended to have them ferried across the deepest part of the water, but when we continued out about waist-deep one of the men told me he thought he felt a path. We found it to be so and concluded that it kept to the highest ground. This proved to be the case, and by taking pains to follow it, we reached the Sugar Camp without the least difficulty. Here we found about half an acre of dry ground, or at any rate, ground not under water, and on it we took up our lodging.

Shortly after sunrise I addressed the men. What I said to them I do not now remember, but it may be easily imagined by anyone who can understand my affection for them at that time. I concluded by informing them that by surmounting the plain, now in full view, and reaching the woods opposite, they would put an end to their suffering and in a few hours would have sight of their long-wished-for goal. Without waiting for any reply, I stepped into the water, and a hurrah was raised. We commonly marched through the water in single file as it was much easier to advance in this way. When about a third of the men had entered, I halted them, and further to prove the men and because I had some suspicion of three or four of them, I called to Major Bowman to fall into the rear with twenty-five men and to put to death any of the men who refused to march, saying that we wished to have no such person among us. The whole force raised a cry of approbation, and on we went. This was the most trying difficulty of all we had experienced. I had fifteen or twenty of the strongest men follow after me, and, judging from my own sensations what must be those of the men, on reaching the middle of the plain where the water was about knee-deep I realized that I was failing. There being no trees or bushes here for the men to support themselves by, I did not doubt but that many of the weaker ones would be drowned. I therefore ordered the canoes to make the land, discharge their loads, and then ply backward and forward with all possible diligence, picking up the men. To encourage the party I sent some of the strongest men ahead with orders to pass the word back when they reached a certain distance that the water was getting shallower and on approaching the woods to cry out "Land." This stratagem produced the desired effect. Encouraged by it, the men exerted themselves to the limit of their ability, the weaker holding on to the stronger ones and frequently one man being upheld by two. This was a great advantage to the weak, but the water, instead of getting shallower, became continually deeper. On reaching the woods, where they expected land, the water was up to my shoulders. Nevertheless, gaining these woods was a matter of great importance. All the weak and short men clung to the trees and floated on logs until they were taken off by the canoes. The strong and tall men got ashore and started fires. Many would reach the bank and fall with their bodies half in the water, not being able to support themselves outside it. This was a delightful spot of dry ground, about ten acres in extent. We soon found, however, that the fires did us no good and that the only way to restore the men was for two strong ones to take a weak one by the arms and exercise him and by this means they soon recovered.

We were now in the situation I had been laboring to attain. The idea of being taken prisoner was foreign to almost all of our men. In the event of capture they looked forward to being tortured by the savages. Our fate was now to be determined, probably within the next few hours, and we knew that nothing but the boldest conduct would insure success. I knew that some of the inhabitants wished us well, while many more were lukewarm to the interest of the British and Americans alike. I also learned that the grand chief, the son of Tobacco, had within a few days openly declared, in council with the British, that he was a brother and friend of the Big Knives. These circumstances were in our favor. . . .

Shortly before sunset we advanced, displaying ourselves in full view of the crowds in the town. We were plunging headlong either to certain destruction or to success.

I ordered Lieutenant Bailey with fourteen men to advance and open fire on the fort while the main body moved in a different direction and took possession of the strongest part of the town. The firing now commenced against the fort, but since drunken Indians often saluted it after nightfall, the garrison did not suppose it to be from an enemy until one of the men, lighting his match, was shot down through a porthole. The drums now sounded and the conflict was fairly joined on both sides. . . .

The garrison was now completely surrounded, and the firing continued without intermission (except for about fifteen minutes shortly before dawn) until nine o'clock the following morning. Our entire force, with the exception of fifty men kept as a reserve in case of some emergency, participated in the attack, being joined by a few young men.

Since we could not afford to lose any of our men, great pains were taken to keep them sufficiently sheltered and to maintain a hot fire against the fort in order to intimidate the enemy as well as to destroy them. The embrasures for their cannon were frequently closed, for our riflemen, finding the true direction, would pour in such volleys when they were open that the artillerymen could not stand to the guns. Seven or eight of them were shot down in a short time. Our men frequently taunted the enemy in order to provoke them into opening the portholes and firing the cannon so that they might have the pleasure of cutting them down with their rifles. Fifty rifles would be leveled the instant the port flew open, and had the garrison stood to their artillery, most of them, I believe, would have been destroyed during the night, as the greater part of our men, lying within thirty yards of the walls and behind some houses, were as well sheltered as those within the fort and were much more expert in this mode of fighting. The enemy fired at the flash of our guns, but our men would change their position the moment they had fired. On the instant of the least appearance at one of their loopholes a dozen guns would be fired at it. At times an irregular fire as hot as could be maintained was poured in from different directions for several minutes. This would be continually succeeded by a scattering fire at the portholes, and a great uproar and laughter would be raised by the reserve parties in different parts of the town to give the impression that they had only fired on the fort for a few minutes for amusement, while those who were keeping up a continuous fire were being regularly relieved.

The firing immediately recommenced with redoubled vigor on both sides, and I do not believe that more noise could possibly have been made by an equal number of men. Their shouting could not be heard amid the discharge of the muskets, and a continual line of fire around the garrison was maintained until shortly before daylight.

Thus the attack continued until nine o'clock on the morning of the 24th.

Toward evening a flag of truce appeared.

GEORGE ROGERS CLARK, Sketch of His Campaign in the Illinois

38. Mutiny in the Pennsylvania Line

Hostilities during 1780 were almost wholly confined to the South, where the British captured Charleston in May, and would soon have subjugated the whole section but for a savage partisan warfare which broke out in upper South Carolina. Washington's army was practically paralyzed during the year by lack of money and adequate supplies, the difficulty of obtaining recruits, and the appalling decline in public spirit. A French expeditionary force which landed under Rochambeau at Newport was at once bottled up there by the British. It was the darkest hour before the final dawn. Washington's troubles came to a crisis when, the pay of his ill-clad, ill-fed troops having fallen into arrears, some of them began to mutiny.

JANUARY 6, 1781.—Be prepared, my dear Eliot, for a shock, and attend to an event which must sensibly affect every honest heart. The accumulated distresses of the army have at length produced most dreadful effects. The noncommissioned officers and privates of the Pennsylvania line, stationed at Morristown, have mutinied, broken up their cantonments, and in a body are marching to Philadelphia, to demand redress of their grievances from Congress.

The particulars of this revolt, as nearly as I have been able to collect them, are as follows. On the 1st instant, the whole line, except three regiments, by a signal given for that purpose, turned out under arms, without their officers, and declared for a redress of grievances. General Wayne and the officers did everything that could be expected to quell the tumult, but in vain. Numbers of them were wounded, and one (a captain) killed. The three regiments above mentioned paraded under their officers, but, being called on by the others to join, threatened with death in case of refusal, and actually fired on, they complied. They then seized upon the fieldpieces, and forcing the artillerymen, who had not yet joined them, to do it instantly under penalty of being every man bayoneted, the mutiny became general.

Besides the many and complicated injuries arising from the want of clothing, pay, and provision which the army at large have for so long a time groaned under, there was one circumstance peculiarly aggravating to the soldiers of the Pennsylvania line, and which conduced not a little to hasten the catastrophe. A deputation from the state had arrived in camp a few days before, with six hundred half joes, to be given three to each man as a bounty to such of the six-months levies, whose times were then expired, as would enlist again for the war. This was too much for veterans who had borne the burden of the day to put up with. They made it the principal article of grievance, and told their officers they neither could nor would be any longer abused; that they were determined, at every hazard, to march in a body to Congress and obtain redress. On General Wayne's cocking his pistols there were a hundred bayonets at his breast. "We love you, we respect you," said they, "but you're a dead man if you fire," and added: "Do not mistake us; we are not going to the enemy; on the contrary, were they now to come out, you should see us fight under your orders with as much resolution and alacrity as ever." They began their march that night, and the next day General Wayne forwarded after them provisions, to prevent the otherwise inevitable depredation which would be made on private property, himself and three principal officers, supposed highest in their esteem, following to mix with them, assist them with their advice, and endeavor to prevent any outrages. They were civilly received, have acquired much of the confidence of the troops, and are conducting them to Pennsylvania.

Immediately on this event the Jersey line were posted in the neighborhood of Elizabethtown, where they are joined by a body of the militia of the state, constituting a force sufficient to frustrate any attempt of the enemy to avail themselves of this unhappy affair.

Thus, my dear friend, is the scene opened; when it will close, and what may be its final consequences, God only knows. At any rate, it is a reproach to our country, and must materially injure, if not totally ruin, the discipline of its armies.

The Journals of Major Samuel Shaw

39. The "Bonhomme Richard" Defeats the "Serapis"

The Scottish-born John Paul Jones had gained ample experience in the British merchant marine before he settled in America; and it was natural for Congress to commission him as a first lieutenant in the new navy when war began. For a time he cruised off the Atlantic coast, preying on British merchantmen and fishing vessels. Then late in 1777 he sailed for France as captain of the war sloop Ranger *with news of Burgoyne's surrender. The late summer of 1779 found him commodore in command of a little squadron fitted out in French ports. On September 23, with three men-of-war, he sighted two British warships, the* Serapis *and* Countess of Scarborough, *off the English coast. One of Jones's vessels, under a French commander, turned tail and fled. But with the two others, the* Bonhomme Richard *and* Pallas, *he fought and won a desperate engagement of three and a half hours. Its strategic consequences were unimportant, but it gave the American Navy a baptism of glory.*

ON THE morning of the 23d [Sept., 1779] we chased a brigantine that appeared laying to, to windward. About noon, we saw and chased a large ship that appeared coming round Flamborough Head, from the northward, and at the same time I manned and armed one of the pilot boats to send in pursuit of the brigantine, which now appeared to be the vessel that I had forced ashore. Soon after this, a fleet of forty-one sail appeared off Flamborough Head, bearing north-northeast. This induced me to abandon the single ship which had then anchored in Burlington Bay; I also called back the pilot boat, and hoisted a signal for a general chase. When the fleet discovered us bearing down, all the merchant ships crowded sail toward the shore. The two ships of war that protected the fleet at the same time steered from the land, and made the disposition for battle. In approaching the enemy, I crowded every possible sail, and made the signal for the line of battle. to which the *Alliance* showed no attention. Earnest as I was for the action, I could not reach the commodore's ship until seven in the evening, being then within pistol-shot, when he hailed the *Bonhomme Richard*. We answered him by firing a whole broadside.

The battle being thus begun, was continued with unremitting fury. Every method was practised on both sides to gain an advantage, and rake each other; and I must confess that the enemy's ship, being much more manageable than the *Bonhomme Richard,* gained thereby several times an advantageous situation, in spite of my best endeavors to prevent it. As I had to deal with an enemy of greatly superior force, I was under the necessity of closing with him, to prevent the advantage which he had over me in point of maneuver. It was my intention to lay the *Bonhomme Richard* athwart the enemy's bow; but as that operation required great dexterity in the management of both sails and helm, and some of our braces being shot away, it did not exactly succeed to my wish. The enemy's bowsprit, however, came over the *Bonhomme Richard's* poop by the mizzenmast, and I made both ships fast together in that situation, which, by the action of the wind on the enemy's sails, forced her stern close to the *Bonhomme Richard's* bow, so that the ships lay square alongside of each other, the yards being all entangled, and the cannon of each ship touching the opponent's. When this position took place, it was eight o'clock, previous to which the *Bonhomme Richard* had received sundry eighteen-pound shots below the water, and leaked very much. My battery of twelve-pounders, on which I had placed my chief dependence, being commanded by Lieutenant Dale and Colonel Weibert, and manned principally with American seamen and French volunteers, was entirely silenced and abandoned. As to the six old eighteen-pounders that formed the battery of the lower gun deck, they did no service whatever, except firing eight shot in all. Two out of three of them burst at the first fire, and killed almost all the men who were stationed to manage them. Before this time, too, Colonel de Chamillard, who commanded a party of twenty soldiers on the poop, had abandoned that station after having lost some of his men. I had now only two pieces of cannon (nine-pounders), on the quarter-deck that were not silenced, and not one of the heavier cannon was fired during the rest of the action. The purser, M. Mease, who commanded the guns on the quarter-deck, being dangerously wounded in the head, I was obliged to fill his place, and with great difficulty rallied a few men, and shifted over one of the lee quarter-deck guns, so that we afterward played three pieces of nine-pounders upon the enemy. The tops alone seconded the fire of this little battery, and held out bravely during the whole of the action, especially the maintop, where Lieutenant Stack commanded. I directed the fire of one of the three cannon against the mainmast, with double-headed shot, while the other two were exceedingly well served with grape and canister shot, to silence the enemy's musketry and clear her decks, which was at last effected. The enemy were, as I have since understood, on the instant of calling for quarter, when the cowardice or treachery of three of my under officers induced them to call to the enemy. The English commodore asked me if I demanded quarter, and I having answered him in the most determined negative, they renewed the battle with double fury. They were unable to stand the deck; but the fire of their cannon, especially the lower battery, which was entirely formed of ten-pounders, was incessant; both ships were set on fire in various places, and the scene was dreadful beyond the reach of language. To account for the timidity of my three under officers, I mean the gunner, the carpenter, and the master-at-arms, I must observe that the two first were slightly wounded, and, as the ship had received various shot under water, and one of the pumps being shot away, the carpenter expressed his fears that she would sink, and the other two concluded that she was sinking, which occasioned the gunner to run aft on the poop, without my knowledge, to strike the colors. Fortunately for me, a cannon ball had done that before, by carrying away the ensign staff; he was therefore reduced to the necessity of sinking, as he supposed, or of calling for quarter, and he preferred the latter.

All this time the *Bonhomme Richard* had sustained the action alone, and the enemy, though much superior in force, would have been very glad to have got clear, as appears by their own acknowledgments, and by their having let go an anchor the instant that I laid them on board, by which means they would have escaped, had I not made them well fast to the *Bonhomme Richard*.

At last, at half past nine o'clock, the *Alliance* appeared, and I now thought the battle at an end; but, to my utter astonishment, he dis-

charged a broadside full into the stern of the *Bonhomme Richard.*
We called to him for God's sake to forbear firing into the *Bonhomme
Richard;* yet they passed along the off side of the ship, and continued
firing. There was no possibility of his mistaking the enemy's ship
for the *Bonhomme Richard,* there being the most essential difference in their appearance and construction. Besides, it was then full
moonlight, and the sides of the *Bonhomme Richard* were all black,
while the sides of the prize were all yellow. Yet, for the greater
security, I showed the signal of our reconnoissance, by putting out
three lanterns, one at the head, another at the stern, and the third
in the middle, in a horizontal line. Every tongue cried that he was
firing into the wrong ship, but nothing availed; he passed round,
firing into the *Bonhomme Richard's* head, stern, and broadside,
and by one of his volleys killed several of my best men, and mortally
wounded a good officer on the forecastle. My situation was really
deplorable; the *Bonhomme Richard* received various shot under
water from the *Alliance;* the leak gained on the pumps, and the
fire increased much on board both ships. Some officers persuaded
me to strike, of whose courage and good sense I entertain a high
opinion. My treacherous master-at-arms let loose all my prisoners
without my knowledge, and my prospects became gloomy indeed.
I would not, however, give up the point. The enemy's mainmast
began to shake, their firing decreased fast, ours rather increased,
and the British colors were struck at half an hour past ten o'clock.

This prize proved to be the British ship of war the *Serapis,* a new
ship of forty-four guns, built on the most approved construction,
with two complete batteries, one of them of eighteen-pounders, and
commanded by the brave Commodore Richard Pearson.

R. C. SANDS, Life and Correspondence of John Paul Jones

40. The World Turned Upside Down at Yorktown

For a brief period before the British commander Rodney annihilated a French fleet in the West Indies, the French navy held the upper hand on the American coast. When Cornwallis in the summer of 1781 placed his small army at the end of the Virginia Peninsula, Washington's quick eye saw the opportunity. By rapid movements the French and American land forces were united before Yorktown, while De Grasse with the French navy closed the Chesapeake. The capitulation of Cornwallis meant the downfall of Lord North's ministry, and the end of the war.

OCTOBER 18, 1781.—It is now ascertained that Lord Cornwallis, to avoid the necessity of a surrender, has determined on the bold attempt to make his escape in the night of the 16th, with a part of his army, into the country. His plan was to leave sick and baggage behind, and to cross with his effective force over to Gloucester Point, there to destroy the French legion and other troops, and to mount his infantry on their horses and such others as might be procured, and thus push their way to New York by land. A more preposterous and desperate attempt can scarcely be imagined. Boats were secretly prepared, arrangements made, and a large proportion of his troops actually embarked and landed on Gloucester Point, when, from a moderate and calm evening, a most violent storm of wind and rain ensued. The boats with the remaining troops were all driven down the river, and it was not till the next day that his troops could be returned to the garrison at York.

At an early hour this forenoon General Washington communicated to Lord Cornwallis the general basis of the terms of capitulation, which he deemed admissible, and allowed two hours for his reply. Commissioners were soon afterward appointed to prepare the particular terms of agreement. The gentlemen appointed by General Washington are Colonel Laurens, one of his aide-de-camps, and

Viscount Noailles of the French army. They have this day held an interview with the two British officers on the part of Lord Cornwallis; the terms of capitulation are settled, and being confirmed by the commanders of both armies, the royal troops are to march out to-morrow and surrender their arms.

19th. — This is to us a most glorious day; but to the English, one of bitter chagrin and disappointment. Preparations are now making to receive as captives that vindictive, haughty commander and that vanquished army who, by their robberies and murders, have so long been a scourge to our brethren of the Southern states. Being on horse-back, I anticipate a full share of satisfaction in viewing the various movements in the interesting scene. The stipulated terms of capitulation are similar to those granted to General Lincoln at Charleston the last year. The captive troops are to march out with shouldered arms, colors cased, and drums beating a British or German march, and to ground their arms at a place assigned for the purpose. The officers are allowed their side arms and private property, and the generals and such officers as desire it are to go on parole to England or New York. The marines and seamen of the King's ships are prisoners of war to the navy of France, and the land forces to the United States. All military and artillery stores to be delivered up unimpaired. The royal prisoners to be sent into the interior of Virginia, Maryland, and Pennsylvania in regiments, to have rations allowed them equal to the American soldiers, and to have their officers near them, Lord Cornwallis to man and dispatch the *Bonetta* sloop of war with dispatches to Sir Henry Clinton at New York without being searched, the vessel to be returned and the hands accounted for.

At about twelve o'clock, the combined army was arranged and drawn up in two lines extending more than a mile in length. The Americans were drawn up in a line on the right side of the road, and the French occupied the left. At the head of the former, the great American commander, mounted on his noble courser, took his station, attended by his aides. At the head of the latter was posted the excellent Count Rochambeau and his suite. The French troops, in complete uniform, displayed a martial and noble appearance; their band of music, of which the timbrel formed a part, is a delightful novelty, and produced while marching to the ground a most enchanting effect. The Americans, though not all in uniform nor their dress so neat, yet exhibited an erect, soldierly air, and every countenance beamed with satisfaction and joy. The concourse of spectators from the country was prodigious, in point of numbers was probably equal to the military, but universal silence and order prevailed. It was about two o'clock when the captive army advanced through the line formed for their reception. Every eye was prepared to gaze on Lord Cornwallis, the object of peculiar interest and solicitude, but he disappointed our anxious expectations; pretending indisposition, he made General O'Hara his substitute as the leader of his army. This officer was followed by the conquered troops in a slow and solemn step, with shouldered arms, colors cased, and drums beating a British march. Having arrived at the head of the line, General O'Hara, elegantly mounted, advanced to his Excellency the Commander-in-Chief, taking off his hat, and apologized for the nonappearance of Earl Cornwallis. With his usual dignity and politeness, his Excellency pointed to Major General Lincoln for directions, by whom the British army was conducted into a spacious field, where it was intended they should ground their arms. The royal troops, while marching through the line formed by the allied army, exhibited a decent and neat appearance, as respects arms and clothing, for their commander opened his store, and directed every soldier to be furnished with a new suit complete, prior to the capitulation. But in their line of march we remarked a disorderly and unsoldierly conduct, their step was irregular, and their ranks frequently broken. But it was in the field, when they came to the last act of the drama, that the spirit and pride of the British soldier was put to the severest test: here their mortification could not be concealed. Some of the platoon officers appeared to be exceedingly chagrined when giving the word, "Ground arms," and I am a witness that they performed this duty in a very unofficerlike manner and that many of the soldiers manifested a *sullen temper,* throwing their arms on the pile with violence, as if determined to render them useless. This irregularity, however, was checked by the authority of General Lincoln. After having grounded their arms and divested themselves of their accouterments, the captive troops were conducted back to Yorktown, and guarded by our troops till they could be removed to the place of their destination.

JAMES THACHER, Military Journal during the American Revolution

41. America the Hope of the World

American pride and optimism in the first flush of secure independence rose to a high pitch. David Ramsay, a South Carolina physician who had performed patriotic political service in the Revolution and had been exiled during the period of British conquest, published in 1789 a two-volume work celebrating the war and its fruits.

THE AMERICAN Revolution, on the one hand, brought forth great vices; but on the other hand, it called forth many virtues, and gave occasion for the display of abilities which, but for that event, would have been lost to the world. When the war began, the Americans were a mass of husbandmen, merchants, mechanics, and fishermen; but the necessities of the country gave a spring to the active powers of the inhabitants, and set them on thinking, speaking, and acting in a line far beyond that to which they had been accustomed. The difference between nations is not so much owing to nature as to education and circumstances. While the Americans were guided by the leading strings of the mother country they had no scope nor encouragement for exertion. All the departments of government were established and executed for them, but not by them. In the years 1775 and 1776, the country being suddenly thrown into a situation that needed the abilities of all its sons, these generally took their places, each according to the bent of his inclination. As they severally pursued their objects with ardor, a vast expansion of the human mind speedily followed. This displayed itself in a variety of ways. It was found that the talents for great stations did not differ in kind, but only in degree, from those which were necessary for the proper discharge of the ordinary business of civil society. In the bustle that was occasioned by the war, few instances could be produced of any persons who made a figure, or who rendered essential services, but from among those who had given specimens of similar talents in their respective professions. Those who from indolence or dissipation had been of little service to the community in time of peace were found equally unserviceable in war. A few young men were exceptions to this general rule. Some of these, who had indulged in youthful follies, broke off from their vicious courses, and on the pressing call of their country became useful servants of the public; but the great bulk of those who were the active instruments of carrying on the revolution were self-made, industrious men. These, who by their own exertions had established, or laid a foundation for establishing, personal independence, were most generally trusted, and most successfully employed in establishing that of their country. In these times of action, classical education was found of less service than good natural parts, guided by common sense and sound judgment.

Several names could be mentioned of individuals who, without the knowledge of any other language than their mother tongue, wrote not only accurately, but elegantly, on public business. It seemed as if the war not only required but created talents. Men whose minds were warmed with the love of liberty, and whose abilities were improved by daily exercise and sharpened with a laudable ambition to serve their distressed country, spoke, wrote, and acted with an energy far surpassing all expectations which could be reasonably founded on their previous acquirements.

The Americans knew but little of one another previous to the Revolution. Trade and business had brought the inhabitants of their seaports acquainted with each other, but the bulk of the people in the interior country were unacquainted with their fellow citizens. A Continental army and Congress composed of men from all the states, by freely mixing together, were assimilated into one mass. Individuals of both, mingling with the citizens, disseminated principles of union among them. Local prejudices abated. By frequent collision asperities were worn off, and a foundation was laid for the establishment of a nation, out of discordant materials. Intermarriages between men and women of different states were much more common than before the war, and became an additional cement to the Union. Unreasonable jealousies had existed between the inhabitants of the Eastern and of the Southern states; but on becoming better acquainted with each other, these in a great measure subsided. A wiser policy prevailed. Men of liberal minds led the way in discouraging local distinctions, and the great body of the people, as soon as reason got the better of prejudice, found that their best interests would be most effectually promoted by such practices and sentiments as were favorable to union. Religious bigotry had broken in upon the peace of various sects, before the American war. This was kept up by partial establishments, and by a dread that the Church of England, through the power of the mother country, would be made to triumph over all other denominations. These apprehensions were done away by the Revolution. The different sects, having nothing to fear from each other, dismissed all religious controversy. A proposal for introducing bishops into America, before the war, had kindled a flame among the dissenters; but the Revolution was no sooner accomplished than a scheme for that purpose was perfected, with the consent and approbation of all those sects who had previously opposed it. Pulpits which had formerly been shut to worthy men, because their heads had not been consecrated by the imposition of the hands of a bishop or of a presbytery, have since the establishment of independence been reciprocally opened to each other, whensoever the public convenience required it. The world will soon see the result of an experiment in politics, and be able to determine whether the happiness of society is increased by religious establishments, or diminished by the want of them.

DAVID RAMSAY, The History of the American Revolution

VIII

Confederation and Constitution

42. The Thirteen States Establish a Confederation

John Dickinson was head of a committee of the Continental Congress which on July 12, 1776, reported the draft of some "Articles of Confederation." They were not formally adopted until more than a year later, were not signed for almost another year, and were not ratified by all the States until 1781. But they were a long first step toward a true Union.

THE STYLE of this confederacy shall be "The United States of America."

Each state retains its sovereignty, freedom, and independence, and every power, jurisdiction, and right, which is not by this confederation expressly delegated to the United States in Congress assembled.

The said states hereby severally enter into a firm league of friendship with each other, for their common defense, the security of their liberties, and their mutual and general welfare, binding themselves to assist each other against all force offered to, or attacks made upon them, or any of them, on account of religion, sovereignty, trade, or any other pretense whatever. . . .

Every state shall abide by the determinations of the United States in Congress assembled, on all questions which by this confederation are submitted to them. And the articles of this confederation shall be inviolably observed by every state, and the union shall be perpetual; nor shall any alteration at any time hereafter be made in any of them; unless such alteration be agreed to in a Congress of the United States, and be afterwards confirmed by the legislature of every state.

And whereas it hath pleased the Great Governor of the World

to incline the hearts of the legislatures we respectively represent in Congress, to approve of, and to authorize us to ratify the said articles of confederation and perpetual union, know ye that we the undersigned delegates . . . do by these presents . . . fully and entirely ratify and confirm each and every of the said articles of confederation and perpetual union, and all and singular the matters and things therein contained. And we do further solemnly plight and engage the faith of our respective constituents, that they shall abide by the determinations of the United States in Congress assembled, on all questions, which by the said confederation are submitted to them. And that the articles thereof shall be inviolably observed by the states we respectively represent, and that the union shall be perpetual.

The Articles of Confederation, 1781

43. Major Pierce Limns the Fathers of the Constitution

When the Constitutional Convention assembled in Philadelphia in May, 1787, it was thought that it would revise and strengthen the weak Articles of Confederation. Instead, it threw them aside and wrote an entirely new instrument. A shrewd Georgia delegate who was called home by business troubles midway in the work of the Convention left some delightfully graphic impressions of his principal associates. They are short, pithy, and memorable.

FROM MASSACHUSETTS

Mr. KING is a man much distinguished for his eloquence and great parliamentary talents. He was educated in Massachusetts, and is said to have good classical as well as legal knowledge. He has served for three years in the Congress of the United States with great and deserved applause, and is at this time high in the confidence and approbation of his countrymen. This gentleman is about thirty-three years of age, about five feet ten inches high, well formed, an handsome face, with a strong expressive eye, and a sweet high-toned voice. In his public speaking there is something peculiarly strong and rich in his expression, clear, and convincing in his arguments, rapid and irresistible at times in his eloquence, but he is not always equal. His action is natural, swimming, and graceful, but there is a rudeness of manner sometimes accompanying it. But take him *tout ensemble,* he may with propriety be ranked among the luminaries of the present age.

Mr. Gorham is a merchant in Boston, high in reputation, and much in the esteem of his countrymen. He is a man of very good sense, but not much improved in his education. He is eloquent and easy in public debate, but has nothing fashionable or elegant in his style; all he aims at is to convince, and where he fails it never is from his auditory not understanding him, for no man is more perspicuous and full. He has been president of Congress and three years a member of that body.

Mr. Gorham is about forty-six years of age, rather lusty, and has an agreeable and pleasing manner.

Mr. Gerry's character is marked for integrity and perseverance. He is a hesitating and laborious speaker, possesses a great degree of confidence, and goes extensively into all subjects that he speaks on, without respect to elegance or flower of diction. He is connected and sometimes clear in his arguments, conceives well, and cherishes as his first virtue a love for his country. Mr. Gerry is very much of a gentleman in his principles and manners; he has been engaged in the mercantile line and is a man of property. He is about thirty-seven years of age.

Mr. Strong is a lawyer of some eminence; he has received a liberal education, and has good connections to recommend him. As a speaker he is feeble, and without confidence. This gentleman is about thirty-five years of age, and greatly in the esteem of his colleagues.

FROM CONNECTICUT

Dr. Johnson is a character much celebrated for his legal knowledge; he is said to be one of the first classics in America, and certainly possesses a very strong and enlightened understanding.

As an orator, in my opinion, there is nothing in him that warrants the high reputation which he has for public speaking. There is something in the tone of his voice not pleasing to the ear, but he is eloquent and clear, always abounding with information and instruction. He was once employed as an agent for the State of Connecticut to state her claims to certain landed territory before the British House of Commons; this office he discharged with so much dignity, and made such an ingenious display of his powers, that he laid the foundation of a reputation which will probably last much longer than his own life. Dr. Johnson is about sixty years of age, possesses the manners of a gentleman, and engages the hearts of men by the sweetness of his temper and that affectionate style of address with which he accosts his acquaintance.

Mr. Sherman exhibits the oddest-shaped character I ever remember to have met with. He is awkward, unmeaning, and unaccountably strange in his manner. But in his train of thinking there is something regular, deep, and comprehensive; yet the oddity of his address, the vulgarisms that accompany his public speaking, and that strange New England cant which runs through his public as well as his private speaking make everything that is connected with him grotesque and laughable; and yet he deserves infinite praise — no man has a better heart or a clearer head. If he cannot embellish he can furnish thoughts that are wise and useful. He is an able politician and extremely artful in accomplishing any particular object; it is remarked that he seldom fails. I am told he sits on the bench in Connecticut and is very correct in the discharge of his judicial functions. In the early part of his life he was a shoemaker, but despising the lowness of his condition, he turned almanac maker, and so progressed upwards to a judge. He has been several years a member of Congress and discharged the duties of his office with honor and credit to himself and advantage to the State he represented. He is about sixty.

Mr. Ellsworth is a judge of the Supreme Court in Connecticut; he is a gentleman of a clear, deep, and copious understanding, eloquent and connected in public debate, and always attentive to his duty. He is very happy in a reply and choice in selecting such parts of his adversary's arguments as he finds make the strongest impressions — in order to take off the force of them, so as to admit the power of his own. Mr. Ellsworth is about thirty-seven years of age, a man much respected for his integrity and venerated for his abilities.

FROM PENNSYLVANIA

Dr. Franklin is well known to be the greatest philosopher of the present age; all the operations of nature he seems to understand; the very heavens obey him, and the clouds yield up their lightning to be imprisoned in his rod. But what claim he has to the politician, posterity must determine. It is certain that he does not shine much in public council — he is no speaker, nor does he seem to let politics engage his attention. He is, however, a most extraordinary man, and tells a story in a style more engaging than anything I ever heard. Let his biographer finish his character. He is eighty-two years old, and possesses an activity of mind equal to a youth of twenty-five years of age.

Mr. Wilson ranks among the foremost in legal and political knowledge. He has joined to a fine genius all that can set him off and show him to advantage. He is well acquainted with man and understands all the passions that influence him. Government seems to have been his peculiar study; all the political institutions of the world he knows in detail, and can trace the causes and effects of every revolution from the earliest stages of the Grecian commonwealth down to the present time. No man is more clear, copious, and comprehensive than Mr. Wilson, yet he is no great orator. He draws the attention not by the charm of his eloquence, but by the force of his reasoning. He is about forty-five years old.

Mr. Gouverneur Morris is one of those geniuses in whom every species of talent combines to render him conspicuous and flourishing in public debate. He winds through all the mazes of rhetoric, and throws around him such a glare that he charms, captivates, and leads away the senses of all who hear him. With an infinite stretch of fancy he brings to view things, when he is engaged in deep argumentation, that render all the labor of reasoning easy and pleasing. But with all these powers he is fickle and inconstant, never pursuing one train of thinking, nor ever regular. He has gone through a very extensive course of reading and is acquainted with all the sciences. No man has more wit, nor can anyone engage the attention more than Mr. Morris. He was bred to the law, but I am told he disliked the profession and turned merchant. He is engaged in some great mercantile matters with his namesake Mr. Robert Morris. This gentleman is about thirty-eight years old; he has been unfortunate in losing one of his legs and getting all the flesh taken off his right arm by a scald, when a youth.

FROM NEW YORK

Colonel Hamilton is deservedly celebrated for his talents. He is a practitioner of the law, and reputed to be a finished scholar. To a clear and strong judgment he unites the ornaments of fancy, and whilst he is able, convincing, and engaging in his eloquence the heart and head sympathize in approving him. Yet there is something too feeble in his voice to be equal to the strains of oratory; it is my opinion that he is rather a convincing speaker than a blazing orator. Colonel Hamilton requires time to think; he inquires into every part of his subject with the searchings of philosophy, and when he comes forward he comes highly charged with interesting matter; there is no skimming over the surface of a subject with him; he must sink to the bottom to see what foundation it rests on. His language is not always equal, sometimes didactic like Bolingbroke's, at others light and tripping like Sterne's. His eloquence is not so diffusive as to trifle with the senses, but he rambles just enough to strike and keep up the attention. He is about thirty-three years old, of small stature, and lean. His manners are tinctured with stiffness, and sometimes with a degree of vanity that is highly disagreeable.

FROM DELAWARE

Mr. Dickinson has been famed through all America for his *Farmer's Letters;* he is a scholar, and said to be a man of very extensive information. When I saw him in the convention I was induced to pay the greatest attention to him whenever he spoke. I had often heard that he was a great orator, but I found him an indifferent speaker. With an affected air of wisdom he labors to produce a trifle; his language is irregular and incorrect; his flourishes (for he sometimes attempts them) are like expiring flames; they just show themselves and go out; no traces of them are left on the mind to cheer or animate it. He is, however, a good writer and will be ever considered one of the most important characters in the United States. He is about fifty-five years old, and was bred a Quaker.

FROM VIRGINIA

General Washington is well known as the Commander-in-Chief of the late American army. Having conducted these States to independence and peace, he now appears to assist in framing a government to make the people happy. Like Gustavus Vasa, he may be said to be the deliverer of his country; like Peter the Great, he appears as the politician and the statesman; and like Cincinnatus, he returned to his farm perfectly contented with being only a plain citizen, after enjoying the highest honor of the confederacy, and now only seeks for the approbation of his countrymen by being virtuous and useful. The General was conducted to the chair as President of the Convention by the unanimous voice of its members. He is in the fifty-second year of his age.

Mr. Wythe is the famous professor of law at the University of William and Mary. He is confessedly one of the most learned legal characters of the present age. From his close attention to the study of general learning he has acquired a complete knowledge of the dead languages and all the sciences. He is remarked for his exemplary life and universally esteemed for his good principles. No man, it is said, understands the history of government better than Mr. Wythe, nor any one who understands the fluctuating condition to which all societies are liable better than he does; yet from his too favorable opinion of men, he is no great politician. He is a neat and pleasing speaker and a most correct and able writer. Mr. Wythe is about fifty-five years of age.

Mr. Madison is a character who has long been in public life, and what is very remarkable, every person seems to acknowledge his greatness. He blends together the profound politician with the scholar. In the management of every great question, he evidently took the lead in the Convention, and though he cannot be called an orator, he is a most agreeable, eloquent, and convincing speaker. From a spirit of industry and application which he possesses in a most eminent degree, he always comes forward the best-informed man of any point in debate. The affairs of the United States, he perhaps has the most correct knowledge of, of any man in the Union. He has been twice a member of Congress and was always thought one of the ablest members that ever sat in that council. Mr. Madison is about thirty-seven years of age, a gentleman of great modesty, with a remarkable sweet temper. He is easy and unreserved among his acquaintance, and has a most agreeable style of conversation.

FROM SOUTH CAROLINA

Mr. Rutledge is one of those characters who was highly mounted at the commencement of the late Revolution; his reputation in the first Congress gave him a distinguished rank among the American worthies. He was bred to the law, and now acts as one of the chancellors of South Carolina. This gentleman is much famed in his own State as an orator, but in my opinion he is too rapid in his public speaking to be denominated an agreeable orator. He is undoubtedly a man of abilities and a gentleman of distinction and fortune. Mr. Rutledge was once Governor of South Carolina. He is about forty-eight years of age.

Mr. Charles Cotesworth Pinckney is a gentleman of family and fortune in his own State. He has received the advantage of a liberal education, and possesses a very extensive degree of legal knowledge. When warm in a debate he sometimes speaks well, but he is generally considered an indifferent orator. Mr. Pinckney was an officer of high rank in the American army, and served with great reputation through the war. He is now about forty years of age.

Mr. Charles Pinckney is a young gentleman of the most promising talents. He is, although only twenty-four years of age, in possession of a very great variety of knowledge. Government, law, history, and philosophy are his favorite studies, but he is intimately acquainted with every species of polite learning and has a spirit of application and industry beyond most men. He speaks with great neatness and perspicuity, and treats every subject as fully, without running into prolixity, as it requires. He has been a member of Congress and served in that body with ability and éclat.

FROM GEORGIA

Mr. Baldwin is a gentleman of superior abilities, and joins in a public debate with great art and eloquence. Having laid the foun-

dation of a complete classical education at Harvard College, he pur-
sues every other study with ease. He is well acquainted with books
and characters, and has an accommodating turn of mind, which
enables him to gain the confidence of men and to understand them
He is a practising attorney in Georgia and has been twice a mem
ber of Congress. Mr. Baldwin is about thirty-eight years of age.

Notes of Major William Pierce in the Federal Convention

44. "A Rising, Not a Setting Sun"

*While George III still ruled the
American colonies, Franklin had tried to bring them into a confederation within the British Empire. He was the principal author
of the Albany Plan of Union in 1754. Twenty-two years later he had
signed the Declaration of Independence. Eleven years later still, he
joyfully signed the new Constitution, and uttered the hopeful prophecy which James Madison — one of the leading framers of the great
document — here records. More than once the convention had seemed
on the point of breaking up amid bitter quarrels; but at last it had finished its colossal work, which went to the thirteen states for rati-
fication.*

THE ENGROSSED Constitution being read [September 17,
1787], Dr. Franklin rose with a speech in his hand, which he had
reduced to writing for his own convenience, and which Mr. Wilson
read in the words following:

"Mr. President: I confess that there are several parts of this Constitution which I do not at present approve, but I am not sure I shall
never approve them. For, having lived long, I have experienced many
instances of being obliged, by better information or fuller consideration, to change opinions, even on important subjects, which I once
thought right, but found to be otherwise. It is therefore that, the

older I grow, the more apt I am to doubt my own judgment, and to pay more respect to the judgment of others. Most men, indeed, as well as most sects in religion, think themselves in possession of all truth, and that wherever others differ from them, it is so far error. Steele, a Protestant, in a dedication, tells the Pope, that the only difference between our churches, in their opinions of the certainty of their doctrines, is, 'the Church of Rome is infallible, and the Church of England is never in the wrong.' But though many private persons think almost as highly of their own infallibility as of that of their sect, few express it so naturally as a certain French lady, who, in a dispute with her sister, said, 'I don't know how it happens, sister, but I meet with nobody but myself that is always in the right — *il n'y a que moi qui a toujours raison.*'

"In these sentiments, sir, I agree to this Constitution, with all its faults, if they are such; because I think a general government necessary for us, and there is no form of government, but what may be a blessing to the people if well administered; and believe further, that this is likely to be well administered for a course of years, and can only end in despotism, as other forms have done before it, when the people shall become so corrupted as to need despotic government, being incapable of any other. I doubt, too, whether any other convention we can obtain may be able to make a better constitution. For, when you assemble a number of men to have the advantage of their joint wisdom, you inevitably assemble with those men all their prejudices, their passions, their errors of opinion, their local interests, and their selfish views. From such an assembly can a perfect production be expected? It therefore astonishes me, sir, to find this system approaching so near to perfection as it does; and I think it will astonish our enemies, who are waiting with confidence to hear that our councils are confounded, like those of the builders of Babel, and that our States are on the point of separation, only to meet hereafter for the purpose of cutting one another's throats. Thus I consent, sir, to this Constitution, because I expect no better, and because I am not sure that it is not the best. The opinions I have had of its errors I sacrifice to the public good. I have never whispered a syllable of them abroad. Within these walls they were born, and here they shall die. If every one of us, in returning to our constituents, were to report the objections he has had to it, and endeavor to gain partisans in support of them, we might prevent its being generally received, and thereby lose all the salutary effects and great advantages resulting naturally in our favor among foreign nations, as well as among ourselves, from our real or apparent unanimity. Much of the strength and efficiency of any government, in procuring and securing happiness to the people, depends on opinion — on the general opinion of the goodness of the government, as well as of the wisdom and integrity of its governors. I hope, therefore, that for our own sakes, as a part of the people, and for the sake of posterity, we shall act heartily and unanimously in recommending this Constitution (if approved by Congress and confirmed by the conventions) wherever our influence may extend, and turn our future thoughts and endeavors to the means of having it well administered.

"On the whole, sir, I cannot help expressing a wish that every member of the Convention, who may still have objections to it, would with me, on this occasion, doubt a little of his own infallibility, and, to make manifest our unanimity, put his name to this instrument." He then moved that the Constitution be signed by the members, and offered the following as a convenient form, viz.: "Done in Convention by the unanimous consent of *the States* present, the 17th of September, etc. In witness whereof, we have hereunto subscribed our names."

This ambiguous form had been drawn up by Mr. Gouverneur Morris, in order to gain the dissenting members, and put into the hands of Dr. Franklin that it might have the better chance of success. . . .

On the question to agree to the Constitution, enrolled, in order to be signed, it was agreed to, all the States answering aye.

Mr. Randolph then rose, and, with an allusion to the observations of Dr. Franklin, apologized for his refusing to sign the Constitution, notwithstanding the vast majority and venerable names that would give sanction to its wisdom and its worth. He said, however, that he did not mean by this refusal to decide that he should oppose the Constitution withoutdoors. He meant only to keep himself free to be governed by his duty, as it should be prescribed by his future judgment. He refused to sign, because he thought the object of the Convention would be frustrated by the alternative which it presented to the people. Nine states will fail to ratify the plan, and confusion must ensue. With such a view of the subject he ought not, he could not, by pledging himself to support the plan, restrain himself from taking such steps as might appear to him most consistent with the public good.

Mr. Gouverneur Morris said, that he too had objections, but, considering the present plan as the best that was to be attained, he should take it with all its faults. The majority had determined in its favor, and by that determination he should abide. The moment this plan goes forth, all other considerations will be laid aside, and the great question will be, shall there be a national government, or not? and this must take place, or a general anarchy will be the alternative. He remarked that the signing, in the form proposed, related only to the fact that the States present were unanimous.

Mr. Williamson suggested that the signing should be confined to the letter accompanying the Constitution to Congress, which might perhaps do nearly as well, and would be found satisfactory to some members who disliked the Constitution. For himself, he did not think a better plan was to be expected, and had no scruples against putting his name to it.

Mr. Hamilton expressed his anxiety that every member should sign. A few characters of consequence, by opposing, or even refusing to sign the Constitution, might do infinite mischief, by kindling the latent sparks that lurk under an enthusiasm in favor of the Convention which may soon subside. No man's ideas were more remote from the plan than his own were known to be; but is it possible to deliberate between anarchy, and convulsion, on one side, and the chance of good to be expected from the plan, on the other? . . .

Whilst the last members were signing, Dr. Franklin, looking towards the president's chair, at the back of which a rising sun happened to be painted, observed to a few members near him, that painters had found it difficult to distinguish, in their art, a rising from a setting sun. "I have," said he, "often and often, in the course of the session, and the vicissitudes of my hopes and fears as to its issue, looked at that behind the president, without being able to tell whether it was rising or setting; but now, at length, I have the happiness to know that it is a rising, and not a setting sun."

Madison's Debates in the Federal Convention

IX

Launching the New Government

45. Washington Is Inaugurated President

Even before the early ratifications of the Constitution, Washington had been designated by public opinion for the first President. He modestly tried to refuse the honor. Fifty-six years old, he declared that he had no "wish but that of living and dying an honest man on my own farm." But the nation insisted, and borrowing some money for traveling expenses, he set out for the temporary capital, New York. He was to take the oath of office April 30, 1789. One of the leading Federalists in New Jersey, Elias Boudinot, helped conduct him to his new duties, and set down an animated narrative of the scenes they encountered.

MY DEAREST WIFE: If it was in my power, I could wish to give you an adequate account of the proceedings of the citizens of this metropolis on the approach and at the reception of our President when he arrived here yesterday *New York, April 24, 1789*.

When we drew near to the mouth of the Kills, a number of boats with various flags came up with us and dropped in our wake. Soon after we opened the bay, General Knox and several generals in a large barge presented themselves, with their splendid colors. Boat after boat and sloop after sloop, added to our train, gaily dressed in all their naval ornaments, made a most splendid appearance. Before we got to Bedloe Island, a large sloop came with full sail on our starboard bow, when there stood up about twenty gentlemen and ladies and with most excellent voices sang an elegant ode prepared for the purpose, to the tune of "God Save the King," welcoming their great chief to the seat of government. On the conclusion we gave them our hats, and then they with the surrounding boats gave us three cheers. Soon after, another boat came under our stern and presented us with a number of copies of another ode, and immediately about a dozen gentlemen began to sing it in parts as we passed along. Our worthy President was greatly affected with these tokens of profound respect.

As we approached the harbor, our train increased, and the huzzaing and shouts of joy seemed to add life to this lively scene. At this moment a number of porpoises came playing amongst us, as if they had risen up to know what was the cause of all this joy. We now discovered the shores covered with thousands of people — men, women, and children — nay, I may venture to say tens of thousands. From the fort to the place of landing although near half a mile, you could see little else along the shores — in the streets and on board every vessel — but heads standing as thick as ears of corn before the harvest. The vessels in the harbor made a most superb appearance indeed, dressed in all the pomp of attire. The Spanish packet in a moment, on a signal given, discovered twenty-seven or twenty-eight different colors of all nations on every part of the rigging and paid us the compliment of thirteen guns, with her yards all manned, as did another vessel in the harbor, displaying colors in the same manner. I have omitted the like compliment from the battery of eighteen-pounders.

We soon arrived at the ferry stairs, where there were many thousands of the citizens waiting with all the eagerness of expectation to welcome our excellent patriot to that shore, which he had regained from a powerful enemy by his valor and good conduct. We found the stairs covered with carpeting and the rails hung with crimson. The President, being preceded by the committee, was received by the Governor and the citizens in the most brilliant manner. Here he was met on the wharf by many of his old and faithful officers and fellow patriots who had borne the heat and burden of the day with him, and who, like him, had experienced every reverse of fortune with fortitude and patience, and who now joined the universal chorus of welcoming their great deliverer (under Providence) from their fears.

It was with difficulty a passage could be made by the troops through the pressing crowds, who seemed to be incapable of being satisfied by gazing at this man of the people. You will see the particulars of the procession, from the wharf to the house appointed for his residence, in the newspapers. The streets were lined with the inhabitants as thick as the people could stand, and it required all the exertions of a numerous train of city officers, with their staffs, to make a passage for the company. The houses were filled with gentlemen and ladies, the whole distance being half a mile, and the windows to the highest stories were illuminated by the sparkling eyes of innumerable companies of ladies, who seemed to vie with each other to show their joy on this great occasion.

It was half an hour before we could finish our commission and convey the President to the house prepared for his residence. As soon as this was done, notwithstanding his great fatigue of both body and mind, he had to receive all the gentlemen and officers to a very large amount who wished to show their respect in the most affectionate manner. When this was finished and the people dispersed, we went, undressed and dined with his Excellency Governor Clinton, who had provided an elegant dinner for the purpose. Thus ended our commission.

The evening, though very wet, was spent by all ranks in visiting the city, street after street being illuminated in a superb manner. I cannot help stating now how highly we were favored in the weather, the whole procession having been completely finished and we had repaired to the Governor's before it began to rain. When the President was on the wharf, an officer came up, and addressing the President, said he had the honor to command his guard, and it was ready to obey his orders. The President answered that as to the present arrangement he should proceed as was directed, but that after that was over, he hoped he would give himself no further trouble, as the affections of his fellow citizens (turning to the crowd) was all the guard he wanted.

Good night. May God bless you.

Elias Boudinot, Letter to His Wife

46. Jefferson and Hamilton Strike a Bargain

The new Federal government was no sooner set up than it became plain that Jefferson and Hamilton held divergent views of its proper functions, and were certain to quarrel. Parties sprang up about them. Jefferson, who was Secretary of State, trusted the people and feared a strong government; Hamilton, the Secretary of the Treasury, trusted in a strong government and feared the people. In order to make the nation more powerful, Hamilton wished the Treasury to assume all the state debts, so that holders of government paper would support it. Jefferson opposed this program, but it was carried by an ingenious bargain which Jefferson later came to regret.

THIS GAME was over, and another was on the carpet at the moment of my arrival; and to this I was most ignorantly and innocently made to hold the candle. This fiscal maneuver is well known by the name of the Assumption [1790]. Independently of the debts of Congress, the States had during the war contracted separate and heavy debts; . . . and the more debt Hamilton could rake up, the more plunder for his mercenaries. This money, whether wisely or foolishly spent, was pretended to have been spent for general purposes, and ought, therefore, to be paid from the general purse. But it was objected that nobody knew what these debts were, what their amount, or what their proofs. No matter; we will guess them to be twenty millions. But of these twenty millions, we do not know how much should be reimbursed to one State, or how much to another. No matter; we will guess. And so another scramble was set on foot among the several States, and some got much, some little, some nothing. But the main object was obtained; the phalanx of the Treasury was reinforced by additional recruits. This measure produced the most bitter and angry contest ever known in Congress before or since the Union of the States. I arrived in the midst of it. But a stranger to the ground, a stranger to the actors on it, so long absent as to have lost all familiarity with the subject, and as yet unaware of its object, I took no concern in it.

The great and trying question, however, was lost in the House of Representatives. So high were the feuds excited by this subject, that on its rejection, business was suspended. Congress met and adjourned from day to day without doing anything, the parties being too much out of temper to do business together. The Eastern members, particularly, who, with Smith from South Carolina, were the principal gamblers in these scenes, threatened a secession and dissolution. Hamilton was in despair. As I was going to the President's one day, I met him in the street. He walked me backwards and forwards before the President's door for half an hour. He painted pathetically the temper into which the legislature had been wrought, the disgust of those who were called the creditor States, the danger of the secession of their members, and the separation of the States. He observed that the members of the administration ought to act in concert; that though this question was not of my department, yet a common duty should make it a common concern; that the President was the center on which all administrative questions ultimately rested, and that all of us should rally around him, and support with joint efforts measures approved by him; and that the question having been lost by a small majority only, it was probable that an appeal from me to the judgment and discretion of some of my friends might effect a change in the vote, and the machine of government, now suspended, might be again set into motion. I told him that I was really a stranger to the whole subject; that not having yet informed myself of the system of finances adopted, I knew not how far this was a necessary sequence; that undoubtedly if its rejection endangered a dissolution of our Union at this incipient stage, I should deem that the most unfortunate of all consequences, to avert which all partial and temporary evils should be yielded. I proposed to him, however, to dine with me the next day, and I would invite another friend or two, bring them into conference together, and I thought it impossible that reasonable men, consulting together coolly, could fail, by some mutual sacrifices of opinion, to form a compromise which was to save the Union.

The discussion took place. I could take no part in it but an exhortatory one, because I was a stranger to the circumstances which should govern it. But it was finally agreed that whatever importance had been attached to the rejection of this proposition, the preservation of the Union and of concord among the States was more important, and that therefore it would be better that the vote of rejection should be rescinded, to effect which, some members should change their votes. But it was observed that this pill would be peculiarly bitter to the Southern States, and that some concomitant measure should be adopted, to sweeten it a little to them. There had before been propositions to fix the seat of government either at Philadelphia, or at Georgetown on the Potomac; and it was thought that by giving it to Philadelphia for ten years, and to Georgetown permanently afterwards, this might, as an anodyne, calm in some degree the ferment which might be excited by the other measure alone. So two of the Potomac members (White and Leem, but White with a revulsion of stomach almost convulsive) agreed to change their votes, and Hamilton undertook to carry the other point. In doing this, the influence he had established over the Eastern members with the agency of Robert Morris with those of the Middle States, effected his side of the engagement; and so the Assumption was passed, and twenty millions of stock divided among favored States, and thrown in as pabulum to the stock-jobbing herd. This added to the number of votaries in the Treasury, and made its chief the master of every vote in the legislature, which might give to the government the direction suited to his political views.

THOMAS JEFFERSON, The Anas

47. Washington Bids Farewell to His Countrymen

Washington's Farewell Address, long and carefully prepared with the aid of Hamilton's pen, was published in September, 1796, six months before he left office. In it he explained the course he had taken as President, set forth some political precepts which he believed the country should follow, and insisted upon the duty of patriotism. "Be united," he said; "be Americans."

FRIENDS and fellow citizens: The period for a new election of a citizen to administer the executive government of the United States being not far distant, and the time actually arrived when your thoughts must be employed in designating the person who is to be clothed with that important trust, it appears to me proper, especially as it may conduce to a more distinct expression of the public voice, that I should now apprize you of the resolution I have formed to decline being considered among the number of those out of whom a choice is to be made. . . .

Here, perhaps, I ought to stop. But a solicitude for your welfare which cannot end with my life, and the apprehension of danger natural to that solicitude, urge me on an occasion like the present to offer to your solemn contemplation and to recommend to your frequent review some sentiments which are the result of much reflection, of no inconsiderable observation, and which appear to me all-important to the permanency of your felicity as a people. . . .

Interwoven as is the love of liberty with every ligament of your hearts, no recommendation of mine is necessary to fortify or confirm the attachment.

The unity of government which constitutes you one people is also now dear to you. It is justly so, for it is a main pillar in the edifice of your real independence, the support of your tranquillity at home, your peace abroad, of your safety, of your prosperity, of that very liberty which you so highly prize. But as it is easy to foresee that from different causes and from different quarters much pains will be taken, many artifices employed, to weaken in your minds the conviction of this truth, as this is the point in your political fortress against which the batteries of internal and external enemies will be most constantly and actively (though often covertly and insidiously) directed, it is of infinite moment that you should properly estimate the immense value of your national union to your collective and individual happiness; that you should cherish a cordial, habitual, and immovable attachment to it; accustoming yourselves to think and speak of it as of the palladium of your political safety and prosperity; watching for its preservation with jealous anxiety; discountenancing whatever may suggest even a suspicion that it can in any event be abandoned, and indignantly frowning upon the first dawning of every attempt to alienate any portion of our country from the rest or to enfeeble the sacred ties which now link together the various parts. . . .

Is there a doubt whether a common government can embrace so large a sphere? Let experience solve it. To listen to mere speculation in such a case were criminal. It is well worth a fair and full experiment. With such powerful and obvious motives to union affecting all parts of our country, while experience shall not have demonstrated its impracticability, there will always be reason to distrust the patriotism of those who in any quarter may endeavor to weaken its bands. . . .

This Government, the offspring of our own choice, uninfluenced and unawed, adopted upon full investigation and mature deliberation, completely free in its principles, in the distribution of its powers, uniting security with energy, and containing within itself a provision for its own amendment, has a just claim to your confidence and your support. Respect for its authority, compliance with its laws, acquiescence in its measures, are duties enjoined by the fundamental maxims of true liberty. The basis of our political systems is the right of the people to make and to alter their constitutions of government. But the constitution which at any time exists, till changed by an explicit and authentic act of the whole people, is sacredly obligatory upon all. The very idea of the power and the right of the people to establish government presupposes the duty of every individual to obey the established government. . . .

I have already intimated to you the danger of parties in the State, with particular reference to the founding of them on geographical discriminations. Let me now take a more comprehensive view, and warn you in the most solemn manner against the baneful effects of the spirit of party generally. . . .

It is important, likewise, that the habits of thinking in a free country should inspire caution in those intrusted with its administration to confine themselves within their respective constitutional spheres, avoiding in the exercise of the powers of one department to encroach upon another. The spirit of encroachment tends to consolidate the powers of all the departments in one, and thus to create, whatever the form of government, a real despotism. . . .

Of all the dispositions and habits which lead to political prosperity, religion and morality are indispensable supports. . . . And let us with caution indulge the supposition that morality can be maintained without religion. Whatever may be conceded to the influence of refined education on minds of peculiar structure, reason and experience both forbid us to expect that national morality can prevail in exclusion of religious principle.

It is substantially true that virtue or morality is a necessary spring of popular government. The rule indeed extends with more or less force to every species of free government. Who that is a sincere friend to it can look with indifference upon attempts to shake the foundation of the fabric? Promote, then, as an object of primary importance, institutions for the general diffusion of knowledge. In proportion as the structure of a government gives force to public opinion, it is essential that public opinion should be enlightened. . . .

Observe good faith and justice toward all nations. Cultivate peace and harmony with all. . . .

In the execution of such a plan nothing is more essential than that permanent, inveterate antipathies against particular nations and passionate attachments for others should be excluded, and that in place of them just and amicable feelings toward all should be cultivated. . . .

So, likewise, a passionate attachment of one nation for another produces a variety of evils. Sympathy for the favorite nation, facilitating the illusion of an imaginary common interest in cases where no real common interest exists, and infusing into one the enmities of the other betrays the former into a participation in the quarrels and wars of the latter without adequate inducement or justification. . . .

Against the insidious wiles of foreign influence (I conjure you to believe me, fellow citizens) the jealousy of a free people ought to be *constantly* awake, since history and experience prove that foreign influence is one of the most baneful foes of republican government. . . .

The great rule of conduct for us in regard to foreign nations is, in extending our commercial relations, to have with them as little *political* connection as possible. So far as we have already formed engagements let them be fulfilled with perfect good faith. Here let us stop.

Europe has a set of primary interests which to us have none or a very remote relation. Hence she must be engaged in frequent controversies, the causes of which are essentially foreign to our concerns. Hence, therefore, it must be unwise in us to implicate ourselves by artificial ties in the ordinary vicissitudes of her politics or the ordinary combinations and collisions of her friendships or enmities.

Our detached and distant situation invites and enables us to pursue a different course. If we remain one people, under an efficient government, the period is not far off when we may defy material injury from external annoyance; when we may take such an attitude as will cause the neutrality we may at any time resolve upon to be scrupulously respected; when belligerent nations, under the impossibility of making acquisitions upon us, will not lightly hazard the giving us provocation; when we may choose peace or war, as our interest, guided by justice, shall counsel.

Why forego the advantages of so peculiar a situation? Why quit our own to stand upon foreign ground? Why, by interweaving our destiny with that of any part of Europe, entangle our peace and prosperity in the toils of European ambition, rivalship, interest, humor, or caprice?

It is our true policy to steer clear of permanent alliances with any portion of the foreign world, so far, I mean, as we are now at liberty to do it; for let me not be understood as capable of patronizing infidelity to existing engagements. I hold the maxim no less applicable to public than to private affairs that honesty is always the best policy. I repeat, therefore, let those engagements be observed in their genuine sense. But in my opinion it is unnecessary and would be unwise to extend them. . . .

Though in reviewing the incidents of my Administration I am unconscious of intentional error, I am nevertheless too sensible of my defects not to think it probable that I may have committed many errors. Whatever they may be, I fervently beseech the Almighty to avert or mitigate the evils to which they may tend. I shall also carry with me the hope that my country will never cease to view them with indulgence, and that, after forty-five years of my life dedicated to its service with upright zeal, the faults of incompetent abilities will be consigned to oblivion, as myself must soon be to the mansions of rest.

Relying on its kindness in this as in other things, and actuated by that fervent love toward it which is so natural to a man who views it in the native soil of himself and his progenitors for several generations, I anticipate with pleasing expectation that retreat in which I promise myself to realize without alloy the sweet enjoyment of partaking in the midst of my fellow citizens the benign influence of good laws under a free government — the ever-favorite object of my heart, and the happy reward, as I trust, of our mutual cares, labors, and dangers.

GEORGE WASHINGTON, Farewell Address, 1796

48. "This Government, the World's Best Hope"

Jefferson was the first President inaugurated in Washington; the first to whom John Marshall administered the oath of office. The President-elect walked from Conrad's boarding-house, where he had been living as Vice-President, to the Capitol. Here, after the ceremonies of the day, he read an address which expressed with noble eloquence, faith in democracy and in republicanism.

FRIENDS and fellow citizens: Called upon to undertake the duties of the first executive office of our country, I will avail myself of the presence of that portion of my fellow citizens which is here assembled to express my grateful thanks for the favor with which they have been pleased to look toward me, to declare a sincere consciousness that the task is above my talents, and that I approach it with those anxious and awful presentiments which the greatness of the charge and the weakness of my powers so justly inspire. A rising nation, spread over a wide and fruitful land, traversing all the seas with the rich productions of their industry, engaged in commerce with nations who feel power and forget right, advancing rapidly to destinies beyond the reach of mortal eye — when I contemplate these transcendent objects, and see the honor, the happiness, and the hopes of this beloved country committed to the issue and the auspices of this day, I shrink from the contemplation, and humble myself before the magnitude of the undertaking. . . .

During the contest of opinion through which we have passed the animation of discussions and of exertions has sometimes worn an aspect which might impose on strangers unused to think freely and to speak and to write what they think; but this being now decided by the voice of the nation, announced according to the rules of the Constitution, all will, of course, arrange themselves under the will of the law, and unite in common efforts for the common good. All, too, will bear in mind the sacred principle, that though the will of the majority is in all cases to prevail, that will to be rightful must be reasonable; that the minority possess their equal rights, which equal law must protect, and to violate would be oppression. Let us, then, fellow citizens, unite with one heart and one mind. Let us restore to social intercourse that harmony and affection without which liberty and even life itself are but dreary things. And let us reflect that, having banished from our land that religious intolerance under which mankind so long bled and suffered, we have yet gained little if we countenance a political intolerance as despotic, as wicked, and capable of as bitter and bloody persecutions. During the throes and convulsions of the ancient world, during the agonizing spasms of infuriated man, seeking through blood and slaughter his long-lost liberty, it was not wonderful that the agitation of the billows should reach even this distant and peaceful shore; that this should be more felt and feared by some and less by others, and should divide opinions as to measures of safety. But every difference of opinion is not a difference of principle. We have called by different names brethren of the same principle. We are all Republicans, we are all Federalists. If there be any among us who would wish to dissolve this Union or to change its republican form, let them stand undisturbed as monuments of the safety with which error of opinion may be tolerated where reason is left free to combat it. I know, indeed, that some honest men fear that a republican government cannot be strong, that this government is not strong enough; but would the honest patriot, in the full tide of successful experiment, abandon a government which has so far kept us free and firm on the theoretic and visionary fear that this government, the world's best hope, may by possibility want energy to preserve itself? I trust not. I believe this, on the contrary, the strongest government on earth. I believe it the only one where every man, at the call of the law, would fly to the standard of the law, and would meet invasions of the public order as his own personal concern. Sometimes it is said that man cannot be trusted with the government of himself. Can he, then, be trusted with the government of others? Or have we found angels in the forms of kings to govern him? Let history answer this question.

Let us, then, with courage and confidence pursue our own Federal and Republican principles, our attachment to union and representative government. Kindly separated by nature and a wide ocean from the exterminating havoc of one quarter of the globe; too high-minded to endure the degradations of the others; possessing a chosen country, with room enough for our descendants to the thousandth and thousandth generation; entertaining a due sense of our equal right to the use of our own faculties, to the acquisitions of our own industry, to honor and confidence from our fellow citizens, resulting not from birth, but from our actions and their sense of them; enlightened by a benign religion, professed, indeed, and practised in various forms, yet all of them inculcating honesty, truth, temperance, gratitude, and the love of man; acknowledging and adoring an overruling Providence, which by all its dispensations proves that it delights in the happiness of man here and his greater happiness hereafter — with all these blessings, what more is necessary to make us a happy and a prosperous people? Still one thing more, fellow citizens — a wise and frugal government, which shall restrain men from injuring one another, shall leave them otherwise free to regulate their own pursuits of industry and improvement, and shall not take from the mouth of labor the bread it has earned. This is the sum of good government, and this is necessary to close the circle of our felicities. . . .

THOMAS JEFFERSON, First Inaugural Address, 1801

49. Burr's Muster at Blenner-hasset Island

Aaron Burr, who tied with Jefferson in 1800 in electoral votes for the Presidency, ruined himself politically in 1804 by killing Alexander Hamilton at Weehawken, New Jersey. In the next two years he developed some hazy plans for a western expedition, one of its objects apparently being an invasion of the Spanish dominions in Mexico. Undoubtedly he entertained dreams of conquest. But in a trip he made from Pittsburgh to New Orleans he aroused suspicion among many that he was also planning to detach western territory from the United States and set up an independent nation. By 1806 he had interested Harman Blennerhasset, a wealthy young Irishman living on an island in the Ohio River, near Marietta, Ohio, in what he represented as speculation in land. Blennerhasset helped provide funds for Burr's hazy and dubious enterprise. He was quite innocent of any evil intent, and Burr's arrest and trial for treason brought on him a disaster that he did not deserve.

THE FIRST I knew of this business was, I was hired on the island to help to build a kiln for drying corn [1806]; and after working some time, Mrs. Blennerhasset told me that Mr. Blennerhasset and Colonel Burr were going to lay in provisions for an army for a year. I went to the mill, where I carried the corn to be ground after it had been dried. I worked four weeks on that business in the island. Last fall (or in September) after Blennerhasset had come home — he had been promising me cash for some time — I stept up to him. He had no money at the time, but would pay me next day, or soon. Says he, "Mr. Allbright, you are a Dutchman." But he asked me first and foremost, whether I would not join with him and go down the river. I told him I did not know what they were upon, and he said, "Mr. Allbright, we are going to settle a new country." And I gave him an answer, that I would not like to leave my family. He said he did not want any families to go along with him. Then he said to me, "You are a Dutchman, and a common man; and as the Dutch are apt to be scared by high men, if you'll go to New Lancaster, where the Dutch live, and get me twenty or thirty to go with us, I will give you as many dollars." New Lancaster was some distance off. I went home then, and gave him no answer upon that. In a few days after, the boats came and landed at the island. The snow was about two or three inches deep, and I went a-hunting. I was on the Ohio side; I met two men; I knew they belonged to the boats, but I wanted to find out; and they asked me whether I had not given my consent to go along with Blennerhasset down the river. As we got into a conversation together they named themselves Colonel Burr's men, belonging to the boats, landed at the island. When they asked me whether I had not consented to go down with Blennerhasset, I put a question to them. I told them I did not know what they were about; and one of the gentlemen told me, they were going to take a silver mine from the Spanish. I asked the gentlemen whether they would not allow that this would raise war with America. They replied, no. These were only a few men; and if they went with a good army, they would give up the country and nothing more said about it. I had all this conversation with the two men. These men showed me what fine rifles they had, going down the river with them. Then I went to the island, and Blennerhasset paid me off in Kentucky notes. People however didn't like these notes very well, and I went over to the bank at Kanawha to change them. I got two of the notes changed; and one, a ten-dollar note, was returned to my hand, for which I wished to get silver from Blennerhasset. I went to the island the day the proclamation came out. But before I went to Blennerhasset's house, I heard he was not at home, but at Marietta. I went on the Virginia side, where I met three other men, belonging to the boats, with three complete rifles. They made a call upon me, to take them to the island in my canoe, and I accepted to it; but afterwards I carried the third man, who stood close by my canoe, over to the island. After being some time on the island, I went down to the four boats. Blennerhasset was not at home yet, and I met some of the boat people shooting at a mark. They had a fire between the bank and boats. I saw this in the daytime. . . .

I waited at the house till Blennerhasset came home. He appeared very much scared. One of the boatmen came up to him for something, and he told him, "Don't trouble me, I have enough trouble already." He went up to his chamber, and I saw no more of him. I asked an old gentleman who was there, and with whom I was well acquainted, to go up to his chamber, and change my note for silver. He did go, and brought me silver. By and by I heard that they were going to start that night. Thinks I, "I'll see the end of it." This was the night of the very day that Blennerhasset got back from Marietta. He got back before night. When night came on, I was among the men and also in the kitchen, and saw the boatmen running bullets. One of them spoke out to the others, "Boys, let's mold as many bullets as we can fire twelve rounds." After that, I saw no more till after twelve o'clock at night. Then Blennerhasset came down from the chamber and called up some of his servants; he had four or five trunks. There were not trusty hands enough to carry them to the boats, and some person called after my name and asked me to help them, and I carried one of the trunks and moved along with them. When we got down, some person, I don't particularly know who, but think it was Blennerhasset himself, asked me to stand by the trunks, till they were put in the boats. When the last of them went off, I saw men standing in a circle on the shore. I went up to them; perhaps they were five or six rods from me. The first thing that I noticed was their laying plans and consulting how Blennerhasset and Comfort Tyler should get safe by Gallipolis. One Nahum Bennett was called forward, and when he came, Blennerhasset asked him whether he had not two smart horses. Nahum Bennett answered no; he had but one. Then Blennerhasset told him to go to Captain Dennie, and get his sorrel horse; and Nahum Bennett told him that the sorrel horse had no shoes on; and Blennerhasset said the roads were soft and would not hurt the horse. Blennerhasset told Nahum Bennett to meet him and Comfort Tyler with the horses, some where about Gallipolis. Bennett inquired how he was to find him out, should he inquire for him. "No." "Have you no friends there?" "No." Mrs. Blennerhasset then came forward, and she told Blennerhasset and Comfort Tyler that they must take a canoe and get into it before they got to Gallipolis, and sail down the stream of the Ohio; for nobody would mind a couple of men going down the stream. She said she'd pay for the canoe. Blennerhasset told Nahum Bennett to take the two horses and pass round Gallipolis before day, and then they might go round Gallipolis. After that, a man by the name of Tupper laid his hands upon Blennerhasset, and said, "Your body is in my hands, in the name of the commonwealth." Some such words as that he mentioned. When Tupper made that motion, there were seven or eight muskets leveled at him. Tupper looked about him and said, "Gentlemen, I hope you will not do the like." One of the gentlemen who was nearest, about two yards off, said, "I'd as lieve as not." Tupper then changed his speech, and said he wished him to escape safe down the river, and wished him luck. Tupper before told Blennerhasset he should stay and stand his trial. But Blennerhasset said no; that the people in the neighborhood were coming down next day to take him, and he would go. Next day after I saw the Wood county militia going down. The people went off in boats that night about one.

Reports of the Trials of Colonel Aaron Burr

50. How Jefferson Lived in the White House

Jefferson was a widower when he began his eight years in the White House in 1801. Tall, loosely built, rather carelessly dressed, informal of manner, full of endless frank, entertaining, shrewd talk, he impressed many observers as lacking in dignity. But his unaffected simplicity was actually one of the virtues of as true a gentleman as ever occupied the Presidential chair. One of his intimate friends was Mrs. Harrison Smith, long a leader in Washington society.

WHEN HE took up his residence in the President's House, he [Jefferson] found it scantily furnished with articles brought from Philadelphia and which had been used by General Washington.

These, though worn and faded, he retained from respect to their former possessor. His drawing room was fitted up with the same crimson damask furniture that had been used for the same purpose in Philadelphia. The additional furniture necessary for the more spacious mansion provided by the government was plain and simple to excess. The large East Room was unfinished and therefore unused. The apartment in which he took most interest was his cabinet; this he had arranged according to his own taste and convenience. It was a spacious room. In the center was a long table, with drawers on each side, in which were deposited not only articles appropriate to the place, but a set of carpenter's tools in one and small garden implements in another, from the use of which he derived much amusement. Around the walls were maps, globes, charts, books, etc. In the window recesses were stands for the flowers and plants which it was his delight to attend, and among his roses and geraniums was suspended the cage of his favorite mockingbird, which he cherished with peculiar fondness, not only for its melodious powers, but for its uncommon intelligence and affectionate disposition, of which qualities he gave surprising instances. It was the constant companion of his solitary and studious hours. Whenever he was alone, he opened the cage and let the bird fly about the room. After flitting for a while from one object to another, it would alight on his table and regale him with its sweetest notes, or perch on his shoulder and take its food from his lips. Often when he retired to his chamber it would hop up the stairs after him and while he took his siesta, would sit on his couch and pour forth its melodious strains. How he loved this bird! How he loved his flowers! He could not live without something to love, and in the absence of his darling grandchildren his bird and his flowers became objects of tender care. In a man of such dispositions, such tastes, who would recognize the rude, un-polished democrat which foreigners and political enemies described him to be? If his dress was plain, unstudied, and sometimes old-fashioned in its form, it was always of the finest materials; in his personal habits he was fastidiously neat; and if in his manners he was simple, affable, and unceremonious, it was not because he was ignorant of but because he despised the conventional and artificial usages of courts and fashionable life. His simplicity never degener-ated into vulgarity, nor his affability into familiarity. On the con-trary, there was a natural and quiet dignity in his demeanor that often produced a degree of restraint in those who conversed with him, unfavorable to that free interchange of thoughts and feelings which constitute the greatest charm of social life. His residence in foreign courts never imparted that polish to his manners which courts require, and though possessed of ease they were deficient in grace. His external appearance had no pretensions to elegance, but it was neither coarse nor awkward, and it must be owned his greatest personal attraction was a countenance beaming with benevolence and intelligence.

He was called, even by his friends, a national man, full of odd fancies in little things, and it must be confessed that his local and domestic arrangements were full of contrivances or *conveniences,* as he called them, peculiarly his own and never met with in other houses. Too often the practical was sacrificed to the fanciful, as was evident to the most superficial observer in the location and structure of his house at Monticello.

The same fanciful disposition characterized all his architectural plans and domestic arrangements, and even in the President's House were introduced some of these favorite contrivances, many of them really useful and convenient. Among these, there was in his dining room an invention for introducing and removing the dinner without the opening and shutting of doors. A set of circular shelves were so contrived in the wall that on touching a spring they turned into the room loaded with the dishes placed on them by the servants without the wall, and by the same process the removed dishes were conveyed out of the room. When he had any persons dining with him with whom he wished to enjoy a free and unrestricted flow of conversation, the number of persons at table never exceeded four and by each individual was placed a *dumb-waiter* containing everything necessary for the progress of the dinner from beginning to end so as to make the attendance of servants entirely unnecessary, believing, as he did, that much of the domestic and even public discord was produced by the mutilated and misconstructed repetition of free conversation at dinner tables by these mute but not inattentive listeners. William McClure and Caleb Lowndes, both distinguished and well-known citizens of Philadelphia, were invited together to one of these dinners. Mr. McClure, who had traveled over a great part of Europe and after a long residence in Paris had just returned to the United States, could of course impart a great deal of important and interesting information with an accuracy and fullness unattainable through the medium of letters. Interesting as were the topics of his discourse, Mr. Jefferson gave him his whole attention, but closely as he listened, Mr. McClure spoke so low that although seated by his side, the President scarcely heard half that was said. "You need not speak so low," said Mr. Jefferson, smiling; "you see we are alone and *our walls have no ears*." "I have so long been living in Paris, where the walls have ears," replied Mr. McClure, "that I have contracted this habit of speaking in an undertone." He then described the system of espionage established throughout France, whose vigilance pervaded the most private circles and retired families, among whose servants one was sure to be in the employment of the police.

At his usual dinner parties the company seldom if ever exceeded fourteen, including himself and his secretary. The invitations were not given promiscuously, or as has been done of late years, alphabetically, but his guests were generally selected in reference to their tastes, habits, and suitability in all respects, which attention had a wonderful effect in making his parties more agreeable than dinner parties usually are; this limited number prevented the company's forming little knots and carrying on in undertones separate conversations, a custom so common and almost unavoidable in a large party. At Mr. Jefferson's table the conversation was general; every guest was entertained and interested in whatever topic was discussed. To each an opportunity was offered for the exercise of his colloquial powers, and the stream of conversation, thus enriched by such various contributions, flowed on, full, free, and animated. Of course he took the lead and gave the tone with a tact so true and discriminating that he seldom missed his aim, which was to draw forth the talents and information of each and all of his guests and to place every one in an advantageous light, and by being pleased with themselves, be enabled to please others. Did he perceive any one individual silent and unattended to, he would make him the object of his peculiar attention and in a manner apparently the most undesigning would draw him into notice and make him a participator in the general conversation. One instance will be given which will better illustrate this trait in Mr. Jefferson's manners of presiding at his table than any verbal description. On an occasion when the company was composed of several distinguished persons and the conversation was eager and animated, one individual remained silent and unnoticed; he had just arrived from Europe, where he had so long been a resident that on his return he felt himself a stranger in his own country and was totally unknown to the present company. After having, seemingly without design, led the conversation to the desired point, Mr. Jefferson, turning to this individual, said, "To you, Mr. C., we are indebted to this benefit; no one more deserves the gratitude of his country." Every eye was turned on the hitherto unobserved guest, who honestly looked as much astonished as any one in the company. The President continued, "Yes, sir, the upland rice which you sent from Algiers and which thus far succeeds, will, when generally adopted by the planters, prove an inestimable blessing to our Southern States." At once Mr. C., who had been a mere cipher in this intelligent circle, became a person of importance and took a large share in the conversation that ensued. . . .

Mr. Jefferson was known in Europe as much, if not more, as a philosopher, than as a politician. Mr. Jefferson's acquaintance in this wide and distinguished circle in Paris made him well known throughout Europe, and when he became President his reputation as a philosopher and man of letters brought many literary and scientific foreigners to our country. Among others, Baron Humboldt one day, in answer to some inquiries addressed to this celebrated traveler, replied, "I have come not to see your great rivers and mountains, but to become acquainted with your great men." Of these, he held Mr. Jefferson in the highest estimation. Soon after the Baron's arrival on our shores, he hastened to Washington and, during his visit to our city, passed many hours of every day with Mr. Jefferson. Baron Humboldt formed not his estimate of men and manners by their habiliments and conventionalisms, and refined as were his tastes and polished as were his manners, he was neither shocked nor disgusted, as was the case with the British minister (Mr. Foster) by the old-fashioned form, ill-chosen colors, or simple material of the President's dress. Neither did he remark the deficiency of elegance in his person or of polish in his manners, but, indifferent to these external and extrinsic circumstances, he easily discerned and most highly appreciated the intrinsic qualities of the philosophic statesman through even the homely costume which had concealed them from the ken of the fastidious diplomat.

His visits at the President's House were unshackled by mere ceremony and not limited to any particular hour. One evening he called about twilight, and being shown into the drawing room without being announced, he found Mr. Jefferson seated on the floor, surrounded by half a dozen of his little grandchildren, so eagerly and noisily engaged in a game of romps that for some moments his entrance was not perceived. When his presence was discovered, Mr. Jefferson rose up and shaking hands with him said, "You have found me playing the fool, Baron, but I am *sure* to you I need make no apology."

Another time he called of a morning and was taken into the cabinet. As he sat by the table, among the newspapers that were scattered about, he perceived one that was always filled with the most virulent abuse of Mr. Jefferson, calumnies the most offensive, personal as well as political. "Why are these libels allowed?" asked the Baron, taking up the paper. "Why is not this libelous journal suppressed, or its editor at least fined and imprisoned?"

Mr. Jefferson smiled, saying: "Put that paper in your pocket, Baron, and should you hear the reality of our liberty, the freedom of our press, questioned, show this paper and tell where you found it."

MRS. SAMUEL HARRISON SMITH, First Forty Years of Washington Society

51. John Marshall Expounds the Constitution

Marshall of Virginia, a staunch Federalist and a believer in a strong national government, was Chief Justice from 1801 to his death in 1835. His great opinions tended to repress state power wherever it encroached upon the field of authority delegated by the Constitution to the Federal government. They also safeguarded property interests and strengthened the Supreme Court as the interpreter of the Constitution.

I

IF ANY one proposition could command the universal assent of mankind, we might expect it would be this: that the government of the Union, though limited in its powers, is supreme within its sphere of action. This would seem to result necessarily from its nature. It is the government of all; its powers are delegated by all; it represents all, and acts for all. Though any one State may be willing to control its operations, no State is willing to allow others to control them. The nation, on those subjects on which it can act, must necessarily bind its component parts. But this question is not left to mere reason: the people have, in express terms, decided it, by saying, "this Constitution, and the laws of the United States, which shall be made in pursuance thereof," "shall be the supreme law of the land," and by requiring that the members of the State legislatures, and the officers of the executive and judicial departments of the States, shall take the oath of fidelity to it.

The government of the United States, then, though limited in its powers, is supreme; and its laws, when made in pursuance of the Constitution, form the supreme law of the land, "anything in the constitution or laws of any State to the contrary notwithstanding."

M'Culloch *v.* Maryland (1819)

II

But a constitution is framed for ages to come and is designed to approach immortality as nearly as human institutions can approach it. Its course cannot always be tranquil. It is exposed to storms and tempests, and its framers must be unwise statesmen indeed if they have not provided it, so far as its nature will permit, with the means of self-preservation from the perils it may be destined to encounter. No government ought to be so defective in its organization as not to contain within itself the means of securing the execution of its own laws against other dangers than those which occur every day. . . .

That the United States form, for many and for most important purposes, a single nation, has not yet been denied. In war we are one people. In making peace we are one people. In all commercial regulations we are one and the same people. In many other respects the American people are one, and the government which is alone capable of controlling and managing their interests in all these respects is the government of the Union. It is their government, and in that character they have no other. America has chosen to be, in many respects, and to many purposes, a nation; and for all these purposes her government is complete; to all these objects it is competent. The people have declared that in the exercise of all the powers given for these objects it is supreme. It can, then, in effecting these objects, legitimately control all individuals or governments within the American territory. The constitution and laws of a State, so far as they are repugnant to the Constitution and laws of the United States, are absolutely void. These States are constituent parts of the United States. They are members of one great empire — for some purposes sovereign, for some purposes subordinate.

Cohens v. Virginia (1821)

III

This instrument contains an enumeration of powers expressly granted by the people to their government. It has been said that these powers ought to be construed strictly. But why ought they to be so construed? Is there one sentence in the Constitution which gives countenance to this rule? In the last of the enumerated powers, that which grants, expressly, the means for carrying all others into execution, Congress is authorized "to make all laws which shall be necessary and proper" for the purpose. But this limitation on the means which may be used is not extended to the powers which are conferred; nor is there one sentence in the Constitution, which has been pointed out by the gentlemen of the bar or which we have been able to discern, that prescribes this rule. We do not, therefore, think ourselves justified in adopting it. What do the gentlemen mean by a strict construction? If they contend only against that enlarged construction which would extend words beyond their natural and obvious import we might question the application of the term, but should not controvert the principle. If they contend for that narrow construction which, in support of some theory not to be found in the Constitution, would deny to the government those powers which the words of the grant, as usually understood, import, and which are consistent with the general views and objects of the instrument; for that narow construction, which would cripple the government, and render it unequal to the objects for which it is declared to be instituted, and to which the powers given, as fairly understood, render it competent; then we cannot perceive the propriety of this strict construction, nor adopt it as the rule by which the Constitution is to be expounded. As men whose intentions require no concealment generally employ the words which most directly and aptly express the ideas they intend to convey, the enlightened patriots who framed our Constitution, and the people who adopted it, must be understood to have employed words in their natural sense, and to have intended what they have said. . . .

Powerful and ingenious minds, taking as postulates that the powers expressly granted to the government of the Union are to be contracted, by construction, into the narrowest possible compass, and that the original powers of the States are to be retained, if any possible construction will retain them, may, by a course of well-digested but refined and metaphysical reasoning, founded on these premises, explain away the Constitution of our country and leave it a magnificent structure indeed, to look at, but totally unfit for use. They may so entangle and perplex the understanding as to obscure principles which were before thought quite plain, and induce doubts where, if the mind were to pursue its own course, none would be perceived. In such a case it is peculiarly necessary to recur to safe and fundamental principles, to sustain those principles, and, when sustained, to make them the tests of the arguments to be examined.

Gibbons *v.* Ogden (1824)

X

The War of 1812

52. A Yankee Privateer Captures a Prize

The second war with Great Britain was begun in part as a war for "sailors' rights." About two hundred and fifty privateers — that is, privately outfitted war vessels — were commissioned to prey upon British commerce. Their crews showed pluck and enterprise, and though few made money, they fought some of the bravest engagements of the war. The authorship of this tale is still something of a mystery.

O UR SHIP was a good one, and in excellent condition for the business in which she was about to be engaged; her armament was effective, being sixteen long six-pounders; and her crew, numbering, all told, one hundred and forty, were for the most part good seamen and able-bodied men. The officers were selected for their knowledge of seamanship or for their reputed bravery.

Thus manned and equipped, we set sail from our port about the middle of September, 1812, with favoring gales and buoyant spirits — making our course to the southward, being destined to cruise near to the coast of Brazil. We had been at sea about twenty days, and had seen no sail since we left the American coast, when, one morning about ten o'clock, word was passed from the foretop of "Sail, oh!" All hands were called, and all sail was set upon our ship, and we stood toward the strange vessel, which our lieutenant, who had gone to the masthead with his spyglass, reported to be a brig standing to the northeastward.

All was now excitement, and the men were contemplating the chance of a prize and calculating their share of the prize money. The guns were well seen to and were double-shotted; matches were lighted; the gunner and his assistants were in the powder maga-zine, the men at their quarters, and everything on board presented a most warlike aspect. My post was with the surgeon in the ward-room, which we used for a cockpit, and after having taken from the medicine chest several rolls of bandages and sticking plasters, to-gether with the tourniquet and amputating instruments, and placed them ready for use, I went on deck to view the progress of the chase.

It was now about one o'clock, and the brig could be distinctly seen from our deck, but the wind was light, and she was far off. She was evidently an English vessel, as those said who were judges of the matter, and a merchantman, deeply laden. Our ship had English colors flying, but the brig displayed none; our officers had on Eng-lish uniforms, and our marines were dressed in red coats. The cap-tain gave the word to "man the sweeps," and all hands turned to with a will to propel our ship toward the object of our anticipated capture.

We now gained upon her fast, and at 5 P.M. she displayed English colors. We could see that she had several guns on a side, but that her crew were not very numerous. In about two hours more we were within hailing distance and ordered her to heave to, but her captain did not choose to comply with this order; we accordingly threw a shot across her forefoot, which the spunky Briton returned without any ceremony. We now gave him a general discharge from our bat-tery; but he was determined to die game, and returned it; but it was no equal match, and in about four minutes he was completely silenced. We then ordered him to send his boat on board us, which order he promptly complied with. She proved to be from Pernam-buco, bound for London, with a valuable cargo of cotton, sugar, and dye woods, and her officers were ignorant that war existed between the United States and Great Britain. We removed her crew into our own vessel, and sent her home, in charge of a prizemaster and seven men, where she arrived in safety.

This capture put new life and animation into our crew, and all our thoughts and conversation were of prizes and fortunes to be made upon the ocean. I shared in the general joy; yet I could not but look with pity upon the captain of the brig, who appeared to be a very worthy man, and who said that he was ruined by our success, as he had all his worldly property in the vessel which was

now on its way to the United States. As for the crew, they appeared
to care nothing about their capture. They were not English, and
felt no allegiance to Great Britain, and they were well treated on
board our ship, as our captain would not permit them to be plundered of the most trifling article. Several of them wished to enlist
among our crew, but this was not permitted.

NATHANIEL HAWTHORNE, ed., The Yarn of a Yankee Privateer

53. The "Constitution" Defeats the "Guerrière"

The Constitution *under Captain
Isaac Hull sailed from Chesapeake Bay on July 12, 1812, and more
than a month later fell in with the British frigate* Guerrière. *In the
battle which followed — the first important naval battle of the war —
the American vessel won a decisive victory. It was superior in guns
and men, but it also showed better seamanship and gunnery.*

I COMMANDED the American brig *Betsey,* in the year 1812,
and was returning home from Naples, Italy, to Boston. When near
the western edge of the Grand Bank of Newfoundland, on the 10th
of August, 1812, I fell in with the British frigate *Guerrière,* Captain
Dacres, and was captured by him. Myself and a boy were taken on
board of the frigate; the remainder of my officers and men were left
in the *Betsey,* and sent into Halifax, N.S., as a prize to the *Guerrière.*

On the 19th of the same month, the wind being fresh from
the northward, the *Guerrière* was under double-reefed topsails during all the forenoon of this day. At 2 P.M. we discovered a large sail
to windward, bearing about north from us. We soon made her out
to be a frigate. She was steering off from the wind, with her head
to the southwest, evidently with the intention of cutting us off as
soon as possible.

Signals were soon made by the *Guerrière,* but as they were not answered, the conclusion of course was that she was either a French or an American frigate. Captain Dacres appeared anxious to ascertain her character, and after looking at her for that purpose, handed me his spyglass, requesting me to give him my opinion of the stranger. I soon saw from the peculiarity of her sails and from her general appearance that she was, without doubt, an American frigate, and communicated the same to Captain Dacres. He immediately replied, that he thought she came down too boldly for an American, but soon after added, "The better he behaves, the more honor we shall gain by taking him."

The two ships were rapidly approaching each other, when the *Guerrière* backed her main topsail, and waited for her opponent to come down and commence the action. He then set an English flag at each masthead, beat to quarters, and made ready for the fight. When the strange frigate came down to within two or three miles distance, he hauled upon the wind, took in all his light sails, reefed his topsails, and deliberately prepared for action. It was now about five o'clock in the afternoon, when he filled away and ran down for the *Guerrière.* At this moment, Captain Dacres politely said to me: "Captain Orme, as I suppose you do not wish to fight against your own countrymen, you are at liberty to go below the waterline." It was not long after this before I retired from the quarterdeck to the cockpit.

Of course I saw no more of the action until the firing ceased, but I heard and felt much of its effects; for soon after I left the deck, the firing commenced on board the *Guerrière,* and was kept up almost constantly until about six o'clock, when I heard a tremendous explosion from the opposing frigate. The effect of her shot seemed to make the *Guerrière* reel and tremble as though she had received the shock of an earthquake. Immediately after this, I heard a tremendous crash on deck, and was told the mizzenmast was shot away. In a few moments afterward the cockpit was filled with wounded men.

At about half past six o'clock in the evening, after the firing had ceased, I went on deck, and there beheld a scene which it would be difficult to describe: all the *Guerrière's* masts were shot away, and as she had no sails to steady her, she lay rolling like a log in the trough of the sea. Many of the men were employed in throwing the dead overboard. The decks were covered with blood and had the appearance of a butcher's slaughterhouse; the gun tackles were not made fast, and several of the guns got loose and were surging to and fro from one side to the other.

Some of the petty officers and seamen, after the action, got liquor, and were intoxicated, and what with the groans of the wounded, the noise and confusion of the enraged survivors on board of the ill-fated ship rendered the whole scene a perfect hell.

The Report of Captain Orme

54. Tecumseh Pledges Support to the British

The Shawnee chief Tecumseh felt outraged by what he considered American aggressions upon the lands of his tribe, and willingly joined with the British to halt them. General Harrison met Tecumseh and his braves at the battle of Tippecanoe, November 1811, and destroyed the Indian confederacy. Two years later Tecumseh was killed at the battle of the Thames.

FATHER, listen to your children! You have them now all before you. The war before this, our British father gave the hatchet to his red children, when old chiefs were alive. They are now dead. In that war our father was thrown on his back by the Americans, and our father took them by the hand without our knowledge; and we are afraid that our father will do so again at this time.

Summer before last, when I came forward with my red brethren, and was ready to take up the hatchet in favor of our British father, we were told not to be in a hurry, that he had not yet determined to fight the Americans.

Listen! When war was declared, our father stood up and gave us the tomahawk, and told us that he was ready to strike the Americans; that he wanted our assistance, and that he would certainly get us our lands back, which the Americans had taken from us.

Listen! You told us, at that time, to bring forward our families to this place, and we did so — and you promised to take care of them, and that they should want for nothing, while the men would go and fight the enemy; that we need not trouble ourselves about the enemy's garrisons; that we knew nothing about them, and that our father would attend to that part of the business. You also told your red children that you would take good care of your garrison here, which made our hearts glad.

Listen! When we were last at the Rapids, it is true we gave you little assistance. It is hard to fight people who live like ground hogs.

Father, listen! Our fleet has gone out; we know they have fought; we have heard the great guns, but know nothing of what has happened to our father with one arm. Our ships have gone one way, and we are much astonished to see our father tying up everything and preparing to run away the other, without letting his red children know what his intentions are. You always told us to remain here and take care of our lands. It made our hearts glad to hear that was your wish. Our great father, the King, is the head, and you represent him. You always told us that you would never draw your foot off British ground; but now, Father, we see you are drawing back, and we are sorry to see our father doing so without seeing the enemy. We must compare our father's conduct to a fat animal that carries its tail upon its back, but when affrighted, it drops it between its legs and runs off.

Listen, Father! The Americans have not yet defeated us by land; neither are we sure that they have done so by water — we therefore wish to remain here and fight our enemy, should they make their appearance. If they defeat us, we will then retreat with our father.

At the battle of the Rapids, last war, the Americans certainly defeated us; and when we retreated to our father's fort in that place, the gates were shut against us. We were afraid that it would now be the case, but instead of that, we now see our British father preparing to march out of his garrison.

Father! You have got the arms and ammunition which our great father sent for his red children. If you have an idea of going away, give them to us, and you may go and welcome, for us. Our lives are in the hands of the Great Spirit. We are determined to defend our lands, and if it is His will, we wish to leave our bones upon them.

FRANK MOORE, *American Eloquence*

55. The British Burn Washing-ton City

In August, 1814, Admiral Cockburn of the British Navy arrived off the Virginia coast with a fleet of twenty-one vessels, bringing General Robert Ross, and a British expeditionary force of 4,000 or 4,500 men. This force dispersed the American militia at Bladensburg, chased Madison and his Cabinet into the Virginia woods, and burned the Capitol in Washington. Neither Americans nor Britons have cared to remember the episode. The only heroic figure in the affair was Dolly Madison, who remained at the White House until the British were at its gates, and then wrenched Stuart's large portrait of Washington from its frame to be carried away. A British veteran of the Napoleonic Wars here tells the story of the capture.

As IT was not the intention of the British government to attempt permanent conquests in this part of America, and as the General was well aware that, with a handful of men, he could not pretend to establish himself for any length of time in an enemy's capital, he determined to lay it under contribution and to return quietly to the shipping.

Such being the intention of General Ross, he did not march the troops immediately into the city, but halted them upon a plain in its immediate vicinity, whilst a flag of truce was sent in with terms. But whatever his proposal might have been, it was not so much as heard, for scarcely had the party bearing the flag entered the street, than they were fired upon from the windows of one of the houses, and the horse of the General himself, who accompanied them, killed. You will easily believe that conduct so unjustifiable, so direct a breach of the law of nations, roused the indignation of every individual, from the General himself down to the private soldier. All thoughts of accommodation were instantly laid aside;

the troops advanced forthwith into the town, and having first put
to the sword all who were found in the house from which the shots
were fired, and reduced it to ashes, they proceeded, without a moment's delay, to burn and destroy everything in the most distant
degree connected with government. In this general devastation were
included the Senate House, the President's palace, an extensive dockyard and arsenal, barracks for two or three thousand men, several
large storehouses filled with naval and military stores, some hundreds of cannon of different descriptions, and nearly twenty thousand
stand of small arms. There were also two or three public rope works
which shared the same fate, a fine frigate pierced for sixty guns and
just ready to be launched, several gun brigs and armed schooners,
with a variety of gunboats and small craft. The powder magazines
were, of course, set on fire, and exploded with a tremendous crash,
throwing down many houses in their vicinity, partly by pieces of
the wall striking them, and partly by the concussion of the air,
whilst quantities of shot, shell, and hand grenades, which could not
otherwise be rendered useless, were thrown into the river.

All this was as it should be, and had the arm of vengeance been
extended no farther, there would not have been room given for so
much as a whisper of disapprobation. But, unfortunately, it did not
stop here; a noble library, several printing offices, and all the national archives were likewise committed to the flames, which, though
no doubt the property of government, might better have been spared.
It is not, however, my intention to join the outcry which will probably be raised against what they will term a line of conduct at once
barbarous and unprofitable. Far from it; on the contrary, I cannot
help admiring the forbearance and humanity of the British troops,
since, irritated as they had every right to be, they spared as far as
was possible all private property, not a single house in the place
being plundered or destroyed, except that from which the General's
horse had been killed and those which were accidentally thrown
down by the explosion of the magazines.

While the third brigade was thus employed, the rest of the army,
having recalled its stragglers and removed the wounded into Bladensburg, began its march towards Washington. Though the battle was
ended by four o'clock, the sun had set before the different regiments
were in a condition to move, consequently this short journey was

performed in the dark. The work of destruction had also begun in the city, before they quitted their ground; and the blazing of houses, ships, and stores, the report of exploding magazines, and the crash of falling roofs informed them, as they proceeded, of what was going forward. You can conceive nothing finer than the sight which met them as they drew near to the town. The sky was brilliantly illuminated by the different conflagrations, and a dark red light was thrown upon the road, sufficient to permit each man to view distinctly his comrade's face. Except the burning of St. Sebastian's, I do not recollect to have witnessed, at any period of my life, a scene more striking or more sublime.

I need scarcely to observe that the consternation of the inhabitants was complete, and that to them this was a night of terror. So confident had they been of the success of their troops, that few of them had dreamed of quitting their houses, or abandoning the city; nor was it till the fugitives from the battle began to rush in, filling every place as they came with dismay, that the President himself thought of providing for his safety. That gentleman, as I was credibly informed, had gone forth in the morning with the army, and had continued among his troops till the British forces began to make their appearance. Whether the sight of his enemies cooled his courage or not, I cannot say, but, according to my informer, no sooner was the glittering of our arms discernible, than he began to discover that his presence was more wanted in the Senate than with the army; and having ridden through the ranks, and exhorted every man to do his duty, he hurried back to his own house, that he might prepare a feast for the entertainment of his officers, when they should return victorious. For the truth of these details, I will not be answerable; but this much I know, that the feast was actually prepared, though, instead of being devoured by American officers, it went to satisfy the less delicate appetites of a party of English soldiers. When the detachment sent out to destroy Mr. Madison's house entered his dining parlor, they found a dinner table spread and covers laid for forty guests. Several kinds of wine, in handsome cutglass decanters, were cooling on the sideboard; plate holders stood by the fireplace, filled with dishes and plates; knives, forks, and spoons were arranged for immediate use; in short, everything was ready for the entertainment of a ceremonious party. Such were the arrangements in the dining room, whilst in the kitchen were others answerable to them in every respect. Spits, loaded with joints of various sorts, turned before the fire; pots, saucepans, and other culinary utensils stood upon the grate; and all the other requisites for an elegant and substantial repast were exactly in a state which indicated that they had been lately and precipitately abandoned.

You will readily imagine that these preparations were beheld by a party of hungry soldiers with no indifferent eye. An elegant dinner, even though considerably overdressed, was a luxury to which few of them, at least for some time back, had been accustomed, and which, after the dangers and fatigues of the day, appeared peculiarly inviting. They sat down to it, therefore, not indeed in the most orderly manner, but with countenances which would not have disgraced a party of aldermen at a civic feast, and, having satisfied their appetites with fewer complaints than would have probably escaped their rival *gourmands,* and partaken pretty freely of the wines, they finished by setting fire to the house which had so liberally entertained them.

But, as I have just observed, this was a night of dismay to the inhabitants of Washington. They were taken completely by surprise; nor could the arrival of the flood be more unexpected to the natives of the antediluvian world than the arrival of the British army to them. The first impulse of course tempted them to fly, and the streets were in consequence crowded with soldiers and senators, men, women, and children, horses, carriages, and carts loaded with household furniture, all hastening towards a wooden bridge which crosses the Potomac. The confusion thus occasioned was terrible, and the crowd upon the bridge was such as to endanger its giving way. But Mr. Madison, having escaped among the first, was no sooner safe on the opposite bank of the river than he gave orders that the bridge should be broken down; which being obeyed, the rest were obliged to return and to trust to the clemency of the victors.

In this manner was the night passed by both parties; and at daybreak next morning, the light brigade moved into the city, while the reserve fell back to a height about a half a mile in the rear. Little, however, now remained to be done, because everything marked out for destruction was already consumed. Of the Senate house, the President's palace, the barracks, the dockyard, etc., nothing could be seen except heaps of smoking ruins; and even the bridge, a noble structure upwards of a mile in length, was almost wholly demolished.

GEORGE ROBERT GLEIG, A Narrative of the Campaigns of the British Army

56. Andrew Jackson Routs the Redcoats at New Orleans

The British force which had taken Washington soon left to join the army of Sir Edward Pakenham, a relative of Wellington who had been sent to capture New Orleans. The military situation of the Americans at the mouth of the Mississippi was very weak. But the government did the one thing needed to save Louisiana when it placed the tall, lanky, hot-tempered, and singularly effective Andrew Jackson in command there. He arrived on the second of December, 1814, and set every man within reach to work throwing up earthworks and mounting guns. Our British officer tells what happened when the battle of New Orleans was fought the following month — eleven days after peace had been signed at Ghent. When Britons and Americans met again on a battlefield just over a century later, it was as comrades facing a common enemy.

THE MORNING of the 1st of January [1815] chanced to be peculiarly gloomy. A thick haze obscured for a long time the rays of the sun, nor could objects be discerned with any accuracy till a late hour.

But, at length, the mist gave way, and the American camp was fully exposed to view. Being at this time only three hundred yards distant, we could perceive all that was going forward with great exactness. The different regiments were upon parade, and being dressed in holiday suits, presented really a fine appearance. Mounted officers were riding backwards and forwards through the ranks, bands were playing, and colors floating in the air; in a word, all seemed jollity and gala, when suddenly our batteries opened, and the face of affairs was instantly changed. The ranks were broken; the different corps, dispersing, fled in all directions, while the utmost terror and disorder appeared to prevail. Instead of nicely-dressed lines, nothing but confused crowds could now be observed; nor was it without much difficulty that order was finally restored.

While this consternation prevailed among the infantry, their artillery remained silent, but as soon as the former rallied, they also recovered confidence, and answered our salute with great rapidity and precision. A heavy cannonade therefore commenced on both sides and continued during the whole of the day, till towards evening our ammunition began to fail, and our fire in consequence to slacken. The fire of the Americans, on the other hand, was redoubled; landing a number of guns from the flotilla, they increased their artillery to a prodigious amount; and, directing at the same time the whole force of their cannon on the opposite bank, against the flank of our batteries, they soon convinced us that all endeavors to surpass them in this mode of fighting would be useless. Once more, therefore, were we obliged to retire, leaving our heavy guns to their fate; but as no attempt was made by the Americans to secure them, working parties were again sent out after dark, and such as had not been destroyed were removed.

All our plans had as yet proved abortive; even this, upon which so much reliance had been placed, was found to be of no avail, and it must be confessed that something like murmuring began to be heard through the camp. And, in truth, if ever an army might be permitted to murmur, it was this. In landing they had borne great hardships, not only without repining, but with cheerfulness; their hopes had been excited by false reports as to the practicability of the attempt in which they were embarked, and now they found themselves entangled amidst difficulties from which there appeared to be no escape except by victory. In their attempts upon the enemy's line, however, they had been twice foiled; in artillery they perceived themselves so greatly overmatched that their own could hardly assist them; their provisions, being derived wholly from the fleet, were both scanty and coarse; and their rest was continually broken. For not only did the cannon and mortars from the main of the enemy's position play unremittingly upon them both day and night, but they were likewise exposed to a deadly fire from the opposite bank of the river, where no less than eighteen pieces of artillery were now mounted and swept the entire line of our encampment. Besides all this, to undertake the duty of a picket was as dangerous as to go into action. Parties of American sharpshooters harassed and disturbed those appointed to that service, from the time they took possession of their post till they were relieved; while to light fires at night was impossible because they served but as certain marks for the enemy's gunners.

It was determined to divide the army, to send part across the river, who should seize the enemy's guns and turn them on themselves, while the remainder should at the same time make a general assault along the whole entrenchment. But before this plan could be put into execution, it would be necessary to cut a canal across the entire neck of land from the Bayou de Catiline to the river, of sufficient width and depth to admit of boats being brought up from the lake. Upon this arduous undertaking were the troops immediately employed.

While these things were going on and men's minds were anxiously turned towards approaching events, fresh spirit was given to the army by the unexpected arrival of Major General Lambert with the Seventh and Forty-third — two fine battalions, mustering each eight hundred effective men. By this reinforcement together with the addition of a body of sailors and marines from the fleet, our numbers amounted now to little short of eight thousand men, a force which in almost any other quarter of America would have been irresistible.

According to the preconcerted plan, Colonel Thornton's detachment was to cross the river immediately after dark. They were to push forward so as to carry all the batteries and point the guns before daylight, when, on the throwing up of a rocket, they were to commence firing upon the enemy's line, which at the same moment was to be attacked by the main of our army.

Thus were all things arranged on the night of the 7th, for the

8th was fixed upon as the day decisive of the fate of New Orleans. . . .

But unfortunately, the loss of time nothing could repair. Instead of reaching the opposite bank, at latest by midnight, dawn was beginning to appear before the boats quitted the canal. It was in vain that they rowed on in perfect silence, and with oars muffled, gaining the point of debarkation without being perceived. It was in vain that they made good their landing and formed upon the beach without opposition or alarm. Day had already broke, and the signal rocket was seen in the air while they were yet four miles from the batteries, which ought hours ago to have been taken.

In the meantime, the main body armed and moved forward some way in front of the pickets. There they stood waiting for daylight, and listening with the greatest anxiety for the firing which ought now to be heard on the opposite bank. But this attention was exerted in vain, and day dawned upon them long before they desired its appearance. Nor was Sir Edward Pakenham disappointed in this part of his plan alone. Instead of perceiving everything in readiness for the assault, he saw his troops in battle array, indeed, but not a ladder or fascine upon the field. The Forty-fourth, which was appointed to carry them, had either misunderstood or neglected their orders, and now headed the column of attack, without any means being provided for crossing the enemy's ditch, or scaling his rampart.

The indignation of poor Pakenham on this occasion may be imagined, but cannot be described. Galloping towards Colonel Mullens, who led the Forty-forth, he commanded him instantly to return with his regiment for the ladders, but the opportunity of planting them was lost, and though they were brought up, it was only to be scattered over the field by the frightened bearers. For our troops were by this time visible to the enemy. A dreadful fire was accordingly opened upon them, and they were mowed down by hundreds, while they stood waiting for orders.

Seeing that all his well-laid plans were frustrated, Pakenham gave the word to advance, and the other regiments, leaving the Forty-fourth with the ladders and fascines behind them, rushed on to the assault. On the left, a detachment of the Ninety-fifth, Twenty-first, and Fourth, stormed a three-gun battery and took it. Here they remained for some time in the expectation of support, but none arriving, and a strong column of the enemy forming for its recovery, they determined to anticipate the attack, and pushed on. The battery which they had taken was in advance of the body of the works, being cut off from it by a ditch, across which only a single plank was thrown. Along this plank did these brave men attempt to pass; but being opposed by overpowering numbers, they were repulsed; and the Americans, in turn, forcing their way into the battery, at length succeeded in recapturing it with immense slaughter. On the right, again, the Twenty-first and Fourth being almost cut to pieces and thrown into some confusion by the enemy's fire, the Ninety-third pushed on and took the lead. Hastening forward, our troops soon reached the ditch; but to scale the parapet without ladders was impossible. Some few, indeed, by mounting one upon another's shoulders, succeeded in entering the works, but these were instantly overpowered, most of them killed, and the rest taken, while as many as stood without were exposed to a sweeping fire, which cut them down by whole companies. It was in vain that the most obstinate courage was displayed. They fell by the hands of men whom they absolutely did not see, for the Americans, without so much as lifting their faces above the rampart, swung their firelocks by one arm over the wall, and discharged them directly upon their heads. The whole of the guns, likewise, from the opposite bank, kept up a well-directed and deadly cannonade upon their flank; and thus were they destroyed without an opportunity being given of displaying their valour or obtaining so much as revenge.

Poor Pakenham saw how things were going and did all that a general could do to rally his broken troops. Riding towards the Forty-fourth which had returned to the ground, but in great disorder, he called out for Colonel Mullens to advance, but that officer had disappeared, and was not to be found. He, therefore, prepared to lead them on himself, and had put himself at their head for that purpose, when he received a slight wound in the knee from a musket ball, which killed his horse. Mounting another, he again headed the Forty-fourth, when a second ball took effect more fatally, and he dropped lifeless into the arms of his aide-de-camp.

GEORGE ROBERT GLEIG, A Narrative of the Campaigns of the British Army

57. "Peace!"

The commercial city of New York, like most of New England, had disliked the war. When on a Saturday evening early in 1815 a British warship anchored in the harbor with news of peace, the populace plunged into a carnival of joy. "For nearly two hours," wrote the editor of the Evening Post, *"it was difficult to make one's way through unnumbered crowds of persons who came to see and to hear and to rejoice."*

NEW YORK, February 7th, 1815.—Peace! Peace! Peace! What a delightful sound. Long may the glad tidings ring in our ears. Oh, what a night was last Saturday to the inhabitants of N.Y.C. We were quietly sitting around the table with our work when the Ogdens came in; the first sounds were "Peace! Peace!" the boys screaming it in the streets, the city in an uproar. The girls tore about like mad creatures. Eliza threw herself in the middle of the floor as soon as the bells began to ring, and they opened the window shutters for me to hear them. I cried, I capered with Caroline Ogden and tore around the room, stepping from chair to chair, till I thought we would have broken their legs. Mr. Ward rushed in, pulled open the window curtains, and put the lamps in the windows. The girls seized hold of candles and tore all over the house, illuminating every window even to the third story. People rushed in one after the other, almost tearing us to pieces for joy. In short, everybody had taken leave of their senses, the girls ran out in the street and then in again, then out again, then into Mrs. Ogden's, screeching and screaming; the boys ran about in a mob with candles, echoing "Peace! Peace!" Mr. Ward made a whisky punch, the girls drank it, and to cut the matter short, we finished by dancing cotillions till half past eleven o'clock. Our family then sat down to supper and drank a bottle of the *best old Madeira* upon the occasion, and went to bed at about twelve. We have hardly come to our senses yet. Yesterday we calculated about the hour you would hear it, and thought of your raptures. . . . I never shall forget that memorable night that brought the glad tidings. I have hardly yet recovered from my rhapsodies. We expect to have a grand time when the President ratifies it. I presume the whole city will be illuminated.

Mrs. Samuel Ward, Letter to Her Mother

XI

The Hardy Frontiersman

58. New Settlements in Connecticut

The pioneer type, the habits and institutions of the frontier, appeared in America in the early decades of English settlement. They were clearly definable before the middle of the eighteenth century. Nothing, not even the Indians, interested foreign observers more. The Marquis de Chastellux, a gallant French officer who had served with Rochambeau in the Revolution, published in 1786 in France one of the best of the early volumes of American travels. It contained his journal written in New England, during a trip from Philadelphia to Saratoga, and in Virginia, where Jefferson entertained him at Monticello.

WHILE I was meditating on the great process of Nature, which employs fifty thousand years in rendering the earth habitable, a new spectacle, well calculated as a contrast to those which I had been contemplating, fixed my attention and excited my curiosity: this was the work of a single man, who, in the space of a year, had cut down several acres of wood, and had built himself a house in the middle of a pretty extensive territory he had already cleared. I saw for the first time what I have since observed a hundred times; for, in fact, whatever mountains I have climbed, whatever forests I have traversed, whatever bypaths I have followed, I have never traveled three miles without meeting with a new settlement, either beginning to take form or already in cultivation.

The following is the manner of proceeding in these improvements or new settlements: any man who is able to procure a capital of five or six hundred livres of our money, or about twenty-five pounds sterling, and who has strength and inclination to work, may go into the woods and purchase a portion of one hundred and fifty or two hundred acres of land, which seldom costs him more than a dollar, or four shillings and six pence, an acre, a small part of which only he pays in ready money. There he conducts a cow, some pigs or a full sow, and two indifferent horses, which do not cost him more than four guineas each. To these precautions he adds that of having a provision of flour and cider. Provided with this first capital, he begins by felling all the smaller trees and some strong branches of the large ones; these he makes use of as fences to the first field he wishes to clear. He next boldly attacks those immense oaks or pines, which one would take for the ancient lords of the territory he is usurping; he strips them of their bark, or lays them open all round with his ax. These trees, mortally wounded, are the next spring robbed of their honors; their leaves no longer spring, their branches fall, and their trunk becomes a hideous skeleton. This trunk still seems to brave the efforts of the new colonist, but where there are the smallest chinks or crevices it is surrounded by fire and the flames consume what the iron was unable to destroy. But it is enough for the small trees to be felled and the great ones to lose their sap. This object completed, the ground is cleared. The air and the sun begin to operate upon that earth which is wholly formed of rotten vegetables and teems with the latent principles of production. The grass grows rapidly. There is pasturage for the cattle the very first year, after which they are left to increase, or fresh ones are bought, and they are employed in tilling a piece of ground which yields the enormous increase of twenty- or thirtyfold. The next year the same course is repeated, when, at the end of two years, the planter has wherewithal to subsist and even to send some articles to market. At the end of four or five years, he completes the payment of his land and finds himself a comfortable planter. Then his dwelling — which at first was no better than a large hut formed by a square of the trunks of trees, placed one upon another, with the intervals filled by mud — changes into a handsome wooden house, where he contrives more convenient, and certainly much cleaner, apartments than those in the greatest part of our small towns. This is the work of three weeks or a month, his first habitation that of eight-and-forty hours. I shall be asked, perhaps, how one man or one family can be so quickly lodged. I answer that in America a man is never alone, never an isolated being. The neighbors, for they are everywhere to be found, make it a point of hospitality to aid the new farmer. A cask of cider drunk in common and with gaiety, or a gallon of rum, are the only recompense for these services.

Marquis de Chastellux, Travels in North America
in 1780, 1781 and 1782

59. Judge Cooper's Settlements in Upstate New York

William Cooper, father of the author of "The Leatherstocking Tales," said with truth in his old age: "I have settled more acres than any other man in America. There are forty thousand souls holding directly or indirectly under me." Such great estate-owners were not uncommon either before or after the Revolution. Cooper held large tracts in both western and northern New York, and had Alexander Hamilton for his attorney. Settling in 1789 on Otsego Lake in south-central New York, he founded Cooperstown there. Little by little he helped build up a remarkable community, with church, seminary, newspaper, and improved roads and bridges. After serving in Congress and on the bench, he died in 1809.

I BEGAN with the disadvantage of a small capital and the encumbrance of a large family, and yet I have already settled more acres than any man in America. There are forty thousand souls now holding directly or indirectly under me, and I trust that no one amongst so many can justly impute to me any act resembling oppression. I am now descending into the vale of life, and I must acknowledge that I look back with self-complacency upon what I have done, and am proud of having been an instrument in reclaiming such large and fruitful tracts from the waste of the creation. And I question whether that sensation is not now a recompense more grateful to me than all the other profits I have reaped. Your good sense and knowledge of the world will excuse this seeming boast; if it be vain, we all must have our vanities, let it at least serve to show that industry has its reward, and age its pleasures, and be an encouragement to others to persevere and prosper.

In 1785 I visited the rough and hilly country of Otsego, where there existed not an inhabitant, nor any trace of a road; I was alone three hundred miles from home, without bread, meat, or food of any kind; fire and fishing tackle were my only means of subsistence. I caught trout in the brook, and roasted them on the ashes. My horse fed on the grass that grew by the edge of the waters. I laid me down to sleep in my watch coat, nothing but the melancholy wilderness around me. In this way I explored the country, formed my plans of future settlement, and meditated upon the spot where a place of trade or a village should afterwards be established.

In May, 1786, I opened the sales of forty thousand acres, which, in sixteen days, were all taken up by the poorest order of men. I soon after established a store and went to live among them, and continued so to do till 1790, when I brought on my family. For the ensuing four years the scarcity of provisions was a serious calamity; the country was mountainous, and there were neither roads nor bridges.

But the greatest discouragement was in the extreme poverty of the people, none of whom had the means of clearing more than a small spot in the midst of the thick and lofty woods, so that their grain grew chiefly in the shade; their maize did not ripen; their wheat was blasted, and the little they did gather they had no mill to grind within twenty miles distance; not one in twenty had a horse, and the way lay through rapid streams, across swamps, or over bogs. They had neither provisions to take with them, nor money to purchase them; nor if they had, were any to be found on their way. If the father of a family went abroad to labor for bread, it cost him three times its value before he could bring it home, and all the business on his farm stood still till his return.

I resided among them and saw too clearly how bad their condition was. I erected a storehouse and during each winter filled it with large quantities of grain, purchased in distant places. I procured from my friend Henry Drinker a credit for a large quantity of sugar kettles; he also lent me some potash kettles, which we conveyed as we best could, sometimes by partial roads on sleighs, and sometimes over the ice. By this means I established potash works among the settlers and made them debtor for their bread and laboring utensils. I also gave them credit for their maple sugar and potash, at a price that would bear transportation, and the first year after the adoption of this plan I collected in one mass forty-three hogsheads of sugar and three hundred barrels of pot- and pearlash, worth about nine thousand dollars. This kept the people together and at home, and the country soon assumed a new face.

I had not funds of my own sufficient for the opening of new roads, but I collected the people at convenient seasons, and by joint efforts we were able to throw bridges over the deep streams, and to make, in the cheapest manner, such roads as suited our then humble purposes.

In the winter preceding the summer of 1789, grain rose in Albany to a price before unknown. The demand swept all the granaries of the Mohawk country. The number of beginners who depended upon it for their bread greatly aggravated the evil, and a famine ensued, which will never be forgotten by those who, though now in the enjoyment of ease and comfort, were then afflicted with the cruelest of wants.

In the month of April I arrived amongst them with several loads of provisions, destined for my own use and that of the laborers I had brought with me for certain necessary operations; but in a few days all was gone, and there remained not one pound of salt meat nor a single biscuit. Many were reduced to such distress as to live upon the roots of wild leeks; some more fortunate lived upon milk, whilst others supported nature by drinking a syrup made of maple sugar and water. The quantity of leeks they eat had such an effect upon their breath, that they could be smelled at many paces distant, and when they came together, it was like cattle that had pastured in a garlic field. A man of the name of Beets, mistaking some poisonous herb for a leek, ate it, and died in consequence. Judge of my feelings at this epoch, with two hundred families about me and not a morsel of bread.

A singular event seemed sent by a good Providence to our relief; it was reported to me that unusual shoals of fish were seen moving in the clear waters of the Susquehanna. I went and was surprised to find that they were herrings. We made something like a small net by the interweaving of twigs, and by this rude and simple contrivance we were able to take them in thousands. In less than ten days each family had an ample supply with plenty of salt. I also obtained from the Legislature, then in session, seventeen hundred bushels of corn. This we packed on horses' backs, and on our arrival made a distribution among the families, in proportion to the number of individuals of which each was composed.

This was the first settlement I made, and the first attempted after the Revolution; it was, of course, attended with the greatest difficulties; nevertheless, to its success many others have owed their origin. It was besides the roughest land in all the state, and the most difficult of cultivation of all that had been settled; but for many years past it has produced everything necessary to the support and comfort of man. It maintains at present eight thousand souls, with schools, academies, churches, meetinghouses, turnpike roads, and a market town. It annually yields to commerce large droves of fine oxen, great quantities of wheat and other grain, abundance of pork, potash in barrels, and other provisions; merchants with large capital and all kinds of useful mechanics reside upon it; the waters are stocked with fish, the air is salubrious, and the country thriving and happy. When I contemplate all this, and above all, when I see these good old settlers meet together and hear them talk of past hardships, of which I bore my share, and compare the misery they then endured with the comforts they now enjoy, my emotions border upon weakness which manhood can scarcely avow.

WILLIAM COOPER, A Guide in the Wilderness

60. "Old America Is Moving Westward"

After the War of 1812 the westward current ran broad and fast; Indiana was admitted to the Union in 1816, Illinois in 1818. A liberal-minded English observer who became greatly interested in Illinois settlement pictures this pioneering advance as he saw it in Pennsylvania, where the great highways to the West converged on the Ohio River.

McCONNEL'S TOWN, May 23, 1817. — The road we have been traveling terminates at this place, where it strikes the great turnpike from Philadelphia to Pittsburgh; and with the road ends the line of stages by which we have been traveling, a circumstance of which we knew nothing until our arrival here, having entered ourselves passengers at George Town for Pittsburgh, by the Pittsburgh stage, as it professed to be.

So here we are, nine in number, one hundred and thirty miles of mountain country between us and Pittsburgh. We learn that the stages which pass daily from Philadelphia and Baltimore are generally full and that there are now many persons at Baltimore waiting for places. No vehicles of any kind are to be hired, and here we must either stay or *walk* off. The latter we prefer, and separating each our bundle from the little that we have of traveling stores, we are about to undertake our mountain pilgrimage — accepting the alternative most cheerfully after the dreadful shaking of the last hundred miles by stage. . . .

We have now fairly turned our backs on the old world and find ourselves in the very stream of emigration. Old America seems to be breaking up and moving westward. We are seldom out of sight, as we travel on this grand track towards the Ohio, of family groups, behind and before us, some with a view to a particular spot, close to a brother, perhaps, or a friend who has gone before and reported well of the country. Many, like ourselves, when they arrive in the wilderness, will find no lodge prepared for them.

A small wagon (so light that you might almost carry it, yet strong enough to bear a good load of bedding, utensils and provisions, and a swarm of young citizens, and to sustain marvelous shocks in its passage over these rocky heights) with two small horses, sometimes a cow or two, comprises their all, excepting a little store of hard-earned cash for the land office of the district, where they may obtain a title for as many acres as they possess half-dollars, being one-fourth of the purchase money. The wagon has a tilt, or cover, made of a sheet or perhaps a blanket. The family are seen before, behind, or within the vehicle, according to the road or weather or perhaps the spirits of the party.

The New Englanders, they say, may be known by the cheerful air of the women advancing in front of the vehicle, the Jersey people by their being fixed steadily within it, whilst the Pennsylvanians creep lingering behind, as though regretting the homes they have left. A cart and single horse frequently afford the means of transfer, sometimes a horse and packsaddle. Often the back of the poor pilgrim bears all his effects, and his wife follows, naked-footed, bending under the hopes of the family. . . .

A blacksmith here earns twenty dollars per month and board, and he lives in a cabin of one room, for which, with a garden, he pays twenty dollars a year. Firewood is two dollars per cord — the price is merely the labor, as is, in fact, a great part of what you pay for everything. Thus, nothing but land is cheap in this country, excepting British goods, and they are not cheap to the consumer, because the storekeeper sells his own labor at a dear rate. Land will long be at a low price, but as produce hardly keeps pace with the population, the latter is proportionably dear. Therefore, agriculture is and will be a safe and profitable occupation. As to manufactures, they will rise as they are wanted, and if they rise spontaneously, they will flourish without extraneous aid.

May 26. — We have completed our third day's march to general satisfaction. We proceed nearly as fast as our fellow travelers in carriages, and much more pleasantly.

This is a land of plenty, and we are proceeding to a land of *abundance,* as is proved by the noble droves of oxen we meet, on their way from the western country to the city of Philadelphia. They are kindly, well-formed, and well-fed animals, averaging about six hundredweight.

A flock of sheep, properly speaking, has not met my eyes in America, nor a tract of good sheep pasture. Twenty or thirty half-starved creatures are seen now and then straggling about in much wretchedness. These supply a little wool for domestic use. Cattle are good and plentiful, and horses excellent.

May 28. — The condition of the people of America is so different from aught that we in Europe have an opportunity of observing that it would be difficult to convey an adequate notion of their character. They are great travelers, and in general, better acquainted with the vast expanse of country spreading over their eighteen states than the English with their little island. They are also a migrating people and even when in prosperous circumstances can contemplate a change of situation which, under our old establishments and fixed habits, none but the most enterprising would venture upon when urged by adversity.

To give an idea of the internal movements of this vast hive, about twelve thousand wagons passed between Baltimore and Philadelphia in the last year, with from four to six horses, carrying from thirty-five to forty hundredweight. The cost of carriage is about seven dollars per hundredweight from Philadelphia to Pittsburgh, and the money paid for the conveyance of goods on this road exceeds three hundred thousand pounds sterling. Add to these the numerous stages, loaded to the utmost, and the innumerable travelers on horseback, on foot, and in light wagons, and you have before you a scene of bustle and business, extending over a space of three hundred miles, which is truly wonderful.

MORRIS BIRKBECK, Notes on a Journey in America

61. "Leave England for America"

While Englishmen like William Cobbett, Morris Birkbeck, and Richard Flower wrote books to encourage their countrymen to migrate to America, others sent enthusiastic letters to friends and relatives. Often these "American letters" found their way into newspapers, whence they have since been exhumed by historical searchers.

THIS IS the country for a man to enjoy himself: Ohio, Indiana, and the Missouri Territory; where you may see prairie sixty miles long and ten broad, not a stick nor a stone in them, at two dollars an acre, that will produce from seventy to one hundred bushels of Indian corn per acre: too rich for wheat or any other kind of grain. I measured Indian corn in Ohio State last September more than fifteen feet high, and some of the ears had from four to seven hundred grains. I believe I saw more peaches and apples rotting on the ground than would sink the British fleet. I was at many plantations in Ohio where they no more knew the number of their hogs than myself. And they have such flocks of turkeys, geese, ducks, and hens as would surprise you; they live principally upon fowls and eggs, and in summer upon apple and peach pies. The poorest family has a cow or two and some sheep and in the fall can gather as many apples and peaches as serve the year round. Good rye whisky; apple and peach brandy, at forty cents per gallon, which I think equal to rum. Excellent cider at three dollars per barrel of thirty-three gallons, barrel included.

There is enough to spare of everything a person can desire; have not heard either man or woman speak a word against the government or the price of provisions.

The poorest families adorn the table three times a day like a wedding dinner — tea, coffee, beef, fowls, pies, eggs, pickles, good bread; and their favorite beverage is whisky or peach brandy. Say, is it so in England?

If you knew the difference between this country and England you would need no persuading to leave it and come hither. It abounds with game and deer; I often see ten or fifteen together; turkeys in abundance, weighing from eighteen to twenty-four pounds. The rivers abound with ducks and fish. There are some elk and bears. We have no hares, but swarms of rabbits: the woods are full of turtledoves, and eight or nine kinds of woodpeckers. Robin redbreast about the size of your pigeon.

SAMUEL CRABTREE, Letter to His Brother (1818)

62. Davy Crockett Runs for the Legislature in Tennessee

The noted Tennessee Indian-fighter, bear-killer, and pioneer, Davy Crockett, was jocularly proposed for Congress, got elected, and served three terms there. His frontier exploits, his exuberant self-confidence, his rough good humor, and his shrewd wit made him a national figure in Jacksonian days. Crockett's "tour of the North" in 1834 resulted in the publication of his so-called autobiography, clearly written by some hand not his own, but authentically reflecting his spirit and retailing many of his adventures. Two years later he was to die in the heroic defense of the Alamo.

I JUST now began to take a rise, as in a little time I was asked to offer for the Legislature in the counties of Lawrence and Heckman.

I offered my name in the month of February, and started about the first of March with a drove of horses to the lower part of the state of North Carolina. This was in the year 1821, and I was gone upwards of three months. I returned and set out electioneering, which was a bran-fire new business to me. It now became necessary that I should tell the people something about the government, and an eternal sight of other things that I knowed nothing more about than I did about Latin and law and such things as that. I have said before that in those days none of us called General Jackson the government, nor did he seem in as fair way to become so as I do now; but I knowed so little about it that if anyone had told me he was "the government," I should have believed it, for I had never read even a newspaper in my life, or anything else, on the subject. But over all my difficulties, it seems to me I was born for luck, though it would be hard for any one to guess what sort. I will, however, explain that hereafter.

I went first into Heckman County to see what I could do among the people as a candidate. Here they told me that they wanted to move their town nearer to the center of the county, and I must come out in favor of it. There's no devil if I knowed what this meant, or how the town was to be moved; and so I kept dark, going on the identical same plan that I now find is called *noncommittal*. About this time there was a great squirrel hunt on Duck River, which was among my people. They were to hunt two days, then to meet and count the scalps and have a big barbecue, and what might be called a tiptop country frolic. The dinner, and a general treat, was all to be paid for by the party having taken the fewest scalps. I joined one side, taking the place of one of the hunters, and got a gun ready for the hunt. I killed a great many squirrels, and when we counted scalps, my party was victorious.

The party had everything to eat and drink that could be furnished in so new a country, and much fun and good humor prevailed. But before the regular frolic commenced, I mean the dancing, I was called on to make a speech as a candidate, which was a business I was as ignorant of as an outlandish Negro.

A public document I had never seen, nor did I know there were any such things; and how to begin I couldn't tell. I made many apologies and tried to get off, for I knowed I had a man to run against who could speak prime, and I knowed too that I wa'n't able to shuffle and cut with him. He was there, and knowing my ignorance as well as I did myself, he also urged me to make a speech. The truth is, he thought my being a candidate was a mere matter of sport, and didn't think for a moment that he was in any danger from an ignorant backwoods bear hunter. But I found I couldn't get off, and so I determined just to go ahead, and leave it to chance what I should say. I got up and told the people I reckoned they knowed what I come for, but if not, I could tell them. I had come for their votes, and if they didn't watch mighty close, I'd get them too. But the worst of all was, that I couldn't tell them anything about government. I tried to speak about something, and I cared very little what, until I choked up as bad as if my mouth had been jammed and crammed chock-full of dry mush. There the people stood, listening all the while, with their eyes, mouths, and years all open to catch every word I would speak.

At last I told them I was like a fellow I had heard of not long before. He was beating on the head of an empty barrel near the road-side when a traveler who was passing along asked him what he was doing that for. The fellow replied that there was some cider in that barrel a few days before and he was trying to see if there was any then, but if there was, he couldn't get at it. I told them that there had been a little bit of speech in me awhile ago, but I believed I couldn't get it out. They all roared out in a mighty laugh and I told some other anecdotes, equally amusing to them; and believing I had them in a first-rate way, I quit and got down, thanking the people for their attention. But I took care to remark that I was as dry as a powder horn and that I thought it was time for us to wet our whistles a little; and so I put off to the liquor stand and was followed by the greater part of the crowd.

I felt certain this was necessary, for I knowed my competitor could open government matters to them as easy as he pleased. He had, however, mighty few left to hear him as I continued with the crowd, now and then taking a horn and telling good-humored stories till he was done speaking. I found I was good for the votes at the hunt, and when we broke up, I went on to the town of Vernon, which was the same they wanted me to move. Here they pressed me again on the subject, and I found I could get either party by agreeing with them. But I told them I didn't know whether it would be right or not, and so couldn't promise either way.

Their court commenced on the next Monday, as the barbecue was on a Saturday, and the candidates for governor and for Congress as well as my competitor and myself all attended.

The thought of having to make a speech made my knees feel mighty weak and set my heart to fluttering almost as bad as my first love scrape with the Quaker's niece. But as good luck would have it, these big candidates spoke nearly all day, and when they quit, the people were worn out with fatigue, which afforded me a good apology for not discussing the government. But I listened mighty close to them, and was learning pretty fast about political matters. When they were all done, I got up and told some laughable story and quit. I found I was safe in those parts, and so I went home and didn't go back again till after the election was over. But to cut this matter short, I was elected, doubling my competitor and nine votes over.

A short time after this, I was in Pulaski, where I met with Colonel Polk, now a member of Congress from Tennessee. He was at that time a member elected to the Legislature as well as myself; and in a large company he said to me, "Well, Colonel, I suppose we shall have a radical change of the judiciary at the next session of the Legislature." "Very likely, sir," says I, and I put out quicker, for I was afraid some one would ask me what the judiciary was; and if I knowed I wish I may be shot. I don't indeed believe I had ever before heard that there was any such thing in all nature, but still I was not willing that the people there should know how ignorant I was about it.

When the time for meeting of the Legislature arrived, I went on, and before I had been there long, I could have told what the judiciary was, and what the government was too; and many other things that I had known nothing about before.

A Narrative of the Life of David Crockett

63. Timothy Flint Appraises the Frontiersmen

Not all accounts of the frontier were exuberantly favorable. Some observers drew harsh pictures of its squalor, hardships, and uncouthness. A balanced description was offered by Timothy Flint, a Harvard graduate and missionary who spent a decade, beginning in 1816, in church work in the Mississippi Valley. He said much about the crudeness, drudgery, and disappointments of life in pioneer communities; but, as the following pages show, he thought these difficulties an excellent school for character.

THE PEOPLE in the Atlantic states have not yet recovered from the horror inspired by the term "backwoodsman." This prejudice is particularly strong in New England, and is more or less felt from Maine to Georgia. When I first visited this country, I had my full share, and my family by far too much for their comfort. In approaching the country, I heard a thousand stories of gougings, and robberies, and shooting down with the rifle. I have traveled in these regions thousands of miles under all circumstances of exposure and danger. I have traveled alone, or in company only with such as needed protection, instead of being able to impart it; and this too, in many instances, where I was not known as a minister, or where such knowledge would have had no influence in protecting me. I never have carried the slightest weapon of defense. I scarcely remember to have experienced anything that resembled insult, or to have felt myself in danger from the people. I have often seen men that had lost an eye. Instances of murder, numerous and horrible in their circumstances, have occurred in my vicinity. But they were such lawless rencounters as terminate in murder everywhere, and in which the drunkenness, brutality, and violence were mutual. They were catastrophes in which quiet and sober men would be in no danger of being involved. When we look round these immense regions and consider that I have been in settlements three hundred miles from any court of justice, when we look at the position of the men and the state of things, the wonder is that so few outrages and murders occur. The gentlemen of the towns, even here, [Louisiana] speak often with a certain contempt and horror of the backwoodsmen. It is true there are worthless people here; it is true there are gamblers and gougers and outlaws; but there are fewer of them than, from the nature of things and the character of the age and the world, we ought to expect. But the backwoodsman of the west, as I have seen him, is generally an amiable and virtuous man. His general motive for coming here is to be a freeholder, to have plenty of rich land, and to be able to settle his children about him. It is a most virtuous motive. And I fully believe that nine in ten of the emigrants have come here with no other motive. You find, in truth, that he has vices and barbarisms peculiar to his situation. His manners are rough. He wears, it may be, a long beard. He has a great quantity of bear- or deerskins wrought into his household establishment, his furniture and dress. He carries a knife or a dirk in his bosom, and when in the woods has a rifle on his back and a pack of dogs at his heels. An Atlantic stranger, transferred directly from one of our cities to his door, would recoil from a rencounter with him. But remember that his rifle and his dogs are among his chief means of support and profit. Remember that all his first days here were passed in dread of the savages. Remember that he still encounters them, still meets bears and panthers. Enter his door and tell him you are benighted and wish the shelter of his cabin for the night. The welcome is indeed seemingly ungracious: "I reckon you can stay," or "I suppose we must let you stay." But this apparent ungraciousness is the harbinger of every kindness that he can bestow and every comfort that his cabin can afford. Good coffee, corn bread and butter, venison, pork, wild and tame fowls, are set before you. His wife, timid, silent, reserved, but constantly attentive to your comfort, does not sit at the table with you, but, like the wives of the patriarchs, stands and attends on you. You are shown to the best bed which the house can afford. When this kind of hospitality has been afforded you as long as you choose to stay, and when you depart and speak about your bill, you are most commonly told with some slight mark of resentment that they do not keep tavern. Even the flaxen-headed urchins will turn away from your money.

In all my extensive intercourse with these people, I do not recollect but one instance of positive rudeness and inhospitality. . . .

I have found the backwoodsmen to be such as I have described — a hardy, adventurous, hospitable, rough, but sincere and upright race of people. I have received so many kindnesses from them that it becomes me always to preserve a grateful and affectionate remembrance of them. If we were to try them by the standard of New England customs and opinions, that is to say, the customs of a people under entirely different circumstances, there would be many things in the picture that would strike us offensively. They care little about ministers and think less about paying them. They are averse to all, even the most necessary, restraints. They are destitute of the forms and observances of society and religion, but they are sincere and kind without professions, and have a coarse but substantial morality, which is often rendered more striking by the immediate contrast of the graceful bows, civility, and professions of their French Catholic neighbors, who have the observances of society and the forms of worship with often but a scanty modicum of the blunt truth and uprightness of their unpolished neighbors.

I have spoken of the movable part of the community, and unfortunately for the western country, it constitutes too great a proportion of the whole community. The general inclination here is too much like that of the Tartars. Next to hunting, Indian wars, and the wonderful exuberance of Kentucky, the favorite topic is new countries. They only make such improvements as they can leave without reluctance and without loss. I have everywhere noted the operation of this impediment in the way of those permanent and noble improvements which grow out of a love for that appropriated spot where we were born and where we expect to die.

> TIMOTHY FLINT, Recollections of the Last Ten
> Years [1815–1825]

64. Milburn Rides the Circuit in Western Virginia

The circuit rider or traveling clergyman and missionary was familiar in America from the earliest years of the Methodist and Baptist churches. Many of these men had little training except what they picked up in "Swamp College and Brush University," but they performed an important cultural and religious work none the less. They met the perils of Indian and outlaw, flood and storm, panther and wolf, without hesitation. They traveled long distances on horseback, slept at night on shuck mattresses, and lived on hog and hominy. No circuit rider was more heroic than William Henry Milburn, born in Philadelphia and reared on the Illinois frontier, who though at first half and then completely blind, in wretched health, and long almost penniless, worked for years in the South and West, and finally became a well-known lecturer. Here he describes his own early days.

BY WAY of administering a sound reproof to him for being handsome and looking well in his clothes, his superiors sent him one year [1847] — the fourth of his ministry — to a region of country where it was thought he would be broken down or broken in. He had already seen hard service; more than once had he ridden at full speed, chased by a pack of yelling Indians, their bullets whistling round him like hail. He had become familiar with all manner of exposure and privation, but it was thought that this circuit would put him to the uttermost test. It was a wild, mountainous tract in western Virginia, sparsely populated by hunters, who were there for the game and peltry.

You may see him riding up some evening to the door of a cabin, where he is to lodge, and as it is a pretty fair specimen of the houses in the country, you may desire a description of it. The cabin is twelve by fourteen feet, and one story high. The spaces between the logs are chinked and then daubed with mud for plaster. The interior consists of one room, one end of which is occupied by a fireplace. In this one room are to sleep the man, his wife, the fifteen or twenty children bestowed upon them by Providence — for Providence is bountiful in this matter upon the border — and as the woods are full of "varmints," hens and chickens must be brought in for safekeeping, and as the dogs constitute an important portion of every hunter's family, they also take potluck with the rest. Fastened to a tree near the door is a clapboard upon which is traced in characters of charcoal a sentence to the following effect — which you may read if you are keen at deciphering hieroglyphics: "Akomidation fur man and Beast."

In this one room the family are to perform their manifold household offices. Here their sleeping, cooking, eating, washing, preaching, and hearing are to be performed. Amid the driving storms of winter, it is of course impossible for our youthful theologian to transform an old log or the shadow of a tree into a study; his book must therefore be carried into the house, where he is surrounded by a motley group. Of course a hunter never swears in bad weather; the lady of the house never scolds; children of all ages never quarrel and raise a row; dogs never bark and fight; nevertheless, you may imagine that if our student is able to confine his attention to the page, deriving mental nutriment from the lettered line, he must possess not a little power of concentration and abstraction. He may obtain permission of his host to pursue his studies after the rest of the family have retired. Lighting a pine knot, he sticks it up in one corner of the huge fireplace, lays himself down on the flat of his stomach in the ashes, glowing with transport over "the thoughts that breathe and words that burn." These are what poets call "midnight oil" and "cloisters pale." Not a few men have I known who acquired a mastery of the Latin and Greek tongue and much valuable and curious lore in such "grottoes and caves" as these.

Possibly there may be another apartment in the cabin. If so, it is denominated the "prophet's chamber." You gain access to it by a rickety stepladder in one corner of the cabin. Toiling up this steep ascent you reach a loft, formed by laying loose clapboards on the rafters. With dubious tread and careful steps you pick your way across the floor. I have said the clapboards are loose, and if you are not cautious, one end will fly up and the other down, in company with which latter you will be precipitated upon the sleepers below. Having reached the opposite end of the loft, the prophet's bed is discovered. It is a bearskin, a buffaloskin, or a tick filled with shucks. Having laid him on his couch, our prophet, if he be thoughtfully inclined, can study astronomy from his resting place, through the rifts in the roof; and when it rains or snows, he has the benefit of the hydropathic treatment without fee or prescription.

Many a time was the bare, bleak mountainside his bed, the wolves yelling a horrid chorus in his ears. Sometimes he was fortunate enough to find a hollow log within whose cavity he inserted his body and found it a good protection from the rain or frost.

Sitting one fine summer afternoon beneath the shadow of a noble tree, intently studying his book, he heard a rustling in the branches above, then a low warning *whist* from some one near at hand, followed by the sharp crack of a rifle. Crashing through the branches there falls upon the ground at his feet a huge panther. The beast had been crouching in preparation for a deadly spring, when a ball from the rifle of his hunter host saved his life.

Once, seated at the puncheon dinner table with a hunter's family, the party is startled by affrighted screams from the dooryard. Rushing out, they behold a great wildcat bearing off the youngest child. Seizing a rifle from the pegs over the door, the preacher raises it to his shoulder, casts a rapid glance along the barrel, and delivers his fire. The aim has been unerring, but too late — the child is dead, already destroyed by the fierce animal.

That same year he had a hand-to-hand fight with a bear, from which conflict he came forth victor, his knife entering the vitals of the creature just as he was about to be enfolded in the fatal hug.

He must ford or swim mountain torrents as they boil and rush along their downward channels, in cold weather as in warm. Often he emerged from the wintry stream, his garments glittering in the clear, cold sunlight, as if they had been of burnished steel armor, chill as the touch of death. During that twelvemonth, in the midst of such scenes, he traveled on foot and horseback four thousand miles, preached four hundred times, and found on casting up the receipts — yarn socks, woolen vests, cotton shirts, and a little silver change — that his salary amounted to twelve dollars and ten cents.

Undaunted by the suspicions of his brethren, their fears that he would not make a preacher, by the hardships and perils of the way, he persevered.

WILLIAM HENRY MILBURN, The Pioneer Preacher

XII

New Settlements in the Wilderness

65. William Howells Remembers Neighborliness in Ohio

William Cooper Howells — father of the novelist William Dean Howells — was one of the notable editors of Ohio in the generation before the Civil War; migrating from town to town, editing one small journal after another, he upheld Whig principles and the antislavery cause. His recollections were later edited by his more famous son, who himself in some of his novels turned to the scenes here described.

I CAN hardly realize how greatly things have changed since that period, and what a primitive and simple kind of life prevailed. Particularly remarkable was the general equality and the general dependence of all upon the neighborly kindness and good offices of others. Their houses and barns were built of logs, and were raised by the collection of many neighbors together on one day, whose united strength was necessary to the handling of the logs. As every man was ready with the ax and understood this work, all came together within the circle where the raising was to be done, and all worked together with about equal skill. The best axmen were given charge of the placing of the logs on the wall, and some one of experience took the general direction. The logs of the width and length of the house were usually of different lengths. Those intended for the two sides were placed in a convenient place, some distance from the foundation; those for the ends, in another place. The first two side logs were put in place at the back and front; then the end logs were notched down in their places; then two side logs would be rolled up on skids, and notched in their places. At the corners the top of the log, as soon as it was put in place, would be dressed up by the cornerman; and when the next logs were rolled up they would be notched, which notch would be turned downwards upon the saddle made to receive it, when the cornerman would saddle that log ready for the next. This kept the logs in their places like a dovetail and brought them together so as to form a closer wall. The ends of the skids would be raised on each new log as it was laid down to make a way for the next. The logs on these skids would be rolled as long as the men could handle them from the ground, but when the wall got too high, then they would use forks, made by cutting a young notched tree, with which the logs would be pushed up. By using a fork at each end of the log, it could be pushed up with ease and safety. The men understood handling timber, and accidents seldom happened, unless the logs were icy or wet or the whisky had gone round too often. I was often at these raisings, because we had raisings of the kind to do, and it was the custom always to send one from a family to help, so that you could claim like assistance in return. At the raisings I would take the position of cornerman, if the building was not too heavy, as it was a post of honor, and my head was steady when high up from the ground. In chopping on the corners we always stood up straight, and it required a good balance.

This kind of mutual help of the neighbors was extended to many kinds of work, such as rolling up the logs in a clearing, grubbing out the underbrush, splitting rails, cutting logs for a house, and the like. When a gathering of men for such a purpose took place there was commonly some sort of mutual job laid out for women, such as quilting, sewing, or spinning up a lot of thread for some poor neighbor. This would bring together a mixed party, and it was usually arranged that after supper there should be a dance or at least plays which would occupy a good part of the night and wind up with the young fellows seeing the girls home in the short hours or, if they went home early, sitting with them by the fire in that kind of interesting chat known as sparking.

The flax crops required a good deal of handling, in weeding, pulling, and dressing, and each of these processes was made the occasion of a joint gathering of boys and girls and a good time. As I look back now upon those times, I am puzzled to think how they managed to make such small and crowded houses serve for large parties, and how they found room to dance in an apartment of perhaps eighteen feet square, in which there would be two large beds and a trundle bed, besides the furniture, which though not of great quantity, took some room. And then, if these were small houses, they often contained large families. I have often seen three or four little heads peeping out from that part of a trundle bed that was not pushed entirely under the big bed, to get their share of the fun going on among the older ones while the big beds were used to receive the hats and bonnets and perhaps a baby or two, stowed away till the mothers were ready to go home.

One of the gatherings for joint work which has totally disappeared from the agriculture of modern times, and one that was always a jolly kind of affair, was the cornhusking. It was a sort of harvest home in its department, and it was the more jolly because it was a gathering with very little respect to persons, and embraced in the invitation men and big boys, with the understanding that no one would be unwelcome. There was always a good supper served at the husking, and as certainly a good appetite to eat it with. It came at a plentiful season, when the turkeys and chickens were fat, and a fat pig was at hand, to be flanked on the table with good bread in various forms, turnips and potatoes from the autumn stores, apple and pumpkin pies, good coffee and the like. And the cooking was always well done, and all in such bountiful abundance that no one feared to eat, while many a poor fellow was certain of a square meal by being present at a husking. You were sure to see the laboring men of the vicinity out, and the wives of a goodly number of farm hands would be on hand to help in the cooking and serving at the table. The cornhusking has been discontinued because the farmers found out that it was less trouble to husk it in the field, direct from the stalk, than to gather in the husk and go over it again. But in that day they did not know that much and therefore took the original method of managing their corn crop, which was this: as soon as the grain began to harden they would cut the stalks off just above the ears and save these tops for fodder, and if they had time they stripped all the blades off the stalks below the ears, which made very nice though costly feed. Then, as barn room was not usually overplenty, they made a kind of frame of poles, as for a tent, and thatched it, sides and top, with the corn tops placed with the tassel downward, so as to shed the rain and snow. This was called the fodder house and was built in the barn-yard. Inside they would store the blades in bundles, the husks, and the pumpkins that were saved for use in the winter. The fodder house was commonly made ten feet high and as long as was neces-sary, and it was used up through the winter by feeding the fodder to the cattle, beginning at the back, which would be temporarily closed by a few bundles of the tops. It would thus serve as a pro-tection for what might be stored in it till all was used up. The fod-der house was, of all things, a favorite place for the children to hide in and play. When the season for gathering the corn came the farmers went through the fields and pulled off the ears and husks together, throwing them upon the ground in heaps, whence they were hauled into the barnyard and there piled up in a neat pile of convenient length, according to the crop, and say four or five feet high, rising to a sharp peak from a base of about six feet. Care was taken to make this pile of equal width and height from end to end, so that it would be easily and fairly divided in the middle by a rail laid upon it.

When the husking party had assembled they were all called out into line, and two fellows, mostly ambitious boys, were chosen cap-tains. These then chose their men, each calling out one of the crowd alternately, till all were chosen. Then the heap was divided, by two judicious chaps walking solemnly along the ridge of the heap of corn, and deciding where the dividing rail was to be laid, and, as this had to be done by starlight or moonlight at best, it took con-siderable deliberation, as the comparative solidity of the ends of the heap and the evenness of it had to be taken into account. This done, the captains placed a good steady man at each side of the rail, who made it a point to work through and cut the heap in two as soon as possible; and then the two parties fell to husking, all standing with the heap in front of them, and throwing the husked corn on to a clear space over the heap, and the husks behind them. From the time they began till the corn was all husked at one end, there would be steady work, each man husking all the corn he could, never stopping except to take a pull at the stone jug of in-spiration that passed occasionally along the line; weak lovers of the stuff were sometimes overcome, though it was held to be a dis-graceful thing to take too much. The captains would go up and down their lines and rally their men as if in a battle, and the whole was an exciting affair. As soon as one party got done, they raised a shout, and hoisting their captain on their shoulders, carried him over to the other side with general cheering. Then would come a little bantering talk and explanation why the defeated party lost, and all would turn to and husk up the remnants of the heap. All hands would then join to carry the husks into the fodder house. The shout at hoisting the captain was the signal for bringing the supper on the table, and the huskers and the supper met soon after. These gatherings often embraced forty or fifty men. If the farmhouse was small it would be crowded, and the supper would be managed by repeated sittings at the table. At a large house there was less crowding and more fun, and if, as was often the case, some occasion had been given for an assemblage of the girls of the neighborhood, and particularly if the man that played the fiddle should attend, after the older men had gone there was very apt to be a good time. There was a tradition that the boys who accidentally husked a red ear and saved it would be entitled to a kiss from somebody. But I never knew it to be necessary to produce a red ear to secure a kiss where there was a disposition to give or take one.

WILLIAM COOPER HOWELLS, Recollections of Life in Ohio from 1813 to 1840

66. Grandmother Brown Recalls Her Ohio Home

Mrs. Maria D. Brown celebrated her hundredth birthday at Fort Madison, Iowa, in 1927. Her parents had told her of events in colonial and Revolutionary days; she vividly remembered the pioneer movement to the Northwest. Born in the Hocking Valley while it was still wild, she herself, as her daughter-in-law writes, "had joined in the great migration down the Ohio, helping to carry forward the customs and ideals of the English-speaking world into the wilderness that lay beyond the Mississippi."

AFTER periods at the Brice House or in Logan or Somerset, we were always glad to get back to our own father's dear old home. Nowhere else did we have the same conveniences. We did most of our work there in the summer kitchen. That was where we had the big brick oven. We used to fire it twice a week and do a sight o' baking all at once. We'd make a hot fire in the oven, and then, when the bricks were thoroughly heated, we'd scrape out all the coals with a big iron scraper, dump the coals into the fireplace, and shove in the roasts and fowls, the pies and bread. At other times we'd use the open fireplace. It wasn't nearly so difficult to work by as people think. When we went to keeping house in 1845, Dan'l and I, he bought me a little iron stove, a new thing in those days. It was no good, and would only bake things on one side. I soon went back to cooking at an open fireplace.

You know the look of andirons, crane, spit, reflectors. Our heavy iron vessels were swung from chains. When we wanted to lift the iron lids off, we'd have to reach in with a hook and swing them off. They had a flange around the edge. Many of our dishes were baked in Dutch ovens on the hearth. We used to bake Indian pone — that is, bread made of rye and corn meal — that way. We would set it off in a corner of the hearth covered with coals and ashes, and there it would bake slowly all night long. In the morning the crust would be thick but soft — oh, *so* good.

For roasting meat we had reflectors. Some joints we roasted in our big iron kettles with a bit of water. And others we put on three-legged gridirons which could be turned. These had a little fluted place for the gravy to run down. Chickens we could split down the back and lay on the gridiron with a plate and flatirons on top to hold them down. Oh, how different, how different, is everything now, encumbered with conveniences!

The difference between those who were naturally clean and orderly and those who were not was perhaps more marked in those days than it is now. It was so easy, for instance, since we had no screens, to let the flies spoil everything. My mother just wouldn't have it so. We weren't allowed to bring apples into the house in summer, because apples attract flies. If any of us dropped a speck of butter or cream on the floor, she had to run at once for a cloth to wipe it up. Our kitchen floor was of ash, and Ma was very proud of keeping it white. In the summer kitchen the floor was of brick, and it was expected to be spotless also. At mealtime someone stood and fanned to keep the flies away while the others ate. When Sister Libbie went to housekeeping, she had little round-topped screens for every dish on her table. That was considered quite stylish. Ma used to set some tall thing in the centre of her table, spread a cloth over it, and slip food under until we were ready to sit down. As soon as the meal was finished, all curtains had to be pulled down and the flies driven from the darkened room.

Our dishes for common use were white with blue edges. The finer ones were a figured blue. I remember, also, a large blue soup tureen with a cover and a blue, long-handled ladle, all very handsome.

Our forks were two-tined. They weren't much good for holding some things. But if we used our knives for conveying food to our mouths it had to be done with the back of the knife towards the face. We had no napkins. We used our handkerchiefs. Tablecloths were made of cotton diaper especially woven for the purpose. The first white bedspread I ever had was made of two widths of that same cotton whitened on the grass.

In warm weather we washed outdoors under the quince bushes. We used our well water. It was so soft, it was just beautiful. We'd draw a barrel of water, put one shovel of ashes into it, and it would just suds up like soft water, so white and clean. We used soft soap, of course. Our starch was of two kinds — either made from a dough of flour worked round and round until it was smooth and fine or made from grated potato cooked to the right consistency.

Ma put us girls to work early. It was taken as a matter of course that we should learn all kinds of housework. I know that before I was seven years old I used to wash the dishes. But our mother had village girls to help her also. I remember one Ann Fierce who was with us for years, but it seems to me that Sister Libbie and I usually did the washing. There was need of many hands to get all the work done. It required more knowledge to do the things for everyday living than is the case nowadays. If one wants light now, all one has to do is pull a string or push a button. Then, we had to pick up a coal with tongs, hold it against a candle, and blow. And one had to make the candles, perhaps.

I remember the first matches that I ever saw. Someone handed me a little bunch of them, fastened together at the bottom in a solid block of wood about a half inch square. "Lucifer matches" they called them. I tore one off and set the whole thing afire.

Some people had tinder boxes. Some kept a kind of punk which would give off a spark when struck with steel or knife. Generally speaking, people kept the fire on their hearthstones going year in and year out.

We did not make our candles at home, but got them usually from Uncle Dean, who made candles for the town. I used to love to watch him and Aunt Maria at work dipping candles — she with the hot tallow in a big kettle on the hearth, he with stillyards beside him, weighing carefully. Occasionally we had some sperm candles made of fine whale tallow. Besides candles, people sometimes burned sperm or whale oil in little lamps that looked like square-topped candlesticks. In the square top was a place for a bowl that would hold perhaps a half pint of oil.

Even without candle making, there was certainly a plenty to do to keep life going in those days. Baking, washing, ironing, sewing, kept us busy. Not to mention the spinning and weaving that had to be done before cloth was available for the seamstress.

My mother used to spin. She made beautiful fine thread. She taught Sister Libbie how to spin, but decided, before my turn came, that spinning was doomed to become a lost art, and that I might be better employed in some other way. I used to love to watch her at the spinning wheel. She had two wheels, lovely big ones. She used a wheel boy to turn her wheel. I can just close my eyes and see Ma standing over there spinning a thread as far as from here to the bed — say, twelve feet long.

My mother and her sister had some beautiful woolen cloth of their own spinning and weaving. Part of the thread was made with the open, part with the crossed, band. They colored it with butternut bark, but the two kinds would never color alike, so that part of it was a light and part a dark brown. They wove it into a plaid and had it pressed, and then they made fine dresses out of it to wear to church. I remember, too, that my mother raised flax, spun it into linen, wove it into cloth, — colored blue in the yarn, — made it up into a dress for me which she embroidered in white above the hem. I wish I had kept that dress to show my children the beautiful work of their grandmother.

Ma used to use Aunt Betsy's loom sometimes. When I was eight years old, she wove me a plaid dress of which I was very proud. I remember the pattern: eight threads of brown, then one of red, one of blue, one of red, then brown again, both in the warp and in the woof. It made the prettiest flannel, and that dress lasted me for years.

Women made their own designs for cloth as well as for dresses in those days. If a woman had taste, she had a chance to show it in her weaving. But, oh, it was hard work. You never saw warping bars, did you? Clumsy things, long as a bed. On them work was prepared for the loom. You had to draw each thread through a reed. I used to love to watch my mother weaving, her shuttle holding the spool with yarn shooting through the warp, then back the other way. When she had woven as far as she could reach, she would bend below the loom and wind the woven cloth into a roll beneath. Blankets made at home used to last a long, long time. Homespun things were good.

We had all the things that were really necessary for our comfort in those days, and we had quite as much leisure as people have now. Always, too, we had time to attend church and Sunday school.

HARRIET CONNOR BROWN, Grandmother Brown's Hundred Years

67. Grandmother Brown Moves to Iowa

The pioneers were rarely content to stay long in one place. Grandmother Brown would have preferred to stay in her Ohio home, but the men were attracted by tales of richer lands to the west. It was an old story, often repeated. It hastened the settlement of the West, but it was cruelly hard on the women.

 AND so it was that the Brown family came to Iowa.

"How did it seem to you when you got over your excitement about the gold and looked around you?" I asked Grandmother Brown.

"Oh, my heart sank. 'Don't let's unpack our goods,' I said to Dan'l. 'It looks so wild here. Let's go home.' But we had bought the farm and there we were.

"We lived there fourteen years, and I was never reconciled to it. I had never lived in the country before. The drudgery was unending. The isolation was worse. In time, we knew a few families with whom we had friendly relations, but they were very few. At first we had the Oliver Browns across the way. They were always great readers, were educated and sent their children away to school. But they were frontiersmen by nature, always moving west, and a couple of years after we came to Iowa they sold their farm and moved on.

"We had a good farm of rich black soil. But it is people that really make a country, not soil. Those who had settled in that neighborhood were of American stock, but it was poor in quality. I like to be with people who know something, who want something. One of our neighbors let three years go by before she came to see us. 'I woulda come before,' she said, 'but I heard you had Brussels carpet on the floor!' Why, she should have come to see what it was like. She was mistaken about the carpet, anyway.

"Soon after we came to our farm there was a Fourth of July celebration not far from us in a grove on Lost Creek. I packed a picnic luncheon and took my children over. Long tables were set for dinner. There was plenty to eat of a kind — but the people had no more manners than so many pigs. They stared not only at us, but particularly at the jelly cake I had set on the table. Without apology, they grabbed at my cake and gobbled it down.

"The nearest town to us was Augusta," continued Grandmother Brown. "It was about two miles away on Skunk River, a narrow winding little stream not entirely without beauty. Augusta once showed some signs of life, though not a very cultivated life. It had two mills and two blacksmith shops, and several stores. But now it's a strip of desolation, all grown up with weeds. You can't find it on the map.

"Denmark was a pretty village, a really charming town in some respects. It had an air of refinement. It had been settled by educated people from the East. They had a fine academy and a good church there. But it was five miles from us, and five miles in days of bad roads was a real barrier. We could not often spare the time or use the horses to drive so far to church. The first Sunday we were at the farm we drove to the poor little church on Lost Creek. It used to have two front doors. Men went in one and women in the other. When a man and wife from town came in and sat beside each other, the children giggled."

"And what a woodsy congregation it was!" sighed Grandmother Brown. "Lizzie kept whispering that first Sunday: 'Oh, Mother, I'd rather be in Ohio. I'd rather hear Aunt Ann sing!' It brought tears to my eyes and a homesick lump to my throat to hear her carry on so. It was just the way I felt. . . . But it was only once in a great while that we could go to church. If the horses were used all week, they needed rest on Sunday. And we were tired ourselves and glad to be quiet at home. It was a lonely life. Practically no close neighbors or associates for fourteen years!"

"Was your land virgin soil?" I asked Grandmother Brown.

"Much of it had never been broken," she answered, "but the farm was twenty years old when we bought it. It had been entered with the Government by old Uncle William, Oliver Brown's father. He sold it to a man named Thompson, and we bought it from him. Dan'l paid $17.50 an acre for that farm. There were two hundred and two acres, which was about the average size of the farms in the neighborhood. The two acres were thrown in extra. Eighty of the two hundred and two acres were timber land, a grove of walnut trees on Skunk River. The timber was used most wastefully. The best logs were cut. There was an old log house on the place that had a siding of walnut boards and a roofing an inch thick made out of walnut logs. The granary and barn were also made of wide walnut boards. Such wastefulness!

"Just think," said Grandmother Brown solemnly, "if Dan'l had only been a financier, those eighty acres of walnut trees would have enabled him to die a rich man. But then, what's the use of fretting about it now? We lived and worked and had our being, and burned that nice walnut wood in our stoves, and kept our house warm and comfortable. Otherwise there was no wastefulness in that house of ours. Four rooms with cellar and attic was all we got. It was a well-built, good house painted white, but without a single extra thing. No shutters, no porch, no closets. Not even a nail to hang a dishrag on! Just house!

"The biggest room was used as joint kitchen and dining room. In it we installed our good St. Louis cookstove. I missed the open fires of Ohio. I remember that I thought it pathetic when Gus asked me one time in his childhood what a 'mantelpiece' was. Across the tiny hallway was a sitting room from which a door opened outdoors. The two other rooms were bedrooms, and sometimes we had a bed in the sitting room, too. In the attic there was a window at either end. On either side of each window we put up beds — those at one end for our boys, those at the other for hired hands, when we had them.

"All about the house, at first, was a tangle of hazel brush. It grew so close about us that the cows couldn't get between it and the house. It was wild enough when we first came there, but when we left, after fourteen years, it was pretty much all under cultivation. All our stock was under shelter. At first we had only a log barn, but later we built two new barns, one with a fine stone basement with room for our carriage and with five stalls for horses. Once we had reached the farm we had very little use for our carriage and for our silver-mounted harness — a rarity in Iowa. One of the first things that Dan'l did was to get me some muslin in Fort Madison, and I made a cover for that beautiful carriage. We set it away on the threshing floor and kept it clean and bright until we had a chance to sell it in later years.

"Another useless luxury in the first years was our Brussels carpet. Until we had walks and fences and an orderly domain, it was folly to spread out carpets. I was thankful if I could keep my bare floors clean. I can remember how Charlie would say in the harvest time: 'Come on, boys, turn down your pants and shake out the chaff; don't carry it upstairs.' But, oh, how Grandpa Brown would stamp in with chunks of mud hanging to his boots! And so it was several years before our Brussels carpet was unrolled. Not until we had a nice board fence all around the house and garden.

"In time the place came to look rather nice. No amount of cultivation could make it beautiful in the sense that the hills around Athens are beautiful. It was doomed to be flat and uninteresting by comparison. We had so many more birds then than we have now. One time I shall never forget. I was washing outdoors on the shady side of the house and I heard a bird with an unfamiliar note. I left my washing and followed it into the orchard, where I saw it quite plainly. I rushed into the house and consulted the bird book I had bought for my children. A Baltimore oriole! They build their nests of thread. Isn't it wonderful how a bird can do that — take thread and weave a nest for its babies and line it soft and nice with feathers from its own breast?

"At night it used to make me so lonesome, sitting at the front door in the dusk — we had supper at five o'clock — to hear the prairie chickens calling over the meadow, 'Boo-hoo! Boo-hoo! Boo-hoo!' Charlie could make a noise exactly like their three calls.

" 'Twas sufficiently settled up in Iowa by the time we got there so that there were no prairie wolves about. We were too late for the Indians, also. They too had gone before we came. But once, driving home from Fort Madison, Dan'l did overtake two braves. He asked them to ride. When he reached home they sat down under a tree in the yard. I fixed up a big trayful of good things to eat and sent it out to them. There they squatted in paint and feathers, showing their nakedness as they ate. They were the first Indians I ever saw.

"One thing we did have in Iowa that was terrifying. That was thunder and lightning. I don't remember that the Iowa storms ever hurt our crops, but the lightning tore a splinter out of a walnut tree and tied it around a little tree in the yard. I never shall forget the crash that shook the house when that happened.

"Oh, those were busy days! Besides the everyday routine of cooking, cleaning, washing, ironing, and baby tending, there were many things to be done that nowadays women might consider extras. I never did any gardening — that was thought to be men's work in our house — and I never milked any cows or made the cheese. But I looked after the chickens and eggs and butter. We stocked up with big Shanghais, but we couldn't afford to live on chickens that first year. I would never sell all our cream, but always saved enough to make good butter. I never made soft, runny butter; you could always cut a slice off *my* butter. Only the other day, Lizzie said to me: 'I can just see how you used to work your butter, Mother. I can see you shaping the roll, tossing it over and over and rolling it, and tapping it at the ends, making it so pretty!'

"I suppose that the most unusual piece of work I ever did while we were living on the farm," continued Grandmother Brown, "was to make a casket for a little dead baby. It was my brother's child, and had been born dead. My brother himself was ill at the time and had little money. 'You can't afford to buy a casket,' I said to him. 'I'll make you one.' 'You! How can you?' he exclaimed. 'What's that dog lying on?' I asked him. 'A pair of old pants!' He shooed the dog away. The pants were of fine broadcloth and were lined. 'Rip out the lining!' I said. The inside was like fine black velvet. I looked about and saw some thin boards that had been laid down to step on, to keep the mud out of the house. Brother John cut them out the proper shape for a little casket and tacked them together, and I covered them with the black broadcloth. I lined the box with cotton batting, tacking it neatly in the corners. I had an old white dress of thin stuff. I folded it in pleats and tacked it over the batting. I covered a board for the top in the same way. Brother had some pretty little white tacks that looked like silver. I tacked them in around the edge like a finish. And then I made a pillow of the white stuff and laid the baby on it. Brother John wept, and said: 'My! Sister! What *can't* you do?' 'Better that,' I told him, 'than buying a casket when you have so little money.' We buried the little baby on our farm.

"It seemed as if the only time when I felt justified in taking up a book or paper was when I sat down to nurse my babies. Anyway, for many years all my household tasks were performed with an ear cocked for the cry of a waking baby. How often I used to think: 'What happiness it would be if I had nothing to do *except* take care of my babies!' There was one terrible period when, for two years, I carried my little sick Carrie around with me on a pillow as I went from stove to table or from room to room, doing my work.

"Such a way of living is hard, *hard,* HARD. The only thing that can make it endurable for a woman is love and plenty of it. I remember one day on the farm when Dan'l was going up to Burlington. I remember that before he left he kissed me — kissed me and my little sick baby lying so white on her pillow. I had many things to do that day. But, my! how the work flew under my hands! What a difference a kiss can make!"

HARRIETT CONNOR BROWN, Grandmother Brown's Hundred Years

68. Martin Chuzzlewit Buys Land in Eden

When young Dickens came to America for his first visit at the beginning of the eighteen-forties, he was received as if he were some great prince or conqueror. His novel, Martin Chuzzlewit (1844), a direct result of the tour, contained some sharply satiric chapters on our democratic ways. These greatly offended Americans, and yet they had much truth in them. Speculation in western lands was to the eighteen-thirties what stock-market speculation was a century later. Eden was Cairo, Illinois, and in his picture of the knavery of real-estate boomers there Dickens did no more than justice to one type of American swindling.

MY GOOD FELLOW," said Martin, "we are no longer master and servant, but friends and partners, and are mutually gratified. If we determine on Eden, the business shall be commenced as soon as we get there, under the name," said Martin, who never hammered upon an idea that wasn't red hot, "under the name of Chuzzlewit and Tapley."

"Lord love you, Sir," cried Mark, "don't have my name in it. I ain't acquainted with the business, Sir. I must be Co., I must. I've often thought," he added, in a low voice, "as I should like to know a Co., but I little thought as ever I should live to be one."

Before they parted for the night it was agreed between them that they should go together to the agent's in the morning, but that Martin should decide the Eden question on his own sound judgment.

Off they all four started for the office of the Eden Settlement, which was almost within rifleshot of the National Hotel.

It was a small place — something like a turnpike. But a great deal of land may be got into a dicebox, and why may not a whole territory be bargained for in a shed? It was but a temporary office too, for the Edeners were "going" to build a superb establishment for the transaction of their business, and had already got so far as to mark out the site, which is a great way in America. The office door was wide open, and in the doorway was the agent, no doubt a tremendous fellow to get through his work, for he seemed to have no arrears, but was swinging backwards and forwards in a rocking chair, with one of his legs planted high up against the doorpost and the other doubled up under him, as if he were hatching his foot.

He was a gaunt man in a huge straw hat and coat of green stuff. The weather being hot, he had no cravat, and wore his shirt collar wide open, so that every time he spoke something was seen to twitch and jerk up in his throat, like the little hammers in a harpsichord when the notes are struck. Perhaps it was the Truth feebly endeavoring to leap to his lips. If so, it never reached them.

Two gray eyes lurked deep within this agent's head, but one of them had no sight in it, and stood stock-still. With that side of his face he seemed to listen to what the other side was doing. Thus each profile had a distinct expression, and when the movable side was most in action the rigid one was in its coldest state of watchfulness. It was like turning the man inside out to pass to that view of his features in his liveliest mood, and see how calculating and intent they were.

Such was the man whom they now approached, and whom the General saluted by the name of Scadder.

"Well, Gen'ral," he returned, "and how are you?"

"Ac-tive and spry, sir, in my country's service and the sympathetic cause. Two gentlemen on business, Mr. Scadder."

He shook hands with each of them — nothing is done in America without shaking hands — then went on rocking.

"I think I know what bis'ness you have brought these strangers here upon, then, Gen'ral?"

"Well, sir. I expect you may."

"You air a tongue-y person, Gen'ral. For you talk too much, and that's a fact," said Scadder. "You speak a-larming well in public, but you didn't ought to go ahead so fast in private. Now!"

"If I can realize your meaning, ride me on a rail!" returned the General, after pausing for consideration.

"You know we didn't wish to sell the lots off right away to any loafer as might bid," said Scadder; "but had con-cluded to reserve 'em for Aristocrats of Natur'. Yes!"

"And they are here, sir!" cried the General, with warmth. "They are here, sir!"

"If they air here," returned the agent, in reproachful accents, "that's enough. But you didn't ought to have your dander riz with *me*, Gen'ral."

The General whispered Martin that Scadder was the honestest fellow in the world, and that he wouldn't have given him offense, designedly, for ten thousand dollars.

"Mr. Scadder," said the General, assuming his oratorical deportment. "Sir! Here is my hand, and here my heart. I esteem you, sir, and ask your pardon. These gentlemen air friends of mine, or I would not have brought 'em here, sir, being well aware, sir, that the lots at present go entirely too cheap. But these air friends, sir; these air partick'ler friends."

Mr. Scadder was so satisfied by this explanation that he shook the General warmly by the hand, and got out of the rocking chair to do it. He then invited the General's particular friends to accompany him into the office. As to the General, he observed, with his usual benevolence, that, being one of the company, he wouldn't interfere in the transaction on any account, so he appropriated the rocking chair to himself and looked at the prospect, like a good Samaritan waiting for a traveler.

"Heyday!" cried Martin, as his eye rested on a great plan which occupied one whole side of the office. Indeed, the office had little else in it, but some geological and botanical specimens, one or two rusty ledgers, a homely desk, and a stool. "Heyday! what's that?"

"That's Eden," said Scadder, picking his teeth with a sort of young bayonet that flew out of his knife when he touched a spring.

"Why, I had no idea it was a city."

"Hadn't you? Oh, it's a city."

A flourishing city, too! An architectural city! There were banks, churches, cathedrals, market places, factories, hotels, stores, mansions, wharves; an exchange, a theater; public buildings of all kinds down to the office of the *Eden Stinger,* a daily journal; all faithfully depicted in the view before them.

"Dear me! It's really a most important place!" cried Martin, turning round.

"Oh! it's very important," observed the agent.

"But I am afraid," said Martin, glancing again at the Public Buildings, "that there's nothing left for me to do."

"Well! it ain't all built," replied the agent. "Not quite."

This was a great relief.

"The market place, now," said Martin, "is that built?"

"That?" said the agent, sticking his toothpick into the weathercock on the top. "Let me see. No, that ain't built."

"Rather a good job to begin with — eh, Mark?" whispered Martin, nudging him with his elbow.

Mark, who with a very stolid countenance had been eying the plan and the agent by turns, merely rejoined "Uncommon!"

A dead silence ensued. Mr. Scadder, in some short recesses or vacations of his toothpick, whistled a few bars of "Yankee Doodle" and blew the dust off the roof of the theater.

"I suppose," said Martin, feigning to look more narrowly at the plan, but showing by his tremulous voice how much depended in his mind upon the answer, "I suppose there are — several architects there?"

"There ain't a single one," said Scadder.

"Mark," whispered Martin, pulling him by the sleeve, "do you hear that? But whose work is all this before us, then?" he asked aloud.

"The soil being very fruitful, public buildings grows spontaneous, perhaps," said Mark.

He was on the agent's dark side as he said it, but Scadder instantly changed his place and brought his active eye to bear upon him.

"Feel of my hands, young man," he said.

"What for?" asked Mark, declining.

"Air they dirty, or air they clean, sir?" said Scadder, holding them out.

In a physical point of view they were decidedly dirty. But it being obvious that Mr. Scadder offered them for examination in a figurative sense, as emblems of his moral character, Martin hastened to pronounce them pure as the driven snow.

"I entreat, Mark," he said, with some irritation, "that you will not obtrude remarks of that nature, which, however harmless and well intentioned, are quite out of place, and cannot be expected to be very agreeable to strangers. I am quite surprised."

Mr. Scadder said nothing, but he set his back against the plan and thrust his toothpick into the desk some twenty times, looking at Mark all the while as if he were stabbing him in effigy.

"You haven't said whose work it is," Martin ventured to observe at length, in a tone of mild propitiation.

"Well, never mind whose work it is or isn't," said the agent, sulkily. "No matter how it did eventuate. P'raps he cleared off, handsome, with a heap of dollars; p'raps he wasn't worth a cent. P'raps he was a loafin' rowdy; p'raps a ring-tailed roarer. Now!"

"All your doing, Mark!" said Martin.

"P'raps," pursued the agent, "them ain't plants of Eden's raising. No! P'raps that desk and stool ain't made from Eden lumber. No! P'raps no end of squatters ain't gone out there. No! P'raps there ain't no such location in the territoary of the Great U-nited States. Oh, no!"

"I hope you're satisfied with the success of your joke, Mark," said Martin.

But here, at a most opportune and happy time, the General interposed, and called out to Scadder from the doorway to give his friends the particulars of that little lot of fifty acres with the house upon it; which, having belonged to the company formerly, had lately lapsed again into their hands.

"You air a deal too open-handed, Gen'ral," was the answer. "It is a lot as should be rose in price. It is."

He grumblingly opened his books notwithstanding, and always keeping his bright side towards Mark, no matter at what amount of inconvenience to himself, displayed a certain leaf for their perusal. Martin read it greedily, and then inquired —

"Now, where upon the plan may this place be?"

"Upon the plan?" said Scadder.

"Yes."

He turned towards it and reflected for a short time, as if, having been put upon his mettle, he was resolved to be particular to the very minutest hair's breadth of a shade. At length, after wheeling his toothpick slowly round and round in the air as if it were a carrier pigeon just thrown up, he suddenly made a dart at the drawing, and pierced the very center of the main wharf through and through.

"There!" he said, leaving his knife quivering in the wall; "that's where it is!"

Martin glanced with sparkling eyes upon his Co., and his Co. saw that the thing was done.

The bargain was not concluded as easily as might have been expected though, for Scadder was caustic and ill-humored, and cast much unnecessary opposition in the way, at one time requesting them to think of it, and call again in a week or a fortnight, at another predicting that they wouldn't like it, at another offering to retract and let them off, and muttering strong imprecations upon the folly of the General. But the whole of the astoundingly small sum total of purchase money — it was only one hundred and fifty dollars, or something more than thirty pounds of the capital brought by Co. into the architectural concern — was ultimately paid down, and Martin's head was two inches nearer the roof of the little wooden office, with the consciousness of being a landed proprietor in the thriving city of Eden.

"If it shouldn't happen to fit," said Scadder, as he gave Martin the necessary credentials on receipt of his money, "don't blame me."

"No, no," he replied, merrily. "We'll not blame you. General, are you going?"

"I am at your service, sir, and I wish you," said the General, giving him his hand with grave cordiality, "joy of your po-session. You air now, sir, a denizen of the most powerful and highly-civilized do-minion that has ever graced the world — a dominion, sir, where man is bound to man in one vast bond of equal love and truth. May you, sir, be worthy of your a-dopted country!" . . .

The wharf was close at hand, and at that instant Mark could hear them shouting out his name — could even hear Martin calling to him to make haste or they would be separated. It was too late to mend the matter, or put any face upon it but the best. He gave the captain a parting benediction, and ran off like a racehorse.

"Mark! Mark!" cried Martin.

"Here am I, sir," shouted Mark, suddenly replying from the edge of the quay, and leaping at a bound on board. "Never was half so jolly, sir. All right. Haul in! Go ahead!"

The sparks from the wood fire streamed upward from the two chimneys as if the vessel were a great firework just lighted, and they roared away upon the dark water. . . .

"Mark," he said then, "are there really none but ourselves on board this boat who are bound for Eden?"

"None at all, sir. Most of 'em, as you know, have stopped short and the few that are left are going further on. What matters that! More room there for us, sir."

"Oh, to be sure!" said Martin. "But I was thinking" — and there he paused.

"Yes, sir?" observed Mark.

"How odd it was that the people should have arranged to try their fortune at a wretched hole like that, for instance, when there is such a much better, and such a very different kind of place near at hand, as one may say."

He spoke in a tone so very different from his usual confidence, and with such an obvious dread of Mark's reply, that the good-natured fellow was full of pity.

"Why, you know, sir," said Mark, as gently as he could by any means insinuate the observation, "we must guard against being too sanguine. There's no occasion for it, either, because we're determined to make the best of everything, after we know the worst of it. Ain't we, sir?"

Martin looked at him, but answered not a word.

"Even Eden, you know, ain't all built," said Mark.

"In the name of Heaven, man," cried Martin, angrily, "don't talk of Eden in the same breath with that place. Are you mad? There — God forgive me! — don't think harshly of me for my temper!"

After that he turned away, and walked to and fro upon the deck full two hours. Nor did he speak again, except to say "Good night," until next day; nor even then upon this subject, but on other topics quite foreign to the purpose.

As they proceeded farther on their track, and came more and more towards their journey's end, the monotonous desolation of the scene increased to that degree, that, for any redeeming feature it presented to their eyes, they might have entered in the body on the grim domains of Giant Despair. A flat morass, bestrewn with fallen timber — a marsh on which the good growth of the earth seemed to have been wrecked and cast away, that from its decomposing ashes vile and ugly things might rise — where the very trees took the aspect of huge weeds, begotten of the slime from which they sprang, by the hot sun that burnt them up; where fatal maladies, seeking whom they might infect, came forth at night in misty shapes and, creeping out upon the water, haunted them like specters until day; where even the blessed sun, shining down on festering elements of corruption and disease, became a horror — this was the realm of Hope through which they moved.

At last they stopped. At Eden too. The waters of the Deluge might have left it but a week before, so choked with slime and matted growth was the hideous swamp which bore that name.

There being no depth of water close inshore, they landed from the vessel's boat, with all their goods beside them. There were a few log houses visible among the dark trees — the best, a cowshed or a rude stable; but for the wharves, the market place, the public buildings —

"Here comes an Edener," said Mark. "He'll get us help to carry these things up. Keep a good heart, sir. Hallo there!"

The man advanced towards them through the thickening gloom, very slowly, leaning on a stick. As he drew nearer they observed that he was pale and worn, and that his anxious eyes were deeply sunken in his head. His dress of homespun blue hung about him in rags, his feet and head were bare. He sat down on a stump halfway, and beckoned them to come to him. When they complied, he put his hand upon his side as if in pain, and while he fetched his breath, stared at them wondering.

"Strangers!" he exclaimed, as soon as he could speak.

"The very same," said Mark. "How are you, sir?"

"I've had the fever very bad," he answered, faintly. "I haven't stood upright these many weeks. Those are your notions, I see," pointing to their property.

"Yes, sir," said Mark, "they are. You couldn't recommend us some one as would lend a hand to help carry 'em up to the — to the town, could you, sir?"

"My eldest son would do it if he could," replied the man; "but today he has his chill upon him, and is lying wrapped up in the blankets. My youngest died last week."

"I'm sorry for it, governor, with all my heart," said Mark, shaking him by the hand. "Don't mind us. Come along with me, and I'll give you an arm back. The goods is safe enough, sir" — to Martin — "there ain't many people about, to make away with 'em. What a comfort that is!"

"No," cried the man. "You must look for such folks here," knocking his stick upon the ground, "or yonder in the bush, towards the north. We've buried most of 'em. The rest have gone away. Them that we have here don't come out at night."

"The night air ain't quite wholesome, I suppose?" said Mark.

"It's deadly poison," was the settler's answer.

Mark showed no more uneasiness than if it had been commended to him as ambrosia; but he gave the man his arm, and as they went along explained to him the nature of their purchase, and inquired where it lay. Close to his own log house, he said — so close that he had used their dwelling as a storehouse for some corn; they must excuse it that night, but he would endeavor to get it taken out upon the morrow. He then gave them to understand, as an additional scrap of local chit-chat, that he had buried the last proprietor with his own hands — a piece of information which Mark also received without the least abatement of his equanimity.

In a word, he conducted them to a miserable cabin, rudely constructed of the trunks of trees, the door of which had either fallen down or been carried away long ago, and which was consequently open to the wild landscape and the dark night. Saving for the little store he had mentioned, it was perfectly bare of all furniture, but they had left a chest upon the landing place, and he gave them a rude torch in lieu of candle. This latter acquisition Mark planted in the hearth, and then, declaring that the mansion "looked quite comfortable," hurried Martin off again to help bring up the chest. And all the way to the landing place and back Mark talked incessantly — as if he would infuse into his partner's breast some faint belief that they had arrived under the most auspicious and cheerful of all imaginable circumstances.

But many a man who would have stood within a home dismantled, strong in his passion and design of vengeance, has had the firmness of his nature conquered by the razing of an air-built castle. When the log hut received them for the second time, Martin lay down upon the ground and wept aloud. . . .

"I ask your forgiveness a thousand times, my dear fellow," said Martin. "I couldn't have helped it if death had been the penalty."

"Ask my forgiveness!" said Mark, with his accustomed cheerfulness, as he proceeded to unpack the chest. "The head partner a asking forgiveness of Co., eh? There must be something wrong in the firm when that happens. I must have the books inspected, and the accounts gone over immediate. Here we are. Everything in its proper place. Here's the salt pork. Here's the biscuit. Here's the whisky — uncommon good it smells too. Here's the tin pot. This tin pot's a small fortun' in itself! Here's the blankets. Here's the ax. Who says we ain't got a first-rate fit out? I feel as if I was a cadet gone out to Indy, and my noble father was chairman of the board of directors. Now, when I've got some water from the stream afore the door and mixed the grog," cried Mark, running out to suit the action to the word, "there's a supper ready, comprising every delicacy of the season. Here we are, sir, all complete. For what we are going to receive, et cetrer. Lord bless you, sir, it's very like a gypsy party!"

It was impossible not to take heart in the company of such a man as this. Martin sat upon the ground beside the box, took out his knife, and ate and drank sturdily.

"Now you see," said Mark, when they had made a hearty meal, "with your knife and mine I sticks this blanket right afore the door, or where, in a state of high civilization, the door would be. And very neat it looks. Then I stops the aperture below, by putting the chest agin it. And very neat *that* looks. Then there's your blanket, sir. Then here's mine. And what's to hinder our passing a good night?"

For all his light-hearted speaking, it was long before he slept himself. He wrapped his blanket round him, put the ax ready to his hand, and lay across the threshold of the door, too anxious and too watchful to close his eyes. . . . Never had the light of day been half so welcome to his eyes as when, awaking from a fitful doze, Mark saw it shining through the blanket in the doorway.

He stole out gently, for his companion was sleeping now; and having refreshed himself by washing in the river, where it flowed before the door, took a rough survey of the settlement. There were not above a score of cabins in the whole — half of these appeared untenanted, all were rotten and decayed. The most tottering, abject, and forlorn among them was called, with great propriety, the Bank and National Credit Office. It had some feeble props about it, but was settling deep down in the mud, past all recovery.

Here and there an effort had been made to clear the land, and something like a field had been marked out, where, among the stumps and ashes of burnt trees, a scanty crop of Indian corn was growing. In some quarters a snake or zigzag fence had been begun, but in no instance had it been completed, and the fallen logs, half hidden in the soil, lay moldering away. Three or four meager dogs, wasted and vexed with hunger, some long-legged pigs, wandering away into the woods in search of food, some children, nearly naked, gazing at him from the huts, were all the living things he saw. A fetid vapor, hot and sickening as the breath of an oven, rose up from the earth, and hung on everything around, and, as his footprints sank into the marshy ground, a black ooze started forth to blot them out.

Their own land was mere forest. The trees had grown so thick and close that they shouldered one another out of their places, and the weakest, forced into shapes of strange distortion, languished like cripples. The best were stunted, from the pressure and the want of room; and high about the stems of all grew long rank grass, dank weeds, and frowsy underwood — not devisable into their separate kinds, but tangled all together in a heap — a jungle deep and dark, with neither earth nor water at its roots, but putrid matter, formed of the pulpy offal of the two, and of their own corruption.

He went down to the landing place where they had left their goods last night, and there he found some half dozen men — wan and forlorn to look at, but ready enough to assist — who helped him to carry them to the log house. They shook their heads in speaking of their settlement, and had no comfort to give him. Those who had the means of going away had all deserted it. They who were left had lost their wives, their children, friends, or brothers there, and suffered much themselves. Most of them were ill then — none were the men they had been once. They frankly offered their assistance and advice, and, leaving him for that time, went sadly off upon their several tasks.

Martin was by this time stirring; but he had greatly changed, even in one night. He was very pale and languid; he spoke of pains and weakness in his limbs, and complained that his sight was dim, and his voice feeble. Increasing in his own briskness as the prospect grew more and more dismal, Mark brought away a door from one of the deserted houses, and fitted it to their own habitation, then went back again for a rude bench he had observed, with which he presently returned in triumph, and having put this piece of furniture outside the house, arranged the notable tin pot and other such movables upon it, that it might represent a dresser or a sideboard. Their blankets, clothes, and the like he hung on pegs and nails. And, lastly, he brought forth a great placard (which Martin in the exultation of his heart had prepared with his own hands at the National Hotel), bearing the inscription CHUZZLEWIT & Co., ARCHITECTS AND SURVEYORS, which he displayed upon the most conspicuous part of the premises, with as much gravity as if the thriving city of Eden had had a real existence, and they expected to be overwhelmed with business.

CHARLES DICKENS, Martin Chuzzlewit, 1844

XIII

Sailing and Whaling

69. A Flogging at Sea

Flogging in the navy was not abolished by Congress until 1850, after a persistent agitation by Senator John P. Hale of New Hampshire. It was common in the merchant marine until that time. Nobody did more to arouse sentiment against it than the young Bostonian, Richard Henry Dana, who dropped his Harvard studies because of eye trouble in 1833, and the following year shipped before the mast on the brig, Pilgrim, *for a voyage to California. The book which resulted from this voyage, lively, fresh, and courageous in its exposure of the maltreatment of common sailors, has become a classic of adventure.*

FOR SEVERAL days the captain seemed very much out of humor. Nothing went right, or fast enough for him. He quarreled with the cook, and threatened to flog him for throwing wood on deck; and had a dispute with the mate about reeving a Spanish burton; the mate saying that he was right, and had been taught how to do it by a man *who was a sailor!* This, the captain took in dudgeon and they were at sword's points at once.

But his displeasure was chiefly turned against a large heavy-molded fellow from the middle States who was called Sam. This man hesitated in his speech, and was rather slow in his motions, but was a pretty good sailor, and always seemed to do his best; but the captain took a dislike to him, thought he was surly and lazy; and "if you once give a dog a bad name" — as the sailor phrase is — "he may as well jump overboard." The captain found fault with everything this man did, and hazed him for dropping a marline-spike from the main yard, where he was at work. This, of course, was an accident, but it was set down against him.

The captain was on board all day Friday, and everything went on hard and disagreeably. "The more you drive a man the less he will do" was as true with us as with any other people. We worked late Friday night and were turned to early Saturday morning. About ten o'clock the captain ordered our new officer, Russell, who by this time had become thoroughly disliked by all the crew, to get the gig ready to take him ashore.

John, the Swede, was sitting in the boat alongside, and Russell and myself were standing by the main hatchway, waiting for the captain, who was down in the hold, where the crew were at work. when we heard his voice raised in violent dispute with somebody, whether it was with the mate or one of the crew I could not tell; and then came blows and scuffling. I ran to the side and beckoned to John, who came up, and we leaned down the hatchway; and though we could see no one, yet we knew that the captain had the advantage, for his voice was loud and clear.

"You see your condition! You see your condition! Will you ever give me any more of your *jaw?*" No answer, and then came wrestling and heaving, as though the man was trying to turn him.

"You may as well keep still, for I have got you," said the captain. Then came the question, "Will you ever give me any more of your jaw?"

"I never gave you any, sir," said Sam; for it was his voice that we heard, though low and half choked.

"That's not what I ask you. Will you ever be impudent to me again?"

"I never have been," said Sam.

"Answer my question, or I'll make a spread eagle of you! I'll flog you, by G—d."

"I'm no Negro slave," said Sam.

"Then I'll make you one," said the captain; and he came to the hatchway, and sprang on deck, threw off his coat, and rolling up his sleeves, called out to the mate: "Seize that man up, Mr. A——! Seize him up! Make a spread eagle of him! I'll teach you all who is master aboard!"

The crew and officers followed the captain up the hatchway, and after repeated orders the mate laid hold of Sam, who made no resistance, and carried him to the gangway.

'What are you going to flog that man for, sir?" said John, the Swede, to the captain.

Upon hearing this, the captain turned upon him, but knowing him to be quick and resolute, he ordered the steward to bring the irons, and calling upon Russell to help him, went up to John.

"Let me alone," said John. "I'm willing to be put in irons. You need not use any force"; and putting out his hands, the captain slipped the irons on, and sent him aft to the quarter-deck. Sam by this time was *seized up,* as it is called, that is, placed against the shrouds, with his wrists made fast to the shrouds, his jacket off, and his back exposed. The captain stood on the break of the deck, a few feet from him, and a little raised, so as to have a good swing at him, and held in his hand the bight of a thick, strong rope. The officers stood round, and the crew grouped together in the waist.

All these preparations made me feel sick and almost faint, angry and excited as I was. A man — a human being, made in God's likeness — fastened up and flogged like a beast! A man, too, whom I had lived with and eaten with for months, and knew almost as well as a brother.

The first and almost uncontrollable impulse was resistance. But what was to be done? The time for it had gone by. The two best men were fast, and there were only two besides myself, and a small boy of ten or twelve years of age. And then there were (besides the captain) three officers, steward, agent, and clerk. But besides the numbers, what is there for sailors to do? If they resist, it is mutiny; and if they succeed and take the vessel, it is piracy. If they ever yield again, their punishment must come; and if they do not yield, they are pirates for life. If a sailor resist his commander, he resists the law, and piracy or submission are his only alternatives. Bad as it was, it must be borne. It is what a sailor ships for.

Swinging the rope over his head, and bending his body so as to give it full force, the captain brought it down upon the poor fellow's back. Once, twice — six times. "Will you ever give me any more of your jaw?" The man writhed with pain, but said not a word. Three times more. This was too much, and he muttered something which I could not hear; this brought as many more as the man could stand; when the captain ordered him to be cut down, and go forward.

"Now for you," said the captain, making up to John and taking his irons off. As soon as he was loose, he ran forward to the forecastle. "Bring that man aft," shouted the captain. The second mate, who had been a shipmate of John's stood still in the waist, and the mate walked slowly forward; but our third officer, anxious to show his zeal, sprang forward over the windlass, and laid hold of John; but he soon threw him from him.

At this moment I would have given worlds for the power to help the poor fellow, but it was all in vain. The captain stood on the quarter-deck, bare-headed, his eyes flashing with rage, and his face as red as blood, swinging the rope, and calling out to his officers, "Drag him aft! — Lay hold of him! I'll *sweeten* him!" etc., etc.

The mate now went forward and told John quietly to go aft, and he, seeing resistance in vain, threw the blackguard third mate from him; said he would go aft of himself, that they should not drag him; and went up to the gangway and held out his hands; but as soon as the captain began to make him fast, the indignity was too much, and he began to resist; but the mate and Russell holding him, he was soon seized up.

When he was made fast, he turned to the captain, who stood turning up his sleeves and getting ready for the blow, and asked him what he was to be flogged for. "Have I ever refused my duty, sir? Have you ever known me to hang back, or to be insolent, or not to know my work?"

"No," said the captain, "it is not that I flog you for; I flog you for your interference — for asking questions."

"Can't a man ask a question here without being flogged?"

"No," shouted the captain; "nobody shall open his mouth aboard this vessel, but myself"; and began laying the blows upon his back, swinging half round before each blow, to give it full effect. As he went on his passion increased and he danced about the deck calling out as he swung the rope: "If you want to know what I flog you for, I'll tell you. It's because I like to do it! — because I like to do it! It suits me! That's what I do it for!"

The man writhed under the pain, until he could endure it no longer, when he called out, with an exclamation more common among foreigners than with us — "Oh, Jesus Christ, oh, Jesus Christ!"

"Don't call on Jesus Christ," shouted the captain. "*He can't help you. Call on Captain T——. He's the man! He can help you! Jesus Christ can't help you now!"*

At these words, which I never shall forget, my blood ran cold. I could look on no longer. Disgusted, sick, and horror-struck, I turned away and leaned over the rail, and looked down into the water. A few rapid thoughts of my own situation, and of the prospect of future revenge, crossed my mind; but the falling of the blows and the cries of the man called me back at once.

At length they ceased, and turning round, I found that the mate, at a signal from the captain, had cut him down. Almost doubled up with pain, the man walked forward and went down into the forecastle. Every one else stood still at his post, while the captain, swelling with rage and with the importance of his achievement, walked the quarter-deck, and at each turn, as he came forward, calling out to us:

"You see your condition! You see where I've got you all, and you know what to expect! You've been mistaken in me — you didn't know what I was! Now you know what I am!" — "I'll make you toe the mark, every soul of you, or I'll flog you all, fore and aft, from the boy up!" — "You've got a driver over you! Yes, a *slave-driver, a Negro driver!* I'll see who'll tell me he isn't a Negro slave!"

With this and the like matter, equally calculated to quiet us and to allay any apprehensions of future trouble, he entertained us for about ten minutes, when he went below. Soon after, John came aft, with his bare back covered with stripes and wales in every direction, and dreadfully swollen, and asked the steward to ask the captain to let him have some salve or balsam to put upon it.

"No," said the captain, who heard him from below; "tell him to put his shirt on, that's the best thing for him, and pull me ashore in the boat. Nobody is going to lay up on board this vessel."

He then called to Mr. Russell to take those two men and two others in the boat and pull him ashore. I went for one. The two men could hardly bend their backs, and the captain called to them to "give way," "give way!" but finding they did their best, he let them alone. The agent was in the stern sheet, but during the whole pull — a league or more — not a word was spoken.

We landed; the captain, agent, and officer went up to the house, and left us with the boat. I, and the man with me, stayed near the boat, while John and Sam walked slowly away, and sat down on the rocks. They talked some time together, but at length separated, each sitting alone.

I had some fears of John. He was a foreigner, and violently tempered, and under suffering; and he had his knife with him, and the captain was to come down alone to the boat. The captain was probably armed, and if either of them had lifted a hand against him, they would have had nothing before them but flight, and starvation in the woods of California, or capture by the soldiers and Indian bloodhounds whom the offer of twenty dollars would have set upon them.

After the day's work was done, we went down into the forecastle and ate our plain supper; but not a word was spoken. It was Saturday night; but there was no song — no "sweethearts and wives." A gloom was over everything.

The two men lay in their berths, groaning with pain, and we all turned in, but, for myself, not to sleep. A sound coming now and then from the berths of the two men showed that they were awake, as awake they must have been, for they could hardly lie in one posture a moment; the dim, swinging lamp of the forecastle shed its light over the dark hole in which we lived; and many and various reflections and purposes coursed through my mind.

I thought of our situation, living under a tyranny; of the character of the country we were in; of the length of the voyage, and of the uncertainty attending our return to America; and then if we should return, of the prospect of obtaining justice and satisfaction for these poor men; and vowed that if God should ever give me the means, I would do something to redress the grievances and relieve the sufferings of that poor class of beings, of whom I then was one.

RICHARD HENRY DANA, Jr., Two Years before the Mast, 1840

70. The First Lowering

Even before the Revolution the skill and courage of the American whalemen were famous abroad, and elicited a famous tribute from Edmund Burke. Whaling reached its height in the period from 1840 to 1860, when never less than 500 and in one year as many as 735 American vessels put out to obtain sperm oil, whale oil, and whalebone. The rugged tars of New Bedford gained a salt-sprayed renown throughout the seven seas. Most famous of all their sailing hands was Herman Melville, who shipped on the Acushnet in 1841. When he could no longer endure the hardships of whaling life, he deserted at the Marquesas Islands; his voyage thus gave him the material for both Moby Dick *and* Typee.

To A landsman, no whale, nor any sign of a herring, would have been visible at that moment; nothing but a troubled bit of greenish white water, and thin scattered puffs of vapor hovering over it, and suffusingly blowing off to leeward, like the confused scud from white rolling billows. The air around suddenly vibrated — and tingled, as it were — like the air over intensely heated plates of iron. Beneath this atmospheric waving and curling, and partially beneath a thin layer of water, also, the whales were swimming. Seen in advance of all the other indications, the puffs of vapor they spouted seemed their forerunning couriers and detached flying outriders.

All four boats were now in keen pursuit of that one spot of troubled water and air. But it bade fair to outstrip them; it flew on and on, as a mass of interblending bubbles borne down a rapid stream from the hills.

"Pull, pull, my good boys," said Starbuck, in the lowest possible but intensest concentrated whisper to his men; while the sharp fixed glance from his eyes, darted straight ahead of the bow, almost seemed as two visible needles in two unerring binnacle compasses. He did not say much to his crew, though, nor did his crew say anything to him; only the silence of the boat was at intervals startingly pierced by one of his peculiar whispers, now harsh with command, now soft with entreaty.

How different the loud little King Post. "Sing out and say something, my hearties. Roar and pull, my thunderbolts! Beach me, beach me on their black backs, boys; only do that for me, and I'll sign over to you my Martha's Vineyard plantation, boys; including wife, and children, boys. Lay me on — lay me on! O Lord, Lord! but I shall go stark, staring mad! See! see that white water!" And so shouting, he pulled his hat from his head, and stamped up and down on it; then picking it up, flirted it far off upon the sea; and finally fell to rearing and plunging in the boat's stern like a crazed colt from the prairie. . . .

Meanwhile, all the boats tore on. The repeated specific allusions of Flask to "that whale," as he called the fictitious monster which he declared to be incessantly tantalizing his boat's bow with his tail — these allusions of his were at times so vivid and lifelike that they would cause some one or two of his men to snatch a fearful look over the shoulder. But this was against all rule, for the oarsmen must put out their eyes, and ram a skewer through their necks, usage pronouncing that they must have no organs but ears, and no limbs but arms, in these critical moments.

It was a sight full of quick wonder and awe! The vast swells of the omnipotent sea; the surging, hollow roar they made, as they rolled along the eight gunwales, like gigantic bowls in a boundless bowling green; the brief suspended agony of the boat, as it would tip for an instant on the knifelike edge of the sharper waves that almost seemed threatening to cut it in two; the sudden profound dip into the watery glens and hollows; the keen spurrings and goadings to gain the top of the opposite hill; the headlong, sledlike slide down its other side — all these, with the cries of the headsmen and harpooners, and the shuddering gasps of the oarsmen, with the wondrous sight of the ivory *Pequod* bearing down upon her boats with outstretched sails, like a wild hen after her screaming brood; all this was thrilling. Not the raw recruit, marching from the bosom of his wife into the fever heat of his first battle; not the dead man's ghost encountering the first unknown phantom in the other world — neither of these can feel stranger and stronger emotions than that man does, who for the first time finds himself pulling into the charmed, churned circle of the hunted sperm whale.

The dancing white water made by the chase was now becoming more and more visible, owing to the increasing darkness of the dun cloud shadows flung upon the sea. The jets of vapor no longer blended, but tilted everywhere to right and left; the whales seemed separating their wakes. The boats were pulled more apart, Starbuck giving chase to three whales running dead to leeward. Our sail was now set. and, with the still rising wind, we rushed along, the boat going with such madness through the water that the lee oars could scarcely be worked rapidly enough to escape being torn from the rowlocks.

Soon we were running through a suffusing wide veil of mist, neither ship nor boat to be seen.

"Give way, men," whispered Starbuck, drawing still farther aft the sheet of his sail; "there is time to kill fish yet before the squall comes. There's white water again! — close to! Spring!"

Soon after, two cries in quick succession on each side of us denoted that the other boats had got fast; but hardly were they overheard, when with a lightninglike hurtling whisper Starbuck said, "Stand up!" and Queequeg, harpoon in hand, sprang to his feet.

Though not one of the oarsmen was then facing the life-and-death peril so close to them ahead, yet with their eyes on the intense countenance of the mate in the stern of the boat, they knew that the imminent instant had come; they heard, too, an enormous wallowing sound as of fifty elephants stirring in their litter. Meanwhile the boat was still booming through the mist, the waves curling and hissing around us like the erected crests of enraged serpents.

"That's his hump. *There, there,* give it to him!" whispered Starbuck.

A short rushing sound leaped out of the boat; it was the darted iron of Queequeg. Then all in one welded commotion came an invisible push from astern, while forward the boat seemed striking on a ledge; the sail collapsed and exploded; a gush of scalding vapor shot up near by; something rolled and tumbled like an earthquake beneath us. The whole crew were half suffocated as they were tossed helter-skelter into the white curdling cream of the squall. Squall, whale, and harpoon had all blended together; and the whale, merely grazed by the iron, escaped.

Though completely swamped, the boat was nearly unharmed. Swimming round it, we picked up the floating oars, and lashing them across the gunwale, tumbled back to our places. There we sat up to our knees in the sea, the water covering every rib and plank, so that to our downward-gazing eyes the suspended craft seemed a coral boat grown up to us from the bottom of the ocean.

The wind increased to a howl; the waves dashed their bucklers together; the whole squall roared, forked, and crackled around us like a white fire upon the prairie, in which, unconsumed, we were burning, immortal in these jaws of death! In vain we hailed the other boats; as well roar to the live coals down the chimney of a flaming furnace as hail those boats in that storm. Meanwhile the driving scud, rack, and mist grew darker with the shadows of night; no sign of the ship could be seen. The rising sea forbade all attempts to bale out the boat. The oars were useless as propellers, performing now the office of life preservers. So, cutting the lashing of the waterproof match keg, after many failures Starbuck contrived to ignite the lamp in the lantern; then stretching it on a waif pole, handed it to Queequeg as the standard-bearer of this forlorn hope. There, then, he sat, holding up that imbecile candle in the heart of that almighty forlornness. There, then, he sat, the sign and symbol of a man without faith, hopelessly holding up hope in the midst of despair.

Wet, drenched through, and shivering cold, despairing of ship or boat, we lifted up our eyes as the dawn came on. The mist still spread over the sea, the empty lantern lay crushed in the bottom of the boat. Suddenly Queequeg started to his feet, hollowing his hand to his ear. We all heard a faint creaking, as of ropes and yards hitherto muffled by the storm. The sound came nearer and nearer; the thick mists were dimly parted by a huge, vague form. Affrighted, we all sprang into the sea as the ship at last loomed into view, bearing right down upon us within distance of not much more than its length.

Floating on the waves we saw the abandoned boat, as for one instant it tossed and gaped beneath the ship's bows like a chip at the base of a cataract; and then the vast hull rolled over it, and it was seen no more till it came up weltering astern. Again we swam for it, were dashed against it by the seas, and were at last taken up and safely landed on board. Ere the squall came close to, the other boats had cut loose from their fish and returned to the ship in good time. The ship had given us up, but was still cruising, if haply it might light upon some token of our perishing, an oar or a lance pole.

HERMAN MELVILLE, Moby Dick

71. Stubb Kills a Whale

Melville's greatest book, Moby Dick, *was a failure, misunderstood and neglected. In 1853, two years after its publication, a fire at Harper's destroyed all the unsold copies. Years passed before it was reprinted. It contains pages of ideal beauty and profound meditation mingled with passages of vivid and almost brutal realism. One of the latter follows.*

THE NEXT day was exceedingly still and sultry, and with nothing special to engage them, the *Pequod's* crew could hardly resist the spell of sleep induced by such a vacant sea. For this part of the Indian Ocean through which we then were voyaging is not what whalemen call a lively ground; that is, it affords fewer glimpses of porpoises, dolphins, flying fish, and other vivacious denizens of more stirring waters, than those off the Rio de la Plata or the inshore ground off Peru.

It was my turn to stand at the foremast head, and with my shoulders leaning against the slackened royal shrouds, to and fro I idly swayed in what seemed an enchanted air. No resolution could withstand it; in that dreamy mood losing all consciousness, at last my soul went out of my body, though my body still continued to sway as a pendulum will, long after the power which first moved it is withdrawn.

Ere forgetfulness altogether came over me, I had noticed that the seamen at the main and mizzenmastheads were already drowsy. So that at last all three of us lifelessly swung from the spars, and for every swing that we made there was a nod from below from the slumbering helmsman. The waves, too, nodded their indolent crests; and across the wide trance of the sea, east nodded to west, and the sun over all.

Suddenly bubbles seemed bursting beneath my closed eyes; like vises my hands grasped the shrouds; some invisible, gracious agency preserved me; with a shock I came back to life. And lo! close under our lee, not forty fathoms off, a gigantic sperm whale lay rolling in the water like the capsized hull of a frigate, his broad, glossy back of an Ethiopian hue, glistening in the sun's rays like a mirror. But lazily undulating in the trough of the sea, and ever and anon tranquilly spouting his vapory jet, the whale looked like a portly burgher smoking his pipe of a warm afternoon. But that pipe, poor whale, was thy last. As if struck by some enchanter's wand, the sleepy ship and every sleeper in it all at once started into wakefulness; and more than a score of voices from all parts of the vessel, simultaneously with the three notes from aloft, shouted forth the accustomed cry, as the great fish slowly and regularly spouted the sparkling brine into the air.

"Clear away the boats! Luff!" cried Ahab. And obeying his own order, he dashed the helm down before the helmsman could handle the spokes.

The sudden exclamations of the crew must have alarmed the whale, and ere the boats were down, majestically turning, he swam away to the leeward, but with such a steady tranquillity, and making so few ripples as he swam, that thinking after all he might not as yet be alarmed, Ahab gave orders that not an oar should be used, and no man must speak but in whispers. So, seated like Ontario Indians on the gunwales of the boats, we swiftly but silently paddled along, the calm not admitting of the noiseless sails being set. Presently, as we thus glided in chase, the monster perpendicularly flitted his tail forty feet into the air, and then sank out of sight like a tower swallowed up.

"There go flukes!" was the cry, an announcement immediately followed by Stubb's producing his match and igniting his pipe, for now a respite was granted. After the full interval of his sounding had elapsed, the whale rose again, and being now in advance of the smoker's boat, and much nearer to it than to any of the others, Stubb counted upon the honor of the capture. It was obvious now that the whale had at length become aware of his pursuers. All silence or cautiousness was therefore no longer of use. Paddles were dropped, and oars came loudly into play. And still puffing at his pipe, Stubb cheered on his crew to the assault.

Yes, a mighty change had come over the fish. All alive to his jeopardy, he was going "head out," that part obliquely projecting from the mad yeast which he brewed.

"Start her, start her, my men! Don't hurry yourselves; take plenty of time — but start her; start her like thunderclaps, that's all," cried Stubb, spluttering out the smoke as he spoke. "Start her, now; give 'em the long and strong stroke, Tashtego. Start her, Tash, my boy — start her, all; but keep cool, keep cool — cucumbers is the word — easy, easy — only start her like grim death and grinning devils, and raise the buried dead perpendicular out of their graves, boys — that's all. Start her!"

"Woo-hoo! Wa-hee!" screamed the Gay-Header in reply, raising some old war whoop to the skies, as every oarsman in the strained boat involuntarily bounced forward with the one tremendous leading stroke which the eager Indian gave.

But his wild screams were answered by others quite as wild. "Kee-hee! Kee-hee!" yelled Daggoo, straining forwards and backwards on his seat like a pacing tiger in his cage.

"Ka-la! Koo-loo!" howled Queequeg, as if smacking his lips over a mouthful of grenadier's steak. And thus with oars and yells the keels cut the sea. Meanwhile Stubb, retaining his place in the van, still encouraged his men to the onset, all the while puffing the smoke from his mouth. Like desperadoes they tugged and they strained till the welcome cry was heard: "Stand up, Tashtego! — give it to him!" The harpoon was hurled. "Stern all!" The oarsmen backed water; the same moment something went hot and hissing along every one of their wrists. It was the magical line. An instant before, Stubb had swiftly caught two additional turns with it round the loggerhead, whence, by reason of its increased rapid circlings, a hempen blue smoke now jetted up and mingled with the steady fumes from his pipe. As the line passed round and round the loggerhead, so also, just before reaching that point, it blisteringly passed through and through both of Stubb's hands, from which the handcloths, or squares of quilted canvas sometimes worn at these times, had accidentally dropped. It was like holding an enemy's sharp two-edged sword by the blade, and that enemy all the time striving to wrest it out of your clutch.

"Wet the line! wet the line!" cried Stubb to the tub oarsman (him seated by the tub), who, snatching off his hat, dashed the sea water into it. More turns were taken, so that the line began holding its place. The boat now flew through the boiling water like a shark all fins. Stubb and Tashtego here changed places — stem for stern — a staggering business truly in that rocking commotion.

From the vibrating line extending the entire length of the upper part of the boat, and from its now being more tight than a harpstring, you would have thought the craft had two keels — one cleaving the water, the other the air — as the boat churned on through both opposing elements at once. A continual cascade played at the bows, a ceaseless whirling eddy in her wake, and at the slightest motion from within, even but of a little finger, the vibrating, cracking craft canted over her spasmodic gunwale into the sea. Thus they rushed, each man with might and main clinging to his seat to prevent being tossed to the foam, and the tall form of Tashtego at the steering oar crouching almost double in order to bring down his center of gravity. Whole Atlantics and Pacifics seemed passed as they shot on their way, till at length the whale somewhat slackened his flight.

"Haul in — haul in!" cried Stubb to the bowsman, and facing round towards the whale, all hands began pulling the boat up to him, while yet the boat was being towed on. Soon ranging up by his flank, Stubb, firmly planting his knee in the clumsy cleat, darted dart after dart into the flying fish, at the word of command the boat alternately sterning out of the way of the whale's horrible wallow, and then ranging up for another fling.

The red tide now poured from all sides of the monster like brooks down a hill. His tormented body rolled not in brine but in blood, which bubbled and seethed for furlongs behind in their wake. The slanting sun, playing upon this crimson pond in the sea, sent back its reflection into every face, so that they all glowed to each other like red men. And all the while, jet after jet of white smoke was agonizingly shot from the spiracle of the whale, and vehement puff after puff from the mouth of the excited headsman, as at every dart, hauling in upon his crooked lance (by the line attached to it), Stubb straightened it again and again by a few rapid blows against the gunwale, then again and again sent it into the whale.

"Pull up — pull up!" he now cried to the bowsman, as the waning whale relaxed in his wrath. "Pull up! — close to!" and the boat ranged along the fish's flank. When reaching far over the bow, Stubb slowly churned his long, sharp lance into the fish and kept it there, carefully churning and churning, as if cautiously seeking to feel after some gold watch that the whale might have swallowed and which he was fearful of breaking ere he could hook it out. But that gold watch he sought was the innermost life of the fish. And now it is struck, for, starting from his trance into that unspeakable thing called his flurry, the monster horribly wallowed in his blood, overwrapped himself in impenetrable, mad, boiling spray, so that the imperiled craft, instantly dropping astern, had much ado blindly to struggle out from that frenzied twilight into the clear air of the day.

And now abating in his flurry, the whale once more rolled out into view, surging from side to side, spasmodically dilating and contracting his spout hole, with sharp, cracking, agonized respirations. At last, gush after gush of clotted red gore, as if it had been the purple lees of red wine, shot into the frighted air, and falling back again, ran dripping down his motionless flanks into the sea. His heart had burst!

"He's dead, Mr. Stubb," said Daggoo.

"Yes; both pipes smoked out!" And withdrawing his own from his mouth, Stubb scattered the dead ashes over the water and for a moment stood thoughtfully eying the vast corpse he had made.

HERMAN MELVILLE, Moby Dick

72. How to Cut and Boil a Whale

Other whaling books than Melville's became almost classic. A justly famous English work was William Scoresby's on the whale fisheries of the Arctic and Greenland, published as early as 1820. Another was Reuben Delano's narrative of twelve years spent in a whaling-ship, issued in Boston in 1846 — fifteen years before the Civil War and the fast-increasing production of petroleum united to kill whaling as an important American industry.

BUT HERE I will digress from my narrative a little to give the reader a plain account of the manner of killing, cutting in, and boiling out a whale.

Whales being raised from the masthead, the hands are at once employed in getting the lines into the boats and "bending on the craft," which consists of two harpoons, one to a short warp and one to the line. They are then placed in the harpooner crotch, which is situated on the starboard bow of the boat, being within a convenient distance for our operations; the main yard is hauled aback, the boats are hoisted and cranes swung, the boat steerer and boat header jump in, the order is given to lower away, and she is followed down the ship's side by the respective crews.

All hands are now seated at the oars, the boat steerer taking the harpooner oar, and the word now is "Pull, my boys, for the whale," whilst those left in charge of the ship are hauling up the davit tackles, bracing, forward the main yard, with one hand aloft, looking out for the boats and whales.

As the boat approaches near the whale, the boat steerer stands up, and when within striking distance, throws his line iron, and then the short warp, and the cry is now "Stern all." This being accomplished, he changes places with the boat header, who takes the lance, and the boat steerer the steering oar, and with the assistance of the crew he manages the boat and wets the line, the bight of which is in the after part of the boat with a round turn round the loggerhead.

The crew is now occupied in hauling the boat on to the whale, while the boat steerer is coiling away the line. When the boat is brought again within a convenient distance the headsman throws his lance and if he be expert kills the whale sometimes at a single dart.

The cry is now, "There she spouts blood." On such an occasion the shark of the Pacific is nearly as attentive as the land sharks of our cities and seaports are to poor Jack on his first arrival, with this difference, that while one is contented with destroying the body, the other destroys both body and soul.

The whale being dead, if the ship is to windward signals are made for her to run down; meanwhile a hole is cut in her head and one in the fluke, and lines made fast for the purpose of hauling alongside.

The captain's boat now comes alongside the ship and is hoisted up, and preparations commence for taking the whale alongside, which is done by hauling aback the head yards, jib hauled down, main- and mizzentopsails braced forward, and the spanker set. The boat which has the whale in tow now takes her line to the ship, and all come on board and commence hauling in the whale. When alongside, she is fluke-roped and made fast to the bowsprit bits, and the boats are all hoisted up to their proper stations. By this time Jack begins to feel the want of a fresh nip, and the welcome sound comes from aft to "Splice the main brace," which causes Jack's eyes to glisten and makes his heart rejoice. This operation being performed, some are employed in reeving the cutting falls and others the guys for heaving in the blubber. The falls being to the windlass, and the guys hauled out, and the hooks lashed on, the stages are over the side and the respective officers for cutting out are at their places, the first mate in the after staging and the second in the forward, which is slung between the gangway and main chesstree. Then comes the boat steerer, who goes over the side on to the whale to put in the hook and raise the piece. The hole is now cut, and the monkey rope on the hook being entered, the word is given to heave away, and the boat steerer comes on board and takes his place in the blubber room for the purpose of stowing away the blubber; while the other two, with two edged knives with blades three feet in length, made for the purpose, stand by to board the piece, which being hove a proper distance above the plank-sheer, a hole is cut close down; a block with strap of sufficient length is put in the hole and toggled on the outside; they surge on one fall and heave on the other till our last fall has sufficient strain. We then lower a bit on the first piece, cut it off, and lower it down into the blubber room. Now commences the process of cutting off the head, which generally takes from an hour to an hour and a half by an expert workman with a sharp blade. We now heave away on the body, which in the operation of heaving and cutting rolls over until the blubber is all peeled off to the tail; which being unjointed, the carcass is let go, and numerous are the ravenous birds and sharks, the dread of the sailor, that attend it. We now lash on our hooks for the purpose of hooking to the head. this being hauled alongside for that purpose. And now the main brace must be spliced again, which agreeable ceremony being performed, we heave away and separate the junk from the case. This being on board, we now hook to the case, which is hove up high enough to bail it without intermixture with the salt water. The hole is now cut in the head of the size of a barrel, a tail block made fast to the cutting falls above with a line, and bucket attached to it. We now commence bailing out the case, which in a large whale often contains from fifteen to twenty barrels of head matter, which is made into spermaceti candles. The whale being now on board, all hands are at their stations; some are cutting, some are mincing, while the boat steerers are lighting the fires for the purpose of boiling out.

The head matter is boiled out first, and we generally calculate that a sixty-barrel whale will yield us twenty barrels of head oil, which is the best.

REUBEN DELANO, Wanderings and Adventures

73. The Mackerel Fleet Fishes off Monhegan Island

The fishing industry in America at an early date developed a new type of vessel. In 1713 Captain Andrew Robinson of the fishing village of Gloucester, Massachusetts, completed a craft entirely novel in style. She had two masts with great fore-and-aft sails in place of the old square sails. Watching her slide down the ways, an approving spectator exclaimed, "Oh, how she scoons!" Robinson heard him. "A scooner let her be!" he ejaculated. All up and down the coasts of Massachusetts, Maine, and Nova Scotia the schooner and her sisters, the chebacco and pinkie, were (and are) used to take mackerel, halibut, and cod.

MACKEREL, and mackerel only, was the object of their ambition. It seemed almost an object in itself, apart from what it would bring. . . . There were three seine boats, owned in shares by their crews, as the custom was. No one on the island could be oblivious to their movements. Its whole life centered round them. They set off for their first trips before daylight, and the voices and turnkeys at the door in the darkness awakened the settlement. At noon and evening the careful housewife had the old spyglass often at her eye and knew how to regulate the laying of the cloth and the lifting of the cover of the boiling pot to the dot of an *i* by their rounding the point at the harbor mouth. But it was their departures by day, often after considerable spells of inaction, that were most animated. . . .

The lookout had been sitting a long time on the cliff. Suddenly he jumped to his feet, shouted, and came running down. The heavy-booted, flannel-shirted, lounging men knew what it meant and were down at the beaches and in their long, swift boats instantly. Each strove for the lead. How the boats leaped through the water under the strokes of the bending hickory!

Seven men throw their weight upon the oars, some standing, some sitting. The Cap, aloft on the poop, surveys the watery field and directs the course with a long steering oar, down to the slight rippled patches which to the experienced eye denote the schooling fish. The great seine, one hundred and fifty fathoms long and twenty-four wide, well sprinkled with salt for preservation, is piled aft, and two veteran hands stand by to pay it out. A boy rows in the dory astern.

The schools are exceeding shy. The trick is to anticipate, if possible, their direction and meet them with the net. Even then they will dive directly under it and disappear. The first shoal is missed, the second, the third, the fourth. The fifth is of great promise, but a single gull comes and hovers over it to pounce upon a victim. "I wish I had a gun for that fellow," says the Cap, but having none, he swings his hat and screams shrilly. Meanwhile the fish have gone down, and the heavy net must be dragged in again without result.

With their many disappointments, they are presently eight to ten miles offshore. All the boats of the fleet are out around them, full of men, as if meditating some warlike descent on the coast. The cloud of fast, yachtlike schooners is tacking and standing off and on in every variety of pose. Dark figures in their tops and shrouds look out for schools; others fling over bait of ground porgies from boxes along the sides, to toll the fish for easier capture. Among the rest are two of the singular "porgy steamers," turned to mackereling. The veterans predict that their career will be brief, saying they will roll too much and their fires be put out.

Yonder, again, is a promising school; there are fifty barrels in it if there is a fish. Give way, all! The *Fidelia's* boat sees it too, and so does the *Watchman's,* the *Excalibur's,* the *Wild Rose's,* and that of the *Light of the Age,* and all race for it. But the Cap and Middleton are there first and have the *pas.*

Over with the net! The dory holds one end of it, while the seine boat rows around the school. Swash! swash! go the corks, drawing a long, agreeable curve on the water. The two ends are brought together and the net pursed up. "Bagged, by the great horn spoon," cries an excited shareholder, and they go to dipping the fish out with a scoop net and loading the dory as full as it will hold. . . .

The fleet at night, with its numerous lanterns, red to port and green to starboard, and watchmen on deck, was like a floating city. There was no commodore and no regular organization, yet accidents from collision were of rare occurrence. All had their heads one way, by tacit agreement. At midnight they reversed this and beat back over the same course.

The schools worked nearer the top at night, and their presence was betrayed by a phosphorescent "firing" in the water, so that it seemed almost like insensate folly that this, instead of the day, should not be the favorite fishing time. But attention to the subject showed that the nets fired the water, too, and gave a warning much more than counterbalancing the advantage.

W. H. BISHOP, Fish and Men in the Maine Islands

XIV

Steamboat Days

74. Launching the First Steamboat on Western Waters

After Robert Fulton proved his Hudson River steamboat an unquestioned success in 1807, the use of such vessels on western waters was only a question of time. As a result of a conference which Fulton and Robert R. Livingston held in 1810 with Governor Claiborne of Louisiana, the legislature of Louisiana Territory early in 1811 passed a law giving the first-named men the sole privilege of using steamboats on the lower Mississippi. As soon as news of this law came, Fulton went to Pittsburgh; and there his able assistant, Nicholas Roosevelt, directed the building and launching of the New Orleans, *the first steamboat to navigate any stream of the interior. She weighed only about a hundred tons, and had two masts as well as a stern-wheel. Roosevelt himself was an inventor, claiming to have originated the vertical paddle wheel.*

PRIOR to the introduction of steamboats on the western waters, the means of transportation thereon consisted of keelboats, barges, and flatboats. Keelboats and barges ascended as well as descended the stream. The flatboat was an unwieldy box and was broken up, for the lumber it contained, on its arrival at the place of destination. The keelboat was long and slender, sharp fore and aft, with a narrow gangway just within the gunwale for the boatmen as they poled or warped up the stream when not aided by the eddies that made their oars available. When the keelboat was covered with a low house lengthwise between the gangways, it was dignified with the name of barge. Keelboats, barges, and flatboats had prodigious steering oars, and oars of the same dimensions were hung on fixed pivots on the sides of the last named, by which the shape-less and cumbrous contrivance was in some sort managed. Ignorant of anything better, the people of the West were satisfied with these appliances of trade in 1810.

Whether steam could be employed on the western rivers was a question that its success between New York and Albany was not regarded as having entirely solved, and after the idea had been suggested of building a boat at Pittsburgh to ply between Natchez and New Orleans, it was considered necessary that investigations should be made as to the current of the rivers to be navigated, in regard to the new system. These investigations Mr. Roosevelt undertook, with the understanding that if his report were favorable, Chancellor Livingston, Mr. Fulton, and himself were to be equally interested in the undertaking. The Chancellor and Fulton were to supply the capital, and Roosevelt was to superintend the building of the boat and engine.

The first thing to be done was to obtain the timber to build the boat, and for this purpose men were sent into the forest, there to find the necessary ribs and knees and beams, transport them to the Monongahela, and raft them to the shipyard. White pine was the only material for planking that could be obtained without a delay that was inadmissible. The sawing that was required was done in the old-fashioned and now long-forgotten saw pits of 1811. Boatbuilders, accustomed to construct the barges of that day, could be obtained in Pittsburgh; but a shipbuilder and the mechanics required in the machinery department had to be brought from New York. Under these circumstances Mr. Roosevelt began the work. . . .

At length all difficulties were overcome by steady perseverance, and the boat was launched — and called, from the place of her ultimate destination, the *New Orleans*. It cost in the neighborhood of thirty-eight thousand dollars.

As the *New Orleans* approached completion and when it came to be known that Mrs. Roosevelt intended to accompany her husband on the voyage, the numerous friends she had made in Pittsburgh united in endeavoring to dissuade her from what they regarded as utter folly, if not absolute madness. Her husband was appealed to. The criticisms that had been freely applied to

the boat by the crowds of visitors to the shipyard were now transferred to the conduct of the builder. He was told that he had no
right to peril his wife's life, however reckless he might be of his
own. . . . But the wife believed in her husband, and in the latter
part of September, 1811, the *New Orleans,* after a short experimental trip up the Monongahela, commenced her voyage.

There were two cabins, one aft for ladies and a larger one forward for gentlemen. In the former there were four berths. It was
comfortably furnished. Of this, Mrs. Roosevelt took possession. Mr.
Roosevelt and herself were the only passengers. There was a captain, an engineer named Baker, Andrew Jack, the pilot, six hands,
two female servants, a man waiter, a cook, and an immense Newfoundland dog named Tiger. Thus equipped, the *New Orleans*
began the voyage which changed the relations of the West — which
may almost be said to have changed its destiny.

The people of Pittsburgh turned out in mass and lined the
banks of the Monongahela to witness the departure of the steamboat, and shout after shout rent the air, and handkerchiefs were
waved and hats thrown up by way of Godspeed to the voyagers
as the anchor was raised; and heading upstream for a short distance, a wide circuit brought the *New Orleans* on her proper
course, and, steam and current aiding, she disappeared behind
the first headlands on the right bank of the Ohio.

Too much excited to sleep, Mr. Roosevelt and his wife passed
the greater part of the first night on deck and watched the shore,
covered then with an almost unbroken forest, as reach after reach
and bend after bend were passed at a speed of from eight to ten
miles an hour. The regular working of the engine, the ample supply of steam, the uniformity of the speed, inspired at last a confidence that quieted the nervous apprehension of the travelers.
Mr. Jack, the pilot, delighted with the facility with which the vessel was steered and at a speed to which he was so little accustomed,
ceased to express misgivings and became as sanguine as Mr. Roosevelt himself in regard to the success of the voyage. The very crew
of unimaginative men were excited with the novelty of the
situation, and when the following morning assembled all hands
on deck to return the cheers of a village whose inhabitants had
seen the boat approaching down a long reach in the river and

turned out to greet her as she sped by, it probably shone upon as jolly a set as ever floated on the Ohio.

On the second day after leaving Pittsburgh the *New Orleans* rounded to opposite Cincinnati and cast anchor in the stream. Levees and wharf boats were things unknown in 1811. Here, as at Pittsburgh, the whole town seemed to have assembled on the bank, and many acquaintances came off in small boats. . . .

Morning after morning, the rise in the river during the night was reported; and finally, in the last week in November, it was ascertained that the depth of water in the shallowest portion of the falls exceeded by five inches the draught of the boat. It was a narrow margin. But the rise had ceased; there was no telegraph in those days to tell hourly what was the weather in the country drained by the Ohio; and Mr. Roosevelt, assuring himself personally of the condition of the falls, determined to take the responsibility and go over them if he could. It was an anxious time. All hands were on deck. Mrs. Roosevelt, whom her husband would willingly have left behind to join him below the falls, refused to remain on shore, and stood near the stern. The two pilots, for an extra one had been engaged for the passage through the rapids, took their places in the bow. The anchor was weighed. To get into the Indiana channel, which was the best, a wide circuit had to be made, bringing her head downstream, completing which, the *New Orleans* began the descent. Steerageway depended upon her speed exceeding that of the current. The faster she could be made to go, the easier would it be to guide her. All the steam the boiler would bear was put upon her. The safety valve shrieked; the wheels revolved faster than they had ever done before; and the vessel, speaking figuratively, fairly flew away from the crowds collected to witness her departure from Louisville. Instinctively each one on board now grasped the nearest object and with bated breath awaited the result. Black ledges of rock appeared, only to disappear as the *New Orleans* flashed by them. The waters whirled and eddied and threw their spray upon the deck as a more rapid descent caused the vessel to pitch forward to what at times seemed inevitable destruction. Not a word was spoken. The pilots directed the men at the helm by motions of their hands. Even the great Newfoundland dog seemed affected by the apprehension of danger and came and crouched at Mrs. Roosevelt's feet. The tension on the nervous system was too great to be long sustained. Fortunately the passage was soon made, and with feelings of profound gratitude to the Almighty at the successful issue of the adventure on the part of both Mr. Roosevelt and his wife, the *New Orleans* rounded to in safety below the falls.

J. H. B. Latrobe, The First Steamboat Voyage
on the Western Waters

75. Mark Twain Learns to Be a Pilot

In 1857 Mark Twain, a restless youth who as itinerant printer had wandered from Missouri as far east as Philadelphia and New York, got himself apprenticed to a Mississippi River pilot. For a year and a half he was learning his craft — a very precise and expert calling — for two years and a half he practised it as a licensed pilot. Then the Civil War closed the river and that chapter of his career. But it was this experience which gave him material for some of his best books — notably the two from which selections are here taken, and Tom Sawyer *and* Huckleberry Finn.

THE "PAUL JONES" was now bound for St. Louis. I planned a siege against my pilot, and at the end of three hard days he surrendered. He agreed to teach me the Mississippi River from New Orleans to St. Louis for five hundred dollars, payable out of the first wages I should receive after graduating. I entered upon the small enterprise of "learning" twelve or thirteen hundred miles of the great Mississippi River with the easy confidence of my time of life. If I had really known what I was about to require of my faculties, I should not have had the courage to begin. I supposed that all a pilot had to do was to keep his boat in the river, and I did not consider that that could be much of a trick, since it was so wide.

The boat backed out from New Orleans at four in the afternoon, and it was "our watch" until eight. Mr. B——, my chief, "straightened her up," plowed her along past the sterns of the other boats that lay at the levee, and then said, "Here, take her; shave those steamships as close as you'd peel an apple." I took the wheel, and my heart went down into my boots; for it seemed to me that we were about to scrape the side off every ship in the line, we were so close. I held my breath and began to claw the boat away from the danger; and I had my own opinion of the pilot who had known no better than to get us into such peril, but I was too wise to express it. In half a minute I had a wide margin of safety intervening between the *Paul Jones* and the ships; and within ten seconds more I was set aside in disgrace, and Mr. B—— was going into danger again and flaying me alive with abuse of my cowardice. I was stung, but I was obliged to admire the easy confidence with which my chief loafed from side to side of his wheel, and trimmed the ships so closely that disaster seemed ceaselessly imminent. When he had cooled a little he told me that the easy water was close ashore and the current outside, and therefore we must hug the bank, upstream, to get the benefit of the former, and stay well out, downstream, to take advantage of the latter. In my own mind I resolved to be a downstream pilot and leave the upstreaming to people dead to prudence.

Now and then Mr. B—— called my attention to certain things. Said he, "This is Six-Mile Point." I assented. It was pleasant enough information, but I could not see the bearing of it. I was not conscious that it was a matter of any interest to me. Another time he said, "This is Nine-Mile Point." Later he said, "This is Twelve-Mile Point." They were all about level with the water's edge; they all looked about alike to me; they were monotonously unpicturesque. I hoped Mr. B—— would change the subject. But no; he would crowd up around a point, hugging the shore with affection, and then say, "The slack water ends here, abreast this bunch of China trees; now we cross over." So he crossed over. He gave me the wheel once or twice, but I had no luck. I either came near chipping off the edge of a sugar plantation, or else I yawed too far from shore, and so I dropped back into disgrace and got abused again.

The watch was ended at last, and we took supper and went to bed. At midnight the glare of a lantern shone in my eyes, and the night watchman said: "Come! turn out!"

And then he left. I could not understand this extraordinary procedure; so I presently gave up trying to, and dozed off to sleep. Pretty soon the watchman was back again, and this time he was gruff. I was annoyed. I said:

"What do you want to come bothering around here in the middle of the night for? Now as like as not I'll not get to sleep again tonight."

The watchman said, "Well, if this an't good, I'm blest."

The "off watch" was just turning in, and I heard some brutal laughter from them and such remarks as "Hello, watchman! an't the new cub turned out yet? He's delicate, likely. Give him some sugar in a rag and send for the chambermaid to sing rockaby-baby to him."

About this time Mr. B—— appeared on the scene. Something like a minute later I was climbing the pilothouse steps with some of my clothes on and the rest in my arms. Mr. B—— was close behind, commenting. Here was something fresh — this thing of getting up in the middle of the night to go to work. It was a detail in piloting that had never occurred to me at all. I knew that boats ran all night, but somehow I had never happened to reflect that somebody had to get up out of a warm bed to run them. I began to fear that piloting was not quite so romantic as I had imagined it was; there was something very real and worklike about this new phase of it.

It was a rather dingy night, although a fair number of stars were out. The big mate was at the wheel, and he had the old tub pointed at a star and was holding her straight up the middle of the river. The shores on either hand were not much more than a mile apart, but they seemed wonderfully far away and ever so vague and indistinct. . . .

Mr. B—— made for the shore and soon was scraping it, just the same as if it had been daylight. And not only that, but singing "Father in heaven the day is declining," etc. It seemed to me that I had put my life in the keeping of a peculiarly reckless outcast. Presently he turned on me and said:

"What's the name of the first point above New Orleans?"

I was gratified to be able to answer promptly, and I did. I said I didn't know.

"Don't *know*?"

This manner jolted me. I was down at the foot again, in a moment. But I had to say just what I had said before.

"Well, you're a smart one," said Mr. B——. "What's the name of the *next* point?"

Once more I didn't know.

"Well, this beats anything. Tell me the name of *any* point or place I told you."

I studied awhile and decided that I couldn't.

"Look-a-here! What do you start out from, above Twelve-Mile Point, to cross over?"

"I — I — don't know."

"You — you — don't know?" mimicking my drawling manner of speech. "What *do* you know?"

"I — I — nothing, for certain."

"By the great Caesar's ghost I believe you! You're the stupidest dunderhead I ever saw or ever heard of, so help me Moses! The idea of *you* being a pilot — *you!* Why, you don't know enough to pilot a cow down a lane."

Oh, but his wrath was up! He was a nervous man, and he shuffled from one side of his wheel to the other as if the floor was hot. He would boil awhile to himself and then overflow and scald me again.

"Look-a-here! What do you suppose I told you the names of those points for?"

I tremblingly considered a moment, and then the devil of temptation provoked me to say: —

"Well — to — to — be entertaining, I thought."

This was a red rag to the bull. He raged and stormed so (he was crossing the river at the time) that I judge it made him blind, because he ran over the steering oar of a trading scow. Of course the traders sent up a volley of red-hot profanity. Never was a man so grateful as Mr. B—— was, because he was brimful, and here were subjects who would *talk back*. He threw open a window, thrust his head out, and such an eruption followed as I never had heard before. The fainter and farther away the scowmen's curses drifted, the higher Mr. B—— lifted his voice and the weightier his adjectives grew. When he closed the window he was empty. You could have drawn a seine through his system and not caught curses enough to disturb your mother with. Presently he said to me in the gentlest way: —

"My boy, you must get a little memorandum book, and every time I tell you a thing, put it down right away. There's only one way to be a pilot, and that is to get this entire river by heart. You have to know it just like A B C."

That was a dismal revelation to me, for my memory was never loaded with anything but blank cartridges. However, I did not feel discouraged long. I judged that it was best to make some allowances, for doubtless Mr. B—— was "stretching." Presently he pulled a rope and struck a few strokes on the big bell. The stars were all gone, now, and the night was as black as ink. I could hear the wheels churn along the bank, but I was not entirely certain that I could see the shore. The voice of the invisible watchman called up from the hurricane deck:

"What's this, sir?"

"Jones's plantation."

I said to myself, I wish I might venture to offer a small bet that it isn't. But I did not chirp. I only waited to see. Mr. B—— handled the engine bells, and in due time, the boat's nose came to the land, a torch glowed from the forecastle, a man skipped ashore, a darky's voice on the bank said, "Gimme de carpetbag, Mars' Jones," and the next moment we were standing up the river again, all serene. I reflected deeply awhile and then said — but not aloud — Well, the finding of that plantation was the luckiest accident that ever happened; but it couldn't happen again in a hundred years. And I fully believed it *was* an accident, too.

By the time we had gone seven or eight hundred miles up the river, I had learned to be a tolerably plucky upstream steersman, in daylight, and before we reached St. Louis, I had made a trifle of progress in night work, but only a trifle. I had a notebook that fairly bristled with the names of towns, "points," bars, islands, bends, reaches, etc.; but the information was to be found only in the notebook — none of it was in my head. It made my heart ache to think I had only got half of the river set down; for as our watch was four hours off and four hours on, day and night, there was a long four-hour gap in my book for every time I had slept since the voyage began.

My chief was presently hired to go on a big New Orleans boat, and I packed my satchel and went with him. She was a grand affair. When I stood in her pilothouse I was so far above the water that I seemed perched on a mountain, and her decks stretched so far away, fore and aft, below me, that I wondered how I could ever have considered the little *Paul Jones* a large craft. There were other differences, too. The *Paul Jones's* pilothouse was a cheap, dingy, battered rattletrap, cramped for room; but here was a sumptuous glass temple; room enough to have a dance in; showy red and gold window curtains; an imposing sofa; leather cushions and a back to the high bench where visiting pilots sit, to spin yarns and "look at the river"; bright, fanciful cuspidors instead of a broad wooden box filled with sawdust; nice new oilcloth on the floor; a hospitable big stove for winter; a wheel as high as my head, costly with inlaid work; a wire tiller rope; bright brass knobs for the bells; and a tidy, white-aproned, black "texas tender" to bring up tarts and ices and coffee during midwatch, day and night. Now this was "something like," and so I began to take heart once more to believe that piloting was a romantic sort of occupation after all. The moment we were under way I began to prowl about the great steamer and fill myself with joy. She was as clean and as dainty as a drawing room; when I looked down her long, gilded saloon, it was like gazing through a splendid tunnel; she had an oil picture, by some gifted sign painter, on every stateroom door; she glittered with no end of prism-fringed chandeliers; the clerk's office was elegant, the bar was marvelous, and the barkeeper had been barbered and upholstered at incredible cost. The boiler deck (i.e. the second story of the boat, so to speak) was as spacious as a church, it seemed to me; so with the forecastle; and there was no pitiful handful of deckhands, firemen, and roustabouts down there, but a whole battalion of men. The fires were fiercely glaring from a long row of furnaces, and over them were eight huge boilers! This was unutterable pomp. The mighty engines — but enough of this. I had never felt so fine before. And when I found that the regiment of natty servants respectfully sirred me, my satisfaction was complete. When I returned to the pilothouse St. Louis was gone and I was lost. Here was a piece of river which was all down in my book, but I could make neither head nor tail of it: you understand, it was turned around. I had seen it, when coming upstream, but I had never faced about to see how it looked when it was behind me. My heart broke again, for it was plain that I had got to learn this troublesome river *both ways*.

The pilothouse was full of pilots, going down to "look at the river." . . .

We had a fine company of these river inspectors along, this trip. There were eight or ten, and there was abundance of room for them in our great pilothouse. Two or three of them wore polished silk hats, elaborate shirt fronts, diamond breastpins, kid gloves, and patent-leather boots. They were choice in their English and bore themselves with a dignity proper to men of solid means and prodigious reputation as pilots. The others were more or less loosely clad and wore upon their heads tall felt cones that were suggestive of the days of the Commonwealth.

I was a cipher in this august company and felt subdued, not to say torpid. I was not even of sufficient consequence to assist at the wheel when it was necessary to put the tiller hard down in a hurry; the guest that stood nearest did that when occasion required — and this was pretty much all the time, because of the crookedness of the channel and the scant water. I stood in a corner, and the talk I listened to took the hope all out of me. One visitor said to another:

"Jim, how did you run Plum Point, coming up?"

"It was in the night, there, and I ran it the way one of the boys on the *Diana* told me; started out about fifty yards above the wood-pile on the false point, and held on the cabin under Plum Point till I raised the reef — quarter less twain — then straightened up for the middle bar till I got well abreast the old one-limbed cottonwood in the bend, then got my stern on the cottonwood and head on the low place above the point, and came through a-booming — nine and a half."

"Pretty square crossing, an't it?"

"Yes, but the upper bar's working down fast."

Another pilot spoke up and said:

"I had better water than that, and ran it lower down; started out from the false point — mark twain — raised the second reef abreast the big snag in the bend, and had quarter less twain."

One of the gorgeous ones remarked: "I don't want to find fault with your leadsmen, but that's a good deal of water for Plum Point, it seems to me."

There was an approving nod all around as this quiet snub dropped on the boaster and settled him. And so they went on talk-talk-talking. Meantime, the thing that was running in my mind was: "Now if my ears hear aright, I have not only to get the names of all the towns and islands and bends, and so on, by heart, but I must even get up a warm personal acquaintanceship with every old snag and one-limbed cottonwood and obscure woodpile that ornaments the banks of this river for twelve hundred miles; and more than that, I must actually know where these things are in the dark, unless these guests are gifted with eyes that can pierce through two miles of solid blackness; I wish the piloting business was in Jericho and I had never thought of it."

At dusk Mr. B—— tapped the big bell three times (the signal to land), and the captain emerged from his drawing room in the forward end of the texas and looked up inquiringly. Mr. B—— said:

"We will lay up here all night, Captain."

"Very well, sir."

That was all. The boat came to shore and was tied up for the night. It seemed to me a fine thing that the pilot could do as he pleased without asking so grand a captain's permission. I took my supper and went immediately to bed, discouraged by my day's observations and experiences. My late voyage's notebooking was but a confusion of meaningless names. It had tangled me all up in a knot every time I had looked at it in the daytime. I now hoped for respite in sleep; but no, it reveled all through my head till sunrise again, a frantic and tireless nightmare.

Next morning I felt pretty rusty and low-spirited. We went booming along, taking a good many chances, for we were anxious to get out of the river (as getting out to Cairo was called) before night should overtake us. But Mr. B——'s partner, the other pilot, presently grounded the boat, and we lost so much time getting her off that it was plain the darkness would overtake us a good long way above the mouth. This was a great misfortune especially to certain of our visiting pilots, whose boats would have to wait for their return, no matter how long that might be. It sobered the pilothouse talk a good deal. Coming upstream, pilots did not mind low water or any kind of darkness; nothing stopped them but fog. But downstream work was different; a boat was too nearly helpless, with a stiff current pushing behind her; so it was not customary to run downstream at night in low water.

There seemed to be one small hope, however: if we could get through the intricate and dangerous Hat Island crossing before night, we could venture the rest, for we would have plainer sailing and better water. But it would be insanity to attempt Hat Island at night. So there was a deal of looking at watches all the rest of the day and a constant ciphering upon the speed we were making; Hat Island was the eternal subject; sometimes hope was high; and sometimes we were delayed in a bad crossing, and down it went again. For hours all hands lay under the burden of this suppressed excitement; it was even communicated to me, and I got to feeling so solicitous about Hat Island, and under such an awful pressure of responsibility, that I wished I might have five minutes on shore to draw a good, full, relieving breath and start over again. We were standing no regular watches. Each of our pilots ran such portions of the river as he had run when coming upstream, because of his greater familiarity with it; but both remained in the pilothouse constantly.

An hour before sunset, Mr. B—— took the wheel and Mr. W—— stepped aside. For the next thirty minutes every man held his watch in his hand and was restless, silent, and uneasy. At last somebody said, with a doomful sigh, "Well, yonder's Hat Island—and we can't make it."

All the watches closed with a snap, everybody sighed and muttered something about its being "too bad, too bad — ah, if we could *only* have got here half an hour sooner!" and the place was thick with the atmosphere of disappointment. Some started to go out, but loitered, hearing no bell-tap to land. The sun dipped behind the horizon; the boat went on. Inquiring looks passed from one guest to another, and one who had his hand on the doorknob and had turned it waited, then presently took away his hand and let the knob turn back again. We bore steadily down the bend. More looks were exchanged, and nods of surprised admiration — but no words. Insensibly the men drew together behind Mr. B—— as the sky darkened and one or two dim stars came out. The dead silence and sense of waiting became oppressive. Mr. B—— pulled the cord, and two deep, mellow notes from the big bell floated off on the night. Then a pause, and one more note was struck. The watchman's voice followed, from the hurricane deck:

"Labboard lead, there! Stabboard lead!"

The cries of the leadsmen began to rise out of the distance and were gruffly repeated by the word-passers on the hurricane deck.

"M-a-r-k three! M-a-r-k three! Quarter-less-three! Half twain! quarter twain! M-a-r-k twain! Quarter-less" —

Mr. B—— pulled two bell ropes and was answered by faint jinglings far below in the engine room, and our speed slackened. The steam began to whistle through the gauge cocks. The cries of the leadsmen went on — and it is a weird sound, always, in the night. Every pilot in the lot was watching, now, with fixed eyes, and talking under his breath. Nobody was calm and easy but Mr. B——. He would put his wheel down and stand on a spoke, and as the steamer swung into her (to me) utterly invisible marks — for we seemed to be in the midst of a wide and gloomy sea — he would meet and fasten her there. Talk was going on, now, in low voices.

"There; she's over the first reef all right!"

After a pause, another subdued voice:

"Her stern's coming down just *exactly* right, by *George!* Now she's in the marks; over she goes!"

Somebody else muttered:

"Oh, it was done beautiful — *beautiful!*"

Now the engines were stopped altogether, and we drifted with the current. Not that I could see the boat drift, for I could not, the stars being all gone by this time. This drifting was the dismalest work; it held one's heart still. Presently I discovered a blacker gloom than that which surrounded us. It was the head of the island. We were closing right down upon it. We entered its deeper shadow, and so imminent seemed the peril that I was likely to suffocate; and I had the strongest impulse to do *something*, anything, to save the vessel. But still Mr. B—— stood by his wheel, silent, intent as a cat, and all the pilots stood shoulder to shoulder at his back.

"She'll not make it!" somebody whispered.

The water grew shoaler and shoaler by the leadsmen's cries, till it was down to —

"Eight-and-a-half! E-i-g-h-t feet! E-i-g-h-t feet! Seven-and" —

Mr. B—— said warningly through his speaking tube to the engineer:

"Stand by, now!"

"Aye, aye, sir."

"Seven-and-a-half! Seven feet! *Six*-and" —

We touched bottom! Instantly Mr. B—— set a lot of bells ringing, shouted through the tube, "*Now* let her have it — every ounce you've got!" then to his partner, "Put her hard down! snatch her! snatch her!" The boat rasped and ground her way through the sand, hung upon the apex of disaster a single tremendous instant, and then over she went! And such a shout as went up at Mr. B——'s back never loosened the roof of a pilothouse before!

There was no more trouble after that, Mr. B—— was a hero that night, and it was some little time, too, before his exploit ceased to be talked about by rivermen.

Fully to realize the marvelous precision required in laying the great steamer in her marks in that murky waste of water, one should know that not only must she pick her intricate way through snags and blind reefs and then shave the head of the island so closely as to brush the overhanging foliage with her stern, but at one place she must pass almost within arm's reach of a sunken and invisible wreck that would snatch the hull timbers from under her if she should strike it, and destroy a quarter of a million dollars' worth of steamboat and cargo in five minutes, and maybe a hundred and fifty human lives into the bargain.

The last remark I heard that night was a compliment to Mr. B——, uttered in soliloquy and with unction by one of our guests. He said:

"By the shadow of Death, but he's a lightning pilot!"

MARK TWAIN, Old Times on the Mississippi

76. Mississippi River Steamboats Race to Destruction

As the boom days of the early Grant period closed with the panic of 1873, Mark Twain joined with Charles Dudley Warner in publishing a satiric novel on the extravagance and follies of the time. But he also included in The Gilded Age *many recollections of the Hannibal of his childhood and the river days of his young manhood. Such races as the one here described were all too frequent.*

EARLY in the morning Squire Hawkins took passage in a small steamboat, with his family and his two slaves, and presently the bell rang, the stage plank was hauled in, and the vessel proceeded up the river. The children and the slaves were not much more at ease after finding out that this monster was a creature of human contrivance than they were the night before when they thought it the lord of heaven and earth. They started, in fright, every time the gauge cocks sent out an angry hiss, and they quaked from head to foot when the mud valves thundered. The shivering of the boat under the beating of the wheels was sheer misery to them.

But of course familiarity with these things soon took away their terrors, and then the voyage at once became a glorious adventure, a royal progress through the very heart and home of romance, a realization of their rosiest wonder dreams. They sat by the hour in the shade of the pilothouse on the hurricane deck and looked out over the curving expanses of the river sparkling in the sunlight. . . .

When the sun went down it turned all the broad river to a national banner laid in gleaming bars of gold and purple and crimson, and in time these glories faded out in the twilight and left the fairy archipelagoes reflecting their fringing foliage in the steely mirror of the stream.

At night the boat forged on through the deep solitudes of the river, hardly ever discovering a light to testify to a human presence

—mile after mile and league after league the vast bends were guarded by unbroken walls of forest that had never been disturbed by the voice or the footfall of man or felt the edge of his sacrilegious ax.

An hour after supper the moon came up, and Clay and Washington ascended to the hurricane deck to revel again in their new realm of enchantment. They ran races up and down the deck; climbed about the bell; made friends with the passenger dogs chained under the lifeboat; tried to make friends with a passenger bear fastened to the verge staff, but were not encouraged; "skinned the cat" on the hog chains; in a word, exhausted the amusement possibilities of the deck. Then they looked wistfully up at the pilothouse, and finally, little by little, Clay ventured up there, followed diffidently by Washington. The pilot turned presently to "get his stern marks," saw the lads, and invited them in. Now their happiness was complete. This cosy little house, built entirely of glass and commanding a marvelous prospect in every direction, was a magician's throne to them, and their enjoyment of the place was simply boundless.

They sat them down on a high bench and looked miles ahead and saw the wooded capes fold back and reveal the bends beyond, and they looked miles to the rear and saw the silvery highway diminish its breadth by degrees and close itself together in the distance. Presently the pilot said:

"By George, yonder comes the *Amaranth!*"

A spark appeared, close to the water, several miles down the river. The pilot took his glass and looked at it steadily for a moment, and said, chiefly to himself:

"It can't be the *Blue Wing*. She couldn't pick us up this way. It's the *Amaranth*, sure."

He bent over a speaking tube and said:

"Who's on watch down there?"

A hollow, unhuman voice rumbled up through the tube in answer:

"*I* am. Second engineer."

"Good! You want to stir your stumps, now, Harry. The *Amaranth's* just turned the point, and she's just a-humping herself too!"

The pilot took hold of a rope that stretched out forward, jerked it twice and two mellow strokes of the big bell responded. A voice out on the deck shouted:

"Stand by, down there, with that labboard lead!"

"No, I don't want the lead," said the pilot, "I want *you*. Roust out the old man — tell him the *Amaranth's* coming. And go and call Jim — tell *him*."

"Aye, aye, sir!"

The old man was the captain — he is always called so, on steamboats and ships; Jim was the other pilot. Within two minutes both of these men were flying up the pilothouse stairway, three steps at a jump. Jim was in his shirt sleeves, with his coat and vest on his arm. He said:

"I was just turning in. Where's the glass?"

He took it and looked:

"Don't appear to be any nighthawk on the jack staff — it's the *Amaranth,* dead sure!"

The captain took a good long look, and only said:

"Damnation!"

George Davis, the pilot on watch, shouted to the night watchman on deck:

"How's she loaded?"

"Two inches by the head, sir."

" 'Tain't enough!"

The captain shouted now:

"Call the mate. Tell him to call all hands and get a lot of that sugar forrard — put her ten inches by the head. Lively, now!"

"Aye, aye, sir!"

A riot of shouting and tramping floated up from below presently, and the uneasy steering of the boat soon showed that she was getting down by the head.

The three men in the pilothouse began to talk in short, sharp sentences, low and earnestly. As their excitement rose their voices went down. As fast as one of them put down the spyglass another took it up, but always with a studied air of calmness. Each time the verdict was:

"She's a-gaining!"

The captain spoke through the tube:

"What steam are you carrying?"

"A hundred and forty-two, sir! But she's getting hotter and hotter all the time."

The boat was straining and groaning and quivering like a monster in pain. Both pilots were at work now, one on each side of the wheel, with their coats and vests off, their bosoms and collars wide open, and the perspiration flowing down their faces. They were holding the boat so close to the shore that the willows swept the guards almost from stem to stern.

"Stand by!" whispered George.

"All ready!" said Jim, under his breath.

"Let her come!"

The boat sprang away from the bank like a deer and darted in a long diagonal toward the other shore. She closed in again and thrashed her fierce way along the willows as before. The captain put down the glass.

"Lord, how she walks up on us! I do hate to be beat!"

"Jim," said George, looking straight ahead, watching the slightest yawing of the boat and promptly meeting it with the wheel, "how'll it do to try Murderer's Chute?"

"Well, it's — it's taking chances. How was the cottonwood stump on the false point below Boardman's Island this morning?"

"Water just touching the roots."

"Well, it's pretty close work. That gives six feet scant in the head of Murderer's Chute. We can just barely rub through if we hit it exactly right. But it's worth trying. *She* don't dare tackle it!" — meaning the *Amaranth*.

In another instant the *Boreas* plunged into what seemed a crooked creek, and the *Amaranth's* approaching lights were shut out in a moment. Not a whisper was uttered, now, but the three men stared ahead into the shadows and two of them spun the wheel back and forth with anxious watchfulness while the steamer tore along. The chute seemed to come to an end every fifty yards, but always opened out in time. Now the head of it was at hand. George tapped the big bell three times; two leadsmen sprang to their posts, and in a moment their weird cries rose on the night air and were caught up and repeated by two men on the upper deck:

"No-o bottom!"

"De-e-p four!"

"Quarter three!"

"Mark under wa-a-ter three!"

"Half twain!"

"Quarter twain! — "

Davis pulled a couple of ropes. There was a jingling of small bells far below, the boat's speed slackened, and the pent steam began to whistle and the gauge cocks to scream:

"By the mark twain!"

"Quar-ter-*her*-er-*less* twain!"

"Eight *and* a half!"

"Eight feet!"

"Seven-and-a-half! — "

Another jingling of little bells, and the wheels ceased turning altogether. The whistling of the steam was something frightful, now — it almost drowned all other noises.

"Stand by to meet her!"

George had the wheel hard down and was standing on a spoke.

"All ready!"

The boat hesitated — seemed to hold her breath, as did the captain and pilots — and then she began to fall away to starboard and every eye lighted:

"*Now* then! — meet her! meet her! Snatch her!"

The wheel flew to port so fast that the spokes blended into a spider-web — the swing of the boat subsided — she steadied herself —

"Seven feet!"

"Sev — six and a *half!*"

"*Six* feet! Six f — "

Bang! She hit the bottom! George shouted through the tube:

"Spread her wide open! *Whale it at her!*"

Pow — wow — chow! The escape pipes belched snowy pillars of steam aloft, the boat ground and surged and trembled — and slid over into —

"M-a-r-k twain!"

"Quarter-*her* — "

"Tap! tap! tap!" (To signify "lay in the leads.")

And away she went, flying up the willow shore, with the whole silver sea of the Mississippi stretching abroad on every hand.

No *Amaranth* in sight!

"Ha-ha, boys, we took a couple of tricks that time!" said the captain.

And just at that moment a red glare appeared in the head of the chute and the *Amaranth* came springing after them!

"Well, I swear!"

"Jim, what *is* the meaning of that?"

"I'll tell you what's the meaning of it. That hail we had at Napoleon was Wash Hastings, wanting to come to Cairo — and we didn't stop. He's in that pilothouse now, showing those mud turtles how to hunt for easy water."

"That's it! I thought it wasn't any slouch that was running that middle bar in Hog-eye Bend. If it's Wash Hastings — well, what he don't know about the river ain't worth knowing — a regular gold-leaf, kid-glove, diamond-breastpin pilot Wash Hastings is. We won't take any tricks off of *him,* old man!"

"I wish I'd 'a' stopped for him, that's all."

The *Amaranth* was within three hundred yards of the *Boreas* and still gaining. The old man spoke through the tube:

"What is she carrying now?"

"A hundred and sixty-five, sir!"

"How's your wood?"

"Pine all out — cypress half gone — eating up cottonwood like pie!"

"Break into that rosin on the main deck — pile it in. The boat can pay for it!"

Soon the boat was plunging and quivering and screaming more madly than ever. But the *Amaranth's* head was almost abreast the *Boreas'* stern.

"How's your steam now, Harry?"

"Hundred and eighty-two, sir!"

"Break up the casks of bacon in the forrard hold! Pile it in! Levy on that turpentine in the fantail — drench every stick of wood with it!"

The boat was a moving earthquake by this time.

"How is she now?"

"A hundred and ninety-six and still a-swelling! Water below the middle gauge cocks! Carrying every pound she can stand! Nigger roosting on the safety valve!"

"Good, how's your draft?"

"Bully! Every time a nigger heaves a stick of wood into the furnace he goes out the chimney with it!"

The *Amaranth* drew steadily up till her jack staff breasted the *Boreas'* wheelhouse — climbed along inch by inch till her chimneys breasted it — crept along farther and farther till the boats were wheel to wheel — and then they closed up with a heavy jolt and locked together tight and fast in the middle of the big river under the flooding moonlight! A roar and a hurrah went up from the crowded decks of both steamers — all hands rushed to the guards to look and shout and gesticulate — the weight careened the vessels over toward each other — officers flew hither and thither cursing and storming, trying to drive the people amidships — both captains were leaning over their railings, shaking their fists, swearing and threatening — black volumes of smoke rolled up and canopied the scene, delivering a rain of sparks upon the vessels — two pistolshots rang out, and both captains dodged unhurt and the packed masses of passengers surged back and fell apart while the shrieks of women and children soared above the intolerable din —

And then there was a booming roar, a thundering crash, and the riddled *Amaranth* dropped loose from her hold and drifted helplessly away!

Instantly the fire doors of the *Boreas* were thrown open and the men began dashing buckets of water into the furnaces — for it would have been death and destruction to stop the engines with such a head of steam on.

As soon as possible the *Boreas* dropped down to the floating wreck and took off the dead, the wounded, and the unhurt — at least all that could be got at, for the whole forward half of the boat was a shapeless ruin, with the great chimneys lying crossed on top of it, and underneath were a dozen victims imprisoned alive and wailing for help. While men with axes worked with might and main to free these poor fellows, the *Boreas'* boats went about, picking up stragglers from the river.

And now a new horror presented itself. The wreck took fire from the dismantled furnaces! Never did men work with a heartier will than did those stalwart braves with the axes. But it was of no use.

The fire ate its way steadily, despising the bucket brigade that fought it. It scorched the clothes, it singed the hair of the axmen — it drove them back, foot by foot — inch by inch — they wavered, struck a final blow in the teeth of the enemy, and surrendered. . . .

The *Boreas* stood away out of danger, and the ruined steamer went drifting down the stream, an island of wreathing and climbing flame that vomited clouds of smoke from time to time, and glared more fiercely and sent its luminous tongues higher and higher after each emission. A shriek at intervals told of a captive that had met his doom. The wreck lodged upon a sand bar, and when the *Boreas* turned the next point on her upward journey it was still burning with scarcely abated fury.

When the boys came down into the main saloon of the *Boreas,* they saw a pitiful sight and heard a world of pitiful sounds. Eleven poor creatures lay dead and forty more lay moaning, or pleading or screaming, while a score of good Samaritans moved among them, doing what they could to relieve their sufferings, bathing their skin-less faces and bodies with linseed oil and limewater, and covering the places with bulging masses of raw cotton that gave to every face and form a dreadful and unhuman aspect. . . .

The head engineer of the *Amaranth,* a grand specimen of physical manhood, struggled to his feet, a ghastly spectacle, and strode toward his brother, the second engineer, who was unhurt. He said:

"You were on watch. You were boss. You would not listen to me when I begged you to reduce your steam. Take that! — take it to my wife and tell her it comes from me by the hand of my murderer! Take it — and take my curse with it to blister your heart a hundred years — and may you live so long!"

And he tore a ring from his finger, stripping flesh and skin with it, threw it down and fell dead!

But these things must not be dwelt upon. The *Boreas* landed her dreadful cargo at the next large town and delivered it over to a multitude of eager hands and warm Southern hearts — a cargo amounting by this time to thirty-nine wounded persons and twenty-two dead bodies. And with these she delivered a list of ninety-six missing persons that had drowned or otherwise perished at the scene of the disaster.

A jury of inquest was impaneled, and after due deliberation and inquiry they returned the inevitable American verdict which has been so familiar to our ears all the days of our lives — "NOBODY TO BLAME."

MARK TWAIN and CHARLES DUDLEY WARNER, The Gilded Age

XV

Social Life in the Early Republic

77. What Is an American?

The best studies of American traits, the best characterizations of the genius of America, have been made by men born and trained abroad. One of the first in this long line of foreign students of American character was Hector St. John de Crèvecœur. Born in Normandy in 1735, Crèvecœur migrated to Canada, fought under Montcalm, reached New York in 1759, and after much drifting about, became a British subject and settled on a farm in Orange County, New York, in 1769. During the Revolution he was a Loyalist; after it he became French consul in New York. He knew pioneer life and the lot of the small farmer and laborer in America thoroughly, and wrought his knowledge into a large number of letters and essays, cast in vigorous English. He had a broad philosophical approach to the questions of his time, and he could depict rural life and general social conditions with graphic and minute detail.

I WISH I could be acquainted with the feelings and thoughts which must agitate the heart and present themselves to the mind of an enlightened Englishman when he first lands on this continent. He must greatly rejoice that he lived at a time to see this fair country discovered and settled. He must necessarily feel a share of national pride when he views the chain of settlements which embellish these extended shores. Here he sees the industry of his native country displayed in a new manner, and traces, in their works, the embryos of all the arts, sciences, and ingenuity which flourish in Europe. Here he beholds fair cities, substantial villages, extensive fields, an immense country filled with decent houses, good roads, orchards, meadows, and bridges, where, a hundred years ago, all was wild, wooded, and uncultivated! What a train of pleasing ideas this fair spectacle must suggest! It is a prospect which must inspire a good citizen with the most heart-felt pleasure!

The difficulty consists in the manner of viewing so extensive a scene. He is arrived on a new continent; a modern society offers itself to his contemplation, different from what he had hitherto seen. It is not composed, as in Europe, of great lords who possess everything and of a herd of people who have nothing. Here are no aristocratical families, no courts, no kings, no bishops, no ecclesiastical dominion, no invisible power giving to a few a very visible one, no great manufactures employing thousands, no great refinements of luxury. The rich and the poor are not so far removed from each other as they are in Europe. Some few towns excepted, we are all tillers of the earth, from Nova Scotia to West Florida. We are a people of cultivators, scattered over an immense territory, communicating with each other by means of good roads and navigable rivers, united by the silken bands of mild government, all respecting the laws without dreading their power, because they are equitable. We are all animated with the spirit of an industry which is unfettered and unrestrained, because each person works for himself. If he travels through our rural districts, he views not the hostile castle and the haughty mansion contrasted with the clay-built hut and the miserable cabin where cattle and men help to keep each other warm and dwell in meanness, smoke, and indigence. A pleasing uniformity of decent competence appears throughout our habitations. The meanest of our log houses is a dry and comfortable habitation. Lawyer or merchant are the fairest titles our towns afford; that of a farmer is the only appellation of the rural inhabitants of our country. It must take some time ere he can reconcile himself to our dictionary, which is but short in words of dignity and names of honor. There, on a Sunday, he sees a congregation of respectable farmers and their wives, all clad in neat homespun, well mounted, or riding in their own humble wagons. There is not among them an esquire, saving the unlettered magistrate. There he sees a parson as simple as his flock, a farmer who does not riot on the labor of others. We have no princes for whom we toil, starve, and bleed. We are the most perfect society now existing in the world. Here man is free as he ought to be; nor is this pleasing equality so transitory as many others are. Many ages will not see the shores of our great lakes replenished with inland nations, nor the unknown bounds of North America entirely peopled. Who can tell how far it extends? Who can tell the millions of men whom it will feed and contain, for no European foot has, as yet, traveled half the extent of this mighty continent?

The next wish of this traveler will be to know whence came all these people. They are a mixture of English, Scotch, Irish, French, Dutch, Germans, and Swedes. From this promiscuous breed, that race now called Americans have arisen. The eastern provinces must indeed be excepted, as being the unmixed descendants of English men. I have heard many wish that they had been more intermixed also; for my part, I am no wisher, and think it much better as it has happened. They exhibit a most conspicuous figure in this great and variegated picture. They too enter for a great share in the pleasing perspective displayed in these thirteen provinces. I know it is fashionable to reflect on them, but I respect them for what they have done, for the activity and wisdom with which they have settled their territory, for the decency of their manners, for their early love of letters, their ancient college, the first in this hemisphere, for their industy, which to me, who am but a farmer, is the criterion of everything. There never was a people, situated as they are, who with so ungrateful a soil have done more in so short a time. Do you think that the monarchical ingredients which are more prevalent in other governments have purged them from all foul stains? Their histories assert the contrary.

In this great American asylum the poor of Europe have by some means met together, and in consequence of various causes. To what purpose should they ask one another what countrymen they are? Alas, two-thirds of them had no country. Urged by a variety of motives, here they came. Everything has tended to regenerate them. New laws, a new mode of living, a new social system. Here they are become men. In Europe they were as so many useless plants, wanting vegetative mold and refreshing showers. They withered and were mowed down by want, hunger, and war; but now, by the power of transplantation, like all other plants, they have taken root and flourished! Formerly they were not numbered in any civil lists of their country except in those of the poor; here they rank as citizens. By what invisible power has this surprising metamorphosis been performed? By that of the laws and that of their industry. The laws, the indulgent laws, protect them as they arrive, stamping on them the symbol of adoption; they receive ample rewards for their labors; these accumulated rewards procure them land; those lands confer on them the title of freemen, and to that title every benefit is affixed which men can possibly require. This is the great operation daily performed by our laws.

What attachment can a poor European emigrant have for a country where he had nothing? The knowledge of the language, the love of a few kindred as poor as himself, were the only cords that tied him. His country is now that which gives him his land, bread, protection, and consequence. . . . What then is the American, this new man? He is neither a European nor the descendant of a European; hence that strange mixture of blood which you will find in no other country. I could point out to you a family whose grandfather was an Englishman, whose wife was Dutch, whose son married a French woman, and whose present four sons have now four wives of different nations. He is an American who, leaving behind him all his ancient prejudices and manners, receives new ones from the new mode of life he has embraced, the new government he obeys, and the new rank he holds. He becomes an American by being received in the broad lap of our great *alma mater*. Here individuals of all nations are melted into a new race of men whose labors and posterity will one day cause great changes in the world. Americans are the western pilgrims, who are carrying along with them the great mass of arts, sciences, vigor, and industry which began long since in the East. They will finish the great circle. The Americans were once scattered all over Europe. Here they are incorporated into one of the finest systems of population which has ever appeared and which will hereafter become distinct by the power of the different climates they inhabit. The American ought therefore to love this country much better than that in which either he or his forefathers were born. Here the rewards of his industry follow with equal steps the progress of his labor. His labor is founded on the basis of nature, *self-interest:* can it want a stronger allurement? Wives and children, who before in vain demanded of him a morsel of bread, now, fat and frolicsome, gladly help their father to clear those fields whence exuberant crops are to rise, to feed and to clothe them all, without any part being claimed either by a despotic prince, a rich abbot, or a mighty lord.

Here religion demands but little of him — a small voluntary salary to the minister, and gratitude to God — can he refuse these? The American is a new man who acts on new principles; he must therefore entertain new ideas and form new opinions. From involuntary idleness, servile dependence, penury, and useless labor, he has passed to toils of a very different nature, rewarded by ample subsistence. This is an American.

CRÈVECŒUR, Letters from an American Farmer, 1782

78. Samuel Goodrich Remembers Life in Connecticut

The once-famous "Peter Parley," author of a large number of books of popular instruction, grew up in Ridgefield, Connecticut, then a quaint and isolated village, now within the suburban belt of New York. Samuel Griswold Goodrich, to give him his full name, was the sixth of ten children, and was well reared, though his father's salary as minister averaged but $400 a year. In those very early years of the nineteenth century rural households were self-sufficing. Goodrich tells us that each family slaughtered its own beeves and hogs; spun and dyed its own cloth; ground its own rye and corn for bread; made its own maple sugar; molded its own candles; cut its own fuel. But Goodrich himself showed how ready the Yankees were to bring in the industrial revolution. After serving in the War of 1812, his first venture was a pocketbook factory at Hartford.

I MUST not fail to give you a portrait of one of our village homes — of the middle class — at this era [1800]. I take as an example that of our neighbor, J—— B——, who had been a tailor, but having thriven in his affairs and now advanced to the age of some fifty years, had become a farmer — such a career, by the way, being common at the time; for the prudent mechanic, adding to his house and his lands, as his necessities and his thrift dictated, usually ended as the proprietor of an ample house, fifty to a hundred acres of land, and an ample barn, stocked with half a dozen cows, one or two horses, a flock of sheep, and a general assortment of poultry.

The home of this, our neighbor B——, was situated on the road leading to Salem, there being a wide space in front occupied by the woodpile, which in these days was not only a matter of great importance, but of formidable bulk. The size of the woodpile was indeed in some sort an index to the rank and condition of the proprietor. The house itself was a low edifice, forty feet long, and of two stories in front, the rear being what was called a breakback, that is, sloping down to a height of ten feet, this low part furnishing a shelter for garden tools and various household instruments. The whole was constructed of wood, the outside being of the dun complexion assumed by unpainted wood exposed to the weather for twenty or thirty years, save only that the roof was tinged of a reddish brown by a fine moss that found sustenance in the chestnut shingles.

To the left was the garden, which in the productive season was a wilderness of onions, squashes, cucumbers, beets, parsnips, and currants, with the neverfailing tansy for bitters, horse-radish for seasoning, and fennel for keeping old women awake in churchtime. A sprig of fennel was, in fact, the theological smelling bottle of the tender sex and not unfrequently of the men, who, from long sitting in the sanctuary after a week of labor in the field, [finding] themselves too strongly tempted to visit the forbidden land of Nod, would sometimes borrow a sprig of fennel and exorcise the fiend that threatened their spiritual welfare.

The interior of the house presented a parlor with plain whitewashed walls, a homemade carpet upon the floor, calico curtains at the window, and a mirror three feet by two against the side, with a mahogany frame; to these must be added eight chairs and a cherry table of the manufacture of Deacon Hawley. The keeping or sitting room had also a carpet, a dozen rush-bottom chairs, a table, etc. The kitchen was large — fully twenty feet square, with a fireplace six feet wide and four feet deep. On one side it looked out upon the garden, the squashes and cucumbers climbing up and forming festoons over the door; on the other a view was presented of the orchard, embracing first a circle of peaches, pears, and plums, and beyond, a widespread clover field, embowered with apple trees. Just by was the well, with its tall sweep, the old oaken bucket dangling from the pole. The kitchen was in fact the most comfortable room in the house, cool in summer and perfumed with the breath of the garden and the orchard; in winter, with its roaring blaze of hickory, it was a cosy resort, defying the bitterest blasts of the season. Here the whole family assembled at meals, save only when the presence of company made it proper to serve tea in the parlor.

The chambers were all without carpets, and the furniture was generally of a simple character. The beds, however, were of ample size and well filled with geese feathers, these being deemed essential for comfortable people. I must say, by the way, that every decent family had its flock of geese, of course, which was picked thrice a year, despite the noisy remonstrances of both goose and gander. The sheets of the bed, though of homemade linen, were as white as the driven snow. Indeed, the beds of this era showed that sleep was a luxury, well understood and duly cherished by all classes. The cellar, extending under the whole house, was a vast receptacle and by no means the least important part of the establishment. In the autumn it was supplied with three barrels of beef and as many of pork, twenty barrels of cider, with numerous bins of potatoes, turnips, beets, carrots, and cabbages. The garret, which was of huge dimensions, at the same time displayed a labyrinth of dried pumpkins, peaches, and apples hung in festoons upon the rafters, amid bunches of summer savory, boneset, fennel, and other herbs, the floor being occupied by heaps of wool, flax, tow, and the like.

The barn corresponded to the house. It was a low brown structure, having abundance of sheds built on to it, without the least regard to symmetry. I need not say it was well stocked with hay, oats, rye, and buckwheat. Six cows, one or two horses, three dozen sheep, and an ample supply of poultry, including two or three broods of turkeys, constituted its living tenants.

In most families the first exercise of the morning was reading the Bible, followed by a prayer, at which all were assembled, including the servants and helpers of the kitchen and the farm. Then came the breakfast, which was a substantial meal, always including hot viands, with vegetables, applesauce, pickles, mustard, horse-radish, and various other condiments. Cider was the common drink for laboring people; even children drank it at will. Tea was common, but not so general as now. Coffee was almost unknown. Dinner was a still more hearty and varied repast, characterized by abundance of garden vegetables; tea was a light supper.

The day began early; breakfast was had at six in summer and seven in winter; dinner at noon — the workpeople in the fields being called to their meals by a conch shell, usually winded by some kitchen Triton. The echoing of this noontide horn, from farm to farm and over hill and dale, was a species of music which even rivaled the popular melody of drum and fife. Tea, the evening meal, usually took place about sundown. In families where all were laborers, all sat at table, servants as well as masters, the food being served before sitting down. In families where the masters and mistresses did not share the labors of the household or the farm, the meals of the domestics were had separate. There was, however, in those days, a perfectly good understanding and good feeling between the masters and servants. The latter were not Irish; they had not as yet imbibed the plebeian envy of those above them which has since so generally embittered and embarrassed American domestic life. The terms democrat and aristocrat had not got into use; these distinctions and the feelings now implied by them had indeed no existence in the hearts of the people. Our servants, during all my early life, were of the neighborhood, generally the daughters of respectable farmers and mechanics, and, respecting others, were themselves respected and cherished. They were devoted to the interests of the family and were always relied upon and treated as friends. In health they had the same food, in sickness the same care, as the masters and mistresses or their children. This servitude implied no degradation, because it did not degrade the heart or manners of those subjected to it.

At the period of my earliest recollections, men of all classes were dressed in long, broad-tailed coats, with huge pockets, long waistcoats, and breeches. Hats had low crowns, with broad brims — some so wide as to be supported at the sides with cords. The stockings of the parson, and a few others, were of silk in summer and worsted in winter; those of the people were generally of wool, and blue and gray mixed. Women dressed in wide bonnets, sometimes of straw and sometimes of silk; the gowns were of silk, muslin, gingham, etc., generally close and short-waisted, the breast and shoulders being covered by a full muslin kerchief. Girls ornamented themselves with a large white Vandyke. On the whole, the dress of both men and women has greatly changed. As to the former, short, snug, close-fitting garments have succeeded to the loose, latitudinarian coats of former times; stovepipe hats have followed broad brims, and panta-loons have taken the place of breeches. With the other sex, little French bonnets set round with glowing flowers flourish in the place of the plain, yawning hats of yore; then it was as much an effort to make the waists short, as it is now to make them long. As to the hips, which now make so formidable a display, it seems to me that in the days I allude to, ladies had none to speak of.

The amusements were then much the same as at present, though some striking differences may be noted. Books and newspapers, which are now diffused even among the country towns, so as to be in the hands of all, young and old, were then scarce and were read respectfully and as if they were grave matters, demanding thought and attention. They were not toys and pastimes, taken up every day, and by everybody, in the short intervals of labor, and then hastily dismissed, like waste paper. The aged sat down when they read, and drew forth their spectacles, and put them deliberately and reverently upon the nose. These instruments were not, as now, little tortoise-shell hoops attached to a ribbon and put off and on with a jerk; but they were of silver or steel, substantially made and calculated to hold on with a firm and steady grasp, showing the gravity of the uses to which they were devoted. Even the young ap-proached a book with reverence and a newspaper with awe. How the world has changed!

S. G. GOODRICH, Recollections of a Lifetime

79. School and Play in Old Salem

We turn back to a girlhood in the New England town that Hawthorne made famous. Salem, early in the nineteenth century, was still a hustling seaport, sending its proud ships over the seven seas. Even the candies, as any Crowningshield recalls, testified to the all-pervading influence of the sea.

ALL THE children of our set were sent to the dame school at a very early age, there to learn sewing, reading, writing, and manners. The schoolroom was upstairs in one of the chambers of the large house that had been her home for many years. It had been turned into a schoolroom, and here the children of our set congregated to be taught by the prim dame.

I have still a sampler that I worked while at the dame school. It is faded with age, and its alphabet in script is very hard to decipher. Like many of the early samplers, it was copied from an approved pattern, the teacher leading my fingers toward perfection. Halfway down is a picture showing water in three shades, holding fish, ducks, and water lilies. Three hills rise behind the water, each one bearing a tree, in one of which a parrot rested happily. It was worked in simple cross-stitch in various shades of silk and expressed my future hopes at the end:

> Amy Kittredge is my name,
> Salem is my dwelling place,
> New England is my nashun,
> And Christ is my salvation.

I wrought this in the twelfth year of my age. These schools are now a thing of the past; their memories linger tenderly in the hearts of those who were fortunate enough to be able to receive invaluable lessons in good breeding through the instructions of the gentle dames. Those tall and dignified spinsters never forgot manners and consequently never overlooked any breaches that were made by their scholars. In a way these schools resembled those in the English homes in that they were kept by gentlewomen whose fortunes had diminished and who had no other way of earning a living. Many of them were intimates of the family and attended social affairs, never forgetting to hold before us the example that they taught at school. Not everybody was admitted as a pupil to one of these schools; not a child but had to have his family history looked up before he could enter the door. Children whose parents or grandparents had always attended a school such as this were the first to be looked after, and their applications for admission were put in almost while in the cradle, so that when the child was grown they would be ahead on the waiting list. Once a pupil of this school, one's standing was established. It was like an introduction at court, and no matter what should happen in afterlife, every pupil was stamped with the insignia of having been a pupil in one of these schools.

It must be remembered that there was not then, as today, progression in teaching. The pupils had it instilled into their minds that to be a gentlewoman was above everything else, and manners were most important. Any breach along these lines was treated with the utmost severity, and the pupil was made to feel her impropriety by sharp looks and a lecture that she did not readily forget. Doubtless many of these people who held the position of instructor were not up in the scientific methods of today and got their appointments through friends who wished to help them in their impoverished condition. The teachers were past middle life, many of them stiff, angular, and prim.

The entrance to the schoolroom was not through the front door but by a side door that opened in the yard. We came up the side staircase and used the back stairs at recess. Religious exercises were the first event of the day, and a tap of the pencil on the desk brought the children to order. An air of good breeding pervaded the schoolroom, and every child was taught that manners were as important as lessons. We entered and behaved generally in the schoolroom in the most decorous manner, our high spirits finding vent in the schoolyard, where we romped to our hearts' content but were never allowed to quarrel. Harry and I managed to have seats close together, and often when the teacher was not looking we passed notes to each other, commenting on the arrival or the departure of some favorite ship.

It was through Harry's helpfulness that I was able to progress as rapidly as I did, for I was behindhand in many studies because of my slower progress at home. We spelled and read from our little reading books, sang our multiplication table to the tune of "Yankee Doodle," and studied arithmetic through the use of wooden beads strung on wire. Punishments were rare, but when they were necessary we were either sent into a closet or punished in some mild way, being forced to make amends possibly by writing our names or by doing a sum on the slate.

Classes consisted generally of but one pupil, as the books varied, mine being one that Mother had used. We learned to read, spell, and sew, after a fashion, but not as it is taught today in the modern schools. Courtesy was considered an accomplishment, and we received instructions in the art just as we did in the three R's. Needlework was also considered the proper thing, and not a child was ever graduated from a school such as this who had not worked one sampler and more often two. Sewing was a fine art in those days, and we were taught to do it so delicately that the stitches were practically invisible. You will find samples of my work hidden away in the old trunk and also a sampler that was worked when Harry was only eleven years of age. It was the ability to sew that gave him occupation later during his long voyages. He took with him material and did beautiful work, some of which I kept.

New Year's was a great day at the school. There was a bustle of excitement, and weeks beforehand certain scholars were chosen to visit the parents to obtain money as a gift for the teachers. It was carefully wrapped up and placed in an envelope bearing on the outside the address of the teacher written in a childish hand by one of the pupils. The rest of us would gather close around to witness the proceedings. The envelope was handed to the teacher with great ceremony and was received in the same manner, being considered a surprise, though in reality it was expected. Each of us received a gift. Among them were quaint little jointed wooden dolls with old-fashioned faces. You will find some of these packed away in a trunk with other gifts that were made to Harry and me.

There was one thing to be said in favor of these schools, and that was that what we learned we remembered, for our lessons were not all from books. The old-fashioned manner of our teachers has been so impressed on my mind that I have never forgotten it, and the breeding of the girls of that day differed essentially from that of the present generation.

Another thing that fascinated me and that I never was tired of doing was to visit the penny shops, like the one kept by Hepzibah Pyncheon in *The House of the Seven Gables*. To my childish mind they contained treasures of the Orient. The copper cent, as big as half a dollar, seemed to us children to possess the compelling power of a fortune, and it was only after consideration worthy of it that it found its way always into the drawer behind the counter in one of these stores.

They were tended by gentlewomen, and there was about them an air of mystery that was fascinating. Standing on the shelves were calicoes and prints to be made up into dresses and aprons, and so honest were these shopkeepers that they even pointed out flaws before selling, a practice not acted on today.

Little dolls, wooden jointed, and all sorts of penny purchases were intermingled under the glass case. One of the favorites was a sheet of white paper on which were dropped with great precision rows of white and pink peppermints. These could be purchased for a penny and were always in demand by the children. Then there were the gingerbread Jim Crows, a triumph of art in our eyes and so tasty and appetizing that we never could get enough for our satisfaction.

Black Jacks and Salem Gibraltars came in later. Their fame has been widespread for many a year. There were no modern confections, for our great-grandfathers disapproved of them. Black Jack never had the fame of Gibraltars. The latter were so stony and flint-hearted that they libeled the rock of that name. They might well be looked upon as the aristocrat of our Salem candies, and so popular did they become and so connected with recollections that it is said that the old sea captains took them on voyages to eat when they felt homesick.

Gibraltars were not all of one flavor. There were lemon and peppermint and checkerberry; the favorite of all those with the older people was the peppermint. I remember Mrs. Spencer, whose son came to Salem in 1822, starting the confection making a little later, driving about in a wagon from shop to shop, to carry supplies to wholesale customers.

The growth in the confection sale was not extensive at first, for they retailed at fourpence halfpenny for seven. Wrapped in soft white paper, they tempted not only the children but the older people, and finally not a house did not include this confection as a necessary part of the serving at afternoon tea. Black Jacks were dark and sticky, tasting as if they had been burnt in the kettle, and the flavor was intentional, not accidental, which was a part of the mystery that surrounded its making.

Harry and I saved our pennies until we got a goodly store and then recklessly invested it all in the four things our hearts desired — we preferring a feast to a dribble. The very last time that Harry went on his voyage, I bought two boxes of Gibraltars for him to take with him. Since he passed away I have never tasted one and could not; they were too closely connected with our life together. The very sight of one in a store brings to mind the lad growing out of boyhood into manhood standing at the edge of the wharf bidding me a last farewell. In his hand was the box of these goodies, the last gift that I presented to him.

MARY HARROD NORTHEND, Memories of Old Salem

80. Josiah Quincy Sees Eclipse Beat Sir Henry

Bostonians are familiar with a daguerreotype taken about 1860, showing four Josiah Quincys in a line of direct descent; the oldest of whom was born in 1772, and the youngest of whom died in 1919. Three of the four were mayors of Boston and one was president of Harvard. It was the second in this group, his career covering the years 1802–1882, who left a delightful sheaf of autobiographic papers dealing with American life in the first third of the century. He described talks with old John Adams, Lafayette's visit to Bunker Hill, visits of John Randolph of Roanoke, and Andrew Jackson's tour of New England. He also had an eye for a horse race.

ON THE 27th of May, 1823, nearly fifty-seven years ago, there was great excitement in the city of New York, for on that day the long-expected race of "Eclipse against the world" was to be decided on the racecourse on Long Island. It was an amicable contest between the North and the South. The New York votaries of the turf, a much more prominent interest than at present, had offered to run Eclipse against any horse that could be produced, for a purse of ten thousand dollars; and the Southern gentlemen had accepted the challenge.

I could obtain no carriage to take me to the course, as every conveyance in the city was engaged. Carriages of every description formed an unbroken line from the ferry to the ground. They were driven rapidly, and were in very close connection, so much so that when one of them suddenly stopped, the poles of at least a dozen carriages broke through the panels of those preceding them. The drivers were naturally much enraged at this accident, but it seemed a necessary consequence of the crush and hurry of the day, and nobody could be blamed for it. The party that I was with, seeing there was no chance of riding, was compelled to foot it. But after plodding some way, we had the luck to fall in with a returning carriage, which we chartered to take us to the course.

On arriving, we found an assembly which was simply overpowering; it was estimated that there were over one hundred thousand persons upon the ground. The conditions of the race were four-mile heats, the best two in three; the course was a mile in length. A college friend, the late David P. Hall, had procured for me a ticket for the jockey box, which commanded a view of the whole field.

There was great difficulty in clearing the track until Eclipse and Sir Henry (the Southern horse) were brought to the stand. They were both in brave spirits, throwing their heels high into the air; they soon effected that scattering of the multitude which all other methods had failed to accomplish. And now a great disappointment fell like a wet blanket on more than half the spectators. It was suddenly announced that Purdy, the jockey of Eclipse, had had a difficulty with his owner and refused to ride. To substitute another in his place seemed almost like giving up the contest, but the man was absolutely stubborn, and the time had come. Another rider was provided, and the signal for the start was given.

I stood exactly opposite the judges' seat, where the mastering excitement found its climax. Off went the horses, every eye straining to follow them. Four times they dashed by the judges' stand, and every time Sir Henry was on the lead. The spirits of the Southerners seemed to leap up beyond control, while the depression of the more phlegmatic North set in like a physical chill. Directly before me sat John Randolph, the great orator of Virginia. Apart from his intense sectional pride, he had personal reasons to rejoice at the turn things were taking, for he had bet heavily on the contest and, it was said, proposed to sail for Europe upon clearing enough to pay his expenses.

Half an hour elapsed for the horses to get their wind, and again they were brought to the stand. But now a circumstance occurred which raised a deafening shout from the partisans of the North. Purdy was to ride. How his scruples had been overcome did not appear, but there he stood before us, and was mounting Eclipse. Again, amidst breathless suspense, the word "Go!" was heard, and again Sir Henry took the inside track, and kept the lead for more than two miles and a half. Eclipse followed close on his heels and, at short intervals, attempted to pass. At every spurt he made to get ahead, Randolph's high-pitched and penetrating voice was heard, each time shriller than before: "You can't do it, Mr. Purdy! You can't do it, Mr. Purdy! You can't do it, Mr. Purdy!"

But Mr. Purdy *did* do it. And as he took the lead, what a roar of excitement went up! Tens of thousands of dollars were in suspense, and although I had not a cent depending, I lost my breath, and felt as if a sword had passed through me. Purdy kept the lead and came in a length or so ahead. The horses had run eight miles, and the third heat was to decide the day. The confidence on the part of the Southern gentlemen was abated. The manager of Sir Henry rode up to the front of our box and, calling to a gentleman, said: "You must ride the next heat; there are hundreds of thousands of Southern money depending on it. That boy don't know how to ride; he don't keep his horse's mouth open!"

The gentleman positively refused, saying that he had not been in the saddle for months. The manager begged him to come down, and John Randolph was summoned to use his eloquent persuasions. When the horses were next brought to the stand, behold, the gentleman appeared, booted and spurred, with a red jacket, and a jockey cap on his head. On the third heat Eclipse took the lead, and by dint of constant whipping and spurring, won by a length this closely-contested race.

There was never contest more exciting. Sectional feeling and heavy pecuniary stakes were both involved. The length of time before it was decided, the change of riders, the varying fortunes, all intensified the interest. I have seen the great Derby races, but they finish almost as soon as they begin, and were tame enough in comparison to this. Here for nearly two hours there was no abatement in the strain. I was unconscious of everything else, and found when the race was concluded that the sun had actually blistered my cheek without my perceiving it. The victors were, of course, exultant, and Purdy, mounted on Eclipse, was led up to the judges' stand, the band playing "See the Conquering Hero Comes."

The Southerners bore their losses like gentlemen, and with a good grace. It was suggested that the comparative chances of Adams and Jackson at the approaching presidential election should be tested by a vote of that gathering. "Ah," said Mr. Randolph, "if the question of the presidency could be settled by this assembly there would be no opposition; Mr. Purdy would go to the White House by acclamation."

JOSIAH QUINCY, Figures of the Past

81. Harriet Martineau Finds a Working Girls' Paradise

The Industrial Revolution had its brutal side in America as in England. But the factories built by Francis Cabot Lowell and other liberal-minded New Englanders made the towns of Lowell, Waltham, and Lynn seem model communities to visiting foreigners. They were placed in attractive sur-

roundings; family life was encouraged; morals protected; the wage scale encouraged thrift; and favorable surroundings attracted a high quality of labor. An eminent Englishwoman here joins in the chorus of praise.

I VISITED [1834] the corporate factory establishment at Waltham, within a few miles of Boston. The Waltham Mills were at work before those of Lowell were set up. The establishment is for the spinning and weaving of cotton alone, and the construction of the requisite machinery. Five hundred persons were employed at the time of my visit. The girls earn two, and sometimes three, dollars a week, besides their board. The little children earn one dollar a week. Most of the girls live in the houses provided by the corporation, which accommodate from six to eight each. When sisters come to the mill, it is a common practice for them to bring their mother to keep house for them and some of their companions, in a dwelling built by their own earnings. In this case, they save enough out of their board to clothe themselves, and have their two or three dollars a week to spare. Some have thus cleared off mortgages from their fathers' farms; others have educated the hope of the family at college; and many are rapidly accumulating an independence. I saw a whole street of houses built with the earnings of the girls, some with piazzas and green Venetian blinds, and all neat and sufficiently spacious.

The factory people built the church, which stands conspicuous on the green in the midst of the place. The minister's salary (eight hundred dollars last year) is raised by a tax on the pews. The corporation gave them a building for a lyceum, which they have furnished with a good library, and where they have lectures every winter — the best that money can procure. The girls have, in many instances, private libraries of some merit and value.

The managers of the various factory establishments keep the wages as nearly equal as possible, and then let the girls freely shift about from one to another. When a girl comes to the overseer to inform him of her intention of working at the mill, he welcomes her, and asks how long she means to stay. It may be six months, or a year, or five years, or for life. She declares what she considers herself fit for, and sets to work accordingly. If she finds that she cannot work so as to keep up with the companion appointed to her, or to please her employer or herself, she comes to the overseer, and volunteers to pick cotton, or sweep the rooms, or undertake some other service that she can perform.

The people work about seventy hours per week, on the average. The time of work varies with the length of the days, the wages continuing the same. All look like well-dressed young ladies. The health is good, or rather (as this is too much to be said about health anywhere in the United States) it is no worse than it is elsewhere.

These facts speak for themselves. There is no need to enlarge on the pleasure of an acquaintance with the operative classes of the United States.

The shoemaking at Lynn is carried on almost entirely in private dwellings, from the circumstance that the people who do it are almost all farmers or fishermen likewise. A stranger who has not been enlightened upon the ways of the place would be astonished at the number of small square erections, like miniature schoolhouses, standing each as an appendage to a dwelling house. These are the shoeshops, where the father of the family and his boys work, while the women within are employed in binding and trimming. Thirty or more of these shoeshops may be counted in a walk of half a mile. When a Lynn shoe manufacturer receives an order, he issues the tidings. The leather is cut out by men on his premises; and then the work is given to those who apply for it — if possible, in small quantities, for the sake of dispatch. The shoes are brought home on Friday night, packed off on Saturday, and in a fortnight or three weeks are on the feet of dwellers in all parts of the Union. The whole family works upon shoes during the winter, and in the summer the father and sons turn out into the fields or go fishing. I know of an instance where a little boy and girl maintained the whole family, while the earnings of the rest went to build a house. I saw very few shabby houses. Quakers are numerous in Lynn. The place is unboundedly prosperous, through the temperance and industry of the people. The deposits in the Lynn Savings Bank in 1834 were about thirty-four thousand dollars, the population of the town being then four thousand. Since that time, both the population and the prosperity have much increased. It must be remembered too that the mechanics of America have more uses for their money than are open to the operatives of England. They build houses, buy land, and educate their sons and daughters.

It is probably true that the pleasures and pains of life are pretty equally distributed among its various vocations and positions, but it is difficult to keep clear of the impression which outward circumstances occasion, that some are eminently desirable. The mechanics of these Northern States appear to me the most favored class I have ever known. In England, I believe the highest order of mechanics to be, as a class, the wisest and best men of the community. They have the fewest base and narrow interests; they are brought into sufficient contact with the realities of existence without being hardened by excess of toil and care; and the knowledge they have the opportunity of gaining is of the best kind for the health of the mind. To them, if to any, we may look for public and private virtue. The mechanics of America have nearly all the same advantages, and some others. They have better means of living; their labors are perhaps more honored; and they are republicans, enjoying the powers and prospects of perfectly equal citizenship. The only respect in which their condition falls below that of English artisans of the highest order is that the knowledge which they have commonly the means of obtaining is not of equal value. The facilities are great; schools, lyceums, libraries, are open to them; but the instruction imparted there is not so good as they deserve. Whenever they have this, it will be difficult to imagine a mode of life more favorable to virtue and happiness than theirs.

There seems to be no doubt among those who know both England and America that the mechanics of the New World work harder than those of the Old. They have much to do besides their daily handicraft business. They are up and at work early about this, and when it is done, they read till late, or attend lectures, or perhaps have their houses to build or repair, or other care to take of their property. They live in a state and period of society where every man is answerable for his own fortunes and where there is therefore stimulus to the exercise of every power.

What a state of society it is when a dozen artisans of one town — Salem — are seen rearing each a comfortable one-story (or, as the

Americans would say, two-story) house, in the place with which they have grown up! when a man who began with laying bricks criticizes, and sometimes corrects, his lawyer's composition; when a poor errand boy becomes the proprietor of a flourishing store before he is thirty; pays off the capital advanced by his friends at the rate of two thousand dollars per month, and bids fair to be one of the most substantial citizens of the place! Such are the outward fortunes of the mechanics of America.

HARRIET MARTINEAU, Society in America

82. Edward Everett Hale Recalls a New England Boyhood

As Goodrich depicted a rural boyhood in New England, so Edward Everett Hale described a Boston boyhood. His father also was a minister, but was a Harvard graduate and was more prosperous than the elder Goodrich. Young Hale was born in 1822; his recollections were penned almost three-quarters of a century later.

So FAR as I remember the houses themselves and the life in them, everything was quite as elegant and finished as it is now. Furniture was stately, solid, and expensive. I use chairs, tables, and a sideboard in my house today which are exactly as good now as they were then. Carpets, then of English make, covered the whole floor, and were of what we should now call perfect quality. In summer, by the way, in all houses of which I knew anything, these carpets were always taken up, and India mattings substituted in the living rooms. Observe that very few houses were closed in summer. Dress was certainly as elegant and costly as it is now; so were porcelain, glass, table linen, and all table furniture. In the earlier days of which I write, a decanter of wine would invariably have stood on a side-board in every parlor, so that a glass of wine could readily be offered at any moment to any guest. All through my boyhood it would have been matter of remark if, when a visitor made an evening call, something to eat or drink was not produced at nine o'clock. It might be crackers and cheese, it might be mince pie, it might be oysters or cold chicken. But something would appear as certainly as there would be a fire on the hearth in winter. Every house, by the way, was warmed by open fires; and in every kitchen cooking was done by an open fire. I doubt if I ever saw a stove in my boyhood except in a school or an office. Anthracite coal was first tried in Boston in 1824. Gas appeared about the same time. I was taken, as a little boy, to see it burning in the shops in Washington Street, and to wonder at an elephant, a tortoise, and a cow, which spouted burning gas in one window. Gas was not introduced into dwelling houses until Pemberton Square was built by the Lowells, Jacksons, and their friends, in the years 1835, 1836, and later. It was a surprise to every one when Papanti introduced it in his new Papanti's Hall. To prepare for that occasion the ground-glass shades had a little rouge shaken about in the interior, that the white gaslight might not be too unfavorable to the complexion of the beauties below. Whether this device is still thought necessary in ballrooms I do not know, but I suggest it as a hint to the wise.

A handsome parlor then differed from a handsome parlor now mostly in the minor matters of decoration. The pictures on the walls were few, and were mostly portraits. For the rest, mirrors were large and handsome. You would see some copies from well-known paintings in European galleries, and anyone who had an Allston would be glad to show it. But I mean that most walls were bare. In good houses, if modern, the walls of the parlors would invariably be painted of one neutral tint; but in older houses there would be paper hangings, perhaps of landscape patterns. The furniture of a parlor would generally be twelve decorous heavy chairs, probably hair-seated, with their backs against the walls; a sofa which matched them, also with its back against the wall; and a heavy, perhaps marble-topped center table. There might be a rocking chair in the room also, but so far as I remember, other easy chairs, scattered as one chose about a room, were unknown.

As the snow melted, and the elms blossomed, and the grass came, the Common opened itself to every sort of game. We played marbles in holes in the malls. We flew kites everywhere, not troubled, as boys would be now, by trees on the cross paths, for there were no such trees. The old elm and a large willow by the Frog Pond were the only trees within the pentagon made by the malls and the burial ground. Kiteflying was, as it is, a science; and on a fine summer day, with southwest winds, a line of boys would be camped in groups, watching or tending their favorite kites as they hung in the air over Park Street. Occasionally a string would break. It was a matter of honor to save your twine. I remember following my falling kite, with no clew but the direction in which I saw it last, till I found that the twine was lying across a narrow court which opened where the Albion Hotel is now. There were two rows of three-story houses which made the court, and my twine festooned it, supported by the ridgepoles of the roofs on either side. I rang a doorbell, stated my case, and ran up, almost without permission, into the attic. Here I climbed out of the attic window, ran up the roof, and drew in the coveted twine. For the pecuniary value of the twine we cared little, but it would have been, in a fashion, disgraceful to lose it.

Boats on the Frog Pond were much what they are now. The bottom of the pond was not paved until 1848. There were no frogs, so far as I know, but some small horned pout were left there, for which boys fished occasionally. The curb around the pond was laid in Mr. Quincy's day, in 1823; I mean when he was mayor. To provide the stone the last of the bowlders on the Common were blasted. In old days, as appears from Sewall, they were plenty; he blasted enough for the foundations of a barn. I think the old Hancock House was built from such bowlders. Among those destroyed was the Wishing Stone. This stood, or so Dr. Shurtleff told me, where two paths now join, a little east of the foot of Walnut Street. If you went round it backward nine times, and repeated the Lord's Prayer backward, whatever you wished would come to pass. I once proposed to the mayor and aldermen to go round the Frog Pond nine times backward and wish that the city debt might be reduced fifty per cent. But they have never had the faith to try. Mr. Quincy proposed that the Frog Pond should be called Crescent Lake. But nobody ever really called it so. I have seen the name on maps, I think, but it is now forgotten.

Charles Street was new in those days, and the handsome elms which shade the Charles Street mall were young trees, just planted, in 1825. By the building of the milldam, about that time, the water was shut out from the southern side of Charles Street. There existed a superstition among the boys that law did not extend to the flat, because it was below high-water mark. On holidays, therefore, there would be shaking of props and other games of mild gambling there, which "Old Reed" [the authorities] did not permit on the upland. This was, of course, a ridiculous boyish superstition. In those days, however, we had a large number of seafaring men, who brought with them foreign customs. Among others was the use of "props," a gambling game which the boys had introduced perfectly innocently as an element in playing marbles. I dare say people played props for money on the dried surface of the Back Bay.

The boys were in touch with the large public in their unauthorized and unrecognized connection with the fire department. Boston was still a wooden town, and the danger of fire was, as it is in all American cities, constantly present. There hung in our front entry two leather buckets; in each of them was certain apparatus which a person might need if he were in a burning house. Strange to say, there was a bedkey, that he might take down a bedstead if it were necessary. These were relics of a time when my father had been a member of one of the private fire companies. In those associations each man was bound to attend at any fire where the property of other members of the association was in danger; and there were traditions of Father's having been present at the great Court Street fire, for instance. But these fire clubs either died out or became social institutions, as the Fire Club in Worcester exists to this day; and nothing was left but the bucket as a sort of memorial of a former existence.

Before our day the volunteer fire department system of Boston had been created, and there were similar systems in all large cities. Of course we boys supposed that ours was the best in the world; each boy in Boston supposed that the engine nearest his house was the best engine in the world, and that, on occasion, it could throw water higher than any other engine. It could likewise, on occasion,

pump dry any engine that was in line with it. I need not say that
these notions of the boys were simply superstitions, wholly un-
founded in fact. Our engine was the *New York*. The enginehouse
was one of a curious mass of public buildings that occupied the
place where Franklin's statue now stands, in front of what was the
courthouse of that day. There was no electric fire alarm in those
early days. The moment a fire broke out everybody who had any
lungs ran up the street or down the street, or both ways, crying
"Fire!" and as soon as the churches could be opened, all the bells
in Boston began to ring. Then the company which was to drag
the *New York* to the fire began to assemble at its house, and naturally there was great pride in seeing that your engine was first in
place. You learned where the fire was, not by any signal, but by the
rumor of the street. It was at the North End, or at the South End,
or on the wharves, or on Nigger Hill. As soon as boys and men,
of whatever connection, arrived, sufficient to drag the engine, it
started, under the direction of such officer of the company as might
be present. The members of the company had no uniforms, so far
as I remember; they joined the lines as quickly as they could, but
there were always enough people to pull. As I have intimated, it
was everybody's business to attend at the fire.

When you arrived at the spot there would be a general caucus
as to the method of attack; yet I think there were people in command. Afterwards a gentleman named Amory, highly respected by
all of us, was chief engineer. Whatever the caucus directed was
done, with as much efficiency as was possible under such democratic
institutions. But, in the first place, the probability was that there
was no water near. The Jamaica Pond aqueduct carried water in
log pipes to the lower levels of the city, but for fully half the city
there was no such supply, and wells had to be relied upon. Every
engine, therefore, which was good for anything was a suction engine, as it was called; that is, it was able to pump from a well, as
well as able to throw water to an indefinite height. The engine that
arrived first repaired to the well best known in that neighborhood,
or, if the occasion were fortunate, to the sea, and began to pump.
The engine that arrived next took station next to this, and pumped
from it through a long line of hose; and so successive engines carried the water to the place where some foreman directed it upon

the flames. It was thus that the different engines attained their celebrity, as one pumped the tub of another dry, while the unfortunate members were "working the brakes" to their best to keep it full.

The buckets of which I have spoken were the remains of a yet earlier period, when people formed themselves in line to the well or to the sea and passed buckets backward and forward — full if they were going toward the fire, empty if they were going away; and the water was thus thrown upon such flames as chose to wait for it.

I need hardly say that the old method interested to the full every boy in town. If his father and mother would let him, he attended the fire, where he could at least scream "Fire!" if he could not do anything else. If a boy were big enough he was permitted almost to kill himself by working at the brakes. This was the most exhausting method for the application of human power that has been contrived, but there was power enough to be wasted, and, until the introduction of steam, it was everywhere used. It is still used on board ships which have no steam power. Every enterprising boy regarded it as the one wish of his life that he might be eighteen years old, so that he could join the company in his particular neighborhood; and even if he had not attained that age, he attached himself to the company as a sort of volunteer aid, and, as I say, was permitted, as a favor, to assist in running through the streets, dragging at the long rope which drew the engine.

EDWARD EVERETT HALE, A New England Boyhood

83. Rebecca Felton Describes Country Life in Georgia

Rebecca Latimer Felton was born while Jackson was still in the White House; she lived to become in 1922 the first woman Senator of the United States. Her girlhood in Georgia embraced experiences typical of the larger and more prosperous ante-bellum plantations.

IT WAS my Georgia grandmother, Mrs. Lucy Talbot Swift, around whom my early recollections cluster. I was often at her home and I was a close observer of her housekeeping methods and of her abounding hospitality. The mother of eleven children, all reaching maturity except two that lived to eleven and twelve years, her industry, her management, and her executive ability in caring for and carrying on her household affairs are still wonderful memories, and have continually lingered with me as examples in the progress of my own extended life. It was a fine specimen of a Southern planter's family and home in ante-bellum times. Grandfather had a plantation, a grain mill and sawmill, which kept him busy with his own duties as a provider, but it was grandmother's skill as a homemaker, with an eye single to her domestic duties and diligent attention to home economies, that impressed me most in that early time of my life when I trotted around after her as she went from the dwelling to the garden and to the milk dairy, to the poultry house, to the loom house, to the big meat house, where rations were issued once a day, and to the flour and meal house where there was always a superabundance of supplies for white and colored.

She had fowls of all domestic kinds to look after, and there were fattening pigs in the pen also. She had geese to raise feathers for the family beds, because there were no mattresses in that early time. When one of the children married there was a substantial outfit prepared to set them up for limited housekeeping. There were no such things as "comforts" eighty years ago, but quilt making was never interrupted, winter or summer, and in early Georgia homes woolen "coverlids" woven at home, and quilts innumerable made by hand, were the bedcoverings in all such well-to-do Georgia homes. I distinctly remember that my own mother made and quilted with her own nimble fingers fifty good, serviceable, and good-looking quilts in the first ten years of her married life.

In that early time, before there was a railroad in Georgia, our own home became a regular stopping place for travelers, and there was urgent need for beds that could meet the demand when people traveled from Savannah and regions lower down south even to Nashville, Tennessee, going north, and after stagecoaches were set going the coach expense was so great, at ten cents a mile, that the bulk of the travel was still made in carriages, carts, gigs, and on horseback. In event of stormy weather these travelers were often detained at our house. Sometimes floods in rivers and washed-out roads intercepted travel. All mules and horses and hogs brought into the state were driven from Kentucky and Tennessee, as there was no railroad in Georgia to furnish markets in southeastern Georgia.

When my grandmother, Lucy Swift, began housekeeping, wool and flax were the dependence of housekeepers for clothing their families. Silk culture was exploited in General Oglethorpe's time, but the use of cotton was handicapped. Before there were any cotton gins the cotton lint was picked from the seed by human fingers. The lint was then carded by hand, spun on homemade wheels, then reeled into what were called "hanks" by use of homemade reels; then the warp was prepared for the homemade loom by a variety of processes, all tedious and slow, and all the work done by the house-mother and her helpers. In this way all the wearing apparel of the masses was constructed. Well-to-do men generally contrived to get a broadcloth coat, maybe once in a lifetime. The rest had coats of plain jeans. Silk dresses were scarce and with scanty lengths and they were only worn occasionally, at weddings or brilliant occasions. A leghorn bonnet would last a woman a lifetime, and kid slippers were the fashionable and expensive footwear of the belles of the period.

The shoe problem was an immense proposition, and the hides were generally tanned in dug-out troughs, stretched out, dressed, and dried at home. The traveling shoemaker made periodic visits, and one pair of shoes per annum was considered a liberal provision for grown-ups. Suffice to say the children as a rule all went bare-footed summer and winter, and how remarkable they were for good health and lusty frame, and their longevity was astonishing. And this perplexing shoemaking problem lasted a long time. I recall with vivid memory the first time the family shoemaker measured my feet for a pair of shoes. He brought along a piece of white pine board, and I stood flat-footed on the board, while he marked a line in front of my toes with his big coarse horn-handled knife. Then he marked another line behind my heel and cautioned me that I must not draw my toes together or try to crumple up the bottom of my foot. I felt quite a somebody when the new shoes came home and I had liberty to lay aside the red-morocco baby shoes to which I had been accustomed. Stumped toes in summer and cracked heels in the winter were always in evidence with pupils during my school days, when the country child had a log cabin for a schoolroom and puncheon benches for seats, and the farmer boys and girls of the rural neighborhood wore coarse home-fashioned clothes spun and woven in looms at home. Towels, tablecloths, and shirts were made in the same slow way, and even the best-fixed families were glad to use "thrums" for towels and soft soap in a gourd to wash hands, and the family had a shelf for the washbasin outside for young and old.

A pretty white complexion was the call of that period. The young women were emphatic on this line. They were constantly busy, often with clothmaking work, but they were scrupulous in care of the skin. They wore gloves for washing dishes or when washing clothes. Tomboy girls were sometimes encountered, but the belles of Georgia enjoyed beautiful complexions. They also laced very tight, and it was fashionable to faint on occasions. Weddings were sumptuous affairs. When my mother married there was a crowded wedding at night and three more days of festivities, with a different dress for each day. "Infares" were popular, where the wedding spreads were transferred to the groom's home. Everything good to eat was bountifully furnished, meats in abundance, all sorts of home collections and concoctions topped off with pound cake and sillabub. There was always a sideboard where gin, rum, and peach brandy held distinction. Loaf sugar brought from Charleston and Augusta by wagons was uniformly present. I can remember with accurate recollection those beautiful snowy cones of white sugar encased in thick bluish-green papers, that were always in request when company came, and the sideboard drinks were set forth in generous array. "Peach and honey" was in reach of everybody that prided in their home. Those primitive farmers had abounding peach orchards, and beehives were generally in evidence more or less on Georgia farms. Everything to eat and to wear that could be grown at home was diligently cultivated, and the early fortunes of Georgians were promoted by such thrift, economy, and conservation of resources. In the summer time the drying of fruit was diligently pursued, and it was a poor and thriftless domicile which failed to supply itself with dried peaches, apples, cherries, pears, etc. My careful grandmother put up bushels of dried white English peaches, of which she often made family preserves for home consumption in the scarcer springtime.

My grandmother made all the starch she used, sometimes from whole wheat, oftener from wheat bran. Her seven girls, big and little, delighted in dainty white muslin frocks, and laundry work for thirteen in family was always going on, and insistent in that large household. She was a rare soapmaker, and every pound was prepared at home with diligent care. The meat scraps and bones were utilized and cooked with lye, drained in ash hoppers. It made perfect soap for domestic uses. Hard soap was prepared for the big house in various ways, tempered with age, and used by young and old alike. For wounds and baby usage there could be bought Castile soap, but the soaps of the multitudes were prepared at home. Except salt, iron, sugar, and coffee, everything was raised by those early Georgia planters necessary for human comfort and sustenance.

REBECCA FELTON, Country Life in Georgia in the Days of My Youth

84. Charles Dickens Travels from Baltimore to Harrisburg

America received the young author of Pickwick Papers, Oliver Twist, *and* Nicholas Nickleby (*he was only twenty-nine when he arrived*) *with almost delirious enthusiasm when he toured the Northern States in 1842. He would not go farther south than Richmond because of his repugnance to slavery. When he published his* American Notes *his critical passages aroused much resentment. Yet he was not really unfair. Americans were merely thin-skinned, and his acute observations hurt in proportion to their truthfulness.*

W E LEFT Baltimore by another railway at half past eight in the morning and reached the town of York, some sixty miles off, by the early dinnertime of the hotel which was the starting place of the four-horse coach wherein we were to proceed to Harrisburg.

This conveyance, the box of which I was fortunate enough to secure, had come down to meet us at the railroad station, and was as muddy and cumbersome as usual. As more passengers were waiting for us at the inn door, the coachman observed under his breath, in the usual self-communicative voice, looking the while at his moldy harness as if it were to that he was addressing himself, "I expect we shall want the *big* coach."

I could not help wondering within myself what the size of this big coach might be, and how many persons it might be designed to hold, for the vehicle which was too small for our purpose was something larger than two English heavy night coaches, and might have been the twin brother of a French diligence. My speculations were speedily set at rest, however, for as soon as we had dined, there came rumbling up the street, shaking its sides like a corpulent giant, a kind of barge on wheels. After much blundering and backing, it stopped at the door, rolling heavily from side to side when its other motion had ceased, as if it had taken cold in its damp stable, and between that and the having been required in its dropsical old age to move at any faster pace than a walk, were distressed by shortness of wind.

"If here ain't the Harrisburg mail at last, and dreadful bright and smart to look at too," cried an elderly gentleman in some excitement, "darn my mother!" . . .

They booked twelve people inside; and the luggage (including such trifles as a large rocking chair and a good-sized dining table) being at length made fast upon the roof, we started off in great state.

At the door of another hotel there was another passenger to be taken up.

"Any room, sir?" cries the new passenger to the coachman.

"Well, there's room enough," replies the coachman, without getting down or even looking at him.

"There ain't no room at all, sir," bawls a gentleman inside. Which another gentleman (also inside) confirms, by predicting that the attempt to introduce any more passengers "won't fit nohow."

The new passenger, without any expression of anxiety, looks into the coach, and then looks up at the coachman.

"Now how do you mean to fix it?" says he after a pause, "for I *must* go."

The coachman employs himself in twisting the lash of his whip into a knot, and takes no more notice of the question, clearly signifying that it is anybody's business but his, and that the passengers would do well to fix it among themselves. In this state of things, matters seem to be approximating to a fix of another kind, when another inside passenger in a corner, who is nearly suffocated, cries faintly, "I'll get out."

This is no matter of relief or self-congratulation to the driver, for his immovable philosophy is perfectly undisturbed by anything that happens in the coach. Of all things in the world the coach would seem to be the very last upon his mind. The exchange is made, however, and then the passenger who has given up his seat makes a third upon the box, seating himself in what he calls the middle — that is, with half his person on my legs and the other half on the driver's.

"Go ahead, cap'n," cries the colonel who directs.

"Gŏ-lāng!" cries the cap'n to his company, the horses, and away we go.

We took up at a rural barroom, after we had gone a few miles, an intoxicated gentleman who climbed upon the roof among the luggage, and subsequently slipping off without hurting himself, was seen in the distant perspective reeling back to the grogshop where we had found him. We also parted with more of our freight at different times, so that when we came to change horses I was again alone outside.

The coachmen always change with the horses, and are usually as dirty as the coach. The first was dressed like a very shabby English baker, the second like a Russian peasant, for he wore a loose purple camlet robe with a fur collar, tied round his waist with a particolored worsted sash, gray trousers, light blue gloves, and a cap of bearskin. It had by this time come on to rain very heavily, and there was a cold, damp mist besides, which penetrated to the skin. I was very glad to take advantage of a stoppage and get down to stretch my legs, shake the water off my greatcoat, and swallow the usual antitemperance recipe for keeping out the cold.

When I mounted to my seat again, I observed a new parcel lying on the coach roof, which I took to be a rather large fiddle in a brown bag. In the course of a few miles, however, I discovered that it had a glazed cap at one end and a pair of muddy shoes at the other; and further observation demonstrated it to be a small boy in a snuff-colored coat with his arms quite pinioned to his sides by deep forcing into his pockets. He was, I presume, a relative or friend of the coachman's, as he lay atop of the luggage with his face towards the rain, and except when a change of position brought his shoes in contact with my hat, he appeared to be asleep. At last, on some occasion of our stopping, this thing slowly upreared itself to the height of three feet six, and fixing its eyes on me, observed in piping accents, with a complaisant yawn half quenched in an obliging air of friendly patronage, "Well, now, stranger, I guess you find this a'most like an English arternoon, hey?" . . .

We crossed this river by a wooden bridge, roofed and covered in on all sides and nearly a mile in length. It was profoundly dark, perplexed with great beams crossing and recrossing it at every possible angle, and through the broad chinks and crevices in the floor the rapid river gleamed, far down below, like a legion of eyes. We had no lamps, and as the horses stumbled and floundered through this place towards the distant speck of dying light, it seemed interminable. I really could not at first persuade myself as we rumbled heavily on, filling the bridge with hollow noises, and I held down my head to save it from the rafters above, but that I was in a painful dream; for I have often dreamed of toiling through such places, and as often argued, even at the time, "This cannot be reality."

At length, however, we emerged upon the streets of Harrisburg, whose feeble lights, reflected dismally from the wet ground, did not shine out upon a very cheerful city. We were soon established in a snug hotel, which, though smaller and far less splendid than many we put up at, is raised above them all in my remembrance by having for its landlord the most obliging, considerate, and gentlemanly person I ever had to deal with.

CHARLES DICKENS, American Notes, 1842

85. Joseph Jefferson Tries Play Acting in Springfield, Illinois

Most beloved of American actors in his time, Joe Jefferson (as a long generation called him) was a scion of a famous Anglo-American family of the stage. His grandfather was said to have been introduced to the theater by Garrick. His father was part painter, part actor, who roved the United States until he died of yellow fever and left little Joe, then thirteen, to support the family. This the lad, who had made his debut in song and dance at the age of four, did right valiantly. He barnstormed the Southern and Western country, and went through many rough experiences until several years before the Civil War he ended his apprenticeship by becoming a member of Laura Keene's company. Here he writes of his early years, when father, mother, and boy played together in halls, barns, log houses even — wherever they could find an audience.

AFTER a short season in Chicago, with the varying success which in those days always attended the drama, the company went to Galena for a short season, [1837] traveling in open wagons over the prairie. Our seats were the trunks that contained the wardrobe — those old-fashioned hair trunks of a mottled and spotted character made from the skins of defunct circus horses: "To what base uses we may return!" These smooth hair trunks, with geometrical problems in brass tacks ornamenting their surface, would have made slippery seats even on a macadamized road; so one may imagine the difficulty we had in holding on while jolting over a rough prairie. Nothing short of a severe pressure on the brass tacks and a convulsive grip of the handles could have kept us in position, and whenever a treacherous handle gave way our company was for the

time being just one member short. As we were not an express mail
train, of course we were allowed more than twenty minutes for refreshments; the only difficulty was the refreshments. We stopped at
farmhouses on the way for this uncertain necessity, and they were far
apart. If the roads were heavy and the horses jaded, those actors who
had tender hearts and tough limbs jumped out and walked to ease
the poor brutes. Often I have seen my father trudging along ahead
of the wagon, smoking his pipe, and I have no doubt thinking of
the large fortune he was going to make in the next town, now and
then looking back with his light blue eyes, giving my mother a
cheerful nod which plainly said: "I'm all right. This is splendid;
nothing could be finer." If it rained he was glad it was not snowing;
if it snowed he was thankful it was not raining. This contented
nature was his only inheritance, but it was better than a fortune
made in Galena or anywhere else, for nothing could rob him of it.

We traveled from Galena to Dubuque on the frozen river in
sleighs — smoother work than the roughly rutted roads of the
prairie, but it was a perilous journey, for a warm spell had set in
and made the ice sloppy and unsafe. We would sometimes hear it
crack and see it bend under our horses' feet — now a long-drawn
breath of relief as we passed some dangerous spot, then a convulsive
grasping of our nearest companion as the ice groaned and shook
beneath us. Well, the passengers arrived safe, but, horror to relate!
the sleigh containing the baggage, private and public, with the
scenery and properties, green curtain and drop, broke through the
ice and tumbled into the Mississippi. My poor mother was in tears,
but my father was in high spirits at his good luck, as he called it —
because there was a sand bar where the sleigh went in! So the things
were saved at last, though in a forlorn condition. The opening had
to be delayed in order to dry the wardrobe and smooth the scenery.

The halls of the hotel were strung with clotheslines, and costumes
of all nations festooned the doors of the bedrooms, so that when an
unsuspicious boarder came out suddenly into the entry he was
likely to run his head into a damp Roman shirt or perhaps have the
legs of a soaking pair of red tights dangling round his neck. Mildew
filled the air. The gilded pasteboard helmets fared the worst. They
had succumbed to the softening influences of the Mississippi and
were as battered and out of shape as if they had gone through the

pass of Thermopylae. Limp leggings of scale armor hung wet and dejected from the lines; low-spirited cocked hats were piled up in a corner; rough-dried court coats stretched their arms out as if in the agony of drowning, as though they would say, "Help me, Cassius, or I sink." Theatrical scenery at its best looks pale and shabby in the daytime, but a well-worn set after a six hours' bath in a river presents the most woebegone appearance that can well be imagined; the sky and water of the marine had so mingled with each other that the horizon line had quite disappeared. My father had painted the scenery, and he was not a little crestfallen as he looked upon the ruins: a wood scene had amalgamated with a Roman street painted on the back of it and had so run into stains and winding streaks that he said it looked like a large map of South America; and pointing out the Andes with his cane, he humorously traced the Amazon to its source. Of course this mishap on the river delayed the opening for a week. In the meantime the scenery had to be repainted and the wardrobe put in order; many of the things were ruined, and the helmets defied repair.

After a short, and, I think, a good season at Dubuque, we traveled along the river to the different towns just springing up in the west — Burlington, Quincy, Peoria, Pekin, and Springfield. In those primitive days, I need scarcely say, we were often put to severe shifts for a theater.

In Quincy the courthouse was fitted up, and it answered admirably. In one town a large warehouse was utilized, but in Pekin we were reduced to the dire necessity of acting in a pork house. This establishment was a large frame building, stilted up on piles about two feet from the ground, and situated in the open prairie just at the edge of the town. The pigs were banished from their comfortable quarters and left to browse about on the common during the day, taking shelter under their former abode in the evening. After undergoing some slight repairs in the roof and submitting to a thorough scouring and whitewashing, the building presented quite a respectable appearance. The opening play was "Clari, the Maid of Milan." This drama was written by John Howard Payne, and his song of "Home, Sweet Home" belongs to the play. My mother, on this occasion, played the part of *Clari* and sang the touching ballad.

Now it is a pretty well-established fact in theatrical history that if an infant has been smuggled into the theater under the shawl of its fond mother, however dormant it may have been during the unimportant scenes of the play, no sooner is an interesting point arrived at, where the most perfect stillness is required, than the dear little innocent will break forth in lamentation loud and deep. On this occasion no youthful humanity disturbed the peace, but the animal kingdom, in the shape of the banished pigs, asserted its right to a public hearing. As soon as the song "Home, Sweet Home" commenced they began by bumping their backs up against the beams, keeping anything but good time to the music; and as my mother plaintively chanted the theme "sweet, sweet home," realizing their own cruel exile, the pigs squealed most dismally. Of course the song was ruined, and my mother was in tears at the failure. My father, however, consoled her by saying that though the grunting was not quite in harmony with the music, it was in perfect sympathy with the sentiment.

Springfield being the capital of Illinois, it was determined to devote the entire season to the entertainment of the members of the Legislature. Having made money for several weeks previous to our arrival here, the management resolved to hire a lot and build a theater. This sounds like a large undertaking, and perhaps with their limited means it was a rash step. I fancy that my father rather shrank from this bold enterprise, but the senior partner (McKenzie) was made of sterner stuff, and his energy being quite equal to his ambition, the ground was broken and the temple erected.

The building of a theater in those days did not require the amount of capital that it does now. Folding opera chairs were unknown. Gas was an occult mystery, not yet acknowledged as a fact by the unscientific world in the West; a second-class quality of sperm oil was the height of any manager's ambition. The footlights of the best theaters in the western country were composed of lamps set in a float with the counterweights. When a dark stage was required or the lamps needed trimming or refilling, this mechanical contrivance was made to sink under the stage. I believe if the theater, or "devil's workshop," as it was sometimes called, had suddenly been illuminated with the same material now in use, its enemies would have declared that the light was furnished from the Old Boy's private gasometer.

The new theater, when completed, was about ninety feet deep

and forty feet wide. No attempt was made at ornamentation, and as it was unpainted, the simple lines of architecture upon which it was constructed gave it the appearance of a large dry-goods box with a roof. I do not think my father or McKenzie ever owned anything with a roof until now; so they were naturally proud of their possession.

In the midst of our rising fortunes a heavy blow fell upon us. A religious revival was in progress at the time, and the fathers of the church not only launched forth against us in their sermons, but by some political maneuver got the city to pass a new law enjoining a heavy license against our unholy calling; I forget the amount, but it was large enough to be prohibitory. Here was a terrible condition of affairs: all our available funds invested, the Legislature in session, the town full of people, and we by a heavy license denied the privilege of opening the new theater!

In the midst of their trouble a young lawyer called on the managers. He had heard of the injustice and offered, if they would place the matter in his hands, to have the license taken off, declaring that he only desired to see fair play, and he would accept no fee whether he failed or succeeded. The case was brought up before the council. The young lawyer began his harangue. He handled the subject with tact, skill, and humor, tracing the history of the drama from the time when Thespis acted in a cart to the stage of today. He illustrated his speech with a number of anecdotes and kept the council in a roar of laughter; his good humor prevailed, and the exorbitant tax was taken off.

This young lawyer was very popular in Springfield, and was honored and beloved by all who knew him. His name was Abraham Lincoln!

Autobiography of Joseph Jefferson

86. Samuel Morse Invents the Telegraph

Few Americans have been as versatile as the brilliant, impetuous, stalwart Samuel Finley Breese Morse, painter, photographer, inventor, politician, and public figure. In 1836 (when president of the National Academy of Design, and Native American candidate for mayor of New York) he was far advanced with his telegraphic apparatus at the University of the City of New York, where he was a professor. In the next half-dozen years, with the aid of Joseph Henry and other scientists, he steadily developed his ideas. He was certain of success — but meanwhile he met poverty and even hunger.

So ENDED the year 1842, a decade since the first conception of the telegraph, and it found the inventor making his last stand for recognition from that government to which he had been so loyal and upon which he wished to bestow a priceless gift. With the dawn of the new year, a year destined to mark an epoch in the history of civilization, his flagging spirits were revived, and he entered with zest on what proved to be his final and successful struggle.

It passes belief that with so many ocular demonstrations of the practicability of the Morse telegraph and with the reports of the success of other telegraphs abroad, the popular mind, as reflected in its representatives in Congress, should have remained so incredulous. Morse had been led to hope that his bill was going to pass by acclamation, but in this he was rudely disappointed.

The alternating moods of hope and despair through which the inventor passed during the next few weeks are best pictured forth by himself in brief extracts from letters to his brother Sidney.

"January 6, 1843. — I sent you a copy of the report on the telegraph a day or two since. I was in hopes of having it called up today, but the House refused to go into committee of the whole on the state of the Union; so it is deferred. The first time they go into committee of the whole on the state of the Union it will probably be called up and be decided upon.

"Everything looks favorable, but I do not suffer myself to be sanguine, for I do not know what may be doing secretly against it. I shall believe it passed when the signature of the President is affixed to it, and not before."

"January 16. — I snatch the moments of waiting for company in the Committee Room of Commerce to write a few lines. Patience is a virtue much needed and much tried here. So far as opinion goes everything is favorable to my bill. I hear of no opposition but should not be surprised if it met with some. The great difficulty is to get it up before the House; there are so many who must *define their position,* as the term is, so many who must say something 'Buncombe,' that a great deal of the people's time is wasted in mere idle, unprofitable speechifying. I hope something may be done this week that shall be decisive, so that I may know what to do. This waiting at so much risk makes me question myself: Am I in the path of duty? When I think that the little money I brought with me is nearly gone, that if nothing should be done by Congress I shall be in a destitute state, that perhaps I shall have again to be a burden to friends until I know to what to turn my hands, I feel low-spirited. I am only relieved by naked trust in God, and it is right that this should be so."

"January 20. — My patience is still tried in waiting for the action of Congress on my bill. With so much at stake you may easily conceive how tantalizing is this state of suspense. . . . At times, after waiting all day and day after day, in the hope that my bill may be called up, and in vain, I feel heartsick, and finding nothing accomplished, that no progress is made, that *precious time* flies, I am depressed and begin to question whether I am in the way of duty. But when I feel that I have done all in my power, and that this delay may be designed by the wise Disposer of all events for a trial of patience, I find relief and a disposition quietly to wait such issue as He shall direct, knowing that, if I sincerely have put my trust in Him, He will not lead me astray, and my way will, in any event, be made plain."

"January 25. — I am still *waiting, waiting*. I know not what the issue will be and wish to be prepared, and have you all prepared, for the worst in regard to the bill. Although I learn of no opposition, yet I have seen enough of the modes of business in the House to know that everything there is more than in ordinary matters uncertain."

"February 21. — I think the clouds begin to break away, and a little sunlight begins to cheer me. The House in committee of the whole on the state of the Union have just passed my bill through committee to report to the House. There was an attempt made to cast ridicule upon it by a very few headed by Mr. Cave Johnson, who proposed an amendment that half the sum should be appropriated to mesmeric experiments. Only twenty-six supported him, and it was laid aside to be reported to the House without amendment and without division.

"I was immediately surrounded by my friends in the House, congratulating me and telling me that the crisis is passed, and that the bill will pass the House by a large majority. Mr. Kennedy, chairman of the Committee on Commerce, has put the bill on the Speaker's calendar for Thursday morning, when the final vote in the House will be taken. It then has to go to the Senate, where I have reason to believe it will meet with a favorable reception. Then to the President, and, if signed by him, I shall return with renovated spirits, for I assure you I have for some time been at the lowest ebb, and can now scarcely realize that a turn has occurred in my favor."

Writing to Alfred Vail, he says after telling of the passage of the bill:

"You can have but a faint idea of the sacrifices and trials I have had in getting the telegraph thus far before the country and the world. I cannot detail them here; I can only say that for two years I have labored all my time and at my own expense, without assistance from the other proprietors (except in obtaining the iron of the magnets for the last instruments obtained of you), to forward our enterprise. My means to defray my expenses, to meet which every cent I owned in the world was collected, are nearly all gone, and if by any means the bill should fail in the Senate, I shall return to New York with the *fraction of a dollar* in my pocket."

And now the final struggle which meant success or failure was on. Only eight days of the session remained, and the calendar was, as usual, crowded. The inventor, his nerves stretched to the breaking point, hoped and yet feared. He had every reason to believe that the Senate would show more broadminded enlightenment than the House, and yet he had been told that his bill would pass the House by acclamation, while the event proved that it had barely squeezed through by a beggarly majority of six. He heard disquieting rumors of a determination on the part of some of the House members to procure the defeat of the bill in the Senate. Would they succeed, would the victory, almost won, be snatched from him at the last moment, or would his faith in an overruling Providence and in his own mission as an instrument of that Providence be justified at last?

Every day of that fateful week saw him in his place in the gallery of the Senate chamber, and all day long he sat there, listening, as we can well imagine, with growing impatience to the senatorial oratory on the merits or demerits of bills which to him were of such minor importance, however heavily freighted with the destinies of the nation they may have been. And every night he returned to his room with the sad reflection that one more of the precious days had passed and his bill had not been reached. And then came the last day, March 3.

He thus describes the events of that fateful night and of the next morning:

"The last days of the last session of that Congress were about to close. A bill appropriating thirty thousand dollars for my purpose had passed the House and was before the Senate for concurrence. On the last day of the session I had spent the whole day and part of the evening in the Senate chamber, anxiously watching the progress of the passing of the various bills, of which there were, in the morning of that day, over one hundred and forty to be acted upon before the one in which I was interested would be reached; and a resolution had a few days before been passed to proceed with the bills on the calendar in their regular order, forbidding any bill to be taken up out of its regular place.

"As evening approached there seemed to be but little chance that the telegraph bill would be reached before the adjournment and consequently I had the prospect of the delay of another year, with the loss of time, and all my means already expended. In my anxiety I consulted with two of my senatorial friends — Senator Huntington, of Connecticut, and Senator Wright, of New York — asking their opinion of the probability of reaching the bill before the close of the session. Their answers were discouraging, and their advice was to prepare myself for disappointment. In this state of mind I retired to my chamber and made all my arrangements for leaving Washington the next day.

"In the morning, as I had just gone into the breakfast room, the servant called me out, announcing that a young lady was in the parlor wishing to speak with me. I was at once greeted with the smiling face of my young friend, the daughter of my old and valued friend and classmate, the Honorable H. L. Ellsworth, the Commissioner of Patents. On my expressing surprise at so early a call, she said:

" 'I have come to congratulate you.'

" 'Indeed, for what?'

" 'On the passage of your bill.'

" 'Oh! no, my young friend, you are mistaken; I was in the Senate chamber till after the lamps were lighted, and my senatorial friends assured me there was no chance for me.'

" 'But,' she replied, 'it is you that are mistaken. Father was there at the adjournment at midnight, and saw the President put his name to your bill, and I asked Father if I might come and tell you, and he gave me leave. Am I the first to tell you?'

"The news was so unexpected that for some moments I could not speak. At length I replied:

" 'Yes, Annie, you are the first to inform me, and now I am going to make you a promise; the first dispatch on the completed line from Washington to Baltimore shall be yours.'

" 'Well,' said she, 'I shall hold you to your promise.' " . . .

And now at last the supreme moment had arrived. The line from Washington to Baltimore was completed, and on the 24th day of May, 1844, the company invited by the inventor assembled in the chamber of the United States Supreme Court to witness his triumph. True to his promise to Miss Annie Ellsworth, he had asked her to indite the first public message which should be flashed over the completed line, and she, in consultation with her good mother, chose the now historic words from the twenty-third verse of the twenty-third chapter of Numbers, "What hath God wrought!" . . . Calmly he seated himself at the instrument and ticked off the inspired words in the dots and dashes of the Morse alphabet. Alfred Vail, at the other end of the line in Baltimore, received the message without an error, and immediately flashed it back again, and the electromagnet telegraph was no longer the wild dream of a visionary, but an accomplished fact.

Letters and Journals of Samuel F. B. Morse

87. Dr. Morton Discovers Anesthesia

William Thomas Green Morton studied dentistry in Baltimore, and after practising in Boston, turned to the study of medicine at Harvard. But to support himself he still had to work as dentist. A Harvard professor, Charles T. Jackson, had proved to his chemistry classes that the breathing of sulphuric ether caused loss of consciousness. Morton, anxious to perform delicate and often painful operations upon the teeth, was seized with the idea whose application is here described. Even before this Dr. Crawford Long, of Georgia, had performed several successful operations with ether, but not until 1849 did Dr. Long publish the results of his experiments.

ATTENDANCE at the clinical lectures and at operations in the Massachusetts General Hospital formed part of the course then pursued by medical students. It was a privilege of which young Morton gladly availed himself. Then was revealed to him how terrible was the sway which pain exercised over sensitive organizations and how utterly incapable of controlling and subduing it were medical science and surgical skill. Again and again the great idea which he had conceived, that there was some way of shackling this awful monster of torture, stirred within him, and urged him to leave nothing undone to discover by what beneficent agency it could be accomplished. . . .

With characteristic intrepidity, Doctor Morton's first experiments were made upon himself. It occurred to him that ether, if combined with such narcotics as he had been in the habit of using in his practice, would probably produce insensibility to pain more speedily and assuredly than if used alone. He placed a mixture of ether and morphine in a retort round which he wrapped a hot towel, and with many misgivings he inhaled the mixture. In a similar way he also inhaled a preparation of ether and opium. He was punished for his temerity by some splitting headaches, but when, emboldened by the discovery that no severer pains or penalties were imposed upon him, he gradually prolonged the periods of inhalation, he was rewarded by the perception of a distinct feeling of numbness pervading his body and limbs.

In the spring of 1846 he again posted off to the country, this time to his own place at Wellesley, to experiment on some denizens of the farmyard. He etherized a hen and cut off its comb, the hen meanwhile making no protest or indicating in any way that it had any personal interest in the proceedings. Still more satisfactory was an experiment tried on a favorite water spaniel.

When Doctor Morton returned to Boston, he was so confident that he would succeed that he determined to turn over the management of his office and practice to other hands, that he might devote himself exclusively to the prosecution of his researches and experiments. . . .

After obtaining some chemically pure sulphuric ether, on September 30, 1846, Doctor Morton returned to his office determined to test its efficacy on himself. He shut himself up alone in a room to make the experiment. It was an act revealing courage of a high order, and a sublime faith. The annals of science and medicine contained no record of the effects of ether when inhaled to the extent of producing complete unconsciousness. Hints there were not a few that to inhale it was to invite grave injuries and possibly death itself.

"Taking my tube and flask [he wrote], I shut myself up in my room, seated myself in the operating chair, and commenced inhaling. I found the ether so strong that it partially suffocated me, but produced no decided effect. I then saturated my handkerchief and inhaled it from that. I looked at my watch and soon lost consciousness. As I recovered, I felt a numbness in my limbs, and a sensation like nightmare, and would have given the world for somebody to come and arouse me. I thought for a moment I should die in that state, and that the world would only pity or ridicule my folly. At length I felt a slight tingling of the blood in the end of my third finger and made an effort to press it with my thumb, but without success. At a second effort I touched it, but there seemed to be no sensation. I gradually raised my arm and pinched my thigh, but I could see that the sensation was imperfect. I attempted to rise from my chair, but fell back. I immediately looked at my watch and found that I had been insensible between seven and eight minutes."

For him rest was impossible until that one step more was taken which would prove that what the world had so long waited for had been discovered — something that could subdue pain.

"I had become much excited, and had determined that I would not leave the office until I had seen something more of the power of this new agent [he wrote]. Twilight came on, but in my present state, I felt it to be impossible to go home to my family. As the evening wore away my anxiety increased. The hour had long passed when it was usual for patients to call. I had just resolved to inhale the ether again and have a tooth extracted under its influence when a feeble ring was heard at the door. Making a motion to one of my assistants who started to answer the bell, I hastened myself to the door, where I found a man with his face bound up, who seemed to be suffering extremely.

" 'Doctor,' said he, 'I have a dreadful tooth, but it is so sore I cannot summon courage to have it pulled. Can't you mesmerize me?'

"I need not say that my heart bounded at this question and that I found it difficult to control my feelings, but putting a great constraint on myself, I expressed my sympathy for the man and invited him to walk into the office. There were no instruments in sight to terrify him, and the ether was close at hand, every arrangement having been previously made in the hope that a similar case might occur. I examined the tooth and in the most encouraging manner told the poor sufferer that I had something better than mesmerism by means of which I could take out his tooth without giving him pain. He gladly consented, and saturating my handkerchief with ether, I gave it to him to inhale. He became unconscious almost immediately. It was dark. Doctor Hayden held the lamp. My assistants were trembling with excitement, apprehending the usual prolonged scream from the patient while I extracted a firmly-rooted bicuspid tooth. I was so much agitated that I came near throwing the instrument out of the window. But now came a terrible reaction. The wrenching of the tooth had failed to rouse him in the slightest degree. Instead of the quick start of relief with which a patient usually leaves the operating chair the moment the instruments are withdrawn, he remained still and motionless as if already in the embrace of death.

"The terrible thought flashed through my mind that he might be dead, that in my zeal to test my new theory I might have gone too far and sacrificed a human life. With the rapidity of lightning my mind ran through the whole process of my investigations up to the present hour. I trembled under the sense of my responsibility to my Maker and to my fellow men. The question, Can I restore him to consciousness? startled me into action. I seized a glass of water and dashed it in the man's face. The result proved most happy. He recovered in a minute, and knew nothing of what had occurred. Seeing us all stand around him he appeared bewildered. I instantly, in as calm a tone as I could command, asked:

"'Are you ready to have your tooth extracted?'

"'Yes,' he answered, in a hesitating tone.

"'It is over,' I said, pointing to a decayed tooth on the floor.

"'No!' he shouted, leaping from the chair. . . ."

After consultation with friends he decided that to gain recognition for his discovery, he must give a demonstration of its efficacy under conditions that would preclude any suspicion of deception, and in the presence of witnesses who would command the confidence of the medical profession of the world.

No more fitting place was there in all Boston for such a work than the Massachusetts General Hospital. Doctor Morton obtained permission from Doctor John C. Warren, the senior surgeon, to make a trial of his pain annihilator at the hospital. On Wednesday, October 14, 1846, he received a note from Doctor Warren, requesting him to be present at the hospital at ten o'clock the next Friday morning to administer his preparation to a patient who was then to be operated on. On that morning he arose at four o'clock, hurried off to the house of an instrument maker, and awaking him, induced him to undertake forthwith the construction of an inhaler, the design for which had been prepared only on the previous evening. As the hour appointed for the test drew near and it was still uncompleted, Doctor Morton snatched it from the maker's hands and hurried off to the hospital.

Meanwhile, within, all necessary preparations for the operation had been made. The patient selected for the trial was Gilbert Abbott, who was suffering from a congenital but superficial vascular tumor just below the jaw on the left side of the neck. The announcement that the operation was to furnish a test of some preparation for which the astounding claim had been made that it would render the person treated with it temporarily incapable of feeling pain had attracted a large number of medical men to the theater. It was inevitable that nearly all of those present should be skeptical as to the result. As the minutes slipped by without any sign of Doctor Morton, the incredulous gave vent to their suspicions concerning him and his discovery.

"As Doctor Morton has not yet arrived," said Doctor Warren, after waiting fifteen minutes, "I presume that he is otherwise engaged."

The response was a derisive laugh, clearly implying the belief that Doctor Morton was staying away simply because he was afraid to submit his discovery to a critical test.

Doctor Warren grasped the knife. At that critical moment Doctor Morton entered. No outburst of applause, no smiles of encouragement, greeted him. Doubt and suspicion were depicted on the faces of those who looked down upon him from the tiers of seats that encircled the room. No actor about to assume a new rôle ever received a more chilling reception.

"Well, sir," exclaimed Doctor Warren, abruptly, "your patient is ready."

Thus aroused from the bewilderment into which the novelty of his position had thrown him, he spoke a few words of encouragement to the young man about to be operated on, adjusted the inhaler, and began to administer the ether. As the subtle vapor gradually took possession of the citadel of consciousness, the patient dropped off into a deep slumber.

Doctor Warren seized the bunch of veins and made the first incision with his knife.

Instead of awakening with a cry of pain, the patient continued to slumber peacefully, apparently as profoundly unconscious as before.

Then the spectators underwent a transformation. All signs of incredulity and indifference vanished. Not a whisper was uttered. As the operation progressed, men began to realize that they were witnessing something the like of which had never been seen before.

When the operation was over and while the patient still lay like a log on the table, Doctor Warren, addressing the spectators, said, with solemn emphasis, "Gentlemen, this is no humbug."

E. L. SNELL, Dr. Morton's Discovery of Anesthesia

88. Philip Hone Views the Passing Show in New York

Having gained moderate wealth as an auctioneer of imported goods, Philip Hone retired from business in early middle life, and devoted himself to politics, society, and letters. He became mayor of New York; an intimate of such Whig chieftains as Webster, Clay, and Seward; a leader of fashion; and a friend of Washington Irving, James K. Paulding, and other literary figures. His diary presents an unrivaled picture of life in old New York from 1830 to 1851. In it he sketches the fires, the riots, the exciting elections, the processions, the most interesting balls and dinners, the foreign visitors of note, the reception given new books, the advent of striking inventions and new fashions; he draws portraits of Presidents, generals, authors, politicians, and actors; he discusses all the ideas of his time. A thoroughgoing conservative in politics,

an Episcopalian in religion, a lover of good old Knickerbocker cus-
toms in daily life, he was deeply alarmed by the growing radicalism
of the masses. The panic of 1837, the arrival of the first regular trans-
atlantic steamships, the bloody clash between followers of a great
English actor and a lesser American stage-idol, were but a few of the
hundreds of events he chronicled.

I

MONDAY, February 13, 1837.—*Riots.* This city was disgraced this morning by a mob regularly convened by public notice
in the park for the notable purpose of making bread cheaper by
destroying the flour in the merchants' warehouses. The following
notice was extensively published on Saturday by placards at the
corners of the streets:

"Bread, meat, rent, fuel—their prices must come down.
"The voice of the people shall be heard, and will prevail.
"The people will meet in the park, rain or shine, at four o'clock
on Monday afternoon to inquire into the cause of the present unexampled distress, and devise a suitable remedy. All friends of humanity determined to resist monopolists and extortioners are invited to attend."

Many thousands assembled on this call. The day was bitter cold
and the wind blew a hurricane, but there was fire enough in the
speeches of Messrs. Windt and Ming to inflame the passions of the
populace. These two men, disciples in the sect of the Locofocos, did
not tell them in so many words to attack the stores of the flour
merchants, but stigmatized them as monopolists and extortioners
who enriched themselves at the expense of the laboring poor. They
said that Eli Hart and Company had fifty thousand barrels of flour
in their store, which they held at an exorbitant price whilst the poor
of the city were starving. This was a firebrand suddenly thrown
into the combustible mass which surrounded the speaker, and away
went the mob to Hart's store in Washington near Cortlandt Street,
which they forced open, threw four or five hundred barrels of flour
and large quantities of wheat into the street, and committed all the

extravagant acts which usually flow from the unlicensed fury of a mob. The mayor and other magistrates, with the police officers, repaired to the spot, and with the assistance of many well-disposed citizens succeeded after a time in clearing and getting possession of the store. From thence the mob went to Herrick and Company in Water Street and destroyed about fifty barrels of flour. The mayor ordered out a military force, which, with the other measures adopted, kept the rioters in check.

Saturday, February 18. — Never yet have I known so dear a market as the Fulton was this morning. It had the appearance of famine, although Saturday, when the country always sends in its produce, there was plenty of beef at eighteen cents per pound, but of poultry and veal and such things there did not appear to be a day's supply for the table of the City Hotel. What is to become of the laboring classes? The mechanic who has a family does not do so well now with eighteen shillings per day as he did when his wages were only twelve shillings. I record for future observation the cost of my marketing this morning. I could not do with less. It may cease to be a wonder hereafter, for aught I know, but it is ruinous now:

A bass weighing 14 pounds	$2.50
Two small turkeys	3.50
Three pairs chickens, 4 pounds each	3.37
One pair partridges (forbidden)	1.00
Ordinary hindquarter veal, 21 lbs.	3.94
Neck and breast mutton, 12 lbs.	1.50
Six sweetbreads	1.50
	$17.31

II

Tuesday, May 9 [1837]. — *Panic.* The Dry Dock Bank was laid under an injunction yesterday morning from the Chancellor. Its doors were not opened. Crowds of exasperated creditors collected and great alarm prevailed. At about ten o'clock the Mayor (who is president of the Bank of the State of New York) addressed the people and told them that an arrangement had been made by which the notes of the Dry Dock Bank would be redeemed by the other

Wall Street banks. This allayed the tumult. But the crowd was great during the day, and a constant run was made for specie on all the other banks, which will inevitably drain them all in a week. *The banks will be compelled to suspend the payment of specie,* and the Legislature must pass an act before they adjourn to suspend for a given period the operation of the law forfeiting the charter of banks refusing to pay specie. Mr. Van Buren's precious safety fund cries "enough" on receiving the first blow; the rotten fabric falls like the walls of Jericho on the first blast of the trumpet.

Wednesday, May 10. — *The Crisis; Banks Suspended.* The *experiment* has succeeded. The volcano has burst and overwhelmed New York; the glory of her merchants is departed. After a day of unexampled excitement and a ruthless run upon all the banks which drew from their vaults $600,000 in specie yesterday, nearly as much having been drawn on Monday, the officers held a meeting last evening and resolved to *suspend specie payments.*

It was inevitable, and the banks will be sustained in this measure by all good citizens. The Legislature must pass an act immediately suspending the operation of that part of the safety-fund law which annuls their charter on a refusal to pay specie; otherwise we shall be worse off than ever, having no circulating medium at all. They must also repeal the law which forbids the issuing of bank notes under five dollars. I regret the necessity for the latter measure, having been always in favor of the law. It worked well and would have continued to do so but for the accursed Jackson and Benton *experiment.* (The word makes me sick. I wish it could be drummed out of the English language.)

The Savings Bank also sustained a most grievous run yesterday. They paid to three hundred and seventy-five depositors eighty-one thousand dollars. The press was awful. The hour for closing the bank is six o'clock, but they did not get through the paying of those who were in at that time till nine. I was there with the other trustees and witnessed the madness of the people. Women were nearly pressed to death, and the stoutest men could scarcely sustain themselves, but they held on, as with a death's grip, upon the evidences of their claims, and exhausted as they were with the pressure, they had strength to cry, "Pay! Pay!"

The trustees met in melancholy conclave and adopted an excellent statement, prepared by Mr. Peter A. Jay, first vice-president, which was published in all the papers this morning. While we were in session, intelligence was brought that the banks had suspended specie payments. Great fears were entertained that these measures would produce serious consequences when they became known, particularly those adopted by the Bank for Savings, where there are twenty-five thousand depositors, and those generally of the poorest and most ignorant classes. I went down this morning; the notice was hung out at the door of the bank. A crowd was collected, which continued during the day, but I do not think there were at any time more than one hundred persons. Some were a little savage, but they seemed to require explanations only. It was a sort of recompense for their disappointment which they were entitled to, and when I addressed them, and some of the other trustees who were present made the explanations they wanted, they were easily pacified, and went away, by the tens and twenties, tolerably well reconciled to their disappointment, and two hours before sunset the street was cleared.

During the day Wall Street was greatly crowded, but there was no riot or tumult; on the contrary, men's countenances wore a more cheerful aspect than for several days past. The suspension of specie payments will restore confidence, the men of capital will suffer by the deterioration of the value of the circulating medium, and John Bull (if he has not been compelled to adopt the same measure ere this) will scold furiously and stigmatize the Yankees as a nation of swindlers. But honest men who are in debt and wish to pay and mechanics who are willing to work will have cause to rejoice. As for myself, I am in the first predicament and cry *laus deo*. The limb is amputated, the symmetry of the body spoiled, but the life of the patient is saved. The new mayor has done his duty like a man. The troops were out during the day, and Major General Hays, with his regiment of *clubadiers,* have shown themselves at various points in strong force. Thus ends this most eventful day.

The events of yesterday caused an astonishing rise in the price of some of the stocks which have been the most depressed. Delaware and Hudson, which sold yesterday at 50, was sold today at 67; Morris Canal rose from 30 to 50. The merchants are the most excitable class of men in the world — in the garret, or in the cellar.

Thursday, May 11. — A dead calm has succeeded the stormy weather of Wall Street and the other places of active business. All is still as death. No business is transacted, no bargains made, no negotiations entered into; men's spirits are better because the danger of universal ruin is thought to be less imminent. A slight ray of hope is to be seen in countenances where despair only dwelt for the last fortnight, but all is wrapped up in uncertainty. Nobody can foretell the course matters will take. The fever is broken, but the patient lies in a sort of syncope, exhausted by the violence of the disease and the severity of the remedies.

Friday, May 12. — The banks of Philadelphia suspended specie payments yesterday, all but the Bank of the United States, and that must follow. It is impossible that that institution, mighty as it is and reluctant to enter into the measure, can stand alone. The Baltimore banks have also suspended. It cannot fail of being general. The commercial distress and financial embarrassment pervade the whole nation. Posterity may get out of it, but the sun of the present generation will never again shine out. Things will grow better gradually, from the curtailment of business, but the glory has departed. Jackson, Van Buren, and Benton form a triumvirate more fatal to the prosperity of America than Caesar, Pompey, and Crassus were to the liberties of Rome.

III

Monday, April 23 [1838]. — *Arrival of the "Sirius."* The British steamer *Sirius,* Lieutenant Richard Roberts of the royal navy, commander, arrived here last evening, having sailed from Cork on the 4th. She has performed the voyage without any accident except the slight one of having grounded at Sandy Hook, from which she will have been extricated at this time. She has on board forty-six passengers.

The *Sirius* comes out as a pioneer to the great steam packet which is preparing to come to this country. She was to have sailed on the second instant from Cork and has been looked for with some anxiety the last three or four days, but the wind has been westerly during her whole voyage, and her passage has been longer than it will be hereafter. The arrival of the *Sirius* is an event of so great an interest that the corporation of the city appointed a joint committee to receive and visit her on her arrival. This committee, of which Alderman Hoxie is chairman, have made arrangements with Mr. Buchanan for that purpose, and they will probably make a jollification on the occasion. It is stated in the morning papers that the *Sirius,* since her departure from Cork, has used only fresh water in her boilers, having on board Mr. Hall's ingenious condensing apparatus.

The "Great Western." It was an agreeable coincidence that the great steamboat of which the *Sirius* was, as I said, the pioneer, should have arrived this morning just in time to have the event celebrated at the anniversary dinner of St. George's Society, the red-cross banner floating from the windows of the banquet hall, the Carlton House.

The *Great Western* (for such is the rather awkward name of this noble steamer) came up from Sandy Hook about two o'clock, passed around the *Sirius,* then lying at anchor off the Battery, and proceeding up the East River, hauled into Pike Slip. She is much larger than her avant-courier, being the largest vessel propelled by steam which has yet made her appearance in the waters of Europe. Her registered measurement is 1604 tons, length 234 feet, breadth from out to out of the paddle boxes 58 feet, with her engines and machinery of 450 horsepower. She is commanded by Lieutenant Hoskin, of the royal navy, and owned by the Great Western Steamship Navigation Company. She sailed from Bristol on the 8th instant, four days later than the departure of the *Sirius* from Cork, performing thus her voyage under the disadvantages of new machinery and a prevalence of head winds, in fifteen days.

The city was in a ferment during the day from the arrival of these two interesting strangers. The Battery and adjacent streets were crowded with curious spectators, and the water covered with boats, conveying obtrusive visitors on board. The committee of arrangements of the Corporation have fixed upon tomorrow at one o'clock for the two Houses, with their guests, to visit the *Sirius,* where a collation will be prepared for them, on which occasion her commander, Lieutenant Roberts, is to receive the freedom of the city.

The passengers on board the two vessels speak in the highest terms of the convenience, steadiness, and apparent safety of the new mode of conveyance across the ocean. Everybody is so enamored of it that for a while it will supersede the New York packets — the noblest vessels that ever floated in the merchant service. Our countrymen, "studious of change and pleased with novelty," will rush forward to visit the shores of Europe instead of resorting to Virginia or Saratoga Springs, and steamers will continue to be the fashion until some more dashing adventurer of the go-ahead tribe shall demonstrate the practicability of balloon navigation and gratify their impatience on a voyage *over* and not *upon* the blue waters in two days instead of as many weeks, thereby escaping the rocks and shoals and headlands which continue yet to fright the minds of timid passengers and cautious navigators. Then they may soar above the dangers of icebergs and look down with contempt upon the Goodwin Sands or Hempstead beach. As for me, I am still skeptical on the subject.

IV

May 8 [1849]. — *Theatrical Riot*. Mr. Macready commenced an engagement last evening at the Opera House, Astor Place, and was to have performed the part of *Macbeth,* whilst his rival, Mr. Forrest, appeared in the same part at the Broadway theater. A violent animosity has existed on the part of the latter theatrical hero against his rival, growing out of some differences in England, but with no cause that I can discover except that one is a gentleman and the other is a vulgar, arrogant loafer with a pack of kindred rowdies at his heels. Of these retainers a regularly organized force was employed to raise a riot at the Opera House and drive Mr. Macready off the stage, in which, to the disgrace of the city, the ruffians succeeded. On the appearance of the Thane of Cawdor, he was saluted with a shower of missiles, rotten eggs, and other unsavory objects, with shouts and yells of the most abusive epithets. In the midst of this disgraceful riot the performance was suspended, the respectable part of the audience dispersed, and the vile band of *Forresters* were left in possession of the house. This cannot end here; the respectable part of our citizens will never consent to be put down by a mob raised to serve the purpose of such a fellow as Forrest. Recriminations will be resorted to, and a series of riots will have possession of the theaters of the opposing parties.

May 10. — *The Riots.* The riot at the Opera House on Monday night was children's play compared with the disgraceful scenes which were enacted in our part of this devoted city this evening and the melancholy loss of life to which the outrageous proceedings of the mob naturally led.

An appeal to Mr. Macready had been made by many highly respectable citizens and published in the papers, inviting him to finish his engagement at the Opera House, with an implied pledge that they would stand by him against the ferocious mob of Mr. Forrest's friends who had determined that Macready should not be allowed to play, whilst at the same time their oracle was strutting, unmolested, his "hour upon the stage" of the Broadway theater. This announcement served as a firebrand in the mass of combustibles left smoldering from the riot of the former occasion. The *Forresters* perceived that their previous triumph was incomplete, and a new conspiracy was formed to accomplish effectually their nefarious designs. Inflammatory notices were posted in the upper ward, meetings were regularly organized, and bands of ruffians, gratuitously supplied with tickets by richer rascals, were sent to take possession of the theater. The police, however, were beforehand with them, and a large body of their force was posted in different parts of the house.

When Mr. Macready appeared he was assailed in the same manner as on the former occasion, but he continued on the stage and performed his part with firmness amidst the yells and hisses of the mob. The strength of the police and their good conduct, as well as that of the mayor, recorder, and other public functionaries, succeeded in preventing any serious injury to the property withindoors, and many arrests were made; but the war raged with frightful violence in the adjacent streets. The mob — a dreadful one in numbers and ferocity — assailed the extension of the building, broke in the windows, and demolished some of the doors. I walked up to the corner of Astor Place, but was glad to make my escape. On my way down, opposite the New York Hotel, I met a detachment of troops, consisting of about sixty cavalry and three hundred infantry, fine-looking fellows, well armed, who marched steadily to the field of action. Another detachment went by the way of Lafayette Place. On their arrival they were assailed by the mob, pelted with stones and brickbats, and several were carried off severely wounded.

Under this provocation, with the sanction of the civil authorities, orders were given to fire. Three or four volleys were discharged; about twenty persons were killed and a large number wounded. It is to be lamented that in the number were several innocent persons, as is always the case in such affairs, a large proportion of the mob being lookers-on who, putting no faith in the declaration of the magistrates that the fatal order was about to be given, refused to retire, and shared the fate of the rioters. What is to be the issue of this unhappy affair cannot be surmised; the end is not yet.

May 11. — *After the Battle.* I walked up this morning to the field of battle in Astor Place. The Opera House presents a shocking spectacle, and the adjacent buildings were smashed with bullet holes. Mrs. Langdon's house looks as if it had withstood a siege. Groups of people were standing around, some justifying the interference of the military, but a large proportion were savage as tigers with the smell of blood.

May 12. — Last night passed off tolerably quietly, owing to the measures taken by the magistrates and police. But it is consolatory to know that law and order have thus far prevailed. The city authorities have acted nobly. The whole military force was under arms all night, and a detachment of United States troops was also held in reserve. All the approaches to the Opera House [were] strictly guarded and no transit permitted. The police force, with the addition of a thousand special constables, were employed in every post of danger; and although the lesson has been dearly bought, it is of great value, inasmuch as the fact has been established that law and order can be maintained under a republican form of government.

V

Saturday, June 30 [1849]. — *Cholera.* Died this morning, Cornelius Low, aged fifty-four years. Dr. Francis says it was a regular case of "blue cholera." This dreadful disease increases fearfully; there are eighty-eight new cases today, and twenty-six deaths. Our visitation is severe, but thus far it falls much short of other places. St. Louis, on the Mississippi, is likely to be depopulated, and Cincinnati, on the Ohio, is awfully scourged. These two flourishing cities are the resort of emigrants from Europe, Irish and Germans coming by Canada, New York, and New Orleans, filthy, intemperate, unused to the comforts of life and regardless of its proprieties. They flock to the populous towns of the great West with disease contracted on shipboard and increased by bad habits on shore. They inoculate the inhabitants of those beautiful cities, and every paper we open is only a record of premature mortality. The air seems to be corrupted, and indulgence in things heretofore innocent is frequently fatal now in these "cholera times."

Tuesday, July 24. — The mortality in the city is greater than was supposed. The report of deaths by cholera made to the Board of Health has not exceeded forty in any one day, while the report of the city inspector of interments for the last week discloses the astounding fact that there were fourteen hundred deaths, of which seven hundred and fourteen are represented as of cholera, and a large proportion of the remainder diseases of the same family. This discrepancy in the reports arises from the negligence or culpable obstinacy of the medical faculty, some of whom will not report, because they do not wish it to be known, how many of their patients slip through their fingers. But there is an increased alarm in the city, and I fancy that the streets are deserted and everything wears a gloomy aspect.

Saturday, July 28. — Poor New York has become a charnel house; people die daily of cholera to the number of two or three hundred — that is, of cholera and other cognate diseases. But this mortality is principally among the emigrants in the eastern and western extremities of the city, where hundreds are crowded into a few wretched hovels, amidst filth and bad air, suffering from personal neglect and poisoned by eating garbage which a well-bred hog on a Westchester farm would turn up his snout at. It is remarkable that the three lower wards of the city, which in yellow-fever times were the seat of the disease, are now nearly exempt from the cholera, and the upper wards, our place of refuge from the pestilence of those days, have become almost exclusively the scene of "death's doings."

Friday, August 3. — This is a day of fasting, humiliation, and prayer, ordered by the President of the United States. May the voice of a nation punished for the sins of the people be heard by the Almighty and serve to avert the dreadful infliction under which we are suffering. It is a sublime and solemn subject of reflection. Millions of people in this vast country, of different sexes, all ages, ranks and professions, and religions and political opinions, simultaneously offering their penitential appeals to heaven for pardon and forgiveness of their sins and a removal of the chastening hand which lies heavy on the nation.

The Diary of Philip Hone

XVI

Man the Reformer

89. "A Fertility of Projects for the Salvation of the World"

As Philip Hone represented the smug conservatism of propertied New Yorkers, Ralph Waldo Emerson represented the eager skepticism, the intellectual emancipation, the social and religious radicalism, of a large group of New England leaders. Unitarianism early in the nineteenth century broke down the religious dogmatism of the Bostonians and opened their minds while Republicanism cleared the way for new social and political ideas. The romanticism of the English poets, Coleridge and Wordsworth, the deeper thought of Carlyle, and the idealism of Goethe and other German thinkers all laid a mark on the New England intellect. As Unitarianism thrived, as transcendentalism reached its height, and as the Abolition agitation began, New England seemed full of yeasty aspirations, of heady ideas, of new causes. Emerson has described the appetite for novelty and "isms," often running to wild extremes.

WHAT a fertility of projects for the salvation of the world! One apostle thought all men should go to farming, and another that no man should buy or sell, that the use of money was the cardinal evil; another that the mischief was in our diet, that we eat and drink damnation. These made unleavened bread and were foes to the death to fermentation. It was in vain urged by the housewife that God made yeast as well as dough and loves fermentation just as dearly as he loves vegetation, that fermentation develops the saccharine element in the grain and makes it more palatable and more digestible. No; they wish the pure wheat, and will die but it shall not ferment. Stop, dear Nature, these incessant advances of thine;

let us scotch these ever-rolling wheels! Others attacked the system of agriculture, the use of animal manures in farming, and the tyranny of man over brute nature; these abuses polluted his food. The ox must be taken from the plow and the horse from the cart, the hundred acres of the farm must be spaded, and the man must walk, wherever boats and locomotives will not carry him. Even the insect world was to be defended — that had been too long neglected, and a society for the protection of ground worms, slugs, and mosquitoes was to be incorporated without delay. With these appeared the adepts of homeopathy, of hydropathy, of mesmerism, of phrenology, and their wonderful theories of the Christian miracles! Others assailed particular vocations, as that of the lawyer, that of the merchant, of the manufacturer, of the clergyman, of the scholar. Others attacked the institution of marriage as the fountain of social evils. Others devoted themselves to the worrying of churches and meetings for public worship, and the fertile forms of antinomianism among the elder puritans seemed to have their match in the plenty of the new harvest of reform.

With this din of opinion and debate there was a keener scrutiny of institutions and domestic life than any we had known; there was sincere protesting against existing evils, and there were changes of employment dictated by conscience.

There was in all the practical activities of New England for the last quarter of a century [1815–1840] a gradual withdrawal of tender consciences from the social organizations. There is observable throughout, the contest between mechanical and spiritual methods, but with a steady tendency of the thoughtful and virtuous to a deeper belief and reliance on spiritual facts.

In politics, for example, it is easy to see the progress of dissent. The country is full of rebellion; the country is full of kings. Hands off! let there be no control and no interference in the administration of the affairs of this kingdom of me. Hence the growth of the doctrine and of the party of free trade and the willingness to try that experiment in the face of what appear incontestable facts. I confess the motto of the *Globe* newspaper is so attractive to me that I can seldom find much appetite to read what is below it in its columns: "The world is governed too much." So the country is frequently affording solitary examples of resistance to the government, solitary nullifiers who throw themselves on their reserved rights; nay, who have reserved all their rights; who reply to the assessor and to the clerk of court that they do not know the State, and embarrass the courts of law by nonjuring and the commander-in-chief of the militia by nonresistance.

The same dispostion to scrutiny and dissent appeared in civil, festive, neighborly, and domestic society. A restless, prying, conscientious criticism broke out in unexpected quarters. Who gave me the money with which I bought my coat? Why should professional labor and that of the countinghouse be paid so disproportionately to the labor of the porter and wood sawyer? This whole business of trade gives me to pause and think, as it constitutes false relations between men, inasmuch as I am prone to count myself relieved of any responsibility to behave well and nobly to that person whom I pay with money; whereas, if I had not that commodity, I should be put on my good behavior in all companies, and man would be a benefactor to man, as being himself his only certificate that he had a right to those aids and services which each asked of the other. Am I not too protected a person? Is there not a wide disparity between the lot of me and the lot of thee, my poor brother, my poor sister? Am I not defrauded of my best culture in the loss of those gymnastics which manual labor and the emergencies of poverty constitute? I find nothing healthful or exalting in the smooth conventions of society; I do not like the close air of saloons. I begin to suspect myself to be a prisoner, though treated with all this courtesy and luxury. I pay a destructive tax in my conformity.

The same insatiable criticism may be traced in the efforts for the reform of education. The popular education has been taxed with a want of truth and nature. It was complained that an education to things was not given. We are students of words; we are shut up in schools, and colleges, and recitation rooms, for ten or fifteen years, and come out at last with a bag of wind, a memory of words, and do not know a thing. We cannot use our hands, or our legs, or our eyes, or our arms. We do not know an edible root in the woods; we cannot tell our course by the stars, nor the hour of the day by the sun. It is well if we can swim and skate. We are afraid of a horse, of a cow, of a dog, of a snake, of a spider. The Roman rule was to teach a boy nothing that he could not learn standing. The old English rule was, "All summer in the field, and all winter in the study." And it seems as if a man should learn to plant, or to fish, or to hunt, that he might secure his subsistence at all events and not be painful to his friends and fellowmen. The lessons of science should be experimental also. The sight of a planet through a telescope is worth all the course on astronomy; the shock of the electric spark in the elbow outvalues all the theories; the taste of the nitrous oxide, the firing of an artificial volcano, are better than volumes of chemistry.

RALPH WALDO EMERSON, The New England Reformers

90. The Lunatic Fringe of Reform

An American libertarian of New Hampshire origin, Thomas Low Nichols was able to write of the intellectual fads of his day from full knowledge. While he was a student at Dartmouth he adopted the food-reform principles of Sylvester Graham, who invented graham flour. A little later he became a follower of Fourier and of John Humphrey Noyes, the founder of the Oneida Community. He married a woman who specialized in the water cure or hydropathy, and the two began crusading for mesmerism, vegetarianism, and woman's rights. Ultimately they turned to the Catholic Church, and found England a pleasanter home than America.

WHEN Doctor Spurzheim, the associate of Gall in the elaboration of the system of phrenology, came to America about 1834, he was received with enthusiasm. Phrenology became the rage. Plaster casts of heads, and lithographs marked with the organs, were sold by thousands. There was a universal feeling of heads. Lecturers went from town to town, explaining the new science and giving public and private examinations. Periodicals were published to promulgate the new philosophy, and a library of phrenological books was rapidly published. I have no doubt that in five years after the event of Doctor Spurzheim there were more believers of phrenology in the United States than in all the world beside.

Mesmerism trod closely on the heels of phrenology. Monsieur Poyen, a French Creole, from one of the West India islands, came to Boston and introduced the new science to the American public. His lectures were succeeded by experiments. At one of the hospitals a patient selected for the experiment was so thoroughly mesmerized that she remained asleep forty-eight hours, though suffering from an acute disease of the heart that usually deprived her of rest. During the trance she appeared placid and free from pain, but it was impossible to awaken her. At the end of the forty-eight hours she awoke of herself, much refreshed, and said she felt better than she had for months. The publication of this and a few similar cases, of course, set a great many people to mesmerizing each other. There were medical mesmerists and clairvoyants everywhere. Distinguished surgeons performed operations on patients who were insensible to pain during the magnetic sleep. Clairvoyants professed to inspect the internal organs of patients, describe their diseases, and prescribe remedies, which were not more varied or dangerous than those given by the regular and irregular faculty.

There were psychometrists, who could tell the lives, characters, fortunes, and diseases of people they had never seen, by holding a sealed letter, scrap of writing, lock of hair, or other connecting relic in their hands. There was one who, when a fossil of some remote geological era was placed in contact with her forehead, would give an animated description of the appearance of the planet at that period.

Mesmerism vulgarly culminated in an exhibition of what was called, absurdly enough, "psychology" or "biology," a process of hallucination by which a number of susceptible persons selected by a lecturer from his audience were made to believe and do the most ridiculous things — to fancy they were swimming, or flying, or drinking, at the will of the operator, and to dance, sing, declaim, and do many things they never thought of doing in their normal condition

The vegetarian system of dietetics was taken up with great zeal and promulgated with singular ability by Sylvester Graham, Doctor Alcott, Professor Muzzy, and other sanitary reformers. The English talk a good deal abou· roast beef, but there are ten persons in England who do not taste flesh meat of any kind oftener than once a week, to one in America. Irish emigrants, who, perhaps, never ate meat a dozen times a year at home, think they must eat it three times a day in America. Some thousands of Americans abandoned the use of flesh entirely, and many never returned to it. These believe that most of the diseases and evils of life are caused by eating flesh and that with its disuse would come health, purity, and happiness.

The spread of hydropathy was another example of the readiness of Americans to accept anything new. The system had scarcely been heard of before several large water-cure establishments were opened in America, and in a few years five or six water-cure journals were published, medical schools of hydropathy opened, and numerous practitioners, male and female, were dispensing packs and douches, with much desirable cleanliness, and much sanitary improvement also, to the American public.

The advocacy of women's rights did not begin in America. Mary Wollstonecraft was an Englishwoman, and so was Frances Wright, who lectured thirty years ago in America on politics, socialism, and deism with considerable success, which, however, did not outlast the novelty of an accomplished woman giving public addresses on such subjects. But many American women have aspired to places in the learned professions of law, physic, and divinity. Women have practised law, been settled as preachers, but this is scarcely a novelty, since female preachers have long been common among the Friends or Quakers and women have founded several denominations.

The attempt on the part of certain American women to assume masculine or semi-masculine habiliments — a movement which received the name of Bloomerism from one of its prominent American advocates — was a bold and energetic one, but not successful. Some thousands of American women adopted what they thought a convenient and healthful costume and were brave to heroism and persevering to fanaticism, but the attempted reform was a failure. America could rebel against a foreign government; she may revolutionize her own; but America is not strong enough to war upon the fashions of civilization. A woman in New York may make a political speech to three or four thousand people, but to wear a Bloomer dress down Broadway is another affair, and a far greater difficulty would be to get others to follow her example.

The land reformers were at one period a pretty formidable organization and had some influence on local and even on national politics. That the earth is the property of its inhabitants, that the land of every country belongs to the people of that country, that no individual can have a right to monopolize great tracts of country and compel others to pay him rent or starve, many Americans believe. Land, said the land reformers, should be as free as air or water. Land is a necessary of life, and all men have an equal right to life and what is necessary to preserve it. A man cannot bottle up the atmosphere. Why claim exclusive possession of square leagues of territory? Who gives any man an exclusive right to earth and sunshine and the food they produce? "Land for the landless!" "No land monopoly!" "Vote yourself a farm."

THOMAS LOW NICHOLS, Forty Years of American Life, 1821–1861

91. Dorothea Dix Pleads the Cause of the Insane

The great humanitarian Dorothea Lynde Dix found her life work when in 1841, undertaking a Sunday school class in a jail in East Cambridge, Massachusetts, she found insane prisoners kept in misery in an unheated room. She gave the rest of her years to the reformation of the care of the insane, the improvement of jails, and the building of hospitals for the mentally diseased, traveling from state to state, and appealing to legislature after legislature. Her memorial to the Massachusetts legislators in 1843, which gained the support of public opinion and brought about the establishment of proper facilities at Worcester, marked the beginning of her great crusade.

GENTLEMEN: I come to present the strong claims of suffering humanity. I come to place before the Legislature of Massachusetts the condition of the miserable, the desolate, the outcast. I come as the advocate of helpless, forgotten, insane, and idiotic men and women; of beings sunk to a condition from which the most unconcerned would start with real horror; of beings wretched in our prisons, and more wretched in our almshouses.

I must confine myself to a few examples, but am ready to furnish other and more complete details, if required.

I proceed, gentlemen, briefly to call your attention to the *present* state of insane persons confined within this Commonwealth, in *cages, closets, cellars, stalls, pens! Chained, naked, beaten with rods,* and *lashed* into obedience.

I offer the following extracts from my notebook and journal.

Springfield: In the jail, one lunatic woman, furiously mad, a state pauper, improperly situated, both in regard to the prisoners, the keepers, and herself. It is a case of extreme self-forgetfulness and oblivion to all the decencies of life, to describe which would be to repeat only the grossest scenes. In the almshouse of the same town is a woman apparently only needing judicious care and some well-chosen employment to make it unnecessary to confine her in solitude in a dreary unfurnished room. Her appeals for employment and companionship are most touching, but the mistress replied "she had no time to attend to her."

Lincoln: A woman in a cage. *Medford:* One idiotic subject chained, and one in a close stall for seventeen years. *Pepperell:* One often doubly chained, hand and foot; another violent; several peaceable now. *Brookfield:* One man caged, comfortable. *Granville:* One often closely confined, now losing the use of his limbs from want of exercise. *Charlemont:* One man caged. *Savoy:* One man caged. *Lenox:* Two in the jail, against whose unfit condition there the jailer protests.

Dedham: The insane disadvantageously placed in the jail. In the almshouse, two females in stalls, situated in the main building, lie in wooden bunks filled with straw; always shut up. One of these subjects is supposed curable. The overseers of the poor have declined giving her a trial at the hospital, as I was informed, on account of expense.

Besides the above, I have seen many who, part of the year, are chained or caged. The use of cages is all but universal. Hardly a town but can refer to some not distant period of using them; chains are less common; negligences frequent; wilful abuse less frequent than sufferings proceeding from ignorance, or want of consideration. I encountered during the last three months many poor creatures wandering reckless and unprotected through the country. . . . But I cannot particularize. In traversing the state, I have found hundreds of insane persons in every variety of circumstance and condition, many whose situation could not and need not be improved; a less number, but that very large, whose lives are the saddest pictures of human suffering and degradation description fades before reality.

Men of Massachusetts, I beg, I implore, I demand pity and protection for these of my suffering, outraged sex. Become the benefactors of your race, the just guardians of the solemn rights you hold in trust. Raise up the fallen, succor the desolate, restore the outcast, defend the helpless, and for your eternal and great reward receive the benediction, "Well done, good and faithful servants, become rulers over many things!"

Injustice is also done to the *convicts:* it is certainly very wrong that they should be doomed day after day and night after night to listen to the ravings of madmen and madwomen. This is a kind of punishment that is not recognized by our statutes, and is what the criminal ought not to be called upon to undergo. The confinement of the criminal and of the insane in the same building is subversive of that good order and discipline which should be observed in every well-regulated prison. I do most sincerely hope that more permanent provision will be made for the pauper insane by the state, either to restore Worcester Insane Asylum to what it was originally designed to be or else to make some just appropriation for the benefit of this very unfortunate class of our fellow beings.

Gentlemen, I commit to you this sacred cause. Your action upon this subject will affect the present and future condition of hundreds and of thousands. In this legislation, as in all things, may you exercise that "wisdom which is the breath of the power of God."

Old South Leaflets

92. A Woman's Declaration of Independence

When Elizabeth Cady, of a well-known New York family, was married in 1840 to Henry B. Stanton, she was already sufficiently interested in woman's rights to insist that the word "obey" be left out of the ceremony. Going to a frontier community, Seneca Falls, to live, she had the hardships and injustices of woman's lot more forcibly impressed upon her. Together with Lucretia Mott, who had been barred out of an antislavery convention because of her sex, she called a woman's rights convention in the Methodist Church in Seneca Falls in the summer of 1848. Mrs. Mott protested when Mrs. Stanton offered a woman-suffrage plank. "Why, Lizzy, thee will make us ridiculous!" she exclaimed. But Mrs. Stanton stuck by her demand.

WHEN, in the course of human events, it becomes necessary for one portion of the family of man to assume among the people of the earth a position different from that which they have hitherto occupied, but one to which the laws of nature and of nature's God entitle them, a decent respect to the opinions of mankind requires that they should declare the causes that impel them to such a course.

We hold these truths to be self-evident: that all men and women are created equal; that they are endowed by their Creator with certain inalienable rights; that among these are life, liberty, and the pursuit of happiness; that to secure these rights governments are instituted, deriving their just powers from the consent of the governed. Whenever any form of government becomes destructive of these ends, it is the right of those who suffer from it to refuse allegiance to it, and to insist upon the institution of a new government, laying its foundation on such principles, and organizing its powers in such form, as to them shall seem most likely to effect their safety and happiness. Prudence, indeed, will dictate that governments long established should not be changed for light and transient causes; and accordingly all experience hath shown that mankind are more disposed to suffer while evils are sufferable, than to right themselves by abolishing the forms to which they are accustomed. But when a long train of abuses and usurpations, pursuing invariably the same object, evinces a design to reduce them under absolute despotism, it is their duty to throw off such government, and to provide new guards for their future security. Such has been the patient sufferance of the women under this government, and such is now the necessity which constrains them to demand the equal station to which they are entitled.

The history of mankind is a history of repeated injuries and usurpations on the part of man toward woman, having in direct object the establishment of an absolute tyranny over her. To prove this, let facts be submitted to a candid world. . . .

Now, in view of this entire disfranchisement of one-half the people of this country, their social and religious degradation — in view of the unjust laws above mentioned, and because women do feel themselves aggrieved, oppressed, and fraudulently deprived of their most sacred rights, we insist that they have immediate admission to all the rights and privileges which belong to them as citizens of the United States.

In entering upon the great work before us, we anticipate no small amount of misconception, misrepresentation, and ridicule; but we shall use every instrumentality within our power to effect our object. We shall employ agents, circulate tracts, petition the state and national legislatures, and endeavor to enlist the pulpit and the press in our behalf. We hope this convention will be followed by a series of conventions embracing every part of the country.

RESOLUTIONS

Resolved, That all laws which prevent woman from occupying such a station in society as her conscience shall dictate, or which place her in a position inferior to that of man, are contrary to the great precept of nature, and therefore of no force or authority.

Resolved, That woman is man's equal — was intended to be so by the Creator, and the highest good of the race demands that she should be recognized as such. . . .

Resolved, That it is the duty of the women of this country to secure to themselves their sacred right to the elective franchise. . . .

Resolved, That the speedy success of our cause depends upon the zealous and untiring efforts of both men and women for the overthrow of the monopoly of the pulpit and for the securing to women an equal participation with men in the various trades, professions, and commerce.

Resolved, therefore, That, being invested by the Creator with the same capabilities and the same consciousness of responsibility for their exercise, it is demonstrably the right and duty of woman, equally with man, to promote every righteous cause by every righteous means; and especially in regard to the great subjects of morals and religion, it is self-evidently her right to participate with her brother in teaching them, both in private and in public, by writing and by speaking, by any instrumentalities proper to be used, and in any assemblies proper to be held; and this being a self-evident truth growing out of the divinely implanted principles of human nature, any custom or authority adverse to it, whether modern or wearing the hoary sanction of antiquity, is to be regarded as a self-evident falsehood, and at war with mankind.

Seneca Falls Declaration of Sentiments, July 19, 1848

93. Bronson Alcott Sows Transcendental Wild Oats

Bronson Alcott, Connecticut farmer's son, Yankee peddler, schoolteacher, and traveling philosopher, was long regarded as a foolish and impractical idealist, and for many years was best known as Louisa M. Alcott's father. But Emerson said that his mind was "the best instrument I have ever met with." His life was one of worldly failure but spiritual success. Having taught school

in various places, married, and visited England, in 1844 he set up
the co-operative community of Fruitlands on a hundred-acre tract
at Harvard, Massachusetts, about thirty miles west of Boston. The
failure of this vegetarian community was swift and ignominious —
it was abandoned early the next year. But his daughter Louisa,
twelve years old at the time, was able to see the humorous side of
the adventure.

O N THE first day of June, 184-, a large wagon drawn by a
small horse and containing a motley load went lumbering over certain New England hills, with the pleasing accompaniments of wind,
rain, and hail. A serene man with a serene child upon his knee was
driving or rather being driven, for the small horse had it all his own
way. A brown boy with a William Penn style of countenance sat
beside him, firmly embracing a bust of Socrates. Behind them was
an energetic-looking woman with a benevolent brow, satirical
mouth, and eyes brimful of hope and courage. A baby reposed upon
her lap, a mirror leaned against her knee, and a basket of provisions
danced about at her feet, as she struggled with a large, unruly umbrella. Two blue-eyed little girls with hands full of childish treasures
sat under one old shawl, chatting happily together.

In front of this lively party stalked a tall, sharp-featured man in
a long blue cloak; and a fourth small girl trudged along beside him
through the mud as if she rather enjoyed it.

The wind whistled over the bleak hills; the rain fell in a despond-
ent drizzle; and twilight began to fall. But the calm man gazed as
tranquilly into the fog as if he beheld a radiant bow of promise
spanning the gray sky. The cheery woman tried to cover every one
but herself with the big umbrella. The brown boy pillowed his head
on the bald pate of Socrates and slumbered peacefully. The little
girls sang lullabies to their dolls in soft, maternal murmurs. The
sharp-nosed pedestrian marched steadily on, with the blue cloak
streaming out behind him like a banner; and the lively infant
splashed through the puddles with a ducklike satisfaction pleasant
to behold.

Thus these modern pilgrims journeyed hopefully out of the old world, to found a new one in the wilderness. This prospective Eden at present consisted of an old red farmhouse, a dilapidated barn, many acres of meadowland, and a grove. Ten ancient apple trees were all the "chaste supply" which the place offered as yet; but, in the firm belief that plenteous orchards were soon to be evoked from their inner consciousness, these sanguine founders had christened their domain Fruitlands.

Here Timon Lion intended to found a colony of latter-day saints, who, under his patriarchal sway, should regenerate the world and glorify his name for ever. Here Abel Lamb [Bronson Alcott], with the devoutest faith in the high ideal which was to him a living truth, desired to plant a Paradise, where Beauty, Virtue, Justice, and Love might live happily together, without the possibility of a serpent entering in. And here his wife, unconverted but faithful to the end, hoped, after many wanderings over the face of the earth, to find rest for herself and a home for her children.

"There is our new abode," announced the enthusiast, smiling with a satisfaction quite undamped by the drops dripping from his hatbrim, as they turned at length into a cart path that wound along a steep hillside into a barren-looking valley.

"A little difficult of access," observed his practical wife, as she endeavored to keep her various household gods from going overboard with every lurch of the laden ark.

"Like all good things. But those who earnestly desire and patiently seek will soon find us," placidly responded the philosopher from the mud, through which he was now endeavoring to pilot the much-enduring horse.

"Truth lies at the bottom of a well, Sister Hope," said Brother Timon, pausing to detach his small comrade from a gate whereon she was perched for a clearer gaze into futurity.

"That's the reason we so seldom get at it, I suppose," replied Sister Hope, making a vain clutch at the mirror, which a sudden jolt sent flying out of her hands.

"We want no false reflections here," said Timon with a grim smile, as he crunched the fragments underfoot in his onward march.

Sister Hope held her peace and looked wistfully through the mist at her promised home. The old red house with a hospitable glimmer at its windows cheered her eyes, and, considering the weather, was a fitter refuge than the sylvan bowers some of the more ardent souls might have preferred.

The newcomers were welcomed by one of the elect — a regenerate farmer, whose idea of reform consisted chiefly in wearing white cotton raiment and shoes of untanned leather. This costume, with a snowy beard, gave him a venerable and at the same time a somewhat bridal appearance.

The goods and chattels of the Society not having arrived, the weary family reposed before the fire on blocks of wood, while Brother Moses White regaled them with roasted potatoes, brown bread, and water, in two plates, a tin pan, and one mug, his table service being limited. But, having cast the forms and vanities of a depraved world behind them, the elders welcomed hardship with the enthusiasm of new pioneers, and the children heartily enjoyed this foretaste of what they believed was to be a sort of perpetual picnic.

During the progress of this frugal meal, two more brothers appeared. One was a dark, melancholy man, clad in homespun, whose peculiar mission was to turn his name hind part before and use as few words as possible. The other was a bland, bearded Englishman, who expected to be saved by eating uncooked food and going without clothes. He had not yet adopted the primitive costume, however, but contented himself with meditatively chewing dry beans out of a basket.

"Every meal should be a sacrament, and the vessels used should be beautiful and symbolical," observed Brother Lamb, mildly, righting the tin pan slipping about on his knees. "I priced a silver service when in town, but it was too costly; so I got some graceful cups and vases of britannia ware."

"Hardest things in the world to keep bright. Will whiting be allowed in the community?" inquired Sister Hope, with a housewife's interest in labor-saving institutions.

"Such trivial questions will be discussed at a more fitting time," answered Brother Timon sharply, as he burnt his fingers with a very hot potato. "Neither sugar, molasses, milk, butter, cheese, nor flesh are to be used among us, for nothing is to be admitted which has caused wrong or death to man or beast."

"Our garments are to be linen till we learn to raise our own cotton or some substitute for woolen fabrics," added Brother Abel, blissfully basking in an imaginary future as warm and brilliant as the generous fire before him.

"Haou abaout shoes?" asked Brother Moses, surveying his own with interest.

"We must yield that point till we can manufacture an innocent substitute for leather. Bark, wood, or some durable fabric will be invented in time. Meanwhile, those who desire to carry out our idea to the fullest extent can go barefooted," said Lion, who liked extreme measures.

"I never will, nor let my girls," murmured rebellious Sister Hope, under her breath.

"Haou do you cattle'ate to treat the ten-acre lot? Ef things ain't 'tended to right smart, we shan't hev no crops," observed the practical patriarch in cotton.

"We shall spade it," replied Abel, in such perfect good faith that Moses said no more, though he indulged in a shake of the head as he glanced at hands that had held nothing heavier than a pen for years. He was a paternal old soul and regarded the younger men as promising boys on a new sort of lark.

"What shall we do for lamps if we cannot use any animal substance? I do hope light of some sort is to be thrown upon the enterprise," said Mrs. Lamb with anxiety, for in those days kerosene and camphene were not, and gas was unknown in the wilderness.

"We shall go without till we have discovered some vegetable oil or wax to serve us," replied Brother Timon, in a decided tone, which caused Sister Hope to resolve that her private lamp should be always trimmed, if not burning.

"Each member is to perform the work for which experience, strength, and taste best fit him," continued Dictator Lion. "Thus drudgery and disorder will be avoided and harmony prevail. We shall rise at dawn, begin the day by bathing, followed by music, and then a chaste repast of fruit and bread. Each one finds congenial occupation till the meridian meal, when some deep-searching conversation gives rest to the body and development to the mind. Healthful labor again engages us till the last meal, when we assemble in social communion, prolonged till sunset, when we retire to sweet repose, ready for the next day's activity."

"What part of the work do you incline to yourself?" asked Sister Hope, with a humorous glimmer in her keen eyes.

"I shall wait till it is made clear to me. Being in preference to doing is the great aim, and this comes to us rather by a resigned willingness than a wilful activity, which is a check to all divine growth," responded Brother Timon.

"I thought so." And Mrs. Lamb sighed audibly, for during the year he had spent in her family Brother Timon had so faithfully carried out his idea of "being, not doing," that she had found his "divine growth" both an expensive and unsatisfactory process. . . .

The furniture arrived next day, and was soon bestowed, for the principal property of the community consisted in books. To this rare library was devoted the best room in the house, and the few busts and pictures that still survived many flittings were added to beautify the sanctuary, for here the family was to meet for amusement, instruction, and worship.

Any housewife can imagine the emotions of Sister Hope when she took possession of a large dilapidated kitchen, containing an old stove and the peculiar stores out of which food was to be evolved for her little family of eleven — cakes of maple sugar, dried peas and beans, barley and hominy, meal of all sorts, potatoes, and dried fruit. No milk, butter, cheese, tea, or meat appeared. Even salt was considered a useless luxury and spice entirely forbidden by these lovers of Spartan simplicity. Her ten years' experience of vegetarian vagaries had been good training for this new freak, and her sense of the ludicrous supported her through many trying scenes.

Unleavened bread, porridge, and water for breakfast; bread, vegetables, and water for dinner; bread, fruit, and water for supper was the bill of fare ordained by the elders. No teapot profaned that sacred stove, no gory steak cried aloud for vengeance from her chaste gridiron; and only a brave woman's taste, time, and temper were sacrificed on that domestic altar.

The vexed question of light was settled by buying a quantity of bayberry wax for candles, and [when it was discovered] that no one knew how to make them, pine knots were introduced, to be used when absolutely necessary. [As it was] summer, the evenings were not long, and the weary fraternity found it no great hardship to retire with the birds. The inner light was sufficient for most of them. But Mrs. Lamb rebelled. Evening was the only time she had to herself; and while the tired feet rested, the skillful hands mended torn frocks and little stockings, or the anxious heart forgot its burden in a book.

So "mother's lamp" burned steadily, while the philosophers built a new heaven and earth by moonlight; and through all the metaphysical mists and philanthropic pyrotechnics of that period Sister Hope played her own little game of "throwing light," and none but the moths were the worse for it.

Such farming probably was never seen before since Adam delved. The band of brothers began by spading garden and field, but a few days of it lessened their ardor amazingly. Blistered hands and aching backs suggested the expediency of permitting the use of cattle till the workers were better fitted for noble toil by a summer of the new life.

The sowing was equally peculiar, for, owing to some mistake, the three brethren who devoted themselves to this graceful task found, when about half through the job, that each had been sowing a different sort of grain in the same field, a mistake which caused much perplexity, as it could not be remedied. But after a long consultation and a good deal of laughter, it was decided to say nothing and see what would come of it.

Slowly things got into order and rapidly rumors of the new experiment went abroad, causing many strange spirits to flock thither, for in those days communities were the fashion and transcendentalism raged wildly. Some came to look on and laugh, some to be supported in poetic idleness, a few to believe sincerely and work heartily. Each member was allowed to mount his favorite hobby and ride it to his heart's content. Very queer were some of the riders, and very rampant some of the hobbies.

One youth, believing that language was of little consequence if the spirit was only right, startled newcomers by blandly greeting them with "Good morning, damn you," and other remarks of an equally mixed order. A second irrepressible being held that all the emotions of the soul should be freely expressed, and illustrated his theory by antics that would have sent him to a lunatic asylum, if, as an unregenerate wag said, he were not already in one. When his spirit soared, he climbed trees and shouted; when doubt assailed him, he lay upon the floor and groaned lamentably. At joyful periods he raced, leaped, and sang; when sad, he wept aloud; and when a great thought burst upon him in the watches of the night, he crowed like a jocund cockerel, to the great delight of the children and the great annoyance of the elders. One musical brother fiddled whenever so moved, sang sentimentally to the four little girls, and put a music box on the wall when he hoed corn.

Transcendental wild oats were sown broadcast that year, and the fame thereof has not yet ceased in the land; for, futile as this crop seemed to outsiders, it bore an invisible harvest, worth much to those who planted it in earnest.

A new dress was invented, since cotton, silk, and wool were forbidden as the products of slave labor, worm slaughter, and sheep robbery. Tunics and trousers of brown linen were the only wear. The women's skirts were longer and their straw hatbrims wider than the men's, and this was the only difference. Some persecution lent a charm to the costume, and the long-haired, linen-clad reformers quite enjoyed the mild martyrdom they endured when they left home.

Money was abjured as the root of all evil. The produce of the land was to supply most of their wants or be exchanged for the few things they could not grow. This idea had its inconveniences, but self-denial was the fashion, and it was surprising how many things one can do without. When they desired to travel, they walked, if possible, begged the loan of a vehicle, or boldly entered car or coach and, stating their principles to the officials, took the consequences. Usually their dress, their earnest frankness, and gentle resolution won them a passage; but now and then they met with hard usage and had the satisfaction of suffering for their principles.

They preached vegetarianism everywhere and resisted all temptations of the flesh, contentedly eating apples and bread at well-spread tables and much afflicting hospitable hostesses by denouncing their food and taking away their appetites, discussing the "horrors of shambles," the "incorporation of the brute in man," and "on elegant abstinence the sign of a pure soul." But when the perplexed or offended ladies asked what they should eat, they got in reply a bill of fare consisting of "bowls of sunrise for breakfast," "solar seeds of the sphere," "dishes from Plutarch's chaste table," and other viands equally hard to find in any modern market.

Reform conventions of all sorts were haunted by these brethren, who said many wise things and did many foolish ones. Unfortunately, these wanderings interfered with their harvest at home; but the rule was to do what the spirit moved, so they left their crops to Providence and went a-reaping in wider and, let us hope, more fruitful fields than their own. . . .

This attempt at regeneration had its tragic as well as its comic side, though the world saw only the former.

Louisa May Alcott, Silver Pitchers

94. Henry Thoreau Builds a Cabin at Walden Pond

To illustrate his doctrine of the simplification of life, to gain leisure to write a book, A Week on the Concord and Merrimac, *and find material for another, and to test some of his theories both of economics and philosophy, Henry David Thoreau spent a little more than two years in his hut on Walden Pond near the village of Concord, Massachusetts. It was the most important episode in the life of a man whose stature in American letters has steadily grown and is still growing.*

NEAR the end of March, 1845, I borrowed an ax and went down to the woods by Walden Pond, the nearest to where I intended to build my house, and began to cut down some tall arrowy white pines, still in their youth, for timber. It is difficult to begin without borrowing, but perhaps it is the most generous course thus to permit your fellow men to have an interest in your enterprise. The owner of the ax, as he released his hold on it, said that it was the apple of his eye; but I returned it sharper than I received it. It was a pleasant hillside where I worked, covered with pine woods through which I looked out on the pond, and a small open field in the woods where pines and hickories were springing up. The ice in the pond was not yet dissolved, though there were some open spaces, and it was all dark-colored and saturated with water. There were some slight flurries of snow during the day that I worked there; but for the most part when I came out on to the railroad on my way home, its yellow sand heap stretched away gleaming in the hazy atmosphere, and the rails shone in the spring sun, and I heard the lark and peewee and other birds already come to commence another year with us. They were pleasant spring days in which the winter of man's discontent was thawing as well as the earth, and the life that had lain torpid began to stretch itself. One day when my ax had come off and I had cut a green hickory for a wedge, driving it with a stone, and had placed the whole to soak in a pond hole in order to swell the wood, I saw a striped snake run into the water, and he lay on the bottom, apparently without inconvenience, as long as I stayed there, or more than a quarter of an hour, perhaps because he had not yet fairly come out of the torpid state. It appeared to me that for a like reason men remain in their low and primitive condition; but if they should feel the influence of the spring of springs arousing them, they would of necessity rise to a higher and more ethereal life. I had previously seen the snakes in frosty mornings in my path with portions of their bodies still numb and inflexible, waiting for the sun to thaw them. On the first of April it rained and melted the ice, and in the early part of the day, which was very foggy, I heard a stray goose groping about over the pond and cackling as if lost, or like the spirit of the fog.

So I went on for some days cutting and hewing timber, and also studs and rafters, all with my narrow ax, not having many communicable or scholarlike thoughts, singing to myself —

> Men say they know many things;
> But lo! they have taken wings —
> The arts and sciences,
> And a thousand appliances;
> The wind that blows
> Is all that anybody knows.

I hewed the main timbers six inches square, most of the studs on two sides only, and the rafters and floor timbers on one side, leaving the rest of the bark on, so that they were just as straight and much stronger than sawed ones. Each stick was carefully mortised or tenoned by its stump, for I had borrowed other tools by this time. My days in the woods were not very long ones; yet I usually carried my dinner of bread and butter, and read the newspaper in which it was wrapped at noon, sitting amid the green boughs which I had cut off, and to my bread was imparted some of their fragrance, for my hands were covered with a thick coat of pitch. Before I had done, I was more the friend than the foe of the pine tree, though I had cut down some of them, having become better acquainted with it. Sometimes a rambler in the wood was attracted by the sound of my ax, and we chatted pleasantly over the chips which I made.

Before I finished my house, wishing to earn ten or twelve dollars by some honest and agreeable method, in order to meet my unusual expenses, I planted about two acres and a half of light sandy soil near it chiefly with beans, but also a small part with potatoes, corn, peas, and turnips. The whole lot contains eleven acres, mostly growing up to pines and hickories, and was sold the preceding season for eight dollars and eight cents an acre. One farmer said that it was "good for nothing but to raise cheeping squirrels on." I put no manure whatever on this land, not being the owner, but merely a squatter, and not expecting to cultivate so much again, and I did not quite hoe it all once. I got out several cords of stumps in plowing, which supplied me with fuel for a long time, and left small circles of virgin mold, easily distinguishable through the summer by the greater luxuriance of the beans there. The dead and for the most part unmerchantable wood behind my house and the driftwood from the pond have supplied the remainder of my fuel. I was obliged to hire a team and a man for the plowing, though I held the plow myself. My farm outgoes for the first season were: for implements, seed, work, etc., $14.72½. The seed corn was given me. This never costs anything to speak of, unless you plant more than enough. I got twelve bushels of beans and eighteen bushels of potatoes, besides some peas and sweet corn. The yellow corn and turnips

were too late to come to anything. My whole income from the farm
was

	$23.44
Deducting the outgoes	14.72½
There are left	$8.71½

beside produce consumed and on hand at the time this estimate was
made of the value of $4.50 — the amount on hand much more than
balancing a little grass which I did not raise. All things considered,
that is, considering the importance of a man's soul and of today,
notwithstanding the short time occupied by my experiment, nay,
partly even because of its transient character, I believe that that was
doing better than any farmer in Concord did that year.

The next year I did better still, for I spaded up all the land which
I required, about a third of an acre, and I learned from the experience of both years, not being in the least awed by many celebrated
works on husbandry, Arthur Young among the rest, that if one
would live simply and eat only the crop which he raised, and raise
no more than he ate, and not exchange it for an insufficient quantity
of more luxurious and expensive things, he would need to cultivate
only a few rods of ground, and that it would be cheaper to spade
that up than to use oxen to plow it, and to select a fresh spot from
time to time than to manure the old, and he could do all his necessary farm work, as it were, with his left hand at odd hours in the
summer; and thus he would not be tied to an ox, or horse, or cow,
or pig, as at present. I desire to speak impartially on this point, and
as one not interested in the success or failure of the present economical and social arrangements. I was more independent than any
farmer in Concord, for I was not anchored to a house or farm, but
could follow the bent of my genius, which is a very crooked one,
every moment. Beside being better off than they already, if my
house had been burned or my crops had failed, I should have been
nearly as well off as before.

I am wont to think that men are not so much the keepers of
herds as herds are the keepers of men, the former are so much the
freer. Men and oxen exchange work; but if we consider necessary
work only, the oxen will be seen to have greatly the advantage, their

farm is so much the larger. Man does some of his part of the exchange work in his six weeks of haying, and it is no boy's play. Certainly, no nation that lived simply in all respects — that is, no nation of philosophers — would commit so great a blunder as to use the labor of animals. True, there never was and is not likely soon to be a nation of philosophers, nor am I certain it is desirable that there should be. However, *I* should never have broken a horse or bull and taken him to board for any work he might do for me, for fear I should become a horse-man or a herdsman merely; and if society seems to be the gainer by so doing, are we certain that what is one man's gain is not another's loss, and that the stableboy has equal cause with his master to be satisfied? Granted that some public works would not have been constructed without this aid, and let man share the glory of such with the ox and horse; does it follow that he could not have accomplished works yet more worthy of himself in that case? When men begin to do, not merely unnecessary or artistic but luxurious and idle work with their assistance, it is inevitable that a few do all the exchange work with the oxen, or, in other words, become the slaves of the strongest. Man thus not only works for the animal within him, but for a symbol of this, he works for the animal without him. Though we have many substantial houses of brick or stone, the prosperity of the farmer is still measured by the degree to which the barn overshadows the house. This town is said to have the largest houses for oxen, cows, and horses hereabouts, and it is not behindhand in its public buildings; but there are very few halls for free worship or free speech in this county.

For more than five years I maintained myself thus solely by the labor of my hands, and I found that by working about six weeks in a year, I could meet all the expenses of living. The whole of my winters, as well as most of my summers, I had free and clear for study. I have thoroughly tried schoolkeeping, and found that my expenses were in proportion, or rather out of proportion, to my income, for I was obliged to dress and train, not to say think and believe, accordingly, and I lost my time into the bargain. As I did not teach for the good of my fellow men, but simply for a livelihood, this was a failure. I have tried trade; but I found that *it* would take ten years to get under way in that, and that then I should probably be on my way to the devil. I was actually afraid that I might by that time be doing what is called a good business. When formerly I was looking about to see what I could do for a living, some sad experience in conforming to the wishes of friends being fresh in my mind to tax my ingenuity, I thought often and seriously of picking huckleberries; that surely I could do, and its small profits might suffice — for my greatest skill has been to want but little — so little capital it required, so little distraction from my wonted moods, I foolishly thought. While my acquaintances went unhesitatingly into trade or the professions, I contemplated this occupation as most like theirs: ranging the hills all day to pick the berries which came in my way, and thereafter carelessly dispose of them; so, to keep the flocks of Admetus. I also dreamed that I might gather the wild herbs, or carry evergreens to such villagers as loved to be reminded of the woods, even to the city, by haycart loads. But I have since learned that trade curses everything it handles; and though you trade in messages from heaven, the whole curse of trade attaches to the business.

As I preferred some things to others, and especially valued my freedom, as I could fare hard and yet succeed well, I did not wish to spend my time in earning rich carpets or other fine furniture, or delicate cookery, or a house in the Grecian or the Gothic style just yet. If there are any to whom it is no interruption to acquire these things and who know how to use them when acquired, I relinquish to them the pursuit. Some are "industrious," and appear to love labor for its own sake, or perhaps because it keeps them out of worse mischief; to such I have at present nothing to say. Those who would not know what to do with more leisure than they now enjoy, I might advise to work twice as hard as they do — work till they pay for themselves, and get their free papers. For myself I found that the occupation of a day laborer was the most independent of any, especially as it required only thirty or forty days in a year to support one. The laborer's day ends with the going down of the sun, and he is then free to devote himself to his chosen pursuit, independent of his labor; but his employer, who speculates from month to month, has no respite from one end of the year to the other.

In short, I am convinced both by faith and experience that to maintain one's self on this earth is not a hardship but a pastime, if we will live simply and wisely; as the pursuits of the simpler nations are still the sports of the more artificial. It is not necessary that a man should earn his living by the sweat of his brow unless he sweats easier than I do.

HENRY DAVID THOREAU, Walden

95. A Shaker Village at Lebanon, Ohio

The Shakers were an American sect which first sprang up in New York State during the Revolution, and soon spread to other parts of the country. Their principal founder was an Englishwoman, Mother Ann Lee, who migrated to America in 1774. While the Shakers did not forbid marriage, they believed it less perfect than a state of celibacy. In general they were pacifists who refused to fight; they declined to take oaths; and they held all their property in common. A number of Shaker communities were established all the way from Maine to Kentucky, and attracted wide attention because of the thrift, the religious fervor, and the peculiar views of the members.

IN CINCINNATI, Ohio, I met one day with a Shaking Quaker. He wore a broad-brimmed hat and shad-bellied coat of a bluish-gray homespun cloth, with his hair cropped short before and falling into the neck behind. He was mild in manner, simple in conversation, and his communications were "yea" and "nay." He conversed freely on the doctrines and polity of the society, and gave me a friendly invitation to visit the Shaker village of Lebanon, twenty miles distant.

The wisdom of the ruling elders could scarcely have selected a finer spot for the domain of a community. The land in the Miami valley is of a wonderful fertility, and the whole region is a rich and well-cultivated country; still the domain of the Shakers was marked by striking peculiarities. The fences were higher and stronger than those on the adjacent farms; the woods were cleared of underbrush; the tillage was of extraordinary neatness; the horses, cattle, and sheep were of the best breeds, and in the best condition.

In the Shaker village are no taverns or shops, but large, plainly-built dwelling houses, barns, workshops, and an edifice for meetings and religious exercises. Simple utility is the only rule of architecture. There is not, in the whole village, one line of ornament. The brown paint is used only to protect the woodwork of the buildings. I did not see so much as an ornamental shrub or flower in the whole domain.

One house is set apart for the entertainment of strangers, who receive attention, food, and lodging as long as they choose to remain. The brethren and sisters who are appointed to fulfill the duties of hospitality neither demand nor refuse payment.

The women, old and young, ugly and pretty, dress in the same neat but unfashionable attire. There are no bright colors, no ruffles or flounces or frills, no embroidery or laces, no ribbons or ornaments of any kind. The hair is combed smoothly back under a plain cap; a three-cornered kerchief of sober brown covers the bosom, and the narrow gored shirt has no room for crinoline.

The rooms and furniture are as plain and homely as the external architecture. There is not a molding nor any colored paper; not a picture nor print adorns the walls, nor is there a vase or statue. The only books are a few of their own religious treatises, collections of hymns, and works of education, science, and utility.

But there is everywhere the perfection of order and neatness. The floors shine like mirrors. Every visible thing is bright and clean. There is a place for everything, and everything is in its place. This order and neatness is carried out in the workshops, the farmyards, everywhere.

A community of two or three hundred industrious persons, all engaged in agriculture and useful manufactures, paying no rents, having no costly vices, producing for themselves all the necessaries of life, and selling their surplus produce, cannot fail to grow rich. I found this community living in comfort and abundance, surrounded with a great wealth of houses and lands, flocks and herds and, as I was told, with large sums invested in the best securities. Men, women, and children all work. There are no idlers, and no time is lost. As the honesty of the Shakers is proverbial, they have the command of the best markets for their wooden wares, agricultural implements, brooms, garden seeds, preserved fruits and vegetables, and the surplus of their cloth, leather, etc. There is nothing, therefore, to hinder them from accumulating property to an immense extent, as can easily be done by an honest community in any country.

As there are no marriages, all the men and women living together like brothers and sisters, their only increase is by the accession of new members from "the world," or by taking orphan and destitute children, sometimes children from the workhouse. People with whom the world has dealt hardly, widows, or wives deserted by drunken husbands, with families of children, go to the Shakers. They are never turned away. So long as they choose to remain and comply with the rules of the society, they have the full enjoyment of all its material and spiritual goods. So the Shakers slowly increase, and new domains are purchased and brought under cultivation.

THOMAS LOW NICHOLS, Forty Years of American Life, 1821–1861

96. How Ralph Waldo Emerson Lectured

Greatest of all the lyceum lecturers was Emerson. The Godfather of half the reforms of his generation, it was through his lectures as well as his writings that he carried the gospel of transcendentalism to the people. Lowell has described the power of his earnest manner, felicitous language, and musical voice. "He somehow managed to combine the charm and unpremeditated discourse with the visible existence of carefully written manuscript lying before him on the desk; and while reciting an oration strictly committed to memory, he had an air of fetching inspiration from the clouds."

MANY years ago the Easy Chair used to hear Ralph Waldo Emerson lecture. Perhaps it was in the small Sunday-school room under a country meetinghouse, on sparkling winter nights, when all the neighborhood came stamping and chattering to the door in hood and muffler, or ringing in from a few miles away, buried under bufflalo skins. The little, low room was dimly lighted with oil lamps, and the boys clumped about the stove in their cowhide boots, and laughed and buzzed and ate apples and peanuts and giggled, and grew suddenly solemn when the grave men and women looked at them. At the desk stood the lecturer and read his manuscript, and all but the boys sat silent and enthralled by the musical spell.

Some of the hearers remembered the speaker as a boy, as a young man. Some wondered what he was talking about. Some thought him very queer. All laughed at the delightful humor or the illustrative anecdote that sparkled for a moment upon the surface of his talk; and some sat inspired with unknown resolves, soaring upon lofty hopes as they heard. A nobler life, a better manhood, a purer purpose, wooed every listening soul. It was not argument, nor description, nor appeal. It was wit and wisdom, and hard sense and poetry, and scholarship and music. And when the words were spoken and the lecturer sat down, the Easy Chair sat still and heard the rich cadences lingering in the air, as the young priest's heart throbs with the long vibrations when the organist is gone.

The same speaker had been heard a few years previously in the Masonic Temple in Boston. It was the fashion among the gay to call him transcendental. Grave parents were quoted as saying, "I don't go to hear Mr. Emerson; I don't understand him. But my daughters do." . . .

As the lyceum or lecture system grew, the philosopher whom "my daughters" understood was called to speak. A simplicity of manner that could be called rustic if it were not of a shy, scholarly elegance; perfect composure; clear, clean, crisp sentences; maxims as full of glittering truth as a winter night of stars; an incessant spray of fine fancies like the November shower of meteors; and the same intellectual and moral exaltation, expansion, and aspiration, were the characteristics of all his lectures.

He was never exactly popular, but always gave a tone and flavor to the whole lyceum course. . . . "We can have him once in three or four seasons," said the committees. But really they had him all the time without knowing it. He was the philosopher Proteus, and he spoke through all the more popular mouths. The speakers were acceptable because they were liberal, and he was the great liberalizer. They were, and they are, the middlemen between him and the public. They watered the nectar, and made it easy to drink.

The Easy Chair heard from time to time of Proteus on the platform — how he was more and more eccentric — how he could not be understood — how abrupt his manner was. But the Chair did not believe that the flame which had once been so pure could ever be dimmer, especially as he recognized its soft luster on every aspect of life around him.

After many years the opportunity to hear him came again; and although the experiment was dangerous the Chair did not hesitate to try it. The hall was pretty and not too large, and the audience was the best that the country could furnish. Every one came solely to hear the speaker, for it was one lecture in a course of his only. It was pleasant to look around and mark the famous men and the accomplished women gathering quietly in the same city where they used to gather to hear him a quarter of a century before. How much the man who was presently to speak had done for their lives, and their children's and the country!

GEORGE WILLIAM CURTIS, From the Easy Chair

XVII

The South and Slavery

97. A Connecticut Yankee
Invents the Cotton Gin

A Massachusetts farmer-boy by origin, Eli Whitney worked his way through Yale in the class of 1792. Then, going to Savannah with the intention of teaching school, he was disappointed in not finding a position. But he went to stay on the plantation of Mrs. Nathanael Greene, widow of the general; and the result was one of the most important of American inventions.

I WENT from N. York with the family of the late Major General Greene to Georgia. I went immediately with the family to their plantation about twelve miles from Savannah with an expectation of spending four or five days and then proceed into Carolina to take the school. During this time I heard much said of the extreme difficulty of ginning cotton; that is, separating it from its seeds. There were a number of very respectable gentlemen at Mrs. Greene's who all agreed that if a machine could be invented which would clean the cotton with expedition, it would be a great thing both to the country and to the inventor. I involuntarily happened to be thinking on the subject and struck out a plan of a machine in my mind, which I communicated to Miller (who is agent to the executors of General Greene and resides in the family, a man of respectability and property); he was pleased with the plan and said if I would pursue it and try an experiment to see if it would answer, he would be at the whole expense; I should lose nothing but my time, and if I succeeded we would share the profits. Previous to this I found I was like to be disappointed in my school;

that is, instead of a hundred, I found I could get only fifty guineas a year. I, however, held the refusal of the school until I tried some experiments. In about ten days I made a little model for which I was offered, if I would give up all right and title to it, a hundred guineas. I concluded to relinquish my school and turn my attention to perfecting the machine. I made one, before I came away, which required the labor of one man to turn it and with which one man will clean ten times as much cotton as he can in any other way before known and also cleanse it much better than in the usual mode. This machine may be turned by water or with a horse, with the greatest ease, and one man and a horse will do more than fifty men with the old machines. It makes the labor fifty times less, without throwing any class of people out of the business.

I returned to the northward for the purpose of having a machine made on a large scale and obtaining a patent for the invention. I went to Philadelphia soon after I arrived, made myself acquainted with the steps necessary to obtain a patent, took several of the steps, and the Secretary of State, Mr. Jefferson, agreed to send the patent to me as soon as it could be made out — so that I apprehended no difficulty in obtaining the patent. . . . I have employed several workmen in making machines . . . I am certain I can obtain a patent in England. As soon as I have got a patent in America I shall go with the machine which I am now making to Georgia, where I shall stay a few weeks to see it at work. From thence I expect to go to England, where I shall probably continue two or three years. How advantageous this business will eventually prove to me, I cannot say. It is generally said by those who know anything about it that I shall make a fortune by it. I have no expectation that I shall make an independent fortune by it but think I had better pursue it than any other business into which I can enter. Something which cannot be foreseen may frustrate my expectations and defeat my plan, but I am now so sure of success that ten thousand dollars, if I saw the money counted out to me, would not tempt me to give up my right and relinquish the object. I wish you, sir, not to show this letter nor communicate anything of its contents to anybody except my brother and sister, enjoining it on them to keep the whole a *profound secret.*

Correspondence of Eli Whitney, Sept. 11, 1793

98. Luxury among the Planters of Louisiana

To an observant traveler like Timothy Flint the Mississippi Valley offered striking contrasts. In the upper valley were the poor but democratic frontiersmen whom he has elsewhere described. In Louisiana, however, and especially at New Orleans, he found an opulence, extravagance and sophistication which was unique in the United States of the eighteen-twenties.

THE OPULENT planters of this state have many amiable traits of character. They are high-minded and hospitable in an eminent degree. I have sojourned much among them and have never experienced a more frank, dignified, and easy hospitality. It is taken for granted that the guest is a gentleman and that he will not make an improper use of the great latitude that is allowed him. If he do not pass over the limits which just observance prescribes, the more liberties he takes and the more ease he feels within those limits, the more satisfaction he will give to his host. You enter without ceremony, call for what you wish, and intimate your wishes to the servants. In short, you are made to feel yourself at home. This simple and noble hospitality seems to be a general trait among these planters, for I have not yet called at a single house where it has not been exercised toward me. Suppose the traveler to be a gentleman, to speak French, and to have letters to one respectable planter, it becomes an introduction to the settlement, and he will have no occasion for a tavern.

It results in some way from their condition, from their ample income, or perhaps, as they would say, from the influence of slavery, that they are liberal in their feelings, as it respects expenditure, and are more reckless of the value of money than any people that I have seen. The ladies no doubt have their tea-table or rather their coffee-table scandal. But I confess that I have seen less of that prying curiosity to look into the affairs of neighbors and have heard less scandal here than in other parts of the United States.

The luxury of the table is carried to a great extent among them. They are ample in their supply of wines, though claret is generally drunk. Every family is provided with claret, as we at the North are with cider. I have scarcely seen an instance of intoxication among the respectable planters. In drinking, the guests universally raise their glasses and touch them together instead of a health. In the morning, before you rise, a cup of strong coffee is offered you. After the dessert at dinner you are offered another. It is but very recently that the ladies have begun to drink tea. During the warm months, before you retire, it is the custom in many places for a black girl to take off your stockings and perform the ancient ceremonial of washing the feet.

They are easy and amiable in their intercourse with one another and excessively attached to balls and parties. They certainly live more in sensation than in reflection. The past and the future are seasons with which they seem little concerned. The present is their day, and "a short life and a merry one" their motto. Their feelings are easily excited. Tears flow. The excitement passes away, and another train of sensations is started. In the pulpit they expect an ardor, an appeal to the feelings, which the calmer and more reflecting manner of the North would hardly tolerate.

An intelligent and instructed planter's family is certainly a delightful family in which to make a short sojourn, and they have many of the lesser virtues, exercised in a way so peculiar and appropriate to their modes of existence as to impress you with all the freshness of novelty. Unhappily, as appertains to all earthly things, there is a dark ground to the picture. The men are "sudden and quick in quarrel." The dirk or the pistol is always at hand. Fatal duels frequently occur. They are profane and excessively addicted to gambling. This horrible vice, so intimately associated with so many others, prevails like an epidemic. Money got easily and without labor is easily lost. Betting and horse racing are amusements eagerly pursued, and oftentimes to the ruin of the parties. A Louisianian will forego any pleasure to witness and bet at a horse race. Even the ladies visit these amusements and bet with the gentlemen.

It is true that there are opulent French planters, reared in the simplicity of the early periods of Louisiana, who can neither read nor write. I have visited more than one such. But it is also true that the improving spirit of the age, the rapid communication by steamboats, which brings all the luxuries, comforts, and instructions of society immediately to their doors, is diffusing among the planters a thirst for information, an earnest desire that their children should have all the advantages of the improved modes of present instruction. They have, in many instances, fine collections of books. A piano is seen in every good house. Their ear, taste, and voice and their excitability of character fit the ladies for excellence in music. In common with those in other parts of the Union, great and too much stress is laid upon accomplishments merely external, and there is not attached sufficient importance to that part of education which fits for rational conversation and usefulness. It is asserted here, even to a proverb, and so far as my observation extends, with great truth, that the Creole ladies are, after marriage, extremely domestic, quiet, affectionate, and exemplary wives and mothers.

TIMOTHY FLINT, Recollections of the Last Ten Years, 1826

99. The Reverend Mr. Walsh Inspects a Slave Ship

England forbade her subjects to engage in the slave trade by a law of 1807, and in the United States a similar prohibition became effective in 1808. Nevertheless, citizens of other lands (as well as some lawless Americans and Britons) continued the detestable traffic. Cuba and Brazil especially received large numbers of slaves. Both British and American warships were vigilant in trying to intercept slave ships. By an agreement in 1842, the two nations provided for the joint support of squadrons to patrol the west coast of Africa. A clergyman here describes a typical capture.

ON FRIDAY, May 22, [1829] we were talking of this pirate at breakfast and the probability of meeting her in this place, when in the midst of our conversation a midshipman entered the cabin and said in a hurried manner that a sail was visible to the northwest on the larboard quarter. We immediately all rushed on deck, glasses were called for and set, and we distinctly saw a large ship of three masts, apparently crossing our course. It was the general opinion that she was either a large slaver or a pirate, or probably both, and Captain Arabin was strongly inclined to believe it was his friend the Spaniard from the coast of Africa, for whom we had been looking out.

All night we were pointing our glasses in the direction in which she lay, and caught occasional glimpses of her, and when morning dawned, we saw her like a speck on the horizon, standing due north. We followed in the same track; the breeze soon increased our way to eight knots, and we had the pleasure to find we were every moment gaining on her. We again sent a long shot after her, but she only crowded the more sail to escape.

We could now discern her whole equipment; her gun streak was distinctly seen along the water, with eight ports of a side; and it was the general opinion that she was a French pirate and slaver, notorious for her depredations. At twelve o'clock we were entirely within gunshot, and one of our long bow guns was again fired at her. It struck the water alongside, and then, for the first time, she showed a disposition to stop. While we were preparing a second she hove to, and in a short time we were alongside her, after a most interesting chase of thirty hours, during which we ran three hundred miles.

The first object that struck us was an enormous gun, turning on a swivel, on deck — the constant appendage of a pirate; and the next were large kettles for cooking, on the bows — the usual apparatus of a slaver. Our boat was now hoisted out, and I went on board with the officers. When we mounted her decks we found her full of slaves. She was called the *Veloz*, commanded by Captain José Barbosa, bound to Bahia. She was a very broad-decked ship, with a mainmast, schooner rigged, and behind her foremast was that large, formidable gun, which turned on a broad circle of iron, on deck, and which enabled her to act as a pirate if her slaving speculation failed. She had taken in, on the coast of Africa, 336 males and 226 females, making in all 562, and had been out seventeen days, during which she had thrown overboard 55. The slaves were all inclosed under grated hatchways between decks. The space was so low that they sat between each other's legs and [were] stowed so close together that there was no possibility of their lying down or at all changing their position by night or day. As they belonged to and were shipped on account of different individuals, they were all branded like sheep with the owner's marks of different forms. These were impressed under their breasts or on their arms, and, as the mate informed me with perfect indifference "burnt with the red-hot iron." Over the hatchway stood a ferocious-looking fellow with a scourge of many twisted thongs in his hand, who was the slave driver of the ship, and whenever he heard the slightest noise below, he shook it over them and seemed eager to exercise it. I was quite pleased to take this hateful badge out of his hand, and I have kept it ever since as a horrid memorial of reality, should I ever be disposed to forget the scene I witnessed.

As soon as the poor creatures saw us looking down at them, their dark and melancholy visages brightened up. They perceived something of sympathy and kindness in our looks which they had not been accustomed to, and, feeling instinctively that we were friends, they immediately began to shout and clap their hands. One or two had picked up a few Portuguese words, and cried out, "*Viva! Viva!*" The women were particularly excited. They all held up their arms, and when we bent down and shook hands with them, they could not contain their delight; they endeavored to scramble up on their knees, stretching up to kiss our hands, and we understood that they knew we were come to liberate them. Some, however, hung down their heads in apparently hopeless dejection; some were greatly emaciated, and some, particularly children, seemed dying.

But the circumstance which struck us most forcibly was how it was possible for such a number of human beings to exist, packed up and wedged together as tight as they could cram, in low cells three feet high, the greater part of which, except that immediately under the grated hatchways, was shut out from light or air, and this when the thermometer, exposed to the open sky, was standing in the shade, on our deck, at 89°. The space between decks was divided into two compartments 3 feet 3 inches high; the size of one was 16 feet by 18 and of the other 40 by 21; into the first were crammed the women and girls, into the second the men and boys: 226 fellow creatures were thus thrust into one space 288 feet square and 336 into another space 800 feet square, giving to the whole an average of 23 inches and to each of the women not more than 13 inches. We also found manacles and fetters of different kinds, but it appears that they had all been taken off before we boarded.

The heat of these horrid places was so great and the odor so offensive that it was quite impossible to enter them, even had there been room. They were measured as above when the slaves had left them. The officers insisted that the poor suffering creatures should be admitted on deck to get air and water. This was opposed by the mate of the slaver, who, from a feeling that they deserved it, declared they would murder them all. The officers, however, persisted, and the poor beings were all turned up together. It is impossible to conceive the effect of this eruption — 517 fellow creatures of all ages and sexes, some children, some adults, some old men and women, all in a state of total nudity, scrambling out together to taste the luxury of a little fresh air and water. They came swarming up like bees from the aperture of a hive till the whole deck was crowded to suffocation from stem to stern, so that it was impossible to imagine where they could all have come from or how they could have been stowed away. On looking into the places where they had been crammed, there were found some children next the sides of the ship, in the places most remote from light and air; they were lying nearly in a torpid state after the rest had turned out. The little creatures seemed indifferent as to life or death, and when they were carried on deck, many of them could not stand.

After enjoying for a short time the unusual luxury of air, some water was brought; it was then that the extent of their sufferings was exposed in a fearful manner. They all rushed like maniacs towards it. No entreaties or threats or blows could restrain them; they shrieked and struggled and fought with one another for a drop of this precious liquid, as if they grew rabid at the sight of it.

It was not surprising that they should have endured much sickness and loss of life in their short passage. They had sailed from the coast of Africa on the 7th of May and had been out but seventeen days, and they had thrown overboard no less than fifty-five, who had died of dysentery and other complaints in that space of time, though they had left the coast in good health. Indeed, many of the survivors were seen lying about the decks in the last stage of emaciation and in a state of filth and misery not to be looked at. Even-handed justice had visited the effects of this unholy traffic on the crew who were engaged in it. Eight or nine had died, and at that moment six were in hammocks on board, in different stages of fever. This mortality did not arise from want of medicine. There was a large stock ostentatiously displayed in the cabin, with a manuscript book containing directions as to the quantities; but the only medical man on board to prescribe it was a black, who was as ignorant as his patients.

While expressing my horror at what I saw and exclaiming against the state of this vessel for conveying human beings, I was informed by my friends, who had passed so long a time on the coast of Africa and visited so many ships, that this was one of the best they had seen. The height sometimes between decks was only eighteen inches, so that the unfortunate beings could not turn round or even on their sides, the elevation being less than the breadth of their shoulders; and here they are usually chained to the decks by the neck and legs. In such a place the sense of misery and suffocation is so great that the Negroes, like the English in the Black Hole at Calcutta, are driven to a frenzy. They had on one occasion taken a slave vessel in the river Bonny; the slaves were stowed in the narrow space between decks and chained together. They heard a horrible din and tumult among them and could not imagine from what cause it proceeded. They opened the hatches and turned them up on deck. They were manacled together in twos and threes. Their horror may be well conceived when they found a number of them in different stages of suffocation; many of them were foaming at the mouth and in the last agonies — many were dead. A living man was sometimes dragged up, and his companion was a dead body; sometimes of the three attached to the same chain, one was dying and another dead. The tumult they had heard was the frenzy of those suffocating wretches in the last stage of fury and desperation, struggling to extricate themselves. When they were all dragged up, nineteen were irrecoverably dead. Many destroyed one another in the hopes of procuring room to breathe; men strangled those next them, and women drove nails into each other's brains. Many unfortunate creatures on other occasions took the first opportunity of leaping overboard and getting rid, in this way, of an intolerable life.

REVEREND R. WALSH, Notices of Brazil

100. Nellie Thomas Recalls Her Grandfather's Plantation in South Carolina

The happiest aspect of slavery was presented on those great plantations of the lower South where the masters were kindly, conscientious, and personally interested in their human property. Had the South shown more of this "patriarchal" type of slaveholding, and less of slave-driving by overseers, attacks on the institution would have been fewer and weaker. Sometimes the master and mistress worked far harder than their servants.

NATHANIEL and Lydia came to South Carolina in 1750. They took up a tract of forest land in Marlboro County, on a stream called Three Creeks. My grandfather's inheritance was part of this land, and he added many acres to the original tract. When he married Deborah Bethea, he had a well-stocked farm, a large body of densely timbered pine land, and a few slaves. As his means justified it, Grandfather bought more land, and occasionally he bought a new slave. The purchase of a Negro was usually to secure a wife desired by one of his men or to get a specially skilled blacksmith or carpenter. It was always to add to the industrial efficiency of the plantation rather than to acquire a large number of slaves.

Grandfather held his slaves as part of his official family. He owned them in families and encouraged the making of family ties among them. By these natural methods of economic conservation there were before very long many Negroes in the "quarters." As Grandfather was his own overseer, he gave his personal attention and supervision to every detail of his business and looked closely after the comfort, health, and moral well-being of his slaves.

Grandfather's discipline with his slaves was mild, but exceedingly firm. There was no rebellion or even an undercurrent of dissatisfaction against his rule. They all obeyed him implicitly. I think the secret of his success and his hold on his employees was the absolute system and order that marked the program of plantation work. No cog ever slipped. The tasks were so dovetailed into each other that there was perfect adjustment and harmony. Amid such conditions — conditions that were their right — the slaves were happy and cheerful and worked willingly and enthusiastically.

Bales and bales of woolen goods and unbleached cotton cloth were bought for clothing the slaves. Grandfather bought all his staple groceries by the wholesale — barrels of sugar and flour, sacks of coffee, chests of tea, kits of salt mackerel, and shoes by the gross. These purchases were made once a year through his factors in Charleston, who bought his cotton. The goods were shipped up the Pee Dee River to Hunt's Bluff, the nearest landing. For days, wagons were hauling the goods to the Three Creeks Plantation.

The commissary where supplies were kept resembled a country store. Every Wednesday at sundown the heads of all the Negro families gathered at this store to get their weekly allowance of provisions. Each allotment had been weighed and measured in advance and was ready to be delivered. It was an interesting sight. Each Negro received his portion, hoisted it to his shoulder, and went off, singing, to his cabin.

Making the clothing for such a large number of Negroes was a never-ending task. Grandmother and a sewing woman cut out the garments from the bales of cloth, and they were made up in the sewing room by women trained for this work under a supervising sewing woman. As a rule the women who sewed were the less robust workers who were not strong enough to work in the fields. On rainy days or in the bitter cold weather of winter all the Negro women on the place were expected to work in the sewing room.

On Christmas Eve, Grandfather presented a new suit of clothes and a new pair of shoes to each of the Negroes. In addition to these substantial gifts, each one, after giving the master a toast, received a glass of eggnog.

If one of the Negroes became ill, his symptoms were reported to Grandfather, who would consult a thick book entitled *Dr. Gunn's Family Physician* and send medicine accordingly; but if the patient continued ill, a physician was called in and the case put in his hands.

There was little sickness on the plantation, and few deaths. Grandmother often went to the quarters to supervise the health and sanitary conditions of the slaves. Sometimes I went with her, but we were never allowed to walk in the quarters alone.

I knew all the Negroes by name and loved to go down to the gate to see them come in with baskets of cotton on their heads. In my imagination I hear them singing now:

> Dese rows am mighty long,
> An' de cotton, hit's so thick,
> Jim an' his poky ol' song
> Needs hittin' with a stick,
> An' sure as he don' move,
> I gwine fetch him a kick!

NELLIE THOMAS McCOLL, Old Folks at Home

101. Southern Planters Sow "Seed from Madagascar"

South Carolina long surpassed all her sisters in the production of rice, though after the War she was surpassed by Texas and Louisiana. Cultivation of the plant began in South Carolina as early as 1700. The low coastal plain, divided from the sea by a belt of marshes, was ideal for rice-growing. Since white men could not labor in the hot, sultry climate, gangs of Negro slaves had to be used. Like the tobacco and later the cotton plantations, the rice plantations often grew very large, and their owners accumulated wealth.

To RECLAIM an inland swamp for rice, the first work to be done was to throw up a strong earth dam across its lower end. The purpose of this dam was to prevent salt water from overflowing the parts of the swamp to be planted. Then, higher up in the swamp, smaller dams were built. The land between these dams was known as "squares," and each square was given a name by which it could be designated. All of the dams extended entirely across the swamp from the highland on one side to the highland on the other. . . .

When the dams had been built and the trunks [sluice gates] installed, the clearing of the swamp was begun. This was not, in most instances, a great undertaking, for very large trees seldom grew in the lower portions of these swamps, nor was the undergrowth very dense. When the land was cleared, canals and ditches were dug. This also was not difficult work, for the dark alluvial soil yielded readily to the shovel. By means of these ditches the lands to be planted were drained to the greatest possible extent. The smaller of the ditches ran across the swamp and were known as "quarter" ditches, while the larger, running in both directions, were called "face" ditches. These names continued to be used during the life of the industry in South Carolina and Georgia.

Nearly equal in size to the large dam at the lower end of the swamp was another dam, the highest up in the swamp. This dam held the water in the upper unreclaimed portion of the swamp and made it a reservoir, to be used for irrigation. These reservoirs were, however, most uncertain, for the amount of water they contained was dependent upon rainfall, and a long dry season meant the failure of a crop.

It was principally this lack of water at one time and too much water at another that caused, in later years, the inland swamp plantations to be gradually abandoned and the cultivation of rice transferred to the much larger swamps adjacent to fresh-water rivers, in which the rise and fall of the tides could be depended upon for irrigation and drainage.

The reclamation of the fresh-water swamps was a great undertaking, considerably greater than that of the inland swamps which bordered on the salt-water marshes. There were many large white-gum, cedar, and cypress trees, and the dark alluvial soil was so soft that one could scarcely walk any distance upon it. To avoid sinking he would have to step from one root to another or trust his weight to some treacherous tussock. Everywhere his progress was impeded by dense undergrowth and his clothes and flesh torn by briars. Half the time the land was under water, which slowly receded when the tide in the river ebbed, but which soon returned.

The first step in reclaiming the swamp lands was to build a bank along the edge of the river, with both ends joined to strips of highland where they approached the river's edge, and through the bank to place trunks, similar to those used in the inland swamps, for the water to pass through.

When the bank had been built and the trunks installed, the digging of canals and ditches in the swamp followed. Then the trees and undergrowth had to be removed, the greatest undertaking of all. The trees were cut down and burned, but their stumps were never completely removed. Some old cedar stumps, level with the ground, are there today and are very hard to get rid of. A modern stump-puller would be useless, for, instead of pulling the stumps up with their long lateral roots, the puller would sink into the soil.

After their crops had been grown and stacked in the barnyards, the planters still had difficult problems to solve. The first was how to remove the grains of rice from the straw, and the second, which required a longer time to solve, was how to find a satisfactory method of preparing the grain for market. To thresh the rice, the planters had, for many years, to resort to flail sticks. The bundles of rice were placed in rows on the ground, with the heads joining each other. The Negroes walked between the rows, swinging the flail sticks above their heads and bringing them down on the heads of rice, thus beating off the grain.

The use of the flail stick was slow work, especially as it could be carried on only during good weather. When the grain was threshed off, it had to be gathered up and carried to what was known as a "winnowing house," a building about twenty feet off the ground, supported on posts. In the floor of the winnowing house a grating was placed through which the rice was dropped to the ground, so that if any breeze were stirring it would blow away the light and unfilled grains and also any short pieces of straw which were mixed with the rice.

After the rice had passed through these two processes resort was made to the ancient method of pounding rice, that of the wooden mortar and pestle, in order to remove the outer hull, and to do this required an even longer time than did threshing and winnowing. It was thus often far into the winter before the crop could be sent to market. In order to prevent these delays, the planters, very soon after the beginning of the industry, adopted an experiment never before tried in this country — the use of the tides as a source of power. While it could not be pronounced an effective method, it was used for many years.

On practically every abandoned rice plantation in South Carolina can be seen today a square known as the mill-pond square, for it was into these squares that the tides were allowed to flow and ebb during the fall and winter months, when the old pounding mills were in operation. Water was let into these squares through a brick raceway, the sides of which can often still be seen, and as it flowed into the field and out it turned an undershot wooden wheel, causing two large stones to revolve, one upon the other, between which the hulls of the rice were rubbed off. The gate to the raceway was not opened until half tide, either flood or ebb, and hence the mill could be operated for only a limited time — for about five hours during the day and the same length of time at night. A simple mechanical rearrangement of the driving belt reversed the direction of the mechanism with the change of the tide. . . .

The first step in the growing of a rice crop was taken in the late fall or early winter after a killing frost. This was to burn the stubble of the preceding crop. Burning stubble was usually done by women, who dragged the fire with their hoes. When the stubble was thoroughly dry and a stiff breeze blowing, they sometimes had to jump across the quarter ditches to avoid the advancing fire. There was considerable excitement in this work, and the women seemed to enjoy it. Their dresses were tied up to their knees and did not hinder them from jumping the ditches when they were caught in a close place by the fire. "Look out, Sister!" they would often call. "Don't let dat fire ketch 'ona. Jump de ditch."

It was unfortunate for the good of the soil that the only way of getting rid of the rice stubble was to burn it, for it was quite thick, and by fall had grown to a considerable height. . . .

When the stubble was burned the blackbirds descended on the fields in large flocks and picked up the unsprouted grains from the past year's crop. During the fall before, when the fields had been under water, the wild ducks had had their chance to feed on the shattered grains and often had come in flocks larger by far than did the blackbirds. Both ducks and blackbirds were thus helping the planters, for they were ridding his land of grains of "volunteer" rice which, when turned under by the plow, would have reduced the yield of his next crop.

During the years of slavery, the Negroes, walking in the alleys of the previous year's crop, turned the soil with eight-inch hoes, set perfectly straight on the handles. This was known as "back sodding." Later, with hoes set at an angle, they chopped up the land exceedingly fine. In fact, they both plowed and harrowed it with their hoes, and from all I have been told they did most excellent work, often better than was later done with disc harrows.

When mules began to be used, rather crude wooden harrows with iron teeth, made on the plantation, took the place of the hoe, and in later years disc harrows were very generally used.

In my great-grandfather's time, after the fields had been turned with hoes, or, in my time, plowed, the next step was to clean the ditches, small as well as large. This work was done by both men and women, and the implements used were long-handled scoops, in which mud which had accumulated in the ditch was dragged out and scattered along its edge. Every year some of the ditches had to be sunk deeper. Only men could do this, walking in the ditches and throwing out the mud with shovels. In cleaning larger ditches and canals, scoops were used.

With us, rice has always been planted in trenches four inches wide and eleven inches apart and very shallow, only enough soil being displaced to cover the seed. From the beginning of the industry, these trenches also were made with hoes, and it is remarkable how straight the Negroes made them. In them the seed was sown by hand. Women always did this work, for the men used to say that this was "woman's wuck," and I do not recall seeing one of the men attempt it. My first two or three crops were planted by hand, and then drills began to be generally used.

There were two periods during which rice might be planted. The first was from the tenth of March to the tenth of April, and the second from the first to the tenth of June. Never was any planting done between the middle of April and the last of May. The reason for not planting after the tenth of April was the coming of the May birds, which, during the month of May, were on their way northward, after wintering in the far South, and could always be depended upon to appear in our rice fields. They seemed to travel on a regular schedule, and were always on time.

I know of no crop which in beauty can be compared with a crop of rice. In my dreams I still see the crops I used to grow, and when I am awake, I am conscious of the fact that my dreams failed to do them justice. This was especially true during the late spring and summer months, when the crop was passing through its successive stages of growth and looked different to me each day as I rode through it.

Until the middle of July the color of the rice never looked the same. Some days it changed as constantly as the colors change on the surface of the sea. As its blades changed their direction with each shifting breeze, they changed their color also. Over the field a breeze often blew, coming inland from the ocean across the salt marshes and up the lower reaches of the river. Thus the crop was kept in constant motion, swaying in one direction and then in another. The result was that the whole field, as far as one could see, appeared to be alive, shifting with the wind, the sunshine, and the shadows of passing clouds.

As the season advanced, a decided change gradually took place in the color of the field, for its green began to be mingled with gold as the heads of rice appeared and its stalks began to be weighted down with the ripening grain. Yellow then predominated over the green until the whole field looked like a mass of gold, as it awaited the hook of the reaper.

Rice planted in March ripened the latter part of August, and, very shortly after, rice planted in April was ready for the sickle.

DUNCAN CLINCH HEYWARD, Seed from Madagascar

102. A Yankee Approves of Slavery

A Maine boy, born in 1809, Joseph Holt Ingraham became a sailor. Later he went south to teach, becoming a member of the faculty of Jefferson College at Washington, Mississippi. He remained a Southerner the rest of his life, dying in Mississippi on the eve of the Civil War. Though he became an Episcopal minister, he is best remembered for his long list of romances. One of them, A Prince of the House of David, is still read. At the age of twenty-six he published a two-volume work on the "South-West" (by which he meant Mississippi and the adjoining areas) which gives a very favorable view of slavery.

PLANTERS, particularly native planters, have a kind of affection for their Negroes, incredible to those who have not observed its effects. If rebellious they punish them — if well behaved, they not infrequently reward them. In health they treat them with uniform kindness, in sickness with attention and sympathy. I once called on a native planter — a young bachelor, like many of his class, who had graduated at Cambridge and traveled in Europe — yet Northern education and foreign habits did not destroy the Mississippian. I found him by the bedside of a dying slave, nursing him with a kindness of voice and manner, and displaying a manly sympathy with his sufferings, honorable to himself and to humanity. On large plantations hospitals are erected for the reception of the sick, and the best medical attendance is provided for them. The physicians of Natchez derive a large proportion of their incomes from attending plantations. On some estates a physician permanently resides, whose time may be supposed sufficiently taken up in attending to the health of from one to two hundred persons. Often several plantations, if the force on each is small, unite and employ one physician for the whole.

Every plantation is supplied with suitable medicines, and generally to such an extent that some room or part of a room in the planter's house is converted into a small apothecary's shop. These, in the absence of the physician in any sudden emergency, are administered by the planter. Hence, the health of the slaves, so far as medical skill is concerned, is well provided for. They are well fed and warmly clothed in the winter, in warm jackets and trousers, and blanket coats enveloping the whole person, with hats or woolen caps and brogans. In summer they have clothing suitable to the season, and a ragged Negro is less frequently to be met with than in Northern cities.

No scene can be livelier or more interesting to a Northerner than that which the Negro quarters of a well-regulated plantation present on a Sabbath morning just before church hour. In every cabin the men are shaving and dressing — the women, arrayed in their gay muslins, are arranging their frizzly hair, in which they take no little pride, or investigating the condition of their children's heads — the old people, neatly clothed, are quietly conversing or smoking about their doors, and those of the younger portion who are not undergoing the affliction of the washtub, are enjoying themselves in the shade of the trees or around some little pond with as much zest as though slavery and freedom were synonymous terms. When all are dressed and the hour arrives for worship, they lock up their cabins, and the whole population of the little village proceeds to the chapel, where divine worship is performed, sometimes by an officiating clergyman and often by the planter himself, if a church member. The whole plantation is also frequently formed into a Sabbath class which is instructed by the planter or some member of his family, and often such is the anxiety of masters that they should perfectly understand what they are taught — a hard matter in the present state of African intellect — that no means calculated to advance their progress are left untried. I was not long since shown a manuscript catechism, drawn up with great care and judgment by a distinguished planter, on a plan admirably adapted to the comprehension of Negroes. The same gentleman, in conjunction with two or three neighboring planters, employs a Presbyterian clergyman to preach to the slaves, paying him a salary for his services. On those plantations which have no chapel and no regular worship on the Sabbath, Negroes are permitted to go to the nearest town to church, a privilege they seldom know how to appreciate, and prefer converting their liberty into an opportunity for marketing or visiting. Experience, however, has convinced planters that no indulgence to their slaves is so detrimental as this, both to the moral condition of the slave and the good order of the plantation, for there is no vice in which many of them will not become adepts, if allowed a temporary freedom from restraint one day in seven. Hence, this liberty, except in particular instances, is denied them on some estates, to which they are confined under easy discipline during the day, passing the time in strolling through the woods, sleeping, eating, and idling about the quarters. The evenings of the Sabbath are passed in little gossiping circles in some of the cabins, or beneath the shade of some tree in front of their dwellings, or at weddings. The Negroes are usually married by the planter, who reads the service from the gallery — the couple with their attendants standing upon the steps or on the green in front. These marriages, in the eye of the slave, are binding. Clergymen are sometimes invited to officiate by those planters who feel that respect for the marriage covenant which leads them to desire its strict observance where human legislation has not provided for it. On nuptial occasions the Negroes partake of fine suppers to which the ladies add many little delicacies and handsome presents of wearing apparel to the married pair. When the Negroes desire a clergyman to perform the ceremony for them, planters seldom refuse to comply with their request.

JOSEPH HOLT INGRAHAM, The South-West by a Yankee, 1835

103. Fanny Kemble Disapproves of Slavery

The gifted Frances Anne Kemble came of a famous English stage family, and her precocious brilliance made her successful in London at the age of twenty. A few years later she went on an American tour, and in 1834, at the age of twenty-five, married a wealthy Southern planter, Pierce Butler. On his Georgia plantation, supposed to be better managed than most, she was horrified by the condition of the slaves. Long afterward, during the Civil War, she published her vigorous and sincere, though perhaps somewhat overdrawn, diary of her impressions. It makes a scathing condemnation of slavery. Her marriage was unsuccessful, and she returned to her remarkable career on the stage.

IN THE afternoon I made my first visit to the hospital of the estate, and found it, as indeed I find everything else here, in a far worse state even than the wretched establishments on the Rice Island dignified by that name; so miserable a place for the purpose to which it was dedicated I could not have imagined on a property belonging to Christian owners. The floor (which was not boarded, but merely the damp hard earth itself) was strewn with wretched women, who, but for their moans of pain and uneasy restless motions, might very well have each been taken for a mere heap of filthy rags. The chimney refusing passage to the smoke from the pine-wood fire, it puffed out in clouds through the room, where it circled and hung, only gradually oozing away through the windows which were so far well adapted to the purpose that there was not a single whole pane of glass in them. My eyes, unaccustomed to the turbid atmosphere, smarted and watered and refused to distinguish at first the different dismal forms from which cries and wails assailed me in every corner of the place. By degrees I was able to endure for a few minutes

what they were condemned to live their hours and days of suffering and sickness through; and, having given what comfort kind
words and promises of help in more substantial forms could
convey, I went on to what seemed a yet more wretched abode of
wretchedness. This was a room where there was no fire because
there was no chimney and where the holes made for windows
had no panes or glasses in them. The shutters being closed, the
place was so dark that, on first entering it, I was afraid to stir
lest I should fall over some of the deplorable creatures extended
upon the floor. As soon as they perceived me, one cry of "Oh,
missis!" rang through the darkness, and it really seemed to me
as if I was never to exhaust the pity and amazement and disgust
which this receptacle of suffering humanity was to excite in me.
The poor, dingy, supplicating sleepers upraised themselves as I
cautiously advanced among them; those who could not rear their
bodies from the earth held up piteous, beseeching hands, and as I
passed from one to the other, I felt more than one imploring
clasp laid upon my dress to solicit my attention to some new form
of misery. One poor woman called Tressa, who was unable to
speak above a whisper from utter weakness and exhaustion, told
me she had had nine children, was suffering from incessant
flooding, and felt "as if her back would split open." There she lay,
a mass of filthy tatters, without so much as a blanket under or
over her, on the bare earth in this chilly darkness.

I promised them help and comfort, beds and blankets, and light
and fire — that is, I promised to ask Mr. —— for all this for them;
and in the very act of doing so I remembered with a sudden pang
of anguish that I was to urge no more petitions for his slaves to
their master. I groped my way out, and emerging on the piazza,
all the choking tears and sobs I had controlled broke forth, and I
leaned there crying over the lot of these unfortunates till I heard
a feeble voice of "Missis, you no cry; missis, what for you cry?"
and looking up, saw that I had not yet done with this intolerable
infliction. A poor crippled old man, lying in the corner of the
piazza, unable even to crawl toward me, had uttered this word of
consolation, and by his side (apparently too idiotic, as he was too
impotent, to move) sat a young woman, the expression of whose
face was the most suffering and at the same time the most horribly repulsive I ever saw. I found she was, as I supposed, half-

witted; and on coming nearer to inquire into her ailments and what I could do for her, found her suffering from that horrible disease — I believe some form of scrofula — to which the Negroes are subject, which attacks and eats away the joints of their hands and fingers — a more hideous and loathsome object I never beheld. Her name was Patty, and she was granddaughter to the old crippled creature by whose side she was squatting.

I wandered home, stumbling with crying as I went, and feeling so utterly miserable that I really hardly saw where I was going.

FRANCES ANNE KEMBLE, Journal of a Residence on a Georgian Plantation in 1838–1839

104. Social Classes among the Slaves

Social gradations among the slaves were as numerous and as nicely drawn as among English servants. The social status of the slave depended in part upon the particular work which he performed, in part upon the social position of his master. These distinctions were of course far more elaborate on the great plantations of the Tidewater and in the Natchez region than in the less aristocratic areas. This description by Ingraham coincides with other Northern observations of the peculiar institution.

THERE are properly three distinct classes of slaves in the South. The first and most intelligent class is composed of the domestic slaves or servants, as they are properly termed, of the planters. Some of these both read and write and possess a great degree of intelligence, and as the Negro, of all the varieties of the human species, is the most imitative, they soon learn the language and readily adopt the manners of the family to which they are attached.

In the more fashionable families Negroes feel it their duty — to show their aristocratic breeding — to ape manners, and to use language, to which the common herd cannot aspire. An aristocratic Negro, full of his master's wealth and importance, which he feels to be reflected upon himself, is the most aristocratic personage in existence. He supports his own dignity and that of his own master, or "family" as he phrases it, which he deems inseparable, by a course of conduct befitting colored gentlemen. Always about the persons of their masters or mistresses, the domestic slaves obtain a better knowledge of the modes of civilized life than they could do in the field, where Negroes can rise but little above their original African state. So identified are they with the families in which they have been "raised," and so accurate, but rough, are the copies which they individually present of their masters, that were all the domestic slaves of several planters' families transferred to Liberia or Haiti, they would there constitute [an] African society whose model would be found in Mississippi. Each family would be a faithful copy of that with which it was once connected, and should their former owners visit them in their new home, they would smile at the resemblance to the original.

The second class is composed of town slaves, which not only includes domestic slaves, in the families of the citizens, but also all Negro mechanics, draymen, hostlers, laborers, hucksters, and washwomen, and the heterogeneous multitude of every other occupation who fill the streets of a busy city — for slaves are trained to every kind of manual labor. The blacksmith, cabinetmaker, carpenter, builder, wheelwright — all have one or more slaves laboring at their trades. The Negro is a third arm to every workingman who can possibly save money enough to purchase one. He is emphatically the "right-hand man" of every man. Even free Negroes cannot do without them; some of them own several, to whom they are the severest masters.

"To whom do you belong?" I once inquired of a Negro whom I had employed. "There's my master," he replied, pointing to a steady old Negro, who had purchased himself, then his wife, and subsequently his three children by his own manual exertions and persevering industry. He was now the owner of a comfortable house, a piece of land, and two or three slaves, to whom he could add one every three years. It is worthy of remark and serves to illustrate one of the many singularities characteristic of the race that the free Negro, who "buys his wife's freedom," as they term it, from her master, by paying him her full value, ever afterward considers her in the light of property.

Many of the Negroes who swarm in the cities are what are called "hired servants." They belong to planters or others who, finding them qualified for some occupation in which they cannot afford to employ them, hire them to citizens, as mechanics, cooks, waiters, nurses, etc., and receive the monthly wages for their services. Some steady slaves are permitted to "hire their own time"; that is, to go into town and earn what they can as porters, laborers, gardeners, or in other ways and pay a stipulated sum weekly to their owners, which will be regulated according to the supposed value of the slave's labor. Masters, however, who are sufficiently indulgent to allow them to "hire their time" are seldom rigorous in rating their labor very high. But whether the slave earn less or more than the specified sum, he must always pay that and neither more nor less than that to his master at the close of each week as the condition of this privilege. Few fail in making up the sum, and generally they earn more, if industrious, which is expended in little luxuries or laid by in an old rag among the rafters of their houses till a sufficient sum is thus accumulated to purchase their freedom. This they are seldom refused, and if a small amount is wanting to reach their value, the master makes it up out of his own purse, or rather, takes no notice of the deficiency. I have never known a planter refuse to aid, by peculiar indulgences, any of his steady and well-disposed slaves who desired to purchase their freedom. On the contrary, they often endeavor to excite emulation in them to the attainment of this end. This custom of allowing slaves to "hire their time," insuring the master a certain sum weekly and the slave a small surplus, is mutually advantageous to both.

The third and lowest class consists of those slaves who are termed field hands. They are, and by necessity always will be, an inferior class to the two former.

It is now popular to treat slaves with kindness, and those planters who are known to be inhumanly rigorous to their slaves are scarcely countenanced by the more intelligent and humane portion of the community. Such instances, however, are very rare, but there are unprincipled men everywhere who will give vent to their ill feelings and bad passions, not with less good will upon the back of an indented apprentice than upon that of a purchased slave. Private chapels are now introduced upon most of the plantations of the more wealthy which are far from any church; Sabbath schools are instituted for the black children and Bible classes for the parents, which are superintended by the planter, a chaplain, or some of the female members of the family. But with all these aids they are still, as I have remarked, the most degraded class of slaves; and they are not only regarded as such by the whites but by the two other classes, who look upon them as infinitely beneath themselves. It is a difficult matter to impress upon their minds moral or religious truths. They generally get hold of some undefined ideas, but they can go no further. Their minds seem to want the capacity to receive intellectual impressions, nor are they capable of reasoning from the simplest principles or of associating ideas. A native planter, who has had the management of between two and three hundred slaves since he commenced planting, recently informed me that if he conveyed an order to any of his field hands which contained two ideas, he was sure it would not be followed correctly.

JOSEPH HOLT INGRAHAM, The South-West by a Yankee. 1835

105. Field Hands on the Combahee

The Heyward family was in colonial days one of the wealthiest in South Carolina, and gave the United States a signer of the Declaration of Independence — Thomas Heyward (1746–1809). Here we have a description of how the slaves were treated on the great Heyward plantation.

EARLY in the morning, except when the weather would not permit, the driver, standing in his door at the head of the street, would awaken the field hands by blowing a horn, though on some plantations a bell was rung. They were awakened early enough to give them time to cook their breakfasts and to put up something for the midday meal. Then they all gathered at some central spot and started for the fields, the driver leading the way. As they went along in a gang there was usually much talking and a good deal of jesting. Some were very voluble, but in reality said nothing, scarcely understanding themselves, while others were quite full of humor and said many witty things. The men rarely joked the women, but the women had much to say to the men, seeming to make fun of their looks, while a few were sullen and morose and had little to say. These had no "Mornin'" for anybody.

In the spring and summer the men and sometimes the women went to the field without shoes, the latter usually wearing cotton leggings fitting closely and coming nearly to their knees. Their dresses came just below their knees and were tied just below the waist with a cord, thus forming a roll. When the dews were heavy, the men rolled up their pants to keep them dry, and some would wear their caps while others left them at home. The women, with few exceptions, wore colored handkerchiefs on their heads.

When the squares where they were to work were reached the line would close up, and all the Negroes would gather in a crowd. Many of them promptly sat down on check-banks, all waiting for their names to be called and to be "set" their tasks, the field having been laid off in half-acre tasks. "Fall en yeh, Lizabet." "You, Scipio, tek dat tas' hed of Tom." "Gal, ona fall en behine Isrul." "Chillun, ona tek de tas' longside ob yo ma, and mine don't fool wid me today." Such orders as these have been heard thousands of times on rice plantations, just as the sun, coming through a bank of clouds in the east, began to dispel the heavy white fog which often lies close to the ground.

The field hands were classed as half hands or full hands, and the work of each, in both character and amount, was what long experience had shown could be done and done thoroughly, for in slavery days great stress was laid on the quality of the work.

It was always the custom during the spring and summer months to allow the field hands to finish their work early enough to give them at least two hours by the sun in order that they might work for themselves, or if they did not care to work, they were allowed to do as they pleased. During the winter months opportunity was given them to gather firewood and to grind corn. To all full field hands who would make use of it, high land was allotted, and they were encouraged to plant crops for themselves; and this many of them did. In fact, on rice plantations probably more Negroes planted their own crops on a small scale when they were slaves than they did after they became free. Negroes who did plant for themselves after freedom usually wanted to plant more land than they could cultivate, thinking that by so doing they would be more independent and could work or not, as they chose. The result was that many of them were continually in debt and at the end of the year had nothing.

Each year during November or December woolen cloth was distributed to the Negroes, and in May or June cloth of a lighter material. This cloth was of Australian wool and was of excellent quality. The color of most of the cloth was gray, though some was blue. All of it was imported from England. Every field hand was given five and a half yards of gray cloth and a smaller quantity for each of his or her children. For a baby a mother received one and a half yards. The drivers, carpenters, and other head men, to distinguish them from the rest, were allotted six and a half yards of blue cloth and one of white. They were also given overcoats and felt hats. The men among the field hands received caps and the women plaid handkerchiefs known as bandannas, which they tied around their heads and wore constantly. Woolen blankets were given to the slaves when needed.

In the fall each Negro was provided with a pair of shoes of substantial quality. There was no haphazard distribution of these shoes; each pair was ordered to fit a certain individual. To accomplish this a small cedar stick, neatly made by a plantation carpenter, was given to every slave. After measuring the length of his or her feet the slave would cut the stick accordingly and notch it to indicate the width of the feet. These sticks were sent to the factor in Charleston along with the order for the shoes.

The slaves set great store by their shoes and usually took the best care of them. I have heard that once on a very cold morning, when the ground was frozen, a Negro was seen walking along the road barefooted and carrying a new pair of shoes in his hand. Asked why he did not wear his shoes, he replied, "Well, oonuh see dese duh me shoesh; me feet dem blonxs tuh Maussuh."

Regularly one day each week the slaves were rationed. They were given corn, sweet potatoes, rice, and syrup. Each adult received four quarts of corn and one-half of this amount for each of his children. When sweet potatoes were given plentifully, the amount of corn was slightly reduced. Until the time of Charles Heyward, they were not given meat; this they were expected to provide for themselves. In order to do so they were allowed to raise their own hogs and were given the privilege of hunting and fishing. Fish were very plentiful in the Combahee, and often a narrow-mouthed black bass could be caught which would furnish as much food as the average Negro family would require in one day. In addition to this, most of the slaves raised poultry and often sold eggs.

One would naturally suppose that since the slaves received no wages they did not have any money, but this was not the case. They always managed in one way or another to have something to sell and to do some trading. Adjacent to every two or three plantations there was a crossroads store, with which the owners of the plantations had nothing to do, but where the Negroes could trade. At these stores they purchased their tobacco and such small articles as they might need or fancy. Although it was the rule that they could not leave the plantation without permission, this was rarely refused, especially to go to the store, and often one Negro would do the buying for several. It was at these little nearby stores, during the days of slavery, that rice-field Negroes formed the habit of buying groceries in very small quantities, and from this habit they never recovered. For many years after the Civil War, though they had enough money in their pockets to buy at one time a week's supply of provisions, they much preferred to buy what they wished each night, by the nickel's or dime's worth. "Gimme tree cent wut tobacco; lemme hab five cent sugar, want ten cent wut butt meat," was the way they generally dealt in the stores, and this they do to a large extent even today. In making their purchases they were quite good at addition, keeping the amount of a number of small items in their heads. They could seldom understand the principle of debit and credit.

On every plantation before the Civil War there was a gristmill for general use, but most of the grinding of corn was done by small grinding mills, which were portable and which the Negroes moved from house to house, one mill being allowed to every five families. These grinding mills consisted of a flat round stone, which was placed on a stand about three feet from the floor. Another stone was laid on top of it and was worked on a pivot by a crank which hung from the ceiling. The crank was a long wooden pole, one end of which was fastened to the ceiling directly over the center of the stone and the other end to the edge of the upper stone, the turning being done by hand. From the corn placed between these stones both grits and flour were made, the flour consisting of the eye of the corn, and the grits of the remainder of the grain.

Sunday was always a day of rest, and frequently church services were held on the plantation by white ministers, whose salaries were supplemented and traveling expenses paid by the planters. There were then not as many local preachers among the slaves as sprang up after they were freed, but the preachers they had were allowed to hold prayer meetings at night, though at these meetings there was not as much loud shouting and promiscuous praying as there was after the Civil War, when many of the men on the plantation became either "class leaders" or "locus pastuhs."

During the days of slavery a considerable number of slaves on the rice plantations of South Carolina were members of the Episcopal Church, as most of the ministers who held services for them belonged to that denomination. When the slaves were declared free and were no longer preached to by white clergymen, they very rapidly established their own churches of other denominations, so that today in South Carolina few Negroes are members of the Episcopal Church.

The rule that the slaves should not leave the plantation without permission, I am sure, was often broken, especially at night. When they were back on time for work in the morning, the drivers said nothing. The Negroes were never kept under guard, and it was not difficult for them to obtain permission occasionally to leave the plantation during the day when it did not interfere with their work. When night came, they were expected to be in their own houses, but no doubt this rule was often violated, by the men especially. The enforcement was left largely to the head drivers, though the overseer would try to see that it was carried out. Usually at night the drivers were in their own houses, and a slave who happened to be interested in their whereabouts knew they were there and realized if he could "ketch back fore day clean" the risk was small, for there were so many of them and all were dressed alike. The county patrols had little or nothing to do, for seldom did a Negro on the Combahee try to run away.

DUNCAN CLINCH HEYWARD, Seed from Madagascar

106. Thomas Dabney Runs a Model Plantation

Before the Civil War, Thomas Dabney was one of the richest of all Mississippi planters. He was a devoted Unionist, but when the war came, he gave his fullest support to the Confederate cause. The conflict cost him losses of more than half a million; and then the failure of a friend saddled him with a heavy debt. He courageously went to work to pay it off, laboring with his own hands. It is said that Gladstone, on reading his biography, called him "one of the very noblest of human characters."

HIS PLANTATION was considered a model one and was visited by planters anxious to learn his methods [c. 1840]. He was asked how he made his Negroes do good work. His answer was that a laboring man could do more work and better work in five and a half days than in six. He used to give the half of Saturdays to his Negroes unless there was a great press of work, but a system of rewards was more efficacious than any other method. He distributed prizes of money among his cotton pickers every week during the season, which lasted four or five months. One dollar was the first prize, a Mexican coin valued at eighty-seven and a half cents the second, seventy-five cents the third, and so on, down to the smallest prize, a small Mexican coin called picayune, which was valued at six and a quarter cents.

The decimal nomenclature was not in use there. The coins were spoken of as bits. Eighty-seven and a half cents were seven bits, fifty cents four bits, twenty-five cents two bits. The master gave money to all who worked well for the prizes, whether they won them or not. When one person picked six hundred pounds in a day, a five-dollar gold piece was the reward. On most other plantations four hundred pounds or three hundred and fifty or three hundred was considered a good day's work, but on the Burleigh place many picked five hundred pounds. All had to be picked free of trash. No one could do this who had not been trained in childhood. To get five hundred pounds a picker had to use both hands at once. Those who went into the cotton fields after they were grown only knew how to pull out cotton by holding on to the stalk with one hand and picking it out with the other. Two hundred pounds a day would be a liberal estimate of what the most industrious could do in this manner. A very tall and lithe young woman, one of mammy's "brer Billy's" children, was the best cotton picker at Burleigh. She picked two rows at a time, going down the middle with both arms extended and grasping the cotton bolls with each hand. Some of the younger generation learned to imitate this. At Christmas Nelly's share of the prize money was something over seventeen dollars. Her pride in going up to the master's desk to receive it, in the presence of the assembled Negroes, as the acknowledged leader of the cotton pickers, was a matter of as great interest to the white family as to her own race.

The Negroes were helped in every way to gather the cotton, not being interrupted or broken down by any other work. Some of the men were detailed to carry the cotton hampers to the wagons that the pickers might lift no weights. Water carriers, with buckets of fresh water, went up and down the rows handing water to the pickers. They would get so interested and excited over the work that they had to be made to leave the fields at night, some of the very ambitious ones wishing to sleep at the end of their rows, that they might be up and at work in the morning earlier than their rivals. The cotton was weighed three times a day and the number of pounds picked by each servant set down opposite to his or her name on a slate. In addition to the cotton crop corn was raised in such abundance that it was not an unusual thing to sell a surplus of a thousand or two bushels or more. A maxim with the master was that no animal grew fat on bought corn. In putting in his corn crop he made full allowance for a bad season; hence there was never a scarcity. A lock on a corn crib was not known. After the mules and horses were fed in the evening the Negroes carried home all that they cared to have. They raised chickens by the hundred. One of the chicken raisers, old Uncle Isaac, estimated that he raised five hundred, unless the season was bad. Uncle Isaac's boast was that he was a child of the same year as the master and that the master's mother had given to him in her own arms some of the baby Thomas's milk, as there was more of it than he wanted. He would draw himself up as he added, "I called marster brother till I was a right big boy, an' I called his mother Ma till I was old enough to know better an' to stop it myself. She never tole me to stop."

The Negroes sold all the chickens they did not eat. They were taken to Raymond or Cooper's Well in a four-mule wagon provided by the master. As he paid the market price and as there was some risk of their getting less than he gave, there was not often a desire to send them off if he would take them.

The thrifty Negroes made so much on their chickens, peanuts, popcorn, molasses cakes, baskets, mats, brooms, taking in sewing, and in other little ways that they were able to buy luxuries. Some of the women bought silk dresses; many had their Sunday dresses made by white mantuamakers. Of course they had the clothes of the master and mistress in addition, and in later years, as the house grew full of young masters and young mistresses, theirs were added. As the family knew that the servants liked nothing so well as the well-made clothes that they laid aside, they wore their clothes but little. They justly considered that those who had labored for them had rights to them while still fresh. Under these circumstances it did not seem wasteful for a daughter of the house to distribute, at the end of a season, as many as a dozen or more dresses that had been made up but a few months before. It was quite funny to see among the gallants three or four swallowtail coats of the master's come in at the gate for the grand promenade on Sunday evenings, escorting the colored belles in all their bravery of hoopskirts, and ruffles, and ribbons, and flowers.

On rainy days all the plantation women were brought into the house. Then Mammy Maria, who was in her way a field marshal on such occasions, gave out the work and taught them to sew. By word and action she stimulated and urged them on until there was not on the Burleigh plantation a woman who could not make and mend neatly her own and her husband's and children's clothes.

She was far more severe in her judgment of misdemeanors than the master and mistress. The place that she had made for herself was one that would, in a character less true and strong, have brought on herself the hatred and the distrust of her race. But they knew her to be just, one who never assailed the innocent, and with so warm and compassionate a heart in real trouble that none were afraid to come to her. From being a confidential servant she grew into being a kind of prime minister, and it was well known that if she espoused a cause and took it to the master it was sure to be attended to at once, and according to her advice.

The nurse who took care of the women when their babies were born received a fee each time. The mothers themselves looked on these seasons as gala times. They were provided with flour, sugar, dried fruit, and often meals from the table, and a woman to do all their cooking, washing, and housework for a month. During the rest of the year they did little more than take care of the babies. Their cabins were clean and orderly, their beds gay with bright quilts, and often the pillows were snowy enough to tempt any head.

When we children were allowed to go to see some of the servants, they delighted in setting out a little feast. If they had nothing else, we were not allowed to go without a new-laid egg or two. Once at Christmas Mammy Harriet gave a high tea to us children. I was at that time about fourteen years of age, the oldest of the invited. A friend of my own age, Arabella Foote, the youngest daughter of Henry S. Foote (Governor and United States Senator), was spending her Christmas holidays with me. Mammy felt some modesty about inviting the young lady into her house, but I took Arabella, and she enjoyed it as much as any of us. Mammy had made a nice cake and hot biscuits and tea for the occasion, set out in choicest cups, some of rare old china, and with sugar in the sugar bowl that she had inherited from her mother. She gave us, besides, sweetmeats, nuts, raisins, fruits of several kinds — indeed, a delightful tea. And she stood behind us waiting on the table, her bright bandanna kerchief towering aloft on her head, and she looked so pleased.

Some of the sons taught those of the plantation Negroes who cared to learn, but very few were willing to take the trouble to study. Virginius was successful with his scholars. Five of them learned to read so well that they became preachers. For this service he got one dozen eggs a month, or occasionally in lieu of this he received a pullet at the end of two months. He taught in the kitchen by the light of pine torches. His method of enforcing discipline on these middle-aged men was truly ludicrous. As his tutor, being one of the old-fashioned sort, did not spare the rod in the morning, so at night Virginius belabored the backs of his sturdy fellows. His beatings were received with shouts of laughter, the whole school would be in an uproar, the scholars dodging about to escape the young peda-gogue's stick, and the cook and other onlookers roaring with laughter. One of his graduates asked his advice as to a course of reading, suggesting history as the branch that he wished to pursue. The youthful teacher promptly advised *Robinson Crusoe* and lent his own handsome copy to this promising pupil. After reading one hundred pages, Joe came to him and said, "Marse Virginius, did you say dat book was history?" Virginius explained as well as he could what fiction was, on which Joe said, "I bin mistrustin' all 'long dat some o' de things what Robinson Crusoe say warn't true."

SUSAN DABNEY SMEDES, Memorials of a Southern Planter

XVIII

Abolition and Fugitive Slaves

107. Garrison Is Mobbed by the Boston Conservatives

Though by no means the first Abolitionist in America, William Lloyd Garrison was the most eloquent and the most famous, as well as the best-hated. After a brief experience with editing an Abolitionist sheet in Baltimore, Garrison moved to Boston and there founded the Liberator. *He soon discovered, however, that the respectable citizens of Boston were no less hostile to anti-slavery agitation than were Southerners. Mr. Nichols here describes the memorable effort of the Bostonians to mob Garrison and his English abolitionist-friend, George Thompson.*

IT WAS, I think, in 1834. George Thompson had been sent to America to preach abolition. He had given lectures in and around Boston, and the newspapers of the South were beginning to protest against an agitation which was increased by the addresses of this emissary of a foreign society. The merchants of Boston were aroused to the dangers of such an agitation, which, it was then believed by many, would eventually cause a dissolution of the Union.

Mr. Garrison, who published the *Liberator* in an office in the lower end of Washington Street, did not care much for that. He said, in his mild way, the "Constitution was an agreement with Death and a covenant with Hell" and that all slaveholders were thieves, robbers, murderers, and other disreputable things too numerous to mention. He wished to abolish slavery, and failing that, to turn the Southern states out of the Union.

The merchants of Boston, whose fathers had, like the merchants of Liverpool and Bristol, made fortunes by the slave trade — the merchants who were then making fortunes by Southern trade and the manufacture of cotton — were opposed to the agitation. They were indignant that the English should send emissaries to stir up sectional strife, perhaps civil war, between the states of the Union.

At that day the abolitionists in Boston and in New England were few and far between. Garrison's most earnest supporters were a few women — Mrs. Child, Mrs. Chapman, and others — good, pious souls, who formed a female Anti-Slavery Society and held prayer meetings for the slaves.

The merchants and bankers of Boston, assembled on 'Change in State Street, got into a great excitement one day about Mr. George Thompson and believing him to be at the office of Garrison's *Liberator,* they gathered tumultuously and came around from State Street into Washington Street, determined to put a stop to the eloquence of the English abolitionist.

I do not remember how it happened, but I was in the editorial office of Mr. Garrison when the crowd began to gather in the street below. It was a wonderful spectacle. There were hundreds — then thousands. It was a mob of people dressed in black broadcloth, a mob of gentlemen — capitalists, merchants, bankers, a mob of the Stock Exchange and of the first people in Boston, which considered itself the nicest of cities, and intellectually the "hub of the universe."

I looked down upon this mob from the front window of the second floor, while the street became black with a dense crowd of people shouting "Thompson! Thompson!" and very evidently intending mischief to that gentleman had they found him. Mr. Garrison was writing at his desk. He was very calm about it; he had been in a state of chronic martyrdom for several years and did not seem to mind a slight exacerbation. He came to the window, however, poked his shining bald head out for a moment, and looked down on the howling mob below, and then advised me not to expose myself to observation, lest the crowd might mistake me for the object of their search.

It happened that some of the ladies I have mentioned were holding a meeting in a room of the building that afternoon. They were interrupted and ordered out. They passed through the crowd, which politely made way for them, content with expressing its feelings by a few groans and hisses.

Meantime the authorities began to bestir themselves. The city marshal made a speech, begging his fellow citizens to quietly disperse and not disgrace their great and noble city. They informed him that the man they wished to see was George Thompson. He told them he would ascertain if he was in the building, and went to Mr. Garrison, who assured him that Mr. Thompson was not in town; he had fortunately left in the morning to visit a friend in the country. The officer reported to the mob and was answered by a howl of disappointed rage and then a cry for Garrison! The whole fury of the crowd — of all Boston there concentrated and represented — seemed in one instant to turn upon the editor of the *Liberator*. Had they all been constant readers of his paper, they could not have been more violent.

The marshal interposed in vain. A more powerful municipal officer now made his appearance — the mayor. He was a Boston merchant — a merchant prince. How well I remember his tall, handsome form, his noble features, his silvery voice and graceful elocution. I have always thought him a man of men. True, he did not read the riot act; he did not bring up the police — there were none to bring. The watchmen were at home asleep, and the constables were serving writs on unwilling debtors. There was no time to call out the militia, and I have a suspicion that the flower of that force was on the spot and foremost in the mischief.

The eloquence of the mayor was of no avail. At best he only gained a little time. At every pause in his speech the cry arose louder and fiercer for Garrison. The mob would have searched the building or torn it down had not the mayor given his pledge that if Garrison was in it he should be forthcoming, but he had the moment before sent the marshal to get him out by a back way and if possible secure his escape; and when Garrison had unwillingly consented to escape the threatened martyrdom, the mayor announced that he was not in the building.

There was a great howl of rage; but, a moment after, it became a yell of triumph. Garrison had been seen to go from the building into a narrow lane behind it. Pursued, he took refuge in a carpenter's shop, only to be dragged out and carried into the midst of the mob, where it seemed for a moment that he would be torn in pieces. I saw him, his hat off, his bald head shining, his scanty locks flying, his face pale, his clothes torn and dusty, with a rope around his neck.

"To the Common!" shouted the mob. "To the Common!" The first thought of the whole vast crowd — all maddened as one man is mad — was to drag the poor man to Boston Common — a beautiful park in front of the State House — there to hang him upon the great elm, the "Tree of Liberty," on which Quakers had been hanged in the early Puritan days and under which Tories had been tarred and feathered before the Revolution — to hang him upon the sacred tree, or at least to give him the traditional coat of tar and feathers. So the whole mob moved toward the Common.

But to get there they had to pass by the City Hall, in which was the mayor's office, at the head of State Street. At the moment Garrison was brought opposite that point, the mayor, with a dozen or so of strong fellows to back him, dashed into the crowd, opened it like a wedge, striking right and left, gallantly seized Garrison, and carried him triumphantly into the mayor's office. The mob surged round the building with cries of rage. The mayor came out upon a balcony, looking nobler and handsomer than ever after his exploit, and told his respected fellow citizens, when they demanded Garrison, that he would shed the last drop of his blood before a hair of his head should be injured; not that he cared for him or his cause — they knew well that he sympathized with neither — but for the honor of Boston and the office he held. Then two coaches drove up to the doors of the building. The crowd was divided. A cry was raised to draw the crowd on one side while Garrison was taken out on the other, shoved into the carriage, and the coachman lashed his horses into the crowd. They grasped the wheels to turn the carriage over, but as they seized both sides at once they only lifted it from the ground. They took out knives to cut the traces. The driver knocked them down with the loaded handle of his whip. The spirited horses dashed forward; the mob opened and then ran yelling after the carriage. It was too fast for them. Up Court Street, down Leverett Street. Ponderous gates swung open — the carriage dashed in. The gates closed with a bang, and Garrison was safe in Leverett Street jail, where he could hear the howling of the pack of human wolves that had pursued him.

THOMAS LOW NICHOLS, Forty Years of American Life, 1821–1861

108. Elijah Lovejoy Is Martyred for His Abolitionism

Elijah Lovejoy, who was born in Maine and educated at Princeton for the Presbyterian ministry, early became a fervent Abolitionist. He went west to set up a weekly journal in St. Louis. When that slave-holding city resented his utterances, he moved his paper twenty-five miles up the river to Alton, Illinois. At that time Alton was one of the most flourishing cities in the Mississippi Valley. But here also men took offense at his antislavery opinions, and he was in constant danger of mob violence.

IT BECAME known [November 7, 1837] that the press had arrived and was secure within the walls of Mr. Gilman's warehouse, guarded from within by an armed force of some fifteen citizens. This knowledge was borne on the wings of the wind to every nook and corner of the city [Alton, Illinois]. The excitement raged with a fury surpassing all others that preceded it, and the call to arms by the leaders of the mob was heard in every street. John M. Krum, Esq., the mayor of the city, had been formally and legally notified by Mr. Gilman of the assembling of the mob for the avowed purpose of making an unlawful and incendiary attack upon his property, as well as upon those who were in possession of it for the sole purpose of defending it from destruction; and he demanded of the mayor the faithful exercise of all his official power and prerogatives which the law had provided for the protection of life, liberty, and property. Soon the air was vocal with the blasphemous shouts of the infuriated mob for vengeance upon the building and all within it. A demand from without was shouted by their brazen-faced leader upon Mr. Gilman to surrender the press stored within his warehouse, or he must take the consequences. Again it was repeated, if possible in more defiant and reckless tones; and, no notice being taken of it by any of the inmates, a fire was opened upon the building by the mob. At last shots from the windows of the second story fronting the street were at intervals returned by the besieged into the crowd, and one of the besiegers fell mortally wounded. This acted like oil poured upon the flames of the excitement, and as the wounded man was carried through the infuriated crowd to a place of safety, there arose from the blood-thirsty mob a shout, "Set the roof of the d——d abolition building on fire, and let no one inside escape!" The mayor, who had been continuously present, becoming alarmed from fear the threat would be put in speedy execution, induced the leaders of the mob to call a halt and stay the hand of the incendiary long enough to enable him to make an effort with the besieged to come to some terms of capitulation with the mob that would save any further loss of life and prevent the wanton sacrifice by fire of the warehouse and its valuable contents. The mayor announced to the mob that such efforts would be made by him as a private citizen and not in his official capacity.

Gaining, without any difficulty, admission to the building, a parley ensued, which promptly resulted in its owner and the associate defenders utterly refusing either to surrender the press or abandon their defense of the property or to make concession involving their constitutional rights as American citizens so long as a man among them was left. When the mayor returned and communicated formally to the mob his utter failure in accomplishing anything looking to peace to be purchased by a surrender of the press, the die was cast. A ladder which had been held in reserve by the mob to accomplish their murderous and incendiary designs was at once brought forward and raised from the vacant lot to a position about midway on the exposed side of the building. Their fiendish leader, with a lighted torch in his hand, ascended the ladder to apply it to the roof, encouraged by the cry of his cohort of outlaws, "Burn up the d——d abolitionists!"

When the brave Lovejoy heard from within that demand from the mob for the lives of the defenders of the building, he comprehended in a moment the situation of himself and the small handful of associates, and grasping a loaded gun from the hands of one of them, determined to make a last struggle to save the lives of his besieged companions and the building with its contents. He quickly threw open the lower door at the river end, stepped to the corner of the building, and facing the mob, deliberately brought his gun to a shoulder and aimed at the miscreant ascending the ladder, and who had nearly reached the roof. But before he had perfected his aim, a volley of a dozen or more shots had been discharged at him, and his body fell where he stood. He was at once got back in the building, the door closed behind him, and the mob believing he had been killed, for the moment the whirlwind and the tempest of their murderous passions were checked. For the brief period this greatest American martyr to human liberty lingered, no word of complaining, no utterances of vengeance or uncharitableness, escaped his lips; but in fullness of a perfect faith, his noble, fearless, pure spirit returned to Him who gave it.

The Autobiography of Colonel George Davis

109. Levi Coffin Runs an Underground-Railroad Depot

Levi Coffin, a leader in operating the "underground railroad," was born of Quaker stock in the slave state of North Carolina. But in 1826 he removed to Newport, Indiana, where he lived for the next twenty years. That town was already on the underground line. In the most fearless way he made his house a depot, receiving passengers every few days, and sending them on — often at the risk of his own life.

IN THE winter of 1826–27 fugitives began to come to our house, and as it became more widely known on different routes that the slaves fleeing from bondage would find a welcome and shelter at our house and be forwarded safely on their journey, the number increased. Friends in the neighborhood who had formerly stood aloof from the work, fearful of the penalty of the law, were encouraged to engage in it when they saw the fearless manner in which I acted and the success that attended my efforts. They would contribute to clothe the fugitives and would aid in forwarding them on their way but were timid about sheltering them under their roof; so that part of the work devolved on us. . . .

I soon became extensively known to the friends of the slaves, at different points on the Ohio River where fugitives generally crossed, and to those northward of us on the various routes leading to Canada. Depots were established on the different lines of the underground railroad, south and north of Newport, and a perfect understanding was maintained between those who kept them. Three principal lines from the South converged at my house, one from Cincinnati, one from Madison, and one from Jeffersonville, Indiana. The roads were always in running order, and the connections were good, the conductors active and zealous, and there was no lack of passengers. Seldom a week passed without our receiving passengers by this mysterious road. We found it necessary to be always prepared to receive such company and properly care for them. We knew not what night or what hour of the night we would be roused from slumber by a gentle rap at the door. Outside in the cold or rain there would be a two-horse wagon loaded with fugitives, perhaps the greater part of them women and children. I would invite them in a low tone to come in, and they would follow me into the darkened house without a word, for we knew not who might be watching and listening. When they were all safely inside and the door fastened, I would cover the windows, strike a light, and build a good fire. By this time my wife would be up and preparing victuals for them, and in a short time the cold and hungry fugitives would be made comfortable. I would accompany the conductor of the train to the stable and care for the horses that had, perhaps, been driven twenty-five or thirty miles that night through the cold and rain. The fugitives would rest on pallets before the fire the rest of the night. Frequently wagonloads of passengers from the different lines have met at our house, having no previous knowledge of each other. The companies varied in number, from two or three fugitives to seventeen.

The pursuit was often very close, and we had to resort to various stratagems in order to elude the pursuers. Sometimes a company of fugitives were scattered and secreted in the neighborhood until the hunters had given up the chase. At other times their route was changed and they were hurried forward with all speed. It was a continual excitement and anxiety to us, but the work was its own reward.

As I have said before, when we knew of no pursuit and the fugitives needed to rest or to be clothed or were sick from exposure and fatigue, we have kept them with us for weeks or months. A case of this kind was that of two young men who were brought to our house during a severe cold spell in the early part of winter. They had been out in the snow and ice, and their feet were so badly frozen that their boots had to be cut off, and they were compelled to lie by for three months, being unable to travel. Doctor Henry H. Way, who was always ready to minister to the fugitives, attended them, and by his skillful treatment their feet were saved, though for some time it was thought that a surgical operation would have to be performed. The two men left us in the spring and went on to Canada. They seemed loath to part from us and manifested much gratitude for our kindness and care. The next autumn one of them returned to our house, saying that he felt so much indebted to us that he had come back to work for us to try to repay us, in some measure, for what we had done for him. I told him that we had no charge against him and could not receive anything for our attention to him while he was sick and helpless, but if he thought he would be safe, I would hire him during the winter at good wages. He accepted this offer and proved to be a faithful servant. He attended night school and made some progress in learning. He returned to Canada in the spring.

Many of the fugitives came long distances, from Alabama, Mississippi, Louisiana, in fact from all parts of the South. Sometimes the poor hunted creatures had been out so long, living in woods and thickets, that they were almost wild when they came in and so fearful of being betrayed that it was some time before their confidence could be gained and the true state of their case learned. Although the number of fugitives that I aided on their way was so large, not one, so far as I ever knew, was captured and taken back to slavery. Providence seemed to favor our efforts for the poor slaves and to crown them with success.

At another time when I was in the city accompanied by my wife and daughter, Hiram S. Gillmore, a noted abolitionist and one of my particular friends, asked me if I knew of any person in from the country with a wagon who would take a fugitive slave girl out to a place of safety. He then gave me the outlines of her story. She had come from Boone County, Kentucky, having run away because she learned that she was to be sold to the far South. Knowing that she would be pursued and probably retaken if she started northward immediately, she conceived a plan like that adopted by Cassie and Emmeline when they ran away from Legree in *Uncle Tom's Cabin*. She hid herself in the interior of a large straw pile near her master's barn, having previously arranged apertures for air and a winding passage with concealed entrance by which her fellow servants who brought her food could enter. Here she remained six weeks, while her master with a posse of men scoured the country in search of her. Like Cassie who looked from her hiding place in the garret and heard the discomfited Legree swearing at his ill luck as he returned from the unsuccessful pursuit, this young woman could hear in her hiding place in the straw pile the noise of horses' feet and the sound of talking as her master and his men returned from their fruitless search for her. When the hunt was over, she stole out and made her way safely to the Ohio River, crossed in a skiff, and reached the house of a family of abolitionists in Cincinnati, where she was kindly received and furnished with comfortable clothing.

In answer to the inquiry of Hiram S. Gillmore I replied that I was there in a carriage and would take her out if she would be ready when I called for her at nine o'clock next morning. At the appointed time we started. The young slave woman was nearly white, was well dressed, and presented quite a ladylike appearance.

At the end of the first day's travel we stopped about four miles above Hamilton, at a private house, the residence of one of my friends — a Democrat, by the way — who had often invited me to call at his house with my wife and pay his family a visit. The gentleman's daughter ran out to meet us and I said to her: "Well, Ellen, I have brought my wife with me this time; now guess which of these ladies she is."

She looked from one to the other, hardly able to decide, but finally, judging perhaps from the Quaker bonnet my wife wore, decided on the right one. The gentleman and his wife now came out to meet us, and when I introduced the young lady with us as a fugitive slave, they were full of surprise and curiosity, having never seen a fugitive slave before.

I told them her story and then said to my friend:

"Will she be safe here tonight, Thomas?"

"I reckon so," was the reply.

"I don't want any *reckon* about it," I rejoined; "I shall put her in thy care, and I don't want thee to let anybody capture her." She was kindly treated.

Next morning — it being the Sabbath day — we went on about eight miles to West Elkton, a Friends' settlement, to attend meeting and spend the day. Meeting had just commenced when we arrived. My wife took the fugitive into meeting with her and seated her by her side. This was the first time the girl had ever attended a Quaker meeting. At its close I introduced her to a number of our friends as a runaway slave from Kentucky. She was the first that had been seen at that place, and a mysterious influence seemed to invest her at once. Men lowered their voices as if in awe when they inquired about her, and some of them seemed alarmed, as if there was danger in the very air that a fugitive slave breathed. I spoke in a loud, cheerful tone and asked: "Why do you lower your voices? Are you afraid of anything? Have you bloodhounds among you? If so, you ought to drive them out of your village."

This public exposition of a fugitive slave at Friends' meeting and in the village seemed to have a good effect in the place, for West Elkton afterward became one of our best underground railroad depots and the timid man first alluded to became one of the most zealous workers on the road.

The Reminiscences of Levi Coffin

110. Anthony Burns Is Sent Back to Slavery

A law to strengthen the hands of Southern masters in recovering runaway slaves was made part of the Compromise of 1850. Most famous of the fugitive slave cases which grew out of this Act — so unpopular in the North — was that of Anthony Burns. He fled from Richmond, Virginia, in February of 1854, and three months later was captured in Boston. The excitement which ensued in that city was said to be the greatest since Revolutionary days. Here the story is told by R. H. Dana, one of the counsel who defended Burns.

MAY 25 [1854], Thursday. — This morning at a little before nine o'clock, as I was going past the courthouse, a gentleman told me that there was a fugitive slave in custody in the United States courtroom. I went up immediately and saw a Negro, sitting in the usual place for prisoners, guarded by a large corps of officers. He is a piteous object, rather weak in mind and body, with a large scar on his cheek, which looks much like a brand, a broken hand from which a large piece of bone projects, and another scar on his other hand. He seemed completely cowed and dispirited. I offered to act as his counsel. He said: "It is of no use. They will swear to me and get me back, and if they do, I shall fare worse if I resist." I told him there might be some flaw in the papers or some mistake and that he might get off. The officers told him he had better have counsel, as it would cost him nothing and could do him no harm. He seemed entirely helpless and could not say what he wished to do, but the great thing on his mind seemed to be the fear that any delay and expense he caused his master would be visited upon him when he got back and that his best policy was to conciliate his master as best he could. I would not press a defense upon him under these circumstances but felt it my duty to address the court and ask for a delay. The commissioner, Edward G. Loring, at my private suggestion, called the prisoner to him and told him what his rights were, and asked him if he wished for time to consider what he would do. The man made no reply and looked round bewildered, like a child. Judge Loring again put the question to him in a kind manner and asked him if he would like to have a day or two and then see him there again. To this he replied faintly, "I would." The judge then ordered a delay until Saturday. . . .

The claimant, one Colonel Suttle of Richmond or Alexandria, Va., was present and sat in full sight of the poor Negro all the time.

May 26. Friday. — Tonight a great meeting is to be held at Faneuil Hall. There is a strong feeling in favor of a rescue, and some of the abolitionists talk quite freely about it. But the most remarkable exhibition is from the Whigs, the Hunker Whigs, the compromise men of 1850. Men who would not speak to me in 1850 and 1851, and who enrolled themselves as special policemen in the Sims affair stop me in the street and talk treason. This is all owing to the Nebraska bill. I cannot respect their feeling at all, except as a return to sanity.

Amos A. Lawrence called to offer any amount of retainer to enable me to employ some eminent Whig counsel. He said he was authorized to do this by a number of active 1850 men who were determined it should be known that it was not the Free Soilers only who were in favor of the liberation of the slaves, but the conservative, compromise men.

May 27. Saturday. — Last night an attempt was made to rescue the slave. It was conducted by a few and failed for want of numbers, the greater part being opposed to an action then. They broke in a door of the courthouse, and a few of them entered, but they were not supported. They killed one man, a truckman named Batchelder, who has volunteered three times to assist in catching and keeping slaves, and the officers retreated. But the men who entered were at first driven back, and the crowd thought themselves repulsed and retreated also. The men who went in first were wounded, and on being driven out, they found that the crowd outside had deserted them. The leader of this mob, I am surprised to hear, in secrecy, was Reverend T. W. Higginson of Worcester. I knew his ardor and courage, but I hardly expected a married man, a clergyman, and a man of education to lead the mob. But Theodore Parker offered to lead a mob to the rescue of Sims, if one hundred men could be got themselves, but they could not get thirty.

Robert Carter tells me that Doctor Samuel G. Howe offered to lead a mob of two hundred to storm the courthouse and that it would probably have been done had not Higginson's attempt led the marshal to call out the military.

Immediately after this mob the marshal sent for a company of United States marines from Charlestown and a company of artillery from Fort Independence. The mayor, too, ordered out two or three companies of volunteer militia to keep the peace but not to aid in the return of the slave.

The hearing began at ten o'clock. The courthouse was filled with hireling soldiers of the standing army of the United States, nearly all of whom are foreigners. The lazy hounds were lounging all day out of the windows and hanging over the stairs, but ready to shoot down good men at a word of command. Some difficulties occurred between them and the citizens, but nothing very serious.

The trial of the Burns case occupied all day of Monday, Tuesday, and Wednesday, 29th, 30th, and 31st of May. Each day the courtroom was filled with the United States marshal's guard, as he called them, a gang of about one hundred and twenty men, the lowest villains in the community. These are all armed with revolvers and other weapons and occupy the rows of seats behind the bar and jury seats. A corps of marines from the navy yard, about sixty in number, commanded by Major Dulany, and two companies of United States artillery, about one hundred and twenty men, commanded by Ridgely, occupy the courthouse and guard all the passages with loaded guns and fixed bayonets. To reach the courthouse one has to pass two or three cordons of police and two of soldiers. Personally I have been well treated, and all whom I desire to have admitted have been admitted; but there has been a great deal of rudeness and violence to others. In one instance a sergeant or corporal, in command of a guard at the foot of the stairs, ordered his men to charge. They did so in good earnest and drove the people down the entry, and it seemed to me, who had just passed them, a wonder that some were not run through.

Beside the general guard which the marshal had to keep his

prisoner, there was a special guard of Southern men, some of them law students from Cambridge, who sat round Colonel Suttle and went in and out with him.

June 2. Friday. — This was a day of intense excitement and deep feeling in the city, in the state, and throughout New England and indeed a great part of the Union. The hearts of millions of persons were beating high with hope, or indignation, or doubt. The mayor of Boston, who is a poor shoat, a physician of a timid, conceited, scatterbrain character, raised by accident to a mayoralty, has vacillated about for several days and at last has done what a weak man almost always does; he has gone too far. He has ordered out the entire military force of the city, from 1500 to 1800 men, and undertaken to place full discretionary power in the hands of General Edmunds. These troops and the three companies of regulars fill the streets and squares from the courthouse to the end of the wharf, where the revenue cutter lies in which it is understood that Burns, if remanded, will be taken to Virginia.

The decision was short. It took no notice of the objections to the admissibility or effect of the record but simply declared it to be conclusive as to title and escape and said that the only point before [the commissioner] was that of identity. On this, upon the evidence of the witnesses there was so much doubt that he could not decide the question and would be obliged to discharge the prisoner. In this dilemma he resorted to the testimony of Brent as to the admissions made by the prisoner to Colonel Suttle on the night of his arrest, which he considered as establishing the identity beyond a reasonable doubt, and on these admissions he was convicted. Convicted on an *ex parte* record, against the actual evidence, and on his own admissions made at the moment of arrest to his alleged master! A tyrannical statute and a weak judge!

The decision was a grievous disappointment to us all, and chiefly to the poor prisoner. He looked the image of despair.

The courtroom was ordered to be cleared at once of all but the prisoner and the guard. I remained with the prisoner, and so did Mr. Grimes, the preacher. We remained in the courtroom a full hour in company with the prisoner and this horrible pack, the guard. Mr. Grimes talked constantly with the prisoner and kept up his spirits as best he could. He told him he thought that it was only a point of honor with the government and the slaveholders to take him to Virginia and that he would be bought as soon as he arrived there. This cheered him. He expressed some fear lest he should be forgotten and said that if sold with his weakened right hand he would be sold "down the river" and, being put to some new work to which he was unaccustomed, would be ill-treated. This was what induced him to run away.

Mr. Grimes and I walked to and fro in front of the courthouse for an hour or so, the entire square being cleared of the people and filled with troops. Every window was filled, and beyond the lines drawn by the police was an immense crowd. Whenever a body of troops passed to or fro, they were hissed and hooted by the people, with some attempts at applause from their favorers. Nearly all the shops in Court and State Streets were closed and hung in black, and a huge coffin was suspended across State Street and flags union down. A brass fieldpiece belonging to the Fourth Artillery was ostentatiously loaded in sight of all the people and carried by the men of that corps in rear of the hollow square in which Burns was placed. Some 1500 or 1800 men of the volunteer militia were under arms, all with their guns loaded and capped, and the officers with revolvers. These men were stationed at different posts in all the streets and lanes that led into Court or State Streets from the courthouse to Long Wharf. The police forced the people back to a certain line, generally at the foot or middle of the lanes and streets leading into the main streets, and wherever there was a passage, there, a few paces behind the police, was a body of troops, from twenty or thirty to fifty or one hundred, according to the size and importance of the passage.

The mayor having given General Edmunds discretionary orders to preserve peace and enforce the laws, General Edmunds gave orders to each commander of a post to fire on the people whenever they passed the line marked by the police in a manner he should consider turbulent and disorderly. So from nine o'clock in the morning until towards night the city was really under martial law. The entire proceeding was illegal. The people were not treated as rioters or ordered to disperse. No civil officers were on the spot to direct the military or to give orders when and how to act. But the people were given their line as on a parade day and the troops were ordered by a military commander to fire upon them at the discretion of the various commanders of posts. In one case, that of Captain Evans of the Boston artillery, the two first orders were actually given, and in a second more the company would have fired but for the fortunate intervention of Colonel Boyd, who ordered their guns to shoulder. Mr. Almon tells me that he heard an officer mounted tell the crowd that if they passed a certain line, the soldiers were ordered to fire and would certainly do so. Professor Wyman says that Captain Young of the Artillery at the head of Franklin Avenue presented his pistol at every man that came to the alley and put two or three persons ridiculously under arrest, with threats to shoot them. I myself saw several men of Company H, First Regiment, at the head of Broad or Kilby Street, on a slight sign of commotion in the crowd at the foot of State Street, such as often is seen in large crowds, cock their guns and present them ready to fire without orders. An accident would have cost lives, and it was with great reluctance and only after repeated orders that these men would uncock their guns and bring them to order. It has been the greatest good fortune in the world that not a gun was fired by accident or design. No one could limit the consequences, and all concerned would have been, in the eye of the law, murderers.

Mr. Grimes and I remained in the courthouse until the vile procession moved. Notwithstanding their numbers and the enormous military protection, the marshal's company were very much disturbed and excited. They were exceedingly apprehensive of some unknown and unforeseen violence.

The guard at length filed out and formed a hollow square. Each man was armed with a short Roman sword and one revolver hanging in his belt. In this square marched Burns with the marshal. The United States troops and the squadron of Boston light horse preceded and followed the square, with the fieldpiece. As the procession moved down, it was met with a perfect howl of "Shame! Shame!" and hisses.

I walked slowly down the streets at a considerable distance in the rear of the procession, and when I heard the news that it had safely reached the end of the wharf and that the cutter was steaming out to sea, I returned to my office.

Diary of Richard Henry Dana

111. John Brown Makes a Speech at Harper's Ferry

"John Brown of Osawatomie" made his famous raid on Harpers Ferry, Virginia — hoping to free the Negroes there and begin a general slave insurrection — in October, 1859. When marines and militia arrived under Colonel Robert E. Lee, he was soon captured. During his trial, and at his execution on December 2, the grim, fanatical Brown gave an impressive exhibition of fortitude.

I HAVE, may it please the Court, a few words to say.

In the first place, I deny everything but what I have all along admitted — the design on my part to free the slaves. I intended certainly to have made a clean thing of that matter, as I did last winter [1858], when I went into Missouri and there took slaves without the snapping of a gun on either side, moved them through the country, and finally left them in Canada. I designed to have done the same thing again, on a larger scale. That was all I intended. I never did intend murder, or treason, or the destruction of property, or to excite or incite slaves to rebellion, or to make insurrection.

I have another objection; and that is, it is unjust that I should suffer such a penalty. Had I interfered in the manner which I admit, and which I admit has been fairly proved . . . had I so interfered in behalf of the rich, the powerful, the intelligent, the so-called great, or in behalf of any of their friends — either father, mother, brother, sister, wife, or children, or any of that class — and suffered and sacrificed what I have in this interference, it would have been all right; and every man in this court would have deemed it an act worthy of reward rather than punishment.

This court acknowledges, as I suppose, the validity of the law of God. I see a book kissed here which I suppose to be the Bible, or at least the New Testament. That teaches me that all things whatsoever I would that men should do to me, I should do even so to them. It teaches me, further, to "remember them that are in bonds, as bound with them." I endeavored to act up to that instruction. I say, I am yet too young to understand that God is any respecter of persons. I believe that to have interfered as I have done — as I have always freely admitted I have done — in behalf of His despised poor, was not wrong but right. Now if it is deemed necessary that I should forfeit my life for the furtherance of the ends of justice and mingle my blood further with the blood of my children and with the blood of millions in this slave country whose rights are disregarded by wicked, cruel, and unjust enactments — I submit; so let it be done!

Let me say one word further.

I feel entirely satisfied with the treatment I have received on my trial. Considering all the circumstances, it has been more generous than I expected. But I feel no consciousness of guilt. I have stated from the first what was my intention and what was not. I never had any design against the life of any person, nor any disposition to commit treason, or excite slaves to rebel, or make any general insurrection. I never encouraged any man to do so, but always discouraged any idea of that kind.

Let me say also a word in regard to the statements made by some of those connected with me. I hear it has been stated by some of them that I have induced them to join me. But the contrary is true. I do not say this to injure them, but as regretting their weakness. There is not one of them but joined me of his own accord, and the greater part of them at their own expense. A number of them I never saw and never had a word of conversation with till the day they came to me, and that was for the purpose I have stated.

Now I have done.

JAMES REDPATH, *The Public Life of Captain John Brown*

XIX

Westward the Course of Empire

112. Trading Furs on the North-west Coast

When the British explorer Captain Cook visited Nootka Sound in the Pacific Northwest in 1778, he found the Indians there eager to sell his men beautiful furs — wolf, bear, marten, fox, sea-otter, beaver, and many others — for bits of iron and brass. His two ships took aboard many pelts. Then when Captain Cook's men reached China, they found the Chinese willing to pay enormous prices for even defective skins. Out of this situation grew a great trade in Northwestern furs. British captains were first on the scene, but soon after the Revolution, Boston skippers appeared. One of these Americans was Richard Jeffry Cleveland, who was born in Salem, Massachusetts, in 1773, who became a full-fledged captain at twenty-four, and who beginning in 1797 carried out a series of daring and profitable voyages. An intrepid, able, and honest mariner, he remained at sea with brief intermissions until 1822, making and losing several fortunes. Here he tells of barter with the Northwestern Indians.

EARLY in the morning of the 30th of March [1799], we saw the usual indications of land — driftwood, kelp, and gulls, — and at ten o'clock perceived the snow-capped hills of the American coast twelve leagues distant. We immediately set all hands to work in bending our cables and getting up a bulwark, which we had been preparing of hides sewed together. These were attached to stanchions of about six feet, and completely screened us from being seen by the natives, whom it was important to our safety to keep in ignorance of our numbers. Towards evening we anchored in a snug harbour at Norfolk Sound, in latitude fifty-seven degrees ten minutes north. Here the smoothness of the water, the feeling of safety, and the silent tranquillity which reigned all round us, formed a striking contrast to the scenes with which we had been familiar since leaving Canton and would have afforded positive enjoyment, had I possessed a crew on whose fidelity I could depend.

The following day was very clear and pleasant. At the first dawn of the morning we discharged a cannon to apprize any natives who might be near of our arrival. We then loaded the cannon and a number of muskets and pistols, which were placed where they could be most readily laid hold of. The only accessible part of the vessel was the stern, and this was exclusively used (while it was necessary to keep up the bulwark) as the gangway. As it was over the stern that we meant to trade, I had mounted there two four-pound cannon and on the tafferel a pair of blunderbusses on swivels, which were also loaded. Soon after the discharge of our cannon several Indians came to us, and before dark some hundreds had arrived, who encamped on the beach near which the vessel was anchored. As we observed them to be loaded with skins, we supposed that we were the first who had arrived this season.

With a view to our own security as well as convenience, I directed my interpreter to explain to the chiefs, and through them to the tribe, that after dark no canoe would be allowed to come near the vessel, and that if I perceived any one approaching I should fire at it; that only three or four canoes must come at a time to trade, and that they must always appear under the stern, avoiding the sides of the vessel. With my own men I neglected no precaution to make escape impossible but at the imminent risk of life. While at anchor they were divided into three watches. One of these I took charge of, and stationing them in such parts of the vessel that no movement could be made undiscovered, obliged them to strike the gong every half hour throughout the night and to call out from each end of the vessel and amidships, "All's well." This practice so amused the Indians that they imitated it by striking a tin kettle and repeating the words as near as they were able.

But a more hideous set of beings in the form of men and women I had never before seen. The fantastic manner in which many of the faces of the men were painted was probably intended to give them a ferocious appearance, and some groups looked really as if they had escaped from the dominions of Satan himself. One had a perpendicular line dividing the two sides of the face, one side of which was painted red, the other black, with the head daubed with grease and red ocher and filled with the white down of birds. Another had the face divided with a horizontal line in the middle and painted black and white. The visage of a third was painted in checkers, etc. Most of them had little mirrors, before the acquisition of which they must have been dependent on each other for those correct touches of the pencil which are so much in vogue and which daily require more time than the toilet of a Parisian belle.

The women made, if possible, a still more frightful appearance. The ornament of wood which they wear to extend an incision made beneath the upper lip so distorts the face as to take from it almost the resemblance to the human; yet the privilege of wearing this ornament is not extended to the female slaves, who are prisoners taken in war. Hence it would seem that distinctive badges have their origin in the most rude state of society. It is difficult, however, for the imagination to conceive of more disgusting and filthy beings than these patrician dames.

It was quite noon before we could agree upon the rate of barter, but when once arranged with one of the chiefs and the exchange made, they all hurried to dispose of their skins at the same rate; and before night we had purchased upwards of a hundred, at the rate of two yards of blue broadcloth each. The Indians assured us that a vessel with three masts had been there a month before, from which they had received four yards of cloth for a skin, but this story was rendered improbable by the number they had on hand, and I considered it as a maneuver to raise the price. As soon as it became dark they retired in an orderly manner to their encampment, abreast the vessel; and some of them appeared to be on the watch all night, as we never proclaimed the hour on board without hearing a repetition of it on shore.

The following morning the natives came off soon after daylight and began without hesitation to dispose of their furs to us at the price fixed upon the day before, and such was their activity in trading that, by night, we had purchased of them more than two hundred sea-otter skins, besides one hundred and twenty tails. Our barter consisted of blue cloth, greatcoats, blankets, Chinese trunks, with beads, China cash, and knives as presents. Canoes were arriving occasionally throughout the day, so that at night there was a very perceptible augmentation of their numbers.

Having observed on the 4th and 5th that their store of furs was nearly exhausted, we weighed anchor the next morning, and parting on good terms with the natives, steered up a narrow passage in an easterly direction till we arrived in that extensive sound which Vancouver has called Chatham's Straits. . . . Several women came off and told us there were no skins in the village; that the men were gone in pursuit of them; and that, if we came there again in twice ten days, they should have plenty. Here we passed a day in filling up our empty water casks and getting a supply of wood.

In the afternoon of the 9th we put out of the snug cover in which we were lying, having been informed by the Indians that there was a ship in sight. This we found to be true, as on opening the sound we saw her not more than a mile distant from us. Soon after, we were boarded by Captain Rowan of ship *Eliza,* of Boston, who had arrived on the coast at least a month before us, and who, having been very successful, was now on his way to the southward to complete his cargo and then to leave the coast. He mentioned that ten vessels would probably be dispatched from Boston for the coast this season.

RICHARD J. CLEVELAND, A Narrative of Voyages and Commercial
Enterprises

113. The Rendezvous of the Mountain Men

The "mountain men" were the trappers who penetrated every nook and corner of the Rocky Mountains for furs — chiefly for beaver pelts. Some were hired trappers who were paid yearly wages by a fur company; some were "skin" trappers who got their outfits from a company, and were merely obligated to sell it what they caught; some were free trappers, who took their pelts where they pleased and sold them wherever they liked. The years from 1820 to 1845 marked the heyday of the trappers; a hardy, daring, rough-mannered, illiterate race of men, who made important contributions to the exploration and conquest of the West. Greatest among the "mountain men" was Kit Carson, though James Bridger and Thomas Fitzpatrick also have a title to fame. Washington Irving in his Adventures of Captain Bonneville *has told the story of a soldier (B. L. E. Bonneville became colonel and bravest brigadier-general) who was fascinated by the commercial possibilities of the fur trade, and spent the years 1832–35 exploring them, and also exploring some new parts of the West.*

THE GREEN RIVER valley was at this time [c. 1832] the scene of one of those general gatherings of traders, trappers, and Indians, that we have already mentioned. The three rival companies, which for a year past had been endeavoring to outtrade, outtrap, and outwit each other, were here encamped in close proximity, awaiting their annual supplies. About four miles from the rendezvous of Captain Bonneville was that of the American Fur Company, hard by which was that also of the Rocky Mountain Fur Company.

After the eager rivalry and almost hostility displayed by these companies in their late campaigns it might be expected that when thus brought in juxtaposition they would hold themselves warily and sternly aloof from each other, and should they happen to come in contact, brawl and bloodshed would ensue.

No such thing! Never did rival lawyers after a wrangle at the bar meet with more social good humor at a circuit dinner. The hunting season over, all past tricks and maneuvers are forgotten, all feuds and bickerings buried in oblivion. From the middle of June to the middle of September all trapping is suspended, for the beavers are then shedding their furs and their skins are of little value. This, then, is the trapper's holiday, when he is all for fun and frolic and ready for a saturnalia among the mountains.

At the present season, too, all parties were in good humor. The year had been productive. Competition, by threatening to lessen their profits, had quickened their wits, roused their energies, and made them turn every favorable chance to the best advantage, so that on assembling at their respective places of rendezvous, each company found itself in possession of a rich stock of peltries.

The leaders of the different companies, therefore, mingled on terms of perfect good-fellowship, interchanging visits and regaling each other in the best style their respective camps afforded. But the rich treat for the worthy captain was to see the "chivalry" of the various encampments engaged in contests of skill at running, jumping, wrestling, shooting with the rifle, and running horses. And then their rough hunters' feastings and carousals. They drank together, they sang, they laughed, they whooped; they tried to outbrag and outlie each other in stories of their adventures and achievements. Here the free trappers were in all their glory; they considered themselves the "cocks of the walk" and always carried the highest crests. Now and then familiarity was pushed too far and would effervesce into a brawl and a rough-and-tumble fight; but it all ended in cordial reconciliation and maudlin endearment.

The presence of the Shoshone tribe contributed occasionally to cause temporary jealousies and feuds. The Shoshone beauties became objects of rivalry among some of the amorous mountaineers. Happy was the trapper who could muster up a red blanket, a string of gay beads, or a paper of precious vermilion with which to win the smiles of a Shoshone fair one.

The caravans of supplies arrived at the valley just at this period of gallantry and good-fellowship. Now commenced a scene of eager competition and wild prodigality at the different encampments. Bales were hastily ripped open and their motley contents poured forth. A mania for purchasing spread itself throughout the several bands — munitions for war, for hunting, for gallantry, were seized upon with equal avidity — rifles, hunting knives, traps, scarlet cloth, red blankets, garish beads, and glittering trinkets were bought at any price, and scores run up without any thought how they were ever to be rubbed off. The free trappers especially were extravagant in their purchases. For a free mountaineer to pause at a paltry consideration of dollars and cents in the attainment of any object that might strike his fancy would stamp him with the mark of the beast in the estimation of his comrades. For a trader to refuse one of these free and flourishing blades a credit, whatever unpaid scores might stare him in the face, would be a flagrant affront, scarcely to be forgiven.

Now succeeded another outbreak of revelry and extravagance. The trappers were newly fitted out and arrayed and dashed about with their horses caparisoned in Indian style. The Shoshone beauties also flaunted about in all the colors of the rainbow. Every freak of prodigality was indulged to its fullest extent, and in a little while most of the trappers, having squandered away all their wages and perhaps run knee-deep in debt, were ready for another hard campaign in the wilderness.

WASHINGTON IRVING, The Adventures of Captain Bonneville, 1837

114. General Wistar Learns Trapping in the Rockies

Isaac Jones Wistar, scion of a prominent Pennsylvania family, played many roles in his adventurous life—a gold hunter in the California rush of 1849, trader, speculator, rancher, and lawyer on the Pacific Coast, cattle dealer in the Mississippi Valley, soldier in the Civil War, and railroad builder after it. For a time he was also trapper and fur trader in the Northern Rockies, where he met with grim hardships and some terrifying adventures.

FOR MYSELF I knew but little of the kind of work laid out for the winter [c. 1850], but my companion had been in the Hudson's Bay Company all his life and was as experienced a trapper, hunter, and traveler as was to be found through all its vast territory. There was no fish, bird, or animal whose habits and resorts he did not know. If there was a deer anywhere within ten miles he was sure to find it, and I doubt whether he had a superior anywhere as a mountain man and hunter. . . .

Before settling down to our winter's work it may be well to describe what a sable trapper's work is like. It is totally different from beaver trapping, which requires an outfit of steel traps and must be pursued along streams and rivers which are also frequented during the winter by Indians, whose hostility is often extremely dangerous. The marten or sable is a small animal of the weasel tribe that lives well up in the middle district of the mountains, where the Indians, unless traveling, rarely come in winter. The trapper, having deposited his livestock in a safe place and laid up either pemmican or smoked dried meat for provisions, sits down on some remote, difficult, and well-concealed stream, well up, though not too high among the mountains, and makes a small brush shelter, open in front, and if possible with plenty of dry, well-felled timber close by. Here he can have as much fire as he chooses at night, when the smoke cannot be seen, but if he is prudent and regards his scalp, he will not risk much of it during the day. Nor will he ever discharge a gun either by night or day except in circumstances of stringent necessity.

Here he is soon snowed in and shut off from all the world, provided he has been sufficiently careful of his trail and the marks and signs he has left behind him. His horses, turned out in some distant valley, may be and often are discovered and stolen, in which event he must, when spring comes, replace them in the same way or abandon all the proceeds of his winter's labor. Having made his quarters comfortable, safely disposed of his provisions, and prepared snowshoes and trapsticks, one of the pair starts off, taking a long leading ridge for forty miles or more, setting traps in favorable places as he goes, crossing over and returning by some similar ridge as far as practicable. Each of such trips may occupy a week or more — sometimes, if fresh snow falls, considerably more — and on his return his partner does the same, of course avoiding the same ridges. Thus they alternate all winter, setting and resetting traps, skinning, and packing in the skins. While in camp there is plenty of work, fleshing, drying, stretching, and packing the skins and trapping small game for fresh provisions when it can be had.

But if a carcajou or, as the Americans call them, wolverine gets on the line of traps, or if quarters have to be moved in mid-winter in consequence of scarcity of martens, or worst of all, should the sign of some prowling Indian be detected, it may become necessary to move the camp and the entire theater of operations far away to another district, in which case the skins already collected must be cached and protected from the weather and from hungry prowlers and every other asset backed on snowshoes through the wildest and roughest intricacies of inhospitable mountains covered deep with snow. Supposing, however, that such accidents and removals can be avoided, the mere routine of trap setting and attendance gives but little trouble except after fresh falls of snow, especially when caught by storms far away from camp. Notwithstanding that in the low temperature of those regions snow frequently falls dry and hard-frozen like sand, it has a constant tendency to settle and pack and can often be traversed without snowshoes, though when these are not worn they must always be carried ready for use, usually over the shoulder with the bag of fire sticks.

Marten traps in themselves are simple enough; it is in the locality, lines, directions, and modes of concealment from uninvited guests that the trapper's skill consists. They are made by arranging a small inclosure of driven stakes with a single opening. Across that is laid as threshold a log, stone, or even a flat chunk of ice, upon which at one end rests the movable deadfall, the other end of the latter supported by some of the various kinds of trap sticks, the common "figure four" being usually preferred. A small bait of fresh or dried meat, the former preferable when it can be had, is carried by the trigger stick inside the inclosure, where the marten can only reach it by introducing his long neck through the entrance. As soon as he seizes it, conscious of the suspicious character of the arrangement, he quickly backs out, bringing down the fall, which breaks his neck or his back on the lower log without marking the skin, which in that climate, even when covered by snow, will keep fresh a long time if not found by the carcajou or other carnivorous prowlers.

After the trapper has laid in his provisions, disposed of his horses, and settled down in his solitary winter quarters, incidents are few; and as none of a pleasant character are likely to occur, the fewer they are, the better for him.

In our case about this time, martens being scarce and the camp, in consequence of the lateness of our arrival, having been badly chosen, it was found necessary to shift it in the dead of winter; for which purpose, taking but little provision from our scanty store and caching the rest of our effects, we pushed out in a northerly direction, hoping to find a better location on some of the other tributaries of the Peace. But with ground covered by heavy snow, streams hard bound with ice, and frequent windstorms which at the low prevailing temperatures none can face and live, our progress was slow and no place looked very attractive. Hence no great time had elapsed before we found our provisions exhausted, in a difficult country with game not to be had. Making a temporary shelter in a bad place and under unfavorable circumstances, we therefore proceeded to devote our whole attention to hunting, till after some days we became awake to the fact that the district was absolutely without game. Every day the weather permitted, we covered long distances in opposite directions, without finding so much as a recent sign or track. Then we set traps for fish in such rapids as remained open, and for birds and small animals, but without success. Travel over the rocky sidehills concealed by snow was exhausting and dangerous, both of us getting some bad falls. Moreover, as one dare not stir from camp in the uncertain weather without carrying a considerable weight and bulk of articles like furs, snowshoes, and so forth, which might at any moment become essential to life, we soon became weak and exhausted.

After trying in vain all the resources practised by trappers in such straits, all of which were well known to François, we ate the grease in our rifle stocks, all the fringes and unnecessary parts of our buck-leather clothes, gun and ammunition bags, and every scrap of eatable material, boiling it down in an Assinaboine basket with hot stones, and were finally reduced to buds and twigs. After many days of this extreme privation, no longer possessing strength to travel or hunt, I became discouraged; and as we lay down one night I determined to abandon the struggle and remain there, enduring with such fortitude as I might the final pangs, which could not be long deferred. At this last stage in the struggle, an event occurred of the most extraordinary character, which cannot seem more strange and incredible to any one than it has always appeared to me on the innumerable occasions when I have since reflected on it. Notwithstanding our exhaustion and desperate conclusion of the night before, François rose at daylight, made up the fire as well as his strength permitted, blazed a tree near by on which he marked with charcoal a large cross, and carefully reloading and standing his gun against that emblem, proceeded to repeat in such feeble whispers as he was yet capable of, all the scraps of French and Latin prayers he could remember, to all of which I was in no condition to give much attention. When he got through he remarked with much cheerfulness that he was now sure of killing something and urged me to make one more effort with him, which I rather angrily refused, and bade him lie down and take what had to come, like a man. With cheerful assurance he replied that he was not afraid to die, but our time had not come. He knew he would find and kill, and we would escape all right. Then desisting from his useless effort to get me up, François, leaving his heavy snowshoes behind, directed himself with weak and uneven steps down the little stream in the deep gorge of which our camp was made; and never expecting to see him again, my mind relapsed into an idle, vacuous condition in which external circumstances were forgotten or disregarded. But scarcely a few minutes had elapsed and he had hardly traversed a couple of hundred yards when I heard his gun, which I knew never cracked in vain.

I had thought myself unable to rise, but at that joyful sound promptly discovered my mistake. I found François in the spot from which he had fired, leaning against a tree in such deep excitement that he could speak with difficulty. On that rugged sidehill apparently destitute of all life, in that most improbable of all places, within sound and smell of our camp, he had seen not a squirrel or a rabbit, but a deer. Attempting to climb for a better shot, the deer jumped, and with terrible misgivings he had fired at it running. He had heard it running after his shot but was sure he had made a killing hit. Scrambling with difficulty up the hill, we found a large clot of blood and a morsel of "lights," which we divided and ate on the spot. After taking up the trail we soon found the animal.

After passing safely through that period of starvation we were glad enough to get back to the old camp and make the best of it during the remainder of the season, which furnished little more of incident to vary the monotony of our solitary occupation. One or the other occasionally got caught in a storm of snow or, still worse,

of wind, but though sometimes thus long delayed on extremely cur-
tailed diet, we always made shift to find or make some shelter and
get back in safety at last. The cold was mostly intense, but being
steadier and drier than on the plains, gave no great trouble till the
diurnal thaws set in toward spring. As when these arrive it is already too late to catch marketable furs, we might have lain quiet but
for our insufficient stock of pemmican and even of jerked meat, both
of which became so reduced that we were obliged to hunt almost
constantly without much regard to weather. . . .

By March, except in extreme northern latitudes, the marten's fur
begins to deteriorate, and those taken after April the Company will
not receive at all, so that in medium latitudes the trapper's work
is over long before he can safely bring up the horses and get away
with his pelts. Much of that interval we passed below in the foothills, where we reclaimed our horses safe, healthy, and fat and
amused ourselves with trapping fish and hunting, enjoying our
liberation from the gloomy mountain fastnesses and the comparative
abundance and variety of the fare. Falling in with friendly As-
sinaboines, who are the ancient friends of the trappers and mostly
engaged in the same pursuit, we also enjoyed the pleasures of society,
which are best appreciated by those who have been totally secluded
during a long and dreary winter. It was perhaps not before the end
of May that the little patches of new grass in sheltered places along
the streams were sufficiently forward to permit of commencing the
long and somewhat risky journey required to dispose of our peltrys.

The Autobiography of General Isaac Wistar

115. Richard Henry Dana, Jr., Visits Spanish California

The author of Two Years Before
the Mast *describes California as he saw it in the last days of Mexican
rule (1836–1837), just ten years before the American conquest.*

By BEING thus continually engaged in transporting passengers with their goods to and fro, we gained a knowledge of the character, dress, and language of the people. The women wore gowns of various texture — silks, crape, calicoes, etc. — made after the European style except that the sleeves were short, leaving the arm bare, and that they were loose about the waist, having no corsets. They wore shoes of kid or satin, sashes or belts of bright colors, and almost always a necklace and earrings. Bonnets they had none. I only saw one on the coast, and that belonged to a wife of an American sea captain who had settled in San Diego and had imported the chaotic mass of straw and ribbon as a choice present to his new wife. They wear their hair (which is almost invariably black or a very dark brown) long on their necks, sometimes loose, and sometimes in long braids, though the married women often do it up on a high comb. Their complexions are various, depending — as well as their dress and manner — upon their rank, or in other words upon the amount of Spanish blood they can lay claim to.

Those who are of pure Spanish blood, having never intermarried with aborigines, have clear brunette complexions and sometimes even as fair as those of Englishwomen. There are but few of these families in California, being mostly those in official stations or who, on the expiration of their offices, have settled here upon property which they have acquired, and others who have been banished for state offenses. These form the aristocracy, intermarrying, keeping up an exclusive system in every respect. They can be told by their complexions, dress, manner, and also by their speech; for calling themselves Castilians, they are very ambitious of speaking the pure Castilian language, which is spoken in a somewhat corrupted dialect by the lower classes.

From this upper class they go down by regular shades, growing more and more dark and muddy, until you come to the pure Indian, who runs about with nothing upon him but a small piece of cloth kept up by a wide leather strap drawn round his waist. Generally speaking, each person's caste is decided by the quality of the blood, which shows itself, too plainly to be concealed, at first sight. Yet the least drop of Spanish blood, if it be only of quadroon or octoroon, is sufficient to raise them from the rank of slaves and entitle them to a suit of clothes — boots, hat, cloak, spurs, long knife, all complete, though coarse and dirty as may be — and to call themselves Españolos and to hold property, if they can get any.

The fondness for dress among the women is excessive and is often the ruin of many of them. A present of a fine mantle or of a necklace or pair of earrings gains the favor of the greater part of them. Nothing is more common than to see a woman living in a house of only two rooms, and the ground for a floor, dressed in spangled satin shoes, silk gown, high comb, and gilt if not gold earrings and necklace. If their husbands do not dress them well enough, they will soon receive presents from others. They used to spend whole days on board our vessel, examining the fine clothes and ornaments, and frequently made purchases at a rate which would have made a seamstress or waiting maid in Boston open her eyes.

Next to the love of dress I was most struck with the fineness of the voices and beauty of the intonations of both sexes. Every common ruffian-looking fellow, with a slouched hat, blanket coat, dirty under-dress, and soiled leather leggings, appeared to me to be speaking elegant Spanish.

Another thing that surprised me was the quantity of silver that was in circulation. I certainly never saw so much silver at one time in my life as during the week that we were at Monterey. The truth is they have no credit system, no banks, and no way of investing money but in cattle. They have no circulating medium but silver and hides — which the sailors call California bank notes. Everything that they buy they must pay for in one or the other of these things. The hides they bring down dried and doubled, in clumsy ox carts or upon mules' backs, and the money they carry tied up in a handkerchief — fifty, eighty, or a hundred dollars and half dollars. . . .

Monterey, as far as my observation goes, is decidedly the pleasantest and most civilized-looking place in California. In the center of it is an open square surrounded by four lines of one-story plastered buildings, with half a dozen cannon in the center, some mounted and others not. This is the presidio or fort. Every town has a presidio in its center, or rather, every presidio has a town built around it; for the forts were first built by the Mexican government, and then the people built near them for protection. The presidio here was entirely open and unfortified.

There were several officers with long titles, and about eighty soldiers, but they were poorly paid, fed, clothed, and disciplined. The governor general, or, as he is commonly called, the general, lives here, which makes it the seat of government. He is appointed by the central government at Mexico and is the chief civil and military officer. In addition to him each town has a commandant, who is the chief military officer and has charge of the fort and of all transactions with foreigners and foreign vessels, and two or three alcaldes and corregidores, elected by the inhabitants, who are the civil officers.

Courts and jurisprudence they have no knowledge of. Small municipal matters are regulated by the alcaldes and corregidores, and everything relating to the general government, to the military, and to foreigners, by the commandants, acting under the governor general. Capital cases are decided by him upon personal inspection if he is near or upon minutes sent by the proper officers if the offender is at a distant place.

No Protestant has any civil rights, nor can he hold any property or indeed remain more than a few weeks on shore unless he belongs to some vessel. Consequently the Americans and English who intend to reside here become Catholics, to a man; the current phrase among them being, "A man must leave his conscience at Cape Horn."

But to return to Monterey. The houses here, as everywhere else in California, are of one story, built of clay made into large bricks about a foot and a half square and three or four inches thick and hardened in the sun. These are cemented together by mortar of the same material, and the whole are of common dirt-color. The floors are generally of earth, the windows grated and without glass; and the doors, which are seldom shut, open directly into the common room, there being no entries.

Some of the more wealthy inhabitants have glass to their windows and board floors, and in Monterey nearly all the houses are plastered on the outside. The better houses, too, have red tiles upon the roofs. The common ones have two or three rooms which open into each other and are furnished with a bed or two, a few chairs and tables, a looking glass, a crucifix of some material or other, and small daubs of paintings inclosed in glass and representing some miracle or martyrdom. They have no chimneys or fireplaces in the houses, the climate being such as to make a fire unnecessary; and all their cooking is done in a small cookhouse, separated from the house.

The Indians, as I have said before, do all the hard work, two or three being attached to each house; and the poorest persons are able to keep one, at least, for they have only to feed them and give them a small piece of coarse cloth and a belt, for the males, and a coarse gown, without shoes or stockings, for the females.

In Monterey there are a number of English and Americans (English or "Ingles" all are called who speak the English language) who have married Californians, become united to the Catholic Church, and acquired considerable property. Having more industry, frugality, and enterprise than the natives, they soon get nearly all the trade into their hands. They usually keep shops, in which they retail the goods purchased in larger quantities from our vessels, and also send a good deal into the interior, taking hides in pay, which they again barter with our vessels.

In every town on the coast there are foreigners engaged in this kind of trade, while I recollect but two shops kept by natives. The people are naturally suspicious of foreigners, and they would not be allowed to remain were it not that they become good Catholics, and by marrying natives and bringing up their children as Catholics and Spaniards and not teaching them the English language, they quiet suspicion and even become popular and leading men. The chief alcaldes in Monterey and Santa Barbara were both Yankees by birth.

The men in Monterey appeared to me to be always on horseback. Horses are as abundant here as dogs and chickens were in Juan Fernandez. There are no stables to keep them in, but they are allowed to run wild and graze wherever they please, being branded and having long leather ropes called lassos attached to their necks and dragging along behind them, by which they can be easily taken. The men usually catch one in the morning, throw a saddle and bridle upon him, and use him for the day, and let him go at night, catching another the next day. When they go on long journeys, they ride one horse down and catch another, throw the saddle and bridle upon him, and after riding him down take a third, and so on to the end of the journey.

There are probably no better riders in the world. They get upon a horse when only four or five years old, their little legs not long enough to come halfway over his sides, and may almost be said to keep on him until they have grown to him. The stirrups are covered or boxed up in front, to prevent their catching when riding through the woods; and the saddles are large and heavy, strapped very tight upon the horse, and have large pommels or loggerheads in front, round which the lasso is coiled when not in use. They can hardly go from one house to another without getting on a horse, there being generally several standing tied to the doorposts of the little cottages. When they wish to show their activity, they make no use of their stirrups in mounting but, striking the horse, spring into the saddle as he starts and, sticking their long spurs into him, go off on the full run. Their spurs are cruel things, having four or five rowels, each an inch in length, dull and rusty. The flanks of the horses are often sore from them, and I have seen men come in from chasing bullocks with their horses' hind legs and quarters covered with blood.

They frequently give exhibitions of their horsemanship in races, bullbaitings, etc.; but as we were not ashore during any holiday we saw nothing of it. Monterey is also a great place for cockfighting, gambling of all sorts, fandangos, and every kind of amusement and knavery. Trappers and hunters, who occasionally arrive here from over the Rocky Mountains with their valuable skins and furs, are often entertained with every sort of amusement and dissipation until they have wasted their time and their money and go back, stripped of everything.

RICHARD HENRY DANA, JR., Two Years before the Mast, 1840

116. Riding the Oregon Trail with the Cow Column

The emigration of American settlers to Oregon in 1843 is called "The Great Emigration" because of its size. Peter H. Burnett was elected captain of the company, but resigned when the men who had no cattle refused to help stand guard over the herds of those who did. The emigrants then split into two groups, the lighter body moving ahead, while those with cattle — "the cow column" — came on behind. Jesse Applegate was chosen to lead the cow column, and in his classic description of a day with it, written long years afterward, he gives a memorable picture of the life and customs of the expedition as it crossed the plains and mountains. He also pays a deserved tribute to the energy and wisdom of Dr. Marcus Whitman, the great Oregon missionary, who accompanied the settlers for most of their journey.

THE MIGRATION of a large body of men, women, and children across the continent to Oregon was, in the year 1843, strictly an experiment not only in respect to numbers, but to the outfit of the migration party.

The migrating body numbered over one thousand souls, with about one hundred and twenty wagons, drawn by six-ox teams, averaging about six yokes to the team, and several thousand loose horses and cattle.

The emigrants first organized and attempted to travel in one body, but it was soon found that no progress could be made with a body so cumbrous and as yet so averse to all discipline. And at the crossing of the Big Blue it divided into two columns, which traveled in supporting distance of each other as far as Independence Rock on the Sweet Water.

From this point, all danger from Indians being over, the emigrants separated into small parties better suited to the narrow mountain paths and small pastures on their front. Some of the emigrants had only their teams, while others had large herds in addition which must share the pastures and be guarded and driven by the whole body. Those not encumbered with or having but few loose cattle attached themselves to the light column; those having more than four or five cows had of necessity to join the heavy or cow column. Hence the cow column, being much larger than the other and encumbered with its large herds, had to use greater exertion and observe a more rigid discipline to keep pace with the more agile consort. It is with the cow or more clumsy column that I propose to journey with the reader for a single day.

It is 4 A.M.; the sentinels on duty have discharged their rifles — the signal that the hours of sleep are over; and every wagon and tent is pouring forth its night tenants, and slow-kindling smokes begin largely to rise and float away on the morning air.

Sixty men start from the corral, spreading as they make through the vast herd of cattle and horses that form a semicircle around the encampment, the most distant perhaps two miles away.

The herders pass to the extreme verge and carefully examine for trails beyond, to see that none of the animals have strayed or been stolen during the night.

This morning no trails lead beyond the outside animals in sight, and by five o'clock the herders begin to contract the great moving circle and the well-trained animals move slowly toward camp, clipping here and there a thistle or tempting bunch of grass on the way.

In about an hour five thousand animals are close up to the encampment, and the teamsters are busy selecting their teams and driving them inside the "corral" to be yoked. The corral is a circle one hundred yards deep, formed with wagons connected strongly with each other, the wagon in the rear being connected with the wagon in front by its tongue and oxchains. It is a strong barrier that the most vicious ox cannot break, and in case of an attack of the Sioux would be no contemptible entrenchment. From six to seven o'clock is a busy time; breakfast is to be eaten, the tents struck, the wagon loaded, and the teams yoked and brought in readiness to be attached to their respective wagons. All know that when, at seven o'clock, the signal to march sounds, those not ready to take their proper places in the line of march must fall into the dusty rear for the day.

There are sixty wagons. They have been divided into fifteen divisions or platoons of four wagons each, and each platoon is entitled to lead in its turn. The leading platoon of today will be the rear one tomorrow and will bring up the rear unless some teamster, through indolence or negligence, has lost his place in the line and is condemned to that uncomfortable post. It is within ten minutes of seven; the corral, but now a strong barricade, is everywhere broken, the teams being attached to the wagons. The women and children have taken their places in them. The pilot (a borderer who has passed his life on the verge of civilization and has been chosen to the post of leader from his knowledge of the savage and his experience in travel through roadless wastes) stands ready in the midst of his pioneers and aids to mount and lead the way.

Ten or fifteen young men, not today on duty, form another cluster. They are ready to start on a buffalo hunt, are well mounted and well armed, as they need be, for the unfriendly Sioux have driven the buffalo out of the Platte, and the hunters must ride fifteen or twenty miles to reach them. The cow drivers are hastening, as they get ready, to the rear of their charges, to collect and prepare them for the day's march.

It is on the stroke of seven; the rushing to and fro, the cracking of the whips, the loud command to oxen, and what seems to be the inextricable confusion of the last ten minutes has ceased. Fortunately every one has been found and every teamster is at his post. The clear notes of the trumpet sound in the front; the pilot and his guards mount their horses, the leading division of wagons moves out of the encampment and takes up the line of march, the rest fall into their places with the precision of clockwork, until the spot so lately full of life sinks back into that solitude that seems to reign over the broad plain and rushing river as the caravan draws its lazy length toward the distant El Dorado. It is with the hunters we will briskly canter toward the bold but smooth and grassy bluffs that bound the broad valley. We have been traveling briskly for more than an hour. . . .

We are full six miles away from the line of march. Though everything is dwarfed by distance, it is seen distinctly. The caravan has been about two hours in motion and is now extended as widely as is prudent. First near the bank of the shining river is a company of horsemen; they seem to have found an obstruction, for the main body has halted while three or four ride rapidly along the bank of the creek or slough. They are hunting a favorable crossing for the wagons; while we look they have succeeded; it has apparently required no work to make it passable, for all but one of the party have passed on, and he has raised a flag, no doubt a signal to the wagons to steer their course to where he stands. The leading teamster sees him though he is yet two miles off, and steers his course directly toward him, all the wagons following in his track. They (the wagons) form a line three quarters of a mile in length; some of the teamsters ride upon the front of their wagons, some walk beside their teams; scattered along the line companies of women and children are taking exercise on foot; they gather bouquets of rare and beautiful flowers that line the way; near them stalks a stately greyhound or an Irish wolf dog, apparently proud of keeping watch and ward over his master's wife and children.

Next comes a band of horses; two or three men or boys follow them, the docile and sagacious animals scarce needing this attention, for they have learned to follow in the rear of the wagons and know that at noon they will be allowed to graze and rest — their knowledge of time seems as accurate as of the place they are to occupy in the line, and even a full-bloom thistle will scarcely tempt them to straggle or halt until the dinner hour has arrived — not so with the large herd of horned beasts that bring up the rear; lazy, selfish, and unsocial, it has been a task to get them in motion, the strong always ready to domineer over the weak, halt in the front, and forbid the weaker to pass them. They seem to move only in fear of the driver's whip; though in the morning full to repletion, they have not been driven an hour before their hunger and thirst seem to indicate a fast of days' duration.

Through all the long day their greed is never sated nor their thirst quenched, nor is there a moment of relaxation of the tedious and vexatious labors of their drivers, although to all the others the march furnishes some season of relaxation or enjoyment. For the cow drivers there is none. But from the standpoint of the hunters the vexations are not apparent; the crack of the whips and loud objurgations are lost in the distance. Nothing of the moving panorama, smooth and orderly as it appears, has more attractions for the eye than that vast square column in which all colors are mingled, moving here slowly and there briskly, as impelled by horsemen riding furiously in front and rear.

But the picture, in its grandeur, its wonderful mingling of colors and distinctness of detail, is forgotten in contemplation of the singular people who give it life and animation. No other race of men with means at their command would undertake so great a journey — none save those could successfully perform it with no previous preparation, relying only on the fertility of their invention to devise the means to overcome each danger and difficulty as it arose. They have undertaken to perform, with slow-moving oxen, a journey of two thousand miles. The way lies over trackless wastes, wide and deep rivers, rugged and lofty mountains, and is beset with hostile savages. Yet, whether it were a deep river with no tree upon its bank, a rugged defile where even a loose horse could not pass, a hill too steep for him to climb, or a threatened attack of an enemy, they are always found ready and equal to the occasion, and always conquerors. May we not call them men of destiny? They are people changed in no essential particulars from their ancestors, who have followed closely on the footsteps of the receding savage from the Atlantic seaboard to the valley of the Mississippi.

The pilot, by measuring the ground and timing the speed of the wagons and the walk of his horse, has determined the rate of each, so as to enable him to select the nooning place as near as the requisite grass and water can be had at the end of five hours' travel of the wagons. Today, the ground being favorable, little time has been lost in preparing the road, so that he and his pioneers are at the nooning place an hour in advance of the wagons; which time is spent in preparing convenient watering places for the animals and digging little wells near the bank of the Platte. As the teams are not unyoked but simply turned loose from the wagons, a corral is not formed at noon, but the wagons are drawn up in columns, four abreast, the leading wagon of each platoon on the left — the platoon being formed with that in view. This brings friends together at noon as well as at night.

Today an extra session of the council is being held to settle a dispute that does not admit of delay, between a proprietor and a young man who has undertaken to do a man's service on the journey for board and bed. Many such engagements exist and much interest is taken in the manner this high court, from which there is no appeal, will define the right of each party in such engagements. The council was a high court in the most exalted sense. It was a senate composed of the ablest and most respected fathers of the emigration. It exercised both legislative and judicial powers, and its laws and decisions proved it equal and worthy of the high trust reposed in it. Its sessions were usually held on days when the caravan was not moving. It first took the state of the little commonwealth into consideration, revised or repealed rules defective or obsolete, and imposed such others as exigencies seemed to require. The commonwealth being cared for, it next resolved itself into a court to hear and settle private disputes and grievances. The offender and aggrieved appeared before it, witnesses were examined. The judges, thus being made fully acquainted with the case and being in no way influenced or cramped by technicalities, decided all cases according to their merits. There was but little use for lawyers before this court, for no plea was entertained which was calculated to defeat the ends of justice. Many of these judges have since won honors in higher spheres. They have aided to establish on the broad basis of right and universal liberty two of the pillars of our great republic in the Occident. Some of the young men who appeared before them as advocates have themselves sat upon the highest judicial tribunals, commanded armies, been governors of states, and taken high positions in the Senate of the nation.

It is now one o'clock; the bugle has sounded and the caravan has resumed its westward journey. It is in the same order, but the evening is far less animated than the morning march; a drowsiness has fallen apparently on man and beast; teamsters drop asleep on their perches and even walking by their teams, and the words of command are now addressed to the slowly creeping oxen in the softened tenor of women or the piping treble of children, while the snores of themselves make a droning accompaniment.

But a little incident breaks the monotony of the march. An emigrant's wife whose state of health has caused Doctor Whitman to travel near the wagon for the day, is now taken with violent illness; the doctor has had the wagon driven out of the line, a tent pitched, and a fire kindled. Many conjectures are hazarded in regard to this mysterious proceeding and as to why this last wagon is to be left behind.

And we must leave it, hasten to the front, and note the proceedings, for the sun is now getting low in the west and at length the painstaking pilot is standing ready to conduct the train in the circle which he has previously measured and marked out, which is to form the invariable fortification for the night. The leading wagons follow him so nearly round the circle that but a wagon length separates them. Each wagon follows in its track, the rear closing on the front, until its tongue and ox chains will perfectly reach from one to the other, and so accurate the measurement and perfect the practice, that the hindmost wagon of the train always precisely closes the gateway as each wagon is brought into position. It is dropped from its team (the teams being inside into position), the team unyoked, and the yokes and chains are used to connect the wagon strongly with that in its front. Within ten minutes from the time the leading wagon halted, the barricade is formed, the teams unyoked and driven out to pasture.

Everyone is busy preparing fires of buffalo chips to cook the evening meal, pitching tents, and otherwise preparing for the night. There are anxious watchers for the absent wagon, for there are many matrons who may be afflicted like its inmate before the journey is over; and they fear the strange and startling practice of the Oregon doctor will be dangerous. But as the sun goes down the absent wagon rolls into camp; the bright, speaking face and cheery look of the doctor, who rides in advance, declares without words that all is well and both mother and child are comfortable. I would fain now and here pay a passing tribute to that noble, devoted man, Doctor Whitman. I will obtrude no other name upon the reader, nor would I his, were he of our party or even living, but his stay with us was transient, though the good he did is permanent, and he has long since died at his post.

From the time he joined us on the Platte until he left us at Fort Hall his great experience and indomitable energy were of priceless value to the migrating column. His constant advice, which we knew was based upon a knowledge of the road before us, was: "Travel, travel, travel — nothing else will take you to the end of your journey; nothing is wise that does not help you along. Nothing is good for you that causes a moment's delay." He was a great authority as a physician, and complete success in the case above referred to saved us many prolonged and perhaps ruinous delays from similar causes, and it is no disparagement to others to say that to no other individual are the emigrants of 1843 so much indebted for the successful conclusion of their journey as to Doctor Mason Whitman.

All able to bear arms in the party have been formed into three companies, and each of these into four watches. Every third night it is the duty of one of these companies to keep watch and ward over the camp, and it is so arranged that each watch takes its turn of guard duty through the different watches of the night. Those forming the first watch tonight will be second not on duty, then third and fourth; which brings them through all the watches of the night. They begin at 8 P.M. and end at 4 A.M.

It is not eight o'clock when the first watch is to be set; the evening meal is just over, and the corral now free from the intrusion of the cattle or horses, groups of children are scattered over it. The larger are taking a game of romps; the wee toddling things are being taught that great achievement that distinguishes man from the lower animals. Before a tent near the river a violin makes lively music, and some youths and maidens have improvised a dance upon the green; in another quarter a flute gives its mellow and melancholy notes to the still air, which as they float away over the quiet river seem a lament for the past rather than a hope for the future. It has been a prosperous day; more than twenty miles have been accomplished of the great journey. The encampment is a good one; one of the causes that threatened much future delay has just been removed by the skill and energy of that good angel Doctor Whitman, and it has lifted a load from the hearts of the elders. Many of these are assembled around the good doctor at the tent of the pilot (which is his home for the time being) and are giving grave attention to his wise and energetic counsel. The careworn pilot sits aloof, quietly smoking his pipe, for he knows the brave doctor is strengthening his hands.

But time passes; the watch is set for the night; the council of old men has broken up, and each has turned to his own quarters. The flute has whispered its last lament to the deepening night; the violin is silent, and the dancers have dispersed. Enamored youths have whispered a tender good night in the ears of blushing maidens or stolen a kiss from the lips of some future bride — for Cupid here as elsewhere has been busy bringing together congenial hearts, and among those simple people he alone is consulted in forming the marriage tie. Even the doctor and the pilot have finished their confidential interview and have separated for the night. All are hushed and repose from the fatigue of the day save the vigilant guard and the wakeful leader, who still has cares upon his mind that forbid sleep.

He hears the ten-o'clock relief taking post and the "all's well" report of the returned guard; the night deepens; yet he seeks not the needed repose. At length a sentinel hurries to him with the welcome report that a party is approaching — as yet too far away for its character to be determined, and he instantly hurries out. This he does both from inclination and duty, for in times past the camp had been unnecessarily alarmed by timid or inexperienced sentinels causing much confusion and fright amongst women and children, and it had been made a rule that all extraordinary incidents of the night should be reported directly to the pilot, who alone had the authority to call out the military strength of the column or so much of it as was in his judgment necessary to prevent a stampede or repel an enemy.

Tonight he is at no loss to determine that the approaching party are our missing hunters and that they have met with success, and he only waits until by some further signal he can know that no ill has happened to them. This is not long wanting. He does not even await their arrival, but the last care of the day being removed and the last duty performed, he too seeks the rest that will enable him to go through the same routine tomorrow.

JESSE APPLEGATE, A Day with the Cow Column in 1843

117. John C. Frémont Conquers the Sierras in Midwinter

Probably the greatest of all the American-born explorers, John C. Frémont had one of the most romantic careers in the nation's history. After some initial training as an explorer in the country between the Mississippi and the Missouri, he led five great exploring expeditions into the wild west; he took a prominent part in the American conquest of California in 1846; he owned for a time the richest of American gold mines; he was Senator from California; the Republican Party nominated him as its first candidate for the Presidency; and he commanded two departments in the Civil War. One of the most striking of his feats was the passage of the high Sierras in midwinter, an exploit that would be full of peril even today.

FEBRUARY 4th, 1844. — I went ahead early with two or three men, each with a lead horse to break the road. We were obliged to abandon the hollow entirely and work along the mountainside, which was very steep, and the snow covered with an icy crust. We cut a footing as we advanced, and trampled a road through for the animals, but occasionally one plunged outside the trail and slid along the field to the bottom, a hundred yards below.

Toward a pass which the guide indicated here, we attempted in the afternoon to force a road, but after a laborious plunging through two or three hundred yards our best horses gave out, entirely refusing to make any further effort, and for the time we were brought to a stand. The guide informed us that we were entering the deep snow, and here began the difficulties of the mountain; and to him, and almost to all, our enterprise seemed hopeless.

Tonight we had no shelter, but we made a large fire around the trunk of one of the huge pines and, covering the snow with small boughs, on which we spread our blankets, soon made ourselves comfortable. The night was very bright and clear, though the thermometer was only at ten degrees. Strong wind, which sprang up at sundown, made it intensely cold, and this was one of the bitterest nights during the journey.

Two Indians joined our party here, and one of them, an old man, immediately began to harangue us, saying that ourselves and animals would perish in the snow, and that if we would go back, he would show us another and a better way across the mountain. He spoke in a very loud voice, and there was a singular repetition of phrases and arrangement of words, which rendered his speech striking and not unmusical.

We had now begun to understand some words and with the aid of signs easily comprehended the old man's simple ideas.

"Rock upon rock — rock upon rock — snow upon snow," said he; "even if you get over the snow, you will not be able to get down from the mountains." He made us the sign of precipices and showed us how the feet of the horses would slip and throw them off from the narrow trails that led along their sides. Our Chinook, who comprehended even more readily than ourselves and believed our situation hopeless, covered his head with his blanket and began to weep and lament. "I wanted to see the whites," said he; "I came away from my own people to see the whites, and I wouldn't care to die among them, but here" — and he looked around into the cold night and gloomy forest and, drawing his blanket over his head, began again to lament.

Seated around the tree, the fire illuminating the rocks and the tall bolls of the pines round about and the old Indian haranguing, we presented a group of very serious faces.

5th. — The night had been too cold to sleep, and we were up very early. Our guide was standing by the fire with all his finery on, and seeing him shiver in the cold, I threw on his shoulders one of my blankets. We missed him a few minutes afterwards and never saw him again. He had deserted. His bad faith and treachery were in perfect keeping with the estimate of Indian character which a long intercourse with this people had gradually forced upon my mind.

While a portion of the camp were occupied in bringing up the baggage to this point, the remainder were busy making sledges and snowshoes. I had determined to explore the mountain ahead, and the sledges were to be used in transporting the baggage.

6th. — Accompanied by Mr. Fitzpatrick, I set out today with a reconnoitering party on snowshoes. We marched all in single file, trampling the snow as heavily as we could. Crossing the open basin, in a march of about ten miles, we reached the top of one of the peaks to the left of the pass indicated by our guide. Far below us, dimmed by the distance, was a large snowless valley, bounded on the western side, at the distance of about a hundred miles, by a low range of mountains, which Carson recognized with delight as the mountains bordering the coast. "There," said he, "is the little mountain — it is fifteen years since I saw it; but I am just as sure as if I had seen it yesterday." Between us, then, and this low coast range, was the valley of the Sacramento, and no one who had not accompanied us through the incidents of our life for the last few months could realize the delight with which at last we looked down upon it.

All our energies are now directed to getting our animals across the snow, and it was supposed that after all the baggage had been drawn with the sleighs over the trail we had made, it would be sufficiently hard to bear our animals. At several points between this point and the ridge we had discovered some grassy spots where the wind and sun had dispersed the snow from the sides of the hills, and these were to form resting places to support the animals for a night in their passage across. On our way across we had set on fire several broken stumps and dried trees to melt holes in the snow for the camps. Its general depth was five feet, but we passed over places where it was twenty feet deep, as shown by the trees.

With one party drawing sleighs loaded with baggage, I advanced today about four miles along the trail and encamped at the first grassy spot, where we expected to bring our horses. Mr. Fitzpatrick, with another party, remained behind, to form an intermediate station between us and the animals.

9th. — During the night the weather changed, the wind rising to a gale, and commencing to snow before daylight; before morning the trail was covered. We remained quiet in camp all day, in the course of which the weather improved. Four sleighs arrived toward evening, with the bedding of the men. We suffer much from the want of salt, and all the men are becoming weak from insufficient food.

10th. — The elevation of the camp, by the boiling point, is 8050 feet. We are now 1000 feet above the level of the South Pass in the Rocky Mountains, and still we are not done ascending. The top of a flat ridge near was bare of snow and very well sprinkled with bunch grass, sufficient to pasture the animals two or three days, and this was to be their main support.

11th. — In the evening I received a message from Mr. Fitzpatrick, acquainting me with the utter failure of his attempt to get our mules and horses over the snow — the half-hidden trail had proved entirely too slight to support them, and they had broken through and were plunging about or lying half buried in the snow. He was occupied in endeavoring to get them back to his camp and in the meantime sent to me for further instructions. I wrote to him to send the animals immediately back to their old pastures and, after having made mauls and shovels, turn in all the strength of his party to open and beat a road through the snow, strengthening it with branches and boughs of the pines.

13th. — We continued to labor on the road, and in the course of the day had the satisfaction to see the people working down the face of the opposite hill, about three miles distant. During the morning we had the pleasure of a visit from Mr. Fitzpatrick, with the information that all was going on well. A party of Indians had passed on snowshoes, who said they were going to the western side of the mountain after fish. This was an indication that the salmon were coming up the streams, and we could hardly restrain our impatience as we thought of them, and worked with increased vigor.

The meat train did not arrive this evening, and I gave Godey leave to kill our little dog (Tlamath), which he prepared in Indian fashion, scorching off the hair and washing the skin with soap and snow, and then cutting it up into pieces, which were laid on the snow. Shortly afterward the sleigh arrived with a supply of horse meat, and we had tonight an extraordinary dinner — pea soup, mule, and dog.

16th. — We had succeeded in getting our animals safely to the first grassy hill, and this morning I started with Jacob on a reconnoitering expedition beyond the mountain. We traveled along the crests of narrow ridges extending down from the mountain in the direction of the valley from which the snow was fast melting away. On the open spots was tolerably good grass, and I judged we should succeed in getting the camp down by way of these. Toward sundown we discovered some icy spots in a deep hollow and, descending the mountain, we encamped on the headwater of a little creek, where at last the water found its way to the Pacific.

The night was clear and very long. We heard the cries of some wild animals which had been attracted by our fire, and a flock of geese passed over during the night. Even these strange sounds had something pleasant to our senses in this region of silence and desolation.

We started again early in the morning. The creek acquired a regular breadth of about twenty feet, and we soon began to hear the rushing of water below the icy surface over which we traveled to avoid the snow; a few miles below we broke through where the water was several feet deep, and halted to make a fire and dry our clothes. We continued a few miles farther, walking being very laborious without snowshoes.

I was now perfectly satisfied that we had struck the stream on which Mr. Sutter lived, and turning about, made a hard push and reached the camp at dark. Here we had the pleasure to find all the remaining animals, fifty-seven in number, safely arrived at the grassy hill near the camp. . . .

On the 19th the people were occupied in making a road and bringing up the baggage; and on the afternoon of the next day, February 20, 1844, we encamped with the animals and all the *matériel* of the camp on the summit of the Pass in the dividing ridge, 1000 miles by our traveled road from the Dalles to the Columbia.

J. C. FRÉMONT, The Exploring Expedition to the Rocky Mountains

118. Starvation and Death at Donner Lake

About five hundred American settlers entered California in 1846, the year that Frémont, Stockton, and Kearny conquered it for the United States. But one party which had set out for the Pacific Coast never reached its goal. This party originated in a group formed at Springfield, Illinois, by George and Jacob Donner and James F. Reed. They were delayed in transit, and did not reach the Sierras until snow was falling and winter was coming on. The deep drifts stopped them at Truckee Lake (since called Donner Lake), their food gave out, and, as members died, some of the survivors turned to cannibalism. Of the original force of eighty-seven, only forty-eight reached California alive.

SNOW was already falling, although it was only the last week in October [1846]. Winter had set in a month earlier than usual. All trails and roads were covered, and our only guide was the summit which it seemed we would never reach. Despair drove many nearly frantic. Each family tried to cross the mountains but found it impossible. When it was seen that the wagons could not be dragged through the snow, their goods and provisions were packed on oxen and another start was made, men and women walking in snow up to their waists, carrying their children in their arms and trying to drive their cattle. The Indians said they could find no road; so a halt was called, and Stanton went ahead with the guides and came back and reported that we could get across if we kept right on, but that it would be impossible if snow fell. He was in favor of a forced march until the other side of the summit should be reached, but some of our party were so tired and exhausted with the day's labor that they declared they could not take another step; so the few who knew the danger that the night might bring yielded to the many, and we camped within three miles of the summit.

That night came the dreaded snow. Around the campfires under the trees great feathery flakes came whirling down. The air was so full of them that one could see objects only a few feet away. The Indians knew we were doomed, and one of them wrapped his blanket about him and stood all night under a tree. We children slept soundly on our cold bed of snow with a soft white mantle falling over us so thickly that every few moments my mother would have to shake the shawl — our only covering — to keep us from being buried alive. In the morning the snow lay deep on mountain and valley. With heavy hearts we turned back to a cabin that had been built by the Murphy-Schallenberger party two years before. We built more cabins and prepared as best we could for the winter. That camp, which proved the camp of death to many in our company, was made on the shore of a lake, since known as Donner Lake. The Donners were camped in Alder Creek Valley below the lake, and were, if possible, in a worse condition than ourselves. The snow came on so suddenly that they had no time to build cabins, but hastily put up brush sheds, covering them with pine boughs.

Three double cabins were built at Donner Lake, which were known as the Breen Cabin, the Murphy Cabin, and the Reed-Graves Cabin. The cattle were all killed, and the meat was placed in snow for preservation. My mother had no cattle to kill, but she made arrangements for some, promising to give two for one in California. Stanton and the Indians made their home in my mother's cabin.

Many attempts were made to cross the mountains, but all who tried were driven back by the pitiless storms. Finally a party was organized, since known as the Forlorn Hope. They made snow-shoes, and fifteen started — ten men and five women — but only seven lived to reach California; eight men perished. They were over a month on the way, and the horrors endured by that Forlorn Hope no pen can describe nor imagination conceive. The noble Stanton was one of the party, and perished the sixth day out, thus sacrificing his life for strangers. I can find no words in which to express a fitting tribute to the memory of Stanton.

The misery endured during those four months at Donner Lake in our little dark cabins under the snow would fill pages and make the coldest heart ache. Christmas was near, but to the starving its memory gave no comfort. It came and passed without observance, but my mother had determined weeks before that her children should have a treat on this one day. She had laid away a few dried apples, some beans, a bit of tripe, and a small piece of bacon. When this hoarded store was brought out, the delight of the little ones knew no bounds. The cooking was watched carefully, and when we sat down to our Christmas dinner, Mother said, "Children, eat slowly, for this one day you can have all you wish." So bitter was the misery relieved by that one bright day that I have never since sat down to a Christmas dinner without my thoughts going back to Donner Lake.

The storms would often last ten days at a time, and we would have to cut chips from the logs inside which formed our cabins in order to start a fire. We could scarcely walk, and the men had hardly strength to procure wood. We would drag ourselves through the snow from one cabin to another, and some mornings snow would have to be shoveled out of the fireplace before a fire could be made. Poor little children were crying with hunger, and mothers were crying because they had so little to give their children. We seldom thought of bread, we had been without it so long. Four months of such suffering would fill the bravest hearts with despair. . . .

Time dragged slowly along till we were no longer on short allowance but were simply starving. My mother determined to make an effort to cross the mountains. She could not see her children die without trying to get them food. It was hard to leave them, but she felt that it must be done. She told them she would bring them bread, so they were willing to stay, and with no guide but a compass we started — my mother, Eliza, Milt Elliott, and myself. Milt wore snowshoes, and we followed in his tracks. We were five days in the mountains; Eliza gave out the first day and had to return, but we kept on and climbed one high mountain after another only to see others higher still ahead. Often I would have to crawl up the mountains, being too tired to walk. The nights were made hideous by the screams of wild beasts heard in the distance. Again, we would be lulled to sleep by the moan of the pine trees, which seemed to sympathize with our loneliness. One morning we awoke to find ourselves in a well of snow. During the night, while in the deep sleep of exhaustion, the heat of the fire had melted the snow and our little camp had gradually sunk many feet below the surface until we were literally buried in a well of snow. The danger was that any attempt to get out might bring an avalanche upon us, but finally steps were carefully made and we reached the surface. My foot was badly frozen, so we were compelled to return, and just in time, for that night a storm came on, the most fearful of the winter, and we should have perished had we not been in the cabins.

We now had nothing to eat but raw hides, and they were on the roof of the cabin to keep out the snow; when prepared for cooking and boiled they were simply a pot of glue. When the hides were taken off our cabin and we were left without shelter, Mr. Breen gave us a home with his family, and Mrs. Breen prolonged my life by slipping me little bits of meat now and then when she discovered that I could not eat the hide. Death had already claimed many in our party, and it seemed as though relief never would reach us. Baylis Williams, who had been in delicate health before we left Springfield, was the first to die; he passed away before starvation had really set in. . . .

On his arrival at Sutter's Fort my father made known the situation of the emigrants, and Captain Sutter offered at once to do everything possible for their relief. He furnished horses and provisions, and my father and Mr. McClutchen started for the mountains, coming as far as possible with horses and then with packs on their backs proceeding on foot; but they were finally compelled to return. Captain Sutter was not surprised at their defeat. He stated that there were no able-bodied men in that vicinity, all having gone down the country with Frémont to fight the Mexicans. He advised my father to go to Yerba Buena, now San Francisco, and make his case known to the naval officer in command. My father was in fact conducting parties there — when the seven members of the Forlorn Hope arrived from across the mountains. Their famished faces told the story. Cattle were killed and men were up all night, drying beef and making flour by hand mills, nearly two hundred pounds being made in one night, and a party of seven, commanded by Captain Reasen P. Tucker, were sent to our relief by Captain Sutter and the alcalde, Mr. Sinclair. On the evening of February 19, 1847, they reached our cabins, where all were starving. They shouted to attract attention. Mr. Breen clambered up the icy steps from our cabin, and soon we heard the blessed words, "Relief, thank God, relief!" There was joy at Donner Lake that night, for we did not know the fate of the Forlorn Hope; and we were told that relief parties would come and go until all were across the mountains. But with the joy sorrow was strangely blended. There were tears in other eyes than those of children; strong men sat down and wept. For the dead were lying about on the snow, some even unburied, since the living had not had strength to bury their dead. When Milt Elliott died — our faithful friend who seemed so like a brother — my mother and I dragged him up out of the cabin and covered him with snow. Commencing at his feet, I patted the pure white snow down softly until I reached his face. Poor Milt! it was hard to cover that face from sight forever, for with his death our best friend was gone.

On the 22d of February the first relief started with a party of twenty-three — men, women, and children. My mother and her family were among the number. It was a bright, sunny morning, and we felt happy; but we had not gone far when Patty and Tommy gave out. They were not able to stand the fatigue, and it was not thought safe to allow them to proceed; so Mr. Glover informed Mama that they would have to be sent back to the cabins to await the next expedition. What language can express our feelings? My mother said that she would go back with her children — that we would all go back together. This the relief party would not permit, and Mr. Glover promised Mama that as soon as they reached Bear Valley he himself would return for her children. . . . Mr. Glover returned with the children and, providing them with food, left them in the care of Mr. Breen.

With sorrowful hearts we traveled on, walking through the snow in single file. The men wearing snowshoes broke the way, and we followed in their tracks. At night we lay down on the snow to sleep, to awake to find our clothing all frozen, even to our shoestrings. At break of day we were again on the road, owing to the fact that we could make better time over the frozen snow. The sunshine, which it would seem would have been welcome, only added to our misery. The dazzling reflection of the snow was very trying to the eyes, while its heat melted our frozen clothing, making [it] cling to our bodies. My brother was too small to step in the tracks made by the men, and in order to travel he had to place his knee on the little hill of snow after each step and climb over. Mother coaxed him along, telling him that every step he took he was getting nearer Papa and nearer something to eat. He was the youngest child that walked over the Sierra Nevada. On our second day's journey John Denton gave out and declared it would be impossible for him to travel, but he begged his companions to continue their journey. A fire was built and he was left lying on a bed of freshly-cut pine boughs, peacefully smoking. He looked so comfortable that my little brother wanted to stay with him, but when the second relief party reached him, poor Denton was past waking. His last thoughts seemed to have gone back to his childhood's home, as a little poem was found by his side, the pencil apparently just dropped from his hand.

Captain Tucker's party on their way to the cabins had lightened their packs of a sufficient quantity of provisions to supply the sufferers on their way out. But when we reached the place where the cache had been made by hanging the food on a tree, we were horrified to find that wild animals had destroyed it; and again starvation stared us in the face. But my father was hurrying over the mountains and met us in our hour of need with his hands full of bread. He had expected to meet us on this day and had stayed up all night, baking bread to give us. He brought with him fourteen men. Some of his party were ahead, and when they saw us coming they called out: "Is Mrs. Reed with you? If she is, tell her Mr. Reed is here." We heard the call; Mother knelt on the snow, while I tried to run to meet Papa.

When my father learned that two of his children were still at the cabins, he hurried on, so fearful was he that they might perish before he reached them. He seemed to fly over the snow, and made in two days the distance we had been five in traveling, and was overjoyed to find Patty and Tommy alive. He reached Donner Lake on the 1st of March, and what a sight met his gaze! The famished little children and the deathlike look of all made his heart ache. He filled Patty's apron with biscuits which she carried around, giving one to each person. He had soup made for the infirm and rendered every assistance possible to the sufferers. Leaving them with about seven days' provisions, he started out with a party of seventeen, all that were able to travel. Three of his men were left at the cabins to procure wood and assist the helpless. My father's party (the second relief) had not traveled many miles when a storm broke upon them. With the snow came a perfect hurricane. The crying of half-frozen children, the lamenting of the mothers, and the suffering of the whole party was heart-rending; and above all could be heard the shrieking of the storm king. One who has never witnessed a blizzard in the Sierra can form no idea of the situation. All night my father and his men worked unceasingly through the raging storm, trying to erect shelter for the dying women and children. At times the hurricane would burst forth with such violence that he felt alarmed on account of the tall timber surrounding the camp. The party were destitute of food, all supplies that could be spared having been left with those at the cabins. The relief party had cached provisions on their way over to the cabins, and my father had sent three of the men forward for food before the storm set in, but they could not return. Thus, again, death stared all in the face. At one time the fire was nearly gone; had it been lost, all would have perished. Three days and nights they were exposed to the fury of the elements. Finally my father became snow-blind and could do no more, and he would have died but for the exertions of William McClutchen and Hiram Miller, who worked over him all night. From this time forward the toil and responsibility rested upon McClutchen and Miller.

The storm at last ceased, and these two determined to set out over the snow and send back relief to those not able to travel. Hiram Miller picked up Tommy and started. Patty thought she could walk, but gradually everything faded from her sight, and she too seemed to be dying. All other sufferings were now forgotten, and everything was done to revive the child. My father found some crumbs in the thumb of his woolen mitten; warming and moistening them between his own lips, he gave them to her and thus saved her life, and afterward she was carried along by different ones in the company. Patty was not alone in her travels. Hidden away in her bosom was a tiny doll which she had carried day and night through all of our trials. Sitting before a nice, bright fire at Woodworth's Camp, she took dolly out to have a talk, and told her of all her new happiness.

VIRGINIA REED MURPHY, Across the Plains in the Donner Party

119. A Frenchman Interviews Brigham Young

In 1847 the Mormons, who had been driven out of Nauvoo, Illinois, set forth from what is now Council Bluffs to found a new community in the Far West. Their leaders had read Frémont's reports, and had concluded that their best home would be found in the valley of the Great Salt Lake. By winter of that year a colony of some 2,800 people had been planted in or near Salt Lake City; and in 1848 a great new concourse joined them. Under the statesmanlike guidance of Brigham Young, the Mormons shortly built up a flourishing new city, which drew curious visitors from all parts of Europe and America.

BRIGHAM YOUNG is the supreme president of the Church of Latter-Day Saints throughout the world. He is the Mormon pope; he is at the same time, by election of the people, a prophet, "revelator," and seer; and still more, he was, at the time of our journey, governor of the Territory of Utah, and recognized in that capacity by the President of the United States. He is a man of fifty-four years of age [1855], fair, of moderate height, stout almost to obesity. He has regular features, a wide forehead, eyes which convey an idea of finesse, and a smiling expression of mouth. His general appearance is that of an honest farmer, and nothing in his manners indicates a man of the higher classes. Of superior intellect, though uneducated, Brigham Young has given proofs of remarkable talent and profound ability, in combining the heterogeneous elements of which his people are made up. . . . As president of the Church, Brigham Young unites in his own hands more power than any potentate in the world. He is the autocrat of thought and action, the omnipotent soul of this rising body already so considerable, but which is looked upon by the Americans merely in the light of a phantom evoked by evil passions which they hope to lay.

To this personage we were about to pay a visit in our miner's costume. We found him in his official cabinet, dictating instructions to his secretaries, and at the same time preparing a quid of Virginia tobacco. He occupied an armchair, in which he rather squatted than sat. On his head he wore a broad-brimmed, fawn-colored felt hat. His coat, of greenish cloth, was of the cut which was called formerly *à la Française,* but of inordinate amplitude. His stockings, visible below his trousers, were clean and white, and his linen tolerably fair. He continued dictating for half an hour, without appearing to take the least notice of our presence. Then, as soon as he had finished, he exchanged a few words with an Indian who had kissed his hand when he entered. Mr. Haws now presented us to his Excellency. Brigham Young shook hands with us, and then retired into an adjoining apartment, from which he returned in about two minutes with a plug of tobacco which he gave to the Indian. He then asked us to take a seat and sat down himself without taking off his hat. Either on account of our introducer or on account of our rough costume, which was by no means adapted to create a favorable impression, he did not appear to pay attention to us and did not condescend to favor us with a word.

We learned afterward that we were looked upon as persons of bad character, sent by the Gentiles to assassinate the leader of the Mormons. . . .

Brigham Young, who much regretted his mistake, excused himself by saying that he distrusted strangers presented to him by persons who scarcely knew them, which was the case with Haws in respect to us. He begged us to return to his house, at the same time expressing his regret in being unable to visit us at Judge Kinney's, and to convince us that he was really sorry, sent us a present of nearly all the works which had been written and published by the Mormons, handsomely bound.

From this moment we were at ease. We were made much of everywhere; we were called Brother Brenchley, Brother Rémy. This tickled us so mightily that we thought it good fun not to undeceive them. Some talked of making us apostles on the first vacancy, or at least bishops; others gave out that we were going to finish the temple with our own good money. Every one spoke of giving us parties; we were invited to dinner and to tea without end. Once the church musicians came and gave us a serenade; a Sicilian named Ballo conducted the orchestra. They played us "La Marseillaise," "God Save the Queen," "Yankee Doodle," "Hail Columbia," sacred pieces from Méhul and Mozart, and bits from the operas of Meyerbeer and Rossini. The music, we should observe to the credit of the Mormons, was very good, and better than what one meets with in most provincial towns in Europe. A ball, too, was given us, at which every gentleman danced with two ladies at once, an ingenious innovation, and not the only one with which Mormonism aspires to endow society with a view to its reformation. All the kindness which was showered upon us was certainly sincere, but at the same time we could not avoid seeing in it a bait by which they sought to catch us poor fish, led astray by a longing after the unknown into the waters of these new fishers of men.

A reception equally flattering was given us by the *Gentiles*. The Mormons give this appellation to all those who do not share their faith, whatever may be their creeds — Catholics, Protestants, Mohammedans, Buddhists, or pagans. The number of gentiles was not very considerable in Utah at the period of our journey; it could not exceed a hundred, which is certainly very few for a population of sixty thousand souls, including the twelve thousand residing in the capital, spread over the surface of the Mormon territory. In this handful of gentiles were merchants, doctors, federal officers, and some vagabonds, coming no one knew whence, living no one knew how, mostly at the expense of travelers and the Mormons themselves. During our sojourn at the Salt Lake we were robbed twice, and each time it was found to be by the gentiles. This fact has a very great importance in our eyes, because it authorizes an impartial mind to believe that very often persons have laid to the charge of the Mormons crimes committed by the intruders who have crept among them. Nevertheless, the Saints acknowledge, with a candor which does them honor, that among their brethren there have been found some unworthy of that appellation, who have on several occasions stolen the cattle of emigrants. This, however, is not owing to the lack of very severe laws; for, independently of those which are contained in the criminal code of Utah, Brigham Young advises his people — and we have heard it with our own ears — to kill without trial all thieves caught in the fact. It will be perceived that there is a clear incompatibility between this excessive severity and communism, which the Mormons have been accused of practising. Nothing in their organization or in their customs approaches to the latter, as will be found further on in the exposition of their doctrine. If there is seen in their remote establishments a sort of transient association, it is due to the necessity which is imposed on them by the Indians, of living under the shelter of the same walls, under pain of being easily surprised and plundered. But property always remains rigidly personal, and every one receives the fruit of his labor. It would be a great mistake to find evidence of communism in the barter to which they are obliged to have recourse when money is deficient or becomes very scarce. This barter is effected in a very simple manner, under the control of a municipal regulation which determines every season the value in money, whether by weight or by measure, of all their commodities. Thus, during the famine of 1855–1856, a pound of butter, which was valued at a dollar, was given in exchange for a pound of tea, which was worth the same money.

It is even our duty to avow that they have qualities and virtues which recommend them in more ways than one. They are industrious, honest, sober, pious, and it is just to say, since we believe it to be the case, even chaste in their polygamic relations.

The valuable qualities we have just enumerated will assist us in understanding how it is the Mormons generally enjoy robust health, notwithstanding the privations to which they have to a certain extent been periodically exposed. One sees but few sick in Utah, so that the want of medical men is little felt. It is, moreover, one of the peculiarities of the Mormon Church to discourage the practice of medicine and to compel all medical men who embrace the faith to select another career, unless they choose to live on the mustard and senna of their own surgeries. An invalid who has recourse to medicine would be suspected of verging on infidelity, and a new baptism alone could efface the pollution. Brother Brigham menaces with celestial wrath those weak enough to employ, in the treatment of diseases, other remedies than olive oil and the herbs of the fields. The power of performing miraculous cures is possessed by the faithful generally, though more especially by those who have received some degree of ordination. We were told of numerous remarkable cures having been effected by the use of oil and prayer, and although we were unable to verify a single instance of the kind, we are disposed to believe the testimony of credible and disinterested persons on the subject. Under the mysterious influence of an energetic faith, imagination may work miracles, even among pagans. Brigham Young told us one day, speaking of medicine, that doctors often wrote to him from California and the Eastern states to know if there was any chance of establishing a practice in Utah, announcing that in case there might be, they would have no objection to becoming converts to Mormonism. The Mormon pope, who now despises such impertinence too much to notice it, used at first to reply that his religion did not seek to purchase adherents.

JULES RÉMY, A Journey to Great-Salt-Lake City

120. The Pony Express

The most famous mail route in American history, the Pony Express, was planned by William M. Gwin, Senator from California. Beginning in 1854 he unsuccessfully tried to induce Congress to provide for a line of fast mail riders across the plains to California. When the Government refused to risk the venture, the firm of Russell, Majors and Waddell undertook it. The first runs were made between St. Joseph, Missouri, and Sacramento, in April, 1860. At the height of its fame, the Pony

Express used 420 horses, 400 station men and helpers, and 125 riders. It was natural for Mark Twain, going West in 1861 to Carson City, where his brother was secretary to the Territorial Governor of Nevada, to study this famous system with keen interest. Each rider spanned from 75 to 125 miles, changing horses at relay stations scattered 10 or 15 miles apart.

IN A little while all interest was taken up in stretching our necks and watching for the "pony rider" — the fleet messenger who sped across the continent from St. Joe to Sacramento, carrying letters nineteen hundred miles in eight days [1860]! Think of that for perishable horse and human flesh and blood to do! The pony rider was usually a little bit of a man, brimful of spirit and endurance. No matter what time of the day or night his watch came on and no matter whether it was winter or summer, raining, snowing, hailing, or sleeting, or whether his beat was a level straight road or a crazy trail over mountain crags and precipices, or whether it led through peaceful regions or regions that swarmed with hostile Indians, he must be always ready to leap into the saddle and be off like the wind! There was no idling time for a pony rider on duty. He rode fifty miles without stopping, by daylight, moonlight, starlight, or through the blackness of darkness — just as it happened. He rode a splendid horse that was born for a racer and fed and lodged like a gentleman; kept him at his utmost speed for ten miles, and then, as he came crashing up to the station where stood two men holding fast a fresh, impatient steed, the transfer of rider and mailbag was made in the twinkling of an eye, and away flew the eager pair and were out of sight before the spectator could get hardly the ghost of a look. Both rider and horse went "flying light." The rider's dress was thin and fitted close; he wore a roundabout and a skullcap and tucked his pantaloons into his boot tops like a race rider. He carried no arms — he carried nothing that was not absolutely necessary, for even the postage on his literary freight was worth *five dollars a letter*. He got but little frivolous correspondence to carry — his bag had business letters in it mostly. His horse was stripped of all unnecessary weight too. He wore light shoes or none at all. The little flat mail pockets strapped under the rider's thighs would each hold about the bulk of a child's primer. They held many and many an important business chapter and newspaper letter, but these were written on paper as airy and thin as gold leaf, nearly, and thus bulk and weight were economized. The stagecoach traveled about a hundred to a hundred and twenty-five miles a day (twenty-four hours), the pony rider about two hundred and fifty. There were about eighty pony riders in the saddle all the time, night and day, stretching in a long, scattering procession from Missouri to California, forty flying eastward and forty toward the west, and among them making four hundred gallant horses earn a stirring livelihood and see a deal of scenery every single day in the year.

We had had a consuming desire, from the beginning, to see a pony rider, but somehow or other all that passed us and all that met us managed to streak by in the night, and so we heard only a whiz and a hail, and the swift phantom of the desert was gone before we could get our heads out of the windows. But now we were expecting one along every moment and would see him in broad daylight. Presently the driver exclaims:

"Here he comes!"

Every neck is stretched farther and every eye strained wider. Away across the endless dead level of the prairie a black speck appears against the sky, and it is plain that it moves. Well, I should think so! In a second or two it becomes a horse and rider, rising and falling, rising and falling — sweeping toward us nearer and nearer — growing more and more distinct, more and more sharply defined — nearer and still nearer, and the flutter of the hoofs comes faintly to the ear — another instant a whoop and a hurrah from our upper deck, a wave of the rider's hand, but no reply, and man and horse burst past our excited faces and go swinging away like a belated fragment of a storm!

So sudden is it all and so like a flash of unreal fancy that, but for the flake of white foam left quivering and perishing on a mail sack after the vision had flashed by and disappeared, we might have doubted whether we had seen any actual horse and man at all, maybe.

MARK TWAIN, Roughing It

XX

The Mining Kingdom

121. James Marshall Discovers Gold in California

James W. Marshall, a wheelwright and farmer, arrived at Sutter's Fort in California with an emigrant train in 1845; he fought the next year in Frémont's California Battalion; and when mustered out of service in 1847, he returned north and went into partnership with Sutter for the construction of a sawmill near the fort. It was while deepening the tailrace that he made the great discovery here recorded. Like Sutter himself, Marshall spent his last years in poverty.

IN MAY, 1847, with my rifle, blanket, and a few crackers to eat with the venison (for the deer then were awful plenty) I ascended the American River, according to Mr. Sutter's wish, as he wanted to find a good site for a sawmill, where we could have plenty of timber and where wagons would be able to ascend and descend the river hills. Many fellows had been out before me, but they could not find any place to suit; so when I left I told Mr. Sutter I would go along the river to the very head and find the place, if such a place existed anywhere upon the river or any of its forks. I traveled along the river the whole way. Many places would suit very well for the erection of the mill, with plenty of timber everywhere, but then nothing but a mule could climb the hills; and when I would find a spot where the hills were not steep, there was no timber to be had; and so it was until I had been out several days and reached this place, which, at first sight, looked like the exact spot we were hunting.

I passed a couple of days examining the hills and found a place where wagons could ascend and descend with all ease. On my return to the fort I went out through the country examining the canyons and gulches and picking out the easiest places for crossing them with loaded wagons.

You may be sure Mr. Sutter was pleased when I reported my success. We entered into partnership; I was to build the mill, and he was to find provisions, teams, tools, and to pay a portion of the men's wages. I believe I was at the time the only millwright in the whole country. In August, everything being ready, we freighted two wagons with tools and provisions, and accompanied by six men I left the fort, and after a good deal of difficulty reached this place one beautiful afternoon and formed our camp.

Our first business was to put up log houses, as we intended remaining here all winter. This was done in less than no time, for my men were great with the ax. We then cut timber and fell to work hewing it for the framework of the mill. The Indians gathered about us in great numbers. I employed about forty of them to assist us with the dam, which we put up in a kind of way in about four weeks. In digging the foundation of the mill we cut some distance into the soft granite. We opened the forebay, and then I left for the fort, giving orders to Mr. Weimar to have a ditch cut through the bar in the rear of the mill, and after quitting work in the evening to raise the gate and let the water run all night, as it would assist us very much in deepening and widening the millrace.

I returned in a few days and found everything favorable, all the men being at work in the ditch. When the channel was opened it was my custom every evening to raise the gate and let the water wash out as much sand and gravel through the night as possible; and in the morning, while the men were getting breakfast, I would walk down and, shutting off the water, look along the race and see what was to be done, so that I might tell Mr. Weimar, who had charge of the Indians, at what particular point to set them to work for the day. As I was the only millwright present, all my time was employed upon the framework and machinery.

One morning in January [1848] — it was a clear cold morning; I shall never forget that morning — as I was taking my usual walk along the race, after shutting off the water my eye was caught by a glimpse of something shining in the bottom of the ditch. There

was about a foot of water running there. I reached my hand down
and picked it up; it made my heart thump, for I felt certain it was
gold. The piece was about half the size and of the shape of a pea.
Then I saw another piece in the water. After taking it out I sat
down and began to think right hard. I thought it was gold, and yet
it did not seem to be of the right color; all the gold coin I had seen
was of a reddish tinge; this looked more like brass. I recalled to
mind all the metals I had ever seen or heard of, but I could find
none that resembled this. Suddenly the idea flashed across my mind
that it might be iron pyrites. I trembled to think of it! This question
could soon be determined. Putting one of the pieces on hard river
stone, I took another and commenced hammering it. It was soft and
didn't break; it therefore must be gold, but largely mixed with some
other metal, very likely silver; for pure gold, I thought, would certainly have a brighter color.

When I returned to our cabin for breakfast I showed the two
pieces to my men. They were all a good deal excited, and had they
not thought that the gold only existed in small quantities they would
have abandoned everything and left me to finish the job alone.
However, to satisfy them, I told them that as soon as we had the
mill finished we would devote a week or two to gold hunting and
see what we could make out of it.

While we were working in the race after this discovery, we always
kept a sharp lookout, and in the course of three or four days we had
picked up about three ounces — our work still progressing as lively
as ever, for none of us imagined at that time that the whole country
was sowed with gold.

In about a week's time after the discovery I had to take another
trip to the fort, and to gain what information I could respecting the
real value of the metal, took all we had collected with me and
showed it to Mr. Sutter, who at once declared it was gold but
thought, with me, it was greatly mixed with some other metal. It
puzzled us a great deal to hit upon the means of telling the exact
quantity contained in the alloy; however, we at last stumbled on an
old American cyclopedia where we saw the specific gravity of all
the metals, and rules given to find the quantity of each in a given
bulk. After hunting over the whole fort and borrowing from some
of the men, we got three dollars and a half in silver, and with a

small pair of scales we soon ciphered it out that there was no silver nor copper in the gold, but that it was entirely pure.

This fact being ascertained, we thought it our best policy to keep it as quiet as possible till we should have finished our mill, but there was a great number of disbanded Mormon soldiers in and about the fort, and when they came to hear of it, why, it just spread like wildfire, and soon the whole country was in a bustle. I had scarcely arrived at the mill again till several persons appeared with pans, shovels, and hoes, and those that had not iron picks had wooden ones, all anxious to fall to work and dig up our mill; but this we would not permit. As fast as one party disappeared another would arrive, and sometimes I had the greatest kind of trouble to get rid of them. I sent them all off in different directions, telling them about such and such places where I was certain there was plenty of gold if they would only take the trouble of looking for it. At that time I never imagined the gold was so abundant. I told them to go to such and such places, because it appeared that they would dig nowhere but in such places as I pointed out; and I believe such was their confidence in me that they would have dug on the very top of [the] mountain if I had told them to do so. . . .

The second place where gold was discovered was in a gulch near the Mountaineer House on the road to Sacramento. The third place was on a bar on the South Fork of the American River a little above the junction of the Middle and South Forks. The diggings at Hangtown [now Placerville] were discovered next by myself, for we all went out for a while as soon as our job was finished. The Indians next discovered the diggings at Kelsey's, and thus in a very short time we discovered that the whole country was but one bed of gold. So there, stranger, is the entire history of the gold discovery in California — a discovery that hasn't as yet been of much benefit to me.

James Marshall's Account of the Discovery of Gold

122. The Gold Fever Reaches Monterey

When the Americans took possession of California, the chaplain of one of the warships on the coast, the Congress was appointed chief judge ("alcalde") of the former capital, Monterey. This was Walter Colton, a Vermonter by birth and a graduate of Yale. Continued in his office by popular vote, he established the first newspaper in California, and built the first school. He was a man of refinement and brains, who had been teacher and editor as well as clergyman, and he left his impress on California society when he returned East in 1849. His book on his three years' experiences on the Pacific Coast is one of the most vivid of the early records of that region.

MONDAY, May 29 [1848].—Our town [Monterey] was startled out of its quiet dreams today by the announcement that gold had been discovered on the American Fork. Then men wondered and talked, and the women too; but neither believed. . . .

Monday, June 5.—Another report reached us this morning from the American Fork. The rumor ran that several workmen, while excavating for a millrace, had thrown up little shining scales of a yellow ore that proved to be gold; that an old Sonorarian who had spent his life in gold mines pronounced it the genuine thing. Still the public incredulity remained, save here and there a glimmer of faith, like the flash of a firefly at night.

Tuesday, June 6.—I determined to put an end to the suspense and dispatched a messenger this morning to the American Fork. He will have to ride, going and returning, some four hundred miles, but his report will be reliable. We shall then know whether this gold is a fact or a fiction—a tangible reality on the earth or a fanciful treasure at the base of some rainbow, retreating over hill and waterfall, to lure pursuit and disappoint hope.

Monday, June 12. — A straggler came in today from the American Fork, bringing a piece of yellow ore weighing an ounce. The young dashed the dirt from their eyes, and the old from their spectacles. One brought a spyglass, another an iron ladle; some wanted to melt it, others to hammer it, and a few were satisfied with smelling it. All were full of tests, and many who could not be gratified in making their experiments declared it a humbug. One lady sent me a huge gold ring in the hope of reaching the truth by comparison, while a gentleman placed the specimen on the top of his gold-headed cane and held it up, challenging the sharpest eyes to detect a difference. But doubts still hovered on the minds of the great mass. They could not conceive that such a treasure could have lain there so long undiscovered. The idea seemed to convict them of stupidity.

Tuesday, June 20. — My messenger, sent to the mines, has returned with specimens of the gold; he dismounted in a sea of upturned faces. As he drew forth the yellow lumps from his pockets and passed them around among the eager crowd, the doubts, which had lingered till now, fled. All admitted they were gold except one old man who still persisted they were some Yankee invention, got up to reconcile the people to the change of flag. The excitement produced was intense, and many were soon busy in their hasty preparations for a departure to the mines. The family who had kept house for me caught the moving infection. Husband and wife were both packing up; the blacksmith dropped his hammer, the carpenter his plane, the mason his trowel, the farmer his sickle, the baker his loaf, and the tapster his bottle. All were off for the mines, some on horses, some on carts, and some on crutches; and one went in a litter. An American woman who had recently established a boardinghouse here pulled up stakes and was off before her lodgers had even time to pay their bills. Debtors ran, of course. I have only a community of women left and a gang of prisoners, with here and there a soldier who will give his captain the slip at the first chance. I don't blame the fellow a whit; seven dollars a month, while others are making two or three hundred a day! That is too much for human nature to stand.

Saturday, July 15. — The gold fever has reached every servant in Monterey; none are to be trusted in their engagement beyond a week, and as for compulsion, it is like attempting to drive fish into a net with the ocean before them. General Mason, Lieutenant Lanman, and myself form a mess; we have a house and all the table furniture and culinary apparatus requisite, but our servants have run, one after another, till we are almost in despair; even Sambo, who we thought would stick by from laziness, if no other cause, ran last night; and this morning, for the fortieth time, we had to take to the kitchen and cook our own breakfast. A general of the United States army, the commander of a man-of-war, and the alcalde of Monterey, in a smoking kitchen, grinding coffee, toasting a herring, and peeling onions! These gold mines are going to upset all the domestic arrangements of society, turning the head to the tail, and the tail to the head. Well, it is an ill wind that blows nobody any good; the nabobs have had their time, and now comes that of the "niggers." We shall all live just as long and be quite as fit to die.

Tuesday, July 18. — Another bag of gold from the mines and another spasm in the community. It was brought down by a sailor from Yuba River and contains a hundred and thirty-six ounces. It is the most beautiful gold that has appeared in the market; it looks like the yellow scales of the dolphin passing through his rainbow hues at death. My carpenters, at work on the schoolhouse, on seeing it, threw down their saws and planes, shouldered their picks, and are off for the Yuba. Three seamen ran from the *Warren,* forfeiting their four years' pay; and a whole platoon of soldiers from the fort left only their colors behind. One old woman declared she would never again break an egg or kill a chicken without examining yolk and gizzard.

Saturday, August 12. — My man Bob, who is of Irish extraction and who had been in the mines about two months, returned to Monterey four weeks since, bringing with him over two thousand dollars as the proceeds of his labor. Bob, while in my employ, required me to pay him every Saturday night in gold which he put into a little leather bag and sewed into the lining of his coat after taking out just twelve and a half cents, his weekly allowance for tobacco. But now he took rooms and began to branch out; he had the best horses, the richest viands, and the choicest wines in the place. He never drank himself, but it filled him with delight to brim the sparkling goblet for others. I met Bob today and asked him how he got on. "Oh, very well," he replied, "but I am off again for the mines." "How is that, Bob? You brought down with you over two thousand dollars; I hope you have not spent all that; you used to be very saving; twelve and a half cents a week for tobacco, and the rest you sewed into the lining of your coat." "Oh, yes," replied Bob, "and I have got *that* money yet; I worked hard for it, and the devil can't get it away; but the two thousand dollars came aisily by good luck, and has gone as aisily as it came." Now Bob's story is only one of a thousand like it in California and has a deeper philosophy in it than meets the eye. Multitudes here are none the richer for the mines. He who can shake chestnuts from an exhaustless tree won't stickle about the quantity he roasts.

Thursday, August 16. — Four citizens of Monterey are just in from the gold mines on Feather River, where they worked in company with three others. They employed about thirty wild Indians who are attached to the ranch owned by one of the party. They worked precisely seven weeks and three days and have divided seventy-six thousand eight hundred and forty-four dollars, nearly eleven thousand dollars to each. Make a dot there, and let me introduce a man, well known to me, who has worked on the Yuba River sixty-four days and brought back as the result of his individual labor five thousand three hundred and fifty-six dollars. Make a dot there, and let me introduce another townsman who has worked on the North Fork fifty-seven days and brought back four thousand five hundred and thirty-four dollars. Make a dot there, and let me introduce a boy, fourteen years of age, who has worked on the Mokelumne fifty-four days and brought back three thousand four hundred and sixty-seven dollars. Make another dot there, and let me introduce a woman, of Sonorarian birth, who has worked in the dry diggings forty-six days and brought back two thousand one hundred and twenty-five dollars. Is not this enough to make a man throw down his ledger and shoulder a pick? But the deposits which yielded these harvests were now opened for the first time; they were the accumulation of ages; only the footprints of the elk and wild savage had passed over them. Their slumber was broken for the first time by the sturdy arms of the American emigrant.

Tuesday, August 28. — The gold mines have upset all social and domestic arrangements in Monterey; the master has become his own servant, and the servant his own lord. The millionaire is obliged to groom his own horse and roll his wheelbarrow, and the hidalgo — in whose veins flows the blood of all the Cortes — to clean his own boots! Here is Lady L——, who has lived here seventeen years, the pride and ornament of the place, with a broomstick in her jeweled hand! And here is Lady B——, with her daughter — all the way from old Virginia, where they graced society with their varied accomplishments — now floating between the parlor and kitchen, and as much at home in the one as the other! And here is Lady S——, whose cattle are on a thousand hills, lifting, like Rachel of old, her bucket of water from the deep well! And here is Lady M. L——, whose honeymoon is still full of soft seraphic light, unhouseling a potato and hunting the hen that laid the last egg. And here am I, who have been a man of some note in my day, loafing on the hospitality of the good citizens and grateful for a meal though in an Indian's wigwam. Why, is not this enough to make one wish the gold mines were in the earth's flaming center from which they sprung? Out on this yellow dust! it is worse than the cinders which buried Pompeii, for there high and low shared the same fate!

WALTER COLTON, Three Years in California

123. Social Life in the California Diggings

"The days of old, and the days of gold, and the days of '49" were a unique interlude of adventure and romance in American history. From all over the world — from Europe, Asia, and Australia as well as from the Eastern States and Mexico — men hurried to California to make their fortunes; and roaring cities and lawless mining-camps sprang into existence almost overnight. Fortunately, many of the adventurers were able to write, and few phases of American history have been better described than this gold rush.

THE WINTER of 1848 and spring of 1849 had brought to our shores an addition of some fifty thousand to our populations. Sacramento City, like Stockton, had sprung up Minervalike, full-grown; Sutter's Fort was nearly deserted, or at least no trade was carried on within its walls; Sacramento and Stockton had then become and ever will remain the great depots for the mining regions.

We continued on to the old diggings from Stockton. When we reached the top of the mountains overlooking Carson's and Angel's Creeks, we had to stand and gaze on the scene before us — the hillsides were dotted with tents, and the creeks were filled with human beings to such a degree that it seemed as if a day's work of the mass would not leave a stone unturned in them. We did not stop but proceeded on to the Wood's Creek, in hopes there to find more room to exercise our digging propensities. But here it was worse — on the long flat we found a vast canvas city under the name of Jamestown, which, similar to a bed of mushrooms, had sprung up in a night. A hundred flags were flying from restaurants, taverns, rum mills, and gaming houses. The gambling tables had their crowds continually, and the whole presented a scene similar to that of San Francisco during the past winter. I have there seen Spaniards betting an *arroba* of gold at a time, and win or lose it as coolly as if it had been a bag of clay. Gold dust had risen in value from what it was in 1848 — as high as ten dollars per ounce was given for gold dust at the monte banks. Wood's Creek was filled up with miners, and I here, for the first time after the discovery of gold, learned what a miner's claim was. In 1848 the miners had no division of the ground into claims — they worked where it was richest, and many times four or five could be seen at work in a circle of six feet in diameter, but here they were now measuring the ground off with tape measures under the direction of the alcaldes so as to prevent disputes arising from the division.

Each day now added thousands to our population, all of whom came intent on making fortunes in a few days and then leaving the country; many came on speculating expeditions; property of every description ran up to rates that set the world to wondering. In San

Francisco, in particular, lots and buildings changed hands at rates unknown before in the annals of trade.

But to return to the diggings. This swarm of human beings laid cold the bright calculations of the old diggers of 1848. They had found gold at every step and looked on the supply as inexhaustible — that for years to come but few would be here and that our rich harvest would continue as it then was. Men who would work could get from one to five hundred dollars per day, and in confidence of this good fortune continuing, these heavy earnings were foolishly spent in drinking and gaming, purchasing fine horses, and dressing in gaudy Indian style. Honesty was the ruling passion of '48. If an *hombre* got broke, he asked the first one he met to lend him such amount as he wanted until he could "dig her out." The loans were always made and always paid according to promise. The writer on one occasion was accosted by name at the old dry diggings by a rough-looking case (with whom I had no acquaintance) for the loan of some dust until a specified time. His rough hands and muscular arms proclaimed him a workingman, which was all the security required. Without asking his name the amount (fifty ounces) was handed to him. On the day appointed it was duly returned, with an additional pound and a pound of brandy for "old acquaintance' sake," as he remarked — telling the lender at the same time that he considered him "a d——d fine feller." It would not be very safe to lend out dust under like circumstances at the present date.

But this honesty, so universal in '48, was not to be found in the crowds that daily thickened around us in '49. Hordes of pickpockets, robbers, thieves, and swindlers were mixed with men who had come with honest intentions. These rascals had lived all their lives by the sleight of hand, and it was evident that they had not come to California with gold rings on their white, soft hands for the purpose of wielding the pick and pan in obtaining their wishes. Murders, thefts, and heavy robberies soon became the order of the day. A panic seized that portion of the diggers who had never before been out of sight of "marm's chimbly" and who went cringing about in fear, though most of them presented the appearance of traveling armories; yet it was evident they wouldn't shoot. But men were to be found who had ridden the elephant of this world all their lives and well knew the course we had to pursue under the change of affairs. Whipping on the bare back, cutting off ears, and hanging soon became matters of as frequent occurrence as those of robbery, theft, and murder.

J. H. CARSON, Early Recollections of the Mines

124. Sarah Royce Braves the Desert and the Mountains

The parents of the philosopher Josiah Royce were among the host of emigrants who braved fatigue, hunger, thirst, disease, and Indians in their quest for California gold. Both were of English birth; and Mrs. Sarah Royce, from whose reminiscences the following narrative is taken, had been born in Stratford-on-Avon. She and her husband, joining an emigrant train, and taking with them a two-year-old daughter, encountered many hardships even before they reached Salt Lake City. From that point onward they traveled with but three men as companions, and with only the manuscript diary of a Mormon who had gone to California and back in 1848 as a guide. In the Carson Valley, they were opportunely met by a detachment from a military relief party, which had been sent out to bring in the last of the year's emigrants.

WE WERE traveling parallel with a placid river on our right, beyond which were trees; and from us to the water's edge the ground sloped so gently it appeared absurd not to turn aside to its brink and refresh ourselves and our oxen.

But as day dawned these beautiful sights disappeared, and we began to look anxiously for the depression in the ground and the holes dug which we were told would mark the Sink of the Humboldt. But it was nearly noonday before we came to them. There was still some passable water in the holes, but not fit to drink clear; so we contrived to gather enough sticks of sage to boil some, made a little coffee, ate our lunch, and thus refreshed, we hastened to find the forking road. Our director had told us that within about two or three miles beyond the Sink we might look for the road, to the left, and we did look and kept looking and going on drearily till the sun got lower and lower and night was fast approaching. Then the conviction which had long been gaining ground in my mind took possession of the whole party. We had passed the forks of the road before daylight that morning and were now miles out on the desert without a mouthful of food for the cattle and only two or three quarts of water in a little cask.

What could be done? Halt we must, for the oxen were nearly worn out and night was coming on. The animals must at least rest, if they could not be fed; and that they might rest, they were chained securely to the wagon, for, hungry and thirsty as they were, they would, if loose, start off frantically in search of water and food and soon drop down exhausted. Having fastened them in such a way that they could lie down, we took a few mouthfuls of food, and then, we in our wagon and the men not far off upon the sand, fell wearily to sleep — a forlorn little company wrecked upon the desert.

The first question in the morning was, "How can the oxen be kept from starving?" A happy thought occurred. We had thus far on our journey managed to keep something in the shape of a bed to sleep on. It was a mattress tick, and just before leaving Salt Lake we had put into it some fresh hay — not very much, for our load must be as light as possible; but the old gentleman traveling with us had also a small straw mattress; the two together might keep the poor things from starving for a few hours. At once a small portion was dealt out to them, and for the present they were saved. For ourselves we had food which we believed would about last us till we reached the gold mines if we could go right on; if we were much delayed anywhere, it was doubtful. The two or three quarts of water in our little cask would last only a few hours, to give moderate drinks to each of the party. For myself I inwardly determined I should scarcely take any of it, as I had found throughout the journey that I could do with less drink than most land travelers. Some of the men, however, easily suffered with thirst, and as to my little girl, it is well known a child cannot do long without either water or milk. Everything looked rather dark and dubious.

Should we try to go on? But there were miles of desert before us, in which we knew neither grass or water could be found. . . . Here we were without water and with only a few mouthfuls of poor feed, while our animals were already tired out and very hungry and thirsty. No, it would be madness to go farther out in the desert under such conditions. Should we then turn back and try to reach the meadows with their wells? But as near as we could calculate, it could not be less than twelve or fifteen miles to them. Would it be possible for our poor cattle to reach there? Their only food would be that pitiful mess still left in our mattresses. It might be divided into two portions, giving them each a few mouthfuls more at noon, and then, if they kept on their feet long enough to reach the holes at the Sink, we might possibly find enough water to give them each a little drink, which with the remainder of the fodder might keep them up till the meadows were reached. It was a forlorn hope, but it was all we had.

The morning was wearing away while these things were talked over. Precious time was being wasted, but the truth was the situation was so new and unexpected that it seemed for a while to confuse — almost to stupefy — most of the little party; and those least affected in this way felt so deeply the responsibility of the next move that they dared not decide upon it hastily. . . . But this would never do. So the more hopeful ones proposed that we should all eat something and as soon as the noon heat abated prepare for a move. So we took some lunch, and soon the men were lying upon the sand at short distances from each other, fast asleep. Soon some of the party awoke and after a little talk concluded that two of them would walk to a bald ridge that rose out of the flat waste about a mile and a half distant and take a view from thence in the faint hope that we might yet be mistaken and the forking road and the meadows might still be in advance. My husband said he would go, and the best of the two young men went with him, while the other two wandered listlessly off again. I made no opposition; I felt no inclination to oppose, though I knew the helplessness and loneliness of the position would thus be greatly increased. But that calm strength, that certainty of One near and all-sufficient, hushed and cheered me. Only a woman who has been alone upon a desert with her helpless child can have any adequate idea of my experience for the next hour or two. But that consciousness of an unseen Presence still sustained me.

When the explorers returned from their walk to the ridge, it was only to report no discovery, nothing to be seen on all sides but sand and scattered sagebrush interspersed with the carcasses of dead cattle. So there was nothing to be done but to turn back and try to find the meadows. Turn back! What a chill the words sent through one. *Turn back,* on a journey like that, in which every mile had been gained by most earnest labor, growing more and more intense until of late it had seemed that the certainty of *advance* with every step was all that made the next step possible. And now for miles we were to *go back.* In all that long journey no steps ever seemed so heavy, so hard to take, as those with which I turned my back to the sun that afternoon of October 4, 1849.

We had not been long on the move when we saw dust rising in the road at a distance and soon perceived we were about to meet a little caravan of wagons. Then a bright gleam of hope stole in. They had doubtless stopped at the meadows and were supplied with grass and water. Might it not be possible that they would have enough to spare for us? Then we could go on with them. My heart bounded at the thought. But the hope was short-lived. We met, and some of the men gathered round our wagon with eager inquiries, while those who could not leave their teams stood looking with wonder at a solitary wagon headed the wrong way.

Our story was soon told. It turned out that they were camping in the meadows at the very time we passed the forking road without seeing it, the morning we so ambitiously started soon after midnight. Ah, we certainly got up too early that day! If we had only seen that road and taken it, we might now have been with this company, provided for the desert, and no longer alone. But when the question was asked whether they could spare sufficient grass and water to get our team over the desert, they shook their heads and unanimously agreed that it was out of the question. Their own cattle, they said, were weak from long travel and too often scant supplies. They had only been able to load up barely enough to get to the Carson River. The season was far advanced, and the clouds hanging of late round the mountain tops looked threatening. It would be like throwing away their own lives without any certainty of saving ours, for, once out in the desert without food, we would all be helpless together. One of the men had his family with him, a wife and two or three children; and while they talked the woman was seen coming toward us. She had not, when they first halted, understood that any but men were with the lone wagon. As soon as she heard to the contrary and what were the circumstances, she hastened, with countenance full of concern, to condole with me; and I think, had the decision depended alone upon her, she would have insisted upon our turning back with them and sharing their feed and water to the last.

But fortunately for them, probably for us all, other counsels prevailed, and we resumed our depressing backward march. . . .

I had now become so impressed with the danger of the cattle giving out that I refused to ride except for occasional brief rests. So, soon after losing sight of the dust of the envied little caravan, I left the wagon and walked the remainder of the day. For a good while I kept near the wagon, but by and by, being very weary, I fell behind. The sun had set before we reached the Sink, and the light was fading fast when the wagon disappeared from my sight behind a slight elevation; and as the others had gone on in advance some time before, I was all alone on the barren waste. However, as I recognized the features of the neighborhood and knew we were quite near the Sink, I felt no particular apprehension, only a feeling that it was a weird and dreary scene, and instinctively urged forward my lagging footsteps in hope of regaining sight of the wagon.

The next morning we resumed our backward march after feeding out the last mouthful of fodder. The water in the little cask was nearly used up in making coffee for supper and breakfast, but if only each one would be moderate in taking a share when thirst impelled him, we might yet reach the wells before any one suffered seriously. We had lately had but few chances for cooking, and only a little boiled rice with dried fruit and a few bits of biscuit remained after we had done breakfast. If we could only reach the meadows by noon! But that we could hardly hope for; the animals were so weak and tired. There was no alternative, however; the only thing to be done was to go steadily on, determined to do and endure to the utmost.

I found no difficulty this morning in keeping up with the team. They went so slowly and I was so preternaturally stimulated by anxiety to get forward that before I was aware of it I would be some rods ahead of the cattle, straining my gaze as if expecting to see a land of promise, long before I had any rational hope of the kind. My imagination acted intensely. I seemed to see Hagar in the wilderness walking wearily away from her fainting child among the dried-up bushes and seating herself in the hot sand. I seemed to become Hagar myself, and when my little one from the wagon behind me called out, "Mamma, I want a drink," I stopped, gave her some, noted that there were but a few swallows left, then mechanically pressed onward again, alone, repeating over and over the words, "Let me not see the death of the child."

Wearily passed the hottest noonday hour, with many an anxious look at the horned heads which seemed to me to bow lower and lower, while the poor tired hoofs almost refused to move. The two young men had been out of sight for some time when all at once we heard a shout and saw, a few hundred yards in advance, a couple of hats thrown into the air and four hands waving triumphantly. As soon as we got near enough, we heard them call out, "Grass and water! Grass and water!" and shortly we were at the meadows.

On Monday morning we loaded up, but did not hurry, for the cattle had not rested any too long; another day would have been better, but we dared not linger. So, giving them time that morning thoroughly to satisfy themselves with grass and water, we once more set forward toward the formidable desert and, at that late season, with our equipment, the scarcely less formidable Sierras. The feeling that we were once more going forward instead of backward gave an animation to every step which we could never have felt but by contrast. By night we were again at the Sink, where we once more camped; but we durst not, the following morning, launch out upon the desert with the whole day before us, for, though it was now the 9th of October, the sun was still powerful for some hours daily, and the arid sand doubled its heat. Not much after noon, however, we ventured out upon the sea of sand, this time to cross or die. . . .

Morning was now approaching, and we hoped, when full day-light came, to see some signs of the river. But for two or three weary hours after sunrise nothing of the kind appeared. The last of the water had been given to the cattle before daylight. When the sun was up we gave them the remainder of their hay, took a little breakfast, and pressed forward. For a long time not a word was spoken save occasionally to the cattle. I had again unconsciously got in advance, my eyes scanning the horizon to catch the first glimpse of any change, though I had no definite idea in my mind what first to expect. But now there was surely something. Was it a cloud? It was very low at first, and I feared it might evaporate as the sun warmed it. But it became rather more distinct and a little higher. I paused and stood till the team came up. Then, walking beside it, I asked my husband what he thought that low dark line could be. "I think," he said, "it must be the timber on Carson River." Again we were silent, and for a while I watched anxiously the heads of the two leading cattle. They were rather unusually fine animals, often showing considerable intelligence, and so faithful had they been, through so many trying scenes, I could not help feeling a sort of attachment to them; and I pitied them as I observed how low their heads drooped as they pressed their shoulders so resolutely and yet so wearily against the bows. Another glance at the horizon. Surely there was now visible a little unevenness in the top of that dark line, as though it might indeed be trees. "How far off do you think that is now?" I said. "About five or six miles, I guess," was the reply. At that moment the white-faced leader raised his head, stretched forward his nose, and uttered a low moo-o-oo. I was startled, fearing it was the sign for him to fall, exhausted. "What is the matter with him?" I said. "I think he smells the water," was the answer. "How can he at such a distance?" As I spoke, the other leader raised his head, stretched out his nose, and uttered the same sound. The hinder cattle seemed to catch the idea, whatever it was; they all somewhat increased their pace and from that time showed renewed animation.

But we had yet many weary steps to take, and noon had passed before we stood in the shade of those longed-for trees beside the Carson River. As soon as the yokes were removed, the oxen walked into the stream and stood a few moments, apparently enjoying its coolness, then drank as they chose, came out, and soon found feed that satisfied them for the present, though at this point it was not abundant. The remainder of that day was spent in much-needed rest. The next day we did not travel many miles, for our team showed decided signs of weakness, and the sand became deeper as we advanced, binding the wheels so as to make hauling very hard. We had conquered the desert.

But the great Sierra Nevada Mountains were still all before us, and we had many miles to make, up Carson River, before their ascent was fairly begun. If this sand continued many miles, as looked probable, when should we ever even begin the real climbing? The men began to talk among themselves about how much easier they could get on if they left the wagon, and it was not unlikely they would try starting out without us if we had to travel too slowly. But they could not do this to any real advantage unless they took with them their pack mule to carry some provisions. All they had was the bacon they found on the desert and some parched corn meal, but they felt sanguine that they could go so much faster than the cattle with the wagon, they could easily make this last them through. But the bargain had been, when we agreed to supply them with flour, that the pack mule, and the old horse if he could be of any use, should be at our service to aid in any pinch that might occur, to the end of the journey. Having shared the perils of the way thus far, it certainly seemed unwise to divide the strength of so small a party when the mountains were to be scaled.

I wished most heartily there was some more rapid way for Mary and me to ride. But it was out of the question, for only a thoroughly-trained mountain animal would do for me to ride, carrying her. Besides this, all the clothing and personal conveniences we had in the world were in our wagon, and we had neither a sufficient number of sound animals nor those of the right kind to pack them across the mountains. So the only way was to try to keep on. But it looked like rather a hopeless case when for this whole day we advanced but a few miles.

The next morning, Friday, the 12th of October, we set out once more, hoping the sand would become lighter and the road easier to travel. But instead of this the wheels sank deeper than yesterday, there was more of ascent to overcome, the sun shone out decidedly hot, and toward noon we saw that we were approaching some pretty steep hills, up which our road evidently led. It did not look as though we could ascend them, but we would at least try to reach their foot. As we neared them we saw dust rising from the road at one of the turns we could distinguish high up in the hills a few miles off. Probably it was some party ahead of us. There was no hope of our overtaking anybody; so when we lost sight of the dust we did not expect to see it again. But soon another section of the road was in sight, and again the dust appeared, this time nearer and plainly moving toward us. Conjecture now became very lively. It was probably Indians, but they could not be of the same tribes we had seen. Were they foes? How many were there? Repeatedly we saw the dust at different points but could make out no distinct figures.

We were now so near the foot of the hills that we could distinctly see a stretch of road leading down a very steep incline to where we were moving so laboriously along. Presently at the head of this steep incline appeared two horsemen clad in loose, flying garments that flapped like wings on each side of them, while their broad-brimmed hats, blown up from their foreheads, revealed hair and faces that belonged to no Indians. Their rapidity of motion and the steepness of the descent gave a strong impression of coming down from above, and the thought flashed into my mind, "They look heaven-sent." As they came nearer we saw that each of them led by a halter a fine mule, and the perfect ease with which all the animals cantered down that steep was a marvel in our eyes. My husband and myself were at the heads of the lead cattle, and our little Mary was up in the front of the wagon, looking with wonder at the approaching forms.

As they came near they smiled, and the forward one said, "Well, sir, you are the man we are after!" "How can that be?" said my husband with surprise. "Yes, sir," continued the stranger, "you and your wife and that little girl are what brought us as far as this. You see, we belong to the relief company sent out by order of the United States Government to help the late emigrants over the mountains. We were ordered only as far as Truckee Pass. When we got there we met a little company that had just got in. They'd been in a snow-storm at the summit — 'most got froze to death themselves, lost some of their cattle, and just managed to get to where some of our men had fixed a relief camp. There was a woman and some children with them, and that woman set right to work at us fellows to go on over the mountains after a family she said they'd met on the desert going back for grass and water 'cause they'd missed their way. She said there was only one wagon, and there was a woman and child in it; and she knew they could never get through them canyons and over them ridges without help. We told her we had no orders to go any farther then. She said she didn't care for orders. She didn't believe anybody would blame us for doing what we were sent out to do, if we did have to go farther than ordered. And she kept at me so, I couldn't get rid of her. You see, I've got a wife and little girl of my own; so I felt just how it was; and I got this man to come with me, and here we are, to give you more to eat, if you want it, let you have these two mules, and tell you how to get right over the mountains the best and quickest way."

While he thus rapidly, in cheery though blunt fashion, explained their sudden presence with us, the thought of their being heaven-sent — that had so lightly flashed into my mind as I at first watched their rapid descent of the hill with flying garments — grew into a sweetly solemn conviction; and I stood in mute adoration, breathing in my inmost heart thanksgiving to that Providential hand which had taken hold of the conflicting movements, the provoking blunders, the contradictory plans, of our lives and those of a dozen other people who a few days before were utterly unknown to each other and many miles apart, and had from those rough, broken materials wrought out for us so unlooked-for a deliverance.

SARAH ROYCE, A Frontier Lady

125. Bayard Taylor Visits the El Dorado of the West

The greatest and most influential American newspaper of the fifties was the New York Tribune; and one of the most famous members of its staff was the traveler, poet, and novelist Bayard Taylor. He was sent out in June, 1849, to report the gold rush. Reaching California by way of Panama, he spent five months there, hugely enjoying the picturesqueness, variety, and energy of life in the gold regions, and sending back to the Tribune *the materials which later made up one of his best books,* El Dorado.

SAN FRANCISCO September, 1849.—We obtained a room with two beds at twenty-five dollars per week, meals being in addition twenty dollars per week. I asked the landlord whether he could send a porter for our trunks. "There is none belonging to the house," said he; "every man is his own porter here." I returned to the Parker House, shouldered a heavy trunk, took a valise in my hand and carried them to my quarters in the teeth of the wind. Our room was in a sort of garret over the only story of the hotel; two cots, evidently of California manufacture and covered only with a pair of blankets, two chairs, a rough table, and a small looking glass constituted the furniture. There was not space enough between the bed and the bare rafters overhead to sit upright, and I gave myself a severe blow in rising the next morning without the proper heed. Through a small roof window of dim glass I could see the opposite shore of the bay, then partly hidden by the evening fogs. The wind whistled around the eaves and rattled the tiles with a cold, gusty sound that would have imparted a dreary character to the place, had I been in a mood to listen.

Many of the passengers began speculation at the moment of landing. The most ingenious and successful operation was made by a gentleman of New York who took out fifteen hundred copies of the *Tribune* and other papers, which he disposed of in two hours at one dollar apiece! Hearing of this, I bethought me of about a dozen papers which I had used to fill up crevices in packing my valise. There was a newspaper merchant at the corner of the City Hotel, and to him I proposed the sale of them, asking him to name a price. "I shall want to make a good profit on the retail price," said he, "and can't give more than ten dollars for the lot." I was satisfied with the wholesale price, which was a gain of just four thousand per cent!

I set out for a walk before dark and climbed a hill back of the town, passing a number of tents pitched in the hollows. The scattered houses spread out below me, and the crowded shipping in the harbor, backed by a lofty line of mountains, made an imposing picture. The restless, feverish tide of life in that little spot and the thought that what I then saw and was yet to see will hereafter fill one of the most marvelous pages of all history rendered it singularly impressive.

I was forced to believe many things which in my communications to the *Tribune* I was almost afraid to write with any hope of their obtaining credence. It may be interesting to give here a few instances of the enormous and unnatural value put upon property at the time of my arrival. The Parker House rented for one hundred and ten thousand dollars yearly, at least sixty thousand dollars of which was paid by gamblers, who held nearly all the second story. Adjoining it on the right was a canvas tent fifteen by twenty-five feet, called El Dorado, and occupied likewise by gamblers, which brought forty thousand dollars. On the opposite corner of the plaza a building called the Miner's Bank, used by Wright and Company, brokers, about half the size of a fire-engine house in New York, was held at a rent of seventy-five thousand dollars. A mercantile house paid forty thousand dollars rent for a one-story building of twenty feet front; the United States Hotel, thirty-six thousand dollars; the Post Office, seven thousand dollars; and so on to the end of the chapter. A friend of mine who wished to find a place for a law office was shown a cellar in the earth, about twelve feet square and six deep, which he could have at two hundred and fifty dollars a month. One of the common soldiers at the battle of San Pasquale was reputed to be among the millionaires of the place, with an income of fifty thousand dollars *monthly*. A citizen of San Francisco died insolvent to the amount of forty-one thousand dollars the previous autumn. His administrators were delayed in settling his affairs, and his real estate advanced so rapidly in value meantime that after his debts were paid his heirs had a yearly income of forty thousand dollars. These facts were indubitably attested; every one believed them; yet, hearing them talked of daily, as matters of course, one at first could not help feeling as if he had been eating of the insane root.

The prices paid for labor were in proportion to everything else. The carman of Mellus, Howard and Company had a salary of six thousand dollars a year, and many others made from fifteen to twenty dollars daily. Servants were paid from one hundred to two hundred dollars a month, but the wages of the rougher kinds of labor had fallen to about eighty dollars. Yet, notwithstanding the number of gold seekers who were returning enfeebled and disheartened from the mines, it was difficult to obtain as many workmen as the forced growth of the city demanded. A gentleman who arrived in April told me he then found but thirty or forty houses; the population was then so scant that not more than twenty-five persons would be seen in the streets at any one time. Now there were probably five hundred houses, tents, and sheds, with a population, fixed and floating, of six thousand. People who had been absent six weeks came back and could scarcely recognize the place. Streets were regularly laid out, and already there were three piers at which small vessels could discharge. It was calculated that the town increased daily by from fifteen to thirty houses; its skirts were rapidly approaching the summits of the three hills on which it is located.

A curious result of the extraordinary abundance of gold and the facility with which fortunes were acquired struck me at the first glance. All business was transacted on so extensive a scale that the ordinary habits of solicitation and compliance on the one hand and stubborn cheapening on the other seemed to be entirely forgotten. You enter a shop to buy something; the owner eyes you with perfect indifference, waiting for you to state your want; if you object to the price, you are at liberty to leave, for you need not expect to get it cheaper; he evidently cares little whether you buy it or not. One who has been some time in the country will lay down the money without wasting words. This disregard for all the petty arts of money-making was really a refreshing feature of society. Another equally agreeable trait was the punctuality with which debts were paid and the general confidence which men were obliged to place perforce in each other's honesty. Perhaps this latter fact was owing in part to the impossibility of protecting wealth, and consequent dependence on an honorable regard for the rights of others.

A better idea of San Francisco in the beginning of September, 1849, cannot be given than by the description of a single day. Supposing the visitor to have been long enough in the place to sleep on a hard plank and in spite of the attacks of innumerable fleas; he will be awakened at daylight by the noises of building, with which the hills are all alive. The air is temperate, and the invariable morning fog is just beginning to gather. By sunrise, which gleams hazily over the Coast Mountains across the bay, the whole populace is up and at work. The wooden buildings unlock their doors; the canvas houses and tents throw back their front curtains; the lighters on the water are warped out from ship to ship; carts and porters are busy along the beach; and only the gaming tables, thronged all night by the votaries of chance, are idle and deserted. The temperature is so fresh as to inspire an active habit of body, and even without the stimulus of trade and speculation there would be few sluggards at this season.

By nine o'clock the town is in the full flow of business. The streets running down to the water and Montgomery Street, which fronts the bay, are crowded with people, all in hurried motion. The variety of characters and costumes is remarkable. Our own countrymen seem to lose their local peculiarities in such a crowd, and it is by chance epithets rather than by manner that the New Yorker is distinguished from the Kentuckian, the Carolinian from the down-Easter, the Virginian from the Texan. The German and Frenchman are more easily recognized. Peruvians and Chilians go by in their brown ponchos, and the sober Chinese, cool and impassive in the midst of excitement, look out of the oblique corners of their long eyes at the bustle, but are never tempted to venture from their own line of business. The eastern side of the plaza in front of the Parker House and a canvas hell called the El Dorado are the general rendezvous of business and amusement — combining exchange, park, club room, and promenade all in one. There everybody not constantly employed in one spot may be seen at some time of the day. The character of the groups scattered along the plaza is oftentimes very interesting. In one place are three or four speculators bargaining for lots, buying and selling "fifty varas square" in towns some of which are canvas and some only paper; in another, a company of miners, brown as leather and rugged in features as in dress; in a third, perhaps, three or four naval officers speculating on the next cruise or a knot of genteel gamblers talking over the last night's operations.

The day advances. The mist which after sunrise hung low and

heavy for an hour or two has risen above the hills, and there will be two hours of pleasant sunshine before the wind sets in from the sea. The crowd in the streets is now wholly alive. Men dart hither and thither as if possessed with a never-resting spirit. You speak to an acquaintance — a merchant, perhaps. He utters a few hurried words of greeting, while his eyes send keen glances on all sides of you; suddenly he catches sight of somebody in the crowd; he is off and in the next five minutes has bought up half a cargo, sold a town lot at treble the sum he gave, and taken a share in some new and imposing speculation. It is impossible to witness this excess and dissipation of business without feeling something of its influence. The very air is pregnant with the magnetism of bold, spirited, unwearied action, and he who but ventures into the outer circle of the whirlpool is spinning, ere he has time for thought, in its dizzy vortex.

About twelve o'clock a wind begins to blow from the northwest, sweeping with most violence through a gap between the hills, opening toward the Golden Gate. The bells and gongs begin to sound for dinner, and these two causes tend to lessen the crowd in the streets for an hour or two. Two o'clock is the usual dinnertime for business men, but some of the old and successful merchants have adopted the fashionable hour of five. Where shall we dine today? The restaurants display their signs invitingly on all sides; we have choice of the United States, Tortoni's, the Alhambra, and many other equally classic resorts, but Delmonico's, like its distinguished original in New York, has the highest prices and the greatest variety of dishes. We enter a little door at the end of the building, ascend a dark, narrow flight of steps, and find ourselves in a long, low room, with ceiling and walls of white muslin and a floor covered with oilcloth.

There are about twenty tables disposed in two rows, all of them so well filled that we have some difficulty in finding places. Taking up the written bill of fare, we find such items as the following:

SOUPS

Mock turtle . . . . $ .75
St. Julien 1.00

FISH

Boiled salmon trout, anchovy sauce . . 1.75

BOILED

Leg mutton, caper sauce	1.00
Corned beef, cabbage	1.00
Ham and tongues	.75

ENTREES

Fillet of beef, mushroom sauce . . .	1.75
Veal cutlets, breaded	1.00
Mutton chop	1.00
Lobster salad	2.00
Sirloin of venison	1.50
Baked macaroni	.75
Beef tongue, *sauce piquante*	1.00

So that, with but a moderate appetite, the dinner will cost us five dollars, if we are at all epicurean in our tastes. There are cries of "Steward!" from all parts of the room — the word waiter is not considered sufficiently respectful, seeing that the waiter may have been a lawyer or merchant's clerk a few months before. The dishes look very small as they are placed on the table, but they are skillfully cooked and very palatable to men that have ridden in from the diggings. The appetite one acquires in California is something remarkable. For two months after my arrival, my sensations were like those of a famished wolf.

The afternoon is less noisy and active than the forenoon. Merchants keep withindoors, and the gambling rooms are crowded with persons who step in to escape the wind and dust. The sky takes a cold gray cast, and the hills over the bay are barely visible in the dense, dusty air. Now and then a watcher who has been stationed on the hill above Fort Montgomery comes down and reports an inward-bound vessel, which occasions a little excitement among the boatmen and the merchants who are awaiting consignments. Toward sunset the plaza is nearly deserted, the wind is merciless in its force, and a heavy overcoat is not found unpleasantly warm. As it grows dark, there is a lull, though occasional gusts blow down the hill and carry the dust of the city out among the shipping.

The only objects left for us to visit are the gaming tables, whose day has just fairly dawned. We need not wander far in search of one. Denison's Exchange, the Parker House, and El Dorado stand side by side; across the way are the Verandah and Aguila de Oro, higher up the plaza the St. Charles and Bella Union, while dozens of second-rate establishments are scattered through the less-frequented streets. The greatest crowd is about the El Dorado; we find it difficult to effect an entrance. There are about eight tables in the room, all of which are thronged; copper-hued Kanakas, Mexicans rolled in their serapes, and Peruvians thrust through their ponchos stand shoulder to shoulder with the brown and bearded American miners. The stakes are generally small, though when the bettor gets into a streak of luck, as it is called, they are allowed to double until all is lost or the bank breaks. Along the end of the room is a spacious bar supplied with all kinds of bad liquors, and in a sort of gallery suspended under the ceiling a female violinist tasks her talent and strength of muscle to minister to the excitement of play.

There are other places where gaming is carried on privately and to a more ruinous extent — rooms in the rear of the Parker House, in the City Hotel and other places, frequented only by the initiated. Here the stakes are almost unlimited, the players being men of wealth and apparent respectability. Frequently in the absorbing interest of some desperate game the night goes by unheeded and morning breaks upon haggard faces and reckless hearts. Here are lost, in a few turns of a card or rolls of a ball, the product of fortunate ventures by sea or months of racking labor on land.

Bayard Taylor, El Dorado

126. "Old Pancake" Discovers the Comstock Lode

Late in 1859 strange news reached San Francisco — news of a great silver discovery in Washoe Valley beyond the Sierras; silver by tons, silver in huge beds, a bonanza strike. In October a pack train of eighty mules brought all the ore they could carry through the Sierra passes into California. It proved to be worth five thousand dollars a ton! The white bars of silver were soon being displayed in a banker's window in San Francisco. Forthwith a motley crowd, first thousands and then tens of thousands, streamed over the mountains into Nevada Territory. Virginia City, built close to the incredibly rich Comstock Ledge, leaped into national fame almost overnight. The great mines — Ophir, Mexican, Central, Gould and Curry — were known all over the world. Within a few years Nevada had given the country a new crop of millionaires, of whom John Mackay, an uneducated and penniless young prospector, and James Fair, a mining superintendent, were the most prominent. One story of the original discovery is here given by an early chronicler.

IN THE spring of 1859, a considerable number of miners returned to Six-Mile Canyon [in Nevada] to work. They now made their headquarters at Gold Hill, where two or three log houses, including a large log boardinghouse, had been erected.

Peter O'Riley and Pat McLaughlin set to work well up at the head of the ravine where the ground began to rise toward the mountain. They used rockers and found small pay. They continued to work at this point until about the 1st of June, 1859, gradually extending their operations up the slope of the hill in the hope of finding something better. Having but a small stream of water, it became necessary for them to dig a hole as a sort of reservoir in which to collect it for use in their rockers.

They set to work a short distance above the little cut in which they were mining to make the needed reservoir or water hole and at a depth of about four feet struck into a stratum of the rich, decomposed ore of the Ophir mine and of the now world-famous Comstock silver lode.

The manner in which the grand discovery was made was much less romantic than in the case of the discovery of the celebrated silver mine of Potosí, Peru. What our miners found was not glittering native silver, but a great bed of black sulphuret of silver — a decomposed ore of silver filled with spangles of native gold. This gold, however, was alloyed with silver to such an extent that it was more the color of silver than of gold. . . .

When the discoverers struck into the odd-looking black dirt, they only thought that it was a sudden and rather singular change from the yellowish gravel and clay in which they had been digging. As any change was welcome, the luck in which they had been working considered, they at once concluded to try some of the curious-looking stuff in their rockers.

The result astounded them. Before, they had only been taking out a dollar or two per day, but now they found the bottoms of their rockers covered with gold as soon as a few buckets of the new dirt had been washed. They found that they were literally taking out gold by the pound.

However, as the gold they were getting was much lighter in color and weight than any they had found below on the canyon or even on the surface in their cut, they began to fear that all was not right. They thought that, after all, what they had found might be some sort of bogus stuff, base metal of some new and strange kind.

It is not strange that these impecunious miners, tinkering away there on the side of a lone, sage-covered mountain with their rockers, should have felt a little alarmed on account of the great quantity of gold they were getting, as in a few weeks after the discovery was made and the work had been advanced farther into the croppings of the lode they were taking out gold at the rate of a thousand dollars per day. This they were doing with the rockers. Taking the harder lumps left on the screens of the rockers, one man was able to pound out gold at the rate of a hundred dollars per day in a common hand mortar.

In the evening of the day on which the grand discovery was made by O'Riley and McLaughlin, H. T. P. Comstock made his appearance upon the scene.

"Old Pancake" [Comstock], who was then looking after his Gold Hill mines, which were beginning to yield largely, had strolled northward up the mountain toward evening in search of a mustang pony that he had out prospecting for a living among the hills. He had found his pony, had mounted him, and with his long legs dragging the tops of the sagebrush, came riding up just as the lucky miners were making the last cleanup of their rockers for the day.

Comstock, who had a keen eye for all that was going on in the way of mining in any place he might visit, saw at a glance the unusual quantity of gold that was in sight.

When the gold caught his eye, he was off the back of his pony in an instant. He was soon down in the thick of it all, hefting and running his fingers through the gold and picking into and probing the mass of strange-looking stuff exposed.

Conceiving at once that a wonderful discovery of some kind had been made, "Old Pancake" straightened himself up as he arose from a critical examination of the black mass in the cut wherein he had observed the glittering spangles of gold and coolly proceeded to inform the astonished miners that they were working on ground that belonged to him. He asserted that he had some time before taken up one hundred and sixty acres of land at this point for a ranch; also that he owned the water they were using in mining, it being from the Caldwell spring in what was afterward known as Spanish Ravine.

Suspecting that they were working in a decomposed quartz vein, McLaughlin and O'Riley had written out and posted up a notice calling for a claim of three hundred feet for each and a third claim for the discovery, which extra claim they were entitled to under the mining laws. Having soon ascertained all this from the men before him, Comstock would have none of it. He boisterously declared that they should not work there at all unless they would agree to locate himself and his friend Manny (Emmanuel) Penrod in the claim. In case he and Penrod were given an interest, there should be no further trouble about the ground.

After consulting together the discoverers concluded that rather than have a great row about the matter, they would put the names of Comstock and Penrod in their notice of location.

This being arranged to his satisfaction, Comstock next demanded that one hundred feet of ground on the lead should be segregated and given to Penrod and himself for the right to the water they were using, he stoutly asserting that he not only owned the land but also the water, and as they had recognized his right to the land, they could not consistently ignore his claim to the water flowing upon it. In short, he talked so loud and so much about his water right that he at last got the hundred feet segregated as he demanded. This hundred feet afterwards became the Spanish or Mexican mine and yielded millions of dollars.

DAN DE QUILLE, History of the Big Bonanza

127. Vigilante Days and Ways in Montana

Gold was discovered at Alder Gulch, Montana, in 1863, and within a few weeks thousands of fortune hunters poured over the mountains into the new El Dorado. For a time the activities of the notorious Henry Plummer and his gang of outlaws threatened the very existence of the new community, but a vigilante organization such as that which arose in California fifteen years earlier restored law and order. Nathaniel Langford, who played an active part in the vigilante movement, became the first superintendent of the Yellowstone National Park.

IN MAY, 1863, a company of miners, while returning from an unsuccessful exploring expedition, discovered the remarkable placer afterward known as Alder Gulch. They gave the name of one of their number, Fairweather, to the district. Several of the company went immediately to Bannack, communicated the intelligence, and returned with supplies to their friends. The effect of the news was electrical. Hundreds started at once to the new placer, each striving to outstrip the other in order to secure a claim. In the hurry of departure, among many minor accidents, a man whose body, partially concealed by the willows, was mistaken for a beaver was shot by a Mr. Arnold. Discovering the fatal mistake, Arnold gave up the chase and bestowed his entire attention upon the unfortunate victim until his death a few days afterward. The great stampede with its numerous pack animals penetrated the dense alder thicket which filled the gulch a distance of eight miles to the site selected for building a town. An accidental fire occurring, swept away the alders for the entire distance in a single night. In less than a week from the date of the first arrival hundreds of tents, brush wakiups, and rude log cabins extemporized for immediate occupancy were scattered at random over the spot, now for the first time trodden by white men. For a distance of twelve miles from the mouth of the gulch to its source in Bald Mountain claims were staked and occupied by the men fortunate enough first to assert an ownership. Laws were adopted, judges selected, and the new community was busy in upheaving, sluicing, drifting, and cradling the inexhaustible bed of auriferous gravel which has yielded under these various manipulations a greater amount of gold than any other placer on the continent.

The Southern sympathizers of the Territory gave the name of Varina to the new town which had sprung up in Alder Gulch, in honor of the wife of President Jefferson Davis. Dr. Bissell, one of the miners' judges of the Gulch, was an ardent Unionist. Being called upon to draw up some papers before the new name had been generally adopted and requested to date them at "Varina City," he declared with a very emphatic expletive he would not do it, and wrote the name "Virginia City," by which name the place has ever since been known. . . .

Of the settlements in Alder Gulch, Virginia City was the principal, though Nevada, two miles below, at one time was of nearly equal size and population. A stranger from the Eastern states entering the gulch for the first time two or three months after its discovery would be inspired by the scene and its associations with reflections of the most strange and novel character. This human hive, numbering at least ten thousand people, was the product of ninety days. Into it were crowded all the elements of a rough and active civilization. Thousands of cabins and tents and brush wakiups, thrown together in the roughest form and scattered at random along the banks and in the nooks of the hills, were seen on every hand. Every foot of the gulch, under the active manipulations of the miners, was undergoing displacement, and it was already disfigured by huge heaps of gravel which had been passed through the sluices and rifled of their glittering contents. In the gulch itself all was activity. Some were removing the superincumbent earth to reach the pay dirt, others who had accomplished that were gathering up the clay and gravel upon the surface of the bedrock, while by others still it was thrown into the sluice boxes. This exhibition of mining industry was twelve miles long. Gold was abundant, and every possible device was employed by the gamblers, the traders, the vile men and women that had come with the miners to the locality, to obtain it. Nearly every third cabin in the towns was a saloon where vile whiskey was peddled out for fifty cents a drink in gold dust. Many of these places were filled with gambling tables and gamblers, and the miner who was bold enough to enter one of them with his day's earnings in his pocket seldom left until thoroughly fleeced. Hurdy-gurdy dance houses were numerous, and there were plenty of camp beauties to patronize them. Not a day or night passed which did not yield its full fruition of fights, quarrels, wounds, or murders. The crack of the revolver was often heard above the merry notes of the violin. Street fights were frequent, and as no one knew when or where they would occur, every one was on his guard against a random shot.

Sunday was always a gala day. The miners then left their work and gathered about the public places in the towns. The stores were all open, the auctioneers specially eloquent on every corner in praise of their wares. Thousands of people crowded the thoroughfares, ready to rush in any direction of promised excitement. Horse racing was among the most favored amusements. Prize rings were formed, and brawny men engaged at fisticuffs until their sight was lost and their bodies pommelled to a jelly, while hundreds of onlookers cheered the victor. Hacks rattled to and fro between the several towns, freighted with drunken and rowdy humanity of both sexes. Citizens of acknowledged respectability often walked, more often perhaps rode side by side on horseback, with noted courtesans in open day through the crowded streets and seemingly suffered no harm in reputation. Pistols flashed, bowie knives flourished, and braggart oaths filled the air, as often as men's passions triumphed over their reason. This was indeed the reign of unbridled license, and men who at first regarded it with disgust and terror, by constant exposure soon learned to become part of it and forget that they had ever been aught else. All classes of society were represented at this general exhibition. Judges, lawyers, doctors, even clergymen, could not claim exemption. Culture and religion afforded feeble protection where allurement and indulgence ruled the hour.

Underneath this exterior of recklessness there was in the minds and hearts of the miners and business men of this society a strong and abiding sense of justice — and that saved the Territory. While they could enjoy what they called sport even to the very borders of crime and indulge in many practices which in themselves were criminal, yet when any one was murdered, robbed, abused, or hurt, a feeling of resentment, a desire for retaliation, animated all. With the ingathering of new men fear of the roughs gradually wore away, but the desire to escape responsibility, to acquire something and leave in peace, prevented any active measures for protection; and so far as organization was concerned, the law-and-order citizens, though in the majority, were as much at sea as ever.

NATHANIEL PITT LANGFORD, Vigilante Days and Ways

XXI

Texas and the Mexican War

128. Noah Smithwick Takes the Road to Texas

As Mexico completed its eleven-year struggle for independence from Spain in 1821, the first Anglo-Saxon groups settled upon Texan soil. This was the year in which Stephen F. Austin established a permanent Anglo-American settlement on the Brazos River. An extensive immigration from the United States began, and by 1830 there were believed to be about twenty thousand Americans in the Texas country. Difficulties soon arose between the Americans and English on one side, and the old Spanish-speaking stock on the other.

WHAT the discovery of gold was to California, the colonization act of 1825 was to Texas. In the following year Sterling C. Robinson, who had obtained a grant for a colony, for each hundred families of which he was to receive a bonus of 23,025 acres of land, went up into Kentucky recruiting. The glowing terms in which he talked of the advantages to be gained by emigration were well calculated to further his scheme. To every head of a family, if a farmer, was promised 177 acres of farming land and 4428 acres of pasture land for stock; colonists to be exempt from taxation six years from date of settlement, with the privilege of importing, duty free, everything they might desire for themselves and families; an abundance of game, wild horses, cattle, turkeys, buffalo; deer and antelope by the drove. The woods abounded in bee trees, wild grapes, plums, cherries, persimmons, haws, and dewberries, while walnuts, hickory nuts, and pecans were abundant along the watercourses. The climate was so mild that houses were not essential; neither was an abundance of clothing or bedding, buffalo robes and bearskins supplying all that was needed for the latter and buckskin the former. Corn in any quantity was to be had for the planting

In short, *there* the primitive curse was set at defiance. Mexican soldiers were stationed on the frontier to keep the Indians in check.

Of the hardships and privations, the ever-increasing danger from the growing dissatisfaction of the Indians, upon whose hunting grounds the whites were steadily encroaching, and the almost certainty of an ultimate war with Mexico, Robinson was discreetly silent. Viewed from that distance, the prospect was certainly flattering, and it should not occasion surprise that men with large families were induced to migrate thither with the hope of securing homes for themselves and children.

I was but a boy in my nineteenth year, and in for adventure. My older brothers talked of going. They abandoned the project, but it had taken complete possession of me. So, early in the following year, 1827, I started out from Hopkinsville, Kentucky, with all my worldly possessions, which consisted of a few dollars in money, a change of clothes, and a gun, of course, to seek my fortune in this lazy man's paradise.

Few steamboats plied the western waters, and none had ventured out to sea. The stagecoach, the only public overland conveyance, took me down to the mouth of the river, where I intended to take steamer for New Orleans; but the steamboat had not arrived, and no one knew when it would. My impatience could brook no delay; so I took passage on a flatboat or, as they were known in river parlance, a Mississippi broadhorn, the poor man's transfer.

Out on the broad bosom of the Father of Waters these boats floated from the Ohio, the Cumberland, the Tennessee, laden with the products of the vast region adjoining, to be floated down to New Orleans and thence distributed around the seaboard by sailing vessels. The flatboat, after serving its purpose, was broken up and sold for lumber and fuel, while the owner pocketed his cash and wended his way home, generally on foot up through Mississippi, where he was liable to be interviewed by footpads and relieved of his money if not of his life.

My transport was loaded with ice, artificial ice being a thing then unheard of. The crew consisted of three men whose principal duty was to look out for sawyers (sunken trees) and to keep clear of eddies, for a boat once drawn into the swirl would go floating around, in danger of colliding with the drift and being sunk. As flatboats never returned and seldom passed each other, the slow, leisurely drifting, day after day, became intolerably monotonous; so I stopped off at Natchez and waited for a steamboat. Very poetical it was, no doubt, this dropping down with the rippling stream; but I had not started out in search of the poetical.

By the time I reached New Orleans my money was running low and mechanics were getting big wages; so I went to work in the old Leeds foundry.

When the sickly season came on and the men began to leave, I again took up the line of march for Texas, this time on board a coasting schooner laden with supplies for the Mexican army. A steam tug towed us out to the mouth of the Mississippi as far as steamers ventured. The weather was lovely as a dream of Venice, and we sped away on the wings of the trade winds. We passed Galveston Island in plain view. There was no sign of human habitation on it, nothing to give promise of the thriving city which now covers it. It was only noted then as having been the headquarters of Lafitte and his pirates and as such was pointed out to me. The trip was a delightful one, and I was in fine spirits. On the third day we threaded the Paso Caballo and ran into Matagorda Bay, having made the run in a little over forty-eight hours, a remarkable record in those days.

We cast anchor in the mouth of the Lavaca River, where we had calculated to find the Mexican troops; but there were no troops, no agent, no one authorized to receive the goods. There was not an American there. The colonization law exempted from settlement all land within twenty-five miles of the coast; so the territory was given over to the Karankawa Indians, a fierce tribe, whose hand was against every man. A few Mexicans came around, but they spoke no English, and I understood no Spanish.

At length two men who had squatted on land six or eight miles up the river sighted the schooner and came down in a dugout. They took me in with them, and I spent my first night in Texas in their cabin. My first meal on Texas soil was dried venison sopped in honey. Next morning I set out on foot for De Witt's colony, ten miles farther up on the Lavaca.

NOAH SMITHWICK, *The Evolution of a State*

129. Davy Crockett Defends the Alamo

The frontiersman Crockett had been dropped from Congress because he opposed many of Jackson's measures in the face of strong Jackson sentiment in his district. Determining to leave Tennessee, he heard of the movement for Texan independence, and his sympathy was fired. He arrived at San Antonio in February, 1836, just in time to share in the gallant defense of the Alamo and to fall under a storm of bullets in the last Mexican assault. The authenticity of this autobiographical fragment is open to doubt, but its accuracy as a picture of the seige is accepted.

I WRITE this on the nineteenth of February, 1836, at San Antonio. We are all in high spirits, though we are rather short of provisions for men who have appetites that could digest anything but oppression; but no matter, we have a prospect of soon getting our bellies full of fighting, and that is victuals and drink to a true patriot any day. We had a little sort of convivial party last evening: just about a dozen of us set to work most patriotically to see whether we could not get rid of that curse of the land, whisky, and we made considerable progress.

This morning I saw a caravan of about fifty mules passing by Bexar and bound for Santa Fé. They were loaded with different articles to such a degree that it was astonishing how they could travel at all, and they were nearly worn out by their labors. They were without bridle or halter, and yet proceeded with perfect regularity in a single line; and the owners of the caravan rode their mustangs with their enormous spurs, weighing at least a pound apiece, with rowels an inch and a half in length, and lever bits of the harshest description, able to break the jaws of their animals under a very gentle pressure. The men were dressed in the costume of Mexicans. Colonel Travis sent out a guard to see that they were not laden with munitions of war for the enemy. I went out with the party.

Finding that the caravan contained nothing intended for the enemy, we assisted the owners to replace the heavy burdens on the backs of the patient but dejected mules and allowed them to pursue their weary and lonely way. For full two hours we could see them slowly winding along the narrow path, a faint line that ran like a thread through the extended prairie; and finally they were whittled down to the little end of nothing in the distance and were blotted out from the horizon.

February 22. — The Mexicans, about sixteen hundred strong, with their president, Santa Anna, at their head, aided by Generals Almonte, Cos, Sesma, and Castrillon, are within two leagues of Bexar. General Cos, it seems, has already forgot his parole of honor and is come back to retrieve the credit he lost in this place in December last. If he is captured a second time, I don't think he can have the impudence to ask to go at large again without giving better bail than on the former occasion. Some of the scouts came in and bring reports that Santa Anna has been endeavoring to excite the Indians to hostilities against the Texans, but so far without effect. The Comanches in particular entertain such hatred for the Mexicans and at the same time hold them in such contempt that they would rather turn their tomahawks against them and drive them from the land than lend a helping hand. We are up and doing and as lively as Dutch cheese in the dog days. Two hunters left the town this afternoon for the purpose of reconnoitering.

February 23. — Early this morning the enemy came in sight, marching in regular order and displaying their strength to the greatest advantage in order to strike us with terror. But that was no go; they'll find that they have to do with men who will never lay down their arms as long as they can stand on their legs. We held a short council of war, and, finding that we should be completely surrounded and overwhelmed by numbers if we remained in the town, we concluded to withdraw to the fortress of Alamo and defend it to the last extremity. We accordingly filed off in good order, having some days before placed all the surplus provisions, arms, and ammunition in the fortress. We have had a large national flag made; it is composed of thirteen stripes, red and white alternately, on a blue ground with a large white star of five points in the center, and between the points the letters TEXAS. As soon as all our little band, about one hundred and fifty in number, had entered and secured the fortress in the best possible manner, we set about raising our flag on the battlements. The enemy marched into Bexar and took possession of the town, a blood-red flag flying at their head, to indicate that we need not expect quarters if we should fall into their clutches. In the afternoon a messenger was sent from the enemy to Colonel Travis, demanding an unconditional and absolute surrender of the garrison, threatening to put every man to the sword in case of refusal. The only answer he received was a cannon shot; so the messenger left us with a flea in his ear, and the Mexicans commenced firing grenades at us, but without doing any mischief. At night Colonel Travis sent an express to Colonel Fanning at Goliad, about three or four days' march from this place, to let him know that we are besieged. The old pirate volunteered to go on this expedition and accordingly left the fort after nightfall.

February 24.— Very early this morning the enemy commenced a new battery on the banks of the river about three hundred and fifty yards from the fort, and by afternoon they amused themselves by firing at us from that quarter. Our Indian scout came in this evening, and with him a reinforcement of thirty men from Gonzales, who are just in the nick of time to reap a harvest of glory; but there is some prospect of sweating blood before we gather it in.

February 25.— The firing commenced early this morning, but the Mexicans are poor engineers, for we haven't lost a single man, and our outworks have sustained no injury. Our sharpshooters have brought down a considerable number of stragglers at a long shot. I got up before the peep of day, hearing an occasional discharge of a rifle just over the place where I was sleeping, and I was somewhat amazed to see Thimblerig mounted alone on the battlement, no one being on duty at the time but the sentries. "What are you doing there?" says I. "Paying my debts," says he, "interest and all." "And how do you make out?" says I. "I've nearly got through," says he; "stop a moment, Colonel, and I'll close the account." He clapped his rifle to his shoulder and blazed away, then jumped down from his perch and said: "That account's settled; them chaps will let me play out my game in quiet next time." I looked over the wall and saw four Mexicans lying dead on the plain. I asked him to explain what he meant by paying his debts, and he told me that he had run the grapeshot into four rifle balls and that he had taken an early stand to have a chance of picking off stragglers. "Now, Colonel, let's go take our bitters," said he; and so we did. The enemy have been busy during the night and have thrown up two batteries on the opposite side of the river. The battalion of Matamoras is posted there, and cavalry occupy the hills to the east and on the road to Gonzales. They are determined to surround us and cut us off from reinforcement or the possibility of escape by a sortie. Well, there's one thing they cannot prevent: we'll still go ahead, and sell our lives at a high price.

February 27. — The cannonading began early this morning, and ten bombs were thrown into the fort, but fortunately exploded without doing any mischief. So far it has been a sort of tempest in a teapot, not unlike a pitched battle in the Hall of Congress, where the parties array their forces, make fearful demonstrations on both sides, then fire away with loud-sounding speeches, which contain about as much meaning as the report of a howitzer charged with a blank cartridge. Provisions are becoming scarce, and the enemy are endeavoring to cut off our water. If they attempt to stop our grog in that manner, let them look out, for we shall become too wrathy for our shirts to hold us. We are not prepared to submit to an excise of that nature, and they'll find it out. This discovery has created considerable excitement in the fort.

February 28. — Last night our hunters brought in some corn and hogs and had a brush with a scout from the enemy beyond gun-shot of the fort. They put the scout to flight and got in without injury. They bring accounts that the settlers are flying in all quarters, in dismay, leaving their possessions to the mercy of the ruthless invader, who is literally engaged in a war of extermination more brutal than the untutored savage of the desert could be guilty of. Slaughter is indiscriminate, sparing neither sex, age, nor condition. Buildings have been burnt down, farms laid waste, and Santa Anna appears determined to verify his threat and convert the blooming paradise into a howling wilderness. For just one fair crack at that rascal even at a hundred yards distance I would bargain to break my Betsey and never pull trigger again. My name's not Crockett if I wouldn't get glory enough to appease my stomach for the remainder of my life.

February 29. — Before daybreak we saw General Sesma leave his camp with a large body of cavalry and infantry and move off in the direction of Goliad. We think that he must have received news of Colonel Fanning's coming to our relief. We are all in high spirits at the prospect of being able to give the rascals a fair shake on the plain. This business of being shut up makes a man wolfish.

I had a little sport this morning before breakfast. The enemy had planted a piece of ordnance within gunshot of the fort during the night, and the first thing in the morning they commenced a brisk cannonade point-blank against the spot where I was snoring. I turned out pretty smart and mounted the rampart. The gun was charged again, a fellow stepped forth to touch her off, but before he could apply the match I let him have it, and he keeled over. A second stepped up, snatched the match from the hand of the dying man, but Thimblerig, who had followed me, handed me his rifle, and the next instant the Mexican was stretched on the earth beside the first. A third came up to the cannon, my companion handed me another gun, and I fixed him off in like manner. A fourth, then a fifth, seized the match, who both met with the same fate, and then the whole party gave it up as a bad job and hurried off to the camp, leaving the cannon ready charged where they had planted it. I came down, took my bitters, and went to breakfast. Thimblerig told me that the place from which I had been firing was one of the snuggest stands in the whole fort, for he never failed picking off two or three stragglers before breakfast when perched up there. And I recollect now having seen him there, ever since he was wounded, the first thing in the morning and the last at night — and at times thoughtlessly playing at his eternal game.

March 1. — The enemy's forces have been increasing in numbers daily, notwithstanding they have already lost about three hundred men in the several assaults they have made upon us. I neglected to mention in the proper place that when the enemy came in sight we had but three bushels of corn in the garrison but have since found eighty bushels in a deserted house. Colonel Bowie's illness still continues, but he manages to crawl from his bed every day, that his comrades may see him. His presence alone is a tower of strength. — The enemy becomes more daring as his numbers increase.

March 2. — This day the delegates meet in general convention at the town of Washington to frame our Declaration of Independence. That the sacred instrument may never be trampled on by the children of those who have freely shed their blood to establish it is the sincere wish of David Crockett.

March 3. — We have given over all hopes of receiving assistance from Goliad or Refugio. Colonel Travis harangued the garrison and concluded by exhorting them, in case the enemy should carry the fort, to fight to the last gasp and render their victory even more serious to them than to us. This was followed by three cheers.

March 4. — Shells have been falling into the fort like hail during the day, but without effect. About dusk in the evening, we observed a man running toward the fort, pursued by about half a dozen Mexican cavalry. The bee hunter immediately knew him to be the old pirate who had gone to Goliad, and calling to the two hunters, he sallied out of the fort to the relief of the old man, who was hard pressed. I followed close after. Before we reached the spot the Mexicans were close on the heel of the old man, who stopped suddenly, turned short upon his pursuers, discharged his rifle, and one of the enemy fell from his horse. The chase was renewed, but finding that he would be overtaken and cut to pieces, he now turned again and, to the amazement of the enemy, became the assailant in his turn. He clubbed his gun and dashed among them like a wounded tiger, and they fled like sparrows. By this time we reached the spot and in the ardor of the moment followed some distance before we saw that our retreat to the fort was cut off by another detachment of cavalry. Nothing was to be done but to fight our way through. We were all of the same mind. "Go ahead!" cried I, and they shouted, "Go ahead, Colonel!" We dashed among them, and a bloody conflict ensued. They were about twenty in number, and they stood their ground. After the fight had continued about five minutes, a detachment was seen issuing from the fort to our relief; and the Mexicans scampered off, leaving eight of their comrades upon the field. But we did not escape unscathed, for both the pirate and the bee hunter were mortally wounded, and I received a saber cut across the forehead. The old man died, without speaking, as soon as we entered the fort. We bore my young friend to his bed, dressed his wounds, and I watched beside him. He lay without complaint or manifesting pain until about midnight, when he spoke, and I asked him if he wanted anything. "Nothing," he replied, but drew a sigh that seemed to rend his heart as he added, "Poor Kate of Nacogdoches!" His eyes were filled with tears as he continued, "Her words were prophetic, Colonel," and then he sang in a low voice that resembled the sweet notes of his own devoted Kate:

> But toom cam' the saddle, all bluidy to see,
> And hame cam' the steed, but hame never cam' he.

He spoke no more and, a few minutes after, died. Poor Kate, who will tell this to thee!

March 5. — Pop, pop, pop! Bom, bom, bom! throughout the day. No time for memorandums now. Go ahead! Liberty and independence forever!

[Here ends Colonel Crockett's manuscript.]

Colonel Crockett's Exploits and Adventures in Texas

130. "I Shall Never Surrender Nor Retreat"

In 1835 the English-speaking settlers in Texas organized for autonomy or independence, holding a convention at San Felipe de Austin and electing Henry Smith governor, and Sam Houston major-general of their army. Fighting soon began. Though a Mexican force was driven out of San Antonio, early in 1836 General Santa Anna returned with a larger army. He laid siege to the city, and the garrison of 183 brave men took up their stand in the Alamo there.

COMMANDANCY of the Alamo, Bexar, February 24, 1836. — To the people of Texas and all Americans in the world.

Fellow citizens and compatriots: I am besieged by a thousand or more of the Mexicans under Santa Anna. I have sustained a continual bombardment and cannonade for twenty-four hours and have not lost a man. The enemy has demanded a surrender at discretion; otherwise the garrison are to be put to the sword if the fort is taken. I have answered the demand with a cannon shot, and our flag still waves proudly from the walls. *I shall never surrender nor retreat.* Then, I call on you in the name of liberty, of patriotism, and everything dear to the American character, to come to our aid with all dispatch. The enemy is receiving reinforcements daily and will no doubt increase to three or four thousand in four or five days. If this call is neglected, I am determined to sustain myself as long as possible and die like a soldier who never forgets what is due to his own honor and that of his country. VICTORY OR DEATH.

WILLIAM BARRET TRAVIS
Lieutenant Colonel Commandant

P.S. The Lord is on our side. When the enemy appeared in sight we had not three bushels of corn. We have since found in deserted houses eighty or ninety bushels and got into the walls twenty or thirty head of beeves.

HENDERSON YOAKUM, History of Texas

131. Sam Houston Whips the Mexicans at San Jacinto

After various reverses to the American cause in Texas, Sam Houston took active command. He retreated before the Mexicans to the San Jacinto River, and then turning suddenly, struck a blow which crushed Santa Anna's army and ended the war. Already a declaration of independence had been adopted; and before autumn of 1836 Houston had been elected the first president of the new republic.

HEADQUARTERS of the Army, San Jacinto. April 25, 1836. — To His Excellency, David G. Burnet, President of the Republic of Texas.

Sir: I regret extremely that my situation, since the battle of the 21st, has been such as to prevent my rendering you my official report of the same previous to this time.

I have the honor to inform you that on the evening of the 18th instant, after a forced march of fifty-five miles, the army arrived opposite Harrisburg. That evening a courier of the enemy was taken, from whom I learned that General Santa Anna with one division of choice troops had marched in the direction of Lynch's Ferry on the San Jacinto, burning Harrisburg as he passed down.

The army was ordered to be in readiness to march early on the next morning. The main body effected a crossing over Buffalo Bayou, below Harrisburg, on the morning of the 19th, having left the baggage, the sick, and a sufficient camp guard in the rear. We continued the march throughout the night, making but one halt in the prairie for a short time, and without refreshments. At daylight we resumed the line of march. In a short distance our scouts encountered those of the enemy, and we received information that General Santa Anna was at New Washington and would that day take up the line of march for Anahuac, crossing at Lynch's Ferry. The Texan army halted within half a mile of the ferry in some timber and were engaged in slaughtering beeves when the army of Santa Anna was discovered approaching in battle array.

About nine o'clock on the morning of the 21st the enemy were reinforced by five hundred choice troops under the command of General Cos, increasing their effective force to upward of fifteen hundred men, whilst our aggregate force for the field numbered seven hundred and eighty-three.

At half past three o'clock in the evening I ordered the officers of the Texan army to parade their respective commands, having in the meantime ordered the bridge on the only road communicating with the Brazos, distant eight miles from our encampment, to be destroyed, thus cutting off all possibility of escape. Our troops paraded down with alacrity and spirit and were anxious for the contest. The conscious disparity in numbers seemed only to increase their enthusiasm and confidence and heighten their anxiety for the conflict.

Our cavalry was first dispatched to the front of the enemy's left for the purpose of attracting notice, whilst an extensive island of timber afforded us an opportunity of concentrating our forces and deploying from that point. Every evolution was performed with alacrity, the whole advancing rapidly in line and through an open prairie, without any protection whatever for our men. The artillery advanced and took station within two hundred yards of the enemy's breastwork and commenced an effective fire with grape and canister.

Colonel Sherman with his regiment having commenced the action upon our left wing, the whole line, advancing in double-quick time, rung the war cry, "Remember the Alamo!" received the enemy's fire, and advanced within point-blank shot before a piece was discharged from our lines.

The conflict lasted about eighteen minutes from the time of close action until we were in possession of the enemy's encampment. We took one piece of cannon (loaded), four stands of colors, all their camp equipage, stores, and baggage. Our cavalry had charged and routed that of the enemy upon the right and given pursuit to the fugitives, which did not cease until they arrived at the bridge which I have mentioned. Captain Karnes, always the foremost in danger, commanded the pursuers. The conflict in the breastwork lasted but a few moments. Many of the troops encountered hand to hand, and not having the advantage of bayonets on our side, our riflemen used their pieces as war clubs, breaking many of them off at the breech.

The rout commenced at half past four, and the pursuit by the main army continued until twilight. A guard was then left in charge of the enemy's encampment, and our army returned with their killed and wounded. In the battle our loss was two killed and twenty-three wounded, six of them mortally. The enemy's loss was six hundred and thirty killed; wounded, two hundred and eight; prisoners, seven hundred and thirty.

About six hundred muskets, three hundred sabers, and two

hundred pistols have been collected since the action. Several hundred mules and horses were taken and near twelve thousand dollars in specie. For several days previous to the action our troops were engaged in forced marches, exposed to excessive rains and the additional inconvenience of extremely bad roads, ill supplied with rations and clothing; yet amid every difficulty, they bore up with cheerfulness and fortitude and performed their marches with spirit and alacrity. There was no murmuring.

For the commanding general to attempt discrimination as to the conduct of those who commanded in the action or those who were commanded would be impossible. Our success in the action is conclusive proof of such daring intrepidity and courage. Every officer and man proved himself worthy of the cause in which he battled, while the triumph received a luster from the humanity which characterized their conduct after victory. Nor should we withhold the tribute of our grateful thanks from that Being who rules the destinies of nations and has in the time of greatest need enabled us to arrest a powerful invader whilst devastating our country.

I have the honor to be, with highest consideration,

Your obedient servant,
SAM HOUSTON, Commander-in-Chief
Official Report.

132. General Winfield Scott Captures Mexico City

The annexation of Texas in 1845 made war between the United States and Mexico almost certain. The Mexican press and government felt outraged by the act, and quickly broke off diplomatic relations. The American Government in June, 1845, ordered Zachary Taylor to western Texas, later informing him that he should consider the Rio Grande the American boundary. When hostilities began Taylor hastened to invade Mexico from the north; while in March, 1847, Winfield Scott landed an expeditionary force at Vera Cruz to march upon Mexico City.

Headquarters of the Army, September 18, 1847. — At the end of another series of arduous and brilliant operations, of more than forty-eight hours' continuance, this glorious army hoisted, on the morning of the 14th, the colors of the United States on the walls of [the National Palace of Mexico].

The first step in the new movement was to carry Chapultepec, a natural and isolated mound of great elevation, strongly fortified at its base [and] on its acclivities and heights. Besides a numerous garrison, here was the military college of the Republic, with a large number of sublieutenants and other students. Those works were within direct gunshot of the village of Tacubaya, and until carried, we could not approach the city on the west without making a circuit too wide and too hazardous.

In the course of the same night (that of the 11th), heavy batteries within easy ranges were established. . . .

To prepare for an assault, it was foreseen that the play of the batteries might run into the second day; but recent captures had not only trebled our siege pieces but also our ammunition, and we knew that we should greatly augment both by carrying the place. I was, therefore, in no haste in ordering an assault before the works were well crippled by our missiles.

The bombardment and cannonade, under the direction of Captain Huger, were commenced early in the morning of the 12th. Before nightfall, which necessarily stopped our batteries, we had perceived that a good impression had been made on the castle and its outworks and that a large body of the enemy had remained outside, toward the city, from an early hour, to avoid our fire, but to be at hand on its cessation in order to reinforce the garrison against an assault. The same outside force was discovered the next morning after our batteries had reopened upon the castle, by which we again reduced its garrison to the minimum needed for the guns.

The signal I had appointed for the attack was the momentary cessation of fire on the part of our heavy batteries. About eight o'clock in the morning of the 13th, judging that the time had arrived by the effect of the missiles we had thrown, I sent an aide-de-camp to Pillow and another to Quitman with notice that the concerted signal was about to be given. Both columns now advanced with an alacrity that gave assurance of prompt success. The batteries, seizing opportunities, threw shots and shells upon the enemy over the heads of our men, with good effect, particularly at every attempt to reinforce the works from without to meet our assault.

Major General Pillow's approach on the west side lay through an open grove filled with sharpshooters who were speedily dislodged; when, being up with the front of the attack and emerging into open space at the foot of a rocky acclivity, that gallant leader was struck down by an agonizing wound.

The broken acclivity was still to be ascended and a strong redoubt midway to be carried before reaching the castle on the heights. The advance of our brave men, led by brave officers, though necessarily slow, was unwavering, over rocks, chasms, and mines, and under the hottest fire of cannon and musketry. The redoubt now yielded to resistless valor, and the shouts that followed announced to the castle the fate that impended. The enemy were steadily driven from shelter to shelter. The retreat allowed not time to fire a single mine without the certainty of blowing up friend and foe. Those who at a distance attempted to apply matches to the long trains were shot down by our men. There was death below- as well as aboveground.

At length the ditch and wall of the main work were reached; the scaling ladders were brought up and planted by the storming parties; some of the daring spirits, first in the assault, were cast down — killed or wounded; but a lodgment was soon made; streams of heroes followed; all opposition was overcome and several of our regimental colors flung out from the upper walls, amidst long-continued shouts and cheers which sent dismay into the capital. No scene could have been more animating or glorious.

Major General Quitman, nobly supported by Brigadier Generals Shields and P. F. Smith, his other officers and men, was up with the part assigned him. Simultaneously with the movement on the west he had gallantly approached the southeast of the same works over a causeway with cuts and batteries and defended by an army strongly posted outside to the east of the works. Those formidable obstacles Quitman had to face with but little shelter for his troops or space for maneuvering. Deep ditches flanking the causeway made it difficult to cross on either side into the adjoining meadows, and these again were intersected by other ditches. Smith and his brigade had been early thrown out to make a sweep to the right, in order to present a front against the enemy's line (outside) and to turn two intervening batteries near the foot of Chapultepec.

Having turned the forest on the west and arriving opposite to the north center of Chapultepec, Worth came up with the troops in the road under Colonel Trousdale and aided, by a flank movement of a part of Garland's brigade, in taking the one-gun breastwork, then under the fire of Lieutenant Jackson's section of Captain Magruder's field battery. Continuing to advance, this division passed Chapultepec, attacking the right of the enemy's line resting on that road, about the moment of the general retreat consequent upon the capture of the formidable castle and its outworks.

Worth and Quitman were prompt in pursuing the retreating enemy, the former by the San Cosme aqueduct and the latter along that of Belén. Each had now advanced some hundred yards. . . .

I proceeded to join the advance of Worth within the suburb and beyond the turn at the junction of the aqueduct with the great highway from the west to the gate of San Cosme.

At this junction of roads we first passed one of those formidable systems of city defenses spoken of above, and it had not a gun! — a strong proof (1) that the enemy had expected us to fail in the attack upon Chapultepec, even if we meant anything more than a feint; (2) that, in either case, we designed, in his belief, to return and double our forces against the southern gates, a delusion kept up by the active demonstrations of Twiggs with the forces posted on that side; and (3) that advancing rapidly from the reduction of Chapultepec, the enemy had not time to shift guns — our previous captures had left him, comparatively, but few — from the southern gates.

Within those disgarnished works I found our troops engaged in a street fight against the enemy posted in gardens, at windows, and on housetops — all flat, with parapets. Worth ordered forward the mountain howitzers of Cadwalader's brigade, preceded by skirmishers and pioneers, with pickaxes and crowbars, to force windows and doors or to burrow through walls. The assailants were soon on an equality of position fatal to the enemy. By eight o'clock in the evening Worth had carried two batteries in this suburb. There was but one more obstacle, the San Cosme gate (customhouse), between him and the great square in front of the cathedral and palace — the heart of the city; and that barrier, it was known, could not by daylight resist our siege guns thirty minutes. . . .

Quitman within the city, adding several new defenses to the position he had won and sheltering his corps as well as practicable, now awaited the return of daylight under the guns of the formidable citadel yet to be subdued.

At about four o'clock next morning (September 14) a deputation of the *ayuntamiento* [city council] waited upon me to report that the federal government and the army of Mexico had fled from the capital some three hours before and to demand terms of capitulation in favor of the church, the citizens, and the municipal authorities. I promptly replied that I would sign no capitulation, that the city had been virtually in our possession from the time of the lodgments effected by Worth and Quitman the day before, that I regretted the silent escape of the Mexican army, that I should levy upon the city a moderate contribution for special purposes, and that the American army should come under no terms not *self*-imposed — such only as its own honor, the dignity of the United States, and the spirit of the age should, in my opinion, imperiously demand and impose.

Memoirs of Lieutenant-General Scott

XXII

Politics

133. How John Quincy Adams Was Made President

The election of 1824 was curiously indecisive. Andrew Jackson received ninety-nine electoral votes; John Quincy Adams eighty-four; William H. Crawford forty-one; and Henry Clay thirty-seven. The contest was thrown into the House of Representatives, where each of the twenty states had one vote. The decision was still close, and New York proved to be the pivotal state.

THE FRIENDS of Crawford lacked but one of being half of the New York delegation so that the diversion of a single vote from Mr. Adams would produce a tie. General Van Rensselaer was, through his first wife, a brother-in-law to General Hamilton and had at an early age imbibed his dislike of the Adamses. He at no time entertained the idea of voting for Mr. Adams and communicated his views to me at an early period and without reserve. On the morning of the election he came to my room and told me he had some thought of voting for General Jackson and asked me whether it would make any difference in the general result, adding that as he had uniformly told me that he intended to vote for Crawford he did not think it proper to change his determination without letting me know it. I told him that as his vote could not benefit Mr. Crawford, it was of no importance to us whether it was given to him or to General Jackson, but submitted whether, as his intention was known to others as well as myself, there was an adequate motive for subjecting himself to the imputation of fickleness of purpose by a change which would produce no beneficial result to any one. He reflected a moment and then said I was right and that he would adhere to Crawford.

As I entered the Chamber, Mr. Cuthbert met me and said that it was not necessary that I should do anything in the matter, as Mr. Van Rensselaer had at that moment assured him that he certainly would not vote for Mr. Adams on the first ballot. I remained to see the voting, which took place presently afterward, and was pained to witness Mr. Van Rensselaer's obvious agitation and distress. When the votes of the New York delegation were counted, it was found that Mr. Adams had a majority of *one*. The vote of the state was of course given to him, and he was elected. Mr. Van Rensselaer at once admitted that he had voted for Mr. Adams and thus changed the anticipated result.

I had asked no explanations of the General nor did I intend to do so, as I was satisfied that he could not give any that it would be agreeable to him to make. But an evening or two after the election, whilst on our way to visit Mrs. Decatur, he volunteered an explanation which he did not make confidential but of which I did not speak until a long time afterward, and, to the best of my recollections, for the first time to Mr. Clay. He said that after what had passed between us, he felt it to be due to me that he should explain the change in his vote which I had so little reason to expect. He then proceeded to inform me that when he arrived at the Capitol, Mr. Clay invited him to the Speaker's room, where he found Mr. Webster; that they took the ground that the question of election or no election would depend upon his vote; that they portrayed to him the consequences that would in all probability result from a disorganization of the government and referred in very impressive terms to the great stake he had in the preservation of order from his large estate and kindred considerations. He said that his mind was much disturbed by these views, which he had not before regarded in so serious a light, but that he returned to the Chamber determined not to vote for Mr. Adams on the first ballot, whatever he might be induced to do ultimately if their anticipations of a failure to make an election should prove to be well founded. He took his seat fully resolved to vote for Mr. Crawford, but before the box reached him, he dropped his head upon the edge of the desk and made a brief appeal to his Maker for His guidance in the matter — a practice he frequently observed on great emergencies — and when he removed his hand from his eyes he saw on the floor directly below him a ticket bearing the name of

John Quincy Adams. This occurrence, at a moment of great excitement and anxiety, he was led to regard as an answer to his appeal; and taking up the ticket, he put it in the box. In this way it was that Mr. Adams was made President.

The Autobiography of Martin Van Buren

134. Andrew Jackson Is Inaugurated President

A new era in American political history began when Jackson was sworn in as President on March 4, 1829. He had refused to pay the customary courtesy call on the retiring executive, John Quincy Adams, for he could not forget that a newspaper believed to be Adams' personal organ had attacked Mrs. Jackson's reputation. With Jackson there came to the Capital a horde of Westerners and Southerners typical of the new Jacksonian Democracy. "The backwoods had boiled over and spilled into Washington." Lean, roughly-dressed, profane backwoodsmen filled the city. Tobacco-chewing patriots from beyond the mountains, with muddy boots, homespun clothes, and fur caps, jostled the Tammany men from New York and the more polished Democrats from Virginia and Maryland. They stormed the inaugural reception at the White House in a way that horrified aristocratic observers.

WASHINGTON, March 11, Sunday [1829]. — The inauguration was not a thing of detail or a succession of small incidents. No, it was one grand whole, an imposing and majestic spectacle, and to a reflective mind one of moral sublimity. Thousands and thousands of people, without distinction of rank, collected in an immense mass round the Capitol, silent, orderly, and tranquil, with their eyes fixed on the front of that edifice, waiting the appearance of the President in the portico. The door from the rotunda opens; preceded by the marshals, surrounded by the judges of the Supreme Court, the old man with his gray locks, that crown of glory, advances, bows to the people who greet him with a shout that rends the air. The cannons from the heights around, from Alexandria and Fort Warburton, proclaim the oath he has taken, and all the hills reverberate the sound. It was grand — it was sublime! An almost breathless silence succeeded, and the multitude was still, listening to catch the sound of his voice, though it was so low as to be heard only by those nearest to him. After reading his speech the oath was administered to him by the Chief Justice. Then Marshall presented the Bible. The President took it from his hands, pressed his lips to it, laid it reverently down, then bowed again to the people — yes, to the people in all their majesty. And had the spectacle closed here, even Europeans must have acknowledged that a free people, collected in their might, silent and tranquil, restrained solely by a moral power, without a shadow around of military force, was majesty rising to sublimity and far surpassing the majesty of kings and princes surrounded with armies and glittering in gold. But I will not anticipate, but will give you an account of the inauguration in more detail. The whole of the preceding day immense crowds were coming into the city from all parts, lodgings could not be obtained, and the newcomers had to go to Georgetown, which soon overflowed, and others had to go to Alexandria. I was told the avenue and adjoining streets were so crowded on Tuesday afternoon that it was difficult to pass.

A national salute was fired early in the morning and ushered in the 4th of March. By ten o'clock the avenue was crowded with carriages of every description, from the splendid coach down to wagons and carts, filled with women and children, some in finery and some in rags, for it was the people's President, and all would see him; the men all walked. Julia, Anna Maria, and I (the other girls would not adventure), accompanied by Mr. Wood, set off before eleven and followed the living stream that was pouring along to the Capitol. The terraces, the balconies, the porticoes, seemed, as we approached, already filled. We rode round the whole square, taking a view of the animated scene. Then, leaving the carriage outside the palisades, we entered the inclosed grounds, where we were soon joined by John Cranet and another gentleman, which offered each of us a protector. We walked round the terrace several times, every turn meeting groups of ladies and gentlemen whom

we knew — all with smiling faces. The day was warm and delightful. From the south terrace we had a view of Pennsylvania and
Louisiana Avenues, crowded with people hurrying toward the Capitol. It was a most exhilarating scene! Most of the ladies preferred
being inside of the Capitol, and the eastern portico, damp and cold
as it was, had been filled from nine in the morning by ladies who
wished to be near the General when he spoke. Every room was filled
and the windows crowded. But as so confined a situation allowed
no general view, we would not coop ourselves up and certainly
enjoyed a much finer view of the spectacle, both in its whole and
in its details, than those within the walls. We stood on the south
steps of the terrace; when the appointed hour came, saw the General and his company advancing up the Avenue, slow, very slow,
so impeded was his march by the crowds thronging around him.
Even from a distance he could be discerned from those who accompanied him, for he only was uncovered (the servant in presence of his sovereign, the people). The south side of the Capitol
Hill was literally alive with the multitude who stood ready to receive the hero and the multitude who attended him. "There, there,
that is he," exclaimed different voices. "Which?" asked others. "He
with the white head," was the reply. "Ah," exclaimed others, "there
is the old man and his gray hair, there is the old veteran, there is
Jackson." At last he enters the gate at the foot of the hill and
turns to the road that leads round to the front of the Capitol. In
a moment every one who until then had stood like statues gazing
on the scene below them rushed onward, to right, to left, to be
ready to receive him in the front. Our party, of course, were more
deliberate. We waited until the multitude had rushed past us and
then left the terrace and walked round to the farthest side of the
square, where there were no carriages to impede us, and entered
it by the gate fronting the Capitol. Here was a clear space, and stationing ourselves on the central gravel walk, we stood so as to
have a clear, full view of the whole scene — the Capitol in all its
grandeur and beauty. The portico and grand steps leading to it
were filled with ladies. Scarlet, purple, blue, yellow, white draper-
ies and waving plumes of every kind and color among the white
pillars had a fine effect. In the center of the portico was a table
covered with scarlet; behind it, the closed door leading into the

rotunda; below the Capitol and all around, a mass of living beings, not a ragged mob but well dressed and well behaved, respectable and worthy citizens. Mr. Frank Key, whose arm I had, and an old and frequent witness of great spectacles, often exclaimed, as well as myself, a mere novice, "It is beautiful, it is sublime!" The sun had been obscured through the morning by a mist or haziness. But the concussion in the air, produced by the discharge of the cannon, dispersed it, and the sun shone forth in all his brightness. At the moment the General entered the portico and advanced to the table the shout that rent the air still resounds in my ears. When the speech was over and the President made his parting bow, the barrier that had separated the people from him was broken down, and they rushed up the steps, all eager to shake hands with him. It was with difficulty he made his way through the Capitol and down the hill to the gateway that opens on the Avenue. Here for a moment he was stopped. The living mass was impenetrable. After a while a passage was opened, and he mounted his horse which had been provided for his return (for he had walked to the Capitol). Then such a cortege as followed him! Country men, farmers, gentlemen, mounted and dismounted, boys, women, and children, black and white. Carriages, wagons, and carts all pursuing him to the President's house. This I only heard of, for our party went out at the opposite side of the square and went to Colonel Benton's lodgings to visit Mrs. Benton and Mrs. Gilmore. Here was a perfect levee, at least a hundred ladies and gentlemen, all happy and rejoicing — wine and cake was handed in profusion. We sat with this company and stopped on the summit of the hill until the avenue was comparatively clear, though at any other time we should have thought it terribly crowded, streams of people on foot and in carriages of all kinds still pouring toward the President's house. We went home; found your papa and sisters at the bank, standing at the upper windows, where they had been seen by the President, who took off his hat to them, which they insisted was better than all we had seen. From the bank to the President's house, for a long while, the crowd rendered a passage for us impossible. Some went into the cashier's parlor, where we found a number of ladies and gentlemen and had cake and wine in abundance. In about an hour the pavement was clear enough for us to walk. Your father, Mr. Wood, Mr. Ward, Mr. Lyon, with us, we set off to the President's house, but on a nearer approach found an entrance impossible; the yard and avenue was compact with living matter. The day was delightful, the scene animating; so we walked backward and forward, at every turn meeting some new acquaintance and stopping to talk and shake hands. Among others we met Zavr. Dickinson with Mr. Frelinghuysen and Doctor Elmendorf, and Mr. Samuel Bradford. We continued promenading here until near three, returned home unable to stand, and threw ourselves on the sofa. Some one came and informed us the crowd before the President's house was so far lessened that they thought we might enter. This time we effected our purpose. But what a scene did we witness! *The majesty of the people* had disappeared, and a rabble, a mob, of boys, Negroes, women, children, scrambling, fighting, romping. What a pity, what a pity! No arrangements had been made, no police officers placed on duty, and the whole house had been inundated by the rabble mob. We came too late. The President, after having been *literally* nearly pressed to death and almost suffocated and torn to pieces by the people in their eagerness to shake hands with Old Hickory, had retreated through the back way or south front and had escaped to his lodgings at Gadsby's. Cut glass and china to the amount of several thousand dollars had been broken in the struggle to get the refreshments. Punch and other articles had been carried out in tubs and buckets, but had it been in hogsheads it would have been insufficient; ice creams and cake and lemonade for twenty thousand people, for it is said that number were there, though I think the estimate exaggerated. Ladies fainted, men were seen with bloody noses, and such a scene of confusion took place as is impossible to describe — those who got in could not get out by the door again but had to scramble out of windows. At one time the President, who had retreated and retreated until he was pressed against the wall, could only be secured by a number of gentlemen forming round him and making a kind of barrier of their own bodies; and the pressure was so great that Colonel Bomford, who was one, said that at one time he was afraid they should have been pushed down or on the President. It was then the windows were thrown open and the torrent found an outlet, which otherwise might have proved fatal.

This concourse had not been anticipated and therefore not provided against. Ladies and gentlemen only had been expected at this levee, not the people en masse. But it was the people's day, and the people's President, and the people would rule. God grant that one day or other the people do not put down all rule and rulers. I fear, enlightened freemen as they are, they will be found, as they have been found in all ages and countries where they get the power in their hands, that of all tyrants, they are the most ferocious, cruel, and despotic. The noisy and disorderly rabble in the President's house brought to my mind descriptions I had read of the mobs in Tuileries and at Versailles. I expect to hear the carpets and furniture are ruined; the streets were muddy, and these guests all went thither on foot.

Mrs. Samuel Harrison Smith, The First Forty Years of Washington Society

135. "Liberty and Union"

Sectional feeling between North and South grew strained in 1828-1830, when Southern planters felt outraged by the "Tariff of Abominations" passed in 1828. Calhoun brought forward his doctrine of the right of the states to nullify any Federal law within their borders. In January, 1830, Daniel Webster joined in debate with Calhoun's mouthpiece, Robert Y. Hayne; and he achieved one of the greatest oratorical triumphs of his career.

I HAVE thus stated the reasons of my dissent to the doctrines which have been advanced and maintained. I am conscious, sir, of having detained you and the Senate much too long. I was drawn into the debate with no previous deliberation such as is suited to the discussion of so grave and important a subject. But it is a subject of which my heart is full, and I have not been willing to suppress the utterance of its spontaneous sentiments. I cannot even now persuade myself to relinquish it without expressing once more my deep conviction that, since it respects nothing less than the Union of the states, it is of most vital and essential importance to the public happiness. I profess, sir, in my career hitherto, to have kept steadily in view the prosperity and honor of the whole country and the preservation of our federal Union. It is to that Union we owe our safety at home and our consideration and dignity abroad. It is to that Union that we are chiefly indebted for whatever makes us most proud of our country. That Union we reached only by the discipline of our virtues in the severe school of adversity. It had its origin in the necessities of disordered finance, prostrate commerce, and ruined credit. Under its benign influence, these great interests immediately awoke as from the dead and sprang forth with newness of life. Every year of its duration has teemed with fresh proofs of its utility and its blessings, and although our territory has stretched out wider and wider and our population spread farther and farther, they have not outrun its protection or its benefits. It has been to us all a copious fountain of national, social, and personal happiness. I have not allowed myself, sir, to look beyond the Union, to see what might lie hidden in the dark recess behind. I have not coolly weighed the chances of preserving liberty when the bonds that unite us together shall be broken asunder. I have not accustomed myself to hang over the precipice of disunion, to see whether, with my short sight, I can fathom the depth of the abyss below; nor could I regard him as a safe counselor, in the affairs of this government, whose thoughts should be mainly bent on considering, not how the Union should be best preserved, but how tolerable might be the condition of the people when it shall be broken up and destroyed. While the Union lasts, we have high, exciting, gratifying prospects spread out before us, for us and our children. Beyond that, I seek not to penetrate the veil. God grant that in my day, at least, that curtain may not rise. God grant that, on my vision, never may be opened what lies behind. When my eyes shall be turned to behold for the last time the sun in heaven, may I not see him shining on the broken and dishonored fragments of a once glorious Union; on states dissevered, discordant, belligerent; on a land rent with civil feuds, or drenched, it may be, in fraternal blood! Let their last feeble and lingering glance rather behold the gorgeous ensign of the republic, now known and honored throughout the earth, still full high advanced, its arms and trophies streaming in their original luster, not a stripe erased or polluted, nor a single star obscured, bearing for its motto no such miserable interrogatory as, What is all this worth? nor those other words of delusion and folly, Liberty first, and Union afterward; but everywhere, spread all over in characters of living light, blazing on all its ample folds, as they float over the sea and over the land, and in every wind under the whole heavens, that other sentiment, dear to every true American heart — Liberty *and* Union, now and forever, one and inseparable!

DANIEL WEBSTER, Reply to Hayne, January 26, 1830

136. "Tippecanoe and Tyler Too"

The Presidential contest of 1840 between William Henry Harrison of Ohio and Martin Van Buren of New York was one of the noisiest and most enthusiastic in American annals. The Whigs rallied behind Harrison with songs, barbecues, and monster mass meetings — "acres of men." One of their silk-stocking leaders in New York, the wealthy ex-mayor and diarist Philip Hone, here describes the mighty Whig procession in Boston.

BOSTON, Thursday, September 8, 1840. — The great day is over, and how shall I attempt to describe it? The weather, which was doubtful last night, was bright this morning, and the delegates from other states and from the different towns in Massachusetts began to assemble on the Common at nine o'clock, with their standards, badges, and other paraphernalia. The scene began to be very soon of the most exciting character. Crowds were pressing toward the spot from every quarter. The windows of the fine houses which surround the Common were filled with well-dressed ladies. Horsemen were galloping to and fro and Old Men of the Revolution tottering toward the places allotted to them. The marquee of the chief marshal, Franklin Dexter, was placed in the center of the Common, from whence issued troops of handsome young men on horseback and on foot, with their badges of office, conveying his orders to distant points and completing the general arrangements. I was directed to join the other invited guests at the State House, where I met Mr. Webster, the president of the day, and many other distinguished men. The procession did not begin to move until twelve o'clock.

It was headed by an escort of men on horseback to the number of two thousand. Then followed forty or fifty carriages containing the Revolutionary soldiers and some others who were too aged to walk; after which the chief marshal and committee of arrangements, the president of the day, members of Congress and invited guests, and then the different delegations, with flags and banners "flouting the skies," devices of all kinds, and mottoes — some excellent, some so-and-so, and others displaying more party zeal than either wit or good sense. Of those I saw I was most pleased with a whaleboat from New Bedford with all the apparatus for taking the whale and extracting the oil; she was manned by six old masters of whale ships and drawn on a car by six gray horses; and with a colossal shoe from Lynn, in which were seated a number of shoemakers from that celebrated town of Massachusetts, in which shoemaking is the sole occupation. The number of persons in the procession is variously estimated by some as high as fifty thousand, but I think about thirty-two thousand is nearest right. In the number of banners and mottoes, which must have amounted to several hundred, the following were noticed as among the best:

Maryland, a representation of Van Buren under the pressure of a screw, turned by the hand of a mechanic. Motto, "No pressure that an honest man need regret." Marblehead, a representation of a mammoth cod, over which was the motto: "A voice from the deep which seemed to say, 'For Benton a rod, And a bounty on cod.'" The banner of the whaleboat which I have described above, representing a pot on the fire, with Van Buren, Woodbury, and Morton in it up to their chins, with the following motto: "We have tried them *in* office — now we mean to *try them out*."

The procession moved up Beacon Street and down the other side of the Common, thence through several of the principal streets in that part of the city, by Faneuil Hall, around which it made a complete circuit, and so by the wharves and streets occupied by working-people to Charlestown bridge, which it crossed; proceeded through Charlestown and arrived at Bunker Hill after a march of two hours and a half. The president and invited guests occupied a stage, and the delegations were marshaled in their allotted places as they severally came on the ground, a work which occupied a long time; and before they all got to it, the ceremonies were commenced by a short address from Mr. Webster. The Bunker Hill declaration (copies of which had been printed and distributed on the route) was then read by Mr. Winthrop, after which several of the distinguished visitors were introduced to the audience, and each in turn made a short speech much to the purpose.

The most remarkable part of this most splendid spectacle was the appearance of the streets through which the procession passed, and the enthusiastic participation of the people in the triumph. It was after all only a party affair, not one of general or national import in which the current of public opinion may have compelled some reluctantly to join. We took nothing by compulsion, nobody was compelled to shout, and yet the whole line of march was enlivened by the cheers of the men and the smiles of the women. The balconies and windows were filled with women, well dressed, with bright eyes and bounding bosoms, waving handkerchiefs, exhibiting flags and garlands, and casting bouquets of flowers upon us; and this, too, was not confined to any particular part of the city or any class of inhabitants. Young children were exhibited in rows with flags in their little hands, and whenever their greetings were returned, mothers and daughters, old women and beautiful young ones, seemed delighted that their share in the jubilee was recognized.

The stores and shops were all closed; flags were suspended over the streets; arches were erected with suitable devices and inscriptions at the entrances into the several wards; and "Welcome, Whigs" met us at the corners of the principal streets. When we had crossed the bridge and entered Charlestown the same cheering spectacles were presented, and an arch of triumph and welcome, with an extract from one of Mr. Webster's speeches, received the procession. It was Whig all over; there are certainly some Locofocos in Boston, but I am puzzled to know what became of them on this occasion.

I returned to town with Mr. Webster in a carriage and went at a late hour with Ogden Hoffman and Prescott Hall to dine with Mr.

Sargent. In pursuance of the directions of the committee of arrangements, I went at seven o'clock to Mr. Webster's lodgings at the United States Hotel, where I found a number of gentlemen, and we accompanied him to Faneuil Hall, where he was to preside. When we came to the Hall it was crowded to suffocation, and it was extremely difficult for him or the speakers to get to their places. Mr. Webster opened the meeting with some remarks, and Mr. Leigh, Governor Pennington, Governor Ellsworth, and others spoke. It was allotted to me also to speak, but I was overcome with fatigue and the crowd and heat of the room, and made my escape before I was called.

New Bedford, Friday, September 11.—This was another day of excitement. At an early hour the committee of arrangements in Boston called upon me to request my attendance at Faneuil Hall, where the Whigs assembled to receive and do honor to the Revolutionary officers and soldiers who had participated in the Bunker Hill jubilee of yesterday. Mr. Webster again presided. The noble hall was filled in every part, and the assemblage was graced with the presence of many ladies. The president opened the meeting with some touching and eloquent remarks. The venerable Asher Robbins of Rhode Island was first called out and made an excellent speech, but in a voice too low to be heard. My turn came next.

We left Boston at half past four o'clock. Judge Warren remained in Boston and Mr. Joseph Grinnell and his wife came on with us. We came on the railroad with an enormous number of cars, having the Whig delegates from this town and Nantucket and a large number of those from New York returning. There was shouting and hurrahing all the way.

The Diary of Philip Hone

137. Mr. Webster Kills Seventeen Roman Proconsuls

Though President Harrison had studied at Hampden-Sidney College in Virginia, he was much more of a military man than a scholar. It was natural that he should turn his inaugural address, a discourse on the rights and duties of the Chief Executive, over to Webster (whom he had selected as his Secretary of State) for revision.

MR. WEBSTER became Secretary of State under General Harrison in 1841. They had no interview before he was appointed. It was done by correspondence, by an offer of the place on the part of General Harrison by letter, and acceptance by letter on that of Mr. Webster. They did not meet until eight or ten days previous to the inauguration. General Harrison arrived at Washington from Cincinnati about the time Mr. Webster arrived from Massachusetts. Mr. Webster was invited by Mr. Seaton, one of the editors of the *National Intelligencer* and a very warm personal friend of his, to come to his house, as he would be more quiet there and less exposed to intrusion than at a hotel, and to stay until he should get a house and move his family into it. He was constantly occupied with General Harrison on matters connected with the formation of the cabinet, from early morning until the dinner hour, which was six o'clock. It seems that he had prepared an inaugural message for General Harrison. One day among other arrangements he suggested to the new President, in as delicate a way as he could, the fact that he had sketched an inaugural, knowing that General Harrison would be overwhelmed with calls and business after his election, and he himself having leisure to write. The General at once replied that it was not necessary; that he had prepared his own inaugural.

"Oh, yes," said he, "I have got that all ready."

"Will you allow me to take it home and read it tonight?" asked Mr. Webster.

"Certainly," the President replied; "and please let me take yours."

So they exchanged the documents, and the next morning, when they met, General Harrison said to Mr. Webster:

"If I should read your inaugural instead of mine, everybody would know that you wrote it, and that I did not. Now this is the only official paper which I propose to write, for I do not intend to interfere with my secretaries, but this is a sort of acknowledgment on my part to the American people of the great honor they have conferred upon me in elevating me to this high office, and although, of course, it is not so suitable as yours, still it is mine, and I propose to let the people have it just as I have written it. I must deliver my own instead of yours."

Mr. Webster told me that he was a good deal annoyed, because the message was, according to his judgment and taste, so inappropriate. It entered largely into Roman history and had a great deal to say about the states of antiquity and the Roman proconsuls and various matters of that kind. Indeed the word "proconsul" was repeated in it a great many times.

When he found that the President was bent upon using his own inaugural, Mr. Webster said that his desire was to modify it and to get in some things that were not there and get out some things that were there, for as it then stood, he said, it had no more to do with the affairs of the American government and people than a chapter in the Koran. Mr. Webster suggested to General Harrison that he should like to put in some things, and General Harrison rather reluctantly consented to let him take it. Mr. Webster spent a portion of the next day in modifying the message. Mrs. Seaton remarked to him, when he came home rather late that day, that he looked fatigued and worried; but he replied that he was sorry that she had waited dinner for him.

"That is of no consequence at all, Mr. Webster," said she, "but I am sorry to see you looking so worried and tired. I hope nothing has gone wrong. I really hope nothing has happened."

"You would think that something had happened," he replied, "if you knew what I have done. I have killed *seventeen Roman proconsuls* as dead as smelts, every one of them!"

PETER HARVEY, Reminiscences and Anecdotes of Daniel Webster

138. "John Quincy Adams Is No More"

John Quincy Adams retired from the Presidency, in 1829, a defeated and discouraged man, but with characteristic willingness to serve his people, he accepted a seat in the lower House of Congress which his constituency tendered him, and served there for seventeen years. The most venerable figure in the House, he was likewise the ablest and most feared debater, and in his seventieth year he fought and won a memorable fight for the right of petition. His death, at his post of duty, was a fitting end to a long and useful life.

FEBRUARY 24, 1848. — *Death of Mr. Adams.* John Quincy Adams is no more. Full of age and honors, the termination of his eventful career accorded with the character of its progress. He died, as he must have wished to die, breathing his last in the Capitol, stricken down by the angel of death on the field of his civil glory — employed in the service of the people, in the people's senate house, standing by the Constitution at the side of its altar, and administering in the temple of liberty the rites which he had assisted in establishing.

At twenty minutes past one o'clock on Monday, the 21st, Mr. Adams, being in his seat in the House of Representatives (from which he was never absent during its session), attempted to rise (as was supposed, to speak), but sank back upon his seat and fell upon his side. Those nearest caught him in their arms. Mr. Grinnell bathed his temples with ice water, when he rallied for an instant. The House immediately adjourned in the utmost consternation, as did the Senate, when informed of the melancholy event. His last words were characterized by that concise eloquence for which he was remarkable: "*This is the last of earth; I am content.*" Dr. Fries of Ohio, a member, raised him in his arms and bore him to the Speaker's room, where he lay, with occasional indications of consciousness, until last evening, a few minutes before seven o'clock, when he breathed his last. The intelligence of his death came to Albany by the telegraph.

Thus has "a great man fallen in Israel" — in many respects the most wonderful man of the age; certainly the greatest in the United States — perfect in knowledge, but deficient in practical results. As a statesman, he was pure and incorruptible, but too irascible to lead men's judgment. They admired him, and all voices were hushed when he arose to speak, because they were sure of being instructed by the words he was about to utter; but he made no converts to his opinions, and when President his desire to avoid party influence lost him all the favor of all parties. In matters of history, tradition, statistics, authorities, and practice he was the oracle of the House, of which he was at the time of his decease a member. With an unfailing memory, rendered stronger by cultivation, he was never mistaken; none disputed his authority. Every circumstance of his long life was "penned down" at the moment of its occurrence; every written communication, even to the minute of a dinner invitation, was carefully preserved, and nothing passed uncopied from his pen. He "talked like a book" on all subjects. Equal to the highest, the planetary system was not above his grasp. Familiar with the lowest, he could explain the mysteries of a mousetrap.

I listened once, at my own table, with a delight which I shall never forget, to his dissertation on the writings of Shakespeare and an analysis of the character of Hamlet — the most beautiful creation (he called it) of the human imagination. At my request he afterward sent me a synopsis of the latter part of this delightful conversation, a paper which has always been a treasure to me and which will be more precious now that its illustrious author is no more. I listened once, with Mr. Webster, for an hour, at Mr. Adams' breakfast table in Washington, to a disquisition on the subject of *dancing girls;* from those who danced before the ark and the daughter of Jairus, whose premature appearance caused so melancholy a termination to her graceful movements in the dance, through the fascinating exhibition of the odalisques of the harem down to the present times of Fanny Ellsler and Taglioni. He was ignorant on no subject and could enlighten and instruct on all; he loved to talk and was pleased with good listeners — vain, no doubt, and not entirely free from prejudices, but preserving his mental faculties to the last. His sudden death, even at the advanced age of eighty years, to which he arrived in July last, will be acutely felt and deeply deplored by those who have habitually enjoyed the refreshing streams which flowed from the copious fountains of his diversified knowledge.

Mr. Adams' name will be recorded on the brightest page of American history, as statesman, diplomatist, philosopher, orator, author, and, above all, Christian.

The Diary of Philip Hone

139. "The Senator from South Carolina Is in His Seat"

Calhoun, Clay, and Webster all played their last great roles in the debates on compromise between South and North in 1850. To express his opinions on Clay's great Omnibus or Compromise Bill, Calhoun wrote his last formal speech, which Mason of Virginia read to the Senate on March 4th. Immediately afterward Calhoun went to hear Webster's great speech of March 7th in favor of compromise. Before the month closed he was dead. Clay died in June of the same year and Webster in October.

WHEN Mr. Webster was about to deliver his 7th of March speech [1850], he invited me to come on to Washington to hear it. He intended to make it a great effort, the crowning address of his later public life; and as he knew beforehand that his actions and motives would be misconstrued and that the speech would bring down upon him condemnation from many quarters, he was resolved that he would make use of all his powers to render it worthy of his really high motives and his fame. Early on the morning of the 7th I was sitting with him in his house when the sergeant-at-arms of the Senate came in. He told Mr. Webster that already not only the Senate chamber itself but all the approaches to it were crowded by an eager multitude. A great speech from Mr. Webster was a national event. Mr. Webster looked at me and in a sad voice spoke of this as being one of the last times that he should ever address listening masses on the floor of the Senate, and of the rapidly approaching close of his public life. . . .

On going to the Senate chamber at the proper time, I found an excellent seat reserved for me, near and a little in front of the spot where Mr. Webster would stand when he made his speech. While he was speaking an affecting incident occurred, which illustrated the warmth of feeling between Mr. Calhoun and himself. It appeared that, several days before, Mr. Webster had paid a visit to Mr. Calhoun in his sickroom at the old Capitol building. The venerable South Carolina senator was very ill, and it was thought that he would never be able to appear in his seat again. The conversation turning upon the speech that Mr. Webster was about to make, the sick statesman expressed an earnest wish to hear it. Mr. Webster replied that he hoped he would be able to get to the Senate, as he himself was anxious that Mr. Calhoun should be present. Mr. Calhoun shook his head sadly and said that he feared he was on his deathbed, and Mr. Webster parted from him, fully impressed with the belief that the venerable invalid must soon pass away.

Mr. Webster had not been speaking long on this occasion when I saw a tall, gaunt figure, wrapped in a long black cloak, with deep, cavernous black eyes and a thick mass of snow-white hair brushed back from the large brow and falling to the shoulders, advance with slow and feeble steps through the lobby behind the Vice-President's chair, and then, aided by one of the senators, approach and sink into a chair on the opposite side of the chamber. I looked at Mr. Webster and observed that as he spoke his face was turned the other way, so that he had not seen the almost ghostly figure come in. He went on speaking in his deep and sonorous tones and at last came to a passage wherein he alluded to something Mr. Calhoun had once said in debate as "the utterance of the distinguished and venerable senator from South Carolina, who, I deeply regret, is prevented by serious illness from being in his seat today." At this I glanced toward the tall, gaunt figure across the chamber. He was moving restlessly in his chair; his head and body were bent eagerly forward, and he made an effort as if trying to rise and interrupt the orator. But the effort seemed to be too much for him, for he sank back in his chair, evidently exhausted. The noble current of Websterian eloquence flowed majestically on, all unconscious of the intended interruption. Presently the speaker once more had occasion to refer to some statement of Mr. Calhoun, and again he alluded to him as "the eminent senator from South Carolina, whom we all regret so much to miss, from such a cause, from his seat today."

The figure again grew restless; the hands nervously grasped both arms of his chair; the black eyes glared and shone in their eagerness;

and now, half rising from his seat and unable any longer to bear the thought that Mr. Webster should remain unconscious of his presence, he exclaimed, in a feeble and hollow voice, which yet was heard throughout the chamber:

"The senator from South Carolina is in his seat!"

Mr. Webster turned toward him with something like a start, and when he saw that his friend had actually risen from the bed of death and had indeed dared death itself to creep to the Capitol and hear his speech, he for a moment betrayed visible signs of deep emotion. Then, acknowledging this touching compliment by a bow and a smile of profound satisfaction, he went on with his speech.

A few days more, and Calhoun lay dead, in state, within those very walls.

PETER HARVEY, Reminiscences and Anecdotes of Daniel Webster

140. William Herndon Remembers Abraham Lincoln

In 1844 William Henry Herndon, who was nearly ten years younger than Lincoln and greatly admired him, accepted his invitation to become junior law partner. That partnership was broken only by Lincoln's death, for on leaving for Washington, Lincoln requested him to keep the old "shingle" standing. Herndon, who was a great reader and strongly opposed to slavery, influenced Lincoln's thinking on many questions, while he labored with unselfish devotion to promote Lincoln's political fortunes. No man knew Lincoln better.

I

SPRINGFIELD, Ill., November 13, 1885. — Friend Weik: There were three noted storytellers, jokers, jesters, in the central part of this state especially from 1840 to 1853: Lincoln of Sangamon County, William Engle of Menard, and James Murray of Logan. They were all men of mark, each in his own way; they were alike in the line of joking, storytelling, jesting. I knew the men for years. From 1840 to 1853 this section was not known for a very high standard of taste, the love for the beautiful or the good. We had not many newspapers; people in all of these counties would attend court at the respective county seats. Lincoln, Engle, and Murray would travel around from county to county with the court, and those who loved fun and sport, loved jokes, tales, stories, jests, would go with the court, too, from county to county. People had not much to do at the time, and the class of people that then lived here are gone, perished. It was a curious state of affairs indeed. As compared with now it was rough, semibarbarous. In the evening, after the court business of the day was over and book and pen had been laid [down] by the lawyers, judges, jurymen, witnesses, etc., the people generally would meet at some barroom, "gentlemen's parlor," and have a good time in storytelling, joking, jesting, etc. The barroom windows, halls, and all passageways would be filled to suffocation by the people, eager to see the "big ones" and to hear their stories told by them. Lincoln would tell his story in his very best style. The people, all present, including Lincoln, would burst out in a loud laugh and a hurrah at the story. The listeners, so soon as the laugh and the hurrah had passed and silence had come in for its turn, would cry out, "Now, Uncle Billy (William Engle), you must beat that or go home." Engle would clear his throat and say, "Boys, the story just told by Lincoln puts me in mind of a story I heard when a boy." He would tell it and tell it well. The people would clap their hands, stamp their feet, hurrah, yell, shout, get up, hold their aching sides. Things would soon calm down. There was politeness and etiquette in it. Each must have his turn, by comity, in which to tell his story. The good people would, as soon as quiet reigned, cry out: "Now is your time; come, Murray, do your level best or never come here again to tell your stories." Murray would prepare himself with his best. At first he would be a little nervous, but he would soon gather confidence, rise up, walk about, telling his tale as he moved in harmony with his story; he would tell it well, grandly, and the people would sometimes before the story was ended catch the point and raise such a laugh and a yell that the village rang with the yells, laughs, and hurrahs, etc. Lincoln and Engle now were nervous and anxious for their turns to come around. Lincoln would tell his story, and then followed Engle, and then came Murray; and thus this storytelling joking, jesting, would be kept up till one or two o'clock in the night, and thus night after night till the court adjourned for that term. In the morning we would all be sore all through from excessive laughing — the judge, the lawyers, jurymen, witnesses, and all. Our sides and back would ache. This was a gay time, and I'll never see it again. This is or was the way we old Westerners passed away our time. We loved fun and sport — anything for amusement. We had no learning but had good common sense with a liberal broad view of things, were generous and as brave as Caesar. When court had adjourned in Sangamon County, we went to Menard and then to Logan County. This storytelling was kept up faithfully from county to county and from term to term and from year to year.

Your friend,
W. H. HERNDON

II

Springfield, Ill., July 19, 1887. — Mr. Bartlett. My dear sir: Mr. Lincoln was six feet and four inches high in his sock feet; he was consumptive by build and hence more or less stoop-shouldered. He was very tall, thin, and gaunt. When he rose to speak to the jury or to crowds of people, he stood inclined forward, was awkward, angular, ungainly, odd, and being a very sensitive man, I think that it added to his awkwardness; he was a diffident man, somewhat, and a sensitive one, and both of these added to his oddity, awkwardness, etc., as it seemed to me. Lincoln had confidence, full and complete confidence in himself, self-thoughtful, self-helping, and self-supporting, relying on no man. Lincoln's voice was, when he first began speaking, shrill, squeaking, piping, unpleasant; his general look, his form, his pose, the color of his flesh, wrinkled and dry, his sensitiveness, and his momentary diffidence, everything seemed to be against him, but he soon recovered. I can see him now, in my mind distinct. On rising to address the jury or the crowd he quite generally placed his hands behind him, the back part of his left hand resting in the palm of his right hand. As he proceeded and grew warmer, he moved his hands to the front of his person, generally interlocking his fingers and running one thumb around the other. Sometimes his hands, for a short while, would hang by his side. In still growing warmer, as

he proceeded in his address, he used his hands — especially and generally his right hand — in his gestures; he used his head a great deal
in speaking, throwing or jerking or moving it now here and now
there, now in this position and now in that, in order to be more
emphatic, to drive the idea home. Mr. Lincoln never beat the air,
never sawed space with his hands, never acted for stage effect; was
cool, careful, earnest, sincere, truthful, fair, self-possessed, not insulting, not dictatorial; was pleasing, good-natured; had great strong
naturalness of look, pose, and act; was clear in his ideas, simple in
his words, strong, terse, and demonstrative; he spoke and acted to
convince individuals and masses; he used in his gestures his right
hand, sometimes shooting out that long bony forefinger of his to
dot an idea or to express a thought, resting his thumb on his middle
finger. Bear in mind that he did not gesticulate much, and *yet it is
true* that every organ of his body was in motion and acted with ease,
elegance, and grace; so it all looked to *me*.

As Mr. Lincoln proceeded further along with his oration, if time,
place, subject, and occasion admitted of it, he gently and gradually
warmed up; his shrill, squeaking, piping voice became harmonious,
melodious, musical, if you please, with face somewhat aglow; his
form dilated, swelled out, and he rose up a splendid form, erect,
straight, and dignified; he stood square on his feet with both legs up
and down, toe even with toe — that is, he did not put one foot before another; he kept his feet parallel and close to and not far from
each other. When Mr. Lincoln rose up to speak, he rose slowly,
steadily, firmly; he never moved much about on the stand or platform when speaking, trusting no desk, table, railing; he ran his
eyes slowly over the crowd, giving them time to be at ease and to
completely recover himself, *as I suppose*. He frequently took hold
with his left hand, his left thumb erect, of the left lapel of his coat,
keeping his right hand free to gesture in order to drive home and
to clinch an idea. In his greatest inspiration he held both of his
hands out above his head at an angle of about fifty degrees, hands
open or clenched according to his feelings and his ideas. If he was
moved in some indignant and half-mad moment against slavery or
wrong in any direction and seemed to want to tear it down, trample
it beneath his feet, and to eternally crush it, thus he would extend
his arms out, at about the above degree angle, with clenched big,
bony, strong hands on them.

If he was defending the right, if he was defending liberty, eulogiz‹
ing the Declaration of Independence, then he extended out his arms,
palms of his hands upward somewhat at about the above degree,
angle, as if appealing to some superior power for assistance and
support; or that he might embrace the spirit of that which he so
dearly loved. It was at such moments that he seemed inspired, fresh
from the hands of his Creator. Lincoln's gray eyes would flash fire
when speaking against slavery or spoke volumes of hope and love
when speaking of liberty, justice, and the progress of mankind.
Such was this great man *to me,* and I think, I know, such he was to
thousands, if not to millions of others.

Your friend,
W. H. HERNDON
EMANUEL HERTZ, The Hidden Lincoln

141. Carl Schurz Hears Lincoln Debate with Douglas

*In the memorable contest for the
Senatorship from Illinois, in 1858, Abraham Lincoln and Stephen
A. Douglas engaged in the most famous series of debates in American history. Traveling from one little prairie town to another, speaking in dusty courthouse squares under a broiling August sun, they
discussed the issues that were imperiling the Union. Douglas won
the senatorship, but Lincoln's was the greater victory, for he made
himself the logical candidate for the Presidency in 1860. Carl Schurz,
who here remembers the Quincy debate, was the leader of the
German-Americans of his generation and a staunch supporter of
Lincoln.*

THE REPUBLICAN State Committee of Illinois asked me to
make some speeches in their campaign, and obeying that call, I
found myself for the first time on a conspicuous field of political

action. One of the appointments called me to Quincy on the day when one of the great debates between Lincoln and Douglas was to take place there, and on that occasion I was to meet Abraham Lincoln myself. On the evening before the day of the debate I was on a railroad train bound for Quincy. The car in which I traveled was full of men who discussed the absorbing question with great animation. A member of the Republican State Committee accompanied me and sat by my side.

All at once, after the train had left a way station, I observed a great commotion among my fellow passengers, many of whom jumped from their seats and pressed eagerly around a tall man who had just entered the car. They addressed him in the most familiar style: "Hello, Abe! How are you?" and so on. And he responded in the same manner: "Good evening, Ben! How are you, Joe? Glad to see you, Dick!" and there was much laughter at some things he said, which, in the confusion of voices, I could not understand. "Why," exclaimed my companion, the committeeman, "there's Lincoln himself!" He pressed through the crowd and introduced me to Abraham Lincoln, whom I then saw for the first time.

I must confess that I was somewhat startled by his appearance. There he stood, overtopping by several inches all those surrounding him. Although measuring something over six feet myself, I had, standing quite near to him, to throw my head backward in order to look into his eyes. That swarthy face with its strong features, its deep furrows, and its benignant, melancholy eyes, is now familiar to every American by numberless pictures. It may be said that the whole civilized world knows and loves it. At that time it was clean-shaven and looked even more haggard and careworn than later when it was framed in whiskers.

On his head he wore a somewhat battered stovepipe hat. His neck emerged long and sinewy from a white collar turned down over a thin black necktie. His lank, ungainly body was clad in a rusty black dress coat with sleeves that should have been longer; but his arms appeared so long that the sleeves of a "store" coat could hardly be expected to cover them all the way down to the wrists. His black trousers, too, permitted a very full view of his large feet. On his left arm he carried a gray woolen shawl, which evidently served him for an overcoat in chilly weather. His left hand held a cotton umbrella of the bulging kind, and also a black satchel that bore the marks of long and hard usage. His right he had kept free for hand-shaking, of which there was no end until everybody in the car seemed to be satisfied. I had seen, in Washington, several public men of rough appearance, but none whose looks seemed quite so uncouth, not to say grotesque, as Lincoln's.

He received me with an offhand cordiality, like an old acquaint-ance, having been informed of what I was doing in the campaign, and we sat down together. In a somewhat high-pitched but pleasant voice he began to talk to me, telling me much about the points he and Douglas had made in the debates at different places and about those he intended to make at Quincy on the morrow.

When, in a tone of perfect ingenuousness, he asked me — a young beginner in politics — what I thought about this and that, I should have felt myself very much honored by his confidence, had he per-mitted me to regard him as a great man. But he talked in so simple and familiar a strain, and his manner and homely phrase were so absolutely free from any semblance of self-consciousness or preten-sion to superiority, that I soon felt as if I had known him all my life and we had long been close friends. He interspersed our con-versation with all sorts of quaint stories, each of which had a witty point applicable to the subject in hand, and not seldom concluding an argument in such a manner that nothing more was to be said. He seemed to enjoy his own jests in a childlike way, for his un-usually sad-looking eyes would kindle with a merry twinkle, and he himself led in the laughter; and his laugh was so genuine, hearty, and contagious that nobody could fail to join in it.

When we arrived at Quincy, we found a large number of friends waiting for him, and there was much handshaking and many familiar salutations again. Then they got him into a carriage, much against his wish, for he said that he would prefer to "foot it to Browning's," an old friend's house, where he was to have supper and a quiet night. But the night was by no means quiet outside. The blare of brass bands and the shouts of enthusiastic, and not in all cases quite sober, Democrats and Republicans, cheering and hurrah-ing for their respective champions, did not cease until the small hours.

The next morning the country people began to stream into town for the great meeting, some singly, on foot or on horseback, or small parties of men and women and even children in buggies or farm wagons, while others were marshaled in solemn procession from outlying towns or districts with banners and drums, many of them headed by maidens in white with tricolored scarfs, who represented the goddess of Liberty and the different states of the Union, and whose beauty was duly admired by every one, including themselves. On the whole the Democratic displays were much more elaborate and gorgeous than those of the Republicans, and it was said that Douglas had plenty of money to spend for such things. He himself also traveled in what was called in those days great style, with a secretary and servants and a numerous escort of somewhat loud companions, moving from place to place by special train with cars specially decorated for the occasion, all of which contrasted strongly with Lincoln's extremely modest simplicity. There was no end of cheering and shouting and jostling on the streets of Quincy that day. But in spite of the excitement created by the political contest, the crowds remained very good-natured, and the occasional jibes flung from one side to the other were uniformly received with a laugh.

The great debate took place in the afternoon on the open square, where a large pine-board platform had been built for the committee of arrangements, the speakers, and the persons they wished to have with them. I thus was favored with a seat on that platform. In front of it many thousands of people were assembled, Republicans and Democrats standing peaceably together, only chaffing one another now and then in a good-tempered way.

As the champions arrived they were demonstratively cheered by their adherents. The presiding officer agreed upon by the two parties called the meeting to order and announced the program of proceedings. Mr. Lincoln was to open with an allowance of one hour. . . . His voice was not musical, rather high-keyed and apt to turn into a shrill treble in moments of excitement, but it was not positively disagreeable. It had an exceedingly penetrating, far-reaching quality. The looks of the audience convinced me that every word he spoke was understood at the remotest edges of the vast assemblage. His gesture was awkward. He swung his long arms sometimes in a very ungraceful manner. Now and then he would, to give particular emphasis to a point, bend his knees and body with a sudden downward jerk, and then shoot up again with a vehemence that raised him to his tiptoes and made him look much taller than he really was — a manner of enlivening a speech which at that time was, and perhaps still is, not unusual in the West, but which he succeeded in avoiding at a later period.

When Lincoln had sat down amid the enthusiastic plaudits of his adherents, I asked myself with some trepidation in my heart, "What will Douglas say now?" Lincoln's speech had struck me as very clear, logical, persuasive, convincing even, and very sympathetic, but not as an overwhelming argument. Douglas, I thought, might not be able to confute it, but by the cunning sophistry at his command and by one of his forceful appeals to prejudice he might succeed in neutralizing its effect. No more striking contrast could have been imagined than that between those two men as they appeared upon the platform. By the side of Lincoln's tall, lank, and ungainly form, Douglas stood almost like a dwarf, very short of stature, but square-shouldered and broad-chested, a massive head upon a strong neck, the very embodiment of force, combativeness, and staying power. I have drawn his portrait when describing my first impressions of Washington City, and I apprehend it was not a flattering one. On that stage at Quincy he looked rather natty and well groomed in excellently fitting broadcloth and shining linen. But his face seemed a little puffy. The deep, horizontal wrinkle between his keen eyes was unusually dark and scowling. While he was listening to Lincoln's speech, a contemptuous smile now and then flitted across his lips, and when he rose, the tough parliamentary gladiator, he tossed his mane with an air of overbearing superiority. His friends were well pleased with his performance and rewarded him with vociferous cheers.

But then came Lincoln's closing speech of half an hour, which seemed completely to change the temper of the atmosphere. He replied to Douglas' arguments and attacks with rapid thrusts so deft and piercing, with humorous retort so quaint and pat, and with witty illustrations so clinching, and he did it all so good-naturedly, that the meeting again and again broke out in bursts of delight by which even many of his opponents were carried away, while the scowl on Douglas' face grew darker and darker.

When the debate at Quincy was over, the champions were

heartily cheered by their partisans, the assemblage dissolved peace-ably, the brass bands began to play again, several of them within hearing of one another, so as to fill the air with discordant sounds, and the country people, with their banners and their maidens in white, got in motion to return to their homes, each party, no doubt, as it usually happens in such cases, persuaded that the result of the day was in its favor.

The Reminiscences of Carl Schurz

142. Abraham Lincoln Is Nominated in the Wigwam

Lincoln's name began to be widely mentioned for the Republican Presidential nomination after his seven joint debates with Douglas in 1858 attracted national attention. It was as a Presidential possibility that he went to New York in February, 1860, and produced a remarkable impression by the logical power of his Cooper Union address. The principal aspirant for the nomination was William H. Seward of New York, but he had many enemies, including the powerful Horace Greeley, and great numbers of Republicans regarded him as too radical. Salmon P. Chase failed to gain the full support of his own state, Ohio, while Edward Bates of Missouri was disliked by the German voters. Lincoln therefore had a good chance from the outset for winning the nomination; and it was increased by the fact that the Republican convention was held in Chicago, and by the skill with which his Illinois supporters set to work. David Davis took charge of the Lincoln forces at Chicago, and labored indefatigably and effectively. Here a journalist of the day tells the story.

THIRD day [May 18, 1860].— After adjournment on Thursday (the second day) there were few men in Chicago who believed it possible to prevent the nomination of Seward. His friends had played their game to admiration and had been victorious on every preliminary skirmish. When the platform had been adopted, inclusive of the Declaration of Independence, they felt themselves already exalted upon the pinnacle of victory. They rejoiced exceedingly, and full of confidence, cried in triumphant tones, "Call the roll of states." But it was otherwise ordered. The opponents of Mr. Seward left the wigwam that evening thoroughly disheartened. Greeley was, as has been widely reported, absolutely "terrified." The nomination of Seward in defiance of his influence would have been a cruel blow. He gave up the ship. . . .

The New Yorkers were exultant. Their bands were playing and the champagne flowing at their headquarters as after a victory.

But there was much done after midnight and before the convention assembled on Friday morning. There were hundreds of Pennsylvanians, Indianians, and Illinoisians who never closed their eyes that night. I saw Henry S. Lane at one o'clock, pale and haggard, with cane under his arm, walking as if for a wager, from one caucus room to another, at the Tremont House. He had been toiling with desperation to bring the Indiana delegation to go as a unit for Lincoln. And then in connection with others, he had been operating to bring the Vermonters and Virginians to the point of deserting Seward.

The Seward men generally abounded in confidence Friday morning. The air was full of rumors of the caucusing the night before, but the opposition of the doubtful states to Seward was an old story; and after the distress of Pennsylvania, Indiana and Company on the subject of Seward's availability had been so freely and ineffectually expressed from the start, it was not imagined their protests would suddenly become effective. The Sewardites marched as usual from their headquarters at the Richmond House after their magnificent band, which was brilliantly uniformed — epaulets shining on their shoulders and white and scarlet feathers waving from their caps — marched under the orders of recognized leaders, in a style that would have done credit to many volunteer military companies. They were about a thousand strong, and protracting their march a little too far, were not all able to get into the wigwam. This was their first misfortune. They were not where they could scream with the best effect in responding to the mention of the name of William H. Seward.

When the convention was called to order, breathless attention was given the proceedings. There was not a space a foot square in the wigwam unoccupied. There were tens of thousands still outside, and torrents of men had rushed in at the three broad doors until not another one could squeeze in.

Everybody was now impatient to begin the work. Mr. Evarts of New York nominated Mr. Seward. Mr. Judd of Illinois nominated Mr. Lincoln.

Everybody felt that the fight was between them and yelled accordingly.

The applause when Mr. Evarts named Seward was enthusiastic. When Mr. Judd named Lincoln, the response was prodigious, rising and raging far beyond the Seward shriek. Presently, upon Caleb B. Smith seconding the nomination of Lincoln, the response was absolutely terrific. It now became the Seward men to make another effort, and when Blair of Michigan seconded his nomination,

> At once there rose so wild a yell,
> Within that dark and narrow dell;
> As all the fiends from heaven that fell
> Had pealed the banner cry of hell.

The effect was startling. Hundreds of persons stopped their ears in pain. The shouting was absolutely frantic, shrill and wild. No Comanches, no panthers, ever struck a higher note or gave screams with more infernal intensity. Looking from the stage over the vast amphitheater, nothing was to be seen below but thousands of hats —a black, mighty swarm of hats—flying with the velocity of hornets over a mass of human heads, most of the mouths of which were open. Above, all around the galleries, hats and handkerchiefs were flying in the tempest together. The wonder of the thing was that the Seward outside pressure should, so far from New York, be so powerful.

Now the Lincoln men had to try it again, and as Mr. Delano of Ohio on behalf "of a portion of the delegation of that state" seconded the nomination of Lincoln, the uproar was beyond description. Imagine all the hogs ever slaughtered in Cincinnati giving their death squeals together, a score of big steam whistles going (steam at a hundred and sixty pounds per inch), and you conceive something of the same nature. I thought the Seward yell could not be surpassed, but the Lincoln boys were clearly ahead and, feeling their victory, as there was a lull in the storm, took deep breaths all round and gave a concentrated shriek that was positively awful, and accompanied it with stamping that made every plank and pillar in the building quiver.

Henry S. Lane of Indiana leaped upon a table, and swinging hat and cane, performed like an acrobat. The presumption is he shrieked with the rest, as his mouth was desperately wide open; but no one will ever be able to testify that he has positive knowledge of the fact that he made a particle of noise. His individual voice was lost in the aggregate hurricane.

The New York, Michigan, and Wisconsin delegations sat together and were in this tempest very quiet. Many of their faces whitened as the Lincoln *yawp* swelled into a wild hosanna of victory.

The convention now proceeded to business. The most significant vote was that of Virginia, which had been expected solid for Seward, and which now gave him but eight and gave Lincoln fourteen. The New Yorkers looked significantly at each other as this was announced. Then Indiana gave her twenty-six votes for Lincoln. This solid vote was a startler. The division of the first vote caused a fall in Seward stock. It was seen that Lincoln, Cameron, and Bates had the strength to defeat Seward, and it was known that the greater part of the Chase vote would go for Lincoln.

The convention proceeded to a second ballot. Every man was fiercely enlisted in the struggle. The partisans of the various candidates were strung up to such a pitch of excitement as to render them incapable of patience, and the cries of "Call the roll" were fairly hissed through their teeth. The first gain for Lincoln was in New Hampshire. The Chase and the Frémont vote from that state were given him. His next gain was the whole vote of Vermont. This was a blighting blow upon the Seward interest. The New Yorkers started as if an Orsini bomb had exploded. And presently the Cameron vote of Pennsylvania was thrown for Lincoln, increasing his strength forty-four votes. The fate of the day was now determined. New York saw "checkmate" next move and sullenly proceeded with the game, assuming unconsciousness of her inevitable doom. On this ballot Lincoln gained seventy-nine votes. Seward had one hundred and eighty-four and a half votes, Lincoln one hundred and eighty-one. . . .

While this [the third] ballot was taken amid excitement that tested the nerves, the fatal defection from Seward in New England still further appeared, four votes going over from Seward to Lincoln in Massachusetts. The latter received four additional votes from Pennsylvania and fifteen additional votes from Ohio. It was whispered about: "Lincoln's the coming man — will be nominated this ballot." When the roll of states and territories had been called, I had ceased to give attention to any votes but those for Lincoln and had his vote added up as it was given. The number of votes necessary to a choice were two hundred and thirty-three, and I saw under my pencil as the Lincoln column was completed the figures 231½ — one vote and a half to give him the nomination. In a moment the fact was whispered about. A hundred pencils had told the same story. The news went over the house wonderfully, and there was a pause. There are always men anxious to distinguish themselves on such occasions. There is nothing that politicians like better than a crisis. I looked up to see who would be the man to give the decisive vote. In about ten ticks of a watch, Cartter of Ohio was up. I had imagined Ohio would be slippery enough for the crisis. And sure enough! Every eye was on Cartter, and everybody who understood the matter at all knew what he was about to do. He said: "I rise (eh), Mr. Chairman (eh), to announce the change of four votes of Ohio from Mr. Chase to Mr. Lincoln." The deed was done. There was a moment's silence. The nerves of the thousands, which through the hours of suspense had been subjected to terrible tension, relaxed, and as deep breaths of relief were taken, there was a noise in the wigwam like the rush of a great wind in the van of a storm — and in another breath, the storm was there. There were thousands cheering with the energy of insanity.

A man who had been on the roof and was engaged in communicating the results of the ballotings to the mighty mass of outsiders now demanded, by gestures at the skylight over the stage, to know what had happened. One of the secretaries, with a tally sheet in his hands, shouted: "Fire the salute! Abe Lincoln is nominated!"

The city was wild with delight. The "Old Abe" men formed processions and bore rails through the streets. Torrents of liquor were poured down the hoarse throats of the multitude. A hundred guns were fired from the top of the Tremont House.

I left the city on the night train on the Fort Wayne and Chicago road. The train consisted of eleven cars, every seat full and people standing in the aisles and corners. I never before saw a company of persons so prostrated by continued excitement. The Lincoln men were not able to respond to the cheers which went up along the road for "Old Abe." They had not only done their duty in that respect, but exhausted their capacity. At every station where there was a village, until after two o'clock, there were tar barrels burning, drums beating, boys carrying rails, and guns, great and small, banging away. The weary passengers were allowed no rest, but plagued by the thundering jar of cannon, the clamor of drums, the glare of bonfires, and the whooping of the boys, who were delighted with the idea of a candidate for the Presidency who thirty years ago split rails on the Sangamon River — classic stream now and forever-more — and whose neighbors named him "honest."

MURAT HALSTEAD, Caucuses of 1860

XXIII

O Captain, My Captain

143. "We Are Not Enemies, but Friends"

When Lincoln was sworn in as President, seven Southern States had already withdrawn from the Union. Delegates had met at Montgomery, Alabama, had formed a provisional Constitution for the "Confederate States of America," and had chosen Jefferson Davis and Alexander H. Stephens as provisional President and Vice-President. Many Northerners believed that the Federal Government ought to acquiesce in secession and "let the erring sisters go in peace." Many others believed that it ought to compel the Southern States, if necessary by force, to return. Lincoln in his inaugural address took a firm stand. He declared that the Union is perpetual, and that all acts of secession were void; he asserted that the Government was determined to maintain its authority. But at the same time he held out an olive branch to the Southern people, urging them to resume their old places in the American household.

THAT THERE are persons in one section or another who seek to destroy the Union at all events and are glad of any pretext to do it, I will neither affirm nor deny; but if there be such, I need address no word to them. To those, however, who really love the Union may I not speak?

Before entering upon so grave a matter as the destruction of our national fabric, with all its benefits, its memories, and its hopes, would it not be wise to ascertain precisely why we do it? Will you hazard so desperate a step while there is any possibility that any portion of the ills you fly from have no real existence? Will you, while the certain ills you fly to are greater than all the real ones you fly from — will you risk the commission of so fearful a mistake?

Physically speaking, we cannot separate. We cannot remove our respective sections from each other, nor build an impassable wall between them. A husband and wife may be divorced and go out of the presence and beyond the reach of each other, but the different parts of our country cannot do this. They cannot but remain face to face, and intercourse, either amicable or hostile, must continue between them. Is it possible, then, to make that intercourse more advantageous or more satisfactory after separation than before? Can aliens make treaties easier than friends can make laws? Can treaties be more faithfully enforced between aliens than laws can among friends? Suppose you go to war, you cannot fight always; and when, after much loss on both sides, and no gain on either, you cease fighting, the identical old questions as to terms of intercourse are again upon you.

This country, with its institutions, belongs to the people who inhabit it. Whenever they shall grow weary of the existing government, they can exercise their constitutional right of amending it or their revolutionary right to dismember or overthrow it.

Why should there not be a patient confidence in the ultimate justice of the people? Is there any better or equal hope in the world? In our present differences is either party without faith of being in the right? If the Almighty Ruler of nations, with His eternal truth and justice, be on your side of the North, or on yours of the South, that truth and that justice will surely prevail by the judgment of this great tribunal of the American people.

By the frame of the government under which we live, this same people have wisely given their public servants but little power for mischief; and have, with equal wisdom, provided for the return of that little to their own hands at very short intervals. While the people retain their virtue and vigilance, no administration, by any extreme of wickedness or folly, can very seriously injure the government in the short space of four years.

My countrymen, one and all, think calmly and well upon this whole subject. Nothing valuable can be lost by taking time. If there be an object to hurry any of you in hot haste to a step which you would never take deliberately, that object will be frustrated by taking time; but no good object can be frustrated by it. Such of you as are now dissatisfied still have the old Constitution unimpaired, and, on the sensitive point, the laws of your own framing under it, while the new administration will have no immediate power, if it would, to change either. If it were admitted that you who are dissatisfied hold the right side in the dispute, there still is no single good reason for precipitate action. Intelligence, patriotism, Christianity, and a firm reliance on Him who has never yet forsaken this favored land, are still competent to adjust in the best way all our present difficulty.

In your hands, my dissatisfied fellow countrymen, and not in mine, is the momentous issue of civil war. The government will not assail you. You can have no conflict without being yourselves the aggressors. You have no oath registered in heaven to destroy the government, while I shall have the most solemn one to "preserve, protect, and defend" it.

I am loath to close. We are not enemies, but friends. We must not be enemies. Though passion may have strained, it must not break, our bonds of affection. The mystic cords of memory, stretching from every battlefield and patriot grave to every living heart and hearthstone all over this broad land, will yet swell the chorus of the Union when again touched, as surely they will be, by the better angels of our nature.

ABRAHAM LINCOLN, First Inaugural Address

144. Mr. Lincoln Hammers Out a Cabinet

Because Lincoln was the first President elected by the Republican Party, he faced peculiar difficulties in making up his Cabinet. It seemed wise to unite the party by giving places to as many of the principal Republican leaders as possible, whether their views agreed with his own or not. He therefore selected two former Democrats of prominence, Salmon P. Chase of Ohio and Gideon Welles of Connecticut. He also chose both a radical antislavery man, William H. Seward of New York, and a very moderate leader, Edward Bates of Missouri, both former Whigs. His weakest appointee, as time proved, was a practical politician, Simon Cameron, taken from Pennsylvania to be Secretary of War. Here a New York editor and political boss describes some of Lincoln's troubles.

M R. LINCOLN remarked, smiling, that he supposed I had had some experience in cabinet-making; that he had a job on hand, and as he had never learned that trade, he was disposed to avail himself of the suggestions of friends. Taking up his figure, I replied that though never a boss cabinet-maker, I had as a journeyman been occasionally consulted about state cabinets, and that although President Taylor once talked with me about reforming his cabinet, I had never been concerned in or presumed to meddle with the formation of an original Federal cabinet, and that he was the first President elect I had ever seen. The question thus opened became the subject of conversation at intervals during that and the following day. I say at intervals, because many hours were consumed in talking of the public men connected with former administrations, interspersed, illustrated, and seasoned pleasantly with Mr. Lincoln's stories, anecdotes, etc. And here I feel called upon to vindicate Mr. Lincoln, as far as my opportunities and observation go, from the frequent imputation of telling indelicate and ribald stories. I saw much of him during his whole presidential term, with familiar friends and alone, when he talked without restraint, but I never heard him use a profane or indecent word or tell a story that might not be repeated in the presence of ladies.

Mr. Lincoln observed that the making of a cabinet, now that he had it to do, was by no means as easy as he had supposed; that he had, even before the result of the election was known, assuming the probability of success, fixed upon the two leading members of his cabinet, but that in looking about for suitable men to fill the other departments, he had been much embarrassed, partly from his want of acquaintance with the prominent men of the day, and partly, he believed, that while the population of the country had immensely increased, really great men were scarcer than they used to be. He then inquired whether I had any suggestions of a general character affecting the selection of a cabinet to make. I replied that, along with the question of ability, integrity, and experience, he ought, in the selection of his cabinet, to find men whose firmness and courage fitted them for the revolutionary ordeal which was about to test the strength of our government, and that in my judgment it was desirable that at least two members of his cabinet should be selected from slave-holding States. He inquired whether, in the emergency which I so much feared, they could be trusted, adding that he did not quite like to hear Southern journals and Southern speakers insisting that there must be no "coercion"; that while he had no disposition to coerce anybody, yet after he had taken an oath to execute the laws, he should not care to see them violated. I remarked that there were Union men in Maryland, Virginia, North Carolina, and Tennessee, for whose loyalty, under the most trying circumstances and in any event, I would vouch. "Would you rely on such men if their states should secede?" "Yes, sir; the men whom I have in my mind can always be relied on." "Well," said Mr. Lincoln, "let us have the names of your white crows, such ones as you think fit for the cabinet." I then named Henry Winter Davis, of Maryland; John M. Botts, of Virginia; John A. Gilmer, of North Carolina; and Bailey Peyton, of Tennessee. As the conversation progressed, Mr. Lincoln remarked that he intended to invite Governor Seward to take the State and Governor Chase the Treasury Department, remarking that, aside from their long experience in public affairs and their eminent fitness, they were prominently before the people and the convention as competitors for the Presidency, each having higher claims than his own for the place which he was to occupy. On naming Gideon Welles as the gentleman he thought of as the representative of New England in the cabinet, I remarked that I thought he could find several New England gentlemen whose selection for a place in his cabinet would be more acceptable to the people of New England. "But," said Mr. Lincoln, "we must remember that the Republican party is constituted of two elements, and that we must have men of Democratic as well as of Whig antecedents in the cabinet."

Acquiescing in this view, the subject was passed over. And then Mr. Lincoln remarked that Judge Blair had been suggested. I in quired, "What Judge Blair?" and was answered, "Judge Montgomery Blair." "Has he been suggested by any one except his father, Francis P. Blair, Sr.?" "Your question," said Mr. Lincoln, "reminds me of a story," and he proceeded with infinite humor to tell a story, which I would repeat if I did not fear that its spirit and effect would be lost. I finally remarked that if we were legislating on the question, I should move to strike out the name of Montgomery Blair and insert that of Henry Winter Davis. Mr. Lincoln laughingly replied, "Davis has been posting you up on this question. He came from Maryland and has got Davis on the brain. Maryland must, I think, be like New Hampshire, a good state to move from." And then he told a story of a witness in a neighboring county, who, on being asked his age, replied, "Sixty." Being satisfied that he was much older, the judge repeated the question, and on receiving the same answer, admonished the witness, saying that the court knew him to be much older than sixty. "Oh," said the witness, "you're thinking about that fifteen year that I lived down on the eastern shore of Maryland; that was so much lost time, and don't count." This story, I perceived, was thrown in to give the conversation a new direction. It was very evident that the selection of Montgomery Blair was a fixed fact, and although I subsequently ascertained the reasons and influences that controlled the selection of other members of the cabinet, I never did find out how Mr. Blair got there.

The Autobiography of Thurlow Weed

145. Nathaniel Hawthorne Sees President Lincoln

The novelist Hawthorne, now near his grave, visited Washington in the spring of 1862 for amusement and health. He saw both Lincoln and General McClellan; was disgusted by some of the politicians and lobbyists he found hanging about the Capitol; and wrote a frank and caustic article upon his observations, which the Atlantic Monthly *published.*

NINE O'CLOCK had been appointed as the time for receiving the deputation, and we were punctual to the moment; but not so the President, who sent us word that he was eating his breakfast and would come as soon as he could. His appetite, we were glad to think, must have been a pretty fair one; for we waited about half an hour in one of the antechambers, and then were ushered into a reception room, in one corner of which sat the Secretaries of War and of the Treasury, expecting, like ourselves, the termination of the presidential breakfast. During this interval there were several new additions to our group, one or two of whom were in a working garb, so that we formed a very miscellaneous collection of people, mostly unknown to each other, and without any common sponsor, but all with an equal right to look our head servant in the face.

By and by there was a little stir on the staircase and in the passageway, and in lounged a tall, loose-jointed figure, of an exaggerated Yankee port and demeanor, whom (as being about the homeliest man I ever saw, yet by no means repulsive or disagreeable) it was impossible not to recognize as Uncle Abe.

Unquestionably, Western man though he be and Kentuckian by birth, President Lincoln is the essential representative of all Yankees and the veritable specimen, physically, of what the world seems determined to regard as our characteristic qualities. It is the strangest and yet the fittest thing in the jumble of human vicissitudes that he, out of so many millions, unlooked for, unselected by any intelligible process that could be based upon his genuine qualities, unknown to those who chose him, and unsuspected of what endowments may adapt him for his tremendous responsibility, should have found the way open for him to fling his lank personality into the chair of state — where, I presume, it was his first impulse to throw his legs on the council table and tell the cabinet ministers a story. There is no describing his lengthy awkwardness nor the uncouthness of his movement, and yet it seemed as if I had been in the habit of seeing him daily and had shaken hands with him a thousand times in some village street; so true was he to the aspect of the pattern American, though with a certain extravagance which, possibly, I exaggerated still further by the delighted eagerness with which I took it in. If put to guess his calling and livelihood, I should have taken him for a country schoolmaster as soon as anything else. He was dressed in a rusty black frock coat and pantaloons, unbrushed, and worn so faithfully that the suit had adapted itself to the curves and angularities of his figure and had grown to be an outer skin of the man. He had shabby slippers on his feet. His hair was black, still unmixed with gray, stiff, somewhat bushy, and had apparently been acquainted with neither brush nor comb that morning, after the disarrangement of the pillow; and as to a night-cap, Uncle Abe probably knows nothing of such effeminacies. His complexion is dark and sallow, betokening, I fear, an insalubrious atmosphere around the White House; he has thick black eyebrows and an impending brow; his nose is large, and the lines about his mouth are very strongly defined.

The whole physiognomy is as coarse a one as you would meet anywhere in the length and breadth of the states, but withal it is redeemed, illuminated, softened, and brightened by a kindly though serious look out of his eyes and an expression of homely sagacity that seems weighted with rich results of village experience. A great deal of native sense; no bookish cultivation, no refinement; honest at heart, and thoroughly so, and yet, in some sort, sly — at least, endowed with a sort of tact and wisdom that are akin to craft, and would impel him, I think, to take an antagonist in flank, rather than to make a bull run at him right in front. But, on the whole, I like this sallow, queer, sagacious visage, with the homely human sympathies that warmed it and, for my small share in the matter, would as lief have Uncle Abe for a ruler as any man whom it would have been practicable to put in his place.

Immediately on his entrance the President accosted our member of Congress, who had us in charge, and with a comical twist of his face made some jocular remark about the length of his breakfast. He then greeted us all round, not waiting for an introduction, but shaking and squeezing everybody's hand with the utmost cordiality, whether the individual's name was announced to him or not. His manner toward us was wholly without pretense, but yet had a kind of natural dignity, quite sufficient to keep the forwardest of us from clapping him on the shoulder and asking him for a story.

NATHANIEL HAWTHORNE, Tales, Sketches, and Other Papers

146. President Lincoln Pardons a Sleeping Sentinel

Lincoln's compassionate nature became famous early in the war; as Bryant later wrote, he was "slow to smite and swift to spare." As Commander in Chief of the Army and Navy, he interfered again and again to prevent the execution of soldiers for what he thought were essentially minor offenses.

ON A dark September morning in 1861, when I reached my office, I found waiting there a party of soldiers, none of whom I personally knew. They were greatly excited, all speaking at the same time, and consequently unintelligible. One of them wore the bars of a captain. I said to them pleasantly: "Boys, I cannot understand you. Pray let your captain say what you want and what I can do for you." They complied, and the captain put me in possession of the following facts.

They belonged to the Third Vermont Regiment, raised, with the exception of one company, on the eastern slope of the Green Mountains, and mustered into service while the battle of Bull Run was progressing. . . .

The story which I extracted from the boys was, in substance, this: William Scott, one of these mountain boys, just of age, had enlisted in Company K. Accustomed to his regular sound and healthy sleep, not yet inured to the life of the camp, he had volunteered to take the place of a sick comrade who had been detailed for picket duty, and had passed the night as a sentinel on guard. The next day he was himself detailed for the same duty and undertook its performance. But he found it impossible to keep awake for two nights in succession and had been found by the relief sound asleep on his post. For this offense he had been tried by a court-martial, found guilty, and sentenced to be shot within twenty-four hours after his trial and on the second morning after his offense was committed.

Scott's comrades had set about saving him in a characteristic way. They had called a meeting [and] appointed a committee with power to use all the resources of the regiment in his behalf. Strangers in Washington, the committee had resolved to call on me for advice because I was a Vermonter, and they had already marched from the camp to my office since daylight that morning.

The captain took all the blame from Scott upon himself. Scott's mother opposed his enlistment on the ground of his inexperience and had only consented on the captain's promise to look after him as if he were his own son. This he had wholly failed to do. He must have been asleep or stupid himself, he said, when he paid no attention to the boy's statement that he had fallen asleep during the day and feared he could not keep awake on the second night on picket. Instead of sending some one or going himself in Scott's place, as he should, he had let him go to his death. He alone was guilty — "if anyone ought to be shot, I am the fellow, and everybody at home would have the right to say so." "There must be some way to save him, Judge!" "He is as good a boy as there is in the army, and he ain't to blame. You will help us, now, won't you?" he said, almost with tears.

The other members of the committee had a definite if not a practicable plan. They insisted that Scott had not been tried and gave this account of the proceeding. He was asked what he had to say to the charge and said he would tell them just how it all happened. He had never been up all night that he remembered. He was "all beat out" by the night before and knew he should have a hard fight to keep awake; he thought of hiring one of the boys to go in his place, but they might think he was afraid to do his duty, and he decided to chance it. Twice he went to sleep and woke himself while he was marching, and then — he could not tell anything about it — all he knew was that he was sound asleep when the guard came. It was very wrong, he knew. He wanted to be a good soldier and do his duty. What else did he enlist for? They could shoot him, and perhaps they ought to, but he could not have tried harder; and if he was in the same place again, he could no more help going to sleep than he could fly.

One must have been made of sterner stuff than I was not to be touched by the earnest manner with which these men offered to devote even their farms to the aid of their comrade. The captain and the others had no words to express their emotions. I saw that the situation was surrounded by difficulties of which they knew nothing.

The more I reflected upon what I was to do, the more hopeless the case appeared. Thought was useless. I must act upon impulse, or I should not act at all.

"Come," I said, "there is only one man on earth who can save your comrade. Fortunately, he is the best man on the continent. We will go to President Lincoln."

I went swiftly out of the Treasury over to the White House and up the stairway to the little office where the President was writing. The boys followed in a procession. I did not give the thought any time to get a hold on me that I, an officer of the government, was committing an impropriety in thus rushing a matter upon the President's attention. The President was the first to speak.

"What is this?" he asked. "An expedition to kidnap somebody or to get another brigadier appointed or furlough to go home to vote? I cannot do it, gentlemen. Brigadiers are thicker than drum majors, and I couldn't get a furlough for myself if I asked it from the War Department."

There was hope in the tone in which he spoke. I went straight to my point. "Mr. President," I said, "these men want nothing for themselves. They are Green Mountain boys of the Third Vermont, who have come to stay as long as you need good soldiers. They don't want promotion until they earn it. But they do want something that you alone can give them — the life of a comrade."

"What has he done?" asked the President. "You Vermonters are not a bad lot, generally. Has he committed murder or mutiny, or what other felony?"

"Tell him," I whispered to the captain.

"I cannot! I cannot! I should stammer like a fool! You can do it better!"

"Captain," I said, pushing him forward, "Scott's life depends on you. You must tell the President the story. I only know it from hearsay."

He commenced like the man by the Sea of Galilee who had an

impediment in his speech, but very soon the string of his tongue was loosened, and he spoke plain. He began to word-paint a picture with the hand of a master. As the words burst from his lips they stirred my own blood. He gave a graphic account of the whole story and ended by saying: "He is as brave a boy as there is in your army, sir. Scott is no coward. Our mountains breed no cowards. They are the homes of thirty thousand men who voted for Abraham Lincoln. They will not be able to see that the best thing to be done with William Scott will be to shoot him like a traitor and bury him like a dog! Oh, Mr. Lincoln, can you?"

"No, I can't!" exclaimed the President. It was one of the moments when his countenance became such a remarkable study. It had become very earnest as the captain rose with his subject; then it took on that melancholy expression which, later in his life, became so infinitely touching. I thought I could detect a mist in the deep cavities of his eyes. Then in a flash there was a total change. He smiled and finally broke into a hearty laugh as he asked me: "Do your Green Mountain boys fight as well as they talk? If they do, I don't wonder at the legends about Ethan Allen." Then his face softened as he said: "But what can I do? What do you expect me to do? As you know, I have not much influence with the departments."

"I have not thought the matter out," I said. "I feel a deep interest in saving young Scott's life. I think I knew the boy's father. It is useless to apply to General Smith. An application to Secretary Stanton would only be referred to General Smith. The only thing to be done was to apply to you. It seems to me that, if you would sign an order suspending Scott's execution until his friends can have his case examined, I might carry it to the War Department and so insure the delivery of the order to General Smith today, through the regular channels of the War Office."

"No! I do not think that course would be safe. You do not know these officers of the regular army. They are a law unto themselves. They sincerely think that it is a good policy occasionally to shoot a soldier. I can see it, where a soldier deserts or commits a crime, but I cannot in such a case as Scott's. They say that I am always interfering with the discipline of the army and being cruel to the soldiers. Well, I can't help it; so I shall have to go right on doing wrong. I do not think an honest, brave soldier, conscious of no crime but sleeping when he was weary, ought to be shot or hung. The country has better uses for him.

"Captain," continued the President, "your boy shall not be shot — that is, not tomorrow, nor until I know more about his case." To me he said: "I will have to attend to this matter myself. I have for some time intended to go up to the [camp]. I will do so today. I shall know then that there is no mistake in suspending the execution."

I remarked that he was undertaking a burden that we had no right to impose, that it was asking too much of the President in behalf of a private soldier.

"Scott's life is as valuable to him as that of any person in the land," he said. "You remember the remark of a Scotchman about the head of a nobleman who was decapitated. 'It was a small matter of the head, but it was valuable to him, poor fellow, for it was the only one he had.'"

Later in the day the President started in the direction of the camp. . . .

Within a day or two the newspapers reported that a soldier sentenced to be shot for sleeping on his post had been pardoned by the President and returned to his regiment.

It was a long time before Scott would speak of his interview with Mr. Lincoln. One night, when he had received a long letter from home, he opened his heart and told Evans the story.

Scott said: "The President was the kindest man I had ever seen; I knew him at once, by a Lincoln medal I had worn. I was scared at first, for I had never before talked with a great man. But Mr. Lincoln was so easy with me, so gentle, that I soon forgot my fright. He asked me all about the people at home, the neighbors, the farm, and where I went to school, and who my schoolmates were. Then he asked me about mother and how she looked, and I was glad I could take her photograph from my bosom and show it to him. He said how thankful I ought to be that my mother still lived and how, if he was in my place, he would try to make her a proud mother and never cause her a sorrow or a tear. I cannot remember it all, but every word was so kind.

"He said nothing yet about that dreadful next morning. I thought it must be that he was so kindhearted that he didn't like to speak of it. But why did he say so much about my mother and my not causing her a sorrow or a tear when I knew that I must die the next morning. But I suppose that was something that would have to go unexplained, and so I determined to brace up and tell him that I did not feel a bit guilty and ask him wouldn't he fix it so that the firing party would not be from our regiment! That was going to be the hardest of all — to die by the hands of my comrades. Just as I was going to ask him this favor, he stood up, and he says to me, 'My boy, stand up here, and look me in the face.' I did as he bade me. 'My boy,' he said, 'you are not going to be shot tomorrow. I believe you when you tell me that you could not keep awake. I am going to trust you and send you back to your regiment. But I have been put to a good deal of trouble on your account. I have had to come up here from Washington when I have a great deal to do; and what I want to know is, how are you going to pay my bill?' There was a big lump in my throat; I could scarcely speak. I had expected to die, you see, and had kind of got used to thinking that way. To have it all changed in a minute! But I got it crowded down, and managed to say: 'I am grateful, Mr. Lincoln! I hope I am as grateful as ever a man can be to you for saving my life. But it comes upon me sudden and unexpected-like. I didn't lay out for it at all. But there is some way to pay you, and I will find it after a little. There is the bounty in the savings bank. I guess we could borrow some money on the mortgage of the farm.' There was my pay was something, and if he would wait until payday, I was sure the boys would help; so I thought we could make it up, if it wasn't more than five or six hundred dollars. 'But it is a great deal more than that,' he said. Then I said I didn't just see how, but I was sure I would find some way out — if I lived.

"Then Mr. Lincoln put his hands on my shoulders and looked into my face as if he was sorry and said: 'My boy, my bill is a very large one. Your friends cannot pay it, nor your bounty, nor the farm, nor all your comrades! There is only one man in all the world who can pay it, and his name is William Scott! If from this day William Scott does his duty, so that, if I was there when he comes to die, he can look me in the face as he does now, and say, "I have kept my promise, and I have done my duty as a soldier," then my debt will be paid. Will you make that promise and try to keep it?'

"I said I would make the promise and with God's help I would keep it. I could not say any more. I wanted to tell him how hard I would try to do all he wanted, but the words would not come; so I had to let it all go unsaid. He went away, out of my sight forever."

L. E. CHITTENDEN, Recollections of President Lincoln and His Administration

147. Lincoln Reads the Emancipation Proclamation

From the very beginning of the war, radical antislavery men urged Lincoln to take immediate steps to liberate the slaves. But conservative opinion was averse to hasty measures. Moreover, Lincoln was afraid of offending the loyal border States of Missouri, Kentucky, Maryland, and Delaware, where many good Union men still held slaves. Not until public opinion had fairly ripened for the step did he issue his famous Emancipation Proclamation on September 22, 1862. Effective January 1, 1863, it declared free all the slaves within any State or part of a State then in rebellion. Carpenter was an artist who painted the reading of the proclamation to the Cabinet, and to whom Lincoln confided.

THE APPOINTED hour found me at the well-remembered door of the official chamber — that door watched daily, with so many conflicting emotions of hope and fear, by the anxious throng regularly gathered there. The President had preceded me and was already deep in Acts of Congress, with which the writing desk was strewed, awaiting his signature. He received me pleasantly, giving me a seat near his own armchair; and after having read Mr. Lovejoy's note, he took off his spectacles and said, "Well, Mr. Carpenter, we will turn you loose in here and try to give you a good chance to work out your idea." Then, without paying much attention to the enthusiastic expression of my ambitious desire and purpose, he proceeded to give me a detailed account of the history and issue of the great proclamation.

"It had got to be," said he, "midsummer, 1862. Things had gone on from bad to worse, until I felt that we had reached the end of our rope on the plan of operations we had been pursuing, that we had about played our last card and must change our tactics or lose the game! I now determined upon the adoption of the emancipation policy, and without consultation with or the knowledge of the cabinet, I prepared the original draft of the proclamation and, after much anxious thought, called a cabinet meeting upon the subject. This was the last of July or the first part of the month of August, 1862." (The exact date he did not remember.) "This cabinet meeting took place, I think, upon a Saturday. All were present, excepting Mr. Blair, the postmaster general, who was absent at the opening of the discussion, but came in subsequently. I said to the cabinet that I had resolved upon this step and had not called them together to ask their advice but to lay the subject matter of a proclamation before them, suggestions as to which would be in order after they had heard it read. . . . Various suggestions were offered. Secretary Chase wished the language stronger in reference to the arming of the blacks. Mr. Blair, after he came in, deprecated the policy on the ground that it would cost the administration the fall elections. Nothing, however, was offered that I had not already fully anticipated and settled in my own mind until Secretary Seward spoke. He said in substance: 'Mr. President, I approve of the proclamation, but I question the expediency of its issue at this juncture. The depression of the public mind, consequent upon our repeated reverses, is so great that I fear the effect of so important a step. It may be viewed as the last measure of an exhausted government, a cry for help; the government stretching forth its hand to Ethiopia instead of Ethiopia stretching forth her hands to the government.' His idea," said the President, "was that it would be considered our last *shriek*, on the retreat." (This was his precise expression.) " 'Now,' continued Mr. Seward, 'while I approve the measure, I suggest, sir, that you postpone its issue until you can give it to the country supported by military success, instead of issuing it, as would be the case now, upon the greatest disasters of the war!'"

Mr. Lincoln continued: "The wisdom of the view of the Secretary of State struck me with very great force. It was an aspect of the case that, in all my thought upon the subject, I had entirely overlooked. The result was that I put the draft of the proclamation aside, as you do your sketch for a picture, waiting for a victory. From time to time I added or changed a line, touching it up here and there, anxiously watching the progress of events. Well, the next news we had was of Pope's disaster at Bull Run. Things looked darker than ever. Finally came the week of the battle of Antietam. I determined to wait no longer. The news came, I think, on Wednesday, that the advantage was on our side. I was then staying at the Soldiers' Home [three miles out of Washington]. Here I finished writing the second draft of the preliminary proclamation, came up on Saturday, called the cabinet together to hear it, and it was published the following Monday."

F. B. CARPENTER, Six Months at the White House

148. Secretary Chase Recalls a Famous Cabinet Meeting

Lincoln's Cabinet had been divided on the advisability of issuing the Emancipation Proclamation. It did not seem possible to bring it out with proper effect while the Union armies were generally unsuccessful. In the spring of 1862 McClellan had been decisively checked in an attempted advance upon Richmond; during the summer General Pope, who succeeded him, was defeated at Manassas. Then in September Lee's troops crossed the Potomac and invaded Maryland. Here they were met and checked by McClellan at Antietam. Although the Union commander failed to follow up his victory by a pursuit of Lee, the success was sufficient to enable Lincoln to publish his proclamation to the world.

SEPTEMBER 22, 1862.—To department about nine. State Department messenger came with notices to heads of departments to meet at twelve. Received sundry callers. Went to the White House. All the members of the cabinet were in attendance. There was some general talk, and the President mentioned that Artemus Ward had sent him his book. Proposed to read a chapter which he thought very funny. Read it and seemed to enjoy it very much; the heads also (except Stanton). The chapter was "High-Handed Outrage at Utica."

The President then took a graver tone and said: "Gentlemen, I have, as you are aware, thought a great deal about the relation of this war to slavery, and you all remember that, several weeks ago, I read to you an order I had prepared upon the subject, which, on account of objections made by some of you, was not issued. Ever since then my mind has been much occupied with this subject, and I have thought all along that the time for acting on it might probably come. I think the time has come now. I wish it was a better time. I wish that we were in a better condition. The action of the army against the rebels has not been quite what I should have liked best. But they have been driven out of Maryland, and Pennsylvania is no longer in danger of invasion. When the rebel army was at Frederick I determined, as soon as it should be driven out of Maryland, to issue a proclamation of emancipation such as I thought most likely to be useful. I said nothing to any one, but I made a promise to myself and (hesitating a little) to my Maker. The rebel army is now driven out, and I am going to fulfill that promise. I have got you together to hear what I have written down. I do not wish your advice about the main matter, for that I have determined for myself. This I say without intending anything but respect for any one of you. But I already know the views of each on this question. They have been heretofore expressed, and I have considered them as thoroughly and carefully as I can. What I have written is that which my reflections have determined me to say. If there is anything in the expressions I use or in any minor matter which any one of you thinks had best be changed, I shall be glad to receive your suggestions. One other observation I will make. I know very well that many others might, in this matter as in others, do better than I can; and if I was satisfied that the public confidence was more fully possessed by any one of them than by me, and knew of any constitutional way in which he could be put in my place, he should have it. I would gladly yield it to him. But though I believe that I have not so much of the confidence of the people as I had some time since, I do not know that, all things considered, any other person has more; and however this may be, there is no way in which I can have any other man put where I am. I am here. I must do the best I can and bear the responsibility of taking the course which I feel I ought to take."

The President then proceeded to read his Emancipation Proclamation, making remarks on the several parts as he went on, and showing that he had fully considered the subject in all the lights under which it had been presented to him.

After he had closed, Governor Seward said: "The general question having been decided, nothing can be said further about that. Would it not, however, make the proclamation more clear and decided to leave out all reference to the act being sustained during the incumbency of the present President; and not merely say that the Government 'recognizes' but that it will maintain the freedom it proclaims?"

I followed, saying: "What you have said, Mr. President, fully satisfies me that you have given to every proposition which has been made a kind and candid consideration. And you have now expressed the conclusion to which you have arrived clearly and distinctly. This it was your right and, under your oath of office, your duty to do. The proclamation does not, indeed, mark out the course I would myself prefer; but I am ready to take it just as it is written and to stand by it with all my heart. I think, however, the suggestions of Governor Seward very judicious, and shall be glad to have them adopted."

The President then asked us severally our opinions as to the modifications proposed, saying that he did not care much about the phrases he had used. Every one favored the modification, and it was adopted. Governor Seward then proposed that in the passage relating to colonization some language should be introduced to show that the colonization proposed was to be only with the consent of the colonists and the consent of the states in which the colonies might be attempted. This, too, was agreed to; and no other modification was proposed. Mr. Blair then said that the question having been decided, he would make no objection to issuing the proclamation; but he would ask to have his paper, presented some days since, against the policy, filed with the proclamation. The President consented to this readily. And then Mr. Blair went on to say that he was afraid of the influence of the proclamation on the border states and on the army and stated at some length the grounds of his apprehensions. He disclaimed most expressly, however, all objections to emancipation *per se,* saying he had always been personally in favor of it — always ready for immediate emancipation in the midst of slave states, rather than submit to the perpetuation of the system.

Diary of S. P. Chase

149. Lincoln Frees the Slaves

Though accomplishing little at the moment (for it applied mainly to slaves within the Confederate lines), the Emancipation Proclamation did show that freedom would be granted to the bondsmen as rapidly as the Union armies advanced; and it made a profound impression upon public opinion in the North and in Europe.

WHEREAS on the 22d day of September, A.D. 1862, a proclamation was issued by the President of the United States, containing, among other things, the following, to wit:

"That on the 1st day of January, A.D. 1863, all persons held as slaves within any state or designated part of a state the people whereof shall then be in rebellion against the United States shall be then, thenceforward, and forever free; and the executive government of the United States, including the military and naval authority thereof, will recognize and maintain the freedom of such persons and will do no act or acts to repress such persons, or any of them, in any efforts they may make for their actual freedom.

"That the executive will on the 1st day of January aforesaid, by proclamation, designate the states and parts of states, if any, in which the people thereof, respectively, shall then be in rebellion against the United States; and the fact that any state or the people thereof shall on that day be in good faith represented in the Congress of the United States by members chosen thereto at elections wherein a majority of the qualified voters of such states shall have participated shall, in the absence of strong countervailing testimony, be deemed conclusive evidence that such state and the people thereof are not then in rebellion against the United States."

Now, therefore, I, Abraham Lincoln, . . . do, on this 1st day of January, A.D. 1863, . . . order and designate . . . the states and parts of states wherein the people thereof, respectively, are this day in rebellion against the United States. . . .

And by virtue of the power and for the purpose aforesaid, I do order and declare that all persons held as slaves within said designated states and parts of states are, and henceforward shall be, free; and that the executive government of the United States, including the military and naval authorities thereof, will recognize and maintain the freedom of said persons.

And I hereby enjoin upon the people so declared to be free to abstain from all violence, unless in necessary self-defense; and I recommend to them that, in all cases when allowed, they labor faithfully for reasonable wages.

And I further declare and make known that such persons of suitable condition will be received into the armed service of the United States to garrison forts, positions, stations, and other places, and to man vessels of all sorts in said service.

And upon this act, sincerely believed to be an act of justice, warranted by the Constitution upon military necessity, I invoke the considerate judgment of mankind and the gracious favor of Almighty God.

The Emancipation Proclamation

150. Lincoln Consoles Mrs. Bixby

Lincoln found time to write letters to some of the plain people he loved so well, and one of these in particular has become a world-famous classic.

DEAR MADAM: I have been shown in the files of the War Department a statement of the Adjutant General that you are the mother of five sons who have died gloriously on the field of battle. I feel how weak and fruitless must be any words of mine which should attempt to beguile you from the grief of a loss so overwhelming. But I cannot refrain from tendering to you the consolation that may be found in the thanks of the Republic they died to save. I pray that our heavenly Father may assuage the anguish of your bereavement and leave you only the cherished memory of the loved and lost and the solemn pride that must be yours to have laid so costly a sacrifice upon the altar of freedom.

Yours very sincerely and respectfully,

ABRAHAM LINCOLN

Letter to Mrs. Bixby, November 21, 1864

151. "With Malice toward None, with Charity for All"

Lincoln's last Inaugural Address, delivered when the Union armies were plainly within sight of final victory, is noteworthy for two qualities in especial: the moderation and kindliness of its references to the Southern people, and its deep religious feeling.

FELLOW COUNTRYMEN: At this second appearing to take the oath of the presidential office there is less occasion for an extended address than there was at the first. Then a statement somewhat in detail of a course to be pursued seemed fitting and proper. Now, at the expiration of four years, during which public declarations have been constantly called forth on every point and phase of the great contest which still absorbs the attention and engrosses the energies of the nation, little that is new could be presented. The progress of our arms, upon which all else chiefly depends, is as well known to the public as to myself, and it is, I trust, reasonably satisfactory and encouraging to all. With high hope for the future, no prediction in regard to it is ventured.

On the occasion corresponding to this four years ago all thoughts were anxiously directed to an impending civil war. All dreaded it, all sought to avert it. While the inaugural address was being delivered from this place, devoted altogether to *saving* the Union without war, insurgent agents were in the city seeking to *destroy* it without war — seeking to dissolve the Union and divide effects by negotiation. Both parties deprecated war, but one of them would *make* war rather than let the nation survive, and the other would *accept* war rather than let it perish, and the war came.

One eighth of the whole population was colored slaves, not distributed generally over the Union, but localized in the southern part of it. These slaves constituted a peculiar and powerful interest. All knew that this interest was somehow the cause of the war. To strengthen, perpetuate, and extend this interest was the object for which the insurgents would rend the Union even by war, while the government claimed no right to do more than to restrict the territorial enlargement of it. Neither party expected for the war the magnitude or the duration which it has already attained. Neither anticipated that the *cause* of the conflict might cease with or even before the conflict itself should cease. Each looked for an easier triumph and a result less fundamental and astounding. Both read the same Bible and pray to the same God, and each invokes His aid against the other. It may seem strange that any men should dare to ask a just God's assistance in wringing their bread from the sweat of other men's faces, but let us judge not, that we be not judged. The prayers of both could not be answered. That of neither has been answered fully. The Almighty has His own purposes. "Woe unto the world because of offenses; for it must needs be that offenses come, but woe to that man by whom the offense cometh." If we shall suppose that American slavery is one of those offenses which, in the providence of God, must needs come, but which, having continued through His appointed time, He now wills to remove, and that He gives to both North and South this terrible war as the woe due to those by whom the offense came, shall we discern therein any departure from those divine attributes which the believers in a living God always ascribe to Him? Fondly do we hope, fervently do we pray, that this mighty scourge of war may speedily pass away. Yet, if God wills that it continue until all the wealth piled by the bondsman's two hundred and fifty years of unrequited toil shall be sunk, and until every drop of blood drawn with the lash shall be paid by another drawn with the sword, as was said three thousand years ago, so still it must be said, "The judgments of the Lord are true and righteous altogether."

With malice toward none, with charity for all, with firmness in the right as God gives us to see the right, let us strive on to finish the work we are in, to bind up the nation's wounds, to care for him who shall have borne the battle and for his widow and his orphan, to do all which may achieve and cherish a just and lasting peace among ourselves and with all nations.

ABRAHAM LINCOLN, Second Inaugural Address

152. President Lincoln Is Assassinated

President Lincoln had entered Richmond the day after its surrender, and had then returned to Washington in time to make a public address on April 11, 1865. On the evening of the 14th he went to Ford's Theater to see Laura Keene in an

English comedy. John Wilkes Booth, of a famous family of actors, had concocted a plot to assassinate all the principal officers of the government; a Southern sympathizer, he was sufficiently crazed to believe that this might undo the work of the Union armies. Stealthily entering Lincoln's box, he sent a pistol ball into the President's brain. Gideon Welles was Lincoln's Secretary of the Navy.

I HAD retired to bed about half past ten on the evening of the 14th of April [1865] and was just getting asleep when Mrs. Welles, my wife, said some one was at our door. Sitting up in bed, I heard a voice twice call to John, my son, whose sleeping room was on the second floor directly over the front entrance. I arose at once and raised a window, when my messenger, James Smith, called to me that Mr. Lincoln, the President, had been shot, and said Secretary Seward and his son, Assistant Secretary Frederick Seward, were assassinated. James was much alarmed and excited. I told him his story was very incoherent and improbable, that he was associating men who were not together and liable to attack at the same time. "Where," I inquired, "was the President when shot?" James said he was at Ford's Theater on Tenth Street. "Well," said I, "Secretary Seward is an invalid in bed in his house yonder on Fifteenth Street." James said he had been there, stopped in at the house to make inquiry before alarming me.

I immediately dressed myself and, against the earnest remonstrance and appeals of my wife, went directly to Mr. Seward's, whose residence was on the east side of the square, mine being on the north. . . .

As we descended the stairs, I asked Stanton what he had heard in regard to the President that was reliable. He said the President was shot at Ford's Theater, that he had seen a man who was present and witnessed the occurrence. I said I would go immediately to the White House. Stanton told me the President was not there but was at the theater. "Then," said I, "let us go immediately there." He said that was his intention and asked me, if I had not a carriage, to go with him. In the lower hall we met General Meigs, whom he requested to take charge of the house and to clear out all who did not belong there. General Meigs begged Stanton not to go down to Tenth

Street; others also remonstrated against our going. Stanton, I thought, hesitated. Hurrying forward, I remarked that I should go immediately; and I thought it his duty also. He said he should certainly go, but the remonstrants increased and gathered around him. I said we were wasting time and, pressing through the crowd, entered the carriage and urged Stanton, who was detained by others after he had placed his foot on the step. Meigs called to some soldiers to go with us, and there was one on each side of the carriage. The streets were full of people. Not only the sidewalks but the carriage-way was to some extent occupied, all or nearly all hurrying toward Tenth Street. When we entered that street we found it pretty closely packed.

The President had been carried across the street from the theater to the house of a Mr. Peterson. We entered by ascending a flight of steps above the basement and passing through a long hall to the rear, where the President lay extended on a bed, breathing heavily. Several surgeons were present, at least six, I should think more. Among them I was glad to observe Doctor Hall, who, however, soon left. I inquired of Doctor Hall, as I entered, the true condition of the President. He replied the President was dead to all intents, although he might live three hours or perhaps longer.

The giant sufferer lay extended diagonally across the bed, which was not long enough for him. He had been stripped of his clothes. His large arms, which were occasionally exposed, were of a size which one would scarce have expected from his spare appearance. His slow, full respiration lifted the clothes with each breath that he took. His features were calm and striking. I had never seen them appear to better advantage than for the first hour, perhaps, that I was there. After that his right eye began to swell and that part of his face became discolored.

Senator Sumner was there, I think, when I entered. If not he came in soon after, as did Speaker Colfax, Mr. Secretary McCulloch, and the other members of the cabinet, with the exception of Mr. Seward. A double guard was stationed at the door and on the sidewalk to repress the crowd, which was of course highly excited and anxious. The room was small and overcrowded. The surgeons and members of the cabinet were as many as should have been in the room, but there were many more, and the hall and other rooms in the front or main house were full. One of these rooms was occupied by Mrs. Lincoln and her attendants, with Miss Harris. Mrs. Dixon and Mrs. Kinney came to her about twelve o'clock. About once an hour Mrs. Lincoln would repair to the bedside of her dying husband and with lamentation and tears remain until overcome by emotion.

A door which opened upon a porch or gallery, and also the windows, were kept open for fresh air. The night was dark, cloudy, and damp, and about six it began to rain. I remained in the room until then without sitting or leaving it, when, there being a vacant chair which some one left at the foot of the bed, I occupied it for nearly two hours, listening to the heavy groans and witnessing the wasting life of the good and great man who was expiring before me.

About 6 A.M. I experienced a feeling of faintness, and for the first time after entering the room a little past eleven I left it and the house and took a short walk in the open air. It was a dark and gloomy morning, and rain set in before I returned to the house some fifteen minutes later. Large groups of people were gathered every few rods, all anxious and solicitous. Some one or more from each group stepped forward as I passed to inquire into the condition of the President and to ask if there was no hope. Intense grief was on every countenance when I replied that the President could survive but a short time. The colored people especially — and there were at this time more of them, perhaps, than of whites — were overwhelmed with grief.

A little before seven I went into the room where the dying President was rapidly drawing near the closing moments. His wife soon after made her last visit to him. The death struggle had begun. Robert, his son, stood with several others at the head of the bed. He bore himself well but on two occasions gave way to overpowering grief and sobbed aloud, turning his head and leaning on the shoulder of Senator Sumner. The respiration of the President became suspended at intervals and at last entirely ceased at twenty-two minutes past seven. . . .

I went after breakfast to the Executive Mansion. There was a cheerless, cold rain, and everything seemed gloomy. On the Avenue in front of the White House were several hundred colored people, mostly women and children, weeping and wailing their loss. This crowd did not appear to diminish through the whole of that cold, wet day; they seemed not to know what was to be their fate since their great benefactor was dead, and their hopeless grief affected me more than almost anything else, though strong and brave men wept when I met them.

Diary of Gideon Welles

XXIV

Behind the Lines

153. Mr. Dicey Watches Recruiting on Boston Common

An English liberal and a warm friend of prominent Northerners, Edward Dicey spent six months in the United States in the midst of the Civil War. He was a close and sympathetic observer of the great wartime effort the American people were then making; and he hastened after his return to England to publish a book giving his countrymen a better appreciation of the Union cause.

AT BOSTON at the same period there were meetings held daily on the Common in order to stimulate volunteering. I was present at several of them, but at none which I came across was there any outburst of popular enthusiasm. A platform was raised in one corner of the park, from which citizens of note daily addressed any hearers whom they could collect together. A brass band performed during the intervals between the speeches, and recruiting officers were in attendance to enlist any recruit whose courage was stirred up to the enlistment point.

The meeting closed with reading an address from the citizens' committee to the people at Boston, which is too long for quotation. In the whole of this proclamation, no allusion whatever was made to the question of slavery, and this omission was common in all the proceedings of this period. An immediate accession of recruits ought to have been the answer made to these appeals, but, somehow or other, the levy did not correspond to the expectations of the nation. There were many causes which were hostile to its progress. Taking in the three months' volunteers, probably near a million of men had been, at one time or other, in the service of the Federal armies since the war began. Now, as the population of the Northern states is about twenty-four millions and the average life of a generation in

America is certainly not over thirty years, there would only be about four millions of men above twenty. One in four of the military population of a country constitutes an enormous proportion. All, and more than all, the men who would have gone naturally to the war had gone already; and the vast majority of the July levy had to be drawn from classes to whom volunteering was a heavy personal sacrifice.

There was no general distress, too, to force the poorer classes into the army for subsistence. The price of living had risen since the war, but wages, owing to the scarcity of labor, had risen in a higher ratio. The call for troops was made under the most dispiriting circumstances. It came on the day after a disaster, at a time when there was little prospect of immediate action, and when the war seemed likely to be prolonged indefinitely.

The harvest was close at hand, and the sons of the Northern farmers and yeomen who formed so large a part of the Federal army could hardly enlist till the crops were got in. The Irish, too, were hanging back. Amongst them the prejudice against the Negro is stronger than amongst any other class, and they believed that the effect of emancipation would be to flood the Northern states with free Negroes and thus lower their own wages. There was a prevalent idea, too, that conscription would be resorted to, and that in this event the price for substitutes would be much higher than any other bounty yet offered. All these causes were more or less local and temporary in their character, but there was one cause which retarded enlistment more widely and more seriously than all of them put together, and that was the want of public confidence in the generalship of the Federal commanders and still more in the administration of the war. There was a general and growing conviction that the temporizing policy of the government had failed. Slavery, the nation was beginning to see, was a fact that must be looked boldly in the face. The time had come for the government to declare openly what it meant to do, and what it meant not to do, with reference to the Negro. The absence of any outspoken profession of faith on this subject paralyzed the enthusiasm of the people. Could Mr. Lincoln have been induced to issue his emancipation edict at this period, the result, I believe, might have been far different; but while the President vacillated between conflicting counsels, the golden opportunity was allowed to pass.

Before I leave the subject of the levy, let me mention one or two incidents out of many connected with it which came under my own notice. In the City Hall Park there were two sheds hastily run up. One was the enlistment office, the other the temporary hospital for wounded soldiers just landed from the peninsula. Alongside of the recruiting sergeant one saw the convalescent soldiers — wounded, haggard, and maimed — tottering about beneath the trees. The arrangement, perhaps, was not a politic one. Flags and drinking booths and bands of music might attract recruits more readily; yet, to my mind, there was an air of resolution and stern purpose given by the contrast of the wounded veteran and the raw recruit, which was not without promise. So, again, I spoke in a former chapter of a house I knew of, where there hung the pictures of three bright, gallant-looking lads who had gone to the war, one of them never to return. I was there a few days after the battle of the Chickahominy, and the second of these portraits was now a remembrance of one who had died in battle. And yet the only change I could see in the conversation of those to whom the likenesses belonged was an increased ardor for the war, a more intense sympathy for the cause in which the dead had fallen. One more anecdote, and I have finished. In traveling up one night from Baltimore, the cars were crowded with sick and wounded soldiers on their way home from the peninsula. On the bench behind me there was a woman in deep black, carrying a sick child in her arms, and beside her there was a discharged soldier whose health had broken down in the swamps. The woman was a widow just returned from the deathbed of her brother, who, like her husband, had been killed in the campaign. The man looked dreadfully worn and ill; he complained, and, I fear, truly, that he should never be fit for a day's work again; he had a grievance, too, of his own against the government, which he considered had behaved shabbily about the amount of bounty paid him on his discharge. Being seated near them, I could hear the soldier and the soldier's widow telling each other of their hardships and their sorrows; and at last the man consoled the woman by saying to her, "Well, after all, it's for our country, and we're bound to do it." The woman answered him, "Yes, that's so"; and though the words might be commonplace, it seemed to me that there was about them something of true heroism.

EDWARD DICEY, Six Months in the Federal States

154. A War Clerk Describes the Confederate Cabinet

A clerk in the War Department of the Confederacy, J. B. Jones took an extremely critical view of leaders and policies of the South. His diary is an invaluable record of official happenings in Richmond, and his comments are lively and vivid though often colored by prejudice.

MAY 17th, 1861. — Was introduced to the President today. He was overwhelmed with papers and retained a number in his left hand, probably of more importance than the rest. He received me with urbanity, and while he read the papers I had given him, as I had never seen him before, I endeavored to scrutinize his features, as one would naturally do, for the purpose of forming a vague estimate of the character and capabilities of the man destined to perform the leading part in a revolution which must occupy a large space in the world's history. His stature is tall, nearly six feet; his frame is very slight and seemingly frail, but when he throws back his shoulders he is as straight as an Indian chief. The features of his face are distinctly marked with character, and no one gazing at his profile would doubt for a moment that he beheld more than an ordinary man. His face is handsome, and [on] his thin lip often basks a pleasant smile. There is nothing sinister or repulsive in his manners or appearance, and if there are no special indications of great grasp of intellectual power on his forehead and on his sharply-defined nose and chin, neither is there any evidence of weakness or that he could be easily moved from any settled purpose. I think he has a clear perception of matters demanding his cognizance, and a nice discrimination of details. As a politician he attaches the utmost importance to *consistency* — and here I differ with him. I think that to be consistent as a politician is to change with the circumstances of the case. When Calhoun and Webster first met in Congress, the first advocated a protective tariff and the last opposed it. This was told me by Mr. Webster himself, in 1842, when he was Secretary of State; and it was confirmed by Mr. Calhoun in 1844, then Secretary of State himself. Statesmen are the physicians of the public weal, and what doctor hesitates to vary his remedies with the new phases of disease?

When the President had completed the reading of my papers, and during the perusal I observed him make several emphatic nods, he asked me what I wanted. I told him I wanted employment with my pen, perhaps only temporary employment. I thought the correspondence of the Secretary of War would increase in volume, and another assistant besides Major Tyler would be required in his office. He smiled and shook his head, saying that such work would be only temporary indeed; which I construed to mean that even he did not then suppose the war to assume colossal proportions.

May 20th. — Mr. Walker, the Secretary of War, is some forty-seven or -eight years of age, tall, thin, and a little bent, not by age, but by study and bad health. He was a successful lawyer and, having never been in governmental employment, is fast working himself down. He has not yet learned how to avoid unnecessary labor, being a man of the finest sensibilities, and exacting with the utmost nicety all due deference to the dignity of his official position. He stands somewhat on ceremony with his brother officials and accords and exacts the etiquette natural to a sensitive gentleman who has never been broken on the wheel of office. I predict for him a short career. The only hope for his continuance in office is unconditional submission to the President, who, being once Secretary of War of the United States, is familiar with all the wheels of the department. But soon, if I err not, the President will be too much absorbed in the fluctuations of momentous campaigns to give much of his attention to any one of the departments. Nevertheless Mr. Walker, if he be an apt scholar, may learn much before that day; and Congress may simplify his duties by enacting a uniform mode of filling the offices in the field. The applications now give the greatest trouble, and the disappointed class give rise to many vexations.

May 21st. — Being in the same room with the Secretary and seen by all his visitors, I am necessarily making many new acquaintances;

and quite a number recognize me by my books which they have read. Among this class is Mr. Benjamin, the Minister of Justice. . . . Mr. Benjamin is of course a Jew, of French lineage, born I believe in Louisiana, a lawyer and politician. His age may be sixty, and yet one might suppose him to be less than forty. His hair and eyes are black, his forehead capacious, his face round and as intellectual as one of that shape can be; and Mr. Benjamin is certainly a man of intellect, education, and extensive reading, combined with natural abilities of a tolerably high order. Upon his lip there seems to bask an eternal smile; but if it be studied, it is not a smile — yet it bears no unpleasing aspect.

May 22nd. — Today I had, in our office, a specimen of Mr. Memminger's oratory. He was pleading for an installment of the claims of South Carolina on the Confederacy; and Mr. Walker, always hesitating, argued the other side, merely for delay. Both are fine speakers, with most distinct enunciation and musical voices. The demand was audited and paid, amounting to, I believe, several hundred thousand dollars.

And I heard and saw Mr. Toombs today, the Secretary of State. He is a portly gentleman, but with the pale face of the student and the marks of a deep thinker. To gaze at him in repose, the casual spectator would suppose, from his neglect of dress, that he was a planter in moderate circumstances and of course not gifted with extraordinary powers of intellect; but let him open his mouth, and the delusion vanishes. At the time alluded to he was surrounded by the rest of the cabinet, in our office, and the topic was the policy of the war. He was for taking the initiative and carrying the war into the enemy's country. And as he warmed with the subject, the man seemed to vanish, and the genius alone was visible. . . . These little discussions were of frequent occurrence; and it soon became apparent that the Secretary of War [Pope Walker] was destined to be the most important man among the cabinet ministers. His position afforded the best prospect of future distinction — always provided he should be equal to the position and his administration attended with success. I felt convinced that Toombs would not be long chafing in the cabinet but that he would seize the first opportunity to repair to the field.

J. B. Jones, A Rebel War Clerk's Diary at the Confederate States Capital

155. Writing "The Battle Hymn of the Republic"

The daughter of a New York banker and the wife of a well-known New England reformer, Julia Ward Howe early made a name for herself in Boston circles by her essays and poems. She was prominent also as an Abolitionist, and she became one of the leaders of the woman-suffrage movement. In her early forties, while at the front, she wrote her most famous poem and the most memorable poem of the war.

I

I DISTINCTLY remember that a feeling of discouragement came over me as I drew near the city of Washington. I thought of the women of my acquaintance whose sons or husbands were fighting our great battle, the women themselves serving in the hospitals, or busying themselves with the work of the Sanitary Commission. My husband was beyond the age of military service, my eldest son but a stripling; my youngest was a child of not more than two years. I could not leave my nursery to follow the march of our armies; neither had I the practical deftness which the preparing and packing of sanitary stores demanded. Something seemed to say to me, "You would be glad to serve, but you cannot help any one; you have nothing to give, and there is nothing for you to do." Yet, because of my sincere desire, a word was given me to say, which did strengthen the hearts of those who fought in the field and of those who languished in the prison.

We were invited one day to attend a review of troops at some distance from the town. While we were engaged in watching the maneuvers, a sudden movement of the enemy necessitated immediate action. The review was discontinued, and we saw a detachment of soldiers gallop to the assistance of a small body of our men who were in imminent danger of being surrounded and cut off from retreat. The regiments remaining on the field were ordered to march to their cantonments. We returned to the city very slowly, of necessity, for the troops nearly filled the road. My dear minister was in the carriage with me, as were several other friends. To beguile the rather tedious drive, we sang from time to time snatches of the army songs so popular at that time, concluding, I think, with:

> John Brown's body lies a-moldering in the ground;
> His soul is marching on.

The soldiers seemed to like this and answered back, "Good for you!" Mr. Clarke said, "Mrs. Howe, why do you not write some good words for that stirring tune?" I replied that I had often wished to do this but had not as yet found in my mind any leading toward it.

I went to bed that night as usual and slept, according to my wont, quite soundly. I awoke in the gray of the morning twilight, and as I lay waiting for the dawn, the long lines of the desired poem began to twine themselves in my mind. Having thought out all the stanzas, I said to myself, "I must get up and write these verses down, lest I fall asleep again and forget them." So with a sudden effort I sprang out of bed and found in the dimness an old stump of a pen which I remembered to have used the day before. I scrawled the verses almost without looking at the paper. I had learned to do this when, on previous occasions, attacks of versification had visited me in the night and I feared to have recourse to a light lest I should wake the baby, who slept near me. I was always obliged to decipher my scrawl before another night should intervene, as it was only legible while the matter was fresh in my mind. At this time, having completed my writing, I returned to bed and fell asleep, saying to myself, "I like this better than most things that I have written."

The poem, which was soon after published in the *Atlantic Monthly,* [February, 1862] was somewhat praised on its appearance, but the vicissitudes of the war so engrossed public attention that small heed was taken of literary matters. I knew and was content to know that the poem soon found its way to the camps, as I heard from time to time of its being sung in chorus by the soldiers.

JULIA WARD HOWE, *Reminiscences*

II

Mine eyes have seen the glory of the coming of the Lord:
He is trampling out the vintage where the grapes of wrath are stored;
He hath loosed the fateful lightning of his terrible swift sword:
   His truth is marching on.

I have seen Him in the watch fires of a hundred circling camps;
They have builded Him an altar in the evening dews and damps;
I can read His righteous sentence by the dim and flaring lamps.
   His day is marching on.

I have read a fiery gospel writ in burnished rows of steel:
"As ye deal with my contemners, so with you my grace shall deal;
Let the Hero, born of woman, crush the serpent with his heel,
   Since God is marching on."

He has sounded forth the trumpet that shall never call retreat;
He is sifting out the hearts of men before his judgment seat:
Oh! be swift, my soul, to answer Him! be jubilant, my feet!
   Our God is marching on.

In the beauty of the lilies Christ was born across the sea,
With a glory in His bosom that transfigures you and me:
As He died to make men holy, let us die to make men free,
   While God is marching on.

156. A Hospital Transport Receives the Wounded

To aid the Government in taking care of soldiers in the field, the Northern people organized the Sanitary Commission, the Christian Commission, and other volun-

tary associations for looking after the physical and moral welfare of the men. Large sums were raised for these bodies by canvassing and by fairs and benefits.

OFF VIRGINIA PENINSULA, June, 1862. — Sunday night. — The *Knickerbocker* had, by estimate, three hundred and fifty on board. The night being fine, many were disposed of on the outer decks, and before I left, at eleven o'clock, nearly all had been washed, dressed, and put to bed decently, and were as comfortable as circumstances would admit of our making them. All had received needed nourishment and such surgical and medical attention as was immediately demanded. Leaving the *Knickerbocker* in this satisfactory condition, I came back in a small boat, at midnight, to the landing, where I found that the *Elm City* already had five hundred wounded on board. I ordered her to run down and anchor near the *Knickerbocker*. The *State of Maine* had been ordered to the landing by the harbor master, and the wounded remaining on shore, excluded from the *Elm City,* were flocking on board of her. Our ladies on the *Elm City* sent them some food, and we put on board from our supply boat bedding and various stores, of which there was evident need, without waiting to be asked and without finding any one to receive them, the surgeons being fully engrossed in performing operations of pressing necessity.

The battle had been renewed in the morning of this day (Sunday), and we had sent a relief party, composed of medical students and male nurses, with supplies of stimulants, lint, etc., to the battlefield hospitals. A portion of this party returned about midnight with another large train of wounded. All our force that could possibly be withdrawn from duty on the boats was immediately employed in distributing drink and in carrying the wounded from the railroad to the boat. Some men died on the cars. I made another visit to the *Knickerbocker* in the morning, and on my return (Monday), found that a train had just arrived, and the wounded men were walking in a throng across the scow to the *Webster* No. 2, government hospital, the only boat remaining at the landing. I knew that she was not prepared for them and sent for Doctor S., the representative of the medical director. Doctor S. could not be found. I inquired for the surgeon in charge of the railroad train but could find none. There was no one in charge of the wounded. Meantime they were taken out of the cars and assisted toward the landing by volunteer bystanders until the gangplanks of the boat, the landing scow, and the adjoining riverbanks were crowded. As many were nearly fainting in the sun, I advised the captain to let them come on board. He did so, and they hobbled on, till the boat was crowded in all parts. The *Small* was outside the *Webster* No. 2, and our ladies administered as far as possible to their relief. Going on shore, I found still a great number, including the worst cases, lying on litters, gasping in the fervid sun. I do not describe such a scene. The worst cases I had brought upon the *Small*. Two died on the forward deck, under the shade of the awning, within half an hour. One was senseless when brought on; the other revived for a moment, while Mrs. G. bathed his head with ice water, just long enough to whisper the address of his father and to smile gratefully, then passed away, holding her hand.

At the time of which I am now writing (Monday afternoon), wounded men were arriving by every train, entirely unattended, or with at most a detail of two soldiers, two hundred or more of them in a train. They were packed as closely as they could be stowed in the common freight cars, without beds, without straw, at most with a wisp of hay under their heads. Many of the lighter cases came on the roof of the cars. They arrived dead and living together, in the same close box, many with awful wounds festering and swarming with maggots. Recollect it was midsummer in Virginia, clear and calm. The stench was such as to produce vomiting with some of our strong men, habituated to the duty of attending the sick. How close they were packed you may infer from a fact reported by my messenger to Doctor Tripler, who, on his return from headquarters, was present at the loading of a car. A surgeon was told that it was not possible to get another man upon the floor of the car. "Then," said he, "these three men must be laid in *across the others,* for they have got to be cleared out from here by this train!" This outrage was avoided, however.

Need I tell you that the women were always ready to press into these places of horror, going to them in torrents of rain, groping their way by dim lantern light, at all hours of night, carrying spirits and ice water; calling back to life those in despair from utter exhaustion, or again and again catching for mother or wife the last faint whispers of the dying?

One Doctor —— was at this time the only man on the ground who claimed to act as a medical officer of the United States. He was without instructions and without authority and, though miraculously active, could do nothing toward bringing about the one thing wanted, orderly responsibility. Captain Sawtelle, at my request, pitched a hospital tent for the ladies at the riverbank by the railroad, behind which a common camp kitchen was established. To this tent quantities of stores have now been conveyed, and soup and tea in camp kettles are kept constantly hot there. Before this arrangement was complete and until other stores arrived, we were for a time very hard put to it to find food of any kind to meet the extraordinary demand upon us. Just as everything was about giving out, B. found a sutler who told him that he had five hundred loaves of bread on board of a boat which had just arrived at Cumberland; but he had no way of getting it immediately up. A conditional bargain was immediately struck, and the *Elizabeth* hastened off to Cumberland to bring up the bread. When it arrived, to our horror, it proved to be so moldy it could not be used. B., almost crying with disappointment, started again to make a search through the exhausted sutler's stores at the post. While doing so, he came upon a heap of boxes and barrels unopened and unaccounted for. "What's all this?" "Sutler's goods." "Who owns them?" "I do. I am the sutler of the —— New York, up to the front. I want to get them up there, but I can't get transportation." "What's in here?" said B. in great excitement. "Mack'rel in them barrels." "What's in the boxes?" "That's wine biscuits. There's two barrels of molasses and a barrel of vinegar. I've got forty barrels of softtack, too." "Where's that?" "That's one of 'em." And B., hardly waiting for leave, seized a musket and jammed a head off. It was aerated bread, and not a speck of mold on it! He bought the sutler's whole stock on the spot, and in half an hour the ladies were dealing out bread spread with molasses, and iced vinegar and water.

The trains with wounded and sick arrive at all hours of the night, the last one before daylight, generally getting in between twelve and one. As soon as the whistle is heard, Doctor Ware is on hand (he has all the hard work of this kind to do), and the ladies are ready in their tent — blazing trench fires, and kettles all of a row, bright lights and savory supplies, piles of fresh bread and pots of coffee — the tent door opened wide, the road leading to it from the cars dotted all along the side with little fires or lighted candles. Then the first procession of slightly wounded, who stop at their tent door on their way to the boat and get cups of hot coffee with as much milk (condensed) as they want, followed by the slow-moving line of bearers and stretchers, halted by our Zouave, while the poor fellows on them have brandy or wine or iced lemonade given them. It makes but a minute's delay to pour something down their throats and put oranges in their hands and saves them from exhaustion and thirst before, in the confusion which reigns on most of the crowded government transports, food can be served them. When the worst cases have been sent on board, those which are to go to the shore hospital the next day are put into the twenty Sibley tents, pitched for the commission along the railroad, and our detail of five men start, each with his own pail of hot coffee or hot milk and crackers and soft bread, with lemonade and ice water, and feed them from tent to tent, a hundred men every night; sometimes one hundred and fifty are thus taken care of, for whom no provision has been made by government. Between two and three thousand wounded have been sent here this week, and at least nine-tenths have been fed and cared for, as long as they remained, exclusively by the commission.

An Officer of U.S. Sanitary Commission in Hospital Transports,
A Memoir of the Embarkation of the Sick and Wounded

157. The Confederates Burn Their Cotton

A powerful Union fleet under the command of David G. Farragut forced the entrance of the Mississippi — which the Confederates had heavily fortified — on April 24,

1862. It immediately brought New Orleans under its guns, and that richest of the Southern cities surrendered to the Federal forces the same week. A Louisiana girl here gives a vivid picture of the destruction of the city's great stores of cotton to prevent them from falling into Union hands.

APRIL 26, 1862. — We went this morning to see the cotton burning — a sight never before witnessed and probably never again to be seen. Wagons, drays — everything that can be driven or rolled — were loaded with the bales and taken a few squares back to burn on the commons. Negroes were running around, cutting them open, piling them up, and setting them afire. All were as busy as though their salvation depended on disappointing the Yankees. Later Charlie sent for us to come to the river and see him fire a flatboat loaded with the precious material for which the Yankees are risking their bodies and souls. Up and down the levee, as far as we could see, Negroes were rolling it down to the brink of the river where they would set the bales afire and push them in to float burning down the tide. Each sent up its wreath of smoke and looked like a tiny steamer puffing away. Only I doubt that from the source to the mouth of the river there are as many boats afloat on the Mississippi. The flatboat was piled with as many bales as it could hold without sinking. Most of them were cut open, while Negroes staved in the heads of barrels of alcohol, whisky, etc., and dashed bucketfuls over the cotton. Others built up little chimneys of pine every few feet, lined with pine knots and loose cotton, to burn more quickly. There, piled the length of the whole levee or burning in the river, lay the work of thousands of Negroes for more than a year past. It had come from every side. Men stood by who owned the cotton that was burning or waiting to burn. They either helped or looked on cheerfully. Charlie owned but sixteen bales — a matter of some fifteen hundred dollars; but he was the head man of the whole affair and burned his own as well as the property of others. A single barrel of whisky that was thrown on the cotton cost the man who gave it one hundred and twenty-five dollars. (It shows what a nation in earnest is capable of doing.) Only two men got on the flatboat with Charlie when it was ready. It was towed to the middle of the river, set afire in every place, and then they jumped into a little skiff fastened in front and rowed to land. The cotton floated down the Mississippi one sheet of living flame, even in the sunlight. It would have been grand at night. But then we will have fun watching it this evening anyway, for they cannot get through today, though no time is to be lost. Hundreds of bales remained untouched. An incredible amount of property has been destroyed today, but no one begrudges it. Every grogshop has been emptied, and gutters and pavements are floating with liquors of all kinds. So that if the Yankees are fond of strong drink, they will fare ill.

SARAH MORGAN DAWSON, A Confederate Girl's Diary

158. The Yankees Sack Sarah Morgan Dawson's Home

After the occupation of New Orleans, the naval and military forces of the Union fixed on the capture of Vicksburg as their next great objective in the West. If it could be seized, the Mississippi would be open from north to south, and the Confederacy cut in two. Union forces at once moved up the river against Baton Rouge. Here the same Confederate diarist describes a typical scene in the destruction which accompanied their advance.

AUGUST 13th, 1862. — I am in despair. Miss Jones, who has just made her escape from town, brings a most dreadful account. She, with seventy-five others, took refuge at Doctor Enders', more than a mile and a half below town, at Hall's. It was there we sent the two trunks containing Father's papers and our clothing and silver. Hearing that guerrillas had been there, the Yankees went down, shelled the house in the night, turning all those women and children out, who barely escaped with their clothing, and let the soldiers loose on it. They destroyed everything they could lay their hands on, if it could not be carried off; broke open armoires, trunks, sacked the house, and left it one scene of devastation and ruin. They even stole Miss Jones's braid! She got here with nothing but the clothes she wore.

This is a dreadful blow to me. Yesterday I thought myself beggared when I heard that our house was probably burnt, remembering all the clothing, books, furniture, etc., that it contained; but I consoled myself with the recollection of a large trunk packed in the most scientific style, containing quantities of nightgowns, skirts, chemises, dresses, cloaks — in short, our very best — which was in safety. Winter had no terrors when I thought of the nice warm clothes; I only wished I had a few of the organdy dresses I had packed up before wearing. And now? It is all gone, silver, Father's law papers, without which we are beggars, and clothing! Nothing left!

August 25th. About twelve at night. — Sleep is impossible after all that I have heard; so, after vainly endeavoring to follow the example of the rest and sleep like a stoic, I have lighted my candle and take to this to induce drowsiness.

Just after supper, when Anna and I were sitting with Mrs. Carter in her room, I talking as usual of home and saying I would be perfectly happy if Mother would decide to remain in Baton Rouge and brave the occasional shellings, I heard a well-known voice take up some sentence of mine from a dark part of the room; and with a cry of surprise, I was hugging Miriam until she was breathless. Such a forlorn creature! — so dirty, tired, and fatigued as to be hardly recognizable. We thrust her into a chair and made her speak. She had just come with Charlie, who went after them yesterday, and had left Mother and the servants at a kind friend's on the road. I never heard such a story as she told. I was heartsick, but I laughed until Mrs. Badger grew furious with me and the Yankees and abused me for not abusing them.

She says when she entered the house she burst into tears at the desolation. It was one scene of ruin. Libraries emptied, china smashed, sideboards split open with axes, three cedar chests cut open, plundered, and set up on end; all parlor ornaments carried off; her desk lay open with all letters and notes well thumbed and scattered around, while Will's last letter to her was open on the floor, with the Yankee stamp of dirty fingers. Mother's portrait, half cut from its frame, stood on the floor. Margaret, who was present at the sacking, told how she had saved Father's. It seems that those who wrought destruction in our house were all officers. One jumped on the sofa to cut the picture down (Miriam saw the prints of his muddy feet) when Margaret cried: "For God's sake, gentlemen, let it be! I'll help you to anything here. He's dead, and the young ladies would rather see the house burn than lose it!" "I'll blow your damned brains out," was the "gentleman's" answer as he put a pistol to her head, which a brother officer dashed away, and the picture was abandoned for finer sport. All the others were cut up in shreds.

Upstairs was the finest fun. Mother's beautiful mahogany armoire, whose single door was an extremely fine mirror, was entered by crashing through the glass, when it was emptied of every article and the shelves half split and half thrust back crooked. Letters, labeled by the boys private, were strewn over the floor; they opened every armoire and drawer, collected every rag to be found, and littered the whole house with them, until the wonder was where so many rags had been found. Father's armoire was relieved of everything, Gibbes's handsome Damascus sword with the silver scabbard included. All his clothes, George's, Hal's, Jimmy's, were appropriated. They entered my room, broke that fine mirror for sport, pulled down the rods from the bed, and with them pulverized my toilet set, taking also all Lydia's china ornaments I had packed in the washstand. The debris filled my basin and ornamented my bed. My desk was broken open. Over it were spread all my letters and private papers, a diary I kept when twelve years old, and sundry tokens of dried roses, etc., which must have been very funny, they all being labeled with the donor's name and the occasion. Fool! how I writhe when I think of all they saw; the invitations to buggy rides, concerts, "compliments of," etc.! Lilly's sewing machine had disappeared, but as Mother's was too heavy to move, they merely smashed the needles.

In the pillaging of the armoires they seized a pink flounced muslin of Miriam's, which one officer placed on the end of a bayonet and paraded round with, followed by the others who slashed it with their swords, crying: "I have stuck the damned Secesh! That's the time I cut her!" and continued their sport until the rags could no longer be pierced. One seized my bonnet, with which he decked himself, and ran in the streets. Indeed, all who found such rushed frantically around town, by way of frolicking, with the things on their heads. They say no frenzy could surpass it. Another snatched one of my calico dresses and a pair of vases that Mother had when she was married, and was about to decamp when a Mrs. Jones jerked them away and carried them to her boardinghouse, and returned them to Mother the other day. Blessed be Heaven! I have a calico dress! Our clothes were used for the vilest purposes and spread in every corner, at least those few that were not stolen.

Aunt Barker's Charles tried his best to defend the property. "Ain't you 'shamed to destroy all dis here that belongs to a poor widow lady who's got two daughters to support?" he asked of an officer who was foremost in the destruction. "Poor? Damn them! I don't know when I have seen a house furnished like this! Look at that furniture! They poor!" was the retort, and thereupon the work went bravely on of making us poor indeed.

It would have fared badly with us had we been there. The servants say they broke into the house, crying: "Where are those damned Secesh women? We know they are hid in here, and we'll make them dance for hiding from federal officers!" And they could not be convinced that we were not there until they had searched the very garret. Wonder what they would have done? Charles caught a Captain Clark in the streets, when the work was almost over, and begged him to put an end to it. The gentleman went readily, but though the devastation was quite evident, no one was to be seen, and he was about to leave when, insisting that there was some one there, Charles drew him into my room, dived under the bed, and drew from thence a Yankee captain by one leg, followed by a lieutenant, each with a bundle of the boys' clothes which they instantly dropped, protesting they were only looking around the house. The gentleman captain carried them off to their superior.

Ours was the most shockingly-treated house in the whole town. We have the misfortune to be equally feared by both sides, because we will blackguard neither. So the Yankees selected the only house in town that sheltered three forlorn women, to wreak their vengeance on. From far and near, strangers and friends flocked in to see the ravages committed. Crowds rushed in before, crowds came in after, Miriam and Mother arrived, all apologizing for the intrusion, but saying they had heard it was a sight never before seen. So they let them examine to their hearts' content, and Miriam says the sympathy all was extraordinary. A strange gentleman picked up a piece of Mother's mirror, which was as thick as his finger, saying: "Madame, I should like to keep this as a memento. I am about to travel through Mississippi and, having seen what a splendid piece of furniture this was and the state your house is left in, should like to show this as a specimen of Yankee vandalism."

Well! I am beggared! Strange to say, I don't feel it. Perhaps it is the satisfaction of knowing my fate that makes me so cheerful that Mrs. Carter envied my stoicism, while Mrs. Badger felt like beating me because I did not agree that there was no such thing as a gentleman in the Yankee army. I know Major Drum for one, and that Captain Clark must be two, and Mr. Biddle is three, and General Williams — God bless him, wherever he is! for he certainly acted like a Christian. The Yankees boasted loudly that if it had not been for him, the work would have been done long ago.

And now I am determined to see my home before Yankee shells complete the work that Yankee axes spared. So by sunrise I shall post over to Mr. Elder's and insist on Charlie taking me to town with him. I hardly think it is many hours off. I feel so settled, so calm!

Thursday, August 28th — I am satisfied. I have seen my home again. Tuesday I was up at sunrise, and my few preparations were soon completed, and before any one was awake I walked over to Mr. Elder's, through mud and dew, to meet Charlie. Fortunate was it for me that I started so early, for I found him hastily eating his breakfast and ready to leave. He was very much opposed to my going, and for some time I was afraid he would force me to remain, but at last he consented, perhaps because I did not insist; and with wet feet and without a particle of breakfast, I at length found myself in the buggy on the road home.

Our house could not be reached by the front; so we left the buggy in the back yard, and running through the lot without stopping to examine the storeroom and servants' rooms that opened wide, I went through the alley and entered by the front door.

Fortunate was it for this record that I undertook to describe the sacking only from Miriam's account. If I had waited until now, it would never have been mentioned; for as I looked around, to attempt such a thing seemed absurd. I stood in the parlor in silent amazement, and in answer to Charlie's "Well?" I could only laugh. It was so hard to realize. As I looked for each well-known article, I could hardly believe that Abraham Lincoln's officers had really come so low down as to steal in such a wholesale manner. The papier-mâché workbox Miriam had given me was gone. The baby sacque I was crocheting, with all knitting needles and wools, gone also. Of all the beautiful engravings of Annapolis that Will Pinckney had sent me there remained a single one. Gentlemen, my name is written on each! Not a book remained in the parlor except *Idyls of the King* that contained my name also and which together with the doorplate, was the only case in which the name of Morgan was spared. They must have thought we were related to John Morgan and wreaked their vengeance on us for that reason. Thanks for the honor, but there is not the slightest connection! Where they did not carry off articles bearing our name, they cut it off, as in the visiting cards, and left only the first name. Every book of any value or interest except Hume and Gibbon was "borrowed" permanently. I regretted Macaulay more than all the rest. Brother's splendid French histories went too, all except *L'Histoire de la Bastille*. However, as they spared Father's law libraries (all except one volume they used to support a flour barrel with, while they emptied it near the parlor door), we ought to be thankful.

The dining room was very funny. I looked around for the cut-glass celery and preserve dishes that were to be part of my *dot*, as Mother always said, together with the champagne glasses that had figured on the table the day that I was born; but there remained nothing. There was plenty of split-up furniture, though. I stood in mother's room before the shattered armoire, which I could hardly believe the same that I had smoothed my hair before as I left home three weeks previously. Father's was split across and the lock torn off, and in the place of the hundreds of articles it contained I saw two bonnets, at the sight of which I actually sat down to laugh. One was Mother's velvet, which looked very much like a football in its present condition. Mine was not to be found, as the officers forgot to return it. Wonder who has my imperial? I know they never saw a handsomer one, with its black velvet, purple silk, and ostrich feathers.

I went to my room. Gone was my small paradise! Had this shocking place ever been habitable? The tall mirror squinted at me from a thousand broken angles. It looked so knowing! I tried to fancy the Yankee officers being dragged from under my bed by the leg, thanks to Charles; but it seemed too absurd; so I let them alone. My desk! What a sight! The central part I had kept as a little curiosity shop with all my little trinkets and keepsakes, of which a large proportion were from my gentlemen friends. I looked for all I had left; found only a piece of the McRae, which as it was labeled in full, I was surprised they had spared. Precious letters I found under heaps of broken china and rags; all my notes were gone, with many letters. I looked for a letter of poor ——, in cipher, with the key attached, and name signed in plain hand. I knew it would hardly be agreeable to him to have it read, and it certainly would be unpleasant to me to have it published; but I could not find it. Miriam thinks she saw something answering the description somewhere, though.

Bah! What is the use of describing such a scene? Many suffered along with us, though none so severely. Indeed, the Yankees cursed loudly at those who did not leave anything worth stealing. They cannot complain of us on that score. All our handsome Brussels carpets, together with Lydia's fur, were taken, too. What did they not take? In the garret, in its darkest corner, a whole gilt-edged china set of Lydia's had been overlooked; so I set to work and packed it up, while Charlie packed her furniture in a wagon to send to her father.

SARAH MORGAN DAWSON, A Confederate Girl's Diary

159. Anna Dickinson Sees Draft Riots in New York City

The Confederate Government early resorted to a sweeping conscription, which finally applied to able-bodied men between seventeen and fifty-five years of age. In 1863 the Federal Government also turned to conscription. The first efforts to enforce the new law encountered resistance in various parts of the North. The worst disturbances were the great "draft riots" in New York City in July, caused partly by the draft, partly by general political discontent, and partly by the resentment which Irish laborers felt over the new competition offered by refugee Negroes. Many Negroes lost their lives before troops restored order. Anna Dickinson, who describes these shocking outbreaks, was at the time a young woman, but already widely known as a writer and lecturer on antislavery and temperance themes. She was of Pennsylvania Quaker stock.

ON THE morning of Monday, the thirteenth of July [1863], began this outbreak, unparalleled in atrocities by anything in American history and equaled only by the horrors of the worst days of the French Revolution. Gangs of men and boys, composed of railroad employees, workers in machine shops, and a vast crowd of those who lived by preying upon others, thieves, pimps, professional ruffians, the scum of the city, jailbirds, or those who were running with swift feet to enter the prison doors, began to gather on the corners and in streets and alleys where they lived; from thence issuing forth, they visited the great establishments on the line of their advance, commanding their instant close and the companionship of the workmen — many of them peaceful and orderly men — on pain of the destruction of one and a murderous assault upon the other, did not their orders meet with instant compliance.

A body of these, five or six hundred strong, gathered about one of the enrolling offices in the upper part of the city, where the draft was quietly proceeding, and opened the assault upon it by a shower of clubs, bricks, and paving stones torn from the streets, following it up by a furious rush into the office. Lists, records, books, the drafting wheel, every article of furniture or work in the room, was rent in pieces and strewn about the floor or flung into the streets, while the law officers, the newspaper reporters — who are expected to be everywhere — and the few peaceable spectators, were compelled to make a hasty retreat through an opportune rear exit, accelerated by the curses and blows of the assailants.

A safe in the room, which contained some of the hated records, was fallen upon by the men, who strove to wrench open its impregnable lock with their naked hands, and, baffled, beat them on its iron doors and sides till they were stained with blood, in a mad frenzy of senseless hate and fury. And then, finding every portable article destroyed — their thirst for ruin growing by the little drink it had had — and believing, or rather hoping, that the officers had taken refuge in the upper rooms, set fire to the house, and stood watching the slow and steady lift of flames, filling the air with demoniac shrieks and yells, while they waited for the prey to escape from some door or window, from the merciless fire to their merciless hands. One of these, who was on the other side of the street, courageously stepped forward and, telling them that they had utterly demolished all they came to seek, informed them that helpless women and little children were in the house and besought them to extinguish the flames and leave the ruined premises — to disperse or at least to seek some other scene.

By his dress recognizing in him a government official, so far from hearing or heeding his humane appeal, they set upon him with sticks and clubs and beat him till his eyes were blind with blood, and he, bruised and mangled, succeeded in escaping to the handful of police who stood helpless before this howling crew, now increased to thousands. With difficulty and pain the inoffensive tenants escaped from the rapidly-spreading fire, which, having devoured the house originally lighted, swept across the neighboring buildings till the whole block stood a mass of burning flames. The firemen came up tardily and reluctantly, many of them of the same class as the miscreants who surrounded them and who cheered at their approach, but either made no attempt to perform their duty or so feeble and farcical a one as to bring disgrace upon a service they so generally honor and ennoble.

At last, when there was here nothing more to accomplish, the mob, swollen to a frightful size, including myriads of wretched, drunken women and the half-grown vagabond boys of the pavements, rushed through the intervening streets, stopping cars and insulting peaceable citizens on their way, to an armory where were manufactured and stored carbines and guns for the government. In anticipation of the attack, this, earlier in the day, had been fortified by a police squad capable of coping with an ordinary crowd of ruffians, but as chaff before fire in the presence of these murderous thousands. Here, as before, the attack was begun by a rain of missiles gathered from the streets, less fatal, doubtless, than more civilized arms, but frightful in the ghastly wounds and injuries they inflicted. Of this no notice was taken by those who were stationed within. It was repeated. At last, finding they were treated with contemptuous silence and that no sign of surrender was offered, the crowd swayed back, then forward, in a combined attempt to force the wide entrance doors. Heavy hammers and sledges which had been brought from forges and workshops, caught up hastily as they gathered the mechanics into their ranks, were used with frightful violence to beat them in at last successfully. The foremost assailants began to climb the stairs but were checked and for the moment driven back by the fire of the officers, who at last had been commanded to resort to their revolvers. A half-score fell wounded, and one who had been acting in some sort as their leader — a big, brutal Irish ruffian — dropped dead.

The pause was but for an instant. As the smoke cleared away there was a general and ferocious onslaught upon the armory; curses, oaths, revilings, hideous and obscene blasphemy, with terrible yells and cries, filled the air in every accent of the English tongue save that spoken by a native American. Such were there mingled with the sea of sound, but they were so few and weak as to be unnoticeable in the roar of voices. The paving stones flew like hail until the street was torn into gaps and ruts and every windowpane and sash and doorway was smashed or broken. Meanwhile divers attempts were made to fire the building but failed through haste or ineffectual materials or the vigilant watchfulness of the besieged. In the midst of this gallant defense word was brought to the defenders from head-quarters that nothing could be done for their support and that if they would save their lives they must make a quick and orderly retreat. Fortunately there was a side passage with which the mob was unacquainted, and one by one they succeeded in gaining this and vanishing.

The work was begun, continued, gathering in force and fury as the day wore on. Police stations, enrolling offices, rooms or build-ings used in any way by government authority or obnoxious as representing the dignity of law, were gutted, destroyed, then left to the mercy of the flames. Newspaper offices whose issues had been a fire in the rear of the nation's armies by extenuating and defend-ing treason and through violent and incendiary appeals stirring up "lewd fellows of the baser sort" to this very carnival of ruin and blood were cheered as the crowd went by. Those that had been faith-ful to loyalty and law were hooted, stoned, and even stormed by the army of miscreants, who were only driven off by the gallant and de-termined charge of the police and in one place by the equally gallant and certainly unique defense which came from turning the boiling water from the engines upon the howling wretches, who, unpre-pared for any such warm reception as this, beat a precipitate and general retreat. Before night fell it was no longer one vast crowd collected in a single section, but great numbers of gatherings, scat-tered over the whole length and breadth of the city, some of them engaged in actual work of demolition and ruin, others, with clubs and weapons in their hands, prowling round apparently with no definite atrocity to perpetrate, but ready for any iniquity that might offer, and, by way of pastime, chasing every stray police officer or solitary soldier or inoffensive Negro who crossed the line of their vision; these three objects — the badge of a defender of the law, the uniform of the Union army, the skin of a helpless and outraged race — acted upon these madmen as water acts upon a rabid dog.

Late in the afternoon a crowd which could have numbered not less than ten thousand, the majority of whom were ragged, frowzy, drunken women, gathered about the Orphan Asylum for Colored Children — a large and beautiful building and one of the most ad-mirable and noble charities of the city. When it became evident from the menacing cries and groans of the multitude that danger, if not destruction, was meditated to the harmless and inoffensive inmates, a flag of truce appeared, and an appeal was made in their behalf, by the principal, to every sentiment of humanity which these beings might possess — a vain appeal! Whatever human feeling had ever, if ever, filled these souls was utterly drowned and washed away in the tide of rapine and blood in which they had been steeping themselves. The few officers who stood guard over the doors and manfully faced these demoniac legions were beaten down and flung to one side, helpless and stunned, whilst the vast crowd rushed in. All the articles upon which they could seize — beds, bedding, carpets, furniture, the very garments of the fleeing inmates, some of these torn from their persons as they sped by — were carried into the streets and hurried off by the women and children who stood ready to receive the goods which their husbands, sons, and fathers flung to their care. The little ones, many of them assailed and beaten — all, orphans and caretakers, exposed to every indignity and every danger — driven on to the street, the building was fired. This had been attempted whilst the helpless children, some of them scarce more than babies, were still in their rooms; but this devilish consummation was prevented by the heroism of one man. He, the chief of the fire department, strove by voice and arm to stay the endeavor; and when, overcome by superior numbers, the brands had been lit and piled, with naked hands and in the face of threatened death he tore asunder the glowing embers and trod them underfoot. Again the effort was made and again failed through the determined and heroic opposition of this solitary soul. Then on the front steps, in the midst of these drunken and infuriated thousands, he stood up and besought them, if they cared nothing for themselves nor for those hapless orphans, that they would not bring lasting disgrace upon the city by destroying one of its noblest charities, which had for its object nothing but good.

He was answered on all sides by yells and execrations and frenzied shrieks of "Down with the nagurs!" coupled with every oath and every curse that malignant hate of the blacks could devise and drunken Irish tongues could speak. It had been decreed that this building was to be razed to the ground. The house was fired in a thousand places, and in less than two hours the walls crashed in, a mass of smoking, blackened ruins, whilst the children wandered through the streets, a prey to beings who were wild beasts in everything save the superior ingenuity of man to agonize and torture his victims.

Frightful as the day had been, the night was yet more hideous, since to the horrors which were seen was added the greater horror of deeds which might be committed in the darkness — or, if they were seen, it was by the lurid glare of burning buildings, the red flames of which, flung upon the stained and brutal faces, the torn and tattered garments, of men and women who danced and howled around the scene of ruin they had caused, made the whole aspect of affairs seem more like a gathering of fiends rejoicing in pandemonium than aught with which creatures of flesh and blood had to do. . . .

The next morning's sun rose on a city which was ruled by a reign of terror. Had the police possessed the heads of Hydra and the arms of Briareus and had these heads all seen, these arms all fought, they would have been powerless against the multitude of opposers. Outbreaks were made, crowds gathered, houses burned, streets barricaded, fights enacted, in a score of places at once. Where the officers appeared they were irretrievably beaten and overcome, their stand, were it ever so short, but inflaming the passions of the mob to fresh deeds of violence. Stores were closed, the business portion of the city deserted, the large works and factories emptied of men, who had been sent home by their employers or were swept into the ranks of the marauding bands. The city cars, omnibuses, hacks, were unable to run and remained under shelter. Every telegraph wire was cut, the posts torn up, the operators driven from their offices. The mayor, seeing that civil power was helpless to stem this tide, desired to call the military to his aid and place the city under martial law, but was opposed by the Governor — a governor who, but a few days before, had pronounced the war a failure and not only predicted but encouraged this mob rule which was now crushing everything beneath its heavy and ensanguined feet. This man, through almost two days of these awful scenes, remained at a quiet seaside retreat but a few miles from the city. Coming to it on the afternoon of the second day, instead of ordering cannon planted in the streets, giving these creatures opportunity to retire to their homes, and, in the event of refusal, blowing them there by powder and ball, he first went to the point where was collected the chiefest mob and proceeded to address them. Before him stood incendiaries, thieves, and murderers, who even then were sacking dwelling houses and butchering powerless and inoffensive beings. These wretches he apostrophized as "my friends," repeating the title again and again in the course of his harangue, assuring them that he was there as a proof of his friendship, which he had demonstrated by "sending his adjutant general to Washington to have the draft stopped," begging them to "wait for his return," "to separate now as good citizens," with the promise that they "might assemble again whenever they wished to so do"; meanwhile he would "take care of their rights." This model speech was incessantly interrupted by tremendous cheering and frantic demonstrations of delight, one great fellow almost crushing the Governor in his enthusiastic embrace.

His allies in newspaper offices attempted to throw the blame upon the loyal press and portion of the community. This was but a repetition of the cry raised by traitors in arms that the government, struggling for life in their deadly hold, was responsible for the war: "If thou wouldst but consent to be murdered peaceably, there could be no strife."

It was absurd and futile to characterize this new reign of terror as anything but an effort on the part of Northern rebels to help Southern ones at the most critical moment of the war, with the state militia and available troops absent in a neighboring commonwealth and the loyal people unprepared. These editors and their coadjutors, men of brains and ability, were of that most poisonous growth — traitors to the government and the flag of their country — renegade Americans.

ANNA DICKINSON, What Answer?

160. President Davis Quells a
Food Riot in Richmond

The blockade established by Northern ships shut off more and more foreign supplies from the South; the absence of men who were in the army made it impossible to grow normal food crops; and by 1863 transportation began to break down. Our diarist-clerk in the Confederate War Department describes the resulting scarcity and distress.

APRIL 2d, 1863. — This morning early a few hundred women and boys met as by concert in the Capitol Square [Richmond], saying they were hungry, and must have food. The number continued to swell until there were more than a thousand. But few men were among them, and these were mostly foreign residents with exemptions in their pockets. About 9:00 A.M. the mob emerged from the western gates of the square and proceeded down Ninth Street, passing the War Department and crossing Main Street, increasing in magnitude at every step, but preserving silence and (so far) good order. Not knowing the meaning of such a procession, I asked a pale boy where they were going. A young woman, seemingly emaciated, but yet with a smile, answered that they were going to find something to eat. I could not for the life of me refrain from expressing the hope that they might be successful, and I remarked they were going in the right direction to find plenty in the hands of the extortioners. I did not follow to see what they did, but I learned an hour after that they marched through Cary Street and entered diverse stores of the speculators, which they proceeded to empty of their contents. They impressed all the carts and drays in the street, which were speedily laden with meal, flour, shoes, etc. I did not learn whither these were driven, but probably they were rescued from those in charge of them. Nevertheless an immense amount of provisions and other articles were borne by the mob, which continued to increase in numbers. An eyewitness says he saw a boy come out of a store with a hat full of money (notes), and I learned that when the mob turned up into Main Street, where all the shops were by this time closed, they broke in the plate-glass windows, demanding silks, jewelry, etc. Here they were incited to pillage valuables, not necessary for subsistence, by the class of residents (aliens) exempted from military duty by Judge Campbell, Assistant Secretary of War, in contravention of Judge Meredith's decision. Thus the work of spoliation went on until the military appeared upon the scene, summoned by Governor Letcher, whose term of service is near its close. He had the Riot Act read (by the mayor) and then threatened to fire on the mob. He gave them five minutes' time to disperse in, threatening to use military force (the city battalion being present) if they did not comply with the demand. The timid women fell back, and a pause was put to the devastation, though but few believed he would venture to put his threat in execution. If he had done so, he would have been hung, no doubt.

About this time the President appeared and, ascending a dray, spoke to the people. He urged them to return to their homes so that the bayonets there menacing them might be sent against the common enemy. He told them that such acts would bring famine upon them in the only form which could not be provided against, as it would deter people from bringing food to the city. He said he was willing to share his last loaf with the suffering people (his best horse had been stolen the night before), and he trusted we would all bear our privations with fortitude and continue united against the Northern invaders, who were the authors of all our sufferings. He seemed deeply moved, and indeed it was a frightful spectacle, and perhaps an ominous one, if the government does not remove some of the quartermasters who have contributed very much to bring about the evil of scarcity. I mean those who have allowed transportation to forestallers and extortioners.

General Elzey and General Winder waited upon the Secretary of War in the morning, asking permission to call the troops from the camps near the city, to suppress the women and children by a summary process. But Mr. Seddon hesitated and then declined authorizing any such absurdity. He said it was a municipal or state duty, and therefore he would not take the responsibility of interfering in the matter. Even in the moment of aspen consternation, he will still be the politician.

I have not heard of any injuries sustained by the women and children. Nor have I heard how many stores the mob visited, and it must have been many.

All is quiet now (3 P.M.), and I understand the government is issuing rice to the people.

J. B. Jones, A Rebel War Clerk's Diary

161. A War Clerk Suffers Scarcity in Richmond

After the Civil War was fairly under way the Confederate Government had to meet nearly all its expenses by issues of paper money. The paper money steadily depreciated, so that every new issue was followed by a rise in prices. This rise had to be met by additional issues, and so the South was caught in a vicious circle. The blockade increased prices by shutting off imports of goods from Europe. The breakdown of the railroads within the South also increased them by making it hard to move merchandise. With the soldiers away in the armies, smaller food crops were grown. By the spring of 1864 a pair of boots in Richmond cost $200, and a coat $350. Of course wages were not pushed up fast enough to meet this rise. This meant that a heavy burden fell upon the poor, and particularly the women and children. Our rebel war clerk vividly pictures the increasing hardship.

NOVEMBER 16, 1861. — It is sickening to behold the corruption of the commercial men which so much wounds our afflicted country. There are large merchants here who come over from Baltimore breathing vengeance against the Northern "despots," and to make a show of patriotism they subscribe liberally to equip some volunteer companies in the city; but now they are sending their agents north and importing large amounts of merchandise, which they sell to the government at the most fabulous prices. I am informed that some of them realize fifty thousand dollars per month profit! And this after paying officials on both sides bonuses to wink at their operations.

After the order of Mr. Benjamin for applicants for passports to leave the country to be arrested, some of these men applied to me, and I reported the facts to General Winder; but they were not molested. Indeed, they came to me subsequently and exhibited passports they had obtained from the Secretary himself.

May 23, 1862. — Oh, the extortioners! Meats of all kinds are selling at fifty cents per pound; butter, seventy-five cents; coffee, a dollar and half; tea, ten dollars; boots, thirty dollars per pair; shoes, eighteen dollars; ladies' shoes, fifteen dollars; shirts, six dollars each. Houses that rented for five hundred dollars last year are a thousand dollars now. Boarding, from thirty to forty dollars per month. General Winder has issued an order fixing the maximum prices of certain articles of marketing, which has only the effect of keeping a great many things out of market. The farmers have to pay the merchants and Jews their extortionate prices and complain very justly of the partiality of the general. It does more harm than good.

October 1st. — How shall we subsist this winter? There is not a supply of wood or coal in the city — and it is said that there are not adequate means of transporting it hither. Flour at sixteen dollars per barrel and bacon at seventy-five cents per pound threaten a famine. And yet there are no beggars in the streets. We must get a million of men in arms and drive the invader from our soil. We are capable of it, and we must do it. Better die in battle than die of starvation produced by the enemy.

The newspapers are printed on half sheets — and I think the publishers make money; the extras (published almost every day) are sold to the newsboys for ten cents and often sold by them for twenty-five cents. These are mere slips of paper, seldom containing more than a column — which is reproduced in the next issue. The matter of the extras is mostly made up from the Northern papers, brought hither by persons running the blockade. The supply is pretty regular, and dates are rarely more than three or four days behind the time of reception. We often get the first accounts of battles at a distance in this way, as our generals and our government are famed for a prudential reticence.

6th. — A Jew store, in Main Street, was robbed of eight thousand dollars' worth of goods on Saturday night. They were carted away. This is significant. The prejudice is very strong against the extortionists, and I apprehend there will be many scenes of violence this winter. And our own people, who ask four prices for wood and coal, may contribute to produce a new reign of terror. The supplies necessary for existence should not be withheld from a suffering people. It is dangerous.

This evening Custis and I expect the arrival of my family from Raleigh, N.C. We have procured for them one pound of sugar, eighty cents; four loaves of bread, as large as my fist, twenty cents each; and we have a little coffee, which is selling at two dollars and a half per pound. In the morning some one must go to market, else there will be short-commons. Washing is two dollars and a half per dozen pieces. Common soap is worth seventy-five cents per pound.

November 7th. — Yesterday I received from the agent of the City Councils fourteen pounds of salt, having seven persons in my family, including the servant. One pound to each member, per month, is allowed at five cents per pound. The extortionists sell it at seventy cents per pound. One of *them* was drawing for his family. He confessed it but said he paid fifty cents for the salt he sold at seventy cents. Profit ten dollars per bushel! I sent an article today to the *Enquirer,* suggesting that fuel, bread, meat, etc. be furnished in the same manner. We shall soon be in a state of siege.

21st. — Common shirting cotton and Yankee calico that used to sell at twelve and a half cents per yard is now a dollar seventy-five! What a temptation for the Northern manufacturers! What a rush of trade there would be if peace should occur suddenly! And what a party there would be in the South for peace (and unity with Northern Democrats) if the war were waged somewhat differently. The excesses of the Republicans *compel* our people to be almost a unit. This is all the better for us. Still, we are in quite a bad way now, God knows!

Mr. Dargan, M.C., writes to the President from Mobile that the inhabitants of that city are in an awful condition — meal is selling for three dollars and a half per bushel and wood at fifteen dollars per cord — and that the people are afraid to bring supplies, apprehending that the government agents will seize them. The President (thanks to him!) has ordered that interference with domestic trade must not be permitted.

26th. — The government has realized fifty thousand pounds of leather from two counties in eastern North Carolina, in danger of falling into the hands of the enemy. This convinces me that there is abundance of leather in the South if it were properly distributed. It is held, like everything else, by speculators, for extortioners' profits. The government might remedy the evils and remove the distresses of the people, but instead of doing so the bureaus aggravate them by capricious seizures and tyrannical restrictions on transportation. Letters are coming in from every quarter, complaining of the despotic acts of government agents.

January 18, 1863. — We are now, in effect, in a state of siege, and none but the opulent, often those who have defrauded the government, can obtain a sufficiency of food and raiment. Calico, which could once be bought for twelve and a half cents per yard, is now selling at two dollars and a quarter, and a lady's dress of calico costs her about thirty dollars. Bonnets are not to be had. Common bleached cotton shirting brings a dollar and a half per yard. All other dry goods are held in the same proportion. Common tallow candles are a dollar and a quarter per pound; soap, one dollar; hams, one dollar; opossum, three dollars; turkeys, four to eleven dollars; sugar, brown, one dollar; molasses, eight dollars per gallon; potatoes, six dollars per bushel, etc.

These evils might be remedied by the government, for there is no great scarcity of any of the substantials and necessities of life in the country, if they were only equally distributed. The difficulty is in procuring transportation, and the government monopolizes the railroads and canals.

February 11th. — Some idea may be formed of the scarcity of food in this city from the fact that, while my youngest daughter was in the kitchen today, a young rat came out of its hole and seemed to beg for something to eat; she held out some bread, which it ate from her hand, and seemed grateful. Several others soon appeared and were as tame as kittens. Perhaps we shall have to eat them!

18th. — One or two of the regiments of General Lee's army were in the city last night. The men were pale and haggard. They have but a quarter of a pound of meat per day. But meat has been ordered from Atlanta. I hope it is abundant there.

All the necessaries of life in the city are still going up higher in price. Butter, three dollars per pound; beef, one dollar; bacon, a dollar and a quarter; sausage meat, one dollar; and even liver is selling at fifty cents per pound.

By degrees, quite perceptibly, we are approaching the condition of famine. What effect this will produce on the community is to be seen. The army must be fed or disbanded, or else the city must be abandoned. How we, "the people," are to live is a thought of serious concern.

General Lee has recommended that an appeal be made to the people to bring food to the army, to feed their sons and brothers; but the commissary general opposes it; probably it will not be done. No doubt the army could be half fed in this way for months. But the red-tape men are inflexible and inscrutable. Nevertheless, the commissaries and quartermasters are getting rich.

March 30th. — The gaunt form of wretched famine still approaches with rapid strides. Meal is now selling at twelve dollars per bushel and potatoes at sixteen. Meats have almost disappeared from the market, and none but the opulent can afford to pay three dollars and a half per pound for butter. Greens, however, of various kinds, are coming in; and as the season advances, we may expect a diminution of prices. It is strange that on the 30th of March, even in the "sunny South," the fruit trees are as bare of blossoms and foliage as at midwinter. We shall have fire until the middle of May — six months of winter!

I am spading up my garden and hope to raise a few vegetables to eke out a miserable subsistence for my family. My daughter Ann reads Shakespeare to me o' nights, which saves my eyes.

31st. — Another stride of the grim specter, and cornmeal is selling for seventeen dollars per bushel. Coal at twenty dollars and a half per ton, and wood at thirty dollars per cord. And at these prices one has to wait several days to get either. Common tallow candles are selling at four dollars per pound. I see that some furnished houses are now advertised for rent, and I hope that all the population that can get away and subsist elsewhere will leave the city.

April 17th. — Pins are so scarce and costly that it is now a pretty general practice to stoop down and pick up any found in the street. The boardinghouses are breaking up, and rooms, furnished and unfurnished, are renting out to messes. One dollar and fifty cents for beef leaves no margin for profit even at a hundred dollars per month, which is charged for board, and most of the boarders cannot afford to pay that price. Therefore they take rooms and buy their own scanty food. I am inclined to think provisions would not be deficient to an alarming extent if they were equally distributed. Wood is no scarcer than before the war, and yet thirty dollars per load (less than a cord) is demanded for it and obtained.

June 16th. — But, while terrible events are daily anticipated in the field, all the civilians seem to have gone wild with speculation, and official corruption runs riot throughout the land. J. M. Seixas, agent of the War Department, writes from Wilmington that while the government steamers can get no cotton to exchange abroad for ordnance stores, the steamers of individuals are laden and depart almost daily. This is said to be partly the work of the Southern Express Company, believed to be Yankees (a portion of them), which contracts to deliver freight and bribes the railroads and monopolizes transportation. This is the company on whose application Judge Campbell, Assistant Secretary of War, granted so many exemptions and details! It takes a great number of able-bodied men from the army, and then, by a peculiar process, absolutely embarrasses, as General Whiting says, the conduct of the war.

Judge Dargan, of Alabama, writes that private blockade runners are ruining the country — supplying the enemy with cotton and bringing in liquors and useless gewgaws.

J. B. JONES, A Rebel War Clerk's Diary

162. Mr. Eggleston Recalls When Money Was Plentiful

Born in Indiana but educated in Virginia, George Cary Eggleston served throughout the Civil War in the Confederate army. He was a younger brother of Edward Eggleston, who wrote The Hoosier Schoolmaster. *Not many years after the war he published in the* Atlantic *chapters of one of the most graphic and interesting of Southern war volumes,* A Rebel's Recollections. *He showed in it just how the plain Southern private, and the citizen, endured the dangers and privations of the conflict.*

THE FINANCIAL system adopted by the Confederate government was singularly simple and free from technicalities. It consisted chiefly in the issue of treasury notes enough to meet all the expenses of the government, and in the present advanced state of the art of printing there was but one difficulty incident to this process; namely, the impossibility of having the notes signed in the Treasury Department as fast as they were needed. There happened, however, to be several thousand young ladies in Richmond willing to accept light and remunerative employment at their homes, and as it was really a matter of small moment whose names the notes bore, they were given out in sheets to these young ladies, who signed and returned them for a consideration. I shall not undertake to guess how many Confederate treasury notes were issued. Indeed, I am credibly informed by a gentleman who was high in office in the Treasury Department that even the secretary himself did not certainly know. The acts of Congress authorizing issues of currency were the hastily formulated thought of a not very wise body of men, and my informant tells me they were frequently susceptible of widely different construction by different officials. However that may be, it was clearly out of the power of the government ever to redeem the notes, and whatever may have been the state of affairs within the treasury, nobody outside its precincts ever cared to muddle his head in an attempt to get at exact figures.

We knew only that money was astonishingly abundant. Provisions fell short sometimes, and the supply of clothing was not always as large as we should have liked, but nobody found it difficult to get money enough. It was to be had almost for the asking. And to some extent the abundance of the currency really seemed to atone for its extreme badness. Going the rounds of the pickets on the coast of South Carolina one day in 1863, I heard a conversation between a Confederate and a Union soldier, stationed on opposite sides of a little inlet, in the course of which this point was brought out.

Union Soldier. Aren't times rather hard over there, Johnny?

Confederate Soldier. Not at all. We've all the necessaries of life.

U.S. Yes, but how about luxuries? You never see any coffee nowadays, do you?

C.S. Plenty of it.

U.S. Isn't it pretty high?

C.S. Forty dollars a pound, that's all.

U.S. Whew! Don't you call that high?

C.S. (after reflecting). Well, perhaps it is a trifle uppish, but then you never saw money so plentiful as it is with us. We hardly know what to do with it and don't mind paying high prices for things we want.

And that was the universal feeling. Money was so easily got and its value was so utterly uncertain that we were never able to determine what was a fair price for anything. We fell into the habit of paying whatever was asked, knowing that tomorrow we should have to pay more. Speculation became the easiest and surest thing imaginable. The speculator saw no risks of loss. Every article of merchandise rose in value every day, and to buy anything this week and sell it next was to make an enormous profit quite as a matter of course. So uncertain were prices, or rather so constantly did they tend upward, that when a cargo of cadet-gray cloths was brought into Charleston once, an officer in my battery, attending the sale, was able to secure enough of the cloth to make two suits of clothes without any expense whatever, merely by speculating upon an immediate advance. He became the purchaser at auction of a case of the goods and had no difficulty, as soon as the sale was over, in finding a merchant who was glad to take his bargain off his hands, giving him the cloth he wanted as a premium. The officer could not possibly have paid for the case of goods, but there was nothing surer than that he could sell again at an advance the moment the auctioneer's hammer fell on the last lot of cloths. . . .

The prices which obtained were almost fabulous, and singularly enough there seemed to be no sort of ratio existing between the values of different articles. I bought coffee at forty dollars and tea at thirty dollars a pound on the same day.

My dinner at a hotel cost me twenty dollars, while five dollars gained me a seat in the dress circle of the theater. I paid one dollar the next morning for a copy of the *Examiner*, but I might have got the *Whig, Dispatch, Enquirer,* or *Sentinel* for half that sum. For some wretched tallow candles I paid ten dollars a pound. The utter absence of proportion between these several prices is apparent, and I know of no way of explaining it except upon the theory that the unstable character of the money superinduced a reckless disregard of all value on the part of both buyers and sellers. A facetious friend used to say prices were so high that nobody could see them and that they "got mixed for want of supervision." He held, however, that the difference between the old and the new order of things was a trifling one. "Before the war," he said, "I went to market with the money in my pocket and brought back my purchases in a basket; now I take the money in the basket and bring the things home in my pocket." . . .

The effects of the extreme depreciation of the currency were sometimes almost ludicrous. One of my friends, a Richmond lady, narrowly escaped very serious trouble in an effort to practise a wise economy. Anything for which the dealers did not ask an outrageously high price seemed wonderfully cheap always, and she, at least, lacked the self-control necessary to abstain from buying largely whenever she found anything the price of which was lower than she had supposed it would be. Going into market one morning with "stimulated ideas of prices," as she phrased it, the consequence of having paid a thousand dollars for a barrel of flour, she was surprised to find nearly everything selling for considerably less than she had expected. Thinking that for some unexplained cause there was a temporary depression in prices, she purchased pretty largely in a good many directions, buying, indeed, several things for which she had almost no use at all and buying considerably more than she needed of other articles. As she was quitting the market on foot — for it had become disreputable in Richmond to ride in a carriage, and the ladies would not do it on any account — she was tapped on the shoulder by an officer who told her she was under arrest, for buying in market to sell again. As the lady was well known to prominent people she was speedily released, but she thereafter curbed her propensity to buy freely of cheap things. Buying to sell again had been forbidden under severe penalties — an absolutely necessary measure for the protection of the people against the rapacity of the hucksters, who, going early into the markets, would buy literally everything there and by agreement among themselves double or quadruple the already exorbitant rates. It became necessary also to suppress the gambling houses in the interest of the half-starved people. At such a time, of course, gambling was a very common vice, and the gamblers made Richmond their headquarters. It was the custom of the proprietors of these establishments to set costly suppers in their parlors every night for the purpose of attracting visitors likely to become victims. For these suppers they must have the best of everything without stint, and their lavish rivalry in the poorly-stocked markets had the effect of advancing prices to a dangerous point. To suppress the gambling houses was the sole remedy, and it was only by uncommonly severe measures that the suppression could be accomplished. It was therefore enacted that any one found guilty of keeping a gambling house should be publicly whipped upon the bare back, and as the infliction of the penalty in one or two instances effectually and permanently broke up the business of gambling, even in the disorganized and demoralized state in which society then was, it may be said with confidence that whipping is the one certain remedy for this evil. Whether it be not, in ordinary cases, worse than the evil which it cures, it is not our business just now to inquire.

GEORGE CARY EGGLESTON, A Rebel's Recollections

163. Nevada Miners Bid on the "Sanitary" Flour Sack

Mark Twain tried mining in a roaring, turbulent Nevada camp called Aurora, on the slopes of the Sierras. He grew poor instead of rich, and presently walked one hundred and thirty miles, blanket on back, to Virginia City. Here he got a post on the local newspaper, the Enterprise, *and began to observe the life of the wildest and most interesting city of the West. In* Roughing It *he has given an unequalled picture of the Comstock Lode — of its desperadoes, its demagogues, its gamblers, its hard-bitten miners, its spendthrifts, its crimes, excesses, and extravagances. Everybody had money and everybody was reckless. But the people showed generosity also in those prodigal days, and they were exuberantly patriotic.*

MONEY was wonderfully plenty. The trouble was not how to get it but how to spend it, how to lavish it, get rid of it, squander it. And so it was a happy thing that just at this juncture the news came over the wires that a great United States Sanitary Commission had been formed and money was wanted for the relief of the wounded sailors and soldiers of the Union languishing in the Eastern hospitals. Right on the heels of it came word that San Francisco had responded superbly before the telegram was half a day old. Virginia [City] rose as one man! A sanitary committee was hurriedly organized, and its chairman mounted a vacant cart in C Street and tried to make the clamorous multitude understand that the rest of the committee were flying hither and thither and working with all their might and main, and that if the town would only wait an hour, an office would be ready, books opened, and the commission prepared to receive contributions. His voice was drowned and his information lost in a ceaseless roar of cheers and demands that the money be received *now* — they swore they would not wait. The chairman pleaded and argued, but, deaf to all entreaty, men plowed their way through the throng and rained checks of gold coin into the cart and scurried away for more. Hands clutching money were thrust aloft out of the jam by men who hoped this eloquent appeal would cleave a road their strugglings could not open. The very Chinamen and Indians caught the excitement and dashed their half dollars into the cart without knowing or caring what it was all about. Women plunged into the crowd, trimly attired, fought their way to the cart with their coin, and emerged again, by and by, with their apparel in a state of hopeless dilapidation. It was the wildest mob Virginia had ever seen and the most determined and ungovernable, and when at last it abated its fury and dispersed, it had not a penny in its pocket. To use its own phraseology, it came there flush and went away busted.

After that the commission got itself into systematic working order, and for weeks the contributions flowed into its treasury in a generous stream. Individuals and all sorts of organizations levied upon themselves a regular weekly tax for the sanitary fund, graduated according to their means, and there was not another grand universal outburst till the famous "Sanitary Flour Sack" came our way. Its history is peculiar and interesting. A former schoolmate of mine, by the name of Reuel Gridley, was living at the little city of Austin in the Reese River country at this time and was the Democratic candidate for mayor. He and the Republican candidate made an agreement that the defeated man should be publicly presented with a fifty-pound sack of flour by the successful one and should carry it home on his shoulder. Gridley was defeated. The new mayor gave him the sack of flour, and he shouldered it and carried it a mile or two from lower Austin to his home in upper Austin, attended by a band of music and the whole population. Arrived there, he said he did not need the flour and asked what the people thought he had better do with it. A voice said:

"Sell it to the highest bidder for the benefit of the sanitary fund."

The suggestion was greeted with a round of applause, and Gridley mounted a drygoods box and assumed the rôle of auctioneer. The bids went higher and higher as the sympathies of the pioneers awoke and expanded, till at last the sack was knocked down to a millman at two hundred and fifty dollars and his check taken. He was asked where he would have the flour delivered, and he said:

"Nowhere — sell it again."

Now the cheers went up royally, and the multitude were fairly in the spirit of the thing. So Gridley stood there and shouted and perspired till the sun went down, and when the crowd dispersed he had sold the sack to three hundred different people and had taken in eight thousand dollars in gold. And still the flour sack was in his possession.

The news came to Virginia and a telegram went back:

"Fetch along your flour sack!"

Thirty-six hours afterward Gridley arrived, and an afternoon mass meeting was held in the opera house, and the auction began. But the sack had come sooner than it was expected; the people were not thoroughly aroused, and the sale dragged. At nightfall only five thousand dollars had been secured, and there was a crestfallen feeling in the community. However, there was no disposition to let the matter rest here and acknowledge vanquishment at the hands of the village of Austin. Till late in the night the principal citizens were at work arranging the morrow's campaign, and when they went to bed they had no fears for the result.

At eleven the next morning a procession of open carriages, attended by clamorous bands of music and adorned with a moving display of flags, filed along C Street and was soon in danger of blockade by a huzzaing multitude of citizens. In the first carriage sat Gridley, with the flour sack in prominent view, the latter splendid with bright paint and gilt lettering; also in the same carriage sat the mayor and the recorder. The other carriages contained the Common Council, the editors and reporters, and other people of imposing consequence. The crowd pressed to the corner of C and Taylor Streets, expecting the sale to begin there, but they were disappointed and also unspeakably surprised; for the cavalcade moved on as if Virginia had ceased to be of importance and took its way over the divide toward the small town of Gold Hill. Telegrams had gone ahead to Gold Hill, Silver City, and Dayton, and those communities were at fever heat and ripe for the conflict. It was a very hot day and wonderfully dusty. At the end of a short half hour we descended into Gold Hill with drums beating and colors flying, and enveloped in imposing clouds of dust. The whole population — men, women, and children, Chinamen and Indians — were massed in the main street, all the flags in town were at the masthead, and the blare of the bands was drowned in cheers. Gridley stood up and asked who would make the first bid for the National Sanitary Flour Sack. General W. said:

"The Yellow Jacket silver mining company offers a thousand dollars, coin!"

A tempest of applause followed. A telegram carried the news to Virginia, and fifteen minutes afterward that city's population was massed in the streets devouring the tidings — for it was part of the program that the bulletin boards should do a good work that day. Every few minutes a new dispatch was bulletined from Gold Hill, and still the excitement grew. Telegrams began to return to us from Virginia beseeching Gridley to bring back the flour sack, but such was not the plan of the campaign. At the end of an hour Gold Hill's small population had paid a figure for the flour sack that awoke all the enthusiasm of Virginia when the grand total was displayed upon the bulletin boards.

Then the Gridley cavalcade moved on, a giant refreshed with new lager beer and plenty of it — for the people brought it to the carriages without waiting to measure it — and within three hours more the expedition had carried Silver City and Dayton by storm and was on its way back covered with glory. Every move had been telegraphed and bulletined, and as the procession entered Virginia and filed down C Street at half past eight in the evening the town was abroad in the thoroughfares, torches were glaring, flags flying, bands playing, cheer on cheer cleaving the air, and the city ready to surrender at discretion.

The auction began; every bid was greeted with bursts of applause, and at the end of two hours and a half a population of fifteen thousand souls had paid in coin for a fifty-pound sack of flour a sum equal to forty thousand dollars in greenbacks! It was at a rate in the neighborhood of three dollars for each man, woman, and child of the population. The grand total would have been twice as large, but the streets were very narrow, and hundreds who wanted to bid could not get within a block of the stand and could not make themselves heard. These grew tired of waiting, and many of them went home long before the auction was over. This was the greatest day Virginia ever saw, perhaps.

Gridley sold the sack in Carson City and several California towns; also in San Francisco. Then he took it east and sold it in one or two Atlantic cities, I think. I am not sure of that, but I know that he finally carried it to St. Louis, where a monster sanitary fair was being held, and after selling it there for a large sum and helping on the enthusiasm by displaying the portly silver bricks which Nevada's donation had produced, he had the flour baked up into small cakes and retailed them at high prices.

It was estimated that when the flour sack's mission was ended it had been sold for a grand total of a hundred and fifty thousand dollars in greenbacks! This is probably the only instance on record where common family flour brought three thousand dollars a pound in the public market.

Mark Twain, Roughing It

164. Suffering in Andersonville Prison

Both Northern and Southern prisons during the Civil War were horrible spots — there being less to choose between them than Northerners liked to think. At Andersonville in southwestern Georgia was one of the largest of the Confederate prison camps. The first captured Northerners arrived there early in 1863. By midsummer more than 32,000 prisoners were huddled inside a stockade which enclosed an area of only some twenty-six acres. The men lived in little huts improvised out of bits of lumber, in tents made of blankets, or in pits dug in the ground. Their food was insufficient in quantity and bad in quality; their water became polluted. Before the war ended about 50,000 prisoners in all had been received at Andersonville, and 13,000 had died. After peace arrived the superintendent, Henry Wirz, was tried and hanged.

JANUARY 25, 1865. — While going our rounds in the morning we found a very important person in Peter Louis, a paroled Yankee prisoner, in the employ of Captain Bonham. The captain keeps him out of the stockade, feeds and clothes him, and in return reaps the benefit of his skill. Peter is a French Yankee, a shoemaker by trade, and makes as beautiful shoes as I ever saw imported from France. My heart quite softened toward him when I saw his handiwork, and little Mrs. Sims was so overcome that she gave him a huge slice of her Confederate fruitcake. I talked French with him, which pleased him greatly, and Mett and I engaged him to make us each a pair of shoes. I will feel like a lady once more, with good shoes on my feet. I expect the poor Yank is glad to get away from Anderson on any terms. Although matters have improved somewhat with the cool weather, the tales that are told of the condition of things there last summer are appalling. Mrs. Brisbane heard all about it from Father Hamilton, a Roman Catholic priest from Macon, who has been working like a good Samaritan in those dens of filth and misery. It is a shame to us Protestants that we have let a Roman Catholic get so far ahead of us in this work of charity and mercy. Mrs. Brisbane says Father Hamilton told her that during the summer the wretched prisoners burrowed in the ground like moles to protect themselves from the sun. It was not safe to give them material to build shanties as they might use it for clubs to overcome the guard. These underground huts, he said, were alive with vermin and stank like charnel houses. Many of the prisoners were stark naked, having not so much as a shirt to their backs. He told a pitiful story of a Pole who had no garment but a shirt, and to make it cover him better, he put his legs into the sleeves and tied the tail around his neck. The others guyed him so on his appearance and the poor wretch was so disheartened by suffering that one day he deliberately stepped over the dead line and stood there till the guard was forced to shoot him. But what I can't understand is that a Pole, of all people in the world, should come over here and try to take away our liberty when his own country is in the hands of oppressors. One would think that the Poles, of all nations in the world, ought to sympathize with a people fighting for their liberties. Father Hamilton said that at one time the prisoners died at the rate of a hundred and fifty a day, and he saw some of them die on the ground without a rag to lie on or a garment to cover them. Dysentery was the most fatal disease, and as they lay on the ground in their own excrements, the smell was so horrible that the good father says he was often obliged to rush from their presence to get a breath of pure air. It is dreadful. My heart aches for the poor wretches, Yankees though they are, and I am afraid God will suffer some terrible retribution to fall upon us for letting such things happen. If the Yankees ever should come to southwest Georgia and go to Anderson and see the graves there, God have mercy on the land! And yet what can we do? The Yankees themselves are really more to blame than we, for they won't exchange these prisoners, and our poor, hard-pressed Confederacy has not the means to provide for them when our own soldiers are starving in the field. Oh, what a horrible thing war is when stripped of all its pomp and circumstance!

ELIZA FRANCES ANDREWS, The War-Time Journal of a Georgia Girl

165. The Disintegration of the Confederate Army

The Confederate armies had reached a total strength of almost, if not quite, 700,000 men at the beginning of 1863. But after the defeats at Gettysburg and Vicksburg discouragement spread steadily, and during 1864 desertions became a steady stream. By March, 1865, when the Union armies were stronger than ever, there were probably not more than 200,000 men in the Confederate forces. The final scenes in the disbandment of the defeated but heroic Southern units are here described by Eliza Frances Andrews, a Georgia woman who, twenty-five years old the year of Appomattox, soon became well known as an educator and author.

APRIL 24, 1865. Monday. — The shattered remains of Lee's army are beginning to arrive. There is an endless stream passing between the transportation office and the depot, and trains are going and coming at all hours. The soldiers bring all sorts of rumors and keep us stirred up in a state of never-ending excitement. Our avenue leads from the principal street on which they pass, and great numbers stop to rest in the grove. Emily is kept busy cooking rations for them, and pinched as we are ourselves for supplies, it is impossible to refuse anything to the men that have been fighting for us. Even when they don't ask for anything the poor fellows look so tired and hungry that we feel tempted to give them everything we have. Two nice-looking officers came to the kitchen door this afternoon while I was in there making some sorghum cakes to send to General Elzey's camp. They then walked slowly through the back yard and seemed reluctant to tear themselves away from such a sweet, beautiful place. Nearly everybody that passes the street gate stops and looks up the avenue, and I know they can't help thinking what a beautiful place it is. The Cherokee rose hedge is white with blooms. It is glorious. A great many of the soldiers camp in the grove, though Colonel Weems (the Confederate commandant of the post) has located a public camping ground for them farther out of town. The officers often ask for a night's lodging, but our house is always so full of friends who have a nearer claim that a great many have to be refused. It hurts my conscience ever to turn off a Confederate soldier on any account, but we are so overwhelmed with company — friends and people bringing letters of introduction — that the house, big as it is, will hardly hold us all, and members of the family have to pack together like sardines. Captain John Nightingale's servant came in this afternoon — the "little Johnny Nightingale" I used to play with down on the old Tallasee plantation — but reports that he does not know where his master is. He says the Yankees captured him (the Negro) and took away his master's horse that he was tending, but as soon as night came on he made his escape on another horse that he took from them, and put out for home. He says he don't like the Yankees because they "didn't show no respec' for his feelin's." He talks with a strong salt-water brogue and they laughed at him, which he thought very ill-mannered. Father sent him round to the Negro quarters to wait till his master turns up.

May 1st, Monday. — The conduct of a Texas regiment in the streets this afternoon gave us a sample of the chaos and general demoralization that may be expected to follow the breaking up of our government. They raised a riot about their rations, in which they were joined by all the disorderly elements among both soldiers and citizens. First they plundered the commissary department and then turned loose on the quartermaster's stores. Paper, pens, buttons, tape, cloth — everything in the building — was seized and strewn about on the ground. Negroes and children joined the mob and grabbed what they could of the plunder. Colonel Weems's provost guard refused to interfere, saying they were too good soldiers to fire on their comrades, and so the plundering went on unopposed. Nobody seemed to care much, as we all know the Yankees will get it in the end, anyway, if our men don't. I was at Miss Maria Randolph's when the disturbance began, but by keeping to the back streets I avoided the worst of the row, though I encountered a number of stragglers running away with their booty. The soldiers were very generous with their "confiscated" goods, giving away paper, pens, tape, etc., to anybody they happened to meet. One of them poked a handful of pen staves at me; another, staggering under an armful of stationery, threw me a ream of paper, saying, "There, take that and write to your sweetheart on it." I took no notice of any of them but hurried on home as fast as I could, all the way meeting Negroes, children, and men loaded with plunder. When I reached home I found some of our own servants with their arms full of thread, paper, and pens which they offered to sell me, and one of them gave me several reams of paper. I carried them to Father, and he collected all the other booty he could find, intending to return it to headquarters, but he was told that there is no one to receive it, no place to send it to — in fact, there seemed to be no longer any headquarters nor any other semblance of authority. Father saved one box of bacon for Colonel Weems by hauling it away in his wagon and concealing it in his smokehouse. All of Johnston's army and the greater portion of Lee's are still to pass through, and since the rioters have destroyed so much of the forage and provisions intended for their use, there will be great difficulty in feeding them. They did not stop at food but helped themselves to all the horses and mules they needed. A band of them made a raid on General Elzey's camp and took nine of his mules. They excused themselves by saying that all government stores will be seized by the Yankees in a few days, anyway, if left alone, and our own soldiers might as well get the good of them while they can. This would be true if there were not so many others yet to come who ought to have their share.

Our back yard and kitchen have been filled all day, as usual, with soldiers waiting to have their rations cooked. One of them, who had a wounded arm, came into the house to have it dressed and said that he was at Salisbury when Garnett was shot and saw him fall. He told some miraculous stories about the valorous deeds of "the Colonel," and although they were so exaggerated that I set them down as apocryphal, I gave him a piece of cake, notwithstanding, to pay him for telling them.

Tuesday. — The disorders begun by the Texans yesterday were continued today, every fresh band that arrived from the front falling into the way of their predecessors. They have been pillaging the ordnance stores at the depot, in which they were followed by Negroes, boys, and mean white men. I don't see what people are thinking about to let ammunition fall into the hands of the Negroes, but everybody is demoralized and reckless and nobody seems to care about anything any more. A number of paroled men came into our grove, where they sat under the trees to empty the cartridges they had seized. Confederate money is of no more use now than so much waste paper, but by filling their canteens with powder they can trade it off along the road for provisions. They scattered lead and cartridges all over the ground. Marshall went out after they left and picked up enough to last him for years. The balls do not fit his gun, but he can remold them and draw the powder out of the cartridges to shoot with. I am uneasy at having so much explosive material in the house, especially when I consider the careless manner in which we have to live. There is so much company and so much to do that even the servants hardly have time to eat. I never lived in such excitement and confusion in my life. Thousands of people pass through Washington [Georgia] every day, and our house is like a free hotel; Father welcomes everybody as long as there is a square foot of vacant space under his roof. Meeting all these pleasant people is the one compensation of this dismal time, and I don't know how I shall exist when they have all gone their ways and we settle down in the mournful quiet of subjugation. Besides the old friends that are turning up every day, there is a continual stream of new faces crossing my path; and I make some pleasant acquaintance or form some new friendship every day. The sad part of it is that the most of them I will probably never meet again, and if I should, where and how? What will they be? What will I be? These are portentous questions in such a time as this.

It seems as if all the people I ever heard of, or never heard of, either, for that matter, are passing through Washington. Some of our friends pass on without stopping to see us because they say they are too ragged and dirty to show themselves. Poor fellows! if they only knew how honorable rags and dirt are now, in our eyes, when endured in the service of their country, they would not be ashamed of them. The son of the richest man in New Orleans trudged through the other day with no coat to his back, no shoes on his feet. The town is full of celebrities, and many poor fugitives whose necks are in danger meet here to concert plans for escape; and I put it in my prayers every night that they may be successful. General Wigfall started for the West some days ago, but his mules were stolen, and he had to return. He is frantic, they say, with rage and disappointment. General Toombs left tonight, but old Governor Brown, it is said, has determined not to desert his post. I am glad he has done something to deserve respect and hope he may get off yet, as soon as the Yankees appoint a military governor. Clement Clay is believed to be well on his way to the Trans-Mississippi, the land of promise now, or rather the city of refuge from which it is hoped a door of escape may be found to Mexico or Cuba. The most terrible part of the war is now to come, the "bloody assizes." "Kirke's lambs," in the shape of Yankee troopers, are closing in upon us; our own disbanded armies, ragged, starving, hopeless, reckless, are roaming about without order or leaders, making their way to their far-off homes as best they can. The props that held society up are broken. Everything is in a state of disorganization and tumult. We have no currency, no law save the primitive code that might makes right. We are in a transition state from war to subjugation, and it is far worse than was the transition from peace to war. The suspense and anxiety in which we live are terrible.

Eliza Frances Andrews, The War-Time Journal of a Georgia Girl

XXV

The Blue and the Gray

166. Mrs. Chesnut Watches the Attack on Fort Sumter

When President Lincoln dispatched an expedition to provision Fort Sumter, Southern leaders resolved to attack. In this spirited excerpt from a diary, the wife of one of the South Carolina Senators describes the feeling in Charleston during the crisis which culminated in the bombardment of April 12th–13th and the opening of the war.

APRIL 8th, 1861. — Allen Green came up to speak to me at dinner in all his soldier's toggery. It sent a shiver through me. Tried to read Margaret Fuller Ossoli, but could not. The air too full of war news, and we are all so restless.

Went to see Miss Pinckney, one of the last of the old-world Pinckneys. Governor Manning walked in, bowed gravely, and seated himself by me. Again he bowed low in mock-heroic style and with a grand wave of his hand said, "Madam, your country is invaded." When I had breath to speak I asked, "What does he mean?" He meant this: There are six men-of-war outside the bar. Talbot and Chew have come to say that hostilities are to begin. Governor Pickens and Beauregard are holding a council of war. Mr. Chesnut then came in and confirmed the story. Wigfall next entered in boisterous spirits and said, "There was a sound of revelry by night." In any stir of confusion my heart is apt to beat so painfully. Now the agony was so stifling I could hardly see or hear. The men went off almost immediately. And I crept silently to my room, where I sat down to a good cry.

Mrs. Wigfall came in, and we had it out on the subject of civil war. We solaced ourselves with dwelling on all its known horrors, and then we added what we had a right to expect with Yankees in front and Negroes in the rear. "The slaveowners must expect a servile insurrection, of course," said Mrs. Wigfall, to make sure that we were unhappy enough. Suddenly loud shouting was heard. We ran out. Cannon after cannon roared. We met Mrs. Allen Green in the passageway, with blanched cheeks and streaming eyes. Governor Means rushed out of his room in his dressing gown and begged us to be calm. "Governor Pickens," said he, "has ordered, in the plenitude of his wisdom, seven cannon to be fired as a signal to the Seventh Regiment. Anderson will hear as well as the Seventh Regiment. Now you go back and be quiet; fighting in the streets has not begun yet."

So we retired. Doctor Gibbes calls Mrs. Allen Green, Dame Placid. There was no placidity today, with cannon bursting and Allen on the island. No sleep for anybody last night. The streets were alive with soldiers, men shouting, marching, singing. Wigfall, the stormy petrel, is in his glory, the only thoroughly happy person I see. Today things seem to have settled down a little. One can but hope still. Lincoln or Seward has made such silly advances and then far sillier drawings back. There may be a chance for peace after all. Things are happening so fast. My husband has been made an aide-de-camp to General Beauregard.

Three hours ago we were quickly packing to go home. The convention has adjourned. Now he tells me the attack on Fort Sumter may begin tonight; depends upon Anderson and the fleet outside. . . .

Mrs. Hayne called. She had, she said, but one feeling — pity for those who are not here. Jack Preston, Willie Alston, "the take-life-easys," as they are called, with John Green, "the big brave," have gone down to the islands — volunteered as privates. Seven hundred men were sent over. Ammunition wagons were rumbling along the streets all night. Anderson is burning blue lights, signs and signals for the fleet outside, I suppose.

Today at dinner there was no allusion to things as they stand in Charleston harbor. There was an undercurrent of intense excitement. There could not have been a more brilliant circle. In addition to our usual quartet, Judge Withers, Langdon Cheves, and Trescott, our two ex-governors dined with us, Means and Manning. These men all talked so delightfully. For once in my life I listened. That over, business began in earnest. Governor Means has rummaged a sword and red sash from somewhere and brought it for Colonel Chesnut, who had gone to demand the surrender of Fort Sumter. And now, patience — we must wait.

Why did that green goose Anderson go into Fort Sumter? Then everything began to go wrong. Now they have intercepted a letter from him, urging them to let him surrender. He paints the horrors likely to ensue if they will not. He ought to have thought of all that before he put his head in the hole.

12th. — Anderson will not capitulate. Yesterday's was the merriest, maddest dinner we have had yet. Men were audaciously wise and witty. We had an unspoken foreboding that it was to be our last pleasant meeting. Mr. Miles dined with us today. Mrs. Henry King rushed in saying: "The news, I come for the latest news! All the men of the King family are on the island," of which fact she seemed proud.

While she was here our peace negotiator or envoy came in — that is, Mr. Chesnut returned. His interview with Colonel Anderson had been deeply interesting, but Mr. Chesnut was not inclined to be communicative. He wanted his dinner. He felt for Anderson and had telegraphed to President Davis for instructions — what answer to give Anderson, etc. He has now gone back to Fort Sumter with additional instructions. When they were about to leave the wharf, A. H. Boykin sprang into the boat in great excitement. He thought himself ill-used, with a likelihood of fighting and he to be left behind!

I do not pretend to go to sleep. How can I? If Anderson does not accept terms at four, the orders are he shall be fired upon. I count four, St. Michael's bells chime out, and I begin to hope. At half past four the heavy booming of a cannon. I sprang out of bed, and on my knees prostrate I prayed as I never prayed before.

There was a sound of stir all over the house, pattering of feet in the corridors. All seemed hurrying one way. I put on my double gown and a shawl and went too. It was to the housetop. The shells were bursting. In the dark I heard a man say, "Waste of ammunition." I knew my husband was rowing a boat somewhere in that dark bay. If Anderson was obstinate, Colonel Chestnut was to order the fort on one side to open fire. Certainly fire had begun. The regular roar of the cannon, there it was. And who could tell what each volley accomplished of death and destruction?

The women were wild there on the housetop. Prayers came from the women and imprecations from the men. And then a shell would light up the scene. Tonight they say the forces are to attempt to land. We watched up there, and everybody wondered that Fort Sumter did not fire a shot. . . .

We hear nothing, can listen to nothing; boom, boom, goes the cannon all the time. The nervous strain is awful, alone in this darkened room. "Richmond and Washington ablaze," say the papers — blazing with excitement. Why not? To us these last days' events seem frightfully great. We were all women on that iron balcony. Men are only seen at a distance now. Stark Means was leaning over and looking with tearful eyes, when an unknown creature asked, "Why did he take his hat off?" Mrs. Means stood straight up and said, "He did that in honor of his mother; he saw me." She is a proud mother and at the same time most unhappy. Her lovely daughter Emma is dying in there, before her eyes, of consumption. At that moment I am sure Mrs. Means had a spasm of the heart.

13th. — Nobody has been hurt after all. How gay we were last night! Reaction after the dread of all the slaughter we thought those dreadful cannon were making. Not even a battery the worse for wear. Fort Sumter has been on fire. Anderson has not yet silenced any of our guns. So the aides, still with swords and red sashes by way of uniform, tell us. But the sound of those guns makes regular meals impossible. None of us goes to table. Tea trays pervade the corridors, going everywhere. Some of the anxious hearts lie on their beds and moan in solitary misery. Mrs. Wigfall and I solace ourselves with tea in my room. These women have all a satisfying faith. "God is on our side," they say. When we are shut in Mrs. Wigfall and I ask, "Why?" "Of course, He hates the Yankees," we are told, "You'll think that well of Him."

Not by one word or look can we detect any change in the demeanor of these Negro servants. Lawrence sits at our door, sleepy and respectful, and profoundly indifferent. So are they all, but they carry it too far. You could not tell that they even heard the awful roar going on in the bay, though it has been dinning in their ears night and day. People talk before them as if they were chairs and tables. They make no sign. Are they stolidly stupid? or wiser than we are; silent and strong, biding their time?

15th. — I did not know that one could live such days of excitement. Some one called: "Come out! There is a crowd coming." A mob it was, indeed, but it was headed by Colonels Chesnut and Manning. The crowd was shouting and showing these two as messengers of good news. They were escorted to Beauregard's headquarters. For Sumter had surrendered! Those upon the housetops shouted to us, "The fort is on fire." That had been the story once or twice before.

When we had calmed down, Colonel Chesnut, who had taken it all quietly enough, if anything more unruffled than usual in his serenity, told us how the surrender came about. Wigfall was with them on Morris Island when they saw the fire in the fort; he jumped in a little boat and, with his handkerchief as a white flag, rowed over. Wigfall went in through a porthole. When Colonel Chesnut arrived shortly after and was received at the regular entrance, Colonel Anderson told him he had need to pick his way warily, for the place was all mined. As far as I can make out the fort surrendered to Wigfall. But it is all confusion. Our flag is flying there. Fire engines have been sent for to put out the fire. Everybody tells you half of something and then rushes off to tell something else or to hear the last news.

In the afternoon Mrs. Preston, Mrs. Joe Heyward, and I drove out around the battery. We were in an open carriage. What a changed scene — the very liveliest crowd I think I ever saw, everybody talking at once. All glasses were still turned on the grim old fort.

Mary Boykin Chesnut, A Diary from Dixie

167. Abner Doubleday Defends Fort Sumter

A New Yorker by birth and a West Point graduate who had fought in the Mexican War, Abner Doubleday was second in command at Fort Sumter when it was

captured by the Confederates in 1861. He served gallantly through-
out the rest of the war, fighting at Antietam, at Fredericksburg, at
Chancellorsville, and at Gettysburg. His other claim to fame is as the
"father" of baseball.

ABOUT 4 A.M. on the 12th I was awakened by some one groping about my room in the dark and calling out my name. It proved
to be Anderson, who came to announce to me that he had just
received a dispatch from Beauregard, dated 3:20 A.M., to the effect that he should open fire upon us in an hour. Finding it was
determined not to return the fire until after breakfast, I remained
in bed. As we had no lights, we could in fact do nothing before
that time except to wander around in the darkness and fire without an accurate view of the enemy's works.

As soon as the outline of our fort could be distinguished, the
enemy carried out their program. It had been arranged, as a special
compliment to the venerable Edmund Ruffin, who might almost
be called the father of secession, that he should fire the first shot
against us from the Stevens battery on Cummings Point. Almost
immediately afterward a ball from Cummings Point lodged in
the magazine wall and by the sound seemed to bury itself in the
masonry about a foot from my head, in very unpleasant proximity
to my right ear. This is the one that probably came with Mr. Ruffin's
compliments. In a moment the firing burst forth in one continuous
roar, and large patches of both the exterior and interior masonry
began to crumble and fall in all directions. The place where I was
had been used for the manufacture of cartridges, and there was still
a good deal of powder there, some packed and some loose. A shell
soon struck near the ventilator, and a puff of dense smoke entered
the room, giving me a strong impression that there would be
an immediate explosion. Fortunately, no sparks had penetrated
inside.

Nineteen batteries were now hammering at us, and the balls and
shells from the ten-inch columbiads, accompanied by shells from
the thirteen-inch mortars which constantly bombarded us, made us
feel as if the war had commenced in earnest.

When it was broad daylight, I went down to breakfast. I found the officers already assembled at one of the long tables in the mess hall. Our party were calm and even somewhat merry. We had retained one colored man to wait on us. He was a spruce-looking mulatto from Charleston, very active and efficient on ordinary occasions, but now completely demoralized by the thunder of the guns and crashing of the shot around us. He leaned back against the wall, almost white with fear, his eyes closed, and his whole expression one of perfect despair. Our meal was not very sumptuous. It consisted of pork and water, but Doctor Crawford triumphantly brought forth a little farina which he had found in a corner of the hospital.

When this frugal repast was over, my company was told off in three details for firing purposes, to be relieved afterward by Seymour's company. As I was the ranking officer, I took the first detachment and marched them to the casemates which looked out upon the powerful ironclad battery of Cummings Point.

In aiming the first gun fired against the rebellion I had no feeling of self-reproach, for I fully believed that the contest was inevitable and was not of our seeking. . . .

Our firing now became regular and was answered from the rebel guns which encircled us on the four sides of the pentagon upon which the fort was built. The other side faced the open sea. Showers of balls from ten-inch columbiads and forty-two-pounders and shells from thirteen-inch mortars poured into the fort in one incessant stream, causing great flakes of masonry to fall in all directions. When the immense mortar shells, after sailing high in the air, came down in a vertical direction and buried themselves in the parade ground, their explosion shook the fort like an earthquake.

The firing continued all day without any special incident of importance and without our making much impression on the enemy's works. They had a great advantage over us as their fire was concentrated on the fort which was in the center of the circle, while ours was diffused over the circumference. Their missiles were exceedingly destructive to the upper exposed portion of the work, but no essential injury was done to the lower casemates which sheltered us.

From 4 to 6:30 A.M. the enemy's fire was very spirited. From 7 to 8 A.M. a rainstorm came on, and there was a lull in the cannonading. About 8 A.M. the officers' quarters were ignited by one of Ripley's incendiary shells or by shot heated in the furnaces at Fort Moultrie. The fire was put out, but at 10 A.M. a mortar shell passed through the roof and lodged in the flooring of the second story, where it burst and started the flames afresh. This too was extinguished, but the hot shot soon followed each other so rapidly that it was impossible for us to contend with them any longer. It became evident that the entire block, being built with wooden partitions, floors, and roofing, must be consumed, and that the magazine, containing three hundred barrels of powder, would be endangered; for even after closing the metallic door sparks might penetrate through the ventilator. The floor was covered with loose powder where a detail of men had been at work manufacturing cartridge bags out of old shirts, woolen blankets, etc.

While the officers exerted themselves with axes to tear down and cut away all the woodwork in the vicinity, the soldiers were rolling barrels of powder out to more sheltered spots and were covering them with wet blankets. The labor was accelerated by the shells which were bursting around us, for Ripley had redoubled his activity at the first signs of a conflagration. We only succeeded in getting out some ninety-six barrels of powder, and then we were obliged to close the massive copper door and await the result. A shot soon after passed through the intervening shield, struck the door, and bent the lock in such a way that it could not be opened again. We were thus cut off from our supply of ammunition but still had some piled up in the vicinity of the guns. Anderson officially reported only four barrels and three cartridges as on hand when we left.

By 11 A.M. the conflagration was terrible and disastrous. One fifth of the fort was on fire, and the wind drove the smoke in dense masses into the angle where we had all taken refuge. It seemed impossible to escape suffocation. Some lay down close to the ground, with handkerchiefs over their mouths, and others posted themselves near the embrasures, where the smoke was somewhat lessened by the draught of air. Every one suffered severely. I crawled out of one of these openings and sat on the outer edge, but Ripley made it lively for me there with his case shot which spattered all around. Had not a slight change of wind taken place, the result might have been fatal to most of us.

Our firing having ceased and the enemy being very jubilant, I thought it would be as well to show them that we were not all dead yet, and ordered the gunners to fire a few rounds more. I heard afterward that the enemy loudly cheered Anderson for his persistency under such adverse circumstances.

The scene at this time was really terrific. The roaring and crackling of the flames, the dense masses of whirling smoke, the bursting of the enemy's shells and our own which were exploding in the burning rooms, the crashing of the shot, and the sound of masonry falling in every direction, made the fort a pandemonium. When at last nothing was left of the building but the blackened walls and smoldering embers, it became painfully evident that an immense amount of damage had been done. There was a tower at each angle of the fort. One of these, containing great quantities of shells upon which we had relied, was almost completely shattered by successive explosions. The massive wooden gates studded with iron nails were burned, and the wall built behind them was now a mere heap of debris, so that the main entrance was wide open for an assaulting party. The sally ports were in a similar condition, and the numerous windows on the gorge side which had been planked up had now become all open entrances.

About 12:48 P.M. the end of the flagstaff was shot down and the flag fell. . . .

About 2 P.M. Senator Wigfall, in company with W. Gourdin Young, of Charleston, unexpectedly made his appearance at one of the embrasures, having crossed over from Morris Island in a small boat rowed by Negroes. He had seen the flag come down, and supposed that we had surrendered in consequence of the burning of the quarters. An artilleryman serving his gun was very much astonished to see a man's face at the entrance and asked him what he was doing there. Wigfall replied that he wished to see Major Anderson. The man, however, refused to allow him to enter until he had surrendered himself as a prisoner and given up his sword. . . . Wigfall, in Beauregard's name, offered Anderson his own terms, which were the evacuation of the fort, with permission to salute our flag and to march out with the honors of war with our arms and private baggage, leaving all other war material behind. As soon as this matter was arranged, Wigfall returned to Cummings Point.

All of the preliminaries having been duly adjusted, it was decided that the evacuation should take place the next morning. Our arrangements were few and simple, but the rebels made extensive preparations for the event in order to give it the greatest éclat and gain from it as much prestige as possible. The population of the surrounding country poured into Charleston in vast multitudes to witness the humiliation of the United States flag. We slept soundly that night for the first time, after all the fatigue and excitement of the two preceding days.

The next morning, Sunday, the 14th, we were up early, packing our baggage in readiness to go on board the transport. The time having arrived, I made preparations, by order of Major Anderson, to fire a national salute to the flag.

The salute being over, the Confederate troops marched in to occupy the fort. The Palmetto Guard, Captain Cuthbert's company, detailed by Colonel De Saussure, and Captain Hollinquist's Company B, of the regulars, detailed by Colonel Ripley, constituted the new garrison under Ripley. Anderson directed me to form the men on the parade ground, assume command, and march them on board the transport. I told him I should prefer to leave the fort with the flag flying and the drums beating "Yankee Doodle," and he authorized me to do so. As soon as our tattered flag came down and the silken banner made by the ladies of Charleston was run up, tremendous shouts of applause were heard from the vast multitude of spectators; and all the vessels and steamers, with one accord, made for the fort.

ABNER DOUBLEDAY, Reminiscences of Forts Sumter and Moultrie

168. "Bull Run Russell" Reports the Rout of the Federals

The English journalist William Howard Russell arrived in America in 1861 with a great and well-merited reputation as war correspondent. He had distinguished himself by his shrewd, careful, and courageous articles on the Crimean

War, in which he had exposed the mismanagement of affairs at the front. From America he began sending the London (Times) equally honest and outspoken accounts of American affairs. He visited both the Federal and Confederate capitals, and drew vivid pictures of Jefferson Davis and Lincoln. Then, having watched the battle of Bull Run, he told just how badly many of the Northern troops had behaved. His account aroused intense criticism, but on the whole it was just and fair.

JULY 20th, 1861. — The great battle which is to arrest rebellion or to make it a power in the land is no longer distant or doubtful. McDowell has completed his reconnaissance of the country in front of the enemy, and General Scott anticipates that he will be in possession of Manassas tomorrow night.

Some senators and many congressmen have already gone to join McDowell's army or to follow in its wake in the hope of seeing the Lord deliver the Philistines into his hands. Every carriage, gig, wagon, and hack has been engaged by people going out to see the fight. The price is enhanced by mysterious communications respecting the horrible slaughter in the skirmishes at Bull Run. The French cooks and hotelkeepers, by some occult process of reasoning, have arrived at the conclusion that they must treble the prices of their wines and of the hampers of provisions which the Washington people are ordering to comfort themselves at their bloody Derby. . . .

It was a strange scene before us. From the hill a densely wooded country, dotted at intervals with green fields and cleared lands, spread five or six miles in front, bounded by a line of blue and purple ridges, terminating abruptly in escarpments toward the left front and swelling gradually towards the right into the lower spines of an offshoot from the Blue Ridge Mountains. On our left the view was circumscribed by a forest which clothed the side of the ridge on which we stood and covered its shoulder far down into the plain. A gap in the nearest chain of the hills in our front was pointed out by the bystanders as the Pass of Manassas by which the railway from the west is carried into the plain, and still nearer at hand before us is the junction of that rail with the line from Alexandria and with the railway leading southward to Richmond. The intervening space was not a dead level; undulating lines of forest marked the course of the streams which intersected it and gave by their variety of color and shading an additional charm to the landscape which, inclosed in a framework of blue and purple hills, softened into violet in the extreme distance, presented one of the most agreeable displays of simple pastoral woodland scenery that could be conceived.

But the sounds which came upon the breeze and the sights which met our eyes were in terrible variance with the tranquil character of the landscape. The woods far and near echoed to the roar of cannon, and thin, frayed lines of blue smoke marked the spots whence came the muttering sound of rolling musketry; the white puffs of smoke burst high above the treetops, and the gunners' rings from shell and howitzer marked the fire of the artillery.

Clouds of dust shifted and moved through the forest, and through the wavering mists of light blue smoke and the thicker masses which rose commingling from the feet of men and the mouths of cannon, I could see the gleam of arms and the twinkling of bayonets.

On the hill beside me there was a crowd of civilians on horseback and in all sorts of vehicles, with a few of the fairer, if not gentler, sex. A few officers and some soldiers, who had straggled from the regiments in reserve, moved about among the spectators and pretended to explain the movements of the troops below, of which they were profoundly ignorant.

The spectators were all excited, and a lady with an opera glass who was near me was quite beside herself when an unusually heavy discharge roused the current of her blood — "That is splendid. Oh, my! Is not that first-rate? I guess we will be in Richmond this time tomorrow." These, mingled with coarser exclamations, burst from the politicians who had come out to see the triumph of the Union arms.

Loud cheers suddenly burst from the spectators as a man dressed in the uniform of an officer, whom I had seen riding violently across the plain in an open space below, galloped along the front, waving his cap and shouting at the top of his voice. He was brought up, by the press of people round his horse, close to where I stood. "We've whipped them on all points," he cried. "We have taken all their batteries. They are retreating as fast as they can, and we are

after them." Such cheers as rent the welkin! The congressmen shook
hands with each other and cried out: "Bully for us! Bravo! Didn't
I tell you so?" The Germans uttered their martial cheers, and the
Irish hurrahed wildly. At this moment my horse was brought up the
hill and I mounted and turned toward the road to the front . . .

I had ridden between three and a half and four miles, as well as
I could judge, when I was obliged to turn for the third and fourth
time into the road by a considerable stream which was spanned
by a bridge, toward which I was threading my way, when my attention was attracted by loud shouts in advance and I perceived
several wagons coming from the direction of the battlefield, the
drivers of which were endeavoring to force their horses past the
ammunition carts going in the contrary direction near the bridge;
a thick cloud of dust rose behind them, and running by the side of
the wagons were a number of men in uniform whom I supposed to
be the guard. My first impression was that the wagons were returning for fresh supplies of ammunition. But every moment the
crowd increased; drivers and men cried out with the most vehement
gestures: "Turn back! Turn back! We are whipped." They seized
the heads of the horses and swore at the opposing drivers. Emerging from the crowd, a breathless man in the uniform of an officer,
with an empty scabbard dangling by his side, was cut off by getting between my horse and a cart for a moment. "What is the
matter, sir? What is all this about?" "Why, it means we are pretty
badly whipped, that's the truth," he gasped, and continued.

By this time the confusion had been communicating itself through
the line of wagons toward the rear, and the drivers endeavored to
turn round their vehicles in the narrow road, which caused the
usual amount of imprecations from the men and plunging and kicking from the horses.

The crowd from the front continually increased, the heat, the uproar, and the dust were beyond description, and these were aug-
mented when some cavalry soldiers, flourishing their sabers and
preceded by an officer, who cried out, "Make way there — make
way there for the General," attempted to force a covered wagon,
in which was seated a man with a bloody handkerchief round his
head, through the press.

I had succeeded in getting across the bridge, with great difficulty, before the wagon came up, and I saw the crowd on the road was still gathering thicker and thicker. Again I asked an officer, who was on foot with his sword under his arm, "What is all this for?" "We are whipped, sir. We are all in retreat. You are all to go back." "Can you tell me where I can find General McDowell?" "No! nor can any one else."

In a few seconds a crowd of men rushed out of the wood down toward the guns, and the artillerymen near me seized the trail of a piece and were wheeling it round to fire when an officer or sergeant called out: "Stop! stop! They are our own men"; and in two or three minutes the whole battalion came sweeping past the guns at the double and in the utmost disorder. Some of the artillerymen dragged the horses out of the tumbrils, and for a moment the confusion was so great I could not understand what had taken place; but a soldier whom I stopped said, "We are pursued by their cavalry; they have cut us all to pieces."

Murat himself would not have dared to move a squadron on such ground. However, it could not be doubted that something serious was taking place; and at that moment a shell burst in front of the house, scattering the soldiers near it, which was followed by another that bounded along the road; and in a few minutes more out came another regiment from the wood, almost as broken as the first. The scene on the road had now assumed an aspect which has not a parallel in any description I have ever read. Infantry soldiers on mules and draft horses with the harness clinging to their heels, as much frightened as their riders; Negro servants on their masters' chargers; ambulances crowded with unwounded soldiers; wagons swarming with men who threw out the contents in the road to make room, grinding through a shouting, screaming mass of men on foot who were literally yelling with rage at every halt and shrieking out: "Here are the cavalry! Will you get on?" This portion of the force was evidently in discord.

There was nothing left for it but to go with the current one could not stem. I turned round my horse . . . I was unwillingly approaching Centerville in the midst of heat, dust, confusion, imprecations inconceivable. On arriving at the place where a small rivulet crossed the road the throng increased still more. The ground over which I had passed going out was now covered with arms, clothing of all kinds, accouterments thrown off and left to be trampled in the dust under the hoofs of men and horses. The runaways ran alongside the wagons, striving to force themselves in among the occupants, who resisted tooth and nail. The drivers spurred and whipped and urged the horses to the utmost of their bent. I felt an inclination to laugh which was overcome by disgust and by that vague sense of something extraordinary taking place which is experienced when a man sees a number of people acting as if driven by some unknown terror. As I rode in the crowd, with men clinging to the stirrup leathers or holding on by anything they could lay hands on, so that I had some apprehension of being pulled off, I spoke to the men and asked them over and over again not to be in such a hurry. "There's no enemy to pursue you. All the cavalry in the world could not get at you." But I might as well have talked to the stones.

It never occurred to me that this was a grand debacle. All along I believed the mass of the army was not broken and that all I saw around was the result of confusion created in a crude organization by a forced retreat, and knowing the reserves were at Centerville and beyond, I said to myself, "Let us see how this will be when we get to the hill."

I was trotting quietly down the hill road beyond Centerville when suddenly the guns on the other side or from a battery very near opened fire, and a fresh outburst of artillery sounded through the woods. In an instant the mass of vehicles and retreating soldiers, teamsters, and civilians, as if agonized by an electric shock, quivered throughout the tortuous line. With dreadful shouts and cursings the drivers lashed their maddened horses and, leaping from the carts, left them to their fate and ran on foot. Artillerymen and foot soldiers and Negroes, mounted on gun horses with the chain traces and loose trappings trailing in the dust, spurred and flogged their steeds down the road or by the side paths. The firing continued and seemed to approach the hill, and at every report the agitated body of horsemen and wagons was seized, as it were, with a fresh convulsion.

Once more the dreaded cry: "The cavalry! cavalry are coming!" rang through the crowd, and looking back to Centerville, I perceived coming down the hill, between me and the sky, a number of mounted men who might at a hasty glance be taken for horse-men in the act of sabering the fugitives. In reality they were sol-diers and civilians, with, I regret to say, some officers among them, who were whipping and striking their horses with sticks or what-ever else they could lay hands on. I called out to the men who were frantic with terror beside me, "They are not cavalry at all; they're your own men" — but they did not heed me. A fellow who was shouting out, "Run! run!" as loud as he could beside me, seemed to take delight in creating alarm; and as he was perfectly collected as far as I could judge, I said: "What on earth are you running for? What are you afraid of?" He was in the roadside below me and, at once turning on me and exclaiming, "I'm not afraid of you," pre-sented his piece and pulled the trigger so instantaneously that had it gone off I could not have swerved from the ball. As the scoundrel deliberately drew up to examine the nipple, I judged it best not to give him another chance and spurred on through the crowd, where any man could have shot as many as he pleased without interruption. The only conclusion I came to was that he was mad or drunken. When I was passing by the line of the bivouacs a battalion of men came tumbling down the bank from the field into the road with fixed bayonets, and as some fell in the road and others tum-bled on top of them, there must have been a few ingloriously wounded.

22d. — I awoke from a deep sleep this morning about six o'clock. The rain was falling in torrents and beat with a dull, thudding sound on the leads outside my window; but louder than all came a strange sound as if of the tread of men, a confused tramp and splashing and a murmuring of voices. I got up and ran to the front room, the windows of which looked on the street, and there, to my intense surprise, I saw a steady stream of men covered with mud, soaked through with rain, who were pouring irregularly, without any semblance of order, up Pennsylvania Avenue toward the Capitol. A dense stream of vapor rose from the multitude, but looking closely at the men, I perceived they belonged to different regiments, New Yorkers, Michiganders, Rhode Islanders, Massa-chusetters, Minnesotans, mingled pellmell together. Many of them were without knapsacks, crossbelts, and firelocks. Some had neither greatcoats nor shoes; others were covered with blankets. Hastily putting on my clothes, I ran downstairs and asked an officer who was passing by, a pale young man who looked exhausted to death and who had lost his sword, for the empty sheath dangled at his side, where the men were coming from. "Where from? Well, sir, I guess we're all coming out of Virginny as far as we can, and pretty well whipped too." "What! the whole army, sir?" "That's more than I know. They may stay that like. I know I'm going home. I've had enough of fighting to last my lifetime."

The news seemed incredible. But there before my eyes were the jaded, dispirited, broken remnants of regiments passing onward, where and for what I knew not, and it was evident enough that the mass of the grand army of the Potomac was placing that river between it and the enemy as rapidly as possible. "Is there any pursuit?" I asked of several men. Some were too surly to reply; others said, "They're coming as fast as they can after us"; others, "I guess they've stopped it now — the rain is too much for them." A few said they did not know and looked as if they did not care.

The rain has abated a little, and the pavements are densely packed with men in uniforms, some with, others without, arms, on whom the shopkeepers are looking with evident alarm. They seem to be in possession of all the spirit houses. Now and then shots are heard down the street or in the distance, and cries and shouting, as if a scuffle or a difficulty were occurring. Willard's is turned into a barrack for officers and presents such a scene in the hall as could only be witnessed in a city occupied by a demoralized army. There is no provost guard, no patrol, no authority visible in the streets. General Scott is quite overwhelmed by the affair and is unable to stir. General McDowell has not yet arrived. The Secretary of War knows not what to do, Mr. Lincoln is equally helpless, and Mr. Seward, who retains some calmness, is, notwithstanding his military rank and militia experience, without resource or expedient. There are a good many troops hanging on about the camps and forts on the other side of the river, it is said; but they are thoroughly disorganized and will run away if the enemy comes in sight without a shot, and then the capital must fall at once. Why Beauregard does not come I know not, nor can I well guess. I have been expecting every hour since noon to hear his cannon. Here is a golden opportunity. If the Confederates do not grasp that which will never come again on such terms, it stamps them with mediocrity.

WILLIAM HOWARD RUSSELL, My Diary North and South

169. The "Monitor" and the "Merrimac"

When reports reached the North hat the Confederates were converting the ship Merrimac, *captured at Norfolk, into an ironclad, the Navy Department asked for bids for the building of armored vessels. The well-known naval engineer John Ericsson, who had been born in Sweden, was among those who replied. His small armored ship the* Monitor *was launched on January 30, 1862, just in time to meet the* Merrimac *when she finally came out to attack the Union fleet. The great duel of March 9, 1862, between these two craft is one of the most famous naval encounters in modern history.*

U. S. STEAMER *Monitor,* Hampton Roads, Va.—At 4 P.M. [March 8, 1862] we passed Cape Henry and heard heavy firing in the direction of Fortress Monroe. As we approached, it increased, and we immediately cleared ship for action. When about halfway between Fortress Monroe and Cape Henry we spoke the pilot boat. He told us the *Cumberland* was sunk and the *Congress* was on fire and had surrendered to the *Merrimac.* We could not credit it at first, but as we approached Hampton Roads, we could see the fine old *Congress* burning brightly; and we knew it must be true. Sad indeed did we feel to think those two fine old vessels had gone to their last homes with so many of their brave crews. Our hearts were very full, and we vowed vengeance on the *Merrimac* if it should be our lot to fall in with her. At 9 P.M. we anchored near the frigate

Roanoke, the flagship, Captain Marston. Captain Worden immediately went on board and received orders to proceed to Newport News and protect the *Minnesota* (then aground) from the *Merrimac.*

We got under way and arrived at the *Minnesota* at 11 P.M. I went on board in our cutter and asked the captain what his prospects were of getting off. He said he should try to get afloat at 2 A.M., when it was high water. I asked him if we could render him any assistance, to which he replied, "No!" I then told him we should do all in our power to protect him from the *Merrimac.* He thanked me kindly and wished us success. Just as I arrived back to the *Monitor* the *Congress* blew up, and certainly a grander sight was never seen; but it went straight to the marrow of our bones. Not a word was said, but deeply did each man think and wish we were by the side of the *Merrimac.* At 1 A.M. we anchored near the *Minnesota.* The captain and myself remained on deck, waiting for the appearance of the *Merrimac.* At 3 A.M. we thought the *Minnesota* was afloat and coming down on us; so we got under way as soon as possible and stood out of the channel. After backing and filling about for an hour, we found we were mistaken and anchored again. At daylight we discovered the *Merrimac* at anchor with several vessels under Sewall's Point. We immediately made every preparation for battle. At 8 A.M. on Sunday the *Merrimac* got under way, accompanied by several steamers, and started direct for the *Minnesota.* When a mile distant she fired two guns at her. By this time our anchor was up, the men at quarters, the guns loaded, and everything ready for action. As the *Merrimac* came close, the captain passed the word to commence firing. I triced up the port, ran out the gun, and fired the *first* gun, and thus commenced the great battle between the *Monitor* and the *Merrimac.*

Now mark the condition our men and officers were in. Since Friday morning, forty-eight hours, they had had no rest and very little food, as we could not conveniently cook. They had been hard at work all night, and nothing to eat for breakfast except hard bread, and were thoroughly worn out. As for myself, I had not slept a wink for fifty-one hours and had been on my feet almost constantly. But after the first gun was fired we forgot all fatigues, hard work, and everything else and fought as hard as men ever fought. We loaded and fired as fast as we could. I pointed and fired the guns myself. Every shot I would ask the captain the effect, and the majority of them were encouraging. The captain was in the pilot-house, directing the movements of the vessel; Acting Master Stodder was stationed at the wheel which turns the tower but, as he could not manage it, was relieved by Steiners. The speaking trumpet from the tower to the pilothouse was broken; so we passed the word from the captain to myself on the berth deck by Paymaster Keeler and Captain's Clerk Toffey. Five times during the engagement we touched each other, and each time I fired a gun at her, and I will vouch the hundred and sixty-eight pounds penetrated her sides. Once she tried to run us down with her iron prow but did no damage whatever. After fighting for two hours we hauled off for half an hour to hoist shot in the tower. At it we went again as hard as we could, the shot, shell, grape, canister, musket, and rifle balls flying in every direction but doing no damage. Our tower was struck several times, and though the noise was pretty loud it did not affect us any. Stodder and one of the men were carelessly leaning against the tower when a shot struck it exactly opposite them and disabled them for an hour or two. At about 11:30 A.M. the captain sent for me. I went forward, and there stood as noble a man as lives, at the foot of the ladder to the pilothouse, his face perfectly black with powder and iron, and apparently perfectly blind. I asked him what was the matter. He said a shot had struck the pilothouse exactly opposite his eyes and blinded him, and he thought the pilothouse was damaged. He told me to take charge of the ship and use my own discretion. I led him to his room, laid him on the sofa, and then took his position. On examining the pilothouse I found the iron hatch on top, on the forward side, was completely cracked through. We still continued firing, the tower being under the direction of Steiners. We were between two fires, the *Minnesota* on one side and the *Merrimac* on the other. The latter was retreating to Sewall's Point, and the *Minnesota* had struck us twice on the tower. I knew if another shot should strike our pilothouse in the same place, our steering apparatus would be disabled, and we should be at the mercy of the batteries on Sewell's Point. We had *strict* orders to act on the defensive and protect the *Minnesota*. We had evidently finished the *Merrimac* as far as the *Minnesota* was concerned. Our pilothouse was damaged, and we had orders *not* to follow the

Merrimac up; therefore, after the *Merrimac* had retreated, I went to the *Minnesota* and remained by her until she was afloat. General Wool and Secretary Fox both commended me for acting as I did and said it was the strict military plan to follow. This is the reason we did not sink the *Merrimac,* and every one here capable of judging says we acted perfectly right.

Soldiers' Letters from Camp, Battle-field and Prison

170. General Wool Takes Norfolk

At the beginning of the Civil War, Norfolk had been abandoned by the Federal forces, and the navy yard there was hastily and partially burned. Virginia troops then held the city for more than a year — until May 10, 1862. It was this occupation which made possible the repair of the Merrimac *and the exploits of that vessel. But when the city and navy yard were recaptured by Union forces under General Wool, the* Merrimac *was lost to the South.*

NO TIME was lost on the following morning in re-embarking the troops for the purpose of marching on Norfolk by the rear. At the last moment General Wool, with much emotion begged the Secretary (Chase) to allow him to command the troops. The Secretary had decided to relieve him of the command of the expedition on account of his advanced age, but finally reversed his decision with the remark that he could not inflict sorrow upon gray hairs. . . .

Starting at once to the front with our escort, we had not gone very far before it became evident that a great deal of confusion existed in the command — in fact, that there was no organization, and an utter absence of definite instructions or orders of any kind. Overtaking a regiment that was scattered along the road — most of the men lying down wherever any shade could be found, as the day was intensely warm — Mr. Chase inquired of the colonel to whose command he belonged and what his orders were. He replied that he had no idea who was his commander, that some said Weber and some said Mansfield. He had received no orders except that when he landed he was told to take a certain road, and he thought he would wait to see what was to be done next. Overtaking another regiment a mile or two beyond, the Secretary received the same answers. Going on still farther, we came upon General Mansfield and his staff, who had dismounted in the shade near a spring of cool water. Farther still, another straggling regiment was found; yet no one had any orders or instructions. Suddenly the booming of cannon was heard immediately in front, and as no artillery had been landed by us, it was evident that the firing proceeded from the enemy. Straggling soldiers now came running toward us with exaggerated rumors of the enemy being in force, burning the bridges, and contesting with artillery the passage of the streams that crossed the road. The ridiculousness of the situation would have been amusing if it had not been for the serious aspect that it was gradually assuming. Two regiments of cavalry had been embarked and two batteries of artillery; yet not a horse or a gun had been sent to the front. Four regiments of infantry were marching along, uncertain what road to take and unassigned to any brigade; two brigadier generals and their staffs, without orders and without commands, were sitting by the roadside waiting for something to turn up. This was the situation with the enemy firing in front. Secretary Chase took it all in at a glance and rose at once to the necessities of the occasion. Tearing some leaves from his memorandum book, he directed me to send one of our escort back to General Wool with a written requisition for artillery and cavalry. This brought the general to the front with two pieces of artillery and some mounted troops. As he rode up, Mr. Chase expressed to him in very strong language his astonishment at the condition of things. General Wool replied by saying that he presumed General Mansfield had felt some delicacy in assuming command over General Weber and that General Weber had hesitated to act while General Mansfield was so near. "Talk of delicacy," exclaimed the Secretary, "with the enemy firing in front! What absurdity! Let General Mansfield go to the rear and bring up reinforcements, and that will settle all questions of delicacy." This

brought about a prolonged discussion between Generals Wool and
Mansfield, which was carried on at a short distance from the rear
under the shade of a large sycamore tree. Losing all patience, the
Secretary exclaimed, "Two cackling hens!" and turning to me with
a voice and manner that would have become Wellington or Soult,
he said:

"Sir! I order you in the name of the President of the United
States to take command of these troops and march them upon
Norfolk."

An infantry regiment was deployed at double-quick as skirmishers
in advance, and the other regiments were soon moving rapidly down
the Norfolk road. They had proceeded some distance before General Wool was aware of the movement. He was not long in overtaking us, however, and on his demand for an explanation from me
Mr. Chase assumed the responsibility, after which we proceeded
harmoniously toward our destination. At the extreme limits of the
city and before the formidable line of intrenched works was reached,
a large deputation headed by the mayor and municipal councils
made its appearance with a flag of truce and performed a most
skillful ruse to gain time for the Confederates to secure their retreat
from the city. The mayor, with all the formality of a medieval
warden, appeared with a bunch of rusty keys and a formidable roll
of papers which he proceeded to read with the utmost deliberation
previous to delivering the "keys of the city." The reading of the
documents — which embraced a large portion of the history of
Virginia, the causes that led to the war, the peculiar position of the
good citizens of Norfolk, and in short a little of everything that
could have the remotest bearing upon the subject and exhaust the
longest possible space of time in reading — was protracted until
nearly dark. In the meantime the Confederates were hurrying with
their artillery and stores over the ferry to Portsmouth, cutting the
water pipes and flooding the public buildings, setting fire to the
navy yard, and having their own way generally, while our General
was listening in the most innocent and complacent manner to the
long rigmarole so ingeniously prepared by the mayor and skillfully
interlarded with fulsome personal eulogium upon himself. . . . And
now another well-devised plan presented itself in the shape of a
number of carriages which the mayor particularly desired should be

used by the officers in taking possession of the city, the troops in the meanwhile to remain where they were. Falling readily into this second little trap, the General accepted and we were driven to the city hall, where some more rusty keys were produced and more formal speeches were made. A collection of several thousand people, some of them in butternut and gray, assembled in front of the building. While the General and mayor were going through their high formalities, Mr. Chase asked for a pen and a piece of paper and wrote an order assigning the command of the city to myself as military governor, which General Wool signed at his direction. Then, bidding me goodbye, he took the General by the arm and departed, leaving me the solitary occupant of the city hall, without a soldier within two miles and with not even an aide-de-camp to assist me. Fortunately an enterprising newspaper correspondent had followed the carriages on foot, and him I appointed an aide and dispatched for the troops. By the time the troops arrived the moon had risen, and by its light they were placed in position. A regiment dispatched to the navy yard was too late to rescue it from almost complete destruction, but it cut off the *Merrimac* from any supplies from either side of the river. It was long after midnight before the final disposition of troops was made, and this had hardly been accomplished when, with a shock that shook the city and with an ominous sound that could not be mistaken, the magazine of the *Merrimac* was exploded, the vessel having been cut off from supplies and deserted by the crew; and thus this most formidable engine of destruction that had so long been a terror not only to Hampton Roads but to the Atlantic coast went to her doom.

EGBERT L. VIELE, A Trip with Lincoln, Chase and Stanton

171. Eating Mules at Port Hudson

When General N. P. Banks led the Union forces from New Orleans up the Mississippi toward Vicksburg, he found his way blocked by heavy fortifications at Port

Hudson (135 miles above New Orleans), with a garrison that was soon increased to 6,000 men. Flanking movements failed, and there was nothing to do but lay siege to the place. The investment was completed on May 26, 1863, and during all of June the Union forces hemmed in the Confederates along a front of seven miles. Both sides suffered severely, the Federal troops from sickness, the Confederates from increasing hunger. By the beginning of July the garrison was literally starving. Here one of the officers describes their straits.

THE LAST quarter ration of beef had been given out to the troops on the 29th of June [1863]. On the 1st of July, at the request of many officers, a wounded mule was killed and cut up for experimental eating. All those who partook of it spoke highly of the dish. The flesh of mules is of a darker color than beef, of a finer grain, quite tender and juicy, and has a flavor something between that of beef and venison. There was an immediate demand for this kind of food, and the number of mules killed by the commissariat daily increased. Some horses were also slaughtered, and their flesh was found to be very good eating, but not equal to mule. Rats, of which there were plenty about the deserted camps, were also caught by many officers and men and were found to be quite a luxury — superior, in the opinion of those who eat them, to spring chicken; and if a philosopher of the Celestial Empire could have visited Port Hudson at the time, he would have marveled at the progress of the barbarians there toward the refinements of his own people.

Mule meat was regularly served out in rations to the troops from and after the 4th of July, and there were very few among the garrison whose natural prejudices were so strong as to prevent them from cooking and eating their share. The stock of corn was getting very low, and besides that nothing was left but peas, sugar, and molasses. These peas were the most indigestible and unwholesome articles that were ever given to soldiers to eat, and that such a large quantity was left on hand was probably accounted for by the fact that most of the troops would not have them on any consideration. To save corn they were issued out to horses and mules and killed a great many of these animals. All of the horses and mules which were not needed for hauling or other imperative duties had been turned out to graze, where numbers of them were killed or disabled by the enemy's cannonade and rain of Minié balls and the rest nearly starved to death.

The sugar and molasses were put to good use by the troops in making a weak description of beer which was constantly kept at the lines by the barrelful and drunk by the soldiers in preference to the miserable water with which they were generally supplied. This was a very pleasant and healthful beverage and went far to recompense the men for the lack of almost every other comfort or luxury. In the same way, after the stock of tobacco had given out, they substituted sumac leaves, which grew wild in the woods. It had always been smoked by the Indians under the name of killickinnic and when properly prepared for the pipe is a tolerably good substitute for tobacco.

There was a small proportion of the garrison who could not, however, reconcile themselves so easily to the hardships and dangers of the siege. Some one hundred and fifty or more men, almost entirely foreigners of a low class or ignorant conscripts from western Louisiana, men who were troubled with none of that common feeling usually styled patriotism, deserted us for the better-provided commissariats of the enemy, slinking away by couples and squads during the night time. Their loss was not wept over, nor could the information they carried with them concerning our position enable the enemy to capture it.

Port Hudson [La.] . . . As Sketched from the Diary of an Officer

172. Blue and Gray Fraternize at Port Hudson

On July 7, 1863, when the Union troops were about to begin a third attempt to storm the works at Port Hudson, news came that Grant had captured Vicksburg. This meant that the Confederates were now cut off on the north as well as on the south. Firing died away as the tidings were conveyed to

*the Confederate garrison. Their surrender was inevitable, and as
soon as it was completed each side showed its eagerness to pay tribute to the other's courage.*

AT TWO o'clock on the morning of the 8th of July [1863]
General Gardner sent to General Banks by flag of truce for confirma-
tion of the fall of Vicksburg, which was accorded him. About nine
o'clock the same morning he dispatched commissioners to treat for
the surrender of the post [Port Hudson]. They did not return until
afternoon and then announced that an unconditional surrender of the
place and garrison had been agreed upon and that the ceremony
would take place at seven o'clock the next morning.

A cessation of hostilities had already taken place, and immediately
that it was known that the capitulation had been agreed upon, a
singular scene was presented to the observer, particularly upon the
extreme right, where the contending parties, almost near enough
to clutch each other by the throat, had been engaged in a desperate
struggle for the mastery.

Soldiers swarmed from their places of concealment on either side
and met each other in the most cordial and fraternal spirit. Here
you would see a group of Federal soldiers escorted round our works
and shown the effects of their shots and entertained with accounts
of such part of the siege operations as they could not have learned
before. In the same way our men went into the Federal lines and
gazed with curiosity upon the work which had been giving them
so much trouble, escorted by Federal soldiers, who vied with each
other in courtesy and a display of magnanimous spirit. The subject
of the attack and defense seemed to be a tireless one with both sides,
and the conversations that ensued between them were of so cheerful
and pleasant a character that one could hardly believe it possible
these men had just before been fighting with the ferocity of tigers
and striving by every art to slaughter the men they were now
fraternizing with.

Not a single case occurred in which the enemy, either officers or
privates, exhibited a disposition to exult over their victory, but on
the contrary. whenever the subject came up in conversation it elicited

from them only compliments upon the skill and bravery of the defense. Nor was their conduct limited to mere expressions. They were liberal in making presents of tobacco and other luxuries, asking of the garrison only such articles as they could retain as relics of the siege. One of their surgeons came in during a heavy rainstorm and brought medicines for our sick, repeating his visit the next morning and bringing a large quantity of quinine, which he dosed out to the fever patients. During the afternoon and evening of the 8th a large number of Federals were within our lines visiting at our camps, whither most of our men had repaired to pack up their little stock of clothing preparatory to an expected departure on the morrow.

Port Hudson . . . As Sketched from the Diary of an Officer

173. General Lee Invades Pennsylvania

After his victories at Fredericksburg and Chancellorsville, General Lee resolved to invade the North. He felt confident in the superior fighting ability of his troops, and over-estimated the effect of successive defeats on the morale of the Northern armies. While he knew that Grant was likely soon to capture Vicksburg, he rejected Longstreet's proposal that he try to save the situation in the West by advancing against Cincinnati. Before the middle of June his army was on the march. On the 24th and 25th Longstreet and Hill crossed the Potomac and pushed toward the heart of Pennsylvania. Before the month ended Lee's troops had captured Chambersburg and York, and were menacing Harrisburg; but the Union army under Meade was coming up rapidly.

CAMP near Greenwood, Pa., June 28, 1863. — My own darling wife: You can see by the date of this that we are now in Pennsylvania. We crossed the line day before yesterday and are resting today near a little one-horse town on the road to Gettysburg, which we will reach tomorrow. We are paying back these people for some of the damage they have done us, though we are not doing them half as bad as they done us. We are getting up all the horses, etc., and feeding our army with their beef and flour, etc., but there are strict orders about the interruption of any private property by individual soldiers.

Though with these orders, fowls and pigs and eatables don't stand much chance. I felt when I first came here that I would like to revenge myself upon these people for the desolation they have brought upon our own beautiful home, that home where we could have lived so happy, and that we loved so much, from which their vandalism has driven you and my helpless little ones. But though I had such severe wrongs and grievances to redress and such great cause for revenge, yet when I got among these people I could not find it in my heart to molest them. They looked so dreadfully scared and talked so humble that I have invariably endeavored to protect their property and have prevented soldiers from taking chickens, even in the main road; yet there is a good deal of plundering going on, confined principally to the taking of provisions. No houses were searched and robbed, like our houses were done by the Yankees. Pigs, chickens, geese, etc., are finding their way into our camp; it can't be prevented, and I can't think it ought to be. We must show them something of war. I have sent out today to get a good horse; I have no scruples bout that, as they have taken mine. We took a lot of Negroes yesterday. I was offered my choice, but as I could not get them back home I would not take them. In fact my humanity revolted at taking the poor devils away from their homes. They were so scared that I turned them all loose.

I dined yesterday with two old maids. They treated me very well and seemed greatly in favor of peace. I have had a great deal of fun since I have been here. The country that we have passed through is beautiful, and everything in the greatest abundance. You never saw such a land of plenty. We could live here mighty well for the next twelve months, but I suppose old Hooker will try to put a stop to us pretty soon. Of course we will have to fight here, and when it comes it will be the biggest on record. Our men feel that there is to be no back-out. A defeat here would be ruinous. This army has never done such fighting as it will do now, and if we can whip the armies that are now gathering to oppose us, we will have everything in our own hands. We must conquer a peace. If we can come out of this country triumphant and victorious, having established a peace, we will bring back to our own land the greatest joy that ever crowned a people. We will show the Yankees this time how we can fight.

Be of good cheer, and write often to your fondly attached husband,

WILLIAM S. CHRISTIAN
FRANK MOORE, The Rebellion Record

174. High Tide at Gettysburg

I

The culminating event of the three-day battle of Gettysburg was the assault of 15,000 Confederate troops under General George Pickett upon the Union lines strongly posted along Cemetery Ridge. The thrust was preceded by a three-hour bombardment by 115 Confederate guns, to which 80 Federal guns replied. At two o'clock in the afternoon the great charge began. Pickett's men had nearly a mile to go; they moved at a walk, keeping their lines as precisely as on parade; and as they came under a withering Union fire the slaughter was terrific. "A thousand fell where Kemper led, a thousand died where Garnett bled." The Confederate battle flags were planted at one point on the crest of the ridge—but they were kept there only a few minutes. Here the story is told by an English observer, and by one of Lee's most gifted but most stubborn generals.

JULY 2, 1863 (Thursday).—I arrived at 5 A.M. at the same commanding position we were on yesterday, and I climbed up a tree in company with Captain Schreibert of the Prussian army. Just below us were seated Generals Lee, Hill, Longstreet, and Hood in consultation, the two latter assisting their deliberations by the truly American custom of whittling sticks. General Heth was also present; he was wounded in the head yesterday, and although not allowed to command his brigade, he insists upon coming to the field.

At 7 A.M. I rode over part of the ground with General Longstreet and saw him disposing of McLaws' division for today's fight. The enemy occupied a series of high ridges, the tops of which were covered with trees, but the intervening valleys between their ridges and ours were mostly open and partly under cultivation. The cemetery was on their right, and their left appeared to rest upon a high rocky hill. The enemy's forces, which were now supposed to comprise nearly the whole Potomac army, were concentrated into a space apparently not more than a couple of miles in length. The Confederates inclosed them in a sort of semicircle, and the extreme extent of our position must have been from five to six miles at least. The enemy was evidently intrenched, but the Southerns had not broken ground at all. A dead silence reigned till 4:45 P.M., and no one would have imagined that such masses of men and such a powerful artillery were about to commence the work of destruction at that hour.

At that time, however, Longstreet suddenly commenced a heavy cannonade on the right. Ewell immediately took it up on the left. The enemy replied with at least equal fury, and in a few moments the firing along the whole line was as heavy as it is possible to conceive. A dense smoke arose for six miles, there was little wind to drive it away, and the air seemed full of shells. Every now and then a caisson would blow up; if a Federal one, a Confederate yell would immediately follow. The Southern troops, when charging or to express their delight, always yell in a manner peculiar to themselves. The Yankee cheer is much more like ours, but the Confederate officers declare that the rebel yell has a particular merit and always produces a salutary and useful effect upon their adversaries. A corps is sometimes spoken of as a good yelling regiment.

So soon as the firing began, General Lee joined Hill just below our tree, and he remained there nearly all the time, looking through his field glass, sometimes talking to Hill and sometimes to Colonel Long of his staff. But generally he sat quite alone on the stump of a tree. What I remarked especially was that during the whole time the firing continued he sent only one message and only received one report. It is evidently his system to arrange the plan thoroughly with the three corps commanders and then leave to them the duty of modifying and carrying it out to the best of their abilities.

When the cannonade was at its height, a Confederate band of music, between the cemetery and ourselves, began to play polkas and waltzes, which sounded very curious, accompanied by the hissing and bursting of shells.

At five-forty-five all became comparatively quiet on our left and in the cemetery, but volleys of musketry on the right told us that Longstreet's infantry were advancing, and the onward progress of the smoke showed that he was progressing favorably. But about six-thirty there seemed to be a check and even a slight retrograde movement. Soon after seven General Lee got a report by signal from Longstreet to say "we are doing well."

A little before dark the firing dropped off in every direction and soon ceased altogether.

3d. — The distance between the Confederate guns and the Yankee position — i.e. between the woods crowning the opposite ridges — was at least a mile, quite open, gently undulating, and exposed to artillery the whole distance. This was the ground which had to be crossed in today's attack. Pickett's division, which had just come up, was to bear the brunt in Longstreet's attack, together with Heth and Pettigrew in Hill's corps. Pickett's division was a weak one (under five thousand), owing to the absence of two brigades.

At noon all Longstreet's dispositions were made; his troops for attack were deployed into line and lying down in the woods; his batteries were ready to open. The General then dismounted and went to sleep for a short time.

Finding that to see the actual fighting it was absolutely necessary to go into the thick of the thing, I determined to make my way to General Longstreet. It was then about two-thirty. After passing General Lee and his staff, I rode on through the woods in the direction in which I had left Longstreet. I soon began to meet many wounded men returning from the front; many of them asked in piteous tones the way to a doctor or an ambulance. The farther I got, the greater became the number of the wounded. At last I came to a perfect stream of them flocking through the woods in numbers as great as the crowd in Oxford Street in the middle of the day. Some were walking alone on crutches composed of two rifles, others supported by men less badly wounded than themselves, and others were carried on stretchers by the ambulance corps; but in no case did I see a sound man helping the wounded to the rear unless he carried the red badge of the ambulance corps. They were still under a heavy fire; the shells were continually bringing down great limbs of trees and carrying further destruction amongst this melancholy procession. I saw all this in much less time than it takes to write it, and although astonished to meet such vast numbers of wounded, I had not seen enough to give me any idea of the real extent of the mischief.

When I got close up to General Longstreet, I saw one of his regiments advancing through the woods in good order; so, thinking I was just in time to see the attack, I remarked to the General that "I wouldn't have missed this for anything." Longstreet was seated at the top of a snake fence at the edge of the wood and looking perfectly calm and unperturbed. He replied, laughing: "The devil you wouldn't! I would like to have missed it very much; we've attacked and been repulsed; look there!"

For the first time I then had a view of the open space between the two positions and saw it covered with Confederates, slowly and sulkily returning toward us in small broken parties, under a heavy fire of artillery. But the fire where we were was not so bad as farther to the rear, for although the air seemed alive with shell, yet the greater number burst behind us. The General told me that Pickett's division had succeeded in carrying the enemy's position and capturing his guns, but after remaining there twenty minutes, it had been forced to retire, on the retreat of Heth and Pettigrew on its left. . . .

Soon afterward I joined General Lee, who had in the meanwhile come to the front on becoming aware of the disaster. If Longstreet's conduct was admirable, that of Lee was perfectly sublime. He was engaged in rallying and in encouraging the broken troops and was raiding about a little in front of the wood, quite alone, the whole of his staff being engaged in a similar manner farther to the rear. His face, which is always placid and cheerful, did not show signs of the slightest disappointment, care, or annoyance; and he was addressing to every soldier he met a few words of encouragement, such as: "All this will come right in the end; we'll talk it over afterwards; but in the meantime, all good men must rally. We want all good and true men just now," etc. He spoke to all the wounded men that passed him, and the slightly wounded he exhorted to "bind up their hurts and take up a musket" in this emergency. Very few failed to answer his appeal, and I saw many badly wounded men take off their hats and cheer him.

He said to me, "This has been a sad day for us, Colonel — a sad day; but we can't expect always to gain victories." I saw General Willcox come up to him and explain, almost crying, the state of his brigade. General Lee immediately shook hands with him and said cheerfully: "Never mind, General, all this has been *my* fault — it is I that have lost this fight, and you must help me out of it in the best way you can."

In this way I saw General Lee encourage and reanimate his somewhat dispirited troops and magnanimously take upon his own shoulders the whole weight of the repulse. It was impossible to look at him or to listen to him without feeling the strongest admiration.

Colonel Fremantle, The Battle of Gettysburg

II

THE SIGNAL guns broke the silence, the blaze of the second gun mingling in the smoke of the first, and salvoes rolled to the left and repeated themselves, the enemy's fine metal spreading its fire to the converging lines, plowing the trembling ground, plunging through the line of batteries, and clouding the heavy air. The two or three hundred guns seemed proud of their undivided honors and organized confusion. The Confederates had the benefit of converging fire into the enemy's massed position, but the superior metal of the enemy neutralized the advantage of position. The brave and steady work progressed. . . .

General Pickett rode to confer with Alexander, then to the ground upon which I was resting, where he was soon handed a slip of paper. After reading it he handed it to me. It read:

"If you are coming at all, come at once, or I cannot give you proper support, but the enemy's fire has not slackened at all. At least eighteen guns are still firing from the cemetery itself.

— Alexander"

Pickett said, "General, shall I advance?"

The effort to speak the order failed, and I could only indicate it by an affirmative bow. He accepted the duty, with seeming confidence of success, leaped on his horse, and rode gaily to his command. I mounted and spurred for Alexander's post. He reported that the batteries he had reserved for the charge with the infantry had been spirited away by General Lee's chief of artillery, that the ammunition of the batteries of position was so reduced that he could not use them in proper support of the infantry. He was ordered to stop the march at once and fill up his ammunition chests. But, alas! there was no more ammunition to be had.

The order was imperative. The Confederate commander had fixed his heart upon the work. Just then a number of the enemy's batteries hitched up and hauled off, which gave a glimpse of unexpected hope. Encouraging messages were sent for the columns to hurry on — and they were then on elastic springing step. The officers saluted as they passed, their stern smiles expressing confidence. General Pickett, a graceful horseman, sat lightly in the saddle, his brown locks flowing quite over his shoulders. Pettigrew's division spread their steps and quickly rectified the alignment, and the grand march moved bravely on. As soon as the leading columns opened the way, the supports sprang to their alignments. General Trimble mounted, adjusting his seat and reins with an air and grace as if setting out on a pleasant afternoon ride. When aligned to their places solid march was made down the slope and past our batteries of position.

Confederate batteries put their fire over the heads of the men as they moved down the slope, and continued to draw the fire of the enemy until the smoke lifted and drifted to the rear, when every gun was turned upon the infantry columns. The batteries that had been drawn off were replaced by others that were fresh. Soldiers and officers began to fall, some to rise no more, others to find their way to the hospital tents. Single files were cut here and there; then the gaps increased, and an occasional shot tore wider openings, but, closing the gaps as quickly as made, the march moved on. . . .

Colonel Latrobe was sent to General Trimble to have his men fill the line of the broken brigades, and bravely they repaired the damage. The enemy moved out against the supporting brigade in Pickett's rear. Colonel Sorrel was sent to have that move guarded, and Pickett was drawn back to that contention. McLaws was ordered to press his left forward, but the direct line of infantry and cross fire of artillery was telling fearfully on the front. Colonel Fremantle ran up to offer congratulations on the apparent success, but the big gaps in the ranks grew until the lines were reduced to half their length. I called his attention to the broken, struggling ranks. Trimble mended the battle of the left in handsome style, but on the right the massing of the enemy grew stronger and stronger. Brigadier Garnett was killed; Kemper and Trimble were desperately wounded; Generals Hancock and Gibbon were wounded. General Lane succeeded Trimble and with Pettigrew held the battle of the left in steady ranks.

Pickett's lines being nearer, the impact was heaviest upon them. Most of the field officers were killed or wounded. Colonel Whittle, of Armistead's brigade, who had been shot through the right leg at Williamsburg and lost his left arm at Malvern Hill, was shot through the right arm, then brought down by a shot through his left leg.

General Armistead, of the second line, spread his steps to supply the places of fallen comrades. His colors cut down, with a volley against the bristling line of bayonets, he put his cap on his sword to guide the storm. The enemy's massing, enveloping numbers held the struggle until the noble Armistead fell beside the wheels of the enemy's battery. Pettigrew was wounded but held his command.

General Pickett, finding the battle broken while the enemy was still reinforcing, called the troops off. There was no indication of panic. The broken files marched back in steady step. The effort was nobly made and failed from blows that could not be fended.

JAMES LONGSTREET, From Manassas to Appomattox

175. "A New Birth of Freedom"

Part of the battlefield at Gettysburg was made a permanent cemetery for the soldiers slain or mortally wounded there. The ground was consecrated in the autumn of 1863 with appropriate ceremonies, Edward Everett delivering the prin-

cipal oration. The superintendent of the enterprise, David Wills, requested Lincoln to deliver "a few appropriate remarks," and the result was these immortal lines.

FOURSCORE and seven years ago our fathers brought forth on this continent a new nation, conceived in Liberty, and dedicated to the proposition that all men are created equal.

Now we are engaged in a great civil war, testing whether that nation or any nation so conceived and so dedicated can long endure. We are met on a great battlefield of that war. We have come to dedicate a portion of that field as a final resting place for those who here gave their lives that that nation might live. It is altogether fitting and proper that we should do this.

But in a larger sense we cannot dedicate — we cannot consecrate — we cannot hallow — this ground. The brave men, living and dead, who struggled here, have consecrated it, far above our poor power to add or detract. The world will little note nor long remember what we say here, but it can never forget what they did here. It is for us the living, rather, to be dedicated here to the unfinished work which they who fought here have thus far so nobly advanced. It is rather for us to be here dedicated to the great task remaining before us — that from these honored dead we take increased devotion to that cause for which they gave the last full measure of devotion — that we here highly resolve that these dead shall not have died in vain — that this nation, under God, shall have a new birth of freedom — and that government of the people, by the people, for the people, shall not perish from the earth.

ABRAHAM LINCOLN, The Gettysburg Address, November 19, 1863

176. V. M. I. Cadets Fight at Newmarket

The son of a Governor of Virginia and Confederate general, John S. Wise was not yet fifteen when the Civil War broke out. He entered the Virginia Military Institute in

1862, and two years later fought with the cadets in the famous battle of Newmarket, here described. A little later he became a second lieutenant in the Confederate army, and in 1865 he carried to Jefferson Davis, then at Danville, Virginia, the news of the imminent surrender of Lee's forces at Appomattox.

IN THE spring of 1864 I was still a cadet at the Virginia Military Institute. "Unrest" is the word to describe the feeling pervading the school. We heard that Grant had been transferred to command in the East, and we all knew that there would be great fighting at the front. Many cadets resigned. Good boys became bad boys for the express purpose of getting "shipped," parents and guardians having refused to permit them to resign. . . .

It was the 10th of May. . . .

The evening gun boomed forth. The garrison flag fell lazily from its peak on the barracks tower. The four companies went springing homeward at double time to the gayest tune the fifes know how to play. Never in all its history looked Lexington more beautiful.

Hark! The drums are beating! Their throbbing bounds through every corner of the barracks, saying to the sleepers, "Be up and doing." It is the long roll.

Grumblingly the cadets hurried down to their places in the ranks, expecting to be soon dismissed and to return to their beds. A group of officers, intently scanning by the light of a lantern a paper held by the adjutant, stood near the statue of George Washington . . . The companies were marched together. The adjutant commanded attention and proceeded to read the orders in his hands.

They announced that the enemy in heavy force was advancing up the Shenandoah Valley, that General Lee could not spare any forces to meet him, that General Breckinridge had been ordered to assemble troops from southwestern Virginia and elsewhere at Staunton, and that the cadets should join him there at the earliest practicable moment. The corps was ordered to march, with four companies of infantry and a section of artillery, by the Staunton pike at break of day.

First sergeants were ordered to detail eight artillerists from each of the four companies to report for duty immediately and man a section of artillery.

As these orders were announced, not a sound was heard from the boys who stood there with beating hearts in the military posture of parade rest.

"Parade's dismissed," piped the adjutant. The sergeants side-stepped us to our respective company parades.

Methinks that even after thirty-three years I once more hear the gamecock voices of the sergeants detailing their artillery and ammunition squads and ordering us to appear with canteens, haversacks, and blankets at 4 A.M. Still silence reigned. Then, as company after company broke ranks, the air was rent with wild cheering at the thought that our hour was come at last.

Elsewhere in the Confederacy, death, disaster, disappointment, may have by this time chilled the ardor of our people; but here, in this little band of fledgelings, the hope of battle flamed as bright as on the morning of Manassas.

We breakfasted by candlelight and filled our haversacks from the mess-hall tables. In the gray of morning we wound down the hill to the river, tramped heavily across the bridge, ascended the pike beyond, cheered the fading turrets of the school; and sunrise found us going at a four-mile gait to Staunton, our gallant little battery rumbling behind.

We made a good day's march and camped that night near Harrisonburg. During the day we met several couriers bearing dispatches; they reported the enemy advancing in heavy force and had left him near Strasburg and Woodstock.

Evidences of the approach of the enemy multiplied on the second day. We passed a great many vehicles coming up the valley with people and farm products and household effects, and a number of herds of cattle and other livestock, all escaping from the Union troops; now and then a weary or wounded cavalryman came by. Their reports were that Sigel's steady advance was only delayed by a thin line of cavalry skirmishers who had been ordered to retard him as best they could until Breckinridge could march his army down to meet him.

Night closed in upon us; for a little while the woodland resounded with the ax stroke or the cheery halloos of the men from campfire to campfire; for a while the firelight danced, the air laden with the odor of cooking food; for a while the boys stood around the campfires for warmth and to dry their wet clothing; but soon all had wrapped their blankets around them and lain down in silence, unbroken save by the champing of the colonel's horse upon his provender or the fall of a passing shower.

An hour past midnight, the sound of hoofs upon the pike caught my ear, and in a few moments the challenge of the sentry summoned me. The newcomer was an aide-de-camp bearing orders for Colonel Shipp from the commanding general. When I aroused the commandant, he struggled up, rubbed his eyes, muttered something about moving at once, and ordered me to arouse the camp without having the drums beaten. Orders to fall in were promptly given, rolls were rattled off, the battalion was formed, and we debouched upon the pike, heading in the darkness and mud for Newmarket. . . .

Day broke gray and gloomy upon us, toiling onward in the mud. The sober course of our reflections was relieved by the light-heartedness of the veterans. We overtook Wharton's Brigade, with smiling "Old Gabe," a Virginia Military Institute boy, at their head. They were squatting by the roadside, cooking breakfast, as we came up. With many good-natured gibes they restored our confidence; they seemed as merry, nonchalant, and indifferent to the coming fight as if it were their daily occupation. A tall, round-shouldered fellow, whose legs seemed almost split up to his shoulder blades, came among us with a pair of shears and a pack of playing cards, offering to take our names and cut off lovelocks to be sent home after we were dead; another inquired if we wanted rosewood coffins, satin-lined, with name and age on the plate. In a word, they made us ashamed of the depressing solemnity of our last six miles of marching and renewed within our breasts the true daredevil spirit of soldiery.

Resuming the march, the mileposts numbered four, three, two, one mile to Newmarket; then the mounted skirmishers hurried past us to their position at the front. We heard loud cheering at the rear, which was caught up by the troops along the line of march. We learned its import as General John C. Breckinridge and staff approached, and we joined heartily in the cheering as that soldierly man, mounted magnificently, galloped past, uncovered, bowing, and riding like a Cid.

Deployed along the crest of an elevation in our front, we could see our line of mounted pickets and the smoldering fires of their last night's bivouac. We halted at a point where passing a slight turn in the road would bring us in full view of the position of the enemy. Echols' and Wharton's brigades hurried past us; this time there was not much bantering between us. "Forward!" was the word once more, and turning the point in the road, Newmarket was in full view and the whole position was displayed. . . .

It was Sunday morning at eleven o'clock. In a picturesque little Lutheran churchyard, under the very shadow of the village spire and among the white tombstones, a six-gun battery was posted in rear of the infantry lines of the enemy. Firing over the heads of their own troops, that battery opened upon us the moment we came in sight.

Away off to the right, in the Luray Gap, we could see our signal corps telegraphing the position and numbers of the enemy. Our cavalry was galloping to the cover of the creek to attempt to turn the enemy's left flank. Echols' brigade, moving from the pike at a double-quick by the right, went into line of battle across the meadow, its left resting on the pike. Simultaneously its skirmishers were thrown forward at a run and engaged the enemy. Out of the orchards and on the meadows, puff after puff of blue smoke rose as the sharp-shooters advanced, the pop, pop, pop of their rifles ringing forth excitingly. Thundering down the pike came McLaughlin with his artillery. Wheeling out upon the meadows, he swung into battery, action left, and let fly with all his guns.

The cadet section of artillery pressed down the pike a little farther, turned to the left, toiled up the slope in front of us, and, going into position, delivered a plunging fire in reply to the Federal battery in the graveyard. We counted it a good omen when, at the first discharge of our little guns, a beautiful blue-white wreath of smoke shot upward and hovered over them. We had their range beautifully. Every shell hit some obstruction and exploded in the streets or on the hillsides. Every man in our army was in sight. Every position of the enemy was plainly visible. His numbers were uncomfortably large, for, notwithstanding his line of battle, already formed, seemed equal to our own, the pike beyond the town was still filled with his infantry. . . .

The command was given to strip for action. Knapsacks, blankets — everything but guns, canteens, and cartridge boxes was thrown upon the ground. Our boys were silent then. Every lip was tight drawn; every cheek was pale, but not with fear. With a peculiar, nervous jerk, we pulled our cartridge boxes round to the front, laid back the flaps, and tightened belts. Whistling rifle shells screamed over us as, tipping the hill crest in our front, they bounded past. To our right, across the pike, Patton's brigade was lying down abreast of us.

"At-ten-*tion-n-n!* Battalion forward! Guide center-r-r!" shouted Shipp, and up the slope we started. From the left of the line, Sergeant Major Woodbridge ran out and posted himself forty paces in advance of the colors as directing guide, as if we had been upon the drill ground. That boy would have remained there, had not Shipp ordered him back to his post; for this was no dress parade. Brave Evans, standing six feet two, shook out the colors that for days had hung limp and bedraggled about the staff, and every cadet leaped forward, dressing to the ensign, elate and thrilling with the consciousness that this was war.

Moving up to the hill crest in our front, we were abreast of our smoking battery and uncovered to the range of the enemy's guns. We were pressing toward him at arms port, moving with the light tripping gait of the French infantry. The enemy's veteran artillery soon obtained our range and began to drop his shells under our very noses along the slope. Echols' brigade rose up and was charging on our right with the well-known rebel yell.

Down the green slope we went, answering the wild cry of our comrades as their muskets rattled out in opening volleys. "Double time!" shouted Shipp, and we broke into a long trot. In another moment, a pelting rain of lead would fall upon us from the blue line in our front.

Then came a sound more stunning than thunder. It burst directly in my face; lightnings leaped, fire flashed, the earth rocked, the sky whirled round. I stumbled, my gun pitched forward, and I fell upon my knees. Sergeant Cabell looked back at me pityingly and called out "Close up, men!" as he passed on. I knew no more.

When consciousness returned, the rain was falling in torrents. I was lying upon the ground, which all about was torn and plowed with shell, and they were still screeching in the air and bounding on the earth. Poor little Captain Hill, the tactical officer of C Company, was lying near me bathed in blood, with a frightful gash over the temple, and was gasping like a dying fish. Cadets Reed, Merritt, and another whose name I forget were near at hand, badly shot. The battalion was three hundred yards in advance of us, clouded in low-lying smoke and hotly engaged. They had crossed the lane which the enemy had held, and the Federal battery in the graveyard had fallen back to the high ground beyond. "How came they there," I thought, "and why am I here?" Then I found I was bleeding from a long and ugly gash in the head. That rifle shell, bursting in our faces, had brought down five of us. "Hurrah," I thought, "youth's dream is realized at last! I've got a wound and am not dead yet."

Another moment found me on my feet, trudging along to the hospital, almost whistling at thought that the next mail would carry the news to the folks at home with a taunting suggestion that, after all the pains they had taken, they had been unable to keep me out of my share in the fun. From this time forth, I may speak of the gallant behavior of the cadets without the imputation of vanity, for I was no longer a participant in their glory. . . .

We had won a victory — not a Manassas or an Appomattox, but, for all that, a right comforting bit of news went up the pike that night to General Lee, whose thoughts, doubtless, from where he lay locked in the death grapple with Grant in the Wilderness, turned wearily and anxiously toward this attempted flank movement in the valley.

A week after the battle of Newmarket, the cadet corps, garlanded, cheered by ten thousand throats, intoxicated with praise unstinted, wheeled proudly around the Washington monument at Richmond to pass in review before the President of the Confederate States, to hear a speech of commendation from his lips, and to receive a stand of colors from the Governor of Virginia.

JOHN S. WISE, The End of an Era

177. General Sherman Marches from Atlanta to the Sea

When in the spring of 1864 Grant went east to take command of all the Union armies, he left William Tecumseh Sherman in charge in the West. The plan of campaign that summer called for an attack in the East upon Lee's forces in front of Richmond; and an attack in the West upon General Johnston's forces in front of Atlanta. Sherman, with about 100,000 men at his back, commenced operations on May 5th. On September 2nd he captured Atlanta. Six weeks later he set out, with some 62,000 men, to march from Atlanta through the heart of Georgia to Savannah. Living on the country as he went, and destroying munitions, public buildings, and railroads, he made the capture of Savannah a Christmas present to the nation.

ABOUT 7 A.M. of November 16th [1864] we rode out of Atlanta by the Decatur road, filled by the marching troops and wagons of the Fourteenth Corps; and reaching the hill, just outside of the old rebel works, we naturally paused to look back upon the scenes of our past battles. We stood upon the very ground whereon was fought the bloody battle of July 22d and could see the copse of wood where McPherson fell. Behind us lay Atlanta, smoldering and in ruins, the black smoke rising high in air and hanging like a pall over the ruined city. Away off in the distance, on the McDonough road, was the rear of Howard's column, the gun barrels glistening in the sun, the white-topped wagons stretching away to the south, and right before us the Fourteenth Corps, marching steadily and rapidly with a cheery look and swinging pace that made light of the thousand miles that lay between us and Richmond. Some band by accident struck up the anthem of "John Brown's soul goes marching on"; the men caught up the strain, and never before or since have I heard the chorus of "Glory, glory, hallelujah!" done with more spirit or in better harmony of time and place.

Then we turned our horses' heads to the east; Atlanta was soon lost behind the screen of trees and became a thing of the past. Around it clings many a thought of desperate battle, of hope and fear, that now seem like the memory of a dream; and I have never seen the place since. The day was extremely beautiful, clear sunlight, with bracing air, and an unusual feeling of exhilaration seemed to pervade all minds — a feeling of something to come, vague and undefined, still full of venture and intense interest. Even the common soldiers caught the inspiration, and many a group called out to me as I worked my way past them, "Uncle Billy, I guess Grant is waiting for us at Richmond!" Indeed, the general sentiment was that we were marching for Richmond and that there we should end the war, but how and when they seemed to care not; nor did they measure the distance or count the cost in life or bother their brains about the great rivers to be crossed and the food, required for man and beast, that had to be gathered by the way. There was a devil-may-care feeling pervading officers and men that made me feel the full load of responsibility, for success would be accepted as a matter of course, whereas should we fail, this march would be adjudged the wild adventure of a crazy fool.

I had no purpose to march direct for Richmond by way of Augusta and Charlotte but always designed to reach the seacoast first at Savannah or Port Royal, South Carolina, and even kept in mind the alternative of Pensacola.

The first night out we camped by the roadside near Lithonia. Stone Mountain, a mass of granite, was in plain view, cut out in clear outline against the blue sky; the whole horizon was lurid with the bonfires of rail ties, and groups of men all night were carrying the heated rails to the nearest trees and bending them around the trunks. Colonel Poe had provided tools for ripping up the rails and twisting them when hot, but the best and easiest way is . . . heating the middle of the iron rails on bonfires made of the crossties and then winding them around a telegraph pole or the trunk of some convenient sapling. I attached much importance to this destruction of the railroad, gave it my personal attention, and made reiterated orders to others on the subject.

The next day we passed through the handsome town of Covington, the soldiers closing up their ranks, the color-bearers unfurling their flags, and the band striking up patriotic airs. The white people came out of their houses to behold the sight, spite of their deep hatred of the invaders, and the Negroes were simply frantic with joy. Whenever they heard my name, they clustered about my horse, shouted and prayed in their peculiar style, which had a natural eloquence that would have moved a stone. I have witnessed hundreds, if not thousands, of such scenes and can now see a poor girl, in the very ecstasy of the Methodist "shout," hugging the banner of one of the regiments and jumping up to the "feet of Jesus."

I remember, when riding around by a bystreet in Covington to avoid the crowd that followed the marching column, that some one brought me an invitation to dine with a sister of Samuel Anderson, who was a cadet at West Point with me; but the messenger reached me after we had passed the main part of the town. I asked to be excused and rode on to a place designated for camp, at the crossing of the Ulcofauhachee River, about four miles to the east of the town. Here we made our bivouac, and I walked up to a plantation house close by, where were assembled many Negroes, among them an old gray-haired man, of as fine a head as I ever saw. I asked him if he understood about the war and its progress. He said he did; that he had been looking for the "angel of the Lord" ever since he was knee-high, and though we professed to be fighting for the Union, he supposed that slavery was the cause and that our success was to be his freedom. I asked him if all the Negro slaves comprehended this fact, and he said they surely did. I then explained to him that we wanted the slaves to remain where they were and not to load us down with useless mouths, which would eat up the food needed for our fighting men, that our success was their assured freedom, that we could receive a few of their young, hearty men as pioneers, but that if they followed us in swarms of old and young, feeble and helpless, it would simply load us down and cripple us in our great task. I think Major Henry Hitchcock was with me on that occasion and made a note of the conversation, and I believe that old man spread this message to the slaves, which was carried from mouth to mouth to the very end of our journey, and that it in part saved us from the great danger we incurred of swelling our numbers so that famine would have attended our progress.

It was at this very plantation that a soldier passed me with a ham on his musket, a jug of sorghum molasses under his arm, and a big piece of honey in his hand, from which he was eating, and catching my eye, he remarked *sotto voce* and carelessly to a comrade, "Forage liberally on the country," quoting from my general orders. On this occasion, as on many others that fell under my personal observation, I reproved the man, explained that foraging must be limited to the regular parties properly detailed and that all provisions thus obtained must be delivered to the regular commissaries to be fairly distributed to the men who kept their ranks.

From Covington the Fourteenth Corps [Davis'], with which I was traveling, turned to the right for Milledgeville via Shady Dale. General Slocum was ahead at Madison with the Twentieth Corps, having torn up the railroad as far as that place, and thence had sent Geary's division on to the Oconee to burn the bridges across that stream when this corps turned south by Eatonton for Milledgeville, the common objective for the first stage of the march. We found abundance of corn, molasses, meal, bacon, and sweet potatoes. We also took a good many cows and oxen and a large number of mules. In all these the country was quite rich, never before having been visited by a hostile army; the recent crop had been excellent, had been just gathered and laid by for the winter. As a rule, we destroyed none but kept our wagons full and fed our teams bountifully.

The skill and success of the men in collecting forage was one of the features of this march. Each brigade commander had authority to detail a company of foragers, usually about fifty men, with one or two commissioned officers selected for their boldness and enterprise. This party would be dispatched before daylight with a knowledge of the intended day's march and camp, would proceed on foot five or six miles from the route traveled by their brigade, and then visit every plantation and farm within range. They would usually procure a wagon or family carriage, load it with bacon, cornmeal, turkeys, chickens, ducks, and everything that could be used as food or forage, and would then regain the main road, usually in advance of their train. When this came up, they would deliver to the brigade commissary the supplies thus gathered by the way. Often would I pass these foraging parties at the roadside, waiting for their wagons to come up, and was amused at their strange collections — mules, horses, even cattle, packed with old saddles and loaded with hams, bacon, bags of cornmeal, and poultry of every character and description. Although this foraging was attended with great danger and hard work, there seemed to be a charm about it that attracted the soldiers, and it was a privilege to be detailed on such a party. Daily they returned mounted on all sorts of beasts which were at once taken from them and appropriated to the general use, but the next day they would start out again on foot, only to repeat the experience of the day before. No doubt, many acts of pillage, robbery, and violence were committed by these parties of foragers, usually called bummers; for I have since heard of jewelry taken from women and the plunder of articles that never reached the commissary; but these acts were exceptional and incidental. I never heard of any cases of murder or rape, and no army could have carried along sufficient food and forage for a march of three hundred miles, so that foraging in some shape was necessary. The country was sparsely settled, with no magistrates or civil authorities who could respond to requisitions, as is done in all the wars of Europe, so that this system of foraging was simply indispensable to our success. By it our men were well supplied with all the essentials of life and health, while the wagons retained enough in case of unexpected delay, and our animals were well fed. Indeed, when we reached Savannah, the trains were pronounced by experts to be the finest in flesh and appearance ever seen with any army.

The Memoirs of General Sherman

178. Eliza Andrews Comes Home to the "Burnt Country"

Sherman believed that the quickest way to end the war was to bring its horrors home to the civilian population of the South by the wholesale destruction of property. His discipline was not sufficiently strict, and a great deal of wanton pillage accompanied his systematic devastation. The consequence was that he left destitution and famine in his wake.

D ECEMBER 24, 1864. — About three miles from Sparta we struck the "burnt country," as it is well named by the natives, and then I could better understand the wrath and desperation of these poor people. I almost felt as if I should like to hang a Yankee myself. There was hardly a fence left standing all the way from Sparta to Gordon. The fields were trampled down and the road was lined with carcasses of horses, hogs, and cattle that the invaders, unable either to consume or to carry away with them, had wantonly shot down, to starve out the people and prevent them from making their crops. The stench in some places was unbearable; every few hundred yards we had to hold our noses or stop them with the cologne Mrs. Elzey had given us, and it proved a great boon. The dwellings that were standing all showed signs of pillage, and on every plantation we saw the charred remains of the ginhouse and packing screw, while here and there lone chimney stacks, "Sherman's sentinels," told of homes laid in ashes. The infamous wretches! I couldn't wonder now that these poor people should want to put a rope round the neck of every red-handed "devil of them" they could lay their hands on. Hayricks and fodder stacks were demolished, corncribs were empty, and every bale of cotton that could be found was burnt by the savages. I saw no grain of any sort except little patches they had spilled when feeding their horses and which there was not even a chicken left in the country to eat. A bag of oats might have lain anywhere along the road without danger from the beasts of the field, though I cannot say it would have been safe from the assaults of hungry man. Crowds of soldiers were tramping over the road in both directions; it was like traveling through the streets of a populous town all day. They were mostly on foot, and I saw numbers seated on the roadside greedily eating raw turnips, meat skins, parched corn — anything they could find, even picking up the loose grains that Sherman's horses had left. I felt tempted to stop and empty the contents of our provision baskets into their laps, but the dreadful accounts that were given of the state of the country before us made prudence get the better of our generosity.

Before crossing the Oconee at Milledgeville we ascended an immense hill, from which there was a fine view of the town, with

Governor Brown's fortifications in the foreground and the river rolling at our feet. The Yankees had burnt the bridge; so we had to cross on a ferry. There was a long train of vehicles ahead of us, and it was nearly an hour before our turn came; so we had ample time to look about us. On our left was a field where thirty thousand Yankees had camped hardly three weeks before. It was strewn with the debris they had left behind, and the poor people of the neighborhood were wandering over it, seeking for anything they could find to eat, even picking up grains of corn that were scattered around where the Yankees had fed their horses. We were told that a great many valuables were found there at first, plunder that the invaders had left behind, but the place had been picked over so often by this time that little now remained except tufts of loose cotton, piles of half-rotted grain, and the carcasses of slaughtered animals, which raised a horrible stench. Some men were plowing in one part of the field, making ready for next year's crop.

ELIZA FRANCES ANDREWS, The War-Time Journal of a Georgia Girl

179. Lee Stops the Federals at the Gates of Richmond

In June, 1864, Grant threw his army across to the south side of the James River and moved on Petersburg, which lies almost directly south of Richmond. Stopped there by the heroic defense of Beauregard, Grant attempted to blast his way through the Confederate lines by exploding a mine, but the "Battle of the Crater" ended with the Confederates in possession of the field. Undiscouraged Grant attempted a lightning thrust on the weak defences of Richmond, north of the James. Had he broken through here, Richmond might have fallen in the summer of '64 instead of April '65, but the hot resistance of the Southerners once again balked him. The battles of the 14th to 18th of August here described were but minor engagements, but were as bitterly fought as any of the major engagements of the war.

Headquarters, Field's Division, Petersburg, Va., August 26, 1864. — My dear mother: Some three weeks have flown by since

I wrote to you from the north side of the James River, whither this division had been sent at the time of Grant's grand subterranean operation before Petersburg, the strategy of which was characterized by the fiendish ingenuity of Yankee warfare; but fortunately the execution was not on a par with the conception of the scheme, and the engineer was hoisted with his own petard. As I told you from my headquarters near Chapin's Bluff, we fully expected to pitch into the Yankees immediately on arriving on the north side of the river; but when our division had got into position the enemy had disappeared from our front. As far as the fighting was concerned, we had a little respite, but the staff did not profit much by it, for General Field having been placed ad interim in command of that division of the Richmond defenses, our duties became very onerous; but we were to a certain extent compensated by the importance it gave us, for we literally became monarchs of all we surveyed.

This comparative repose was, however, of short duration. Our scouts, a few days after, brought us the intelligence that the enemy had thrown a pontoon bridge across the river and that a large force was moving across it. We had but few troops with us, but preparations were made for a resolute defense of the line committed to our care. On Sunday they drove our skirmishers in, and in the afternoon they attempted to carry a portion of our intrenchments. For that purpose they hurled against us two divisions of their Second Corps, which rushed toward our position with yells, banners flying and bands playing. When they advanced to within about seven hundred yards of our line two twelve-pounders loaded with canister blazed away at them. Our artillery is not considered by any means the most efficient branch of our service and of late has been rather sneered at in this army, but on this occasion it did terrible execution. The Yanks advanced in four lines of battle, and a magnificent spectacle it was to witness that mighty host bearing down upon our thinly-manned breastworks. Notwithstanding my emotion, I could not refrain from admiring the sight. Our fire made wide breaches in their ranks, and after the third discharge the whole line wavered and fluttered like a flag in the wind; another shell exploding in their midst, they broke and fled in every direction without retaining a shadow of their former organization. In their frantic haste to get out of range of our murderous shots they threw away guns, equipment, and all their warlike paraphernalia. Deserters told us that they lost very heavily in that abortive charge. They again renewed the attack, but with less vigor, on our left, and were driven back with great loss by our dismounted cavalry. This was the last of that day's fighting — with the shades of night there came a cessation of hostilities.

In the morning of Tuesday the Yankees attacked us in heavy force, but we repulsed them very handsomely. Finding that these repeated assaults on that part of the line did not pay, General Hancock felt for a more vulnerable point, which he discovered on our left. After riding about ever since dawn, the general and his staff halted in a field in the rear of Wright's brigade of A. P. Hill's corps. The day was a sultry one, and the heat, superadded to other exertions, made us so weary that we got off our horses and lay down for a few moments on the grass. We had not been there many seconds when we were aroused by a terrific cannonade followed by heavy volleys of musketry. We mounted horses in a trice; presently squads of frightened men came from the front in anything but a leisurely manner. They informed us that the whole Yankee army had charged them and that they had been obliged to give way. The firing increased; the air was alive with Minié balls; the ground was torn up by shells and cannonballs, and in a few minutes the whole of Wright's brigade was stampeding toward us. We strove to rally them by entreaties and by menaces, and with pistols drawn we threatened to shoot them if they did not go back, but it was of no avail; you might as well try to argue with a flock of affrighted sheep as with a crowd of panic-stricken soldiers. Up to this time we cannot account for this stampede. The attack, it was true, was sudden and unexpected and the force of the enemy enormous; but the men who were now flying before the Yankees had always beaten them and had invariably borne themselves on every battlefield with distinguished bravery. We are therefore much puzzled to find out what caused them to disgrace the name of their brigade in that manner. My poor comrade, Captain Mason, was shot through the body during our fruitless efforts to rally the men; he fell into the hands of the enemy. We have since heard that he is not likely to live, although General Hancock, who was an old friend and classmate of General Field at West Point, promises to have him well attended to. The General, finding that nothing can be got out of these men, decided to fall back, for the Federals were swooping down upon us in overwhelming numbers; it seemed as though forty thousand men would be an underestimate of the force. I was sent by him for reinforcements. I had orders to bring up without delay two brigades of our own division, viz. Laws's Alabama and Binning's Georgians. They came up at a double-quick amid a very galling fire; they were formed right under the guns of the enemy, and then they rushed in with a deafening war-whoop. It was really splendid to witness the dash of these gallant fellows. I was so carried away with enthusiasm that I cantered alongside of them, but, alas! I did not accompany them during the whole of their triumphant advance, for my faithful charger, poor Palmetto, fell under me, pierced in the left hip by a Minié ball. I was a little stunned by the fall, and when I managed to extricate myself from under him our brave boys had beaten back the foe and recaptured the position which they had taken from us. I am happy to say that our loss was relatively small, whilst that of the enemy must have been very heavy — the battlefield was literally blue with their dead and wounded; we, moreover, captured seven hundred prisoners. The fight was not a long one, not having lasted over an hour and a half, but old veterans tell me that for the time it lasted the battle of Darbytown was one of the hottest affairs they had ever been in. The shelling was positively infernal; all the woods at the rear of the battlefield were torn and chopped to pieces by the enemy's artillery; it is a wonder that any one should have survived such a tempest of shot and shell, but our brave soldiers did not mind it any more than if it had been a summer shower. I cannot say that I like these Yankee shells, but I have got used to them, for since I joined the army I have been plentifully regaled with them. But what I strongly object to are the Minié balls. Some buzz like hornets, others mew like cats, when they pass you; all these sounds indicate a great proximity to your knowledge-box, and if I was not afraid of being afraid I think I would skedaddle like Wright's men. On the whole, notwithstanding the misbehavior of that brigade of Hill's corps, our achievement was a very brilliant one; for with a handful of men, say seven thousand at the outside, we drove back three of the enemy's largest corps; and as usual our division won for itself and its commander golden opinions. General Lee, toward the close of the fight, rode up and congratulated the general on the able manner in which he had handled his troops. At one time it was touch and go, and it required great coolness and skill on the part of our general to parry the attempts of the Yankees to turn our flanks; had they succeeded in accomplishing that, the consequences might have been very serious. The reverse was a very heavy one to the enemy; by sending over the best troops they evidently counted on a success. We had several small artillery and picket engagements during the rest of the week, but finally they sloped off without trumpet or drum, and on Sunday morning Hancock and Company had vamosed. Desertions from the Yankee army have been so frequent during this campaign that General Lee has desired to encourage them by circulating throughout Grant's army a paper in which kind treatment and protection is promised to those soldiers who come over to us voluntarily. This has produced the desired effect, for deserters flock into our lines at a monstrous rate, and the cry is "still they come."

Letters of a Confederate Officer [Richard W. Corbin]

180. General Lee Surrenders at Appomattox

By March, 1865, the Confederate forces under Lee in front of Petersburg and Richmond were reduced to about 50,000 men, while Grant had 124,000, far better fed and equipped. On April 2, by a series of fierce attacks, Grant finally broke the Confederate lines before Petersburg. That night Lee, abandoning the capital, began to march his army toward Danville and the mountainous country of western Virginia. But Sheridan cut off his retreat and Grant brought him to bay at Appomattox. The story of the surrender is here told by Grant himself.

WHEN the white flag was put out by Lee I was moving toward Appomattox Courthouse and consequently could not be communicated with immediately and be informed of what Lee had done. Lee, therefore, sent a flag to the rear to advise Meade and one to the front to Sheridan, saying that he had sent a message to me for the purpose of having a meeting to consult about the surrender of his army, and asked for a suspension of hostilities until I could be communicated with. As they had heard nothing of this until the fighting had got to be severe and all going against Lee, both of these commanders hesitated very considerably about suspending hostilities at all. They were afraid it was not in good faith, and we had the Army of Northern Virginia where it could not escape except by some deception. They, however, finally consented to a suspension of hostilities for two hours to give an opportunity of communicating with me in that time, if possible. It was found that, from the route I had taken, they would probably not be able to communicate with me and get an answer back within the time fixed unless the messenger should pass through the rebel lines.

Lee, therefore, sent an escort with the officer bearing this message through his lines to me.

April 9, 1865

GENERAL: I received your note of this morning on the picket line, whither I had come to meet you and ascertain definitely what terms were embraced in your proposal of yesterday with reference to the surrender of this army. I now request an interview in accordance with the offer contained in your letter of yesterday for that purpose.

R. E. LEE, General

Lieutenant General U. S. Grant,
    Commanding U.S. Armies

When the officer reached me I was still suffering with the sick headache, but the instant I saw the contents of the note I was cured. I wrote the following note in reply and hastened on:

April 9, 1865

GENERAL R. E. LEE,
    Commanding C.S. Armies:

Your note of this date is but this moment (11:50 A.M.) received, in consequence of my having passed from the Richmond and Lynchburg road to the Farmville and Lynchburg road. I am at this writing about four miles west of Walker's Church and will push forward to the front for the purpose of meeting you. Notice sent to me on this road where you wish the interview to take place will meet me.

U. S. GRANT
Lieutenant General

I was conducted at once to where Sheridan was located with his troops drawn up in line of battle facing the Confederate army near by. They were very much excited and expressed their view that this was all a ruse employed to enable the Confederates to get away. They said they believed that Johnston was marching up from North Carolina now, and Lee was moving to join him; and they would whip the rebels where they now were in five minutes if I would only let them go in. But I had no doubt about the good faith of Lee and pretty soon was conducted to where he was. I found him at the house of a Mr. McLean, at Appomattox Courthouse, with Colonel Marshall, one of his staff officers, awaiting my arrival. The head of his column was occupying a hill, on a portion of which was an apple orchard, beyond a little valley which separated it from that on the crest of which Sheridan's forces were drawn up in line of battle to the south. . . .

I had known General Lee in the old army and had served with him in the Mexican War but did not suppose, owing to the difference in our age and rank, that he would remember me, while I would more naturally remember him distinctly, because he was the chief of staff of General Scott in the Mexican War.

When I had left camp that morning I had not expected so soon the result that was then taking place and consequently was in rough garb. I was without a sword, as I usually was when on horseback on the field, and wore a soldier's blouse for a coat, with the shoulder straps of my rank to indicate to the army who I was. When I went into the house I found General Lee. We greeted each other and, after shaking hands, took our seats. I had my staff with me, a good portion of whom were in the room during the whole of the interview.

What General Lee's feelings were I do not know. As he was a man of much dignity, with an impassible face, it was impossible to say whether he felt inwardly glad that the end had finally come or felt sad over the result and was too manly to show it. Whatever his feelings, they were entirely concealed from my observation; but my own feelings, which had been quite jubilant on the receipt of his letter, were sad and depressed. I felt like anything rather than rejoicing at the downfall of a foe who had fought so long and valiantly and had suffered so much for a cause, though that cause was, I believe, one of the worst for which a people ever fought and one for which there was the least excuse. I do not question, however, the sincerity of the great mass of those who were opposed to us.

General Lee was dressed in a full uniform which was entirely new and was wearing a sword of considerable value, very likely the sword which had been presented by the State of Virginia; at all events, it was an entirely different sword from the one that would ordinarily be worn in the field. In my rough traveling suit, the uniform of a private with the straps of a lieutenant general, I must have contrasted very strangely with a man so handsomely dressed, six feet high, and of faultless form. But this was not a matter that I thought of until afterward.

We soon fell into a conversation about old army times. He remarked that he remembered me very well in the old army, and I told him that as a matter of course I remembered him perfectly, but from the difference in our rank and years (there being about sixteen years' difference in our ages), I had thought it very likely that I had not attracted his attention sufficiently to be remembered by him after such a long interval. Our conversation grew so pleasant that I almost forgot the object of our meeting. After the conversation had run on in this style for some time, General Lee called my attention to the object of our meeting and said that he had asked for this interview for the purpose of getting from me the terms I proposed to give his army. I said that I meant merely that his army should lay down their arms, not to take them up again during the continuance of the war unless duly and properly exchanged. He said that he had so understood my letter.

Then we gradually fell off again into conversation about matters foreign to the subject which had brought us together. This continued for some little time, when General Lee again interrupted the course of the conversation by suggesting that the terms I proposed to give his army ought to be written out. I called to General Parker, secretary on my staff, for writing materials, and commenced writing out the following terms:

Appomattox Courthouse, Va.
April 9th, 1865

GENERAL R. E. LEE,
    Comd'g C.S.A.

GENERAL: In accordance with the substance of my letter to you of the 8th instant, I propose to receive the surrender of the Army of Northern Virginia on the following terms, to wit: Rolls of all the officers and men to be made in duplicate. One copy to be given to an officer designated by me, the other to be retained by such officer or officers as you may designate. The officers to give their individual paroles not to take up arms against the Government of the United States until properly exchanged, and each company or regimental commander sign a like parole for the men of their commands. The arms, artillery, and public property to be parked and stacked and turned over to the officer appointed by me to receive them. This will not embrace the sidearms of the officers nor their private horses or baggage. This done, each officer and man will be allowed to return to their homes, not to be disturbed by United States authority so long as they observe their paroles and the laws in force where they may reside.

Very respectfully,
U. S. GRANT
Lieutenant General

When I put my pen to the paper I did not know the first word that I should make use of in writing the terms. I only knew what was in my mind, and I wished to express it clearly, so that there could be no mistaking it. As I wrote on, the thought occurred to me that the officers had their own private horses and effects, which were important to them but of no value to us; also that it would be an unnecessary humiliation to call upon them to deliver their sidearms.

No conversation, not one word, passed between General Lee and myself, either about private property, sidearms, or kindred subjects. He appeared to have no objections to the terms first proposed, or if he had a point to make against them he wished to wait until they were in writing to make it. When he read over that part of the terms about sidearms, horses, and private property of the officers, he remarked, with some feeling, I thought, that this would have a happy effect upon his army.

Then, after a little further conversation, General Lee remarked to me again that their army was organized a little differently from the army of the United States (still maintaining by implication that we were two countries), that in their army the cavalrymen and artillerists owned their own horses; and he asked if he was to understand that the men who so owned their horses were to be permitted to retain them. I told him that as the terms were written they would not, that only the officers were permitted to take their private property. He then, after reading over the terms a second time, remarked that that was clear.

I then said to him that I thought this would be about the last battle of the war — I sincerely hoped so; and I said further I took it that most of the men in the ranks were small farmers. The whole country had been so raided by the two armies that it was doubtful whether they would be able to put in a crop to carry themselves and their families through the next winter without the aid of the horses they were then riding. The United States did not want them, and I would, therefore, instruct the officers I left behind to receive the paroles of his troops to let every man in the Confederate army who claimed to own a horse or mule take the animal to his home. Lee remarked again that this would have a happy effect.

He then sat down and wrote out the following letter:

> Headquarters, Army of Northern Virginia
> April 9, 1865
>
> GENERAL: I received your letter of this date containing the terms of the surrender of the Army of Northern Virginia as proposed by you. As they are substantially the same as those expressed in your letter of the 8th instant, they are accepted. I will proceed to designate the proper officers to carry the stipulations into effect.
>
> R. E. LEE, General
>
> Lieutenant General U. S. Grant

While duplicates of the two letters were being made, the Union generals present were severally presented to General Lee.

The much-talked-of surrendering of Lee's sword and my handing it back, this and much more that has been said about it is the purest romance. The word sword or sidearms was not mentioned by either of us until I wrote it in the terms. There was no premeditation, and it did not occur to me until the moment I wrote it down. If I had happened to omit it and General Lee had called my attention to it, I should have put it in the terms precisely as I acceded to the provision about the soldiers retaining their horses.

General Lee, after all was completed and before taking his leave, remarked that his army was in a very bad condition for want of food and that they were without forage, that his men had been living for some days on parched corn exclusively, and that he would have to ask me for rations and forage. I told him "certainly" and asked for how many men he wanted rations. His answer was about twenty-five thousand, and I authorized him to send his own commissary and quartermaster to Appomattox station, two or three miles away, where he could have, out of the trains we had stopped, all the provisions wanted. As for forage, we had ourselves depended almost entirely upon the country for that.

Personal Memoirs of U. S. Grant

181. The Stars and Stripes Are Raised over Fort Sumter

Midway in the Civil War the Confederate guns at Fort Sumter were silenced by a Union fleet under Admiral John A. B. Dahlgren; and thereafter Union warships kept the harbor of Charleston tightly sealed. When the Confederate forces evacuated Charleston in February, 1865, and Union troops entered, the first thought of the captors was to hold a ceremonial reraising of the flag over the fort. The event was set for April 14th, the anniversary of the surrender four years before, and the flag was hoisted by Robert Anderson, who was in command in 1861. This moving scene is described by Mary Cadwalader Jones, daughter of a well-known Philadelphia attorney, and granddaughter of Horace Binney.

ON APRIL 18, 1861, Simon Cameron, President Lincoln's first Secretary of War, received a dispatch from the steamer *Baltic* off Sandy Hook:

"Having defended Fort Sumter for thirty-four hours, until the quarters were entirely burned, the main gates destroyed by fire, the gorge walls seriously impaired, the magazine surrounded by flames and its door closed from the effects of the heat, four barrels and three cartridges of powder only being available and no provisions remaining but pork, I accepted terms of evacuation offered by General Beauregard (being the same offered by him on the 11th instant, prior to the commencement of hostilities) and marched out of the fort on Sunday afternoon, the 14th instant, with colors flying and drums beating, bringing away company and private property, and saluting my flag with fifty guns.

"ROBERT ANDERSON, Major First Artillery"

Four years later, on March 18, 1865, Edwin M. Stanton, Lincoln's last Secretary of War, wrote to brevet Major General Robert Anderson:

"I have the pleasure of communicating to you the inclosed order of the President, directing the flag of the United States to be raised and planted upon the ruins of Fort Sumter by your hands, on the 14th day of April next, the fourth anniversary of the evacuation of that post by the United States forces under your command."

It was my good fortune to be there. . . .

Sailing from New York in the end of February, 1865, we landed at Hilton Head and reached Charleston by way of Savannah in the last days of March or beginning of April. To one who had never seen the actual effects of war, the city was a melancholy spectacle. Our bombardment had left its marks everywhere, even on church steeples and on gravestones in the cemeteries. One heavy Parrott gun, called by our men the "Swamp Angel" which had been planted in a marsh five miles inland, did a great deal of damage before she burst, and was looked upon by the Charlestonians with a mixture of wrath and amazement.

Every one who could possibly get away had left the city before our troops entered it; the streets were deserted except for our sentries, strolling soldiers and sailors, and bands of Negroes who had floated down on flatboats from distant plantations, many of them never having seen a large town before in their lives. Almost without exception the house and body servants had stuck to their masters and mistresses; these were field hands, and they gaped and laughed like careless children. As their new freedom did not feed them, they lived chiefly on the good-natured charity of our troops and at night camped in the empty cotton warehouses, with the natural result of frequent fires.

Heavy cloth-of-gold roses hung over garden walls and on the porches of closely-shuttered houses; occasionally an old servant would creep furtively from a back door; but there was no sign of ordinary everyday life — the men were all at the war and the women and children either away or in hiding. It had been different in the less aristocratic Savannah, which the Federal troops had occupied since December; when I walked about there, always with an officer or an orderly, the girls would run up their high steps and turn their backs sharply on the hated blue uniform, but if I looked round quickly after I had gone a little farther I usually caught them gazing eagerly at the back of my frock. Fashions were four years old in the Confederacy; it was worth while to run the blockade for rifles or quinine, but not for furbelows. Charleston was, however, too proud and too sad to care about fashions.

The ceremony was to be at noon punctually; four or five thousand people wanted to go, and there was no regular communication between Sumter and the town. The big visiting steamship ferried her own passengers, and the boats belonging to the blockading squadron plied busily to and fro, as temporary landings and steps had been put up on all sides of the fort walls. The entire management was in the hands of the Navy, and everything went like clockwork.

The ceremony began with a short prayer by the old army chaplain who had prayed when the flag was hoisted over Fort Sumter on December 27, 1860. Next a Brooklyn clergymen read parts of several Psalms, expecting the company to read alternate verses, as in church; but that was not very effective, because if any copies were printed, there were not enough of them to go round. Then Sergeant Hart, who had held up the flag when its staff was shot through in the first attack, came forward quietly and drew the selfsame flag out of an ordinary leather mail bag. We all held our breath for a second, and then we gave a queer cry, between a cheer and a yell; nobody started and nobody led it; I never heard anything like it before or since, but I can hear it now. It stopped suddenly, for we saw that a couple of the sailors who had been in the first fight were fastening the flag to its new halyards with a little wreath of laurel on top. General Anderson stood up, bareheaded, took the halyards in his hands, and began to speak. At first I could not hear him, for his voice came thickly, but in a moment he said clearly, "I thank God that I have lived to see this day," and after a few more words he began to hoist the flag. It went up slowly and hung limp against the staff, a weatherbeaten, frayed, and shell-torn old flag, not fit for much more work, but when it had crept clear of the shelter of the walls a sudden breath of wind caught it, and it shook its folds and flew straight out above us, while every soldier and sailor instinctively saluted.

I don't know just what we did next, but I remember looking on either side of me and seeing my father's eyelids brimming over and that Admiral Dahlgren's lips were trembling. I think we stood up, somebody started "The Star-Spangled Banner," and we sang the first verse, which is all that most people know. But it did not make much difference, for a great gun was fired close to us from the fort itself, followed, in obedience to the President's order, "by a national salute from every fort and battery that fired upon Fort Sumter." The measured, solemn booming came from Fort Moultrie, from the batteries on Sullivan and Folly Islands, and from Fort Wagner . . . When the forts were done it was the turn of the fleet, and all our warships from the largest — which would look tiny today — down to the smallest monitor, fired and fired in regular order until the air was thick and black with smoke and one's ears ached with the overlapping vibrations.

MARY CADWALADER JONES, Lantern Slides

XXVI

Reconstruction

182. "Bury Contention with the War"

Paroled as a prisoner of war, General Lee returned to Richmond when hostilities ended. He had no home, for his old seat "Arlington" had been sold in 1863 for taxes. But he shortly accepted the presidency of Washington College (now Washington and Lee University) at Lexington, Virginia. There in the next five years he did his utmost to help the South recuperate economically and culturally from its exhausting ordeal, and to promote good will between the two sections.

I HAVE received your letter of [August 23, 1865] and in reply will state the course I have pursued under circumstances similar to your own and will leave you to judge of its propriety. Like yourself, I have since the cessation of hostilities advised all with whom I have conversed on the subject, who come within the terms of the President's proclamations, to take the oath of allegiance and accept in good faith the amnesty offered. But I have gone further and have recommended to those who were excluded from their benefits to make application, under the *proviso* of the proclamation of the 29th of May, to be embraced in its provisions. Both classes, in order to be restored to their former rights and privileges, were required to perform a certain act, and I do not see that an acknowledgment of fault is expressed in one more than the other. The war being at an end, the Southern states having laid down their arms, and the questions at issue between them and the Northern states having been decided, I believe it to be the duty of every one to unite in the restoration of the country and the re-establishment of peace and harmony. These considerations governed me in the counsels I gave to others and induced me on the 13th of June to make application to be included in the terms of the amnesty proclamation. I have not received an answer and cannot inform you what has been the decision of the President. But whatever that may be, I do not see how the course I have recommended and practised can prove detrimental to the former President of the Confederate States. It appears to me that the allayment of passion, the dissipation of prejudice, and the restoration of reason will alone enable the people of the country to acquire a true knowledge and form a correct judgment of the events of the past four years. It will, I think, be admitted that Mr. Davis has done nothing more than all the citizens of the Southern states and should not be held accountable for acts performed by them in the exercise of what had been considered by them unquestionable right. I have too exalted an opinion of the American people to believe that they will consent to injustice, and it is only necessary, in my opinion, that truth should be known for the rights of every one to be secured. I know of no surer way of eliciting the truth than by burying contention with the war. . . .

ROBERT E. LEE

J. WILLIAM JONES, Personal Reminiscences, Anecdotes, and Letters of General Robert E. Lee

183. Thomas Dabney Does the Family Wash

We have previously met Thomas Dabney, the great Mississippi planter, in the days of his affluence; here we see him in adversity. He might have escaped hardship by pleading bankruptcy and cheating his creditors, but he preferred to work with his own hands until he could pay off his debts.

HE WAS at Burleigh when he heard of General Lee's surrender. On the day that the news reached him he called his son Thomas to him, and they rode together to the field where the Negroes were at work. He informed them of the news that had reached him and that they were now free. His advice was that they should continue to work the crop as they had been doing. At the end of the year they should receive such compensation for their labor as he thought just.

From this time till January 1, 1866, no apparent change took place among the Burleigh Negroes. Those who worked in the fields went out as usual and cultivated and gathered in the crops. In the house they went about their customary duties. We expected them to go away or to demand wages or at least to give some sign that they knew they were free. But, except that they were very quiet and serious and more obedient and kind than they had ever been known to be for more than a few weeks at a time of sickness or other affliction, we saw no change in them.

At Christmas such compensation was made them for their services as seemed just. Afterward fixed wages were offered and accepted. Thomas called them up now and told them that as they no longer belonged to him they must discontinue calling him master.

"Yes, marster," "Yes, marster," was the answer to this. "They seem to bring in 'master' and say it oftener than they ever did," was his comment as he related the occurrence to his children. This was true. The name seemed to grow into a term of endearment. As time went on and under the changed order of things Negroes whom he had never known became tenants on his plantation, these new people called him master also. This was unprecedented in the South, I think. They were proud of living on his place on account of the good name that he had won for himself as a master. Not infrequently they were heard to express a regret that they had not belonged to him, when they saw the feeling that existed between himself and his former slaves. Sometimes he came to us with a puzzled look to ask who those Negroes were who had just called him "old master" and shaken hands with him.

"I cannot recall their faces," he would say; "surely I never owned them."

Finally the Negroes on the neighboring plantations and wherever he went came to call him "old master." They seemed to take pride in thus claiming a relationship with him, as it were; and he grew accustomed to the voluntary homage.

He had come home to a house denuded of nearly every article of furniture and to a plantation stripped of the means of cultivating any but a small proportion of it. A few mules and one cow comprised the stock. We had brought a few pieces of common furniture from Georgia, and a very few necessary articles were bought. In the course of time some homemade contrivances and comforts relieved the desolate appearance of the rooms, but no attempt was ever made to refurnish the house.

He owned nothing that could be turned into money without great sacrifice but five bales of cotton. There were yet two sons and two daughters to be educated. He decided to get a tutor for them and to receive several other pupils in his house in order to make up the salary. The household was put on an economical footing. The plantation Negroes were hired to work in the fields, and things seemed to promise more prosperous days. So the first year was passed. . . .

His chivalrous nature had always revolted from the sight of a woman doing hard work. He determined to spare his daughters all such labor as he could perform. General Sherman had said that he would like to bring every Southern woman to the washtub. "He shall never bring my daughters to the washtub," Thomas Dabney said. "I will do the washing myself." And he did it for two years. He was in his seventieth year when he began to do it.

This may give some idea of the labors, the privations, the hardships, of those terrible years. The most intimate friends of Thomas, nay, his own children who were not in the daily life at Burleigh, have never known the unprecedented self-denial, carried to the extent of acutest bodily sufferings, which he practised during this time. A curtain must be drawn over this part of the life of my lion-hearted father!

When he grew white and thin and his frightened daughters prepared a special dish for him, he refused to eat the delicacy. It would choke him, he said, to eat better food than they had, and he yielded only to their earnest solicitations. He would have died rather than ask for it. When the living was so coarse and so ill prepared that he could scarcely eat it, he never failed, on rising from the table, to say earnestly and reverently as he stood by his chair, "Thank the Lord for this much."

During a period of eighteen months no light in summer and none but a fire in winter, except in some case of necessity, was seen in the house. He was fourteen years in paying the debts that fell on him in his sixty-ninth year. He lived but three years after the last dollar was paid.

When he was seventy years of age he determined to learn to cultivate a garden. He had never performed manual labor, but he now applied himself to learn to hoe as a means of supplying his family with vegetables. With the labor of those aged hands he made a garden that was the best ordered that we had ever seen at Burleigh. He made his garden, as he did everything that he undertook, in the most painstaking manner, neglecting nothing that could insure success. The beds and rows and walks in that garden were models of exactness and neatness. It was a quarter of a mile from the house and from water, on the top of a long, high hill, and three-quarters of an acre in extent. In a time of drought or if he had set out anything that needed watering, he toiled up that long, precipitous hill with bucket after bucket of water. "I never look at the clouds" had been a saying of his in cultivating his plantation, and he carried it out now. That garden supplied the daily food of his family nearly all the year round. He planted vegetables in such quantities that it was impossible to consume all on the table, and he sold barrels of vegetables of different kinds in New Orleans.

Oftentimes he was so exhausted when he came in to dinner that he could not eat for a while. He had his old bright way of making every one take an interest in his pursuits — sympathy was as necessary and sweet to him as to a child — and he showed with pride what he had done by his personal labor in gardening and in washing. He placed the clothes on the line as carefully as if they were meant to hang there always, and they must be admired, too! He said, and truly, that he had never seen snowier ones.

Oh, thou heroic old man! Thou hast a right to thy pride in those exact strokes of the hoe and in those superb potatoes, "the best ever seen in the New Orleans market," and in those long lines of snowy drapery! But those to whom thou art showing these things are looking beyond them, at the man! They are gazing reverently and with scarce suppressed tears on the hands that have been in this world for threescore and ten years and are beginning today to support a houseful of children!

At the end of the hard day's work he would say sometimes: "General Sherman has not brought my daughters to the washtub. I could not stand that."

SUSAN DABNEY SMEDES, Memorials of a Southern Planter

184. Sidney Andrews Views the War-Torn South

Much of the South at the close of the war was a shocking scene of confusion and ruin. With buildings destroyed, railroads torn up, farms devastated, and bridges down, with no capital to repair their losses, and with their labor system suddenly revolutionized, the Southern people faced a gloomier future than any considerable body of Americans had ever before known. Sidney Andrews, who here gives us a glimpse of their losses, was a New England journalist who visited the Carolinas and Georgia in the autumn of 1865, and sent his impressions to Boston and Chicago newspapers.

I

CHARLESTON, S.C., September 4, 1865. — A city of ruins, of desolation, of vacant houses, of widowed women, of rotting wharves, of deserted warehouses, of weed-wild gardens, of miles of grass-grown streets, of acres of pitiful and voiceful barrenness — that is Charleston, wherein Rebellion loftily reared its head five years ago, on whose beautiful promenade the fairest of cultured women gathered with passionate hearts to applaud the assault of ten thousand upon the little garrison of Fort Sumter!

Who kindled the greedy fire of December, 1861, whereby a third of the city was destroyed? No one yet knows. "It was de good Jesus Hisself," said an old Negro to me when I asked him the question — "it was de Almighty Hand workin' fru de man's hand." Certain it is that the people were never able to discover the agency of the fire, though, so far as I can learn, no one doubts that it was the work of an incendiary, "some man," say the ex-Rebels, "who wanted to do you Federals a good turn."

We never again can have the Charleston of the decade previous to the war. The beauty and pride of the city are as dead as the glories of Athens. Five millions of dollars could not restore the ruin of these four past years, and that sum is so far beyond the command of the city as to seem the boundless measure of immeasurable wealth. Yet, after all, Charleston was Charleston because of the hearts of its people. St. Michael's Church, they held, was the center of the universe; and the aristocracy of the city were the very elect of God's children on earth. One marks now how few young men there are, how generally the young women are dressed in black. The flower of their proud aristocracy is buried on scores of battlefields. If it were possible to restore the broad acres of crumbling ruins to their foretime style and uses, there would even then be but the dead body of Charleston.

The Charleston of 1875 will doubtless be proud in wealth and intellect and rich in grace and culture. Let favoring years bring forward such fruitage! Yet the place has not in itself recuperative power for such a result. The material on which to build that fair structure does not here exist and, as I am told by dozens, cannot be found in the state. If Northern capital and Northern energy do not come here, the ruin, they say, must remain a ruin.

Business is reviving slowly, though perhaps the more surely. The resident merchants are mostly at the bottom of the ladder of prosperity. They have idled away the summer in vain regrets for vanished hopes, and most of them are only just now beginning to wake to the new life. Some have already been north for goods, but more are preparing to go, not heeding that, while they vacillate with laggard time, Northern men are springing in with hands swift to catch opportunity. It pains me to see the apathy and indifference that so generally prevail, but the worst feature of the situation is that so many young men are not only idle but give no promise of being otherwise in the immediate future.

Many of the stores were more or less injured by the shelling. A few of these have been already repaired and are now occupied, very likely by Northern men. A couple of dozen, great and small, are now in process of repair; and scores stand with closed shutters or gaping doors and windows. The doubt as to the title of property and the wise caution of the President in granting pardons unquestionably has something to do with the stagnation so painfully apparent, but very much of it is due to the hesitating shiftlessness of even the Southern merchant, who forever lets *I dare not* wait upon *I would*. Rents of eligible storerooms are at least from one-fourth to one-third higher than before the war, and resident business men say only Northern men who intend staying but a short time can afford to pay present prices. I'm sure I can't see how any one can afford to pay them, but I know the demand is greater than the supply.

I queried of the returning merchants on the steamship how they were received in the North. An Augusta man complained that he could get no credit and that there was a disposition to be grinding and exacting. One Charleston man said he asked for sixty days and got it without a word of objection. Another told me that he asked for four months, was given three, and treated like a gentleman everywhere.

It would seem that it is not clearly understood how thoroughly Sherman's army destroyed everything in its line of march — destroyed it without questioning who suffered by the action. That this wholesale destruction was often without orders and often against most positive orders does not change the fact of destruction. The rebel leaders were, too, in their way, even more wanton and just as thorough as our army in destroying property. They did not burn houses and barns and fences as we did, but during the last three months of the war they burned immense quantities of cotton and rosin.

The action of the two armies put it out of the power of men to pay their debts. The values and the bases of value were nearly all destroyed. Money lost about everything it had saved. Thousands of men who were honest in purpose have lost everything but honor. The cotton with which they meant to pay their debts has been burned, and they are without other means. What is the part of wisdom in respect to such men? It certainly cannot be to strip them of the last remnant. Many of them will pay in whole or in part if proper consideration be shown them. It is no question of favor to any one as a favor, but a pure question of business — how shall the commercial relations of the two sections be re-established? In determining it, the actual and exceptional condition of the state with respect to property should be constantly borne in mind.

The city is under thorough military rule, but the iron hand rests very lightly. Soldiers do police duty, and there is some nine-o'clock regulation; but so far as I can learn, anybody goes anywhere at all hours of the night without molestation. "There never was such good order here before," said an old colored man to me. The main street is swept twice a week, and all garbage is removed at sunrise. "If the Yankees was to stay here always and keep the city so clean, I don't reckon we'd have yellow jack here any more," was a remark I overheard on the street. "Now is de fust time sence I can 'mem'er when brack men was safe in de street af'er nightfall," stated the Negro tailor in whose shop I sat an hour yesterday.

On the surface Charleston is quiet and well behaved, and I do not doubt that the more intelligent citizens are wholly sincere in their expressions of a desire for peace and reunion. The city has been humbled as no other city has been, and I can't see how any man, after spending a few days here, can desire that it be further humiliated merely for revenge. Whether it has been humiliated enough for health is another thing. Said one of the Charlestonians on the boat: "You won't see the real sentiment of our people, for we are under military rule; we are whipped, and we are going to make the best of things; but we hate Massachusetts as much as we ever did." This idea of making the best of things is one I have heard from scores of persons. I find very few who hesitate to frankly own that the South has been beaten. "We made the best fight we could, but you were too strong for us, and now we are only anxious to get back into the old Union and live as happily as we can," said a large cotton factor. I find very few who make any special profession of Unionism, but they are almost unanimous in declaring that they have no desire but to live as good and quiet citizens under the laws.

For the first two months of our occupancy of the city scarcely a white woman but those of the poorer classes was seen on the street, and very few were even seen at the windows and doors of the residences. That order of things is now happily changed. There doesn't yet appear to be as much freedom of appearance as would be natural, but very many of what are called the first ladies are to be seen shopping in the morning and promenading in the evening. They, much more than the men, have contemptuous motions for the Negro soldiers; and scorn for Northern men is frequently apparent in the swing of their skirts when passing on the sidewalk.

One doesn't observe so much pleasantness and cheerfulness as would be agreeable, but the general demeanor is quite consonant with the general mourning costume. A stroller at sunset sees not a few pale and pensive-faced young women of exquisite beauty, and a rambler during the evening not infrequently hears a strain of touching melody from the darkened parlor of some roomy old mansion, with now and then one of the ringing, passionate airs with which the Southern heart has been fired during the war.

II

Atlanta, Ga., November 23, 1865. — Coming here has dispelled two illusions under which I rested: first, that Atlanta was a small place; and second, that it was wholly destroyed. It was a city of about fourteen thousand inhabitants two years ago, and it was not more than half burned last fall. The entire business portion, excepting the Masonic Hall building and one block of six stores and a hotel, was laid in ruins, and not a few of the larger residences in all parts of the city were also burned. But the City Hall and the Medical College, and all the churches, and many of the handsomer and more stylish private dwellings, and nearly all the houses of the middling and poorer classes, were spared; and on the first of last June there was ample shelter here for at least six or eight thousand persons. Of course, however, when the entire business portion of the place had disappeared, the city had been practically put out of the way for the time being, even if nothing be said of the fact that it was depopulated by military orders.

The marks of the conflict are everywhere strikingly apparent. The ruin is not so massive and impressive as that of Columbia and Charleston, but as far as it extends it is more complete and of less value. The city always had a mushroom character, and the fire king must have laughed in glee when it was given over into his keeping. There is yet abundant evidence of his energy, not so much in crumbling walls and solitary chimneys as in thousands of masses of brick and mortar, thousands of pieces of charred timber, thousands of half-burned boards, thousands of scraps of tin roofing, thousands of car and engine bolts and bars, thousands of ruined articles of hardware, thousands upon thousands of tons of debris of all sorts and shapes. Moreover, there are plenty of cannonballs and long shot lying about the streets, with not a few shell-struck houses in some sections; and from the courthouse square can be seen a dozen or more forts and many a hillside from which the timber was cut so that the enemy might not come upon the city unawares.

From all this ruin and devastation a new city is springing up with marvelous rapidity. The narrow and irregular and numerous streets are alive from morning till night with drays and carts and hand barrows and wagons, with hauling teams and shouting men, with loads of lumber and loads of brick and loads of sand, with piles of furniture and hundreds of packed boxes, with mortar makers and hod carriers, with carpenters and masons, with rubbish removers and housebuilders, with a never-ending throng of pushing and crowding and scrambling and eager and excited and enterprising men, all bent on building and trading and swift fortune-making.

Chicago in her busiest days could scarcely show such a sight as clamors for observation here. Every horse and mule and wagon is in active use. The four railroads centering here groan with the freight and passenger traffic and yet are unable to meet the demand of the nervous and palpitating city. Men rush about the streets with little regard for comfort or pleasure and yet find the days all too short and too few for the work in hand. The sound of the saw and plane and hammer rings out from daylight to dark, and yet master builders are worried with offered contracts which they cannot take. Rents are so high that they would seem fabulous on Lake Street, and yet there is the most urgent cry for storeroom and office room. Four thousand mechanics are at work, and yet five thousand more could get immediate employment if brick and lumber were to be had at any price. There are already over two hundred stores, so called, and yet every day brings some trader who is restless and fretful till he secures a place in which to display another stock of goods.

Where all this eagerness and excitement will end, no one seems to care to inquire. The one sole idea first in every man's mind is to make money. That this apparent prosperity is real, no outsider can believe. That business is planted on sure foundations, no merchant pretends. That there will come a pause and then a crash, a few prudent men prophesy.

Meantime Atlanta is doing more than Macon and Augusta combined. The railroad from here to Chattanooga clears over one hundred thousand dollars per month and could add fifty thousand more to that enormous sum if it had plenty of engines and rolling stock. The trade of the city is already thirty per cent greater than it was before the war, and it is limited only by the accommodations afforded and has even now spread its wings far out on streets heretofore sacred to the privacy of home.

III

Columbia, S. C., September 12, 1865. — Columbia is in the heart of Destruction. Being outside of it, you can only get in through one of the roads built by Ruin. Being in it, you can only get out over one of the roads walled by Desolation. You go north thirty-two miles and find the end of one railroad; southeast thirty miles and find the end of another; south forty-five miles and find the end of a third; southwest fifty miles and meet a fourth; and northwest twenty-nine miles and find the end of still another. Sherman came in here, the papers used to say, to break up the railroad system of the seaboard states of the Confederacy. He did his work so thoroughly that half a dozen years will nothing more than begin to repair the damage, even in this regard.

Certain bent rails are the first thing one sees to indicate the advent of his army. They are at Branchville. I looked at them with curious interest. "It passes my comprehension to tell what became of our railroads," said a traveling acquaintance; "one week we had passably good roads, on which we could reach almost any part of the state, and the next week they were all gone, — not simply broken up, but gone; some of the material was burned, I know, but miles and miles of iron have actually disappeared, gone out of existence." Branchville, as I have already said, was flanked, and the army did not take it in the line of march, but some of the boys paid it a visit.

At Orangeburg there is ample proof that the army passed that way. About one third of the town was burned. I found much dispute as to the origin of the fire; and while certain fellows of the baser sort loudly assert that it was the work of the Yankee, others of the better class express the belief that it originated with a resident who was angry at the Confederate officers. Thereabouts one finds plenty of railroad iron so bent and twisted that it can never again be used. The genius which our soldiers displayed in destroying railroads seems remarkable. How effectually they did it, when they undertook the work in earnest, no pen can make plain. "We could do something in that line, we thought," said an ex-Confederate captain, "but we were ashamed of ourselves when we saw how your men could do it."

We rode over the road where the army marched. Now and then we found solitary chimneys, but on the whole comparatively few houses were burned, and some of those were fired, it is believed, by persons from the Rebel army or from the neighboring locality. The fences did not escape so well, and most of the planters have had these to build during the summer. This was particularly the case near Columbia. Scarcely a tenth of that destroyed appears to have been rebuilt, and thousands of acres of land of much richness lie open as a common.

There is a great scarcity of stock of all kinds. What was left by the Rebel conscription officers was freely appropriated by Sherman's army, and the people really find considerable difficulty, not less in living than in traveling. Milk, formerly an article much in use, can only be had now in limited quantities; even at the hotels we have more meals without than with it. There are more mules than horses, apparently; and the animals whether mules or horses, are all in ill condition and give evidence of severe overwork.

Columbia was doubtless once the gem of the state. It is as regularly laid out as a checkerboard — the squares being of uniform length and breadth and the streets of uniform width. What with its broad streets, beautiful shade trees, handsome lawns, extensive gardens, luxuriant shrubbery, and wealth of flowers, I can easily see that it must have been a delightful place of residence. No South Carolinian with whom I have spoken hesitates an instant in declaring that it was the most beautiful city on the continent; and, as already mentioned, they charge its destruction directly to General Sherman.

It is now a wilderness of ruins. Its heart is but a mass of blackened chimneys and crumbling walls. Two thirds of the buildings in the place were burned, including, without exception, everything in the business portion. Not a store, office, or shop escaped; and for a distance of three fourths of a mile on each of twelve streets there was not a building left. . . .

Every public building was destroyed, except the new and unfinished Statehouse. This is situated on the summit of tableland whereon the city is built, and commands an extensive view of the surrounding country, and must have been the first building seen by the victorious and on-marching Union army. From the summit of the ridge, on the opposite side of the river, a mile and a half away, a few shells were thrown at it, apparently by way of reminder, three or four of which struck it, without doing any particular damage. With this exception, it was unharmed, though the workshops, in which were stored many of the architraves, caps, sills, etc., were burned — the fire, of course, destroying or seriously damaging their contents. The poverty of this people is so deep that there is no probability that it can be finished, according to the original design, during this generation at least.

The ruin here is neither half so eloquent nor touching as that at Charleston. This is but the work of flame, and might have mostly been brought about in time of peace. Those ghostly and crumbling walls and those long-deserted and grass-grown streets show the prostration of a community — such prostration as only war could bring.

SIDNEY ANDREWS, The South Since the War

185. Hard Times among the Planters

The defeat of the South meant the destruction of the plantation system and the impoverishment of the planter class. The want and distress that prevailed throughout the South in the summer and autumn of 1865 was very acute, and but for the spirit of mutual helpfulness and the work of the Freedmen's Bureau, it would have had tragic consequences.

WE DID anything and everything we could to make a living. Prominent citizens became piesellers. Colonel Cary, of General Magruder's staff, came home to find his family desperately poor, as were all respectable folks. He was a brave soldier, an able officer — before the war, principal of a male academy at Hampton. Now he did not know to what he could turn his hand for the support of himself and family. He walked around his place, came in, and said to his wife: "My dear, I have taken stock of our assets. You pride yourself on your apple pies. We have an apple tree and a cow. I will gather the apples and milk the cow, and you will make the pies, and I will go around and sell them."

Armed with pies, he met his aforetime antagonists at Camp Grant and conquered them quite. The pies were delicious; the seller was a soldier, an officer of distinction, in hard luck; and the men at Camp Grant were soldiers too. There was sharp demand and good price; only the élite — officers of rank — could afford to indulge in these confections. Well it was that Yankee mothers had cultivated in their sons an appetite for pies. One Savannah lady made thirty dollars selling pies to Sherman's soldiers; in Georgia's aristocratic "city by the sea" highbred dames stood at basement windows selling cakes and pies to whoever would buy.

Colonel Cary had thrifty rivals throughout Dixie. A once-rich planter near Columbia made a living by selling flowers; a Charleston aristocrat peddled tea by the pound and molasses by the quart to his former slaves. General Stephen Elliott sold fish and oysters which he caught with his own hands. His friend, Captain Stoney, did likewise. Gentlemen of position and formerly of wealth did not pause to consider whether they would be discredited by pursuing occupations quite as humble. Men of high attainments, without capital, without any basis upon which to make a new start in life except "grit," did whatever they could find to do and made merry over it.

For months after the surrender, Confederates were passing through the country to their homes, and hospitality was free to every ragged and footsore soldier; the poor best the larder of every mansion afforded was at the command of the grayjacket. How diffidently proud men would ask for bread, their empty pockets shaming them! When any man turned them off with cold words, it was not well for his neighbors to know; for so he was like to have no more respectable guests. The soldiers were good company, bringing news from far and wide. Most were cheerful, glad they were going home, undaunted by long tramps ahead. The soldier was used to hard marches. Now that his course was set toward where loved ones watched for his coming, life had its rosy outlook that turned to gray for some who reached the spot where home had stood to find only a bank of ashes. Reports of country through which they came were often summed up: "White folks in the fields, Negroes flocking to towns. Freedmen's Bureau offices everywhere thronged with blacks."

A man who belonged to the crippled squad, not one of whom had a full complement of arms and legs, told this story: As four of them were limping along near Lexington, they noticed a gray-headed white man in rough, mud-stained clothes turning furrows with a plow and behind him a white girl dropping corn. Taking him for a hired man, they hallooed: "Hello, there!" The man raised his head. "Say," they called, "can you tell us where we can get something to eat?" He waved them towards a house where a lady who was on the porch asked them to have a seat and wait while she had food cooked.

They had an idea that she prepared with her own hands the dinner to which they presently sat down, of hot hoecakes, buttermilk, and a little meat so smothered in lettuce leaves that it looked a great deal. When they had cleared up the table, she said: "I am having more bread cooked if you can wait a few minutes. I am sorry we have not more meat and milk. I know this has been a very light repast for hungry men, but we have entertained others this morning, and we have not much left. We hate to send our soldiers hungry from the door; they ought to have the best of everything when they have fought so long and bravely and suffered so much." The way she spoke made them proud of the arms and legs they didn't have.

Now that hunger was somewhat appeased, they began to note surroundings. The dwelling was that of a military man, and a man of piety and culture. A lad running in addressed the lady as Mrs. Pendleton and said something about "where General Pendleton is plowing."

They stumbled to their crutches! and in blushing confusion made humble apologies, all the instincts of the soldier shocked at the liberties they had taken with an officer of such high grade and at the ease of manner with which they had sat at his table to be served by his wife. They knew their host for William Nelson Pendleton, late brigadier general, C.S.A., chief of artillery of the Army of Northern Virginia, a fighting preacher. She smiled when they blundered out the excuse that they had mistaken him for a day laborer.

"The mistake has been made before," she said. "Indeed, the General is a day laborer in his own field, and it does not mortify him in the least now that all our people have to work. He is thankful his strength is sufficient, and for the help that the schoolboys and his daughters give him." She put bread into their haversacks and sent them on their way rejoicing. The day laborer and his plow were close to the roadside, and as they passed, they drew themselves up in line and brought all the hands they had to their ragged caps in salute.

Doctor Robert G. Stephens, of Atlanta, tells me of a Confederate soldier who, returning armless to his Georgia home, made his wife hitch him to a plow which she drove; and they made a crop. A Northern missionary said in 1867, to a Philadelphia audience, that he had seen in North Carolina a white mother hitch herself to a plow which her eleven-year-old son drove, while another child dropped into the furrows seeds Northern charity had given.

Myrta Lockett Avary, Dixie After the War

186. Pike Attends a Black Parliament in South Carolina

No one could accuse James S. Pike of being biased in favor of the Southern whites. Born in Maine, he had given many years of service as Washington correspondent and editorial writer to Greeley's New York Tribune. *He was an uncompromising antislavery man, and Lincoln rewarded him for his work in behalf of the Republican Party by appointment in 1861 as Min-*

ister to Holland. In the midst of Reconstruction he made a trip to South Carolina to view the workings of the "black and tan" government there; and in his famous book The Prostrate State *he showed vividly and eloquently the tyranny under which the carpetbag regime had placed the Southern whites.*

YESTERDAY, about 4 P.M., the assembled wisdom of the state, whose achievements are illustrated on that theater, issued forth from the Statehouse. About three-quarters of the crowd belonged to the African race. They were of every hue, from the light octoroon to the deep black. They were such a looking body of men as might pour out of a market house or a courthouse at random in any Southern state. Every Negro type and physiognomy was here to be seen, from the genteel servingman to the roughhewn customer from the rice or cotton field. Their dress was as varied as their countenances. There was the secondhand black frock coat of infirm gentility, glossy and threadbare. There was the stovepipe hat of many ironings and departed styles. There was also to be seen a total disregard of the proprieties of costume in the coarse and dirty garments of the field, the stub jackets and slouch hats of soiling labor. In some instances rough woolen comforters embraced the neck and hid the absence of linen. Heavy brogans and short, torn trousers it was impossible to hide. The dusky tide flowed out into the littered and barren grounds and, issuing through the coarse wooden fence of the inclosure, melted away into the street beyond. These were the legislators of South Carolina.

We will enter the House of Representatives. Here sit one hundred and twenty-four members. Of these, twenty-three are white men, representing the remains of the old civilization. These are good-looking, substantial citizens. They are men of weight and standing in the communities they represent. They are all from the hill country. The frosts of sixty and seventy winters whiten the heads of some among them. There they sit, grim and silent. They feel themselves to be but loose stones, thrown in to partially obstruct a current they are powerless to resist. They say little and do little as the days go by. They simply watch the rising tide and mark the progressive steps of the inundation. They hold their places reluctantly. They feel themselves to be in some sort martyrs, bound stoically to suffer in behalf of that still great element in the state whose prostrate fortunes are becoming the sport of an unpitying fate. Grouped in a corner of the commodious and well-furnished chamber, they stolidly survey the noisy riot that goes on in the great black Left and Center, where the business and debates of the House are conducted and where sit the strange and extraordinary guides of the fortunes of a once proud and haughty state. In this crucial trial of his pride, his manhood, his prejudices, his spirit, it must be said of the Southern Bourbon of the Legislature that he comports himself with a dignity, a reserve, and a decorum that command admiration. He feels that the iron hand of destiny is upon him. He is gloomy, disconsolate, hopeless. The grayheads of this generation openly profess that they look for no relief. They see no way of escape. The recovery of influence, of position, of control in the state, is felt by them to be impossible. They accept their position with a stoicism that promises no reward here or hereafter. They are the types of a conquered race. They staked all and lost all. Their lives remain; their property and their children do not. War, emancipation, and grinding taxation have consumed them. Their struggle now is against complete confiscation. They endure, and wait for the night.

This dense Negro crowd they confront do the debating, the squabbling, the lawmaking, and create all the clamor and disorder of the body. These twenty-three white men are but the observers, the enforced auditors, of the dull and clumsy imitation of a deliberative body whose appearance in their present capacity is at once a wonder and a shame to modern civilization.

Deducting the twenty-three members referred to, who comprise the entire strength of the opposition, we find one hundred and one remaining. Of this one hundred and one, ninety-four are colored, and seven are their white allies. . . .

One of the things that first strike a casual observer in this Negro assembly is the fluency of debate, if the endless chatter that goes on there can be dignified with this term. The leading topics of discussion are all well understood by the members, as they are of a practical character and appeal directly to the personal interests of every legislator as well as to those of his constituents. When an appropriation bill is up to raise money to catch and punish the Ku Klux, they know exactly what it means. They feel it in their bones. So too with educational measures. The free school comes right home to them; then the business of arming and drilling the black militia — they are eager on this point. Sambo can talk on these topics and those of a kindred character and their endless ramifications day in and day out. There is no end to his gush and babble. The intellectual level is that of a bevy of fresh converts at a Negro camp meeting. Of course this kind of talk can be extended indefinitely. It is the doggerel of debate and not beyond the reach of the lowest parts. Then the Negro is imitative in the extreme. He can copy like a parrot or a monkey, and he is always ready for a trial of his skill. He believes he can do anything and never loses a chance to try and is just as ready to be laughed at for his failure as applauded for his success. He is more vivacious than the white, and being more volatile and good-natured, he is correspondingly more irrepressible. His misuse of language in his imitations is at times ludicrous beyond measure. He notoriously loves a joke or an anecdote and will burst into a broad guffaw on the smallest provocation. He breaks out into an incoherent harangue on the floor just as easily, and being without practice, discipline, or experience and wholly oblivious of Lindley Murray or any other restraint on composition, he will go on repeating himself, dancing as it were to the music of his own voice, forever. He will speak half a dozen times on one question and every time say the same things without knowing it. He answers completely to the description of a stupid speaker in Parliament given by Lord Derby on one occasion; it was said of him that he did not know what he was going to say when he got up, he did not know what he was saying while he was speaking, and he did not know what he had said when he sat down.

But the old stagers admit that the colored brethren have a wonderful aptness at legislative proceedings. They are quick as lightning at detecting points of order, and they certainly make incessant and extraordinary use of their knowledge. No one is allowed to talk five minutes without interruption, and one interruption is the signal for another and another until the original speaker is smothered under an avalanche of them. Forty questions of privilege will be raised in a day. At times nothing goes on but alternating questions of order and of privilege. The inefficient colored friend who sits in the Speaker's chair cannot suppress this extraordinary element of the debate. Some of the blackest members exhibit a pertinacity of intrusion in raising these points of order and questions of privilege that few white men can equal. Their struggles to get the floor, their bellowings and physical contortions, baffle description. The Speaker's hammer plays a perpetual tattoo, all to no purpose. The talking and the interruptions from all quarters go on with the utmost license. Every one esteems himself as good as his neighbor and puts in his oar, apparently as often for love of riot and confusion as for anything else. It is easy to imagine what are his ideas of propriety and dignity among a crowd of his own color, and these are illustrated without reserve. The Speaker orders a member whom he has discovered to be particularly unruly to take his seat. The member obeys and, with the same motion that he sits down, throws his feet on to his desk, hiding himself from the Speaker by the soles of his boots. In an instant he appears again on the floor. After a few experiences of this sort, the Speaker threatens, in a laugh, to call "the gemman" to order. This is considered a capital joke, and a guffaw follows. The laugh goes round, and then the peanuts are cracked and munched faster than ever, one hand being employed in fortifying the inner man with this nutriment of universal use while the other enforces the views of the orator. This laughing propensity of the sable crowd is a great cause of disorder. They laugh as hens cackle — one begins and all follow.

But underneath all this shocking burlesque upon legislative proceedings, we must not forget that there is something very real to this uncouth and untutored multitude. It is not all sham nor all burlesque. They have a genuine interest and a genuine earnestness in the business of the assembly which we are bound to recognize and respect unless we would be accounted shallow critics. They have an earnest purpose, born of a conviction that their position and condition are not fully assured, which lends a sort of dignity to their proceedings. The barbarous, animated jargon in which they so often indulge is on occasion seen to be so transparently sincere and weighty in their own minds that sympathy supplants disgust. The whole thing is a wonderful novelty to them as well as to observers. Seven years ago these men were raising corn and cotton under the whip of the overseer. Today they are raising points of order and questions of privilege. They find they can raise one as well as the other. They prefer the latter. It is easier and better paid. Then, it is the evidence of an accomplished result. It means escape and defense from old oppressors. It means liberty. It means the destruction of prison walls only too real to them. It is the sunshine of their lives. It is their day of jubilee. It is their long-promised vision of the Lord God Almighty.

JAMES SHEPHERD PIKE, The Prostrate State

187. Southern Negroes Join the Union League

One of the most famous of carpetbag officials in the South was Albion W. Tourgée, an Ohioan by birth who did good service for the Union cause in the Civil War, and then in the fall of 1865 removed to Greensboro, North Carolina, to make his fortune. He soon entered politics, founded a newspaper, and in 1868 was elected a judge of the superior court, where he served for six years. The radical Republicans found him a faithful servant, though in all personal — as distinguished from political — matters he was entirely honest. After the carpetbag regime had been overthrown he published a novel, A Fool's Errand, *which gives vivid and accurate pictures of the turmoil of the period, and from which this passage is taken. The Union League was a Northern-promoted organization for giving the Negroes and carpetbaggers political strength in the South.*

"WE'S GOT a little league down h'yer to Verdenton at de schoolhouse fer de culled folks, an' we'd be mighty proud tu hev ye come down some Chuseday night. Dat we would!" said Andy.

"What! You have got a chapter of the Union League there? How did you get it?"

"Wal, I don't jes' 'zactly know. Dar's some culled men belongs to it as was soldiers in de Union army, an' I 'lowed dey might hev fotch it wid 'em when dey come h'yer."

"Who belongs to it? Are they all colored members?"

"Wal, de heft ob 'em is culled, ob co'se; but der's a right smart sprinklin' ob white folks, arter all. . . . I reckon der's ez much ez a dozen white folks in all. Some ez you wouldn't 'spect on't, tu. You'd du us proud ef you'd come down, Mars' Kunnel."

"Who's your president, Andy?"

"Wal, sometimes one, an' sometimes anudder, jes' accordin' tu who's scholar enuff tu take de lead," answered Andy, with ready pride in his new toy.

The idea was very amusing to the Fool, and the more he thought of it, the more he was convinced that it might be a valuable training school to the inchoate citizens of the lately rebellious states. Even while he was discussing the facts which surrounded him, he could not realize them; and he quite forgot, in giving his assent to this idea, the fact that he was living at the South, among a people who did not kindly brook differences of opinion among equals and who would be sure to resent with an implacable hostility any society which not only recognized the political autonomy of the recently subject race but also encouraged that race to look up to the government their masters had failed to destroy as *their* government, *their* guardian, *their* protector — which not only promoted ideas not in harmony with those of the former rulers of this section, but promoted the elevation of the freedman, prepared him for civil life, and gave him confidence in himself as a political integer. Had he thought of this, it is certain that he would not have consented so readily to go and see Andy's society; for what he most feared was a conflict or permanent antagonism between the freedmen and their former masters, and he thought that any sacrifice not going to the substance of their liberties ought to be made rather than that such a conflict should be risked.

However, stumbling over these apparent facts, he went on the next Tuesday night to the schoolhouse in the suburbs of Verdenton. It was a long, low building, made for service — one of that numerous array of buildings which was mainly furnished to the recently emancipated seeker after knowledge by the systematic bounty of that much-abused institution, the Freedmen's Bureau. Acting in conjunction with various religious and benevolent societies of the North, it furnished a class of buildings better adapted to the needs of those for whom they were designed and affording greater results than was ever done in all history with like means. In every village of the South was erected one or more of these rough wooden buildings, consisting only of roof, rafter walls, and floor of undressed plank. The minimum of cost and the maximum of space were the objects kept constantly in view and usually attained beyond all question. These houses became to the colored people what the court of the temple was to the Jews — the place of assembly and worship as well as of instruction. They were usually unsectarian, and it was no unusual spectacle to see two or three denominations worshiping in the same house, while the school was under the management and control of still another.

To them thronged with wondrous eagerness the old and young alike of the recently emancipated race. The building to which Comfort Servosse went that night was an imposing structure in its dimensions. In it seven ladies who had come from far Northern homes, filled with the genuine spirit of the missionary and no doubt thinking themselves endowed with the spirit of that Redeemer who taught publicans in the market or in the desert despite the frowns of the Pharisees, held sway. These seven fair, pure-hearted Northern girls taught within its walls each day and oftentimes at night six hundred and more of the race which had just now its first chance at the tree of knowledge since our common mother persisted in eating the mystic apple. They, no doubt, thought they were doing God's service and wondered why the earnest Christians who dwelt about them should regard the inhabitants of the Mission House with such open aversion and apparent hate. Sometimes they wrote indignant letters to their friends at home, but it was fortunate that the greater part of the evil things which were said of them by the neighboring Christians never came to their knowledge and that their hearts were too pure to comprehend the foul innuendoes which floated by them. So they went on teaching as they had been taught those who had been all their lives thitherto untaught, and the others went on hating and defaming them because such a course was counter to their traditions and those who did it were their hereditary enemies. And both, no doubt, felt that they were doing God's service with their might.

Servosse found a cordon of watchers about the schoolhouse, by one of whom he was challenged and, after learning who he was, taken to the house, where he was carefully examined to ascertain whether he were a member or not, after which he was admitted into the room where the meeting was held. It was a large classroom in the second story, capable of seating, perhaps, two hundred people. It was about half full when he arrived, as the meeting had not yet been called to order; and constant arrivals were fast increasing the number. The great bulk of those who were present were colored men, but in a little group at the right of the platform were perhaps a dozen white men. . . .

"The meetin' will come to order," commanded the president in a thin, stridulous voice, as he rapped upon the rough deal table with one of the teacher's rulers instead of a gavel. The room was crowded by this time, and an instantaneous hush fell upon the dusky crowd at this command. Every one sank into his seat, and those who had no other seats ranged themselves in front and along the aisles upon the floor. About the little group of white men was an open space, and immediately in front of the president was a small table, draped with a Union flag and surmounted by a Bible and the Constitution of the United States.

"The officers will take their appointed stations," said the president.

Then the ceremonies of opening the meeting went on. Each officer was instructed as to his duty, and the general principles of the order were recapitulated in easy dialogue between them and the president.

"Will Colonel Servosse conduct the religious exercises?" asked the president.

Thus called upon, the ex-Union soldier arose and approached the altar, opened the Bible and read and called upon Uncle Jerry to pray. All stood reverentially silent during prayer, and then the business of the meeting went on. Names were proposed for membership, committees reported on former propositions, and the usual business of a secret order was disposed of. There was much awkwardness, no little bad grammar, but the most attentive interest and an evident pride and desire to improve on the part of all. Resuming his seat by Walters, the Fool watched the proceedings with interest.

"Is the League organized to any great extent in the South?" asked Comfort.

"I don't know," responded Walters. "Just before the close of the war I went up into East Tennessee on a little business that took me through the lines, and I joined it there. I don't like it."

"Why not?"

"It's too cumbrous. Our people ain't educated enough to run it well. Besides that, I don't like these big meetings."

"But is it not an educator for the colored men?"

"I've thought of that, and it's the great redeeming feature of the institution. I'm thinking we shall need something more practical and that don't make so much show before we have done with the matters rising out of the war."

"You do not take a hopeful view of the future, then?"

"Well, that depends altogether on the view of the present that the government and the Northern people take. If they get the notion that rebellion has transformed those engaged in it into sanctified and glorified saints, as they seem in a way to do, why, the war will not amount to any certain sum, so far as liberty and progress are concerned. Then Union men an' niggers will have to hunt their holes and will be worse off in fact than they were during the war. I'm 'fraid it's going to be so, Colonel; and I feel as if I ought to go to the West, where I and my children can be free and safe."

"I hope you will not think of that, Mr. Walters," said the Fool.

"Well, I *have* thought of it strongly; but I have decided to stay," was the reply, "chiefly because so many of you Northern men have come down here. I think that if you can stand it, I can. At least I don't think we native Unionists ought to run away and leave you."

A dozen dusky candidates were instructed in the semipublic secrets of the order; one or two songs were sung with great enthusiasm; a few addresses were made; and the meeting adjourned. As he rode back through the moonlit woods to Warrington, the Fool recounted what he had seen to Metta — who had come with him and stopped at the Mission House visiting with the teachers, while the meeting was in progress — and told her that it gave him more hope for a peaceful and prosperous future than anything he had yet seen. The enthusiasm of a soldier for his colors had not yet died out in his breast, and he could not conceive that any organization which cultivated only an unbounded devotion for the flag in the breasts of the embryonic citizens and kept alive the fire of patriotism in the hearts of the old Union element should be a source of evil to any one.

ALBION TOURGÉE, A Fool's Errand

188. The Ku Klux Klan Rides

The insecurity of the Southern whites in Reconstruction days, and their desire to shake off the domination of the Negroes and the carpetbaggers who had come down from the North, led to a rapid growth of secret organizations. The most powerful of these bodies, the Ku Klux Klan, was founded in Tennessee in 1865 and quickly spread throughout most of the section. At the head of this "Invisible Empire" was a Grand Wizard, while under him each State or "Realm" was ruled by a Grand Dragon. It is said that nearly all the Southern whites (except the "Scalawags," who helped the carpetbaggers gain power) aided the Klan in some way. In general, the society tried to intimidate the Negroes and their white allies by threats and demonstrations alone; but particularly in the later years of its short history, a good deal of violence was used. Negroes and carpetbag politicians were whipped, and some were murdered. Stern Federal action finally broke up the last vestiges of the Klan, but not before it had accomplished most of its purposes.

IT WAS a chill, dreary night. A dry, harsh wind blew from the north. The moon was at the full and shone clear and cold in the blue vault.

There was one shrill whistle, some noise of quietly moving horses; and those who looked from their windows saw a black-gowned and grimly masked horseman sitting upon a draped horse at every corner of the streets and before each house — grim, silent, threatening. Those who saw dared not move or give any alarm. Instinctively they knew that the enemy they had feared had come, had them in his clutches, and would work his will of them, whether they resisted or not. So, with the instinct of self-preservation, all were silent — all simulated sleep.

Five, ten, fifteen minutes the silent watch continued. A half hour passed, and there had been no sound. Each masked sentry sat his horse as if horse and rider were only some magic statuary with which the bleak night cheated the affrighted eye. Then a whistle sounded on the road toward Verdenton. The masked horsemen turned their horses' heads in that direction and slowly and silently moved away. Gathering in twos, they fell into ranks with the regularity and ease of a practised soldiery and, as they filed on toward Verdenton, showed a cavalcade of several hundred strong; and upon one of the foremost horses rode one with a strange figure lashed securely to him.

When the few who were awake in the little village found courage to inquire as to what the silent enemy had done, they rushed from house to house with chattering teeth and trembling limbs, only to find that all were safe within, until they came to the house where old Uncle Jerry Hunt had been dwelling alone since the death of his wife six months before. The door was open.

The house was empty. The straw mattress had been thrown from the bed, and the hempen cord on which it rested had been removed.

The Sabbath morrow was well advanced when the Fool was first apprized of the raid. He at once rode into the town, arriving there just as the morning services closed, and met the people coming along the streets to their homes. Upon the limb of a low-branching oak not more than forty steps from the Temple of Justice hung the lifeless body of old Jerry. The wind turned it slowly to and fro. The snowy hair and beard contrasted strangely with the dusky pallor of the peaceful face, which seemed even in death to proffer a benison to the people of God who passed to and fro from the house of prayer, unmindful both of the peace which lighted the dead face and of the rifled temple of the Holy Ghost which appealed to them for sepulture. Over all pulsed the sacred echo of the Sabbath bells. The sun shone brightly. The wind rustled the autumn leaves. A few idlers sat upon the steps of the courthouse and gazed carelessly at the ghastly burden on the oak. The brightly dressed churchgoers enlivened the streets. Not a colored man was to be seen. All except the brown cadaver on the tree spoke of peace and prayer — a holy day among a godly people, with whom rested the benison of peace.

The Fool asked of some trusty friends the story of the night before. With trembling lips one told it to him:

"I heard the noise of horses — quiet and orderly, but many. Looking from the window in the clear moonlight, I saw horsemen passing down the street, taking their stations here and there like guards who have been told off for duty at specific points. Two stopped before my house, two opposite Mr. Haskin's, and two or three upon the corner below. They seemed to have been sent on before as a sort of picket guard for the main body, which soon came in. I should say there were from a hundred to a hundred and fifty still in line. They were all masked and wore black robes. The horses were disguised, too, by drapings. There were only a few mules in the whole company. They were good horses, though; one could tell that by their movements. Oh, it was a respectable crowd! No doubt about that, sir. Beggars don't ride in this country. I don't know when I have seen so many good horses together since the Yankee cavalry left here after the surrender. They were well drilled too. Plenty of old soldiers in that crowd. Why, everything went just like clockwork. Not a word was said — just a few whistles given. They came like a dream and went away like a mist. I thought we should have to fight for our lives, but they did not disturb any one here. They gathered down by the courthouse. I could not see precisely what they were at but from my back upper window saw them down about the tree. After a while a signal was given, and just at that time a match was struck, and I saw a dark body swing down under the limb. I knew then they had hanged somebody, but had no idea who it was. To tell the truth, I had a notion it was you, Colonel. I saw several citizens go out and speak to these men on the horses. There were lights in some of the offices about the courthouse and in several of the houses about town. Everything was as still as the grave — no shouting or loud talking and no excitement or stir about town. It was evident that a great many of the citizens expected the movement and were prepared to co-operate with it by manifesting no curiosity or otherwise endangering its success. I am inclined to think a good many from this town were in it. I never felt so powerless in my life. Here the town was in the hands of two or three hundred armed and disciplined men, hidden from the eye of the law, and having friends and co-workers in almost every house. I knew that resistance was useless."

"But why," asked the Fool, "has not the body been removed?"

"We have been thinking about it," was the reply; "but the truth is, it don't seem like a very safe business. And after what we saw last night, no one feels like being the first to do what may be held an affront by those men. I tell you, Colonel, I went through the war and saw as much danger as most men in it; but I would rather charge up the heights of Gettysburg again than be the object of a raid by that crowd."

After some parley, however, some colored men were found and a little party made up who went out and saw the body of Uncle Jerry cut down and laid upon a box to await the coming of the coroner, who had already been notified. The inquest developed only these facts, and the sworn jurors solemnly and honestly found the cause of death unknown. One of the colored men who had watched the proceedings gave utterance to the prevailing opinion when he said: "It don't do fer niggers to know *too much!* Dat's what ail Uncle Jerry!"

And indeed it did seem as if his case was one in which ignorance might have been bliss.

ALBION TOURGÉE, A Fool's Errand

189. George Julian Regrets the Johnson Impeachment

Andrew Johnson, favoring the same mild policy of Reconstruction that Lincoln had preached, soon quarreled with the vindictive members of Congress who wished to punish the Southerners. The quarrel became bitter, involving important constitutional questions. One of President Johnson's opponents was George Julian of Indiana, an Indiana lawyer and an

Abolitionist, who had been elected to Congress in 1860. He favored Negro suffrage, and the seizure of the lands of all the Confederate leaders. In 1867 he was one of the committee of seven members of the House of Representatives who prepared the formal impeachment of Johnson. But within a few years Julian broke with his party, and in 1872 joined the Liberal Republicans who opposed Grant's re-election. He repented his hostility to Johnson, and makes this plain in his "Recollections."

ON THE 24th of February, 1868, the House, by a vote of one hundred and twenty-six to forty-seven, declared in favor of impeachment. The crowds in the galleries, in the lobbies, and on the floor were unprecedented and the excitement at high tide. The fifty-seven who had voted for impeachment in December were now happy. They felt at last that the country was safe. The whole land seemed to be electrified, as they believed it would have been at any previous time if the House had had the nerve to go forward, and they rejoiced that the madness of Johnson had at last compelled Congress to face the great duty. A committee of seven was appointed by the Speaker to prepare articles of impeachment, of whom Thaddeus Stevens was chairman. He was now rapidly failing in strength and every morning had to be carried upstairs to his seat in the House, but his humor never failed him, and on one of these occasions he said to the young men who had him in charge, "I wonder, boys, who will carry me when you are dead and gone." He was very thin, pale, and haggard. His eye was bright, but his face was "scarred by the crooked autograph of pain." He was a constant sufferer, and during the sessions of the committee kept himself stimulated by sipping a little wine or brandy; but he was its ruling spirit and greatly speeded its work by the clearness of his perceptions and the strength of his will. His mental force seemed to defy the power of disease. The articles of impeachment were ready for submission in a few days and adopted by the House on the second of March by a majority of considerably more than two-thirds, when the case was transferred to the Senate.

The popular feeling against the President was now rapidly nearing its climax and becoming a sort of frenzy. Andrew Johnson was no longer merely a "wrongheaded and obstinate man" but a "genius in depravity," whose hoarded malignity and passion were unfathomable. He was not simply "an irresolute mule," as General Schenck had styled him, but was devil-bent upon the ruin of his country; and his trial connected itself with all the memories of the war, and involved the nation in a new and final struggle for its life. Even so sober and unimaginative a man as Mr. Boutwell, one of the managers of the impeachment in the Senate, lost his wits and completely surrendered himself to the passions of the hour.

No extravagance of speech or explosion of wrath was deemed out of order during this strange dispensation in our politics.

The trial proceeded with unabated interest, and on the afternoon of the eleventh of May the excitement reached its highest point. Reports came from the Senate, then in secret session, that Grimes, Fessenden, and Henderson were certainly for acquittal, and that other senators were to follow them. An indescribable gloom now prevailed among the friends of impeachment, which increased during the afternoon and at night when the Senate was again in session. At the adjournment there was some hope of conviction, but it was generally considered very doubtful. On meeting my old antislavery friend, Doctor Brisbane, he told me he felt as if he were sitting up with a sick friend who was expected to die. His face was the picture of despair. To such men it seemed that all the trials of the war were merged in this grand issue and that it involved the existence of free government on this continent.

The final vote was postponed till the sixteenth, owing to Senator Howard's illness, and on the morning of that day the friends of impeachment felt more confident. The vote was first taken on the eleventh article. The galleries were packed, and an indescribable anxiety was written on every face. Some of the members of the House near me grew pale and sick under the burden of suspense. Such stillness prevailed that the breathing in the galleries could be heard at the announcement of each senator's vote. This was quite noticeable when any of the doubtful senators voted, the people holding their breath as the words "guilty" or "not guilty" were pronounced and then giving it simultaneous vent. Every heart throbbed more anxiously as the name of Senator Fowler was reached and the

Chief Justice propounded to him the prescribed question: "How say you, is the respondent, Andrew Johnson, President of the United States, guilty or not guilty of a high misdemeanor, as charged in this article of impeachment?" The senator, in evident excitement, inadvertently answered "guilty," and thus lent a momentary relief to the friends of impeachment; but this was immediately dissipated by correcting his vote on the statement of the Chief Justice that he did not understand the Senator's response to the question. Nearly all hope of conviction fled when Senator Ross of Kansas voted "not guilty," and a long breathing of disappointment and despair followed the like vote of Van Winkle, which settled the case in favor of the President.

It is impossible now to realize how perfectly overmastering was the excitement of these days. The exercise of calm judgment was simply out of the question. As I have already stated, passion ruled the hour and constantly strengthened the tendency to one-sidedness and exaggeration. The attempt to impeach the President was undoubtedly inspired mainly by patriotic motives, but the spirit of intolerance among Republicans toward those who differed with them in opinion set all moderation and common sense at defiance. Patriotism and party animosity were so inextricably mingled and confounded that the real merits of the controversy could only be seen after the heat and turmoil of the strife had passed away. Time has made this manifest. Andrew Johnson was not the devil incarnate he was then painted, nor did he monopolize entirely the wrongheadedness of the times. No one will now dispute that the popular estimate of his character did him very great injustice. It is equally certain that great injustice was done to Trumbull, Fessenden, Grimes, and other senators who voted to acquit the President and gave proof of their honesty and independence by facing the wrath and scorn of the party with which they had so long been identified. The idea of making the question of impeachment a matter of party discipline was utterly indefensible and preposterous.

GEORGE W. JULIAN, *Political Recollections*

190. Walt Whitman Scans
Democratic Vistas

The Grant Administrations, 1869–1877, were filled with political corruption. Scandals were so numerous and so shocking that by the centennial year, 1876, all patriotic Americans hung their heads in shame. Thomas Carlyle had recently indicted democracy in his essay Shooting Niagara. *Walt Whitman in his pamphlet* Democratic Vistas, *published just as the unhappy Grant era was fully opening, indicated a clear understanding of the weaknesses of and perils to democracy, but sturdily defended it none the less.*

FOR MY part, I would alarm and caution even the political and business reader, and to the utmost extent, against the prevailing delusion that the establishment of free political institutions, and plentiful intellectual smartness, with general good order, physical plenty, industry, etc. (desirable and precious advantages as they all are), do of themselves determine and yield to our experiment of democracy the fruitage of success. With such advantages at present fully, or almost fully, possessed — the Union just issued victorious from the struggle with the only foes it need ever fear (namely, those within itself, the interior ones), and with unprecedented materialistic advancement — society in these states is cankered, crude, superstitious, and rotten. Political or law-made society is, and private or voluntary society is also. In any vigor, the element of the moral conscience, the most important, the vertebra to state or man, seems to me either entirely lacking or seriously enfeebled or ungrown.

I say we had best look our times and lands searchingly in the face, like a physician diagnosing some deep disease. Never was there, perhaps, more hollowness at heart than at present and here in the United States. Genuine belief seems to have left us. The underlying principles of the states are not honestly believed in (for all this hectic glow and these melodramatic screamings), nor is humanity itself believed in. What penetrating eye does not everywhere see through the mask? The spectacle is appalling. We live in an atmosphere of hypocrisy throughout. The men believe not in the women, nor the women in the men. A scornful superciliousness rules in literature. The aim of all the *littérateurs* is to find something to make fun of. A lot of churches, sects, etc., the most dismal phantasms I know, usurp the name of religion. Conversation is a mass of badinage. From deceit in the spirit, the mother of all false deeds, the offspring is already incalculable. An acute and candid person in the revenue department in Washington, who is led by the course of his employment to regularly visit the cities, north, south, and west, to investigate frauds, has talked much with me about his discoveries. The depravity of the business classes of our country is not less than has been supposed but infinitely greater. The official services of America, national, state, and municipal, in all their branches and departments except the judiciary, are saturated in corruption, bribery, falsehood, maladministration; and the judiciary is tainted. The great cities reek with respectable as much as nonrespectable robbery and scoundrelism. In fashionable life, flippancy, tepid amours, weak infidelism, small aims, or no aims at all, only to kill time. In business (this all-devouring modern word, business) the one sole object is, by any means, pecuniary gain. The magician's serpent in the fable ate up all the other serpents, and money-making is our magician's serpent, remaining today sole master of the field. The best class we show is but a mob of fashionably dressed speculators and vulgarians. True, indeed, behind this fantastic farce, enacted on the visible stage of society, solid things and stupendous labors are to be discovered, existing crudely and going on in the background, to advance and tell themselves in time. Yet the truths are none the less terrible. I say that our New World democracy, however great a success in uplifting the masses out of their sloughs, in materialistic development, products, and in a certain highly deceptive superficial popular intellectuality, is so far an almost complete failure in its social aspects and in really grand religious, moral, literary, and esthetic results. In vain do we march with unprecedented strides to empire so colossal, outvying the antique, beyond Alexander's, beyond the proudest sway of Rome. In vain have we annexed Texas, California, Alaska, and reach north for Canada and south for Cuba. It is as if we were somehow being endowed with a vast and more and more thoroughly appointed body and then left with little or no soul.

WALT WHITMAN, Democratic Vistas. 1871

XXVII

The Last West

191. General Dodge Builds the Union Pacific

The Pacific Railway Act of 1862 provided for the construction of a transcontinental railroad to be undertaken by the Central Pacific and Union Pacific Railway companies, the first building eastward from the California line, the second westward from Council Bluffs, Iowa. General Grenville M. Dodge, who had proved his talents as Sherman's engineer in the Atlanta campaign, was made chief engineer of the Union Pacific and was largely responsible for the rapidity and efficiency with which the road was constructed. The juncture of the Union Pacific with the Central Pacific at Promontory Point, Utah, was an event of national importance.

THE ORGANIZATION for work on the plains away from civilization was as follows: Each of our surveying parties consisted of a chief who was an experienced engineer, two assistants, also civil engineers, rodmen, flagmen, and chainmen, generally graduated civil engineers but without personal experience in the field, besides ax men, teamsters, and herders. When the party was expected to live upon the game of the country, a hunter was added. Each party would thus consist of from eighteen to twenty-two men, all armed. When operating in a hostile Indian country they were regularly drilled, though after the Civil War this was unnecessary, as most of them had been in the army. Each party entering a country occupied by hostile Indians was generally furnished with a military escort of from ten men to a company under a competent officer. The duty of this escort was to protect the party when in camp. In the field the escort usually occupied prominent hills commanding the territory in which the work was to be done, so as to head off sudden attacks by the Indians. Notwithstanding this protection the parties were often attacked, their chief or some of their men killed or wounded, and their stock run off. . . .

The location part in our work on the Union Pacific was followed by the construction corps, grading generally a hundred miles at a time. That distance was graded in about thirty days on the plains, as a rule, but in the mountains we sometimes had to open our grading several hundred miles ahead of our track in order to complete the grading by the time the track should reach it. All the supplies for this work had to be hauled from the end of the track, and the wagon transportation was enormous. At one time we were using at least ten thousand animals, and most of the time from eight to ten thousand laborers. The bridge gangs always worked from five to twenty miles ahead of the track, and it was seldom that the track waited for a bridge. To supply one mile of track with material and supplies required about forty cars, as on the plains everything — rails, ties, bridging, fastenings, all railway supplies, fuel for locomotives and trains, and supplies for men and animals on the entire work — had to be transported from the Missouri River. Therefore, as we moved westward, every hundred miles added vastly to our transportation. Yet the work was so systematically planned and executed that I do not remember an instance in all the construction of the line of the work being delayed a single week for want of material. Each winter we planned the work for the next season. By the opening of spring, about April 1st, every part of the machinery was in working order, and in no year did we fail to accomplish our work. After 1866 the reports will show what we started out to do each year and what we accomplished.

Our Indian troubles commenced in 1864 and lasted until the tracks joined at Promontory. We lost most of our men and stock while building from Fort Kearney to Bitter Creek. At that time every mile of road had to be surveyed, graded, tied, and bridged under military protection. The order to every surveying corps, grading, bridging, and tie outfit, was never to run when attacked. All were required to be armed, and I do not know that the order was disobeyed in a single instance, nor did I ever hear that the Indians had driven a party permanently from its work. I remember one occasion when they swooped down on a grading outfit in sight of the temporary fort of the military some five miles away and right in sight of the end of the track. The government commission to examine that section of the completed road had just arrived, and the commissioners witnessed the fight. The graders had their arms stacked on the cut. The Indians leaped from the ravines and, springing upon the workmen before they could reach their arms, cut loose the stock and caused a panic. General Frank P. Blair, General Simpson, and Doctor White were the commissioners; and they showed their grit by running to my car for arms to aid in the fight. We did not fail to benefit from this experience, for on returning to the East the commission dwelt earnestly on the necessity of our being protected.

The Union Pacific and Central Pacific were allowed to build, one east and the other west, until they met. The building of five hundred miles of road during the summers of 1866 and 1867, hardly twelve months' actual work, had aroused great interest in the country and much excitement, in which the government took a part. We were pressed to as speedy a completion of the road as possible, although ten years had been allowed by Congress. The officers of the Union Pacific had become imbued with this spirit, and they urged me to plan to build as much road as possible in 1868. . . . The reaching of the summit of the first range of the Rocky Mountains, which I named Sherman, in honor of my old commander, in 1867, placed us comparatively near good timber for ties and bridges which, after cutting, could be floated down the mountain streams at some points to our crossing and at others within twenty-five or thirty miles of our work. This afforded great relief to the transportation.

We made our plans to build to Salt Lake, four hundred and eighty miles, in 1868, and to endeavor to meet the Central Pacific at Humboldt Wells, two hundred and nineteen miles west of Ogden, in the spring of 1869. I had extended our surveys during the years 1867 and 1868 to the California state line and laid my plans before the company, and the necessary preparations were made to commence work as soon as frost was out of the ground, say about April 1st. Material had been collected in sufficient quantities at the end of the track to prevent any delay. During the winter ties and bridge material had been cut and prepared in the mountains to bring to the line at convenient points, and the engineering forces were started to their positions before cold weather was over, that they might be ready to begin their work as soon as the temperature would permit. I remember that the parties going to Salt Lake crossed the Wasatch Mountains on sledges and that the snow covered the tops of the telegraph poles. We all knew and appreciated that the task we had laid out would require the greatest energy on the part of all hands. About April 1st, therefore, I went on to the plains myself and started our construction forces, remaining the whole summer between Laramie and the Humboldt Mountains. I was surprised at the rapidity with which the work was carried forward. Winter caught us in the Wasatch Mountains, but we kept on grading our road and laying our track in the snow and ice, at a tremendous cost. I estimated for the company that the extra cost of thus forcing the work during that summer and winter was over ten million dollars, but the instructions I received were to go on, no matter what the cost. Spring found us with the track at Ogden, and by May 1st we had reached Promontory, five hundred and thirty-four miles west of our starting point twelve months before. Work on our line was opened to Humboldt Wells, making in the year a grading of seven hundred and fifty-four miles of line.

The Central Pacific had made wonderful progress coming east, and we abandoned the work from Promontory to Humboldt Wells, bending all our efforts to meet them at Promontory. Between Ogden and Promontory each company graded a line, running side by side, and in some places one line was right above the other. The laborers upon the Central Pacific were Chinamen, while ours were Irishmen, and there was much ill feeling between them. Our Irishmen were in the habit of firing their blasts in the cuts without giving warning to the Chinamen on the Central Pacific working right above them. From this cause several Chinamen were severely hurt. Complaint was made to me by the Central Pacific people, and I endeavored to have the contractors bring all hostilities to a close; but for some reason or other they failed to do so. One day the Chinamen, appreciating the situation, put in what is called a "grave" on their work and, when the Irishmen right under them were all at work, let go their blast and buried several of our men. This brought about a truce at once. From that time the Irish laborers showed due respect for the Chinamen, and there was no further trouble.

When the two roads approached in May, 1869, we agreed to connect at the summit of Promontory Point; and the day was fixed so that trains could reach us from New York and California. We laid the rails to the junction point a day or two before the final closing. . . . The two trains pulled up facing each other, each crowded with workmen who sought advantageous positions to witness the ceremonies and literally covered the cars. The officers and invited guests formed on each side of the track, leaving it open to the south. The telegraph lines had been brought to that point, so that in the final spiking as each blow was struck the telegraph recorded it at each connected office from the Atlantic to the Pacific. Prayer was offered; a number of spikes were driven in the two adjoining rails, each one of the prominent persons present taking a hand, but very few hitting the spikes, to the great amusement of the crowd. When the last spike was placed, light taps were given upon it by several officials, and it was finally driven home by the chief engineer of the Union Pacific Railway. The engineers ran up their locomotives until they touched, the engineer upon each engine breaking a bottle of champagne upon the other one, and thus the two roads were wedded into one great trunk line from the Atlantic to the Pacific. Spikes of silver and gold were brought specially for the occasion and later were manufactured into miniature spikes as mementoes of the occasion. It was a bright but cold day. After a few speeches we all took refuge in the Central Pacific cars, where wine flowed freely and many speeches were made.

GRENVILLE M. DODGE, How We Built the Union Pacific

192. Robert Louis Stevenson Travels across the Plains

The journey which Stevenson here chronicles marked the opening of the second period in his adventurous life. He had left his home in Edinburgh with very slender means

in his pocket, and under the disadvantage of very bad health, to
marry a lady of whom he believed his parents would disapprove.
This was a Mrs. Osbourne, whom he intended to join in San
Francisco. He sailed from the Clyde in August, 1879, and within
twenty-four hours of his arrival in New York was on his way west
as an emigrant. The trip across the continent required almost two
weeks, under conditions of the greatest discomfort, and when
Stevenson reached the Pacific he "looked like a man at death's door."
Indeed, at Monterey, where he went to recuperate, he promptly
broke down. But his history of the journey makes light of its hard-
ships. Emigrants who did not know the language, who were not
acquainted with Anglo-Saxon ways, and who lacked his cheeriness
and breadth of sympathy, would have suffered far more.

I T WAS about two in the afternoon of Friday that I found myself in front of the Emigrant House [Council Bluffs, Iowa], with
more than a hundred others, to be sorted and boxed for the journey.
A white-haired official with a stick under one arm and a list in the
other hand stood apart in front of us and called name after name in
the tone of a command. At each name you would see a family gather
up its brats and bundles and run for the hindmost of the three cars
that stood awaiting us, and I soon concluded that this was to be set
apart for the women and children. The second or central car,
it turned out, was devoted to men traveling alone, and the third to
Chinese. The official was easily moved to anger at the least delay,
but the emigrants were both quick at answering their names and
speedy in getting themselves and their effects on board.

The families once housed, we men carried the second car without
ceremony by simultaneous assault. I suppose the reader has some
notion of an American railroad car, that long, narrow wooden
box like a flat-roofed Noah's ark, with a stove and a convenience,
one at either end, a passage down the middle, and transverse benches
upon either hand. Those destined for emigrants on the Union
Pacific are only remarkable for their extreme plainness, nothing
but wood entering in any part into their constitution, and for the
usual inefficacy of the lamps, which often went out and shed but
a dying glimmer even while they burned. The benches are too

short for anything but a young child. Where there is scarce elbow-
room for two to sit, there will not be space enough for one to lie.
Hence the company, or rather, as it appears from certain bills
about the transfer station, the company's servants, have conceived
a plan for the better accommodation of travelers. They prevail on
every two to chum together. To each of the chums they sell a board
and three square cushions stuffed with straw and covered with thin
cotton. The benches can be made to face each other in pairs, for the
backs are reversible. On the approach of night the boards are laid
from bench to bench, making a couch wide enough for two and
long enough for a man of the middle height; and the chums lie
down side by side upon the cushions with the head to the conductor's van and the feet to the engine. When the train is full, of course
this plan is impossible, for there must not be more than one to
every bench; neither can it be carried out unless the chums agree.
It was to bring about this last condition that our white-haired official now bestirred himself. He made a most active master of ceremonies, introducing likely couples and even guaranteeing the
amiability and honesty of each. The greater the number of happy
couples the better for his pocket, for it was he who sold the raw
material of the beds. His price for one board and three straw cushions
began with two dollars and a half, but before the train left and,
I am sorry to say, long after I had purchased mine, it had fallen to
one dollar and a half.

The day faded; the lamps were lit; a party of wild young men,
who got off next evening at North Platte, stood together on the
stern platform, singing "The Sweet By-and-by" with very tuneful
voices; the chums began to put up their beds; and it seemed as if
the business of the day were at an end. But it was not so, for, the
train stopping at some station, the cars were instantly thronged
with the natives, wives and fathers, young men and maidens, some
of them in a little more than night gear, some with stable lanterns,
and all offering beds for sale. Their charge began with twenty-five
cents a cushion but fell, before the train went on again, to fifteen,
with the bed board gratis, or less than one-fifth of what I had paid
for mine at the transfer. This is my contribution to the economy of
future emigrants.

A great personage on an American train is the newsboy. He sells books (such books!), papers, fruit, lollipops, and cigars, and on emigrant journeys soap, towels, tin washing dishes, tin coffee pitchers, coffee, tea, sugar, and tinned eatables, mostly hash or beans and bacon. Early next morning the newsboy went around the cars, and chumming on a more extended principle became the order of the hour. It requires but a copartnery of two to manage beds, but washing and eating can be carried on most economically by a syndicate of three. I myself entered a little after sunrise into articles of agreement and became one of the firm of Pennsylvania, Shakespeare, and Dubuque. Shakespeare was my own nickname on the cars, Pennsylvania that of my bedfellow, and Dubuque, the name of a place in the state of Iowa, that of an amiable young fellow going west to cure an asthma and retarding his recovery by incessantly chewing or smoking and sometimes chewing and smoking together. Shakespeare bought a tin washing dish, Dubuque a towel, and Pennsylvania a brick of soap. The partners used these instruments, one after another, according to the order of their first awaking; and when the firm had finished there was no want of borrowers. Each filled the tin dish at the water filter opposite the stove and retired with the whole stock in trade to the platform of the car. There he knelt down, supporting himself by a shoulder against the woodwork or one elbow crooked about the railing, and made shift to wash his face and neck and hands — a cold, an insufficient, and, if the train is moving rapidly, a somewhat dangerous toilet.

On a similar division of expense, the firm of Pennsylvania, Shakespeare, and Dubuque supplied themselves with coffee, sugar, and necessary vessels; and their operations are a type of what went on through all the cars. Before the sun was up the stove would be brightly burning; at the first station the natives would come on board with milk and eggs and coffee cakes; and soon from end to end the car would be filled with little parties breakfasting upon the bed boards. It was the pleasantest hour of the day. . . .

Many conductors, again, will hold no communication with an emigrant. As you are thus cut off from the superior authorities, a great deal of your comfort depends on the character of the newsboy. He has it in his power indefinitely to better and brighten the emigrant's lot. The newsboy with whom we started from the transfer was a dark, bullying, contemptuous, insolent scoundrel, who treated is like dogs. On the other hand, the lad who rode with us in this capacity from Ogden to Sacramento made himself the friend of all and helped us with information, attention, assistance, and a kind countenance. He told us where and when we should have our meals and how long the train would stop, kept seats at table for those who were delayed, and watched that we should neither be left behind nor yet unnecessarily hurried. You who live at home at ease can hardly realize the greatness of this service, even had it stood alone. When I think of that lad coming and going, train after train, with his bright face and civil words, I see how easily a good man may become the benefactor of his kind. Perhaps he is discontented with himself, perhaps troubled with ambitions; why, if he but knew it, he is a hero of the old Greek stamp; and while he thinks he is only earning a profit of a few cents, and that perhaps exorbitant, he is doing a man's work and bettering the world. . . .

I had been suffering in my health a good deal all the way, and at last, whether I was exhausted by my complaint or poisoned in some wayside eating house, the evening we left Laramie, I fell sick outright. That was a night which I shall not readily forget. The lamps did not go out; each made a faint shining in its own neighborhood, and the shadows were confounded together in the long, hollow box of the car. The sleepers lay in uneasy attitudes — here two chums alongside, flat upon their backs like dead folk, there a man sprawling on the floor with his face upon his arm, there another half seated, with his head and shoulders on the bench. The most passive were continually and roughly shaken by the movement of the train; others stirred, turned, or stretched out their arms like children; it was surprising how many groaned and murmured in their sleep; and as I passed to and fro, stepping across the prostrate, and caught now a snore, now a gasp, now a half-formed word, it gave me a measure of the worthlessness of rest in that unresting vehicle. Although it was chill, I was obliged to open my window, for the degradation of the air soon became intolerable to one who was awake and using the full supply of life. Outside, in a glimmering night, I saw the black, amorphous hills shoot by unweariedly into our wake. They that long for morning have never longed for it more earnestly than I.

And yet when day came, it was to shine upon the same broken

and unsightly quarter of the world. Mile upon mile, and not a tree, a bird, or a river. Only down the long, sterile canyons the train shot hooting and awoke the resting echo. That train was the one piece of life in all the deadly land; it was the one actor, the one spectacle fit to be observed in this paralysis of man and nature. And when I think how the railroad has been pushed through this unwatered wilderness and haunt of savage tribes and now will bear an emigrant for some twelve pounds from the Atlantic to the Golden Gates; how at each stage of the construction roaring, impromptu cities, full of gold and lust and death, sprang up and then died away again, and are now but wayside stations in the desert; how in these uncouth places pigtailed Chinese pirates worked side by side with border ruffians and broken men from Europe, talking together in a mixed dialect, mostly oaths, gambling, drinking, quarreling, and murdering like wolves; how the plumed hereditary lord of all America heard, in this last fastness, the scream of the "bad medicine wagon" charioting his foes; and then when I go on to remember that all this epical turmoil was conducted by gentlemen in frock coats and with a view to nothing more extraordinary than a fortune and a subsequent visit to Paris, it seems to me, I own, as if this railway were the one typical achievement of the age in which we live, as if it brought together into one plot all the ends of the world and all the degrees of social rank, and offered to some great writer the busiest, the most extended, and the most varied subject for an enduring literary work. If it be romance, if it be contrast, if it be heroism that we require, what was Troy town to this?

At Ogden we changed cars from the Union Pacific to the Central Pacific line of railroad.

The cars on the Central Pacific were nearly twice as high, and so proportionally airier; they were freshly varnished, which gave us all a sense of cleanliness as though we had bathed; the seats drew out and joined in the center, so that there was no more need for bed boards; and there was an upper tier of berths which could be closed by day and opened at night.

I had by this time some opportunity of seeing the people whom I was among. They were in rather marked contrast to the emigrants I had met on board ship while crossing the Atlantic. They were mostly lumpish fellows, silent and noisy, a common combination, somewhat sad, I should say, with an extraordinary poor taste in humor, and little interest in their fellow creatures beyond that of a cheap and merely external curiosity.

There were no emigrants direct from Europe save one German family and a knot of Cornish miners who kept grimly by themselves, one reading the New Testament all day long through steel spectacles, the rest discussing privately the secrets of their old-world, mysterious race.

The rest were all American born, but they came from almost every quarter of that continent. All the states of the North had sent out a fugitive to cross the plains with me. From Virginia, from Pennsylvania, from New York, from far western Iowa and Kansas, from Maine that borders on the Canadas, and from the Canadas themselves — some one or two were fleeing in quest of a better land and better wages. The talk in the train, like the talk I heard on the steamer, ran upon hard times, short-commons, and hope that moves ever westward. I thought of my shipful from Great Britain with a feeling of despair. They had come three thousand miles, and yet not far enough. Hard times bowed them out of the Clyde and stood to welcome them at Sandy Hook. Where were they to go? Pennsylvania, Maine, Iowa, Kansas? These were not places for immigration, but for emigration, it appeared — not one of them, but I knew a man who had lifted up his heel and left it for an ungrateful country. And it was still westward that they ran. Hunger, you would have thought, came out of the east like the sun, and the evening was made of edible gold. And meantime, in the car in front of me, were there not half a hundred emigrants from the opposite quarter? Hungry Europe and hungry China, each pouring from their gates in search of provender, had here come face to face. The two waves had met; east and west had alike failed; the whole round world had been prospected and condemned; there was no El Dorado anywhere; and till one could emigrate to the moon, it seemed as well to stay patiently at home. Nor was there wanting another sign, at once more picturesque and more disheartening; for as we continued to steam westward toward the land of gold, we were continually passing other emigrant trains upon the journey east; and these were as crowded as our own. Had all these return voyagers made a fortune in the mines? Were they all bound for Paris and to be in Rome by Easter? It would seem not, for whenever we met them, the passengers ran on the platform and cried to us through the windows, in a kind of wailing chorus, to "come back." On the plains of Nebraska, in the mountains of Wyoming, it was still the same cry and dismal to my heart: "Come back!" That was what we heard by the way "about the good country we were going to." And at that very hour the sand lot of San Francisco was crowded with the unemployed and the echo from the other side of Market Street was repeating the rant of demagogues.

ROBERT LOUIS STEVENSON, Across the Plains

193. Albert Richardson Sees the Tricks of Homesteaders

The Homestead Act, which became law in May 1862, ended the long controversy over the disposition of the public lands of the United States by providing for grants of one hundred and sixty acres to bona fide settlers. The requirement that homesteaders should reside upon or cultivate the land for a period of five years was designed to eliminate speculators but, as Richardson here points out, that requirement was easily circumvented by the speculators. When Richardson made his trip across the continent less than one million acres of homesteads had been patented; since that time the total has risen to almost two hundred and fifty-million acres. But, notwithstanding additional legislation, the trickery and chicanery which he describes continued throughout the nineteenth century.

IN AUGUST [1857] I became a squatter and made a claim. This is the frontier term for the one hundred and sixty acres which the real or constructive settler improves and claims for his future home.

Only after pre-emption and a perfect title from the government is it called his farm.

With several companions whose eyes were dazzled by visions of landed proprietorship, I started from Quindaro on a tour through the unsettled county of Johnson, one of the fairest and richest regions of Kansas. In the belt of deep woods eight or ten miles wide along the Missouri, the summer tints were of wonderful beauty and variety. Purple wild plums of delicate flavor, half the size of apples, abounded; from tree and bush hung vines heavy with ripening grapes, not larger than peas, but plump, palatable, and much used in cooking; wild cherries and crab apples grew in profusion; and the thickets bent under heavy loads of elderberries, of which a bushel could be gathered in a few minutes. They lack pungency, but in the absence of other fruits frontier wives convert them into tasteless preserves and insipid pies.

Crossing the Kansas, we reached the prairies and left the woods behind. Here and there were scattered trees along the far-apart streams, but they were like angel visits. This lack of timber was the most serious drawback of pioneers; yet the farmer would far better settle where he must go twenty-five miles for house and fence lumber and firewood than where he must clear away forests to make room for his corn and grass fields. The latter is the work of one or two generations, but in this rich Kansas soil the locust grows like Jonah's gourd, and the cottonwood attains a trunk diameter of five or six inches in six years. Its feathery seed floats on the wind and takes root in plowed fields miles away from the mother tree.

Toward evening we passed several parties of immigrants, chiefly from Missouri. Come to this encampment and see how kindly frontier families take to a roving life. The long, heavy wagon, its roof covered with white cotton cloth, stands a few yards from the road. It is packed with provisions and household utensils, and two or three pots and kettles are suspended from the hind axle. The tired oxen graze upon the neighboring prairie. The white-haired children are playing hard by — five or six in number, for these new countries are marvelously prolific. The husband is milking the patient cows; the wife is preparing a supper of griddlecakes, bacon, and coffee, in the open air, at the camp stove; the hens are cackling socially from their coop, while the old family dog wags his tail approvingly, but watches with solicitous care the baby creeping about the wagon.

When crossing the great deserts to Utah or California, they toil wearily along from twelve to twenty miles per day. The long-bearded, shaggy drivers, tanned to the hue of Arapahoes, look like animated pillars of earth, and seem under the perpetual sentence: Dust thou art and unto dust shalt thou return. Each keeps his trusty rifle or shotgun within grasp, and at night the wagons are parked in a circle and the cattle driven into the extemporized yard which they inclose, as a protection against Indian surprises. Eternal vigilance is the price of travel. The children of the immigrants revel in dirt and novelty, but their mothers cast eager, longing eyes toward their new homes. There is profound truth in the remark that plains travel and frontier life are peculiarly severe upon women and oxen.

During this fall many residents were pre-empting their claims. The law contemplates a homestead of one hundred and sixty acres at a nominal price for each actual settler and no one else, but land is plenty and everybody pre-empts. A young merchant, lawyer, or speculator rides into the interior to the unoccupied public lands, pays some settler five dollars to show him the vacant claims, and selects one upon which he places four little poles around a hollow square upon the ground, as children commence a cob house. Then he files a notice in the land office that he has laid the foundation of a house upon this claim and begun a settlement for actual residence. He does not see the land again until ready to "prove up," which he may do after thirty days. Then he revisits his claim, possibly erects a house of rough slabs, costing from ten to twenty dollars, eats one meal, and sleeps for a single night under its roof. More frequently, however, his improvements consist solely of a foundation of four logs.

In three cases out of four, after proving up, the pre-emptor never visits his land again unless for the purpose of selling it. Says the Spanish proverb, "Oaths are words, and words are wind." Thus this unequivocal perjury is regarded upon the frontier. The general feeling is that it wrongs no one and that the settlers have a right to the land.

Hundreds of men whose families are still in the East find witnesses to testify that their wives and children are residing upon the land. I have known men to pre-empt who had never been within twenty miles of their claims, facile witnesses swearing with the utmost indifference that they were residing upon them.

The pre-emptors must state under oath that they have made no agreement direct or indirect for selling any part of the land. But in numberless instances these statements are falsehoods connived at by the officers.

In most land offices a man cannot pre-empt unless he has a house at least twelve feet square. I have known a witness to swear that the house in question was twelve by fourteen when actually the only building upon the claim was one whittled out with a pen-knife, twelve *inches* by fourteen.

Some offices require that the house must have a glass window. While traveling in the interior I stopped at a little slab cabin where I noticed a window sash without lights hanging upon a nail. As I had seen similar frames in other cabins, I asked the owner what it was for.

"To pre-empt with," was the reply.

"How?"

"Why, don't you understand? To enable my witness to swear that there is a *window in my house!*"

Sometimes the same cabin is moved from claim to claim until half a dozen different persons have pre-empted with it. In Nebraska a little frame house, like a country Daguerrean car, was built for this purpose *on wheels* and drawn by oxen. It enabled the pre-emptor to swear that he had a bona fide residence upon his claim. It was let at five dollars a day, and scores of claims were proved up and pre-empted with it. The discovery of any such malpractice and perjury would invalidate the title. But I never knew of an instance where the pre-emptor was deprived of his land after once receiving his title.

No woman can pre-empt unless she is a widow or the "head of a family." But sometimes an ambitious maiden who wishes to secure one hundred and sixty acres of land *borrows* a child, signs papers of adoption, swears that she is the head of a family, and pre-empts her claim, then annuls the papers and returns her temporary offspring to its parents with an appropriate gift.

ALBERT D. RICHARDSON, *Beyond the Mississippi*

194. Plenty-Coups Fights Three-Stars on the Rosebud

The building of the transcontinental railroads, the invasion of their hunting grounds by miners and cattlemen, and the destruction of the buffalo, threatened the Plains Indians with extinction. The decades of the sixties and the seventies were marked by continuous Indian unrest, punctuated by open warfare. Of all the Plains Indians the Sioux were the most formidable, and when, late in 1875, the Indian Department ordered them to retire to their reservations, Chief Crazy-Horse of the Oglala Sioux led his braves on the warpath. General Crook hastily enlisted the aid of the Crows and Shoshones, ancient enemies of the Sioux, and in May 1876 won an indecisive victory over Crazy-Horse. One month later came the battle on the upper Rosebud, in southern Montana, which Plenty-Coups here describes. A few days later came the Custer massacre; after that Indian resistance was broken and in September 1877 Crazy-Horse himself was killed.

ONE DAY in the springtime [1876], when our village was on the Rosebud, the Limping Soldier [General Gibbon] came to talk to our chiefs about going to war with him against the Sioux, Cheyennes, and Arapahoes, who had been fighting his soldiers. We agreed, and when he asked us for some Wolves we gave him twenty men. These went away with him to his camp, where he told us he was waiting for The-Other-One [General Terry] and Son-of-the-Morning-Star [General Custer]. . . .

One hundred and thirty-five young men offered themselves, and we got ready at once. Alligator-Stands-Up was our war chief, and besides him there were many good men in our party. The Big Horn River was bank-full, but we were happy and before night were across it, with camp made, to kill buffalo for supplies. Two days after this we came to the hills that looked down on the flat on Goose Creek. I shall never forget what I saw there. It was nearly midday, and countless little tents were in straight rows in the green grass, and there were nearly as many little fires. Blue soldiers were everywhere. I could not count the wagons and horses and mules. They looked like the grass on the plains — beyond counting.

The Wolves of Three-Stars [General Crook] had seen us and had told him we were coming. Even before we dismounted to dress up and paint ourselves for war a bugle sang a war song in the soldiers' village, after which many blue men began running about. Then, under our very eyes and so quickly we could scarcely believe them, countless blue legs were walking together; fine horses in little bands that were all of one color were dancing to the songs of shining horns and drums. Oh, what a sight I saw there on Goose Creek that day in the sunlight! My heart sang with the shining horns of the blue soldiers in Three-Stars' village.

Our faces painted, we put on our war bonnets and sprang upon our horses. We gave the Crow war whoop and, firing our guns in the air, dashed down the hill. . . .

Whoooooo! Our guns were cracking, and we raised a big dust. We threw our bodies first one way and then another on our horses, just as we do when fighting. Some of us sprang to the ground and back again without even staggering our horses, and all the time our beautiful bonnets were blowing in the wind. Ah, that was a great day! . . .

Many of us had cartridge guns now, and the soldiers gave us whole boxes of cartridges, cans of powder, and more balls than we could carry. I had never before seen plenty of ammunition. My own people were always out of either powder or lead. We could make arrows for our bows, but we could not make powder or lead for our guns. But now everybody had more than he needed, more than he could use. And besides cartridges and powder, the soldiers gave us hard bread and bacon — too much of it. They had wagons filled with such things, and the soldiers were generous men. We had everything we wanted, and we were in good condition to fight.

I suppose Three-Stars had his Wolves out on the hills. I know mine were out and had already seen the enemy. The country was alive with Sioux, Cheyennes, and Arapahoes. I told Three-Stars about it, because I did not know his ways. He only said: "We shall move in the morning. I hope to get a message from Elk River tonight."

I am certain no message came to him that night or any other time. None could have reached him. No messenger could have lived between us and Elk River. The enemy were like lice on a robe there, and hot for battle. That night when I was sleeping Left-Hand came to me and said Three-Stars wanted me. I rose and went to his lodge.

"Select nine good men and begin to scout at once toward the Rosebud," he ordered me. "I expect to meet The-Other-One, the Limping Soldier, and Son-of-the-Morning-Star within two days," he said, "I wish you to lead your scouts yourself. We will follow you at daybreak and will march without resting from sun to sun," he finished.

I do not know why Three-Stars believed he would meet those other soldier chiefs within two days unless a message had reached him before we came to Goose Creek. He heard nothing from his friends after our arrival, I am certain. And if he had perfectly understood all that the Crow Wolves told him I am sure he would not have tried to go down the Rosebud at all. Crazy-Horse was there, the Oglala chief, with his warriors, on their way to join the big war village on the little Big-Horn. Three-Stars had been told all this many times and must have known the way was very bad, if Left-Hand talked straight.

We camped that night, all of us, on the Rosebud. I thought it a bad place to choose when trouble was so near, and there was a worse place below, where Crazy-Horse was waiting to trap us. Three-Stars had left all his wagons on Goose Creek, packing his mules, and these were the last to reach our camp. The horse soldiers came in first, next the walking soldiers, and finally, when we were in our robes, the packers came. I had been out looking around before dark. I did not believe the night would pass without a fight, and I did not like our position. I told Three-Stars we were near big trouble, hoping he would move to a better camp; but he did not.

All night long the enemy gathered. Coyote yelps and wolf howls in the hills told me he was closing in on us, while I waited in my robe. I kept thinking about the bad canyon just below us and of our poor stand for a big fight until I began to hear Owls; then I left my robe. I realized that Sioux, Cheyennes, and Arapahoes were thick about us, like ants on a freshly killed buffalo's hide. We were going to have a hard fight in a very bad place.

Before daybreak (three o'clock) Three-Stars was moving, with the Crows divided into parties ahead, and before the sun had been long in the sky we ran into the enemy. I fell back to be with Three-Stars, for the big fight, I knew, was on our hands. He stopped when he heard the first shots, setting his men in position. This is the way I saw them: the pack train was facing south; the walking soldiers were among the bushes in the gulch; the horse soldiers, afoot now, were facing east and north. There were two flags, one with the walking soldiers and one with the horse soldiers. Everybody was ready for the trouble that was following us Crows as fast as it could.

We swung in between Three-Stars and the advancing enemy, facing west and a little north, with the Shoshones. Then, seeing that Three-Stars was ready, we Indians charged the enemy, driving him back and breaking his line. But he divided and turned his ends around ours to get at Three-Stars. When we saw this we turned back with our wounded, because Three-Stars needed us now. His horse soldiers were backing up, leaving their position, when we got there; but his walking soldiers in the willows were holding their ground. Sioux, Cheyenne, and Arapahoe were pressing them hard. I saw horse after horse go down and many a soldier go under before the horse soldiers began to run, so mixed up with Indians and plunging horses we dared not shoot that way. The enemy was clubbing the soldiers, striking them down, with but scattering shots speaking, when we charged.

Our war whoop, with the Shoshones', waked the Echo-People! We rode *through* them, over the body of one of Three-Stars' chiefs who was shot through the face under his eyes so that the flesh was pushed away from his broken bones. Our charge saved him from being finished and scalped.

The enemy fell back. He was fighting desperately, but losing when suddenly I felt my horse break in two behind me. His front part staggered, slid a little way, and then fell. A bullet had broken his back. I struck the ground hard, and I rolled myself away from the many wild hoofs around my head, the Sioux yell in my ears. They thought they had me. I can hear them yet. They believed they were going to count coup on me, but I fooled them.

Discovering a hole in a ledge of rim rock, I worked my way there as fast as I could. Bullets slapped the stone, and dust flew up around the hole when I was going in. But I had kept my gun and did some good shooting from that hole in the rocks until finally everybody got out of range. Then I crawled out to look for a horse to ride and caught a fine bay with a black mane and tail.

The Crows and Shoshones had now turned and were coming back, with the enemy pressing them very hard. I thought I had better try to reach the walking soldiers, because I saw that we should all have to make a stand with them or lose the fight. But before I could get to them they began backing up. They were whipped and likely to run any time. While bullets were cutting the air around me, striking the ground, glancing to whine away, I made up my mind to ride for the walking soldiers in the willows. I leaned low over my horse, lashing him to his best, till I felt him tremble like a leaf in the wind. Before I could even straighten myself on his back he went head first to the ground, dead. A bullet was in his heart. How the enemy did yell!

I realized I was in a bad fix, but instantly I saw a gray horse with a saddle on his back. In less time than I am using to tell it I was in that saddle and away. The horse was no good. I had to beat him to make him even walk. Yet if he had not been so slow and lazy, I suppose I might have been killed. A Crow would not own such a horse as that Sioux gray.

Just then I saw Alligator-Stands-Up, our war chief, make the sign to form wings; so I turned with the nearest Crows. This was the end of the fight on Rosebud. We Indians drove the enemy away down the creek.

The poor soldiers had suffered. They were whipped and wanted no more to do with Crazy-Horse just then.

FRANK B. LINDERMAN, American

195. Andy Adams Herds Texas Cattle on the Long Drive

For generations cattle had grazed wild on the plains of the Southwest, too far distant from market to have any value. In 1867 the Kansas Pacific Railway began to reach out into the Plains, and in that year J. G. McCoy established the first of the cow-towns, Abilene, Kansas, from which live cattle could be shipped to the stock markets of the East. Then began the "long drive," northward along the Goodnight or the Chisholm or other trails to one of the roaring cattle towns on the Kansas Pacific or the Union Pacific railroads. Andy Adams, one of the greatest of the Texas cattlemen, here describes some of the perils of the "long drive."

THE NEXT morning by daybreak the cattle were thrown off the bed ground and started grazing before the sun could dry out what little moisture the grass had absorbed during the night. The heat of the past week had been very oppressive, and in order to avoid it as much as possible, we made late and early drives. Before the wagon passed the herd during the morning drive, what few canteens we had were filled with water for the men. The *remuda* was kept with the herd, and four changes of mounts were made during the day, in order not to exhaust any one horse. Several times, for an hour or more, the herd was allowed to lie down and rest; but by the middle of the afternoon thirst made them impatient and restless, and the point men were compelled to ride steadily in the lead in order to hold the cattle to a walk. A number of times during the afternoon we attempted to graze them, but not until the twilight of evening was it possible. . . .

We were handling the cattle as humanely as possible under the circumstances. The guards for the night were doubled, six men on the first half and the same on the latter, Bob Blades being detailed to assist Honeyman in night-herding the saddle horses. If any of us got more than an hour's sleep that night, he was lucky. Flood, McCann, and the horse wranglers did not even try to rest. To those of us who could find time to eat, our cook kept open house. Our foreman knew that a well-fed man can stand an incredible amount of hardship and appreciated the fact that on the trail a good cook is a valuable asset. Our outfit, therefore, was cheerful to a man, and jokes and songs helped to while away the weary hours of the night.

The second guard, under Flood, pushed the cattle off their beds an hour before dawn, and before they were relieved had urged the herd more than five miles on the third day's drive over this waterless mesa. In spite of our economy of water, after breakfast on this third morning there was scarcely enough left to fill the canteens for the day. In view of this, we could promise ourselves no midday meal — except a can of tomatoes to the man; so the wagon was ordered to drive through to the expected water ahead, while the saddle horses were held available as on the day before for frequent changing of mounts. The day turned out to be one of torrid heat, and before the middle of the forenoon, the cattle lolled their tongues in despair, while their sullen lowing surged through from rear to lead and back again in piteous yet ominous appeal. The only relief we could offer was to travel them slowly, as they spurned every opportunity offered them either to graze or to lie down.

It was nearly noon when we reached the last divide and sighted the scattering timber of the expected watercourse. The enforced order of the day before — to hold the herd in a walk and prevent exertion and heating — now required four men in the lead, while the rear followed over a mile behind, dogged and sullen. Near the middle of the afternoon McCann returned on one of his mules with the word that it was a question if there was water enough to water even the horse stock. The preceding outfit, so he reported, had dug a shallow well in the bed of the creek, from which he had filled his kegs, but the stock water was a mere loblolly. On receipt of this news, we changed mounts for the fifth time that day; and Flood, taking Forrest, the cook, and the horse wrangler, pushed on ahead with the *remuda* to the waterless stream.

The outlook was anything but encouraging. Flood and Forrest scouted the creek up and down for ten miles in a fruitless search for water. The outfit held the herd back until the twilight of evening, when Flood returned and confirmed McCann's report. It was twenty miles yet to the next water ahead, and if the horse stock could only be watered thoroughly, Flood was determined to make the attempt to nurse the herd through to water. McCann was digging an extra well, and he expressed the belief that by hollowing out a number of holes, enough water could be secured for the saddle stock. Honeyman had corralled the horses and was letting only a few go to the water at a time, while the night horses were being thoroughly watered as fast as the water rose in the well.

Holding the herd this third night required all hands. Only a few men at a time were allowed to go into camp and eat, for the herd refused even to lie down. What few cattle attempted to rest were prevented by the more restless ones. By spells they would mill, until riders were sent through the herd at a breakneck pace to break up the groups. During these milling efforts of the herd, we drifted over a mile from camp; but by the light of moon and stars and the number of riders, scattering was prevented. As the horses were loose for the night, we could not start them on the trail until daybreak gave us a change of mounts; so we lost the early start of the morning before.

Good cloudy weather would have saved us, but in its stead was a sultry morning without a breath of air, which bespoke another day of sizzling heat. We had not been on the trail over two hours before the heat became almost unbearable to man and beast. Had it not been for the condition of the herd, all might yet have gone well; but over three days had now elapsed without water for the cattle, and they became feverish and ungovernable. The lead cattle turned back several times, wandering aimlessly in any direction, and it was with considerable difficulty that the herd could be held on the trail. The rear overtook the lead, and the cattle gradually lost all semblance of a trail herd. Our horses were fresh, however, and after about two hours' work, we once more got the herd strung out in trailing fashion; but before a mile had been covered, the leaders again turned, and the cattle congregated into a mass of unmanageable animals, milling and lowing in their fever and thirst. The milling only intensified their sufferings from the heat, and the outfit split and quartered them again and again, in the hope that this unfortunate outbreak might be checked. No sooner was the milling stopped than they would surge hither and yon, sometimes half a mile, as ungovernable as the waves of an ocean. After wasting several hours in this manner, they finally turned back over the trail, and the utmost efforts of every man in the outfit failed to check them. We threw our ropes in their faces, and when this failed, we resorted to shooting; but in defiance of the fusillade and the smoke they walked sullenly through the line of horsemen across their front. Six-shooters were discharged so close to the leaders' faces as to singe their hair; yet under a noonday sun they disregarded this and every other device to turn them and passed wholly out of our control. In a number of instances wild steers deliberately walked against our horses, and then for the first time a fact dawned on us that chilled the marrow in our bones — *the herd was going blind.*

The bones of men and animals that lie bleaching along the trails abundantly testify that this was not the first instance in which the plain had baffled the determination of man. It was now evident that nothing short of water would stop the herd, and we rode aside and let them pass. As the outfit turned back to the wagon, our foreman seemed dazed by the sudden and unexpected turn of affairs but rallied and met the emergency.

"There's but one thing left to do," said he, as we rode along, "and that is to hurry the outfit back to Indian Lakes. The herd will travel day and night, and instinct can be depended on to carry them to the only water they know. It's too late to be of any use now, but it's plain why those last two herds turned off at the lakes; some one had gone back and warned them of the very thing we've met. We must beat them to the lakes, for water is the only thing that will check them now. It's a good thing that they are strong, and five or six days without water will hardly kill any. It was no vague statement of the man who said if he owned hell and Texas, he'd rent Texas and live in hell, for if this isn't Billy hell, I'd like to know what you call it."

We spent an hour watering the horses from the wells of our camp of the night before, and about two o'clock started back over the trail for Indian Lakes. We overtook the abandoned herd during the afternoon. They were strung out nearly five miles in length and were walking about a three-mile gait. Four men were given two extra horses apiece and left to throw in the stragglers in the rear, with instructions to follow them well into the night, and again in the morning as long as their canteens lasted. The remainder of the outfit pushed on without a halt except to change mounts and reached the lakes shortly after midnight. There we secured the first good sleep of any consequence for three days.

It was fortunate for us that there were no range cattle at these lakes, and we had only to cover a front of about six miles to catch the drifting herd. It was nearly noon the next day before the cattle began to arrive at the water holes in squads of from twenty to fifty. Pitiful objects as they were, it was a novelty to see them reach the water and slack their thirst. Wading out into the lakes until their sides were half covered, they would stand and low in a soft moaning voice, often for half an hour before attempting to drink. Contrary to our expectation, they drank very little at first, but stood in the water for hours. After coming out, they would lie down and rest for hours longer and then drink again before attempting to graze, their thirst overpowering hunger. That they were blind there was no question, but with the causes that produced it once removed, it was probable their eyesight would gradually return.

Andy Adams, The Log of a Cowboy

196. Looting a Kansas County

The construction of railroads, speculation in town sites, in land, timber, and minerals, offered golden opportunities for graft. Many long-suffering communities in the last west were infested with the type of grafters here described and saddled for a generation with a heavy debt for which there was nothing to show. The experience of Barber County, described by a Kansas editor, was by no means unique.

IF EVER there was a municipal organization conceived in sin and brought forth in iniquity it was the organization of Barber County. During the early seventies, it occurred to a number of enterprising thieves that the organization of counties in central and western Kansas offered an inviting field for exploitation at comparatively little risk to the exploiters. There were practically no permanent residents in that part of the state at that time and consequently few who had a personal interest in preventing the robbery consummated under forms of law.

The statute governing the organization of new counties required at that time at least six hundred bona fide inhabitants within the territory to be organized. In 1872 there were probably not more than one hundred bona fide inhabitants in the territory included within the boundaries of the proposed county, but that fact presented no impediment to the predatory gang which had perfected its plan of loot. A census taker was appointed, who was void of either conscience or fear of future punishment, and from convenient hotel registers he copied the requisite number of names, swore that they were bona fide residents within the territory of the proposed county, and the preliminaries were arranged with an ease and speed which would have excited the envy of a professional highwayman.

There were some honest men even then living in the territory which now composes the county of Barber, but as I have intimated, they had no vested interest in the country. They were the possessors of herds of cattle of varying size, grazing on the native grasses, but they did not expect to remain permanently in that country. Unfortunately most men are so constituted that they do not become deeply concerned about graft unless that graft touches them in some way. So the conditions were particularly favorable for the highbinders who figured out a scheme of organizing counties, loading them with bonds, selling the bonds to supposed innocent purchasers, pocketing the proceeds, and, when the harvest of loot had been gathered, folding their tents like the Arab and silently stealing away.

The first meeting of the new board of county commissioners, so far as the records show, was held in Medicine Lodge on July 7, 1873. These commissioners were not the master spirits in the conspiracy, but they were willing servants and showed the industry of the busy bee, which flits from flower to flower, gathering honey as it flits. About the first business of importance transacted was to issue twenty-five thousand dollars in county warrants to one C. C.

Beemis, in consideration of which he was supposed to build a court-house. It, of course, showed great confidence in the integrity of Mr. Beemis to issue to him the contract price before he had furnished a brick, a board, or a nail that was to go into the building, but the confidence seemed to have been misplaced, as Mr. Beemis did not even commence the erection of the courthouse. His failure, however, did not interfere with the friendly relations or confidence of the board of commissioners, who made no effort to compel him to fulfill his contract or return the warrants which had been issued. In fact the commissioners acted on the theory that if at first you don't succeed try, try again and next time proposed to vote bonds to build a courthouse to the extent of forty thousand dollars. By that time some of the residents of the county, although temporary, objected to the issuance of more bonds or warrants to build a courthouse, in view of the fact that twenty-five thousand dollars had already been stolen, and they rallied enough votes to defeat the bonds. This, however, did not dash or discourage the commissioners, who issued the warrants anyhow, and then through an act of Legislature put through by the leader of the gang, the first legislative member from Barber, they issued funding bonds to cover the debt. Still no court-house was built. Not a brick was laid or a single foundation stone. The busy board had also issued some forty or fifty thousand dollars in warrants to build bridges, and considering the number of streams there are in the county, I have no doubt they were astonished at their own moderation.

The bridges were not built, but then they might have stolen more. At the instance of members of the gang a railroad corporation called the Nebraska, Kansas and Southwestern was organized. Not only, in the language of a former member of the Kansas Legislature, did this road "not terminate at either end," but it had no existence except on paper. Yet the looters managed to put over an alleged bond election by which the new county voted one hundred thousand dollars' ten-per-cent bonds to this mythical corporation, and then, in violation of the spirit, if not the letter, of the law, under which the road was supposed to be built before the bonds were issued, the board of commissioners issued and sold the bonds without there being a single mile of road constructed. The bonds passed into the hands of an English capitalist, a member of the British Parliament

Afterward the taxpayers of Barber resisted payment of the bonds and carried the litigation through the courts up to the Supreme Court; but they lost in the end and are today paying the principal and interest of that utterly fraudulent obligation.

Finally the shameless stealings of the looters roused the fury of the settlers, who were coming to look on the county with its clear streams, its beautiful valleys, its sweet hills and groves and canyons as their permanent abiding place. So they formed their vigilance committee, with the avowed and laudable purpose of hanging the thieves. They did round up a part of the gang but made the fatal error of permitting them to talk. The spokesman for the gang offered to restore the loot already taken and to leave the county forever. They did leave the county but took with them the county warrant books and county seal, and from the safe retreat of Hutchinson they proceeded to issue new evidence of indebtedness against the sorely plundered municipality. Of course, it is unnecessary to say that they never restored any of the plunder they had garnered under forms of law. A member of the vigilance committee was heard afterward to remark, "If we hadn't been a passel of dam fools we would 'a' hung them blank-blank sons of blank first and then listened to what they had to say afterwards."

T. A. McNEAL, When Kansas Was Young

197. The Grasshopper Plague Hits the High Plains

The region of the High Plains — roughly from the one hundredth meridian to the Rocky Mountains — suffered from insufficient rainfall and from recurrent insect plagues which made farming highly hazardous. Dry farming and irrigation in part solved the problem of aridity, but no method was known of dealing with the grasshopper plagues. When the locusts came, they denuded a field in a few moments, and the farmers stood by helpless as they watched the labor of a year wasted.

IN 1874 came a gigantic calamity in the form of a raid of grasshoppers which ate up every bit of green vegetation from the Rocky Mountains to and beyond the Missouri River. I recall that when coming home late one afternoon for supper I stepped back surprised to see what became known as Rocky Mountain locusts covering the side of the house. Already inside, they feasted on the curtains. Clouds of them promptly settled down on the whole country — everywhere, unavoidable. People set about killing them to save gardens, but this soon proved ridiculous. Specially contrived machines, pushed by horses, scooped up the hoppers in grain fields by the barrelful to burn them. This, too, was then nonsensical. Vast hordes, myriads. In a week grain fields, gardens, shrubs, vines, had been eaten down to the ground or to the bark. Nothing could be done. You sat by and saw everything go.

When autumn came with the country devastated, the population despaired again when seeing the insects remaining for the winter with the apparent plan of being on hand for the next season. It seemed that they could be counted on as a curse for all time, since the Rocky Mountain locusts, as the name indicates, appeared new to science, to the civilized world. No one, accordingly, knew of their habits. And their ingenuity confounded close observers. As if intending to stay permanently on the plains, they bored holes only in hard ground, in roads and other firm places, for their winter occupancy. Intelligently did they avoid soft ground, since tenancy there would be more easily, more apt to be, disturbed.

To add to the terror of the locust invasion was the general accompaniment of weather tending always to be dry. Kansans — "people of the south wind." This poetic Indian meaning might bear a still more distinctive signification if it ran "people of the hot southwest wind." For continental western Kansas, lying in the exact center of the United States, turned out to be subject in summer to burning south or southwest winds untempered by cooling salt breezes creeping up from the Gulf of Mexico or cooling zephyrs descending from Canada. The middle area often missed the relief that either the southern or northern areas might experience. And a steady hot current of air, though mild in velocity, brought the dreaded dry times.

How one hated to see the heavens seal their cisterns and the plains to be sear! A few showers would dash upon the ground and run to cover in the creek and river beds, not stopping to penetrate to roots. Matters seemed, indeed, to be made worse by these spurts of moisture, the blazing sun promptly coming out afterward, baking the earth harder.

Almost hilarious, many of the old-timers during such months! They underwent the stark privations in very fair style, having been shown to be prophets with honor in their own land.

"Hee-hee! Didn't I tell you so? This ain't no farmin' country. Too droughty. Lucky fer cattle if lucky fer anything. An' these 'ere Easterners ruinin' the buffalo grass by plowin' it up! Spilin' everything. Yaps that want to farm better stay back East where there ain't anything better to do. They have driv' out the Texas cattle trade. What have they got left? Mighty little, by cracky!"

People still often considered the plains fit at best for very light spring crops. If these shrank up just before harvest, there would be left after June nothing to fall back upon during the rest of the year. The small corn areas along the streams then resembled patches of sticks. The local livestock in 1874 had to be disposed of, fodder lacking. Pitiful little vegetable gardens shriveled. The few flower plots planted by housewives were at first bravely watered. Like tiny, ghastly totem poles did the scarred stalks afterward look.

In a hot droughty summer most of the wells and springs gave out early. Water in creeks trickled so shallowly that dogs lay panting in them while hardly able to immerse more than their paws. Then the burning spell! The southwest wind blew at frequent intervals out of its Sahara ovens, sweeping the land with a flinty dust. You thought of it as a finely textured burial shroud. People told the old joke: "We'd have had to soak our pigs overnight so that they could hold swill." The nights proved as debilitating as the days, since humanity couldn't sleep for the heat. This was the worst of it — they couldn't sleep. No part of each twenty-four hours furnished forgetfulness of the nightmare of failure.

In that country of poor farming and upon a population heedless about laying by supplies for a scarce period, the disaster of 1874 doubled its effect. One conceded: Of what use to work? Farmers, of course, stood out of a job. They loafed in town from midsummer on. For many said they could hardly have plowed or broken prairie

The lumps of sod needed to be knocked up by axes. Seven months before there would be a thing to do. Locusts and scanty rainfall together!

One watched the office men in towns lounging day after day at their doors or hanging out of their windows, with nothing on hand. Business collapsed. It looked like an idiotic insult to ask any one for what he owed. Tillers of soil could not be counted on to pay anyhow till after harvest, once a year, and now, in 1874, no harvest. The merchants, townsmen in general, were expected to cash up from month to month. They stared blankly at the streets, trying to figure how they could get through the winter with their money and credit mostly gone up the spout. The sight of farmers dawdling in stores and saloons added to the dismalness. What if *next* year brought a blank? Too awful to contemplate! Meanwhile — it looked like sheer unavoidable starvation.

Moral stamina? One knew how the women slouched around red-hot cookstoves three times a day for the regular if skimpy meals. Some strength *must* be kept up, some flesh *must* be kept on bones. Even wives who had had a little pardonable vanity left quit trying to save their complexions. They let their tresses go dry and stick out any way. Hair got crinkly, few bothering much about brushes and combs. Hollow-eyed, fagged out, the fair sex came to care little how they looked, what they wore. The story was told of seeing on a street a woman in a garment she had sewed together from the halves of different flour sacks without taking the pains to remove their brands, the result being shocking. Men swore and played poker no more. Fathers dreaded to face their children, who grew raggeder. As for their dirtiness, who, you might almost ask, hardly dared spare water to wash them? Husbands hated to go home to meals, for they must meet the appeals of their wives to climb on wagons and strike out for back home.

"Sell for what you can get, John — give it away — leave it — only let's get out. I don't have to ride on a railroad. A schooner headed east looks awful good to me."

Prayer meetings being held, a few of the men who had not gone to church dropped in and sat before pulpits, heads bowed, humbled in respect. They wondered now if there might be some virtue in supplication. At least they risked no money nor chances by attending meeting. Anything, even prayer, to see mud puddles drowning out the hoppers! But the believers in the great god luck — the majority — stood, in the main, by their guns. They didn't think petitions by four-hundred-dollar-a-year ministers had enough breeze behind them to be shot clear up to Heaven so that the yelpings could be heard there. Wouldn't luck bring a favorable year next time, since this one could be called a ripper? Herein lay the dependable thing about luck: It always changes. . . .

What with federal and other public aid and a steady immigration with money in larger sums, the population lived through the great grasshopper year mainly from necessity as well as pluck. It was a close call. But the locusts or a drought or both the next year would practically wipe out this early folk. A mighty and unsuspected blessing, however, intervened. Since low and moister regions than the Rocky Mountains cause its grasshopper progeny to die before maturity, one raid will not continue elsewhere its severest damage into the following years. This is what took place on the plains in the spring of 1875, though it could not have been foreseen by the disheartened people. In that year and the year or two afterward this insect did not cause the harm suffered in 1874.

Also the seed grain supplied by Eastern charity made good, and the fortunate season in 1875 brought ample crops to meet good prices. Buoyant faith at once re-established itself. . . . The god luck had again veered. The plains now reigned in prosperity and was freely wagered on in terms of a wet, though glowing, future.

STUART HENRY, Conquering Our Great American Plains

198. Hamlin Garland Harvests Wheat on an Iowa Farm

The reaper was invented by Cyrus McCormick of Virginia in 1831, but it did not begin to revolutionize American agriculture until it was applied to the farming of the prairie country. At the time the reaper was invented it took a man approximately three days to harvest twenty bushels of grain; at the time of which Garland writes, he could perform the same work in about three hours. But though machinery saved labor, it did not release the farmer, or his wife and his boys, from drudgery, and no one has described the drudgery of farm life more realistically than has Hamlin Garland, the son of the Middle Border who went East to become a distinguished man of letters.

As I look back over my life on that Iowa farm the song of the reaper fills large place in my mind. We were all worshipers of wheat in those days. The men thought and talked of little else between seeding and harvest, and you will not wonder at this if you have known and bowed before such abundance as we then enjoyed.

Deep as the breast of a man, wide as the sea, heavy-headed, supple-stocked, many-voiced, full of multitudinous, secret, whispered colloquies — a meeting place of winds and of sunlight — our fields ran to the world's end.

We trembled when the storm lay hard upon the wheat, we exulted as the lilac shadows of noonday drifted over it! We went out into it at noon when all was still — so still we could hear the pulse of the transforming sap as it crept from cool root to swaying plume. We stood before it at evening when the setting sun flooded it with crimson, the bearded heads lazily swirling under the wings of the wind, the mousing hawk dipping into its green deeps like the eagle into the sea, and our hearts expanded with the beauty and the mystery of it — and back of all this was the knowledge that its abundance meant a new carriage, an addition to the house, or a new suit of clothes.

Haying was over, and day by day we boys watched with deepening interest while the hot sun transformed the juices of the soil into those stately stalks. I loved to go out into the fairy forest of it, and lying there, silent in its swaying deeps, hear the wild chickens peep and the wind sing its subtle song over our heads. Day by day I studied the barley as it turned yellow, first at the root and then at the neck (while the middle joints, rank and sappy, retained their blue-green sheen), until at last the lower leaves began to wither and the stems to stiffen in order to uphold the daily increasing weight of the milky berries, and then almost in an hour — lo! the edge of the field became a banded ribbon of green and yellow, languidly waving in and out with every rush of the breeze.

Now we got out the reaper, put the sickles in order, and Father laid in a store of provisions. Extra hands were hired, and at last, early on a hot July morning, the boss mounted to his seat on the self-rake McCormick and drove into the field. Frank rode the lead horse, four stalwart hands and myself took stations behind the reaper, and the battle was on!

Reaping generally came about the 20th of July, the hottest and dryest part of the summer, and was the most pressing work of the year. It demanded early rising for the men, and it meant an all-day broiling over the kitchen stove for the women. Stern, incessant toil went on inside and out from dawn till sunset, no matter how the thermometer sizzled. On many days the mercury mounted to ninety-five in the shade, but with wide fields all yellowing at the same moment, no one thought of laying off. A storm might sweep it flat, or if neglected too long it might crinkle.

Our reaper in 1874 was a new model of the McCormick self-rake — the Marsh harvester was not yet in general use. The Woods dropper, the Seymour and Morgan hand-rake contraptions, seemed a long way in the past. True, the McCormick required four horses to drag it, but it was effective. It was hard to believe that anything more cunning would ever come to claim the farmer's money. Weird tales of a machine on which two men rode and bound twelve acres of wheat in ten hours came to us, but we did not potently believe these reports — on the contrary we accepted the self-rake as quite the final word in harvesting machinery and cheerily bent to the binding of sheaves with their own straw in the good old time-honored way.

No task save that of cradling surpassed in severity binding on a station. It was a full-grown man's job, but every boy was ambitious to try his hand, and when at fourteen years of age I was promoted from bundle boy to be one of the five hands to bind after the reaper, I went to my corner with joy and confidence. For two years I had been serving as binder on the corners (to keep the grain out of the way of the horses), and I knew my job.

I was short and broad-shouldered, with large, strong hands admirably adapted for this work, and for the first two hours easily held my own with the rest of the crew; but as the morning wore on and the sun grew hotter my enthusiasm waned. A painful void developed in my chest. My breakfast had been ample, but no mere stomachful of food could carry a growing boy through five hours of desperate toil. Along about a quarter to ten I began to scan the field with anxious eye, longing to see Harriet and the promised luncheon basket.

Just when it seemed that I could endure the strain no longer she came bearing a jug of cool milk, some cheese, and some deliciously fresh friedcakes. With keen joy I set a couple of tall sheaves together like a tent and flung myself down flat on my back in their shadow to devour my lunch.

Tired as I was, my dim eyes apprehended something of the splendor of the shining clouds which rolled like storms of snow through the deep blue spaces of sky, and so, resting silently as a clod, I could hear the chirp of the crickets, the buzzing wings of flies, and the faint, fairylike tread of smaller unseen insects hurrying their way just beneath my ear in the stubble. Strange green worms, grasshoppers, and shining beetles crept over me as I dozed.

This delicious, dreamful respite was broken by the far-off approaching purr of the sickle, flicked by the faint snap of the driver's whip, and out of the low rustle of the ever-stirring Lilliputian forest came the wailing cry of a baby wild chicken lost from its mother — a falling, thrilling, piteous little pipe.

Such momentary communion with nature seemed all the sweeter for the work which had preceded it as well as that which was to follow it. It took resolution to rise and go back to my work, but I did it, sustained by a kind of soldierly pride.

At noon we hurried to the house, surrounded the kitchen table, and fell upon our boiled beef and potatoes with such ferocity that in fifteen minutes our meal was over. There was no ceremony and very little talking till the hid wolf was appeased. Then came a heavenly half hour of rest on the cool grass in the shade of the trees, a siesta as luxurious as that of a Spanish monarch — but alas! — this "nooning," as we called it, was always cut short by Father's words of sharp command: "Roll out, boys!" and again the big white jugs were filled at the well, the horses, lazy with food, led the way back to the field, and the stern contest began again.

All nature at this hour seemed to invite to repose rather than to labor, and as the heat increased I longed with wordless fervor for the green woods of the Cedar River. At times the gentle wind hardly moved the bended heads of the barley, and the hawks hung in the air like trout sleeping in deep pools. The sunlight was a golden, silent, scorching cataract — yet each of us must strain his tired muscles and bend his aching back to the harvest.

Supper came at five, another delicious interval — and then at six we all went out again for another hour or two in the cool of the sunset. However, the pace was more leisurely now, for the end of the day was near. I always enjoyed this period, for the shadows lengthening across the stubble and the fiery sun veiled by the gray clouds of the west had wondrous charm. The air began to moisten and grow cool. The voices of the men pulsed powerfully and cheerfully across the narrowing field of unreaped grain, the prairie hens led forth their broods to feed, and at last, Father's long-drawn and musical cry: "Turn out! All hands TURN OUT!" rang with restful significance through the dusk. Then, slowly, with low-hung heads the freed horses moved toward the barn, walking with lagging steps like weary warriors going into camp. . . .

My father did not believe in serving strong liquor to his men and seldom treated them to even beer. While not a teetotaler he was strongly opposed to all that intemperance represented. He furnished the best of food, and tea and coffee, but no liquor, and the men respected him for it.

The reaping on our farm that year lasted about four weeks. Barley came first, wheat followed, the oats came last of all. No sooner was the final swath cut than the barley was ready to be put under cover, and stacking, a new and less exacting phase of the harvest, began.

This job required less men than reaping; hence a part of our hands were paid off; only the more responsible ones were retained. The rush, the strain, of the reaping gave place to a leisurely, steady, day-by-day garnering of the thoroughly seasoned shocks into great conical piles, four in a place in the midst of the stubble, which was already growing green with swiftly springing weeds.

A full crew consisted of a stacker, a boy to pass bundles, two drivers for the heavy wagon racks, and a pitcher in the field who lifted the sheaves from the shock with a three-tined fork and threw them to the man on the load.

At the age of ten I had been taught to handle bundles on the stack, but now at fourteen I took my father's place as stacker, whilst he passed the sheaves and told me how to lay them. This exalted me at the same time that it increased my responsibility. It made a man of me — not only in my own estimation, but in the eyes of my boy companions, to whom I discoursed loftily on the value of "bulges" and the advantages of the stack over the rick.

No sooner was the stacking ended than the dreaded task of plowing began for Burton and John and me. Every morning while our fathers and the hired men shouldered their forks and went away to help some neighbor thrash ("changing works"), we drove our teams into the field, there to plod round and round in solitary course. Here I acquired the feeling which I afterward put into verse —

> A lonely task it is to plow!
> All day the black and shining soil
> Rolls like a ribbon from the moldboard's
> Glistening curve. All day the horses toil,
> Battling with savage flies, and strain
> Their creaking singletrees. All day
> The crickets peer from wind-blown stacks of grain.

Franklin's job was almost as lonely. He was set to herd the cattle on the harvested stubble and keep them out of the corn field. A little later, in October, when I was called to take my place as corn husker, he was promoted to the plow. Our only respite during the months of October and November was the occasional cold rain which permitted us to read or play cards in the kitchen.

The crops on our farms in those first years were enormous, and prices were good; and yet the homes of the neighborhood were slow in taking on grace or comfort. I don't know why this was so, unless it was that the men were continually buying more land and more machinery. Our own stables were still straw-roofed sheds, but the trees which we had planted had grown swiftly into a grove, and a garden, tended at odd moments by all hands, brought small fruits and vegetables in season. Although a constantly improving collection of farm machinery lightened the burdens of the husbandman, the drudgery of the housewife's dishwashing and cooking did not correspondingly lessen. I fear it increased, for with the widening of the fields came the doubling of the harvest hands, and my mother continued to do most of the housework herself — cooking, sewing, washing, churning, and nursing the sick from time to time. No one in trouble ever sent for Isabelle Garland in vain, and I have many recollections of neighbors riding up in the night and calling for her with agitated voices.

Of course I did not realize, and I am sure my father did not realize, the heavy burden, the endless grind, of her toil. Harriet helped, of course, and Frank and I churned and carried wood and brought water; but even with such aid, the round of Mother's duties must have been as relentless as a treadmill. Even on Sunday, when we were free for a part of the day, she was required to furnish forth three meals and to help Frank and Jessie dress for church. She sang less and less, and the songs we loved were seldom referred to. If I could only go back for one little hour and take her in my arms and tell her how much I owe her for those grinding days! . . .

Threshing time, which was becoming each year less of a bee and more of a job (many of the men were mere hired hands), was made distinctive by David, who came over from Orchard with his machine — the last time as it turned out — and stayed to the end. As I cut bands beside him in the dust and thunder of the cylinder I regained something of my boyish worship of his strength and skill. The tireless easy swing of his great frame was wonderful to me, and when, in my weariness, I failed to slash a band he smiled and tore the sheaf apart — thus deepening my love for him. I looked up at him at such times as a sailor regards his captain on the bridge. His handsome immobile bearded face, his air of command, his large gestures as he rolled the broad sheaves into the howling maw of the machine, made of him a chieftain. — The touch of melancholy which even then had begun to develop added to his manly charm.

One day in late September as I was plowing in the field at the back of the farm I encountered a particularly troublesome thicket of weeds and vines in the stubble and decided to burn the way before the colter. We had been doing this ever since the frost had killed the vegetation but always on lands after they had been safeguarded by strips of plowing. On this particular land no fire had been set for the reason that four large stacks of wheat still stood waiting the thresher. In my irritation and self-confidence I decided to clear away the matted stubble on the same strip, though at some distance from the stacks. This seemed safe enough at the time, for the wind was blowing gently from the opposite direction.

It was a lovely golden day, and as I stood watching the friendly flame clearing the ground for me, I was filled with satisfaction. Suddenly I observed that the line of red was moving steadily against the wind and *toward* the stacks. My satisfaction changed to alarm. The matted weeds furnished a thick bed of fuel, and against the progress of the flame I had nothing to offer. I could only hope that the thinning stubble would permit me to trample it out. I tore at the ground in desperation, hoping to make a bare spot which the flame could not leap. I trampled the fire with my bare feet. I beat at it with my hat. I screamed for help. Too late I thought of my team and the plow with which I might have drawn a furrow around the stacks. The flame touched the high-piled sheaves. It ran lightly, beautifully up the sides — and as I stood watching it, I thought: "It is all a dream. It can't be true."

But it was. In less than twenty minutes the towering piles had melted into four glowing heaps of ashes. Four hundred dollars had gone up in that blaze.

Slowly, painfully I hobbled to the plow and drove my team to the house. Although badly burned, my mental suffering was so much greater that I felt only part of it. Leaving the horses at the well, I hobbled into the house to my mother. She, I knew, would sympathize with me and shield me from the just wrath of my father, who was away but was due to return in an hour or two.

Mother received me in silence, bandaged my feet, and put me to bed, where I lay in shame and terror.

At last I heard father come in. He questioned; Mother's voice replied. He remained ominously silent. She went on quietly but with an eloquence unusual in her. What she said to him I never knew, but when he came up the stairs and stood looking down at me his anger had cooled. He merely asked me how I felt, uncovered my burned feet, examined them, put the sheet back, and went away, without a word either of reproof or consolation.

None of us except little Jessie ever alluded to this tragic matter

again; she was accustomed to tell my story as she remembered it —
"an 'nen the moon changed — the fire ran up the stacks and burned
'em all down — "

HAMLIN GARLAND, A Son of the Middle Border

199. Opening up Oklahoma

*For half a century what is now
Oklahoma had been set aside as a reservation for the Five Civilized
Tribes of Indians. By the decade of the eighties the pressure for good
land became acute and the demand that the government throw open
part of the Indian Territory for settlement proved irresistible. By
Presidential proclamation the territory was opened to settlers in 1889.
So rapid was the influx of settlers that within a decade the Territory
had a population of almost four hundred thousand.*

ARKANSAS CITY, Kan., April 22, 1889. — Few of the thousands of seekers of something for nothing, who have used this city as
their last halting place prior to making the rush into Oklahoma, went
to bed last night. They spent the night on the street, at the depot,
and in and out of hotel lobbies. Yesterday's influx of visitors was
enormous. The regular trains have had to run in sections. And this
extra accommodation has not sufficed. The aisles have been crowded
to excess, and the suffering of the cooped-up speculators and boomers
must have been great. Fortunately there were very few women in
the crowds.

The depot was crowded all night, and the sale of tickets kept
steadily on, nine-tenths of those issued being to Guthrie and most
of the balance to Arthur. This latter is just five miles over the line,
and as all trains will stop before leaving the Cherokee strip, the
holders of tickets to Arthur propose to jump off at the line. Every
one seemed to be talking, and there was a perfect babel, but the
grand rush commenced about six, when the people who had slept
uptown joined their less fortunate brethren. Some carried absolutely
nothing in their hands, evidently thinking they could do the rushing

better for not being handicapped. But a marked characteristic of the crowd was the great number of spades and axes carried. The [railroad] company's arrangements to prevent a general rush to one train was to so arrange matters that no one could know which train could pass first, and the secret has been admirably kept.

The trip south commenced amid shouting and cheering. There could not have been less than five thousand men who failed to secure seats, although a score of flatcars had been fitted up with plank seats, which were crowded with eager boomers.

Two men got on the cowcatcher of a locomotive but had to be removed. On a later train, however, a man rode the whole journey of eighty-nine miles on the cowcatcher. There were only two ladies on the train. Each had a light boomer's outfit and expressed confidence in the gallantry of the men to enable them to locate claims. The conductor collected ten hundred and twenty-four tickets on this train.

At twelve-fifteen precisely there was a loud whistle from the engine, answered by a shout from the train, and we were in Oklahoma at last. Before the train had crossed the line fifty yards a man sprang off, regardless of the danger. He fell pretty heavily but was on his feet in a few seconds, collected his baggage, which he had thrown out ahead, and was turning sods before the train was out of sight. A little farther south a man had evidently just alighted from the mule which was standing by him and whose pack he was unloading. So far it was just possible that every boomer seen had waited till twelve o'clock before he crossed the line, but squatters pure and simple now came in view. They sprang out of the woods on every side, and it was evident from the appearance of some of them that they had been in hiding for weeks. . . .

When the word was given to advance at the north line, the boomers started forward at various rates of speed. All who desired to locate anywhere near the track in the north end of the Territory found themselves forestalled. Some turned back in disgust, and others pushed farther on into the interior. But for absolute contempt of the President's reminder of the dangers of premature occupation, Guthrie takes the lead. It could not legally be reached by road in advance of the train; yet when the town site came in view, it was literally covered with lot claimants. The location is well suited for a town.

The railroad runs along a valley on the west of which is a creek which forms a picturesque background to the depot. The town, or town site, is on the other side of the track; and the ground slopes gradually up to the summit of a little ridge. At the summit is the land office.

What happened when the train began to slacken beggars all description. Boys, middle-aged men, and old fellows threw themselves off the platform and commenced a wild rush. They fell upon each other, scrambled to their feet, and made off, some carrying their grips and others dropping everything in the eagerness of the chase. As the train went on toward the depot the passengers kept jumping off. The town-lot craze seemed to lend speed even to cripples. A man with a wooden leg was among the first to make the dangerous jump, and he held his own in the race. Not a passenger by this first train went past Guthrie, so that the population of the new city was increased by this rush to the extent of nearly a thousand. All roads seemed to lead to the land office at which a line over one hundred yards long was already formed. For a second the runners paused.

Then they commenced a wild tear out east, and each man, as he found an unclaimed lot, proceeded to stake it out and hold it down. The process of securing the lots, as in general adoption, is simple in the extreme. First of all a stake is driven in the ground, with or without a placer attached, setting forth the name of the claimant. Then the new owner paces off the ground he proposes to occupy for a residence or business house. There is at least a charm of variety about the laying out of Guthrie. Some people contented themselves with twenty-five feet frontage, others took forty feet, and others fifty; but most of the claimants had a fair idea of where the streets ought to be and left the necessary space for them. By the time the men on Train No. 1 had each selected his lot the town site had extended away beyond the half section reserved, and long before the majority had quit running, Train No. 2 pulled in, quite as heavily loaded as its predecessor. The same process was carried out to the letter.

Among those hurrying up the hill were two ladies who succeeded in securing a claim each and will hold it. These ladies are from California. They are going into business at once.

There was a considerable interval before another train arrived, but the third and fourth came in close together, each discharging its cargo of passengers to add to the astounding crush. The limits of the city kept on increasing, and by the time the fifth and sixth trains had unloaded, the city extended far away to the distance. Altogether ten trains got in before three o'clock, and making allowance for those who went on to Oklahoma City, there must have been at least six thousand people in Guthrie three hours after the Territory was legally opened for settlement. It was wonderful, the manner in which disputes among the newcomers were settled in this early part of the proceedings. Sometimes half a dozen men would pounce on a lot simultaneously or nearly so. Each would commence to stake out, but after a little while a general agreement would be come to, and every applicant but one would rush off and secure an undisputed lot. There has been so far no unpleasantness of any kind.

Speculation in town lots commenced at once. Hacks met the trains and drivers shouted, "This way for lots at a dollar apiece!"

For a dollar lot hunters were driven to vacant lots and left to get their dollar's worth themselves.

St. Louis Globe Democrat, 1889

200. Mover Wagons Head East

With brave hopes hundreds of thousands of farmers had streamed onto the High Plains of western Kansas, Nebraska and the Dakotas during the seventies and the eighties. But beginning in 1887 came a prolonged drought which spelled ruin to many of the settlers and poverty and discouragement to most of them. Thousands, unable to hold out against drought, insect plagues, and low farm prices, pulled up stakes and turned back eastward; whole towns disappeared and some counties lost half their population. The young editor who describes the situation came later to be nationally known as "the Sage of Emporia."

THERE came through Emporia yesterday two old-fashioned mover wagons headed east. The stock in the caravan would invoice four horses, very poor and very tired, one mule, more disheartened than the horses, and one sad-eyed dog that had probably been compelled to rustle his own precarious living for many a long and weary day. A few farm implements of the simpler sort were loaded in the wagon, but nothing that had wheels was moving except the two wagons. All the rest of the impedimenta had been left upon the battlefield, and these poor stragglers, defeated but not conquered, were fleeing to another field, to try the fight again. These movers were from western Kansas — from one of those counties near the Colorado line which holds a charter from the state to officiate as the very worst, most desolate, Godforsaken, man-deserted spot on the sad old earth. They had come from that wilderness only after a ten years' hard, vicious fight, a fight which had left its scars on their faces, had beaten their bodies, had taken the elasticity from their steps and left them crippled to enter the battle anew. For ten years they had been fighting the elements. They had seen it stop raining for months at a time. They had heard the fury of the winter wind as it came whining across the short burned grass and cut the flesh from their children huddling in the corner. These movers have strained their eyes, watching through the long summer days for the rain that never came. They have seen that big cloud roll up from the southwest about one in the afternoon, hover over the land, and stumble away with a few thumps of thunder as the sun went down. They have tossed through hot nights, wild with worry, and have arisen only to find their worst nightmares grazing in reality on the brown stubble in front of their sun-warped doors. They had such high hopes when they went out there; they are so desolate now — no, not now, for now they are in the land of corn and honey. They have come out of the wilderness, back to the land of promise. They are now in God's own country down on the Neosho, with their wife's folks, and the taste of apple butter and good corn bread and fresh meat and pie — pieplant pie like Mother used to make — gladdened their shrunken palates last night; and real cream, curdling on their coffee saucers last night for supper, was a sight so rich and strange that it lingered in their dreams, wherein they walked beside the still waters and lay down in green pastures.

WILLIAM ALLEN WHITE, Emporia (Kan.) *Gazette*, 1895

XXVIII

The Rise of the City

201. Horace White Sees the Great Chicago Fire

The spectacularly rapid growth of Chicago had involved the almost universal use of wood for construction purposes and made it peculiarly vulnerable to fire. Older cities, to be sure, like Boston, had been swept by fires, but the Great Chicago Fire of 1871 was the most catastrophic thing of its kind in nineteenth century America. Horace White, whose report of the fire is the most vivid that we have, was editor of the Chicago Tribune *and later of the* New York Evening Post.

I HAD retired to rest, though not to sleep (Sunday, October 8, 1871), when the great bell struck the alarm, but fires had been so frequent of late and had been so speedily extinguished that I did not deem it worth while to get up and look at it or even to count the strokes on the bell to learn where it was. The bell paused for fifteen minutes before giving the general alarm which distinguishes a great fire from a small one. When it sounded the general alarm I rose and looked out. There was a great light to the southwest of my residence, but no greater than I had frequently seen in that quarter, where vast piles of pine lumber have been stored all the time I have lived in Chicago, some eighteen years. But it was not pine lumber that was burning this time. It was a row of wooden tenements in the south division of the city, in which a few days ago were standing whole rows of the most costly buildings which it hath entered into the hearts of architects to conceive. I watched the increasing light for a few moments. Red tongues of light began to shoot upward; my family were all aroused by this time, and I dressed myself for the purpose of going to the *Tribune* office to write something about the catastrophe. Once out upon the street, the magnitude of the fire was suddenly disclosed to me.

The dogs of hell were upon the housetops of La Salle and Wells Streets, just south of Adams, bounding from one to another. The fire was moving northward like ocean surf on a sand beach. It had already traveled an eighth of a mile and was far beyond control. A column of flame would shoot up from a burning building, catch the force of the wind, and strike the next one, which in turn would perform the same direful office for its neighbor. It was simply indescribable in its terrible grandeur. Vice and crime had got the first scorching. The district where the fire got its first firm foothold was the Alsatia of Chicago. Fleeing before it was a crowd of blear-eyed, drunken, and diseased wretches, male and female, half naked, ghastly, with painted cheeks, cursing and uttering ribald jests as they drifted along.

I went to the *Tribune* office, ascended to the editorial rooms, took the only inflammable thing there, a kerosene lamp, and carried it to the basement, where I emptied the oil into the sewer. This was scarcely done when I perceived the flames breaking out of the roof of the courthouse, the old nucleus of which, in the center of the edifice, was not constructed of fireproof material as the new wings had been. As the flames had leaped a vacant space of nearly two hundred feet to get at this roof, it was evident that most of the business portion of the city must go down, but I did not reflect that the city waterworks, with their four great pumping engines, were in a straight line with the fire and wind. Nor did I know then that this priceless machinery was covered by a wooden roof. The flames were driving thither with demon precision.

Billows of fire were rolling over the business palaces of the city and swallowing up their contents. Walls were falling so fast that the quaking of the ground under our feet was scarcely noticed, so continuous was the reverberation. Sober men and women were hurrying through the streets from the burning quarter, some with bundles of clothes on their shoulders, others dragging trunks along the sidewalks by means of strings and ropes fastened to the handles, children trudging by their sides or borne in their arms. Now and then a sick man or woman would be observed half concealed in a mattress doubled up and borne by two men. Droves of horses were in the streets, moving by some sort of guidance to a place of safety. Vehicles of all descriptions were hurrying to and fro, some laden with trunks and bundles, others seeking similar loads and immediately finding them, the drivers making more money in one hour than they were used to see in a week or a month. Everybody in this quarter was hurrying toward the lake shore. All the streets crossing that part of Michigan Avenue which fronts on the lake (on which my own residence stood) were crowded with fugitives hastening towards the blessed water. . . .

There was still a mass of fire to the southwest, in the direction whence it originally came, but as the engines were all down there and the buildings small and low, I felt sure that the firemen would manage it. As soon as I had swallowed a cup of coffee and communicated to my family the facts that I had gathered, I started out to see the end of the battle. Reaching State Street, I glanced down to Field, Leiter and Company's store and to my surprise noticed that the streams of water which had before been showering it, as though it had been a great artificial fountain, had ceased to run. But I did not conjecture the awful reality, viz., that the great pumping engines had been disabled by a burning roof falling upon them. I thought perhaps the firemen on the store had discontinued their efforts because the danger was over. But why were men carrying out goods from the lower story? This query was soon answered by a gentleman who asked me if I had heard that the water had stopped! The awful truth was here! The pumping engines were disabled, and though we had at our feet a basin sixty miles wide by three hundred and sixty long and seven hundred feet deep, all full of clear green water, we could not lift enough to quench a cooking stove. Still the direction of the wind was such that I thought the remaining fire would not cross State Street nor reach the residences on Wabash and Michigan Avenues and the terrified people on the lake shore. I determined to go down to the black cloud of smoke which was rising away to the southwest, the course of which could not be discovered on account of the height of the intervening buildings, but thought it most prudent to go home again and tell my wife to get the family wearing apparel in readiness for moving. I found that she had already done so. I then hurried toward the black cloud, some ten squares distant, and there found the rows of wooden houses on Third and Fourth Avenues falling like ripe wheat before the reaper. At a glance I perceived that all was lost in our part of the city, and I conjectured that the *Tribune* building was doomed too, for I had noticed with consternation that the fireproof post office had been completely gutted, notwithstanding it was detached from other buildings. The *Tribune* [building] was fitted into a niche, one side of which consisted of a wholesale stationery store and the other of McVicker's Theater. But there was now no time to think of property. Life was in danger. The lives of those most dear to me depended upon their getting out of our house, out of our street, through an infernal gorge of horses, wagons, men, women, children, trunks, and plunder.

My brother was with me, and we seized the first empty wagon we could find, pinning the horse by the head. A hasty talk with the driver disclosed that we could have his establishment for one load for twenty dollars. I had not expected to get him for less than a hundred unless we should take him by force, and this was a bad time for a fight. He approved himself a muscular as well as a faithful fellow, and I shall always be glad that I avoided a personal difficulty with him. One peculiarity of the situation was that nobody could get a team without ready money. I had not thought of this when I was revolving in my mind the offer of one hundred dollars, which was more greenbacks than our whole family could have put up if our lives had depended upon the issue. This driver had divined that, as all the banks were burned, a check on the Commercial National would not carry him very far, although it might carry me to a place of safety. All the drivers had divined the same. Every man who had anything to sell perceived the same. "Pay as you go" had become the watch word of the hour. Never was there a community so hastily and so completely emancipated from the evils of the credit system.

With some little difficulty we reached our house, and in less time than we ever set out on a journey before, we dragged seven trunks, four bundles, four valises, two baskets, and one hamper of provisions into the street and piled them on the wagon. The fire was still more than a quarter of a mile distant, and the wind, which was increasing in violence, was driving it not exactly in our direction. The low wooden houses were nearly all gone, and after that the fire must make progress, if at all, against brick and stone. Several churches of massive architecture were between us and harm, and the great Palmer House had not been reached and might not be if the firemen, who had now got their hose into the lake, could work efficiently in the ever-increasing jam of fugitives.

My wife thought we should have time to take another load; my brother thought so; we all thought so. We had not given due credit either to the savage strength of the fire or the firm pack on Michigan Avenue. Leaving my brother to get the family safely out if I did not return in time and to pile the most valuable portion of my library into the drawers of bureaus and tables ready for moving, I seized a bird cage containing a talented green parrot and mounted the seat with the driver. For one square southward from the corner of Monroe Street we made pretty fair progress. The dust was so thick that we could not see the distance of a whole square ahead. It came not in clouds but in a steady storm of sand, the particles impinging against our faces like needle points. Pretty soon we came to a dead halt. We could move neither forward nor backward nor sidewise. The gorge had caught fast somewhere. Yet everybody was good-natured and polite. If I should say I didn't hear an oath all the way down Michigan Avenue, there are probably some mule drivers in Cincinnati who would say it was a lie. But I did not. The only quarrelsome person I saw was a German laborer (a noted exception to his race, who was protesting that he had lost everything and that he would not get out of the middle of the road although he was on foot. He became obstreperous on this point and commenced beating the head of my horse with his fist. My driver was preparing to knock him down with the butt end of his whip when two men seized the insolent Teuton and dragged him to the water's edge, where it is to be hoped he was ducked.

Presently the jam began to move, and we got on perhaps twenty paces and stuck fast again. By accident we had edged over to the east side of the street, and nothing but a board fence separated us from the lake park, a strip of ground a little wider than the street itself. A benevolent laborer on the park side of the fence pulled a loose post from the ground and with this for a catapult knocked off the boards and invited us to pass through. It was a hazardous undertaking, as we had to drive diagonally over a raised sidewalk, but we thought it was best to risk it. Our horse mounted and gave us a jerk which nearly threw us off the seat and sent the provision basket and one bundle of clothing whirling into the dirt. The eatables were irrecoverable. The bundle was rescued, with two or three pounds of butter plastered upon it. We started again, and here our parrot broke out with great rapidity and sharpness of utterance, "Get up, get up, get up, hurry up, hurry up, it's eight o'clock," ending with a shrill whistle. These ejaculations frightened a pair of carriage horses close to us on the other side of the fence, but the jam was so tight they couldn't run.

By getting into the park we succeeded in advancing two squares without impediment, and we might have gone farther had we not come upon an excavation which the public authorities had recently made. This drove us back to the Avenue, where another battering-ram made a gap for us at the intersection of Van Buren Street, the north end of Michigan Terrace. Here the gorge seemed impassable. The difficulty proceeded from teams entering Michigan Avenue from cross streets. Extempore policemen stationed themselves at these crossings and helped as well as they could, but we were half an hour passing the terrace. From this imposing row of residences the millionaires were dragging their trunks and their bundles, and yet there was no panic, no frenzy, no boisterousness, but only the haste which the situation authorized. There was real danger to life all along this street, but nobody realized it, because the park was ample to hold all the people. None of us asked or thought what would become of those nearest the water if the smoke and cinders should drive the whole crowd down to the shore or if the vast bazaar of luggage should itself take fire, as some of it afterward did. Fortunately for those in the street, there was a limit to the number of teams available in that quarter of the city. The contributions from the cross streets grew less, and soon we began to move on a walk without interruption. Arriving at Eldridge Court, I turned into Wabash Avenue, where the crowd was thinner. Arriving at the house of a friend, who was on the windward side of the fire, I tumbled off my load and started back to get another. Halfway down Michigan Avenue, which was now perceptibly easier to move in, I perceived my family on the sidewalk with their arms full of light household effects. My wife told me that the house was already burned, that the flames burst out ready-made in the rear hall before she knew that the roof had been scorched, and that one of the servants, who had disobeyed orders in her eagerness to save some article, had got singed, though not burned, in coming out. My wife and mother and all the rest were begrimed with dirt and smoke, like blackamoors; everybody was. The "bloated aristocrats" all along the streets, who supposed they had lost both home and fortune at one swoop, were a sorry but not despairing congregation. They had saved their lives at all events, and they knew that many of their fellow creatures must have lost theirs. I saw a great many kindly acts done as we moved along. The poor helped the rich, and the rich helped the poor (if anybody could be called rich at such a time) to get on with their loads. I heard of cartmen demanding one hundred and fifty dollars (in hand, of course) for carrying a single load. Very likely it was so, but those cases did not come under my own notice. It did come under my notice that some cartmen worked for whatever the sufferers felt able to pay, and one I knew worked with alacrity for nothing. It takes all sorts of people to make a great fire.

HORACE WHITE, in Cincinnati Commercial

202. The Panic of 1873 Hits New York

The panic of 1873 was the worst which the United States had experienced up to that time, and bore with particular severity upon labor, then almost entirely unorganized. The Tompkins Square "outrage" was significant not only as one of the earliest examples of official repression of labor, but because of its profound influence upon Samuel Gompers who was to be, for some forty years, the spokesman of American labor.

CHRISTMAS in New York was not festive that year. The whole city stirred uneasily under the burden heaped up by conscienceless speculators. Many street meetings followed to burn into the hearts of all tragic demonstrations of human need. . . . The unemployed filled the city's streets and squares and marched to conferences with aldermen and mayor at the City Hall. It was a folk movement born of primitive need — so compelling that even politicians dared not ignore. There is something about a marching folk group that rouses dread. Those in authority did not rest comfortably. The press began hinting at the "Commune."

Meanwhile, plans were moving forward for a big out-of-door mass meeting in Tompkins Square on January 13, 1874. Mayor Havemeyer had promised to be present and to address the meeting.

Several times before that day groups of unemployed, ranging from hundreds to thousands in numbers, accompanied their spokesman to the City Hall. They remained outside listening to speakers, while suggestions were submitted to city authorities. Their physical presence gave urgency to their needs and demand for relief. The police commissioner granted a permit for the mass meeting and parade as far as Canal Street, thus protecting the City Hall from unpleasant personal contacts. This restriction blunted the effectiveness of the plan for the demonstration. Banks and McGuire protested but without avail. Elliot telephoned to Governor Dix, who declared he had no authority to intercede and referred the whole matter to the mayor. The mayor left all to the police commission, which was controlled by a former associate of Boss Tweed. Dissension developed within the ranks of workingmen. The group of radicals, so-called communists, saw in the situation an opportunity for propaganda. Propaganda was for them the chief end of life. They were perfectly willing to use human necessity as propaganda material. Practical results meant nothing in their program. They were young heroes determined to play a great part; hence they were unwilling to do the unostentatious, quiet, orderly things that make for constructive progress. This group got control by self-appointment to a provisional committee of the Safety Committee. They got money for their campaign from Mr. Kayser, ex-member of the Tammany ring. They issued circulars that had artistic and literary merit. They made speeches that contained good headline stuff. They painted the skies with "true" revolutionary plans and extravagant ideals.

The daily press played up the picturesque and made the city feel that communists were in control and that they were on the verge of a revolutionary uprising. On the day before that set for the Tompkins Square demonstration, the park commissioners sent an order to the police commissioner forbidding the gathering because it "threatened public peace." The police commissioner sent an order to the Safety Committee demanding the return of the permit. But the Safety Committee was not to be found — none of them went to their homes that night.

But some of the labor men not on the Safety Committee, who learned of the situation, feared the results for those who would go to Tompkins Square the next morning. Laurrell was among this number. On the night of the 12th he went to union meetings and wherever he knew that working people would be gathered together, told them of the withdrawal of the permit, and warned them against going to the Square on the morrow. That was not a pleasant task and required courage of a very real sort. As it was not generally known that the permit had been withdrawn, Laurrell was unjustly derided as a renegade.

Next morning people began assembling early in the Square. I reached the Square a little after ten. It had been a drill field and playground and, though a bit out of repair, was commonly used by the working people for general gatherings and speeches. A high iron fence surrounded the park, with wide gate entrances. Soon the park was packed and all the avenues leading to it crowded. The people were quiet. There was nothing out of harmony with the spirit of friendly conferences between the chief public official and workless and breadless citizens. The gathering was planned as visible proof of suffering and destitution among New York unemployed. A paper was edited for this special meeting by Lucien Sanial and P. J. McGuire. The paper, widely circulated among the unemployed, the working people, and the city authorities, contained the program proposed by the workers. The *Volcano* was also conspicuously for sale. Tom-ri-John, everybody in New York in the early seventies will remember as a communist or socialist or a reformer of some kind. Tom was also a journalistic reformer. He ran a newspaper called the *Volcano*. It was printed on bright yellow paper and its articles set up in red ink. In accord with their distribution of family responsibility, it was Mrs. Tom-ri-John's business to sell these papers, and her working dress (masculine garb) served to attract attention while the big stick she always carried was her rod and staff of defense and support. The couple had three children — Eruptor, Vesuvia, and Emancipator.

It was about ten-thirty when a detachment of police surrounded the park. Hardly had they taken their position before a group of workers marched into the park from Avenue A. They carried a banner bearing the words, "TENTH WARD UNION LABOR." Just after they entered the park a police sergeant led an attack on them. He was followed by police mounted and on foot with drawn night sticks. Without a word of warning they swept down the defenseless workers, striking down the standard bearer and using their clubs right and left indiscriminately on the heads of all they could reach.

Shortly afterward the mounted police charged the crowd on Eighth Street, riding them down and attacking men, women, and children without discrimination. It was an orgy of brutality. I was caught in the crowd on the street and barely saved my head from being cracked by jumping down a cellarway. The attacks of the police kept up all day long — wherever the police saw a group of poorly dressed persons standing or moving together. Laurrell went to Tompkins Square and received a blow from the police across his back, the effect of which remained with him for several months.

The next few days disclosed revolting stories of police brutality inflicted on the sick, the lame, the innocent bystander. Mounted police and guards had repeatedly charged down crowded avenues and streets. A reign of terror gripped that section of the city. To this day I cannot think of that wild scene without my blood surging in indignation at the brutality of the police on that day. They justified their policy by the charge that communism was rearing its head.

The Tompkins Square outrage was followed by a period of extreme repression. The New York police borrowed Continental methods of espionage. Private indoor meetings were invaded and summarily ended by the ejection of those present. The police frustrated several meetings held to protest against police brutality and in defense of the right of free assemblage for a lawful purpose.

I was in no way connected with the arrangement of this demonstration and was present as an intensely interested workingman, and the import of the situation bore in upon me. As the fundamentals came to me, they became guideposts for my understanding of the labor movement for years to come. I saw how professions of radicalism and sensationalism concentrated all the forces of organized society against a labor movement and nullified in advance normal, necessary activity. I saw that leadership in the labor movement could be safely entrusted only to those into whose hearts and minds had been woven the experiences of earning their bread by daily labor. I saw that betterment for workingmen must come primarily through workingmen. I saw the danger of entangling alliances with intellectuals who did not understand that to experiment with the labor movement was to experiment with human life. I realized too that many of those of the radical, revolutionary, impatient group were of the labor movement and just as sincere as many of those whose judgment was more dependable. The labor movement is made up of men and women of all sorts of natures and experiences. Their welfare depends on solidarity — one group cannot sit in judgment upon others or condemn publicly, but all must do what they can for mutual protection. Division is the great hazard of the labor movement.

SAMUEL GOMPERS, Seventy Years of Life and Labor

203. Ward McAllister Views Life Among the Idle Rich

The Industrial Revolution, the Civil War, railroads, and the opening up of the West created a large group of parvenu millionaires who promptly undertook to buy culture, pleasure, and social standing with their new money. They moved on to the East, built themselves mansions on Fifth Avenue, summered in Newport, traveled abroad, imported works of art, and bought their way into some of the "first families." Ward McAllister, who went everywhere and knew everybody, made himself the social arbiter of this society; his lively autobiographical book is the best description of life among the "idle rich" of New York which has come down to us.

WE HERE reach a period when New York society turned over a new leaf. Up to this time for one to be worth a million of dollars was to be rated as a man of fortune, but now bygones must be bygones. New York's ideas as to values, when fortune was named, leaped boldly up to ten millions, fifty millions, one hundred millions; and the necessities and luxuries followed suit. One was no longer content with a dinner of a dozen or more, to be served by a couple of servants. Fashion demanded that you be received in the hall of the house in which you were to dine by from five to six servants, who, with the butler, were to serve the repast — the butler, on such occasions, to do alone the headwork, and under him he had these men in livery to serve the dinner, he to guide and direct them. Soft strains of music were introduced between the courses, and in some houses gold replaced silver in the way of plate; and everything that skill and art could suggest was added to make the dinners not a vulgar display but a gastronomic effort evidencing the possession by the host of both money and taste.

The butler, from getting a salary of forty dollars a month, received then from sixty to seventy-five dollars a month. The second man jumped up from twenty to thirty-five and forty dollars, and the extra men, at the dinner of a dozen people or more, would cost twenty-four dollars. Then the orchids, being the most costly of all flowers, were introduced in profusion. The canvasback that we could buy at two dollars and a half a pair went up to eight dollars a pair; the terrapin were four dollars apiece. Our forefathers would have been staggered at the cost of the hospitality of these days.

The six quadrilles were really the event of the ball, consisting of the hobbyhorse quadrille, the men who danced in it being dressed in "pink" and the ladies wearing red hunting coats and white satin skirts, all of the period of Louis XIV. In the Mother Goose quadrille were Jack and Jill, Little Red Riding Hood, Bo-Peep, Goody Two-Shoes, Mary, Mary, Quite Contrary, and My Pretty Maid. The opéra bouffe quadrille was most successful, but of all of them, the star quadrille, containing the youth and beauty of the city, was the most brilliant. The ladies in it were arrayed as twin stars in four different colors, yellow, blue, mauve, and white. Above the forehead of each lady, in her hair, was worn an electric light, giving a fairy and elflike appearance to each of them. The Dresden quadrille, in which the ladies wore white satin with powdered hair and the gentlemen white satin knee breeches and powdered wigs, with the Dresden mark, crossed swords, on each of them, was effective. The hostess appeared as a Venetian princess, with a superb jeweled peacock in her hair. The host was the Duke de Guise for that evening. The host's eldest brother wore a costume of Louis XVI. His wife appeared as the electric light in white satin trimmed with diamonds, and her head one blaze of diamonds. The most remarkable costume and one spoken of to this day was that of a cat, the dress being of cats' tails and white cats' heads, and a bell with "Puss" on it in large letters. A distinguished beauty dressed as a phoenix, adorned with diamonds and rubies, was superb, and with the Capuchin monk, with hood and sandals, inimitable. But to name the most striking would be to name all.

The great social revolution that had occurred in New York this winter, like most revolutionary waves, reached Newport. Our distinguished New York journalist then made Newport his summer home, buying the fine granite house that for years had been first known as the Middleton mansion, afterward the Sidney Brooks residence, and filling it with distinguished Europeans. His activity and energy gave new life to the place.

One fine summer morning one of his guests, an officer in the English army, a bright spirit and admirable horseman, riding on his polo pony up to the Newport Reading Room, where all the fossils of the place, the nobs and the swells, daily gossiped, he was challenged to ride the pony into the hall of this revered old club, and being bantered to do it, he actually did ride the pony across the narrow piazza and into the hall of the club itself. This was enough to set Newport agog. What sacrilege! an Englishman to ride in upon us, not respecting the sanctity of the place. It aroused the old patriots, who were members of that institution, with the spirit of '76; and a summary note was sent to the great journalist, withdrawing the invitation the club had previously given his guest. The latter in turn felt aggrieved and retaliated with this result: building for Newport a superb casino, embracing a club, a ballroom, and a restaurant, opposite his own residence. All this evidencing that agitation of any kind is as beneficial in social circles as to the atmosphere we breathe.

Then our journalist conceived and gave a handsome domino ball, all the ladies in domino, much after the pattern of the one previously given by the Duchess de Dino and in many respects resembling it, having a huge tent spread behind the house, and all the rooms on the first floor converted into a series of charming supper rooms, each table decorated most elaborately with beautiful flowers — as handsome a ball as one could give. I took the wife of the attorney general to it in domino, who, after her life in Washington, was amazed at the beauty of the scene. The grounds, which were very handsome, were all, even the plants themselves, illuminated with electric lights — that is, streams of electric light were cunningly thrown under the plants, giving an illumination *a giorno* and producing the most beautiful effect.

At this ball there appeared a blue domino that set all the men wild. Coming to the ball in her own carriage (her servants she felt she could not trust not to betray her) she dashed into the merry throng, and gliding from one to the other, whispered airy nothings into men's ears. But they contained enough to excite the most intense curiosity as to who she was. She was the belle of the evening; she became bold and daring at times, attacking men about the inmost secrets of their hearts, so as to alarm them; and when she had worked them all up to a fever heat, she came to me to take her to the door that she might make good her escape. A dozen men barricaded the way, but with the rapidity of a deer she dashed through them, reached the sidewalk, and her footman literally threw her into the carriage. Her coachman, well drilled, dashed off at a furious rate, and to this day no one has ever found out who the fair creature was.

Just at this time a man of wealth who had accumulated a fortune here resolved to give New Yorkers a sensation, to give them a banquet which should exceed in luxury and expense anything before seen in this country. As he expressed it, "I knew it would be a folly, a piece of unheard-of extravagance, but as the United States government had just refunded me ten thousand dollars, exacted from me for duties upon importations (which, being excessive, I had petitioned to be returned me, and had quite unexpectedly received this sum back), I resolved to appropriate it to giving a banquet that would always be remembered." Accordingly he went to Charles Delmonico, who in turn went to his *cuisine classique* to see how they could possibly spend this sum on this feast. Success crowned their efforts. The sum in such skillful hands soon melted away, and a banquet was given of such beauty and magnificence that even New Yorkers, accustomed as they were to every species of novel expenditure, were astonished at its lavishness, its luxury. The banquet was given at Delmonico's in Fourteenth Street. There were seventy-two guests in the large ballroom looking on Fifth Avenue.

The table covered the whole length and breadth of the room, only leaving a passageway for the waiters to pass around it. It was a long extended oval table, and every inch of it was covered with flowers, excepting a space in the center, left for a lake, and a border around the table for the plates. This lake was indeed a work of art; it was an oval pond, thirty feet in length, by nearly the width of the table, inclosed by a delicate golden wire network reaching from table to ceiling, making the whole one grand cage; four superb swans, brought from Prospect Park, swam in it, surrounded by high banks of flowers of every species and variety, which prevented them from splashing the water on the table. There were hills and dales; the modest little violet carpeting the valleys, and other bolder sorts climbing up and covering the tops of those miniature mountains. Then, all around the enclosure and in fact above the entire table, hung little golden cages with fine songsters who filled the room with their melody, occasionally interrupted by the splashing of the waters of the lake by the swans and the cooing of these noble birds and at one time by a fierce combat between these stately, graceful, gliding white creatures. The surface of the whole table, by clever art, was one unbroken series of undulations, rising and falling like the billows of the sea, but all clothed and carpeted with every form of blossom. It seemed like the abode of fairies, and when surrounding this fairyland with lovely young American womanhood, you had indeed an unequaled scene of enchantment. But this was not to be alone a feast for the eye; all that art could do, all that the cleverest men could devise to spread before the guests, such a feast as the gods should enjoy, was done, and so well done that all present felt, in the way of feasting, that man could do no more! The wines were perfect. Blue seal Johannisberger flowed like water. Incomparable '48 claret, superb Burgundies, and amber-colored Madeira, all were there to add to the intoxicating delight of the scene. Then soft music stole over one's senses; lovely women's eyes sparkled with delight at the beauty of their surroundings, and I felt that the fair being who sat next to me would have graced Alexander's feast.

The next great event in the fashionable world was a Newport ball. A lady who had married a man of cultivation and taste, a member of one of New York's oldest families, who had inherited from her father an enormous fortune, was at once seized with the ambition to take and hold a brilliant social position, to gratify which she built one of the handsomest houses in this city, importing interiors from Europe for it and such old Spanish tapestries as had never before been introduced into New York; after which she went to Newport and bought a beautiful villa on Bellevue Avenue and there gave, in the grounds of that villa, the handsomest ball that had ever been given there. The villa itself was only used to receive and sup the guests in, for a huge tent capable of holding fifteen hundred people had been spread over the entire villa grounds; and in it was built a platform for dancing. The approaches to this tent were admirably designed and produced a great effect. On entering the villa itself you were received by the hostess and then directed by liveried servants to the two improvised salons of the tent. The one you first entered was the Japanese room, adorned by every conceivable kind of old Japanese objects of art, couches, hangings of embroideries, cunning cane houses, all illuminated with Japanese lanterns, and the ceiling canopied with Japanese stuffs, producing, with its soft reddish light, a charming effect; then behind tables scattered in different parts of the room stood Japanese boys in costume, serving fragrant tea. Every possible couch, lounge, and easy chair was there to invite you to sit and indulge yourself in ease and repose.

Leaving this anteroom, you entered still another salon, adorned with modern and Parisian furniture but furnished with cunningly devised corners and nooks for "flirtation couples"; and from this you were ushered into the gorgeous ballroom itself—an immense open tent whose ceiling and sides were composed of broad stripes of white and scarlet bunting; then, for the first time at a ball in this country, the electric light was introduced with brilliant effect. Two grottoes of immense blocks of ice stood on either side of the ball-room, and a powerful jet of light was thrown through each of them, causing the ice to resemble the prisms of an illuminated cavern and fairly to dazzle one with their coloring. Then as the blocks of ice would melt, they would tumble over each other in charming glacierlike confusion, giving you winter in the lap of summer; for every species of plant stood around this immense floor as a flowering border, creeping quite up to these little improvised glaciers. The light was thrown and spread by these two powerful jets sufficiently strong to give a brilliant illumination to the ballroom. The only criticism possible was that it made deep shadows.

All Newport was present to give brilliancy to the scene. Everything was to be European; so one supped at small tables as at a ball in Paris all through the night. Supper was ready at the opening of the ball and also as complete and as well served at the finish by daylight. Newport had never seen before, and has never seen since, anything as dazzling and brilliant, as well conceived, and as well carried out in every detail.

WARD McALLISTER, Society as I Have Found It. 1890

204. Jacob Riis Discovers How the Other Half Lives

A Danish immigrant, Jacob Riis brought to his adopted country not only intelligence and industry, but faith in the possibility of creating here a more just and more humane social order. As a newspaper reporter he was familiar with life in the slums and the tenements of New York, and as a reformer he was determined to improve the lot of the poor and the under-privileged. How the Other Half Lives *was a powerful piece of journalism, which did more to dramatize the problem of tenement-house reform than did anything else at that time. President Theodore Roosevelt called Jacob Riis "the best American I ever knew."*

NEW YORK'S wage earners have no other place to live, more is the pity. They are truly poor for having no better homes; waxing poorer in purse as the exorbitant rents to which they are tied, as ever was serf to soil, keep rising. The wonder is that they are not all corrupted, and speedily, by their surroundings. If on the contrary there be a steady working up, if not out of the slough, the fact is a powerful argument for the optimist's belief that the world is after all growing better not worse, and would go far toward disarming apprehension were it not for the steadier growth of the sediment of the slums and its constant menace. Such an impulse toward better things there certainly is. The German ragpicker of thirty years ago, quite as low in the scale as his Italian successor, is the thrifty tradesman or prosperous farmer of today.

The Italian scavenger of our time is fast graduating into exclusive control of the corner fruit stands, while his black-eyed boy monopolizes the bootblacking industry in which a few years ago he was an intruder. The Irish hod carrier in the second generation has become a bricklayer, if not the alderman of his ward, while the Chinese coolie is in almost exclusive possession of the laundry business. The reason is obvious. The poorest immigrant comes here with the purpose and ambition to better himself and, given half a chance, might be reasonably expected to make the most of it. To the false plea that he prefers the squalid homes in which his kind are housed there could be no better answer. The truth is his half chance has too long been wanting, and for the bad result he has been unjustly blamed.

As emigration from east to west follows the latitude, so does the foreign influx in New York distribute itself along certain well-defined lines that waver and break only under the stronger pressure of a more gregarious race or the encroachments of inexorable business. A feeling of dependence upon mutual effort, natural to strangers in a strange land, unacquainted with its language and customs, sufficiently accounts for this.

The Irishman is the true cosmopolitan immigrant. All-pervading, he shares his lodging with perfect impartiality with the Italian, the Greek, and the "Dutchman," yielding only to sheer force of numbers, and objects equally to them all. A map of the city, colored to designate nationalities, would show more stripes than on the skin of a zebra and more colors than any rainbow. The city on such a map would fall into two great halves, green for the Irish prevailing in the West Side tenement districts and blue for the Germans on the East Side. But intermingled with these ground colors would be an odd variety of tints that would give the whole the appearance of an extraordinary crazy quilt. From down in the Sixth Ward, upon the site of the old Collect Pond that in the days of the fathers drained the hills which are no more, the red of the Italian would be seen forcing its way northward along the line of Mulberry Street to the quarter of the French purple on Bleecker Street and south Fifth Avenue, to lose itself and reappear, after a lapse of miles, in the Little Italy of Harlem, east of Second Avenue. Dashes of red, sharply defined, would be seen strung through the annexed district northward to the city line. On the West Side the red would be seen overrunning the old Africa of Thompson Street, pushing the black of the Negro rapidly uptown, against querulous but unavailing protests, occupying his home, his church, his trade and all, with merciless impartiality. There is a church in Mulberry Street that has stood for two generations as a sort of milestone of these migrations. Built originally for the worship of staid New Yorkers of the old stock, it was engulfed by the colored tide when the draft riots drove the Negroes out of reach of Cherry Street and the Five Points. Within the past decade the advance wave of the Italian onset reached it, and today the arms of United Italy adorn its front. The Negroes have made a stand at several points along Seventh and Eighth Avenues, but their main body, still pursued by the Italian foe, is on the march yet, and the black mark will be found overshadowing today many blocks on the East Side, with One Hundredth Street as the center, where colonies of them have settled recently.

Hardly less aggressive than the Italian, the Russian and Polish Jew, having overrun the district between Rivington and Division Streets, east of the Bowery, to the point of suffocation, is filling the tenements of the old Seventh Ward to the river front and disputing with the Italian every foot of available space in the back alleys of Mulberry Street. The two races, differing hopelessly in much, have this in common; they carry their slums with them wherever they go, if allowed to do it. Little Italy already rivals its parent, the "Bend," in foulness. Other nationalities that begin at the bottom make a fresh start when crowded up the ladder. Happily both are manageable, the one by rabbinical, the other by the civil law. Between the dull gray of the Jew, his favorite color, and the Italian red, would be seen squeezed in on the map a sharp streak of yellow marking the narrow boundaries of Chinatown. Dovetailed in with the German population, the poor but thrifty Bohemian might be picked out by the somber hue of his life as of his philosophy, struggling against heavy odds in the big human beehives of the East Side. Colonies of his people extend northward, with long lapses of space, from below the Cooper Institute more than three miles. The Bohemian is the only foreigner with any considerable representation in the city who counts no wealthy man of his race, none who has not to work hard for a living or has got beyond the reach of the tenement.

Down near the Battery, the West Side emerald would be soiled by a dirty stain, spreading rapidly like a splash of ink on a sheet of blotting paper, headquarters of the Arab tribe that in a single year has swelled from the original dozen to twelve hundred, intent, every mother's son, on trade and barter. Dots and dashes of color here and there would show where the Finnish sailors worship their *Djumala* (God), the Greek pedlars the ancient name of their race, and the Swiss the goddess of thrift. And so on to the end of the long register, all toiling together in the galling fetters of the tenement. Were the question raised who makes the most of life thus mortgaged, who resists most stubbornly its leveling tendency — knows how to drag even the barracks upward a part of the way at least toward the ideal plane of the home — the palm must be unhesitatingly awarded the Teuton. The Italian and the poor Jew rise only by compulsion. The Chinaman does not rise at all; here, as at home, he remains stationary. The Irishman's genius runs to public affairs rather than domestic life; wherever he is mustered in force the saloon is the gorgeous center of political activity. The German struggles vainly to learn his trick; his Teutonic wit is too heavy, and the political ladder he raises from his saloon usually too short or too clumsy to reach the desired goal. The best part of his life is lived at home, and he makes himself a home independent of the surroundings, giving the lie to the saying, unhappily become a maxim of social truth, that pauperism and drunkenness naturally grow in the tenements. He makes the most of his tenement, and it should be added that whenever and as soon as he can save up money enough, he gets out and never crosses the threshold of one again.

Hamilton Street, like Water Street, is not what it was. The missions drove from the latter the worst of its dives. A sailors mission has lately made its appearance in Hamilton Street, but there are no dives there, nothing worse than the ubiquitous saloon and tough tenements.

Enough of them everywhere. Suppose we look into one, No. -- Cherry Street. Be a little careful, please! The hall is dark, and you might stumble over the children pitching pennies back there. Not that it would hurt them; kicks and cuffs are their daily diet. They have little else. Here where the hall turns and dives into utter darkness is a step, and another, another. A flight of stairs. You can feel your way if you cannot see it. Close? Yes! What would you have? All the fresh air that ever enters these stairs comes from the hall door that is forever slamming and from the windows of dark bedrooms that in turn receive from the stairs their sole supply of the elements God meant to be free but man deals out with such niggardly hand. That was a woman filling her pail by the hydrant you just bumped against. The sinks are in the hallway, that all the tenants may have access — and all be poisoned alike by their summer stenches. Hear the pump squeak! It is the lullaby of tenement house babes. In summer, when a thousand thirsty throats pant for a cooling drink in this block, it is worked in vain. But the saloon, whose open door you passed in the hall, is always there. The smell of it has followed you up. Here is a door. Listen! That short, hacking cough, that tiny, helpless wail — what do they mean? They mean that the soiled bow of white you saw on the door downstairs will have another story to tell — oh! a sadly familiar story — before the day is at an end. The child is dying with measles. With half a chance it might have lived, but it had none. That dark bedroom killed it.

"It was took all of a suddint," says the mother, smoothing the throbbing little body with trembling hands. There is no unkindness in the rough voice of the man in the jumper who sits by the window grimly smoking a clay pipe, with the little life ebbing out in his sight, bitter as his words sound: "Hush, Mary! If we cannot keep the baby, need we complain — such as we?"

Such as we! What if the words ring in your ears as we grope our way up the stairs and down from floor to floor, listening to the sounds behind the closed doors — some of quarreling, some of coarse songs, more of profanity. They are true. When the summer heats come with their suffering they have meaning more terrible than words can tell. Come over here. Step carefully over this baby — it is a baby, spite of its rags and dirt — under these iron bridges called fire escapes, but loaded down, despite the incessant watchfulness of the firemen, with broken household goods, with washtubs and barrels, over which no man could climb from a fire. This gap between dingy brick walls is the yard. That strip of smoke-colored sky up there is the heaven of these people. Do you wonder the name does not attract them to the churches? That baby's parents live in the rear tenement here. She is at least as clean as the steps we are now climbing. There are plenty of houses with half a hundred such in. The tenement is much like the one in front we just left, only fouler, closer, darker — we will not say more cheerless. The word is a mockery. A hundred thousand people lived in rear tenements in New York last year. Here is a room neater than the rest. The woman, a stout matron with hard lines of care in her face, is at the washtub. "I try to keep the childer clean," she says, apologetically, but with a hopeless glance around. The spice of hot soapsuds is added to the air already tainted with the smell of boiling cabbage, of rags and uncleanliness all about. It makes an overpowering compound. It is Thursday, but patched linen is hung upon the pulley line from the window. There is no Monday cleaning in the tenements. It is washday all the week round, for a change of clothing is scarce among the poor. They are poverty's honest badge, these perennial lines of rags hung out to dry, those that are not the washerwoman's professional shingle. The true line to be drawn between pauperism and honest poverty is the clothesline. With it begins the effort to be clean that is the first and the best evidence of a desire to be honest.

What sort of an answer, think you, would come from these tenements to the question "Is life worth living?" were they heard at all in the discussion?

JACOB A. RIIS, How the Other Half Lives. 1890

205. Jacob Riis Avenges His Dog

Riis did many things more important than the elimination of police lodging houses, but none of his achievements ever gave him greater satisfaction. He could not have succeeded even in this without the aid of Theodore Roosevelt, and the story which Riis here tells explains in part why "T.R." was so popular with Americans of his generation.

THERE was until last winter a doorway in Chatham Square, that of the old Barnum clothing store, which I could never pass without recalling those nights of hopeless misery with the policeman's periodic "Get up there! move on!" reinforced by a prod of his club or the toe of his boot. I slept there, or tried to when crowded out of the tenements in the Bend by their utter nastiness. Cold and wet weather had set in, and a linen duster was all that covered my back. There was a woolen blanket in my trunk which I had from home — the one, my mother had told me, in which I was wrapped when I was born; but the trunk was in the "hotel" as security for money I owed for board, and I asked for it in vain. I was now too shabby to get work, even if there had been any to get. I had letters still to friends of my family in New York who might have helped me, but hunger and want had not conquered my pride. I would come to them, if at all, as their equal, and lest I fall into temptation I destroyed the letters. So, having burned my bridges behind me, I was finally and utterly alone in the city, with the winter approaching and every shivering night in the streets reminding me that a time was rapidly coming when such a life as I led could no longer be endured.

Not in a thousand years would I be likely to forget the night when it came. It had rained all day, a cold October storm, and night found me, with the chill downpour unabated, down by the North River, soaked through and through, with no chance for a supper, forlorn and discouraged. I sat on the bulwark, listening to the falling rain and the swish of the dark tide, and thinking of home. . . .

And even then help came. A wet and shivering body was pressed against mine, and I felt rather than heard a piteous whine in my ear. It was my companion in misery, a little outcast black-and-tan, afflicted with fits, that had shared the shelter of a friendly doorway with me one cold night and had clung to me ever since with a loyal affection that was the one bright spot in my hard life. As my hand stole mechanically down to caress it, it crept up on my knees and licked my face as if it meant to tell me that there was one who understood; that I was not alone. And the love of the faithful little beast thawed the icicles in my heart. I picked it up in my arms and fled from the tempter; fled to where there were lights and men moving, if they cared less for me than I for them — anywhere so that I saw and heard the river no more.

In the midnight hour we walked into the Church Street police station and asked for lodging. The rain was still pouring in torrents. The sergeant spied the dog under my tattered coat and gruffly told me to put it out if I wanted to sleep there. I pleaded for it in vain. There was no choice. To stay in the street was to perish. So I left my dog out on the stoop, where it curled up to wait for me. Poor little friend! It was its last watch. The lodging room was jammed with a foul and stewing crowd of tramps. A loud-mouthed German was holding forth about the war in Europe and crowding me on my plank. Cold and hunger had not sufficed to put out the patriotic spark within me. It was promptly fanned into flame, and I told him what I thought of him and his crew. Some Irishmen cheered and fomented trouble, and the doorman came in, threatening to lock us all up. I smothered my disgust at the place as well as I could, and slept, wearied nearly to death.

In the middle of the night I awoke with a feeling that something was wrong. Instinctively I felt for the little gold locket I wore under my shirt, with a part of the precious curl in it that was my last link with home. It was gone. I had felt it there the last thing before I fell asleep. One of the tramp lodgers had cut the string and stolen it. With angry tears I went up and complained to the sergeant that I had been robbed. He scowled at me over the blotter, called me a thief, and said that he had a good mind to lock me up. How should I, a tramp boy, have come by a gold locket? He had heard, he added, that I had said in the lodging room that I wished the French would win, and he would only be giving me what I deserved if he sent me to the Island. I heard and understood. He was himself a German. All my sufferings rose up before me, all the bitterness of my soul poured itself out upon him. I do not know what I said. I remember that he told the doorman to put me out. And he seized me and threw me out of the door, coming after to kick me down the stoop.

My dog had been waiting, never taking its eyes off the door, until I should come out. When it saw me in the grasp of the doorman, it fell upon him at once, fastening its teeth in his leg. He let go of me with a yell of pain, seized the poor little beast by the legs, and beat its brains out against the stone steps.

At the sight a blind rage seized me. Raving like a madman, I stormed the police station with paving stones from the gutter. The fury of my onset frightened even the sergeant, who saw, perhaps, that he had gone too far, and he called two policemen to disarm and conduct me out of the precinct, anywhere so that he got rid of me. They marched me to the nearest ferry and turned me loose. The ferry master halted me. I had no money, but I gave him a silk handkerchief, the last thing about me that had any value, and for that he let me cross to Jersey City. I shook the dust of New York from my feet, vowing that I would never return, and, setting my face toward the west, marched straight out the first railroad track I came to.

And now, right here, begins the part of my story that is my only excuse for writing down these facts, though it will not appear for a while yet. The outrage of that night became, in the providence of God, the means of putting an end to one of the foulest abuses that ever disgraced a Christian city and a mainspring in the battle with the slum as far as my share in it is concerned. My dog did not die unavenged.

Typhus fever broke out in the city [New York] in the winter of 1891-92. The wonder was that it did not immediately center in the police lodging rooms. There they lay, young and old, hardened tramps and young castaways with minds and souls soft as wax for their foulness to be stamped upon, on bare floors of stone or planks. Dirty as they came in from every vile contact, they went out in the morning to scatter from door to door, where they begged their breakfast, the seeds of festering disease. Turning the plank was making the bed. Typhus is a filth disease, of all the most dreaded. If ever it got a foothold in those dens, there was good cause for fear. I drew up at once a remonstrance, had it signed by representatives of the united charitable societies — some of them shrugged their shoulders, but they signed — and took it to the Board of Health.

I warned them that there would be trouble with the lodging rooms, and within eleven months the prophecy came true. The typhus broke out *there*. The night after the news had come I took my camera and flashlight and made the round of the dens, photographing them all with their crowds. Of the negatives I had lantern slides made and with these under my arm knocked at the doors of the Academy of Medicine, demanding to be let in. That was the place for that discussion, it seemed to me, for the doctors knew the real extent of the peril we were then facing. Typhus is no respecter of persons, and it is impossible to guard against it as against the smallpox. They let me in, and that night's doings gave the cause of decency a big push. I think that was the first time I told the real story of my dog. I had always got around it somehow; it choked me even then, twenty years after and more, anger boiled up in me so at the recollection.

In another year reform came, and with it came Roosevelt. The committee on vagrancy, a volunteer body of the Charity Organization Society, of which I was a member, unlimbered its guns again and opened fire, and this time the walls came down. For Tammany was out.

We had been looking the police over by night, Roosevelt and I. We had inspected the lodging rooms while I went over the long fight with him, and had come at last, at 2 A.M., to the Church Street Station. It was raining outside. The light flickered, cold and cheerless, in the green lamps as we went up the stone steps. Involuntarily I looked in the corner for my little dog, but it was not there, or any one who remembered it. The sergeant glanced over his blotter grimly; I had almost to pinch myself to make sure I was not shivering in a linen duster, wet to the skin. Down the cellar steps to the men's lodging room I led the president of the police board. It was unchanged — just as it was the day I slept there. Three men lay stretched at full length on the dirty planks, two of them young lads from the country. Standing there, I told Mr. Roosevelt my own story. He turned alternately red and white with anger as he heard it.

"Did they do that to you?" he asked when I had ended. For an answer I pointed to the young lads then asleep before him.

"I was like this one," I said.

He struck his clenched fists together. "I will smash them to-morrow."

He was as good as his word. The very next day the police board took the matter up. Provision was made for the homeless on a barge in the East River until plans could be perfected for sifting the tramps from the unfortunate, and within a week, on recommendation of the chief of police, orders were issued to close the doors of the police lodging rooms on February 15, 1896, never again to be unbarred.

The battle was won. The murder of my dog was avenged and forgiven after twenty-five years.

Jacob A. Riis, The Making of an American

206. Carl Christian Jensen Becomes an American

Carl Christian Jensen was another Danish immigrant who dreamed of America as a better world and contributed much to the realization of that dream. His autobiography is valuable throughout for what it tells of the adjustment of an immigrant to the American environment.

I WAS a man and stronger than most men. Yet my second childhood began the day I entered my new country [1906]. I had to learn life over in a brand-new world. And I could not talk. My first desire was for chocolate drops, and I pointed my finger at them. My second was for fishing tackle, and I pointed my finger at a wrapping cord and heaved up an imaginary fish. I used baby talk. "Price?" I asked. And later in the day, "Vatsprice?" Saleswomen answered with motherly grimaces.

I never quite got over my second childhood. I doubt that any immigrant ever does — with his hasty, often harsh attuning to the new world. My first birth was distant and dim and unreal, for I was almost three years old when I awoke, and most of the shock had disappeared. The old world and I grew up together. We just grew in blissful ignorance of one another's growing pains. And my first childhood stole upon me softly.

Not so my second childhood. I was born full-grown, so to speak, and therefore was aware of my new birth. I regressed to the greed of infancy. My curiosity was that of a child. My manners lacked the poise of adulthood. My angers, fears, and joys were fleeting and childish and divided the new world into absolute categories — into good and evil. The new world cut into my clay and chronicled something which was not there before — another code of thoughts and feelings.

The moment I put foot ashore I dropped my sailor bag from my shoulder, awe-struck at my own puniness. For Battery Park lay like a deep valley under the towering cliffs and mountain crags of Broadway. A glance up at the columns of the Custom House and at the skyscrapers impressed me as no other world wonder could. The dome of heaven sighed over the crags and coulees like a huge sea-shell, and snow covered the majestic peaks of these man-made mountains. . . .

I found shelter in Mill's Hotel — a slender skyscraper on Bleecker Street, where I occupied a cell with a shelf to sleep on and a rope strung up for clothes. There I rested myself the first night, already quite detached from the past and stunned with a crazy feeling that I was somebody else.

At early dawn I was out on the street again to gaze at the buildings, one of which was large enough to house the people of my home town, and at Brooklyn Bridge, which was thrice as broad as the King's Highway running through Denmark, and at the trains above my head and under my feet that were ten times speedier than the narrow-gauge train of the dunes.

Frantic streams of sweatshop workers climbed the subway stairs, leaped out of street cars, poured forth from ferries, rushed down from elevated stations. Children carried box wood home from whole-sale stores and market places. Bent old men carted bulky sacks of rags to their junk shops. Sailor tramps told doleful stories of ship-wrecks in which they had lost their belongings, from the gold they had dug in Alaska to their mother's Bible. Years later I found one of the same tramps on the same spot, telling the same tale. But only the first time did I urge him to accept a loan.

On West Street tangled teams and trucks and peddlers' carts blocked the horse cars that clanged their bells with yowling petulance, while teamsters cursed, peddlers sang, ferries tooted. On one side of the street rows on rows of immigrant liners lay moored. On the other side old tilting rooming houses were crowded with dark-eyed children, and with women with Mona Lisa faces, and with men lamenting in strange tongues.

Labor bureaus shipped away immigrants to mines and mills and factories. The labor market was flooded. Weeping with gratitude they went. Every day brought fresh hordes ashore. For every man who found work a hundred others stepped ashore from the Ellis Island ferry.

I descended into a subway excavation, far beneath the traffic, where laborers ran in continuous gallop, balancing their wheelbarrows on narrow planks, and throwing mud and granite into steam shovels. When a man stumbled or rested to regain his breath, his foreman's curses reverberated against the walls. My ambition was to build a sub-way. But foremen drove me away from their gangs of toilers, watch-men threatened me with arrest, explosives endangered my life.

My next ambition — and one that is not yet dead — was to drive an elevated train. But where could I find the owner? I rode to the end of the lines and stepped off at every station to find the owner. I pestered passengers, ticket takers, conductors, and the men that repaired the tracks. But never did I find the owner.

Along thirty miles of water front I wandered in search of work — around Manhattan Island, on the Brooklyn, Jersey City, Hoboken, and Staten Island wharves — waiting through rain and sleet and snow with gangs of longshoremen to reach the boss before he finished picking the men he wanted. It took strength, when a steamer arrived, to break the brawny barriers and stem the tides of human muscles. Strong men crushed each other to the ground in their passion for work.

Thirty hours these longshoremen worked without a rest while thousands of envious idlers watched from ashore. Their eyes were wild with lust for work. Tobacco juice mingled with sweat from their brows and froze into icicles on their horned mustaches. Cargoes of wheat and fruit, coal and brick, boxes, bales, and barrels, these tireless toilers carried, while their gang boss, yelling like a demon, drove them in a continual trot.

Accidents they ignored in their great urge for work. The paw of a hoisting boom struck a toiler to instant death; a cable swept a row of men off the deck, down on the drifting ice floes; a scaffold gave way under a dozen men, who tumbled down with their barrels in a bleeding heap.

On my arrival I was in possession of a twenty-dollar gold piece, five silver dollars, a pocket Bible, and a good watch. My sailor bag was full of working clothes. A six-shooter and a Spanish pistol, which I had bought in Buenos Aires the previous year, and a linen shirt which I had worn at the age of one, lay hidden on top among a dozen handkerchiefs. The next day sailor tramps borrowed my gold piece. And when the rest of my money was spent I took refuge in the open, cuddling up in a pile of straw that kept the cement from freezing on the foundation of a new skyscraper. There my sailor bag was stolen the first night. My baby shirt I saved, finding it in my pocket the next morning. I had mistaken it for a handkerchief. . . .

When a watchman drove me away from the straw pile, I took refuge in a Bowery hotel, where I was packed on the floor with other vagrants like herrings in a barrel. These were dime and nickel lodgings, and we lay sleeping, not only on floors and benches, but also in the halls and on the stairs, from roof to sidewalk. My watch I pawned for fifty cents. Many a night I was grateful to sleep on the stairs among drunken Bowery bums. We lay or sat intermingled in a solid mass that formed a large, sluggish organism with limbs stretching into every nook, whose breath was strong, and whose coughs and grunts, moans, and snoring were the weirdest music that ever touched my ear.

At dawn we disentangled ourselves from one another's grip. And weaklings who during the night succumbed were shipped to the morgue and to the potter's field — two places I followed friends to that first winter.

The Bowery hotels welcomed me whether I had my nickel or no. They saved me from freezing to death. Why should I not be grateful? Yet they were like slave ships with cargoes of slaves sealed up under the hatches.

And there were other wonders on the Bowery: the daily bread line with its soup, the Bowery Mission with its midnight teas, and the saloon free-lunch counters — traps with cheese, where many a hungry rat was fed. . . .

I joined the bread line on the Bowery, which wound around the block and diminished, when the soup was served, like a roll of wire chopped off into nails. Shabby were the men, gloomy their spirits. Like homeless dogs they were, skulking around for bones in back alleys, snapping and snarling if I stepped on their toes or squeezed them out of line.

At the Bowery Mission the pastor and his wife fed a strange family. I became a frequent visitor there, and among ex-convicts, drunkards, dope fiends, and not infrequently demented youths, testified in baby English about a benevolent Providence. We bragged about our sins, especially on Saturday nights, when wealthy American women went slumming. Here the blackest sinner was the hero.

I hoarded words like a coin collector, and the language of my second childhood grew. Every day I found new words, for all the things and acts that I beheld in the new world had a name, and every name had many modifiers. I talked to myself as I had done in the rope spinnery during my first childhood — playing with my collection during all my leisure hours. I remember distinctly the day when four words which had grown familiar to my ear attached themselves to things that had grown familiar to my eye. "Was the boss *satisfied?*" "This is a *rush* job." "The whistle blew *long ago*." "I'll *O.K.* your time slip." I was less of a child and more grown-up when these four words became part of my own living flesh. We had become partners, the new world and I, for we owned something in common.

My childish responses to the new world uttered themselves in my emotions. A bartender giving me a plate of corned beef and cabbage filled my heart with a rare joy. A park cop poking my ribs with his club made me angry enough to kill. A watchman pointing his gun at me gave me a fear that literally tasted salty. The new world, with its new words and new feelings, grew into a corporation — like the Trinity almost. First in rank came the new world; second, the new words — which were only symbols and were a kind of "substituting vicar"; third, the new feelings — which were like a "spirit" that revealed and appraised its two triumviral peers, a sort of guardian ghost that told me the difference between good and evil. For the new world was neither all good nor all evil. I worshiped it with the faith of a child — that is, selfishly.

In Brooklyn I joined a public night school where immigrants gathered to learn the language of their new country. The teacher was a young American woman of wit and refinement. She handled her forty husky pupils well. There was in the class an old, half-blind Italian doctor who never learned to say "I" instead of "me." There was also an English teamster, with black teeth and clothes that smelled of horses, who was learning a more limber handwriting. And there were many Swedes who after the day's work at the water front were tired and sleepy and always lost the page in their primers when they were called on to read. A German would leap up like a jack-in-the-box to show them the page and paragraph. . . .

Voltage and amperage were the mystery of the age. What else, therefore, should I choose than the trade of an electrician? I was a humble helper, cleaning motors in hundreds of sweatshops of lower Manhattan, hauling new motors from the repair shop, and carrying burned-out armatures back to Prince Street. Even after I had learned the rudimentary tricks of this semimystical trade — such as the methodical waste of time and material on repair jobs and the short cuts of contract jobs — new wonders continued to thrill me.

The part of Manhattan that I learned to know best was the sweatshop district. Between Canal Street and Greenwich Village I worked in several hundred shops: glove shops with rows on rows of sewing machines, and purring shuttles gliding out of and into thread loops, and the mad dance of glinting needles around a thousand tiny leather fingers; lace shops with looms growling appallingly, gears and pinions gnawing one another's teeth, spindles and spools whirring, and shrieks from a jungle of belts; trouser shops with forty layers of cloth cut by a pair of creeping scissors, and long, clattering needle races along the inseams; handbag shops with dies, punches, and curved knives, bronze, silver, and gold hinges, and a cargo of warty alligator skins; feather shops with cellars of vats and blowers, airy drying lofts, and downy assortment rooms — all the shops crowded with bright-eyed immigrant girls.

And there were the rag shops on Hudson and Water Streets where old, hawklike witches squatted on the floor and examined the rags and ripped them apart — piece by piece — and with clairvoyant gaze read a story in each.

There were also shops with old, old men stitching fur caps by day and sleeping on their sewing tables at night — red-eyed, under-nourished dreamers, some of whom seldom, if ever, ventured down into the street except on the Sabbath day.

And I found an artistic hat shop owned and managed by a bearded Talmudic scholar. There was no rush in this shop; young girls had time to steal a glance at me and I at them, the air was cooled by exhaust fans, and there was a cozy, tranquil atmosphere as though I had entered a temple. Etchings and epigrams decorated the walls. The boss was like a peaceful prophet pouring forth wisdom and holiness. Even the motors, unlike the whizzing overworked ones in other shops, hummed harmoniously and pulled the belts with ease.

One day I came upon a man bent over a sewing machine in a dingy sweatshop, a pale, thinly bearded Jew with the melancholy glow of his race burning in his eye. He had suffered his share in this life, having been driven from Moscow into the Siberian ice, during his student days, from whence he had made his escape to America. At noon we lunched together at a sidewalk counter, devouring — and relishing — a glass of synthetic lemonade and a nickel's worth of doughnuts. I treated to ice-cream cones, though this extravagance was more severe on my resources than if during my sailor days I had treated a crew. My apprentice wage of a dollar a day barely covered the four essentials of Manhattan — carfare, clothes, housing, food.

My new friend was in a hurry to return. He was tutoring a youngster in mathematics, he told me. I held him back. Mathematics! The only language that made natural forces obey its command!

The bridge between earth and the stars! The essence of voltage and amperage! He was preparing a youth for entrance examination to Cooper Union on the Bowery. "If I took lessons, could I also enter Cooper Union?" I asked eagerly. "One dollar I'll pay you every week." He looked me over from head to foot — especially my head. "Yes," he said. "I'll teach you."

That spring and summer I studied algebra and geometry with exuberant joy and tenacity. My books were always with me. In the morning on the trains from Brooklyn I studied mathematics. And when I walked along Broadway from City Hall to the shop on Prince Street I solved quadratic equations, often colliding with people on the crowded sidewalk. When I hauled a motor to a sweat-shop and the wagon got stuck in a tie-up, I would ponder over circles and triangles. When my foreman forbade me to hurry a repair job and kept me loafing for days at a time in the cellars of Manhattan, my book was under a plumber's candle, ready at a moment's notice to be tossed into my tool bag. Even when I rode on top of an office elevator the day long, repairing the bellwire cable between stops, my book lay hidden in my tool bag. And the diagrams I drew in my notebook were not of the broken-down bell system but were geometric demonstrations.

Short circuits blew my screwdriver into molten drippings, my pliers into clouds of smoke, and my wrench into meteoric dust. Invisible currents swept through my tissue, some gripping me with ecstatic thrills, some taking hold as a surge seizes a ship, and some hitting me a hammer blow that stunned my senses. But I mastered my trade and my mathematics.

What a glorious second childhood!

CARL CHRISTIAN JENSEN, An American Saga

207. Jane Addams Establishes Hull House

Inspired by the example of Toyn-bee Hall in London, social workers began, around the close of the century, to establish settlement houses in the slums of the great

*cities. The most famous of these were the Henry Street Settlement,
in New York, the South End House in Boston, and Hull House in
Chicago, which first opened its hospitable doors in September 1889.
Jane Addams was largely responsible for its establishment and was its
guide for over forty years. Her broadening activities, which eventually
brought her the Nobel Peace Prize, made her by common consent
the most distinguished of American social workers of her generation.*

As SOCIAL reformers gave themselves over to discussion of
general principles, so the poor invariably accused poverty itself of
their destruction. I recall a certain Mrs. Moran who was returning
one rainy day from the office of the county agent with her arms
full of paper bags containing beans and flour which alone lay between her children and starvation. Although she had no money, she
boarded a street car in order to save her booty from complete destruction by the rain; and as the burst bags dropped "flour on the ladies'
dresses" and "beans all over the place," she was sharply reprimanded
by the conductor, who was further exasperated when he discovered
she had no fare. He put her off, as she had hoped he would, almost
in front of Hull House. She related to us her state of mind as she
stepped off the car and saw the last of her wares disappearing; she
admitted she forgot the proprieties and "cursed a little," but curiously
enough, she pronounced her malediction not against the rain nor the
conductor, nor yet against the worthless husband who had been sent
up to the city prison, but, true to the Chicago spirit of the moment,
went to the root of the matter and roundly "cursed poverty.". . .

I remember one family in which the father had been out of work
for this same winter, most of the furniture had been pawned, and
as the worn-out shoes could not be replaced the children could not
go to school. The mother was ill and barely able to come for the
supplies and medicines. Two years later she invited me to supper
one Sunday evening in the little home which had been completely
restored, and she gave as a reason for the invitation that she couldn't
bear to have me remember them as they had been during that one
winter, which she insisted had been unique in her twelve years of
married life. She said that it was as if she had met me, not as I am
ordinarily, but as I should appear misshapen with rheumatism or

with a face distorted by neuralgic pain; that it was not fair to judge poor people that way. She perhaps unconsciously illustrated the difference between the relief station's relation to the poor and the Settlement's relation to its neighbors, the latter wishing to know them through all the varying conditions of life, to stand by when they are in distress, but by no means to drop intercourse with them when normal prosperity has returned, enabling the relation to become more social and free from economic disturbance.

Possibly something of the same effort has to be made within the Settlement itself to keep its own sense of proportion in regard to the relation of the crowded city quarter to the rest of the country. It was in the spring following this terrible winter, during a journey to meet lecture engagements in California, that I found myself amazed at the large stretches of open country and prosperous towns through which we passed day by day, whose existence I had quite forgotten.

In the latter part of the summer of 1895 I served as a member on a commission appointed by the mayor of Chicago to investigate conditions in the county poorhouse, public attention having become centered on it through one of those distressing stories which exaggerates the wrong in a public institution while at the same time it reveals conditions which need to be rectified. However necessary publicity is for securing reformed administration, however useful such exposures may be for political purposes, the whole is attended by such a waste of the most precious human emotions, by such a tearing of live tissue, that it can scarcely be endured. Every time I entered Hull House during the days of the investigation I would find waiting for me from twenty to thirty people whose friends and relatives were in the suspected institution, all in such acute distress of mind that to see them was to look upon the victims of deliberate torture. In most cases my visitor would state that it seemed impossible to put their invalids in any other place, but if these stories were true, something must be done. Many of the patients were taken out, only to be returned after a few days or weeks to meet the sullen hostility of their attendants and with their own attitude changed from confidence to timidity and alarm.

This piteous dependence of the poor upon the good will of public officials was made clear to us in an early experience with a peasant woman straight from the fields of Germany, whom we met during our first six months at Hull House. Her four years in America had been spent in patiently carrying water up and down two flights of stairs and in washing the heavy flannel suits of iron foundry workers. For this her pay had averaged thirty-five cents a day. Three of her daughters had fallen victims to the vice of the city. The mother was bewildered and distressed, but understood nothing. We were able to induce the betrayer of one daughter to marry her; the second, after a tedious lawsuit, supported his child; with the third we were able to do nothing. This woman is now living with her family in a little house seventeen miles from the city. She has made two payments on her land and is a lesson to all beholders as she pastures her cow up and down the railroad tracks and makes money from her ten acres. She did not need charity, for she had an immense capacity for hard work, but she sadly needed the service of the state's attorney's office, enforcing the laws designed for the protection of such girls as her daughters.

We early found ourselves spending many hours in efforts to secure support for deserted women, insurance for bewildered widows, damages for injured operators, furniture from the clutches of the installment store. The Settlement is valuable as an information and interpretation bureau. It constantly acts between the various institutions of the city and the people for whose benefit these institutions were erected. The hospitals, the county agencies, and state asylums are often but vague rumors to the people who need them most. Another function of the Settlement to its neighborhood resembles that of the big brother whose mere presence on the playground protects the little one from bullies.

We early learned to know the children of hard-driven mothers who went out to work all day, sometimes leaving the little things in the casual care of a neighbor, but often locking them into their tenement rooms. The first three crippled children we encountered in the neighborhood had all been injured while their mothers were at work; one had fallen out of a third-story window, another had been burned, and the third had a curved spine due to the fact that for three years he had been tied all day long to the leg of the kitchen table.

JANE ADDAMS, Forty Years of Hull House

XXIX

School and Society

208. Mary Antin Arrives in the Promised Land

An eager thirst for education and a desire for Americanization has characterized most of the many million immigrants who have come to our shores. Mary Antin, who later made notable contributions to American letters, here presents some of the difficulty and some of the pathos of the immigrant's search for education.

OUR INITIATION into American ways began with the first step on the new soil. My father found occasion to instruct or correct us even on the way from the pier to Wall Street, which journey we made crowded together in a rickety cab. He told us not to lean out of the windows, not to point, and explained the word greenhorn. We did not want to be greenhorns and gave the strictest attention to my father's instructions. I do not know when my parents found opportunity to review together the history of Polotzk in the three years past, for we children had no patience with the subject; my mother's narrative was constantly interrupted by irrelevant questions, interjections, and explanations.

The first meal was an object lesson of much variety. My father produced several kinds of food, ready to eat, without any cooking, from little tin cans that had printing all over them. He attempted to introduce us to a queer, slippery kind of fruit which he called banana, but had to give it up for the time being. After the meal he had better luck with a curious piece of furniture on runners which he called rocking chair. There were five of us newcomers, and we found five different ways of getting into the American machine of perpetual motion and as many ways of getting out of it. One born and bred to the use of a rocking chair cannot imagine how ludicrous people can make themselves when attempting to use it for the first time. We laughed immoderately over our various experiments with the novelty, which was a wholesome way of letting off steam after the unusual excitement of the day.

In our flat we did not think of such a thing as storing the coal in the bathtub. There was no bathtub. So in the evening of the first day my father conducted us to the public baths. As we moved along in a little procession, I was delighted with the illumination of the streets. So many lamps, and they burned until morning, my father said, and so people did not need to carry lanterns. In America, then, everything was free, as we had heard in Russia. Light was free; the streets were as bright as a synagogue on a holy day. Music was free; we had been serenaded, to our gaping delight, by a brass band of many pieces, soon after our installation on Union Place.

Education was free. That subject my father had written about repeatedly, as comprising his chief hope for us children, the essence of American opportunity, the treasure that no thief could touch, not even misfortune or poverty. It was the one thing that he was able to promise us when he sent for us; surer, safer than bread or shelter. On our second day I was thrilled with the realization of what this freedom of education meant. A little girl from across the alley came and offered to conduct us to school. My father was out, but we five between us had a few words of English by this time. We knew the word school. We understood. This child, who had never seen us till yesterday, who could not pronounce our names, who was not much better dressed than we, was able to offer us the freedom of the schools of Boston! No application made, no questions asked, no examinations, rulings, exclusions; no machinations, no fees. The doors stood open for every one of us. The smallest child could show us the way.

This incident impressed me more than anything I had heard in advance of the freedom of education in America. It was a concrete proof—almost the thing itself. One had to experience it to understand it.

It was a great disappointment to be told by my father that we were not to enter upon our school career at once. It was too near the end of the term, he said, and we were going to move to Crescent

Beach in a week or so. We had to wait until the opening of the schools in September. What a loss of precious time — from May till September!

Not that the time was really lost. Even the interval on Union Place was crowded with lessons and experiences. We had to visit the stores and be dressed from head to foot in American clothing; we had to learn the mysteries of the iron stove, the washboard, and the speaking tube; we had to learn to trade with the fruit peddler through the window and not to be afraid of the policeman; and, above all, we had to learn English.

The kind people who assisted us in these important matters form a group by themselves in the gallery of my friends. If I had never seen them from those early days till now, I should still have remembered them with gratitude. When I enumerate the long list of my American teachers, I must begin with those who came to us on Wall Street and taught us our first steps. To my mother, in her perplexity over the cookstove, the woman who showed her how to make the fire was an angel of deliverance. A fairy godmother to us children was she who led us to a wonderful country called uptown, where, in a dazzlingly beautiful palace called a department store, we exchanged our hateful homemade European costumes, which pointed us out as greenhorns to the children on the street, for real American machine-made garments, and issued forth glorified in each other's eyes.

With our despised immigrant clothing we shed also our impossible Hebrew names. A committee of our friends, several years ahead of us in American experience, put their heads together and concocted American names for us all. Those of our real names that had no pleasing American equivalents they ruthlessly discarded, content if they retained the initials. My mother, possessing a name that was not easily translatable, was punished with the undignified nickname of Annie. Fetchke, Joseph, and Deborah issued as Frieda, Joseph, and Dora, respectively. As for poor me, I was simply cheated. The name they gave me was hardly new. My Hebrew name being Maryashe in full, Mashke for short, Russianized into Marya (Mar-ya), my friends said that it would hold good in English as Mary, which was very disappointing, as I longed to possess a strange-sounding American name like the others.

I am forgetting the consolation I had in this matter of names from the use of my surname, which I have had no occasion to mention until now. I found on my arrival that my father was Mr. Antin on the slightest provocation, and not, as in Polotzk, on state occasions alone. And so I was Mary Antin and I felt very important to answer to such a dignified title. It was just like America that even plain people should wear their surnames on week days.

As a family we were so diligent under instruction, so adaptable, and so clever in hiding our deficiencies that when we made the journey to Crescent Beach in the wake of our small wagonload of household goods, my father had very little occasion to admonish us on the way; and I am sure he was not ashamed of us. So much we had achieved toward our Americanization during the two weeks since our landing.

MARY ANTIN, The Promised Land

209. Booker T. Washington Tours Alabama

Born a slave, Booker T. Washington became the greatest leader of the Negro race in America. Trained at Hampton Institute he early became convinced that the Negro must achieve economic independence before he could attain political equality. Idolized by his own people, he was trusted too by the whites, and the great Kentucky editor, Henry Watterson, said of him that "no man, since the war of sections, has exercised such beneficent influence and done such real good for the country — especially to the South."

I REACHED Tuskegee, as I have said, early in June, 1881. The first month I spent in finding accommodations for the school and in traveling through Alabama, examining into the actual life of the people, especially in the country districts, and in getting the school advertised among the class of people that I wanted to have

attend it. The most of my traveling was done over the country roads
with a mule and a cart or a mule and a buggy wagon for conveyance.
I ate and slept with the people in their little cabins. I saw their farms,
their schools, their churches. Since in the case of the most of these
visits there had been no notice given in advance that a stranger was
expected, I had the advantage of seeing the real, everyday life of
the people.

In the plantation districts I found that as a rule the whole family
slept in one room and that in addition to the immediate family
there sometimes were relatives, or others not related to the family,
who slept in the same room. On more than one occasion I went outside the house to get ready for bed or to wait until the family had
gone to bed. They usually contrived some kind of place for me to
sleep, either on the floor or in a special part of another's bed. Rarely
was there any place provided in the cabin where one could bathe
even the face and hands, but usually some provision was made for
this outside the house, in the yard.

The common diet of the people was fat pork and corn bread.
At times I have eaten in cabins where they had only corn bread and
black-eye peas cooked in plain water. The people seemed to have
no other idea than to live on this fat meat and corn bread, the meat
and the meal of which the bread was made having been bought at
a high price at a store in town, notwithstanding the fact that the
land all about the cabin homes could easily have been made to
produce nearly every kind of garden vegetable that is raised anywhere in the country. Their one object seemed to be to plant nothing but cotton, and in many cases cotton was planted up to the very
door of the cabin.

In these cabin homes I often found sewing machines which had
been bought, or were being bought, on instalments, frequently at a
cost of as much as sixty dollars, or showy clocks for which the occupants of the cabins had paid twelve or fourteen dollars. I remember
that on one occasion when I went into one of these cabins for dinner,
when I sat down to the table for a meal with the four members of
the family, I noticed that, while there were five of us at the table,
there was but one fork for the five of us to use. Naturally there was
an awkward pause on my part. In the opposite corner of that same
cabin was an organ for which the people told me they were paying

sixty dollars in monthly instalments. One fork and a sixty-dollar organ! . . .

With a few exceptions I found that the crops were mortgaged in the counties where I went and that the most of the colored farmers were in debt. The state had not been able to build school-houses in the country districts, and as a rule the schools were taught in churches or in log cabins. More than once while on my journeys I found that there was no provision made in the house used for school purposes for heating the building during the winter, and consequently a fire had to be built in the yard and teacher and pupils passed in and out of the house as they got cold or warm. With few exceptions I found the teachers in these country schools to be miser-ably poor in preparation for their work and poor in moral character. The schools were in session from three to five months. There was practically no apparatus in the schoolhouses except that occasionally there was a rough blackboard. I recall that one day I went into a schoolhouse — or rather into an abandoned log cabin that was being used as a schoolhouse — and found five pupils who were studying a lesson from one book. Two of these, on the front seat, were using the book between them; behind these were two others peeping over the shoulders of the first two, and behind the four was a fifth little fellow who was peeping over the shoulders of all four.

What I have said concerning the character of the schoolhouses and teachers will also apply quite accurately as a description of the church buildings and the ministers.

Booker T. Washington, Up From Slavery

210. Booker T. Washington Builds a School

The greatest monument to the genius of Booker T. Washington is the Tuskegee Institute which first opened its doors in midsummer 1881. From the humble be-ginnings here described the Institute has grown to be one of the greatest and most flourishing Negro educational institutions, but it has never abandoned its original policy of combining vocational and cultural education nor lost its character as a distinctly Negro institution.

ON THE morning that the school opened [1881] thirty students reported for admission. I was the only teacher. The students were about equally divided between the sexes. Most of them lived in Macon County, the county in which Tuskegee is situated and of which it is the county seat. A great many more students wanted to enter the school, but it had been decided to receive only those who were above fifteen years of age and who had previously received some education. The greater part of the thirty were public school teachers, and some of them were nearly forty years of age. With the teachers came some of their former pupils, and when they were examined it was amusing to note that in several cases the pupil entered a higher class than did his former teacher. It was also interesting to note how many big books some of them had studied and how many high-sounding subjects some of them claimed to have mastered. The bigger the book and the longer the name of the subject, the prouder they felt of their accomplishment. Some had studied Latin and one or two Greek. This they thought entitled them to special distinction.

The students who came first seemed to be fond of memorizing long and complicated rules in grammar and mathematics but had little thought or knowledge of applying these rules to the everyday affairs of their life. One subject which they liked to talk about and tell me that they had mastered in arithmetic was "banking and discount," but I soon found out that neither they nor almost any one in the neighborhood in which they lived had ever had a banking account. In registering the names of the students I found that almost every one of them had one or more initials. When I asked what the J. stood for in the name of John J. Jones, it was explained to me that this was a part of his "entitles." Most of the students wanted to get an education because they thought it would enable them to earn more money as schoolteachers.

Notwithstanding what I have said about them in these respects,

I have never seen a more earnest and willing company of young men and women than these students were. They were all willing to learn the right thing as soon as it was shown them what was right. I was determined to start them off on a solid and thorough foundation, so far as their books were concerned. I soon learned that most of them had the merest smattering of the high-sounding things that they had studied. While they could locate the Desert of Sahara or the capital of China on an artificial globe, I found out that the girls could not locate the proper places for the knives and forks on an actual dinner table, or the places on which the bread and meat should be set.

I had to summon a good deal of courage to take a student who had been studying cube root and "banking and discount" and explain to him that the wisest thing for him to do first was thoroughly to master the multiplication table.

The number of pupils increased each week until by the end of the first month there were nearly fifty. Many of them, however, said that, as they could remain only for two or three months, they wanted to enter a high class and get a diploma the first year if possible. . . .

We found that the most of our students came from the country districts, where agriculture in some form or other was the main dependence of the people. We learned that about eighty-five per cent of the colored people in the Gulf states depended upon agriculture for their living. Since this was true, we wanted to be careful not to educate our students out of sympathy with agricultural life, so that they would be attracted from the country to the cities and yield to the temptation of trying to live by their wits. We wanted to give them such an education as would fit a large proportion of them to be teachers and at the same time cause them to return to the plantation districts and show the people there how to put new energy and new ideas into farming as well as into the intellectual and moral and religious life of the people.

All these ideas and needs crowded themselves upon us with a seriousness that seemed well-nigh overwhelming. What were we to do? We had only the little old shanty and the abandoned church which the good colored people of the town of Tuskegee had kindly lent us for the accommodation of the classes. The number of students was increasing daily. The more we saw of them and the more we traveled through the country districts, the more we saw that our efforts were reaching to only a partial degree the actual needs of the people whom we wanted to lift up through the medium of the students whom we should educate and send out as leaders. . . .

About three months after the opening of the school and at the time when we were in the greatest anxiety about our work, there came into the market for sale an old and abandoned plantation which was situated about a mile from the town of Tuskegee. The mansion house or "big house," as it would have been called, which had been occupied by the owners during slavery, had been burned. After making a careful examination of this place, it seemed to be just the location that we wanted in order to make our work effective and permanent.

But how were we to get it? The price asked for it was very little — only five hundred dollars — but we had no money, and we were strangers in the town and had no credit. The owner of the land agreed to let us occupy the place if we could make a payment of two hundred and fifty dollars down, with the understanding that the remaining two hundred and fifty dollars must be paid within a year. Although five hundred dollars was cheap for the land, it was a large sum when one did not have any part of it.

In the midst of the difficulty I summoned a great deal of courage and wrote to my friend General J. F. B. Marshall, the treasurer of the Hampton Institute, putting the situation before him and beseeching him to lend me the two hundred and fifty dollars on my own personal responsibility. Within a few days a reply came to the effect that he had no authority to lend me money belonging to the Hampton Institute but that he would gladly lend me the amount needed from his own personal funds. . . .

I lost no time in getting ready to move the school on to the new farm. At the time we occupied the place there were standing upon it a cabin, formerly used as the dining room, an old kitchen, a stable, and an old henhouse. Within a few weeks we had all of these structures in use. The stable was repaired and used as a recitation room, and very presently the henhouse was utilized for the same purpose.

I recall one morning, when I told an old colored man who lived near and who sometimes helped me that our school had grown so large that it would be necessary for us to use the henhouse for school

purposes and that I wanted him to help me give it a thorough cleaning out the next day, he replied in the most earnest manner: "What
you mean, boss? You sholy ain't gwine clean out de henhouse in
de *daytime?*"

A canvass was also made among the people of both races for
direct gifts of money, and most of those applied to gave small sums.
It was often pathetic to note the gifts of the older colored people,
most of whom had spent their best days in slavery. Sometimes they
would give five cents, sometimes twenty-five cents. Sometimes the
contribution was a quilt or a quantity of sugar cane. I recall one
old colored woman, who was about seventy years of age, who came
to see me when we were raising money to pay for the farm. She
hobbled into the room where I was, leaning on a cane. She was
clad in rags, but they were clean. She said: "Mr. Washin'ton, God
knows I spent de bes' days of my life in slavery. God knows I's
ignorant an' poor, but," she added, "I knows what you an' Miss
Davidson is tryin' to do. I knows you is tryin' to make better men an'
better women for de colored race. I ain't got no money, but I wants
you to take dese six eggs what I's been savin' up, an' I wants you to
put dese six eggs into de eddication of dese boys an' gals."

Since the work at Tuskegee started, it has been my privilege to
receive many gifts for the benefit of the institution, but never any,
I think, that touched me so deeply as this one.

BOOKER T. WASHINGTON, Up From Slavery

211. Herbert Quick Studies the McGuffey Readers

*It was in 1836 that William Holmes
McGuffey, clergyman, lecturer, and college President, published the
first of the* McGuffey Eclectic Readers; *by the end of the century
something over one hundred million copies of the* Readers *had been
sold. By introducing children to "selections" from the best of English
and American literature, the* Readers *performed a service of immense*

*value and helped to set the popular literary standard for a whole
generation. Herbert Quick, who here recalls the* Readers *with affection, was the author of a series of novels dealing with the settlement
of Iowa.*

I HAVE just looked at a copy of a twenty-year-old edition of the
McGuffey's First Reader. It has not a single lesson that was in the
one I took in my trembling hand when Maggie Livingstone called
me to her to begin learning my letters. Mine had a green cover, but
it was hidden by the muslin which my mother had stitched over it
to save the wear on a book that cost thirty cents. It was filled with
illustrations which I now know were of British origin, for all the
men wore knee breeches, the girls had on fluffy pantalets and sugar-
scoop bonnets, and the ladies huge many-flounced skirts. One boy
had a cricket bat in his hand, and the ruling passions of the
youngsters seemed to be to shoot with the bow and to roll the hoop.
"Can you hop, Tom? See, I can hop! Tom, hop to me." How
easily does the English language lend itself to early lessons of such
simplicity!

These books were intensely moral, soundly religious, and addicted
to the inculcation of habits of industry, mercy, and most of the
virtues. Lucy was exhorted to rise because the sun was up. "Mary
was up at six," she was assured; and then was added the immortal
line, "Up, up, Lucy, and go out to Mary," which scoffers perverted
to "Double up, Lucy." Most of the words were of one syllable, but
"How doth the little busy bee" was in it, I am certain, and "I like
to see a little dog and pat him on the head." It was an easy book,
and if it fell short of the power in the moral and religious fields
of the more advanced volumes — why, so did its students in the
practice of the vices and the need for reproof or warning.

My mastery of the First and Second Readers — just the opening
of the marvels of the printed page — was a poignant delight. The
reading of anything gave me a sort of ecstasy. These books did not,
however, set in operation the germinant powers of actual literary
treasure hunting. They did give to the mind of the writer and to
the world some things of universal knowledge. We learned that

George Washington could not tell a lie about the cherry tree and that his father proved to him the existence of God by the device of sowing lettuce in a trench which spelled George's name. "It might have grown so by chance," said the elder Washington in this Second Reader lesson, but George saw clearly that it could not have come by chance. Some one sowed those seeds in that way. And his father assured him that this world of wonderful adaptations could not have come as it has by chance. There were many fables and lessons about insects, birds, and beasts. Most of the scenes were British. Our habits, our morals, and our faith were carefully kept in mind, and we grew to know Mary's lamb by heart.

In the Third Reader Mr. McGuffey began to give to my young mind some tastes of real literature. It had several beautiful selections from the Bible. Croly's description of the burning of the amphitheater at Rome, which I have never run across anywhere since, was one of the lessons. There was an analysis of How a Fly Walks on the Ceiling, which gave me as much of an urge toward natural philosophy as if it had been a correct one — which it was not. One gets a glimpse into the McGuffey character from the treatment which the Indian received in these books. The author, whose father was an Indian fighter of renown and who must have sat entranced at fireside stories of Indian wars, in several lessons in these Readers treated the Indian with great respect. There was Logan's great speech in the Fifth, for instance. I can see it before my eyes still: "I appeal to any white man to say, if ever he entered Logan's cabin hungry, and he gave him not meat; if ever he came cold and naked and he clothed him not." I wonder how much of the persistent sentiment among Americans favoring justice to the Indians comes from these old Readers. It has not saved the race from exploitation and oppression, but it has always persisted and it has done much good.

The Third Reader introduced me to such writers as Croly, Irving, Woodworth, through "The Old Oaken Bucket," Scott, and others, but not by their names. In the Fourth we had William Wirt, Wendell Phillips, Lord Bacon, Eliphalet Nott, Addison, Samuel Rogers in his "Ginevra," Willis, Montgomery, Milton and Shakespeare, Campbell, and a variety of lesser and anonymous authors. The Fifth Reader carried me on to longer and more mature selections, all chosen by the same rules — the rules of gradually introducing the child to the best of English literature with no letting down of the requirements as to morality and religious sentiment. There was more of Shakespeare, some of Byron, Milton, Johnson, Bryant, Addison, more of the Bible, and much British matter now lost — to me at least. Every selection was classic English.

But the old Fifth Reader of 1844 we never used in our school. My brother's copy was a wonderful mine for me. The front cover was gone, and a part of the Rhetorician's Guide, which told us when to let our voices fall, when they should rise, and when the circumflex was required. I never regretted the loss. But the text consisted of some hundreds of pages of closely printed selections made by Alexander McGuffey with all the family judgment and taste. There was Pope with "Hector's Attack on the Grecian Walls," from that version of the Iliad of which a critic said, "A very pretty poem, Mr. Pope, but don't call it Homer!" There was "How the Water Comes Down at Lodore." There was oratory — Pitt, Burke, Fox, Barré, Otis, Adams, Webster, Hayne. I had the volume all to myself. There were months when it was my only resource in my favorite dissipation of reading.

A small ration, these McGuffey Readers, for an omnivorous mind, but by no means a negligible one. I did not use them with any intelligence. I simply enjoyed them. I found a tune to which I could sing Browning's "How They Brought the Good News from Ghent to Aix" and sang it at the top of my voice as I followed my cows or the plow or harrow. I shouted "Ivry" to the vastnesses of the prairie. I deepened my boyish voice to orotund on "Now godlike Hector and his troops descend" and "They tug, they sweat, but neither gain nor yield, One foot, one inch, of the contested field!"

And somehow I was inoculated with a little of the virus of good literature. I gained no knowledge that it was anything of the sort. I got not the slightest glimpse into the world of letters as a world. Nobody ever said a word to me about that. I read nothing about it for years and years afterward. But when I did come to read the English classics, I felt as one who meets in after years a charming person with whom he has had a chance encounter on the train. I had already met the gentlemen.

HERBERT QUICK, One Man's Life

212. The Chautauqua Comes to South Dakota

The Chautauqua was originally a Bible School located at Chautauqua Lake, New York; as it grew in popularity, other so-called Chautauquas were established throughout the country. In 1904 the traveling Chautauqua was inaugurated, innumerable companies, of which the Redpath was probably the best known, offering varied entertainment — musical, dramatic, educational — to small-town audiences. At its height — before the days of radio — the Chautauquas reached over ten thousand towns and perhaps five million people annually.

WE LIVED in Howard, South Dakota. When our town paper, the *Miner County Democrat,* came out with a long piece telling about the Chautauqua which was to open at Lake Madison, Mother said it was an opportunity for culture that no right-minded person should miss. Daddy didn't care much about culture, but he said Mother could go for a week and take us children.

There was a great deal of excitement when the program was announced and the posters put up in the store windows. Mother said she was going to hear Reverend T. De Witt Talmage if she had to walk. For weeks nothing was talked of but Chautauqua, and it seemed as if every one were planning to go.

The paper told about how the first Chautauqua had been founded by Dr. John H. Vincent in 1874 on the shores of beautiful Lake Chautauqua and how people came from all over the United States to spend their summers at the assembly and hear the great speakers and entertainers. It said hundreds of Chautauquas were being established and we were fortunate to have one "in our midst."

The next Sunday our minister spoke about the Lake Madison Chautauqua in his sermon. He said it would "uplift the community and bring inspiration, education, and pure wholesome entertainment into our starved lives."

When it came time for us to go to Chautauqua, Daddy killed Old John. Mother cooked him a whole day and then packed him in a big basket together with fresh loaves of bread, baked beans, jelly, and cake. We took the ten o'clock train, but before we got to Winfred, three miles away, Vern wanted a drumstick and Mother had to unpack the basket. Madison was only twenty miles from Howard; so we got there before noon.

At the station we took a bus and rode up Main Street. I could see the Normal School at the end of the street with a flag floating from the cupola. It was the largest building I had ever seen. The streets were crowded with people all dressed up as if it were the Fourth of July, and there were flags and banners everywhere. The banners had the word Chautauqua printed across them in colored letters. Farmers' wagons piled high with bedding, cooking utensils, and children rattled along the dusty roads leading out to the Chautauqua grounds. A frying pan fell out of the wagon ahead of us, and the bus horses stepped on it.

A street car ran out to the Chautauqua from town. The bus driver loaded our trunks on the little car, then helped Mother with the basket and valises and lifted Dess and me up the steps. As we came in sight of the Chautauqua grounds, I could see the flag on top of the auditorium waving over the tree tops and the lake beyond. The grounds seemed to be dotted with little white spots which turned out, as we came nearer, to be small white tents set up among the trees.

Mother paid our admission fee, and as soon as we were inside the gates a man from the assembly headquarters showed us which one of the little tents we were to occupy. The springs and mattress were already down on the dirt floor. The only other furniture was an oil stove, two chairs, and a small pine table. We had brought our bedding from home in a trunk. The tents were rented by the Chautauqua Association to people who could not afford to stay at the hotel by the lake.

As soon as our things were in the tent, we set out for the Administration Building to get the tickets which would admit us to the auditorium for the entertainments.

On our way we came to a rough shack built of pine boards, across the front of which was a large banner announcing, "Headquarters of the C.L.S.C." Mother said the letters meant the Chautauqua Literary and Scientific Circle and she must go in and register, because she intended to organize a reading circle in Howard when we got back.

From the C.L.S.C. we walked down past the hotel. People were sitting on the porches and strolling along the paths by the lake. Some distance farther on there were a number of little tents set up close to the water's edge. Wagons were driving up to the tents and unloading boxes and trunks. The minute the children were set down, they would pull off their shoes and stockings and go wading. We didn't have any lakes at home; so I wished our tent had been pitched by the water, but Mother said those cost more and we couldn't afford it. However, she told us that the lake was free to all, and Vern and I could go wading some day even if our tent wasn't by the lake. . . .

On first sight the auditorium appeared to be a large circular building open all the way around. But on closer inspection it proved to be little more than a dome-shaped roof supported by heavy columns.

The space underneath had been excavated to form a large circular pit, making it possible for the tiers of seats encircling the slanting sides to rest securely in the earth rather than on scaffolding.

The seats, made of rough planks without backs, were arranged in graduated sections divided by sawdust-covered aisles. Each of these groups of seats converged toward a broad path at the bottom like the section of an orange. The level space in the center arena was divided by another sawdust trail leading to the platform. On each side were groups of plank seats.

With such a seating arrangement the building could be filled or emptied in a few moments. In case of rain canvas curtains could be let down to cover the opening all the way around. It was all very crude, but it seemed wonderful to us. Mother said there would be something going on in the auditorium both afternoon and evening and our tickets would admit us to everything.

The Chautauqua was to last two weeks. During that time people would come and go. Some could afford only a day or two and others a week or the entire season. Our stay was limited to one week, but Mother said it was to be a week of "culture, education, and inspiration." It looked like a great deal to me, because most of the shows that came to Howard stayed only one night. Even the Kickapoo Indian Sagwaw Company played but three nights, and the Man with the Bear who came every spring was gone before the bell rang for school.

On the way back to our tent Mother stopped at the Methodist Dining Tent for some fresh milk and doughnuts. All the church ladies had dining tents. There were the Baptist ladies, the Presbyterian ladies, the Methodist ladies, and so on. Vern had a fight with the boy in the tent next to us because he said the Presbyterian doughnuts were better than the Methodist doughnuts.

The Chautauqua wasn't to begin until next day. As soon as we had our supper, Mother said we must go to bed, because we would be at the auditorium every night during the next week and we must have a good sleep. We didn't rest very well, because we had visitors. Some toads hopped into the tent in the middle of the night and thumped around on the dirt floor until Mother had to get up and chase them out with the broom.

We were up early the next morning. Vern went to the well for water while Mother made toast on the oil stove. At ten o'clock we started for the auditorium to hear the morning-hour lecturer. His subject was "Your Boy."

The man talked to parents about how they should raise their boys so they would grow up to be good men. Vern didn't seem very much interested, and about halfway through the lecture he asked Mother if we couldn't go down to the lake and go in wading. Mother said we could if we would go out quietly. When we got outside where no one could see, Vern turned around and made a face at the lecturer. He said he didn't want to be a good boy — that he wanted to chew tobacco and brake on a freight train.

After the lecture Mother went to a round table at the Hall of Science and then to a meeting of the C.L.S.C.; so we had a long time to play. We took off our shoes and stockings and waded in the water and hunted for bright pebbles along the beach.

The afternoon program was given by the Chautauqua Ladies' Quartet. We liked them much better than "Your Boy." One of the ladies had a mustache and a long gold chain and sang bass.

When they got through singing the people crowded around the back of the auditorium to shake hands with them. I wanted to go, but there was such a crowd that we couldn't get through.

After supper we went to the auditorium again, and Mother allowed Vern and Dess and me to sit down on the front seat with the other children. The same ladies sang again. One song was called "Sweet and Low." The bass lady kept on going down until it seemed to me she would never get to where she was going. After they got through singing, they went off the platform and a man came on and introduced the chalk talker. The Chautauqua Ladies' Quartet had been the prelude, he said, but the chalk talker was the main entertainment.

His name was Mr. Frank Beard. He had a large easel on which there were big squares of white paper. While he talked, he drew pictures with colored chalk. Then he threw the pictures out into the audience for any one who could catch them. Vern got Abraham Lincoln, but Willie Matson and Jimmy Greely fought over George Washington and tore him all to pieces. The chalk talker said if they didn't behave he wouldn't throw any more pictures. Then he drew the superintendent of the schools and the president of the bank, and everybody laughed.

That evening a company of ladies dressed in white robes gave tableaux, but I didn't like them as well as the family band, because there were no children with them. The next day there was a blind senator from Washington, and a lady in a spangly dress who recited "The Charge of the Light Brigade" and "The Maniac." Dess got so scared that she cried and ran back to sit with Mother.

But every one seemed to be waiting for Reverend T. De Witt Talmage. I remembered how Mother had said she was going to hear him if she had to walk, and I felt sure that the reason Daddy had bought us tickets on the train was because he didn't want Mother to walk all the way to Lake Madison.

Besides the people who were already at Chautauqua, staying at the hotel or camping out, many more came just for Talmage day. He was to speak in the afternoon, and the auditorium was crowded to hear him. It was so terribly hot and so many people were standing around the outside that no air could get in, and we were almost smothered from the dust the horses kicked up. We had gone early because Mother said she didn't want to miss a word. The children were not allowed on the front seat for Talmage day. We had to sit with our parents. The platform manager said Dr. Talmage was very nervous and we should disturb him.

Some of the speakers were cross at us children if we didn't pay attention. One time Freddie Kelly put a peanut in his slingshot and hit the lecturer right in the middle of his watch charm. Freddie's mother came down the aisle and spanked him before everybody and made him go back and sit with her. The music ladies were nice to us, and one time a man who recited pieces said if we would be good he would buy us some ice cream at the Christian Endeavor ice cream tent afterward. When he got through his speaking, he said we were the best children he had ever seen.

We were at the auditorium so early for Talmage day that I got tired. After everybody was in who could get in, we kept on waiting, and every little while people would start clapping their hands. I think the horses hitched outside got tired too, because they began to neigh, and one horse ran away.

After people stopped clapping, they began to whisper, and one woman told Mother that she had heard that Doctor Talmage was in the habit of not coming. "I heard that he left an audience waiting while he went off and got married," she said.

Just then the platform manager came out with a telegram in his hand. He said he was very sorry, but Doctor Talmage couldn't come because he had "missed his connection." The people all began to talk at once, and some of them acted as if they were angry. Mother said she was just sick. The next day, the platform manager announced that Doctor Talmage was coming on Saturday; so they got ready for another Talmage day, and this time he came.

But by that time I was so excited over Opal May that I wasn't interested in Doctor Talmage. I listened as long as I could, but it was so hot that I got sleepy and put my head on Mother's lap and went to sleep. A big horsefly bit me, and I woke up just as he was finishing his speech. He was yelling awfully loud, and I felt sorry for him because his collar was melted down around his neck and he looked all worn out.

"No matter what others may choose," he said, "give me a Christian's life, a Christian's death, a Christian's burial, and a Christian's immortality."

Then he took a drink of water, bowed, and went off the platform. I looked at Mrs. Turner and she was crying. Rufus tugged at her dress. "What are you crying for, Ma?" he asked.

"Oh, just because I'm — I'm so happy," she said with a sob in her voice. I thought she meant she was happy because Rufus had stayed awake. After selling her butter and eggs so he could hear "The Winning Man," he had slept all through the lecture.

When I looked at Mother, she was crying too, but she was clapping her hands. Pretty soon Doctor Talmage came out on the platform again. Then the people stopped clapping and began to wave their handkerchiefs. At first there were only two or three, but soon everybody, even the farmers, were waving. Their red handkerchiefs looked pretty among the white ones. I unpinned my birthday handkerchief from my dress and waved it too.

Mother said it was the greatest honor that could be given to a Chautauqua speaker. The handkerchief waving, she said, was the Chautauqua salute.

Gay MacLaren, Morally We Roll Along

XXX

Business and Labor

213. Cyrus Field Lays the Atlantic Cable

The idea of a cable across the Atlantic connecting the American and the European continents had long tantalized the minds of engineers and business men, but it was not until Cyrus Field of New York addressed himself actively to the engineering and financial problems involved in so colossal an enterprise that it became a reality. Cyrus Field subsequently interested himself in cable lines to the Orient, in elevated railroads, in railroading and in journalism, but his affairs did not prosper and he died in impoverished circumstances. The laying of the Atlantic cable was one of the great engineering feats of modern times and had an incalculable effect on international relations.

IT IS nearly thirteen years since half a dozen gentlemen met at my house for four successive evenings and around a table covered with maps and charts, and plans and estimates, considered a project to extend a line of telegraph from Nova Scotia to St. John's in Newfoundland, thence to be carried across the ocean. It was a very pretty plan on paper. There was New York, and there was St. John's, only about twelve hundred miles apart. It was easy to draw a line from one point to the other — making no accounts of the forests and mountains, and swamps and rivers and gulfs, that lay in our way. Not one of us had ever seen the country or had any idea of the obstacles to be overcome. We thought we could build the line in a few months. It took two years and a half. Yet we never asked for help outside our own little circle. Indeed, I fear we should not have got it if we had — for few had any faith in our scheme. Every dollar came out of our own pockets.

You perceive that in the beginning this was wholly an American enterprise. It was begun, and for two years and a half was carried on, solely by American capital. Our brethren across the sea did not even know what we were doing away in the forests of Newfoundland. Our little company raised and expended over a million and a quarter of dollars before an Englishman paid a single pound sterling. And in preparing for an ocean cable, the first soundings across the Atlantic were made by American officers in American ships. Our scientific men — Morse, Henry, Bache, and Maury — had taken great interest in the subject. The United States ship *Dolphin* discovered the telegraphic plateau as early as 1853, and the United States ship *Arctic* sounded across from Newfoundland to Ireland in 1856, a year before Her Majesty's ship *Cyclops,* under command of Captain Dayman, went over the same course. This I state, not to take aught from the just praise of England, but simply to vindicate the truth of history.

It was not till 1856 — ten years ago — that the enterprise had any existence in England. Science had begun to contemplate the necessity of such an enterprise, and the great Faraday cheered us with his lofty enthusiasm.

With the history of the expedition of 1857–58 you are familiar. On the third trial we gained a brief success. The cable was laid, and for four weeks it worked, though never very brilliantly, never giving forth such rapid and distinct flashes as the cables of today. It spoke, though only in broken sentences. But while it lasted, no less than four hundred messages were sent across the Atlantic. You all remember the enthusiasm which it excited. It was a new thing under the sun, and for a few weeks the public went wild over it. Of course, when it stopped, the reaction was very great. People grew dumb and suspicious. Some thought it was all a hoax, and many were quite sure that it never worked at all. That kind of odium we have had to endure for eight years, till now, I trust, we have at last silenced the unbelievers.

After the failure of 1858 came our darkest days. When a thing is dead, it is hard to galvanize it into life. It is more difficult to revive an old enterprise than to start a new one. The freshness and novelty are gone, and the feeling of disappointment discourages further effort.

When the scientific and engineering problems were solved, we took heart again and began to prepare for a fresh attempt. This was in 1863. In this country — though the war was still raging — I went from city to city, holding meetings and trying to raise capital, but with poor success. Men came and listened and said it was all very fine and hoped I would succeed, but did nothing. In one of the cities they gave me a large meeting and passed some beautiful resolutions and appointed a committee of "solid men" to canvass the city, but I did not get a solitary subscriber! In this city [New York] I did better, though money came by the hardest effort. By personal solicitations, I succeeded in raising seventy thousand pounds. It was plain that our main hope must be in England, and I went to London. There, too, it dragged heavily. There was a profound discouragement. Many had lost before and were not willing to throw more money into the sea. We needed six hundred thousand pounds, and with our utmost efforts we had raised less than half, and there the enterprise stood in a deadlock. It was plain that we must have help from some new quarter. I looked around to find a man who had broad shoulders and could carry a heavy load and who would be a giant in the cause.

It was at this time I was introduced to a gentleman whom I would hold up to the American public as a specimen of a great-hearted Englishman, Mr. Thomas Brassey. In London he is known as one of the men who have made British enterprise and British capital felt in all parts of the earth. I went to see him, though with fear and trembling. He received me kindly but put me through such an examination as I never had before. I thought I was in the witness box. He asked me every possible question, but my answers satisfied him, and he ended by saying it was an enterprise which ought to be carried out and that he would be one of ten men to furnish the money to do it. This was a pledge of sixty thousand pounds sterling! Encouraged by this noble offer, I looked about to find another such man, though it was almost like trying to find two Wellingtons. But he *was* found in Mr. John Pender, of Manchester. I went one day to his office in London, and we walked together to the House of Commons, and before we got there he said he would take an equal share with Mr. Brassey.

A few days after, half a dozen gentlemen joined together and bought the *Great Eastern* to lay the cable.

Thus organized, the work of making a new Atlantic cable was begun. The core was prepared with infinite care, under the able superintendence of Mr. Chatterton and Mr. Willoughby Smith, and the whole was completed in about eight months. As fast as ready, it was taken on board the *Great Eastern* and coiled in three enormous tanks, and on the 15th of July, 1865, the ship started on her memorable voyage.

I will not stop to tell the story of that expedition. For a week all went well; we had paid out twelve hundred miles of cable and had only six hundred miles farther to go, when, hauling in the cable to remedy a fault, it parted and went to the bottom. That day I can never forget — how men paced the deck in despair, looking out on the broad sea that had swallowed up their hopes; and then how the brave Canning for nine days and nights dragged the bottom of the ocean for our lost treasure and, though he grappled it three times, failed to bring it to the surface. We returned to England defeated, yet full of resolution to begin the battle anew. Measures were at once taken to make a second cable and fit out a new expedition, and with that assurance I came home last autumn.

In December I went back again, when lo! all our hopes had sunk to nothing. The Attorney General of England had given his written opinion that we had no legal right, without a special act of Parliament (which could not be obtained under a year), to issue the new twelve per cent. shares on which we relied to raise our capital. This was a terrible blow. It was finally concluded that the best course was to organize a new company, which should assume the work, and so originated the Anglo-American Telegraph Company. Then the work began again and went on with speed. Never was greater energy infused into any enterprise. It was only the first day of March that the new company was formed, and was registered as a company the next day; and yet such was the vigor and dispatch that in five months from that day the cable had been manufactured, shipped on the *Great Eastern,* stretched across the Atlantic, and was sending messages, literally swift as lightning, from continent to continent.

Yet this was not "a lucky hit" — a fine run across the ocean in calm weather. It was the worst weather I ever knew at that season of the year. We had fogs and storms almost the whole way. Our success was the result of the highest science combined with practical experience. Everything was perfectly organized to the minutest detail. . . .

But our work was not over. After landing the cable safely at Newfoundland, we had another task — to return to midocean and recover that lost in the expedition of last year. This achievement has perhaps excited more surprise than the other. Many even now "don't understand it," and every day I am asked how it was done. Well, it does seem rather difficult to fish for a jewel at the bottom of the ocean two and a half miles deep. But it is not so very difficult when you know how. You may be sure we did not go a-fishing at random, nor was our success mere luck. It was the triumph of the highest nautical and engineering skill. We had four ships and on board of them some of the best seamen in England — men who knew the ocean as a hunter knows every trail in the forest. There was Captain Moriarty, who was in the *Agamemnon* in 1857-58. He was in the *Great Eastern* last year [1865] and saw the cable when it broke, and he and Captain Anderson at once took their observations, so exact that they could go right to the spot. After finding it, they marked the line of the cable by a row of buoys; for fogs would come down and shut out sun and stars so that no man could take an observation.

These buoys were anchored a few miles apart. They were numbered, and each had a flagstaff on it, so that it could be seen by day, and a lantern by night. Having thus taken our bearings, we stood off three or four miles so as to come broadside on; and then, casting over the grapnel, drifted slowly down upon it, dragging the bottom of the ocean as we went. At first it was a little awkward to fish in such deep water, but our men got used to it and soon could cast a grapnel almost as straight as an old whaler throws a harpoon. Our fishing line was of formidable size. It was made of rope twisted with wires of steel so as to bear a strain of thirty tons. It took about two hours for the grapnel to reach bottom, but we could tell when it struck. I often went to the bow and sat on the rope and could feel by the quiver that the grapnel was dragging on the bottom two miles under us. But it was a very slow business. We had storms and calms and fogs and squalls.

Still we worked on, day after day. Once, on the 17th of August we got the cable up and had it in full sight for five minutes, a long, slimy monster, fresh from the ooze of the ocean's bed; but our men began to cheer so wildly that it seemed to be frightened and suddenly broke away and went down into the sea. This accident kept us at work two weeks longer, but finally on the last night of August we caught it. We had cast the grapnel thirty times. It was a little before midnight on Friday night that we hooked the cable, and it was a little after midnight Sunday morning when we got it on board. What was the anxiety of those twenty-six hours! The strain on every man's life was like the strain on the cable itself. When finally it appeared, it was midnight; the lights of the ship and in the boats around our bows, as they flashed in the faces of the men, showed them eagerly watching for the cable to appear on the water.

At length it was brought to the surface. All who were allowed to approach crowded forward to see it. Yet not a word was spoken — only the voices of the officers in command were heard giving orders. All felt as if life and death hung on the issue. It was only when it was brought over the bow and on to the deck that men dared to breathe. Even then they hardly believed their eyes. Some crept toward it to feel of it, to be sure it was there. Then we carried it along to the electricians' room, to see if our long-sought treasure was alive or dead. A few minutes of suspense, and a flash told of the lightning current again set free. Then did the feeling long pent up burst forth. Some turned away their heads and wept. Others broke into cheers, and the cry ran from man to man and was heard down in the engine rooms, deck below deck, and from the boats on the water and the other ships, while rockets lighted up the darkness of the sea. Then with thankful hearts we turned our faces again to the west.

But soon the wind rose, and for thirty-six hours we were exposed to all the dangers of a storm on the Atlantic. Yet in the very height and fury of the gale, as I sat in the electricians' room, a flash of light came up from the deep which, having crossed to Ireland, came back to me in midocean, telling that those so dear to me, whom I had left on the banks of the Hudson, were well and following us with their wishes and their prayers. This was like a whisper of God from the sea, bidding me keep heart and hope. The *Great Eastern* bore herself proudly through the storm, as if she knew that the vital cord which was to join two hemispheres hung at her stern; and so, on Saturday, the 7th of September, we brought our second cable safely to the shore.

CYRUS FIELD, Speech, 1866

214. Andrew Carnegie Gets a Start in Life

Andrew Carnegie, who here recalls his first modest ventures into business, turned his great talents eventually to the manufacture of iron and steel and became, within a few years, the greatest industrialist of his generation. At the height of his power he sold his interests to the new United States Steel Corporation and retired to spend the enormous fortune which he had accumulated. It is as a philanthropist that he is probably best known. Most of his money went to public libraries, but other millions were given to the cause of peace and education.

IT IS a great pleasure to tell how I served my apprenticeship as a business man. But there seems to be a question preceding this: Why did I become a business man? I am sure that I should never have selected a business career if I had been permitted to choose.

The eldest son of parents who were themselves poor, I had, fortunately, to begin to perform some useful work in the world while still very young in order to earn an honest livelihood, and was thus shown even in early boyhood that my duty was to assist my parents and, like them, become as soon as possible a breadwinner in the family. What I could get to do, not what I desired, was the question.

When I was born [1837] my father was a well-to-do master weaver in Dunfermline, Scotland. He owned no less than four damask looms and employed apprentices. This was before the days of steam factories for the manufacture of linen. A few large merchants took orders and employed master weavers such as my father to weave the cloth, the merchants supplying the materials.

As the factory system developed, hand-loom weaving naturally declined, and my father was one of the sufferers by the change. The first serious lesson of my life came to me one day when he had taken in the last of his work to the merchant and returned to our little home greatly distressed because there was no more work for him to do. I was then just about ten years of age, but the lesson burned into my heart, and I resolved then that the wolf of poverty should be driven from our door some day if I could do it.

The question of selling the old looms and starting for the United States came up in the family council, and I heard it discussed from day to day. It was finally resolved to take the plunge and join relatives already in Pittsburgh. I well remember that neither Father nor Mother thought the change would be otherwise than a great sacrifice for them, but that "it would be better for the two boys."

In after life, if you can look back as I do and wonder at the complete surrender of their own desires which parents make for the good of their children, you must reverence their memories with feelings akin to worship.

On arriving in Allegheny City (there were four of us: Father, Mother, my younger brother, and myself), my father entered a cotton factory. I soon followed and served as a "bobbin boy," and this is how I began my preparation for subsequent apprenticeship as a business man. I received one dollar and twenty cents a week and was then just about twelve years old.

I cannot tell you how proud I was when I received my first week's own earnings. One dollar and twenty cents made by myself and given to me because I had been of some use in the world! No longer entirely dependent upon my parents, but at last admitted to the family partnership as a contributing member and able to help them! I think this makes a man out of a boy sooner than almost anything else, and a real man, too, if there be any germ of true manhood in him. It is everything to feel that you are useful. . . .

For a lad of twelve to rise and breakfast every morning except the blessed Sunday morning and go into the streets and find his way to the factory and begin to work while it was still dark outside, and not be released until after darkness came again in the evening, forty minutes' interval only being allowed at noon, was a terrible task.

But I was young and had my dreams, and something within always told me that this would not, could not, should not last — I should some day get into a better position. Besides this, I felt myself no longer a mere boy, but quite a little man, and this made me happy.

A change soon came, for a kind old Scotsman, who knew some of our relatives, made bobbins, and took me into his factory before I was thirteen. But here for a time it was even worse than in the cotton factory, because I was set to fire a boiler in the cellar and actually to run the small steam engine which drove the machinery. The firing of the boiler was all right, for fortunately we did not use coal, but the refuse wooden chips; and I always liked to work in wood. But the responsibility of keeping the water right and of running the engine and the danger of my making a mistake and blowing the whole factory to pieces caused too great a strain, and I often awoke and found myself sitting up in bed through the night, trying the steam gauges. But I never told them at home that I was having a hard tussle. No, no! everything must be bright to them.

This was a point of honor, for every member of the family was working hard, except, of course, my little brother, who was then a child, and we were telling each other only all the bright things. Besides this, no man would whine and give up — he would die first.

There was no servant in our family, and several dollars per week were earned by the mother by binding shoes after her daily work was done! Father was also hard at work in the factory. And could I complain?

My kind employer, John Hay — peace to his ashes! — soon relieved me of the undue strain, for he needed some one to make out bills and keep his accounts, and finding that I could write a plain schoolboy hand and could cipher, he made me his only clerk. But still I had to work hard upstairs in the factory, for the clerking took but little time. . . .

I come now to the third step in my apprenticeship, for I had already taken two, as you see — the cotton factory and then the bobbin factory; and with the third — the third time is the chance, you know — deliverance came. I obtained a situation as messenger boy in the telegraph office of Pittsburgh when I was fourteen. Here I entered a new world.

Amid books, newspapers, pencils, pens and ink and writing pads, and a clean office, bright windows, and the literary atmosphere, I was the happiest boy alive.

My only dread was that I should some day be dismissed because I did not know the city, for it is necessary that a messenger boy should know all the firms and addresses of men who are in the habit of receiving telegrams. But I was a stranger in Pittsburgh. However, I made up my mind that I would learn to repeat successively each business house in the principal streets and was soon able to shut my eyes and begin at one side of Wood Street and call every firm successively to the top, then pass to the other side and call every firm to the bottom. Before long I was able to do this with the business streets generally. My mind was then at rest upon that point.

Of course every ambitious messenger boy wants to become an operator, and before the operators arrive in the early mornings the boys slipped up to the instruments and practised. This I did and was soon able to talk to the boys in the other offices along the line who were also practising.

One morning I heard Philadelphia calling Pittsburgh and giving the signal, "Death message." Great attention was then paid to "death messages," and I thought I ought to try to take this one. I answered and did so, and went off and delivered it before the operator came. After that the operators sometimes used to ask me to work for them.

Having a sensitive ear for sound, I soon learned to take messages by the ear, which was then very uncommon — I think only two persons in the United States could then do it. Now every operator takes by ear, so easy is it to follow and do what any other boy can — if you only have to. This brought me into notice, and finally I became an operator and received the, to me, enormous recompense of twenty-five dollars per month — three hundred dollars a year!

This was a fortune — the very sum that I had fixed when I was a factory worker as the fortune I wished to possess, because the family could live on three hundred dollars a year and be almost or quite independent. Here it was at last! But I was soon to be in receipt of extra compensation for extra work.

The six newspapers of Pittsburgh received telegraphic news in common. Six copies of each dispatch were made by a gentleman who received six dollars per week for the work, and he offered me a gold dollar every week if I would do it, of which I was very glad indeed, because I always liked to work with news and scribble for newspapers.

The reporters came to a room every evening for the news which I had prepared, and this brought me into most pleasant intercourse with these clever fellows, and besides, I got a dollar a week as pocket money, for this was not considered family revenue by me.

I think this last step of doing something beyond one's task is fully entitled to be considered "business." The other revenue, you see, was just salary obtained for regular work; but here was a little business operation upon my own account, and I was very proud indeed of my gold dollar every week.

The Pennsylvania Railroad shortly after this was completed to Pittsburgh, and that genius, Thomas A. Scott, was its superintendent. He often came to the telegraph office to talk to his chief, the general superintendent, at Altoona; and I became known to him in this way.

When that great railway system put up a wire of its own, he asked me to be his clerk and operator; so I left the telegraph office — in which there is great danger that a young man may be permanently buried, as it were — and became connected with the railways.

The new appointment was accompanied by what was to me a tremendous increase of salary. It jumped from twenty-five to thirty-five dollars per month. Mr. Scott was then receiving one hundred and twenty-five dollars per month, and I used to wonder what on earth he could do with so much money.

I remained for thirteen years in the service of the Pennsylvania Railroad Company and was at last superintendent of the Pittsburgh division of the road, successor to Mr. Scott, who had in the meantime risen to the office of vice-president of the company.

One day Mr. Scott, who was the kindest of men and had taken a great fancy to me, asked if I had or could find five hundred dollars to invest.

Here the business instinct came into play. I felt that as the door was opened for a business investment with my chief, it would be willful flying in the face of Providence if I did not jump at it; so I answered promptly:

"Yes, sir; I think I can."

"Very well," he said, "get it; a man has just died who owns ten shares in the Adams Express Company which I want you to buy. It will cost you fifty dollars per share, and I can help you with a little balance if you cannot raise it all."

Here was a queer position. The available assets of the whole family were not five hundred dollars. But there was one member of the family whose ability, pluck and resource never failed us; and I felt sure the money could be raised somehow or other by my mother.

Indeed, had Mr. Scott known our position he would have advanced it himself; but the last thing in the world the proud Scot will do is to reveal his poverty and rely upon others. The family had managed by this time to purchase a small house and pay for it in order to save rent. My recollection is that it was worth eight hundred dollars.

The matter was laid before the council of three that night, and the oracle spoke: "Must be done. Mortgage our house. I will take the steamer in the morning for Ohio and see Uncle and ask him to arrange it. I am sure he can." This was done. Of course her visit was successful — where did she ever fail?

The money was procured, paid over; ten shares of Adams Express Company stock was mine; but no one knew our little home had been mortgaged "to give our boy a start."

Adams Express stock then paid monthly dividends of one per cent., and the first check for five dollars arrived. I can see it now, and I well remember the signature of "J. C. Babcock, Cashier," who wrote a big "John Hancock" hand.

The next day being Sunday, we boys — myself and my ever-constant companions — took our usual Sunday afternoon stroll in the country, and sitting down in the woods, I showed them this check, saying: "Eureka! We have found it."

Here was something new to all of us, for none of us had ever received anything but from toil. A return from capital was something strange and new.

How money could make money, how, without any attention from me, this mysterious golden visitor should come, led to much speculation upon the part of the young fellows; and I was for the first time hailed as a "capitalist."

You see, I was beginning to serve my apprenticeship as a business man in a satisfactory manner.

A very important incident in my life occurred when one day in a train a nice, farmer-looking gentleman approached me, saying that the conductor had told him I was connected with the Pennsylvania Railroad, and he would like to show me something. He pulled from a small green bag the model of the first sleeping car. This was Mr. Woodruff, the inventor.

Its value struck me like a flash. I asked him to come to Altoona the following week, and he did so. Mr. Scott, with his usual quickness, grasped the idea. A contract was made with Mr. Woodruff to put two trial cars on the Pennsylvania Railroad. Before leaving Altoona, Mr. Woodruff came and offered me an interest in the venture, which I promptly accepted. But how I was to make my payments rather troubled me, for the cars were to be paid for in monthly instalments after delivery, and my first monthly payment was to be two hundred and seventeen dollars and a half.

I had not the money, and I did not see any way of getting it. But I finally decided to visit the local banker and ask him for a loan, pledging myself to repay at the rate of fifteen dollars per month. He promptly granted it. Never shall I forget his putting his arm over my shoulder, saying, "Oh, yes, Andy; you are all right!"

I then and there signed my first note. Proud day this, and surely now no one will dispute that I was becoming a business man. I had signed my first note, and most important of all — for any fellow can sign a note — I had found a banker willing to take it as good.

My subsequent payments were made by the receipts from the sleeping cars, and I really made my first considerable sum from this investment in the Woodruff Sleeping Car Company, which was afterward absorbed by Mr. Pullman, a remarkable man whose name is now known over all the world.

Shortly after this I was appointed superintendent of the Pittsburgh division and returned to my dear old home, smoky Pittsburgh. Wooden bridges were then used exclusively upon the railways, and the Pennsylvania Railroad was experimenting with a bridge built of cast iron. I saw that wooden bridges would not do for the future and organized a company in Pittsburgh to build iron bridges.

Here again I had recourse to the bank, because my share of the capital was twelve hundred and fifty dollars, and I had not the money; but the bank lent it to me, and we began the Keystone Bridge Works, which proved a great success. This company built the first great bridge over the Ohio River, three hundred feet span, and has built many of the most important structures since.

This was my beginning in manufacturing, and from that start all our other works have grown, the profits of one building the other. My apprenticeship as a business man soon ended, for I resigned my position as an officer of the Pennsylvania Railroad Company to give exclusive attention to business.

I was no longer merely an official working for others upon a salary, but a full-fledged business man working upon my own account.

And so ends the story of my apprenticeship and graduation as a business man.

ANDREW CARNEGIE, The Gospel of Wealth

215. John Spargo Hears the Bitter Cry of the Children

Despite the coming of millions of unskilled laborers from southern and eastern Europe and the invention of labor-saving machinery, American industry and agriculture drew more and more upon children for its labor force. At the time when John Spargo was writing — about 1900 — there were approximately two million children under fifteen years of age numbered among those "gainfully employed" and almost half of these

were in industry. Industry profited by cheap labor, but society suf-
fered, and the writings of social reformers like Mr. Spargo drama-
tized the need for a reform which came slowly in the ensuing decades.

I SHALL never forget my first visit to a glass factory at night.
It was a big wooden structure, so loosely built that it afforded little
protection from drafts, surrounded by a high fence with several rows
of barbed wire stretched across the top. I went with the foreman of
the factory, and he explained to me the reason for the stockade-like
fence. "It keeps the young imps inside once we've got 'em for the
night shift," he said. The young imps were, of course, the boys employed, about forty in number, at least ten of whom were less than
twelve years of age. It was a cheap bottle factory, and the proportion
of boys to men was larger than is usual in the higher grades of
manufacture. Cheapness and child labor go together — the cheaper
the grade of manufacture, as a rule, the cheaper the labor employed.
The hours of labor for the night shift were from 5:30 P.M. to 3:30 A.M.
I stayed and watched the boys at their work for several hours and,
when their tasks were done, saw them disappear into the darkness
and storm of the night. That night, for the first time, I realized
the tragic significance of cheap bottles.

In the middle of the room was a large round furnace with a
number of small doors, three or four feet from the ground, forming
a sort of belt around the furnace. In front of these doors the glass
blowers were working. With long wrought-iron blowpipes the
blowers deftly took from the furnace little wads of waxlike molten
"metal" which they blew into balls and then rolled on their rolling
boards. These elongated rolls they dropped into molds and then
blew again, harder than before, to force the half-shaped mass into
its proper form. With a sharp, clicking sound they broke their
pipes away and repeated the whole process. There was not, of
course, the fascination about their work that the more artistic forms
of glass blowing possess. There was none of that twirling of the
blowpipes till they looked like so many magic wands which for
centuries has made the glass blower's art a delightful, half-mys-
terious thing to watch. But it was still wonderful to see the exactness

of each man's "dip" and the deftness with which they manipulated the balls before casting them into the molds.

Then began the work of the boys. By the side of each mold sat a take-out boy, who with tongs took the half-finished bottles — not yet provided with necks — out of the molds. Then other boys, called snapper-ups, took these bodies of bottles in their tongs and put the small ends into gas-heated molds till they were red-hot. Then the boys took them out with almost incredible quickness and passed them to other men, finishers, who shaped the necks of the bottles into their final form. Then the carrying-in boys, sometimes called carrier pigeons, took the red-hot bottles from the benches, three or four at a time, upon big asbestos shovels to the annealing oven, where they are gradually cooled off to insure even contraction and to prevent breaking in consequence of too rapid cooling. The work of these carrying-in boys, several of whom were less than twelve years old, was by far the hardest of all. They were kept on a slow run all the time from the benches to the annealing oven and back again. I can readily believe what many manufacturers assert, that it is difficult to get men to do this work, because men cannot stand the pace and get tired too quickly. . . . The distance to the annealing oven in the factory in question was one hundred feet, and the boys made seventy-two trips per hour, making the distance traveled in eight hours nearly twenty-two miles. Over half of this distance the boys were carrying their hot loads to the oven. The pay of these boys varies from sixty cents to a dollar for eight hours' work.

Work in the coal breakers is exceedingly hard and dangerous. Crouched over the chutes, the boys sit hour after hour, picking out the pieces of slate and other refuse from the coal as it rushes past to the washers. From the cramped position they have to assume most of them become more or less deformed and bent-backed like old men. When a boy has been working for some time and begins to get round-shouldered, his fellows say that "he's got his boy to carry round wherever he goes." The coal is hard, and accidents to the hands, such as cut, broken, or crushed fingers, are common among the boys. Sometimes there is a worse accident; a terrified shriek is heard, and a boy is mangled and torn in the machinery or disappears in the chute to be picked out later, smothered and dead. Clouds of dust fill the breakers and are inhaled by the boys, laying the foundations for asthma and miners' consumption. I once stood in a breaker for half an hour and tried to do the work a twelve-year-old boy was doing day after day, for ten hours at a stretch, for sixty cents a day. The gloom of the breaker appalled me. Outside the sun shone brightly, the air was pellucid, and the birds sang in chorus with the trees and the rivers. Within the breaker there was blackness; clouds of deadly dust enfolded everything; the harsh, grinding roar of the machinery and the ceaseless rushing of coal through the chutes filled the ears. I tried to pick out the pieces of slate from the hurrying stream of coal, often missing them; my hands were bruised and cut in a few minutes; I was covered from head to foot with coal dust, and for many hours afterward I was expectorating some of the small particles of anthracite I had swallowed.

I could not do that work and live, but there were boys of ten and twelve years of age doing it for fifty and sixty cents a day. Some of them had never been inside of a school; few of them could read a child's primer. . . .

From the breakers the boys graduate to the mine depths, where they become door tenders, switch boys, or mule drivers. Here, far below the surface, work is still more dangerous. At fourteen or fifteen the boys assume the same risks as the men and are surrounded by the same perils. Nor is it in Pennsylvania only that these conditions exist. In the bituminous mines of West Virginia boys of nine or ten are frequently employed. I met one little fellow ten years old in Mt. Carbon, W. Va., last year, who was employed as a trap boy. Think of what it means to be a trap boy at ten years of age. It means to sit alone in a dark mine passage hour after hour with no human soul near; to see no living creature except the mules as they pass with their loads, or a rat or two seeking to share one's meal; to stand in water or mud that covers the ankles, chilled to the marrow by the cold drafts that rush in when you open the trap door for the mules to pass through; to work for fourteen hours — waiting — opening and shutting a door — then waiting again — for sixty cents; to reach the surface when all is wrapped in the mantle of night, and to fall to the earth exhausted and have to

be carried away to the nearest shack to be revived before it is possible
to walk to the farther shack called home.

JOHN SPARGO, The Bitter Cry of the Children

216. Jurgis Works in a Fertilizer Plant

*The Jungle, first published in 1906,
is one of the few novels that has made history. So shocking were
the revelations of conditions that existed in the stockyards that public
opinion rallied to the support of the pending pure-food legislation
and Congress promptly enacted a Meat Inspection Law and a Pure
Food Act.* The Jungle *was important, too, because it launched upon
his long career the most vigorous polemicist of our time.*

THE FERTILIZER works of Durham's lay away from the rest
of the plant. Few visitors ever saw them, and the few who did
would come out looking like Dante, of whom the peasants declared
that he had been into hell. To this part of the yards came all the
"tankage" and the waste products of all sorts; here they dried out
the bones — and in suffocating cellars where the daylight never
came you might see men and women and children bending over
whirling machines and sawing bits of bone into all sorts of shapes,
breathing their lungs full of the fine dust, and doomed to die, every
one of them, within a certain definite time. Here they made the
blood into albumen and made other foul-smelling things into
things still more foul-smelling. In the corridors and caverns where
it was done you might lose yourself as in the great caves of Kentucky. In the dust and the steam the electric lights would shine like
far-off twinkling stars — red and blue, green and purple stars, according to the color of the mist and the brew from which it came.
For the odors in these ghastly charnel houses there may be words
in Lithuanian, but there are none in English. The person entering

would have to summon his courage as for a cold-water plunge. He would go on like a man swimming under water; he would put his handkerchief over his face and begin to cough and choke; and then, if he were still obstinate, he would find his head beginning to ring and the veins in his forehead to throb, until finally he would be assailed by an overpowering blast of ammonia fumes and would turn and run for his life and come out half dazed.

On top of this were the rooms where they dried the "tankage," the mass of brown stringy stuff that was left after the waste portions of the carcasses had had the lard and tallow dried out of them. This dried material they would then grind to a fine powder, and after they had mixed it up well with a mysterious but inoffensive brown rock which they brought in and ground up by the hundreds of carloads for that purpose, the substance was ready to be put into bags and sent out to the world as any one of a hundred different brands of standard bone phosphate. And then the farmer in Maine or California or Texas would buy this, at say twenty-five dollars a ton, and plant it with his corn; and for several days after the operation the fields would have a strong odor, and the farmer and his wagon and the very horses that had hauled it would all have it too. In Packingtown the fertilizer is pure instead of being a flavoring, and instead of a ton or so spread out on several acres under the open sky there are hundreds and thousands of tons of it in one building, heaped here and here in haystack piles, covering the floor several inches deep, and filling the air with a choking dust that becomes a blinding sandstorm when the wind stirs.

It was to this building that Jurgis came daily as if dragged by an unseen hand. The month of May was an exceptionally cool one, and his secret prayers were granted; but early in June there came a record-breaking hot spell, and after that there were men wanted in the fertilizer mill.

The boss of the grinding room had come to know Jurgis by this time and had marked him for a likely man, and so when he came to the door about two o'clock this breathless hot day he felt a sudden spasm of pain shoot through him — the boss beckoned to him! In ten minutes more Jurgis had pulled off his coat and overshirt and set his teeth together and gone to work. Here was one more difficulty for him to meet and conquer!

His labor took him about one minute to learn. Before him was one of the vents of the mill in which the fertilizer was being ground — rushing forth in a great brown river, with a spray of the finest dust flung forth in clouds. Jurgis was given a shovel, and along with half a dozen others it was his task to shovel this fertilizer into carts. That others were at work he knew by the sound, and by the fact that he sometimes collided with them; otherwise they might as well not have been there, for in the blinding dust storm a man could not see six feet in front of his face. When he had filled one cart he had to grope around him until another came, and if there was none on hand he continued to grope till one arrived. In five minutes he was, of course, a mass of fertilizer from head to feet; they gave him a sponge to tie over his mouth, so that he could breathe, but the sponge did not prevent his lips and eyelids from caking up with it and his ears from filling solid. He looked like a brown ghost at twilight — from hair to shoes he became the color of the building and of everything in it, and, for that matter, a hundred yards outside it. The building had to be left open, and when the wind blew Durham and Company lost a great deal of fertilizer.

Working in his shirt sleeves and with the thermometer at over a hundred, the phosphates soaked in through every pore of Jurgis' skin, and in five minutes he had a headache and in fifteen was almost dazed. The blood was pounding in his brain like an engine's throbbing; there was a frightful pain in the top of his skull, and he could hardly control his hands. Still, with the memory of his four months' siege behind him, he fought on in a frenzy of determination; and half an hour later he began to vomit — he vomited until it seemed as if his inwards must be torn into shreds. A man could get used to the fertilizer mill, the boss had said, if he would only make up his mind to it; but Jurgis now began to see that it was a question of making up his stomach.

At the end of that day of horror he could scarcely stand. He had to catch himself now and then and lean against a building and get his bearings. Most of the men, when they came out, made straight for a saloon — they seemed to place fertilizer and rattlesnake poison in one class. But Jurgis was too ill to think of drinking — he could only make his way to the street and stagger on to a car. He had a sense of humor, and later on, when he became an old hand, he used to think it fun to board a street car and see what happened. Now, however, he was too ill to notice it — how the people in the car began to gasp and sputter, to put their handkerchiefs to their noses and transfix him with furious glances. Jurgis only knew that a man in front of him immediately got up and gave him a seat, and that half a minute later the two people on each side of him got up, and that in a full minute the crowded car was nearly empty — those passengers who could not get room on the platform having got out to walk.

Of course Jurgis had made his home a miniature fertilizer mill a minute after entering. The stuff was half an inch deep in his skin — his whole system was full of it, and it would have taken a week not merely of scrubbing, but of vigorous exercise, to get it out of him. As it was, he could be compared with nothing known to men, save that newest discovery of the savants, a substance which emits energy for an unlimited time, without being itself in the least diminished in power. He smelt so that he made all the food at the table taste and set the whole family to vomiting; for himself it was three days before he could keep anything on his stomach — he might wash his hands and use a knife and fork, but were not his mouth and throat filled with the poison?

And still Jurgis stuck it out! In spite of splitting headaches he would stagger down to the plant and take up his stand once more and begin to shovel in the blinding clouds of dust. And so at the end of the week he was a fertilizer man for life — he was able to eat again, and though his head never stopped aching, it ceased to be so bad that he could not work.

Upton Sinclair, The Jungle

217. James Davis Learns to Be an Iron Puddler

James Davis, who contributes this recollection of life in the steel mills, became later Secretary of Labor under Presidents Harding, Coolidge, and Hoover, but is perhaps better known as founder of the Mooseheart School for the education of orphans.

THE ROLLING mill where Father worked was life's big circus tent to me, and like a kid escaped from school, eager to get past the tent flap and mingle with the clowns and elephants, I chucked my job sorting nails when I found an opening for a youngster in the rolling mill. Every puddler has a helper. Old men have both a helper and a boy. I got a place with an old man, and so at the age of twelve [1886] I was part of the big show whose performance is continuous, whose fire-eaters have real flame to contend with, and whose snake charmers risk their lives in handling great hissing, twisting, red-hot serpents of angry iron.

In this mill there is a constant din by day and night. Patches of white heat glare from the opened furnace doors like the teeth of some great dark, dingy devil grinning across the smoky vapors of the Pit. Half-naked, soot-smeared fellows fight the furnace hearths with hooks, rabbles, and paddles. Their scowling faces are lit with fire like sailors manning their guns in a night fight when a blazing fire ship is bearing down upon them. The sweat runs down their backs and arms and glistens in the changing lights. Brilliant blues and rays of green and bronze come from the coruscating metal, molten yet crystallizing into white-hot frost within the furnace puddle. Flaming balls of woolly iron are pulled from the oven doors, flung on a two-wheeled serving tray, and rushed sputtering and flamboyant to the hungry mouth of a machine which rolls them upon its tongue and squeezes them in its jaw like a cow mulling over her cud. The molten slag runs down red-hot from the jaws of this squeezer and makes a luminous rivulet on the floor like the water from the rubber rollers when a washerwoman wrings out the saturated clothes. Squeezed dry of its luminous lava, the white-hot sponge is drawn with tongs to the waiting rollers — whirling anvils that beat it into the shape they will. Everywhere are hurrying men, whirring flywheels, moving levers of steam engines, and the drum-like roar of the rolling machines, while here and there the fruits of this toil are seen as three or four fiery serpents shoot forth from different trains of rollers and are carried away, wrought iron fit for bridging the creek, shoeing the mule, and hooping the barrel that brings the farmer's apples into town.

"Life in these mills is a terrible life," the reformers say. "Men are ground down to scrap and are thrown out as wreckage." This may be so, but my life was spent in the mills, and I failed to discover it. I went in a stripling and grew into manhood with muscled arms big as a bookkeeper's legs. The gases, they say, will destroy a man's lungs, but I worked all day in the mills and had wind enough left to toot a clarinet in the band. I lusted for labor; I worked hard, and I liked it. And so did my forefathers for generations before me. It is no job for weaklings.

An iron puddler is a pig boiler. The pig boiling must be done at a certain temperature (the pig is iron), just as a farmer butchering hogs must scald the carcasses at a certain temperature. . . . And so the metal pig boiler ages ago learned by experience how to make the proper heat to boil the impurities out of the pig iron or forge iron and change it into that finer product, wrought iron. Pig iron contains silicon, sulphur, and phosphorus; and these impurities make it brittle so that a cast-iron teakettle will break at a blow like a china cup. Armor of this kind would have been no good for our ironclad ancestors. When a knight in iron clothes tried to whip a leather-clad peasant, the peasant could have cracked him with a stone, and his clothes would have fallen off like plaster from the ceiling. So those early ironworkers learned to puddle forge iron and make it into wrought iron, which is tough and leathery and cannot be broken by a blow. This process was handed down from father to son and in the course of time came to my father and so to me. None of us ever went to school and learned the chemistry of it from books. We learned the trick by doing it, standing with our faces in the scorching heat while our hands puddled the metal in its glaring bath.

Today there are books telling just how many degrees of heat make the water right for scalding hogs, and the metallurgists have written down the chemical formula for puddling iron. But the man who learns it from a book cannot do it. The mental knowledge is not enough; it requires great muscular skill like that of the heavyweight wrestler, besides great physical endurance to withstand the terrific heat.

When I became my father's helper he began teaching me to handle the machinery of the trade. The puddling furnace has a working door on a level with a man's stomach. The working door of a puddling furnace is the door through which the puddler does his work. It is a porthole opening upon a sea of flame. The heat of these flames would wither a man's body, and so they are inclosed in a shell of steel. Through this working door I put in the charge of pigs that were to be boiled. These short pieces of mill iron had been smelted from iron ore; they had taken the first step on their journey from wild iron to civilized iron. There isn't much use for pig iron in this world. You've got to be better iron than that.

Six hundred pounds was the weight of pig iron we used to put into a single hearth. Much wider than the hearth was the fire grate, for we needed a heat that was intense. The flame was made by burning bituminous coal. Vigorously I stoked that fire for thirty minutes with dampers open and the draft roaring while that pig iron melted down like ice cream under an electric fan. You have seen a housewife sweating over her oven to get it hot enough to bake a batch of biscuits. Her face gets pink, and a drop of sweat dampens her curls. Quite a horrid job she finds it. But I had iron biscuits to bake; my forge fire must be hot as a volcano. There were five bakings every day, and this meant the shoveling in of nearly two tons of coal. In summer I was stripped to the waist and panting while the sweat poured down across my heaving muscles. My palms and fingers, scorched by the heat, became hardened like goat hoofs, while my skin took on a coat of tan that it will wear forever.

What time I was not stoking the fire, I was stirring the charge with a long iron rabble that weighed some twenty-five pounds. Strap an Oregon boot of that weight to your arm and then do calisthenics ten hours in a room so hot it melts your eyebrows, and you will know what it is like to be a puddler.

After melting down the pig iron as quickly as possible, which took me thirty minutes, there was a pause in which I had time to wipe the back of my hand on the driest part of my clothing (if any spot was still dry) and with my sweat cap wipe the sweat and soot out of my eyes. For the next seven minutes I thickened the heat up by adding iron oxide to the bath. This was in the form of roll scale. The furnace continued in full blast till that was melted. The liquid metal in the hearth is called slag. The iron oxide is put in it to make it more basic for the chemical reaction that is to take place. Adding the roll scale had cooled the charge, and it was thick like hoecake batter. I now thoroughly mixed it with a rabble, which is like a long iron hoe. . . .

My purpose in slackening my heat as soon as the pig iron was melted was to oxidize the phosphorus and sulphur ahead of the carbon. Just as alcohol vaporizes at a lower heat than water, so sulphur and phosphorus oxidize at a lower heat than carbon. When this reaction begins I see light flames breaking through the lake of molten slag in my furnace. Probably from such a sight as this the old-time artists got their pictures of Hell. The flames are caused by the burning of carbon monoxide from the oxidation of carbon. The slag is basic and takes the sulphur and phosphorus into combination, thus ending its combination with the iron. The purpose now is to oxidize the carbon too, without reducing the phosphorus and sulphur and causing them to return to the iron. We want the pure iron to begin crystallizing out of the bath like butter from the churning buttermilk.

More and more of the carbon gas comes out of the puddle, and as it bubbles out the charge is agitated by its escape and the "boil" is in progress. It is not real boiling like the boiling of a teakettle. When a teakettle boils the water turns to bubbles of vapor and goes up in the air to turn to water again when it gets cold. But in the boiling iron puddle a chemical change is taking place. The iron is not going up in vapor. The carbon and the oxygen are. This formation of gas in the molten puddle causes the whole charge to boil up like an ice cream soda. The slag overflows. Redder than strawberry sirup and as hot as the fiery lake in Hades it flows over the rim of the hearth and out through the slag hole. My helper has pushed up a buggy there to receive it. More than an eighth and sometimes a quarter of the weight of the pig iron flows off in slag and is carted away.

Meanwhile I have got the job of my life on my hands. I must stir my boiling mess with all the strength in my body. For now is my chance to defeat nature and wring from the loosening grip of her hand the pure iron she never intended to give us.

For twenty-five minutes while the boil goes on I stir it constantly with my long iron rabble. A cook stirring gravy to keep it from scorching in the skillet is done in two minutes and backs off blinking, sweating, and choking, having finished the hardest job of getting dinner. But my hardest job lasts not two minutes but the better part of half an hour. My spoon weighs twenty-five pounds, my porridge is pasty iron and the heat of my kitchen is so great that if my body was not hardened to it, the ordeal would drop me in my tracks.

Little spikes of pure iron like frost spars glow white-hot and stick out of the churning slag. These must be stirred under at once; the long stream of flame from the grate plays over the puddle, and the pure iron if lapped by these gases would be oxidized — burned up.

Pasty masses of iron form at the bottom of the puddle. There they would stick and become chilled if they were not constantly stirred. The whole charge must be mixed and mixed as it steadily thickens so that it will be uniform throughout. I am like some frantic baker in the Inferno kneading a batch of iron bread for the Devil's breakfast.

The charge which I have been kneading in my furnace has now "come to nature," the stringy sponge of pure iron is separating from the slag. The "balling" of this sponge into three loaves is a task that occupies from ten to fifteen minutes. The particles of iron glowing in this spongy mass are partly welded together; they are sticky and stringy and as the cooling continues they are rolled up into wads like pop-corn balls. The charge, which lost part of its original weight by the draining off of slag, now weighs five hundred and fifty to six hundred pounds. I am balling it into three parts of equal weight. If the charge is six hundred pounds, each of my balls must weigh exactly two hundred pounds.

But the iron worker does not guess his pigs. He knows exactly how much pig iron he put into the boil. His guessing skill comes into play when with a long paddle and hook he separates six hundred pounds of sizzling fireworks into three fire balls each of which will weigh two hundred pounds.

The balls are rolled up into three resting places, one in the fire-bridge corner, one in the flue-bridge corner, and one in the jam, all ready for the puddler to draw them.

My batch of biscuits is now done and I must take them out at once and rush them to the hungry mouth of the squeezing machine. A bride making biscuits can jerk them out of the oven all in one pan. But my oven is larger and hotter. I have to use long-handled tongs, and each of my biscuits weighs twice as much as I weigh. Suppose you were a cook with a fork six feet long, and had three roasting sheep on the grid at once to be forked off as quickly as possible. Could you do it? Even with a helper wouldn't you probably scorch the mutton or else burn yourself to death with the hot grease? That is where strength and skill must both come into play.

One at a time the balls are drawn out on to a buggy and wheeled swiftly to the squeezer. This machine squeezes out the slag which flows down like the glowing lava running out of a volcano. The motion of the squeezer is like the circular motion you use in rolling a bread pill between the palms and squeezing the water out of it. I must get the three balls, or blooms, out of the furnace and into the squeezer while the slag is still liquid so that it can be squeezed out of the iron.

From cold pig iron to finished blooms is a process that takes from an hour and ten minutes to an hour and forty minutes, depending on the speed and skill of the puddler, and the kind of iron. I was a fast one, myself. But you expected that, from the fact that I am telling the story.

JAMES J. DAVIS, The Iron Puddler

218. Henry Ford Constructs a Gasoline Buggy

Henry Ford did not invent the automobile, but it was his engineering skill and business acumen that was largely responsible for changing the automobile from a rich man's luxury to a common necessity, and the famous Model T Ford was the evidence of that change. Less than forty years after the experiments here described the automobile industry was first in the country in the value of its products.

EVEN before that time [1879] I had the idea of making some kind of a light steam car that would take the place of horses — more especially, however, as a tractor to attend to the excessively hard labor of plowing. It occurred to me, as I remember somewhat vaguely, that precisely the same idea might be applied to a carriage or a wagon on the road. A horseless carriage was a common idea. People had been talking about carriages without horses for many years back — in fact, ever since the steam engine was invented — but the idea of the carriage at first did not seem so practical to me as the idea of an engine to do the harder farm work, and of all the work on the farm plowing was the hardest. Our roads were poor, and we had not the habit of getting around. One of the most remarkable features of the automobile on the farm is the way that it has broadened the farmer's life. We simply took for granted that unless the errand were urgent we would not go to town, and I think we rarely made more than a trip a week. In bad weather we did not go even that often.

Being a full-fledged machinist and with a very fair workshop on the farm, it was not difficult for me to build a steam wagon or tractor. In the building of it came the idea that perhaps it might be made for road use. I felt perfectly certain that horses, considering all the bother of attending them and the expense of feeding, did not earn their keep. The obvious thing to do was to design and build a steam engine that would be light enough to run an ordinary wagon or to pull a plow. I thought it more important first to develop the tractor. To lift farm drudgery off flesh and blood and lay it on steel and motors has been my most constant ambition. It was circumstances that took me first into the actual manufacture of road cars. I found eventually that people were more interested in something that would travel on the road than in something that would do the work on the farms. In fact, I doubt that the light farm tractor could have been introduced on the farm had not the farmer had his eyes opened slowly but surely by the automobile. But that is getting ahead of the story. I thought the farmer would be more interested in the tractor.

I built a steam car that ran. It had a kerosene-heated boiler, and it developed plenty of power and a neat control — which is so easy with a steam throttle. But the boiler was dangerous. To get the requisite power without too big and heavy a power plant required that the engine work under high pressure; sitting on a high-pressure steam boiler is not altogether pleasant. To make it even reasonably safe required an excess of weight that nullified the economy of the high pressure. For two years I kept experimenting with various sorts of boilers — the engine and control problems were simple enough — and then I definitely abandoned the whole idea of running a road vehicle by steam.

A few years before — it was while I was an apprentice — I read in *The World of Science,* an English publication, of the silent gas engine which was then coming out in England. I think it was the Otto engine. It ran with illuminating gas, had a single large cylinder, and the power impulses being thus intermittent, required an extremely heavy flywheel. As far as weight was concerned, it gave nothing like the power per pound of metal that a steam engine gave, and the use of illuminating gas seemed to dismiss it as even a possibility for road use. It was interesting to me only as all machinery was interesting. I followed in the English and American magazines which we got in the shop the development of the engine and most particularly the hints of the possible replacement of the illuminating gas fuel by a gas formed by the vaporization of gasoline. The idea of gas engines was by no means new, but this was the first time that a really serious effort had been made to put them on the market. They were received with interest rather than enthusiasm, and I do not recall any one who thought that the internal combustion engine could ever have more than a limited use. All the wise people demonstrated conclusively that the engine could not compete with steam. They never thought that it might carve out a career for itself.

The gas engine interested me, and I followed its progress, but only from curiosity, until about 1885 or 1886, when, the steam engine being discarded as the motive power for the carriage that I intended some day to build, I had to look around for another sort of motive power. In 1885 I repaired an Otto engine at the Eagle Iron Works in Detroit. No one in town knew anything about them. There was a rumor that I did, and although I had never before been in contact with one, I undertook and carried through the job. That gave me a chance to study the new engine at first hand, and in 1887 I built one on the Otto four-cycle model just to see if I understood the principles. "Four cycle" means that the piston traverses the cylinder four times to get one power impulse. The first stroke draws in the gas, the second compresses it, the third is the explosion or power stroke, while the fourth stroke exhausts the waste gas. The little model worked well enough; it had a one-inch bore and a three-inch stroke, operated with gasoline, and while it did not develop much power, it was slightly lighter in proportion than the engines being offered commercially. I gave it away later to a young man who wanted it for something or other and whose name I have forgotten; it was eventually destroyed. That was the beginning of the work with the internal combustion engine.

I was then on the farm to which I had returned, more because I wanted to experiment than because I wanted to farm, and now, being an all-around machinist, I had a first-class workshop to replace the toy shop of earlier days. My father offered me forty acres of timber land, provided I gave up being a machinist. I agreed in a provisional way, for cutting the timber gave me a chance to get married. I fitted out a sawmill and a portable engine and started to cut out and saw up the timber on the tract. Some of the first of that lumber went into a cottage on my new farm, and in it we began our married life. It was not a big house — thirty-one feet square and only a story and a half high — but it was a comfortable place. I added to it my workshop, and when I was not cutting timber I was working on the gas engines — learning what they were and how they acted. I read everything I could find, but the greatest knowledge came from the work. A gas engine is a mysterious sort of thing — it will not always go the way it should. You can imagine how those first engines acted!

It was in 1890 that I began on a double-cylinder engine. It was quite impractical to consider the single cylinder for transportation purposes — the flywheel had to be entirely too heavy. Between making the first four-cycle engine of the Otto type and the start on a double cylinder I had made a great many experimental engines out of tubing. I fairly knew my way about. The double cylinder, I thought, could be applied to a road vehicle, and my original idea was to put it on a bicycle with a direct connection to the crankshaft and allowing for the rear wheel of the bicycle to act as the balance wheel. The speed was going to be varied only by the throttle. I never carried out this plan because it soon became apparent that the engine, gasoline tank, and the various necessary controls would be entirely too heavy for a bicycle. The plan of the two opposed cylinders was that while one would be delivering power the other would be exhausting. This naturally would not require so heavy a flywheel to even the application of power. The work started in my shop on the farm. Then I was offered a job with the Detroit Electric Company as an engineer and machinist at forty-five dollars a month. I took it because that was more money than the farm was bringing me, and I had decided to get away from the farm life anyway. The timber had all been cut. We rented a house on Bagley Avenue, Detroit. The workshop came along, and I set it up in a brick shed at the back of the house. During the first several months I was in the night shift at the electric light plant — which gave me very little time for experimenting — but after that I was in the day shift, and every night and all of every Saturday night I worked on the new motor. I cannot say that it was hard work. No work with interest is ever hard. I always am certain of results. They always come if you work hard enough. But it was a very great thing to have my wife even more confident than I was. She has always been that way.

I had to work from the ground up — that is, although I knew that a number of people were working on horseless carriages, I could not know what they were doing. The hardest problems to overcome were in the making and breaking of the spark and in the avoidance of excess weight. For the transmission, the steering gear, and the general construction, I could draw on my experience with the steam tractors. In 1892 I completed my first motor car, but it was not until the spring of the following year that it ran to my satisfaction. This first car had something of the appearance of a buggy. There were two cylinders, with a two-and-a-half-inch bore and a six-inch stroke, set side by side and over the rear axle. I made them out of the exhaust pipe of a steam engine that I had bought. They developed about four horsepower. The power was transmitted from the motor to the countershaft by a belt and from the countershaft to the rear wheel by a chain. The car would hold two people, the seat being suspended on posts and the body on elliptical springs. There were two speeds — one of ten and the other of twenty miles per hour — obtained by shifting the belt, which was done by a clutch lever in front of the driving seat.

Thrown forward, the lever put in the high speed; thrown back, the low speed; with the lever upright the engine could run free. To start the car it was necessary to turn the motor over by hand with the clutch free. To stop the car one simply released the clutch and applied the foot brake. There was no reverse, and speeds other than those of the belt were obtained by the throttle. I bought the iron-work for the frame of the carriage and also the seat and the springs. The wheels were twenty-eight-inch wire bicycle wheels with rubber tires. The balance wheel I had cast from a pattern that I made, and all of the more delicate mechanism I made myself. One of the features that I discovered necessary was a compensating gear that permitted the same power to be applied to each of the rear wheels when turning corners. The machine altogether weighed about five hundred pounds. A tank under the seat held three gallons of gasoline, which was fed to the motor through a small pipe and a mixing valve. The ignition was by electric spark. The original machine was air-cooled — or to be more accurate, the motor simply was not cooled at all. I found that on a run of an hour or more the motor heated up, and so I very shortly put a water jacket around the cylinders and piped it to a tank in the rear of the car over the cylinders.

Nearly all of these various features had been planned in advance. That is the way I have always worked. I draw a plan and work out every detail on the plan before starting to build. For otherwise one will waste a great deal of time in makeshifts as the work goes on and the finished article will not have coherence. It will not be rightly proportioned. Many inventors fail because they do not distinguish between planning and experimenting. The largest building difficulties that I had were in obtaining the proper materials. The next were with tools. There had to be some adjustments and changes in details of the design, but what held me up most was that I had neither the time nor the money to search for the best material for each part. But in the spring of 1893 the machine was running to my partial satisfaction and giving an opportunity further to test out the design and material on the road.

My gasoline buggy was the first and for a long time the only automobile in Detroit. It was considered to be something of a nuisance, for it made a racket and it scared horses. Also it blocked traffic. For if I stopped my machine anywhere in town a crowd was around it before I could start up again. If I left it alone even for a minute some inquisitive person always tried to run it. Finally, I had to carry a chain and chain it to a lamp post whenever I left it anywhere. And then there was trouble with the police. I do not know quite why, for my impression is that there were no speed laws in those days. Anyway, I had to get a special permit from the mayor and thus for a time enjoyed the distinction of being the only licensed chauffeur in America. I ran that machine about one thousand miles through 1895 and 1896 and then sold it to Charles Ainsley of Detroit for two hundred dollars. That was my first sale. I had built the car not to sell but only to experiment with. I wanted to start another car.

HENRY FORD, My Life and Work

219. Rockefeller Founds the Standard Oil Company

It was in 1859 that oil was struck in western Pennsylvania; within a few years oil and its products were transforming American industry and transportation, and profoundly influencing American social life. It was John D. Rockefeller who organized this industry — often by methods which excited the disapproval of socially minded critics — who created the greatest "trust" of our times, who accumulated the greatest fortune of his day, and who gave more to philanthropic causes than any man in history.

THE STORY of the early history of the oil trade is too well known to bear repeating in detail. The cleansing of crude petroleum was a simple and easy process, and at first the profits were very large. Naturally, all sorts of people went into it; the butcher, the baker, and the candlestick maker began to refine oil, and it was only a short time before more of the finished product was put on the market than could possibly be consumed. The price went down and down until the trade was threatened with ruin. It seemed absolutely necessary to extend the market for oil by exporting to foreign countries, which required a long and most difficult development, and also to greatly improve the processes of refining so that oil could be made and sold cheaply, yet with a profit, and to use as by-products all of the materials which in the less efficient plants were lost or thrown away.

These were the problems which confronted us almost at the outset, and this great depression led to consultations with our neighbors and friends in the business in the effort to bring some order out of what was rapidly becoming a state of chaos. To accomplish all these tasks of enlarging the market and improving the methods of manufacture in a large way was beyond the power or ability of any concern as then constituted. It could only be done, we reasoned, by increasing our capital and availing ourselves of the best talent and experience.

It was with this idea that we proceeded to buy the largest and best refining concerns and centralize the administration of them with a view to securing greater economy and efficiency. The business grew faster than we anticipated.

This enterprise, conducted by men of application and ability working hard together, soon built up unusual facilities in manufacture, in transportation, in finance, and in extending markets. We had our troubles and setbacks; we suffered from some severe fires; and the supply of crude oil was most uncertain. Our plans were constantly changed by changed conditions. We developed great facilities in an oil center, erected storage tanks, and connected pipe lines; then the oil failed and our work was thrown away. At best it was a speculative trade, and I wonder that we managed to pull through so often, but we were gradually learning how to conduct a most difficult business. . . .

I ascribe the success of the Standard Oil Company to its consistent policy of making the volume of its business large through the merit and cheapness of its products. It has spared no expense in utilizing the best and most efficient method of manufacture. It has sought for the best superintendents and workmen and paid the best wages. It has not hesitated to sacrifice old machinery and old plants for new and better ones. It has placed its manufactories at the points where they could supply markets at the least expense. It has not only sought markets for its principal products but for all possible by-products, sparing no expense in introducing them to the public in every nook and corner of the world. It has not hesitated to invest millions of dollars in methods for cheapening the gathering and distribution of oils by pipe lines, special cars, tank-steamers, and tank-wagons. It has erected tank stations at railroad centers in every part of the country to cheapen the storage and delivery of oil. It has had faith in American oil and has brought together vast sums of money for the purpose of making it what it is and for holding its market against the competition of Russia and all the countries which are producers of oil and competitors against American products.

JOHN D. ROCKEFELLER, Random Reminiscences of Men and Events

XXXI

Cuba Libre

220. Theodore Roosevelt Takes Charge of the Navy

Influenced by Admiral Mahan, Theodore Roosevelt had for some years advocated the strengthening of the American Navy and the adoption of a policy of aggressive imperialism. His enthusiastic support of McKinley in 1896 brought him the post of Assistant Secretary of the Navy, and from this vantage point he labored to put into effect his ideas about American foreign policy and naval preparedness. When the war with Spain came, Roosevelt resigned from the Navy Department and organized a regiment of Rough Riders which saw active service in Cuba.

FEBRUARY 25, 1898 — These are trying times. In the evening Roosevelt, whom I had left as Acting Secretary during the afternoon, came around. He is so enthusiastic and loyal that he is in certain respects invaluable; yet I lack confidence in his good judgment and discretion. He goes off very impulsively, and if I have a good night tonight I shall feel that I ought to be back in the Department rather than take a day's vacation.

February 26. — I had a splendid night last night and return to the office both because I feel so much better and because I find that Roosevelt, in his precipitate way, has come very near causing more of an explosion than happened to the *Maine*. His wife is very ill, and his little boy is just recovering from a long and dangerous illness; so his natural nervousness is so much accentuated that I really think he is hardly fit to be entrusted with the responsibility of the Department at this critical time. He is full of suggestions, many of which are of great value to me, and his spirited and force-

ful habit is a good tonic for one who is disposed to be as conservative and careful as I am. He seems to be thoroughly loyal, but the
very devil seemed to possess him yesterday afternoon.

Having the authority for that time of Acting Secretary, he immediately began to launch peremptory orders: distributing ships;
ordering ammunition, which there is no means to move, to places
where there is no means to store it; sending for Captain Barker
to come on about the guns of the *Vesuvius,* which is a matter that
might have been arranged by correspondence; sending messages to
Congress for immediate legislation authorizing the enlistment of
an unlimited number of seamen; and ordering guns from the Navy
Yard at Washington to New York, with a view to arming auxiliary
cruisers which are now in peaceful commercial pursuit. The only
effect of this last order would be to take guns which are now carefully stored, ready for shipment any moment, and which could
be shipped in ample time to be put on any vessel, and dump them
in the open weather in the New York Navy Yard, where they would
be only in the way and under no proper care.

He has gone at things like a bull in a china shop, and with the
best purposes in the world has really taken what, if he could have
thought, he would not for a moment have taken; and that is the
one course which is most discourteous to me, because it suggests that
there had been a lack of attention which he was supplying. It shows
how the best fellow in the world — and with splendid capacities —
is worse than no use if he lack a cool head and careful discretion.

Journal of John Davis Long

221. Admiral Dewey Wins the Battle of Manila Bay

*The war with Spain was designed,
supposedly, to liberate the Cubans from Spanish misrule, and few
Americans had contemplated action in the Far East. The Navy men,
imperialists, and merchants, however, had long foreseen the opportunity which such a war would give for the establishment of*

American power in the Orient. The battle of Manila Bay proved to be one of the decisive battles of history. It effectively ended Spain's century-long dominion in the Pacific, made possible if not inevitable the American acquisition of the Philippines, and dramatized the advent of the United States to world power. Dewey's spectacular victory made him, for a short time, the great popular hero of the American people.

BEFORE me now was the object for which we had made our arduous preparations and which indeed must ever be the supreme test of a naval officer's career. I felt confident of the outcome, though I had no thought that victory would be won at so slight a cost to our own side. Confidence was expressed in the very precision with which the dun, war-colored hulls of the squadron followed in column behind the flagship, keeping their distance excellently. All the guns were pointed constantly at the enemy, while the men were at their stations waiting the word. There was no break in the monotone of the engines save the mechanical voice of the leadsman or an occasional low-toned command by the quartermaster at the conn or the roar of a Spanish shell. The Manila batteries continued their inaccurate fire, to which we paid no attention.

The misty haze of the tropical dawn had hardly risen when at five-fifteen, at long range, the Cavite forts and Spanish squadron opened fire. Our course was not one leading directly toward the enemy, but a converging one, keeping him on our starboard bow. Our speed was eight knots, and our converging course and ever-varying position must have confused the Spanish gunners. My assumption that the Spanish fire would be hasty and inaccurate proved correct.

So far as I could see, none of our ships was suffering any damage, while in view of my limited ammunition supply it was my plan not to open fire until we were within effective range and then to fire as rapidly as possible with all of our guns.

At five-forty, when we were within a distance of five thousand yards (two and one-half miles), I turned to Captain Gridley and said: "You may fire when you are ready, Gridley."

While I remained on the bridge with Lamberton, Brumby, and

Stickney, Gridley took his station in the conning tower and gave the order to the battery. The very first gun to speak was an eight-inch from the forward turret of the *Olympia,* and this was the signal for the other ships to join the action. . . .

When the flagship neared the five-fathom curve off Cavite, she turned to the westward, bringing her port batteries to bear on the enemy, and followed by the squadron, passed along the Spanish line until north of and only some fifteen hundred yards distant from the Sangley Point battery, when she again turned and headed back to the eastward, thus giving the squadron an opportunity to use their port and starboard batteries alternately and to cover with their fire all the Spanish ships as well as the Cavite and Sangley Point batteries. While I was regulating the course of the squadron, Lieutenant Calkins was verifying our position by cross bearings and by the lead.

Three runs were thus made from the eastward and two from the westward, the length of each run averaging two miles and the ships being turned each time with port helm. . . . The fifth run past the Spaniards was farther inshore than any preceding run. At the nearest point to the enemy our range was only two thousand yards.

There had been no cessation in the rapidity of fire maintained by our whole squadron, and the effect of its concentration, owing to the fact that our ships were kept so close together, was smothering, particularly upon the two largest ships, the *Reina Cristina* and *Castilla.* The *Don Juan de Austria* first and then the *Reina Cristina* made brave and desperate attempts to charge the *Olympia,* but becoming the target for all our batteries, they turned and ran back. In this sortie the *Reina Cristina* was raked by an eight-inch shell which is said to have put out of action some twenty men and to have completely destroyed her steering gear. Another shell in her forecastle killed or wounded all the members of the crews of four rapid-fire guns; another set fire to her after orlop; another killed or disabled nine men on her poop; another carried away her mizzen-mast, bringing down the ensign and the admiral's flag, both of which were replaced; another exploded in the after ammunition room; and still another exploded in the sick bay, which was already filled with wounded.

Though in the early part of the action our firing was not what I should have liked it to be, it soon steadied down, and by the time the *Reina Cristina* steamed toward us it was satisfactorily accurate. The *Castilla* fared little better than the *Reina Cristina*. All except one of her guns were disabled; she was set on fire by our shells and finally abandoned by her crew after they had sustained a loss of twenty-three killed and eighty wounded. The *Don Juan de Austria* was badly damaged and on fire, the *Isla de Luzón* had three guns dismounted, and the *Marqués del Duero* was also in a bad way. Admiral Montojo, finding his flagship no longer manageable, half her people dead or wounded, her guns useless, and the ship on fire, gave the order to abandon and sink her and transferred his flag to the *Isla de Cuba* shortly after seven o'clock.

Victory was already ours, though we did not know it. . . .

Feeling confident of the outcome, I now signaled that the crews, who had had only a cup of coffee at 4:00 A.M., should have their breakfast. The public at home, on account of this signal, to which was attributed a nonchalance that had never occurred to me, reasoned that breakfast was the real reason for our withdrawing from action. Meanwhile I improved the opportunity to have the commanding officers report on board the flagship.

There had been such a heavy flight of shells over us that each captain, when he arrived, was convinced that no other ship had had such good luck as his own in being missed by the enemy's fire and expected the others to have both casualties and damages to their ships to report. But fortune was as pronouncedly in our favor at Manila as it was later at Santiago. To my gratification not a single life had been lost, and considering that we would rather measure the importance of an action by the scale of its conduct than by the number of casualties, we were immensely happy. On the *Baltimore* two officers and six men were slightly wounded. None of our ships had been seriously hit, and every one was still ready for immediate action.

At 11:16 A.M. we stood in to complete our work. There remained to oppose us, however, only the batteries and the gallant little *Ulloa*. Both opened fire as we advanced. But the contest was too unequal to last more than a few minutes. Soon the *Ulloa,* under our concentrated fire, went down valiantly with her colors flying.

At 12:30 the *Petrel* signaled the fact of the surrender and the firing ceased. But the Spanish vessels were not yet fully destroyed. Therefore the executive officer of the *Petrel*, Lieutenant E. M. Hughes, with a whaleboat and a crew of only seven men, boarded and set fire to the *Don Juan de Austria, Isla de Cuba, Isla de Luzón, General Lezo, Coreo,* and *Marqués del Duero,* all of which had been abandoned in shallow water and left scuttled by their deserting crews. This was a courageous undertaking, as these vessels were supposed to have been left with trains to their magazines and were not far from the shore, where there were hundreds of Spanish soldiers and sailors, all armed and greatly excited. The *Manila,* an armed transport, which was found uninjured after having been beached by the Spaniards, was therefore spared. Two days later she was easily floated and for many years did good service as a gunboat. The little *Petrel* continued her work until 5:20 P.M., when she rejoined the squadron, towing a long string of tugs and launches, to be greeted by volleys of cheers from every ship.

The order to capture or destroy the Spanish squadron had been executed to the letter. Not one of its fighting vessels remained afloat. That night I wrote in my diary: "Reached Manila at daylight. Immediately engaged the Spanish ships and batteries at Cavite. Destroyed eight of the former, including the *Reina Cristina* and *Castilla.* Anchored at noon off Manila."

GEORGE DEWEY, Autobiography

222. Sampson Defeats Cervera in Santiago Harbor

Shortly after the declaration of war against Spain, the Spanish Admiral, Cervera, steamed out of the Cape Verde Islands to destinations unknown. There was panic all along the Atlantic Coast, but Cervera was not bound on offensive operations. On May nineteenth he sneaked into the narrow landlocked harbor of Santiago on the southern shore of Cuba and was

*promptly bottled up by the American navy under Admiral Sampson
and Commodore Schley. As the American army closed in on
Santiago Cervera had no alternatives but surrender or escape, and he
chose the latter. The complete destruction of the Spanish fleet outside Santiago practically ended the war, but it inaugurated a conflict between the followers of Sampson and those of Schley over the
conduct of the battle that was almost as bitter and far more prolonged.*

SUNDAY morning, July 3 [1898], dawned clear and hot. A fair,
light northwest breeze rippled a smooth sea. The blockading vessels
lay idly off the harbor of Santiago, waiting patiently, as they had
waited thirty-three days, for the coming of the Spanish fleet, penned
up within. No signs but those of peaceful inaction marked shore
and sea.

Day by day the hope that Cervera would dash out had been
growing fainter and fainter. And this morning the consensus of
opinion was that the end of all this weary waiting would only come
when Cervera, desperate, should blow up his own ships inside the
harbor and thus to some extent cheat the blockaders of their
prey. . . .

Rear Admiral Sampson stood on the quarterdeck of the *New
York* as that vessel neared the brown hills of Siboney, wearing his
leggings and all ready for the long, hot ride that lay before him.
He was not in very good health and was well-nigh worn out with
the tremendous strain of the past month. He held himself personally
responsible for the destruction of every ship inside that harbor, and
the Navy Department appeared to take a similar view.

"Smoke in the harbor!" sang out a man on the *New York's*
signal bridge. Sampson turned his glass on Morro. Hearts beat
quicker, and in a second the port side of the flagship was crowded
with anxious men, who gazed as if for dear life at the faint brown
hill which Morro marked.

"The fleet's coming out!" yelled a man from the signal bridge.
And those who heard that cry will never forget it. Sampson took
his glass down and without a trace of excitement said to his assistant chief of staff:

"Yes; they're coming out. Hoist two-fifty." (This signal meant: "Close in toward harbor entrance and attack vessels.")

When Sampson said, "Yes; they're coming out," it was between 9:35 and 9:40 A.M. The inspection lines broke in a second; "general quarters" was sounded; fires were started under all boilers; the helm was put over; and the *New York* swung around and headed for the enemy. But before this was done we saw the white lines vanish, as ours had vanished, from the quarterdecks of the ships that lay in front of the harbor, seven miles away. Puffs of smoke from the shore batteries and the water jets of exploding shells were the first sign of hostilities. Then, suddenly, out from the harbor mouth came the fighting tops of the *Maria Teresa,* the flagship of the Spanish admiral. Her hull was quite hidden by the curling rolls of her own gun smoke, and the fighting tops sailed gracefully, swiftly to sea on a bed of clouds. But from those clouds, rifted every few seconds by the flash of a bigger gun, we knew were coming a hail of shells, for around our own ships the water was alive with geysers. Before the *Maria Teresa* was well out of the shadow of Morro every vessel on the blockade line except the *Vixen* was closing in toward the shore and firing away as fast as the batteries could be manned.

Out they came, gallantly, these fine cruisers, the pride of Spain's navy, round the hill of Morro, pushing their gun smoke before them in thick, tumbling clouds like the chariot of Vulcan. Shells from the *Iowa, Oregon, Brooklyn, Indiana, Texas,* and *Gloucester* fell all around them. One, two, three, four — we counted them as they came and could place them fairly well in their right order — the *Maria Teresa, Viscaya, Colón,* and *Oquendo.* They lost no time in their desperate effort, swinging around the western point with only about five hundred yards between ships. They sped swiftly in the direction of the *Brooklyn.* Against the dull background of the western shore and amid the drifting smoke we could scarcely follow their movements. When the fourth ship had headed off after her sisters and when it was clear that none of them was coming our way, to our amazement there came flying out from the harbor first one and then another torpedo-boat destroyer. We had scarcely hoped that these fragile craft would dare give battle in daytime, and we had never dreamed that they would tempt fate by themselves instead, as they should have been, in the lee of one of the big vessels. With a curious, almost pitiful bravado these boats banged away at the fleet with their fourteen- and six-pounders. It was as if marionettes now occupied the stage where a few minutes before great actors had played tragedy.

A few minutes before we saw the last of the Spanish fleet take the sea the *Resolute* had dashed past us, going for safety to the eastward. Commander Eaton of that vessel sang out, "The Spanish fleet is escaping to the westward!" The answer to this was an order to the *Resolute* to telegraph the news to Guantanamo and to tell the *Massachusetts* to return at once to her blockading station. The *New York* was now plowing through the water at about twelve knots. Smoke was pouring from her funnels, and in the firerooms men worked as they never worked before to get full steam into the boilers. The honor of the ship, it seemed to most of us, was at stake. With frantic energy men poured fuel into cold furnaces and cursed the black coals that would not glow. When a fireman appeared anywhere on deck a hundred eager Jackies would surround him. "For God's sake," they shouted, "get those engines going. Make us move. Burn any old damn thing. Get us there! Get us there!" The spoken and unspoken cry from all hands was "Steam! More steam!" And the engines and their force answered nobly.

When we were abreast the harbor mouth the forts opened on us. Shells came flying over us and for about fifteen minutes kept whizzing by us, but we never made reply. "Shall we answer them?" asked Chadwick. "No," said Sampson, never taking his glass from his eye, "let us get on — on after the fleet! Not one must get away!" Ahead, still about seven miles away, the battle, panoramalike, was stretched before us. The four Spanish cruisers had clung to the outward curve of the western shore, and our battleships had headed in toward them. This maneuvering had brought the fleets to within about a mile of each other. At first it seemed as if our ships and the Spaniards were all mixed up, engaging each other at short ranges, fighting terrible duels, and all formation gone. Then, as the smoke momentarily lifted from first one and then another vessel — we saw all this through good glasses — we made them out, slowly and doubtfully, and saw they were in two lines, running on parallel courses. The ships inshore were the Spaniards; those outside our own. The Spaniards were ahead. The roar of the cannonade could only be heard faintly. Beyond the terrific smoke and flame that belched forth from every ship and the spouting of the water as the shells exploded, there was nothing to show that a battle was in progress; still less was there anything to show how the day was going. Though a long way off, we had a better view than the ships closely engaged, because we had none of our own smoke to contend against. The Spanish ships were bunched together. Masses of flame frequently burst out from them, but whether it was an American shell exploding aboard them or merely the fire of their own guns we knew not.

"The *Brooklyn's* gone!" shouted a man beside me. A smoky mass headed out from our ships. At first I thought it must be a Spanish ship that had broken through our line and was escaping to the southward. Then the three smokestacks of Schley's flagship showed up clearly. Our hopes fell, for the *Brooklyn* was the only ship we had besides the *New York* that in point of supposed speed could cope with the enemy. Now it looked as if she had been disabled. We watched her closely. After going out from the shore she again headed after the Spaniards, though now farther away and to the southward of the enemy. We took hope again, for it was evident that she would not continue on the chase if badly hurt.

From the scene directly ahead of us our eyes now turned to a fight that we were close approaching on our starboard bow. Out of the trailing smoke clouds of the four Spanish cruisers there appeared, as suddenly and as unexpectedly as if dropped from the sky, the little *Gloucester*. How she ever escaped from the melee no one to this day can quite understand. She was headed for the destroyers and blazing away at them as if she possessed the battery of a battleship instead of being of inferior armament to either the *Plutón* or *Furór*. The battleships, especially the *Indiana* and *Iowa,* had already directed a heavy fire against these boats, but both were steaming after the fleet when we first noticed the *Gloucester*. Regardless of the parting shots from our own ships, regardless of the rapid fire kept up from the destroyers themselves or of the danger of torpedoes, Lieutenant Commander Wainwright, the plucky captain of the *Gloucester* and formerly executive officer of the *Maine,* made straight for his two antagonists. In a few minutes we saw that the leading boat was on the beach — it was the *Plutón* — about four miles west of Morro. An explosion broke her in two. The other destroyer, the *Furór,* still kept going, though apparently in distress and as if trying to reach the beach. The *New York* closed in toward the shore, and the Socapa battery landed several shells close aboard. To insure the destruction of the *Furór,* we fired three shots from one of the forward four-inch guns. One struck, but the fate of the *Furór* had already been sealed by the *Gloucester.* The smoke from our guns had scarcely cleared away before we saw that the *Furór* was burning and that a boat from the *Gloucester* was being lowered to go over and take possession of the helpless craft. As the flagship passed, Captain Chadwick, standing on the fo'c'sle, waving his cap, led the crew in wild cheers for the plucky little *Gloucester.*

I have related what we saw of the destruction of the destroyers connectedly, but during that period our attention was divided between this phase of the fight and things of even greater import that were happening ahead. The first intimation we had of how the battle went was when we saw flames shooting out of the stern of one of Spain's ships. A shout went up: "She's on fire!" Scarcely had we realized this before the now blazing vessel slowly turned. Was she going to come around and face us in a desperate effort to regain Santiago harbor? Our excitement during those few moments was intense. Then we saw her cease firing and head for the beach. She passed behind a slight promontory out of our sight, but the smoke from her burning hull mounted above the hill and marked her grave. It was the *Maria Teresa.* Scarcely had our shouts died away before great red flames and black smoke curled up from the stern of another Spanish ship, and she, too, turned toward the Cuban hills, a blazing, helpless mass. It was the *Oquendo.* This was between ten-fifteen and ten-thirty, or less than an hour after we had left Siboney.

On we went, now making about sixteen knots an hour, on after our own gallant ships and after the two Spanish vessels that still forged ahead and still returned the terrible fire. The water around us was strewn with floating wreckage and ammunition boxes.

As we rounded the smoking promontory we came in full sight

of the *Maria Teresa* and *Oquendo*. They were only about half a mile apart and were so near the beach that the surf broke around their bows. From the after part of both ships smoke and flames leaped out, licking up the masts and circling round the smokestacks. On their fo'castles were gathered the white-clad crews. At the bows of the *Maria Teresa* was a long white line. Another look showed it was composed of men sliding down a rope and dropping, one after the other, into the water. Many of them had already reached the beach and stood there in pitiful groups. The sight of these burning ships was inexpressibly sad. The awfulness of it killed, for the time being, the exaltation of victory, and as the *New York* sped by not a shout or a cheer came from her crowded decks. Men simply gazed in silence.

Gradually we gained on the enemy ahead, making seventeen knots despite our foul bottom. About eleven o'clock flames burst out from the *Viscaya* and she turned for the beach. That left but one Spanish ship, the *Colón*. On after her went the *Oregon,* the *Texas,* and the *Vixen,* while outside and ahead of them was the *Brooklyn*. The *Colón* must have been over ten miles ahead of the *New York* at this time, and all we could see of her was her smoke. The *Iowa* followed the *Viscaya*. . . . At the stern of the *Iowa* stood Captain Evans. Behind him, massed over turrets, superstructure, and decks, were his officers and crew, dirty, grimy, and many half naked. As they saw Sampson these men yelled and yelled again for their old captain. It reminded one of the first day of the war, when Sampson had refused to let the *Iowa* fire a salute in his honor, and the men, not to be denied, had cheered him instead. Several times Captain Evans waved to his men to keep still. At last they were quiet, and through the megaphone Evans shouted, "Nobody hurt." To us this message was a revelation. That a ship having so much to do with the utter destruction of those three splendid vessels should escape without any casualties seemed almost impossible. It was more than a repetition of Manila. But even then no one dreamed that the other ships would have fared equally as well as the *Iowa*.

With the three smoking beacons of victory behind us, we pressed on after the last of Cervera's fleet. Knot after knot we covered, and the outlines of the *Colón* grew plainer. At first we thought this was imagination; it seemed impossible. But there was no mistake; we were surely gaining, both on our own ships and upon the enemy. Soon after noon we could clearly make out the positions of the pursuing ships. The *Colón* was well inland, as close as we were to the shore, and dead ahead of us. On our port bow were the *Vixen* and the *Texas*. Well ahead of them was the *Oregon,* apparently keeping pace with the *Colón,* and at this we marveled; for the *Oregon* is a battleship with a maximum speed of sixteen knots, and she had traveled many miles since she last saw dry dock. Away outside the *Oregon,* whether ahead or abeam we could not tell, was the *Brooklyn*. Now and again Schley's flagship fired and now and again the *Colón* replied, but the shells fell more than a mile short. The *Oregon,* with her big thirteen-inch guns, blazed away. It seemed ten minutes, though it was really only about ten seconds, before a big splash near the *Colón* showed us that the Pacific coast battleship still had the enemy within range. Twenty miles farther on, the coast formed a great promontory. To pass this the *Colón* must come out within good range of the *Brooklyn* and the *Oregon*. Should she double on her tracks, she had to count with the *Texas* and ourselves. So by one o'clock we knew that unless some unforeseen accident occurred the entire Spanish fleet was ours.

I have no recollection of what any one said at this moment when we saw the *Colón* turn shoreward. All I know is that there was a great deal of handshaking and cheering and shouting and that everybody felt very proud of the American navy. The *Brooklyn* and *Oregon* turned in after the big Spaniard, and the *Texas* and *Vixen* converged toward her. For her grave she had sought a little inlet under the shadow of a great, green mountain — Rio Tarquino we afterward found it was called. Fifteen minutes after the *Colón* went ashore we had caught up with the *Texas* and *Vixen*. Their crews cheered, and ours answered. We saw a boat being lowered from the *Brooklyn* and rowed over to the *Colón*. We had one ready for the same purpose. From the *Brooklyn,* which stopped a few minutes before ourselves, there fluttered the signal: "We have won a great victory; details later." . . . What we all wanted to know was how many brave men had lost their lives in securing this great victory. So from the *New York's* signal yard there was run the hoist: "Report your casualties." And to our amazement there came a negative from every ship except the *Brooklyn,* and she reported only one killed. It was past all understanding.

W. A. M. GOODE, With Sampson through the War

223. The Bluejackets Charge San Juan Hill

With almost two hundred thousand men on the island of Cuba, the Spanish Captain-General allowed the American expeditionary army of fifteen thousand to land on the beach at Daiquiri, a few miles from Santiago, without opposition. Yet the Spaniards put up a stiff fight for the defense of the city; the battles of Las Guásimas, El Caney and San Juan — the only important land battles of the war — were by no means as one-sided as the naval battles of Manila Bay and Santiago: the fighting of July 1st took a toll of almost fifteen hundred American casualties. San Juan Hill is historically important, too, because it helped to promote Theodore Roosevelt from a colonelcy to the Presidency.

WHEN the line was nearly formed and the last of his men were coming up, General Hawkins, accompanied by Schroeder, the gallant bugler, stepped forward into the open field and, standing by the wire fence, surveyed the slopes which he had never seen plainly before, up which he was now to send his handful of men upon their desperate errand. While engaged in this he noticed half a dozen of his men crouching for cover in the thicket near by. Suddenly one of the men got up and walked away from the group in the cover, though the other men tried to detain him. Hawkins heard the brave fellow say: "No, I'll be blanked if I do; I won't lie down when a general and a better man is standing!" And so he stood up, with his rifle before him, with muscles taut and neck outstretched, only awaiting the order for the rush which was momentarily expected. When Hawkins turned around, he saw that the others were following this man's example. Walking over to where they stood, he said: "Our duties are different here, my men. I must see all I can, and you must be seen as little as possible. Lie down!" And then he resumed his survey of the Spanish positions.

The word was given, and Schroeder put it to the shrill clarion music, and the men of the two little, decimated regiments rushed across the field of guinea grass in a race which lay between victory and death, and, as any military man would have said, with the odds decidedly in favor of death. General Hawkins stood out in the open field, a shining mark indeed, urging the men up on the heights as fast as they emerged from the forest, with their eyes blinking as they came out into the sunlight. Not that they required much urging — they went up the heights to avenge the cruel losses they had met in their advance and because they knew the capture of the blockhouse offered the only hope of turning the adverse tide of battle. When they reached the foothills of the heights, they secured some protection and a better footing and crept up the heights in little bunches, availing themselves of what shelter the inequalities of the ground offered, while Hawkins by his presence and his voice spurred them on to attempt the impossible. Now the three regiments of the Third Brigade (Wikoff's) emerged from the forest, swarmed up the heights some distance to the left of the blockhouse, and overlapping the Spanish line and flanking the Spanish trenches as they did, contributed to the fire of the men of the Sixth and Sixteenth in making the blockhouse untenable.

The Spanish blockhouses, wreathed in the gorgeous red flowers of the flame-tree, rose straight before our advancing columns. Now and again a gleam of the sunlight upon a rifle and the high-crowned guano hat of a Spanish soldier fascinate your gaze. You listen as in a dream to the quick, insistent tone of the orders, for the Spaniards are firing in volleys and not at will; and again you rub your eyes and smile incredulously, for the sun is shining peacefully on the heights, and there is not a speck of smoke anywhere to be seen to tell you from whence the firing comes. And yet, as the little clumps of blue coats that dot the fields and the roadside reveal to you only too truly, this is the stern reality of war. From every trench and blockhouse — you can only guess where they all are in a general way — the volleys are delivered as though by some quick-firing automaton. You hear the mechanical click of the rifle and often the very words of command. As the First Brigade (Hawkins') starts up the hill to the left of the fort, you see that the Spaniards who have been holding the blue house on Kettles Hill to the right with such stubborn resistance are wavering. Then they hurry out of the trenches and run swiftly away down the hill to the right of the little lagoon, and the yellow flag of the Cavalry Division rises over the hill and bursts upon our gaze like a harvest moon; and then appear, like satellites in its wake, the innumerable troop guidons of red and white and yellow. The Spaniards have lost their advanced position, and we have gained one.

The cavalry do not rest long, and some forward spirits rush down the hill and are pretty well mixed up with the infantry brigades before that final charge is delivered which leaves the bullet-swept heights in our possession. Far from relaxing, the fire from the Spanish trenches, which our artillery has utterly failed to keep down, redoubles in vigor. The Spaniards fully recognize that the critical moment has come, and from their vantage they pour a leaden stream down into the valley, where our second line is coming up to the charge. Perhaps, over and above the rattle of the musketry, they also hear and understand the bugle call of the white-haired brigadier as he passes with the bugler along the line, feeling the heartbeat of his men, as it were, and collecting them for the charge he is soon to lead. It is certainly magnificent, it is certainly not war, and had it failed, it would have been called quixotic. These two thin, depleted brigades, the First and Third, are absolutely unsupported by artillery save the Gatling guns, while from the Spanish right they are swept by the shrapnel fire of the heavy batteries. This fire in itself is destructive and upon men of less sturdy fiber could not have failed to exert a depressing effect.

And now, right in front, as if the small-arms fire with all its automatic regularity were not enough, you see the bushes shattered and whole lines of the guinea grass lose their tassels as though falling under the mighty sweep of a scythe in the grasp of some strong, invisible hand. You do not need to hear the turning of the cogwheel crank faster and ever faster to recognize that the Spaniards are pouring upon our men a steady stream of missiles from their machine guns. Then, over the roar of musketry and the booming of the great guns and the quick moans of those who fall, you hear a sharp note of the bugle, and every man steps out, putting into word and into action the trumpet note which spells in martial music the words, "To the charge!"

From right to left one little band rushes fifty yards, crouches, and fires; the platoon on the left passes them, crouches, and fires. And so they go, platoon after platoon. You have no eyes for the writhing masses of blue which mark their progress, particularly by the wire fences where the advance is slow; you only follow that line which rises and falls with the mechanical regularity of a piston rod. In a moment they are under the hill and with a short, breathless cheer commence to swarm up the slope. The fire of the Spaniards almost ceases, then begins again, wild, irregular, and dies away in a desultory pitter-patter. The Spaniards sullenly retire, while the five infantry regiments swarm over the crest of the hill and take possession of the blockhouse and the trenches which the Spaniards fought for with such obstinacy and relinquished with such reluctance. The red and yellow flag disappears, and soon the blue flag of the infantrymen and the Stars and Stripes of us all float over the blockhouse. On the right the six regiments of the cavalry division sweep around the right of the lagoon, all except some of the Third Cavalry who come around the left and have fought almost shoulder to shoulder with the doughboys. The cavalry climb the heights before them in open skirmish order under the hacienda a quarter of a mile to the right of the fort; the Spaniards give way all along the line; and we hold the heights of San Juan. But you cannot please everybody. The fire-eating major of the Second Infantry, Major S——, of the first regiment of the reserve brigade, crouching behind a little foothill five hundred yards away, heaves a mighty sigh as he swings his men out into the open and leads them around to the left. "We were to go in, boys, the moment they wavered; but they didn't waver worth a cent. And so you've all missed being in the greatest charge that our army has ever made."

STEPHEN BONSAL, The Fight for Santiago

XXXII

The Progressive Era

224. Frances Willard Embarks on the Temperance Crusade

The origins of the temperance crusade date back to the early years of the Republic and by mid-nineteenth century the cause of temperance had made impressive headway. Immigration and the growth of cities, however, gave a new impetus to the liquor traffic: between 1860 and 1880 the liquor business increased sevenfold, and the temperance gave way to the prohibition movement. For this change Frances Willard of Evanston, Illinois, was largely responsible. In 1874 she founded the Woman's Christian Temperance Union and thereafter devoted her life to this cause.

THE FIRST saloon I ever entered was Sheffner's, on Market Street, Pittsburgh. In fact that was the only glimpse I ever personally had of the crusade [1874]. It had lingered in this dun-colored city well nigh a year, and when I visited my old friends at the Pittsburgh Female College I spoke with enthusiasm of the crusade and of the women who were, as I judged from a morning paper, still engaged in it here. They looked upon me with astonishment when I proposed to seek out those women and go with them to the saloons, for in the two years that I had taught in Pittsburgh these friends associated me with the recitation room, the Shakespeare Club, the lecture course, the opera, indeed all the haunts open to me that a literary-minded woman would care to enter. However, they were too polite to desire to disappoint me; and so they had me piloted by some of the factotums of the place to the headquarters of the crusade, where I was warmly welcomed and soon found my-

self walking downstreet arm in arm with a young teacher from
the public school who said she had a habit of coming in to add one
to the procession when her day's duties were over. We paused in
front of the saloon that I have mentioned. The ladies ranged themselves along the curbstone, for they had been forbidden in any wise
to incommode the passers-by, being dealt with much more strictly
than a drunken man or a heap of dry-goods boxes would be. At a
signal from our gray-haired leader a sweet-voiced woman began to
sing, "Jesus the water of life will give," all our voices soon blending
in that sweet song. I think it was the most novel spectacle that I
recall. There stood women of undoubted religious devotion and
the highest character, most of them crowned with the glory of
gray hairs. Along the stony pavement of that stoniest of cities
rumbled the heavy wagons, many of them carriers of beer; between us and the saloon in front of which we were drawn up in
line passed the motley throng, almost every man lifting his hat
and even the little newsboys doing the same. It was American manhood's tribute to Christianity and to womanhood, and it was significant and full of pathos. The leader had already asked the saloonkeeper if we might enter, and he had declined; else the prayer
meeting would have occurred inside his door. A sorrowful old lady
whose only son had gone to ruin through that very deathtrap knelt
on the cold, moist pavement and offered a brokenhearted prayer
while all our heads were bowed. At a signal we moved on, and
the next saloonkeeper permitted us to enter. I had no more idea
of the inward appearance of a saloon than if there had been no
such place on earth. I knew nothing of its high, heavily corniced
bar, its barrels with the ends all pointed toward the looker-on, each
barrel being furnished with a faucet; its floors thickly strewn with
sawdust, and here and there a round table with chairs — nor of
its abundant fumes, sickening to healthful nostrils. The tall, stately
lady who led us placed her Bible on the bar and read a psalm,
whether hortatory or imprecatory I do not remember, but the spirit
of these crusaders was so gentle, I think it must have been the former. Then we sang "Rock of Ages" as I thought I had never heard
it sung before, with a tender confidence to the height of which one
does not rise in the easy-going regulation prayer meeting, and then
one of the older women whispered to me softly that the leader

wished to know if I would pray. It was strange, perhaps, but I felt not the least reluctance, and kneeling on that sawdust floor, with a group of earnest hearts around me, and behind them, filling every corner and extending out into the street, a crowd of unwashed, unkempt, hard-looking drinking men, I was conscious that perhaps never in my life save beside my sister Mary's dying bed had I prayed as truly as I did then. This was my crusade baptism. The next day I went on to the West and within a week had been made president of the Chicago W.C.T.U.

FRANCES E. WILLARD, Glimpses of Fifty Years

225. John Peter Altgeld Pardons the Anarchists

The year 1886 was one of labor unrest, and the center of that unrest was in Chicago. On May 4th, while police were watching a meeting of labor sympathizers at Haymarket Square, some one threw a bomb: seven persons were killed, and over sixty injured. Though the actual perpetrator of the outrage could not be found, police rounded up anarchists and radicals. Eight of these were put on trial for murder and found guilty; four were executed and three sentenced to life imprisonment. Six years later Governor Altgeld reopened the case, and on examining the evidence concluded that the Haymarket "anarchists" were innocent of the crime for which they had been convicted and pardoned them. His act brought down upon him a flood of denunciation and vilification, but it brought him, too, the respect and affection of men like Brand Whitlock who here tells the story of the pardon.

INJUSTICE was never for long out of the mind of John P. Altgeld, and during all those first months of his administration he had been brooding over this notable instance of injustice; and he had come to his decision. He knew the cost to him; he had just come to the governorship of his state and to the leadership of his party after its thirty years of defeat, and he realized what powerful interests would be frightened and offended if he were to turn three forgotten men out of prison; he understood how partisanship would turn the action to its advantage.

It mattered not that most of the thoughtful men in Illinois would tell you that the anarchists had been improperly convicted, that they were not only entirely innocent of the murder of which they had been accused, but were not even anarchists; it was simply that the mob had convicted them in one of the strangest frenzies of fear that ever distracted a whole community, a case which all the psychologists of all the universities in the world might have tried without getting at the truth of it — much less a jury in a criminal court.

And so, one morning in June, very early, I was called to the governor's office and told to make out pardons for Fielden, Neebe, and Schwab. "And do it yourself," said the governor's secretary, "and don't say anything about it to anybody."

I cannot tell in what surprise, in what a haze, or with what emotions I went about that task. I got the blanks and the records, and before the executive clerk whose work it was had come down, I made out those three pardons, in the largest, roundest hand I could command, impressed them with the Great Seal of State, had the secretary of state sign them, and took them over to the governor's office. I was admitted to his private room, and there he sat at his great flat desk. The only other person in the room was Dreier, a Chicago banker, who had never wearied, it seems, in his efforts to have those men pardoned. He was standing and was very nervous; the moment evidently meant much to him. The governor took the big sheets of imitation parchment, glanced over them, signed his name to each, laid down the pen, and handed the papers across the table to Dreier. The banker took them and began to say something. But he only got as far as "Governor, I hardly —— " when he broke down and wept. Altgeld made an impatient gesture; he was gazing out of the window in silence, on the elm trees in the yard. He took out his watch, told Dreier he would miss his train — Dreier was to take the Alton to Joliet, deliver the pardons to the men in person, and go on into Chicago with them that night — and Dreier nervously rolled up the pardons, took up a little valise, shook hands, and was gone.

On the table was a high pile of proofs of the document in which Governor Altgeld gave the reasons for his action. It was an able paper; one might well rank it among state papers, and I suppose no one now, in these days, when so many of Altgeld's democratic theories are popular, would deny that his grounds were just and reasonable or that he had done what he could to right a great wrong, though he would regret that so great a soul should have permitted itself to mar the document by expressions of hatred of the judge who tried the case. But perhaps it is not so easy to be calm and impersonal in the midst of the moving event as it is given to others to be long afterward.

But whatever feelings he may have had, he was calm and serene ever after. I saw him as I was walking down to the Capitol the next morning. It was another of those June days which now and then are so perfect on the prairies. The governor was riding his horse — he was a gallant horseman — and he bowed and smiled that faint, wan smile of his, and drew up to the curb a moment. There was, of course, but one subject then, and I said:

"Well, the storm will break now."

"Oh, yes," he replied, with a not wholly convincing air of throwing off a care, "I was prepared for that. It was merely doing right."

I said something to him then to express my satisfaction in the great deed that was to be so willfully, recklessly, and cruelly misunderstood. I did not say all I might have said, for I felt that my opinions could mean so little to him. I have wished since that I had said more — said something, if that might have been my good fortune, that could perhaps have made a great burden a little easier for that brave and tortured soul. But he rode away with that wan, persistent smile. And the storm did break, and the abuse it rained upon him broke his heart; but I never again heard him mention the anarchist case.

BRAND WHITLOCK, *Forty Years of It*

226. Sam Jones Preaches the Golden Rule in Toledo

"Golden Rule" Jones was one of a number of reform mayors who, at the turn of the last century, attempted to end what Lincoln Steffens called "the shame of the cities." In this task he had the loyal support of young Brand Whitlock, who, on Jones's death, succeeded him as mayor of Toledo. Whitlock later achieved fame as a novelist, historian, and as minister to Belgium during the World War.

THERE was in Toledo one man who could sympathize with my attitude, and that was a man whose determination to accept literally and to try to practise the fundamental philosophy of Christianity had so startled and confounded the Christians everywhere that he at once became famous throughout Christendom as Golden Rule Jones. I had known of him only as the eccentric mayor of our city, and nearly every one whom I had met since my advent in Toledo spoke of him only to say something disparaging of him. The most charitable thing they said was that he was crazy. All the newspapers were against him and all the preachers. My own opinion, of course, could have been of no consequence, but I had learned in the case of Altgeld that almost universal condemnation of a man is to be examined before it is given entire credit. I do not mean to say that there was universal condemnation of Golden Rule Jones in Toledo in those days; it was simply that the institutional voices of society, the press and the pulpit, were thundering in condemnation of him. When the people came to vote for his re-election, his majorities were overwhelming, so that he used to say that everybody was against him but the people. But that is another story.

In those days I had not met him. I might have called at his office, to be sure, but I did not care to add to his burdens.

One day suddenly, as I was working on a story in my office, in he stepped with a startling, abrupt manner, wheeled a chair up to my desk, and sat down. He was a big Welshman with a sandy complexion and great hands that had worked hard in their time, and he had an eye that looked right into the center of your skull. He wore, and all the time he was in the room continued to wear, a large cream-colored slouch hat, and he had on the flowing cravat which for some inexplicable reason artists and social reformers wear, their affinity being due, no doubt, to the fact that the reformer must be an artist of a sort; else he could not dream his dreams. I was relieved, however, to find that Jones wore his hair clipped short, and there was still about him that practical air of the very practical businessman he had been before he became mayor. He had been such a practical business man that he was worth half a million, a fairly good fortune for our town; but he had not been in office very long before all the business men were down on him and saying that what the town needed was a business man for mayor, a statement that was destined to ring in my ears for a good many years.

They disliked him, of course, because he would not do just what they told him to — that being the meaning and purpose of a business man for mayor — but insisted that there were certain other people in the city who were entitled to some of his service and consideration; namely, the working people and the poor. The politicians and the preachers objected to him on the same grounds: the unpardonable sin being to express in any but a purely ideal and sentimental form sympathy for the workers or the poor. It seemed to be particularly exasperating that he was doing all this in the name of the Golden Rule, which was for the Sunday school; and they even went so far as to bring to town another Sam Jones, the Reverend Sam Jones, to conduct a revival and to defeat the Honorable Sam Jones. The Reverend Sam Jones had big meetings and said many clever things and many true ones, the truest among them being his epigram, "I am for the Golden Rule myself, up to a certain point, and then I want to take the shotgun and the club." I think that expression marked the difference between him and our Sam Jones, in whose philosophy there was no place at all for the shotgun or the club. The preachers were complaining that Mayor Jones was not using shotguns or at least clubs on the bad people in the town; I suppose that since their own persuasions had in a measure failed, they felt that the mayor with such instruments might have made the bad people look as if they had been converted, anyway.

It was our interest in the disowned, the outcast, the poor, and the criminal that drew us first together, that and the fact that we are gradually assuming the same attitude toward life.

He was always going down to the city prisons or to the workhouses and talking to the poor devils there quite as if he were one of them, which indeed he felt he was and as all of us are, if we only knew it. And he was working all the time to get them out of prison, and finally he and I entered into a little compact by which he paid the expenses incident to their trials — the fees for stenographers and that sort of thing — if I would look after their cases. Hard as the work was and sad as it was, and grievously as my law partners complained of the time it took and of its probable effect on business (since no one wished to be known as a criminal lawyer!), it did pay in the satisfaction there was in doing a little to comfort and console — and, what was so much more, to compel in one city, at least, a discussion of the grounds and the purpose of our institutions. For instance, if some poor girl were arrested and a jury trial were demanded for her and her case were given all the care and attention it would have received had she been some wealthy person, the police, when they found they could not convict, were apt to be a little more careful of the liberties of individuals; they began to have a little regard for human rights and for human life.

We completely broke up the old practice of arresting persons on suspicion and holding them at the will and pleasure of the police without any charge having been lodged against them; two or three trials before juries, the members of which could very easily be made to see, when it was pointed out to them a few times in the course of a three days' trial, that there is nothing more absurd than that policemen should make criminals of people merely by suspecting them and sending them to prison on that sole account, wrought a change. Jones managed to get himself fined for contempt one day, and he immediately turned the incident to his own advantage and made his point by drawing out his checkbook with a flourish, writing his check for the amount of his fine, and declaring that this proved his contention that the only crime our civilization punishes is the crime of being poor.

But he was most in his element when the police judge was absent, as he was now and then. In that exigency the law gave Jones as mayor the power to appoint the acting police judge, and when Jones did not go down and sit as magistrate himself he appointed me, and we always found some reason or other for letting all the culprits go. The foundations of society were shaken, of course, and the editorials and sermons were heavy with all the predictions of disaster. One might have supposed that the whole wonderful and beautiful fabric of civilization which man had been so long in rearing was to fall forever into the awful abyss because a few miserable outcasts had not been put in prison. But nothing happened after all; the poor *misérables* were back again in a few days and made to resume their hopeless rounds through the prison doors. But the policemen of Toledo had their clubs taken away from them, and they became human and learned to help people and not to hurt them if they could avoid it; and that police judge who once fined Jones became in time one of the leaders in our city of the new social movement that has marked the last decade in America. . . .

I regard it as Jones's supreme contribution to the thought of his time that by the mere force of his own original character and personality he compelled a discussion of fundamental principles of government. Toledo today is a community which has a wider acquaintance with all the abstract principles of social relations than any other city in the land — or in the world, since when one ventures into generalities one might as well make them as sweeping as one can.

Jones's other great contribution to the science of municipal government was that of nonpartisanship in local affairs. That is the way he used to express it; what he meant was that the issues of national politics must not be permitted to obtrude themselves into municipal campaigns and that what divisions there are should be confined to local issues. There is, of course, in our cities, as in our land or any land, only one issue, that which is presented by the conflict of the aristocratic or plutocratic spirit and the spirit of democracy.

Jones used to herald himself as a man without a party, but he was a great democrat, the most fundamental I ever knew or imagined; he summed up in himself, as no other figure in our time since Lincoln, all that the democratic spirit is and hopes to be. Perhaps in this characterization I seem to behold his figure larger than it was in relation to the whole mass, but while his work may appear at first glance local, it was really general and universal. No one can estimate the peculiar and lively forces of such a personality; certainly no one can presume to limit his influence, for such a spirit is illimitable and irresistible.

He was elected in that last campaign for the fourth time, but he did not live very long. When he died the only wounds he left in human hearts were because he was no more. They understood him at last, those who had scoffed and sneered and abused and vilified; and I who had had the immense privilege of his friendship and thought I knew him — when I stood that July afternoon, on the veranda of his home, beside his bier to speak at his funeral and looked out over the thousands who were gathered on the wide lawn before his home — I realized that I too had not wholly understood him.

I know not how many thousands were there; they were standing on the lawns in a mass that extended across the street and into the yards on the farther side. Down to the corner and into the side streets they were packed, and they stood in long lines all the way out to the cemetery. In that crowd there were all sorts of that one sort he knew as humanity without distinction — judges and women of prominence and women whom he alone would have included in humanity; there were thieves and prizefighters — and they all stood there with the tears streaming down their faces.

BRAND WHITLOCK, Forty Years of It

227. Robert M. La Follette Stops a Railroad Land Grab

Altogether a generous Congress gave to railroads something over one hundred million acres of public lands, and the States added fifty million more. These princely gifts did not, however, satisfy the roads; the spectacle of rich timber and mineral lands excited their continued cupidity and inspired repeated efforts to obtain from Congress additional grants. With men like Senators Sawyer and Payne this was easy enough. Young Robert La Follette who took his seat in the lower House in 1885 and served there three terms had different notions of public morality, however, and made things difficult for the Old Guard and for the railroads.

A VOLUMINOUS bill was before the Committee on Indian Affairs [1886] providing for the opening for settlement of eleven million acres of the Sioux Indian Reservation in Dakota. As it was being read in committee, we came to a provision to ratify an agreement made by the Chicago, Milwaukee and St. Paul and Chicago and Northwestern Railroads with the Indians for rights of way through the reservation. My previous study of documents on Indian affairs here became useful. I discovered that in addition to the rights of way one company was given the exclusive right to acquire seven hundred and fifteen acres and the other eight hundred and twenty-eight acres of land, ostensibly for terminal facilities, and that each road was to have at intervals of every ten miles an additional hundred and sixty acres of land, presumably for station privileges. I stopped the reading at this point.

"This looks to me like a town-site job," I said. "I cannot see why these railroads should have so much more land than is necessary to use directly in connection with their business as common carriers."

I had no sooner uttered these words than the member of the committee sitting upon my right nudged me and whispered: "Bob, you don't want to interfere with that provision. *Those are your home corporations.*"

But I did interfere and had the paragraphs laid over, and we adjourned the session of the committee at twelve o'clock to attend the meeting of the House. I had not been in my seat half an hour when a page announced that Senator Sawyer wanted to see me. I found him waiting for me near the cloakroom. We sat on a settee and talked of general matters for some time. As the senator rose to go he said, apparently as an afterthought:

"Oh, say, La Follette, your committee will have coming up before long the Sioux Indian bill. There is a provision in it for our folks up in Wisconsin, the Northwestern and St. Paul Railroads. I wish you'd look after it."

"Senator Sawyer," I said, "we have already reached that provision in the bill, and I am preparing an amendment to it. I don't think it's right."

"Is that so," said the Senator, in apparent surprise. "Come and sit down and let's talk it over."

We argued for an hour, Sawyer presenting every point in favor of granting the railroads the prior right to acquire all the land they wanted. This was the first time Sawyer had directly and personally attempted to influence me in a matter of legislation. I was respectful to him but could not yield to his view. I told him that I thought it right to permit the railroads to acquire the land necessary for rights of way, yards, tracks, sidings, depots, shops, roundhouses, and indeed all they needed solely for transportation purposes, and should favor such a provision. But as framed, the provision plainly allowed them to get prior and exclusive rights to much more land for townsite and other speculative uses; that besides, they were not required to build their lines within any definite time and might hold the land to the exclusion of all others indefinitely without turning a sod or laying a rail; that it was unjust to the Indians and the public, and I could not support it. He was not ill-tempered and said he would see me again about it.

Forty-eight hours later Henry C. Payne arrived in Washington. He was secretary of the Republican State Central Committee, political manager of the Wisconsin machine, lobbyist for the St. Paul Railroad and the beef trust, and had the backing of the important corporate interests of the state. Obviously he had been summoned to Washington by Sawyer.

Everybody was taught to believe that Payne had some occult and mysterious power as a political manager and that when he said a thing would happen in politics or legislation it always did happen. He was a perfect ideal of that union of private business and politics that carried on its face apparent devotion to the public interest. A fine head and figure, meditative, introspective eyes, a quiet, clearcut, convincing way of stating his views, he was certainly the most accomplished railroad lobbyist I ever saw. His intimate friendship and business relation with the chairman of the Democratic State

Central Committee in Wisconsin came to be one of the best-known amenities in the politics of the day in that state. It was said that there was a well-worn pathway between the back doors of their private offices.

Well, Sawyer and Payne came to see me night after night for a week or more. Payne was rather stiff and harsh, but Sawyer was fatherly — much like a parent reasoning with a wayward child.

Nils P. Haugen, congressman from the tenth district, occupied a seat near me. One day he said:

"I want to tell you something. I saw Payne last night at the Ebbitt House, and he went for you. He said: 'La Follette is a crank; if he thinks he can buck a railroad company with five thousand miles of line, he'll find out his mistake. We'll take care of him when the time comes.'"

Payne was as good as his word. He fought me ever afterward.

But I got my amendment through, allowing the railroad to acquire the necessary right of way, twenty acres of land for stations, and only such additional land as the Secretary of the Interior should find to be a necessary aid to transportation, prohibiting the use or sale of any of said lands for town-site or other purposes, and providing that each of said roads should within three years locate, construct, and operate their lines or forfeit the lands so acquired to the government.

ROBERT M. LA FOLLETTE, Autobiography

228. A Railroad Lobby Licks Governor La Follette

In 1890 La Follette was retired from Congress, and turned at once to the task of cleaning up his own state, Wisconsin. After ten years of incessant labor he was elected to the governorship and proceeded to make Wisconsin the best governed state in the Union, and to write upon the statute books a body of progressive social legislation that profoundly influenced the course of national politics. The going, however, was not always easy, and from time to time he suffered such setbacks as are

here recounted. As a national figure, La Follette ranks with Bryan,
Wilson, and Theodore Roosevelt, and he was the only one of that
group to have founded a political dynasty.

IN ORDER to make very clear the methods employed, I shall here relate in detail the stories of several of the cases which came directly under my own observation [1901–1903]. I shall withhold the real names of the senators and assemblymen concerned because many of them were the victims of forces and temptations far greater than they could resist. If I could also give the names of the men really responsible for the corruption, bribery, and debauchery — the men higher up, the men behind the lobbyists — I would do it without hesitation.

How did the lobby get them? Various ways. There was Senator A. He was a poor fellow from a northern district, a lawyer without much practice — rather a weak fellow. I can't remember just on what bill it was, but they got him. When he returned to his district after the session he built an expensive home, to the amazement of all his friends, and then came down to Washington to a Federal position.

We depended on Senator B. He made a statement that he could be relied upon to support the direct primary bill. We figured him on our list until about the time that Spooner visited Madison and *he* got away. Senator C. was another man we had counted upon as one of the old reliables in the movement. He was an Irishman and a good talker and debater. They finally got him too. I remember he came to me one night and said:

"Well, I don't know but what I'm going to disappoint you in my vote on the direct primary bill."

I could not at first think of a word to say — it was a staggering blow.

"Why, C.," I said finally, "if you were to go over to the other side on these measures, it would seem to me like the end of everything. You couldn't do a thing like that. You have been one of the pillars of the movement."

I don't believe I tried to reason with him. It simply was not a case for argument. There was only one side to it, for he himself had been one of our ablest speakers on the stump in favor of the direct primary.

Well, he voted against us, and it is significant that a few months after the legislature adjourned he was appointed to a Federal office and is, I believe, still in the service.

Another instance was that of Assemblyman D., who had been for some time quite an active supporter of the reform movement. He was a small business man and came to the legislature from a county in which I was personally very strong. When the committees were being formed, he was counted so much the friend of our measures that he was placed upon one of the most important committees.

He stood with us in the vote on direct primaries, but some little time after that, Assemblyman E., who was one of our leaders in the assembly, came into my office one morning. E. was a fine young fellow and regarded as thoroughly reliable. He was often in the executive office and I trusted him absolutely. Upon the occasion to which I refer he said:

"Governor, I have changed my boarding place" — he had been boarding with some private family, I think. "I have moved over to the Park Hotel."

The Park Hotel was the principal hotel in Madison and the head-quarters of all the lobbyists. I was somewhat surprised and asked him why he had moved.

"Well," he said, "I propose to be where I can watch the game that these lobbyists are playing. I am satisfied that they are working on some of our weak members, and I am going right into their camp to see what they are doing."

Not long after that he came to me and said:

"How much do you know about D.? I notice him about the Park Hotel a great deal talking with lobbyists. There's something about it that I don't like."

Finally in one of his talks about D. he said:

"You want to look out for D.; they've got him; you will find him going back on railroad taxation."

I was disturbed about it. We were up pretty close, as I remember it, to final committee action on the bill. I therefore telephoned to one of the leading bankers in the town in which D. lived and asked him to come to Madison. This banker had been a university chum of mine — a man of the highest standing and a constant and loyal supporter of the Progressive movement. He came to Madison and brought with him a prominent merchant of the town, but before they could reach D. the vote had been taken and the result was so close that it was found that D. had cast the decisive vote against the bill. The banker and his friends took D. into a room in the Capitol and had a very earnest talk with him. They told him he would never be able to make the people believe that he didn't have the money of the railroads in his pocket for his betrayal of our cause. He never got back to the legislature.

A few days later — when this same bill was before the assembly — we were to have another and still worse shock. I have said that we trusted E. implicitly. He was one of the most enthusiastic men we had, and being a high-spirited, energetic young fellow, he was of great assistance in our fights. Whenever we gathered a little group of the members in the executive office to talk over any critical situation in the legislature, E. was always with us. He was an active young manufacturer. He often talked with us about his business. I think he had some special machine which enabled him to make his product more cheaply than other manufacturers.

One day Ray Stevens came into my office and said: "Governor, I wish you would send up and ask E. to come down here. I don't just like the way he talks."

"Why," I said, "Ray, there can't be anything wrong with E." Then I began to think that he had not been in to see me for three or four days. "Well," I said, "I will send up."

When he came through the door he did not meet me with his characteristic frankness. But I greeted him exactly as usual and said, "E., I want to have a little talk with you." I moved my chair right up to his, placed my hands on his knees and looked him in the eye a moment before I spoke. Then I asked, "E., what's the matter?"

The tears started in his eyes, and the response came at once.

"Governor, I can't help it. I've got to vote against the railroad taxation bill." After a moment he added: "I haven't slept any for two or three nights. I have walked the floor. I have thought of resigning and going home."

"Tell me all about it, E.," I said.

"Well," he replied, "you know that all I have in the world I have put into that factory of mine. I have told you about how proud I was of the thing. Now," he said, "this railroad lobby tells me that if I vote for that railroad taxation bill they will ruin me in business. They can take away everything I've got. They have threatened to give my competitors advantages over me in railroad rates that will offset any advantages I have made with my new machinery. Now I can't beggar my family. I have a wife and babies."

I said: "E., you can't do this wrong. You can't violate your conscience." I talked to him quite a bit. He got up and walked the floor. He said he would always be for our measures, but he could not risk being driven to the wall. And then he left the office.

A few minutes before the roll call on the bill, E., who sat next to Lenroot, turned to him and said, "Lenroot, in five minutes I am going to violate my oath of office." Lenroot was shocked and said, "What do you mean?" He replied: "It is a question between my honor and my bread and butter, and I propose to vote for my bread and butter." And he voted against the bill.

ROBERT M. LA FOLLETTE, Autobiography

229. Judge Lindsey Saves Boys in the Children's Court

The growth of great cities, with slums, crime, and vice, enormously complicated the problem of juvenile delinquency. When Ben Lindsey came to the bench, in 1900, boys of fourteen or fifteen were tried by the same laws as were applied to adults. When convicted, the boys were jailed with adult prisoners and thus all too often schooled in crime. Judge Lindsey determined to remedy this situation, and the success of the experiment which he here describes went far to secure reforms in the treatment of child offenders throughout the country.

I HAD begun merely with a sympathy for children and a conviction that our laws against crime were as inapplicable to children as they would be to idiots. I soon realized that not only our laws but our whole system of criminal procedure was wrong. It was based upon fear, and fear, with children as with their elders, is the father of lies. I found that when a boy was brought before me, I could do nothing with him until I had taken the fear out of his heart; but once I had got rid of that fear, I found — to my own amazement — that I could do anything with him. I could do things that seemed miraculous, especially to the police, who seldom tried anything but abuse and curses, and the more or less refined brutalities of the sweat box and the third degree. I learned that instead of fear we must use sympathy, but without cant, without hypocrisy, and without sentimentalism. We must first convince the boy that we were his friends, but the determined enemies of his misdeeds; that we wished to help him to do right, but could do nothing for him if he persisted in doing wrong. We had to encourage him to confess his wrongdoing, teach him wherein it had been wrongdoing, and strengthen him to do right thereafter.

Take, for example, the case of Lee Martin and his river-front gang. He was a boy burglar, a sneak thief, a pickpocket, a jail breaker, and a tramp; and his gang was known to the newspapers as the most desperate band of young criminals in Denver. Lee Martin and another member of the gang named Jack Heimel were one night caught in a drugstore into which they had broken, and when I went to see them in jail, I found them strapped to the benches in their cells, bruised and battered from an interview with the police, in which they had been punished for refusing to snitch on their fellow members of the gang. This was before the passage of our juvenile court laws, and I wished to have an opportunity to try what I could do with these two boys. The police did not wish me to have them.

I told the boys that I intended to try to help them, and they sneered at me. I told them that I thought they had not been given a square deal — which was true — but they did not respond. I used what tact and sympathy I could to draw them out and get their side of the story of their war with society, but it took me something like a month of frequent visits to get them to trust me and to believe that I wished to help them. In the end I was successful. I got their story — a story too long to repeat here; but it proved to me that the boys had been as much sinned against as sinning. They had begun as irresponsible little savages, and they had been made desperate young criminals. Their parents had failed to civilize them, and the school and the church had never had an opportunity to try. I resolved to see if it was too late to begin.

The police captain assured me that it was. "You can't baby Lee Martin," he said. "He's been in jail thirteen times, and it hasn't done him any good."

"Well, I'd like to see what we can do," I replied. "If we fail, we'll still have twelve times the best of the jail. It has cost this city, in officers' fees alone, over a thousand dollars to make a criminal of him. Let us see how much it will cost to turn him into an honest boy."

The officer reeled off a long list of Martin's offenses, and I retorted by showing a typewritten record of them, twice as long. "How in the world did you get 'em, Judge?" he said. "We couldn't *sweat* 'em out of him."

After a week of such argument we got the case referred to our court. The boys were tried, and of course their guilt was clear. I sent them back to the jail under suspended sentence and thought the matter over.

One night I had them brought to my chambers under guard, and after a talk with Heimel I sent him and the guard away and concentrated on Martin. I decided to put my influence over him to the test. I told him of the fight I was making for him, showed him how I had been spending all my spare time trying to straighten things out for him and Heimel, and warned him that the police did not believe I could succeed. "Now, Lee," I said "you can run away if you want to and prove me a liar to the cops. But I want to help you, and I want you to stand by me. I want you to trust me, and I want you to go back to the jail there and let me do the best I can."

He went. And he went alone — unguarded.

Then I put him and Heimel on probation, and in a few days they came to see me and brought Red Mike and Tommie Green, of the river-front gang. I talked to them about their offenses against the law and told them I wanted to help them do what was right and live honest lives, unpersecuted by the police; and I praised Martin for his moral strength in going back to the jail alone. Before they left me, Red and Tommie had snitched on themselves, and I had two new probationers. One by one the others followed until I had all seven members of the gang on my list, all confessed wrongdoers pledged to give up crime and make an honest effort to be straight. Six of the seven are today honest young workmen; Lee Martin failed, after a long and plucky fight, and is now in the penitentiary. The river-front gang, to my knowledge, has been responsible for the reformation of thirty boys in Denver; and Lee Martin in his time did more to discourage crime than any policeman in the city.

For example: one day a boy — whom I knew — stole a pocketbook from a woman in a department store. I told Lee that something ought to be done for that boy, and Lee brought him to me — from a cheap theater where he had been treating the gang. We worked on him together, and we straightened him up. He has since become a trusted employee in the very store in which he stole the pocketbook.

In another instance I sent Lee after a boy, arrested for stealing a watch, who had sawed his way out of jail and had not been recaptured by the police. Lee got him — in El Paso — and brought him to me. After a talk with him I gave him a twenty-dollar bill and sent him alone, unshadowed, to redeem the watch, which he had pawned for three dollars. He returned with the watch and the seventeen dollars change. Then I persuaded him to return the watch to the man from whom he had stolen it, and of course, the prosecution against him was dropped. We have never since had a complaint against that boy, although he had been one of the worst boy thieves in the city.

Another lesson about boys I learned from little Mickey when I was investigating his charge that the jailer had beaten him. The jailer said: "Some o' those kids broke a window in there, and when I asked Mickey who it was he said he didn't know. O' course he knew. D'you think I'm goin' to have kids lie to me?" A police commissioner who was present turned to Mickey. "Mickey," he said, "why did you lie?" Mickey faced us in his rags. "Say," he asked, "do yuh t'ink a fullah ought to snitch on a kid?" And the way he asked it made me ashamed of myself. Here was a quality of loyalty that we should be fostering in him instead of trying to crush it out of him. It was the beginning, in the boy, of that feeling of responsibility to his fellows on which society is founded. Thereafter no child brought before our court was ever urged to turn state's evidence against his partners in crime — much less rewarded for doing so or punished for refusing to do so. Each was encouraged to snitch on himself and himself only.

Still another lesson I learned from an inveterate little runaway named Harry. After several attempts to reform him I sentenced him to the Industrial School in Golden; and this being before the days of the Detention School, he was returned to the jail until a sheriff could take him up. That night the jailer telephoned me that Harry was in hysterics, screaming in his cell and calling wildly to me to help him. "You'd better come down, Judge," the jailer said, "an' see if you can get him quiet." I went to the jail. Inside, the steel doors were opened and the steel bolts withdrawn, one by one, with a portentous clanking and grating. It was as if we were about to penetrate to some awful dungeon in which a murderous giant was penned — so formidable were the iron obstacles that were swung back before us and clashed shut on our heels. And when I reached at the end of a guarded corridor the barred door of Harry's cell, there, in the dim glow of a light overhead, the boy lay asleep on the floor, his round little legs drawn up, his head pillowed on his tiny arm, his baby face pale under the prison lamp. The sight was so pitifully ridiculous that I choked up at it. It seemed such a folly — such a cruel folly — to lock up a child in such a place of lonely terror.

The jailer opened the cell door for me, and I began to raise the boy to put him on his prison stretcher. His head fell back over my arm like an infant's. He woke with a start and clutched me in a return of the hysterical fear that had been mercifully forgotten in sleep. And then when he recognized me, "Judge," he pleaded, "Judge, gi' me another chance. I'll be good, Judge! Just once — once more, Judge!" I had to sit down beside him on the floor and try to reassure him.

I tried to be stern with him. I told him that I had trusted him and trusted him again and again, and he had failed me every time. I explained that we were sending him to the Industrial School for his own good, to make a strong boy of him; that he was weak, untrustworthy. "I can help you, Harry," I said. "But you've got to carry yourself. If I let boys go when they do bad things, I'll lose my job.

The people'll get another judge in my place to punish boys if *I* don't do it. I can't let you go."

We went over it and over it, and at last I thought I had him feeling more resigned and cheerful and I got up to leave him. But when I turned to the door, he fell on his knees before me, and stretching out his little arms to me, his face distorted with tears, he cried: "Judge! Judge! If you let me go, *I'll never* get you into trouble again!"

I had him! It was the voice of loyalty. "Mac," I said to the jailer, "this boy goes with me. I'll write an order for his release."

I took him to his home that night, but his mother did not wish to have him back. Her husband had deserted her; she worked all day in a hotel kitchen; she could not take proper care of her boy, and she was afraid that he would be killed on some of his long bumming trips in the freight cars. But she finally consented to give him another trial, and this time he stuck. "Judge," she told me long afterward, "I asked Harry the other day how it was he was so good for *you* when he wouldn't do it for me or the policeman. And he says: 'Well, Maw, you see, if I gets bad agin, the judge he'll lose his job. I've got to stay with him 'cause he stayed with me.'" I have used that appeal to loyalty hundreds of times since in our work with the boys, and it is almost infallibly successful.

I saw too, from Harry's case, that if we were to reform children we must help parents who were unable to keep a close watch on their children. And nowadays if one of our probationers fails to arrive at school the teacher is required to telephone the Juvenile Court immediately, and a probation officer starts out at once to find the delinquent. Every two weeks, on report day, the probationers must bring us reports on their behavior from the school, the home, and the neighborhood; and by praising those who have good reports and censuring those who have bad ones, we are not only able to prevent wrongdoing but to encourage right doing. We impress on the children the need of doing right because it *is* right, because it hurts to do wrong, because only weak kids do wrong—*not* because wrong is punished; for *that* teaching, I believe, is the great error of our ethics. The fear of punishment, I find, makes weak children liars and hypocrites; and with strong ones it adds to the entice· ment of evil all the proverbial sweetness of forbidden fruit.

One evening a probationer brought four boys to my chambers with the announcement that they wished to snitch on themselves. They had been stealing bicycles — making a regular practice of it — and they had five such thefts to their discredit. I investigated their story and found it to be true. The police had a complete record of the thefts, and I tried — and got the boys to try — to recover the wheels, but we could not; they had been sold and resold and quite lost track of. A police officer with whom I consulted insisted that the boys should be arrested and sentenced to jail, and while I listened to him it dawned upon me what the difference was between the criminal procedure and the methods of our court. "Officer," I said, "you are trying to save bicycles. I am trying to save boys. The boys are more important than the bicycles. And if we can save the boys we can save bicycles in the future that we could not save in the past." I put the boys on probation with the understanding that if they did not live up to their new resolve to be honest, I should be allowed to use their confessions against them. Not one of them failed me. The court helped them to get work and they are honest and useful members of society today.

In one year two hundred and one boys came in this way to our court, voluntarily, and confessed their wrongdoing, and promised to cut it out.

One evening after I had adjourned court and the room had emptied, I saw a youngster sitting in a chair by the rear wall, apparently forgotten by his parents. He was no bigger than a baby. I sent the bailiff to ask him if he knew his name or address. He came up to the bench — to my chair on the platform — and hiding his face against my shoulder, he began to cry. He had been "swipin' things," he said, and wanted to "cut it out." And would I give him a chance — as I had another boy he knew? We gave him a chance. He reported regularly for more than a year and proved to be an honest, sturdy boy. Another boy who came to my chambers with a similar confession was so small that I said to him: "You're a mighty little boy. How did you find your way down here?" "Well," he replied, "'most every kid I seed knew the way." I found that nearly all these boys were members of neighborhood gangs, that some member of the gang had been in court, had gone back to the gang with the lessons we had tried to teach him, and had used his influence to send the other boys to us. We began to reach for this gang spirit and to turn it to our uses instead of against us, and we succeeded there too in time. I could relate scores of stories that came to us of how the gangs threatened to beat up some young delinquent if he did not play square with the judge. We taught the boys who had been doing wrong that they should try to overcome the evil they had done by now doing something good, and they practised that doctrine by persuading their companions to desist from some mischief they had planned.

I even had a little newsboy come to me with the assurance that if I wanted the street kids to stop shooting craps, I need only go down and tell them so. "Dere ain't a kid in de whole push," he said, "dat won't go down the line wit' yuh, Judge. De cops can't make 'em stop craps, but I bet dey'd do it fer *you*." I did not try it. I did not believe that I could permanently stop street boys shooting craps; it is as natural for them to gamble as for schoolboys to play marbles. But I rejoiced in the loyalty, the spirit of co-operation, shown by these street gamins. Therein lies the success of the Juvenile Court.

JUDGE BEN B. LINDSEY, The Beast

XXXIII

Modern Politics

230. The Populists Defy the Old Parties

Hard times on the farms in the late eighties aroused a nationwide revolt which found expression first in the Farmer's Alliances and later in the Populist Party. That party made its first bid for support in 1892 when its candidate, General James B. Weaver, polled over a million votes; four years later it was absorbed by the Democratic Party. The Populist platform of 1892 was looked upon, at the time, as dangerously radical, but most of its proposals have since been enacted into law. The preamble to that platform was written by Ignatius Donnelly of Minnesota, one of the most colorful politicians of his generation.

ASSEMBLED upon the one hundred and sixteenth anniversary of the Declaration of Independence [1892], the People's Party of America, in their first national convention, invoking upon their action the blessing of Almighty God, put forth in the name and on behalf of the people of this country the following preamble and declaration of principles:

PREAMBLE

The conditions which surround us best justify our co-operation; we meet in the midst of a nation brought to the verge of moral, political, and material ruin. Corruption dominates the ballot box, the legislatures, the Congress, and touches even the ermine of the bench. The people are demoralized; most of the states have been compelled to isolate the voters at the polling places to prevent universal intimidation and bribery. The newspapers are largely subsidized or muzzled, public opinion silenced, business prostrated, homes covered with mortgages, labor impoverished, and the land concentrating in the hands of capitalists. The urban workmen are denied the right to organize for self-protection, imported pauperized labor beats down their wages, a hireling standing army, unrecognized by our laws, is established to shoot them down, and they are rapidly degenerating into European conditions. The fruits of the toil of millions are boldly stolen to build up colossal fortunes for a few, unprecedented in the history of mankind; and the possessors of these in turn despise the Republic and endanger liberty. From the same prolific womb of governmental injustice we breed the two great classes — tramps and millionaires. . . .

We have witnessed for more than a quarter of a century the struggles of the two great political parties for power and plunder, while grievous wrongs have been inflicted upon the suffering people. We charge that the controlling influences dominating both these parties have permitted the existing dreadful conditions to develop without serious effort to prevent or restrain them. Neither do they now promise us any substantial reform. They have agreed together to ignore in the coming campaign every issue but one. They propose to drown the outcries of a plundered people with the uproar of a sham battle over the tariff so that capitalists, corporations, national banks, rings, trusts, watered stock, the demonetization of silver, and the oppressions of the usurers may all be lost sight of. They propose to sacrifice our homes, lives, and children on the altar of mammon; to destroy the multitude in order to secure corruption funds from the millionaires.

Assembled on the anniversary of the birthday of the nation and filled with the spirit of the grand general and chief who established our independence, we seek to restore the government of the Republic to the hands of the plain people, with which class it originated. We assert our purposes to be identical with the purposes of the national Constitution; to form a more perfect union and establish justice, insure domestic tranquillity, provide for the common defense, promote the general welfare, and secure the blessings of liberty for ourselves and our posterity.

We declare that this Republic can only endure as a free government while built upon the love of the people for each other and for the nation; that it cannot be pinned together by bayonets; that the Civil War is over, and that every passion and resentment which grew out of it must die with it, and that we must be in fact, as we are in name, one united brotherhood of free men.

Our country finds itself confronted by conditions for which there is no precedent in the history of the world; our annual agricultural production amounts to billions of dollars in value, which must, within a few weeks or months, be exchanged for billions of dollars' worth of commodities consumed in their production; the existing currency supply is wholly inadequate to make this exchange; the results are falling prices, the formation of combines and rings, the impoverishment of the producing class. We pledge ourselves that if given power we will labor to correct these evils by wise and reasonable legislation in accordance with the terms of our platform.

We believe that the power of government — in other words, of the people — should be expanded (as in the case of the postal service) as rapidly and as far as the good sense of an intelligent people and the teachings of experience shall justify, to the end that oppression, injustice, and poverty shall eventually cease in the land.

While our sympathies as a party of reform are naturally upon the side of every proposition which will tend to make men intelligent, virtuous, and temperate, we nevertheless regard these questions, important as they are, as secondary to the great issues now pressing for solution, and upon which not only our individual prosperity but the very existence of free institutions depend; and we ask all men to first help us to determine whether we are to have a republic to administer before we differ as to the conditions upon which it is to be administered, believing that the forces of reform this day organized will never cease to move forward until every wrong is righted and equal rights and equal privileges securely established for all the men and women of this country.

Populist Party Platform, 1892

231. "Crucify Mankind upon a Cross of Gold"

In 1896 the great issue before the American people was the "money question." The Republican Party had committed itself to the gold standard, but the Democrats, under the leadership of men like "Silver Dick" Bland and young William Jennings Bryan broke away from the Cleveland leadership and endorsed free silver. The "Cross of Gold" speech, delivered before the Democratic Convention at Chicago, insured the adoption of a silver platform by that party, but it did more: it insured the nomination of Bryan himself as the party's candidate for the Presidency. The "Cross of Gold" speech is an excellent example of the eloquence for which he was famous.

I WOULD be presumptuous, indeed, to present myself against the distinguished gentlemen to whom you have listened if this were a mere measuring of abilities; but this is not a contest between persons. The humblest citizen in all the land, when clad in the armor of a righteous cause, is stronger than all the hosts of error. I come to speak to you in defense of a cause as holy as the cause of liberty — the cause of humanity. . . .

Never before in the history of this country has there been witnessed such a contest as that through which we have just passed. Never before in the history of American politics has a great issue been fought out as this issue has been, by the voters of a great party. On the fourth of March, 1893, a few Democrats, most of them members of Congress, issued an address to the Democrats of the nation, asserting that the money question was the paramount issue of the hour; declaring that a majority of the Democratic party had the right to control the action of the party on this paramount issue; and concluding with the request that the believers in the free coinage of silver in the Democratic party should organize, take charge of, and control the policy of the Democratic party. Three months later, at Memphis, an organization was perfected, and the silver Democrats went forth openly and courageously proclaiming their belief and declaring that if successful they would crystallize into a platform the declaration which they had made. Then began the struggle. With a zeal approaching the zeal which inspired the Crusaders who followed Peter the Hermit, our silver Democrats went forth from victory unto victory until they are now assembled, not to discuss, not to debate, but to enter up the judgment already rendered by the plain people of this country. In this contest brother has been arrayed against brother, father against son. The warmest ties of love, acquaintance, and association have been disregarded; old leaders have been cast aside when they have refused to give expression to the sentiments of those whom they would lead, and new leaders have sprung up to give direction to this cause of truth. Thus has the contest been waged, and we have assembled here under as binding and solemn instructions as were ever imposed upon representatives of the people. . . .

When you [turning to the gold delegates] come before us and tell us that we are about to disturb your business interests, we reply that you have disturbed our business interests by your course.

We say to you that you have made the definition of a business man too limited in its application. The man who is employed for wages is as much a business man as his employer; the attorney in a country town is as much a business man as the corporation counsel in a great metropolis; the merchant at the crossroads store is as much a business man as the merchant of New York; the farmer who goes forth in the morning and toils all day, who begins in the spring and toils all summer, and who by the application of brain and muscle to the natural resources of the country creates wealth, is as much a business man as the man who goes upon the Board of Trade and bets upon the price of grain; the miners who go down a thousand feet into the earth or climb two thousand feet upon the cliffs and bring forth from their hiding places the precious metals to be poured into the channels of trade are as much business men as the few financial magnates who, in a back room, corner the money of the world. We come to speak of this broader class of business men.

Ah, my friends, we say not one word against those who live upon the Atlantic coast, but the hardy pioneers who have braved all the dangers of the wilderness, who have made the desert to bloom as the rose — the pioneers away out there [pointing to the west] who rear their children near to Nature's heart, where they can mingle their voices with the voices of the birds — out there where they have erected schoolhouses for the education of their young, churches where they praise their Creator, and cemeteries where rest the ashes of their dead — these people, we say, are as deserving of the consideration of our party as any people in this country. It is for these that we speak. We do not come as aggressors. Our war is not a war of conquest; we are fighting in the defense of our homes, our families, and posterity. We have petitioned, and our petitions have been scorned; we have entreated, and our entreaties have been disregarded; we have begged, and they have mocked when our calamity came. We beg no longer; we entreat no more; we petition no more. We defy them! . . .

And now, my friends, let me come to the paramount issue. If they ask us why it is that we say more on the money question than we say upon the tariff question, I reply that if protection has slain its thousands the gold standard has slain its tens of thousands. If they ask us why we do not embody in our platforms all the things that we believe in, we reply that when we have restored the money of the Constitution, all other necessary reform will be possible; but that until this is done, there is no other reform that can be accomplished.

Why is it that within three months such a change has come over the country? Three months ago when it was confidently asserted that those who believed in the gold standard would frame our platform and nominate our candidates, even the advocates of the gold standard did not think that we could elect a President. And they had good reason for their doubt, because there is scarcely a state here today asking for the gold standard which is not in the absolute control of the Republican party. But note the change. Mr. McKinley was nominated at St. Louis upon a platform which declared for the maintenance of the gold standard until it can be changed into bimetallism by international agreement. Mr. McKinley was the most popular man among the Republicans, and three months ago everybody in the Republican party prophesied his election. How is it today? Why, the man who was once pleased to think that he looked like Napoleon — that man shudders today when he remembers that he was nominated on the anniversary of the battle of Waterloo.

Not only that, but as he listens he can hear with ever-increasing distinctness the sound of the waves as they beat upon the lonely shores of St. Helena.

Why this change? Ah, my friends, is not the reason for the change evident to any one who will look at the matter? No private character however pure, no personal popularity however great, can protect from the avenging wrath of an indignant people a man who will declare that he is in favor of fastening the gold standard upon this country or who is willing to surrender the right of self-government and place the legislative control of our affairs in the hands of foreign potentates and powers. . . .

You come to us and tell us that the great cities are in favor of the gold standard; we reply that the great cities rest upon our broad and fertile prairies. Burn down your cities and leave our farms, and your cities will spring up again as if by magic; but destroy our farms, and the grass will grow in the streets of every city in the country.

My friends, we declare that this nation is able to legislate for its own people on every question, without waiting for the aid or consent of any other nation on earth; and upon that issue we expect to carry every state in the Union. I shall not slander the inhabitants of the fair state of Massachusetts nor the inhabitants of the state of New York by saying that, when they are confronted with the proposition, they will declare that this nation is not able to attend to its own business. It is the issue of 1776 over again. Our ancestors when but three million in number had the courage to declare their political independence of every other nation; shall we their descendants, when we have grown to seventy millions, declare that we are less independent than our forefathers?

No, my friends, that will never be the verdict of our people. Therefore we care not upon what lines the battle is fought. If they say bimetallism is good but that we cannot have it until other nations help us, we reply that instead of having a gold standard because England has, we will restore bimetallism and then let England have bimetallism because the United States has it. If they dare to come out in the open field and defend the gold standard as a good thing, we will fight them to the uttermost. Having behind us the producing masses of this nation and the world, supported by the commercial interests, the laboring interests, and the toilers everywhere, we will answer their demand for a gold standard by saying to them: You shall not press down upon the brow of labor this crown of thorns, you shall not crucify mankind upon a cross of gold.

W. J. BRYAN, Speech in the Democratic Convention, 1896

232. W. J. Bryan Campaigns in the Rain

Bryan's 1896 campaign was the most brilliant in the history of American politics, but his superb oratorical talents were not sufficient to overcome the handicaps under which he labored. His defeat, however, did not cost him leadership of his party. He was renominated for the Presidency in 1900 and again in 1908, and he dominated the convention of 1912. G. W. Steevens was an Englishman who toured the United States in 1896 and wrote one of the more intelligent books about it.

IN THE course of his pilgrimage Bryan arrived yesterday (September 19) at Washington. When I walked down to the station five minutes before his train was due I found it dense with men and women, white, whitey-brown, and black, who overflowed into the streets. In a torrid wind that fanned them lazily off the baked bricks and pavements they waited with a crowd's usual mixture of expectancy and listlessness. A large force of police, on foot and mounted, kept the street clear; by way of precaution they had brought a white and gray van which I take to be the American equivalent of Black Maria. "I suppose they are going to take Bryan away in that," remarked a Republican cynic. The police of this country have not the best of reputations for tact, but these Washington men did their duty admirably. "Why don't ye get on to the sidewalk?" pleaded a persuasive mounted Irishman. "Ye'll have to do ut; why don't ye do ut when I tell ye? Ye'll all see him." "See him for four years yet," sang out a gentleman with a twelve-inch crimson confession of Democracy streaming from his coat. In the moments of waiting there trickled along a discussion of the usual silver question. This being the political capital of the Union, the inhabitants are dis franchised, and the mass of them appear to know and care very little about the subject. Most of them seem to think that if Bryan gets in they will somehow get more silver and if McKinley gets in they will somehow get some gold — and if all I hear of electoral methods is true their expectation is not wholly unwarranted. "I'm for gold," said a yellow man; "I don't want fifty cents instead of a dollar." "Why, we've got silver," said a cabman, as he pulled out a dime, "and we've got paper," producing a dollar; "what's Bryan making all the fuss about?" The cogent argument had a great success.

From inside the station arose a piercing sound, something between a whoop and a scream. This was the American cheer. Our cheer is produced by people shouting in unison; the American by the combination of an infinite number of short, discordant noises. The difference is not, perhaps, without its analogy to national character. Ours is the more disciplined and falls the more roundly on the ear, but to convey a head-splitting impression of enthusiasm their method is the more direct and effective.

There was a trembling in the crowd by the door. An open carriage with four horses and two colossal Negroes in livery swung up to the pavement. Next moment William J. Bryan was standing bareheaded inside it. A compact, black-coated figure, a clean-shaven, clear-cut face, a large, sharp nose, and a square mouth and jaw. With the faint blue stubble on this face and his long grizzly hair he suggests an actor to the English mind. But you could not mistake him for a bad actor. Cheers rang out down the street, and hats flew in the air; and so he drove off, serene and upright, pleased but not surprised, with a smile on his lips and a light in his eye — the very type of a great demagogue.

Not necessarily a demagogue in any reproachful sense. Demagogue means leader of the people, and you may lead people by straight ways or crooked, to good destinies or bad. In a free country every politician must be something of a demagogue. Disraeli and Gladstone were both finished demagogues, and until we have two more great demagogues in England politics will continue to be as ditchwater.

As for Mr. Bryan, not one questioning word have I ever heard as to the purity of his motives. And in this country where charges of gross corruption are volleyed to and fro across the net of party politics until you wonder what has become of the law of libel, the absence of accusation may be taken as conclusive proof of innocence. But demagogue — one who knows how to lead the people and who enjoys it — he is from the crown of his thinning hair to the dust of travel on his boots.

I wandered up to the park where the great meeting was to be held and drifted into the crowd. The platform was built in front of a large stage whereon sat perhaps a thousand people. It was draped with bunting, flags flew from every corner, and it was festooned with hundreds of incandescent lights. Along to the speaker's left was another stand. At one end of this a brazen-lunged band punctuated the speeches with "Shouting out the battle cry of freedom" and similar appropriate airs. In front of the platform was massed the dense company, about ten thousand strong; this was not an extraordinarily large meeting for America. Out of the sea of soft felt hats rose an occasional club banner, and parts of the crowd were as thick with American ensigns as a wheat field with poppies. A speaker was declaiming with vigor and eloquence from the platform, but the crowd took not the least notice. In the pauses of their conversation they occasionally caught a phrase and whooped commendingly. But they were not there to hear arguments; they were there to hear Bryan, and Bryan at the moment was dining. Now and again an enthusiast threw into the air a sheaf of bills bearing the opinions of Abraham Lincoln on the money power, and the ominous hot wind, which was plainly bringing up a thunderstorm, distributed them over the crowd. The crowd was only languidly interested in free silver, but it was down on the money power. That is the kernel of this election. It is the first stirring of a huge revolt against plutocracy — against the trusts and rings that take their toll out of every man's dollar. Free silver happens to be the hallmark of revolt, but free copper or free mercury or free arsenic would do just as well.

Suddenly, above the periods of the orator and the whistling of the wind, the band crashed out "See the conquering hero comes." Instantly the whole park awoke. A forest of little American flags sprang up on the stand and waved furiously. A deafening scream went up from the whole ground. "Unfurl," said a voice at my elbow; I looked up, and behold! I was standing under the flaunting standard of the North Carolina Bryan Club. I felt the position was a false one — the more so when the staff snapped in the wind and the banner extinguished me; but nobody had leisure to think of such things. The mass of heads and flags in the stand was still heaving tumultuously; it took the candidate a matter of minutes to swim through to the platform; yet the piercing quality of the shrieking never varied. Then he appeared, calm but radiant. Ten thousand hats flew in the air — ten thousand and one, counting mine, which with the stolidity of my race I merely waved — and the screams rose yet more shrilly. A little girl in silver tripped along the platform rail and presented a bunch of silver roses. The shrieks became delirium. For a moment the square, black figure stood absolutely still. Then slowly he reached forth the hand like St. Paul in the Bible. The din went on unabated. Still very slowly he raised an arm above his head and made passes — one, two, three — in each direction of the crowd. Gradually silence crept over the mass of heads, and then the orator opened his lips. In a voice low but plain, hoarse but very rich, he began. He was glad to see once more those among whom he had spent four years of official life. "We'll give you four years more," shrieked my friend from the station. A broad and winning smile broke over the candidate's mouth, and again the mob screamed. A most admirable demagogue! "That's smart," said a little man behind me; "did ye see how it made him laugh?" Everybody saw; everybody was meant to see. Then again, when rain began to fall, somebody held up an umbrella over the orator's head. The wind blew it inside out. But the orator crammed a broad felt hat on to his head, turned up his coat collar with a sturdy gesture, and then spread out his arms to his hearers. Once more they cracked their throats with applause. "They won't get him down from there so easy," cried a delighted elector. Nature herself, turned goldbug, was powerless to deter the people's hero from his mission.

As for the matter of the speech, why trouble to inquire about it? It reads well in this morning's newspaper, but I thought it smacked of platitude and tautology. Certainly it was most effectively delivered, and telling gestures drove every point hard home. But the matter — 'twas no matter what he said. They had come to see and hear, but not to reason. Each man was more concerned to set his own little radius laughing with a smart bit of comment than to hear what the man they cheered had to say. "Did ye see him?" was the question one put to another — not "What did he say?" Both for good and evil, the free American citizen is no disciple of anybody; it would take a smart man to teach him. So the whole meeting was just a spectacular effect. And nobody knew and acted on that truth better than William J. Bryan.

Then came the storm. First a clap of thunder, then a cloud of dust, then flagstaffs cracking, and finally such a fusillade of heavy raindrops as England never sees. Three-quarters of the audience took to their heels like a routed army. The rest squatted down close to the ground in bunches of two or three under an umbrella till the park might have been dotted with toads under toadstools. Minute by minute the pitiless downpour went on. Then the remaining quarter split asunder from the center. "He's gone!" and in fifteen seconds the park was as bare as if Bryan had never been. But as I splashed home I saw the four-horsed carriage, with the nodding helmets of mounted police, driving rapidly off, with a further running, yelling escort of devotees. And I saw the black, square figure turn from side to side, buoyant and elastic, glad and exultant over the popular applause.

G. W. STEEVENS, The Land of the Dollar

233. T.R. Makes Up with Mark Hanna

Mark Hanna, a Cleveland, Ohio, industrialist, had managed McKinley's campaign in 1896, and his success had made him one of the "bosses" of the Republican Party. In 1900 the leaders of the party, against Hanna's judgment, had named Governor Roosevelt of New York for the Vice-Presidency — largely,

it was alleged, to get rid of him. The assassination of McKinley,
shortly after his second inauguration, made Roosevelt President.
Despite mutual suspicion Roosevelt and Hanna managed to patch
up their differences and work together during the few remaining
years of the latter's life.

ROOSEVELT occupied a drawing room. He asked me to sit
with him. His mind was working like a trip hammer. He talked
of many things he was going to do.

Part of the time I was in the second Pullman. An hour or two
after leaving Buffalo, Mark Hanna came to my seat. He was in an
intensely bitter state of mind. He damned Roosevelt and said:
"I told William McKinley it was a mistake to nominate that wild
man at Philadelphia. I asked him if he realized what would happen
if he should die. Now look, that damned cowboy is President of the
United States!"

I tried to reason with him, told him Roosevelt did not want to be
"shot into the Presidency," but could not mollify him.

A little later I asked Roosevelt how he and Mark Hanna got along.
He said: "Hanna treats me like a boy. He calls me Teddy." I
asked him if he realized what it meant if he and Hanna quarreled
and told him Hanna held the Republican organization in the hollow
of his hand, that he was the leader in the Senate and could defeat
any measure that he, Roosevelt, proposed and make his administration a failure. I cited the Garfield-Conkling row.

Roosevelt said: "What can I do about it? Give him complete
control of the patronage!" I said, "Hanna would resent any such
suggestion." I told him Hanna was heartbroken. He saw his best
friend gone, all his hopes crushed.

Finally I made the suggestion he invite Hanna to take supper
with him alone in his drawing room; that he must not say anything
in the presence of the waiter that could be repeated, as the newspaper
men would pounce upon the poor colored boy when they arrived
in Washington; that after the plates and cloth were removed, to let

the table remain, calling his attention to the awful gap between the front and back seat of a Pullman sleeper; when they were alone, to say: "Old man, I want you to be my friend. I know you cannot give me the love and affection you gave McKinley, but I want you to give me just as much as you can. I need you. Will you be my friend?" "Then put your hands, palms up, on the table. If he puts his hands in his pockets you are a goner, but if he puts his hands in yours you can bet on him for life." Roosevelt said, "All right, I'll try it!"

Later, as I sat in the forward coach, I saw the waiter whisper in Senator Hanna's ear. He hesitated a moment and then nodded his head. He came to my seat at the other end of the car and said: "That damned cowboy wants me to take supper with him alone. Damn him!" I said: "Mark, you are acting like a child. Go and meet him halfway."

Shortly after, he disappeared into Roosevelt's car. I was very nervous, but as an hour passed and thirty minutes more, Hanna came in; and I knew by his face, as he limped toward my seat, that it was all right. With a smile which the late Volney Foster said would grease a wagon, Hanna said, "He's a pretty good little cuss after all!" When I asked him what took place, he told of Roosevelt's putting his hands on the table, and as near as one man can quote another, he told what Roosevelt said, repeating what I had told Roosevelt to say. "What did you do, Mark?" He answered: "Putting my hands in his I said: 'I will be your friend on two conditions: first that you carry out McKinley's policies, as you promised.' Roosevelt answered, 'All right, I will.' 'Second, that you quit calling me "old man." If you don't I'll call you Teddy.' 'All right. You call me Teddy and I'll call you "old man."'" From that moment Roosevelt and Hanna were staunch, loyal friends. The only rift was for a few weeks late in 1903, when some anti-Roosevelt people tried to get Mark Hanna into the race for the Presidency.

All of Roosevelt's own writings and his numerous biographers tell of his friendly relations with Hanna but are silent as to how it came about.

HERMANN H. KOHLSAAT, From McKinley to Harding

234. The Roosevelts Take Over the White House

The youngest of American Presidents, impetuous, temperamental, colorful, Roosevelt brought life and gusto into official Washington which it had long lacked, and in this his family eagerly aided and abetted him. Ike Hoover who describes the change was White House usher for some forty years.

ONE MIGHT have expected that the Roosevelts, coming in under such tragic conditions, would have been hesitant and subdued. On the contrary, from the day of their arrival they displayed the characteristics which were to distinguish their entire administration.

To those around the White House who had a personal recollection of Mr. Roosevelt as Civil Service Commissioner and later as Assistant Secretary of the Navy, his bold step of taking up his residence in the place so soon after the funeral of Mr. McKinley was no surprise. They vividly pictured him coming in — as he had on many occasions as commissioner and as assistant secretary — and going upstairs two steps at a time, expounding his positive ideas in a manner that permitted of no contradiction. As had been expected, it was a continual two-step and spirited waltz for seven and one half years. The music varied, but the pace never ceased.

After the McKinley funeral Mr. Roosevelt himself did not appear for several days, but in the meantime Mrs. Roosevelt and her son Teddy arrived. After looking the place over they sent word to the others to join them, and in less than a week all the family were living in their new quarters. Then began the wildest scramble in the history of the White House. The children, hearty and full of spirits, immediately proceeded to cut loose.

The life of the employees who took their responsibilities too seriously was made miserable. The children left no nook or corner unexplored. From the basement to the flagpole on the roof, every channel and cubbyhole was thoroughly investigated. Places that had not seen a human being for years were now made alive with the howls and laughter of these newcomers. The house became one general playground for them and their associates. Nothing was too sacred to be used for their amusement, and no place too good for a playroom. The children seemed to be encouraged in these ideas by their elders, and it was a brave man indeed who dare say no or suggest putting a stop to these escapades.

One of the favorite stunts of the children was to crawl through the space between ceilings and floors where no living being but rats and ferrets had been for years. They took delight also in roller-skating and bicycle-riding all over the house, especially on the smooth hardwood floors. Practically every member of the family, with the exception of the President and Mrs. Roosevelt, had a pair of wooden stilts, and no stairs were too well carpeted or too steep for their climbing, no tree too high to scramble to the top, no fountain too deep to take a dip, no furniture too good or too high to use for leapfrog and horseplay, no bed was too expensive or chair too elegantly upholstered to be used as a resting place for the various pets in the household.

Giving the pony a ride in the elevator was but one of many stunts. This little fellow, spotted and handsome, had free access to any of the children's bedrooms. By means of the elevator he would be conveyed to the bedroom floor from the basement, a distance of two complete floors. As the children grew, there grew with them the idea on the part of the staff that such a situation was really necessary to the proper conduct of things. In fact it seemed as natural to the daily life of the White House as it was for an officer to arrest a crank or for the cook to prepare the meals.

These indeed were interesting days. The two smaller children, Archie and Quentin, were mere babies. Ethel and Kermit were about the same age and were inseparable, one just as daring as the other, and Ethel not willing to permit Kermit to outdo her in any respect. The escapades of these two alone would set any household agog.

Alice and Teddy completed the younger part of the household, and while both had their share of fun, it must be said they were the more subdued upon their arrival. Alice appeared more sedate than in after years. Ted seemed quiet enough, but as time wore on he too got his share in the way of sport and amusement.

But to leave the younger set and proceed to the daily life of these exciting times. Immediately upon the Roosevelts' arrival, the usual household changes were begun, only in this case they were more numerous and more radical than ever before. Instead of moving a piece of furniture here and there whole rooms were changed outright. Where one bed might have been before, two were now placed, and vice versa. The children were assigned to convenient apartments, and all settled down to enjoy the White House to the utmost. As the President was heard to remark just before finally leaving, "Perhaps others have lived longer in the place and enjoyed it quite as much, but none have ever really had more fun out of it than we have."

That describes best the everyday life of the Roosevelts. From the hour of rising in the morning plans were immediately prepared as to how best to enjoy the day. Meal hours, office hours, school hours, were all subject to change to fit in with these plans. Nothing was ever known to interfere — neither weather, company, business, nor anything else.

These pastimes took on all forms. First and foremost, of course, were the horseback rides. Every member of the family was an expert rider, and the President never seemed so happy as when either Mrs. Roosevelt or one of the children accompanied him on his ride. Next perhaps might be mentioned his lawn tennis games. It was great sport for him to figure just whom he preferred to play with in the afternoon. Of course none dared refuse the invitation, but it was well known that a poor player was never invited a second time. His favorites seemed to be Garfield, Pinchot, and Murray, but Bacon, Jusserand, and Meyer were close up, while experts like McCawley and Hurstman were only invited when he was feeling especially good. No sport seemed to be amiss in this family. Boxing, wrestling, fencing, running, and walking were among the President's favorite diversions.

Entering upon the daily routine, we found the entire family down to breakfast at eight o'clock. After breakfast the President spent an hour or so in his study, perhaps reading, while Mrs. Roosevelt arranged the details of the day's program. The President went to his office at nine-thirty or ten o'clock, and Mrs. Roosevelt for a walk or shopping, often accompanied by her secretary or one of her many friends.

All returned just about in time for lunch. Those famous lunches! Something indeed was wrong when there were not two or more guests for this meal. To prepare properly for a certain number was almost a physical impossibility, for notice was continually coming from the office that some one had been invited at the last minute, and many times the family and guests had to wait until the table was made larger before they could be seated. The place was really a transient boardinghouse, and how every one got enough to eat was the wonder of the household. Lunch being over, the rest of the afternoon was given over to sport — "exercise" as the President used to call it.

At one time it would be the famous Mike Donovan engaging in battles royal with the President and taking on one of the boys for a side issue. Then again it would be Joe Grant, the famous District champion wrestler, who would spend two or three hours at a time trying his prowess with the head of the nation and giving his points to the younger ones. Then again there would be broadsword battles with General Wood and others and games of medicine ball with Garfield and Pinchot.

Not content with these ordinary playtimes, the President took up jujitsu and put in two full seasons learning this famous art of self-defense. Upon one occasion, not knowing just which was preferable from a defensive standpoint, he decided to try out the two schemes of American wrestling and Japanese jujitsu. The most expert exponent of the Japanese art and the wrestler Grant were to test their respective merits before the President and a few especially invited guests.

On another occasion famous Chinese wrestlers gave an exhibition of their prowess in the East Room, which had been especially prepared for the occasion. These were the big fellows, and, quite different from the jujitsu people, they depended upon their strength alone. It was a very interesting affair and was witnessed by fifty or sixty guests, including cabinet members, senators, and a few others. This was a wholly Chinese contest, and while Mr. Roosevelt expressed offhandedly a wish to take on one of the big fellows, he did not try it.

So it went. Nothing seemed too absurd in the way of exercise and sport. Those employed around the house vied with each other to be the first to get the information of the day's doings.

In more serious matters great stress was laid on the fact that everything must be just right down to the smallest detail. No excuse would be accepted for the slightest error of omission or commission. Everything must be perfect. This led to a state of efficiency that was a pleasure to behold. While the demand was in a measure severe, still the thanks were so profuse that one felt amply repaid for both work and worry.

The Roosevelt family did not care a great deal about elaborate entertaining. Yet the most minute details were gone into in arranging the necessary social affairs. The formalities were so keenly observed that they were sometimes tiresome to every one rather than pleasant or brilliant.

It was more to the liking of the family to spend a quiet evening in the library, either playing cards or reading the current magazines. The whole family were fiends when it came to reading. No newspapers. Never a moment was allowed to go to waste; from the oldest to the youngest they always had a book or a magazine before them. The President, in particular, would just devour a book, and it was no uncommon thing for him to go entirely through three or four volumes in the course of an evening. Likewise we frequently saw one of the children stretched out on the floor flat on his stomach eating a piece of candy and with his face buried deep in a book. The current magazines were entirely too slow coming out, and we were kept busy trying to get them for the different members of the family the moment they appeared. And yet the Roosevelts were early birds, both in retiring and arising. Very seldom, unless something special was on hand, did they go to bed later than ten-thirty. In going out to dinner they made it a rule to make their departure promptly at ten o'clock, then home and immediately to their bedrooms.

IKE HOOVER, Forty-two Years in the White House

235. Taft and Roosevelt Come to a Parting of Ways

Roosevelt might have had another term, in 1908, but preferred to install as his successor his Secretary of War, William Howard Taft. Taft, however, proved less liberal and more independent than Roosevelt had expected, and gradually the two men drifted into opposite camps. By 1912 the break was complete; Roosevelt headed a revolt, split his party, and ran for the Presidency on his own Progressive platform. Archie Butt, whose letters reveal the course of the historic break, was military aide to both Presidents, and was torn between his affection for Roosevelt and his loyalty to Taft.

JULY 6, 1910. — The press this morning carried a report from Oyster Bay that Mr. Roosevelt had had an interview with Representative Poindexter of Washington State and had pledged him his support against Secretary Ballinger, who is an applicant for the Senate. I went for the President at nine o'clock and found him sitting on the porch. He had no sooner started to Myopia than he said to me:

"Archie, I am very distressed. I do not see how I am going to get out of having a fight with President Roosevelt."

"You refer to the Poindexter matter?" I asked.

"Yes. He seems to have thrown down the gauntlet in this matter, for what was given to the press he gave out himself. I have doubted up to the present time whether he really intended to fight my administration or not, but he sees no one but my enemies, and if by chance he sees any supporters of the administration, he does not talk intimately with any of them. Poindexter is one of the most bitter political opponents and always has been. Mr. Roosevelt's support of him seems most gratuitous and unnecessary. I confess it wounds me very deeply. I hardly think the prophet of the square deal is playing it exactly square with me now."

"Don't you think it possible that he intends to support the insurgent wing of the party up to a certain point and then unite it against the Democratic?"

"I should like to think so. But I think if he intended to do that, he would at least take into his confidence some other members of the party than those who have fought me and whom I have had to fight. But I shall do nothing. I shall let matters shape themselves in his mind and give him every chance to whip around if he sees he is making a mistake. I shall take no notice of it until it absolutely forces itself on me or the administration." . . .

I asked the President if he thought it possible that Mr. Roosevelt really contemplated forming a third party.

"I do not know. I have thought sometimes he did, and then I don't see how he can. In his mind, however, it may be the only logical way of reaching a third term. Then, too, his tour of Europe, his reception there, and the fact that every crowned head seemed to take it for granted that he would be elected to another term may have caused him to think that he should be, so as to realize the prophecies of so many people."

I felt his talk with me had had some especial significance, for as we neared Myopia he said to me:

"You may hear me say some bitter things of our old chief at times, and I fear it may distress you, but as long as I confine my criticism of him to my immediate official family you will have to put up with it, Archie, and I want you to know that it will be quite as distressing to me to break with him as it will be to you to see this break come." . . .

The view of the President at this moment is of interest and marks one more step which so many people think will end in the disruption of the old Republican party and the overthrow of the present administration.

August 25.— The President told me yesterday that the whole trouble between him and Mr. Roosevelt started, he feared, with that letter which I carried to the ex-President when he was sailing for Europe.

"Something offended him in that letter," said the President, "but I was never certain what it was until recently when some one who was with him on the steamer told me. It seems that I said that I would never forget what he and my brother Charlie had done for me. He became very angry and said how dared I couple him with my brother, and he would teach me to compare what he had done for me with what my brother had done, at the same time using some rather objectionable terms in description of old Charlie. I was sure there was some offense taken, because, as you remember, he has never answered it, after telling you that he would do so. Of course he does not think that Charlie was a factor in my nomination, and for this very reason he does not understand my desire to recognize what my brother did."

The President is in a little better frame of mind, but he is still pretty thoughtful. Mr. Roosevelt has made no acknowledgment at all of his letter in which he stated that he was not a party to the program to humiliate him in New York. The letter was addressed to Lloyd Griscom, but it was really intended for the ex-President, and the President feels that Mr. Roosevelt might have at least sent him some word which would indicate to him that he accepted the truth of the statement.

September 20. — It did not take long for the bomb to explode. Mr. Roosevelt is out in a statement tonight denying that he sought the interview, and both he and Griscom charge Norton and inferentially the President with giving false statements as to who asked for it and what was done there. . . .

Colonel Roosevelt, whatever his object was in coming to the conference, acted squarely and gave to the President every opportunity to get nearer to him. The conference was a great, serious thing, not only to the two men concerned, but for the party and the country. Mr. Roosevelt treated it seriously, and the President did not. That is the truth of the matter, and in consequence the two men are further apart than ever. But facts are more interesting now than comments.

The President told us just what occurred.

He said that Roosevelt was not genial and quite offish, he thought, and talked on matters of a general nature. He said they did not touch on Federal matters, but that he, in order to bring things to a head, brought up the New York matter and volunteered to help Mr. Roosevelt in his fight on bossism in that state. So, strictly speaking, Mr. Roosevelt did not ask for any assistance.

"But that was what he was there for," said the President, "and I went to the point at once, but Roosevelt said the conference was necessary to help bring the party together — that both of us owed that much to the party."

"The fact of the matter is," said the President, "if you were to remove Roosevelt's skull now, you would find written on his brain '1912.' But he is so purely an opportunist that should he find conditions changed materially in another year and you were to open his brain, you would not find there 1912, and Roosevelt would deny it was ever there."

"That makes it all the more important," said Schmidlapp, "that you say nothing which will widen the breach so that he cannot support you should you be renominated. If your administration is a success, the party will have to renominate you; if it is a failure, no Republican can be elected, and Roosevelt will be the first one to recognize this fact."

It was not a very cheerful meal.

October 19. — We had rather a scene at the breakfast table this morning. Mrs. Henry Taft told the President that the Troy *Times* was owned by a Mr. Francis, an old friend of hers, who had always written to her, but he had stopped writing, and she felt certain that he was attacking the administration bitterly, and she was able to account for it. Troy, I think, is her old home. She said that Francis had told her two years ago that he was to be appointed ambassador to Italy, that President Roosevelt had got the promise from Mr. Taft, who was then just elected, to send him to Rome. Later some one else had been appointed, and Francis looked upon the matter as an intentional insult both to himself and the ex-President, and he was now taking it out on the administration.

The President was indignant and proceeded to hit out right and left. He said that Mr. Roosevelt had never asked it of him as a favor but merely expressed the hope that Francis would be named to Italy. He then said:

"I meet this sort of thing everywhere. One day just after I was nominated I told Roosevelt that, should I be elected, I did not see how I could do anything else but retain all the old members of the cabinet who had been associated with me. I thought nothing more about it, but I learned later that Roosevelt had practically told every member of his cabinet that he was going to be retained should I be elected. The only one he made it a point to ask me to retain was Meyer, and I retained him. I am now placed in the attitude of breaking a promise to each of these men."

He said much more of a character to show how deeply he felt, but this gives the gist of what he said.

January 19, 1911. — I had a conversation with the President about Colonel Roosevelt. I repeated to him what Mr. Griscom had said to me the night before at the diplomatic dinner, which had saddened me very much. I could not get out of my mind all day the picture he drew of Colonel and Mrs. Roosevelt at Oyster Bay. He and Mrs. Griscom had gone down to spend Sunday, and he said that he had found the Colonel in a most depressed state of mind; all his old buoyancy was gone, and he really seemed to him to be a changed man. Mrs. Roosevelt, he said, seemed more depressed than the Colonel, and this I realized came from the state he must be in, for if she could have her wish it would be never to hear of politics again. But if he is wounded she shows her distress just in this way. Her depression told me, better than anything else which Mr. Griscom could have said, the state of the Colonel's mind.

At any rate I told the President just what Griscom had told me, and when he got to the White House he asked me to come in, as he wanted to talk, and while I took off my things he walked ahead of me and turned on the lights in the Red Room and sat down with his overcoat on.

"Tell me again what Griscom said. It is strange he never told me any of this."

I told the President that Griscom had said he would not repeat it to any one else but myself, for he knew my interest in and love for the family.

"Archie," said the President, "I don't see what I could have done to make things different. Somehow people have convinced the Colonel that I have gone back on him, and he does not seem to be able to get that out of his mind. But it distresses me very deeply, more deeply than any one can know, to think of him sitting there at Oyster Bay alone and feeling himself deserted. I know just what he feels. It is a dreary spot in winter, and the surroundings must have a bad effect on both of them."

The President stopped talking and looked hard ahead of him. He reached up and wiped his eye. I don't know whether a tear had formed there or not, but I could see that something of a big nature was going on in his mind. He may have been reviewing all those years of intimacy and come face to face with some thought of disloyalty on his own part. I started to rise, but he waved me back, and he sat for some time longer in absolute silence. When he broke it again, it was to say:

"It may be that a break had to come. The situation was a most difficult one for both of us, but no harder for him than for me, and I don't think he ever saw my side of it. What he is undergoing now may be the thing most needed to get him back to a normal frame of mind. The American people are strange in their attitudes toward their idols. This is not the first time this sort of thing has happened. They have even led their idols on and on, to cut their legs from under them later and apparently to make their fall all the greater.

"Where I do blame Roosevelt is for allowing them to get him in this position. He should have kept aloof and not given the people an opportunity to do what they have done. But I don't know when I have had anything affect me as deeply as the picture which this conversation brings to my mind. To feel everything slipping away from him, all the popularity, the power which he loved, and above all the ability to do what he thought was of real benefit to his country, to feel it all going and then to be alone! I hope the old boy has enough philosophy left to take him through this period; that is all. If he could only fight! That is what he delights in, and that is what is denied to him now. The papers in the East have adopted a policy of ignoring him, of never mentioning him. I had heard that this was done with a view of driving home the iron. This robs him of the right to hit back, to fight, and leaves him in a way without an audience. I hear Pinchot has deserted him and that his old allies are weakening. It is all sad! Well, do you see where I could have acted differently?"

He appealed to me for comfort, for in his mind there was the still small voice saying I know not what, but enough to make the quiver in his voice genuine.

"I don't see how you could have done differently," I said.

February 14. — The President and I took a long walk in the afternoon. He was most talkative all the way. He could not get Roosevelt off his mind and kept saying that if Roosevelt succeeded in defeating him for the nomination, he [Roosevelt] would be the most bitterly discredited statesman ever in American politics.

"The humiliation which will be meted out to him in November and during the campaign will cause any humiliation I may feel at the convention to seem as nothing."

He told me he felt certain that Roosevelt would become in the near future a declared candidate. He believes every story brought to him, from whatever source, and is growing more bitter every hour toward the man who nominated him before. He thinks that the Colonel has no cause for resentment at all, and it is not for me to say now that he is right, for I remember too much in the past. The clash which must follow between these two men is tragic. It is moving now from day to day with the irresistible force of the Greek drama, and I see no way for anything save divine Providence to interpose to save the reputation of either should they hurl themselves at each other. Their most intimate friends are all mutually intimate with both, and every one of us feels involved in the outcome.

21st. — I went walking with the President this afternoon. President Roosevelt had delivered his much-advertised speech in Columbus, Ohio, coming out for the initiative, referendum, and recall, and the reports show that he had been given an overwhelming reception. When asked if he were to be a candidate he answered:

"My hat is in the ring. I will answer all such questions Monday."

The President had long told me that Roosevelt would be a candidate, and he simply dreaded the issue. I saw that he was worried from the moment we left the White House and so said hardly a word to him. Finally as we neared Dupont Circle he said to me:

"Well, Archie, what do you think of the recall of judges as announced by the Colonel today?"

"I have always been opposed to the recall of the judiciary, Mr. President."

We took a long walk, being out nearly two hours. When we were nearly home he turned to me and stopped and said:

"Archie, I am going to say something which may surprise you, and therefore you must not say anything about it. Do you know those presentiments which sometimes come over one, even against his reasoning? Well, I have a strong presentiment that the Colonel is going to beat me in the convention. It is almost a conviction with me. I shall continue to fight to the last moment, but when you see me claiming victory or my friends claiming victory for me, remember that I feel that I am losing a battle and that I am not blind myself, no matter what my friends may put out."

"My presentiment is all the other way," I said, to show some cheerful side.

"No, that is because you want to see me win. But don't think me capable of quitting. I can fight just as well when losing as when certain of victory, and I have made up my mind to answer that speech of Theodore's and answer it in Ohio, where he dared to deliver it. He has drawn the line now, and I hope we can keep the fight from becoming personal. He has leaped far ahead of the most radical leaders of the Progressive Party, and his heart is not with them, but he deludes himself that he will be able to guide it and stem it when he gets in power. He can't do it. He has gone too far. He will either be a hopeless failure if elected or else destroy his own reputation by becoming a socialist, being swept there by force of circumstances just as the leaders of the French Revolution were swept on and on, all their individual efforts failing to stem the tide until it had run itself out."

It was a nasty and wet afternoon, and I don't know whether that had anything to do with the President's mood, but I never saw him quite so pessimistic before.

25th. — I was at the White House tonight when the President received the announcement of Colonel Roosevelt's candidacy. There was nothing very dramatic about it, and little to be remembered except the simple way it was received.

Job Hedges and Crawford Hill, the latter from Denver, were spending the night at the White House. Mrs. Taft ordered dinner at half past seven in order that we might be on time at the Belasco to hear Buffalo Jones describe in a ludicrous way his catching of live animals in Africa. Just as we were going in to dinner a short note was handed to the President. He read it and passed it to each one of us. It was merely an announcement of the Associated Press that it had the Colonel's letter to the governors, the gist of which was hat he would accept the nomination if offered to him.

We had sat down to the table before any one made a comment. Mrs. Taft was the first to break the silence.

"I told you so four years ago, and you would not believe me."

The President laughed good-naturedly and said:

"I know you did, my dear, and I think you are perfectly happy now. You would have preferred the Colonel to come out against me than to have been wrong yourself."

"Well, she is a better guesser than I," said Jacob Hedges, "for only last week I was predicting that under no conditions would the Colonel be a declared candidate."

Conversation became general, and we tried to rattle Helen about always coming in late to dinner. She said:

"I don't see why Father and Mother don't scold me for being late, as I always am, but they take it very good-naturedly."

"One of the saddest things that can come to a parent is to see his own faults coming out in his own children," said the President.

Just at this time there was sent from the office the entire letter of Colonel Roosevelt, which was short, clear-cut, and a plain statement that the Colonel was a candidate for the nomination. The President read it aloud. Every one took a whack at it, but the President regarded it as much stronger than he had thought it would be. He explained that he had believed it would come out loaded with conditions and explanations, whereas it was a short, brief announcement and direct to the people.

"No, he could not have made it stronger," said the President. "It is characteristic of him, and it will be a rallying cry to the Progressives of the country and to the discontented, but I think you will find that in a week or ten days it will have lost much of its clarion note, and there will be a great sag in the sentiment which will at first be aroused by it."

Taft and Roosevelt, The Intimate Letters of Archie Butt

236. Woodrow Wilson Is Nominated at Baltimore

The split in the Republican Party, in 1912, made the Democratic nomination tantamount to election, and the contest for the nomination was therefore unusually keen. Woodrow Wilson, who had made a national reputation as a reform governor of New Jersey, was favored by the liberal element in the party. The support of Bryan, still the most powerful man in the party, brought him the nomination and the election; Bryan was rewarded with the Secretaryship of State.

WHEN Beatrice and I left the train at Baltimore, our friends crowded the platform and called after us, "Be sure to nominate Clark," and we answered: "No, we won't. We want Wilson. We want Wilson." Arrived at the Emerson Hotel, where the queue at the registry ran in tedious loops, we ran into more friends, among them Mr. Henry Morgenthau, whom I had learned to respect through various municipal enterprises in New York. Baltimore was hotter than Chicago, or so it seemed, and I began to think Mr. Dooley had been right when he said at Chicago, "Us Dimmycrats won't know the worst till our own convention meets." Worse it might be, but like an old war horse smelling powder, I only felt myself at home and, on meeting Charles Murphy for the first time that night, jumped in roughshod with "Why aren't you for Wilson?" He turned his mask to me and said, "The boys don't want him."

Some of the Independent members of the New York delegation, McAdoo, George Foster Peabody, Morgenthau, and others, came up, and the big question was asked at once: "What is Bryan going to do? What is Bryan going to do?" Chicago had been gloomy. Baltimore was the Donnybrook Fair all over, housed in the armory under a canopy of yellow and white cheesecloth festooned there for some acoustic purpose. "You got to quit kicking my houn' around," the

Clark men set up their tune, "quit a-kicking my houn' dog around," and into the middle of the drawling chant would cut the staccato, "We want Wilson—we want Wilson—we want Wilson."

The fight over temporary chairman ended in the election of jovial, perspiring Senator James from Kentucky. This was good, for Judge Parker had too much about him of the flavor of Elihu Root, and his defeat gave a feeling to the convention that Chicago never had. In Chicago the machine could say who should be nominated. In Baltimore the machine knew from the first that the most it could do was to block action. It could not hope to lead. There was Ollie James on the platform; seated in the midst of the Nebraska delegation on the floor was the man in the alpaca coat, a man who really believed in democracy, who was ready to let the country exert pressure from without on convention in session. Here the nomination would be made in response to what "the people," busy on the farms and in the mills, were wanting. Beatrice and I had had an orchestra seat in Chicago. However, here in Baltimore the worst seats were the best. Politicians from the floor climbed the stairs to gossip with us.

Champ Clark was put in nomination. Pandemonium broke loose —cheers and cheers and more nasal celebration of the houn' dog. Then just as we were almost wilted by speech after speech from incurably eloquent throats, Judge Westcott, of New Jersey, rose and put Woodrow Wilson in nomination. After its flowery predecessors his speech was electric and to the point. He captured and carried his crowd because he was so terribly in earnest and the speech was so dramatically delivered. He told me afterward one day, when we were lunching with the governor at Sea Girt, that he had felt so ill the day of the nomination that he had walked about outside the hall, feeling that he couldn't possibly get up on the platform. When his turn came the audience so inspired him that he entirely forgot everything but the fact that he was urging the nomination of Woodrow Wilson. "New Jersey believes," he said, "that there is omniscience in national instinct. That instinct centers in her governor. He is that instinct. We want Wilson." Crowds in the gallery took it up. I turned to a woman sitting near, wife of a delegate on the floor below. "How do you know about him? What makes you want him?" She was from Iowa. "Oh, we've heard. We've read. Long winter evenings on the farm I've been making his acquaintance in the magazines. Wilson's an ideal to us." "We want Wilson, we want Wilson." The absolutely stirring quality of Judge Westcott's speech was particularly interesting to me because he had been a political foe of Wilson's in 1910, when it was he who was chosen by the New Jersey progressive Democrats to place in nomination for the governorship Mayor Katzenbach of Trenton. After Mr. Wilson's speech of acceptance at that time the judge sought out the nominee, although he had left the hall in disgust when Wilson was nominated. The two became great friends, and when chosen by the governor to make the nominating speech at Baltimore the judge had been delighted.

I don't mean to say that the galleries were all for Wilson. Clark flags flapped there too, and the houn' dog tune was always in our ears. I sat not far from a pretty Southern woman who was very strong for Underwood and was one of a group who let white doves out of baskets when he was put in nomination. By the end of the convention she had prattled to me about her whole life history, including a love match with an elderly congressman husband, and ended with an appeal: "Mrs. Harriman, you seem to know all the powerful people among the Wilson backers. I just wish that you'd tell them to make my husband vice-president. He is such a good man and such a clever man, and his selection would please so many people."

The balloting began: "Alabama, Arkansas" — echoes of Chicago, — "Kansas, Kentucky." The Texas delegation, forty strong, plumped for Wilson. So the ghost story was true. The little colonel from Texas was not there, but the shadowy myth that he had sewed up Texas solid and had stolen away to Europe, knowing that from the first ballot to the last the Texas delegation would never waver, was so. At the end of the first ballot Clark was leading with nearly four hundred. The balloting went on. There was a dark moment three evenings later when Clark forged ahead and it looked as if he were going to get the two-thirds necessary for nomination. McAdoo went on giving statements to the press that the nomination of Wilson was inevitable. George Marvin leaned over my shoulder in the gallery. "McAdoo looks like an American eagle," he said, "and that ought to be an asset to him in politics." "Certainly," I said, making a speech *en tête-à-tête*. "He is an eagle. He is a fierce fighter. He knows what he wants, goes straight after it, and usually gets it. He has dash and boldness." Anyhow none could say that Mr. McAdoo was just an ordinary man.

Rumors flew about. Champ Clark had come to Baltimore. His followers were divided; some wanted to bring the old man into the hall, some thought the chances would be better if he stayed away. Balloting went on. On the eleventh ballot Clark reached his zenith. Then Mr. Luke Lea, of Tennessee, asked that the Tennessee delegation be polled. That made the Clark vote drop from five hundred and fifty-four to five hundred and forty-seven and a half, and from then on Wilson picked off a vote here and a vote there. It was like a crew gaining inch by inch on its opponent in a boat race. Every time they polled a delegation they found scattered Wilson votes. There were six hundred Wilson votes under cover, a fact the Wilson leaders knew from the first. The excitement and the pandemonium grew more intense. We never left the galleries even for a meal. We hung over the railing, nibbling Peters chocolate and drinking sarsaparilla out of bottles.

I had met a newspaper editor from North Carolina, a Mr. Daniels, who was a slow talker, a cross between a thoroughly unassuming, old-fashioned character and a very courtly Southern politician. He had promised to introduce me to Mr. and Mrs. Bryan if I would come to the Bellevue Hotel at nine-thirty the next morning.

We arrived before Mr. and Mrs. Bryan were ready to receive and found the hall outside their room jammed like the assembling point of a Fourth of July parade with men wearing Bryan buttons, "longhorns from Texas, jayhawks from Kansas," Lindsay would say, a nice hot Western crowd. Then the door opened, and I was presented to Mrs. Bryan, a handsome woman with a motherly, encompassing smile, serene as the prairie on a fine spring morning. Behind me the "Bryan boys," as they called themselves, made a rush at the Commoner, who stood in the center of his bedroom, wearing the inevitable alpaca deacon's coat with panama hat and clasping a palm leaf fan which he pressed to his chest when there was a pause in its steady breeze making. Over on one side of the room Mrs. Bryan and I talked. She reminded me that Eastern people had been unfair always to her husband. I nodded; she was right, I knew. Here was I, the wife of a broker, living in a Wall Street atmosphere, remembering how I had been carried away by the general furore about free silver and how I used to watch Bordie walk in "sound money parades" and go with him to hear Bourke Cockran hymn the gold standard in Madison Square Garden. Mrs. Bryan talked quietly, and I was echoing, "True." Most of the progressive measures in American politics that other people had adopted had originally been sponsored by the prophet from Nebraska.

When there was a chance to get near to Mr. Bryan we moved over, and I asked him if he were a candidate; the newspapers had kept printing that "Bryan plays the grandmother game and is really seeking the nomination for himself." He looked me straight in the eye and gave the same answer that he gave Judge Westcott later in the week, giving it with great earnestness and positive sincerity:

"I can never again be the candidate for the presidency for three reasons: first, my stand on prohibition; second, my attitude toward the Roman Catholic Church; and third, because I have run unsuccessfully so many times that by some people I am considered a hoodoo to the party."

I then said what I had come to say, that the real progressive Democrats from New York wanted Wilson. If Clark were nominated and elected we felt he would be controlled by Hearst. That we didn't want. "If Wilson gets in you will be secretary of state, a fine combination." I no sooner had the idea than it popped out of my mouth, and I couldn't tell whether there wasn't just a little flicker of amusement around his crow's-footed eyes. We talked. Mr. Bryan ended the conversation with the very direct "I will never cast another vote for Clark." When I reported my conversation to my New York friends I deleted one sentence. They listened and then exclaimed when I told them about his never voting for Clark again: "If he leaves Clark he'll have to come to Wilson." They were satisfied. Then I confessed my fault — "I've done something dreadful"; and I repeated my bright idea blurted to Mr. Bryan about the secretaryship of state. "Well, your saying it doesn't make cabinet members." I heaved a sigh of relief, delighted to be a person of no importance and particularly not a culprit impulsively offering eggs that hadn't been hatched and that never would belong to me in any case.

At the next ballot Bryan switched; things were coming our way. There were little incidents; a group of Clark men brought in a banner on standards, quoting from an old speech of Bryan's in which he had praised Clark, and held it in front of Bryan. This maneuver made it hard for the hundreds of eyes constantly seeking the face of the Commoner for their leadership. Presently the banner was disposed of, and Governor Francis of Missouri, who afterward became ambassador to Russia, apologized in courtly fashion for the ill-temper of his fellow delegates.

By this time Clark's "houn' dog" song had faded out of the picture, and Wilson, by picking off votes like currants, was far ahead. The tired delegates sprawled across a field of varnished chairs as we watched them in the hot, pale blue fog of the armory.

Just in a line with my eye every little while, a lean, stoop-shouldered, shirt-sleeved figure would stand on his chair, leaning against a pillar, and hold out his hand for recognition. This was "Alfalfa Bill" Murray of Oklahoma; the first time he had particularly drawn people's attention was the night that he drawled out: "There's one thing I know, Oklahoma ain't going to follow Tammany Hall."

On the sixty-third ballot the machine gave up: Wilson nine hundred and ninety, Clark eighty-four, and Harmon twelve. McCombs, Wilson's manager, was happy, nervous, haggard. All sorts of people began to say they had known it all along. I never took my eyes off Bryan; it was he and he alone who had made possible the choosing of the people's own candidate. Queer, looking at him and saying, "So far so good." I never doubted once but what Wilson was destined to be the next President of the United States.

Mrs. J. Borden Harriman, *From Pinafores to Politics*

XXXIV

The World War

237. Herbert Hoover Feeds the Belgians

The German invasion of Belgium in August, 1914, brought ruin and starvation to that hapless country, and in October a Commission for Relief in Belgium was organized in London with semiofficial support from the United States. Herbert Clark Hoover, a consulting engineer then living in London, was placed in charge of relief work, and within less than a month the first food-ship docked at Rotterdam. Hoover's achievement as director of relief work brought him world renown as a humanitarian and an administrator, and paved the way for his subsequent political career in the United States.

SUNDAY, November 29, 1914. — Took a walk this morning, and I have seldom worked so hard as I did in the afternoon, preparing the courier who goes out early in the morning with letters to London, and so on. Then at four arrived Shaler with Hoover, Doctor Rose, and Bicknell. Doctor Rose and Bicknell represent the Rockefeller Foundation and are here to investigate conditions in Belgium. Doctor Rose is the great hookworm specialist, and Bicknell is the Red Cross expert; Rose a little man who looks something like a preacher; Bicknell tall, fine-looking, with white hair and a sense of humor. Hoover just as Francqui described him, the type of American business man, a face somewhat *fruste,* very direct, positive, able, speaks little, but everything he says counts. I talked to him for a while and explained the situation to him here and learned what has been going on outside. The usual amount of quarreling in America between rival committees, Catholics and Protestants, and so forth. Nothing so sweet and charming and altogether lovely as to see rival religions in each other's hair over some question of sweet charity!

The poor man has had many troubles but seems to surmount them all bravely.

The Rockefeller representatives, with the right by money to ask questions, cross-examined me for two hours; and for two hours I answered questions explaining the situation here and when I was through felt that I had made out my case. Hoover thought so too, and so did Shaler and so did the Rockefeller men; but I was as tired as though I had been making an argument before the Supreme Court. We had them here to dinner and still more talk. Then at ten Madame Carton de Wiart came in. Francqui had been here at noon to see me. He had known Hoover in China and admired him immensely and wished to have an hour with Hoover before Hoover saw any of the others. We discussed Heineman somewhat, but agreed that we had great need of him since he has influence with the Germans. Hoover speaks no French and Francqui pigeon English; so it is amusing to hear them.

30th. — I showed to Kaufmann the figures that Hoover had given me, namely twenty-seven hundred thousand pounds, which translated into German means fifty-four million marks, the amount of the value of foodstuffs already imported into Belgium from America! "*Sapristi!*" said Kaufmann.

This afternoon a long session with Hoover, Francqui, Heineman, Rose, Bicknell, and Shaler about the problem of financing the scheme. Six hundred thousand pounds furnished by the English and French governments to the Belgian government are to be turned over by the Belgian government to our committee, credited to the Comité National here, and by them distributed among the communes. The Rockefeller men are much impressed by our organization and by conditions in Belgium. They start in a day or two on a tour, to be accompanied by Gibson and probably Francqui. To-morrow we go to see the soup kitchens; in the afternoon a session of the Comité National. The consul general was in, and I asked him to go with us.

December 1. — This morning Hoover, Bell, Doctor Rose, Bicknell, Francqui, Shaler, Gibson, Leval, Watts, and I drove about in the rain to see the soup kitchens, a doleful morning's business, though not without its reassurance of the goodness that still is in human nature. We went first to the Boulevard Anspach, and there in a great circular dome that was once used by an express company was a wire ring of caldrons with cooks bending over them brewing the savory soup that is sent out to the various kitchens and there served to the poor. We then drove to some of these stations, notably one in the Rue Blaes near the Boulevard du Midi, in the very heart of the Quartier des Marolles. Long lines of poor women and men crowding the sidewalks and inside the hall, once a kind of theater and café, its garish decorations full of mockery. Each poor soul entered with a ticket and there was given a bit of coffee, a bit of chicory, a loaf of bread. Each person receives enough for the day's nourishment, a noble answer to the prayer, "Give us this day our daily bread."

Each person has a card from his commune with a number. The numbers are checked off. The lines are inspected in groups by persons connected with the neighborhoods whence they come. If one is missing, the absence is instantly detected: "Where is Jeanne today? Is she sick? Or what?"

The admirable organization deeply impressed Hoover and Rose. We stayed some time there watching this line of poor march by. Each one, as he or she received his or her ration, said "Thank you," and I had to turn away to hide my tears.

I came back to the Legation, wrote letters for Hoover to take to Page, very tired and worn out by the day, and then Madame Carton de Wiart came, wishing to see the Rockefeller men, and then Hoover to bid me good-bye. He was very much moved by the sight of suffering he saw today, and very cordial and very fine. A remarkable man indeed. His last thought was to place enough money on deposit here to pay all expenses. The Belgians, he said, must not be put to a pennyworth of expense. His meeting with Francqui in this work is quite interesting. Years ago Hoover was in China managing a profitable business, a veritable king of a little province. One morning Francqui arrived and said Belgian capital had bought the control. So Hoover was displaced, though he stayed and worked with Francqui for some time. Now after all these years they meet and are friends again, working in a great cause. I was proud today to think that my country was doing this noble work amidst all this rage, this brutal and ignorant destruction, but one's thoughts are almost drowned these days, and it is difficult to express them.

The Journal of Brand Whitlock

238. Woodrow Wilson Breaks with Germany

It was the German submarine warfare that caused a crisis in her relations with the United States. On May 4, 1916, Germany promised that no more merchant vessels would be sunk without warning, but by the end of that year her condition was so desperate that she found it necessary to repudiate that promise and to inaugurate unrestricted submarine warfare. It was this shift in Germany's policy which precipitated the final crisis that led directly to the rupture of relations. Robert Lansing, who tells the story of the break, had succeeded Bryan as Secretary of State.

DURING the forenoon of Wednesday, January 31, 1917, the German ambassador telephoned my office and arranged an interview for four o'clock that afternoon. He did not indicate his purpose, and my own idea was that he probably desired to talk over confidentially the terms on which Germany would make peace.

When he entered my room at ten minutes after four I noticed that, though he moved with his usual springy step, he did not smile with his customary assurance. After shaking hands and sitting down in the large easy chair by the side of my desk he drew forth from an envelope which he carried several papers. Selecting one, he held it out, saying that he had been instructed to deliver it to me. As I took the paper he said that for convenience he had prepared an English translation. He then handed me three documents in English, consisting of a note and two accompanying memoranda.

He asked me if he should read them to me or if I would read them to myself before he said anything about them. I replied that I would read the papers, which I did slowly and carefully; for as the nature of the communication was disclosed I realized that it was of very serious import and would probably bring on the gravest crisis which this government had had to face during the war. The note announced the renewal *on the next day* of indiscriminate submarine warfare and the annulment of the assurances given this government by Germany in the note of May 4, 1916, following the *Sussex* affair.

While I had been anticipating for nearly three months this very moment in our relations with Germany and had given expression to my conviction in the public statement which I made concerning our note of December 18, for which I had been so generally criticized, I was nevertheless surprised that Germany's return to ruthless methods came at this time. I knew that all her shipyards had been working to their full capacity in constructing submarines for the past seven months and that thousands of men were being trained to handle their complex mechanism, but I assumed that on account of the difficulties of using submarines in northern waters during midwinter the campaign would not begin before March and probably not until April. It was therefore with real amazement that I read the note and memoranda handed me. I can only account for the premature announcement of indiscriminate warfare on the ground that the food situation in Germany had reached such a pass that the Imperial Government had to do something to satisfy public opinion.

As I finished my deliberate perusal of the papers, I laid them on the desk and turned toward Count von Bernstorff. "I am sorry," he said, "to have to bring about this situation, but my government could do nothing else."

I replied, "That is of course the excuse given for this sudden action, but you must know that it cannot be accepted."

"Of course, of course," he said, "I understand that. I know it is very serious, very, and I deeply regret that it is necessary."

"I believe you do regret it," I answered, "for you know what the result will be. But I am not blaming you personally."

"You should not," he said with evident feeling; "you know how constantly I have worked for peace."

"I do know it," I said. "I have never doubted your desire or failed to appreciate your efforts."

"I still hope," he said, speaking with much earnestness, "that with a full realization of Germany's situation your government will in justice decide that the notification of blockade is entirely warranted."

I answered him that I could not discuss the merits until I had thoroughly digested the documents, but I would say that the first reading had made a very bad impression and that to give only eight hours' notice without any previous warning of intention was in my opinion an unfriendly and indefensible act.

He exclaimed: "I do not think it was so intended; I am sure it was not."

"I regret that I must differ with you," I replied, "but this has come so suddenly that I am sure you will understand I do not wish to discuss the matter further."

"Of course, of course; I quite understand," he said, rising and extending his hand, which I took with a feeling almost of compassion for the man, whose eyes were suffused and who was not at all the jaunty, carefree man-of-the-world he usually was. With a ghost of a smile he bowed as I said "Good afternoon," and turning, left the room.

Immediately on his departure I called in Polk and Woolsey and read the communication which I had received. We all agreed that the only course which seemed open was to break off diplomatic relations.

I telephoned to the White House and found the President was out. I then wrote him a short letter transmitting the papers and sent it by Sweet to the White House, who between five and five-thirty left it with the usher to be put in the President's hands as soon as he returned. Through some confusion with other papers the President did not get the papers until after eight o'clock. He then telephoned me to come to the White House.

From a quarter to nine until half past ten we conferred in his study. Throughout the conference I maintained that we must pursue the course which he had declared we would pursue in our *Sussex* note of April 18, 1916, namely to break off relations with Germany if she practiced ruthless submarine warfare, that any lesser action would be impossible, and that the only question in my mind was whether we ought not to go further and declare that the actual renewal of indiscriminate submarine attack affecting our citizens or ships would be considered by us to be an act of war.

The President, though deeply incensed at Germany's insolent notice, said that he was not yet sure what course we must pursue and must think it over; that he had been more and more impressed with the idea that "white civilization" and its domination over the world rested largely on our ability to keep this country intact, as we would have to build up the nations ravaged by the war. He said that as this idea had grown upon him he had come to the feeling that he was willing to go to any lengths rather than to have the nation actually involved in the conflict.

I argued with him that if the break did not come now, it was bound to do so in a very short time and that we would be in a much stronger position before the world if we lived up to our declared purpose than if we waited until we were further humiliated. I said that if we failed to act I did not think we could hold up our heads as a great nation and that our voice in the future would be treated with contempt by both the Allies and Germany.

The President said that he was not sure of that; that, if he believed it was for the good of the world for the United States to keep out of the war in the present circumstances, he would be willing to bear all the criticism and abuse which would surely follow our failure to break with Germany; that contempt was nothing unless it impaired future usefulness; and that nothing could induce him to break off relations unless he was convinced that, viewed from every angle, it was the wisest thing to do.

I replied to this that I felt that the greatness of the part which a nation plays in the world depends largely upon its character and the high regard of other nations, that I felt that to permit Germany to do this abominable thing without firmly following out to the letter what we had proclaimed to the world we would do would be to lose our character as a great power and the esteem of all nations, and that to be considered a bluffer was an impossible position for a nation which cherished self-respect.

There was, of course, much more said during our conference. The President showed much irritation over the British disregard for neutral rights and over the British plan (asserted by Germany) to furnish British merchant ships with heavy guns. I told him that . . . proof of this we had none, but it seemed to me that Germany's declaration in any event justified such a practice. He replied that he was not certain that the argument was sound, but he did not think it worth while to discuss it now in view of the present crisis.

After some further talk it was agreed that I should prepare a note to Bernstorff setting out the breach of faith by Germany and breaking off diplomatic relations. . . .

On returning home I immediately prepared a draft in rough form, and the next morning (Thursday) I redrew it in my own hand-writing, using for the quoted parts clippings from the printed correspondence. (This note, with practically no changes, was the one finally sent.)

Although many diplomats called at the Department, I denied myself to them all as I did not care to discuss the situation. However, I had to see Senator Hitchcock, who was the ranking Democrat on the Committee on Foreign Relations. He suggested that we ask the belligerents of both sides for a ten-day armistice. I asked him what good that would do. He said, "To gain time." "Well, and then what?" I asked. He had nothing to offer, and I told him that I did not think that it would get us anywhere, but that even if there were some benefit to be gained, I was sure that Germany would decline and the Allies would probably do the same. He went away in a dispirited frame of mind, saying that he saw no other way of avoiding trouble.

At noon on Thursday (the first of February) I went over to the White House and, with Colonel House, who had arrived early that morning, conferred with the President for about an hour in his study. We went over substantially the same ground which the President and I had covered the night before. The Colonel, as is customary with him, said very little, but what he did say was in support of my views.

I went further in this conference than I did in the previous one by asserting that in my opinion peace and civilization depended on the establishment of democratic institutions throughout the world and that this would be impossible if Prussian militarism after the war controlled Germany. The President said that he was not sure of this, as it might mean the disintegration of German power and the destruction of the German nation. His argument did not impress me as very genuine, and I concluded that he was in his usual careful way endeavoring to look at all sides of the question.

When I left the conference I felt convinced that the President had almost reached a decision to send Bernstorff home. It was not any particular thing which he said but rather a general impression gained from the entire conversation. At any rate I felt very much better than I had the night before, when the President's tone of indecision had depressed me. Probably I misjudged him because he did not at once fall in with my views, which were certainly radical. . . .

At two-thirty Friday afternoon the cabinet met and sat until four forty-five. The entire time was given to a discussion of the crisis with Germany. The discussion was very general, although it was chiefly confined to the subjects which the President and I had been over in our conference.

Friday was a day of extreme tension. From morning till night officials and newspaper men were fairly on tiptoe with suppressed excitement. Fully eighty of the correspondents were present at my interview in the morning, and they were swarming in the corridors when I returned to the Department at five o'clock. I slept soundly that night, feeling sure the President would act vigorously.

Saturday morning (the third), soon after I reached the Department, Polk and I discussed the situation. He was doubtful and distressed, and I assured him that I was certain the President would act that day. . . .

At ten-thirty I reached the President's study, and we conferred for half an hour. He told me that he had decided to hand Bernstorff his passports and to recall Gerard and that at two o'clock that afternoon he would address Congress, laying before them in a little more elaborate form the substance of the note which I had drafted, together with a statement that he would come before them again and ask for powers in case Germany should carry out her threats. I congratulated him on his decision, saying I was sure that he was right and that the American people almost to a man would stand behind him.

War Memoirs of Robert Lansing

239. "The World Must Be Made Safe for Democracy"

During the month of March, 1917, German submarines torpedoed five American merchant vessels, and President Wilson felt that the time had come to proclaim the existence of war. Unwilling to lead the country into war merely in defense of technical rights or even of the lives of those who insisted on taking risks by ocean travel, Wilson attempted to justify our entry into the war on the larger issue of making the world safe for democracy. His war speech is one of the most eloquent of American state papers.

I HAVE called the Congress into extraordinary session because there are serious, very serious, choices of policy to be made, and made immediately, which it was neither right nor constitutionally permissible that I should assume the responsibility of making. . . .

With a profound sense of the solemn and even tragical character of the step I am taking and of the grave responsibilities which it involves, but in unhesitating obedience to what I deem my constitutional duty, I advise that the Congress declare the recent course of the imperial German government to be in fact nothing less than war against the government and people of the United States, that it formally accept the status of belligerent which has thus been thrust upon it, and that it take immediate steps not only to put the country in a more thorough state of defense but also to exert all its power and employ all its resources to bring the government of the German Empire to terms and end the war.

We have no quarrel with the German people. We have no feeling toward them but one of sympathy and friendship. It was not upon their impulse that their government acted in entering this war. It was not with their previous knowledge or approval. It was a war determined upon as wars used to be determined upon in the old, unhappy days when peoples were nowhere consulted by their rulers and wars were provoked and waged in the interest of dynasties or of little groups of ambitious men who were accustomed to use their fellow men as pawns and tools. . . .

We are accepting this challenge of hostile purpose because we know that in such a government, following such methods, we can never have a friend, and that in the presence of its organized power, always lying in wait to accomplish we know not what purpose, there can be no assured security for the democratic governments of the world. We are now about to accept gauge of battle with this natural foe to liberty and shall, if necessary, spend the whole force of the nation to check and nullify its pretensions and its power. We are glad, now that we see the facts with no veil of false pretense about them, to fight thus for the ultimate peace of the world and for the liberation of its peoples, the German peoples included: for the rights of nations great and small and the privilege of men everywhere to choose their way of life and of obedience. The world must be made safe for democracy. Its peace must be planted upon the tested foundations of political liberty. We have no selfish ends to serve. We desire no conquest, no dominion. We seek no indemnities for ourselves, no material compensation for the sacrifices we shall freely make. We are but one of the champions of the rights of mankind. We shall be satisfied when those rights have been made as secure as the faith and the freedom of nations can make them. . . .

It is a distressing and oppressive duty, gentlemen of the Congress, which I have performed in thus addressing you. There are, it may be, many months of fiery trial and sacrifice ahead of us. It is a fearful thing to lead this great peaceful people into war, into the most terrible and disastrous of all wars, civilization itself seeming to be in the balance. But the right is more precious than peace, and we shall fight for the things which we have always carried nearest our hearts — for democracy, for the right of those who submit to authority to have a voice in their own governments, for the rights and liberties of small nations, for a universal dominion of right by such a concert of free peoples as shall bring peace and safety to all nations and make the world itself at last free. To such a task we can dedicate our lives and our fortunes, everything that we are and everything that we have, with the pride of those who know that the day has come when America is privileged to spend her blood and her might for the principles that gave her birth and happiness and the peace which she has treasured. God helping her, she can do no other.

WOODROW WILSON, Address to Congress, April 2, 1917

240. Torpedoed!

There had been experiments with submarines even as early as the American Civil War, but the World War was the first war in which the submarine was used with effectiveness. This new weapon changed the whole character of naval warfare and, as used by Germany, for a time seriously threatened England's supremacy on the seas.

THE FIRST torpedo struck us at a few minutes past ten o'clock in the morning. I was down below in the saloon with E. We had both kept a boat watch during the night and were the last officers to come to breakfast.

The saloon was a fine, large place, with lots of glass and tables and white-jacketed stewards. Above, on the decks, the men and most of the officers had fallen in at dawn and were to remain alert during our passage through the danger zone. A couple of Japanese destroyers, one to port and one to starboard, formed our escort. Our course was a series of zigzags at fourteen knots per hour by day and rather more at night.

E. and I ate our bacon and eggs and drank our coffee. The steward waiting on us was a clean-shaven little fellow who looked much like a low comedian. When the torpedo struck, there was no mistaking it for anything else. E. and I laughed, as much as to say: "Here she is!" Then I put on my cork belt, asked myself whether any part of me had suffered in the explosion, and received a confident answer, and next I leaped up the three flights of stairs that led to the liner's deck and my own boat station.

E. raced with me. I have never seen him since. He had a lovable habit of mothering people. I dare say it cost him his life. There is something specially tragical about this officer's disappearance. He was the last of three brothers. Two had died gallantly in France, and so that one of her boys might be spared to the bereaved mother, E. had been taken out of the trenches and given a safe job at the base; yet even so the fates had followed him.

The stewards and cooks raced with us too. There was something theatrical and cinema-ish about that picture — so many white jackets and blue uniform trousers and white overalls.

All this time — it might have been a couple of minutes — the greater part of me was so active that I have no recollection of any instant devoted to fear. Crude and horrible as it may sound, there was a large portion of my consciousness which was most vividly and delightedly enjoying itself. . . .

Just picture us, on a great liner, cozy as a grand hotel. Everything was remote from war and death as I have seen them so constantly on land these last three years. No mud, no dirt, no continuity. And we were all at ease and leading civilian lives, with bathrooms, linen sheets, and even an American bar! I don't know why, but I had imagined it all quite differently.

As one rushed upstairs one thought of things one had valued yesterday — two brand-new pairs of boots, one's field glasses, some money — they seemed now so utterly of no account. Providence must have been with me, for, arrived on deck, I stood flush before my boat, Number 13. I stood there and took charge. To left of me the right people were busy with our sixty-six sisters. These ladies were part of the staff of a new hospital unit. Safely they were put into their boats, safely lowered, and safely rowed away from us. We cheered them as they left, and they cheered back. Then Tommy, lined on deck, struck up a song. He always does in moments of emotion.

I had filled my boat as full as it would go. All was ready. I stepped on board and gave the signal. Then slowly we descended. Above our heads one of the ship's officers was seeing to it that we went down all right. Immediately below us was another boat. It pushed off at last, and now we were free to hit the water. Before we pushed off I took on five of the crew who had helped to lower us. They swarmed down the ropes and reached us safely. Then I refused to take anybody else, and we got the oars out and rowed away. Only then did I notice that the ship had stopped dead. She looked perfectly steady, like a ship anchored.

On leaving her I had thought of the other two officers who should have been with me and of the long rows of men I had seen drawn up on the decks. A moment I had hesitated, feeling very like a rat; but it was my duty to leave them, and I had no choice. Three more boats were waiting to follow mine. I pointed this out to the men I had to leave behind. And still I felt rather like a rat. Now, with a fuller knowledge, I am glad I went. . . .

So we floated, one of many little units, on those waters; and for a long time we were kept passionately interested by what we saw. Speaking for myself, I have never lived through moments so tense, so big, so charged with all extremes and textures of emotion.

The big ship — she was near to fifteen thousand tons — stood like an island and as if she could stand forever. While one of our destroyers went away on an unknown quest, the other drew alongside. We saw the little khaki figures swarm into her, and to be frank, we envied them. Then the destroyer maneuvered, and there was a flash and an explosion. A second torpedo had struck, and the Japanese commander had just dodged it. We now saw that his mast was broken and his wireless installation was sagging. But still the great ship stood there like an island.

I remember especially seeing another boat with only five men on board, four rowing gaily past us, the fifth baling. It seemed to us a horrible injustice, and several of my men said so aloud. I negatived the proposition, however, that we should get alongside and in part transfer. We seemed all right, and it struck me as best to leave well enough alone.

There followed next the most dramatic period of that spectacle. So far the great ship had stood firm, as if anchored. We noticed now that she had a definite list to starboard. The angle grew steeper, and then suddenly her bow dropped, her stern lifted, and next she slid to the bottom like a diver. It was as though a living thing had disappeared beneath the waves. We watched her, open-mouthed, a tightness at our hearts. We missed the comfort of her presence; we felt the tragedy of her surrender. In her death and engulfment there was a something more than human. So might a city built by countless hands and quick with life pass suddenly away. From somewhere in the middle of her bled a great puff of smoke, and I noticed that her deck as she stood on end, one half of her submerged, was bare and naked. It might have been a ballroom floor.

You must picture us now on an empty sea, for with the going of our ship, although some thousands of us were floating, struggling, and, alas, drowning, we made no great impression on that immensity. We felt very small and we felt very much alone and neglected.

ALBERT KINROSS, Torpedoed, *Atlantic Monthly*

241. The Navy Sows a Mine Barrage in the North Sea

> *By spring of 1917 German submarines were destroying Allied shipping faster than it could be replaced, and there was real danger that the submarine would give the Central Powers victory in the war. The most effective weapon against the U-boats, as they were called, was the mine, and it was the American Admiral Sims who was largely responsible for laying a barrage of mines in the North Sea — from the Orkneys to the Norwegian coast — through which few submarines could penetrate.*

THESE Americans had come this long distance to do their part in laying the mighty barrage [March, 1918] which was to add one more serious obstacle to the illegal German submarine campaign. Though the operation was a joint one of the American and British navies, our part was much the larger. The proposal was to construct this explosive impediment from the Orkney Islands to the coast of Norway, in the vicinity of Udsire Light, a distance of about two hundred and thirty nautical miles. Of this great area about a hundred and fifty miles, extending from the Orkneys to three degrees east longitude, was the American field, and the eastern section, which extended fifty nautical miles to Norway, was taken over by the British.

The mines were laid in a series of thirteen expeditions or excursions, as our men somewhat cheerfully called them. The ten mine layers participated in each excursion, all ten together laying about fifty-four hundred mines at every trip. Each trip to the field of action was practically a duplicate of the others; a description of one will, therefore, serve for all. After days and sometimes after weeks of preparation the squadron, usually on a dark and misty night, showing no lights or signals, would weigh anchor, slip by the rocky palisades of Moray Firth, and stealthily creep out to sea. As the ships passed through the nets and other obstructions and reached open waters, the speed increased, the gunners took their stations at their batteries, and suddenly from a dark horizon came a group of low, rapidly moving vessels; these were the British destroyers from the Grand Fleet which had been sent to escort the expedition and protect it from submarines. The absolute silence of the whole proceeding was impressive; not one of the destroyers showed a signal or a light; not one of the mine layers gave the slightest sign of recognition; all these details had been arranged in advance, and everything now worked with complete precision. The swishing of the water on the sides and the slow churning of the propellers were the only sounds that could possibly betray the ships to their hidden enemies. After the ships had steamed a few more miles the dawn began to break, and now a still more inspiring sight met our men. A squadron of battleships with scout cruisers and destroyers suddenly appeared over the horizon. This fine force likewise swept on, apparently paying not the slightest attention to our vessels. They steamed steadily southward and in an hour or so had entirely disappeared. The observer would hardly have guessed that this squadron from Admiral Beatty's fleet at Scapa Flow had anything to do with the American and British mine layers. Its business, however, was to establish a wall of steel and shotted guns between these forces and the German battle fleet at Kiel. At one time it was believed that the mine forces on the northern barrage would prove a tempting bait to the German dreadnaughts and that indeed it might induce the enemy to risk a second general engagement on the high seas. At any rate a fleet of converted excursion steamers laying mines in the North Sea could hardly be left exposed to the attacks of German raiders; our men had the satisfaction of knowing that while engaged in their engrossing if unenviable task a squadron of British or American battleships — for Admiral Rodman's forces took their regular turn in acting as a screen in these excursions — was standing a considerable distance to the south, prepared to make things lively for any German surface vessels which attempted to interfere with the operation.

Now in the open seas, the ten mine layers formed in two columns, abreast of each other and five hundred yards apart, and started for the waters of the barrage. Twelve destroyers surrounded them, on the lookout for submarines, for the ships were now in the track of the U-boats bound for their hunting ground or returning to their home ports. At a flash from the flagship all slackened speed and put out their paravanes — those underwater outrigger affairs which protected the ships from mines, for it was not at all unlikely that the Germans would place some of their own mines in this field for the benefit of the barrage builders. This operation took only a few minutes; then another flash, and the squadron again increased its speed. It steamed the distance across the North Sea to Udsire Light, then turned west again and headed for that mathematical spot on the ocean which was known as the start point — the place, that is, where the mine laying was to begin. In carrying out all these maneuvers — sighting the light on the Norwegian coast — the commander was thinking not only of the present but of the future, for the time would come, after the war had ended, when it would be necessary to remove all these mines, and it was therefore wise to fix them as accurately as possible in reference to landmarks, so as to know where to look for them. All this time the men were at their stations, examining the mines to see that everything was ready, testing the laying mechanism, and mentally rehearsing their duties. At about four o'clock an important signal came from the flagship:

"Have everything ready, for the squadron will reach start point in an hour and mine laying will begin."

Up to this time the ships were sailing in two columns; when they came within seven miles of start point another signal was broken out; the ships all wheeled like a company of soldiers, each turning sharply to the right, so that in a few minutes, instead of two columns, we had eight ships in line abreast, with the remaining two, also in line abreast, sailing ahead of them. This splendid array, keeping perfect position, approached the starting point like a line of race horses passing under the wire. Not a ship was off this line by so much as a quarter length; the whole atmosphere was one of eagerness; the officers all had their eyes fixed upon the stern of the flagship for the glimpse of the red flag which would be the signal to begin. Suddenly the flag was hauled down, indicating: "First mine over."

If you had been following one of these ships, you would probably have been surprised at the apparent simplicity of the task. The vessel was going at its full speed; at intervals of a few seconds a huge black object, about five feet high, would be observed gliding toward the stern; at this point it would pause for a second or two, as though suspended in air; it would then give a mighty lurch, fall head first into the water, sending up a great splash, and then sink beneath the waves. By the time the disturbance was over the ship would have advanced a considerable distance; then in a few seconds another black object would roll toward the stern, make a similar plunge, and disappear. You might have followed the same ship for two or three hours, watching these mines fall overboard at intervals of about fifteen seconds. There were four planters, each of which could and did on several trips lay about eight hundred and sixty mines in three hours and thirty-five minutes, in a single line about forty-four miles long. These were the *Canandaigua,* the *Canonicus,* the *Housatonic,* and the *Roanoke.* Occasionally the monotony of this procedure would be enlivened by a terrible explosion, a great geyser of water rising where a mine had only recently disappeared; this meant that the egg, as the sailors called it, had gone off spontaneously, without the assistance of any external contact; such accidents were part of the game, the records showing that about four per cent. of all the mines indulged in such initial premature explosions. For the most part, however, nothing happened to disturb the steady mechanical routine. The mines went over with such regularity that to an observer the whole proceeding seemed hardly the work of human agency. Yet every detail had been arranged months before in the United States; the mines fell into the sea in accordance with a time-table which had been prepared in Newport before the vessels started for Scotland. Every man on the ship had a particular duty to perform, and each performed it in the way in which he had been schooled under the direction of Captain Belknap.

The spherical mine case which contains the explosive charge and the mechanism for igniting it is only a part of the contrivance. While at rest on board the ship this case stands upon a boxlike affair about two feet square, known as the anchor; this anchor sinks to the bottom after launching, and it contains an elaborate arrangement for maintaining the mine at any desired depth beneath the surface. The bottom of the anchor has four wheels on which it runs along the little railroad track on the launching deck to the jumping-off place at the stern. All along these railroad tracks the mines were stationed one back of another; as one went overboard, they would all advance a peg, a mine coming up from below on an elevator to fill up the vacant space at the end of the procession. It took a crew of hard-working, begrimed, and sweaty men to keep these mines moving and going over the stern at the regularly appointed intervals. After three or four hours had been spent in this way and the ships had started back to their base, the decks would sometimes be covered with the sleeping figures of these exhausted men. It would be impossible to speak too appreciatively of the spirit they displayed; in the whole summer there was not a single mishap of any importance. The men all felt that they were engaged in a task which had never been accomplished before, and their exhilaration increased with almost every mine that was laid. "Nails in the coffin of the Kaiser" the men called these grim instruments of vengeance.

WILLIAM SOWDEN SIMS AND BURTON J. HENDRICK,
The Victory at Sea

242. The A.E.F. Reduces the Saint-Mihiel Salient

The summer of 1918 was the turning point of the war. Late in March of that year the Germans had launched their great offensive, designed to end the war, and in a series of brilliant assaults had pushed back the Allies to the gates of Paris. Allied man power was depleted and morale low, when General Pershing placed the American troops at the disposal of Generalissimo Foch who, in May, inaugurated a counterattack. First at Château-Thierry, then at Belleau Wood, Americans took the offensive and drove back the Germans, and in the Second Battle of the Marne, July 15 to 18, "the tide of war was definitely turned in favor of the Allies." Next month the American army was assigned the task of reducing the Saint-Mihiel salient, south of Verdun, and on the 12th of September the attack began. How successfully it was completed is here told by the commander of the American armies, General Pershing.

THE SAINT–MIHIEL salient lay between the Meuse and the Moselle Rivers and was roughly outlined by the triangle Pont-à-Mousson, Saint-Mihiel, Verdun. On the western side of this area the wooded heights of the Meuse extend along the east bank of the river. Beyond these heights lies the broad plain of the Woëvre with its large forest areas and numerous lakes and swamps. High wooded bluffs follow both banks of the Moselle, and the deep ravines and heavy forests on the western bank offer difficult terrain for extensive operations. Between the Moselle and Meuse Rivers the only stream of any importance is the Rupt de Mad, which flows northeast through Thiaucourt and empties into the Moselle. . . .

During the period of four years' occupation the Germans had strengthened the natural defensive features by elaborate fortifications and by a dense network of barbed wire that covered the entire front. There were four or five defensive positions, the first of which included the outpost system, the fourth being the Hindenburg Line, back of which were a series of detached works, and in rear the permanent fortifications of Metz and Thionville. The strength of the defenses had been fully demonstrated earlier in the war, when powerful efforts by the French against various points of the line had been defeated with heavy losses.

The salient was practically a great field fortress. It had, however, the characteristic weakness of all salients in that it could be attacked from both flanks in converging operations. Our heaviest blow was to be from the south, where there were no great natural features to be overcome, while the secondary attack was to come from the west and join the main drive in the heart of the salient.

In our original plans it had been my purpose after crushing the salient to continue the offensive through the Hindenburg Line and as much farther as possible, depending upon the success attained and the opposition that developed.

However, the agreement reached in conference on September 2d

[1918] limited the operations to the reduction of the salient itself. The basic features of the plan were not altered, but its objectives were defined and the number of troops to be employed was reduced.

A tactical surprise was essential to success, as the strength of the position would permit small forces of the enemy to inflict heavy losses on attacking troops. The sector had been quiet for some time and was usually occupied by seven enemy divisions in the front line, with two in reserve. It was estimated that the enemy could reinforce it by two divisions in two days, two more in three days, and as many divisions as were available in four days.

From captured documents and other sources of information, it seemed reasonable to conclude that the enemy had prepared a plan for withdrawal from the salient to the Hindenburg Line in case of heavy Allied pressure. There was no doubt he was aware that an American attack was impending. Therefore it was possible that he might increase his strength on our front. In that case our task would be more difficult, and as anything short of complete success would undoubtedly be seized upon to our disadvantage by those of the Allies who opposed the policy of forming an American army, no chances of a repulse in our first battle could be taken. These considerations prompted the decision to use some of our most experienced divisions along with the others.

As the plans for the battle neared completion, the duration of the preliminary artillery bombardment came up for consideration as affecting the element of surprise. Practically all previous attacks by the Allies had been preceded by severe bombardments, in some instances lasting for days. In the event that we should pursue the same method the enemy would, of course, be fully warned of our intentions. I decided, therefore, that there should be only enough preliminary artillery fire to disconcert the enemy and still not leave him time to withdraw or bring up reserves in any number before we could strike. A reasonable amount of firing would give encouragement to our own troops and would be especially advantageous in case rain should make the ground difficult for the tanks.

The attack on the southern face of the salient started at five o'clock on the morning of the twelfth, and before that hour I went with several staff officers to old Fort Gironville, situated on a commanding height overlooking the battlefield from the south. The secondary attack on the west was launched at 8:00 A.M. as an element of surprise and in order to give more time for artillery preparation there.

A drizzling rain and mist prevented us from getting a clear view, but the progress of our troops could be followed by the barrage which preceded them. Notwithstanding a heavy rainfall on the night of the 11th–12th, the weather gave us an advantage, as the mist partially screened our movements from the enemy. There was a chill breeze blowing, and its direction was such that no sound of firing could be heard from the artillery in our immediate front, although the more distant artillery bombardment on the western face was heard distinctly.

The sky over the battlefield, both before and after dawn, aflame with exploding shells, star signals, burning supply dumps and villages, presented a scene at once picturesque and terrible. The exultation in our minds that here, at last, after seventeen months of effort, an American army was fighting under its own flag was tempered by the realization of the sacrifice of life on both sides; and yet fate had willed it thus and we must carry through. Confidence in our troops dispelled every doubt of ultimate victory.

As we returned from Gironville, groups of prisoners were already being marched to stockades in the rear. About nine o'clock reports began to come in to army headquarters at Ligny from all portions of the twenty-five mile front that everything was going well, with losses light.

Mr. Baker returned from his observation point near the battlefield much elated over the success of the troops. He had been a witness to the first effort of an American army, and it was a proud day for him to feel that as Secretary of War his directing hand had led to such results. He took much pleasure in going about to all parts of the army and scorned being treated as a guest.

Thanks to the thorough preparation beforehand, the wire entanglements were more easily overcome than we had expected. Trained teams of pioneers and engineers, with bandalore torpedoes, wire cutters, and axes, assisted in opening gaps in the masses of barbed wire protecting the German positions. The leading troops themselves carried along rolls of chicken wire which was thrown across entanglements here and there, forming a kind of bridge for the infantry. In all their offensives the Allies had spent days in destroying these obstructions with artillery fire or had used a large number of heavy tanks, which were ineffective for such work. The fact that we had smothered the enemy artillery was an advantage, as it enabled the leading waves deliberately to do their work without serious loss.

The quick passage through these entanglements by our troops excited no little surprise among the French, who sent a large number of officers and noncommissioned officers to Saint-Mihiel several days later to see how it had been done. One of these officers after his reconnaissance remarked in all seriousness that the Americans had the advantage over Frenchmen because of their long legs and large feet.

In making our dispositions for battle, our older divisions, the First, Second, and Forty-second, had been given positions on the southern face opposite the open spaces to enable them to flank the wooded areas quickly, thus aiding the advance of less experienced units assigned to these areas. The whole line, pivoting as planned on the Eighty-second Division on the right, advanced resolutely to the attack. The entire operation was carried through with dash and precision.

By afternoon the troops had pushed beyond their scheduled objectives and by evening had reached the second day's objective on most of the southern front. The divisions of the Fourth Corps and those on the left of the First Corps overwhelmed the hostile garrisons and quickly overran their positions, carrying the fighting into the open. The German resistance on this part of the front was disorganized by the rapidity of our advance and was soon overcome.

When the First Division on the marching flank of the southern attack had broken through the hostile forward positions, the squadron of cavalry attached to the Fourth Corps was passed through the breach. At 1:45 P.M. it pushed forward to reconnoiter the roads toward Vigneulles, but encountering machine guns in position, was forced to retire. . . .

On the afternoon of the twelfth, learning that the roads leading out of the salient between the two attacks were filled with retreating enemy troops with their trains and artillery, I gave orders to the commanders of the Fourth and Fifth Corps to push forward without delay. Using the telephone myself, I directed the commander of the Fifth Corps to send at least one regiment of the Twenty-sixth Division toward Vigneulles with all possible speed. That evening a stronge force from the Fifty-first Brigade pushed boldly forward and reached Vigneulles at 2:15 A.M. on the 13th. It immediately made dispositions that effectively closed the roads leading out of the salient west of that point. In the Fourth Corps the Second Brigade of the First Division advanced in force about dawn of the thirteenth, its leading elements reaching Vigneulles by 6:00 A.M. The salient was closed, and our troops were masters of the field.

The troops continued to advance on the thirteenth, when the line was established approximately along the final objectives set for this offensive. In view of the favorable situation that had been developed just west of the Moselle River by our successes farther to the left, a limited attack, in accordance with our previous plans, was made on that part of the front by elements of the Eighty-second and Ninetieth Divisions with good results. During the night our troops were engaged in organizing their new positions for defense, preparatory to the withdrawal of divisions and corps troops for participation in the Meuse-Argonne battle. On September 14, 15, and 16, local operations continued, consisting of strong reconnaissances and the occupation of better ground for defensive purposes. Beginning on the thirteenth, several counterattacks were repulsed. The line as finally established was: Haudiomont–Fresnes-en-Woëvre–Doncourt–Jaulny–Vandières.

Reports received during the thirteenth and fourteenth indicated that the enemy was retreating in considerable disorder. Without doubt an immediate continuation of the advance would have carried us well beyond the Hindenburg Line and possibly into Metz, and the temptation to press on was very great, but we would probably have become involved and delayed the greater Meuse-Argonne operation, to which we were wholly committed.

Nearly sixteen thousand prisoners were taken, and some four hundred and fifty enemy guns had fallen into our hands. Our casualties numbered about seven thousand. As the enemy retreated, he set fire to many large supply dumps and several villages. The few remaining French inhabitants who found themselves within our lines were overjoyed to be released from the domination of the enemy, but many were left destitute by the burning of their homes at the very moment of deliverance.

On the thirteenth, General Pétain came by my headquarters, and we went together to Saint-Mihiel, where the people, including the children carrying French flags, gave us a welcome which may well be imagined when one realizes that they had been held as prisoners entirely out of touch with their own countrymen for four years, though always within sight of the French lines. They had heard only such vague reports of the war as their captors cared to furnish them, which were mainly accounts of German successes, and they were quite ignorant of the momentous events that had taken place during the previous two months.

JOHN J. PERSHING, My Experiences in the World War

243. "To Fight You Must Be Brutal and Ruthless"

President Wilson was anxious to justify the World War as being one for the preservation of liberty and democracy, but he knew well the dangers to which war exposed these very things at home. Despite his realization of this danger, he permitted, or acquiesced in, a lamentable violation of the rights of free speech and free press in this country during and after the war. Frank Cobb, to whom the President here unburdens himself, was the great liberal editor of the old New York World.

THE NIGHT before [Wilson] asked Congress for a declaration of war against Germany he sent for me [Frank Cobb, of the New York *World*]. I was late getting the message somehow and didn't reach the White House till one o'clock in the morning. "The old man" was waiting for me, sitting in his study with the typewriter on his table, where he used to type his own messages.

I'd never seen him so worn down. He looked as if he hadn't slept, and he said he hadn't. He said he was probably going before

Congress the next day to ask a declaration of war, and he'd never been so uncertain about anything in his life as about that decision. For nights, he said, he'd been lying awake going over the whole situation — over the provocation given by Germany, over the probable feeling in the United States, over the consequences to the settlement and to the world at large if we entered the melee.

He tapped some sheets before him and said that he had written a message and expected to go before Congress with it as it stood. He said he couldn't see any alternative, that he had tried every way he knew to avoid war. "I think I know what war means," he said, and he added that if there were any possibility of avoiding war he wanted to try it. "What else can I do?" he asked. "Is there anything else I can do?"

I told him his hand had been forced by Germany, that so far as I could see we couldn't keep out.

"Yes," he said, "but do you know what that means?" He said war would overturn the world we had known; that so long as we remained out there was a preponderance of neutrality but that if we joined with the Allies the world would be off the peace basis and on to a war basis.

It would mean that we should lose our heads along with the rest and stop weighing right and wrong. It would mean that a majority of people in this hemisphere would go war-mad, quit thinking, and devote their energies to destruction. The President said a declaration of war would mean that Germany would be beaten and so badly beaten that there would be a dictated peace, a victorious peace.

"It means," he said, "an attempt to reconstruct a peacetime civilization with war standards, and at the end of the war there will be no bystanders with sufficient power to influence the terms. There won't be any peace standards left to work with. There will be only war standards."

The President said that such a basis was what the Allies thought they wanted and that they would have their way in the very thing America had hoped against and struggled against. W.W. was uncanny that night. He had the whole panorama in his mind. He went on to say that so far as he knew he had considered every loophole of escape, and as fast as they were discovered Germany deliberately blocked them with some new outrage.

Then he began to talk about the consequences to the United States. He had no illusions about the fashion in which we were likely to fight the war.

He said when a war got going it was just war, and there weren't two kinds of it. It required illiberalism at home to reinforce the men at the front. We couldn't fight Germany and maintain the ideals of government that all thinking men shared. He said we would try it, but it would be too much for us.

"Once lead this people into war," he said, "and they'll forget there ever was such a thing as tolerance. To fight you must be brutal and ruthless, and the spirit of ruthless brutality will enter into the very fiber of our national life, infecting Congress, the courts, the policeman on the beat, the man in the street." Conformity would be the only virtue, said the President, and every man who refused to conform would have to pay the penalty.

He thought the Constitution would not survive it, that free speech and the right of assembly would go. He said a nation couldn't put its strength into a war and keep its head level; it had never been done.

"If there is any alternative, for God's sake, let's take it," he exclaimed. Well, I couldn't see any, and I told him so.

The President didn't have illusions about how he was going to come out of it, either. He'd rather have done anything else than head a military machine. All his instincts were against it. He foresaw too clearly the probable influence of a declaration of war on his own fortunes, the adulation certain to follow the certain victory, the derision and attack which would come with the deflation of excessive hopes and in the presence of world responsibility. But if he had it to do over again he would take the same course. It was just a choice of evils.

JOHN L. HEATON, Cobb of "The World"

244. Frederic Howe Deplores Wartime Hysteria

Wilson's melancholy prophecies came true; for a short time after the war the American people "forgot there ever was such a thing as tolerance." One phase of intolerance was the drive against alien "reds" which resulted in the deportation of thousands of aliens, many of them quite inoffensive. Frederic Howe, who here describes his experiences as commissioner of immigration at Ellis Island, had a long and honorable record as a progressive reformer.

HYSTERIA over the immoral alien was followed by a two-year panic over the "Hun." Again inspectors, particularly civilian secret service agents, were given carte blanche to make arrests on suspicion. Again Ellis Island was turned into a prison, and I had to protect men and women from a hue and cry that was but little concerned over guilt or innocence. During these years thousands of Germans, Austrians, and Hungarians were taken without trial from their homes and brought to Ellis Island. Nearly two thousand officers and seamen from sequestered German ships were placed in my care. Many of them had married American wives. They conducted themselves decently and well. They were obedient to discipline. They accepted the situation, and they gave practically no trouble. They were typical of the alien enemies the country over that were arrested under the hysteria that was organized and developed into a hate that lingers on . . .

Again I had either to drift with the tide or assume the burden of seeing that as little injustice as possible was done. I realized that under war conditions convincing evidence could not be demanded. I accepted that fact but not the assumption that "the Hun should be put against the wall and shot." From our entrance into the war until after the armistice my life was a nightmare. My telephone rang constantly with inquiries from persons seeking news of husbands and fathers who had been arrested. On my return home in the evening I would often find awaiting me women in a state of nervous collapse whose husbands had mysteriously disappeared and who feared that they had been done away with. I furnished them with such information as was possible. On the island I had to stand between the official insistence that the German should be treated as a criminal and the admitted fact that the great majority of them had been arrested by persons with little concern about their innocence or guilt and with but little if any evidence to support the detention.

Within a short time I was branded as pro-German. I had to war with the local staff to secure decent treatment for the aliens and with the army of secret service agents to prevent the island from being filled with persons against whom some one or other had filed a suspicious inquiry.

The final outbreak of hysteria was directed against the reds, the winter of 1918–19. It started in the state of Washington in the lumber camps and was directed against members of the I.W.W. organizations which had superseded the more conservative craft unions affiliated with the American Federation of Labor. There was a concerted determination on the part of employers to bring wages back to the prewar conditions and to break the power of organized labor. The movement against alien labor leaders had the support of the Department of Justice. Private detective agencies and strikebreakers acted with assurance that in any outrages they would be supported by the government itself. The press joined in the cry of red revolution and frightened the country with scare headlines of an army of organized terrorists who were determined to usher in revolution by force. The government borrowed the *agent provocateur* from old Russia; it turned loose innumerable private spies. For two years we were in a panic of fear over the red revolutionists, anarchists, and enemies of the Republic who were said to be ready to overthrow the government.

I had to stand against the current. Men and women were herded into Ellis Island. They were brought under guard and in special trains, with instructions to get them away from the country with as little delay as possible. Most of the aliens had been picked up in raids on labor headquarters; they had been given a drumhead trial by an inspector, with no chance for the defense; they were held incommunicado and often were not permitted to see either friends or attorneys before being shipped to Ellis Island. In these proceedings the inspector who made the arrest was prosecutor, witness, judge, jailer, and executioner. He was clerk and interpreter as well. This was all the trial the alien could demand under the law. In many instances the inspector hoped that he would be put in charge of his victim for a trip to New York and possibly to Europe at the expense of the government. Backed by the press of his city and by the hue and cry of the pack, he had every inducement to find the alien guilty and arrange for his speedy deportation.

I was advised by the commissioner general to mind my own business and carry out orders, no matter what they might be. Yet such obvious injustice was being done that I could not sit quiet. Moreover, I was an appointee of the President and felt that I owed responsibility to him whose words at least I was exemplifying in my actions. My words carried no weight with my superior officials, who were intoxicated with the prominence they enjoyed and the publicity which they received from the press. The bureaucratic organization at the island was happy in the punishing powers which all jailers enjoy and resented any interference on behalf of its victims. Members of Congress were swept from their moorings by an organized business propaganda and demanded that I be dismissed because I refused to railroad aliens to boats made ready for their deportation. I took the position from which I would not be driven, that the alien should not be held incommunicado and should enjoy the right of a writ of habeas corpus in the United States courts, which was the only semblance of legal proceedings open to him under the law.

In maintaining this position I had to quarrel with my superiors and the official force at the island. I faced a continuous barrage from members of Congress, from the press, from business organizations and prosecuting attorneys. Yet day by day aliens, many of whom had been held in prison for months, came before the court; and the judge, after examining the testimony, unwillingly informed the immigration authorities that there was not a scintilla of evidence to support the arrest. For in deportation cases it is not necessary to provide a preponderance of testimony or to convince the court of the justice of the charge; all that the government needs to support its case is a scintilla of evidence, which may be any kind of evidence at all. If there is a bit of evidence, no matter how negligible it may be, the order of deportation must be affirmed.

Again the pack was unleashed. No one took the trouble to ascertain the facts. The press carried stories to the effect that I had released hundreds of persons ordered deported. I had released aliens, but in each case I had been ordered to do so by the courts or the bureau. I had observed the law when organized hysteria demanded that it be swept aside. I had seen to it that men and women enjoyed their legal rights, but evidently this was the worst offense I could have committed. A congressional committee came to Ellis Island and held protracted hearings. It listened to disaffected officials, it created scare headlines for the press, it did everything in its power to convince the country that we were on the verge of a nationwide revolution, of which the most hard-boiled inspectors sent out by the bureau had reported they could not find a trace. When I went to the hearings and demanded the right to be present, to cross-examine witnesses and see the records, when I demanded that I be put on the witness stand myself, the committee ordered the sergeant-at-arms to eject me from the rooms.

As I look back over these years, my outstanding memories are not of the immigrants. They are rather of my own people. Things that were done forced one almost to despair of the mind, to distrust the political state. Shreds were left of our courage, our reverence. The Department of Justice, the Department of Labor, and Congress not only failed to protest against hysteria; they encouraged these excesses; the state not only abandoned the liberty which it should have protected, it lent itself to the stamping out of individualism and freedom. It used the *agent provocateur,* it permitted private agencies to usurp government powers, turned over the administration of justice to detective agencies, card-indexed liberals and progressives. It became frankly an agency of employing and business interests at a time when humanity — the masses, the poor — were making the supreme sacrifice of their lives.

I had fondly imagined that we prized individual liberty; I had believed that to Anglo-Saxons human rights were sacred and they would be protected at any cost.

Latin peoples might be temperamental, given to hysteria; but we were hard-headed, we stood for individuality. But I found that we were lawless, emotional, given to mob action. We cared little for freedom of conscience, for the rights of men to their opinions. Government was a convenience of business. Discussion of war profiteers was not to be permitted. The Department of Justice lent itself to the suppression of those who felt that war should involve equal sacrifice. Civil liberties were under the ban. Their subversion was not, however, an isolated thing; it was an incident in the ascendancy of business privileges and profits acquired during the war — an ascendancy that did not bear scrutiny or brook the free discussion which is the only safe basis of orderly popular government.

FREDERIC C. HOWE, Confessions of a Reformer

245. "Free Trade in Ideas"

One of the most consistent defenders of freedom of speech and of personal liberty was Oliver Wendell Holmes, Associate Justice of the United States Supreme Court from 1902 to 1932. A son of the famous author of The Autocrat of the Breakfast-Table, *Mr. Justice Holmes had, in the opinion of many of his contemporaries, the most distinguished mind of his generation and the most profound learning of any man who ever sat upon the Supreme Court bench. The following opinion is from one of the most notable of his numerous dissents.*

PERSECUTION for the expression of opinions seems to me perfectly logical. If you have no doubt of your premises or your power and want a certain result with all your heart you naturally express your wishes in law and sweep away all opposition. To allow opposition by speech seems to indicate that you think the speech impotent, as when a man says that he has squared the circle, or that you do not care wholeheartedly for the result, or that you doubt either your power or your premises. But when men have realized that time has upset many fighting faiths, they may come to believe even more than they believe the very foundations of their own conduct that the ultimate good desired is better reached by free trade in ideas — that the best test of truth is the power of the thought to get itself accepted in the competition of the market, and that truth is the only ground upon which their wishes safely can be carried out. That at any rate is the theory of our Constitution. It is an experiment, as all life is an experiment. Every year if not every day we have to wager our salvation upon some prophecy based upon imperfect knowledge. While that experiment is part of our system I think that we should be eternally vigilant against attempts to check the expression of opinions that we loathe and believe to be fraught with death, unless they so imminently threaten immediate interference with the lawful and pressing purposes of the law that an immediate check is required to save the country.

OLIVER WENDELL HOLMES, Dissenting Opinion
in Abrams *v*. United States, 1919

XXXV

From Normalcy to New Deal

246. President Harding Helps
His Friends

*The nomination of Warren G.
Harding by the Republican Convention of 1920 was not a response
to popular demand but to the demands of a group of political bosses,
of whom Boies Penrose was the most notorious. Harding was well-
intentioned, but he found it difficult to refuse a friend anything
within his power to give. With Harding's election the "Ohio gang"
took over national politics and for three years had things pretty
much their own way. Mrs. McLean, who here describes the Hardings, was a woman of great wealth and the wife of the editor of the
Washington* Post.

THE ONE time in our life when I thought that Ned McLean
was going to be saved from a disastrous end in dissipation was
when he was going around with Warren Gamaliel Harding. Good
heavens! I had cause enough for hope, because that friend of my
husband and of mine became the President and thus possessed not
only the power but the will to confer on us some great distinction
that would fully gratify the most ambitious appetite for dignity. I
have the President's written word that he was alert to recognize be-
comingly our "valued and devoted friendship."

In that stage of the 1920 campaign when the Republican candidate
was leaving his front porch from time to time to make speeches from
the rear platform of his train and in auditoriums before vast gatherings of cheering people whom he addressed as his "fellow countrymen," Ned and I were with the Hardings for a while and found out
that the Hardings we had known as poker-playing friends were
quite unchanged. However, out-of-doors or any place where others
might observe us, Mrs. Harding was clutched by a set of the strangest

fears that I ever encountered; and so, to a less degree, was her husband.

I stood beside her one day as photographers prepared to take our picture in a group with several others. I was engaged at the time in what for thirty years or more has been one of the least compromising of my habits — I was smoking a cigarette. Suddenly, aware of its smoke, she whirled on me and snatched the cigarette from my lips. She was as much concerned as if its tip had been hovering over a powder barrel.

"Evalyn," she chided me a little later, "you've got to help us by being circumspect. The Lord knows *I* don't mind your cigarettes, or jewels. You know how much I think of you; but you must give a thought to what we now are doing."

"But the senator smokes cigarettes," I said.

"Not when he is having his picture taken," said Mrs. Harding grimly. "Just let me catch him light a cigarette where any hostile eye might see him! He can't play cards until the campaign is over, either."

"But does he smoke tobacco?"

"A pipe, cigars, yes; but a cigarette is something that seems to infuriate swarms of voters who have a prejudice against cigarettes. He can chew tobacco, though." When she added that bit of information Mrs. Harding grimaced with a twinkle in her cornflower-blue eyes.

I learned that golf was something else that seemed to upset the stomachs of great masses of the voters, of factory laborers, of farmers, and of others who dwelt by myriads in those states where the campaign would be won or lost. Altogether the candidate had to shape himself, or seem to, just to fit the convolutions of the voters' minds.

I began to understand how sincere Warren Harding had been when he told us one time when we played poker that he really did not want to run for President.

"I'm satisfied with being senator," he said. "I'd like to go on living here in Washington and continue to be a member of the world's most exclusive club. I'm sure I can have six years more; I may have twelve or eighteen. If I have to go on and live in the White House I won't be able to call my soul my own. I don't want to be spied on every minute of the day and night. I don't want secret-service men trailing after me." He meant it, and it is my conviction that his wife meant it, too, when she said she preferred that they should be to the end of their days Senator and Mrs. Harding. The one who nagged and coaxed them to change their course was Harry M. Daugherty.

I remembered that Mr. Cox, who owned a newspaper in Dayton, Ohio, and one or two other small city newspapers, came to see us in Washington almost before the campaign was under way. He wanted to make sure that Ned would put the *Cincinnati Enquirer* wholeheartedly on the side of the Democratic party — and Cox. The *Enquirer* always had been Democratic.

"We've got to make up our minds," said Ned. "We're for Harding, you and me, but the readers of the *Enquirer* and the *Post* may be less ready for a shift than we should like to have them."

The fact is, I suppose, that old John R. [McLean] would have walked the earth as Hamlet's father did if he had known how lightly Ned was flipping back and forth with the idea of altering overnight the political complexion of two big, money-making papers. The question was especially vital with the *Enquirer*. Always under John R.'s direction it had been devoted to the Democratic party, which was natural since he himself was a party boss out in Ohio.

Just what to do came to me clearly in the night! Harding was going to win hands down, and everybody loves a winner. I put it plainly up to Ned, and he to me; we convinced each other (and I think so still) that as between Harding and Cox for President my choice to the end of time would be Warren G. Harding. There was no open break with the party, but Ned made it clear that he wanted nothing printed that would interfere even a little with the success of the Harding campaign.

The constant adulation of people was beginning to have an effect on Senator Harding. He was more and more inclined to believe in himself. He cherished an idea that when a man was elevated to the presidency his wits by some automatic mental chemistry were increased to fit the stature of his office. We, his friends, could see him, during that vacation, as a young Aladdin testing experimentally the terrific power of the mighty engine called the presidency.

"Hey, Ed," we would hear him call in a loud tone, as a king in olden times called for a jester. He really loved Ed Scobey, and it was fun for Harding to be able to announce to him that he should become the Director of the Mint and to know that what he promised would, by reason of his great power, come to pass.

Ned, before long, was to learn that he had been made chairman of the inaugural committee, which would have full charge of all arrangements for the celebration in connection with the ceremony whereby Woodrow Wilson would relinquish power and Warren Harding take it. A few other acts of powered graciousness were revealed to us on that trip, or just a few weeks later, as, one by one, all of Harding's well-liked friends received some kind of title. Dick Crissinger, for example, had been Harding's playmate when they were barefoot country boys. He grew up to be a Democrat of consequence in Marion, but it was his old pal Harding who made him governor of the Federal Reserve Board. These were not bad appointments; as good, no doubt, as needed for the jobs; but it seems significant to me, now, that they were made as they were — because Warren Harding had received the presidency by chance, without having expected until late in life that he had even, as he might have said, a Chinaman's chance to win the office. The office of president was hardly a subject that he had studied. I think it was a thing he had merely dreamed about, as we all dream when we wish we had power to fix everything. It is my opinion that Warren Harding, if he could have looked ahead when he was young and seen a vision of the time when he would be selected to go and live in the White House, would have lived quite differently. As it happened, he was a loyal friend who was, unhappily, loyal sometimes to the wrong people.

Guns, dogs, and horses were the instruments with which my husband had much of his fun; a duck blind on a raw and foggy morning was for him a place rich with excitement, and I think he liked nothing better than to see some horse he owned racing — out in front. However, when Senator Harding was elected Ned took up golf. He was well equipped to play at poker, but not so well equipped as the President-elect at bridge. Upon deciding to become a better golfer Ned did not merely buy a book; he hired the full-time services of a first-rate professional, Freddie McLeod. When that was done we had at Friendship all the appurtenances of a splendid country club, but this was a club where none paid dues nor any other fees — except we two McLeans. We had our money's worth in providing entertainment for those who came. As for me, there was an added value in the chance I seemed to sense that Ned McLean would stir with fine ambitions as he watched our friend, President-elect Harding, wield power and change the destinies of other men.

Certainly when Harding started in to pick his cabinet some of his selections were of a kind to make other men envy him his power. Charles Evans Hughes, Herbert Hoover, John W. Weeks, were names that aroused my enthusiasm when I heard they were slated for the Harding cabinet. There was a special thrill for me in those choices, because one afternoon during his post-election vacation at Brownsville, Texas, Senator Harding talked to me about that first big job he had to do.

"I want to have a really great cabinet," he said. Saying this, he was looking out the window of our private car. His shaggy brows were knit, and under them his blue-gray eyes were tender as he let them peer beyond the flatness of the Texas landscape until he took into his mind some concept of the whole of that country of which he had become the leader. Even there and then, however, one might have seen that troubles were in store for a man so easy-going with his friends. He was himself a loyal friend and could not think that treachery could mask itself behind the eyes of those he looked upon as friends of his. Unhappily, for many persons he had become something other than a friend; he was to all of these no less a thing than Opportunity. In consequence, if he talked alone with one man for five or ten minutes some others became uncomfortable, fearful of losing an expected favor.

EVALYN WALSH McLEAN, Father Struck It Rich

247. Calvin Coolidge Takes the Oath of Office

Calvin Coolidge, who had long been an obscure figure in Massachusetts politics, vaulted to national fame by his handling of the Boston police strike of 1919, and was nominated to the Vice-Presidency by the Republican Convention of 1920 against the wishes of the bosses and in response to popular demand. His frugality and simplicity were genuine, but the peculiar appropriateness of his accession to the Presidency was largely Coolidge "luck"; had President Harding died twenty-four hours later Coolidge would have taken the oath of office in the home of a multimillionaire friend whom he was planning to visit!

On THE night of August 2, 1923, I was awakened by my father coming up the stairs, calling my name. I noticed that his voice trembled. As the only times I had ever observed that before were when death had visited our family, I knew that something of the gravest nature had occurred.

His emotion was partly due to the knowledge that a man whom he had met and liked was gone, partly to the feeling that must possess all of our citizens when the life of their President is taken from them.

But he must have been moved also by the thought of the many sacrifices he had made to place me where I was, the twenty-five mile drives in storms and in zero weather over our mountain roads to carry me to the academy, and all the tenderness and care he had lavished upon me in the thirty-eight years since the death of my mother, in the hope that I might sometime rise to a position of importance, which he now saw realized.

He had been the first to address me as President of the United States. It was the culmination of the lifelong desire of a father for the success of his son.

He placed in my hands an official report and told me that President Harding had just passed away. My wife and I at once dressed.

Before leaving the room I knelt down and, with the same prayer with which I have since approached the altar of the church, asked God to bless the American people and give me power to serve them.

My first thought was to express my sympathy for those who had been bereaved and after that was done to attempt to reassure the country with the knowledge that I proposed no sweeping displacement of the men then in office and that there were to be no violent changes in the administration of affairs. As soon as I had dispatched a telegram to Mrs. Harding, I therefore issued a short public statement declaratory of that purpose.

Meantime I had been examining the Constitution to determine what might be necessary for qualifying by taking the oath of office. It is not clear that any additional oath is required beyond what is taken by the vice president when he is sworn into office. It is the same form as that taken by the president.

Having found this form in the Constitution, I had it set up on the typewriter, and the oath was administered by my father in his capacity as a notary public, an office he had held for a great many years.

The oath was taken in what we always called the sitting room, by the light of the kerosene lamp, which was the most modern form of lighting that had then reached the neighborhood. The Bible which had belonged to my mother lay on the table at my hand. It was not officially used, as it is not the practice in Vermont or Massachusetts to use a Bible in connection with the administration of an oath.

Besides my father and myself, there were present my wife, Senator Dale, who happened to be stopping a few miles away, my stenographer, and my chauffeur. . . .

Where succession to the highest office in the land is by inheritance or appointment, no doubt there have been kings who have participated in the induction of their sons into their office, but in republics, where the succession comes by an election, I do not know of any other case in history where a father has administered to his son the qualifying oath of office which made him the chief magistrate of a nation. It seemed a simple and natural thing to do at the time, but I can now realize something of the dramatic force of the event.

This room was one which was already filled with sacred memories for me. In it my sister and my stepmother passed their last hours. It was associated with my boyhood recollections of my own mother, who sat and reclined there during her long invalid years, though she passed away in an adjoining room, where my father was to follow her within three years from this eventful night.

The Autobiography of Calvin Coolidge

248. Charles Lindbergh Flies to Paris

"God never intended man to fly" was a serious conviction in 1900, but before the end of the decade the vision of Samuel P. Langley and the perseverance of the Wright brothers proved that the airplane was a practical invention. As early as 1919 two Englishmen, Alcock and Brown, made a nonstop flight from Newfoundland to Ireland, and throughout the twenties other aviators had revealed the almost limitless possibilities of aviation. But no feat of that generation caught the imagination of Americans as did Lindbergh's solo flight from New York to Paris, and the modesty with which Lindbergh received the universal acclaim further endeared him to his countrymen.

ON THE morning of May nineteenth, a light rain was falling and the sky was overcast. Weather reports from land stations and ships along the great circle course were unfavorable and there was apparently no prospect of taking off for Paris for several days at least. But at about six o'clock I received a special report from the New York Weather Bureau. A high pressure area was over the entire North Atlantic and the low pressure area over Nova Scotia and Newfoundland was receding. It was apparent that the prospects of the fog clearing up were as good as I might expect for some time to come. The North Atlantic should be clear with only local storms on the coast of Europe. The moon had just passed full and the percentage of days with fog over Newfoundland and the Grand Banks was increasing so that there seemed to be no advantage in waiting longer.

We went to Curtiss Field as quickly as possible and made arrangements for the barograph to be sealed and installed, and for the plane to be serviced and checked.

We decided partially to fill the fuel tanks in the hangar before towing the ship on a truck to Roosevelt Field which adjoins Curtiss on the east, where the servicing would be completed.

I left the responsibility for conditioning the plane in the hands of the men on the field while I went into the hotel for about two and one-half hours of rest; but at the hotel there were several more details which had to be completed and I was unable to get any sleep that night.

I returned to the field before daybreak on the morning of the twentieth. A light rain was falling which continued until almost dawn; consequently we did not move the ship to Roosevelt Field until much later than we had planned, and the take off was delayed from daybreak until nearly eight o'clock.

At dawn the shower had passed, although the sky was overcast, and occasionally there would be some slight precipitation. The tail of the plane was lashed to a truck and escorted by a number of motorcycle police. The slow trip from Curtiss to Roosevelt was begun.

The ship was placed at the extreme west end of the field heading along the east and west runway and the final fueling commenced.

About 7:40 A.M. the motor was started and at 7:52 I took off on the flight for Paris.

The field was a little soft due to the rain during the night and the heavily loaded plane gathered speed very slowly. After passing the halfway mark, however, it was apparent that I would be able to clear the obstructions at the end. I passed over a tractor by about fifteen feet and a telephone line by about twenty, with a fair reserve of flying speed. I believe that the ship would have taken off from a hard field with at least five hundred pounds more weight.

I turned slightly to the right to avoid some high trees on a hill directly ahead, but by the time I had gone a few hundred yards I had sufficient altitude to clear all obstructions and throttled the engine down to 1750 R.P.M. I took up a compass course at once and soon reached Long Island Sound where the Curtiss Oriole with its photographer, which had been escorting me, turned back.

The haze soon cleared and from Cape Cod through the southern half of Nova Scotia the weather and visibility were excellent. I was flying very low, sometimes as close as ten feet from the trees and water.

On the three-hundred-mile stretch of water between Cape Cod and Nova Scotia I passed within view of numerous fishing vessels.

The northern part of Nova Scotia contained a number of storm areas and several times I flew through cloudbursts.

As I neared the northern coast, snow appeared in patches on the ground and far to the eastward the coastline was covered with fog.

For many miles between Nova Scotia and Newfoundland the ocean was covered with caked ice, but as I approached the coast the ice disappeared entirely and I saw several ships in this area.

I had taken up a course for St. John's, which is south of the great circle from New York to Paris, so that there would be no question of the fact that I had passed Newfoundland in case I was forced down in the North Atlantic.

I passed over numerous icebergs after leaving St. John's, but saw no ships except near the coast.

Darkness set in about 8:15 and a thin, low fog formed over the sea through which the white bergs showed up with surprising clearness. This fog became thicker and increased in height until within two hours I was just skimming the top of storm clouds at about ten thousand feet. Even at this altitude there was a thick haze through which only the stars directly overhead could be seen.

There was no moon and it was very dark. The tops of some of the storm clouds were several thousand feet above me and at one time, when I attempted to fly through one of the larger clouds, sleet started to collect on the plane and I was forced to turn around and get back into clear air immediately and then fly around any clouds which I could not get over.

The moon appeared on the horizon after about two hours of darkness; then the flying was much less complicated.

Dawn came at about 1 A.M., New York time, and the temperature had risen until there was practically no remaining danger of sleet.

Shortly after sunrise the clouds became more broken, although some of them were far above me and it was often necessary to fly through them, navigating by instruments only.

As the sun became higher, holes appeared in the fog. Through one the open water was visible, and I dropped down until less than a hundred feet above the waves. There was a strong wind blowing from the northwest and the ocean was covered with white caps.

After a few miles of fairly clear weather the ceiling lowered to zero and for nearly two hours I flew entirely blind through the fog at an altitude of about 1500 feet. Then the fog raised and the water was visible again.

On several more occasions it was necessary to fly by instrument for short periods; then the fog broke up into patches. These patches took on forms of every description. Numerous shorelines appeared, with trees perfectly outlined against the horizon. In fact, the mirages were so natural that, had I not been in mid-Atlantic and known that no land existed along my route, I would have taken them to be actual islands.

As the fog cleared I dropped down closer to the water, sometimes flying within ten feet of the waves and seldom higher than two hundred.

There is a cushion of air close to the ground or water through which a plane flies with less effort than when at a higher altitude, and for hours at a time I took advantage of this factor.

Also it was less difficult to determine the wind drift near the water. During the entire flight the wind was strong enough to produce white caps on the waves. When one of these formed, the foam would be blown off, showing the wind's direction and approximate velocity. This foam remained on the water long enough for me to obtain a general idea of my drift.

During the day I saw a number of porpoises and a few birds but no ships, although I understand that two different boats reported me passing over.

The first indication of my approach to the European Coast was a small fishing boat which I first noticed a few miles ahead and slightly to the south of my course. There were several of these fishing boats grouped within a few miles of each other.

I flew over the first boat without seeing any signs of life. As I circled over the second, however, a man's face appeared, looking out of the cabin window.

I have carried on short conversations with people on the ground by flying low with throttled engine, and shouting a question, and receiving the answer by some signal. When I saw this fisherman I decided to try to get him to point towards land. I had no sooner made the decision than the futility of the effort became apparent. In all likelihood he could not speak English, and even if he could he would undoubtedly be far too astounded to answer. However, I circled again and closing the throttle as the plane passed within a few feet of the boat I shouted, "Which way is Ireland?" Of course the attempt was useless, and I continued on my course.

Less than an hour later a rugged and semi-mountainous coastline appeared to the northeast. I was flying less than two hundred feet from the water when I sighted it. The shore was fairly distinct and not over ten or fifteen miles away. A light haze coupled with numerous storm areas had prevented my seeing it from a long distance.

The coastline came down from the north and curved towards the east. I had very little doubt that it was the southwestern end of Ireland, but in order to make sure I changed my course towards the nearest point of land.

I located Cape Valencia and Dingle Bay, then resumed my compass course towards Paris.

After leaving Ireland I passed a number of steamers and was seldom out of sight of a ship.

In a little over two hours the coast of England appeared. My course passed over southern England and a little south of Plymouth; then across the English Channel, striking France over Cherbourg.

I was flying at about a fifteen-hundred-foot altitude over England and as I crossed the Channel and passed over Cherbourg, France, I had probably seen more of that part of Europe than many native Europeans. The visibility was good and the country could be seen for miles around.

The sun went down shortly after passing Cherbourg and soon the beacons along the Paris-London airway became visible.

I first saw the lights of Paris a little before 10 P.M., or 5 P.M., New York time, and a few minutes later I was circling the Eiffel Tower at an altitude of about four thousand feet.

The lights of Le Bourget were plainly visible, but appeared to be very close to Paris. I had understood that the field was farther from the city, so continued out to the northeast into the country for four or five miles to make sure that there was not another field farther out which might be Le Bourget. Then I returned and spiralled down closer to the lights. Presently I could make out long lines of hangars, and the roads appeared to be jammed with cars.

I flew low over the field once, then circled around into the wind and landed.

CHARLES A. LINDBERGH, "We"

249. Mrs. McLean Sees the Bonus Army

Congress, in 1924, had provided for a soldier's bonus to be paid at death or after twenty years. The depression stimulated a demand for immediate payment of this bonus, and after repeated failure to get satisfaction through ordinary political pressure, a bonus army of veterans marched on Washington, June 1932, to present a "petition on boots." After some procrastination, President Hoover directed the National Guard to break up the bonus army camp and drive out the veterans. This task the army performed with an efficiency that shocked public opinion, largely destroyed Hoover's reputation as a humanitarian, and contributed to his defeat at the polls that fall.

ON A day in June, 1932, I saw a dusty automobile truck roll slowly past my house. I saw the unshaven, tired faces of the men who were riding in it standing up. A few were seated at the rear with their legs dangling over the lowered tailboard. On the side of the truck was an expanse of white cloth on which, crudely lettered in black, was a legend, BONUS ARMY.

Other trucks followed in a straggling succession, and on the sidewalks of Massachusetts Avenue where stroll most of the diplomats and the other fashionables of Washington were some ragged hikers, wearing scraps of old uniforms. The sticks with which they strode along seemed less canes than cudgels. They were not a friendly-looking lot, and I learned they were hiking and riding into the capital along each of its radial avenues; that they had come from every part of the continent. It was not lost on me that those men, passing any one of my big houses, would see in such rich shelters a kind of challenge.

I was burning, because I felt that crowd of men, women, and children never should have been permitted to swarm across the continent. But I could remember when those same men, with others, had been cheered as they marched down Pennsylvania Avenue. While I recalled those wartime parades, I was reading in the newspapers that the bonus army men were going hungry in Washington.

That night I woke up before I had been asleep an hour. I got to thinking about those poor devils marching around the capital. Then I decided that it should be a part of my son Jock's education to see and try to comprehend that marching. It was one o'clock, and the Capitol was beautifully lighted. I wished then for the power to turn off the lights and use the money thereby saved to feed the hungry.

When Jock and I rode among the bivouacked men I was horrified to see plain evidence of hunger in their faces; I heard them trying to cadge cigarettes from one another. Some were lying on the side-walks, unkempt heads pillowed on their arms. A few clusters were shuffling around. I went up to one of them, a fellow with eyes deeply sunken in his head.

"Have you eaten?"

He shook his head.

Just then I saw General Glassford, superintendent of the Washington police. He said, "I'm going to get some coffee for them."

"All right," I said, "I am going to Childs'."

It was two o'clock when I walked into that white restaurant. A man came up to take my order. "Do you serve sandwiches? I want a thousand," I said. "And a thousand packages of cigarettes."

"But, lady—"

"I want them right away. I haven't got a nickel with me, but you can trust me. I am Mrs. McLean."

Well, he called the manager into the conference, and before long they were slicing bread with a machine; and what with Glassford's coffee also (he was spending his own money) we two fed all the hungry ones who were in sight.

Next day I went to see Judge John Barton Payne, head of the Red Cross, but I could not persuade him that the bonus army men were part of a national crisis that the Red Cross was bound to deal with. He did promise a little flour, and I was glad to accept it.

Then I tried the Salvation Army and found that their girls were doing all they could. I asked the officer in charge, a worried little man, if he would undertake to find out how I could help the men. With enthusiasm he said he would, and the next day he came to my house to tell me that what the bonus army leaders said they most needed was a big tent to serve as a headquarters in which fresh arrivals could be registered. At once I ordered a tent sent over from Baltimore. After that I succeeded in getting Walter Waters to come to my house. He was trying to keep command of that big crowd of men. I talked to him, and before long we were friends. I sent books and radios to the men. I went to the house in Pennsylvania Avenue that Glassford had provided for the women and children. There was not a thing in it. Scores of women and children were sleeping on its floors. So I went out and bought them army cots. Another day I took over some of my sons' clothing, likewise some of my own, and dresses of my daughter. One of the women held up one of little Evalyn's dresses and examined it on both sides. Then she said, "I guess my child can starve in a fifty-dollar dress as well as in her rags."

One day Waters, the so-called commander, came to my house and said: "I'm desperate. Unless these men are fed, I can't say what won't happen to this town." With him was his wife, a little ninety-three-pounder, dressed as a man, her legs and feet in shiny boots. Her yellow hair was freshly marceled.

"She's been on the road for days," said Waters, "and has just arrived by bus."

I thought a bath would be a welcome change; so I took her upstairs to that guest bedroom my father had designed for King Leopold. I sent for my maid to draw a bath, and told the young woman to lie down.

"You get undressed," I said, "and while you sleep I'll have all your things cleaned and pressed."

"Oh, no," she said, "not me. I'm not giving these clothes up. I might never see them again."

Her lip was out, and so I did not argue. She threw herself down on the bed, boots and all, and I tiptoed out.

That night I telephoned to Vice-President Charlie Curtis. I told him I was speaking for Waters, who was standing by my chair. I said: "These men are in a desperate situation, and unless something is done for them, unless they are fed, there is bound to be a lot of trouble. They have no money, nor any food."

Charlie Curtis told me that he was calling a secret meeting of senators and would send a delegation of them to the House to urge immediate action on the Howell bill, providing money to send the bonus army members back to their homes.

Those were times when I often wished for the days of Warren Harding. Harding would have gone among those men and talked in such a manner as to make them cheer him and cheer their flag. If Hoover had done that, I think, not even troublemakers in the swarm could have caused any harm.

Nothing I had seen before in my whole life touched me as deeply as what I had seen in the faces of those men of the bonus army. Their way of righting things was wrong — oh, yes; but it is not the only wrong. I had talked with them and their women. Even when the million-dollar home my father built was serving as a sort of headquarters for their leader, I could feel and almost understand their discontent and their hatred of some of the things I have represented.

I was out in California when the United States army was used to drive them out of Washington. In a moving-picture show I saw in a news reel the tanks, the cavalry, and the gas-bomb throwers running those wretched Americans out of our capital. I was so raging mad I could have torn the theater down. They could not be allowed to stay, of course; but even so I felt myself one of them.

EVALYN WALSH McLEAN, Father Struck It Rich

250. Franklin D. Roosevelt
Promises a New Deal

Confident of victory, the Democrats, in their convention at Chicago in 1932 nominated Franklin D. Roosevelt for their standard-bearer and adopted a platform calling for far-reaching reforms. Democratic confidence was justified. Roosevelt carried every state but six, and Democratic control of both Houses of Congress was complete. In his Inaugural Address the new President promised "a new deal" to the "forgotten man" — a promise which he proceeded to carry out with breath-taking rapidity in the early months of his administration.

THIS is a day of national consecration, and I am certain that my fellow Americans expect that on my induction into the Presidency I will address them with a candor and a decision which the present situation of our nation impels.

This is pre-eminently the time to speak the truth, the whole truth, frankly and boldly. Nor need we shrink from honestly facing conditions in our country today. This great nation will endure as it has endured, will revive and will prosper.

So first of all let me assert my firm belief that the only thing we have to fear is fear itself — nameless, unreasoning, unjustified terror which paralyzes needed efforts to convert retreat into advance.

In every dark hour of our national life a leadership of frankness and vigor has met with that understanding and support of the people themselves which is essential to victory. I am convinced that you will again give that support to leadership in these critical days.

In such a spirit on my part and on yours we face our common difficulties. They concern, thank God, only material things. Values have shrunken to fantastic levels; taxes have risen; our ability to pay has fallen; government of all kinds is faced by serious curtailment of income; the means of exchange are frozen in the currents of trade; the withered leaves of industrial enterprise lie on every side; farmers find no markets for their produce; the savings of many years in thousands of families are gone.

More important, a host of unemployed citizens face the grim problem of existence, and an equally great number toil with little return. Only a foolish optimist can deny the dark realities of the moment.

Yet our distress comes from no failure of substance. We are stricken by no plague of locusts. Compared with the perils which our forefathers conquered because they believed and were not afraid, we have still much to be thankful for. Nature still offers her bounty and human efforts have multiplied it. Plenty is at our doorstep, but a generous use of it languishes in the very sight of the supply.

Primarily, this is because the rulers of the exchange of mankind's goods have failed through their own stubbornness and their own incompetence, have admitted their failure and abdicated. Practices of the unscrupulous money-changers stand indicted in the court of public opinion, rejected by the hearts and minds of men.

True, they have tried, but their efforts have been cast in the pattern of an outworn tradition. Faced by failure of credit, they have proposed only the lending of more money.

Stripped of the lure of profit by which to induce our people to follow their false leadership, they have resorted to exhortations, pleading tearfully for restored confidence. They know only the rules of a generation of self-seekers.

They have no vision, and when there is no vision the people perish.

The money-changers have fled from their high seats in the temple of civilization. We may now restore that temple to the ancient truths. . . .

Restoration calls, however, not for changes in ethics alone. This nation asks for action, and action now.

Our greatest primary task is to put people to work. This is no unsolvable problem if we face it wisely and courageously.

It can be accomplished in part by direct recruiting by the government itself, treating the task as we would treat the emergency of a war, but at the same time, through this employment, accomplishing greatly needed projects to stimulate and reorganize the use of our natural resources.

Hand in hand with this, we must frankly recognize the overbalance of population in our industrial centers and, by engaging on a national scale in a redistribution, endeavor to provide a better use of the land for those best fitted for the land.

The task can be helped by definite efforts to raise the values of agricultural products and with this the power to purchase the output of our cities.

It can be helped by preventing realistically the tragedy of the growing loss, through foreclosure, of our small homes and our farms.

It can be helped by insistence that the Federal, state, and local governments act forthwith on the demand that their cost be drastically reduced.

It can be helped by the unifying of relief activities which today are often scattered, uneconomical, and unequal. It can be helped by national planning for and supervision of all forms of transportation and of communications and other utilities which have a definitely public character.

There are many ways in which it can be helped, but it can never be helped merely by talking about it. We must act, and act quickly. . . .

Action in this image and to this end is feasible under the form of government which we have inherited from our ancestors.

Our Constitution is so simple and practical that it is possible always to meet extraordinary needs by changes in emphasis and arrangement without loss of essential form.

That is why our constitutional system has proved itself the most superbly enduring political mechanism the modern world has produced. It has met every stress of vast expansion of territory, of foreign wars, of bitter internal strife, of world relations.

It is to be hoped that the normal balance of executive and legislative authority may be wholly adequate to meet the unprecedented task before us. But it may be that an unprecedented demand and need for undelayed action may call for temporary departure from that normal balance of public procedure.

I am prepared under my constitutional duty to recommend the measures that a stricken nation in the midst of a stricken world may require.

These measures, or such other measures as the Congress may build out of its experience and wisdom, I shall seek, within my constitutional authority, to bring to speedy adoption.

But in the event that the Congress shall fail to take one of these two courses, and in the event that the national emergency is still critical, I shall not evade the clear course of duty that will then confront me.

I shall ask the Congress for the one remaining instrument to meet the crisis — broad executive power to wage a war against the emergency as great as the power that would be given me if we were in fact invaded by a foreign foe.

For the trust reposed in me I will return the courage and the devotion that befit the time. I can do no less.

We face the arduous days that lie before us in the warm courage of national unity; with the clear consciousness of seeking old and precious moral values; with the clean satisfaction that comes from the stern performance of duty by old and young alike.

We aim at the assurance of a rounded and permanent national life.

We do not distrust the future of essential democracy. The people of the United States have not failed. In their need they have registered a mandate that they want direct, vigorous action.

They have asked for discipline and direction under leadership. They have made me the present instrument of their wishes. In the spirit of the gift I take it.

In this dedication of a nation we humbly ask the blessing of God. May He protect each and every one of us! May He guide me in the days to come!

FRANKLIN D. ROOSEVELT, First Inaugural Address, 1933

251. "We Too Are the People"

When Roosevelt came to office in March 1933, there were some twelve million unemployed, private charity was well-nigh exhausted, many states on the verge of bankruptcy, and it was imperative for the Federal Government to take over the burden of relief. The Works Progress Administration, established with an appropriation of almost five billion dollars in

1935, was one of the many agencies which the New Deal set up to cope with the task of putting men and women to work on useful projects.

THERE are at least fifty men in the big room, but the group is constantly changing. Three just went out one door as five came in another. Here is a new arrival, a big fellow in boots with his wife and three small children. In spite of the lumberjack boots, these men are not lumberjacks, though some of them have been in their earlier years. The costume of those roaring, rollicking days still persists more or less as it was because it is the costume of the north country, the only one possible for those who have to brave the snow and ice and the bitter winds of such a wintry world. The boots are called high-tops now when you buy them at the store. The best ones come up almost to the knee, but some are lower, and there is an endless variety of rubber boots and high overshoes. Most of the boots responsible for this particular thumping undertone are old, worn out, patched and muddy. In some cases only the leather tops remain, and high red farm rubbers have been sewed on for the feet. The rest of this typical north country costume consists of a short, heavy jacket of some kind, rarely an overcoat, overalls or shabby patched trousers, sometimes corduroy, worn inside the boots, heavy stockings pulled up over the trousers, with gay colored tops turned down over the top of the boots, and nondescript caps of many kinds. The jackets are plaid mackinaws, making bright patches of color in the crowd even though they are old and faded, sheepskin-lined jackets in varying shades of earth color, leather jackets, some so tattered that they suggest fur or fringe, and heavy sweaters, dingy, ragged, or darned in many places. The caps are mostly the kind which pull over the ears, with here and there a bright-colored knitted one of the typical lumberjack style, like a small tight-fitting stocking cap with a tassel on top.

These men form the solid background of this picture of human life. Against this mottled background other colorful figures stand out, taking the spotlight for a moment, and passing on as others take their places. An old Ottawa Indian stands at the far end of the room, leaning on a long staff. In spite of his dingy, furry, ragged clothing, he is the most dignified figure in the room. With his white hair hanging to his shoulders, head erect, eyes narrowed, he looks like some ancient prophet. A handsome young Indian stands beside him. What a model for a sculptor! As you look at him, his forlorn cap and patched overalls seem to melt away, and you see him with eagle feather war bonnet and blanket, for the glory of the past still lives in that bronze face, a glory which he himself has never known. An attractive blonde trained nurse makes her way through the crowd, a charming highlight in the picture with her white uniform and dark blue cape. A burly truck driver lurches in, slapping his leather-mittened hands together. His genial face, bright red from the stinging cold, breaks into a grin as a swarthy brown-eyed boy of twenty strides across the room to him with his hands full of papers. A drugstore clerk in a starched white linen coat is talking to the pretty girl who sits at the desk near the door. A tall blond squaw man smiles down at his dusky wife as their beautiful baby holds out her arms to him. He has taken the baby now, and her tiny hands are gripping the sheepskin collar of his jacket. That huge man with the perfect Viking face is the highway commissioner. He is the only man in the room who is wearing an overcoat. His wide blue eyes search the crowd. A road foreman steps forward to join him, a picturesque type — tawny hair, a strong face above that gaudy mackinaw. He speaks with a Southern drawl, unfamiliar in this north country. They make their way to a very thin man sitting at a desk piled with papers.

A halfwit mumbles to himself near the window. A drunken man utters maudlin protests as he is quietly but firmly ushered out the door. A white-haired, trimly dressed woman doctor has entered. As her keen eyes glance about the crowd, she smiles and nods a greeting here and there. She stops to speak to an old man. Dear old fellow, his wrinkled cheeks are apple-red from the cold, and his whole face seems to twinkle as he talks. What a Santa Claus he would make if he only had whiskers! Now the doctor has turned to speak to a motherly-looking woman holding a frail little boy by the hand. This mother has almost a Madonna face. Perhaps the smooth dark hair gives that effect. Her blue cotton dress is clean and starched, but her old black coat is shabby and worn. Can this be another mother standing beside her? It is a woman, but she is dressed like the men — muddy high-tops, trousers, a dirty, ragged mackinaw, and a stocking cap. Her thin face is scarred on one side. Those might be acid burns that show through the rouge. It is a hard, predatory face, the face of a gunman's moll, but she is holding a beautiful little girl by the hand. An elderly Jew stands a little apart from the crowd. That white face with its deep-sunk eyes arrests one's attention. He is perhaps the most tragic figure in the group. A sergeant of the state police has come in, his shining black puttees a contrast to the many shabby boots. Keen face, trim uniform, quick, decisive movements, make him seem like a high-geared machine, ready to function on the instant. He is all modern, this trooper, in this crowd of men where many seem somehow of the past.

A wave of merriment drifts over the group near the door as a laughing, dancing black man stops to speak to the girl at the desk. In his tattered overalls he looks like a scarecrow in the wind. As he talks his feet keep time to his words and his body sways in a syncopated rhythm. He has the girl at the desk laughing now. Black, so black — but he is a bright spot in the picture, this Negro with dancing feet and a dancing soul. A United States army officer and two CCC boys are talking to a striking-looking dark woman in a brown sport dress. The captain's handsome tan boots put all the other boots in the room to shame, even the trooper's. He is a dashing figure in his smart uniform. So are the boys in their khaki outfits. Their ruddy young faces glow with health. Now an official of the National Forest Service has joined the group, his dark green uniform an added color note in the picture. A fat Polish woman is wailing complaints now to the girl at the desk. A prim old lady is looking daggers of disapproval at her. Is this creature who just shambled in a man? That hairy face, those half-closed, shifty eyes, are hardly human. He might be one of Peer Gynt's trolls — and that slatternly wench beside him the Troll King's daughter. Certainly he is a different species from these stalwart men in boots and mackinaws. But there is another like him leaning against the wall, scratching his head. That matted hair has never known a comb. Over yonder is another. Were those rags, tied about his middle with a string, ever a coat? These creatures are out of the picture. This scene is set in the present. This is civilization and the age of progress. They must be trolls.

Is this Hollywood? Is the scene set for some feature film? Are these the extras made up for character parts? No, gentle readers (if any), this is the Emergency Relief office in a rural county of some eighteen thousand souls in northern Michigan. I was administrator of relief in that county for three years.

The little Golinski boy is worse. Pneumonia. . . . Yes, certainly we'll O.K. the drugstore order. . . . Old Mrs. Peterson's chimney has fallen down, and she can't build a fire in her stove. That's too bad. No. Of course we won't let the poor old lady freeze to death. We'll send a man right over. . . . Ten more men for the highway project near Mousetown. That's good news. Better have Elsie look over the list. That's her territory. Tell her not to forget that poor Collins chap. His wife is sick and his cow died and he's in an awful state of mind. . . . Good morning! The baby gets prettier every time I see her. Did she get over her cold? Look at her smile! Bless her heart! Yes, she probably needs more cod liver oil. The young lady over there will get it for you. . . . Yes. What did you want to see me about? Oh, you haven't been here before. Your landlord is going to evict you. Well, you leave your name and address with the young lady at the desk there and fill out a blank. We'll send a case worker over to see you. The sheriff? Oh, you don't need to worry. They can't put you out for a few days at least. We'll call up the sheriff. . . . Old Peter needs coal. He had half a ton the fifteenth of last month. That's doing pretty well for this weather. Yes. Give it to him. . . . Good morning! A note for me? Oh, from the school nurse. She says his eyes are very bad. Yes, indeed. We'll be very glad to. Margaret, please make out an order for an office call to the oculist for this little boy. . . . Yes. Oh, yes, I remember you. You're from up north in the county, aren't you? Your daughter. How old is she? Is she married? Who is the father? Does she know? Well, I'll send your case worker up to see you right away. . . . Yes. What is it? Everybody gets work but you! Why, we mailed you a work card yesterday. You're to report on the city sidewalk project next Monday. Yes, absolutely sure. You'd better go home and watch for the postman.

Charlie, do you reckon I have time to talk to chuckleheaded black rascals with this crowd waiting? Well, stop laughing then and tell me what you want. Another sack of flour. That depends on when you had the last one. You don't know! Well, you go ask Miss Grace over there. She'll look it up in the book and find out. . . . What does Myrtle want? Shoes for Nita. Does she need them? Did you look at her shoes? Yes. Give them to the poor little soul. She ought to have galoshes too. Be sure to mark the order "for child." You know Myrtle. . . . Good morning, Sergeant! What's the news today? Goldie's arrested again. Well, I certainly want to hear about that. Can you wait a minute? The doctor's ahead of you. . . . Good morning, Doctor! We'll go in my office. . . . What is it? A call from out in the county. Is it urgent? All right. I'll take it on this phone. . . . Just a minute please, Doctor. . . . Yes. Talking. Wait a minute. I'll write that down. Give me a pencil, Marie. Yes. Farm family — burned out last night. Father, mother, and six children. Any of them hurt? That's good. No insurance, I suppose. Where do they live? Two miles east of the schoolhouse in Brookdale Township. One of our case workers started up that way about half an hour ago. Maybe we can catch him. Oh, yes. We'll take care of it today. Good-bye. . . . Marie, call Pop Skelton's store in Brookdale and tell him to watch for Elmer. He ought to be passing that way any minute now. Tell him to have Elmer call the office. . . . Where's Bud? Don't let him get away! The truck will have to go up to Brookdale with food, clothing and bedding as soon as we hear from Elmer. . . . Now, Doctor! Come in! I guess we can talk in peace for a few minutes. . . . Oh, goodness! That phone! . . . Yes. Yes. Talking. . . . All right. . . . Sit down, please, Doctor. This is a long-distance call from our state office.

"What do you find to do up there in the country?" my old friends in the city used to ask. "Don't you get awfully bored sometimes?"

I usually found plenty to do. Keeping our home, puttering

with our garden, exploring these hills and woods, kept me busy. But it was rather lonely, marooned up here, so far away from the city which had always been our home, and I was bored at times, until I found myself in the maelstrom of the relief office. After that life was not dull for a single minute. And it came so suddenly — this great adventure. I felt as if one of our northwest gales had picked me up bodily off my own front terrace, whizzed me through the air, and dropped me into a whirlpool.

Some months after I had started my work, a Chicago woman asked: "Do you conduct this relief work you are doing in your home or do you have an office?" I answered: "I wish you could be in my office for just half an hour." At the moment it had seemed to me such a foolish question, but of course she didn't know — she couldn't know. That is the pity of it.

Only the social workers and people in close contact with them have any correct idea of what has been going on these past three years. Hundreds of thousands of the general public, and the intelligent general public at that, have absolutely no conception of what this tremendous emergency has meant and of what conditions of life have come to light in trying to cope with it. If the lady who asked me that natural but seemingly foolish question had been able to visit my office, she would have witnessed something very like the impressions I have tried to give in the preceding pages. Exaggerated? Not at all. That might have been any half hour of any day during the winter months of the first two years. After WPA started and the work program was taken out of the hands of Emergency Relief, the picture changed considerably; and even during the years we had charge of the work program, the summer months were a little less strenuous, though we never lacked thrills. The cast of characters was the same in summer, but of course the costumes were different. However, here in the north country summer makes only a hasty visit and dashes away, sometimes returning very briefly in October, when the forests are crimson and gold. Winter settles down and about and over us for a good eight months cf the year. There are stretches of time when the polar ice cap itself seems to have descended upon us. Snow, snow, and more snow, but of course the snow is beautiful. Worse than the snow by far are the ice and the fearful winds, the terrible, howling gales that bring the blizzards. Chicago — the Windy City? I laugh at that now. I lived in Chicago most of my life, and I never knew what wind was until the first winter I spent in the northland. But I had little time to think of the weather after the work began. We all fought our way down to the office, which — thank heaven! — was well heated, and carried on. Many and many a day, during those first two winters, I personally interviewed well over a hundred people.

Louise V. Armstrong, We Too Are the People

252. The Farm Security Administration Pulls the Farmer Out of Trouble

Nowhere was distress more acute when Roosevelt became President than on the farms. Farm owners were promptly assisted by the AAA, and later by the Soil Conservation and Domestic Allotment Act. Farm tenants offered a more difficult problem. To help them, Congress created the Farm Security Administration and appropriated funds from which tenants could borrow money at very low rates to improve their position and to purchase land. Within 3 years about 750,000 "rehabilitation loans" had been made — and the most impoverished class of farming people were winning their way back to safety.

THE relocation agent was driving me out past the steaming gray buildings of the chemical factories, over the hill that gave us, as the road looped, a backward view of the whole busy little northern Alabama industrial town with its trainyards and warehouses and the great pile of the steel mill and the long corrugated iron sheds of the pipe works lying in the bowl-shaped valley under a ceiling of soft-coal smoke. We passed a few tourist cabins turned into permanent residences and a last row of temporary shacks for chemical industry workers and turned onto a country road through a bleak shallow valley between scrubby pine woods. Counting all the war dislocations in together, the agent was telling me six hundred and ninety-nine families had had to move off farms in this county alone. Of these Farm Security Administration had helped five hundred and twenty-three. Of these only a hundred and fifty-seven had gone back on farms. So far as he knew those figures were about average for the dislocated areas in the Southeast.

Of the families Farm Security had helped, thirty-four had been set up in dairying (he hoped to raise that figure to ninety-six before long), twenty-seven in the chicken business, fifteen in beef cattle and the rest were raising cotton as they were accustomed to. Seemed a drop in the bucket, didn't it? But you had to begin slowly in a thing like this. If the experiment worked, it would be easy enough to multiply the number of farms.

The agent was a ruddy-faced young man immensely absorbed in what he was doing. He stopped the car on the side of the road and pointed proudly to a one-story white house on a little knoll of red clay barely fuzzed with new green grass. "This is the first of our dairy farms. These places are already making cash money every two weeks selling milk to the army camp through the cooling plant. Let's take a look."

Across the road beyond the new barbed wire fence oats were sprouting in even rows in the red land. "That'll be our permanent pasture."

The house was clean and new with screened windows and a screened porch. The milking shed with its concrete floor was clean and new. The small cows, by a Jersey bull out of local scrub stock, looked clean and new. Only the farmer and his wife, a lanky weather-beaten pair, the man in overalls, the woman in Mother Hubbard and poke bonnet, had the old-time back-country look. Their clothes were clean though patched like crazy quilts, they were keeping the place clean all right, but they still looked ill at ease as if they hadn't settled down yet to feel this was really their home. The man kept talking about his water pump in a worried way, kept saying he was afraid it was going to break down. His wife was complaining about the faucet in the sink in the milking shed.

"It's not his pump that's worrying him," the agent said, grinning as he drove off. "It's the loan he had to make to buy the cows. He's accustomed to making a crop loan of a couple of hundred dollars and twelve hundred seems a terrible lot. When I tell him that he's selling a hundred dollars worth of milk every two weeks the figures just don't sink in. He's doing fine but he can't believe it . . . Of course the high price of feed isn't doing us any good. About half of what we make on the milk goes into feed. Even so we are making out. The project's making out and the dairymen are making out."

In another county there were colored people living in the small new low white houses. At the place where we stopped the mother and father had gone to town because it was Saturday afternoon. We looked at the young chicks and the hogs and the neat hills of earth the man's sweet potatoes were stored in. "This feller's going to be all right," the agent said. "There's one across the railroad tracks that isn't turning out so good, spends all his time working off his farm."

A little barefooted black girl in a clean pink dress had been following us around timidly. "How much preserving did your mother do last year?" the agent asked. "Let's see them . . . Oh yes, canning is part of the program. Every client has a pressure kettle and is shown how to use it."

The little girl was too scared to open her mouth but she ran on the tips of her toes to the kitchen door and opened it and beckoned us in. The kitchen looked as if it had just been scrubbed that morning. With a look of reverence as if she were showing off some sacred magical object in a niche the little girl pulled open the door of the closet opposite the back door. From floor to ceiling clear shining jars of corn and beans and tomatoes and okra packed every carefully scrubbed shelf. They looked like the bright-colored vegetables you see winning prizes at country fairs.

"They look all right," said the agent. He couldn't help puffing out his chest, you could see, as he showed them off. "That means they've been eating something more than white meat and sweet potatoes this winter. That means a balanced diet."

As we drove back down the scrawny back road where Negro families lived in identically the same demountable white houses that were put up in other regions for the whites I couldn't help thinking that maybe in the electric brooders for chicks, in the electric pumps and the preserving kettles and the boilers for sterilizing the pails in the dairies and the vegetable patches and the clean hog pens there was the germ of a new way of life for the countryside.

"Is this sort of thing going to catch on?" I asked.

"Is Congress going to let us go ahead with it?" the agent asked me back . . .

When we drove out of town the hoarfrost still sugared the henna-colored sage grass along the sides of the road and lay in a shining mist over the pallid green drifts of winter oats. The sun was rising dim as the yolk of a poached egg in the steaming sky. Crows perched on the scraggly bare limbs of locust trees and flapped cawing over undulant pasturelands where the red white-faced cattle grazed in groups. The road curved out of the rolling land and cut straight across a level plain until it was lost in the frosty haze. At the beginning of the straightaway the Farm Security man drove the car to the side of the road and brought it to a stop and made a broad sweep with his hand above the wheel. "Now this is where the Black Belt begins," he said. "My people moved in here from Savannah way back in the last century with a wagon load of old English furniture and a barrel of French crockery and a couple of blooded horses and a bunch of Negroes. They used to say nobody but a Negro could work this heavy land. This was the empire of the cotton barons. Now it's all going into stock farming and dairying, going back into the prairie it came from. The boll weevil started the process and the war has speeded it up." He gave a short laugh. "Looks like the war has speeded up every kind of process, good and bad, in this country."

"That means less hands to work. What are you going to do with the people?"

"Of course we think resettlement's the answer, resettlement on family-sized farms."

"Why do you suppose there's so much opposition? Why is the Farm Bureau so dead set against it?"

He gave a little chuckle. "I used to work for the Farm Bureau myself. I reckon some of it is institutional jealousy. Then they are scared of high wages."

"I can understand why the communists should be against it. They are all for collectivization. But why hasn't it got more friends among the liberals?"

"I guess liberals are city people mostly . . . Let's go talk to a real successful farmer. This feller's a college graduate and a man of really considerable learning. He runs a very successful farm." He started up the car again.

We found the college graduate just coming out of the door of his henhouse pushing before him a shovelful of chicken droppings and rusty feathers. He was a tall silvery-haired man with a narrow head and long, sharply marked features ruddy from the weather. He was wearing overalls and an old sweater worn out at the elbows. "You find us in a mess," he said apologetically. "We're cleaning out the henhouse . . . But I've never seen a time yet when this place was fit for visitors."

We asked him what he thought of the Farm Bureau policies. "To tell the truth," he answered, "I haven't had time to read up on them . . . I'm probably a member. I believe somebody did come around and got five dollars off me. In general the farmer likes the Farm Bureau because it's agin the government. Now, mind you, I don't go with them all the way, but they are good practical talkers and there's been so much inefficiency and red tape and unnecessary regulation . . . I don't mean you, George, you know that," he said aside to the Farm Security man. "I think you boys are doing a real good job, but all this war food program has been so bungled up that I don't blame the farmers for following the men who'll wade in and try to get 'em what they think they're entitled to . . . People don't look far ahead in this country, they just see what they've got in front of their noses . . . And the farmer he's just too busy running his farm to keep up with trends . . . Want to see the chickens?"

We walked through the long tar-paper building the shape of a greenhouse that had an alley down the middle and layers and layers of chickens on wire floors on either side. Near the entrance the chicks were yellow and peeping fresh from the egg. Further on they had pinfeathers and at the end they were clucking broilers.

The air was choking with the warm sour reek of crowded fowls. "They come in one end from the incubator and go out the other to market," said the college graduate. "Works fine if you don't slip up on something. I guess you have to do so much regulating yourself running a farm that the farmers get sick of regulations. Right now we feel the whole system of regulations is a nuisance. We don't care whether the purpose is good or bad . . . Then too, we are getting prosperous. A prosperous farmer's the most conservative man on earth. We were plenty sick for a while. Now we feel about ready to throw away our crutches. Just leave us alone. Get us good prices and let us produce, that's what we say."

"What about the feller who still needs a crutch?"

"We'll hire him. By God, we've got work for him to do! I'm not so bad off as some for labor, but I could use three good men right now. My wife and I wouldn't have to break our backs cleaning out these henhouses if we could hire somebody to do it . . . Good-by." He packed us off hurriedly but genially. "I got to get back to my business."

"Well, this isn't exactly the moving picture idea of life on the old plantation, is it?" asked the Farm Security man, laughing as we climbed back into his car. . . .

The office of Farm Security was over an implement store on the other side of the courthouse. When I walked in the door a six-foot lantern-jawed backwoodsman in stained overalls with a quid of tobacco as big as an apple in his cheek stood leaning over the desk counting out ten-dollar bills while the administrator made out a receipt.

"Well, that jest about clars me up," he said as he slapped down the last greenback on the pile on the desk. He lifted the window a little with a long leathery flipper and spat delicately out into the yellow branches of a willow tree just feathered with early green.

"Feel better?" asked the administrator.

"Right smart . . . Good-day, gentlemen . . . I'll be goin'," said the man gravely and stalked out of the office.

"To go by the speeches in Congress I've just seen something that never happens, a Farm Security client paying off his loan."

"A very high percentage pay off their loans," said the administrator sharply; "higher all the time."

He was a quiet, studious-looking man with a long, closely cropped head. He wore a leather jacket and boots. He sat there at his desk for some time without speaking. Then he said suddenly, "I'll tell you a funny thing," and threw himself back in his chair and stared up at the peeling ceiling above his head. "You know when we started this relocation work we picked our clients very carefully, made all sorts of investigations of their character and background to see if they'd be a good risk or not. Now we just take them as they come. Statistically the random clients work out as well or better than the hand-picked clients."

"What do you figure it means?"

"You tell me what it means."

While I sat there trying to figure out an answer he straightened himself up at his desk and picked up a pencil in a businesslike way as if he were going to start writing with it. "What it means to me is that the great majority of people will turn out all right if you give them the proper chance . . . I said the proper chance." He paused again and smiled. "Maybe that was the sort of thing the men who founded this country figured on." He jumped to his feet in a hurry as if he were afraid he'd said too much. "Suppose you and me go across the street and get us some dinner before they run out of everything," he said in a voice suddenly warm and good-natured.

JOHN DOS PASSOS, State of the Nation

253. David Lilienthal Describes the Work of the TVA

One of the first acts of the New Deal was the creation of the Tennessee Valley Authority. The primary purpose of the TVA was to construct dams for hydroelectric power, but the terms of the act were broadly drawn, and TVA early embarked upon a program of regional reconstruction. The TVA region embraces

*an area of some 40,000 square miles in 7 states, works closely with
state and local authorities in this region for such things as public health,
recreation, the improvement of agriculture, and rural electrification. The
story of its accomplishments is here told by its director, David Lilienthal, who was later appointed director of the Atomic Energy Commission.*

THIS is an entirely different region from what it was ten years
ago. You can see the change almost everywhere you go. You can
see it in the copper lines strung along back-country roads, in the
fresh paint on the houses those electric lines were built to serve.
You can see it in new electric water pumps in the farmyards, in the
community refrigerators at the crossroads, in the feed grinders in
the woodsheds. You can see the factories that stand today where
there were worn-out cotton fields and rows of tenant shacks a few
years ago. You can see new houses, by the thousands, on the edges
of the towns — new houses of the men who take away as much cash
from a few trips to the payroll window as they used to earn in a year.

You can see the change best of all if you have flown down the
valley from time to time, as I have done so frequently during these
past ten years. From five thousand feet the great change is unmistak-
able. There it is, stretching out before your eyes, a moving and exciting picture. You can see the undulation of neatly terraced hillsides,
newly contrived to make the beating rains "walk, not run, to the
nearest exit"; you can see the gray bulk of the dams, stout marks
across the river now deep blue, no longer red and murky with its
hoard of soil washed from the eroding land. You can see the barges
with their double tows of goods to be unloaded at new river terminals. And marching toward every point on the horizon you can
see the steel crisscross of electric transmission towers, a twentieth-
century tower standing in a cove beside an eighteenth-century
mountain cabin, a symbol and a summary of the change. These are
among the things you can see as you travel through the Tennessee
Valley today. And on every hand you will also see the dimensions of
the job yet to be done, the problem and the promise of the valley's
future. . . .

The story of the change begins with the river. On the map the river's five mountain tributaries, each a considerable stream — the French Broad, the Holston, the Hiwassee, the Little Tennessee, the Clinch — are clearly set off from the broad main stem, the Tennessee itself, a major river of great volume, fed by the heaviest rainfall in eastern America. The map shows that main stem as a deep crescent, its source and eastern tip in the Appalachian Mountains, the dip of the crescent slicing off the northern third of Alabama, the western tip arching northward through the flat red lands of western Tennessee and Kentucky. The river flows not in one general direction, but in three; it moves southward first, then its middle course is westward, and its lower reaches turn back toward the north. A river that "flows up the map," as visitors to TVA almost invariably remark, seems to be water flowing perversely uphill, making its way more than 650 miles from Knoxville in Tennessee, in sight of the virgin timber in the Great Smoky Mountains, the highest peaks in eastern North America, to Paducah in the lowlands of Kentucky where across the broad Ohio you can see the fields of Illinois.

The valley through which the river flows actually lies in seven historic states of the Old South: the western part of the seacoast states of North Carolina and Virginia; the northern parts of Georgia, Alabama, and Mississippi; the western half of Kentucky from its southern jointure with Tennessee north to the Ohio River; and almost the whole of the wide reaches of the state of Tennessee. Less exactly, the region reaches from the mountains about Asheville west to the sluggish Mississippi at Memphis, and north and south from the old steamboat whistle landings on Ohio's shores to the cotton fields of Mississippi and the flambeau of the furnaces at Birmingham — an area all told about the size of England and Scotland, with a population of about 4,500,000 persons.

This is the river system that twenty-one dams of the TVA now control and have put to work for the people. To do that job sixteen new dams, several among the largest in America, were designed and constructed. Five dams already existing have been improved and modified. One of TVA's carpenters, a veteran who worked on seven of these dams, described this to me as "one hell of a big job of work." I cannot improve on that summary. It is the largest job of engineering and construction ever carried out by any single organization in all our history.

In heat and cold, in driving rain and under the blaze of the August sun, tens of thousands of men have hewed and blasted and hauled with their teams and tractors, clearing more than 175,000 acres of land, land that the surface of the lakes now covers. They have built or relocated more than 1200 miles of highway and almost 140 miles of railroad. With thousands of tons of explosives and great electric shovels they have excavated nearly 30,000,000 cubic yards of rock and earth to prepare the foundations of these dams — an excavation large enough to bury 20 Empire State buildings. To hold the river the men of the TVA have poured and placed concrete, rock fill, and earth in a total quantity of 113 million cubic yards.

To comprehend these figures requires a few comparisons. This 113 million cubic yards of material is more than twelve times the bulk of the seven great pyramids of Egypt. Of these materials, the concrete alone poured into the TVA dams is two and a half times as much as used in all the locks and structures of the Panama Canal; is four times as much as in Boulder Dam, 1,200,000 cubic yards greater than in the Grand Coulee Dam; would build more than seven dams as large as Soviet Russia's great Dnieprostroy Dam. The Grand Coulee Dam is the largest single masonry structure yet built, and Boulder Dam the second largest. Boulder was in the process of construction for five years and took the combined efforts of six of our largest private building contractor firms. Grand Coulee took eight years to build, and ten major private construction firms were engaged on it.

Thirty-five Boulder dams or ten Grand Coulee dams could have been built with the total materials required for completion of this valley's dams, the work of a single organization. The TVA's employees in 1942 were simultaneously designing and building a dozen dams and improving four others, were erecting the South's largest steam-electric plant, and building large chemical and munitions factories, with a total of 40,000 men and women at work.

The work of the builders has made of the river a highway that is carrying huge amounts of freight over its deep watercourses. In 1942 more than 161 million ton-miles of traffic moved through locks, designed in co-operation with the Army Corps of Engineers and operated by them, which raise the barges from one lake's level to another. But in 1928 only a little more than 46 million ton-miles of traffic moved on the river; in 1933 the figure was 32 million. This was mostly sand and gravel moving in short hauls between adjacent areas, and some forest products.

Today huge modern towboats, powered by great Diesel engines, move up and down the channel, pushing double columns of barges, and the cargo is no longer limited to raw materials. Billets of steel and cotton goods come from Birmingham headed north, grain from Minneapolis, millions of gallons of gasoline, oil, machinery, merchandise, automobiles, military ambulances and jeeps. It is estimated that in 1945, when the channel will be fully completed for all the year and for the river's total length, the savings to shippers will be about three and a half million dollars each year.

Quiet cotton towns of yesterday are now busy river ports. And, as always has been true of water transportation, new industries are rising along its course. Millions of dollars have been invested and thousands of jobs created as new grain elevators, flour mills, and oil terminals have been erected along the river's banks. At Decatur in Alabama, on land where a few years ago farmers were raising corn and cotton, now newly built ocean-going vessels go down the ways into "Wheeler Lake" and thence to their North Atlantic job.

And on these same lakes are thousands of new pleasure craft of every kind — costly yachts, sailboats, homemade skiffs. Nine thousand miles of shoreline — more than the total of the seacoast line of the United States on the Atlantic, the Pacific, and the Gulf of Mexico — are available for the recreation of the people. Thousands of acres along the shore are devoted to public parks, operated by the states, by counties, cities, and by the TVA. More than fifty boat docks serve the needs of fishermen from all parts of the United States. By patient scientific methods designed to give nature a chance, the number of fish has been increased fortyfold in the storage reservoirs, fifteen times in the main stream reservoirs. More than forty species of fish have been caught in these lakes — a variety comparable to that of the Great Lakes. Here is the basis of a thriving industry that in 1943 produced six million pounds of edible fish, and is expected to increase to twenty-five million pounds a year.

Before the men of the Tennessee Valley built these dams, flooding was a yearly threat to every farm and industry, every town and village and railroad on the river's banks, a barrier to progress. To-day there is security from that annual danger in the Tennessee Valley. With the erection of local protective works at a few points this region will be completely safe, even against a flood bigger than anything in recorded history. A measure of protection resulting from the Tennessee's control extends even beyond this valley; for no longer will the Tennessee send her torrents at flood crest to add what might be fatal inches to top the levees and spread desolation on the lower Ohio and the Mississippi.

In others of the earth's thousand valleys people live under the shadow of fear that each year their river will bring upon them damage to their property, suffering, and death. Here the people are safe. In the winter of 1942 torrents came raging down this valley's two chief tributaries, in Tennessee and Virginia. Before the river was controlled this would have meant a severe flood; the machinery of vital war industries down the river at Chattanooga would have stopped, under several feet of water, with over a million dollars of direct damage resulting.

But in 1942 it was different. Orders went out from the TVA office of central control to every tributary dam. The message came flashing to the operator in the control room at Hiwassee Dam, deep in the mountains of North Carolina: "Hold back all the water of the Hiwassee River. Keep it out of the Tennessee." The operator pressed a button. Steel gates closed. The water of the tributary was held. To Cherokee Dam on the Holston went the message: "Keep back the flow of the Holston." To Chickamauga Dam just above the industrial danger spot at Chattanooga: "Release water to make room for the waters from above."

Day by day till the crisis was over the men at their control instruments at each dam in the system received their orders. The rate of water release from every tributary river was precisely controlled. The Tennessee was kept in hand. There was no destruction, no panic, no interruption of work. Most of the water, instead of wreck-ing the valley, actually produced a benefit in power, when later it was released through the turbines.

DAVID LILIENTHAL, Democracy on the March

XXXVI

The Second World War

254. Senator Borah Knows More than the State Department

On the eve of the new war in Europe, in the summer of 1939, the Roosevelt Administration urgently desired to have the fetters of the existing neutrality legislation loosed. It was so bound by the laws placed on the statute books in 1935–1938 that it could do nothing to give encouragement to the threatened European democracies, or to deter Hitler and Mussolini. The President and Secretary of State Hull urged the Senate Foreign Relations Committee to report suitable amendments. But the isolationists were still too strong. They refused point-blank — until events showed them the folly of their stand.

ON July 11, the day the committee was to vote, I restated at a press conference the recommendations I had made in my May 27 letter to Pittman and Bloom. That afternoon the President backed me up by saying that what I had said was "a very good statement." But when Pittman brought the question to a vote, the committee voted, 12 to 11, to postpone all consideration of neutrality legislation until the next session of Congress, in January, 1940.

January, 1940! What might not happen before then! In those six months the fate of the civilized world might be at stake.

The issues were so great that I still refused to accept defeat. There was yet a hope that the Senate might vote to overrule Pittman's committee. My associates and I at the State Department therefore prepared another statement to Congress, to be sent to the Capitol by the President. Mr. Roosevelt duly sent this to Congress on July 14 with a brief accompanying letter of approval in which he said: "It has been abundantly clear to me for some time that for the cause of peace and in the interests of American neutrality and security, it is highly advisable that the Congress at this session should take certain much needed action. In the light of present world conditions, I see no reason to change that opinion."

In my statement I emphasized, among other points, the peace possibilities of lifting the arms embargo. We, I said, "are convinced that the arms embargo plays into the hands of those nations which have taken the lead in building up their fighting power. It works directly against the interests of the peace-loving nations, especially those which do not possess their own munitions plants. It means that, if any country is disposed towards conquest, and devotes its energy and resources to establish itself as a superior fighting power, that country may be more tempted to try the fortunes of war if it knows that its less well-prepared opponents would be shut off from those supplies which, under every rule of international law, they should be able to buy in all neutral countries, including the United States.

"It means also that some of those countries which have only limited facilities for the production of arms, ammunition, and implements of war are put in a position of increased dependence. During peacetime they would feel the compulsion of shaping their political as well as their economic policy to suit the military strength of others; and during wartime their powers of defense would be limited."

I underlined as strongly as I could my belief that "the present embargo encourages a general state of war both in Europe and Asia. Since the present embargo has this effect, its results are directly prejudicial to the highest interests and to the peace and to the security of the United States."

I intensified my discussions with the President and with leading Senators. Mr. Roosevelt agreed to call a White House meeting of the Senate leaders of both parties for the evening of July 18. At this meeting the President and I intended to make a final appeal for support of the bill, or, failing in this, to make the opposition take the responsibility for what would happen if the legislation were not passed. In view of the action already taken by the Senate and the

House, it was a desperate effort. But both the President and I felt we had to make one last, supreme attempt to prevail on the Senate leaders to recognize fully and clearly the perils to our own nation that were just ahead if war should come to Europe.

As the meeting came to order in the President's upstairs study, a reasonable cordiality was apparent on the surface, but the feeling underneath was tense. Among those attending were Vice President Garner, Majority Leader Barkley, Pittman, Minority Leader Mc-Nary, Deputy Minority Leader Warren Austin, and William E. Borah, ranking minority member of the Foreign Relations Committee.

The President opened the discussion by referring to Senator Nye's extreme isolationist views which were blocking the passage of our measure in the Senate. Borah rather quickly interrupted and, with a sweeping gesture, said, "There are others, Mr. President." The President, somewhat taken back, turned to him and asked, "What did you say, Senator Borah?" Borah thereupon repeated, "There are others, Mr. President." A dialogue followed between the President and Borah, during which Borah emphasized his opposition to repeal of the arms embargo and stated emphatically his view that no war would occur at least in the near future.

The President thereupon turned to me and said, "Cordell, what do you think about the possibility of danger ahead?"

I replied earnestly, restraining myself as much as I could: "If Senator Borah could only see some of the cables coming to the State Department about the extremely dangerous outlook in the international situation, I feel satisfied he would modify his views."

Thereupon Borah, in a tone of emphasis and absolute finality, said he had access to information from abroad which satisfied him in his judgment. This information was that there would be no war in Europe in the near future. He implied that it was more reliable information than that received at the State Department.

More recently I have noticed publication of what purported to be Senator Borah's written memorandum of this conversation. I shall not enter into a discussion of the precise verbiage of the conversation, but I must say that Borah's language created the definite, fixed understanding in my mind as to what occurred, as I have just related it. President Roosevelt made clear on more than one occasion that he had derived the same understanding as I had from Borah's utterances.

Never in my experience had I found it nearly so difficult to restrain myself and refrain from a spontaneous explosion. I knew from masses of official facts piled high on one another at the State Department that Borah was everlastingly wrong, and that we were looking squarely at a state of imminent danger of a general outbreak of war before the end of summer — and I said so. Borah's statement, giving more credit to his private sources of information than to the official State Department dispatches, was a disparagement of our whole diplomatic service.

After other leaders of both parties had unanimously expressed their view that it was impossible to secure the passage of our embargo repeal through Congress, the President turned to me and asked: "Cordell, what do you think about the situation?"

I had been on the verge of an explosion during the minutes that followed Borah's reflection of myself and the State Department. My agitation was probably not concealed as I replied to the President: "I scarcely know what to think about anything in the light of the complacent way Senator Borah has brushed aside the whole mass of facts we have at the State Department, which completely disprove his theory that there will be no war." I could scarcely proceed further without losing my self-control, so deeply was I convinced of the dangers just ahead and so greatly did I feel outraged at the brusque manner in which all these facts and considerations were ignored.

At midnight, as the meeting ended on this tone, the White House issued two communiqués. One stated the consensus of the Senators present, Democrat and Republican, that no action on neutrality legislation could be obtained at this session of Congress, but that it would be considered at the next session. The other stated: "The President and the Secretary of State maintained the definite position that failure by the Senate to take action now would weaken the leadership of the United States in exercising its potent influence in the cause of preserving peace among other nations in the event of a new crisis in Europe between now and next January."

Only five weeks later we had to exert that influence in a final effort to prevent a European war. Our influence, so far as Hitler was concerned, was undoubtedly weakened by his realization that Congress had refused to follow the lead of the Administration, and by his belief that Britain and France could not obtain arms, ammunition, or airplanes in the United States.

Immediately after the meeting Senator Borah, followed by Senator McNary, disclaimed to me the least idea of reflecting on me or on my official position in any way. But it was not possible to apologize for reflecting on the State Department, which I headed. I received these disclaimers coldly. I give Borah credit for the best of intentions, but I am forced to conclude that he was so terribly wrought up as not to think clearly.

I had frequently invited Borah to come to the State Department where I could show him dispatches from our diplomatic missions in Europe and Asia and talk over the general foreign situation with him, but he never did me this courtesy. What could I have shown if he had come to the department during the discussions on neutrality? Among dozens of other references, there were these:

Our Chargé in Berlin, Alexander Kirk, cabled me on May 13 that the diplomatic representatives of many other nations, although not expecting immediate German action against Poland, were very pessimistic about the chances of avoiding a conflict. The prevailing impression in Berlin foreign military circles was that Germany was militarily able to move against Poland at any time. On June 24 Kirk reported that rumors of unusual troop movements and continued military activity in Germany had created the general impression that preparations were being made for some eventuality.

Ambassador Bullitt cabled from Paris on May 16 that Premier Daladier had expressed the opinion that peace would probably continue through June but he was not, on the whole, optimistic. One month later Bullitt cabled that Foreign Minister Bonnet had told him that, while he did not expect any immediate aggression by Germany, he was certain of a major crisis before the end of the summer. On June 28 Bullitt cabled the opinion of the Polish Ambassador to France that the chances were eighty out of a hundred that war would come between Poland and Germany by the middle of August. On June 30 Bullitt cabled the belief of Alexis Léger, of the French Foreign Office, that a crisis of the gravest character was inevitable before the middle of August.

Polish Ambassador Count Potocki said to me on May 31 that Hitler would be obliged to make a move in some direction during the coming months. On June 26 Potocki informed me that his country was preparing increasingly to fight in case Germany should start a war. I commented to him that conditions in Europe were not favorable. Increasing signs and circumstances of an ominous nature were appearing. Sooner or later — no one could say when — with Europe so highly geared to a war basis, something very serious was likely to occur unless in the meantime steps were taken to avoid it.

From London Ambassador Kennedy cabled me on June 27 Lord Halifax's thought that the German situation was very uneasy and that there was ample opportunity for trouble before the end of the next month. On July 5 Kennedy cabled that Halifax had told him the British were calling up their reserves of ships and Navy personnel, ostensibly for maneuvers in August, but actually in order to have the Navy ready a month before trouble might come, on the assumption that this would be in September.

Our Chargé at the Hague, J. Webb Benton, reported to me on June 3 the opinion of Admiral Furstner, Chief of the Netherlands Naval Staff, that Hitler might resort to war between the middle and end of August, after the harvest, and Furstner referred to known German efforts to harvest the crops as rapidly as possible.

Moreover, we were receiving from our diplomatic missions abroad constant reports on developments in Europe indicating continued German pressure on Poland and maneuvers to get possession of Danzig, and on difficulties in the way of any immediate conclusion of an Anglo-Soviet agreement toward which British diplomacy had been working for several months.

All these dispatches Borah and his associates could have seen if they had wanted to. But Borah chose instead to rely for his information on what was later reported to be a minor press service in London.

Here was the last effective stand of the powerful isolation movement in the United States. The movement continued its fight by every means at hand and it remained a danger, but after war came in Europe it was never again able to thwart an Administration proposal.

No one can say definitely that the failure of our efforts to lift the arms embargo was a final, or even an important, factor in Hitler's ultimate decision to go to war. I am certain, however, that if the arms embargo had been lifted in May, June, or even July, 1939, he would inevitably have had to take this factor into his calculations. I am equally certain that the failure to lift the embargo encouraged him to go ahead, stimulated by Ribbentrop's assurances that Britain and France would not really come to the assistance of Poland and that, if they did, they would be unable to do so effectively because American material help would be withheld from them. On July 20 Bullitt, in a cable from Paris for the President, said the opinion in both London and Paris was that the probability of Hitler's deciding to make war in August had been increased by Congress's decision to postpone action on neutrality legislation, and that British Foreign Undersecretary Vansittart was betting two to one that war would come in August.

The Memoirs of Cordell Hull

255. Roosevelt Finds a Variety of Intimates

The circle of White House confidants and counselors changed rapidly in the first and second administrations of Franklin D. Roosevelt. One of them, Raymond B. Moley, has written that Roosevelt chose him on the basis of "common ideals." When disagreement came, one figure after another (like Moley) left the favored group. These men helped the President carry heavy burdens. They handled correspondence, talked with officials, diplomats, and businessmen, helped write speeches, and furnished expert information and advice. With one or two exceptions, Roosevelt entrusted none of them with any great power. Great interest was taken in them by such Democratic politicians as the one writing here.

IF Colonel House may have been the first of the White House courtiers, and possibly the one who most influenced the policies of Franklin Roosevelt, he must yield in point of permanency to the eminence of Harry Hopkins. That welfare worker has been on top — or near the top — ever since he came to Washington to administer the WPA, that organization charged with putting to work those who but for its offices would have been on direct relief. He perhaps did as good a job there as anybody could have done, notwithstanding the jibes at the leaf rakers, and the boondoggle stories, and the reiterated charges from the Republicans that he was using his huge agency to promote Democratic election success.

His first big blunder was when he announced one day when Gillette and Wearin were contesting for the Iowa senatorship that if he had a vote in Iowa he would cast it for Wearin. That gave point to the charge of partisanship, for Gillette was one of those on the purgee list by reason of his position during the Supreme Court fight, and the Republicans construed Administrator Hopkins's utterance as a warning to the reliefers that they had better vote for the administration candidate. His role, in view of his particular job, should have been to steer as wide from a political comment as he could get. Whether in his ingenuous mind he conceived the idea that flaunting his colors would help the administration candidate, or whether he failed to realize the possible imputations of an inconsequential remark, it was stupid politically. Hopkins probably had nothing more in mind than to illustrate his loyalty to his chief, but it indicated his lack of political wisdom, as it compelled certain awkward and not quite convincing explanations.

Organization Democrats were generally hostile to him anyhow, for they said he preferred Republicans to Democrats when he was appointing his key men to the big jobs under him both as relief administrator and as boss of WPA. Actually it must be assumed that he was politically nonpartisan in these matters and named his individual friends and associates — which may or may not be an improvement on the more conventional spoils system. During his New York career in various relief activities he was credited to no party. Indeed the apparent type of his mind when he came to Washington seemed to preclude definite devotion to any set of economic principles beyond a shadowy faith that virtue was inherent in poverty and absent from wealth. In his later environment he seems to have drifted far from those unstable mental moorings.

The hostility of the political regulars did not diminish during his term as secretary of commerce but did not interfere with the President's high regard for him and for his abilities. When the cabinet was shuffled again, he emerged as chief of the lend-lease activities, and finally moved into the White House as special assistant to the President. Once there was a move to make him the Democratic candidate for governor of New York. Farley is credited with having spiked that.

Hopkins has done nothing to increase his popularity with Congressmen or other Democratic officials — rather the reverse, as they complain that he will not answer his telephone calls, even when the caller tells his secretary that the President had directed him to talk to Hopkins. Whether this manifestation is due to exaggerated ego or to preoccupation with his official duties, the effect is the same.

There is nothing new about the lack of cordiality at the Capitol for the President's contact men. Hopkins is perhaps no more anathema up there than was Tommy Corcoran, whom, by the way, the present special assistant is credited with eliminating from the White House circle.

The President's liking for Corcoran was quite understandable. Tommy is able, witty, companionable, entertaining, and, when he cares to be, courteous and obliging. His trouble with Congress was that he did not bother to exercise his pleasant qualities on the members thereof. They resented his phoning them orders without even sugar-coating the dose. They were irked at the idea that it would be wise to consult him about patronage. There was no question as to his influence; and whether that came to him with authority or whether he was running a tremendous — and successful — bluff, nobody was quite sure. The White House people insisted that he was merely useful to the President as confidential messenger and as an aide with a gift for speech writing, but even the underlings there were not so certain that that was the limit of his status as to cross him. He is a capable lawyer, though in the writing of laws delivered to Congress Ben Cohen did the heavy work.

Whatever is the truth — or rather whatever was the truth — about his authority, there is no question that he not only had but exercised the power. Under the guise of supplying real experts where they were needed at the beginning of the Roosevelt regime, he made Jim Farley look like a tyro in staffing the offices. In this way he had his key men in every branch of the government — a circumstance invaluable to his present sphere of activity, that of "practicing law" in the district. No man looking for a fat contract, and no one who is having difficulties with the government, could employ a more useful attorney.

Lest there be some suspicion in the lay mind that his activities while he was the star member of the White House inner circle were those of the common or garden variety of lobbyist, it is only just to say that there was no immediate money profit for himself involved. He was after power, not pecuniary gains. Whether he had in mind what would come when he departed from the palace guard, nobody knows but himself. As brilliant a mind as Corcoran's could hardly have failed to look that far ahead. He is reputed to have piled up a fortune — and not a small fortune — in fees during the year or so that he has been in private practice.

As to his qualifications it is sufficient to state that he was picked by Felix Frankfurter, and was taken into the office of Justice Holmes in conformity with that great jurist's habit of choosing as his law secretary the banner graduate of the Harvard Law School. He worked indefatigably at his strange job. He is credited with keeping the brain trust of his period harmonious but felt no call to exercise his skill in that direction on persons who could not be of use to him. . . .

He served the President longer than anybody with a similar relationship except Harry Hopkins. Those two were supposed to have an understanding that so long as their activities did not clash there would be no hostility.

. . . General Hugh Johnson was a disturbing member. The old cavalryman, with his pyrotechnic expletives and his blistering comparisons, jarred the professors. His roaring voice dominated their meetings. His tone was that of a commander of troops ordering a charge. There was no disrespect involved; it was simply the emphasis of an intensely positive man, and behind the bluster was a lot of good hard common sense. The General's appointment as head of the NRA was enthusiastically applauded by the remainder of the group. They always regarded him, as an economist, with much the same attitude as a regular physician regards a faith healer. I am afraid their enthusiasm for the NRA was more because it took him from their midst than for its promise as a recovery measure.

Perhaps a better comparison of their estimate of the General would be the feeling at Democratic headquarters toward the professorial approach to political questions.

Contrary to the popular estimate of Hugh Johnson as merely a violent master of brimstony epigrams and pungent allegories, always in a furious temper, he was, or had been, a deep student of the abstruse problems of the day. Perhaps he overestimated the depth of his researches and covered too wide a field in his dogmatic dissertations.

Rex Tugwell and Adolph Berle, of the original brain trust, graduated into serious official posts. Berle showed a capacity to mold himself into the classical officeholder status with only a few more controversies than are normal to men so circumstanced; but poor Tugwell seems to be always in hot water. Perhaps nobody could have made Puerto Rico happy, considering that that island is still in the throes of democratic birth pains, with a heavy hang-over of the old *hacendero* philosophy, and with an inherited Latin tendency to direct methods in politics superimposed on its economic misery. Incidentally, the situation was not helped by the mainland habit of calling every exponent of liberalism a communist or socialist — Puerto Rico is prone to believe that we mean our epithets and that they are not merely campaign currency.

It appears that in appraising the qualifications of the "integrated body" grouped about the President, I have been rather fulsome as to the abilities of the individual members. There were among them, of course, stargazers as well as stuporous bookworms, but each had the stuff the President wanted. Ray Moley was, in my estimation, the ablest of them, even though, when he had ceased to be the Rasputin of the administration, he showed a startling indifference to the sacredness of confidences and backtracked from his symbolism of liberalism into the advocacy of the causes against which Roosevelt had, with his assistance, ranged himself. So we find him critical of

Frankfurter's law, and Brandeis's assay of bigness of corporations as a menace to the nation's welfare.

CHARLES MICHELSON, The Ghost Talks

256. Japan Strikes at Pearl Harbor

To most Americans in the closing weeks of 1941 it seemed likely that the United States would soon be in the great new world war, and most people believed the country would enter by some blow in the Atlantic area. But in the Far East, where Japan had been on the aggressive for twenty years, the leaders in Tokyo deemed the moment ripe for decisive action. They thought that the United States could never fight a successful war on two great fronts. Even while their envoys in Washington parleyed with Secretary Hull they were planning a sudden treacherous effort to put the Pacific fleet of the United States out of commission — and temporarily they almost succeeded.

SUNDAY MORNING December 7, 1941, I went to my office, as I had done almost every Sunday since I entered the State Department in 1933. I first conferred with Far Eastern experts Hornbeck, Hamilton, and Ballantine, and then had a lengthy conference with Secretaries Stimson and Knox. The faces of my visitors were grim. From all our reports it appeared that zero hour was a matter of hours, perhaps minutes.

During the morning I received a series of decoded intercepts consisting of fourteen parts of a long telegram from Foreign Minister Togo to Nomura and Kurusu. This was the answer to our proposals of November 26. There was also a short message instructing the Ambassadors to present this to our Government, if possible to me, at one o'clock that afternoon. Here then was the zero hour.

The Japanese note was little more than an insult. It said that our proposal "ignores Japan's sacrifices in the four years of the China affair, menaces the Empire's existence itself, and disparages its honor and prestige." It accused us of conspiring with Great Britain and other countries "to obstruct Japan's efforts toward the establishment of peace through the creation of a new order in East Asia." It concluded by saying that, in view of the attitude of the American Government, the Japanese Government considered it impossible to reach an agreement through further negotiations.

The note did not declare war. Neither did it break off diplomatic relations. Japan struck without such preliminaries.

Toward noon Ambassador Nomura telephoned my office to ask for an appointment with me at one o'clock for himself and Kurusu. I granted his request.

A few minutes after one, Nomura telephoned again to ask that the appointment be postponed until 1:45. I agreed.

The Japanese envoys arrived at the Department at 2:05 and went to the diplomatic waiting room. At almost that moment the President telephoned me from the White House. His voice was steady but clipped.

He said, "There's a report that the Japanese have attacked Pearl Harbor."

"Has the report been confirmed?" I asked.

He said, "No."

While each of us indicated his belief that the report was probably true, I suggested that he have it confirmed, having in mind my appointment with the Japanese Ambassadors.

With me in my office were Green H. Hackworth, Legal Adviser, and Joseph W. Ballantine who had been with me during most of my conversations with the Japanese. I turned to them, saying:

"The President has an unconfirmed report that the Japanese have attacked Pearl Harbor. The Japanese Ambassadors are waiting to see me. I know what they want. They are going to turn us down on our note of November 26. Perhaps they want to tell us that war has been declared. I am rather inclined not to see them."

As I thought it over, however, I decided that, since the President's report had not been confirmed and there was one chance out of a hundred that it was not true, I would receive the envoys. After a brief discussion, Hackworth left the room, and Ballantine remained as I called for the Ambassadors.

Nomura and Kurusu came into my office at 2:20. I received them coldly and did not ask them to sit down.

Nomura diffidently said he had been instructed by his Government to deliver a document to me at one o'clock, but that difficulty in decoding the message had delayed him. He then handed me his Government's note.

I asked him why he had specified one o'clock in his first request for an interview.

He replied that he did not know, but that was his instruction.

I made a pretense of glancing through the note. I knew its contents already but naturally could give no indication of this fact.

After reading two or three pages, I asked Nomura whether he had presented the document under instructions from his Government.

He replied that he had.

When I finished skimming the pages, I turned to Nomura and put my eye on him.

"I must say," I said, "that in all my conversations with you during the last nine months I have never uttered one word of untruth. This is borne out absolutely by the record. In all my fifty years of public service I have never seen a document that was more crowded with infamous falsehoods and distortions — infamous falsehoods and distortions on a scale so huge that I never imagined until today that any Government on this planet was capable of uttering them."

Nomura seemed about to say something. His face was impassive, but I felt he was under great emotional strain. I stopped him with a motion of my hand. I nodded toward the door. The Ambassadors turned without a word and walked out, their heads down.

I have seen it stated that I "cussed out" the Japanese envoys in rich Tennessee mountain language, but the fact is I told them exactly what I said above. No "cussing out" could have made it any stronger.

Ballantine took notes of what I said. The moment the Ambassadors left, I called in a stenographer and dictated from memory what I had told them. This is the statement as issued to the press.

Nomura's last meeting with me was in keeping with the ineptitude that had marked his handling of the discussions from the beginning.

His Government's intention, in instructing him to ask for the meeting at one o'clock, had been to give us their note a few minutes in advance of the attack at Pearl Harbor. Nomura's Embassy had bungled this by its delay in decoding. Nevertheless, knowing the importance of a deadline set for a specific hour, Nomura should have come to see me precisely at one o'clock, even though he had in his hand only the first few lines of his note, leaving instructions with the Embassy to bring him the remainder as it became ready.

It was therefore without warning that the Japanese struck at Pearl Harbor, more than an hour before Nomura and Kurusu delivered their note.

I talked with the President on the telephone shortly after the Ambassadors left my office, and repeated to him what I had told them. He said he was pleased that I had spoken so strongly. By then he had received further reports on the attack at Pearl Harbor.

Shortly after three o'clock I went to the White House, where I talked with the President and others for forty minutes. Mr. Roosevelt was very solemn in demeanor and conversation. The magnitude of the surprise achieved by the Japanese at Pearl Harbor was already becoming evident. But neither he nor any of us lost faith for a moment in the ability of the United States to cope with the danger.

We had a general discussion preparatory to a conference that the President decided to hold that evening with Stimson, Knox, myself, General Marshall, Admiral Stark, and other principal advisers. We discussed in a tentative way the many different steps that would have to be taken, when and by whom. The President early determined to go to Congress with a message asking for a declaration of a state of war with Japan.

The Memoirs of Cordell Hull

257. The Marines Cross a River Under Fire on Guadalcanal

The Japanese, driving forward far and fast after Pearl Harbor, established themselves on a wide perimeter, reaching almost to Australia and the New Hebrides on the south, to the central archipelagoes in the middle Pacific, and to the Aleutians in the north. In 1942 and the first half of 1943 the American forces could only nibble at this defensive perimeter. But two notable attacks, on the island of Guadalcanal in the south and on Attu in the Aleutians, proved that man for man the Americans could outfight the best Japanese troops. No story of the war was more heroic than that of Guadalcanal.

WHEN the runner returned, he reported just what Rigaud's lieutenants had guessed — that George and Easy Companies had moved up to make contact with our right, and that they were to try to help force the river. He also reported that we were only about a hundred yards from the river.

Captain Rigaud passed this whispered order: "Advance and watch out for friendly troops on the right."

The men who were carrying machine gun parts seemed to bunch up together as we moved forward this time. They wanted to be ready to assemble their guns on shortest notice.

Occasional whispering, which had been visible though not audible along the line when we moved before, now stopped.

Men picked their footsteps carefully now.

Captain Rigaud's small back and stooped shoulders hardly moved up and down at all. His knees were a little bent, like those of a cat about to leap.

We crossed and recrossed the stream very carefully but rather hurriedly: no one wanted to be caught in the water. It was much wider now, much browner and more sluggish. We were apparently quite near the Matanikau.

Up ahead, as a matter of fact, some of Rigaud's men and a few of the men of George and Easy Companies had already crossed the river. No shots had been fired. There seemed to be no opposition: there was reason to hope that Whaling had already swept around behind whatever was on the other side and cleaned it out (we had heard some firing from the other side during the morning), so that now our job would be a pushover. Maybe, if we were lucky, just a sniper or two to hunt down and kill.

The trail left the stream, turned off to the right, and climbed up onto a spur. Up there, on the spur, we could see the thinning of the trees which meant the Matanikau. In a moment we would be at the river and, if Whaling had been as successful as we hoped, across it.

The captain and I were about seventy-five feet from the river when we found out how wrong our hope was.

The signal was a single shot from a sniper.

It came from somewhere behind us, but probably not as far as the first shots we had heard. The high flat snap was easily recognizable as a Japanese sound, and immediately after it, overhead, went the sound of the bullet, like a supercharged bee.

After a couple of too quick seconds, snipers all around us opened up. There would be the snap, and the whine, and then the tuck when the bullet went into the ground. There was no way of knowing where the next was coming from. The only thing you could be certain of was that it would come soon enough to take your eye off the place where you thought you might spot the last one.

Then machine guns from across the river opened up.

But the terrible thing was that Jap mortars over there opened up, too.

The first thing a green man fixes upon in his mind is the noise of these weapons. This was the first time I had ever been surrounded this way by the tight-woven noise of war.

Its constant fabric was rifle fire; this sounded like Bucks County, Pennsylvania, on the first day of the pheasant season, only near by and not an amusement. Like a knife tearing into the fabric, every once in a while, there would be the short bursts of machine gun fire. The noise of the mortars was awful, a thump which vibrated not just your eardrums, but your entrails as well. Forward we could still hear our aviation — dive bombs fumbling into the jungle, and the laughter of strafing P-39s. And every once in a while the soft, fluttery noise of our artillery shells making a trip. The noise alone was enough to scare a new man, to say nothing of the things which were done by the things which were making the noise.

The Japs had made their calculations perfectly. There were only three or four natural crossings of the river; this was one of them. And so they had set their trap.

They had machine guns all mounted, ready to pour stuff into the jungle bottleneck at the stream's junction with the river. They had snipers scattered on both sides of the river. And they had their mortars all set to lob deadly explosions into the same area. Their plan was to hold their fire and let the enemy get well into the trap before snapping it, and this they had done with too much success.

Apparently the single sniper shot had given the command to the other snipers; when the machine gunners across the river heard all the snipers firing, they let go; and when the Jap mortar batteries farther back heard the machine gun bursts, they in turn opened up.

Had we been infantry, the trap might not have worked. Brave men with rifles and grenades could have wiped out the enemy nests. Captain Rigaud's helplessness was that he could not bring his weapons to bear. Heavy machine guns take some time to be assembled and mounted. In that narrow defile his men, as brave as any, never succeeded in getting more than two guns firing.

As soon as the firing broke out, the men with the machine gun parts rushed together, and regardless of cover put their weapons together. Then the crews felt their way along, trying to find a place where they could both have a little cover and do some harm. As they went they approach-fired, throwing out little fifty caliber exclamations, as if the guns could say: "Look out, you Japs."

But they never had a chance. The enemy had his guns in position, with nothing to do but aim and squeeze the trigger. And even if the enemy had had no machine guns, his mortar fire had Rigaud's men boxed.

The mortar fire was what was terrifying. Beside it the Japs' sniper fire and even machine gun fire, with its soprano, small-sounding report, seemed a mere botheration. It is hard to think of death as having anything but a deep bass voice. Each roar of mortar certainly seemed to be a word spoken by death.

Having seen Lou Diamond's mortar battery in action, I had a clear picture of what was happening to us. In some small clearing about a half a mile beyond the river, four little tubes, looking like stubby stove pipes, were set up at a high angle on a tripod. Somewhere behind them a Japanese officer stood. A man beside him gave him reports from a telephone or from runners. After each report he would bark out brief orders. A swarm of intelligent little animals would fuss around each tube, changing the angle a hair, turning the aim a trifle. Then the officer would shout to stand by. Some of the animals would step back, one or two at each tube would put their fingers in their ears. Then one, in the attitude of a small boy setting punk to a giant firecracker, would reach out over the mouth of each tube, holding in his hand a thing which looked very much like a miniature aerial bomb, complete with fins. At the order to fire, he would drop the thing, fins first, down the tube. As soon as it struck the bottom there would be a huge thump, and the thing was off on its uncertain flight.

Mortars send their shells in an exceedingly high toss. Consequently their aim is by guess and by God. You will understand this if you have ever seen the job an outfielder has judging a high fly, or if you are an inexpert tennis player and often have been embarrassed by trying to smash a high lob and misjudging it.

That was what made being on the receiving end of mortar fire so terrible: the next thing that those little tubes gave off might land anywhere. We would almost have felt more comfortable if something which could aim was aiming right at us.

When the first bolts of this awful thunder began to fall among Rigaud's men, we hit the ground. We were like earthy insects with some great foot being set down in our midst, and we scurried for little crannies — cavities under the roots of huge trees, little gullies, dead logs. I found a good spot to the left of the trail. It was the combination of a small embankment and a big tree; I grew very affectionate toward the spot; I embraced it. Captain Rigaud, I noticed, took little or no cover. He kept darting back and forth to see what was happening to his men.

What was happening to his men was something terrible. The mortar shells were exploding among them and bleaching some of the bravery out of them. The noise and seeing friends hurt were not things to be dismissed.

The reports were about ten seconds apart, and the shells burst erratically all around us, now fifty yards away, now twenty feet.

And all the while snipers and machine gunners wrote in their nasty punctuation. Our own guns answered from time to time with good, deep, rich sound, but not enough.

We heard one of our guns knocked out. If you have never heard a conversation between two machine guns which are trying to knock each other out, you cannot imagine what a terrible debate it is. At first they talk back and forth equally. Then as in most human arguments, one begins to get the upper hand and finally winds up doing all the talking. That was how it was when our gun was knocked out. It sounded like this:

"Tatatatatatatatatatatat," said the Jap gun, in a high Japanese voice.

"Bubububububububububub," said ours, deeply.

"Tatatatatatatatatatatatat," the Jap insisted.

"Bubububububububububub," said ours.

"Tatatatatatatatat," the Jap said, sure of itself.

"Bubububub . . . . bubub," ours said, uncertainly.

"Tatatatatatatatatatatat," the Jap reiterated.

"Bubub." Ours seemed almost to have been convinced.

"Tatatatatatatatat," said the Jap, to clinch the matter.

"Bub," ours said, in pathetic protest.

"Tatatatatatatatat . . .

"Tatatatatatatatatatatat."

And then silence. It was awful. (I have heard some conversations in which our guns talked theirs down. Then it is not awful; it makes you cheer.)

I don't believe that this was one of Captain Rigaud's guns. It was a gun belonging to George or Easy Company, and it was manned to the end by a brave man named Sergeant Bauer.

*   *   *

We could not see the enemy, either on our side of the river or the other. All this hatred was pouring out of jungle too thick to see more than twenty or thirty feet.

This was advantageous, in a way. It meant that the enemy no longer seemed animate. There was no excuse for feelings such as I had had when I picked up the head net. The firing over there was coming from the enemy as an idea, something easy to hate.

But this invisibility was also unsettling. You might have thought that the jungle itself had grown malevolent, and hated us. The trees were hurling little pellets at us; the vines were slinging great explosions.

But even if we had been able to see the enemy, we could not have done anything to him. We couldn't get our weapons to work. We were helpless. Our men were being killed and wounded. We were trapped, hopelessly trapped.

Individually the marines in that outfit were as brave as any fighters in any army in the world, I am positive; but when fear began to be epidemic in that closed-in place, no one was immune. No one could resist it.

The first sign of flight among those men was in their eyes. At first they watched what was going on as calmly as an audience at some play. Then suddenly they were looking around for the nearest exit. They would look at Captain Rigaud's face, looking for some sign that he would order them to retire; or their eyes would dart along the trail back, as they wished they could.

I myself kept looking at Captain Rigaud, to see what he would do with us. His expression had not changed. It had the same look of desperate vigilance that it had worn all along the trail.

The next sign of the growing fear was the way the men started moving around. When a mortar shell would go off near by, they would scramble away from the vicinity to new cover, as if the thing could explode a second time.

The men began to think that it was time to get away from that whole place.

Any men who were men would have taken flight from that impossible place. Some Japanese might not have, if they had had specific orders to stay there; but they would no longer have been much use to the Emperor. I think even most Japanese would have fled. Certainly Germans would have: they are good fighters: they have the sense to live and fight more advantageously another day. I think it is safe to say that Italians would have fled.

The Marines had been deeply enough indoctrinated so that even flight did not wipe out the formulas, and soon the word came whispering back along the line:

"Withdraw."

"Withdraw."

"Withdraw. . . ."

Then they started moving back, slowly at first, then running wildly, scrambling from place of cover to momentary cover.

This was a distressing sight, and though I myself was more than eager to be away from that spot, I had a helpless desire to do something to stop the flight. It seemed wrong. One had heard so much about how the Marines kill ten Japs for every man they lose (which is true), of the callousness of the Marines (true in a way), and of our endless successes against the Japs (true in sum total). Captain Rigaud had told me that this would probably be an easy job. It sounded so. And yet here were our men running away.

I couldn't do anything about it because I was caught up in the general feeling. It is curious how this feeling communicated itself. Except for the hard knot which is inside some men, courage is largely the desire to show other men that you have it. And so, in a large group, when a majority have somehow signalled to each other a willingness to quit acting, it is very hard indeed not to quit. The only way to avoid it is to be put to shame by a small group of men to whom this acting is life itself, and who refuse to quit; or by a naturally courageous man doing a brave deed.

It was at this moment that Charles Alfred Rigaud, the boy with tired circles under his eyes, showed himself to be a good officer and grown man.

Despite snipers all around us, despite the machine guns and the mortar fire, he stood right up on his feet and shouted out: "Who in Christ's name gave that order?"

This was enough to freeze the men in their tracks. They threw themselves on the ground, in attitudes of defense; they took cover behind trees from both the enemy and the anger of their captain.

Next, by a combination of blistering sarcasm, orders and cajolery, he not only got the men back into position: he got them in a mood to fight again.

"Where do you guys think you're going?" he shouted. And: "Get back in there. . . . Take cover, you. . . . What do you guys do, just invent orders? . . . Listen, it's going to get dark and we got a job to do. . . . You guys make me ashamed. . . ."

But the most telling thing he said was: "Gosh, and they call you Marines."

JOHN HERSEY, Into the Valley

258. American Airplanes Raid Tokyo

The first blow in the air offensive against Japan was the famous raid of April 18, 1942. Lieutenant-Colonel James H. Doolittle's force of sixteen medium bombers was carried by the Hornet *to within striking range of the Japanese capital. Few of those on board knew that Tokyo would be the target. The Chinese airfields were so far distant that Doolittle's fliers could not hope to make safe landings there. Not only Tokyo but five other cities were hit in the raid. Captain Ted W. Lawson tells the story.*

WE skimmed along. We went over the rooftops of a few small villages, and I began to worry. Twenty minutes was what it was supposed to take to reach Tokyo from the point where we came in. Now we had been over land for nearly thirty minutes, and no sign of the city. I saw one fairly large town off to the left, however, and I said to myself that if worst came to worst and we couldn't find Tokyo, I'd come back there and do at least some damage.

But just then we came up over a hill, dusting the top of another temple, and there before us, as smooth as glass, lay Tokyo Bay.

It was brilliant in the mid-day sun and looked as limitless as an ocean. I came down to within about fifteen feet, while McClure checked our course. I kept the same slow speed, gas-saving but nerve-racking when I thought occasionally of the 400 mph plus diving speed of the Zeros.

We were about two minutes out over the bay when all of us seemed to look to the right at the same time and there sat the biggest, fattest-looking aircraft carrier we had ever seen. It was a couple of miles away, anchored, and there did not seem to be a man in sight. It was an awful temptation not to change course and drop one on it. But we had been so drilled in what to do with our four bombs, and Tokyo was now so close, that I decided to go on.

There were no enemy planes in sight. Ahead, I could see what must have been Davey Jones climbing fast and hard and running into innocent-looking black clouds that appeared around his plane.

It took about five minutes to get across our arm of the bay, and, while still over the water, I could see the barrage balloons strung between Tokyo and Yokohama, across the river from Tokyo. . . .

In days and nights of dreaming about Tokyo and thinking of the eight millions who live there, I got the impression that it would be crammed together, concentrated, like San Francisco. Instead it spreads all over creation, like Los Angeles. There is an aggressively modern sameness to much of it and now, as we came in very low over it, I had a bad feeling that we wouldn't find our targets. I had to stay low and thus could see only a short distance ahead and to the sides. I couldn't go up to take a good look without drawing anti-aircraft fire, which I figured would be very accurate by now because the planes that had come in ahead of me all had bombed from 1500 feet. The buildings grew taller. I couldn't see people.

I was almost on the first of our objectives before I saw it. I gave the engines full throttle as Davenport adjusted the prop pitch to get a better grip on the air. We climbed as quickly as possible to 1500 feet in the manner which we had practiced for a month and had discussed for three additional weeks.

There was just time to get up there, level off, attend to the routine of opening the bomb bay, make a short run and let fly with the first bomb. The red light blinked on my instrument board, and I knew the first 500-pounder had gone.

Our speed was picking up. The red light blinked again, and I knew Clever had let the second bomb go. Just as the light blinked, a black cloud appeared about 100 yards or so in front of us and rushed past at great speed. Two more appeared ahead of us, on about the line of our wing tips, and they too swept past. They had our altitude perfectly, but they were leading us too much.

CAPTAIN TED W. LAWSON, *Thirty Seconds Over Tokyo*

259. Yanks and Australians Fight for New Guinea

General Douglas MacArthur, after his flight from the Philippines, set up headquarters in Australia. Large American forces were gradually collected on that island continent. The Japanese had entrenched themselves in eastern New Guinea, just to the north, which they held as a barrier to any advance in the Southwest Pacific. It was necessary to drive them out as a preliminary to an attack on the Bismarck Archipelago, and movement further north toward the Philippines. In gallant fighting, the Americans and Australians made good their control of New Guinea.

THE rainy season was now on in earnest and the daily downpours made life miserable for everybody, turned streams into raging torrents, wiped out bridges, transformed swamps into lakes and made the few existing roads impassable. Most of the boys were unshaven, and it was not long before they all became hollow-eyed. They had cold bully beef and biscuits to eat and wet mud for a bed.

The Japs were trapped with their backs to the sea in a triangular area that stretched from Cape Endaiadere, three miles below Buna, to a point beyond Gona, fourteen miles above Buna, and inland for distances that varied from mere yards to a mile or more. Americans formed the spearhead of the thrust against Buna, while Australians concentrated on knocking out the Japs entrenched at Gona.

It was difficult to distinguish our own and the Japs' positions at any time because there was no such thing as a front line. But there were pockets of resistance everywhere. Sometimes the enemy were in foxholes or machine-gun pits only ten yards from us. For instance, around Sanananda Point the Japs were along the shore. Farther inland there was a strong force of Australians. Still farther inland was still another force of Japs, who in turn were sandwiched in between two groups of Americans. . . .

The main body of our forces, laying direct siege to Buna itself, encountered a heavy barrage of enemy artillery and mortar fire. Our own 75 mm. guns replied in kind. Jap barrages often appeared pointless, but they were effective nevertheless. They would try to knock out our artillery, of course, but they also seemed to fire aimlessly all over the landscape. And enemy planes, taking advantage of the thick weather which held our own airmen on the other side of the mountains, swooped down on our positions in strafing attacks. At one point seven Zeros raked our positions with machine-gun fire. There is nothing more trying than to face a plane traveling more than 300 miles an hour only 20 feet over your head with all its guns spraying the earth with bullets.

The enemy troops were as quick to take advantage of weather conditions as were their brothers in the Jap Air Corps, and they repeatedly sought to infiltrate our positions with small guerrilla bands. Once along the Giriwu River near Saputs they tried to slip in under cover of a fog to wipe out an Australian company in a surprise attack, but the Australians had long since become wise to every Jap trick; they met the Japs this time with a withering blast of rifle fire. . . .

By December 3rd the Australians and Yanks had cut off Gona and had infiltrated into the defenses around Buna. The end was in sight for the Japs, but they never stopped trying to land reinforcements. They made their fifth attempt on December 9th, when six destroyers tried to send troops ashore on barges. Our bombers and pursuit planes suddenly swooped down on them, sank all the barges and routed the destroyers.

The Japs were being trapped in an ever-narrowing beachhead and they made repeated attempts to break through the encircling ring of steel. Near Sanananda Point a large force of Australians surrounded ninety-five Japs and called on them to surrender. It was a case of surrender or die. These Japs, all tough Marines, chose death. They not only would not surrender but they wouldn't even dig in. They attacked, and every one of them was killed. . . .

Gona fell to the Australians on December 10th, and the next day the Japs were hemmed in on a thin fringe of beach and coastal jungle around Buna. Every foot of that defense line bristled with guns.

Then the torrential rains came. The fighting almost ceased for a day or two, and we took advantage of the weather-enforced truce to bury 638 Japs. These dead men had been lying outside Jap positions for days and the enemy had had no chance to bury them under the constant avalanche of mortar, machine-gun and artillery fire from our side, to say nothing of a steady downpour of bombs and bullets from our airmen. The stench was unbearable, and we wondered how the live Japs had borne it until we discovered they were wearing gas masks as protection against their own dead.

PAT ROBINSON, The Fight for New Guinea

260. Labor Mobilizes for the War

Many Americans, including President Roosevelt, were greatly impressed with the universal call-up of the whole working population in Great Britain. In the war crisis every man and woman over eighteen (with many younger) was enrolled and assigned to a job. No such drastic measure could be undertaken in the United States. But the workers had to be stimulated to put their utmost effort into the tasks of war production. Frances W. Perkins, the Secretary of Labor under Roosevelt, helped him in the undertaking.

ONE of the earliest acts indicating that the President foresaw the likelihood of war was his revival of the National Defense Council. By an Executive Order in May 1940 he declared that an emergency existed and revived this council provided for under law.

The idea of reviving the National Defense Council seemed wise to all of us. A lot of planning and thinking would be necessary. The President's ingenuity led him to make the National Defense Council the effective core. The cabinet officers who were, under the law, members of the Council, were to be on it, he said, but the Advisory Commission to the Council was to advise us and we were to do whatever they requested.

When he announced the members of the Advisory Commission, there was a mild protest from cabinet officers who thought he might have done a great deal better.

One cabinet officer spoke up to say that William Knudsen was a mighty fine manufacturer of automobiles but as an organizer of the resources of the country there were a lot of better people. The President, however, liked Bill Knudsen. He had confidence in him. The fact that he had a following and a certain amount of affection in American business life was not lost on the President. There was bound to be a willingness by business to do whatever good old Bill Knudsen asked it to do. That was the important factor in Roosevelt's decision, and he gauged it correctly.

I commented upon the President's selection of Sidney Hillman as the labor member. Hillman was an old and valued friend of mine. However, there was the split between the AF of L and the CIO, and Hillman was in the CIO, which made his name anathema in AF of L circles, which were inclined to blame him rather than John L. Lewis for the whole CIO. There was also a split brewing inside the CIO which, although not known to the public, was perfectly clear to those of us who knew the inside story. Moreover, Hillman was an officer of a rather small union not engaged in heavy industry. I strongly recommended that the President appoint two labor men, one from the CIO and one from the AF of L.

The President replied he had thought of all that and wasn't going to have two labor men; too much trouble to have two. This sounded a lot like Harry Hopkins to me.

"Anyhow," said the President, "in times like these people can't bother about their private quarrels, they just have to work together. We know Hillman to be a good man. He knows about labor development in the United States. We know he is honest and trustworthy. I am not going to bother with two labor men, and besides I haven't a place for two labor men."

I pointed out that he didn't need an economist on the Advisory Commission. He had listed Leon Henderson in that role. I said he could get Leon Henderson on loan as an adviser.

No, he had made up his mind about having an economist.

"Well," I said, "you don't absolutely need Miss Elliott."

"No, we have to have a woman," he said. "Got to pacify the women. If there is a woman, you won't have women's protests against actions that are too military, against giving too much help to the allies. The presence of a woman on the Commission will stop all that."

He was adamant. I never knew him to be so stubborn. It has always been my thought that somebody prepared the plan, sold it to him in toto, and even selected the personnel. At any rate, he went through with it and the rest of us did our part. Labor was angry but as usual came around in the end, because they loved and had confidence in the President and because the times were serious.

The appointment of the Advisory Commission of the Defense Council was the beginning of the administrative confusion which has been pointed out so often by critics of Roosevelt and his administration. . . .

Hillman began to have great influence in the Government. In addition to [Daniel] Tracy, I lent him Isador Lubin, head of the Bureau of Labor Statistics, a man of vast comprehension of economics and ingenuity in finding ways to do things. Hillman built up a large staff, as was almost inevitable, and some were people with their own ideas and ambitions, which, I think, was not anticipated by the President. Some made confusion and conflict within Hillman's own organization. Others developed secretive habits and tried to cut corners around old-line Government establishments, even when they were operating in the same field.

Conciliators from the Department of Labor going about their customary duties ran into bright young men sent to settle a strike from Hillman's office — often self-assigned. Often Hillman knew nothing about it. The "troubleshooters," as they called themselves, kept turning up in the most unexpected places. It wouldn't have mattered, except that we were short of people to do this work, and the customers sometimes got angry and confused over multiple advice.

Into the melee sprang the Army and Navy. The armed services appointed labor advisers and labor relations adjusters. These young men, most of them out of industry or law offices and suddenly clapped into uniform, were well meaning, and many were good. But they too would turn up, without notice, to adjust a complaint or threatened dispute. Sometimes three or four adjusters would meet in the same place. First they would glower at each other. Then it took persuasion to get them to settle things among themselves as well as with the firm. Finally, the fellow who could handle it best took over. . . .

A good many agencies in Washington equipped themselves with labor advisers. This was in no way the fault of the President. A well-intentioned man with a particular job to do would think of all the problems he would have to deal with and get someone to assist him on each. He thought of labor as one of the problems and tended to get himself a labor adviser. There weren't enough good labor advisers to go around. Competent labor leaders were taken away from important work in the field with their unions and brought to Washington, and as labor advisers outside their own industry and sphere of experience they often were not particularly good. There is no magic formula.

No one asked the President's advice, nor should the President have had to give advice on the details of a job someone had been asked to do. But when these labor advisers began to get into conflict and to give conflicting advice which brought the heads of their units into conflict, there was a snarl. In such cases the agency heads often would come to me. Sometimes they went to the President. Always astonished at such conflict, he would say, "Go straighten it out. See the Secretary of Labor. Confer with Hillman. Come to an agreement. That is your job, not mine."

He had a serene belief that his whole administration should work like a team and that his associates should find ways of adjusting their problems. When I once talked with him about these conflicts, about which complaints were reaching the public ear, he gave me a little philosophical dissertation.

"This is the way I have always looked at it," he said. "We have new and complex problems. We don't really know what they are. Why not establish a new agency to take over the new duty rather than saddle it on an old institution? Of course, a great many mistakes are going to be made. They are bound to be made in anything so new and enormous as supplying our allies, training our Army and Navy, and recruiting the necessary industrial reserve. Mistakes in military strategy are made. They just absorb them. There will be mistakes in domestic and supply strategy. We have to be prepared to absorb and correct them quickly. We have to be prepared to abandon bad practices that grow up out of ignorance. It seems to me it is easier to use a new agency which is not a permanent part of the structure of government. If it is not permanent, we don't get bad precedents that will carry over into the days of peace. We can do anything that needs to be done and then discard the agency when the emergency is over.

"I think that there is something to be said for this," he went on. "There is something to be said too for having a little conflict between agencies. A little rivalry is stimulating, you know. It keeps everybody going to prove that he is a better fellow than the next man. It keeps them honest too. An awful lot of money is being handled. The fact that there is somebody else in the field who knows what you are doing is a strong incentive to strict honesty.

"You take the lead," he wound up, "in getting them together and keeping them together."

That became my principal wartime job. At his direction I sat in on so many interdepartmental committees and held so many conferences that the Department of Labor had the air of a service agency for the war activities.

FRANCES PERKINS, *The Roosevelt I Knew*

261. Henry Kaiser Builds Liberty Ships

Very early in the war it became clear that victory would depend, in large measure, on the American ship-building program. German submarines were sinking British and American ships at a terrifying rate, and Winston Churchill later ad-

mitted that the submarine was a greater danger to Britain than the German air force. President Roosevelt called for an all-out ship-building program, and a large share of it was assigned to Henry Kaiser, a new industrialist who had proved his ability to accomplish near-miracles of construction during the thirties and who had helped build, among other things, Bonneville, Boulder, and Grand Coulee dams. The American shipbuilding program, spearheaded by Kaiser, succeeded beyond expectations. John Gunther, one of the ablest of all American reporters and interpreters, here describes part of that program.

WE went out to Richmond, across the bay from San Francisco, on the day that Kaiser's 732nd ship was launched. The first thing I noticed: a chain of cars from the old Sixth Avenue El in New York, which Kaiser used to help move his workers to where they slept and back.

Richmond consists of four yards, built by Kaiser for the U.S. Maritime Commission, on a fee basis in conjunction with other companies. Yards No. 1 and No. 2 were operated by the Permanente Metals Corporation, No. 3 by Kaiser Co., Inc., No. 4 by Kaiser Cargo Co., Inc. For the four together, the peak of wartime employment was 91,000. As of V-J Day the yards had built $1,800,000,000 worth of ships, mostly Liberties and Victories, amounting to about 7,000,000 tons which is 20 per cent of the entire American production of merchant shipping during the war. One fifth of the American merchant navy was, in other words, built by Kaiser in this single area. Count in the Oregon yards, and the proportion goes up to one third.

Kaiser turned out combat ships too; in fact his Vancouver, Washington, yards built fifty baby flattops, small aircraft carriers, in eighteen months. Not only did the Navy say that this could not be done; it fought the project with embittered stubbornness, holding that ships built so fast could not be seaworthy; Kaiser got the program started only by going to Roosevelt over the heads of both admirals and Navy Department. For a time he was delivering carriers at the unprecedented and seemingly impossible rate of one a week.

The Liberties rolled off at Richmond even faster. At peak, a ship could be built in four and one half days, that is the various prefabricated parts and sections were put together in that time, and launchings once reached a rate of thirty-two per month, or one million-dollar ship a day. We visited yard No. 2, and I began dimly to see how the job was done. Part of the secret lay in prefabrication, part in the astute application of new techniques. Take deck houses. These were the toughest problem to solve, because they are the soul and brain of the ship and complex to make. In World War I it took 180 days to build a ship; most of the delay came from deck houses. So a method was contrived to build them in sections — upside down! They proceed down a monstrously large assembly line just like an automobile; then, when finished, they are cut into four huge parts, and each part is carted to the ship on an enormous specially-built eighty-five-ton trailer; finally the deck house is welded together again on the ship itself.

Richmond trained something like three hundred thousand welders out of soda clerks and housewives. Normally it takes two to three months to make a tolerable welder. The Kaiser technique turned them out in ten days, because they were only taught "down-hand" welding, which means welding below the waist, so that the weld itself flows by gravity. To make a good weld overhead takes skill, but practically anybody can do it on the lower level. So forepeaks were built sideways, and the actual sides of ships, cut, shaped and welded to predetermined patterns, were built flat, rather than inside a tall and costly scaffolding. The Kaiser principle was to fit the job to the man, instead of vice versa.

Richmond expanded so fast that a near-by mountain once got in the way. So three million cubic feet of it were moved.

A fancy explosion came in 1946 when Congress began an investigation of huge wartime profits by the shipbuilding industry in general. Nineteen firms, it was charged, had made $365,000,000 profit on a capital investment of $22,979,275. Six Kaiser companies were cited in the complaint drawn up by the General Accounting Office; this asserted that Kaiser and his associates, on an investment of only $2,510,000, had realized profits of more than $190,000,000. The sight — and sound — of Kaiser on the witness stand was stimulating. His rebuttal stated that his firms' combined net profits amounted to only one-tenth of 1 per cent on dollar volume.

JOHN GUNTHER, Inside U.S.A.

262. The Fifth Army Fights It Out on the Winter Line

The American offensive against Germany and Italy began with the landings on the shores of North Africa in November 1942. By the following spring all Africa was cleared of the enemy, and the Allies prepared to assault Sicily and Italy. The invasion of Sicily was an unqualified success, and by August 1943 the American Fifth and the British Eighth Armies stood poised for an invasion of Italy itself. At this juncture the tyrant Mussolini was deposed, and Italy prepared to surrender. The surrender took place September 3, but before the Allies could take over Italy the German Army moved into key positions and prepared to fight it out, mile by mile and yard by yard. There followed some of the toughest fighting of the whole war. The famous war correspondent, Ernie Pyle, describes the hardships of fighting on the Winter Line — the Apennines — in 1944.

THE war in Italy was tough. The land and the weather were both against us. It rained and it rained. Vehicles bogged down and temporary bridges washed out. The country was shockingly beautiful, and just as shockingly hard to capture from the enemy. The hills rose to high ridges of almost solid rock. We couldn't go around them through the flat peaceful valleys, because the Germans were up there looking down upon us, and they would have let us have it. So we had to go up and over. A mere platoon of Germans, well dug in on a high, rock-spined hill, could hold out for a long time against tremendous onslaughts.

I know the folks back home were disappointed and puzzled by the slow progress in Italy. They wondered why we moved northward so imperceptibly. They were impatient for us to get to Rome. Well, I can say this — our troops were just as impatient for Rome. But on all sides I heard: "It never was this bad in Tunisia." "We ran into a new brand of Krauts over here." "If it would only stop raining." "Every day we don't advance is one day longer before we get home."

Our troops were living in almost inconceivable misery. The fertile black valleys were knee-deep in mud. Thousands of the men had not been dry for weeks. Other thousands lay at night in the high mountains with the temperature below freezing and the thin snow sifting over them. They dug into the stones and slept in little chasms and behind rocks and in half-caves. They lived like men of prehistoric times, and a club would have become them more than a machine gun. How they survived the dreadful winter at all was beyond us who had the opportunity of drier beds in the warmer valleys.

That the northward path was a tedious one was not the fault of our troops, nor of their direction either. It was the weather and the terrain and the weather again. If there had been no German fighting troops in Italy, if there had been merely German engineers to blow the bridges in the passes, if never a shot had been fired at all, our northward march would still have been slow. The country was so difficult that we formed a great deal of cavalry for use in the mountains. Each division had hundreds of horses and mules to carry supplies beyond the point where vehicles could go no farther. On beyond the mules' ability, mere men — American men — took it on their backs.

On my way to Italy, I flew across the Mediterranean in a cargo plane weighted down with more than a thousand pounds beyond the normal load. The cabin was filled with big pasteboard boxes which had been given priority above all other freight. In the boxes were packboards, hundreds of them, with which husky men would pack 100, even 150, pounds of food and ammunition, on their backs, to comrades high in those miserable mountains.

But we could take consolation from many things. The air was almost wholly ours. All day long Spitfires patrolled above our fighting troops like a half dozen policemen running up and down the street watching for bandits.

What's more, our artillery prevailed — and how! We were prodigal with ammunition against those rocky crags, and well we might be, for a $50 shell could often save 10 lives in country like that. Little by little, the fiendish rain of explosives upon the hillsides softened the Germans. They always were impressed by and afraid of our artillery, and we had concentrations of it there that were demoralizing.

And lastly, no matter how cold the mountains, or how wet the snow, or how sticky the mud, it was just as miserable for the German soldier as for the American.

Our men were going to get to Rome all right. There was no question about that. But the way was cruel. No one who had not seen that mud, those dark skies, those forbidding ridges and ghost-like clouds that unveiled and then quickly hid the enemy, had the right to be impatient with the progress along the road to Rome.

The mountain fighting went on week after dreary week. For a while I hung around with one of the mule-pack outfits. There was an average of one mule-packing outfit for every infantry battalion in the mountains. Some were run by Americans, some by Italian soldiers.

The pack outfit I was with supplied a battalion that was fighting on a bald, rocky ridge nearly four thousand feet high. That battalion fought constantly for ten days and nights, and when the men finally came down less than a third of them were left.

All through those terrible days every ounce of their supplies had to go up to them on the backs of mules and men. Mules took it the first third of the way. Men took it the last bitter two thirds, because the trail was too steep even for mules.

The mule skinners of my outfit were Italian soldiers. The human packers were mostly American soldiers. The Italian mule skinners were from Sardinia. They belonged to a mountain artillery regiment, and thus were experienced in climbing and in handling mules. They were bivouacked in an olive grove alongside a highway at the foot of the mountain. They made no trips in the daytime, except in emergencies, because most of the trail was exposed to artillery fire. Supplies were brought into the olive grove by truck during the day, and stacked under trees. Just before dusk they would start loading the stuff onto mules. The Americans who actually managed the supply chain liked to get the mules loaded by dark, because if there was any shelling the Italians instantly disappeared and could never be found.

There were 155 skinners in this outfit and usually about 80 mules were used each night. Every mule had a man to lead it. About

ten extra men went along to help get mules up if they fell, to re-
pack any loads that came loose, and to unpack at the top. They
could be up and back in less than three hours. Usually a skinner
made just one trip a night, but sometimes in an emergency he made
two.

On an average night the supplies would run something like this —
85 cans of water, 100 cases of K ration, 10 cases of D ration, 10 miles
of telephone wire, 25 cases of grenades and rifle and machine-gun
ammunition, about 100 rounds of heavy mortar shells, 1 radio, 2
telephones, and 4 cases of first-aid packets and sulfa drugs. In addition, the packers would cram their pockets with cigarettes for the
boys on top; also cans of Sterno, so they could heat some coffee once
in a while.

Also, during that period, they took up more than five hundred of
the heavy combat suits we were issuing to the troops to help keep
them warm. They carried up cellophane gas capes for some of the
men to use as sleeping bags, and they took extra socks for them too.

Mail was their most tragic cargo. Every night they would take up
sacks of mail, and every night they'd bring a large portion of it
back down — the recipients would have been killed or wounded the
day their letters came.

On the long man-killing climb above the end of the mule trail they
used anywhere from twenty to three hundred men a night. They
rang in cooks, truck drivers, clerks, and anybody else they could lay
their hands on. A lot of stuff was packed up by the fighting soldiers
themselves. On a big night, when they were building up supplies for
an attack, another battalion which was in reserve sent three hundred
first-line combat troops to do the packing. The mule packs would
leave the olive grove in bunches of twenty, starting just after dark.
American soldiers were posted within shouting distance of each
other all along the trail, to keep the Italians from getting lost in the
dark.

Those guides — everybody who thought he was having a tough
time in this war should know about them. They were men who had
fought all through a long and bitter battle at the top of the mountain.
For more than a week they had been far up there, perched behind
rocks in the rain and cold, eating cold K rations, sleeping without
blankets, scourged constantly with artillery and mortar shells, fight-

ing and ducking and growing more and more weary, seeing their comrades wounded one by one and taken down the mountain.

Finally sickness and exhaustion overtook many of those who were left, so they were sent back down the mountain under their own power to report to the medics there and then go to a rest camp. It took most of them the better part of a day to get two thirds of the way down, so sore were their feet and so weary their muscles.

And then — when actually in sight of their haven of rest and peace — they were stopped and pressed into guide service, because there just wasn't anybody else to do it. So there they stayed on the mountainside, for at least three additional days and nights that I know of, just lying miserably alongside the trail, shouting in the darkness to guide the mules.

They had no blankets to keep them warm, no beds but the rocks. And they did it without complaining. The human spirit is an astounding thing.

ERNIE PYLE, Brave Men

263. General Eisenhower Describes the Great Invasion

So successful was Eisenhower's management of the African and Sicilian campaigns that he was appointed to the Supreme Command of American and British forces in the European theater. Transferring his headquarters to London, in 1943, he began preparations for the greatest of all military gambles — the cross-channel invasion of France. Although the enemy had expected the invasion for months, they miscalculated both the time and the place, and the Allies scored a strategic, though not a tactical, surprise. Only the weather surprised the Allies: just before the scheduled invasion the worst June gale in forty years struck the treacherous British Channel and threatened, for a moment, to upset all carefully laid plans. Eisenhower, however, took the responsibility of ordering the invasion to go ahead.

THE final conference for determining the feasibility of attacking on the tentatively selected day, June 5, was scheduled for 4:00 A.M. on June 4. However, some of the attacking contingents had already been ordered to sea, because if the entire force was to land on June 5, then some of the important elements stationed in northern parts of the United Kingdom could not wait for final decision on the morning of June 4.

When the commanders assembled on the morning of June 4 the report we received was discouraging. Low clouds, high winds, and formidable wave action were predicted to make landing a most hazardous affair. The meteorologists said that air support would be impossible, naval gunfire would be inefficient, and even the handling of small boats would be rendered difficult. Admiral Ramsay thought that the mechanics of landing could be handled, but agreed with the estimate of the difficulty in adjusting gunfire. His position was mainly neutral. General Montgomery, properly concerned with the great disadvantages of delay, believed that we should go. Tedder disagreed.

Weighing all factors, I decided that the attack would have to be postponed. This decision necessitated the immediate dispatch of orders to the vessels and troops already at sea and created some doubt as to whether they could be ready twenty-four hours later in case the next day should prove favorable for the assault. Actually the maneuver of the ships in the Irish Sea proved most difficult by reason of the storm. That they succeeded in gaining ports, refueling, and readying themselves to resume the movement a day later represented the utmost in seamanship and in brilliant command and staff work.

The conference on the evening of June 4 presented little, if any, added brightness to the picture of the morning, and tension mounted even higher because the inescapable consequences of postponement were almost too bitter to contemplate.

At three-thirty the next morning our little camp was shaking and shuddering under a wind of almost hurricane proportions and the accompanying rain seemed to be traveling in horizontal streaks. The mile-long trip through muddy roads to the naval headquarters was anything but a cheerful one, since it seemed impossible that in such conditions there was any reason for even discussing the situation.

When the conference started the first report given us by Group Captain Stagg and the Meteorologic Staff was that the bad conditions predicted the day before for the coast of France were actually prevailing there and that if we had persisted in the attempt to land on June 5 a major disaster would almost surely have resulted. This they probably told us to inspire more confidence in their next astonishing declaration, which was that by the following morning a period of relatively good weather, heretofore completely unexpected, would ensue, lasting probably thirty-six hours. The long-term prediction was not good but they did give us assurance that this short period of good weather would intervene between the exhaustion of the storm we were then experiencing and the beginning of the next spell of really bad weather.

The prospect was not bright because of the possibility that we might land the first several waves successfully and then find later build-up impracticable, and so have to leave the isolated original attacking forces easy prey to German counteraction. However, the consequences of the delay justified great risk and I quickly announced the decision to go ahead with the attack on June 6. The time was then 4:15 A.M., June 5. No one present disagreed and there was a definite brightening of faces as, without a further word, each went off to his respective post of duty to flash out to his command the messages that would set the whole host in motion.

A number of people appealed to me for permission to go aboard the supporting naval ships in order to witness the attack. Every member of a staff can always develop a dozen arguments why he, in particular, should accompany an expedition rather than remain at the only post, the center of communications, where he can be useful. Permission was denied to all except those with specific military responsibility and, of course, the allotted quotas of press and radio representatives.

Among those who were refused permission was the Prime Minister. His request was undoubtedly inspired as much by his natural instincts as a warrior as by his impatience at the prospect of sitting quietly back in London to await reports. I argued, however, that the chance of his becoming an accidental casualty was too important from the standpoint of the whole war effort and I refused his request. He replied, with complete accuracy, that while I was in sole command of the operation by virtue of authority delegated to me by both governments, such authority did not include administrative control over the British organization. He said, "Since this is true it is not part of your responsibility, my dear General, to determine the exact composition of any ship's company in His Majesty's Fleet. This being true," he rather slyly continued, "by shipping myself as a bona fide member of a ship's complement it would be beyond your authority to prevent my going."

All of this I had ruefully to concede, but I forcefully pointed out that he was adding to my personal burdens in this thwarting of my instructions. Even, however, while I was acknowledging defeat in the matter, aid came from an unexpected source. The King had learned of the Prime Minister's intention and, while not presuming to interfere with the decision reached by Mr. Churchill, the King sent word that if the Prime Minister felt it necessary to go on the expedition he, the King, felt it to be equally his duty and privilege to participate at the head of his troops. This instantly placed a different light upon the matter and I heard no more of it.

Nevertheless, my sympathies were entirely with the Prime Minister. Again I had to endure the interminable wait that always intervenes between the final decision of the high command and the earliest possible determination of success or failure in such ventures. I spent the time visiting troops that would participate in the assault. A late evening visit on the fifth took me to the camp of the U.S. 101st Airborne Division, one of the units whose participation had been so severely questioned by the air commander. I found the men in fine fettle, many of them joshingly admonishing me that I had no cause for worry, since the 101st was on the job and everything would be taken care of in fine shape. I stayed with them until the last of them were in the air, somewhere about midnight. After a two-hour trip back to my own camp, I had only a short time to wait until the first news should come in. . . .

The first report came from the airborne units I had visited only a few hours earlier and was most encouraging in tone. As the morning wore on it became apparent that the landing was going fairly well. Montgomery took off in a destroyer to visit the beaches and to find a place in which to set up his own advanced headquarters. I promised to visit him on the following day.

Operations in the Utah area, which involved the co-ordination of the amphibious landing with the American airborne operation, proceeded satisfactorily, as did those on the extreme left flank. The day's reports, however, showed that extremely fierce fighting had developed in the Omaha sector. That was the spot, I decided, to which I would proceed the next morning.

We made the trip in a destroyer and upon arrival found that the 1st and 29th Divisions, assaulting on Omaha, had finally dislodged the enemy and were proceeding swiftly inland. Isolated centers of resistance still held out and some of them sustained a most annoying artillery fire against our beaches and landing ships. I had a chance to confer with General Bradley and found him, as always, stouthearted and confident of the result. In point of fact the resistance encountered on Omaha Beach was at about the level we had feared all along the line. The conviction of the Germans that we would not attack in the weather then prevailing was a definite factor in the degree of surprise we achieved and accounted to some extent for the low order of active opposition on most of the beaches. In the Omaha sector an alert enemy division, the 352d, which prisoners stated had been in the area on maneuvers and defense exercises, accounted for some of the intense fighting in that locality.

DWIGHT D. EISENHOWER, Crusade in Europe

264. Ernie Pyle Describes Hedgerow Fighting in Normandy

Within five days of the original landings the Allies had landed sixteen divisions in Normandy. By June 12 Omaha and Utah beachheads had been joined by the capture of Carentan, and the Allies controlled eighty miles of the Normandy coast. Another week and they swept across the Cotentin Peninsula, seized the great port of Cherbourg, and prepared to swing inland to the heart of France and to Paris. As the fighting moved deeper into Normandy our troops met a new obstacle, the age-old hedgerows of the Normandy farms. Ernie Pyle tells how they overcame this formidable obstacle.

I want to describe to you what the weird hedgerow fighting in northwestern France was like. This type of fighting was always in small groups, so let's take as an example one company of men. Let's say they were working forward on both sides of a country lane, and the company was responsible for clearing the two fields on either side of the road as it advanced. That meant there was only about one platoon to a field, and with the company's understrength from casualties, there might be no more than twenty-five or thirty men.

The fields were usually not more than fifty yards across and a couple of hundred yards long. They might have grain in them, or apple trees, but mostly they were just pastures of green grass, full of beautiful cows. The fields were surrounded on all sides by the immense hedgerows — ancient earthen banks, waist high, all matted with roots, and out of which grew weeds, bushes, and trees up to twenty feet high. The Germans used these barriers well. They put snipers in the trees. They dug deep trenches behind the hedgerows and covered them with timber, so that it was almost impossible for artillery to get at them. Sometimes they propped up machine guns with strings attached so that they could fire over the hedge without getting out of their holes. They even cut out a section of the hedgerow and hid a big gun or a tank in it, covering it with bush. Also they tunneled under the hedgerows from the back and made the opening on the forward side just large enough to stick a machine gun through. But mostly the hedgerow pattern was this: a heavy machine gun hidden at each end of the field and infantrymen hidden all along the hedgerow with rifles and machine pistols.

We had to dig them out. It was a slow and cautious business, and there was nothing dashing about it. Our men didn't go across the open fields in dramatic charges such as you see in the movies. They did at first, but they learned better. They went in tiny groups, a squad or less, moving yards apart and sticking close to the hedgerows on either end of the field. They crept a few yards, squatted, waited, then crept again.

If you could have been right up there between the Germans and the Americans you wouldn't have seen many men at any one time — just a few here and there, always trying to keep hidden. But you would have heard an awful lot of noise. Our men were taught in training not to fire until they saw something to fire at. But the principle didn't work in that country, because there was very little to see. So the alternative was to keep shooting constantly at the hedgerows. That pinned the Germans to their holes while we sneaked up on them. The attacking squads sneaked up the sides of the hedgerows while the rest of the platoon stayed back in their own hedgerow and kept the forward hedge saturated with bullets. They shot rifle grenades too, and a mortar squad a little farther back kept lobbing mortar shells over onto the Germans. The little advance groups worked their way up to the far ends of the hedgerows at the corners of the field. They first tried to knock out the machine guns at each corner. They did this with hand grenades, rifle grenades and machine guns. . . .

Usually, when the pressure was on, the German defenders of the hedgerow started pulling back. They would take their heavier guns and most of the men back a couple of fields and start digging in for a new line. They left about two machine guns and a few riflemen scattered through the hedge to do a lot of shooting and hold up the Americans as long as they could. Our men would then sneak along the front side of the hedgerow, throwing grenades over onto the other side and spraying the hedges with their guns. The fighting was close — only a few yards apart. . . .

This hedgerow business was a series of little skirmishes like that clear across the front, thousands and thousands of little skirmishes. No single one of them was very big. Added up over the days and weeks, however, they made a man-sized war — with thousands on both sides getting killed. But that is only a general pattern of the hedgerow fighting. Actually each one was a little separate war, fought under different circumstances. For instance, the fight might be in a woods instead of an open field. The Germans would be dug in all over the woods, in little groups, and it was really tough to get them out. Often in cases like that we just went around the woods and kept going, and let later units take care of those surrounded and doomed fellows. Or we might go through a woods and clean it out, and another company, coming through a couple of hours later, would find it full of Germans again. In a war like this everything was in such confusion that I never could see how either side ever got anywhere. . . .

In a long drive an infantry company often went for a couple of days without letting up. Ammunition was carried up to it by hand, and occasionally by jeep. The soldiers sometimes ate only one K ration a day. They sometimes ran out of water. Their strength was gradually whittled down by wounds, exhaustion cases and straggling. Finally they would get an order to sit where they were and dig in. Then another company would pass through, or around them, and go on with the fighting. The relieved company might get to rest as much as a day or two. But in a big push such as the one that broke us out of the beachhead, a few hours' respite was about all they could expect.

The company I was with got its orders to rest about five o'clock one afternoon. They dug foxholes along the hedgerows, or commandeered German ones already dug. Regardless of how tired a man might be, he always dug in the first thing. Then they sent some men looking for water. They got more K rations up by jeep, and sat on the ground eating them. They hoped they would stay there all night, but they weren't counting on it too much. Shortly after supper a lieutenant came out of a farmhouse and told the sergeants to pass the word to be ready to move in ten minutes. They bundled on their packs and started just before dark. Within half an hour they had run into a new fight that lasted all night. They had had less than four hours' rest in three solid days of fighting. . . .

There in Normandy the Germans went in for sniping in a wholesale manner. There were snipers everywhere: in trees, in buildings, in piles of wreckage, in the grass. But mainly they were in the high, bushy hedgerows that form the fences of all the Norman fields and line every roadside and lane.

It was perfect sniping country. A man could hide himself in the thick fence-row shrubbery with several days' rations, and it was like hunting a needle in a haystack to find him. Every mile we advanced there were dozens of snipers left behind us. They picked off our soldiers one by one as they walked down the roads or across the fields. It wasn't safe to move into a new bivouac area until the snipers had been cleaned out. The first bivouac I moved into had shots ringing through it for a full day before all the hidden gunmen were rounded up. It gave me the same spooky feeling that I got on moving into a place I suspected of being sown with mines.

ERNIE PYLE, Brave Men

265. The Americans Seize a Bridge at Remagen and Cross the Rhine

By the end of August the Allies had won the battle of France, liberated Paris, and were swinging eastward towards Germany. British and Canadian forces under General Montgomery raced along the coast through Lille, into Belgium, and to the Dutch border. The American Seventh Army, which had landed on the south coast of France, was sweeping northward to join forces with the armies of the north. Yet there was the hardest kind of fighting ahead — at Aachen, along the Roer River, in the Hürtgen forest, in the rugged forests of the Ardennes where in mid December the Germans broke through with a fierce counteroffensive. Not until February, 1945, were the Allies ready to resume the offensive into Germany proper. On March 7 the great city of Cologne fell to the Allies, and they prepared to cross the Rhine. But how to get across that formidable barrier? A task force of the 9th Armored Division moved up the left bank of the Rhine to the old university town of Bonn and to the little town of Remagen, where, to their amazement, they found a bridge intact.

THE Germans had, of course, made elaborate advance preparations to destroy the Rhine bridges. The Ludendorff Bridge was no exception. However, so rapid was the advance of the American troops and so great was the confusion created among the defenders that indecision and doubt overtook the detachment responsible for detonation of the charges under the bridge. Apparently the defenders could not believe that the Americans had arrived in force and possibly felt that destruction of the bridge should be delayed in order to permit withdrawal of German forces which were still west of the river in strength.

The 9th Armored Division, under General Leonard, was leading the advance toward the bridge. Without hesitation a gallant detachment of the division rushed the bridge and preserved it against complete destruction, although one small charge under the bridge was exploded.

This news was reported to Bradley. It happened that a SHAEF staff officer was in Bradley's headquarters when the news arrived, and a discussion at once took place as to the amount of force that should be pushed across the bridge. If the bridgehead force was too small it would be destroyed through a quick concentration of German strength on the east side of the river. On the other hand, Bradley realized that if he threw a large force across he might occasion damaging interference to further development of my basic plan. Bradley instantly telephoned me.

I was at dinner with the corps and division commanders of the American airborne forces when Bradley's call came through. When he reported that we had a permanent bridge across the Rhine I could scarcely believe my ears. He and I had frequently discussed such a development as a remote possibility but never as a well-founded hope.

I fairly shouted into the telephone: "How much have you got in that vicinity that you can throw across the river?"

He said, "I have more than four divisions but I wanted to call you up to make sure that pushing them over would not interfere with your plans."

I replied, "Well, Brad, we expected to have that many divisions tied up around Cologne and now those are free. Go ahead and shove over at least five divisions instantly, and anything else that is necessary to make certain of our hold."

His answer came over the phone with a distinct tone of glee: "That's exactly what I wanted to do but the question had been raised here about conflict with your plans, and I wanted to check with you."

That was one of my happy moments of the war. Broad success in war is usually foreseen by days or weeks, with the result that when it actually arrives higher commanders and staffs have discounted it and are immersed in plans for the future. This was completely unforeseen. We were across the Rhine, on a permanent bridge; the traditional defensive barrier to the heart of Germany was pierced. The final defeat of the enemy, which we had long calculated would be accomplished in the spring and summer campaigning of 1945, was suddenly now, in our minds, just around the corner.

My guests at the dinner table were infected by my enthusiasm. Among them were veterans of successful aerial jumps against the enemy and of hard fighting in every kind of situation. They were unanimous in their happy predictions of an early end to the war. I am sure that from that moment onward every one of them went into battle with the *élan* that comes only from the joyous certainty of early and smashing victory.

By March 9 the First Army had enlarged the Remagen bridgehead area until it was more than three miles deep. It took the enemy a considerable time to recover from his initial surprise and confusion, and by the time he could bring up reinforcements against our bridgehead troops we were too strong to fear defeat. As usual the enemy attacked piecemeal with every unit as soon as it could arrive in the area but such feeble tactics were unable to combat our steady enlargement of the hold we had on his vitals.

From the day we crossed the river the enemy initiated desperate efforts to destroy the Ludendorff Bridge. Long-range artillery opened fire on it and the German Air Force concentrated every available plane for bombing attacks upon the structure. None of these was immediately successful and we continued to pour troops across the bridge, but at the same time we established floating Treadway bridges over the river.

The Treadway bridge was one of our fine pieces of equipment, capable of sustaining heavy military loads. It was comparatively easy to transport and was quickly installed. After General Collins and his VII Corps crossed the Rhine he was of course concerned with getting his floating bridges established as quickly as possible. He called in his corps engineer, Colonel Mason J. Young, and said, "Young, I believe you can put a bridge across this river in twelve hours. What kind of a prize do you want me to give you for doing it in less time than that?" Young reflected a second and then said, "I don't want anything but if you can promise a couple of cases of champagne to my men we shall certainly try to win them." "All right," said Collins, "I'll get the champagne if you get me a bridge in less than twelve hours."

In 10 hours and 11 minutes the 330-yard bridge was completed and the first load crossed the river. Collins gladly paid off. I heard that even this creditable record was later broken.

DWIGHT D. EISENHOWER, Crusade in Europe

266. Stalin Agrees to War on Japan

Despite pledges of nonaggression, the Nazis had invaded Russia in midsummer 1941. Thereafter the major battles of the European war were fought on Russian soil. President Roosevelt promptly extended lend-lease aid to Russia, and beginning in 1942 an ever-increasing stream of supplies and munitions flowed from the United States to Russia either through the Persian Gulf route or along the Arctic Ocean to Murmansk. Could Russia, in turn, be counted on to help the Western Powers? Would she join the United States and Britain in the war on Japan; would she co-operate to build an international order after the war? These questions were uppermost all through the war. Late in 1943 President Roosevelt sent his Secretary of State, Cordell Hull, to Moscow to discuss these and other questions with Marshal Stalin. Secretary Hull gives us an account of the conference.

THE Catherine the Great Hall of the Kremlin was the scene of a banquet given to the delegations by Marshal Stalin on the night of the last day of the conference, October 30. This was the first social event of the conference I attended. Immediately on arriving in Moscow, I had told Molotov that in my state of health I could not combine social activity and work. At the beginning he did not seem to believe me and pressed upon me invitations to the theater and to other gala functions. When I persisted in my refusal he seemed impressed, and I was later told that this emphasized to him the intensity of purpose I had in traveling all the way to Moscow in my uncertain health so as to help lay the foundations for a better postwar world.

I was seated at Stalin's right. This gave me a wonderful opportunity to talk to him during the long dinner and the entertainment that followed. I utilized it to the utmost in an effort to discuss our relations and future, knowing this would be the last chance I would have before leaving Moscow. I approached him somewhat in circles to draw him out.

Stalin was in a most agreeable state of mind. No matter what subject was discussed, he seemed to overlook nothing that might make clearer my understanding of his situation, present and prospective. He opened the conversation by saying: "You have had a successful conference." I at once replied that the credit was entirely his, that he had authorized his great country to take the decisive step of joining with Great Britain and the United States in a world program based on co-operation. This seemed to please him. Throughout the conversation he expressed himself as unqualifiedly for a broad program of international co-operation — military, political, and economic — for peace.

In the strongest way possible I presented to Stalin all the considerations calling for his joining in personal co-operation and leadership with the President and the Prime Minister. As for meeting them at Basra, however, he definitely stated his conclusion that he could not leave his military-emergency situation at present. He said we should give him credit for being sincere in this regard.

He then said he would send Molotov in his stead, since under the Soviet law Molotov was his duly constituted second-ranking man in the Government, designated to take his place when he himself might be absent. He asked what I thought of this idea.

I promptly replied that, of course, if he should find it absolutely impossible to go, Molotov would make a good representative. But in the minds of the President and myself, the main point was that, if Stalin himself were to go, it would have a tremendous psychological effect that would extend throughout the world. I said I desired still to plead with him to go himself if at all possible.

I got nowhere with this. His conclusion seemed to be final. I inferred that he had talked this over with his advisers and they felt that the time had not yet come when either the military situation or the necessity for a conference was such as to warrant his leaving. I decided to press the point no further, since to do so might hurt rather than help our purposes.

But I did say that he and the people of Russia had a tremendous prestige in many parts of the world, and there was an extremely compelling need for leadership such as he, in conjunction with President Roosevelt and Prime Minister Churchill, could offer. I remarked that he had no idea how great was his prestige in the world and therefore how necessary it was for him to exert leadership without delay, and that failure to do so would be serious and damaging.

"Through all past history," I said, "more than three fourths of the human race until very recently have simply had to have leadership. Real leaders appear in the world only every one or two centuries. You yourself have demonstrated that leadership both at home and abroad, and you have a responsibility to exercise it in this stage of the gravest possible world crisis by immediately appearing out in the world in close conjunction with President Roosevelt and Prime Minister Churchill."

He agreed that I was correct about the course of human affairs in the past and about the need for leadership now, but made no further response about meeting Roosevelt and Churchill.

Then, however, he did make a statement of transcendent importance. He astonished and delighted me by saying clearly and unequivocally that, when the Allies succeeded in defeating Germany, the Soviet Union would then join in defeating Japan.

Stalin had brought up this subject entirely on his own, although he may have had in mind the conversations I had had on this subject with Ambassador Litvinov. He finished by saying that I could inform President Roosevelt of this in the strictest confidence. I thanked him heartily.

The Marshal's statement of his decision was forthright. He made it emphatically, it was entirely unsolicited, and he asked nothing in return.

At the Yalta Conference in February, 1945, Stalin made this same promise to the President in writing, but then only as a result of the President's agreement to numerous territorial concessions to the Soviet Union in Asia, including the Kurile Islands and part of Sakhalin Island. I had resigned in November, 1944, hence do not know what changed situation might have rendered these concessions necessary — but when Stalin made his promise to me, for transmission to the President, it had no strings attached to it.

Later in the evening Stalin said the Soviet Union was not for isolation. I emphasized the soundness of that view by pointing out that isolation had almost ruined my country and his.

The Marshal stressed the necessity for collaboration and cooperation between the United States and Russia in the most sympathetic manner. I replied that this was a wonderful program to be carried out, that our two peoples were very much alike in many respects, that each was a great people, and that there need be no serious difficulty at all in promoting close understanding, trust and friendship — and, based on these, a spirit of co-operation — to all of which he agreed.

I concluded that patience on the part of both countries, and especially of their leaders in key positions, would be necessary in dealing with a mistake made here and there, and with intemperate individuals who would try to give trouble in both countries.

During the dinner innumerable toasts were drunk. Stalin and I drank them in red wine, though many of the guests preferred vodka. General Deane stole the show when, in answer to Stalin's toast to the American armed forces, he offered a toast to the day when American and British forces would meet Russian forces in Berlin. Stalin rose from his chair beside me and paid Deane alone the high honor of walking around the table to clink glasses with him.

When we left the dinner table Stalin led me and two or three others to an adjoining room for a few minutes before going to another room for a motion picture. He proceeded on his own initiative to speak in the most sarcastic terms about reports circulated in the past that the Soviet Union and Germany might agree on a separate peace. I remarked that any person who knew the Russian people and their relation to Germany in this war knew they would not make a separate peace with Germany. To this he heartily subscribed. . . .

When the Chinese Ambassador to the Soviet Union called on me
. . . to thank me again for what our Government had done for
China during the conference, I made it clear to him that neither
my associates nor I had intimated anything to the press about
China's difficulties in being permitted to become one of the original
signatories of the Four-Nation Declaration. The Ambassador said he
had cautioned his Government to say nothing about it, although he
had given Chiang Kai-shek the facts as to just what had occurred.

I said to the Ambassador that throughout the conference all Russian officials had been exceedingly cordial and that, when matters
of difference were under discussion, they had talked them out with
us in a thoroughly agreeable spirit.

"This," I said, "is a splendid state of mind with which to launch
our great forward movement of international co-operation, with
Russia for the first time a full-fledged member of it without reservations of any kind. All signs indicate that Mr. Stalin and his Government are opposed to isolation and are wholeheartedly in favor of the
movement of international co-operation launched by this conference,
with Russia as a full partner with the United States, Great Britain,
and China."

As I boarded the plane for home, I felt very strongly that great
things had been accomplished at Moscow. We had agreed on the
creation of the international organization that became the United
Nations. Russia agreed to be a member of that organization and to
work closely with the Western Powers in many other respects. We
had agreed on a policy toward Italy and toward Austria. We had
created the European Advisory Commission and the Advisory
Council for Italy. We had exchanged numerous ideas on the postwar
treatment of Germany, on our attitudes toward France, and on the
economic policies to pursue after the war. And, apart from the conference, Stalin had agreed to enter the war against Japan, once Hitler
was defeated.

Russia, moreover, never once raised the question that had disturbed us the previous year; namely, the settlement at this time of
postwar frontiers.

The Memoirs of Cordell Hull

267. Americans Seize a
Beachhead on Okinawa

Early in April, 1945, the German High Command signed an unconditional surrender, and the great war that had ravaged the continent since September 1939 came to an end. There was still Japan to deal with. Already the Americans, aided by their British allies, were closing in on the doomed Nipponese. The Japanese Navy was all but annihilated in the battle of the Philippines. From near-by islands — notably Iwo Jima, giant B29's rained death and destruction on the Japanese homeland. Some 800 miles west of Iwo Jima lay the great island of Okinawa, part of the Japanese homeland. Late in March a vast American armada of more than 1400 ships of all types converged on the doomed island. April 1 came the first landings, to be followed by a month of some of the hardest fighting of the entire war. This account of fighting on the beachhead is part of the official story of the war, written from the records, and from interviews with those who participated in the fight.

Dawn of Easter Sunday, 1 April 1945, disclosed an American fleet of 1300 ships in the waters adjacent to Okinawa, poised for invasion. Most of them stood to the west in the East China Sea. The day was bright and cool — a little under 75°; a moderate east-northeast breeze rippled the calm sea; there was no surf on the Hagushi beaches. Visibility was 10 miles until 0600, when it lowered to from 5 to 7 miles in the smoke and haze. More favorable conditions for the assault could hardly be imagined.

The Japanese doubtless marveled at the immensity of the assemblage of ships, but they could not have been surprised at the invasion itself. The Kerama Islands had been seized; Okinawa had been heavily bombarded for days; and underwater demolition teams had reconnoitered both the Hagushi beaches and the beaches above Minatoga on the southeast coast, indicating that landings were to be expected at either place or both. Moreover, Japanese air and submarine reconnaissance had also spotted the convoys en route.

The Japanese had been powerless to interfere with the approach to the Ryukyus. Bad weather, however, had caused not only seasickness among the troops but also concern over the possibility that a storm might delay the landings. It was necessary for some convoys to alter their courses to avoid a threatening typhoon. The rough seas caused delays and minor damage and resulted in other deflections from planned courses. Thus on the evening before L Day various task forces converging on Okinawa were uncertain of their own positions and those of other forces. All arrived on time, however, and without mishap.

For the men, observing the outline of the strange island in the first rays of light before the beaches became shrouded in the smoke and dust of naval and air bombardment, this Easter Sunday was a day of crisis. From scale models of Okinawa studied on shipboard they had seen that the rising ground behind the landing beaches, and even more the island's hills and escarpments, were well suited for defense. They had read of the native houses, each protected by a high wall, and of the thousands of strange Okinawan tombs which might serve the enemy as pillboxes and dugouts. They had been encouraged by the weakness of Kerama Retto's defenses, but the generally held expectations of an all-out defense of the beaches on the first Japanese "home" island to be invaded was one to appall even the dullest imagination. And behind the beaches the men were prepared to meet deadly snakes, awesome diseases, and a presumably hostile civilian population.

H Hour had been set for 0830. At 0406 Admiral Turner, Commander of Task Force 51, signaled, "Land the Landing Force." At 0530, 20 minutes before dawn, the fire support force of 10 battleships, 9 cruisers, 23 destroyers, and 177 gunboats began the pre-H-Hour bombardment of the beaches. They fired 44,825 rounds of 5-inch or larger shells, 33,000 rockets, and 22,500 mortar shells. This was the heaviest concentration of naval gunfire ever to support a landing of troops. About 70 miles east of Okinawa, Task Force

58 was deployed to furnish air support and to intercept attacks from Kyushu. In addition, support carriers had arrived with troop convoys. At 0745 carrier planes struck the beaches and near-by trenches with napalm.

Meanwhile LSTs and LSMs, which had carried to the target both the men composing the first assault forces and the amphibian vehicles in which they were to ride, spread their yawning jaws and launched their small craft, loaded and ready for the shore. Amphibian tanks formed the first wave at the line of departure, 4,000 yards from the beach. Flagged on their way at 0800, they proceeded toward land at 4 knots. From five to seven waves of assault troops in amphibian tractors followed the tanks at short intervals.

Opposite each landing beach, control craft, with pennants flying from the mast, formed the assault waves of amphibious vehicles in rotating circles. At 0815 the leading wave of amtracks uncoiled and formed a line near their mother control craft. Five minutes later the pennants were hauled down and an almost unbroken 8-mile line of landing craft moved toward the beaches.

Gunboats led the way in, firing rockets, mortars, and 40-mm. guns into prearranged target squares, on such a scale that all the landing area for 1,000 yards inland was blanketed with enough 5-inch shells, 4.5-inch rockets, and 4.2-inch mortars to average 25 rounds in each 100-yard square. Artillery fire from Keise added its weight. After approaching the reef, the gunboats turned aside and the amphibian tanks and tractors passed through them and proceeded unescorted, the tanks firing their 75-mm. howitzers at targets of opportunity directly ahead of them until landing. Simultaneously, two 64-plane groups of carrier planes saturated the landing beaches and the areas immediately behind with machine-gun fire while the fire from supporting ships shifted inland. When the assault wave moved in, the landing area had been under constant bambardment for three hours.

As the small boats made their way steadily toward the shore the men kept expecting fire from the Japanese. But there was no sign of the enemy other than the dropping of an occasional mortar or artillery shell, and the long line of invasion craft advanced as though on a large-scale maneuver. The offshore obstacles had either been removed by the underwater demolition teams or were easily pushed over by the amphibian tractors. Some concern had been felt as to whether, despite the rising tide, the Navy landing boats would be able to cross the coral reef, and the first waves were to inspect the reef and send back information. The reef did not hinder the first waves, in amphibian vehicles, but those who followed in boats had difficulty and were therefore ordered to transfer at the edge of the reef and cross in LVTs.

Beginning at 0830, the first waves began to touch down on their assigned beaches. None was more than a few minutes late. The volume of supporting fire had increased until a minute or two before the first wave landed; then suddenly the heavy fire on the beach area ended and nothing was to be heard except the rumble of the shells that were shifted inland. Quickly the smoke and dust that had shrouded the landing area lifted, and it became possible for the troops to see the nature of the country directly before them. They were on a beach which was generally about 20 yards in depth and which was separated by a 10-foot sea wall from the country beyond. There were a few shell holes on the beach itself, but naval gunfire had blown large holes in the sea wall at frequent intervals to provide adequate passageways. Except at the cliff-bordered Bishi River mouth, in the center of the landing area, the ground rose gradually to an elevation of about 50 feet. There was only sparse natural vegetation, but from the sea wall to the top of the rise the coastal ground was well cultivated. In the background, along the horizon, hills showed through the screen of artillery smoke. Farther inland, in many places, towns and villages could be seen burning and the smoke rising above them in slender and twisted spires. These evidences of devastation, however, made less impression upon the men than did the generally peaceful and idyllic nature of the country, enhanced by the pleasant warmth, the unexpected quiet, and the absence of any sign of human life.

New waves of troops kept moving in. Before an hour had passed III Amphibious Corps had landed the assault elements of the 6th and 1st Marine Divisions abreast north of the Bishi River, and XXIV Corps had put ashore those of the 7th and 96th Infantry Divisions abreast south of that river. The 6th Marine Division and the 96th

Division were on the flanks. Two battalion landing teams from each of two assault regimental combat teams in the four divisions, or more than 16,000 troops, came ashore in the first hour.

The assault troops were followed by a wave of tanks. Some were equipped with flotation devices, others were carried by LCM(6)s which had themselves been transported by LSDs, and still others were landed by LSMs. After debarking the assault waves, the amphibian tractors returned to the transfer line to ferry support troops, equipment, and supplies across the reef onto the beach. LVT, DUKW, and small-boat control points were established at the transfer line. Amphibian vehicles preloaded with ammunition and supplies proceeded inland as needed.

The entire landing on Okinawa had taken place with almost incredible ease. There had been little molestation from enemy artillery, and on the beaches no enemy and few land mines had been encountered. The operation had taken place generally according to plan; there was little disorganization and all but a few of the units landed at the beaches assigned to them. The absence of any but the most trivial opposition, so contrary to expectation, struck the men as ominous and led them to reconnoiter suspiciously. After making certain that they were not walking into a trap, the troops began moving inland, according to plan, a very short time after they had landed.

Spirits rose as the marines and soldiers easily pushed up the hill-sides behind the beaches. The land was dry and green with conifers and the air bracing — a welcome change from the steaming marshes and palm trees of the islands to the south. An infantryman of the 7th Division, standing atop a hill just south of the Bishi River soon after the landing, expressed the common feeling when he said, "I've already lived longer than I thought I would."

ROY E. APPLEMAN, JAMES M. BURNS, RUSSELL A. GUGELER, AND JOHN STEVENS, Okinawa: The Last Battle

268. An American Plane Ushers in the Atomic Age

By mid-summer of 1945 Japan was reeling under repeated blows. Great cities like Tokyo and Yokohama were charred ruins; Admiral Halsey's Third Fleet cruised at will up and down the coast; submarines cut off Japanese access to the Asiatic mainland. Meeting at Potsdam, Germany, in July the Allied leaders served notice on Japan to get out of the war. But the Japanese ignored the Potsdam declaration. On August 6 a lone B–29 flew over the great industrial city of Hiroshima and dropped a single atomic bomb. A vast explosion shattered the city, and when the smoke blew away it was seen that over half of the city had been destroyed. To the stunned Japanese President Truman gave a new ultimatum, which was once more ignored. On August 8 a second, improved, atomic bomb was released on the city of Nagasaki. William E. Laurence, consultant to the War Department, went on the flight which dropped the bomb and here describes it for us.

WE flew southward down the channel and at 11:33 crossed the coastline and headed straight for Nagasaki about 100 miles to the west. Here again we circled until we found an opening in the clouds. It was 12:01 and the goal of our mission had been reached.

We heard the prearranged signal on our radio, put on our arc-welder's glasses and watched tensely the maneuverings of the strike ship about half a mile in front of us.

"There she goes!" someone said.

Out of the belly of *The Great Artiste* what looked like a black object went downward.

Captain Bock swung around to get out of range; but even though we were turning away in the opposite direction, and despite the fact that it was broad daylight in our cabin, all of us became aware of a giant flash that broke through the dark barrier of our arc-welder's lenses and flooded our cabin with intense light.

We removed our glasses after the first flash, but the light still lingered on, a bluish-green light that illuminated the entire sky all around. A tremendous blast wave struck our ship and made it tremble from nose to tail. This was followed by four more blasts in rapid succession, each resounding like the boom of cannon fire hitting our plane from all directions.

Observers in the tail of our ship saw a giant ball of fire rise as though from the bowels of the earth, belching forth enormous white smoke rings. Next they saw a giant pillar of purple fire, 10,000 feet high, shooting skyward with enormous speed.

By the time our ship had made another turn in the direction of the atomic explosion, the pillar of purple fire had reached the level of our altitude. Only about forty-five seconds had passed. Awestruck, we watched it shoot upward like a meteor coming from the earth instead of from outer space, becoming ever more alive as it climbed skyward through the white clouds. It was no longer smoke, or dust, or even a cloud of fire. It was a living thing, a new species of being born before our incredulous eyes.

At one stage of its evolution, covering millions of years in terms of seconds, the entity assumed the form of a giant square totem pole, with its base about three miles long, tapering off to about a mile at the top. Its bottom was brown, its center was amber, its top white. But it was a living totem pole, carved with many grotesque masks grimacing at the earth.

Then, just when it appeared as if the thing had settled down into a state of permanence, there came shooting out of the top a giant mushroom that increased the height of the pillar to a total of 45,000 feet. The mushroom top was even more alive than the pillar, seething and boiling in a white fury of creamy foam, sizzling upward and then descending earthward, a thousand Old Faithful geysers rolled into one.

It kept struggling in an elemental fury, like a creature in the act of breaking the bonds that held it down. In a few seconds it had freed itself from its gigantic stem and floated upward with tremendous speed, its momentum carrying into the stratosphere to a height of about 60,000 feet.

But no sooner did this happen than another mushroom, smaller in size than the first one, began emerging out of the pillar. It was as though the decapitated monster were growing a new head.

As the first mushroom floated off into the blue, it changed its shape into a flower-like form, its giant petal curving downward, creamy white outside, rose-colored inside. It still retained that shape when we last gazed at it from a distance of about 200 miles.

WILLIAM E. LAURENCE, in the *New York Times*

269. "Sail, Sail Thy Best, Ship of Democracy"

Sail, sail thy best, ship of Democracy,
Of value is thy freight, 'tis not the Present only,
The Past is also stored in thee,
Thou holdest not the venture of thyself alone, not of the Western
    Continent alone,
Earth's *résumé* entire floats on thy keel O ship, is steadied by thy
    spars,
With thee Time voyages in trust, the antecedent nations sink or
    swim with thee,
With all their ancient struggles, martyrs, heroes, epics, wars, thou
    bear'st the other continents,
Theirs, theirs as much as thine, the destination-port triumphant;
Steer then with good strong hand and wary eye O helmsman, thou
    carriest great companions,
Venerable priestly Asia sails this day with thee,
And royal feudal Europe sails with thee.

*   *   *

Beautiful world of new superber birth that rises to my eyes,
Like a limitless golden cloud filling the western sky,
Emblem of general maternity lifted above all,
Sacred shape of the bearer of daughters and sons,
Out of thy teeming womb thy giant babes in ceaseless procession
    issuing,
Acceding from such gestation, taking and giving continual strength
    and life,
World of the real -- world of the twain in one,

World of the soul, born by the world of the real alone, led to
    identity, body, by it alone,
Yet in beginning only, incalculable masses of composite precious
    materials,
By history's cycles forwarded, by every nation, language, hither sent,
Ready, collected here, a freer, vast electric world, to be constructed
    here,
(The true New World, the world of orbic science, morals, literatures
    to come,)
Thou wonder world yet undefined, unform'd, neither do I define
    thee,
How can I pierce the impenetrable blank of the future?
I feel thy ominous greatness evil as well as good,
I watch thee advancing, absorbing the present, transcending the
    past,
I see thy light lighting, and thy shadow shadowing, as if the entire
    globe,
But I do not undertake to define thee, hardly to comprehend thee,
I but thee name, thee prophesy, as now,
I merely thee ejaculate!
Thee in thy future,
Thee in thy only permanent life, career, thy own unloosen'd mind,
    thy soaring spirit,
Thee as another equally needed sun, radiant, ablaze, swift-moving,
    fructifying all,
Thee risen in potent cheerfulness and joy, in endless great hilarity,
Scattering for good the cloud that hung so long, that weigh'd so
    long upon the mind of man,
The doubt, suspicion, dread, of gradual, certain decadence of man;
Thee in thy larger, saner brood of female, male — thee in thy
    athletes, moral, spiritual, south, north, west, east,
(To thy immortal breasts, Mother of All, thy every daughter, son,
    endear'd alike, forever equal,)
Thee in thy own musicians, singers, artists, unborn yet, but certain,
Thee in thy moral wealth and civilization (until which thy proud-
    est material civilization must remain in vain),
Thee in thy all-supplying, all-inclosing worship — thee in no single
    bible, saviour, merely,

Thy saviours countless, latent within thyself, thy bibles incessant
    within thyself, equal to any, divine as any,
(Thy soaring course thee formulating, not in thy two great wars,
    nor in thy century's visible growth,
But far more in these leaves and chants; thy chants, great Mother!)
Thee in an education grown of thee, in teachers, studies, students,
    born of thee,
Thee in thy democratic fêtes-en-masse, thy high original festivals,
    operas, lecturers, preachers,
Thee in thy ultimata (the preparations only now completed, the
    edifice on sure foundations tied),
Thee in thy pinnacles, intellect, thought, thy topmost rational joys,
    thy love and godlike aspiration,
In thy resplendent coming literati, thy full-lung'd orators, thy
    sacerdotal bards, cosmic savants,
These! these in thee (certain to come) today I prophesy.

*   *   *

Land tolerating all, accepting all, not for the good alone, all good
    for thee,
Land in the realms of God to be a realm unto thyself,
Under the rule of God to be a rule unto thyself.

(Lo, where arise three peerless stars,
To be thy natal stars my country, Ensemble, Evolution, Freedom,
Set in the sky of Law.)

*   *   *

Land of unprecedented faith, God's faith,
Thy soul, thy very subsoil, all upheav'd,
The general inner earth so long so sedulously draped over, now hence
    for what it is boldly laid bare,
Open'd by thee to heaven's light for benefit or bale.
Not for success alone,
Nor to fair-sail unintermitted always,
The storm shall dash thy face, the murk of war and worse than war
    shall cover thee all over,
(Wert capable of war, its tug and trials? be capable of peace, its trials,

For the tug and mortal strain of nations come at last in prosperous
    peace, not war;)
In many a smiling mask death shall approach beguiling thee, thou
    in disease shalt swelter,
The livid cancer spread its hideous claws, clinging upon thy breasts,
    seeking to strike thee deep within,
Consumption of the worst, moral consumption, shall rouge thy
    face with hectic,
But thou shalt face thy fortunes, thy diseases, and surmount them all,
Whatever they are today and whatever through time they may be,
They each and all shall lift and pass away and cease from thee,
While thou, Time's spirals rounding, out of thyself, thyself still
    extricating, fusing,
Equable, natural, mystical Union thou, (the mortal with immortal
    blent,)
Shalt soar toward the fulfilment of the future, the spirit of the body
    and the mind,
The soul, its destinies.

The soul, its destinies, the real real,
(Purport of all these apparitions of the real;)
In thee America, the soul, its destinies,
Thou globe of globes! thou wonder nebulous!
By many a throe of heat and cold convuls'd (by these thyself so-
    lidifying),
Thou mental, moral orb — thou New, indeed new, Spiritual World!
The Present holds thee not — for such vast growth as thine,
For such unparallel'd flight as thine, such brood as thine,
The FUTURE only holds thee and can hold thee.

                        WALT WHITMAN, Leaves of Grass

Bibliography

We have listed below, in numerical order, the sources from which the selections for the *Heritage of America* have been taken. In most, but not in all, cases we have made our selections from the original edition of the source, but as this book is designed for general use, we have thought it desirable to indicate the existence of later editions where they are available. Needless to say, the editors assume no responsibility for the accuracy with which these sources were originally printed. Some, such as the so-called *Journal of Columbus,* were badly translated; others, such as Miss Post's *Soldiers' Letters from Camp, Battle-field and Prison,* were poorly edited; still others, such as *A Narrative of the Life of David Crockett,* are of dubious authenticity. Any extended bibliographical commentary, however, would seem to be out of place in a book of this nature. This list, therefore, is neither critical nor annotated; it is included for the convenience of the reader, not for the edification of the scholar.

1. *The Voyages of the Northmen to America,* edited by the Reverend Edmund F. Slafter. Printed for the Prince Society. Boston, 1877.
2. *The Journal of Christopher Columbus,* edited by Clements R. Markham. Translated for the Hakluyt Society. London, 1893. There are several other editions of this journal, of which that by Cecil Jane is perhaps the most satisfactory.
3. *Narratives of the Career of Hernando de Soto in the Conquest of Florida, as Told by a Knight of Elvas. . . .* Translated by Buckingham Smith. N.Y., The Bradford Club, 1866. This translation is also available in Theodore H. Lewis, editor, *Spanish Explorers in the Southern United States, 1528–1543,* one of the volumes of the *Original Narratives of American History.*
4. *The Jesuit Relations and Allied Documents. Travels and Explorations of the Jesuit Missionaries in New France, 1610–1791,* Vol. LIX, edited by Reuben Gold Thwaites. Cleveland, 1900. By kind permission of The Burrows Brothers Company.

5. I. *A True Relation of Such Occurrences and Accidents of Noate as Hath Hapned in Virginia,* by John Smith. London, 1608, and many later editions.

II. *The Generall Historie of Virginia, New England, and the Summer Isles,* by Captaine John Smith. London, 1624, and many later editions. The best edition of the works of John Smith is that by Edward Arber, published in two volumes.

6. *Bradford's History "Of Plimoth Plantation."* From the original manuscript. Published by the Commonwealth of Massachusetts, Boston, 1899. There are various other editions.

7. *Richard Mather's Journal.* 1635. Collections of the Dorchester Antiquarian and Historical Society, Number 3. Boston, 1850.

8. *A History of New York. From the Beginning of the World to the End of the Dutch Dynasty* . . . , by Diedrich Knickerbocker [Washington Irving]. 2 vols. N.Y., 1809. There are innumerable later editions.

9. I. *The Wonders of the Invisible World* . . . , by Cotton Mather. Boston, 1693.

II. *Brief and True Narrative of Some Remarkable Passages* . . . , by Deodat Lawson. Boston, 1692.

III. *More Wonders of the Invisible World* . . . , by Robert Calef. London, 1700.

The best collection of sources on witchcraft is that by George Lincoln Burr, editor, *Narratives of the Witchcraft Cases,* in *Original Narratives of American History.* N.Y., 1914.

10. *Beginning, Progress and Conclusion of Bacon's Rebellion in Virginia in the Years 1675 and 1676.* [By T. M.] Reprinted by G. P. Humphrey, Rochester, N.Y., 1897.

11. *An Account of Two Voyages to New England* . . . , by John Josselyn. London, 1675.

12. *The History of the Dividing Line and Other Tracts. From the Papers of William Byrd of Westover, in Virginia,* edited by Thomas H. Wynne. Richmond, Va., 1866. There are several later editions, the most satisfactory of which is that by William K. Boyd.

13. *The Journals of Madam Knight, etc.,* edited by Timothy Dwight. N.Y., 1825.

14. *Gottlieb Mittelberger's Journey to Pennsylvania in the Year 1750, and Return to Germany in the Year 1754,* edited by Carl Theodore Eben. Philadelphia, 1898. By kind permission of the John J. McVey Company, Philadelphia.

15. *The Autobiography of Benjamin Franklin.* There are innumerable editions; that in two volumes by John Bigelow is perhaps the most useful.

16. *The Life of George Mason,* by Kate Rowland. 2 vols. N.Y., 1892. By kind permission of G. P. Putnam's Sons.

17. *The History of Carolina . . . ,* by John Lawson. Raleigh, N.C., 1860. Reprinted by Garrett and Massie, Richmond, Va., 1937.

18. *The History of King Philip's War,* by Benjamin Church. With an introduction and notes by Henry Martyn Dexter. 2 vols. Boston, 1865.

19. *Narrative of the Captivity and Restoration of Mrs. Mary Rowlandson.* Cambridge, Mass., 1682. Reprinted, Lancester, Mass., 1903.

20. *Memoirs of Odd Adventures, Strange Deliverances, Etc.,* by John Giles. Cincinnati, 1869.

21. *Account of the Remarkable Occurrences in the Life and Travels of Colonel James Smith,* edited by W. A. Darlington. Cincinnati, 1870.

22. *The Writings of George Washington,* Vol. I, edited by Worthington C. Ford. N.Y., 1889. By kind permission of G. P. Putnam's Sons.

23. *The Autobiography of Benjamin Franklin.* See No. 15.

24. *Montcalm and Wolfe,* Vol. II, by Francis Parkman. Boston, 1884, and many later editions. By kind permission of Little, Brown and Company.

25. *A Retrospect of the Boston Tea-Party with a Memoir of George R. T. Hewes.* N.Y., 1834.

26. *The Works of John Adams,* edited by Charles Francis Adams. Vol. II, *The Diary.* Boston, 1850.

27. *Sketches of the Life and Character of Patrick Henry,* by William Wirt. Philadelphia, 1817, and many later editions.

28. *Reminiscences of an American Loyalist, 1738–1789. Being the Autobiography of the Reverend Jonathan Boucher . . . ,* edited by his grandson, Jonathan Bouchier. Boston, 1925. By kind permission of Houghton, Mifflin Company.

29. *The Works of John Adams,* edited by Charles Francis Adams. Vol. II, *The Diary.* Boston, 1850.

30. *General Gage's Informers,* by Allen French. Ann Arbor, Mich., 1932. By kind permission of Mr. French and the University of Michigan Press.

31. *The Works of John Adams,* edited by Charles Francis Adams. Vol. II, *The Diary,* Boston, 1850.

32. *Documents of American History,* edited by Henry Steele Commager. N.Y., 1934.

33. *A Narrative of Colonel Ethan Allen's Captivity. . . .* Boston, 1779, and many later editions, the most accessible that by John Pell.

34. *A Journal Kept by William Humphrey of Captain Thayer's Company on a March to Quebec. . . . The Magazine of History,* Extra Number 166. William Abbatt, Tarrytown, N.Y., 1931.

35. *The Journals of Major Samuel Shaw,* edited by Josiah Quincy. Boston, 1847.

36. *A French Volunteer of the War of Independence,* by the Chevalier de Pontgibaud, edited by Robert B. Douglas. N.Y., 1898. By kind permission of the D. Appleton-Century Company.

37. *The Capture of Old Vincennes,* edited by Milo M. Quaife. Indianapolis, 1927. By kind permission of the Bobbs-Merrill Company.

38. *The Journals of Major Samuel Shaw,* edited by Josiah Quincy. Boston, 1847.

39. *Life and Correspondence of John Paul Jones,* by Robert C. Sands. N.Y., 1830.

40. *Military Journal during the American Revolutionary War, from 1775 to 1783,* by James Thacher, M.D. Hartford, 1854.

41. *History of the American Revolution,* 2 vols., by David Ramsay. Philadelphia, 1789.

42. *Documents of American History,* edited by Henry Steele Commager. N.Y., 1934.

43. *Documents Illustrative of the Formation of the Union of the United States,* edited by C. C. Tansill. Washington, 1927.

44. *Documents Illustrative of the Formation of the Union of the United States,* edited by C. C. Tansill. Washington, 1927. There are various other editions of Madison's notes, of which that by Max Farrand is the most comprehensive.

45. *History of the Centennial Celebration of the Inauguration of George Washington,* edited by Clarence W. Bowen. N.Y., 1892.

46. *The Writings of Thomas Jefferson,* edited by Albert Ellery Bergh, Vol. I. Washington, 1903.

47. *A Compilation of the Messages and Papers of the Presidents,* edited by James D. Richardson, Vol. I. Various editions. "Washington's Farewell Address" can likewise be readily found in any edition of the writings of Washington; the most elaborate edition of the Address itself is that by Victor H. Paltsits.

48. *The Writings of Thomas Jefferson,* edited by Albert Ellery Bergh, Vol. III. Washington, 1903. "The First Inaugural" can likewise be found in any edition of Jefferson's writings, in Commager's *Documents,* and in Richardson's *Messages and Papers.*

49. *Reports of the Trials of Colonel Aaron Burr for Treason and for a Misdemeanor,* Vol. I. Philadelphia, 1808.

50. *The First Forty Years of Washington Society. Portrayed by Family Letters of Mrs. Samuel Harrison Smith from the Collection of Her Grandson, J. Henley Smith,* edited by Gaillard Hunt. N.Y., 1906. By permission of Charles Scribner's Sons.

51. "McCulloch *v.* Maryland" is in *4 Wheaton's Reports, 316;* "Cohens *v.* Virginia" in *6 Wheaton's Reports, 264;* "Gibbons *v.* Ogden" in *9 Wheaton's Reports, 1.* All three cases may be found conveniently in *Documents of American History,* edited by H. S. Commager, or in more extensive form in the editions of Marshall's decisions by J. M. Dillon and by J. P. Cotton.

52. *The Yarn of a Yankee Privateer* [by Benjamin F. Browne], edited by Nathaniel Hawthorne, introduction by Clifford Smyth. N.Y., 1926. By kind permission of Funk & Wagnalls Company.

53. *A History of the American Privateers and Letters of Marque,* by George Coggeshall. N. Y., 1856.

54. *American Eloquence,* Vol. II, edited by Frank Moore. N.Y., 1864.

55. *A Narrative of the Campaigns of the British Army at Washington and New Orleans* [By George Robert Gleig]. London, 1826.

56. *A Narrative of the Campaigns of the British Army at Washington and New Orleans* [By George Robert Gleig]. London, 1826.

57. *Uncle Sam Ward and His Circle,* by Maud Howe Elliott. N.Y., 1928. By permission of The Macmillan Company, publishers.

58. *Travels in North America, in the Years 1780, 1781 and 1782,* 2 vols., by the Marquis de Chastellux. London, 1787.

59. *A Guide in the Wilderness. A Series of Letters Addressed by Judge Cooper of Coopers-town to William Sampson, Barrister.* Dublin, 1810. Reprinted, Rochester, N.Y., 1897.

60. *Notes on a Journey in America from the Coast of Virginia to the Territory of Illinois,* by Morris Birkbeck. London, 1818.

61. *Important Extracts from Original and Recent Letters Written by Englishmen, in the United States of America, to Their Friends in England.* Second Series. Manchester, 1818. Reprinted in *Historical Aspects of the Immigration Problem,* by Edith Abbott, Chicago, 1926.

62. *A Narrative of the Life of David Crockett . . . Written by Himself.* Philadelphia, 1834, and many later editions, the most accessible of which is that by Hamlin Garland.

63. *Recollections of the Last Ten Years,* by Timothy Flint. Boston, 1826, and later editions, the most accessible of which is that by C. Hartley Grattan.

64. *The Pioneer Preacher, or Rifle, Axe and Saddle-Bags, and other Lectures,* by [William] Henry Milburn, edited by the Reverend J. McClintock. N.Y., 1857.

65. *Recollections of Life in Ohio from 1813 to 1840,* by William Cooper Howells. Cincinnati, 1895. By kind permission of John G. Kidd and Son, Inc.

66. *Grandmother Brown's Hundred Years, 1827–1927,* by Harriet Con-

nor Brown. Boston, 1931. By kind permission of Little, Brown and Company.

67. *Grandmother Brown's Hundred Years, 1827–1927*, by Harriet Connor Brown. Boston, 1931. By kind permission of Little, Brown and Company.

68. *The Life and Adventures of Martin Chuzzlewit*, by Charles Dickens. Innumerable editions.

69. *Two Years Before the Mast*, by Richard H. Dana. Boston, 1840, and numerous later editions.

70. *Moby Dick*, by Herman Melville. Innumerable editions.

71. *Moby Dick*, by Herman Melville. Innumerable editions.

72. *Wanderings and Adventures of Reuben Delano, Being a Narrative of Twelve Years' Life in a Whale Ship*. Worcester, Mass., 1846.

73. *Fish and Men in the Maine Islands*, by W. H. Bishop. N.Y., 1885.

74. *The First Steamboat on the Western Waters*, by J. H. B. Latrobe. Maryland Historical Society Fund, Publication No. 6. Baltimore, 1871.

73. *Fish and Men in the Maine Islands*, by W. H. Bishop. N.Y., 1885.

75. *Life on the Mississippi* and "Old Times on the Mississippi," by Mark Twain. The *Atlantic Monthly*, Volume 35. February, 1875. By kind permission of Harper and Brothers and The Atlantic Monthly Press.

76. *The Gilded Age*, by Mark Twain and Charles Dudley Warner. N.Y., 1873, and many later editions. By permission of Harper and Brothers.

77. *Letters from an American Farmer. Written for the Information of a Friend in England*, by J. Hector St. John. London, 1782. The letters of Michel G. St. Jean de Crèvecœur are available in many editions, the most convenient of which are those by Ernest Rhys in the Everyman's Library and by Ludwig Lewisohn.

78. *Recollections of a Lifetime*, by Samuel G. Goodrich. 2 vols. Auburn, New York, 1856.

79. *Memories of Old Salem, Drawn from the Letters of a Great-Grandmother*, by Mary Harrod Northend. N.Y., 1917. By kind permission of Francis S. Benjamin.

80. *Figures of the Past*, by Josiah Quincy. Boston, 1883. There is a more recent edition, edited by M. A. DeWolfe Howe, published by Little, Brown and Company.

81. *Society in America*, by Harriet Martineau. 2 vols. N.Y., 1837, and other editions.

82. *A New England Boyhood*, by Edward Everett Hale. N.Y., 1893. By kind permission of Little, Brown and Company.

83. *Country Life in Georgia in the Days of My Youth*, by Rebecca L. Felton. Atlanta, Georgia, 1919.

84. *American Notes,* by Charles Dickens. Innumerable editions.

85. *The Autobiography of Joseph Jefferson.* New York, 1890. By kind permission of the D. Appleton-Century Company.

86. *Samuel F. B. Morse, His Letters and Journals,* 2 vols., edited by Edward Lind Morse. Boston, 1914. By kind permission of Houghton Mifflin Company.

87. "Dr. Morton's Discovery of Anesthesia," by E. L. Snell. The *Century Magazine,* Vol. XLVIII (New Series, Vol. XXVI), 1894.

88. *The Diary of Philip Hone,* edited by Allan Nevins. N.Y., 1936. By kind permission of Dodd, Mead and Company.

89. *The Essays of Ralph Waldo Emerson,* Second Series. Boston, 1883, and many later editions. By kind permission of Houghton Mifflin Company.

90. *Forty Years of American Life,* by Thomas Low Nichols. London, 1874. Reprinted, N.Y., 1937.

91. *Memorial to the Legislature of Massachusetts, January, 1843,* by Dorothea Dix. Old South Leaflets, No. 148. Boston, no date.

92. *The History of Woman Suffrage,* Vol. I, edited by E. C. Stanton, S. B. Anthony and M. J. Gage. Rochester, N.Y., 1881. Available also in Commager's *Documents of American History.*

93. *Silver Pitchers,* by Louisa May Alcott. Boston, 1876. By kind permission of Little, Brown and Company.

94. *Walden, or Life in the Woods,* by Henry David Thoreau. Boston, 1854, and innumerable later editions. By kind permission of Houghton Mifflin Company.

95. *Forty Years of American Life, 1821–1861,* by Thomas Low Nichols. London, 1874. Reprinted, N.Y., 1937.

96. *From the Easy Chair,* by George William Curtis. N.Y., 1892.

97. "The Correspondence of Eli Whitney," edited by M. B. Hammond. The *American Historical Review,* Vol. III, 1897–98.

98. *Recollections of the Last Ten Years,* by Timothy Flint. Boston, 1826, and later editions, the most accessible of which is that by C. Hartley Grattan.

99. *Notices of Brazil,* 2 vols., by the Reverend R. Walsh. London, 1830.

100. *Old Folks at Home,* by Nellie Thomas McColl. Privately printed, 1921.

101. *Seed from Madagascar,* by Duncan Clinch Heyward. Chapel Hill, North Carolina, 1937. By kind permission of the University of North Carolina Press.

102. *The South-West by a Yankee* [Joseph Holt Ingraham], 2 vols., N.Y., 1835.

103. *Journal of a Residence on a Georgian Plantation in 1838–1839,* by Frances Anne Kemble. London, 1863.

104. *The South-West by a Yankee* [Joseph Holt Ingraham], 2 vols. N.Y., 1835.

105. *Seed from Madagascar,* by Duncan Clinch Heyward. Chapel Hill, North Carolina, 1937. By kind permission of the University of North Carolina Press.

106. *Memorials of a Southern Planter,* by Susan Dabney Smedes. Baltimore, 1887.

107. *Forty Years of American Life, 1821–1861,* by Thomas Low Nichols. London, 1874. Reprinted, N.Y., 1937.

108. *The Autobiography of Colonel George Thomas Davis.* N.Y., 1891.

109. *The Reminiscences of Levi Coffin.* Cincinnati, 1877.

110. *Richard Henry Dana, A Biography.* 2 vols., by Charles Francis Adams. Boston, 1891. By kind permission of Houghton Mifflin Company.

111. *The Public Life of Captain John Brown,* by James Redpath. Boston, 1860. Also in Commager's *Documents of American History.*

112. *A Narrative of Voyages and Commercial Enterprises,* by Richard Jeffry Cleveland. Boston, 1842, and later editions.

113. *The Adventures of Captain Bonneville, U. S. A., in the Rocky Mountains and the Far West* . . . , by Washington Irving. Innumerable editions.

114. *The Autobiography of Isaac Jones Wistar,* Philadelphia, 1937. By kind permission of The Wistar Institute of Anatomy and Biology.

115. *Two Years Before the Mast,* by Richard Henry Dana, Jr. Boston, 1840, and numerous later editions.

116. "With the Cow Column on the Oregon Trail," by Jesse Applegate. *Quarterly* of the Oregon Historical Society, Vol. I, December, 1900. Also in *Recollections of My Boyhood,* by Jesse Applegate, various editions.

117. *The Exploring Expedition to the Rocky Mountains, Oregon and California,* by J. C. Frémont. Buffalo, 1849.

118. "Across the Plains in the Donner Party," by Virginia Reed Murphy. The *Century Magazine,* Vol. XLII (New Series, Vol. XX) 1891.

119. *A Journey to Great-Salt-Lake City,* by Jules Rémy. 2 vols., London, 1861.

120. *Roughing It,* by Mark Twain. 2 vols., Hartford, Conn., 1871. By permission of Harper and Brothers.

121. "James Marshall's Account of the Discovery of Gold in California," by Charles B. Gillespie. The *Century Magazine,* Vol. XLI, February, 1891.

122. *Three Years in California*, by Reverend Walter Colton. N.Y., 1852.

123. "Early Recollections of the Mines," by J. H. Carson, Esq., Stockton, 1852. Reprinted in The *Magazine of History*, Extra Number 164, William Abbott, Tarrytown, N.Y.

124. *A Frontier Lady: Recollections of the Gold Rush and Early California*, by Sarah Royce, edited by R. H. Gabriel. New Haven, Conn., 1932. By permission of the Yale University Press.

125. *El Dorado*, by Bayard Taylor. N.Y., 1850.

126. *History of the Big Bonanza*, by Dan de Quille (William Wright). Hartford, Conn., 1877.

127. *Vigilante Days and Ways in Montana*, by Nathaniel Pitt Langford. 2 vols., Boston, 1890. Reprinted, Chicago, 1912. By kind permission of A. C. McClurg and Company.

128. *The Evolution of a State, or Recollections of Old Texas Days*, by Noah Smithwick, compiled by Nanna Smithwick Donaldson. Austin, Texas, 1900. Reprinted, Austin, 1935.

129. *Colonel Crockett's Exploits and Adventures in Texas* . . . , London, 1837, and various later editions, the most accessible of which is that by Hamlin Garland.

130. *History of Texas*, by Henderson Yoakum. 2 vols. N.Y., 1856.

131. "Official Report of General Sam Houston to David Burnet, President of the Republic of Texas," in *History of Texas*, by Henderson Yoakum. N.Y. 1856.

132. *The Memoirs of Lieutenant-General Scott*. 2 vols. N.Y., 1864.

133. *The Autobiography of Martin Van Buren*, edited by John C. Fitzpatrick. Annual Report of the American Historical Association, 1918, Vol. II. Washington, 1920.

134. *The First Forty Years of Washington Society, Portrayed by Family Letters of Mrs. Samuel Harrison Smith from the Collection of Her Grandson, J. Henley Smith*, edited by Gaillard Hunt. N.Y., 1906. By permission of Charles Scribner's Sons.

135. *The Works of Daniel Webster*, Vol. III. Boston, 1851.

136. *The Diary of Philip Hone*, edited by Allan Nevins, N.Y., 1936. By kind permission of Dodd, Mead and Company.

137. *Reminiscences and Anecdotes of Daniel Webster*, by Peter Harvey. Boston, 1921. By kind permission of Little, Brown and Company.

138. *The Diary of Philip Hone*, edited by Allan Nevins. N.Y., 1936. By kind permission of Dodd, Mead and Company.

139. *Reminiscences and Anecdotes of Daniel Webster*, by Peter Harvey. Boston, 1921. By kind permission of Little, Brown and Company.

140. *The Hidden Lincoln, From the Letters and Papers of William H. Herndon*, edited by Emanuel Hertz. N.Y., 1938. By kind permission of The Viking Press, Inc.

141. *Reminiscences,* by Carl Schurz, Vol. II, copyright 1906, 1907. Reprinted by permission from Doubleday, Doran & Company, Inc.

142. *Caucuses of 1860. A History of the National Political Conventions of the Current Presidential Campaign,* by Murat Halstead. Columbus, Ohio, 1860.

143. *A Compilation of the Messages and Papers of the Presidents,* by James D. Richardson. Vol. VI. Various editions. This address can likewise be found in any collection of the works of Abraham Lincoln, and in Commager's *Documents of American History.*

144. *The Autobiography of Thurlow Weed,* edited by his daughter, Harriet A. Weed. N.Y., 1883.

145. *Tales, Sketches and Other Papers. The Complete Works of Nathaniel Hawthorne,* edited by George Parsons Lathrop. Vol. XII. Boston, 1883. By kind permission of Houghton Mifflin Company.

146. *Recollections of President Lincoln and His Administration,* by L. E. Chittenden. N.Y., 1891. By permission of Harper & Brothers.

147. *Six Months at the White House with Abraham Lincoln,* by F. B. Carpenter. N.Y., 1867.

148. *The Life and Public Services of Salmon Portland Chase,* by J. W. Schuckers. N.Y., 1874.

149. *Abraham Lincoln's Complete Works,* edited by John G. Nicolay and John Hay, Vol. II, N.Y., 1902. The Proclamation can be found in any edition of Lincoln's works or in Commager's *Documents of American History.*

150. *Abraham Lincoln's Complete Works,* edited by John G. Nicolay and John Hay, Vol. II, N.Y., 1902.

151. *Abraham Lincoln's Complete Works,* edited by John G. Nicolay and John Hay, Vol. II, N.Y., 1902.

152. *The Diary of Gideon Welles,* edited by John T. Morse, Jr., Vol. II, Boston, 1911. By kind permission of Houghton Mifflin Company.

153. *Six Months in the Federal States,* by Edward Dicey. Vol. II. London, 1863.

154. *A Rebel War Clerk's Diary at the Confederate States Capital,* by J. B. Jones. 2 vols. Philadelphia, 1866. A new edition of the diary, edited by Howard Swiggett, was published in 1935.

155. *Reminiscences of Julia Ward Howe, 1819–1899.* Boston, 1899. By kind permission of Houghton Mifflin Company.

156. *Hospital Transports. A Memoir of the Embarkation of the Sick and Wounded from the Peninsula of Virginia in the Summer of 1862.* Boston, 1863.

157. *A Confederate Girl's Diary,* by Sarah Morgan Dawson. Boston, 1913. By permission of Houghton Mifflin Company.

158. *A Confederate Girl's Diary,* by Sarah Morgan Dawson. Boston, 1913. By permission of Houghton Mifflin Company.

159. *What Answer?,* by Anna Elizabeth Dickinson. Boston, 1868.

160. *A Rebel War Clerk's Diary at the Confederate States Capital,* by J. B. Jones. 2 vols. Philadelphia, 1866.

161. *A Rebel War Clerk's Diary at the Confederate States Capital,* by J. B. Jones. 2 vols. Philadelphia, 1866.

162. *A Rebel's Recollections,* by George Cary Eggleston. N.Y., 1874.

163. *Roughing It,* by Mark Twain. 2 vols. Hartford, Conn., 1871. By permission of Harper and Brothers.

164. *The War-Time Journal of a Georgia Girl,* by Eliza Frances Andrews. N.Y., 1908. By kind permission of D. Appleton-Century Company.

165. *The War-Time Journal of a Georgia Girl,* by Eliza Frances Andrews. N.Y., 1908. By kind permission of D. Appleton-Century Company.

166. *A Diary from Dixie,* by Mary Boykin Chesnut, edited by Isabella D. Martin and Myrta Lockett Avary. N.Y., 1905. By kind permission of D. Appleton-Century Company.

167. *Reminiscences of Forts Sumter and Moultrie,* by Abner Doubleday. N.Y., 1876.

168. *My Diary North and South,* by William Howard Russell. 2 vols. London, 1863.

169. *Soldiers' Letters from Camp, Battle-field and Prison,* edited by Lydia Minturn Post. N.Y., 1865.

170. "A Trip with Lincoln, Chase and Stanton," by Egbert L. Viele. *Scribner's Monthly,* Vol. XVI, 1878.

171. *Port Hudson — Its History from an Interior Point of View, as Sketched from the Diary of an Officer.* St. Francisville, La., 1938. By kind permission of Elrie Robinson.

172. *Port Hudson — Its History from an Interior Point of View, as Sketched from the Diary of an Officer.* St. Francisville, La., 1938. By kind permission of Elrie Robinson.

173. *The Rebellion Record,* edited by Frank Moore. Vol. VII. N.Y., 1864.

174. I. "The Battle of Gettysburg and the Campaign in Pennsylvania. Extract from the Diary of an English Officer Present with the Confederate Army." (Arthur J. L. Fremantle.) *Blackwood's Edinburgh Magazine,* Vol. XCIV, 1863.

II. *From Manassas to Appomattox,* by James Longstreet. Philadelphia, 1896.

175. *Abraham Lincoln's Complete Works,* edited by John G. Nicolay and John Hay, Vol. II, N.Y., 1902. The Address can be found in any

edition of Lincoln's works, in Commager's *Documents of American History,* and in countless other compilations.

176. *The End of an Era,* by John S. Wise. Boston, 1899. By permission of Houghton Mifflin Company.

177. *Memoirs of General William T. Sherman, By Himself.* Vol. II, N.Y., 1875.

178. *The War-Time Journal of a Georgia Girl,* by Eliza Frances Andrews. N.Y., 1908. By kind permission of D. Appleton-Century Company.

179. "Letters of a Confederate Officer to His Family in Europe during the Last Year of the War." [By Richard W. Corbin] The *Magazine of History,* with notes and queries. Extra Number 24. N.Y., 1913.

180. *Personal Memoirs of U. S. Grant,* Vol. II, N.Y., 1885, and later editions.

181. *Lantern Slides,* by Mary Cadwalader Jones. Privately printed, Boston, 1937. By kind permission of Mrs. Max Farrand.

182. *Personal Reminiscences, Anecdotes and Letters of General Robert E. Lee,* by the Reverend J. William Jones, N.Y., 1875.

183. *Memorials of a Southern Planter,* by Susan Dabney Smedes. Baltimore, 1887.

184. *The South Since the War,* by Sidney Andrews. Boston, 1866.

185. *Dixie After the War,* by Myrta Lockett Avary. N.Y., 1906. Reprinted, Boston, 1937. By permission of Houghton Mifflin Company.

186. *The Prostrate State,* by James Shepherd Pike. N.Y., 1874. Reprinted, N.Y., 1935.

187. *A Fool's Errand, by One of the Fools* (Albion Tourgée). N.Y., 1879.

188. *A Fool's Errand, by One of the Fools* (Albion Tourgée). N.Y., 1879.

189. *Political Recollections, 1840 to 1872,* by George W. Julian. Chicago, 1884.

190. *Democratic Vistas,* by Walt Whitman. Innumerable editions.

191. "How We Built the Union Pacific Railway, and Other Railway Papers and Addresses," by G. M. Dodge. Pamphlet, no place, no date.

192. *Across the Plains, with Other Memories and Essays,* by Robert Louis Stevenson. Numerous editions. By permission of Charles Scribner's Sons.

193. *Beyond the Mississippi,* by Albert D. Richardson. Hartford, Conn., 1869.

194. *American,* by Frank B. Linderman. N.Y., 1930. By permission of The John Day Company, Inc.

195. *The Log of a Cowboy,* by Andy Adams. Boston, 1927. By permission of Houghton Mifflin Company.

196. *When Kansas Was Young,* by T. A. McNeal. N.Y., 1922. By permission of The Macmillan Company, publishers.

197. *Conquering Our Great American Plains,* by Stuart Henry, published by E. P. Dutton and Company, Inc., New York.

198. *A Son of the Middle Border,* by Hamlin Garland. N.Y., 1917. By permission of The Macmillan Company, publishers.

199. The *St. Louis Globe Democrat,* April 22, 1889. Reprinted in *America Goes to Press,* by Laurence Greene, Indianapolis, 1936.

200. Editorial by William Allen White in the *Emporia Gazette,* June 20, 1895. Reprinted in *American Press Opinion,* edited by Allan Nevins. N.Y., 1928.

201. "The Great Chicago Fire," by Horace White, special report to the *Cincinnati Commercial,* October 14, 1871. Reprinted in *A Library of American Literature,* compiled and edited by Edmund Clarence Stedman and Ellen Mackay Hutchinson, Vol. IX. N.Y., 1889.

202. *Seventy Years of Life and Labor,* by Samuel Gompers, Vol. I, published and copyrighted by E. P. Dutton & Company, Inc., New York.

203. *Society as I Have Found It,* by Ward McAllister. N.Y., 1890.

204. *How the Other Half Lives,* by Jacob Riis. N.Y., 1890, and later editions. By permission of Charles Scribner's Sons.

205. *The Making of an American,* by Jacob A. Riis. N.Y., 1901. By permission of The Macmillan Company, publishers.

206. *An American Saga,* by Carl Christian Jensen. Boston, 1927. By kind permission of Little, Brown and Company.

207. *Forty Years at Hull House,* by Jane Addams. N.Y., 1935. By permission of The Macmillan Company, publishers.

208. *The Promised Land,* by Mary Antin. Boston, 1912. By permission of Houghton Mifflin Company.

209. *Up from Slavery, an Autobiography,* by Booker T. Washington, copyright 1901, 1929. Reprinted by permission from Doubleday, Doran & Company, Inc.

210. *Up from Slavery, an Autobiography,* by Booker T. Washington, copyright 1901, 1929. Reprinted by permission from Doubleday, Doran & Company, Inc.

211. *One Man's Life, an Autobiography,* by Herbert Quick, copyright 1925. Used by special permission of the publishers, The Bobbs-Merrill Company.

212. *Morally We Roll Along,* by Gay MacLaren. Boston, 1938. By kind permission of Little, Brown and Company.

213. "Report of the Proceedings at a Banquet Given to Mr. Cyrus W. Field by the Chamber of Commerce of New York at the Metropolitan Hotel, November 15, 1866." N.Y., 1866.

214. "How I Served My Apprenticeship," by Andrew Carnegie, *The Youth's Companion*, April 23, 1896. Reprinted in *The Gospel of Wealth*, N.Y., 1906. By kind permission of Mrs. Andrew Carnegie.

215. *The Bitter Cry of the Children*, by John Spargo. N.Y., 1906. By permission of The Macmillan Company, publishers.

216. *The Jungle*, by Upton Sinclair. Numerous editions. By kind permission of Mr. Upton Sinclair.

217. *The Iron Puddler*, by James J. Davis, copyright 1922. Used by special permission of the publishers, The Bobbs-Merrill Company.

218. *My Life and Work*, by Henry Ford in collaboration with Samuel Crowther, copyright 1922, by Doubleday, Doran & Company, Inc.

219. *Random Reminiscences of Men and Events*, by John D. Rockefeller, copyright 1908, 1909, by Doubleday, Doran & Company, Inc.

220. *America of Yesterday: the Diary of John Davis Long*, edited by Lawrence Shaw Mayo. Boston, 1923. By kind permission of Little, Brown and Company.

221. *The Autobiography of George Dewey*. N.Y., 1913. By permission of Charles Scribner's Sons.

222. *With Sampson Through the War*, by W. A. M. Goode, copyright 1899-1927, by Doubleday, Doran & Company, Inc.

223. *The Fight for Santiago*, by Stephen Bonsal, copyright 1899-1927, by Doubleday, Doran & Company, Inc.

224. *Glimpses of Fifty Years, the Autobiography of an American Woman*, by Frances E. Willard. N.Y., 1889.

225. *Forty Years of It*, by Brand Whitlock. N.Y., 1914. By kind permission of D. Appleton-Century Company.

226. *Forty Years of It*, by Brand Whitlock. N.Y., 1914. By kind permission of D. Appleton-Century Company.

227. *The Autobiography of Robert La Follette*. Madison, Wis., 1913. By kind permission of Fola La Follette.

228. *The Autobiography of Robert La Follette*. Madison, Wis., 1913. By kind permission of Fola La Follette.

229. *The Beast*, by Judge Ben B. Lindsey and Harvey J. O'Higgins. N.Y., 1910. By kind permission of the sole copyright owner, Judge Ben B. Lindsey.

230. *Documents of American History*, edited by Henry Steele Commager. N.Y., 1934.

231. *The First Battle, A Story of the Campaign of 1896*, by William J. Bryan. Chicago, 1896.

232. *The Land of the Dollar*, by G. W. Steevens. N.Y., 1897. By kind permission of Dodd, Mead and Company, Inc.

233. *From McKinley to Harding*, by Hermann H. Kohlsaat. N.Y., 1923. By permission of Charles Scribner's Sons.

234. *Forty-Two Years in the White House*, by Irwin Hood (Ike) Hoover. Boston, 1934. By permission of Houghton Mifflin Company.

235. *Taft and Roosevelt: the Intimate Letters of Archie Butt, Military Aide*, Vol. II, copyright 1930, by Doubleday, Doran & Company, Inc.

236. *From Pinafores to Politics*, by Mrs. J. Borden Harriman. N.Y., 1923. By permission of Henry Holt and Company, Inc.

237. *The Journal of Brand Whitlock*, edited by Allan Nevins. N.Y., 1936. By kind permission of the D. Appleton-Century Company.

238. *War Memoirs of Robert Lansing*, copyright 1935. Used by special permission of the publishers, The Bobbs-Merrill Company.

239. *Documents of American History*, edited by Henry Steele Commager. N.Y., 1934.

240. "Torpedoed," by Albert Kinross. The *Atlantic Monthly*, Vol. CXX, December, 1917. By kind permission of the Atlantic Monthly Press.

241. *The Victory at Sea*, by William Snowden Sims, copyright 1921, by Doubleday, Doran & Company, Inc.

242. *My Experiences in the World War*, by John J. Pershing. Vol. II. N.Y., 1931. By kind permission of General Pershing.

243. *Cobb of "The World,"* by John L. Heaton, published by E. P. Dutton & Company, Inc., New York.

244. *Confessions of a Reformer*, by Frederic C. Howe. N.Y., 1925. By permission of Charles Scribner's Sons.

245. *250 United States Reports, 616* (1919). This opinion is reprinted in Commager's *Documents of American History*.

246. *Father Struck It Rich*, by Evalyn Walsh McLean with Boyden Sparkes. Boston, 1936. By kind permission of Little, Brown and Company.

247. *The Autobiography of Calvin Coolidge*, copyright 1929. Reprinted by permission of Farrar & Rinehart, Inc.

248. *"We,"* by Charles A. Lindbergh. N.Y., 1927. By kind permission of Charles Lindbergh and G. P. Putnam's Sons.

249. *Father Struck It Rich*, by Evalyn Walsh McLean with Boyden Sparkes. Boston, 1936. By permission of Little, Brown and Company.

250. *Documents of American History*, edited by Henry Steele Commager. N.Y., 1934.

251. *We Too Are the People*, by Louise V. Armstrong. Boston, 1938. By kind permission of Little, Brown and Company.

252. *State of the Nation,* by John Dos Passos. Boston, 1943. By permission of Houghton Mifflin Company.

253. *Democracy on the March,* by David Lilienthal. N.Y., 1944. By permission of Harper and Brothers.

254. *The Memoirs of Cordell Hull.* 2 vols. N.Y., 1948. Copyright 1948, by Cordell Hull. Used by permission of The Macmillan Company.

255. *The Ghost Talks,* by Charles Michelson. N.Y., 1944. By permission of G. P. Putnam's Sons. Copyright 1944 by Charles Michelson.

256. *The Memoirs of Cordell Hull.* 2 vols. N.Y., 1948. Copyright 1948, by Cordell Hull. Used by permission of The Macmillan Company.

257. *Into the Valley; A Skirmish of the Marines,* by John Hersey. N.Y., 1943. By permission of Alfred A. Knopf, Inc.

258. *Thirty Seconds Over Tokyo,* by Captain Ted W. Lawson. N.Y., 1943. By permission of Random House.

259. *The Fight for New Guinea,* by Pat Robinson. N.Y., 1943. By permission of Random House.

260. *The Roosevelt I Knew,* by Frances Perkins. N.Y., 1946. By permission of The Viking Press, Inc.

261. *Inside U.S.A.,* by John Gunther. N.Y., 1947. By permission of Harper and Brothers.

262. *Brave Men,* by Ernie Pyle. N.Y., 1944. By permission of Henry Holt and Company, Inc. Copyright 1944, by Henry Holt and Company, Inc.

263. *Crusade in Europe,* by Dwight D. Eisenhower. N.Y., 1948. By permission of Doubleday & Company, Inc. Copyright 1948, by Doubleday & Company, Inc.

264. *Brave Men,* by Ernie Pyle. N.Y., 1944. By permission of Henry Holt and Company, Inc. Copyright 1944, by Henry Holt and Company, Inc.

265. *Crusade in Europe,* by Dwight D. Eisenhower. N.Y., 1948. By permission of Doubleday & Company, Inc. Copyright 1948, by Doubleday & Company, Inc.

266. *The Memoirs of Cordell Hull.* 2 vols. N.Y., 1948. Copyright 1948, by Cordell Hull. Used by permission of The Macmillan Company.

267. *Okinawa: The Last Battle,* by Roy E. Appleman, James M. Burns, Russell A. Gugeler, and John Stevens. Washington, D.C., Government Printing Office, 1948.

268. "An American Plane Ushers in the Atomic Age," by William E. Laurence. The *New York Times,* September 9, 1945.

269. *Leaves of Grass,* by Walt Whitman. Numerous editions.

Index